Introduction

Thrash Metal

Thrash Metal, upon its inception during the early '80s, had media scorn poured upon it almost from the word go. Thrash = Trash. It was just too easy. Rather than stifling this bastard child of the NWoBHM movement, for that indeed is what Thrash was really all about, the ridicule and jeering of the established Rock press was like gasoline to a bonfire. Thrash Metal simply exploded and the Metal magazines swiftly accomplished a face saving about turn. Thrash Metal not only rejuvenated the Heavy Metal scene, it probably saved its neck.

Thrash is rooted firmly and squarely in the NWoBHM. As that new generation of lean, hungry and often amateurish acts gave the Heavy Metal old guard a much needed kick up its complacent rear, over in America – or California's Bay Area to be more exact, things were stirring too. Legions of Metalheads fresh out of school, armed with acne, flying Vs and record collections stuffed with SAXON, JUDAS PRIEST and UFO woke up to the NWoBHM at rapid speed. And 'Speed' was the operative word.

There were a number of key figures fuelling this burgeoning phenomenon. Two of the most significant were Brian Slagel of Metal Blade Records in Los Angeles and Ron Quintana of KUSF 'Rampage' radio and 'Metal Mania' fanzine in San Francisco. These two individuals provided the impetus and creative drive for bands to get out of their garages and onto vinyl, the airwaves and into newsprint.

Brian Slagel had been flying the flag for new Metal at his day job in Oz Records and his fanzine 'The New Heavy Metal Revue'. Transforming the printed word into positive action, Slagel's illustrious 'Metal Massacre' compilation gave Thrash the head start It needed, simply by including one band going by the name of METALLICA. Once committed to vinyl it's nigh on impossible for a band's momentum to wane in pursuit of greater goals and one look at the roster displayed on the succeeding 'Metal Massacre' series is testament to that.

Ron Quintana, the man who may very well have actually thought of the name METALLICA, championed the new cutting edge European Metal as well as guitar supremos such as the SCORPIONS' Uli Jon Roth and UFO's Michael Schenker in his highly influential fanzine 'Metal Mania'. The traffic was a two way street, Quintana providing the upcoming bands with new records from MERCYFUL FATE, ACCEPT and ANGELWITCH and enthusiastically giving exposure to demos and records from the Californian new breed of METALLICA, EXODUS, METAL CHURCH, ANVIL CHORUS, HIRAX and MEGADETH.

When examining Thrash and its upbringing one should not forget also the cold and simple fact that Lars Ulrich, drummer and prime motivator of

i

METALLICA, also played a huge part in the story. Without METALLICA there would be no Thrash, even if today, without Thrash there is still a METALLICA.

But just where did Thrash come from? Obviously these bands were entrenched in the history and lore of the '70s Rock giants. So much so in fact that James Hetfield's formative act was titled OBSESSION in honour of UFO's classic 1978 album. The supercharged fury of JUDAS PRIEST's 'Exciter' too has a lot to answer for (…and not just the Canadian EXCITER… or the Dutch EXCITER…)

Punk also played a major part in the rise of Thrash in that there was an emphasis on keeping things as raw as possible and a pervading gung ho 'do it yourself" attitude. It was the old school though that was the major inspiration. Thrash's guitarists still had a yearning to accomplish similar technical feats achieved by the masters like Blackmore, Schenker and Roth. They just wanted to do it twice as fast.

It was to be the elite of the NWoBHM that pushed them over the edge from Metal to Thrash Metal. ANGELWITCH's esoterica and penchant for galloping riffs certainly played a big part, BLITZKRIEG's eponymous single, VENOM's complete rawness had an influence as did DIAMOND HEAD's sheer musical ambition. Another band, sorely – indeed deliberately – overlooked is SAVAGE.

One listen to the opening track on SAVAGE's seminal 'Let It Loose' album tells you all you need to know about Thrash Metal. Stripped to the bone, no frills Speed Metal pure and simple. Recorded in the back room of a terraced house in Hull, SAVAGE never matched it again. METALLICA did though, recording two SAVAGE songs on their very earliest demos they learnt fast. METALLICA also had everything SAVAGE did not, they had the image, they had the drive and they had American zeal.

When Thrash exploded the Rock world was simply knocked off its complacent axis. It hit the youth market just right, giving vent for teenagers bored with a stale Punk scene. Soon the pecking order had been established and the frontrunners had broken away from the pack. The 'Big four' tag was given to METALLICA, New York's ANTHRAX, Dave Mustaine's State of the art speed Metal band MEGADETH and the uncompromising, Satanically charged SLAYER. The lead these acts stretched out in such a short time caught virtually everyone else off guard. Other, equally worthy outfits, such as METAL CHURCH, EXODUS, TESTAMENT, OVERKILL and FLOTSAM & JETSAM just could not catch up. In the blink of an eye a second generation of Thrashers had risen up headed by AGENT STEEL, DARK ANGEL, SACRED REICH and ANNIHILATOR. However, those 'Big four' bands, some 20 years later and despite Mustaine's recent announcement that MEGADETH are to fold, are still the undisputedly the 'Big Four'.

Many Metal bands in this book were, so to speak, caught in the glare of Thrash. Just as METALLICA are no longer a Thrash band artists such as VICIOUS RUMORS, ICED EARTH, ARMORED SAINT and JAG PANZER

A-Z *of* THRASH METAL

GARRY SHARPE-YOUNG

www.rockdetector.com

This edition published in Great Britain
in 2002 by Cherry Red Books Ltd.,
Unit 17, 1st Floor, Elysium Gate West,
126–128 New King's Road,
London SW6 4LZ

All you need to know about the author:
Born: Münchengladbach 1964
Raised: On Judas Priest
Status: Decade of wedlock
Raising: Kerr, Krystan, Kjaric
Hair: By Vikernes

Typeset by Sarah reed.
Printed and bound in Great Britain by
Biddles Ltd., Guildford and King's Lynn.
Cover Design by Jim Phelan at Wolf Graphics Tel: 020 8299 2342

ISBN 1–901447–09–X

were not ploughing the Thrash furrow but got caught up in the whole shooting match. In their formative years many straightforward Heavy Metal bands took on a new injection of Speed simply in order to compete. Hardcore acts too became embroiled, with bands such as D.R.I., AGNOSTIC FRONT, SUICIDAL TENDENCIES and C.O.C. discovering a whole new marketplace.

Paradoxically the ignition of Thrash Metal on American shores did not bounce back to the homeland of Great Britain. Post the Bay Area explosion the UK's attempts at Thrash fell fat short of the mark and reeked of copycatting. Naturally the British major labels reaction was traditionally sheep like, sluggish and misguided. They signed the wrong bands and signed them too late. SLAMMER, ONSLAUGHT and TORANAGA barely made a dent. The independent scene in the UK was simply too weak to make a difference and bands such as XENTRIX, AVENGER and ATOMKRAFT duly suffered. Only SABBAT, signed to a German label, kept Britain's pride afloat.

Britain did boast 'Metal Forces' magazine, a bastion of Thrash Metal from the very beginning. Led by the towering Bernard Doe, 'Metal Forces' got behind METALLICA, SLAYER, MEGADETH and SEPULTURA way before the mainstream caught on.

Roadrunner Records, nowadays transformed into a hugely successful Nu-Metal label, started life by importing an unending stream of budget Thrash into European stores. So awash with Thrash was Roadrunner's seemingly tireless catalogue that reviewers in the UK lined up their albums for decimation like ducks on a fairground shooting gallery. Nevertheless, artists such as RAZOR, ATTACKER and SLAYER all benefited from the exposure. Also not to be underestimated was the prolific Christian Thrash scene as exemplified by TOURNIQUET, VENGEANCE RISING and DELIVERANCE.

The London based Music For Nations label, and its offshoot Under One Flag, enjoyed its glory years courtesy of Thrash. The label was groundbreaking in its astuteness at licensing METALLICA, ANTHRAX, HOLY TERROR and NUCLEAR ASSAULT. Oddly, the only British Thrash acts of note MFN put its muscle behind were less than serious in their pursuit of the craft.

In Germany it was a different story though. Bolstered by a thriving independent scene, with SPV and Noise Records leading the way, Thrash thrived. Magazines like Metal Mike's 'Aardschok' and Germany's 'Rock Hard' understood. Not only did Thrash Metal prosper with numerous bands and quickfire release schedules, but it paved the way for new threads of Thrash. Acts such as KREATOR, CELTIC FROST and HELLOWEEN took Metal into new realms. It seemed like the European Festland was awash with Thrash – ARTILLERY, RAGE, SODOM, DESTRUCTION, RUNNING WILD, GRAVE DIGGER, VECTOM, et al reaped huge album sales and completely revitalised the Rock scene. Naturally the bulk of the British Media sat back and laughed – until it was too late. Only perceptive journalists such as the mighty Bernard Doe of 'Metal Forces' magazine, Dave Constable at 'Shades' record store, the late Paul Miller and the oddly perceptive Xavier Russell actually got a handle on what was going on.

What should not be forgotten is that Thrash's plague like tentacles spanned the entirety of the globe. South America became a breeding ground for bands such as VODU, TRANSMETAL, VULCANO and OVERDOSE. This geographic − and linguistic isolation actually aided in fostering a leaner, hungrier and more inventive form of Thrash, which was to transform the Metal world when SEPULTURA broke out of Brazil and onto the international stage.

As Thrash peaked it naturally spawned offshoots with Canadians VOIVOD and the Swiss eccentrics CELTIC FROST pushing the boundaries of avant-garde 'Art' Thrash. Other experiments, such as 'Funk Thrash', were less than successful. As METALLICA slowed their pace the pretenders quickened theirs and, just as the Bay Area instigators had transformed NWoBHM into a brand new animal, these up and coming acts took it to even deadlier extremes, ultimately resulting in Death Metal. This genre would outgrow and swamp Thrash in time, spawning in turn even more frightening branches with Grindcore and Black Metal.

Thrash, naturally, changed. METALLICA engendered the 'great debate' by cutting their hair; applying make up and quite surreally going on to sell more albums than ever. MEGADETH gambled on their own 'Risk' and ANTHRAX discovered that the wearing of shorts onstage can drastically affect a whole career. SLAYER? Well, they just stayed the same. Same speed, same Satan, same trend defying Billboard chart entries. A lesson to be learned perhaps? Thrash was to be given a new lease of life with the advent of PANTERA and MACHINE HEAD. These two bands reaped commercial reward by applying a slightly different angle on an otherwise tried and trusted Thrash formula.

So where is Thrash Metal today? If you've bought this book for some old time nostalgia, to read up on fond headbanging MEGADETH memories, you may be surprised to learn that Thrash has weathered the storms and is surprisingly healthy. It has, in fact, been enjoying a genuine renaissance of late as both Black and Death Metal bands, vocal in their appreciation of Thrash, have kick-started Thrash Metal projects such as WITCHERY, THE HAUNTED, SCARIOT and THE CROWN. Thrash is not only back, it's selling albums and firing up the Metal youth. Germany, Belgium, Holland and Sweden are all producing teen Thrash acts of high quality.

In particular, Germany's love of all things Thrash has provided enough impetus for many '80s cult acts such as TYRANT, HIRAX and BROCAS HELM to reform. For over a decade stoic acts such as FLOTSAM & JETSAM, TESTAMENT, OVERKILL and VICIOUS RUMORS have found Germany not only a safe haven but a lifeline.

I have been immensely privileged over the years to have interviewed many of the major artists in this book. Amongst personal highlights are interviewing Cliff Burton (only because Lars was late) in what turned out to be an enthusiastic insider journey through the fledgling Bay Area Thrash scene. Sadly I was to discover that was Cliff's last ever interview.

I also sat in on METAL CHURCH rehearsals, got very drunk with FLOTSAM & JETSAM in Germany, caught POSSESSED's only UK shows, SLAYER's first spit drenched UK tour and witnessed the most pissed off Dave Mustaine ripping through the most angry debut show I've ever seen at the Hammersmith Odeon. I interviewed ANTHRAX so many times that I simply ran out of questions to ask them and got the full scam on the early MEGADETH history direct from the man himself. I also saw the originals in action – ANGELWITCH, DIAMOND HEAD and SAVAGE.

This book will be back and bigger. There's more Thrash where that came from!

Garry Sharpe-Young

Your life of Thrash is not complete without these albums. Both this book and the Rockdetector website only succeed if, after reading, you actually LISTEN. In no particular order:

METALLICA 'Ride The Lightning'
SAVAGE 'Loose n' Lethal'
METAL CHURCH 'The Dark'
MEGADETH 'Peace Sells... But Who's Buying'
HELLOWEEN 'Keeper Of The Seven Keys Part II'
EXODUS 'Bonded By Blood'
ANNIHILATOR 'Never Neverland'
FLOTSAM & JETSAM 'Doomsday For The Deceiver'
OVERKILL 'I Hear Black'
SLAYER 'South Of Heaven'
DESTRUCTION 'Eternal Devastation'
SABBAT 'History Of A Time To Come'

ABOUT ROCKDETECTOR

www.rockdetector.com is the world's largest Rock devoted website. These pages are taken directly from the website. As I write it hosts information, including unique biographies and full global discographies, on over 11,800 bands. When you pick up this book tomorrow it will have even more.

We're on a mission at Rockdetector to document Rock music of all genres, persuasions and nationalities, old and new and of every persuasion.

We try to do this in a non-biased, non-opinionated manner. It matters to us that we get our facts straight and aid the promotion of all Rock artists.

We thrive on information. If you have any fact, album cover, band history or discography detail we're presently missing then contribute. If we've got anything wrong – tell us.

We are also actively looking for dedicated Rock fans with specialist knowledge of genres or territories to contribute. If you're the man who knows all the ins and outs on the Bangladeshi Emocore scene then we need to hear from you. Seriously – we're looking for quality writers.

Where do we get our information from? We're often asked this. Fortunately 15 years of journalism has helped. Very often facts are gleaned from face to face interviews with bands. Day to day stuff we get from record companies from all over the world, bands and fans.

We include ALL submissions. There is only one criteria – the band has to Rock. That covers everything in our scheme of things from AOR, Prog Rock, Classic Rock right through to Nu-Metal, Rap Metal and onto Death & Black Metal. We want it all.

Here's the address for submissions:

Musicdetector Websites Ltd,
P.O. Box 3138,
New Plymouth,
Taranaki,
New Zealand

For inclusion on the site we need one of each product format, a full biography and a high quality photo. Information regarding linking to your URLs is also of benefit to you.

If you want a record reviewing we need two copies as we send these out for review.

Here's our e-mail address: info@rockdetector.com

Bands / Labels: DON'T send us an e-mail asking for us to look at your website. We simply don't have time. Be proactive and send the stuff in. Then we'll contact you.

THANKS:

Marco Barberei at Century Media, Bernard Doe, Olly Hahn at SPV, Peter Klapproth at CMM, Kelli Malella & Jim Mills at Metal Blade, Metal Sludge, Sabiene at Season Of Mist, Michael 'Tim' Langbein, Jochen Maas and Markus Wosgein at Nuclear Blast, Ron Quintana, Matt Sampson, Nico Wobben, Cam & Gal of Wrath, Grant & Kevin at Efinity. All especially all the many, many bands who contributed. Respect due to Martin Popoff and Phil Casey.

And, of course, not forgetting the Cherry Red crew – Iain, Tim, Adam, Sarah & Jim.

Many thanks to the industrious Joshua Wood. Many of the Canadian entries are directly attributable to Joshua. Also to Dave Reynolds for his invaluable help.

The ever expanding catalogue of family & friends: Grace-Anne, Kerr, Krystan, Kjaric, Mum, JimJam & Martin, Peter, Shazbat, Chris, Stevie, Phillip, Lucy, Marisa, Sonia, Barry, Jane + 2, Eddie & Helen, Bill & Zay, Ruth & Chris, Simon & Diana Meadows, Adam & Kim Parsons, Debbie & Aaron, Karen Geoghegan, Nell Sully, Andy Southwell, Andy Pyke, Andy Dawson, Greg Russell, Pete Way, Martin Walkyier.

There are of course people my feeble, Metal addled brain has forgotten. I apologise. Get in touch, one and all.

Marshall Law are NOT a Thrash Metal band.

As ever, dedicated to my Dad (who hated Thrash Metal!)

Paul Baloff R.I.P.

AARDVARKS
(GERMANY)
Line-Up: Guido Meyer De Voltaire (vocals / guitar), Hernan Andres Martinez Riveros (guitar), Sven Krautkrämer (bass), Nick Holmfeldt (drums)

A Bonn based Thrash Metal unit forged in 1993 by the Meyer De Voltaire siblings; vocalist Guido of AUGERY and guitarist Andreas along with ex-DERB man Sven Krautkrämer on bass and Nick Holmfeldt of HEATRASH and ARTIFICIAL TEETH on drums. The band debuted with the 'Eyes' demo in 1994, following this with a second session 'Farka's Lemma' two years later. Andreas Meyer De Voltaire would decamp in February of 1998 to be replaced by Daniel Hauenstein.

Hauenstein would make his exit during 2001, duly supplanted by DAKRIA man Nardi Ramirez. Further ructions saw Krautkrämer too opting out in May, this last loss putting AARDVARKS on hold, as a suitable replacement could not be found. During the interim Holmfeldt deputised for Death Metal act SYRE and Meyer De Voltaire cut session lead vocals for the high profile avant-Black Metal act BETHLEHEM.

Much to AARDVARKS' relief Krautkrämer was persuaded to rejoin and the new face of Colombian guitarist Hernan Andres Martinez Riveros also entered the fold.

Singles/EPs:
Profundo Rosso / Grey / Meat / Too Many Puppies, (2001) ('Profundo Rosso' EP)

ABATTOIR (Los Angeles, CA, USA)
Line-Up: Steve Gaines (vocals), Mark Caro (guitar), Danny Oliverio (guitar), Mel Sanchez (bass), Danny Anaya (drums)

Cut-throat metal act ABATTOIR surfaced in Los Angeles during 1978. The band bowed in with a two track demo in 1983, with an inaugural line-up of vocalist Raul Preston, guitarists Mark Caro and Juan Garcia, bassist Mel Sanchez and drummer Danger Wayne. The band debuted live at the notorious Troubadour, but by ABATTOIR's studio session for the track 'Screams From The Grave' (included on the now illustrious 'Metal Massacre IV' compilation) Preston was ousted in favour of erstwhile SCEPTRE frontman John Cyriis. This valuable exposure led to support slots for W.A.S.P. and METALLICA.
Line-up ructions beset the band, with both

Cyriis and Garcia quitting to form AGENT STEEL and Danny Amaya coming in as a new face on the drum stool. ABATTOIR were brought up to strength with the addition of vocalist Steve Gaines (brother of STRYPER bassist Tim Gaines) and guitarist Danny Oliverio.

ABBATOIR's debut album, released on Combat Records in America and Roadrunner in Europe, featured a cover of the MOTÖRHEAD classic 'Ace Of Spades'. Gaines departed to form BLOODLUST releasing the 'Terminal Velocity' single in 1988. His replacement was ex-HERETIC singer Mike Towers (nee Torres) who appears on the slightly tamer 'Only Safe Place' album, which was released on Noise Records in Europe, although they retained a deal with Combat in America. Sanchez quit in 1988 to create EVIL DEAD.

Eventually scuttled by continuous line-up hassles ABATTOIR finally split. However, more than a decade later the band came out of retirement with cover versions for tribute albums.

ABATTOIR lent their touch to Dwell Records IRON MAIDEN tribute 'Call To Irons', W.A.S.P.'s 'School Daze' and SAXON's 'Motorcycle Man'. With interest resurgent in mainland Europe, German label Century Media re-released both albums as ABATTOIR, now comprising Gaines, Sanchez, Caro and drummer Kevin McShane, prepared for a full blown return. ABATTOIR would bounce back in October of 2001 with the live album 'No Sleep 'Til Kalamazoo'. Not only did the band give a nod to MOTÖRHEAD's infamous live album but confirmed their appreciation with a cover version of 'Ace Of Spades'. The album, a strictly limited edition, was only made available through the band's website.

ABATTOIR were busying themselves with recording of a fresh studio album provisionally entitled 'Evil Incarnate' during the latter half of 2001.

Albums:
VICIOUS ATTACK, Roadrunner RR 9788 (1985)
Screams From The Grave / Vicious Attack (Maniac) / The Enemy / Ace Of Spades / The Living And The Dead / Don't Walk Alone / Stronger Than Evil / Game Of Death
THE ONLY SAFE PLACE, Noise N0045 (1986)
Intro: Beyond The Altar / Bring On The Damned / The Only Safe Place / Hammer Of The Godz / Back To Hell / Temptations Of The Flesh / Under My Skin / S.B.D. (Feel The Fire) / Night Of The Knife / Piano Outro

NO SLEEP 'TIL KALAMAZOO, Abattoir (2001)
Vicious Return / The Enemy / Under My Skin / Vicious Attack / Everybody Dies / Stronger Than Evil / Off / Screams From The Grave / Ace Of Spades

ABHORRENT (BRAZIL)
Line-Up: Robson Blake (vocals), Marcus Vireoli (guitar), Hudson Andre (guitar), Leandro Soares (bass), Carlos Fibrian (drums)

Thrash infused Death Metal act ABHORRENT was forged during 1988. However, this original inception of the band would collapse after issuing the 'Horrible Slaughter' demo.
ABHORRENT was reconvened in 1992 for a further session 'Blood On Your Lips'. With guitarist Marcus Vireoli handling bass the band cut album tracks in 1994. Bass player Leandro Soares would be inducted shortly after but these songs would take a full three years to be issued as the 'Rage' album. ABHORRENT did manage to put in a set of European dates to promote the album.
Another tape 'Live In Rage' arrived which included a version of SLAYER's 'Reign In Blood'.

Albums:
RAGE, (1997)
Intro / Let Me Live / Eternal Doubt / Blood On Your Lips / No Chance / Prelude Of The End / The Witch / One Step / Face Of Terror
CAUTION: STRONG IRRITANT, (2000)

ABOMINATION (IL, USA)
Line-Up: Paul Speckmann (vocals / bass / guitar), Dean Chioles (guitar), Aaron Nickeas (drums)

ABOMINATION is another weapon in MASTER vocalist Paul Speckmann's arsenal of Thrash and Death Metal projects.
Speckmann, initially just handling bass guitar duties, had begun his journey into the world of Metal with the 1983 act WARCRY. This unit issued the 'Trilogy Of Terror' demo and also scored a track on Metal Blade's 'Metal Massacre IV' compilation. Speckmann then forged a union with Chris Middlebrunt to create DEATHSTRIKE. After a solitary demo DEATHSTRIKE would evolve into MASTER by 1984. A deal was struck for a proposed album with the Combat label but in the midst of negotiations MASTER splintered.
In 1987 Speckmann resolved to start afresh, enlisting drummer Aaron Nickeas for the formation of ABOMINATION. A brace of

demos ensued as Speckmann consecutively kick started another project band FUNERAL BITCH. ABOMINATION would sign to the German Nuclear Blast concern to release their eponymous debut.
1993 would see ABOMINATION members guitarist Dean Chioles and drummer Aaron Nickeas founding another extreme Metal unit entitled BODY BAG. However, sadly Chioles would soon after be diagnosed with Amyotrophic Lateral Sclerosis and was forced to give up the guitar.
In February of 2000 Speckmann joined Czech Deathsters KRABATHOR.

Singles/EPs:
Split, Nuclear Blast (1990) (Split 7" single with MASTER)

Albums:
ABOMINATION, Nuclear Blast (1989)
The Choice / Murder, Rape, Pillage And Burn / Reformation / Redeem Deny / Possession / Suicidal Dreams / Life And Death / Victim Of The Future / Tunnel Of Damnation
TRAGEDY STRIKES, Nuclear Blast NB050 (1991)
Blood For Oil / They're Dead / Pull The Plug / Will They Bleed / Industrial Sickness / Soldier / Kill Or Be Killed / Oppression
CURSES OF THE DEADLY SIN, (1999)

ABSURD (SWITZERLAND)
Line-Up: Patrick Arn (vocals), Raphael Schneider (guitar), Philipp Gerber (guitar), Jean-Claude Wirth (bass), Ronny Gerber (drums)

Swiss Metal band led by Patrick 'Onkel' Arn formed in 1990. It was six years before ABSURD unleashed their debut album, a record that displayed their preference for technical Thrash Metal. Following the 'Shadows' effort ABSURD would enroll keyboard player Patrick Schaad.

Albums:
SHADOWS, Absurd (1996)
Shadows / Name Of God / Dawn Of The Dead / Moribund / Am Ende Der Straße / No Jesus / Lost Generation / Silence / Nice Day

ABSURDUS (FINLAND)
Line-Up: Aki Martin Kauppi (vocals / guitar), Juha Moilanen (guitar), Taneli Nyholm (bass), Matti Roiha (drums)

Black Thrash act founded by school friends vocalist / guitarist Aki Martin Kauppi, guitarist Juha Moilanen, bass player Taneli Nyholm and drummer Matti Roiha. During 1996 both

Taneli and Roiha would deputize for RAVENSFALL (later CRYHAVOC) but would return to ABSURDUS for recording of the 'No Heaven In Sight' album.

Released on the British Candlelight label, 'No Heaven In Sight' included a version of MOTÖRHEAD's seminal 'Bomber'.

A second album was planned but ABSURDUS opted for a more basic Rock n' Roll approach and were dropped by their label. ABSURDUS would later evolve into PANDEMONIUM OUTCASTS with all members adopting the revised names of guitarist J. 'Aki' Boa (also 'Snake'), bassist Daniel Rock (also 'Daniel Stuka' and 'Serpent') and drummer Matt C. (also 'Dragon').

Bassist Taneli Nyholm (as 'Daniel Stuka') would join Death n' Rollers BABYLON WHORES in late 1999.

Albums:
NO HEAVEN IN SIGHT, Candlelight CANDLE024CD (1998)
Ad Absurdum (One Hell Of An Introduction) / On The Way To Hell / Devil's Ride / My Kingdom / You're Below Everything / Concord In Diablo / Joyreaper / Pure Pleasure / Blood Drive / Life Is Agony / Bomber

ACCELERATOR (SWITZERLAND)
Line-Up: Fredi Zaugg (vocals / guitar), Sascha Von Arx (guitar / keyboards), Roger Friedrich (bass), Adi Krebs (drums)

ACCELERATOR's 1997 debut album 'The Prophecy' saw guest vocals from Patrick Schaad with female vocals from Esther Hofer. The band, created in late 1993 as a trio of vocalist / guitarist Fredi Zaugg, ex-GOMORRHA bassist Roger Friedrich and drummer Adi Krebs, had previously gone under the titles of DEAD END and APOPLEXY. As ACCELERATOR they had made their mark with the 1995 demo session 'The Dark Side'.

Following the release of 'The Prophecy' Von Arx departed and Esther Hofer took over the role of guitarist / keyboard player.

Albums:
THE PROPHECY, (1997)
The Prophecy / Trapped In Insanity / Wasted / Gone / The End Of Your Time / Loneliness / The Sparrow / Final Journey / In Eternal Bliss

ACCUSED (USA)
Line-Up: Blaine 'Fart' Cook (vocals), Tommy 'Accused' Niemeyer (guitar), Alex Maggot Brain (bass), Dana Collins (drums)

Seattle Thrash-Hardcore sons ACCUSED date back to their inception in 1981 with an initial line-up of vocalist John, guitarist Tom Niemeyer, bassist Chewy and drummer Dana Collins. First product was a 1981 split album with THE REJECTORS on Fatal Rejection Records.

John departed in 1984 to be replaced by erstwhile FARTZ man Blaine Cook, the band issuing their first album the same year. The 'Martha Splatterhead' album, released on Condor Records, only saw a limited run of 500 copies.

During a 1986 American tour bassist Chewy was asked to leave and was duly replaced by Alex 'Maggot Brain' Sibbald who was a veteran of Punk acts MAGGOT BRAINS, ITCHY BROTHER and CHEATING DEATH. They toured America with British Punks G.B.H. in 1987.

The 1988 album boasts a guest appearance from METAL CHURCH guitarist Kurdt Vanderhoof. 1990's 'Hymns For The Deranged' album, with new drummer Josh, features live renditions of DEEP PURPLE's 'Highway Star', THIN LIZZY's 'Cold Sweat' and BLACK SABBATH's 'Symptom Of The Universe'.

The ACCUSED hit the cover trail once more in 1991 with their Jack Endino produced 'Straight Razor' offering including a take on LYNYRD SKYNYRD's 'Saturday Night Special'.

Post-ACCUSED the individual band members made their presence felt on the burgeoning Seattle Grunge scene. Sibbald and Niemeyer created GRUNTRUCK before the drummer founded RED HOT LUNATIC.

Niemeyer would journey through HELLCAT, LYE and MONA DIESEL.

Singles/EPs:
Split, Empty (1989) (split single with MORPHIUS)

Albums:
PLEASE PARDON OUR NOISE - IT IS A SOUND OF FREEDOM, Condor (1981) (Split album with THE REJECTORS)
MARTHA SPLATTERHEAD, Condor (1984)
RETURN OF MARTHA SPLATTERHEAD, Subcore 8197-1 (1985)
Martha Splatterhead / Wrong Side Of The Grave / Take My Time / Distractions / Buried Alive / No Mercy / Slow Death / Autopsy / She's The Killer / In A Death Bed / Lonely Place / Fuckin' 4 Bucks / Martha's Revenge
MORE FUN THAN AN OPEN CASKET FUNERAL, Rough Justice JUST 11 (1987)

Halo Of Flies / WCALT / Rape / Lifeless Zone / Scotty / Devil Woman / Bethany Home / Mechanized Death / Take No Prisoners / Splatter Rock / Septi-Child / I'll Be Glad When You're Dead, You Rascal You
MARTHA SPLATTERHEAD'S MADDEST STORIES EVER TOLD, Combat Core (1988)
Psychomania / The Bag Lady Song / Inherit The Earth (The Day Of Wreckoning) / Deception (The Impostors) / Molly's Xmas '72 / I'd Love To Change The World / You Only Die Once / Sick Boy / Chicago / Starved To Death (Eat Yer Buddies) / War + Death '88 (And Beyond) / The Maddest Story Ever Told / Intro (From The Tingler) / Scared Of The Dark / Losing Your Mind / Smothered Her Trust / Lights Out / The Hearse (Traditional Nursery Rhyme)
HYMNS FOR THE DERANGED, Musical Tragedies LP15747 (1990)
Grinning / Brutality And Corruption / Tapping The Vein / Barracuda / Our Way / Cold Sweat / Highway Star / Symptom Of The Universe
GRINNING LIKE AN UNDERTAKER, Nasty Mix NMR 702201 (1990)
Pounding Nails (Into The Lid Of Your Coffin) / Bullet Ridden Bodies / The Corpse Walks / Grinning (Like An Undertaker) / Down And Out (Featuring The Mad Poet) / Cut And Dried / Dropping Like Flies / M Is For Martha / Room 144 / When I Was A Child / The Night / Voices / Boris The Spider / Tapping The Vein
STRAIGHT RAZOR, Nasty Mix (1991)
No Hope For Relief / Close Insight / The Corpse Walks / Straight Razor / Down And Out / Saturday Night Special / Blind Hate - Blind Rage / Voices
SPLATTER ROCK, Nasty Mix (1992)
Two Hours Till Sunrise / Stick In A Hole / No Choice / Lettin' Go / Blind Hate-Blind Rage / Greenwood House Of Medicine-Don't You Have A Woman / She's Back / Tearin' Me Apart / Green Eyed Lady / Brutality And Corruption / Living, Dying, Living - In A Zombie World

ACCUSER (GERMANY)

Line-Up: Eberhard Weyel (vocals / bass), Rene Schutz (guitar), Frank Thoms (guitar), Volker Borchet (drums)

A Speed Metal band that specialized in long drawn out 'Techno-Thrash' material, ACCUSER was formed in 1986 by ex BREAKER men Eberhard Weyel and Volker Borchert together with ex EXPECT NO MERCY guitarist Frank Thoms. Original bassist Thomas Kircher departed before the first album.
Following the release of debut album 'The Conviction', ACCUSER toured Europe with MUCKY PUP and then released a mini-album 'Experimental Errors'.
For the tour to promote the 'Who Dominates Who?' album of 1989 vintage ACCUSER toured on a bill with GRINDER and DESPAIR. However, by the time the ensuing 'Double Talk' was released, guitarist Rene Schutz had been replaced with Milan Peschel.
Frontman Weyel departed in 1991 leaving Thoms to take over lead vocals. Members of ACCUSER would then hook up with noted German Industrial Metal act DIE KRUPPS resulting in the experimental 'Metal Machine Music' album. Borchert would actually be enrolled as live drummer for DIE KRUPPS and both Thoms and Schütz would session on the album '1'.
ACCUSER promptly went through a series of bassists prior to settling on Guido Venzlaff in 1993.
Two of ACCUSER's more recent albums, 'Reflections' and 'Taken By The Throat' were produced by the noted American recording engineer Alex Perialis.
The band signed to Koch International for 1995's 'Taken By The Throat' album but were unable to achieve as high sales figures as they had anticipated the switch would give them.

Singles/EPs:
The Persuasion / Black Suicide / Terroristic Violence / Technical Excess / F.H.W.C. / Ratouli, Atom H 006 (1988) ('Experimental Errors' EP)

Albums:
THE CONVICTION, Atom H 003 (1988)
Evil Liar / Sadistic Terror / Down By Law / Law Of War / Accuser / The Conviction / Screaming For Guilt
WHO DOMINATES WHO?, Atom H 008 (1989)
Master Of Disaster / Who Pulls The Wire? / Elected To Suffer / Symbol Of Hate / Who Dominates Who? / Bastard / Called To The Bench
DOUBLE TALK, Atom H AH014 (1991)
Double Talk / The Freeze / Money / Flag Waver / Why Me / Indistinct Articulation / Revolution / Alcowhore
REPENT, Our Choice RTD 195 1178 3 (1992) (with DIE KRUPPS)
Rotting From Within / Repent / Get Saved / Sacrifice Machine / The Living Dead / The Drones / Judgement Gone Blind / Nosferatu / Metal Machine Music
REFLECTIONS, Major LC6249 (1994)
The Wreckage / Misery / Cowboy On A String / The Jack Of All Trades / Reflections /

Unite-divide / Into The Void / Burn / Manic Ride
CONFUSION ROMANCE, C&C 025052-2 (1994)
Head Like A Hole / Confusion Romance / Cowboy On A String / Driver's Seat / Misery / Repent
TAKEN BY THE THROAT, Koch International 341 682 (1995)
Healium / Taken By The Throat / Fatal Vision / Fire Ignites / Obey! / Condemnation / Blasting In Progress / The Slug / Stonefaced / Amnesia

ACID (BELGIUM)
Line-Up: Kate (vocals), Demon (guitar), Dizzy Lizzy (guitar), T-Bone (bass), Anvill (drums)

Thrash band based in Bruges. Female fronted ACID formed in 1980 with the trio of Demon, Kate and T-Bone splintering from PRECIOUS PAGE and recruiting drummer Anvill. Second guitarist Dizzy Lizzy was added in 1981 in time to record their debut single 'Hooked On Metal', of which 2,000 copies were pressed, and its success led to a deal with the independent Giant label, resulting in three albums between 1983 and 1985.
ACID played throughout Belgium, France and Holland with the likes of BLACK SABBATH, MANOWAR, VENOM, LOUDNESS, PICTURE, BODINE and MOTÖRHEAD, but would ultimately fold after the third album 'Engine Beast'.
1988's 'Acidify' and 1989's 'Don't Lose Your Dreams' are from a German ACID although many publications have mistaken them for their Belgian predecessors.

Singles/EPs:
Hooked On Metal / Hell On Wheels, Acid ACID001 (1981)
Lucifera / Ghostriders, Giant GS 501 (1983)
Black Car / Drop Dead / The Day You Die / Exterminator, Hartdog (1983)

Albums:
ACID, Giant 6711 (1983)
Acid / Ghostriders / Hell On Wheels / Anvil / Demon / Hooked On Metal / Woman At Last / Five Days Hell / Heaven's Devils / Satan
MANIAC, Bullet Megaton 007 (1983)
Max Overload / Maniac / Black Car / America / Lucifera / No Time / Prince Of Hell And Fire / Bottoms Up
ENGINE BEAST, Giant G713 (1985)
STC / Lost In Hell / Halloween Queen / Big Ben / Lady Death / Warriors Of The Dark / Let Me Die / She Loves You / Engine Beast /

Satan's Delivery

ACID DRINKERS (POLAND)
Line-Up: Titus (vocals / bass), Litza (guitar), Popcorn (guitar), Mangood (drums)

A Thrash Heavy Metal act disinclined to take themselves too seriously and blessed with strong Crossover influences, ACID DRINKERS began as a three piece prior to original guitarist Woytek quitting after the debut album was released. ACID DRINKERS duly drafted not one but two guitarists in his place.
ACID DRINKERS garnered an international profile courtesy of the Music For Nations Thrash offshoot label Under One Flag who would license their initial three albums, released domestically by Metal Mind, for Western consumption.
The oddly titled 'Fishdick' album witnessed the band delving deep into covers territory offering forth their renditions of PINK FLOYD's 'Another Brick In The Wall', KISS's 'Deuce', MOTÖRHEAD's 'Ace Of Spades', AC/DC's 'Whole Lotta Rosie', BLACK SABBATH's 'N.I.B.' and DEEP PURPLE's 'Highway Star'.
ACID DRINKERS attempted a Black Metal pastiche with the less than serious 'Infernal Connection' album. The band would have a crack at covering the hoary anthem 'Wild Thing' by THE TROGGS on their 1996 effort 'The State Of Mind Report'. 'High Proof Cosmic Milk' issued in March 1998, included a cover of CREEDANCE CLEARWATER REVIVAL's staple 'Proud Mary'.
By 2001 ACID DRINKERS line-up comprised of vocalist / bassist Tomasz 'Titus' Pukacki, guitarists Dariusz 'Popcorn' Popowicz and Robert 'Litza' Friedrich along with drummer Maciej 'Slimak' Staorsta.
Besides their activities with ACID DRINKERS various members also operate numerous side project acts such as ARMIA, ALBERT ROSENFIELD, KAZIK, FLAPJACK and the PARA WINO BAND.

Albums:
ARE YOU A REBEL?, Under One Flag FLAG45 (1990)
Del Rocca / Barmy Army / I Mean Acid (Do Ya Like It?) / Waitin' For The Hair / Lammin', Obtrusive, Vulgar, Emasculatin' Machine / Fuck The Violence (I'm Sure I'm Right) / I Am The Mystic / Woman With Dirty Feet / Megalopolis / Nagasaki Baby / Moshin' In The Night / Mike Cwel
DIRTY MONEY, DIRTY TRICKS, Under One Flag FLAG 59 (1991)
Are You A Rebel? / Too Many Cops / Acid

Drinker / Smoke On The Water / Yahoo / Max-He Was Here Again / Ziomas / Traditional Birthday / Dirty Money, Dirty Tricks / Angry And Bloody / Street Rockin' / WGFS Power / Don't Touch Me / Zorba / Flooded With Wine

STRIP TEASE, Under One Flag FLAG76 (1992)
Striptease / King Kong Bless You / Seek And Destroy / Rock n' Roll Beast / Rats / Feeling Naughty / Poplin' Twist / Masterhood Of Hearts Devouring / You Are Lost My Dear / Menel Song / Always Look On The Bright Side Of Life / Blood Is Boiling / My Caddish Promise / Mentally Deficient / Hell It Is A Place On Earth / Ronnie And The Brotherspider / I'm A Rocker

VILE VICIOUS VISION, Loud Out Records LOR 050 (1993)
Zero / (Voluntary) Kamikaze Club / Vile Vicious Vision / Pizza Driver / Under The Gun / Marian Is A Metal Guru / Murzyn Mariusz / Balbilator Edzy / Then She Kissed Me / Hats Off (2 This Lady) / Polish Blood / Freeze Me / Midnight Visitor

FISHDICK, Loud Out Records LOR 100 (1994)
Ace Of Spades / Oh No! Bruno / Deuce / N.I.B. / Another Brick In The Wall / Whole Lotta Rosie / Run Run Away / Fuckin' The Tiger / Highway Star / Balada

INFERNAL CONNECTION, Mega Czad CSO777 (1994)
Hiperenigmatic Stuff Of Mr. Nothing / Anybody Home??!! / The Joker / Track Time 66.6 Sec. / Drug Dealer / Slow And Stoned (Method Of Yonash) / Dancing In The Slaughterhouse / IQ Cyco / Backyard Bandit / Infernal Connections / Consument

ACID DRINKERS 1985: ACIDS ON THE DANCE FLOOR, Stage Diving Club Records SDC001 (1995)
Bonarowski Mix Gitarowy / Hrohomyloh Mix / Versya Spoko / Running With The Devil / Konsument / OK! I Fell Alright / Ill Wojna

THE STATE OF MIND REPORT, Polton Warner Music Poland PC176 (1996)
Private Ego / Two Be One / 24 Radical Questions / Solid Rock / United Suicidal Legion / Pump The Plastic Heart / Maximum Overload / Solid Rock Part II / Wild Thing / Walkway To Heaven

AMAZING ATOMIC ACTIVITY, (1997)
Amazing Atomic Activity / You Better Shoot Me / Satisfaction / Cops Broke My Beer / Wake Up! Here Come The Acids / My Pick / She's Gonna Be A Porno Star / Justify Me (I Was So Hungry) / Home Submarine / House Full Of Reptiles / What A Day / Cigarettes / The Last Lap

HIGH PROOF COSMIC MILK, Metal Mind MMP050 (1998)

Rattlesnake Blues / Human Bazooka / High Proof Cosmic Milk / What's Happenin' In The Heart Of A Pacifist / More Life / Be My Godzilla / Dementia Blvd. / Blind Leadin' The Blind / Gain On Shit / Proud Mary

BROKEN HEAD, Metal Mind (2001)
Superstitious Motherfucker / Dog Rock / El Pecado / Calista / Don't Go To Where I Sleep / A Rubber Hammer And A Broken Head / There's So Much Hatred In The Air / The Wildest Planet In Space / Youth / Red And Grey

ACID REIGN (UK)

Line-Up: H (vocals), Kev (guitar), Gaz Jennings (guitar), Ian Gangwer (bass), Mark Ramsey (drums)

Harrogate Thrash band that injected a rather twisted sense of humour into the proceedings. ACID REIGN was created in 1985 by frontman H and guitarist Gaz who later enlisted drummer Ramsey and bassist Ian Gangwer. Their inaugural recording was the 'Moshkinstein' demo, which was laid down before the group had taken the decision of bringing in second guitarist Kev. These recordings secured them management with LITTLE ANGELS' mentor Kevin Nixon and subsequently a label deal with Under One Flag, a subsidiary of Music For Nations.

After releasing the 'Moshkinstein' mini album ACID REIGN guested for a visiting FLOTSAM AND JETSAM at London's Astoria, although a subsequent European tour was put in jeopardy when Gangwer was unable to travel due to insufficient documentation. HOLOSADE's Macc filled in on bass in the interim.

In late 1988 the band underwent a line-up shuffle, with Jennings and Gangwer leaving. Gangwer's departure enabled temporary bassist Macc to join the band on a permanent basis. Jennings place was taken by former LORD CRUCIFER guitarist Adam Lehan.

With the Thrash scene faltering ACID REIGN issued a cover single of 'Hangin' On The Telephone' (made famous by BLONDIE) although this was not enough to save them.

Sadly, ACID REIGN split in mid 1991 citing the flagging fortunes of the British Thrash scene as the deciding factor. Vocalist H formed STRANGE THING then DULLABYE.

Lehan formed BITTER AND TWISTED with ex-DEADLINE and SLAMMER bass player Russell Bertram.

Jennings, Lehan and Ramsey all joined premier retro-Doom mongers CATHEDRAL. Unsurprisingly, Kev teamed up with Nottingham Spoof Thrashers LAWNMOWER DETH.

Singles/EPs:
Goddess / Suspended Sentence / Freedom Of Speech / Motherly Love / Respect The Dead / Chaos (Lambs To The Slaughter), Under One Flag FLAG20 (1988) ('Moshkinstein' EP)
Humanoia, Under One Flag FLAG 106 (1989)
Hangin' On The Telephone / Bad News (Live) / Warriors Of Genghis Khan (Live) / Motherly Love (Live), Under One Flag FLAG 109 (1990)

Albums:
THE FEAR, Under One Flag FLAG31 (1989)
You Never Know / Reflection Of Truths / Insane Ecstasy / Humanoia / The Fear / Blind Aggression / Life In Forms / All I See / Lost In Solitude
OBNOXIOUS, Under One Flag FLAG39 (1990)
Creative Restraint / Joke Chain / Thoughtful Sleep / You Are Your Enemy / Phantasm / My Open Mind / Codes Of Conformity / This Is Serious
THE WORST OF, Under One Flag FLAG 60 (1991)
Billy Boy / Lucifer's Hammer / Motherly Love / Two Minded Takeover / R.F.Y.S. / Amnesiac / Magic Roundabout / The Argument / Sabbath Medley / Reflections Of Truths / Hangin' On The Telephone / Warriors Of Genghis Khan / Three Year War / The Joke's On Us / Big White Teeth

ACRIDITY (Victoria, TX, USA)
Line-Up: Darrin Carroll (vocals), Mel Langenberg (guitar), Anthony Pedone (guitar), Mark Cox (bass), Mark Soto (drums)

Thrash Metal band ACRIDITY heralded their arrival with the 1987 demo 'Countdown To Terror'. At the time of their inaugural effort ACRIDITY could boast two 17 year old guitarists in Mel Langenberg and Anthony Pedone as well as a 14 year old drummer Mark Soto. A further demo, 'For Freedom I Cry', surfaced in 1989.
A solitary album, also titled 'For Freedom I Cry', arrived the same year courtesy of Prophecy Records. ACRIDITY would also donate the track 'Whisper Of Reality' to a Texas scene compilation album issued by Saturn Records 'Voices Of A Red God'. A later variant of ACRIDITY would witness the introduction of a keyboard player Coby Cardosa.

Albums:
FOR FREEDOM I CRY, Prophecy (1989)
Beyond / The Verdict / Exist In Misery / For Freedom I Cry / Countdown To Terror / Denied Right / Lethal Idol / Nothing Held Sacred / Vigilante

ACROPHET (Brookfield, WI, USA)
Line-Up: Dave Baumann (vocals / bass), Todd Saike (guitar), Dave Pelino (guitar), Jason Mooney (drums)

Wisconsin's ACROPHET were to be judged 'Intelligent Speedcore'. The second album was released on the Triple X label in America. Following the issue of 1990's 'Faded Glory' album the band inducted guitarist Rob Anthony. Touring then ensued across America and Mexico but although plans for a third album were laid ACROPHET folded in 1993. Anthony and vocalist / bassist Dave Baumann forged a fresh non-Metal act titled SOUL CITY. This unit, together with the addition of erstwhile VIOGRESSION drummer Barry Jaeger, would develop into the ROB ANTHONY BAND. As such a much lauded acoustic Rock album 'Hard To Believe' surfaced in the late '90s.

Albums:
CORRUPT MINDS, Roadrunner RR 9523 (1988)
Intro To Corruption / Lifeless Image / Crime For Loving / Holy Spirit / Ceremonial Slaughter / Forgotten Faith / Corrupt Minds / Slaves Of Sin / From The Depths / Living In Today / Warped Illusions / Victims Of The Holocaust
FADED GLORY, Roadracer RO9404 (1990)
When Time Stands Still / Dependency / Silent Insanity / Legend Has It / Dead Cell Day / The American Zone 1990 / Independence At It's Finest / Return To Me Life / Innocent Blood / Forever The Fall / Haunting Once Again

ADDICTIVE (AUSTRALIA)
Line-Up: Greg Smith (vocals / bass), Joe Buttigiey (guitar), Mick Sultana (guitar), Matt Coffey (drums)

Thrash Metal act from Sydney evolving in 1988 with a line-up of vocalist / bassist Greg Smith, guitarists Joe Buttigiey and Mick Sultana with drummer Matt Coffey. ADDICTIVE debuted with the 1988 demo 'Ward 74'.
After the issue of debut album 'Pity Of Man' in 1989 Coffey lost his place to former ENTICER drummer Steve Moore.
The veteran bassist Bob Daisley, a man who lists OZZY OSBOURNE, RAINBOW and MOTHERS ARMY to his credit, produced the band's second album 'Kick 'Em Hard'.

Apparently the master tapes of these recordings went astray and it was to be 1993 before the album was finally issued.

Albums:
PITY OF MAN, Survival (1989)
KICK 'EM HARD, Survival (1993)

ADRAMELCH (ITALY)

Line-Up: Vittorio Ballerio (vocals), Gianluca A. Corona (guitar), Sandro Fremiot (guitar), Franco Avalli (bass), Luca Moratti (drums)

ADRAMELCH had developed a good name for themselves on the Underground Metal scene thanks to the 'Irae Melanox' album, a record that displayed strong melodies and intelligent songwriting, but the group split up soon after it emerged.
Some ex-ADRAMELCH members are still playing the Milanese Rock circuit playing in trad-Rock bands.
Vocalist Vittorio Ballerio and guitarist Gianluca Corona reformed ADRAMELCH in early 2000.

Albums:
IRAE MELANOX, Metal Master MET104 (1988)
Fearful Visions / Zephirus / Irae Melanox / Lamento / Decay (Saver Comes) / Was Called Empire / Eyes Of Alabaster / Dreams Of A Jester

ADRENALIN O.D. (USA)

Line-Up: Paul Richards (vocals / guitar), Bruce Wingate (guitar), Jack Steeples (bass), Dave Scott (drums)

Crossover Thrash act ADRENALIN O.D. arrived on the scene with the now extremely rare and sought after 1983 'Let's Barbecue' EP, with a line-up of vocalist / guitarist Paul Richards, guitarist Jim Foster, bass player Jack Steeple and drummer Dave Scott. A split 7" single in union with BEDLAM followed.
Steeples was replaced by Keith Hartel for 1988's 'Cruising with Elvis in Bigfoot's UFO' album. The EP 'Theme From An Imaginary Midget Western' features a B side containing covers of the KISS classic 'Detroit Rock City' and the SKULLS song 'Coffincruiser'.
1990's 'Ishtar' release would see a band roster of Richards, Scott, guitarist Bruce Wingate and bassist Wayne Garcia. The 1995 Grand Theft Audio retrospective includes numerous unreleased demos.
Ex-ADRENALIN O.D. founder and guitarist Jim Foster later founded industrious Punk band ELECTRIC FRANKENSTEIN.

Singles/EPs:
Status Symbol / Hijack / Suburbia / Old People Talk Loud / Trans Am / House Husband / Scare Tactics / Mischief Night, Buy Our Records BOR-7-001 (1983) ('Let's Barbecue' EP)
Caught In The Act / , Buy Our Records (1984) (Split 7" single with BEDLAM)
Theme From An Imaginary Midget Western / Detroit Rock City / Coffin Cruiser, Buy Our Records BOR12016 (1988)
A Nice Song In The Key Of D, Buy Our Records (1988)

Albums:
HUMONGOUS FUNGUS AMONGUS, Buy Our Records BOR 001 (1987)
AOD vs Godzilla / Office Building / Yuppie / Answer / Pope On A Rope / Fishin' Musician / Pizza n' Beer / Bugs / Youth Blimp / Commercial Cuts / Survive / Masterpiece / Crowd Control / Velvet Elvis / Fuck The Neighbours / Surfin' Jew / Bruce's Lament / The Nice Song
THE WACKY HI-JINKS OF ADRENALIN OD, Buy Our Records BOR 002 (1987)
AOD vs Godzilla / White Hassle / New Years Eve / Small Talk / Going To A Funeral / Corporate Disneyland / Trans Am (The Saga Continues) / Sightseeing / Middle Aged Whore / World War IV / Clean And Jerk / Sleep / Rah-Jah! / Rock n' Roll Gas Station / Paul's Not Home
CRUISING WITH ELVIS IN BIGFOOT'S UFO, Buy Our Records (1988)
If It's Tuesday... It Must Be Walla-Walla / Bulimec Food Fight / Swindel / Slow / Second To None/ My Mother Can't Drive / Theme From An Imaginary Midget Western / Something About... Amy Carter / Flipside Unclassified / Baby Elephant Walk
ISHTAR, Restless 7 72380-2 (1990)
My Achin' Back / Twenty Dollar Bill / Sheer Heart Attack / Obvious Toupee / Tiny Fingers / What A Way To Go / Big Time Major Love Thang / Paul A Roid / All Right Tokyo / Joe From Lodi / Dave A Roid / Bad Karma Merchant
SITTIN' PRETTY, Grand Theft Audio GTA-009 (1995)
Status Symbol / Hijack / Suburbia / Old People Talk Loud / Trans Am / House Husband / Scare Tactics / Status Symbol / World War 4 / Hijack / White Hassle / Brady Bunch / A.O.D. vs. Godzilla / White Hassle / New Years Eve / Small Talk / Going To A Funeral / Corporate Disneyland / Trans Am / Sightseeing / Middle-aged Whore / World War 4 / Clean and Jerk / Sleep / Rah-Jah / Rock-n-Roll Gas Station / Paul's Not Home / Surburbia / Trans Am / Going To A Funeral / New Years Eve / World War 4 / Middle-aged

Whore / Clean and Jerk / Infiltrate The State / Masterpiece / Status Symbol / Velvet Elvis / Crowd Control / Rah-Jah / Rather Be Asleep / Sightseeing / We Will Rock You

ADVERSITY (CANADA)
Line-Up: Kyle (vocals), Phillipe (guitar), Franz (guitar), Brendan (drums)

Thrash-Hardcore band ADVERISTY were formed in 1986, releasing the 'You Can Run But You Can't Hide' demo the following year.

Albums:
LOST IT ALL, Manic Ears ACHE 13 (1988)
Wasted Life / Jester / Destinized / Religions For Sale / No More Wars / Smash The Odds / Lost It All / Total Extremes / Metaphysics / Fight Back / Angel To Bread

ADX (FRANCE)
Line-Up: Phil (vocals), Herve Marquis (guitar), Pascal Betov (guitar), Deuch (bass), Didier (drums.)

ADX came to being in 1982 and have surprisingly managed to retain a stable line-up. All their albums until 'Weird Visions' are sung in their native tongue. 'Le Terrieur' was produced by Laurent Thibault.
ADX, with new guitarist Yves Louis XV, would reform for the 1999 'Resurrection' opus.

Albums:
EXECUTION, Madrigal MAD2009 (1984)
Dresse Du Crime / Prisonnier De La Nuit / L'Etranger / Execution / Le Fleau De Dieu / Piere De Satan / Vampire / Caligula
CHAPIRE II - LE TERRIEUR, Sydney Music (1986)
Les Enfants De L'Ombre / Marquis Du Mal / Alesia / Le Terreur / Memoire De L'Eternal / Le Blason De La Monte / Tourmente Et Passion
SUPREMATIE, Sydney Music (1987)
Nostromo / Suprematie / Le Judgement De Salem / Notre Dame De Paris / Victime / Les Secrets De L'Olympe / Broceliende / La Peur Et L'Oubli / L'Order Sacre
EXECUTION PUBLIQUE, Sydney / Musidisc 191101 (1989)
Memoire De L'Eternal / Le Judgement De Salem / Broceliande / Caligula / Les Enfants De L'Ombre / L'Etranger / L'Ordre Sacre / Tourmente Et Passion
WEIRD VISIONS, Noise N0161 (1991)
Weird Visions / King Of Pain / Lost Generation / Sacrifice In The Ice / Mystical Warfare / Fortune Telling / Behind The Mirror / Sign Of The Time / Trouble / Invasion / Kill The King

IN MEMORIUM, XIII Bis 187962 (1997)
Le Fleau De Dieu / Notre Dame De Paris / Fortune Telling / L'Etranger / Memoire De L'Eternal (Live) / L'Ordre Sacre / Deesse Du Crime / Sign Of The Time / Suprematie / Les Enfants De L'Ombre (Live) / Marquis Du Mal (1998 version) / King Of Pain / Broceliande (Live) / Caligula / Lost Generation / Tourmente Et Passion
RESURRECTION, XIII Bis 187882 (1999)
Intro: VII / Resistance / L'Ombre Du Desespoir / Le Maudit / Sniper / L'Esprit Malade / De L'Autre Cote / La Dame En Noire / Jeux De Chair / Resurrection / Marquis Du Mal
HUITIEME SENTENCE, (2000)

AFTERMATH (Tuczon, AZ, USA)
Line-Up: Richard Shayka (vocals), Cliff Finney (guitar), John E. January (guitar), Joe Nutt (bass), Rick Von Glahn (drums)

Arizona Thrash act AFTERMATH bowed in with the 'Straight From Hell' EP. A self-titled demo cassette released in 1987 saw a band line-up of vocalist Richard Shayka, guitarist Cliff Finney, bass player Joe Nutt and drummer Rick Von Glahn.
AFTERMATH signed up with Dutch label Moshroom for the 1988 'Don't Cheer Me Up' record.

Singles/EPs:
Mask Of Deception / You're Never Gonna Wake Me Up / Pandemonium / Straight From Hell, Aftershock (1985) ('Straight from Hell' EP)

Albums:
DON'T CHEER ME UP, Moshroom (1988)
Lines Of Horror / Black And Yellow / Daemynspeke / Straight From Hell / Beast Of Wrath / Luci's Dance / Aftermath

AFTERMATH (Chicago, IL, USA)
Line-Up: Charlie Tsiolis (vocals), Steve Sacco (guitar), John Lazerty (guitar), Pat Delagarza (bass), Ray Schmidt (drums)

Chicago based AFTERMATH, fronted by the Greek born Kyriakas 'Charlie' Tsiolis, formed in October 1985, issuing the five track demo 'Killing The Future'. This featured the tracks 'When Will You Die', 'Going No Place', 'Chaos', 'Meltdown' and 'War For Freedom'. AFTERMATH added bassist John Lazerty following the demo release but then switched Lazerty to second guitar, recruiting Pat Delagarza on bass. The demo excited 'Metal Forces' magazine editor Bernard Doe enough to warrant inclusion on his 'Demolition' compilation album issued in 1988.

A further demo 'Words That Echo Fear' featuring new guitarist John Lovette was released prior to the band demoing for Roadracer Records. Negotiations broke down however and AFTERMATH signed to New York's Big Chief Records. However, this label collapsed forcing AFTERMATH to issue the album under their own steam on the private Thermometer imprint.

AFTERMATH added bassist Chris Waldron in 1990 and released a live four track demo featuring the songs 'Eyes of Tomorrow', 'Afraid Of Time', 'The Act Of Unspoken Wisdom' and 'Reflecting Pictures'.

In January of 1997 the group, retaining a stable line up but augmenting their sound with the addition of DJ Delta 9 and female vocalist Roxanne, retitled themselves MOTHER GOD MOVIESTAR, opting to pursue an alternative Rock direction.

Quite famously as AFTERMATH the act lost a notable court case with high profile millionaire rapper DR. DRE over the ownership of the name. The Rapper reportedly made a conciliatory offer of some $50,000 for rights to use the name but would go ahead and use it regardless. Fortunately for the band this period of turmoil had built bridges with Interscope Records. After the name change to MOTHER GOD MOVIESTAR they signed to Interscope for the eponymous Electro-Metal debut of March 1998

Albums:

THE EYES OF TOMORROW, Thermometer (1992)
Words That Echo Fear / Eyes Of Tomorrow / Being / Experience / Afraid Of Time / Reflecting Pictures / Change Of Mood / The Act Of Unspoken Wisdom / Whisper Of A Dream / Proud Reflex / Snuff

AFTERSHOK (Pittsburgh, PA, USA)
Line-Up: Vic Hex (vocals), George Mihalovich (guitar), Nick Griska (bass), George B. (drums)

Heavy Metal band founded in 1996 by former SHOK PARIS and BANGER singer Vic Hex. Bass player Nick Griska is ex-NIGHTSTALKER, BANGER and SHOCKWAVE. The band debuted live on October 29th 2000 guesting for TENSION at the Attic venue in Barnesville, Ohio. Later gigs included a landmark show with BREAKER at the Cleveland Odeon Club at which a sampler CD, featuring recordings of 'War Machine' and 'Armed And Dangerous', were distributed to fans.

AFTERSHOK have latterly supported LIZZY BORDEN, DORO, BRITNY FOX, YNGWIE MALMSTEEN, NEVERMORE and SAVATAGE. A self financed album was geared up for release in late 2001.

AGENT STEEL
(Los Angeles, CA, USA)
Line-Up: Bruce Hall (vocals), Juan Garcia (guitar), Bernie Versailles (guitar), Karlos Medina (bass), Rigo Amezcua (drums)

Created by ex-SCEPTRE / ABBATOIR frontman John Cyriis, AGENT STEEL soon forged a reputation for surgically precise intense Metal honed by Cyriis' distinct high altitude vocal range. AGENT STEEL's reputation in the Metal world is also undoubtedly enhanced by the band's Sci-Fi apocalyptic lyrical stance.

The roots of AGENT STEEL lay in the SCEPTRE track 'Taken By Force' contributed to the Metal Blade Record compilation album 'Metal Massacre IV'. The guitarist for SCEPTRE, the Brazilian born John Camps, would capitalize on this exposure with a further three track demo. Camps, renaming himself 'John Syriis' - later 'Cyriis' - auditioned for the position of lead vocalist with ABATTOIR. Cyriis, demonstrating an impressive multi-octave range, secured the position easily.

However, within six months Cyriis was ousted and along with drummer Chuck Profus engineered a new proposition billed as SANCTUARY. This band, rounded out by guitarists Sill Simmons and Mark Marshall with bassist George Robb soon evolved into AGENT STEEL. This inaugural line-up cut the '144,000 Gone' demo in 1984.

AGENT STEEL had a complete switch of guitarists when Marshall and Simmons were ejected. Marshall would later make his mark with SAVAGE GRACE.

John Gott briefly occupied the six string position before ex-ABBATOIR man Juan Garcia and Kurt 'Kiltelt' Colfelt were inducted as permanent members for the groundbreaking 'Skeptics Apocalypse' album. This album would make an immediate impact globally. The leading Thrash Metal journal of the time, Britain's 'Metal Forces' magazine, would see editor Bernard Doe citing 'Skeptics Apocalypse' as one of his favourite albums of the year whilst readers voted Cyriis fourth best Metal vocalist.

The band made their first live appearance opening for SLAYER in September 1984 at the Los Angeles Country Club. A brace of headliners later and AGENT STEEL were invited to open dates for British metallers RAVEN. Colfelt would bow out, later gaining recognition with HOLY TERROR, and in his stead would come the teen protégé of Bernie 'Versaille' Versye. Robb too made his exit in favour of bassist Michael Zaputil.

With Thrash Metal riding a high AGENT STEEL put in a notable show at the infamous Dutch 'Aardschok Dag' festival and toured Europe as support to OVERKILL and ANTHRAX during May of 1986. The band released a highly praised EP the same year titled 'Mad Locust Rising' which featured an extreme cover version of JUDAS PRIEST's 'The Ripper'. The band's media profile would be raised during this period with stories that Cyriis, convinced that a Mayan end times theory was set to signal the end of the world, started to sign his autograph as "2011" - the supposed date of the impending apocalypse. The 'Unstoppable Force' album, produced by Dan Johnson, only served to heighten the band's reputation although critics did note a mellowing of Cyriis' vocal delivery. AGENT STEEL were by now the subject of numerous major label inquiries and in November of 1986 reports leaked out that Capitol Records were showing a serious desire to sign the band. AGENT STEEL showcased successfully for the label but as negotiations dragged on the proposed deal withered.

Garcia quit to form EVIL DEAD with his ex-ABBATOIR colleague bassist Mel Sanchez. Garcia, alongside future TESTAMENT and SLAYER drummer John Dette, would also found the Spanish language Metal band TERROR cutting the Mexican release album 'Hijos De Los Cometas'.

Cyriis and Profus, now relocated to Florida, conducted a European tour by drafting in hired hands. Guitarists JAMES MURPHY and Jay Weslord figuring among their number. Another musician to be included in the AGENT STEEL ranks would be ex-PURGATORY bassist Richard Bateman, added to NASTY SAVAGE in 1989. A decade later Bateman founded AFTER DEATH with ex-MORBID ANGEL / NOCTURNUS / INCUBUS man Mike Browning. (Bateman would later tragically be killed in a car accident).

This variant of AGENT STEEL put in a London Hammersmith Odeon gig supported by NUCLEAR ASSAULT and ONSLAUGHT.

In December 1987 members of AGENT STEEL were arrested in Arizona on charges of aggravated assault on a youth. The bizarre allegations centred upon a 17 year old male (actually a band roadie) the band had allegedly tied to a bed whilst they subsequently urinated on him and exploded firecrackers on his chest. Charges were dropped, but the group folded shortly after following another strange incident in which

Cyriis allegedly tried to force band members to get AGENT STEEL tattoos. Whether the rumours of forced tattooing are true or not are unclear but the fact remains that many of Cyriis' former associates sport AGENT STEEL tattoos!

In 1988 AGENT STEEL officially disbanded. Whilst Cyriis and Profus joined PONTIUS PROPHET, guitarist JAMES MURPHY later joined HALLOWS EVE, DEATH, OBITUARY and CANCER. He would also figure in the ever fluid TESTAMENT line up, record with Danes KONKHRA and release solo product. Cyriis would declare his intention to retire in 1988. Profus would put his efforts into a new venture billed as MALFEITOR in union with ex-PONTIUS PROPHET guitarist Michael Hill. Intriguingly it was soon revealed that MALFEITOR's vocalist 'Max Kobol' was in truth none other than John Cyriis.

Cyriis / Kobol would next be spotted as frontman for Tampa, Florida band LEMEGETON appearing on their 'Evil Against Evil' demo. Cyriis re-emerged in 1990 fronting New York's BLACK REIGN.

AGENT STEEL reformed in 1999 prompted by an offer to perform at the annual German 'Wacken Open Air' festival. German label Century Media would aid their cause by re-issuing their entire back catalogue.

AGENT STEEL's reformation line-up now comprised ex-SYBIL singer Bruce Hall, guitarists Juan Garcia and Bernie Versailles, erstwhile EVIL DEAD bassist Karl Medina and drummer Chuck Profus. Versailles also contributed the ENGINE project album assembled by ARMOURED SAINT's Joey Vera and FATES WARNING's Ray Alder.

The band cut another JUDAS PRIEST track 'Beyond The Realms Of Death' for the Dwell Records tribute album 'Hell Bent For Metal'. This track would also be included as a bonus track on American release versions, on the Metal Blade label, of the band's uncompromisingly intense comeback album 'Omega Conspiracy'.

The band toured Germany in early 2000 on a package bill with RIOT, ANVIL and DOMINE. Cyriis, apparently now going under the title of 'Havlock', resurfaced again in 2000 with a fresh act titled OUTER GATEWAYS.

AGENT STEEL would re-title themselves ORDER OF THE ILLUMINATI for new recording projects in 2001. As such the band laid down a cover of BLACK SABBATH's 'Hole In The Sky' for donation to a tribute album.

The same year would witness the retirement of Profus with Rigo Amezcua taking over the drum stool for the band's appearance at the 'Kalamazoo Metal' festival. Versaille would also find time to act as producer for Death Metal band SADISTIC INTENT.

As 2002 dawned it appeared that the relationship between Cyriis and the ongoing band had had defrosted somewhat with a possibility that the next studio album may emerge under the AGENT STEEL banner after all. In March the band performed the second annual 'Hellfest' event in Whittier, California ranked alongside fellow vets EXODUS.

Albums:
SKEPTICS APOCALYPSE, Roadrunner RR 9759 (1985)
Calling / Taken By Force / Bleed For The Godz / 144'000 Gone / Back To Reign / Agents Of Steel / Evil Eye / Children Of The Sun / Guilty As Charged
MAD LOCUST RISING, Music For Nations KUT124 (1986)
The Swarm Is Upon Us / Mad Locust Rising / The Ripper / Let It Be Done / The Day At Guyana
THE UNSTOPPABLE FORCE, Music For Nations MFN 66 (1987)
Unstoppable Force / Never Surrender / Indestructive / Chosen To Stay / Still Searchin' / Rager / The Day At Guyana / Nothing Left / Traveller
OMEGA CONSPIRACY, Candlelight (1999)
Destroy The Hush / Illuminati Is Machine / Fighting Backwards / New Godz / Know Your Master / Infinity / Awaken the Swarm / Into The Nowhere / Bleed Forever / It's Not What You Think

AGENTZ (Flushing, NY, USA)
Line-Up: Patrick Dubs (vocals), Jason Sabo (guitar), Jose Ferro (bass), Tommy Tindall (keyboards), John Cappadona (drums)

AGENTZ touted a heady combination of raw guitars and scorching keyboards.
Unfortunately, despite some promising reviews for their demo material and later French released debut album, 'Stick To Your Guns', the group split with drummer John Cappadona later joining BEGGARS OPERA. The AGENTZ album is now quite sought after by collectors.

Albums:
STICK TO YOUR GUNS, Dream DRE 18 364 (1987)
Stick To Your Guns / Don't Tread On Me / Time Will Tell / Take A Chance On Love / Bite The Bullet / Fire In My Heart / When The Axe Falls / Waiting In Vain

AGGRESSION (CANADA)
Line-Up: Butcher (vocals), Sasquatch Barth (guitar), Burn (guitar), Dug Bugger (bass), Gate (drums)

Originally formed as ASYLUM in late 1985, this Quebec five piece was based in Montreal. After a four track demo in 1986 and another 5 track demo later that year the band managed to get a track on the Greenworld Records, 'Speed Metal Hell II' compilation and another 2 tracks on the New Renaissance compilation 'Thrash Metal Attack'.
In 1987 Cactus Pete replaced Butcher on vocals and Stephan Prudhomme replaced Gate on drums shortly after. The band recorded a couple of solid albums and, offering little in terms of a unique sound, disbanded shortly after.

Albums:
FORGOTTEN SKELETON, Facemelt (1986)
THE FULL TREATMENT, Banzai (1988)

AGNOSTIC FRONT
(New York, NY, USA)
Line-Up: Roger Miret (vocals), Vinnie Stigma (guitar), Alex Kinon (guitar), Rob Kabula (bass), Joe Montanero (drums)

New York's Crossover legends AGNOSTIC FRONT date back to 1982 and debuted with the heavily Hardcore influenced 'Victim Of Pain' album. Strangely a lot of the lyrical content of this album was the work of CARNIVORE's Pete Steele. The initial recording line-up comprised the heavily tattooed front man Roger Miret, guitarists Vinnie Stigma and Alex Kinon, bassist Rob Kabula and drummer Louie 'Raybeez' Beatto. Guitarist Alex Kinon departed after the release of 1986's 'Cause For Alarm' to have his position filled by ex-NYC MAYHEM guitarist Gordon Ancis. AGNOSTIC FRONT added drummer Joe 'Fish' Montanero at this juncture. Ancis having left to form ZERO HOUR, a short-lived act that also involved ex-WHIPLASH drummer T.J. Scaglione and DEATHRASH bassist Pat Burns.
Vinnie Stigma also quit shortly after but returned to record 'Liberty And Justice' as the band completely re-evolved itself. AGNOSTIC FRONT drafted Alan Peterson bass guitar, drummer Will Sheplar and ex-STRAW DOGS guitarist Steve Martin. However, the album was overshadowed by Miret's imprisonment on drug charges.
AGNOSTIC FRONT added ex-SMEGMA, MAYHEM, YOUTH OF TODAY and REST IN PIECES bassist Craig Setari, coming into the fold after recording of the album on which Alan Peters performs drum duties. Montanero had joined British Punks GBH for their 1992 record 'Church Of The Truly Warped'.

The 1991 album 'One Voice', recorded with guitarist Matt Henderson, has a central theme based on Miret's sojourn in prison.

By late 1992 AGNOSTIC FRONT had splintered yet again. Stigma, Sheplar and Matt soon had MADBALL up and running whilst Miret opted for a day job as a motorbike mechanic. In a surreal twist of fate Miret broke his back within a month, stagediving at a show by his younger brother's band. Eventually Stigma opted out of MADBALL to concentrate on family life.

AGNOSTIC FRONT was drawn together in 1997 quite by coincidence when Miret and Stigma were invited onstage to jam at a MADBALL show. With MADBALL guitarist Hoya handing his guitar over to Miret AGONSTIC FRONT were reunited. Kabula was drawn away from his act AGAINST THE GRAIN for the reunion.

Miret guested on RANCID's 1998 album 'Life Won't Wait' guesting on two tracks. RANCID returned the favour when Tim Armstrong and Lars Fredericksen showed up on AGNOSTIC FRONT's 'Something's Gotta Give' album.

FEAR FACTORY covered 'Your Mistake' for inclusion on their 1998 limited edition 'Revolution' album.

1999 found Miret guesting on the track 'Faster Than The World' on fellow New York Hardcore mongers H2O's 'FTTW' album. The singer also produced the debut album from UNDER THE GUN.

AGNOSTIC FRONT meanwhile released a three track single 'Puro De Madre' all sung in Spanish and their first album for Epitaph 'Something's Gotta Give'.

By 2000 Sheplar had created AMONG THIEVES with erstwhile LIFE OF AGONY bassist Alan Robert and SPUDMONSTERS man Scott Roberts.

Roger Miret turns up with his kin Denise Miret on the 2000 album by LADY LUCK 'Life In Between'.

Singles/EPs:
United Blood, Core (1983)
Puro De Madre, Epitaph 0414-7 (1998)

Albums:
VICTIM IN PAIN, Combat Core 88561-8181-1 (1986)
Victim In Pain / Remind Them / Blind Justice / Last Warning / United And Strong / Hiding Inside / Power / Fascist Attitude / Society Sucker / Your Mistake / With Time
CAUSE FOR ALARM, Rough Justice JUST 3 (1986)
The Eliminator / Existence Of Hate / Time Will Come / Growing Concern / Your Mistake / Out For Blood / Toxic Shock / Bomber Zee /

Public Assistance / Shoot His Load / Liberty And Justice / Crucial Moment / Strength / Genesis / Anthem / Another Side / It Happened Yesterday / Lost Land / Hypocrisy / Crucified / Censored
LIBERTY AND JUSTICE, Rough Justice JUST 8 (1987)
Liberty And Justice / Crucial Moment / Strength / Genesis / Anthem / Another Side / Happened Yesterday / Lost / Hypocrisy / Crucified / Censored
LIVE AT CBGB'S, Combat 3001 (1988)
Victim In Pain / Public Assistance / United Blood / Friend Or Foe / Strength / Blind Justice / Last Warning / Toxic Shock / United And Strong / Crucified / Liberty And Justice / Discriminate Me / Your Mistake / Anthem / With Time / Genesis / Pain Song / Fascist Attitudes / Eliminator
TO BE CONTINUED ... THE VERY BEST OF AGNOSTIC FRONT, Rough Justice JUST 20 (1992)
Victim In Pain / Your Mistake / Hypocrisy / New Jack / Liberty And Justice / Time Will Come / Power / Society Sucker / Toxic Shock / Public Assistance / Blind Justice / The Eliminator / One Voice / Crucified / United And Strong / Your Mistake / Fascist Attitudes (Live) / Anthem (Live) / Last Warning (Live)
ONE VOICE, Relativity RO 9222 (1992)
New Jack / One Voice / Infiltrate / The Tombs / The Fall / My Faith / Undertow / Now And Then / Todd's Song / Retaliate / Forcefeed / Bastard
LAST WARNING - LIVE, Roadrunner RR 90782 (1993)
Undertow / Your Mistake / Victim In Pain / One Voice / Infiltrate / Strength / United Blood / Public Assistance / Over The Edge / Blind Justice / Last Warning / Crucified / Toxic Shock / United And Strong / Fascist Attitudes / Anthem / The Eliminator / No One Rules / Final War / Last Warning / Traitor / Friend Or Foe / United Blood / Fight / Discriminate / In Control / Crucial Changes
RAW UNRELEASED, Grand Theft Auto GTA 002R051 (1995)
SOMETHING'S GOTTA GIVE, Epitaph 65362 (1998)
Something's Gotta Give / Believe / Gotta Go / Before My Eyes / No Fear / Blinded / Voices / Do Or Die / My War / Bloodsucker / Blame / Today, Tomorrow, Forever / Rage / Pauly The Dog / Crucified
RIOT RIOT UPSTART, Epitaph (1999)

AGONY (SWEDEN)
Line-Up: Peter Lündstrom (vocals), Magnus Sjölin (guitar), Conny Wigström (guitar), Polo Ström (guitar), Nappe Benschemsi (bass), Tommy Moberg (drums)

A Stockholm act originating in August 1984 when their Punk influences prevailed, the group was originally titled AGONI and found themselves going in a more Thrash Metal oriented direction following the addition of drummer Tommy Moburg and guitarist Magnus Sjölin.

The group, still spelling the name AGONI, toured in Britain with Swedish Punk outfit ANTI CIMEX in June and July 1986 having released the 'The Future Is Ours' demo the previous March.

Following a second demo, 'Execution Of Mankind' (August 1986), AGONY obtained a deal with Music For Nations in 1987.

Although the debut album, 'The First Defiance', was recorded with two guitarists, Pelle Ström was fired before Christmas 1987 and was to later join KRIXJÄLTERS, OMNITRON and COMECON. After AGONY broke up Tommy Moberg joined RUBBERMEN.

Albums:
THE FIRST DEFIANCE, Under One Flag (1988)
Storm Of The Apocalypse / The First Defiance / Execution Of Mankind / Mass Manipulation / Night Of The Emperor / Shadows Of Fear / Madness Reigns / Deadly Legacy

AGONY COLUMN (TX, USA)
Line-Up: Richie Turner (vocals), Stuart Lawrence (guitar), Pawl Willis (bass), Charlie Brownell (drums)

Texan 'Hillbilly' Thrash! The 'Way Back In The Woods' album features Billy Dansfiell on bass

Singles/EPs:
Comes Alive EP - Live, Big Chief (1990)

Albums:
GOD, GUNS AND GUTS, Big Chief (1989)
God, Guns And Guts / Snakebite / 4X4 / Vicious Pack Of Lies / Fiendish Plots / 66 Six Guns / Cars, Sex And Violence / Walk The Night / Scarred For Life / Blackjack / Dead By Dawn / Bag O' Bones
BRAVE WORDS AND BLOODY KNUCKLES, Metal Blade 26460 (1991)
Brave Words And Bloody Knuckles / Angel Of Def / Lord Almighty / Ultraviolet Rays / Bayou Road / No Time To Kill / Crime And Punishment / Big Two Hearted Sammy / Hellbilly Blues / Rain Comes Down / Suppertime / Hole To Hell / Mississippi Queen
WAY BACK IN THE WOODS, No Bull 34174-2 (1996)

The Spirit Rises / Way Back In The Woods / Flying Sorceress / Obey The Command / The Night Has 1000 Eyes / Silver Spoon / Whiskey Bottle / Collywog / Small Black Toad / When The Dark Clouds Return / The Devils Carnival

AGRESSOR (FRANCE)
Line-Up: Alex Colin-Tocquaine (vocals / guitar), Thierry (bass), Laurent (drums)

Antibes Thrash Metal trio that recorded their first demo in November 1986, AGRESSOR released a couple more demos and played dates with APOCALYPSE and LIVING DEATH. The band signed to Black Mark for one album, subtly titled 'Satan's Sodomy', graced with an album cover showing the immediate after effects of buggery with the devil!

AGRESSOR's line-up at this juncture was as a trio of vocalist / guitarist Alex Colin-Tocquaine, bassist J.M. Libeer and drummer Jean Luc Falsini. This incarnation recorded the first two demos 'Merciless Onslaught' and 'Satan's Sodomy'.

Things swiftly changed for the group when AGRESSOR added new drummer Thierry and ex-HELLRAISER bassist Laurent in 1988.

The group then signed to Noise, recording 'Neverending Destiny', after which both new men split leaving Alex Colin-Tocquaine to soldier on alone! Thierry joined LOUDBLAST. Undaunted, Alex put together a brand new line-up of his band, thus the 1992 version of AGRESSOR (which recorded the 'Towards Beyond' album) consisted of Colin-Tocquaine, ex-OUTBURST guitarist Patrick Gibelin, ex-OUTBURST bassist Joel Guigon and ex-DEATHPOWER drummer Stephan Gwegwam.

Gibelin had quit by the time AGRESSOR returned to the studio to cut the ensuing 'Symposium Of Rebirth' album, his place being taken by new guitarist Manu Ragot. The TERRORISER cover track 'After World Obliteration', incidentally, features a guest vocal performance from NAPALM DEATH's Barney Greenaway.

AGRESSOR toured as guests to CRADLE OF FILTH on their British tour of June 1996. The band returned to the studio for the 'Medieval Rites' album. Employing a vast array of traditional instrumentation the multi-faceted release would see both Krell and Christina from Norwegians BLOODTHORN guesting. Also donating their services would be former MERCYFUL FATE drummer Morten Neilsen, ROTTEN SOUND and ENOCHIAN CRESCENT drummer Kai Hahto and the journeyman Death Metal guitarist

JAMES MURPHY.
November of 1999 found AGRESSOR on the road in Europe on a package billing in collusion with BLOODTHORN and Finns AND OCEANS. The line up for these shows would see Colin-Tocquaine and Guigon joined by WITCHES guitarist Bernard Queral and Kai Hahto on drums.

Colin-Tocquaine would also session for touring purposes with American occult ancestral Metal act ABSU.

Albums:
LICENSED TO THRASH, New Wave 024 (1987) (Split LP with LOUDBLAST)
Satan's Sodomy / Brainstorm / Bloodfeast / Uncontrolled Desire / Black Church / It's Pandemonium
SATAN'S SODOMY, Black Mark BMCD 36 (1987)
Satan's Sodomy / Brainstorm / Blood Feast / Uncontrolled Desire / Black Church / It's Pandemonium
NEVERENDINGDESTINY, Black Mark (1990)
Paralytic Disease / The Unknown Spell / Element Decay / Voices From Below / Blood Feast / Neverending Destiny / Prince Of Fire / Dark Power / The Arrival / Brainstorm / Bloody Corps
TOWARDS BEYOND, Black Mark BMCD 23 (1992)
Intro / Primeval Transubtantion / The Fortress / Positionic Showering / Antediluvian / Epileptic Alra / Hyaldid / The Crypt / Future Past- Eldest Things / Turkish March
SYMPOSIUM OF REBIRTH, Black Mark BMCD 55 (1994)
Barabas / Rebirth / Negative Zone / Apocalyptic Prophecies / Erga Meam Salutem / Overloaded / Theology / Civilization / Wheel Of Pain / Abhuman Dreadnought / Torture / Dor Fin-I-Guinar / After World Obliteration
MEDIEVAL RITES, Season Of Mist (1999)
Medieval Rites / Bloodshed / The Woodguy vs. The Black Beast / The Sorcerer / Spirit Of Evil / Wandering Soul / Tye-Melane Melda / God From The Sky / Welcome Home / Ondolinde / Burial Desecration / Tribal Dance / At Night

AIRDASH (FINLAND)
Line-Up: Juha Laine (vocals), Roope Siren (guitar), Tommy Dolivo (guitar), Kirka Sainio (bass), Ykä (drums)

Speed Metal act AIRDASH has supported both SUICIDAL TENDENCIES and ANTHRAX in their home country. Prior to the release of third album 'Both Ends Of The Path' original guitarist Nirri was replaced by Tommy Dolivio. Both Nirri and Roope Siren subsequently joined STONE.

In later years Siren would make his mark with SUB-URBAN TRIBE and with Power Metal band SINERGY. Bassist Kirka Sainio would team up with GANDALF for their 1995 demo session 'The Cradle'.

Singles/EPs:
Vengeance Through Violence / Blow Under The Belt / Cable Terror, Diablo NADAX 1 (1989) ('Vengeance Through Violence' EP)

Albums:
THANK GOD IT'S MONDAY, Diablo (1989)
Give Up / Helluva Noise / Another Day / White Lies / Spit Your Guts / Without It / Reaper / Thank God It's Monday / Eat Shit
HOSPITAL HALLUCINATIONS TAKE ONE, RCA PL74586 (1990)
If.. / Youth Hostel (Burial Side) / Jungle Jim / Decent Citizen / Vengeance Through Violence (No Bullshit) / Trigger Happy / Forbidden Thoughts / Sleepwalk
BOTH ENDS OF THE PATH, Black Mark BMCD 14 (1991)
Liquid Bliss / Hollow Men / Savage Ritual / So It Goes / Soul Of A Renegade / Silent Wall / Deeper Shades / Letter Of Indulgence / Choking Child / View / Take A Look At Me / Got No Blues

AIRWOLF (GERMANY)
Line-Up: Frank Zellmann (vocals / guitar), Guido Braun (guitar), Andreas Rohschak (bass), Thomas Alkamper (drums)

AIRWOLF follow true to expected form in the fine traditions set by fellow Teutonic Speed Metal bands.

Albums:
VICTORY BELLS, Powerline 807305-938 (1988)
Legion Of Doom / Through The Fire / Swordbreaker / Death Metal Rain / Victory Bells / Starfire / (Take Off) Atlantis / Schizomania

AKILLA (USA)

Albums:
THE CURSE, Akilla (1987)
AS FOR ME AS FOR YOU, Undamaged (1988)

ALASTOR (PORTUGAL)

Not to be confused with the Polish Death

Metal and Costa Rican Black Metal outfits sharing the same name. These Lusitanians, signed to the German Barbarian Wrath label, deliver retro Thrash inspired music with Black lyrical overtones.

ALASTOR made their entrance with the 'Gates Of Darkness' album, a split affair with DECAYED. A deal was scored with the Swedish label Iron Fist Productions for the 'Crushing Christendom' opus but never concluded. The album subsequently arrived courtesy of Barbarian Wrath.

The December 2001 album 'Hellward' was not only notable for including a cover version IRON ANGEL's 'Sinner' but for reputedly being the very first Black Metal record with Portuguese lyrics.

Albums:
GATES OF DARKNESS, (1996) (Split album with DECAYED)
Through The Gates / Sacrifice To Satan / Hell On Earth / No Exorcism / Bestial Wrath Of The Antichrist / Possessed By Darkness / Children Of The Grave
CRUSHING CHRISTENDOM, Barbarian Wrath WRATH666-004 (2000)
The Return Of Alastor / Spawn Of Evil / Infernal Power / Witch Hammer / Necronomicunt / The Fall Of God / Total Devastation / Black Mass / Power Thrashing Death
HELLWARD, Barbarian Wrath WRATH666-014 (2001)
Para O Mundo Inferior / Ataque Final Do Inferno / Rainha Dos Mortos / Demonios Antigos / Sacrificio Em Golgota / Serva De Satanas / (Metal) Blasfemia Eterna / Sinner

ALLEGIENCE (AUSTRALIA)
Line-Up: Conrad Higson (vocals), Tony Campo (guitar), Jason Stone (guitar), Dave Harrison (bass), Glenn Butcher (drums)

Aggressive Perth Metal band created in 1990. ALLEGIENCE, featuring ex-INFA RED / INQUISITION bassist Dave Harrison, originally saw John Mihos behind the microphone but when he quit drummer Conrad Higson took over lead vocals and his drum stool was occupied by Glenn Butcher. ALLEGIENCE built up an enviable live reputation in Australia backed with a succession of demos 'Make The Pledge', 'Torn Between Two Worlds' and 'Studio Live'. ALLEGIENCE also contributed the cut 'Morally Justified' to the Roadrunner 1993 compilation 'Redrum'.

ALLEGIENCE caught the eye of ex-JUDAS PRIEST vocalist ROB HALFORD who duly signed them to his E.M.A.S. Management organization. This union resulted in a deal with major label Polygram and ALLEGIENCE bowed in proper with the 1994 'Destitution' album.

ALLEGIENCE supported KREATOR, FEAR FACTORY, Rob Halford's FIGHT and MORBID ANGEL in support of the record. Although a second album 'Skinman' received excellent reviews ALLEGIENCE found themselves labelless soon after. A live album 'Time To React' marked their end of passage. Harrision founded BLACK STEEL.

Albums:
DESTITUTION, Polygram (1994)
Intro / Chaos Dies / One Step Beyond / Hate Frenzy / Torn Between Two Worlds / Destitution / Morally Justified / Pack Of Lies / Dealt The Cruel Hands / Downward Spiral / Twisted Minds / Tranquility
TIME TO REACT - LIVE, Polygram (1995)
Chaos Dies / Pity / Trapped Behind A Shadow / Hate Frenzy / Time To React / Taken By Force / Torn Between Two Worlds / One Step Beyond / Downward Spiral
SKINMAN, Polygram (1996)
Ripped To Shreds / Face Reality / Give Yourself / Scorn / Time To React / Trapped Behind A Shadow / Wasted Life / Taken By Force / Pity / Hands Of Fate

ALLEGIANCE (SWEDEN)
Line-Up: Bogge (vocals / guitar), Pära (guitar), Mickael Almgren (bass), Fredrik Andersson (drums)

ALLEGIANCE, founded in 1989, ply old style trad Thrash on their debut demo 'Sick World'. The band had got decidedly more brutal by second attempt the aptly named 'Eternal Hate'. The band shifted direction undergoing a radical line-up shuffle to emerge as out and out Black Metal merchants on their third tape 'Odin Äge Er Alle'. A fourth stab at the demo scene with 1994's 'Hafdingadrapa' pursued more Viking Metal leanings.

Drummer Frederik Andersson of ALLEGIANCE also has an interest in premier Black Metal act MARDUK.

Albums:
HYMN TILLHANGAGUD, No Fashion NFR 014 (1996)
Höfdingadrapa / De Nordiska Lagren / The Third Raven / Himmelen Rämnar / Den Krisnes Död / The March Of Warlike Damned / Stridsärd / Spjutsängen
BLODÖRNSOFFER, No Fashion NFR021 (1997)
Intag / Med Svard I Hand / Likbal / En Svunnen Tid / Heimdal / Yggdrasil / Korpen

Skall Leda Oss / Blodornsoffer / Blot / Uttag
VREDE, No Fashion NFR031 (1998)
Hofdingadrapa / De Nordiska Lagren / The
Third Raven / Himmlen Rämnar / Den
Kristnes Död / The March Of Warlike
Damned / Stridsfard / Spjutsangen

ALLIGATOR (ITALY)
Line-Up: Gianluca Melino (vocals),
Francesco Capasso (guitar), Tiziano Colombi
(guitar), Dario Zanaboni (bass), Andrea
Bellazzi (drums)

Northern Italian Thrash Metal act founded in
1988. The band, heavily influenced by Bay
Area Thrash, debuted with a 1990 demo 'Bog
Of Horrors'.

Albums:
CEREBRAL IMPLOSION, Last Scream
SCREAM003CD (1994)
Cerebral Implosion / Beyond The Reach Of
Fate / The Cage / Decimation / Help /
Lullaby For The Unborn / Skeleton's Beach /
Tarantula / Drinking Milk From My Knees /
Fetching Fear / Natural Dreams
RULES, Last Scream (1996)

AMAYMON (FRANCE)
Line-Up: Sebastien (vocals / guitar), Christian
Bivel (guitar), Vincent (bass), Fred (drums)

AMAYMON is the Thrash Metal band of
Adipocere label boss Christian Bivel. The
album was a split affair with Canadians
PURULENCE.

Albums:
AMAYMON, Adipocere AR016 (1993) (Split
CD with PURULENCE)
Intro / Buried And Forgotten / Evil Prevails /
The Rapture / Shemhamphorash / The Goetic
Belief

AMEBIX (UK)
Line-Up: The Baron (vocals / bass), Stig Da
Pig (guitar), A. Droid (keyboards), Spider
Arachno Blaster (drums)

AMEBIX offered up Thrash Metal with heavy
doses of caustic Punk rawness. The band, led
by vocalist / bassist The Baron and guitarist
Stig Da Pig, formed at the tail end of 1978
originally dubbed THE BAND WITH NO
NAME. One of these formative tracks,
'University Challenged', turned up on the
renowned compilation album 'Bullshit
Detctor 1'.
A series of line up fluxes eventually saw
keyboard player Norman being enrolled in
1981 as the group relocated to Bristol.

Another inductee would be drummer Virus
from local act DISORDER and in this
incarnation AMEBIX signed to Spiderleg
Records issuing three EPs.
More line up changes saw AMEBIX making
do as a trio for a tour of Italy before the
quickfire changes in the keyboard department
settled when George came in during
November of 1984 for dates in Holland.
Spider Arachno Blaster took the drum mantle
from Virus as AMEBIX signed to Alternative
Tentacles for the 1985 album 'Arise'.
Sophomore effort 'Monolith' arrived on the
Wolverhampton Heavy Metal label but the
band folded in late 1987. Spider, George and
Stig stuck together to forge ZYGOTE. In later
years Spider would be found in
MUCKSPREADER. According to reports The
Baron lives on the Isle of Skye manufacturing
swords!
In 2002 Canadian Black Metal band
MEGIDDO delivered tribute by covering 'Last
Will And Testament' on a split 7" single on the
German Iron Bonehead label.

Singles/EPs:
Who's The Enemy? / Carnage, Spiderleg
SDL 6 (1982)
Winter / Beginning Of The End, Spiderleg
SDL 10 (1983)

Albums:
NO SANCTUARY, Spiderleg SDL14 (1983)
ARISE, Alternative Tentacles VIRUS 46
(1984)
The Moor / Axeman / Fear Of God / Largactyl
/ Drink And Be Merry / Spoils Of Victory /
Arise! / Slave / The Darkest Hour
MONOLITH, Heavy Metal HMR99 (1987)
Monolith / Nobody's Driving / The Power
Remains / Time Bomb / Last Will And
Testament / ICBM / Chain Reaction / Fallen
From Grace / Coming Home

AMNESIA (UK)
Line-Up: Simon Rose (vocals), Clive Heeley
(guitar), Simon Fairhurst (guitar), Matt Foster
(bass), Michael Vincent (drums)

A Melodic Thrash band formed in Barnsley
during 1988 with ex SACRAMENT vocalist
Simon Rose joining in 1990.
Prior to the release of the debut album
AMNESIA supported TORANAGA,
SLAMMER and XENTRIX. The 'Unknown
Entity' album was recorded in a mere nine
days and produced by TORANAGA guitarist
Andy Mitchell.
In 1991 the band supported both METAL
CHURCH and SABBAT.

Albums:
UNKNOWN ENTITY, Major WADES 3 (1991)
Solution / Memories Of Me / Final Revelation / Epitaph / Unknown Entity / No More Tomorrow / One Below Zero / Perish

AMULANCE (IL, USA)
Line-Up: Rik Baez (vocals), Vince Varriale (guitar), Bob Luman (guitar), Tom Braddish (bass), Kent Wagner (drums)

A self styled "Bash Metal" outfit out of Aurora, Illinois. The band was convened during the early '80s, citing a line up of founder and guitarist Bob Luman, vocalist Rik Baez, bassist Tom Braddish and drummer Eric Wedow. Adding second guitar player Vince Varriale in January of 1986 AMULANCE issued a six track demo 'The Rage Within' to positive response. An album, 'Feel The Pain' on New Renaissance Records, followed before Wedow departed. His place would be taken by Tony 'T-Bone' DiVozzo. However, AMULANCE had folded by 1989.
DiVozzo would later join DARKLIN REACH for the 'Where Evil Dwells' album and later BLACK CUNTRY ROCK.

Singles/EPs:
Holocaust, New Renaissance (1989) (Promotion)

Albums:
FEEL THE PAIN, New Renaissance NRR56 (1989)
Holocaust / Schizophrenia / Violent Victory / Witch's Sin / Feel The Pain / Black Moon Rising / Shark Attack / Death Wish / 7th Son

ANACRUSIS (St. Charles, MO, USA)
Line-Up: Ken Nardi (vocals / guitar), Kevin Heidbreder (guitar), John Emery (bass), Mike Owen (drums)

Highly rated ANACRUSIS date from 1984 and are based in St. Louis, Missouri. Frontman Ken Nardi had previously operated with HEAVEN'S FLAME. ANACRUSIS debuted with the 1987 'Annihilation Complete' demo. Featured a track on the Metal Forces magazine compilation 'Demolition' in 1988.
The band would record the inaugural 'Suffering Hour' album self financing it to the tune of $1200. The European Axis label, headed by 'Metal Forces' magazine editor Bernard Doe, would be quick to snap the band up.
1989's 'Reason' would be issued on the Active imprint, actually an evolvement of the Axis concern. However, an American issue licensed to Metal Blade witnessed completely different artwork. Touring in the States found ANACRUSIS as openers to DIRTY ROTTEN IMBECILES.
As the band signed to the Metal Blade concern on a global basis for the 'Manic Impressions' outing drummer Mike Owen was superseded by Chad Smith for the 'Manic Impressions' album. Promotion included a 38 date American tour in the Autumn of 1991 third on the bill to GALACTIC COWBOYS and OVERKILL. The group would then secure further supports stepping up to larger venues with MEGADETH.
The fourth and final ANACRUSIS effort 'Screams And Whispers' would herald another change on the drum stool with Paul Miles taking on duties.

Albums:
SUFFERING HOUR, Axis LP4 (1988)
Present Tense / Imprisoned / ROT / Butcher's Block / A World To Gain / Frigid Bitch / Fighting Evil / Twisted Cross / Annihilation Complete / Disemboweled
REASON, Active ATV9 (1989)
Stop Me / Terrified / Not Forgotten / Wrong / Silent Crime / Misshapen Intent / Afraid To Feel / Child Inside / Vital / Quick To Doubt / Killing My Mind / Injustice
MANIC IMPRESSIONS, Metal Blade ZORRO23 (1990)
Paint A Picture / I Love The World / Something Real / Dream Again / Explained Away / Still Black / What You Became / Our Reunion / Idle Hours / Far Too Long
SCREAMS AND WHISPERS, Metal Blade ZORRO59 (1991)
Sound The Alarm / Sense Of Will / Too Many Prophets / Release / Division / Tools Of Separation / Grateful / A Screaming Breath / My Soul's Affliction / Driven / Brotherhood? / Release

ANATA (SWEDEN)
Line-Up: Fredrik Schälin (vocals / guitar), Andreas Allenmark (guitar), Henrik Drake (bass), Robert Petersson (drums)

Varberg act ANATA began life as a Thrash / Crossover quartet boon soon evolved into a fully fledged lethal Death Metal machine. The band started life in 1993 comprising vocalist / guitarist Fredrik Schälin, guitarist Matthias Svensson, bass player Martin Sjöstrand and drummer Robert Petersson. ANATA released the 1996 demo session 'Bury Forever The Garden Of Lie'.
During 1996 both Svensson and Sjöstrand bade their farewell and new recruits guitarist Andreas Allenmark and bass player Henrik Drake were welcomed into the fold for the

1997 demo 'Vast Lands Of My Infernal Dominion'. ANATA signed with French label Season Of Mist for the debut album 'The Infernal Depths Of Hatred'.

ANATA's second effort formed part of the Seasons Of Mist 'War' series pitching the band up against BETHZAIDA. The band covered BETHZAIDA's 'The Tranquility Of Your Last Breath' and MORBID ANGEL's 'Day Of Suffering' whilst BETHZAIDA reciprocated with their take on ANATA's 'Under Azure Skies'.

ANATA pulled in former ETERNAL LIES drummer Conny Petersson during early 2001.

Albums:
THE INFERNAL DEPTHS OF HATRED,
Seasons Of Mist (1998)
Released When You Are Dead / Let The Heavens Hate / Under Azure Skies / Vast Lands Infernal Gates / Slain Upon His Altar / Those Who Lick The Wounds Of Christ / Dethroned The Hypocrites / Aim Not At The Kingdom High
WAR VOLUME III: VS. BETHZAIDA,
Seasons Of Mist (1999) (Split album with BETHZAIDA)
Let Me Become Your Fallen Messiah / With Me You Shall Fall / Day Of Suffering / The Tranquility Of Your Last Breath
DREAMS OF DEATH AND DISMAY,
Seasons Of Mist (2001)
Die Laughing / Faith, Hope, Self Deception / God Of Death / Metamorphosis By The Well Of Truth / Dreamon / Can't Kill What's Already Dead / Insurrection / The Enigma Of Number Three / Drain Of Blood / The Temple - Erratic

ANDRALLS BRAZIL)
Line-Up: Alex Coelho (vocals / guitar), Denis Di Lallo (guitar), Eddie C. (bass), Alexandre Brito (drums)

Sao Paul retro Thrashers forged in 1998. Original drummer Junior was replaced by Alexandre Brito in July of 2000. ANDRALLS, so called after a building disaster in the city during 1972, self-financed their September 2000 album 'Massacre, Corruption, Destruction', subsequently landing a distribution deal with Century Media.

During 2001 ANDRALLS scored the valuable support slot to JUDAS PRIEST's Rio De Janeiro and Sao Paulo shows.

Albums:
MASSACRE, CORRUPTION, DESTRCTION, Andralls (2000)
Hate / Chaotic World / Shadows In The Mirror / The Future Of Life / Andralls On Fire

/ No Chance To Escape / Behind The Light / Fury In Your Eyes / Lady Death / The Truth

ANESTHESY (BELGIUM)
Line-Up: Frank Libeert (vocals / guitar), Werner Vanlaere (guitar), Chris Decaesteker (bass), Diego Denorme (drums)

A Thrash Metal act with distinct Death overtones dating to 1986 and formed by ex-VENDETTA guitarist Frank "Liberty" Libeert, ANESTHESY debuted with their 'Seasons Of The Witch' demo. A further demo tape 'Overdose', released in 1989, led to a deal with English label C.M.F.T. Unfortunately, after recording their debut album the record label went bust and the tracks seemed destined to remain unreleased.

Undeterred, ANESTHESY re-recorded some of these songs, releasing them as the self financed 'Just Married' EP in 1991. The band would lose their original drummer Ringo around this juncture pulling in Diego Denorme as replacement. Soon after the release of 'Just Married' ANESTHESY would also induct bassist Chris Decaessteker then second guitarist Werner Vanlaere into the fold.

Further recordings were submitted to the Tessa Records compilation 'Demolition' which led in turn to an album deal with the Black Mark label. Recording of the 1994 'Exaltation Of The Eclipse' record would take its toll on the band though witnessing the departure of Decaesteker. A substitute was duly located in Stefaan Vanijzere.

Tragedy would strike the band on the 15th of July 1994. A horrific car crash would injure Vanijzere and kill Libeert. The remaining members vowed to continue and built the band back up to strength with the addition of singer Sven Houfflijn and guitarist David Vandewalle.

This unit prepared the way for their next release 'The Fifth Season' but would be disappointed to find Black Mark failing to renew their option. Vanlaere broke ranks to be replaced by Guy Commeene. Shortly after Vandewalle bade farewell too. His position would be taken by Jason Masschelein and this variant of ANESTHESY eventually committed 'The Fifth Season' to tape for new label Midas Productions.

The group would capitalize on this release by self financing a third effort 1999's 'Let The Mayhem Begin'. Wouter Nottebaert would now assume bass duties and with the recordings completed Reiner Schenk usurped Masschelein.

ANESTHESY have, in their time, supported the likes of NAPALM DEATH, KREATOR, GOREFEST and MORGOTH.

19

Albums:
JUST MARRIED, Anesthesy (1991)
Ace Of Death / Inflammation Of The Bowels /
The Ballad Of Jimmy F. / Rerisin' Humanist /
Desbelieve / Just Married
EXALTATION OF THE ECLIPSE, Black
Mark BMCD 54 (1994)
Primal Exaltation / Beyond Sadness / The
Defector / Guardian / Survival Of The Fittest
/ Intestinal Haemorrahage / The Change /
The Ultimate Reincarnatior / Enstrangled
Minds / The Sun, The Red, The Blood /
Eclipticus Finale Exclinatum
THE FIFTH SEASON, Midas Productions
(1998)
Black Soul / Tears Of A Mortal / Cruelty /
Brutal Expressions / Forgotten Epitaph /
Across The Burning Fields / Retribution /
Those Left Behind / Perishable
Considerations
LET THE MAYHEM BEGIN, Anesthesy
(1999)
Introduction / The Pain I Hide / Darknight
Slaughter / The Chaos Path / The Final
Sleep / Forever Silent / A Walk Through
Infinity / The Last Straw

ANGEL BEAST (CANADA)
Line-Up: Tim Landon (vocals), Curtis
Vaselenak (guitar), Craig French, (bass),
Steve B. (drums)

This little known, yet competent Toronto
Thrash band churned out two or three
independent releases and even managed to
produce a low budget video.

Singles/EPs:
Dead Child's Eyes, / It's Insane, / Fleshy
Eye, Metal Rage (1990) ('In The Meantime'
EP)

ANGEL DUST (GERMANY)
Line-Up: Dirk Thurisch (vocals), Bernd
Aufermann (guitar), Frank Banx (bass),
Steven Banx (keyboards), Dirk Assmuth
(drums)

Dortmund's ANGEL DUST have proven to be
stoic Thrash flagbearers since their inception
in 1984. The band has made no less than
three reunion attempts, all more successful
than the last. Enduring numerous line-up
changes, ANGEL DUST have stuck to their
guns, watching musical trends come and go.
With the close of the millennium ANGEL
DUST are still reaching out to an ever
appreciative and growing international
fanbase.

ANGELDUST, founded by bass player Frank
Banx and drummer Dirk Assmuth, created

ripples outside of Germany with their
uncompromising Speed Metal debut album
'Into The Dark Past'. The record would sell
over 30,000 copies in Germany alone.
However, the band were never totally capable
of promoting the product other than a few
European gigs as guitarists Andreas Lohrum
and Romme Keymer were committed to their
homeland's military service.

ANGEL DUST folded in November 1989, only
to be resurrected by Coe, Banx and Assmuth
with two new guitarists Vinni Lynn and Stefan
K. Nauer. The ensuing 'To Dust You Will
Decay' album being produced by the highly
regarded veteran Kit Woolven.

Vocalist S.L. Coe later joined SCANNERS
and REACTOR. He was later to issue a
creditable solo album in 2000 titled 'Metal'.

Banx meantime joined Speed Metal band
CROWS in 1991 alongside the future
SODOM duo of guitarist Bernd Kost and
drummer Bobby Schottkowski together with
SCANNER's Leczek Szpigiel. The CROWS
issued the Century Media album 'The Dying
Race' but folded in 1993.

1998 saw the reformation of ANGEL DUST
with the 'Border Of Reality' album for new
label Century Media. Joining Banx was his
sibling Steven on keyboards, vocalist /
guitarist Dirk Thurisch and guitarist Bernd
Aufermann.

ANGEL DUST toured Europe in the Spring of
1998 on a package bill with OVERKILL,
NOCTURNAL RITES and NEVERMORE. A
later jaunt found the band sharing European
stages with JAGPANZER and the comeback
was completed with appearances at the
'Wacken Open Air' and 'Rock Hard' festivals.

The 'Bleed' album, produced by Siggi Bemm
and crafted in less than three weeks, would
spread word of ANGEL DUST's resurrection
globally. American variants of the album
would come complete with differing artwork
and no less than three bonus tracks.

ANGEL DUST, marking their growing
maturity, issued the 2000 album 'Enlighten
The Darkness'. Touring in September to
promote the release had the band as part of
a package billing in Europe alongside STEEL
PROPHET, LEFAY and STORMHAMMER.
The following month founder member Dirk
Assmuth announced his departure as the
band inducted former HOUSE OF SPIRITS
man Michael Sticken for live work.

In November ANGEL DUST retired to the
recording studio to commit to tape tracks for
tribute albums, namely 'Believe' by
SAVATAGE and URIAH HEEP's seminal
'Easy Livin'. Thurisch would also find time to
guest on the GB ARTS album 'The Lake'.

Aufermann would find his services requested
by DEMONS & WIZARDS for live work but

turned this offer down. In June of 2001 as the guitarist busied himself with a solo side project dubbed THE SHINING he would find himself ejected from the band. Ironically his quickfire replacement would be none other than DEMONS & WIZARDS touring guitarist Ritchie Wilkinson. Assmuth would also be welcomed back into the fold as ANGEL DUST got to grips with their debut American shows billed alongside NEVERMORE, OPETH and GOD FORBID.

ANGEL DUST would perform at the 2001 'ProgPower' festival utilising drummer Nick Seelinger of Colorado act SILENCER as stand in. The 2002 album 'Of Human Bondage' would surprisingly include a cover of the SEAL tune 'Killer'.

Albums:
INTO THE DARK PAST, Disaster 10004 (1987)
Into The Dark Past / I'll Come Back / Legions Of Destruction / Gambler / Fighters Return / Atomic Roar / Victims Of Madness / Marching For Revenge
TO DUST YOU WILL DECAY, Disaster 10008 (1988)
Third Challenge / Mr. Inferno / Wings Of An Angel / Into The Dark Past (Chapter II) / The King / To Dust You Will Decay / Stranger / The Duel / Hold On
BORDER OF REALITY, Century Media CD 77220-2 (1998)
Border Of Reality / No More Faith / Nightmare / Centuries / When I Die / Where The Wind Blows / Spotlight Kid / Behind The Mirror / Coming Home
BLEED, Century Media (1999)
Bleed / Black Rain / Never / Follow Me (Part I) / Follow Me (Part II) / Addicted To Serenity / Surrender / Sanity / Liquid Angel
ENLIGHTEN THE DARKNESS, Century Media (2000)
Let Me Live / The One You Are / Enjoy! / Fly Away / Come Into Resistance / Beneath The Silence / Still I'm Bleeding / I Need You / First In Line / Cross of Hatred / Oceans Of Tomorrow
OF HUMAN BONDAGE, Century Media (2002)
The Human Bondage / Inhuman / Unreal Soul / Disbeliever / Last Forever / Unite / Got This Evil / The Cultman / Freedom Awaits / Killer

ANGELWITCH (UK)
Line-Up: Kevin Heybourne (vocals / guitar), Kevin Riddles (bass), Dave Dufort (drums)

A band that generated a cult following among the Metalheads of the American West coast based upon the occult overtones and marked speed and heaviness of their original album recorded with drummer Dave Hogg. ANGELWITCH were founded in 1977 by guitarist Kevin Heybourne. Originally titled LUCIFER, Heybourne switched to ANGELWITCH when he heard of another LUCIFER doing the rounds. The band went through numerous line-ups before the classic power trio.

The band's official debut on record was the cut 'Baphomet' on the now legendary 'Metal For Muthas' compilation in early 1980. ANGELWITCH also submitted a track 'Extermination Day' to the 1980 BBC compilation album 'Metal Explosion'. Sadly, Hogg was found to be suffering from leukemia necessitating Ex-E.F. BAND drummer Dave Dufort stepping in as replacement after the album's release.

Dufort actually has a lengthy history in rock n' roll being an ex-member of 1965's THE VOICE, THE SCENERY and PAPER BLITZ ISSUE. All of these mid '60s acts featured latter day SAVOY BROWN, DOG SOLDIER and CHICKENSHACK guitarist MILLER ANDERSON. Dufort then moved on to EAST OF EDEN in the late '60s (he appears on the 1969 album 'Mercator Projected'), as well as being a member of KEVIN AYERS band.

At the height of their popularity ANGELWITCH ranked alongside IRON MAIDEN and SAXON at the forefront of the NWoBHM. The band's success was relatively short lived though, as gigs became few and far between. British shows were limited to London Marquee appearances and one off events, whilst the only date abroad was at the East German Erfurt Festival.

At one point Polydor were due to release a live album culled from a 1982 show, but this never surfaced. The original band split after the debut with Riddles and Dufort going on to form TYTAN. Riddles was last spotted in a covers band with ex-ONSLAUGHT, TORINO and HIGHWIRE vocalist Tony O'Hora.

The beginning of 1982 saw Heybourne flirting briefly with DEEP MACHINE before persevering by playing the odd club gig as ANGELWITCH featuring DEEP MACHINE members, namely bassist Gerry Cunningham and drummer Micky Bruce.

ANGELWITCH became Heyborne's full time act once more in early 1982 as Cunningham and Bruce were enticed away from DEEP MACHINE along with vocalist Roger Marsden. The line-up was merely a brief tenure, however as Heybourne eventually ended up in BLIND FURY.

Marsden joined Swedish band E.F. BAND then in 1984 forged a union with another ex-ANGELWITCH and E.F. BAND man drummer

KEVIN HEYBOURNE of ANGELWICH
Photo: Nico Wobben

Dave Dufort to create NEVADDA FOXX.

ANGELWITCH surfaced again in 1985 with Heybourne and Gordelier splitting from BLIND FURY and enrolling original drummer Dave Hogg together with vocalist Dave Tattum. With this incarnation of the band they laid down the quite commercial edged 'Screamin And Bleedin" album. Hogg left the band once more after its release and was replaced by former DEXYS MIDNIGHT RUNNERS drummer Spencer Hollman. Gigs were still few and far between.

Third album 'Frontal Assault' saw ANGELWITCH return to their former heaviness but Tattum left upon its completion to join the acclaimed Melodic Rock outfit NIGHTWING leaving Heybourne to assume vocal duties.

In 1989 the band added a second guitarist Grant Dennison. A short tour of Holland followed with support act SATAN, but Heybourne eventually relocated to America where nostalgia for early ANGELWITCH reaped the reward of a live set of 'classics'. The band recorded a demo with EXODUS drummer Tom Hunting and Lee Altus of HEATHEN but failed to secure a new deal.

Although ANGELWITCH failed to live up to the legend that was created around the band early on the band remained an influence with groups that arrived on the scene in later years with both ONSLAUGHT and TROUBLE covering the ANGELWITCH classic 'Confused'.

Interest was renewed in the late '90s by the release of a live album on High Vaultage Records. ANGELWITCH themselves were far from dormant issuing a CD compilation of various demos including the 1987 'Psychopathic' tapes and 1999's set 'Twist Of The Knife'. The resulting album 'Resurrection' was only available via the internet.

ANGELWITCH were back in 2000 for live gigs and a projected new album. Alongside Heybourne the fresh look band comprised guitarist Keith Herzberg, bass player Richie Wicks - a former lead vocalist of SONS OF EDEN and VIOLENTLY FUNKY, and drummer Scott Higham. The band bounced back in quite spectacular style with a performance at the prestigious 'Wacken Open Air' Metal festival in Germany before setting to work on fresh studio material.

The list of bands to have covered 'Confused' increased in 2001 as Americans SIX FEET UNDER cut a grindingly heavy take for their latest album. In August of 2001 it was announced that Higham had decamped to join the highly regarded SHADOWKEEP. Ace Finchum, a former member of Glam band TIGERTAILZ, took his place.

In November the ANGELWITCH ranks splintered further with Weeks opting to resume his former role as a lead singer and opting to join fellow NWoBHM resurrectees TYGERS OF PAN TANG. Statements issued by band members in January would confirm the fact that ANGELWITCH had folded once again, Wicks resuming action with SONS OF EDEN.

Singles/EPs:
Sweet Danger / Flight Nineteen, EMI 5064 (1980) **75 UK**
Sweet Danger / Flight Nineteen / Hades Paradise, EMI 12 EMI 5064 (1980) (12" single)
Angelwitch / Gorgon, Bronze BRO 108 (1980)
Loser / Suffer / Dr Phibes, Bronze BRO 121 (1981)
Goodbye / Reawakening, Killerwatt KIL 3001(1985)

Albums:
ANGELWITCH, Bronze BRON532 (1981)
Angelwitch / Atlantis / White Witch / Confused / Sorcerers / Gorgon / Sweet Danger / Free Man / Angel Of Death / Devil's Tower
SCREAMIN' AND BLEEDIN', Killerwatt KILP4001 (1985)
Who's To Blame / Child Of The Night / Evil Games / Afraid Of The Dark / Screamin' And Bleedin' / Reawakening / Waltz The Night / Goodbye / Fatal Kiss / UXB
FRONTAL ASSAULT, Killerwatt Records (1986)
Frontal Assault / Dreamworld / Rendezvous With The Blade / Religion (Born Again) / Straight From Hell / She Don't Lie / Take To The Wing / Something Wrong / Undergods
DOCTOR PHIBES, Rawpower RAWLP025 (1986)
Angelwitch / Atlantis / White Witch / Confused / Sorceress / Loser / Dr. Phibes / Gorgon / Sweet Danger / Free Man / Angel Of Death / Devil's Tower / Suffer
LIVE, Metal Blade ZORRO 1 (1990)
Angel Of Death / Sweet Danger / Confused / Sorceress / Gorgon / Baphomet / Extermination Day / Atlantis / Flight 19 / Angel Witch / White Witch
'82 REVISITED (LIVE), High Vaultage HV-1005 (1996)
Gorgon / Nowhere To Run / They Wouldn't Dare / Sorceress / Evil Games / White Witch / Angel Of Death / Angel Witch / Evil Games (Studio Version) / They Wouldn't Dare (Studio Version) / Nowhere To Run (Studio Version)
RESURRECTION, Angelwitch (1998)
Psychopathic I / Time To Die / Violence /

Silent But Deadly / Twist Of The Knife / Psychopathic II / Slowly Sever / Worm / Scrape The Well / Inertia

ANGKOR WAT (TX, USA)
Line-Up: Dee (vocals), Edith Bunker (guitar), King Bunnie (guitar), Titty (bass), Bambi (drums)

Intelligent Thrash Metal with innovative twists. ANGKOR WAT members created Industrialists SKREW in 1991. Although operating under pseudonyms for ANGKOR WAT vocalist Adam Grossman and guitarist Danny Lohner went on to SKREW, the latter under yet another nom de guerre of 'Opposum'.
Lohner joined NINE INCH NAILS in 1996.

Albums:
WHEN OBSCENITY BECOMES THE NORM - AWAKE, Roadracer RR 94571 (1989)
Innocence '89 / Something To Cry About / Seat Of Power / Prolonged Agony / Ricky / The Search / Awake! / Under Lock And Key / Emotional Blackmail / Warsaw / Died Young / Circus Of Horrors / Civilized
CORPUS CHRISTI, Metal Blade ZORRO 5 (1990)
Indestructible: Innocence '90 / Corpus Christi / Turn Of The Screw / Golden / Anne Marie / Birdsong (Earth) / Ordinary Madness / Sinking / Schizophrenic / Barracuda / Sour Born

ANIALATOR (TX, USA)
Line-Up: Mark Olivio (vocals / guitar), David Trevino (guitar), Alex Dominguez (bass), Alonzo Garcia (drums)

ANIALATOR bassist Alex Dominguez is ex-DEVASTATION. During 1990 the band switched titles to SUFFERANCE.

Single/EPs:
Anialator / Nuclear Destruction, Wild Rags (1988)

Albums:
ANIALATOR, Wild Rags WRR012 (1989)
Filicide / No Future / Fatal Decision / Anialator (Live) / Mission Of Death (Live)

ANIHILATED (UK)

A British Thrash Metal formation.

Albums:
PATH TO DESTRUCTION, Brew 001 (1987)
CREATED IN HATE, Metalworks VOV668

(1988)
Chase The Dragon / Slaughter / Power Is The Path / Anihilated (Part Two) / Final Dawn / Nightmare / Aftermath / Seventh Veil
THE ULTIMATE DESECRATION, Metalworks (1989)

ANIMOSITY (USA)

ANIMOSITY were a Colorado Thrash Metal band.

Albums:
PIT FIEND, Mosh Pit (1987)
GET OFF MY BACK, Mosh Pit MLP01 (1990)

ANNIHILATOR (CANADA)
Line-Up: Randy Rampage (vocals), Jeff Waters (guitar), Anthony Greenham (guitar), Wayne Darley (bass), Ray Hartmann (drums)

Vancouver based straight down the line Speed Metal band first coming to attention with their 1984 'Psycho Metal Kids' tape. At this stage ANNIHILATOR was basically a duo of vocalist / guitarist Jeff Waters and bassist David Scott. In 1985 the band demoed again resulting in 'Welcome To Your Death' which saw John Bates on vocals and Richard Death on drums. This line-up soon folded and a further demo 'Phantasmogoria' with Paul Malek on drums landed the band a deal with Roadrunner Records.
ANNIHILATOR's traditional approach to Metal gave them prominence toward the end of the Thrash boom and their debut 1989 album 'Alice In Hell' won them many converts. The band's main personalities were the peroxide maned hard drinking ex-D.O.A. bassist RANDY RAMPAGE and songwriter Waters.
D.O.A. had been a renowned act which also provided the launch platform for BLACK FLAG and DANZIG drummer Chuck Biscuits. Pre-ANNIHILATOR Rampage had also issued a solo album.
Although guitarist Anthony Greenham, bassist Wayne Darley and former ASSAULT drummer Ray Hartmann are credited on the debut ANNIHILATOR album they did not take part in recording as Waters himself laid down all the instrumentation. Previous to the album a rhythm guitarist Casey Toews joined ANNIHILATOR but was out within days.
Despite rapid progress ructions within the band found Rampage out much to fans chagrin. Second guitarist Anthony Greenham also made way for Dave Scott Davis for 1990's 'Never Neverland'. PANTHER singer Coburn Pharr took the vocal position, as

ANNIHILATOR
Photo: Nico Wobben

ANNIHILATOR seemed poised on the edge of becoming a major act.

Waters still had his eye on potential recognition outside of the band though as he auditioned for MEGADETH in 1990. According to Dave Mustaine Waters came close to securing the position but it was not to be.

ANNIHILATOR grabbed the much sought after support slot to JUDAS PRIEST's 'Painkiller' British tour. Further line-up changes slowed their progress, with 1993's 'Set The World On Fire' seeing another singer in Aaron Randall (Pharr now fronting OMEN) and Neil Goldberg supplanting Davis. The single from the album featured a reworking of JUDAS PRIEST's 'Hell Bent For Leather'.

Mike Mangini occupied the drum stool during this period of flux before he bailed out to join EXTREME in time for their 1994 Castle Donington festival appearance.

The line-up shuffles continued and ANNIHILATOR in 1994, now minus their deal with Roadrunner, had Waters with a reunited Davis, bassist Cam Dixon and drummer Randy Black.

By 1996 ANNIHILATOR had effectively trimmed down to a duo of Waters and Black. Contributing musicians to the 'Refresh The Demon' album included guitarist Davis and bassist Lou Bujdoso.

Waters took time out from his main act to guest on rather more mellow outings including POKERFACE's 1996 album 'Life's A Gamble' and the following year's self-titled effort from THE DISTANCE.

By the 1997 effort the suitably titled 'Remains' ANNIHILATOR had become Waters' solo project. Contributing musicians included guitarist John Bates.

1999 had the band bowing to fan pressure and reinstating Rampage for the much lauded 'Criteria For A Black Widow' album. Randell meantime had founded SPEEED with SEVEN WITCHES / FROSTBITE guitarist Jack Frost for their 1999 album 'Powertrip Pigs'.

Ex LIEGE LORD and OVERKILL man Joe Comeau joined the band in 2000. Comeau would divert himself in late 2000 for a one off reunion with his erstwhile LIEGE LORD guitar partner Paul Nelson to cut a version of 'Too Scared To Run' for a URIAH HEEP tribute album.

February of 2001 found ANNIHILATOR on a headlining tour of Germany supported by a strong billing of NEVERMORE, SOILWORK and HAWHEAD REXX. Drummer Ray Hartman would bow out in favour of a returning Randy Black. The returning drummer had also been busying himself with

JEFF WATERS of ANNIHILATOR
Photo: Nico Wobben

an ambitious German based conceptual project band entitled REBELLION. Fronted by erstwhile XIRON and BLACK DESTINY vocalist Michael Seifert REBELLION had been established by ex-GRAVE DIGGER men guitarist Uwe Lulis and bassist Tommi Göttlich, Black as drummer and with WARHEAD's Bjorn Eilen on second guitar. This unit issued the Shakespeare inspired 'A Tragedy In Steel' debut in March of 2002.

Throughout the latter half of 2001 ANNIHILATOR would be in preparation for a new studio album provisionally billed 'Waking The Fury' and slated for a March 2002 release through SPV/ Steamhammer. Japanese variants added a live version of 'Refresh The Demon' recorded in Rumania. During November guitarist Curran Murphy of AGGRESSION CORE and NEVERMORE joined the ranks. ANNIHILATOR announced European tour dates for April, commencing in Vienna, Austria, backed up with strong support from SEVEN WITCHES and DEBASE.

Singles/EPs:
Stonewall / W.T.Y.D. (Live) / Word Salad (Live), Roadrunner RR 24256 (1991)
Set The World On Fire / Hell Bent For Leather, Roadrunner RR 23856 (1993)
I'll Show You My Gun, Mokum (1994)

Albums:
ALICE IN HELL, Roadrunner (1989)
Crystal Ann / W.T.Y.D. / Burns Like Buzzsaw Blade / Schizos (Are Never Alone) (Parts I & II) / Human Incesticide / Alison Hell / Wicked Mystic / Word Salad / Ligeia
NEVER NEVERLAND, Roadrunner RR 93742 (1990) 48 UK
The Fun Palace / Road To Ruin / Sixes And Sevens / Stonewall / Never, Neverland / Imperiled Eyes / Kraf Dinner / Phantasmagoria / Reduced To Ash / I Am In Command
SET THE WORLD ON FIRE, Roadrunner RR 92002 (1993)
Set The World On Fire / No Zone / Bats In The Belfry / Snake In The Grass / Phoenix Rising / Knight Jumps Queen / Sounds Good To Me / The Edge / Don't Bother Me / Brain Dance
BAG OF TRICKS, Roadrunner RR 8997-2 (1994)
Alison Hell / Phantasmagoria / Back To The Crypt / Gallery / Human Insecticide / Fun Palace / WTYD / Word Salad / Live Wire / Knight Jumps Queen / Fantastic Things / Bats In The Belfry / Evil Appetite / Gallery '86 / Alison Hell '86 / Phantasmagoria '86
KING OF THE HILL, Music For Nations

MFN171 (1994)
Box / King Of The Hill / Hell Is A War / Bliss / Second To None / Annihilator / 21 / In The Blood / Fiasco (Slate) / Fiasco / Catch The Wind / Speed / Bad Child
REFRESH THE DEMON, Music For Nations MFNCD 197 (1996)
Refresh The Demon / Syn. Kill 1 / Awaken / The Pastor Of Disaster / A Man Called Nothing / Ultraparanoia / City Of Ice / Anything For Money / Hunger / Voices And Victims / Innocent Eyes
IN COMMAND LIVE 1989, Roadrunner RR 8852-2 (1996)
W.T.Y.D. / Wicked Mystic / Ligeia / Alison Hell / Word Salad / W.T.Y.D. / The Fun Palace / Never, Neverland / I Am In Command / Stonewall / Road To Ruin / Sixes And Sevens / Alison Hell / Live Wire
REMAINS, Music For Nations CDMFN 228 (1997)
Murder / Sexecution / No Love / Never / Human Remains / Dead Wrong / Wind / Tricks And Traps / I Want / Reaction / Bastiage
CRITERIA FOR A BLACK WIDOW, Roadrunner RR 8640 (1999)
Bloodbath / Back To The Palace / Punctured / Criteria For A Black Widow / Schitzo / Nothing Left / Loving The Sinner / Double Dare / Sonic / Mending
CARNIVAL DIABLO, Roadrunner (2000)
Time Bomb / Battered / The Perfect Virus / Carnival Diablo / Shallow Grave / Denied / The Rush / Insomniac / Liquid Oval / Epic Of War / Hunter Killer / Chicken And Corn
WAKING THE FURY, Roadrunner (2002)
My Precious Lunatic Asylum / Nothing To Me / Ritual / Striker / The Blackest Day / Cold Blooded / Torn / Fire Power / Ultra-Motion / Prime-Time Killing

ANONYMUS (CANADA)
Line-Up: Marco Calliari (guitar / vocals), Daniel Souto (guitar), Oscar Souto (bass / vocals), Carlos Araya (drums)

ANONYMUS is a Thrash band that does not deserve to be anonymous! They have been around for many years and are a strong part of the Quebec metal scene, which is the strongest in Canada and arguably one of the strongest in the world.

Formed in Montreal in January 1989 ANONYMUS unleashed an independent debut called 'Ni Connu, Ni Vu'. After paying their dues for two years gigging, practicing and touring around Quebec they caught the attention of the small label MPV Records. MPV re-issued their debut in 1996 and quickly followed it up with their second CD simply called 'Stress'. What followed was another two years of touring, practicing always growing in strength and popularity. The band can easily draw 1000 fans in their hometown of Montreal and has appeared on a number of Quebec Metal compilations.

The first two CDs caught some big name attention because the producer on their third CD, 'Instinct', was none other than Colin Richardson. Again following a pattern that had brought them success the band hit the road across Canada and into the US building show by show on their loyal following. Performing at small festivals and opening for such luminaries as ANTHRAX and BIOHAZARD has given this band experience and raw edge necessary to compete in a tough genre. The band has a chemistry that is flawless giving them the enviable stability of never having had a line-up change as of early 2002. The band had the good fortune to be handpicked by BLIND GUARDIAN to open for a few select dates in Mexico, where they were reportedly well received.

The band has a cosmopolitan feel with lyrics being written and sung by two vocalists in English, French and Spanish. The band has a strong do-it-yourself ethic and has produced a number of videos. ANONYMOUS is still active.

Albums:

NI VU, NI CONNU, Anonymous (1994)
Cyclope / Cremoecremoepas / Choisor ou Mosisor / Mer Noire / X / Ni Vu, Ni Connu / Amen Tote / Prosternez-vous / Balle D'or / Obstinato / Demonamane
STRESS, MPV, (1997)
Sous Pression / Un Poing C'est Tout / Questo E'L Destin / La Verite Choc / This Life / Ad Vitam Aeternam / Un Pied Dans La Tombe / Sans Dessein / Maquinas, / Casse-Tete / F.L.Y. / In Extremis
INSTINCT, MPV (2000)

ANTHRAX (New York, NY, USA)
Line-Up: Joey Belladonna (vocals), Scott Ian (guitar), Danny Spitz (guitar), Frank Bello (bass), Charlie Benante (drums)

New York Thrash act ANTHRAX formed part of the mid '80s Thrash 'Big Four' alongside METALLICA, MEGADETH and SLAYER. The band was without a doubt the most adventurous in terms of crossing musical boundaries and experimentation.

Formed by FOUR X guitarist Scott Ian Rosenfeld and WHITE HEAT bassist Dan Lilker, ANTHRAX featured vocalist John Connolly during 1981-82. HITTMAN vocalist Dirk Kennedy and drummer Greg D'Angelo (later of WHITE LION) formed part of the fledgling line up. The band's first tracks committed to tape, with Neil Turbin now on vocals, would be a three song demo comprising 'Sin', 'Antichrist' and 'Haunting Dog'.

The band captured the interest of Megaforce Records guru Johnny Zazula with the track 'Soldiers Of Metal' from their second demo. ANTHRAX also registered their first single, produced by none other than MANOWAR guitarist Ross The Boss, 'Soldiers of Metal' backed by 'Howling Furies'. Three thousand copies of the single were sold in a mere two weeks.

Playing a variety of shows locally and as far afield as Boston (where they opened for KROKUS) earnt the band an ever increasing following and contributed to the initial success of their 'Fistful Of Metal' debut album produced by Carl Canedy of THE RODS. Although the album cover, a fist punching out of a mouth, forced many critics to baulk the music gave fans of the burgeoning Thrash scene reason to celebrate.

ANTHRAX toured the American heartland for the first time on a 40-date trek with RAVEN. Following the release of 'Fistful Of Metal' Dan Lilker left ANTHRAX and was replaced in the bass slot by Charlie Benante's cousin and Scott Ian's roadie, Frank Bello. Lilker went on to form the Thrash-Hardcore act NUCLEAR ASSUALT.

Neil Turbin quickly parted company with ANTHRAX due to differences both musical and personal with his new band mates. (He would later turn up on Japanese guitar God KUNI's 1986 album 'Masque'). The band operated minus a vocalist for some two months before Turbin was briefly replaced by Matt Fallon. However, he too departed causing a delay to recording of a planned EP, 'Raise Hell', which was due to include a live version of 'Metal Thrashing Mad' and a cover of the SEX PISTOLS' 'God Save The Queen'. Fallon became part of New Jersey's SKID ROW, being ousted from that band previous to their debut multi-platinum album.

Having added him to the band in late '84 / early '85, ANTHRAX debuted their new vocalist ex-BIBLE BLACK and MEGAFORCE man Joey Belladonna (real name Joseph Bellardini) on the 'Armed And Dangerous' EP. This stopgap release featured re-worked songs from 'Fistful Of Metal' plus a version of the SEX PISTOLS 'God Save The Queen'.

Ian and Benantes side project with METHOD OF DESTRUCTION's vocalist Billy Milano and erstwhile ANTHRAX member Dan Lilker – S.O.D. (STORMTROOPERS OF DEATH) – released their debut album 'Speak English Or Die' two months prior to the second ANTHRAX album 'Spreading The Disease'.

The sophomore effort, issued in February 1985, carved out a distinctive niche for the band as ANTHRAX, while firmly in the Thrash Metal camp, set themselves apart from other contenders with a unique edge. Roadwork in Europe during May of 1985 saw the band billed on the 'Metal Hammer Road Shows' alongside OVERKILL and AGENT STEEL.

During 1987 the band's increasing popularity in Japan led to the re-issue of the 'Fistful Of Metal' album in new packaging with the addition of a couple of live tracks featuring Joey Belladonna singing 'Panic' and 'Raise Hell'.

Meantime ANTHRAX's ascendancy had been duly noted by the major labels and Island Records took the band on for future product. The 'Among The Living' album proved the band's popularity was on the way up achieving sales figures of 400,000 plus. Lyrically ANTHRAX delved into the imaginative realms of horror writer Stephen King for the title track, the plight of native Americans for 'Indians' and even Judge Dredd comics for 'I Am The Law'. The latter two of these tracks would be issued as singles and make valuable impressions on the charts. 'I Am The Law' soon became a crowd favourite as did 'Indians', often performed onstage by Belladonna in full chieftain feathered headdress.

ANTHRAX toured America supporting KISS during 1987 and also appeared at the British Castle Donington 'Monsters Of Rock' festival. ANTHRAX would guest to METALLICA on European dates too, these shows being curtailed with the tragic death of METALLICA bassist Cliff Burton. Further British shows saw TESTAMENT supporting whilst a nationwide tour of America, supported by EXODUS and CELTIC FROST, rounded off the year.

ANTHRAX received huge crossover appeal with their Rap Metal single 'I'm The Man' which became certified gold in America with 500,000 sales. The September 1988 album 'State Of Euphoria' included a version of TRUST's 'Antisocial'. ANTHRAX also recorded various other cover versions during these sessions as intended B sides including TRUST's 'Sex', SEX PISTOLS 'Friggin' In The Riggin', KISS's 'Parasite' and VENTURES' 'Pipeline'.

Touring was once again intensive as ANTHRAX opened arena shows for OZZY OSBOURNE in late 1988. Dates in Britain with guests LIVING COLOR followed prior to a lengthy headlining jaunt sponsored by MTV and supported by EXODUS once more and Germans HELLOWEEN. Live work did not end there though and ANTHRAX returned to Britain with guests KINGS X.

ANTHRAX also featured as guest musicians on the rap single by New Yorkers UFTO in 1988.

The band opened for IRON MAIDEN on a European tour at the close of 1990, but returned to America to find a radical reshaping of their label Island Records, as a consequence of its buy out by Polygram had effectively severed the ties between label and band. In spite of this upward struggle 'Persistence Of Time' went on to gold status shifting more than 600,000 copies as Island and ANTHRAX parted company.

ANTHRAX toured as part of the 'Clash Of The Titans' package during 1991 sharing a co-headlining bill with MEGADETH, SLAYER and ALICE IN CHAINS. The original intention of this touring project was to have been an awesome combination of Thrash's 'big four' (including METALLICA) but nevertheless the assembled bill drew in sizeable crowds. For the European leg ALICE IN CHAINS were replaced by SUICIDAL TENDENCIES but attendances remained almost sell out status throughout.

ANTHRAX's next move was a brave endeavour following their recent full on metal tour. The 'Bring The Noise' track, recorded originally by rappers PUBLIC ENEMY, and originally part of the 'Attack Of The Killer B's' album had found its way onto mainstream radio giving ANTHRAX an airing to fans outside of the hard rock sphere. With such exposure ANTHRAX and PUBLIC ENEMY teamed up to tour America as a unique pairing with support act YOUNG BLACK TEENAGERS, a band that Benante had given his drumming services to on their debut album.

The groundbreaking tour encountered problems from reluctant promoters but in the end over twenty highly successful shows were performed in America. British dates saw PRONG as third band on the bill.

Despite riding on an undoubted high Belladonna shocked fans by leaving. For many years the rumour machine had suggested differences between the singer and the core of the band regarding musical tastes.

ANTHRAX drafted John Bush, a man who had carved his reputation with Californian Metal act ARMORED SAINT. Bush's debut with ANTHRAX 'Sound Of White Noise' entered the Billboard top ten and broke the million sales mark in America.

During 1995 ANTHRAX hit an all time low. Spitz left the band upfront of recording and although a fine album 'Stomp 442' proved to be the nadir for the band sales wise. Undaunted ANTHRAX teamed up with the MISFITS for yet another successful tour of

America.

Ian and Benante resurrected the original line up of S.O.D. for a 1997 American tour culminating in a slot at the Milwaukee Metalfest. Other offbeat endeavours included one of the more interesting interpretations lent to the JUDAS PRIEST tribute album 'Legends Of Metal'. DOOM SQUAD, a one-off band, convened for a very much tongue-in-cheek rendition of 'Burnin' Up'. Those involved included ANTHRAX men Scott Ian and John Bush, ARMORED SAINT bassist Joey Vera and drummer Gonzo with ACCEPT's Jörg Fischer on guitar.

Strangely, a full two years after Danny Spitz had quit ANTHRAX his guitar tech Paul Crook was still temping on a live basis. Lead guitar duties on the 'Volume 8: The Threat Is Real' album were shared by Ian, Benante and Crook.

PANTERA's Dimebag Darrell guested on 'Inside Out' and 'Born Again Idiot' whilst his band mate, vocalist Phil Anselmo, guested on 'Killing Box'. Frank Bello sang lead vocals on the 'hidden' bonus track 'Pieces' that closed the record. Outside of ANTHRAX Ian sessioned on TRICKY's 'Angels With Dirty Faces' album.

ANTHRAX returned to Britain for a one off show in London during October 1998 and by the following year had bounced back with a best of album 'Return Of The Killer A's'. The CD had both Belladonna and Bush uniting to record 'Ball Of Confusion' and remixes by Al Jourgenson of MINISTRY. Former bassist Dan Lilker also puts in an appearance.

Bush returned temporarily to ARMOURED SAINT during 1999 for their much lauded 'Revelation' album but maintained his position with ANTHRAX. Bush also guested on a version of the SCORPIONS' 'Blackout' on SIX FEET UNDER's 'Graveyard Classics' album.

The band's 2000 American tour found SKID ROW guitarist Snake filling in. ANTHRAX went out as guests to MÖTLEY CRÜE but were unable to fulfill all of the shows and bailed out before the tour's completion.

In the summer of 2001 a TWISTED SISTER tribute album 'Twisted And Strange' would witness ANTHRAX offering up their take on the Glamsters 'Destroyer'.

Bush's focus in mid 2001 would be on promoting an ARMORED SAINT archive album upfront of recording a new album with ANTHRAX. Later in the year ANTHRAX, complete with new guitarist Rob Caggiano of New York's BOILER ROOM, would jump on the high profile 2001 American tour of Metal legends JUDAS PRIEST for the late summer. The act also announced the inking of a new deal with Beyond Records, a subsidiary of BMG. First fruits of this liaison was the re-issue of 'Stomp 442' and 'Sound Of White Noise', both complete with a glut of rare foreign B side tracks.

However, just upfront of the JUDAS PRIEST tour the terrorist attacks on America on September 11th forced the cancellation of all shows. The terrorist actions would not only disrupt their plans but put the very nature of ANTHRAX's existence into jeopardy. With America assailed by fears of biological and chemical warfare an Anthrax virus scare in October put the spotlight firmly on the band. In a Washington Post article Scott Ian confessed to having stocked up on supplies of the Anthrax virus antidote Cipro vowing "I will not die an ironic death." Meantime fans were asked to consider if the band should change its name.

As the Anthrax virus terror campaign worsened paradoxically the group found themselves afforded the kind of heavyweight press exposure on TV, radio and newsprint it had been lacking for so long. Indeed, the band's official website scored a massive three million hits in just under two weeks.

Amidst all this publicity former vocalist Neil Turbin announced his comeback with the 'Threat Con Delta' album. Involved in the studio sessions for a forthcoming album from Turbin's crew would be AMSTERDAM's Ronnie Borchert, erstwhile MICHAEL SCHENKER GROUP, HEAVEN and TALAS guitarist MITCH PERRY and Kurt James of STEELER and DR. MASTERMIND.

ANTHRAX finally got to tour with JUDAS PRIEST in January of 2002 as the re-scheduled dates got back under way. An early untoward incident on the sold out tour being when Caggiano was arrested and jailed for throwing a hot dog at a taxi driver in Denver! Amongst the traditional cover versions laid down by the band for the new album would be takes on 'Next To You' by THE POLICE, the RAMONES 'We're A Happy Family' and U2's 'Exit'.

ANTHRAX would head up a Thrash billing of MACHINE HEAD, TESTAMENT and EXODUS in Sao Paolo, Brazil on April 20th.

Singles/EPs:

Soldiers Of Metal / Howling Furies, Megaforce (1983)

Madhouse/ A.I.R., Island (1986)
(7" single)

Madhouse / A.I.R. / God Save The Queen, Island 12IS 285 (1986)
(12" single)

I Am The Law / I'm The Man/ Bud E Luvbomb And Satan's Lounge Band / Madhouse (Live), Island IS LAW1 (1987) **32 UK**

Indians / Sabbath Bloody Sabbath / Taint,

Island IS325 (1987) **44 UK**
I'm The Man (Censored Version) / I'm The
Man (Def uncensored version) / Sabbath
Bloody Sabbath / I'm The Man (Live &
Extremely Def II uncensored version)/
Caught In A Mosh (Live) / I Am The Law
(Live), Megaforce Island (1987) **42**
SWEDEN, 53 USA
I'm The Man / Caught In A Mosh / I Am The
Law (Live), Island IS338 (1987)
20 UK
Make Me Laugh / Anti- Social (Live), Island
(1988) **26 UK** (7" red vinyl single)
Make Me Laugh / Anti-Social (Live) /
Friggin' In The Riggin', Island IS379 (1988)
(12" single)
Anti-Social / Parasite, Island (1989)
(7" single) **44 UK**
Anti-Social / Parasite / Le Sect, Island
IS409 (1989) (12" single)
In My World / Keep It In The Family, Island
IS470 (1990) **29 UK**
In My World / Keep It In The Family / In My
World (Extended version) / Keep It In The
Family (Extended version, Island (1990) (12"
single)
Got The Time / Who Put This Together,
Island (1990) (7" single) **16 UK**
Got The Time / Who Put This Together / I'm
The Man (Live), Island IS 475 (1990) (12"
single)
Bring The Noise / I Am The Law '91 / Keep
It In The Family (Live), Island (1991) (with
CHUCK D) **14 UK**
Only / Only (Mix), Elektra EKR 166 (1993)
36 UK
Only / Cowboy Song / Sodium Pentaghol,
Elektra EKR 166CD1 (1993) (CD single)
Only / Auf Wiedersehn / Noisegate, Elektra
EKR 166CD2 (1993) (CD single)
Black Lodge / Potters Field / Love Her All I
Can, Elektra EKR 171CD (1993)
53 UK
Black Lodge (Black strings mix) / Black
Lodge (Tremelo mix) / Black Lodge (Mellow
to Mad mix) / Black Lodge (LP version),
Elektra EKR 171TP (1993) (Picture disc)
Hy Pro Glo / London, Elektra EKR 178
(1993)
Hy Pro Glo / London / Room For One More
(Live), Elektra EKR 171T (1993) (12" single)
Nothing / Fuelled (Remix) / Remember
Tomorrow / Grunt And Click, Elektra EKR
216CD1 (1996) (CD single)
Nothing / Dethroned Emperor / No Time
This Time, Elektra EKR 216CD2 (1996) (CD
single)

Albums:
FISTFUL OF METAL, Music For Nations
MFN 14 (1985)

Deathrider / I'm Eighteen / Subjagator /
Howling Furies / Death From Above / Across
The River / Metal Thrashing Mad / Panic /
Soldiers Of Metal / Anthrax
ARMED AND DANGEROUS, Megaforce
MRS 05 (1985)
Armed And Dangerous / Raise Hell / God
Save / LIVING, Island ILPS 9865 (1987)
43 SWEDEN, 18 UK, 62 USA
Among The Living / Caught in A Mosh / I Am
The Law / Efinkufsin (N.F.L.) / Skeleton In
The Closet / Indians / One World / ADI
Horror Of It All / Imitation Of Life
STATE OF EUPHORIA, Island ILKPS 9916
(1988)
21 SWEDEN, 12 UK, 30 USA
Be All, End All / Out Of Sight, Out Of Mind /
Make Me Laugh / Antisocial / Who Cares
Wins / Now it's Dark / Schism / Misery Loves
Company / 13 / Finale
PERSISTENCE OF TIME, Island ILPS 9967
(1990)
46 SWEDEN, 13 UK, 24 USA
Time / Blood / Keep It In The Family / In My
World / Gridlock / Intro To Reality / Belly Of
The Beast / Got The Time / H8 Red / One
Man Stands / Discharge
ATTACK OF THE KILLER B'S, Island
ILPS9980 (1991)
38 SWEDEN, 13 UK, 27 USA
Milk (Ode To Billy) / Bring The Noise / Keep
It In The Family (Live) / Startin' Up A Posse /
Protest And Survive / Chromatic Death / I'm
The Man '91 / Parasite / Pipeline / Sects /
Belly Of The Beast (Live) / NFB
(Dallabnikufesin)
SOUND OF WHITE NOISE, Elektra
755961430-2 (1993)
21 SWEDEN, 14 UK, 7 USA
Potters Field / Only / Room For One More /
Packaged Rebellion / Hy Pro Glo / Invisible /
1000 Points Of Hate / Black Lodge / C11
H17 / Burst / This Is Not An Exit
LIVE - THE ISLAND YEARS, Island CID
8027 (1994)
Efilnikufesin NFL / AIR / Parasite / Keep It In
The Family / Caught In A Mosh / Indians /
Antisocial / Bring The Noise / I Am The Law /
Metal Thrashing Mad / In My World / Not It's
Dark
STOMP 442, Elektra 7559-61856-2 (1995)
47 USA
Random Acts Of Senseless Violence /
Fueled / King Size / Riding Shotgun /
Perpetual Motion / In A Zone / Nothing /
American Pompeii / Drop The Ball / Tester /
Bare
MOSHERS... 1986-1991, Connoisseur
Collection VSOP CD 252 (1998)
A.I.R. / Madhouse / Caught In A Mosh / I Am
The Law / Efilnikufesin (NFL) / Indians / I'm

The Man / Make me Laugh / Anti-Social / Now It's Dark / Keep It In The Family / In My World / Belly Of The Beast / Got The Time / Bring The Noise

VOLUME 8 - THE THREAT IS REAL, Ignition - Tommy Boy IGNPRO74036-2 (1998) **73 UK**
Crush / Catharsis / Inside Out / Piss & Vinegar / 604 / Toast / Born Again Idiot / Killing Box / Harm's Way / Hog Tied / Big Fat / Cupajoe / Alpha Male / Stealing From A Thief / Pieces

RETURN OF THE KILLER A'S, Spitfire SPITCD057 (1999)
Bring The Noise / Only / Potters Field (Hypo Luxa Hermes Pan Remix) / Ball Of Confusion / Crush / Room For One More / Inside Out / Hy Pro Glo (Hy Pro Luxa Mix) / Fueled / Among The Living / Got The Time / Indians / Antisocial / I'm The Man / Madhouse / I Am The Law / Metal Thrashing Mad

ANTIDOTE (FINLAND)
Line-Up: Nino Laurenne (vocals / guitar), Tuomo Louhio (guitar), Pete Peltonen (bass), Mika Arnkil (drums)

Thrashers dating back to 1986. Various demo sessions led up to the 1990 tape 'Epoch Of Insanity' capitalized on by the following year's 'Spaced Out'. Promoting the release of their debut album 'The Truth' on the German Shark label ANTIDOTE toured with ACCUSER and HEADHUNTER.

The sophomore outing 'Total', mixed by Timmo Tolkki of STRATOVARIOUS, was recorded utilizing Pete Eloranta as the main songwriter in place of Tuomo Louhio.

In 1996 ANTIDOTE pulled in erstwhile INCREDIBLE BRAINSHELLS man Titus Hjelm on bass.

In later years Laurenne and Hjelm would unite with members of Progressive metal band TUNNELVISION to create the Symphonic Metal band THUNDERSTONE.

Albums:
THE TRUTH, Shark 026 (1992)
Symphony Of Death / Within His Power / Act Of Violence / Melancolia / 3rd Time In Greenland / Rose Machine / Grandiloguent Passaway / Subordinated People / Spaced Out
TOTAL, Shark 100 (1994)
Cold / Woe Betide Them / Life For A Lie / Rain / Multiverse / My Million Years / You Medicate / Slow Motion / Life Recall / Into The Dreamside
MIND ALIVE, Radiation 110572 (1996)
Books Of The Moon / Attitude / Masked Dance / In The Land Of Nod / Bridges / Wallow In Vice / Dying To Be Dead / Icon Of Hate / The Agressor Within / Fall From Disgrace / The Mind Alive

ANTIMON (GERMANY)
Line-Up: Fede (vocals), Michael Vetter (guitar), Claudia (guitar), Toni Kolla (bass), Alex Tröndle (drums)

ANTIMON issued three Thrash Metal demos 'Evil Dead', 'Mistress' and 'The Cult Returns' prior to issuing their 1992 mini-album.

Singles/EPs:
Screaming Skulls / Jesus Babys / Children Of The Day / United In Flames / One For The Angels, Sonic Abus (1992) ('Children Of Today' EP)

ANTITHESIS (Cleveland, OH, USA)
Line-Up: Ty Cook (vocals), Sean Perry (guitar), Tom Guignette (guitar), Jim Lewis (bass), Paul Kostyack (drums)

Cleveland Christian Heavy Metal act of some repute dating back to 1997. Although far from shy in delivering technically inclined, thundering Progressive Heavy Metal ANTITHESIS steer clear of any war mongering, hatred, the occult or negativity in their lyrics. The band was convened by guitarists Sean Perry and Paul Konjicija, the remaining members being recruited through musician want ads in a local free newspaper. By October of the same year, St. Louis native bass player Jim Lewis had joined. Vocalist Ty Cook was the next onboard, ANTITHESIS being rounded off with the addition of drummer Paul Kostyack in February of 1998. Later that year the band entered the recording studio to self-finance their eponymous debut album. The record would be issued through the Danish Intromental Management concern during February of 1999 with a print run of 1000 copies which soon sold out. However, in April Konjicija decamped, ANTITHESIS drafting Tom Guignette as substitute. With their new guitarist in place the band quite remarkably re-recorded the entire album, gave the record an entirely new packaging and re-marketed it in November of the same year.

Guignette left the band in October 1999, his replacement being none other than former member Paul Konjicija.

Albums:
ANTITHESIS, Voice Of Wonder (1999)
Netherworld / Breeding The Beast / Limbo / Sword Of Mouth / The Web / Secret Fires /

Plastic / The Curse / Descend
DYING FOR LIFE, Massacre (2001)
Consequence / Soul Of Ice / Times Of Trial /
Deceiver Within / Distanced / Mad Poet /
Politicide / Dying For Life / Netherworld /
Secret Fires

ANTROPOMORPHIA (HOLLAND)
Line-Up: Ferry Damen (vocals / guitar),
Vincetit Van Boxtel (guitar), Marc Van
Stiphout (bass), Marco Stubbe (drums)

Although originally a Thrash Death Metal act
ANTROPOMORPHIA would evolve into the
Nu-Metal band ANTRO. Both bass player
Marc Van Stiphout and drummer Marco
Stubbe would form part of Thrash Metal act
FLESH MADE SIN convened in 1999 by
SAURON vocalist Twan Van Geel and
SPLATTER guitarist Bjorn Van Hamond.

Albums:
NECROMANTIC LOVE SONGS, Blackend
(1994)
Crack The Casket / The Carnal Pit / Birth
Through Dead / Chunks Of Meat

ANVIL (CANADA)
Line-up: Lips (vocals / guitar), Dave Allison
(guitar), Ian Dickson (bass), Robb Reiner
(drums)

Originally known as LIPS upon their formation
in 1978, the first ANVIL album was originally
issued under the LIPS handle. ('Lips' is the
stage name of frontman Steve Kudlow). The
debut album was in fact intended to be purely
demo material but as an enterprising unit and
eager to recoup their recording costs the
band issued 1,000 vinyl copies on their own
Splash label.
Still as LIPS the outfit's initiative came to the
attention of Attic records who quickly re-
released the album although now under the
band name of ANVIL due to protestations
from disco act LIPPS INC.
An uncompromising slab of heaviness, 'Hard
And Heavy' was the first in line not only to
demonstrate the band's adherence to full on
metal but also their obsession with sex. Tracks
such as 'Bondage' and 'School Love' being
prime examples. Onstage Lips would cultivate
press coverage too by performing lead guitar
solos with the aid of a vibrator!
ANVIL made their first foray onto the live
scene in Canada with a bunch of club shows
leading to the nationwide support to
GIRLSCHOOL. Mainman Lips did take time
out though to produce a demo for KRAKEN.
1982's 'Metal On Metal' boasted the unique
honour of having the track 'Mothra' being

recorded by Lips using a vibrator on his guitar
rather than the more usual plectrum. The
follow up 'Forged In Fire', an equally
heavyweight offering, increased the band's
stature worldwide.
ANVIL went into the studio in 1985 to cut
demos with producer Ric Browde. A strange
choice for ANVIL as Browde's credits include
lighter acts such as POISON. Songs recorded
were 'Rockin', 'Mad Dog', 'World's Apart' and
'Straight Between The Eyes'.
Allison, after recording the 'Pound For Pound'
album, quit in 1989 prompting a period of
inactivity for the band. They bounced back
signed to the Belgian label Mausoleum and
Canadian label Maximum for the 1992 'Worth
The Weight' album with new guitarist
Sebastian Marino in tow. Following the album
release ANVIL pulled in bassist Mike Duncan.
Guitarist Sebastian Marino made himself
busy with RAMROD cutting two demos in
1994 prior to teaming up with cult New York
Speed Metal merchants OVERKILL for their
1997 effort 'From The Underground And
Below'. Marino had also found time to
produce the 1996 album by DEVESTATOR.
With Germany's fascination in the late '90s for
early '80s cult metal acts ANVIL made a
return to the touring circuit undertaking dates
with FLOTSAM AND JETSAM and fellow
Canucks EXCITER. The band rounded off
1998 by performing at the long established
'Wacken Open-Air' festival in Germany.
ANVIL at this juncture in their career included
the lynchpin of Lips, original drummer Rob
Reiner and new faces guitarist Ivan Hurd and
bassist Glenn Five (real name Gyorffy).
Meantime English Metal crew BENEDICTION
had covered 'Forged In Fire' for their 1992
album 'Dark Is The Season'. TUNGSTEN also
paid tribute to the same song on their 1996
album '183.85'.
ANVIL toured Germany in early 2000 sharing
a package bill with RIOT, AGENT STEEL and
DOMINE.
German Massacre label variants of the 2001
album 'Plenty Of Power' differed to Canadian
distributed CDs in having the final exclusive
track as 'Dirty Dorothy'. The Hypnotic
Canadian imprint replaced this song with 'Left
Behind'.
Marino and his colleagues in the RAMROD
rhythm section took to the stage at the
German 'Wacken Open Air' festival the same
year as part of a reunion line up of LIEGE
LORD.
ANVIL have scheduled a new album, 'Still
Going Strong', for release through Massacre
Records in June of 2002.

Singles/EPs:
School Love / Paint It Black, Polydor (1981)
(Japanese Release)
Steamin' / Tease Me, Please Me /
Jackhammer / Stop Me, Noir MET 12 001
(1982)
Make It Up To You / Metal On Metal, Noir
MET12 002 (1983)

Albums:
HARD AND HEAVY, Attic LAT 1100 (1981)
School Love / AC/DC / At The Apartment / I
Want You Both (With Me) / Bedroom Game /
Ooh Baby / Paint It Black / Oh Jane / Hot
Child / Bondage
METAL ON METAL, Attic LAT 1130 (1982)
Metal On Metal / Mothra / Stop Me / March
Of The Crabs / Jackhammer / Heat Sink /
Tag Team / Scenery / Tease Me, Please Me /
666
FORGED IN FIRE, Attic LAT 1170 (1983)
Forged In Fire / Shadow Zone / Free As The
Wind / Never Deceive Me / Butter Bust Jerky
/ Future Wars / Hard Times - Fast Ladies /
Make It Up To You / Motormount / Winged
Assassins
BACKWAXED, Roadrunner RR 9776 (1985)
Pussy Poison / Back Waxed / Steamin' /
You're A Liar / Fryin' Cryin' / Metal On Metal /
Butter Bust Jerky / Scenery / Jackhammer /
School Love
STRENGTH OF STEEL, Roadrunner RR
9618 (1987)
Strength Of Steel / Concrete Jungle / 9-2-5 /
I Dreamed It Was The End Of The World /
Flight Of The Bumble Beast / Cut Loose /
Mad Dog / Straight Between The Eyes / Wild
Eyes / Kiss Of Death / Paper General
POUND FOR POUND, Metal Blade 73336
(1988)
Blood On The Ice / Corporate Preacher / Toe
Jam / Safe Sex / Where Does All The Money
Go? / Brain Burn / Senile King / Machine
King / Fire In The Night / Cramps
PAST AND PRESENT LIVE, Roadracer RO
94532 (1989)
Concrete Jungle / Toe Jam / Motornaut /
Forged In Fire / Blood On The Ice / March Of
The Crabs / Jack Hammer / Metal On Metal /
Winged Assassins / 666 / Mothra
WORTH THE WEIGHT, Mausoleum 904
004-2 (1991)
Infanticide / On The Way To Hell / Bushpig /
Embalmer / Pow Wow / Sins Of The Flesh /
AZ 85 / Sadness / Love Me When I'm Dead
PLUGGED IN PERMANENT, Massacre
(1996)
Racial Hostility / Doctor Kevorkian / Smokin'
Green / Destined For Doom / Killer Hill /
Face Pull / I'm Trying To Sleep / Five Knuckle
Shuffle / Truth Or Consequence / Guilty
ABSOLUTELY NO ALTERNATIVE,

Massacre MASCD0134 (1997)
Old School / Green Jesus / Show Me Your
Tits / No One To Follow / Hair Pie / Rubber
Neck / Piss Test / Red Light / Black Or White
/ Hero By Death
SPEED OF SOUND, Massacre MAS
C00173 (1998)
Speed Of Sound / Blood In The Playground /
Deadbeat Dad / Man Over Board / No Evil /
Bullshit / Mattress Mambo / Secret Agent /
Life To Lead / Park That Truck
CLASSIX SHAPE VOL. 10, Massacre MAS
SH0204 (1999)
Blood On The Ice / Doctor Kevorkian / Old
School / Speed Of Sound / Metal On Metal
(Live)
ANTHOLOGY OF ANVIL, Hypnotic (2000)
Metal On Metal / Smokin' Green / Winged
Assassins / Free As The Wind / Old School /
Bushpig / Blood On The Ice / March Of The
Crabs / Jackhammer / Speed Of Sound /
666 / Stolen / Paper General / Forged In Fire
(Live) / School Love / Motormount / Doctor
Kevorkian / Mothra
PLENTY OF POWER, Hypnotic HYP 1079
(2001)
Plenty Of Power / Grrove Science / Ball Of
Fire / The Creep / Computer Drone / Beat
The Law Pro Wrestling / Siren Of The Sea /
Disgruntled / Real Metal / Left Behind

ANVIL

ANVIL BITCH (PA, USA)
Line-Up: Gary Cappriotti (vocals), John
Plumley (guitar), Dave Carr (bass), Chuck
Stadulis (drums)

Albums:
RISE TO OFFEND, New Renaissance
NRR13 (1987)
Rise To Offend / Lie Through Your Teeth /
Vengeance Of The Sword / Life After Death /
Time To Die / Argue With A Sick Mind /
Maggot Infestation / Neckbreaker / Arsenic
And Cyanide / Fight For Your Life / Shark
Attack / Anvil Bitch

ANVIL CHORUS

(San Francisco, CA, USA)
Line-Up: Aaron Zimpel (vocals), Thaen Rassmussen (guitar), Douglas Piercy (guitar), Bill Skinner (bass), Gere Fennelly (keyboards), Joe Bennett (drums)

Formed from the ashes of the Progressive Rock band LEVIATHAN and other Bay Area groups, assorted members of the defunct San Franciscan bands began jamming with another local act HEAD ON.

The story has it that HEAD ON's manager was impressed enough to offer the guys a support slot to HEAD ON in 1982.

Adopting the name ANVIL CHORUS, the new group not only played the HEAD ON show but also opened up for MÖTLEY CRÜE's earliest forays into Northern California. Other ANVIL CHORUS gigs had METALLICA as the opening act.

Early rehearsals were held with Rasmussen, Piercy bassist Grant Williams, drummer Michael Hegos and vocalist Tim Montana.

By early 1982 ANVIL CHORUS comprised ex-LEVIATHAN vocalist Aaron Zimpel, guitarists Thaen Rassmussen (ex-VY-KING) and Doug Piercy (ex-COBRA and DELTA), bassist Bill Skinner and drummer Ken Farragen (both previously with LEVIATHAN). The latter was eventually replaced by Joe Bennett, Farragen seemingly having ideas to become a policeman. Gere Fennelly, Rasmussen's girlfriend and a member of BLEU FOOD, was brought in on keyboards.

There were strong links between ANVIL CHORUS and the Seattle Metal band METAL CHURCH, Aaron Zimple (a.k.a. Aaron Whymer) having played drums on some early demos. Both bands would also play the old LEVIATHAN track 'Red Skies' in their live sets.

METAL CHURCH mainman Kurdt Vanderhoof had once been in the San Franciscan Punk band THE LEWD and had formed METAL CHURCH with ex-LEVIATHAN guitarist Rick Condran, Aaron Whymer and bassist Steve Haat. For the group's first demo the act was titled ANVIL CHORUS - THE CHURCH OF METAL. When this early incarnation of METAL CHURCH folded Whymer took the name ANVIL CHORUS. The links between the two acts remained though as ANVIL CHORUS paid homage with their track 'Bow To The Church Of Metal'.

Despite strong sales of the ANVIL CHORUS single 'Blondes In Black', especially in Europe as an import, ANVIL CHORUS never released further product and drifted into a more keyboard orientated direction. Although Warner Brothers expressed some interest, the Bay Area band faded into oblivion.

Fennelly and Zimpel quit in 1985. Piercy, having produced demos for LEGACY (later to be retitled TESTAMENT) and EXODUS wished to pursue harder material and joined CONTROL. After CONTROL's second guitarist Dino Carvosia bailed out Rasmussen joined the ranks of CONTROL too in a line-up comprising the two ex-ANVIL CHORUS guitarists with vocalist Ed Bull, bassist Michael Thinger and drummer Eric Rasmussen (no relation). When the latter departed another ANVIL CHORUS refugee Joe Bennett joined.

Doug Piercy would appear with HEATHEN. For HEATHEN's second album the band recut the ANVIL CHORUS track 'Guitarmony' with a guesting Rasmussen. Percy quit HEATHEN in 1991 for ANGEL WITCH and the German based THE COMPANY. Gere Fennelli toured with RED KROSS circa the band's 'PhaseShifter' tour.

ANVIL CHORUS reformed for a one off San Francisco gig in 1987 opening for EXODUS and MEGADETH at the Kabuki venue. Rasmussen founded an ANVIL CHORUS II in the '90s with ex-RELEASE man Steve Kilgore, bassist Ryan Connor and the now jailed Dan Brian. Later work included Pop act PORCELAIN.

Rasmussen and Piercy formed part of the HEATHEN reformation in 2000.

Singles/EPs:
Blondes In Black / Once Again, Leviathan (1982)

APOCALYPTIC RAIDS (BRAZIL)

Line-Up: Nekromaniac (vocals / guitar), Sub Umbra (bass), Adrameleck (drums)

Trio founded in 1997 and massively influenced by the genre defining HELLHAMMER right down to the band name and album cover artwork. Following the self issued 1999 EP, APOCALYPTIC RAIDS signed to the Demise label for 2000's full length 'Only Death Is Real...'

The band - Gustavo Belo, Leon Manssur and A. Aguinaga credit themselves as 'Adrameleck' (Witch Hunts & Machine Guns), 'Necromaniac' (6-String Damnation & Vokills) and 'Sub Umbra' (Low Frequency Armageddon).

Singles/EPs:
Evil / The Impaler / Tyrant, Emperor / Apocalyptic Raids, (1999) ('Apocalyptic Raids' EP)

Albums:
ONLY DEATH IS REAL..., Demise (2000)

The Enemy (Intro) / Evil / Forgotten Tales / Into The Twilight Zone / Eternal Gloom / Angels Of Hell / Humankind Dies / Tyrant, Emperor / Apocalyptic Raids / Tales of Horror (Outro)

APOCALYPSE
(SWITZERLAND)
Line-Up: Carlos Sprenger (vocals), Julien Brocher (guitar), Zurich Zurcher (guitar), Jean Claude Schneider (bass), Momos Domenjoz (drums)

Thrash Metal act APOCALYPSE's debut, originally released on Out Of Tune in Switzerland, was later picked up by Music For Nations, who released it through their Under One Flag imprint.
APOCALYPSE returned in the mid '90s.

Albums:
APOCALYPSE, Out Of Tune DT277-1 (1988)
Digital Life / A Tale Of A Nightmare / Crash! / F**k Off And Die / The Night Before / Apocalypse / Back To The Fire / Dark Sword / Cemetery
FAITHLESS, Phonag MMP007-M (1995)
House Of Confusion / Slay For Play / Division / Unwanted / Extreme Sensation / Faithless / Reason To Live / Shoot You Down / Bad Breath

APOCALYPTICA (FINLAND)
Line-Up: Antero Manninen (cello), Max Lilja (cello), Paavo Lötjönen (cello), Eicca Toppinen (cello)

An unexpected hit from an unlikely source. Four Finnish cellists re-interpreted METALLICA tunes in a sparse classical format. The album was such a success APOCALYPTICA undertook live dates.
A second album emerged in 1998 which alongside more METALLICA renditions included reworkings by contemporaries SEPULTURA, FAITH NO MORE and PANTERA.

Albums:
PLAYS METALLICA BY FOUR CELLOS, Mercury 532 707-2 (1996)
Enter Sandman / Master Of Puppets / Harvester Of Sorrow / The Unforgiven / Sad But True / Creeping Death / Wherever I May Roam / Welcome Home (Sanitorium)
INQUISITION SYMPHONY, Mercury 558 300-2 (1998)
Harmageddon / From Out Of Nowhere / For Whom The Bell Tolls / Nothing Else Matters / Refuse-Resist / M.B. / Inquisition Symphony

/ Fade To Black / Domination / Toreador / One
CULT, Mercury (2000) **31 GERMANY**
Path / Struggle / Romance / Pray! / In Memoriam / Hyperventilation / Beyond Time / Hope / Kaamos / Coma / Hall Of The Mountain King / Until It Sleeps / Fight Fire With Fire

APOCRYPHA (Las Vegas, NV, USA)
Line-Up: Steve Plocica (vocals), Tony Friedanelli (guitar), Al Rumley (bass), Mike Poe (drums)

APOCRYPHA were viewed by many as the vehicle to promote guitarist Tony Friedanelli. The band's debut album line-up comprised Friedanelli, vocalist Steve Plocica, bassist Al Rumley and drummer Mike Poe. Of note is that 'The Forgotten Scroll' is produced by MARTY FRIEDMAN, then a member of CACOPHONY.
APOCRYPHA added second guitarist Chip Chrovian for 1988's 'The Eyes Of Time' album.
Third album 'Area 54' saw the recruitment of a new rhythm section of bassist Breck Smith and drummer Dave Schiller.
Friedanelli issued a solo album 'Breakneck Speed'. He also performed with covers band LOVESHACK before a stint in MAJIK ALEX. By 2000 he was guitarist with multi platinum artists THIRD EYE BLIND.

Albums:
THE FORGOTTEN SCROLL, Roadrunner RR9568 (1987)
Penance (Keep The Faith) / Lost Children Of Hope / Holy Wars (Only Lock The Doors) / Fall Of The Crest / Tablet Of Destiny / Look To The Sun / Riding In The Night / Distorted Reflections / Broken Dream
THE EYES OF TIME, Roadrunner RR 9507-2 (1988)
Father Time / West World / Twilight Of Modern Man / Alexander The King / The Day Time Stood Still / The Hour Glass / H.G. Wells / The Man Who Saw Tomorrow / Mystic
AREA 54, Roadrunner RR 9345 (1990)
Terrors Holding On To You / Catch 22 / A Night In Fog / The Power Elite / Instrubation No 3 / Area 54 / Tiananmen Square / The Detriment Of Man / Refuse The Offer That You Can't Refuse / Born To This World

ARBITRATOR (UK)
Line-Up: Tony Martin (vocals), Tony Ingrams (guitar), Dominic Jeaves (guitar), Neil Henderson (bass), Dave Barrows (drums)

A Warwick based Thrash outfit dating from 1987 that included ex-SACRILIGE drummer Andy Barker in an earlier incarnation (playing in a line-up also featuring vocalist Tony Martin, guitarist Dominic Jeaves, bassist Gavin Ward and guitarist P.M.), before he quit in late 1988.

ARBITRATOR submitted the track 'Memories Of Yesterday' to the 'Taste of Armageddon' compilation in 1989 and released a three track demo featuring 'Deadly Assassin', 'Evil Emperor' and 'Time For Destiny' in 1990.

The quintet finally released product in 1991 with the 'Balance Of Power' album, following it up three years later with 'Darkened Reality'.

Albums:

BALANCE OF POWER, Cyclone 101 (1991)
Allegiance / The Treaty / Evil Emperor / Conquest / Life Line / Graveyard Of Fools / Time For Destiny / Deadly Assassin
DARKENED REALITY, Cyclone 2 (1994)

ARCANE (Arlington, TX, USA)

Line-Up: Oscar Barbour (vocals), Doug Judah (guitar), Byron Hawk (guitar), Kurt Joye (bass), Kelly Sanford (drums)

Progressive Thrash Metal band ARCANE, founded in 1987, debuted with the 1989 'Mirror Deception' demo. Drummer Kelly Sanford was previously a member of BANG GANG.

Albums:

DESTINATION UNKNOWN, Wild Rags (1991)
Recurrent Inception / Enshrouded Crypt / Infernal Domicile / Ancient Internecine / Life's Illusion / Impasse Of Humanity / Mirror Of Deception / Agaememnon

ARCH ENEMY (SWEDEN)

Line-Up: Angela Gossow (vocals), Mike Amott (guitar), Christopher Amott (guitar), Sharlee D'Angelo (bass), Daniel Erlandsen (drums)

Old style Extreme Metal band ARCH ENEMY features ex-members of CARNAGE, CARCASS and EUCHARIST. Despite ploughing a niche market ARCH ENEMY have managed to attain a degree of commercial success, particularly in Japan. Their opening album 'Black Earth', a mix of Thrash and Death elements delivered in a quite unique style, would prove to be a genuine groundbreaking release, the resulting word of mouth amongst the Metal cognoscenti prompting huge world wide sales and respect.

Frontman Johan Liiva previously played with CARNAGE and FURBOWL whilst guitarist Mike Amott, best known for his role in CARCASS, was also once a CARNAGE member early on and, in addition to ARCH ENEMY, currently also plays in SPIRITUAL BEGGARS.

Christopher Amott, Mike's younger brother, would appear to be following his brother's example by not keeping all his eggs in one basket, contributing to his side band ARMAGEDDON, whilst ex-EUCHARIST drummer Daniel Erlandsson occasionally with IN FLAMES.

The band contributed a cover of 'Aces High' to the Toys Factory Records tribute to IRON MAIDEN, namely the cheesily titled compilation album 'Made In Tribute'.

Christopher Amott shifted to bass as the six string position was filled by the esteemed figure of Sharlee D'Angelo on bass, also an active member of WITCHERY and MERCYFUL FATE as well as citing credits with SINERGY and DISMEMBER.

ARCH ENEMY built up quite a global reputation with tours of Japan and Europe. The band also opened for CRADLE OF FILTH in 1999, a support slot gained by admitted nepotism, Erlandsson, older brother having gained the CRADLE OF FILTH drummer's job.

The band would perform at the prestigious 2001 Japanese 'Beast Feast' Festival during August at the 30,000 capacity Yokohama Arena alongside SLAYER, V.O.D., STATIC X and SEPULTURA among others.

Liiva announced the formation of a new endeavour in late 2001 billed as NONEXIST. However, by early 2002 the man had made a re-appearance in HEARSE alongside drummer Max Thornell and guitarist Mattias Ljung.

ARCH ENEMY would transform into a completely new beast for the next studio outing. The Amott siblings would be joined by German singer Angela Gossow, previously with ASMODINA and MISTRESS.

The ARCH ENEMY 'Wages Of Sin' album would see a belated American release, but come with not only a bonus track 'Lament Of A Mortal Soul' and a video clip for 'Ravenous' but a whole separate CD of rarities. Included on the latter would be a previously unreleased version of JUDAS PRIEST's 'Starbreaker' plus covers of IRON MAIDEN's 'Aces High', EUROPE's 'Scream Of Anger' and a glut of bonus tracks originally only to be found on Japanese albums.

ARCH ENEMY toured Japan once more in March of 2002 and put in British debut shows, as support to OPETH, in May.

Burning Angel / Lament Of A Mortal Soul / Starbreaker / Ravenous (Video), Teichiku TFCK-87281 (2002)

Albums:
BLACK EARTH, Wrong Again WAR011CD (1996)
Bury Me An Angel / Dark Insanity / Eureka / Idolatress / Cosmic Retribution / Demoniality / Transmigration Macabre / Time Capsule / Fields Of Desolation
STIGMATA, Century Media CD 77212-2 (1998)
Beast Of Man / Stigmata / Sinister Mephisto / Dark Of The Sun / Let The Killing Begin / Black Earth / Tears Of The Dead / Vox Stellarum / Bridge Of Destiny
BURNING BRIDGES, Century Media 77276-2 (1999)
The Immortal / Dead Inside / Pilgrim / Silverwing / Demonic Science / Seed Of Hate / Angelclaw / Burning Bridges
BURNING JAPAN LIVE 1999, Toys Factory (2000)
The Immortal / Dark Insanity / Dead Inside / Diva Satanica / Pilgrim / Silverwing / Beast Of Man / Bass Intro / Tears Of The Dead / Bridge Of Destiny / Transmigration Macabre / Angelclaw
WAGES OF SIN, Century Media (2001)
Enemy Within / Burning Angel / Heart Of Darkness / Ravenous / Savage Messiah / Dead Bury Their Dead / Web Of Lies / The First Deadly Sin / Behind The Smile / Snow Bound / Shadows And Dust

ARCH RIVAL (OH, USA)
Line-Up: Aaron Wallace (vocals), Michael Harris (guitar), Jeff Dennis (guitar), Gary Rigmaiden (bass), Greg Martin (drums)

Ohio's ARCH RIVAL released a self-financed EP prior to an 8 track demo in 1988. Guitarist Michael Harris featured in Mike Varney's 'Guitar player' magazine spotlight.
The Japanese label Alfa released ARCH RIVAL's new album 'Third Degree Burns' prior to its European release on Bossy Ogress Records. The album features the line-up of Steve Snyder (vocals), Michael Harris (guitar), Gary Rigmaiden (bass) and Greg Martin (drums).
Harris would team up with the ever prolific DAVID T. CHASTAIN to create a new act ZANISTER debuting with the 1999 album 'Symphonica Millennia'.

Singles/EPs:
God Bless America, Arch Rival (1987)

Albums:
THIRD DEGREE BURNS, Alfa ALCB 3176 (1997)
Soul Of Your Machine / Heaven's Kiss / Enter The Dragon / Ultra-Violence (Will Break The Silence) / Drowning In Pain / Tough Love / Silence Is A Word / Writing On The Wall / Third Degree Burns / Minds Of Madness

A.R.G. (FINLAND)
Line-Up: Tepa (vocals / guitar), Vesa (guitar), Jari (bass), Pasi (drums)

Finnish Thrash Metal act A.R.G. hit the scene with a 1988 demo 'Heathenism In Penitentiary'.

Albums:
ENTRANCE, Megamania (1989)
ONE WORLD WITHOUT THE END, Black Mark (1991)
Intro: Last Dawn Of Humanity / Died For What / In The Depths Of Sanity / Adoration Of The Kings / Happy Times / Misfortune Along My Side (R.I.P. II) / Back For Life / One World Without The End / Straybullet

ARIA (RUSSIA)
Line-Up: Valery Kipilov (vocals), Sergey Mavrin (guitar), Vladimir Holstinin (guitar), Vitaly Dubinin (bass), Maxim Udalov (drums)

Russian Metal combo ARIA have released numerous albums, many of which have sold over a million copies.
ARIA were formed in 1984 by guitarist Vladimir Holstinin, previously with ALPHA. Another erstwhile ALPHA member bassist Alik Granovsky joined him and in 1985 vocalist Valery Kipelov was recruited.
ARIA's first recordings, the 'Megalomania' ('Mania Welichia') cassette, was laid down with the aid of drummer Lvov and keyboard player Kirill Pokrovsky. For live work ARIA pulled in second guitarist Andrey Bolshakov as Lvov became a full time member.
In 1986 ARIA, now with a strong fan base dubbed "Arians", performed at the Russian 'Rock Panorama '86' festival. The state Record label Melodia issued a double live album featuring bands from the event but pointedly missed out ARIA. Live shows by the band were attracting hardened fans and also protesters making ARIA a constant thorn in the side of the authorities. ARIA's logo was even banned making it difficult to advertise live shows.
ARIA knuckled down to business with their second tape album 'Whom Are You With' which featured a fresh line-up. ARIA had split down the middle with band members wishing

41

to go more in a Thrash direction and left. Joining Holstinin and Kipilov in the new look ARIA were guitarist Sergey Mavrin, bass player Vitaly Dubinin and drummer Maxim Udalov.

Such was the band's popularity Melodia Records picked up the band for their next release. The band delivered their album titled 'Serving Evil Force' but were horrified to find that Melodia had retitled it without consulting them 'Hero Of A Speedway'. Not only had the record company changed the title but had ruined the sound quality. ARIA dubbed the album 'Hero Of Asphalt' ('Geroj Asfalta'). Nevertheless, despite the problems the album sold over a million copies.

In the winter of 1988 ARIA played their first dates in the West with shows in Germany. Udalov quit after a tour of Bulgaria and in came Alexander Manyakin on drums for the 'Play With Fire' album. However, Dubinin and Mavrin left to join a German band.

ARIA regrouped with ex-GALACTICA / KRASNAYA PLOSHAD guitarist Dimitry Gorbatikov and bassist Alexes Bulkin. By August of 1990 Dubinin and Mavrin returned to the fold.

1991's 'Blood For Blood' was issued on Syntez Records then ARIA signed a lengthy contract with Moraz Records who promptly reissued the first two cassettes onto vinyl.

Just when they had secured a new deal and were setting to work on a fresh album Kipilov quit to join MASTER. Seeing no future for ARIA without the vocalist Mavrin also walked out. Guitarist Sergey Teretvev, who had been recording his own solo album in the same studio took Mavrin's place. The album was finished as Kipolov returned and 'Night Is Shorter Than Day' finally saw a release in 1995.

A double live album followed before band members set about projects outside of ARIA. Dubinin and Holstinin created AVARIA whilst Kipilov and ex-guitarist Mavrin formed DARK AGE.

ARIA returned with 1998's 'Generator Of Evil'.

Singles/EPs:
The Time Has Come / Easy Angel / Hero Of Asphalt '99 / Easy Angel (Karoake version), Moraz (1999) ('A Tribute To Harley Davidson' EP)

Albums:
MANIA WELICHIA, (1985) (Cassette release)
This Is Doom / Torero / Volunteer / Tusks Of Black Rock / Megolomania / Life For Free / Dreams / America Is Behind
S KEM TY, (1986) (Cassette release)
Will And Reason / Stand Up, Subdue Your Fear / Metal Is Being Made Here / Whom Are You With? / Without You / Memory About… / Icarus / Games Not For Us
HERO OF A SPEEDWAY, Melodia (1987)
Serving Evil Powers / Hero Of A Speedway / Dead Zone / Almost 1000 / Rose Street / Ballad Of Old Wars
PLAYING WITH FIRE, Melodia (1989)
What Have You Done To Your Dreams? / We'll Rock The World / Slave Of Fear / Temptation / Playing With Fire / The War Goes On / Power Up!
KROW SA KROW, Syntez (1991)
Farewell Norfolk! / Zombie / Antichrist / If You Don't Want - Don't Believe Me / Blood For Blood / Demons / All, That Have Been / Follow Me
MEGOLOMANIA, Moroz (1994)
This Is Doom / Torero / Volunteer / Tusks Of Black Rock / Megolomania / Life For Free / Dreams / America Is Behind
NOCHJ KOROCHE DNJA, Moroz (1995)
Slavery Of Illusions / Paranoia / Angels Dust / Go Away And Don't Return / Road King / Take My Heart / Beast / Spirit Of War / Night Is Shorter Than Day
MADE IN RUSSIA - LIVE, Moraz (1996)
Slavery Of Illusions / Paranoia / Let's Rock This World / Road King / Angel's Dust / Go away And Don't return / Antichrist / Take My Heart / Follow Me / Night Is Shorter Than Day / Farewell Norfolk! / Volunteer / Spirit Of war / Torero / Fight Is Going On / All, What Have Been / Hero Of Asphalt / Rose Street / Kick Some Ass
RUSSIAN ROCK LEGENDS, Moroz (1997)
Volunteer / Torero / Will And Reason / Give Me A Hand / Hero Of Asphalt / Rose Street / Fight Is Goin On / Play With Fire / Farewell Norfolk! / Antichrist / Blood For Blood / Take My Heart / Road King
GENERATOR OF EVIL, Moraz (1998)
Behold! / Dirt / Deserter / Torture With Silence / Run For The Sun / Deseption / Hermit / Sunset / Diabolic Heart / Closed Circle
2000 AND ONE NIGHT (LIVE), Moraz (2000)
Rose Street / Lost Paradise / Without You / Dirt / All, What Have Been / Take My Heart / Go Away And Don't Return / Who Are You / Torture With Silence / Temptation / Dreams / Sunset

ARISE (SWEDEN)
Line-Up: Erik Ljungvist (vocals / guitar), L.G. Jonasson (guitar), Patrick Skoglow (bass), Daniel Bugno (drums)

ARISE, founded in Alingsas during 1994 and titled in honour of the SEPULTURA album of the same name, blend traditional Swedish style Death Metal with retro Thrash influences.

The group was assembled by a triumvirate of erstwhile HOLOCAUST members guitarist Erik Ljungqvist, bassist Patrick Skoglow and drummer Daniel Bugno. Second guitars were on hand from L.G. Jonasson, an ex-member of FUTURE DEVELOPMENT.

Initially the band was fronted by vocalist Jorgen Sjolander who was in turn replaced by Bjorn Andvik. When Andvik decamped Ljungvist took over the lead vocal role as ARISE switched from playing covers to writing original material. They then proceeded to issue a rush of demos including 'Hell's Retribution', 'Resurrection' and 1999's 'Statues'.

ARISE cut an April 2000 session 'Abducted Intelligence' with KING DIAMOND man Andy LaRocque at the production helm. This last tape duly secured a deal with the Finnish Spinefarm label.

ARISE would also contribute a version of 'Communication Breakdown' to the Dwell Records LED ZEPPELIN Death Metal tribute album 'Dead Zeppelin'.

Japanese issues of the debut album 'A Godly Work Of Art' include an extra track, namely of cover a METALLICA's 'Motorbreath'.

Albums:
THE GODLY WORK OF ART, Spinefarm (2001)
A Godly Work Of Art / Generations For Sale / Within / Delusion Of Life / Haterush / Cellbound / Wounds / Abducted Intelligence / ...And The Truth Is Lies

ARMAGEDOM (BRAZIL)
Line-Up: Eduardo (vocals), Javier (guitar), Claudinei (bass), Barrigo (drums)

A Sao Paulo Thrashcore act heavy on the Punk influences. ARMAGEDOM date back as far as 1982 under their formation as ULTIMA CHANCE with a line up of Javier on vocals, Barriga on guitar, Zero on bass and Ricardo on drums. The act, adding bassist Eduardo, evolved into ARMAGEDOM during 1983.

ARMAGEDOM debuted with a track included on the 1985 compilation 'Ataque Sonoro', following this with a 1986 full length album 'Silencio Funebre'. The band would then undergo a radical shift with band members swapping instruments. Javier took to guitar, Eduardo became lead vocalist whilst Barrigo became drummer. New face Beto took the bass mantle.

ARMAGEDOM welcomed in another bassist, Claudinei, in 1999.

Albums:
SILENCIO FUNEBRE, Rainbow (1986)
ARMAGEDOM, Six Weeks (1999) (Split album with FORCA MACABRE)
DAS CINZAS AO INFERNO, Mothra (2001)

ARMEGEDDON (USA)
Line-Up: Mike Vance (vocals), Bobby Lee (guitar), Charlie Phillips (guitar), Dan Wilkinson (bass), Janusz Smulski (keyboards), Mark Miley (drums)

Albums:
THE MONEY MASK, REX (1990)
The Money Mask / Mercenaries Of Injustice / More Than Conquerors / Looking Out For You / The Ship Of Changes / (Liberation From) Blazing Wasteland / Nightlight / Giving It To You / The Judge / We're Outta Here

ARMED FORCE (USA)
Line-Up: Blazin' Burns (vocals), Flash Blakk (guitar), Torch Tetro (bass), Dante 'Madman' Renzi (drums)

Essentially the Glam Metal new line-up of New York Thrashers ARMED FORCES. The band originally recorded this album under the impression it would spark off a fierce bidding war amongst the labels before deciding to drop the 's' in their name and let the Iron Works label have the 'Heavy Artillery' album. By 1988 Dante Renzi had linked up with N.R.G. vocalist Les Brown and ex BLACK LACE members Carl and Anthony Fragnito to form DAMN CHEETAH. Ronzi's later bands included GREEN DEVIL INDUSTRY and by 2000 the Nu-Metal crew REACH.

Albums:
HEAVY ARTILLERY, Iron Works (1986)
Take No More / Machine Gun Alley / Another Day's Gone / Outraged / Soldier Of Fortune / Land Of Destiny / Ninth Day Be Damned / Heavy Artillery

ARMED FORCES
(New York, NY, USA)
Line-Up: Scotty Knight (vocals), Michael Manne (guitar), Tommy Bolan (guitar), Steve A. Tetro (bass), Joey Cussamano (drums)

NWoBHM Thrash influenced quintet from Brooklyn, New York, ARMED FORCES were originally formed in 1980 and went through the usual phase of having to play covers (in this instance songs by JUDAS PRIEST and IRON MAIDEN) in order to get the gigs and pay the bills.

By the time the band recorded their debut offering, the mini-LP 'Let There Be Metal', lead guitarist Michael Manne was the only original member of the band.

Whilst the band's demos had publications such as Britain's 'Metal Forces' magazine proclaiming the band to be the future of Metal, the actual record once released turned out to be a rather disappointing, muted affair.

By 1985 the band had undergone severe line-up changes and, almost overnight, turned themselves into a Glam band, much to the horror of some of their strongest supporters, with only Manne and Tetro remaining from the band that recorded the mini-album. Joining the revamped line-up came vocalist Kevin Burns, guitarist Billy 'Flash' Blakk and drummer Dante 'Madman' Renzi.

It was with this bunch that the New Yorkers changed their name to ARMED FORCE and signed to the Iron Works label for the release of the 'Heavy Artillery' album.

The band, adopting an almost Glam image, changed names to ARMED FORCE for their second release. Tommy Bolan later joined WARLOCK. Post-ARMED FORCE Dante Renzi teamed up with DAMN CHEETAH and by 2000 was ensconced in Nu-Metal unit REACH.

Albums:
LET THERE BE METAL, Metallic Flame (1984)
The Night Rider / Let There Be Metal / Into The Darkness / The Intruder / Teaze Me

ARMORED SAINT (USA)
Line-Up: John Bush (vocals), Dave Pritchard (guitar), Phil E. Sandoval (guitar), Joey Vera (bass), Gonzo (drums)

Officially formed in the summer of 1982, ARMORED SAINT immediately attracted attention for the quality of a five track demo tape and the headbanging nature of the quintet's live show. The band was initially founded in 1981, yet only fully completed in mid 1982. The individuals concerned had all played in other bands, but none had recorded with anybody previously. Bassist JOEY VERA had played with MÖTLEY CRÜE's Tommy Lee and then OZZY OSBOURNE guitarist JAKE E. LEE during his formative years.

Joey Vera (then a guitarist) and vocalist John Bush first got together in their El Sereno school band RHAPSODY. A covers band, including songs by the likes of FOREIGNER and DEEP PURPLE in their act, RHAPSODY also included guitarist David Avila, bassist Channing, keyboard player Mark Patton and drummer Martin Zuniga.

Vera and Bush stuck together to create their next school band ROYAL DECREE in an

alliance with drummer Gonzo and guitarist Phil E. Sandoval. Vera was now on bass after Bush initially made an attempt but got bored with the instrument. Upon ROYAL DECREE's demise Bush and Vera hooked up with SAPPHIRE but shortly after Bush was ousted by vocalist Brad Parker. The band underwent numerous line-up changes but toward the end of the band's career Vera found himself playing alongside Tommy Lee.

Vera joined ex-DOKKEN guitarist Greg Leon in his GREG LEON INVASION following Lee's departure to MÖTLEY CRÜE. During this time Gonzo, Sandoval and Vera were jamming in a garage, latter day MX MACHINE / MOTOFURY man Diego Negrate having a brief stint on bass. This untitled unit pulled John Bush in on vocals although were quite happy to inform the front man the only reason he got to join was because he owned an impressive PA system. This line-up began to formulate early ARMORED SAINT material as well as covering IRON MAIDEN tunes. One song that didn't make it to any official release was subtly titled 'You Suck My Anal Dry'.

Vera continued his bass duties with the GREG LEON INVASION whilst the mysterious Mike took his role in the garage band. In April of 1982 Vera officially joined the newly titled ARMORED SAINT.

As legend has it, ARMORED SAINT's demo tape was paid for from compensation arising from injuries sustained by Joey Vera in an automobile accident whilst a passenger in a car driven by Tommy Lee.

ARMORED SAINT's first recorded appearance came with a contribution to Metal Blade's 'Metal Massacre II' album. The group offered 'Lesson Well Learned'.

Naturally, Metal Blade then stepped in with a deal for an EP, resulting in the 3 track 12" single issued the following year. The record included 'Lesson Well Learned' with 'False Alarm' and 'On The Way'.

Chrysalis stepped in to snap the group up, placing them in the studio with producer Michael James Jackson (fresh from his work on KISS' 'Creatures Of The Night' album) to deliver the 'March Of The Saint' record. Most fans agree that whilst the material couldn't be faulted, the production left a good deal to be desired, not capturing the intensity of the group at all.

'March Of The Saint' was released in 1984, the band touring America opening for METALLICA soon afterwards, the two bands now sharing management.

The group's second album, 'Delirious Nomad' surfaced a year later. Produced by Max Norman, the record found ARMORED SAINT a quartet following the exit of guitarist Dave

PHIL SANDOVAL of ARMORED SAINT
Photo: Nico Wobben

Sandoval during recording.

A third album, 'Raising Fear', was recorded with Chrysalis before the two parties split after its release in 1987. For touring with KING DIAMOND in America during 1988 ARMORED SAINT drafted former ODIN guitarist Jeff Duncan as the band also parted company with Q-Prime Management.

The 1988 live album, recorded at Cleveland's Agorra Ballroom in October 1987, provided the band with a useful stopgap product and included a brand new studio recording featuring Phil Sandoval 'No Reason To Live'.

As ARMORED SAINT floundered Duncan quit, having his position taken by Alan Barlam. Duncan put together BIRD OF PREY with his brother and ex-ODIN colleague Shawn on drums, vocalist Kyle Michaels (later of MASI and GEEZER BUTLER BAND) and Paul Puljiz (later of KILLING KULTURE). Vera meantime joined LIZZY BORDEN for their 1989 album 'Master Of Disguise'.

ARMORED SAINT guitarist Dave Pritchard died from Leukemia in February 1990. His life was celebrated in the video 'A Trip Thru' Red Times'.

The 'Symbol Of Salvation' comeback album was graced with Pritchard's guitar parts on the track 'Tainted Past'.

Having resisted overtures from the likes of METALLICA in the past, John Bush decided to take up an offer from ANTHRAX to become the New York outfit's new vocalist in the wake of Joey Belladonna's departure in 1992. With Bush gone ARMORED SAINT ceased to exist.

Following the band's split Joey Vera released a solo album, 'A Thousand Faces', through Metal Blade. He then joined FATES WARNING and was involved in the recording of new band colleague Mark Zonder's side project CHROMA KEY in 1998.

ARMORED SAINT with the Sandoval brothers, Vera, Bush and Duncan had the opportunity to reform during 1999 as Bush's career with ANTHRAX appeared on the wane. The comeback album 'Revelation' garnered heady praise from the European Metal press and proved to be a return to former glories. Duncan also issued his solo project band DC4's first outing the same year. In 2001 a highly collectable compilation 'Nod To The Old School' was issued featuring a glut of early demo tracks, three new songs, covers of JUDAS PRIEST's 'Never Satisfied' and ROBIN TROWER's 'Day Of The Eagle' and live cuts. Also included were the tracks from the bands very first EP.

In March of 2002 Joey Vera, still maintaining his posts in both ARMORED SAINT and FATES WARNING, would team up with SAVATAGE guitarist Jack Frost's side

JEFF DUNCAN & JOEY VERA of ARMORED SAINT
Photo: Nico Wobben

endeavour SEVEN WITCHES for European touring. The bassist would also handle production chores for ENGINE's 'Superholic' album.

The other ARMORED SAINT personnel maintained their sense of industry too, Jeff Duncan readying a Joey Vera produced DC4 album release for Europe and Gonzo busying himself with his MONSTER G venture in alliance with Phil Sandoval.

Singles/EPs:
Lesson Well Learned / False Alarm / On The Way, Metal Blade MBR 1009 (1983)
Can U Deliver, Chrysalis (1984)
Take A Turn, Chrysalis (1984)
Long Before I Die, Chrysalis (1985)
Over The Edge, Chrysalis (1985)
Isolation, Chrysalis (1987)

Albums:
MARCH OF THE SAINT, Chrysalis CHR 1479 (1984)
March Of The Saint / Can U Deliver / Mad House / Take A Turn / Seducer / Mutiny On The World / Glory Hunter / Stricken By Fate / Envy / False Alarm
DELIRIOUS NOMAD, Chrysalis CHR 1516 (1985)
Long Before I Die / Nervous Man / Over The Edge / The Laugh / Conqueror / For The Sake / Aftermath / In The Hole / You're Never Alone / Released
RAISING FEAR, Chrysalis CHR 1610 (1987)
Raising Fear / Saturday Night Special / Out On A Limb / Isolation / Chemical Euphoria / Frozen Wil l- Legacy / Human Vulture / Book Of Blood / Terror / Underdogs / Crisis Of Life
SAINTS WILL CONQUER - LIVE, Metal Blade ZORRO 28 (1988)
Raising Fear / Nervous Man / Book Of Blood / Can U Deliver / Mad House / No Reason To Live
SYMBOL OF SALVATION, Metal Blade ZORRO20 (1991)
Reign Of Fire / Dropping Like Flies / Last Train Home / Tribal Dance / The Truth Always Hurts / Half Drawn Bridge / Another Day / Symbol Of Salvation / Hanging Judge / Warzone / Burning Question / Tainted Past / Spineless
REVELATION, Metal Blade 3984-14288-2 (2000)
Pay Dirt / The Pillar / After Me, The Flood / Tension / Creepy Feelings / Damaged / Den Of Thieves / Control Issues / No Me Digas / Deep Rooted Anger / What's Your Pleasure / Upon My Departure
NOD TO THE OLD SCHOOL, Metal Blade (2001)

Real Swagger / Unstable / March Of The Saint / Day Of The Eagle / Never Satisfied / Tainted Past / After Me The Flood (Live) / Creepy Feelings (Live) / Lesson Well Learned / False Alarm / On The Way / Stricken By Fate / Reign Of Fire (Demo) / Betty 79,15 People (Demo) / Get Lost (Demo) / Nothing Between The Ears (Demo) / Pirates (Demo) / Medieval Nightmare (Demo)

ARMOURED ANGEL (AUSTRALIA)
Line-Up: Yuri Ward (guitar / vocals), Glen 'Lucy' Luck (bass), Steve Luff (drums)

Canberra Thrash Metal act ARMOURED ANGEL dating back to their formation by bassist Glen 'Lucy' Luck in 1984. By 1987 Lucy had been joined by guitarist Matt Green and vocalist / drummer Joel Green, this version of the band cutting the 1988 demo session 'Wings Of Death'. 1990 saw the release of the 'Communion' demo and a subsequent East coast tour of Australia that scored the group a deal with ID Records.

'Wings Of Death' would later be issued as a vinyl EP by English label C.C.G. during the early '90s. The sophomore 'Stigmartyr' album was issued in 1992 with 'Mysterium' some two years later. Australian tours found the band treading the boards with international running mates BOLT-THROWER and MORBID ANGEL. European and American tour dates saw the band into 1995.

ARMOURED ANGEL would then score the services of KILLING JOKE's Jaz Coleman as producer for their next album. However, these sessions were never completed. The Green siblings made their exit and the act duly folded.

ARMOURED ANGEL finalized their reunion line-up in January of 1997 as a trio of PSYCHRIST man vocalist / guitarist Yuri Ward, bassist Lucy and drummer Steve Luff. This unit cut the 'Angel Of The Sixth Order' album for Warhead Records.

In April of 2001 Lucy joined Death Metal band REIGN OF TERROR.

Albums:
WINGS OF DEATH, C.C.G. (1989)
STIGMARTYR, Armoured Angel (1992)
Hymn Of Hate / Beyond The Sacrament / Stigmartyr / Ordained In Darkness
MYSTERIUM, ID Records (1994)
Myth Of Creation / Heir To Evil / Enigmatize / Carved In Sin / Pray For Me / Elegy
ANGEL OF THE SIXTH ORDER, Warhead WHCD27 (1998)
Whore Of Babylon / Eve Of Temptation / Seven Angels / Crucifiction / Gadarene Swine / Spear Of Destiny / Cervical Slut /

Thy Blood Eterne / Carved In Sin

ARTILLERY (DENMARK)
Line-Up: Flemming Ronsdorf (vocals), Michael Styzter (guitar), Jorgen Sandau (guitar), Morten Stytzer (bass), Carsten Neilson (drums)

Formed in 1982, with original vocalist Per Oninkin ranks, from various obscure Danish bands. Following a riot at one of ARTILLERY's early gigs Onink was given his marching orders and replaced by Carsten Lohmann.

With their new vocalist ARTILLERY issued the impressive demos, 'Shellshock' and 'Deeds Of Darkness' and succeeded in grabbing a lot of attention from the underground Metal press. Lohmann left shortly after and in came Flemming Ronsdorf. ARTILLERY's next demo secured them a deal with the Newcastle Upon Tyne based Neat Records to release the debut album 'Fear Of Tomorrow' in 1985.

The band's subsequent album, 'Terror Squad', received similar rave reviews to the debut despite having probably one of the worst album covers of all time due to Neat asking the band to design their own record sleeve.

Following the record's release the band suffered the loss of bassist Morten Stytzer, who left the band for a period before re-entering the fold in 1988.

ARTILLERY would, without much fanfare in the Western world, become one of the first outside Rock acts to perform in the Soviet Union. As part of the cultural 'Next Stop' programme ARTILLERY, alongside Danish Punks SORT SOL, performed a number of sold out Russian gigs. However, over enthusiastic fans incited a vicious backlash from security forces and ARTILLERY were duly banished as being a decadent influence. The group took a five day train journey on the Trans Siberian Express back to Europe immortalized later on the song '7am From Tashkent'.

ARTILLERY struggled on, but eventually broke up the same year with Morten Stytzer joining FURIOUS TRAUMA. ARTILLERY folded shortly after and the Styzer brothers then founded MISSING LINK.

However, within nine months the brothers had left their respective bands to reform ARTILLERY with Ronsdorf and ex-URIOUS TRAUMA bassist Michael Rasmussen.

Before too long Rasmussen was out in favour of ex-FORCE MAJEUR / APOCALYPSE bass player Peter Thorslund which enabled Morten Stytzer to switch to guitar. The band toured Denmark and even slotted in a show in

Russia before recording a new demo with METALLICA producer Flemming Rasmussen. With their influence on the European Metal scene being recognized ARTILLERY returned in 2000 for the 'B.A.C.K.' album. Session drums would be handled by Per Jensen of THE HAUNTED, KONKHRA and INVOCATOR fame.

Singles/EPs:
Khomaniac, Roadracer (1990)

Albums:
FEAR OF TOMORROW, Neat (1985)
Time Has Come / The Almighty / Show Your Hate / Ring / Thy Name Is Slayer / Out Of The Sky / Into The Universe / The Eternal War / Fear Of Tomorrow / Deeds Of Darkness
TERROR SQUAD, Neat 1038 (1987)
The Challenge / In The Thrash / Terror Squad / Let There Be Sin / Hunger And Greed / Therapy / At War With Science / Decapitation Of Deviants
BY INHERITANCE, Roadrunner RR9397 (1990)
Khomaniac / Bombfood (Nothing But A Tool) / By Inheritance / R.I.P. (Beneath The City) / Allergic To Knowledge / Back In The Trash / Life In Bondage / Don't Believe / 7am From Tashkent / Prelude To Life
B.A.C.K., Die Hard PCD 33 (1999)
Cybermind / How Do You Fell / Out Of The Trash / Final Show / WWW / Violent Breed / Theatrical Exposure / B.A.C.K. / The Cure / Paparazzi
DEADLY RELICS, Gutter (2001)
Artilleristic Prelude MCMXCVIII / Khomaniac / Don't Believe / Out Of The Sky / Fear Of Tomorrow / Deeds Of Darkness / Too Late To Regret / Deserter / Hey Woman / Time Has Come / All For You / Bitch / Blessed Are The Strong

ASPHYXIA (BELGIUM)
Line-Up: Carlos (vocals), Yves (guitar), Leo (guitar), Calo (bass), Da (drums)

A Belgian Thrash Metal band. ASPHYXIA released the 1991 'Capital Punishment'.

Albums:
EXIT REALITY, Rumble RUMCD 1005 (1991)
Capital Punishment / Violence First / Slice Of Death / Health For Sale / Paranoia Time / The One Who Minds The Worm / One Big Family / Where Shadows Are Dark / No Thanks

ASPID (RUSSIA)

Russian Thrash Metal band ASPID issued the 'Krovoyliyanie' demo in 1991.

Albums:
ASPID, R.U.D. (1993)

AS SAHAR (SINGAPORE)

Line-Up: Barchiel (vocals / guitar), Hanael (bass), Iblyss (drums)

AS SAHAR started out as a straight Thrash Metal trio during the mid '80s with founder members vocalist / guitarist Barchiel and bassist Hanael joined by drummer Uriel. At this stage AS SAHAR were a covers act.

The band dissolved but reformed a few years later opting for a new Black Metal lyrical direction, evident on their 1995 demo 'Santau'.

A further demo 'Meditas Embun Pagi' was recorded and subsequently released as a cassette EP by Nebiula Productions. However, following these sessions Uriel jumped ship. His replacement was former ABHORRER and IMPIETY man Iblyss.

Sales of the previous cassette were strong enough to warrant recording of the debut album 'Phenomistik'. A split album with HAYAGRIVA kept up the momentum prior to the departure of Iblyiss.

Barchiel and Hanael persevered as a duo changing tack once again into Gothic Electronica for the 'Baku Karmi' album.

Albums:
PHENOMISTIK, Shivadarshana (1997)
Nadayage (Ashore) / Depressive Monsoon / Silomanial Dansecration / Tinggam / Sinfonie Jimbalang / Fandeyian Okultika Hymnology / Meditas Embun Pagi / Foleraftty Melo-Harvest / Nadaynde (Adrift)
BEYOND FIRMAMENT, Memories (1998)
(Split Album With HAYAGRIVA)
Berwahi (Dalem Tuntut) / As Sahar / Wijaya Kesuma Buat Susuhunanan / My Hymns, In The East
EKSTASI TEKSTONIS, Nebiula Productions (1999)
Tuju Tuju Opus / Tinggam / Meditasti Embun Pagi / Folkerafty Melo-Harvest / Silumamial Dansecration / Santau Tuju Angin / Stroll In Kafan / Meditation Embun Pagi / My Hymns, In The East / Fandeyian Okultika Hymnology / Sinfonie Jimbalang / Repressive / Nadayaga II (Adrift)
BAKU KARMI, Nebiula Productions (2000)

ASSASSIN (GERMANY)

Line-Up: Robert Gonnella (vocals), Scholli (guitar), Dinko Vekie (guitar), Markus 'Lulle' Ludwig (bass), Psycho (drums)

ASSASSIN arrived upon the scene with a 1986 demo 'Holy Terror', swiftly followed by 'The Saga Of Nemesis' tape.

ASSASSIN recruited two new members to the cause in time to record 'Interstellar Experience' - guitarist Michael Hoffman and drummer Frank Nellen.

For a short spell ASSASSIN ranked as one of the German Thrash hopefuls.

Albums:
THE UPCOMING TERROR, Steamhammer 18951 (1987)
Forbidden Reality / Nemesis / Fight (To Stop The Tyranny) / The Last Man / Assassin / Holy Terror / Bullets / Speed Of Light
INTERSTELLAR EXPERIENCE, Steamhammer SHLP 7011 (1988)
Abstract War / AGD / A Message To Survive / Pipeline / Resolution 598 / Junk Food / Interstellar Experience / Baka

ASSAILANT (Buffalo, NY, USA)

Line-Up: Greg Reynard (vocals), Kenneth London (guitar), Mark Stro (guitar), Jay Sharpe (bass), Jim O'Donnel (drums)

ASSAILANT were founded in April 1983 by bassist Jay Sharpe and guitarist Kenneth London later augmenting the band with second guitarist Mark Stro, vocalist Greg Reynard and drummer Kenny Brand.

ASSAILANT supported the likes of EXCITER, ROUGH CUTT, SAVATAGE and TALAS and a 1984 demo tape was capitalized on by the 'First Offense' EP the following year. However, after the record was released Brand lost his place to Jim O'Donnel.

Singles/EPs:
First Offense, (1985)

ATHEIST (FL, USA)

Line-Up: Kelly Shaefer (vocals / guitar), Rand Burkey (guitar), Roger Patterson (bass), Steve Flynn (drums)

Florida's "Jazz-Thrash" outfit ATHEIST started out life originally titled RAVAGE under which title the band contributed tracks 'Brain Damage' and 'On They Slay' to the 1987 'Raging Death' compilation album. As ATHEIST the band excelled in highly complex innovation taking Thrash into uncharted realms. Although held in awe by their peers ATHEIST found it tough going on the commercial circuit.

Guitarist Rand Burkey's distinction came from not only playing his guitar left handed but performing this feat on a regular but upside down guitar with the strings aligned for a right handed player.

ATHEIST issued a 1988 demo featuring the tracks 'No Truth', 'Choose Your Death', 'Beyond', 'On They Slay' and Brain Damage'. They would support the likes of TESTAMENT, SNFU, DEATH ANGEL and OBITUARY prior to signing to European label Active Records. Scott Burns produced debut album 'Piece Of Time'.

In February 1991 ATHEIST suffered a huge blow when bassist Roger Patterson was killed. They added ex-CYNIC bassist Tony Choy to record 'Unquestionable Presence'. Flynn would opt out after completion of dates with CANNIBAL CORPSE. Choy exited too accompanying Dutch Death Metal crew PESTILENCE for their 1991 world tour. He would later re-emerge as a Jazz musician on a cruise boat!

The 'Elements' album was, at the band's admission, thrown together in haste but would still prove a worthy effort. Josh Greenbaum would handle drums in the studio. A European set of dates ensued alongside BENEDICTION which saw Shaefer joined by guitarist Frank Emmi and drummer Marcel Dissantos.

Shaefer's NEUROTICA side project would blossom into a full time venture. The ex ATHEIST man was still at it in 2001 launching the 'Living In Dry Years' album produced by none other than Brian Johnson of AC/DC fame. Schaefer has recently acquired the rights to all ATHEIST material for a round of long overdue CD re-releases.

Emmi would later figure in GENTLEMEN DEATH. Burkey would hook up with erstwhile CRIMSON GLORY vocalist Midnight for a project band.

In 2001 Shaefer, Burkey, Emmi and Flynn announced the reformation of ATHEIST.

Albums:
PIECE OF TIME, Active ATV8 (1989)
Piece Of Time / Unholy War / Room With A View / On They Slay / Beyond / I Deny / Why Bother? / Life / No Truth
UNQUESTIONABLE PRESENCE, Active ATV20 (1991)
Mother Man / Unquestionable Presence / Your Life's Retribution / Enthralled In Essence / An Incarnation's Dream / The Formative Years / Brains / And The Psychic Saw
ELEMENTS, Music For Nations MFN 150 (1993)
Green/ Water / Samba Briza / Air /

Displacement / Animal / Mineral / Fire / Fractal Point / Earth / See You Again / Elements

ATOM GOD (UK)

Line-Up: Trev Toms (vocals), Billy Liesegang (guitar), Algy Ward (bass), Steve Clark (drums).

A distinctly British Rock outfit with Thrash leanings. ATOM GOD was conceived upon the demise of INNER CITY UNIT in the spring of 1988.

The band's initial line-up comprised frontman Trev Toms, ex-FASTWAY drummer Steve Clark, bassist Hiro Sasaki and guitarist Billy Liesegang. For the second album, 'History Re-Written', ATOM GOD replaced Sasaki with the notable figure of erstwhile DAMNED and TANK bassist Algy Ward. A short British club tour was planned, but wound up being shelved and the band split.

Ward formed WARHEAD with ex-MOTÖRHEAD guitarist WURZEL and ex-WARFARE vocalist / drummer Evo before rejoining THE DAMNED in 1995. The bassist then wound up getting back into action with TANK, touring Germany in 1997 with HAMMERFALL and RAVEN.

Both Ward and Liesegang re-united in 1997 as part of the Death Metal project act NECROPOLIS.

Albums:
WOW, GWR GWLP30 (1989)
Camden Town / Dolphins / Bashin' Up The Rich / Atlantic Waves / Dog Rot / Oh Yea / **HISTORY RE-WRITTEN**, Communique CMG 004 (1991)
History Rewritten Part One / Welcome To The Kingdom Of Doom / History Rewritten Part Two / Radio Death / Atom Bomb / Cesspit (Cauldron Of Death) / Virgin Blood / (Death Will Come From) China

ATOMIZER (AUSTRALIA)

Extreme Australian Metal act founded in 1998. An initial demo 'Atomic Metal Power' led to an album deal split between the French concerns End All Life and Drakkar productions, the former issuing the vinyl format of 'The End Of Forever' and Drakkar the CD. In Australia, Melbourne's The Devil's Own took the album on for domestic release. ATOMIZER toured both Australia and New Zealand during October of 2000. ATOMIZER's next release, for the Norwegian Nihilist Void label, was the 'Gimme Natural Selection' EP featuring two originals alongside covers of MOTÖRHEAD's 'Ace Of

Spades' and 'I Wish You Were A Beer' by the CYCLE SLUTS FROM HELL.

ATOMIZER's March 2002 album 'Death Mutilation Disease Annihilation', released by the French End All Life label, came as a limited edition of 500 gatefold sleeve vinyl issue. ATOMIZER, with support from MALEVOLENCE and Christchurch's MEATYARD, would tour New Zealand the same month.

Singles/EPs:
Gimmie Natural Selection / Death Mutilation Disease Annihilation / Ace Of Spades / I Wish You Were A Beer, Nihilist Void (2001)

Albums:
THE END OF FOREVER, End All Life (1999)
DEATH MUTILATION DISEASE ANNIHILATION, End All Life (2002)
Intro - Incubation / Hesitation Wounds / In The Mortal Realm You Roam No More / For Blood! For Blood! / Black Heart Epiphany / When The Demons Come / Death Mutation Disease Annihilation / He Couldn't Save Himself (How Do You Expect Him To Save You?) / Unit 731 / The End! The End! / Shadenfreude / Ritual

ATOMKRAFT (UK)
Line-Up: Ian Davidson Swift (vocals), Tony Dolan (guitars), Rob Mathews (guitar), D.C. Rage (bass), Ged Wolf (drums)

Newcastle's ATOMKRAFT were in fact one of the first speed metal band forming in 1979 at a time when METALLICA were yet to record their seminal 'No Life Til Leather' demo.

The band was rooted in the late '70s Punk act MORAL FIBRE which comprised bassist Tony 'Demolition' Dolan, drummer Paul Spillett and guitarists Ian Legg and Chris Taylor. With Legg decamping Ian Drew took over the vacant six string position but he too would soon leave. At this juncture Taylor made a trip to Germany and came back sporting a button badge with the environmental message "Atomkraft Nein Danke!"

The band duly re-christened themselves ATOMKRAFT believing it to be more in keeping with their new Metal sound. The band, now minus Taylor, would also undergo a line up shift drafting in guitarist Steve White and bassist Mark Irvine alongside Dolan and Spillett. However, after their inaugural gig Irvine's parents persuaded him there was no future with the act and he left.

ATOMKRAFT demoed two sets of four song demos prior to entering the Neat Records

studios Impulse for the 'Total Metal' / 'Death Valley' session in 1983. ATOMKRAFT at this point had a fluid line up and despite the tape attracting interest on the American underground metal scene the band broke up with Tony relocating to Canada to try his luck. Dolan soon returned home and set about reforming ATOMKRAFT with drummer Ged Wolf (ex-TYSONDOG and brother of VENOM manager Eric Cook) and teenage guitarist Rob Mathews. A further demo 'Pour The Metal In' secured a deal with Neat records for the 'Future Warriors' album.

The band secured their first European shows opening for VENOM and also supported SLAYER at the Marquee. This inaugural London show did not go without incident though as equipment breakages forced the band to cut their set to a mere three songs. Further shows in Europe had ATOMKRAFT supporting EXODUS and VENOM.

Trouble struck when Dolan left the band mid way through recording of a proposed EP to be entitled 'Your Mentor' leaving Wolf and Mathews to pick up the pieces. A new line-up was quickly assembled with new additions being ex-SATAN and AVENGER vocalist Ian Davidson Swift and bassist D.C. Rage.

This line up recorded the re-titled 'Queen Of Death' mini-album. The original version of the title track, the only variant to include Tony Dolan lead vocals, would be included on the Neat Metal 'Powertrax' compilation album.

The band invited Dolan back on board as a guitarist for the 'Conductors Of Noise' EP. ATOMKRAFT were due to play a co-headlining tour of Britain in 1987 but this was cancelled. They fared better in Europe where they played the Dynamo festival in Holland and toured as support to NUCLEAR ASSAULT and AGENT STEEL.

The band had a switch of personnel when bassist D.C. Rage rejoined the band and Dolan moved back to rhythm guitar. 1988 saw ATOMKRAFT touring Europe alongside NASTY SAVAGE and EXHUMER, including the 'Metal Battle' festival in Katowice, Poland and the Dutch 'Dynamo' festival.

ATOMKRAFT were due to release another album 'Atomized' on a different label to Neat but this never materialized.

Dolan later joined VENOM for a series of albums. Following his exit from VENOM in 1994 Dolan became an actor, even scoring a part in the Sylvester Stallone movie 'Judge Dredd'.

Singles/EPs:
Queen Of Death / Protector / Demolition / Funeral Pyre / Mode III, Neat 53-12 (1986) ('Queen Of Death' EP)
Rich Bitch / Teutonic Pain / Vision Of

Belshazzar / Foliage / Requiem / The Cage, Neat 1039 (1987) ('Conductors Of Noise' EP)

Albums:
FUTURE WARRIORS, Neat 1028 (1985)
Future Warriors / Starchild / Dead Man's Hands / Total Metal / Pour The Metal In / Death Valley / This Planet's Burning / Warzone / Burn In Hell / Heat And Pain

ATROPHY (Tucson, AZ, USA)
Line-Up: Brian Zimmerman (vocals), Rick Skowron (guitar), Chris Lykins (guitar), James Gulotta (bass), Tim Kelly (drums)

This Tucson, Arizona based metal act created in 1986 debuted with six track demo 'Chemical Dependency'. Toured as support to SACRED REICH in America during 1988. ATROPHY featured a track on the Metal Forces magazine compilation album 'Demolition' in 1988.
Lykins departed in early 1991 for a career in medicine at Yale University.
ATROPHY was apparently still active on the live circuit as late as November 1999, retaining guitarist Rick Skowron, bassist James Gulotta and drummer Tim Kelly.

Singles/EPs:
Puppies And Friends, Roadracer (1990)

Albums:
SOCIALISED HATE, Roadrunner RR 9518-2 (1988)
Chemical Dependency / Matter Of Attitude / Socialized Hate / Urban Decay / Preacher, Preacher / Rest In Pieces / Best Defense / Product Of The Past / Killing Machine
VIOLENT BY NATURE, Roadracer RO 9450-2 (1990)
Puppies And Friends / Violent By Nature / In Their Eyes / Too Late To Change / Slipped Through the Cracks / Forgotten But Not Gone / Process Of Elimination / Right To Die / Things Change

ATTACKER (Hoboken, NJ, USA)
Line-Up: Bob Mitchell (vocals), Pat Marinelli (guitar), Jim Mooney (guitar), Lou Ciarlo (bass), Michael Sabatini (drums)

Founded by guitarist Pat Marinelli and drummer Mike Sabatini under the handle of WARLOC at the beginning of 1983, the line-up was swiftly completed by Bob Mitchell (real name Bob Nunez) on vocals, John Joseph on bass and Jim Mooney on guitar.
Mitchell earned a good deal of praise for his performances on the group's first demo tape,

a three track affair consisting of '(Call On) The Attacker', 'Slayer's Blade' and 'Disciple'. This tape was recorded shortly before a name change to ATTACKER due to the emergence of the debut album from the Doro Pesch fronted WARLOCK on import from Germany. Mitchell was often compared favourably to major name vocalists with the twin pronged guitar attack of Mooney and Marinelli likened to better known European counterparts.
Joseph was replaced by ex-HADES bassist Lou Ciarlo during the recording of debut album 'Battle At Helm's Deep' for Metal Blade Records, who had picked up on the underground buzz developing around the New Jerseyites. Ciarlo re-recorded all Joseph's bass tracks prior to the release of the album. As coincidence would have it, Joseph went on to replace Ciarlo in HADES! A mixing problem delayed the album's release further and the band's original choice for the album cover was rejected by Metal Blade for a less than satisfactory affair.
There was some interest from Dan Johnson's PAR Records label around the time ATTACKER were making plans to record their second album, a more aggressive affair all round.
Vocalist John Leone and guitarist Tom D'Amico (replacing Mooney) were recruited for the album that aptly wound up being titled 'Second Coming' (the original, tentative title was 'The Deadly Blessing', however)
The choice of Leone was an inspired one as the new man had a similar style to Mitchell, so the switch was incredibly smooth.
The album was produced by Alex Perialis and RAVEN drummer Rob Hunter and eventually emerged through the newly formed Mercenary label in 1988. Prior to the album's release the label had included the track 'Emanon' on the 'L'Amour Rocks' compilation album in 1987.
In late 1988 Sabatini and Ciarlo quit to form JERSEY DOGS with Lou Ciarlo taking over a frontman's role. An EP 'Don't Worry, Get Angry' was issued the following year. Mitchell formed SLEEPY HOLLOW and NIGHTHUNTER.
The specialist label Sentinel Steel reissued both albums in the late '90s which invigorated renewed interest in ATTACKER in Europe. Mitchell, who had been operating side project ALCHEMY X, created a new version of ATTACKER comprising of Rolando Marcias, John Armstrong, Tommy Ackel and erstwhile DARK VENGEANCE and KEVORKIAN HOUSECALL guitarist Rob Oriani to put in a live show at the 2000 'Powermad' festival. This version of ATTACKER put in a total of three live performances all told.
Matters became extremely confusing when in

August 2000 Sabatini, Marinelli and Ciarlo, together with ex-JERSEY DOGS and SLEEPY HOLLOW guitarist Mike Benetatos, also reformed ATTACKER! (Sadly Mooney had recently passed away).

Unable to use the name ATTACKER Mitchell and Oriani assembled a new unit entitled VYNDYKATOR. Other members included guitarist William G. Peria of PSYCHODRAMA and KEVORKIAN HOUSECALL, bassist Steven Ratchen from ALCHEMY X, TRINITY, DOMINION and THE FRIGID EARTH and drummer Mark Mari, who had played with SNEAK ATTACK, DOG EAT DOG and THE FRIGID EARTH. This new band would score a deal with King Fowley's Battle Zone Records for a projected 2001 album release.

Albums:
BATTLE AT HELMS DEEP, Metal Blade (1986)
The Hermit / The Wrath Of Nevermore / Disciple / Downfall / Slayer's Blade / Battle At Helms Deep / Kick Your Face / Dance Of The Crazies / (Call On) The Attacker
THE SECOND COMING, Mercenary (1988)
Lords Of Thunder / Desecration / Zero Hour / Revelations Of Evil / The Madness / Captives Of Babylon / Octagon / Emanon

ATTAKK (USA)
Line-Up: Dave Anthony (vocals), Kuma (guitar), Gary Lee (bass), Phillip Wolfe (keyboards), Steve Pokory (drums)

Featuring ex-SHIRE vocalist Dave Anthony, ATTAKK originally released their debut album through the Japanese Monster Productions concern and possessed Japanese guitarist Kuma in their ranks.
The album was later re-issued by Mandrake Root Records.

Albums:
ATTAKK, Monster Productions ATK 1001 (1988)
Thunder In The Night (Private Hell) / Without A Word / Not Your Man / Never Apart / Ride The Dragon / Attakk

AT THE GATES (SWEDEN)
Line-Up: Tomas Lindberg (vocals), Anders Bjorler (guitar), Martin Larsson (guitar), Jonas Bjorler (bass), Adrian Elandsson (drums)

A very aggressive technical Thrash act in the vein of America's AT HEIST, but with added twists and a touch of the avant garde. This Gothenburg based, quintet formed in August 1990, was initially known as GROTESQUE,

under which name they released the 'Incantation' album in 1991.

As AT THE GATES, the first product to emerge was the mini-album 'Gardens Of Grief' on Dolores Records. The outfit's line-up at this time consisted of vocalist Tomas Lindberg, guitarists Alf Svensson and Anders Bjorler, bassist Jonas Bjorler and drummer Adrian Erlandsson.

Svensson's involvement with AT THE GATES would be ended by his colleagues as the man soon departed, later going on to form OXIPLEGATZ and releasing the 'Worlds And Worlds' album in 1996.

'The Red In The Sky Is Ours' features guest violinist Jesper Jarold. AT THE GATES toured Europe in 1992 opening for MY DYING BRIDE. Their third album 'With Fear I Kiss The Burning Darkness' was produced by noted Death Metal producer Tomas Skogsberg and again received solid reviews. AT THE GATES appeared at the MTV/Peaceville show at Nottingham's Rock City alongside ANATHEMA and MY DYING BRIDE before once more touring Europe with ANATHEMA and CRADLE OF FILTH.

'Terminal Spirit Disease' was produced by Fredrik Nordstrom and includes a selection of live tracks culled from the previous three releases alongside new studio material. To back up its release the band once more hit the road with ANATHEMA and MY DYING BRIDE. Toured Europe in early 1995 with SEANCE.

AT THE GATES switched labels moving to Earache Records, First product of this liaison was the 'Slaughter Of The Soul' album, which featured a version of Australian act SLAUGHTERLORD's track 'Legion'. KING DIAMOND guitarist Andy La Rocque guests on the track 'Cold'.

AT THE GATES also contributed their rendition of 'Captor Of Sin' to the SLAYER tribute album 'Slatanic Slaughter'.

Despite 'Slaughter Of The Soul' proving to be their highest selling effort, AT THE GATES split in late 1996. Various ex-members of AT THE GATES created THE HAUNTED fronted by former FACEDOWN singer Marco Aro.

Erlandsson founded H.E.A.L. and later joined premier British Black Metal act CRADLE OF FILTH in 1999.

Lindberg became vocalist for GREAT DECEIVER releasing the 2000 album 'Jet Black Art'. Lindberg joined DISINCARNATE in 1999, the band assembled by former DEATH / TESTAMENT / CANCER guitarist JAMES MURPHY.

By mid 2000 Lindberg was fronting LOCK UP, the side project of NAPALM DEATH men Shane Embury and Jesse Pintado with DIMMU BORGIR drummer Nick Barker.

Souls Of The Evil Departed / At The Gates / All Life Ends / City Of The Screaming Statues, Dolores DOL 005 (1991)
Souls Of The Evil Departed / All Life Ends, Peaceville Collectors CC7 (1994) (7" yellow vinyl single)

Albums:
THE RED IN THE SKY IS OURS, Peaceville DEAF 10 (1992)
The Red In The Sky Is Ours / The Season To Come / Kingdom Gone / Through Gardens Of Grief / Within / Windows / Claws Of Laughter Dead / Neverwhere / The Scar / Night Comes, Blood Black / City Of Screaming Statues
WITH FEAR I KISS THE BURNING DARKNESS, Peaceville DEAF14 (1993)
Beyond Good And Evil / Raped By The Light Of Christ / The Break Of Autumn / Non-Divine / Primal Breath / The Architects / Stardrowned / Blood Of The Sunsets / The Burning Darkness / Ever-Opening Flower / Through The Red
TERMINAL SPIRIT DISEASE, Peaceville VILE 47 (1994)
The Swarm / Terminal Spirit Disease / And The World Returned / Forever Blind / The Fevered Circle / The Beautiful Wound / All Life Ends (Live) / The Burning Darkness (Live) / Kingdom Gone (Live)
SLAUGHTER OF THE SOUL, Earache MOSH 143 (1995)
Blinded By Fear / Slaughter Of The Soul / Cold / Under A Serpent Sun / Into The Dead Sky / Suicide Nation / World Of Lies / Unto Others / Nausea / Need / The Flames Of The End / Legion

ATTILA (USA)
Line-Up: Vincent Paul (vocals / bass), John DeLeon (guitar), A.T. Soldier (drums)

A New York trio who once featured HITTMAN main-men Jim Bachi and Michael Buccell in the original line up.

Albums:
ROLLING THUNDER, Shattered (1986)
Turn Up The Power / Urban Commandos / March Of Kings / Defcon 1 / Thermonuclear Warrior / Rolling Thunder / Wild / School's Out / Chains Around Heaven / Tryst

AT WAR (Virginia Beach, VA, USA)
Line-Up: Paul Arnold (vocals / bass), Shaun Helsel (guitar), Dave Stone (drums)

A trio formed in 1984, the group issued a two track demo 'Rapechase' a year later prior to appearing on New Renaissance Records' 'Speed Metal Hell II' compilation.
Awarded with a two album deal by New Renaissance, AT WAR released their debut album, 'Ordered To Kill' in 1986. The album was released in Germany on the US Metal label and on Rock Brigade in Brazil.
The three-piece toured America with AGNOSTIC FRONT in December '86 following the release of 'Ordered To Kill' and opened at L'Amours in Brooklyn, New York for SLAYER and POSSESSED.
AT WAR's second album 'Retaliatory Strike' is produced by Alex Perialas and ex RAVEN drummer Rob Hunter.

Albums:
ORDERED TO KILL, GWD 90550 (1987)
Ordered To Kill / Dawn Of Death / Capitulation / Rapechase / The Hammer / Mortally Wounded / Ilsa (She Wolf Of The SS) / Eat Lead
RETALITORY STRIKE, New Renaissance NRR41 (1988)
FYI / Conscientious Objector / Creed Of The Sniper / Covert Sins / Crush Your Life / Gutless Sympathizer / Church And State / Felon's Guilt/ Thinkin' / The Example

AURA NOIR (NORWAY)
Line-Up: Apollyon, Blasphemer, Aggressor (drums)

AURA NOIR is the Thrash Metal side project of Black Metal musicians Carl 'Agressor' Michael Eide from ULVER, CADAVER INC. and VED BUENS ENDE in partnership with DØDHEIMSGARD's Ole 'Apollyon' Jorgen and MAYHEM's Blasphemer.
As 'Aggressor' Carl Michael Eide is also a member of INFERNÖ having debuted with the 1996 album 'Utter Hell'. The man has also deputized for DIMMU BORGIR's Tjodalv whilst the latter was on paternity leave from his band.
Eide guested on FLEURETY's 2000 album 'Department Of Apocalyptic Affairs' and has sessioned for WHITE WILLOW. Apollyon also has links with LAMENTED SOULS.

Albums:
DREAMS LIKE DESERTS, Hot HR002 (1996)
The Rape / Forlorn Blessings To The Dreamking / Angel Ripper / Snake / Mirage
BLACK THRASH ATTACK, Malicious (1997)
Sons Of Hades / Conqueror / Caged Wrath / Wretched Face Of Evil / Black Thrash Attack / The Pest / The One Who Smite / Eternally Your Shadow / Destructor / Fighting For Hell

DEEP TRACTS OF HELL, Malicious (1999)
Deep Tracts Of Hell / Released Damnation / Swarm Of Vultures / Blood Unity / Slasher / Purification Of Hell / The Spiral Scar / The Beautiful, Darkest Path / Broth Of Oblivion
INCREASED DAMNATION, Hammerheart (2001)
The Mirage / Towers Of Limbs And Fever / Released Damnation / Broth Of Oblivion / Swarms Of Vultures / The One Who Smite / Wretched Face Of Evil / Fighting For Hell / The Rape / Forlorn Blessing To The Dreamking / Dreams Like Deserts / Angel Ripper / Snake / Mirage / Towers Of Limbs And Fever

AUTOPSIA (ITALY)
Line-Up: Diego Grossi (vocals), Leo Balocco (guitar), Andrea Bernini (bass), Teo Mazzotti (drums)

Thrashers dating back to 1994. AUTOPSIA began life with a distinct Bay Area sound but have progressed to include Death and even technical, Progressive elements.
The original incarnation of AUTOPSIA was fronted by Dio Demicheli with guitars from Leo Balocco, bass delivered by Ivan Grecchi and drums in the hands of Teo Mazzotti.
A series of line-up shuffles saw the departure of Demicheli in 1995 and Diego Grossi taking the lead vocal mantle. The same year Lobo Ruscitti would be inducted as second guitarist but the following year both Ruscitti and Grecchi decamped. Bass was given over to Ricky Toselli in 1997 and then to Charly Danzi in 1998. By 2000 the four string position was covered by Andrea Bernini and AUTOPSIA bowed in with their first demo 'What Are You Looking For?', made up of four studio cuts and a live track. Further exposure was reaped when a song from this session was included on the Sony Music compilation 'Tendenze'.
A second demo, 'I Lied' produced by Tommy Talamanca of SADIST, arrived in 2000. AUTOPSIA would then put in a round of touring in the Czech Republic.
Drummer Teo Mazzotti also cites membership of infamous Grindcore act CRIPPLE BASTARDS.

AVALANCHE (USA)
Line-Up: Nikki Van Welden (vocals / bass), Michael Cloe (guitar), Barry Nicholson (drums)

Albums:
PRAY FOR THE SINNER, Roadrunner (1985)
They Won't Take Me / We Will Fight / Tortured Defender / This Love I Feel / Devil's Door / Pray For The Sinner / Sorcerer / Child Of Damnation / When The Thunder Roars / Rock Hard And Heavy

AVENGER (GERMANY)
Line-Up: Peter Wagner (vocals / bass), Guiness (guitar), Jörg Michael (drums)

AVENGER later adopted the name RAGE to avoid confusion with the British act of the same name. Under their new guise RAGE, led by Peter 'Peavey' Wagner, would go on to become one of Germany's premier Metal acts and are still a powerful force to this day.
Drummer Jörg Michael would, post-RAGE, find himself in great demand appearing with MEKONG DELTA, LAOS, HEADHUNTER, SCHWARZ ARBEIT, GRAVE DIGGER, STRATOVARIUS, AXEL RUDI PELL and RUNNING WILD.

Singles/EPs:
Depraved To Black / Down To The Bone / Prayers Of Steel (Live) / Faster Than Hell (Live), Wishbone WBLP 4 (1985) ('Depraved To Black' EP)

Albums:
PRAYERS OF STEEL, Wishbone WB 1412 (1984)
Battlefield / Southcross Union / Prayers Of Steel / Halloween / Faster Than Hell / Adoration / Rise Of The Creature / Sword Made Of Steel / Blood Lust / Assorted By Satan

AVENGER (UK)
Line-Up: Ian Swift (vocals), Lez Cheetham (guitar), Mick Moore (bass), Gary Young (drums)

The first incarnation of AVENGER evolved when ex-BLITZKRIEG vocalist Brian Ross teamed up with former AXE ViCTIM bassist Mick Moore, drummer Gary Young and guitarist Steve Bird in September 1982. The band contributed the track 'Hot And Heavy Express' to the Neat 'One Take No Dubs' EP. Shortly after Bird left due to hearing problems (!) to be replaced by John Brownless.
This line-up recorded the 'Too Wild To Tame' single before Brownless was sacked and in came Cheetham. Ross left to fill the vacant slot as SATAN's vocalist when Ian Swift left and, in a bizarre turn of events, Swift joined AVENGER.
In 1985 AVENGER toured Europe with an additional guitarist Ginger, a former member of IPANEMA KATZ. However, after a handful of shows Ginger was allegedly sacked for taking too long in the dressing room applying

make up! Ginger journeyed through ZIG ZAG, THE QUIREBOYS, THE THROBS and THE WILDHEARTS.

AVENGER contributed promo footage for three tracks 'Under The Hammer', 'Run For Your Life' and 'Revenge Attack' to the Neat video compilation 'Metal City' in 1985.

American ex-guitarist GREG REITER replaced Lez Cheetham prior to recording 'Killer Elite'. Cheetham would later figure in the VENOM's history.

Reiter's pedigree pre-AVENGER included stints with HOT ICE, TELEPATH, PSYCHOPATH (at one time fronted by a pre - CINDERELLA Tom Kiefer) and METALWOLF. Young was superseded by another American Darren Kurland.

The band toured the East coast of America, including dates opening for LIEGE LORD, but disintegrated midway through the dates. Towards the end there were plans to add an American vocalist.

Whilst Swift joined another Newcastle Upon Tyne Thrash act ATOMKRAFT, Reiter founded GHOST DANCE with ex-SYCHOPATH man Billy Gram and PRETTY POISON drummer Bobby Corea. By 1990 Reiter had joined Dutch Rockers HIGHWAY CHILE for the 'High Noon' album. Later work had Reiter as part of the Glammed up BITCH BOY alongside ex-PLASMATICS / WENDY O WILLIAMS drummer T.C. Tolliver. The guitarist would cut a solo album 'Fireflies' in 1996.

AVENGER were set to reform in 1995 with a line up of Moore, Reiter and ex-AVEN drummer Joe Hasselvander but this liaison never materialized.

Moore spent most of the nineties in a legal battle with Neat Records in a dispute over royalty statements and payments allegedly winning an out of court cash settlement and the reversion of his rights to the AVENGER back catalogue in 1997. To date these recordings have still not been reissued.

Singles:
One Take No Dubs EP, Neat 25 (1982)
Too Wild To Tame / On The Rocks, Neat 31 (1983)

Albums:
BLOOD SPORTS, Neat 1018 (1984)
Death Race 2000 / Warfare / You'll Never Take Me Alive / Rough Ride / Victims Of Force / N.O.T.J. / On The Rocks / Enforcer / Matriarch
KILLER ELITE, Neat 1026 (1985)
Revenge Attack / Run For Your Life / Brand Of Torture / Steel On Steel / Right To Rock / Hard Times / Under The Hammer / Face To The Ground / Dangerous Games /

Yesterday's Hero / M.M. 85 / Sawmill

AVERSION (CA, USA)
Line-Up: Christian Fuhrer (vocals), Dash (guitar), Edward Tatar (bass), Joe Tatar (drums)

AVERSION debuted with the 1988 demo 'Demo '88' before a second tape 'In Dead Of Night' secured the band a deal for the Randy Burns produced 'The Ugly Truth'. For this release the band comprised vocalist Christian Fuhrer, guitarist Dash, bassist Slelly Cason and drummer Mick Palmesano.

AVERSION toured Europe as openers to GWAR before returning to America for shows with D.O.A. and SUICIDAL TENDENCIES.

Albums:
THE UGLY TRUTH, Armageddon 008-36151 (1990)
Death Trip Picture Show / Wig / Uzi / Welcome To Society / Modern Day Martyr / Injection / G.O.D. C.O.D. / In Dead Of Night / Inertia / Do Or Die / Forward March / No Trouble In Paradise
FIT TO BE TIED, Restless (1993)
FALL FROM GRACE, Bulletproof CDVEST41 (1995)
What Is Mine / I Want More / The Weed, The Tree, The Tree And Me / Drag The Lake / Way Back / Heretic / Kill A Queer For Christ / Dignity / Waco Jesus / Retro-Active Mistake / Self Destructo Man / Psycho Babble / Make It Go Away / The Very End / Leaving

AXEGRINDER (UK)
Line-Up: Trev (vocals), Matt (bass), Steve (guitar), Daryn (drums)

An underground British Metal band that was created in 1986 from various Punk bands, including STONE THE CROWS, the band were originally titled TYRANTS OF HATE with drummer Jel at the drumstool.

As the band began to lean towards more slower, Metal material, a change of name to AXEGRINDER came about. In 1987 they recorded their 'Grind The Enemy' demo which led to interest from Peaceville Records guru Hammy. AXEGRINDER subsequently appeared on the 'A Vile Peace' compilation album which, in turn, led to an offer of a full album. AXEGRINDER later recruited guitarist Cliff Evans, who after the band's demise, formed Death Metal band FLESH.

Trev, Steve and Daryn created WARTECH enlisting bassist Chris.

Albums:
RISE OF THE SERPENT MEN, Peaceville

VILE7 (1989)
Never Ending Winter / Hellstorm / Life Chain /
War Machine / Evilution / Rise Of The Serpent
Men / The Final War

AXEMASTER (Kent, OH, USA)
Line-Up: Christopher Michael (vocals / bass),
Joe Sims (guitar),
Brian Henderson (drums)

Ohio NWoBHM influenced Thrash Metal.
AXEMASTER guitarist Joe Sims would later
figure as a member of Progressive Metal act
THE AWAKENING for the 'Invictus' album. He
would still be flying the flag in 2001 with a new
outfit DREAM OR NIGHTMARE comprising
Sims, fellow guitarist Jim Arnold, vocalist
Javier Colon, bassist Dave Rhynard and
drummer Russ Kirk.
The 1999 album of archive material released
by Greek label Unisound comprises both
AXEMASTER and THE AWAKENING
material.

Singles/EPs:
The Vision / Crusades / Warrior (Live), Azra
(1988)

Albums:
BLESSING IN THE SKIES, Azra A33 (1987)
The Prophecy / Golgotha / Blood Of The
Temple / Rock Forever / Without A Trace /
Crusades / Demon Machine / The Reaper /
Slave To The Blade / The Predator
THE AWAKENING (1985-1995), Unisound
(1999)
Golgotha / Blood Of The Temple / Crusades
/ Demon Machine / Slave To The Blade / The
Predator / Phantom Armies / Black
Dungeons / Secrets Untold / False
Consciousness / Naked Eye / As The Wind
Blows / Flowers For The Dead / Farewell To
A Friend

BABYLON WHORES
(FINLAND)
Line-Up: Ike Vil (vocals / keyboards), Antti Litmanen (guitar), Ewo Meichem (guitar), Jake Babylon (bass), Kouta (drums)

Noted exponents of "Death Rock" BABYLON WHORES mix a heady brew of Gothic Rock, '80s Thrash and Black Metal in a unique combination that has set the band apart from the pack.

The band's debut single 'Devil's Meat' released on their own Sugar Cult label saw the group comprising vocalist Ike Vil, guitarists Jussi Konittinen and Ewo Meichem, bassist M. Ways and drummer Pete Liha. Follow up 'Sloane 313' saw the bass player's job going to the suitably titled Jake Babylon. Further changes were afoot for BABYLON WHORES third release 'Trismegistos' with guitarist Antti Litmanen taking Konittinen's position and Kouta coming in on drums.

In late 1999 Babylon Jake bailed out to found a new act DEATH FIX and was replaced by Taneli Nyholm of ABSURDUS, CRYHAVOC and PANDEMONIUM OUTCASTS. Nyholm also goes under the pseudonyms of 'Serpent', 'Daniel Rock' and 'Daniel Stuka'.

BABYLON WHORES toured America in 2000 as guests to KING DIAMOND.

Singles/EPs:
Cool / Third Eye / East Of Earth, Sugar Cult SUGAR 666 (1994) ('Devil's Meat' 7" single)
Of Blowjobs And Cocktails / Cold Hummingbird / Babylon Astronaut / Silver Apples, Sugar Cult SUGAR 667 (1995) ('Sloane 313' EP)
Love Under Will / Hellboy / Speed Doll / Beyond The Sun / Trismegistos, Sugar Cult SUGAR 668 (1996) ('Trismegistos' EP)
Errata Stigmata / Errata Stigmata (Version) / Fey (Version) Sol Niger (Video), Necropolis NR067 CD (2000)

Albums:
COLD HEAVEN, Heroine - Music For Nations MFN 226 (1997)
Deviltry / Omega Therion / Beyond The Sun / Metatron / Enchirdion For A Common Man / In Arcadia Ego / Babylon Astronaut / Flesh Of A Swine / Cold Heaven
DEGGAEL, Spinefarm SPI62CD (1998)
Dog Star A / Sol Niger / Somniferum / Omega Therion (V2) / Emerald Green / Deggael: A Rat's God
KING FEAR, Necropolis (2000)
Errata Stigmata / Radio Werewolf / Hand Of Glory / Veritas / Skeleton Farm / To Behold

The Suns / Exit Eden / Sol Niger / Fey / King Fear - Song Of The Damned

BAD BRAINS (USA)
Line-Up: H.R. (vocals), Dr. Know (guitar), Darryl Aaron Jenifer (bass), Earl Hudson (drums)

Cult underground and highly influential Rastafarian Crossover Hardcore. The original band comprised vocalist H.R. (real name Paul Hudson), guitarist Dr. Know (real name Gary Wayne Miller), bassist Darryl Aaron Jenifer and drummer Earl Hudson. All the members had been seasoned in Jazz Rock acts on the local Washington D.C. club scene. Their early adventurous endeavours would come to the fore with the high profile Hardcore Punk and Reggae combination BAD BRAINS.

The band's debut album was produced by THE CARS guitarist Rik Ocasek. An attempt was made to support THE DAMNED on a tour of Britain but BAD BRAINS had their work permits refused.

In 1986 H.R. decamped to go solo. Following the 'I Against I' album BAD BRAINS drafted former FAITH NO MORE and CEMENT vocalist Chuck Moseley. His tenure was brief though and Moseley was ousted before recording anything.

The band added ex-CRO MAGS and BLITZSPEER drummer Jason Mackie in 1988. BAD BRAINS' line-up was stabilized when both Hudson brothers returned to the fold for the 'Quickness' record. Both Hudson's jumped ship once more and BAD BRAINS enlisted singer Israel Joseph-I and a returning Mackie.

The 1995 album, recorded for the MADONNA owned Maverick label, saw BAD BRAINS back with producer Rik Ocasek and also H.R. Predictably the latter's term was short. A mid tour band bust up led to H.R.'s permanent dismissal, the ex singer also having to face up to drug charges to boot.

The B-side to Brazilian Metal band SEPULTURA's 'Choke' featured reworks of BAD BRAINS tracks 'Gene Machine' and 'Don't Bother Me'.

A 1999 tribute album 'Never Give In' featured such heavyweight acts as SEPULTURA, ENTOMBED, DOWNSET, MOBY, WILLHAVEN, IGNITE and SKINLAB paying homage.

H.R. would put in a high profile guest appearance on the 2001 P.O.D. no. 1 album 'Satellite', rapping on the track 'Without Jah, Nothin'

Singles/EPs:
Pay To Cum / Stay Close To Me, Bad Brains

BB001 (1980) (7" single)
Big Take Over, (1981)
Bad Brains / Sailin' On / Big Takeover,
Alternative Tentacles VIRIS 13 (1982) (12"
single) ('I Love Jah' EP)
I And I Survive / Destroy Babylon, Food For
Thought YUMT 101 (1983) (12" single)
Spirit Electricity, S.S.T. SST 228 (1989)

Albums:
BAD BRAINS, R.O.I.R. A 106 (1982)
Sailin' On / Don't Need It / Attitude / The
Regulator / Banned In D.C. / Jah Calling /
Supertouch / F.V.K. / Big Take Over / Pay To
Cum / Right Brigade / I Love Jah / Intro /
Leaving Babylon
I AGAINST I, S.S.T. SST 065 (1986)
Intro / I Against I / House Of Suffering / Re-
Ignition / Secret '77 / Let Me Help / She's
Calling You / Sacred Love / Hired Gun /
Return To Heaven
ROCK FOR LIGHT, PVC PVCCD 8933
(1987)
Big Takeover / Attitude / Right Brigade /
Joshua's Song / I And I Survive / Banned In
D.C. / Supertouch / Destroy Babylon / F.V.K.
(Fearless Vampire Killers) / Meek / I / Coptic
Times / Sailin' On / Rock For Light / Rally
Round Jah Throne / At The Movies / Riot
Squad / How Low Can A Punk Get / We Will
Not / Jam
BAD BRAINS LIVE, S.S.T. SST 160 LP
(1988)
I Cried / At The Movies / The Regulator /
Right Brigade / I Against I / I And I Survive /
House Of Suffering / Re-Ignition / Sacred
Love / She's Calling You / Coptic Times /
F.V.K. / secret '77 / Day Tripper
QUICKNESS, Caroline CARCD 4 (1989)
Soul Craft / Voyage Into Infinity / Messengers
/ With The Quickness / Gene Machine /
Don't Bother Me / Don't Blow Bubbles /
Sheba / Your Juice / No Conditions / Silent
Tears / Prophets Eye / Endtro
ATTITUDE - THE ROIR SESSIONS, We Bite
WB 056 (1989)
Sailin' On / Don't Need It / Attitude / The
Regulator / Banned In D.C. / Jah Calling /
Supertouch / Leaving Babylon / Fearless
Vampire Killers / Big Take Over / Pay To Cum
/ Right Brigade / I Luv Jah / Intro
**YOUTH ARE GETTING RESTLESS - LIVE
AT THE PARADISO**, AMSTERDAM 1987,
Caroline CARCD 8 (1990)
Rock For Light / Right Brigade / House Of
Suffering / Day Tripper / She's A Rainbow /
Coptic Times / Sacred Love / Re-Ignition /
Let Me Help / Youth Are Getting Restless /
Banned In D.C. / Sailin' On / Fearless
Vampire Killers / At The Movies / Revolution
(Dub) / Pay To Cum / Big Takeover
RISE, Epic 474265-2 (1993)

Rise / Miss Freedom / Unidentified / Love Is
The Answer / Free / Hair / Coming In
Numbers / Yes Jah / Take Your Time / Peace
Of Mind / Without You / Outro
BAD BRAINS, Reach Out International DEI
2001-1 (1993)
GOD OF LOVE, Maverick 9362 45882-2
(1995)
Cool Mountaineer / Justice Keepers / Long
Time / Rights Of A Child / God Of Love /
Over The Water / Tongue Tee Tie / Darling I
Need You / To The Heavens / Thank JAH /
Big Fun / How I Love Thee
BLACK DOTS, Caroline PCAROL 005CD
(1996)
Don't Need It / At The Atlantis / Pay To Cum
/ Supertouch-Shitfit / Regulator / You're A
Migraine / Don't Bother Me / Banned In D.C.
/ Why'd You Have To Go? / The Man Won't
Annoy Ya / Redbone In The City / Black Dots
/ How Low Can A Punk Get? / Just Another
Damn Song / Attitude / Send You No Flowers
**SOUL BRAINS - A BAD BRAINS
REUNION**, (2000)
SPIRIT ELECTRICITY - LIVE, S.S.T. (2001)

BAL SAGOTH (UK)
Line-Up: Byron A. Roberts (vocals), Chris
Maudling (guitar), Mark Greenwell (bass),
Jonny Maudling (keyboards), Dave
Mackintosh (drums)

A Dark, Black neo-Pagan "Battle" Metal band
out of Yorkshire with a predilection for lengthy
song titles. BAL SAGOTH was formulated as
an idea by vocalist Byron Roberts as early as
1989 but it would not be until July of 1993 that
the involvement of the Maudling siblings
guitarist Christopher and drummer Jonny
took the concept into a band format. Further
draftees in September of the same year,
bassist Jason Porter and keyboard player
Vincent Crabtree brought BAL SAGOTH up to
full strength and by the close of the year an
inaugural demo had been cut.
The band duly signed a three album deal with
the Cacophonous label but delays held back
the issue of the tantalising debut album 'A
Black Moon Broods Over Lemuris' until May
of 1995. During this timeframe Crabtree
departed and was duly replaced by Leon
Forrest. BAL SAGOTH was scheduled to put
in their first live performances supporting
CRADLE OF FILTH but Roberts sustained an
injury whilst stagediving at a CANNIBAL
CORPSE concert which scotched these
plans.
It would be April of 1995 that BAL SAGOTH
finally embarked on the live trail with a gig at
the Dublin Castle in London. Upon the
album's eventual release support dates to
Portuguese Gothic Black Metal act

BAL SAGOTH

MOONSPELL were put in during July, upfront of a tour of the UK and Ireland with labelmates PRIMORDIAL and SIGH in September. However, BAL SAGOTH would pull out of these shows due to disagreements with the promoter. The band's stature was already ascendant in mainland Europe though and BAL SAGOTH headlined the Belgian 'Ragnarok' festival in November.

The following month bassist Jason Porter was ousted by the recruitment of Alastair McLatchy. The band toured Europe for the first time on a package billing with DARK FUNERAL and ANCIENT in February of 1997. BAL SAGOTH supported EMPEROR at the London Astoria and SINISTER in Belgium before completing a second round of European shows in alliance with EMPEROR and NOCTURNAL BREED in October of the same year.

As 1998 broke Forrest announced his exit for a career in the police. Jonny Maudling manouevered over to keyboards to plug the gap and Dave Mackintosh took the drum stool. During the summer MacLatchy broke ranks too and Mark Greenwell took over on bass.

Jonny Maudling found himself on loan to MY DYING BRIDE for European touring during 1999. The band signed to Nuclear Blast during 1999 for 'The Power Cosmic' album. BAL SAGOTH supported arch-Black Metal Swedes MARDUK at the London Dome in December of 2001.

Albums:

A BLACK MOON BROODS OVER LEMURIA, Cacophonous NIHIL 4CD (1995)
Hatheg Kla / Dreaming Of Atlantean Spires / Spellcraft And Moonfire (Beyond The Citadel Of Frosts) / A Black Moon Broods Over Lemuria / Enthroned In The Temple Of The Serpent Kings / Shadows 'neath The Black Pyramid / Witch-Storm / The Ravening / Into The Silent Chambers Of The Sapphirean Throne (Sagas From The Untedelivian Scrolls) / Valley Of Silent Paths

STARFIRE BURNING OVER THE ICE VEILED THRONE OF ULTIMA THULE, Cacophonous NIHL 18 CD (1996)
Black Dragons Soar Above The Mountain Of Shadows (Epilogue) / To Dethrone The Witch-Queen Of Mytos K'unn (The Legend Of The Battle Of Blackhelm Vale) / As The Vortex Illumines The Crystalline Walls Of Kor-Avul-Thaa / Starfire Burning Upon The Ice - Veiled Throne Of Ultima Thule / Journey To The Isle Of Sists (Over The Moonless Depths Of Night-Dark Seas) / The Splendour Of A Thousand Swords Gleaming Beneath

The Blazon Of The Hyperborean Empire / And Lo, When The Imperium Marches Against Gul-Kothoth, Then Dark Sorceries Shall Enshroud The Citadel Of The Obsidian Crown / Summoning The Guardians Of The Astral Gate / In The Raven-Hunted Forests Of Darkenhold, Where Shadows Reign And The Hues Of Sunlight Never Dance / At The Altar Of The Dreaming Gods (Epilogue)
BATTLE MAGIC, Cacophonous NIHIL (1998)
Battle Magic / Naked Steel (The Warrior's Saga) / A Tale From The Deep Woods / Return To The Praesidium Of Ys / Crystal Shards / The Dark Liege Of Chaos Is Unleashed At The Ensorcelled Shrine Of A'Zura-Kai (The Splendour Of A Thousand Swords Gleaming Beneath The Blazon Of The Hyperborean Empire Part II) / When Rides The Scion Of The Storms / Blood Slakes The Sand At The Circus Maximus / Thwarted By The Dark (Blade Of The Vampyre Hunter) / And Atlantis Falls
THE POWER COSMIC, Nuclear Blast NB 421-2 (1999)
The Awakening Of The Stars / The Voyagers Beneath The Mare Imbrium / The Empyreal Lexicon / Of Carnage And A Gathering Of Wolves / Callisto Rising / The Scourge Of The Fourth Celestial Host / Behold, The Armies Of War Descend Screaming From The Heavens! / The Thirteen Cryptical Prophecies Of Mu
ATLANTIS ASCENDANT, Nuclear Blast NB 584-2 (2001)
The Epsilon Exordium / Atlantis Ascendant / Draconis Albionensis / Star-Maps Of The Ancient Cosmographers / The Ghost Of Angkor Wat / The Splendour Of A Thousand Swords Gleaming Beneath The Blazon Of The Hyperborean Empire (Part III) / The Dreamer In Catacombs Of Ur / In Search Of The Lost Cities Of Antarctica / The Chronicle Of Shadows / Six Keys To The Onyx Pyramid

BALISTIK KICK (Bayonne, NJ, USA)
Line-Up: Joe Adrignola (vocals), Mike Marino (guitar), Vinnie Valdes (bass), Mike Paradine (drums)

Albums:
BALISTIK KICK, (1993)
WARHEAD, Zombie Wolf, (1997)
Warhead / Twilights Last Gleaming / March Of Crimes / Ssa / When Worlds Collide / Train Of Pain / Alive / Dying Day / Once Comes The Crow / Help Me / No Pain / Angel Of Mercy / Stonehouse
DESTROY, Brennus (1999)
A.M. Terror / Absence Of Light / Atmosfear /

Deliver The Kill / Sons Of Bitches / Black Hammer Jet / Powerhead / Psychic Domain / In The Devil's Ire / Death From Above

BATHORY (SWEDEN)
Line-Up: Quorthon (vocals / guitar), Kothaar (bass), Vvornth (drums)

A one man Extreme Metal project based around the enigmatic Quorthon (previously known as 'Ace Shot'), who was at one time rumoured to be the son of Black Mark label boss Borje Forsberg. With BATHORY Quorthon prides himself on overblown epic chunks of Metal that has attracted a loyal fan base.
BATHORY came to attention of the masses via the tracks 'The Return Of Darkness And Evil' and 'Sacrifice' that were both featured on the 'Scandinavian Metal Attack' compilation album of 1984. BATHORY was actually created a year before by Black Spade on vocals and guitar, bassist Hanoi and drummer Vans (real name Jonas Akerlund). The band toyed with various band names including NOSFERATU, MEPHISTO, ELIZABETH BATHORY and COUNTESS BATHORY before settling on BATHORY. For the 'Scandinavian Metal Attack' album Black Spade retitled himself Ace Shot and later Quorthon.
BATHORY performed only a handful of gigs before resolving never to perform again in a deliberate intention to compound the mystique surrounding the act. An early bass player was DRILLER KILLER's Cliff. Carsten Nielsen, drummer for Danes ARTILLERY, was offered a position in BATHORY during 1985 but declined. The band nearly relented in 1986 when a European tour with CELTIC FROST and DESTRUCTION was planned. Despite Witchhunter of SODOM rehearsing with the band the touring plans were scrapped.
The rhythm section of Kothaar and Vvornth appeared on 1988's 'Blood Fire Death'.
Quorthon issued a solo album, simply titled 'Album' (Black Mark 666-9), during 1993. For reasons best known to himself Quorthon consistently refuses to take the BATHORY experience out on tour.
1995's 'Octagon' suffered a setback at the last minute before release. It was deemed that lyrics to two tracks 'Resolution Greed' and 'Genocide' were too extreme hence a cover version of the KISS classic 'Deuce' was included instead. The missing two tracks were later issued on the 'Jubileum Volume III' compilation.
A BATHORY record entitled 'Raise The Dead' was planned for release through Music For Nations, but this proposed record never

appeared.

BATHORY are without doubt highly influential in the Scandinavian Black Metal scene with many later artists offering cover versions in homage.

In 1997 various Greek Black Metal acts including KAWIR, EXHUMATION and DEVISER contributed to the 'Hellas Salutes The Vikings' tribute effort. A more substantial album came the following year featuring heavyweight names such as MARDUK, GEHENNAH, DARK FUNERAL, EMPEROR, NECROPHOBIC and SATYRICON titled 'In Conspiracy With Satan'.

BATHORY made a welcome return to the scene with a new album 'Destroyer Of Worlds' during 2001.

Singles/EPs:

The Sword / The Lake, The Woodman, Black Mark (1988) (Promotion)
Twilight Of The Gods / Under The Runes / Hammerheart, Black Mark BM CD666P (1991) (Promotion release)

Albums:

BATHORY, Tyfon / Black Mark BMCD 666-1(1984)
Hades / Reaper / Necromancy / Sacrifice / In Conspiracy With Satan / Armageddon / Raise The Dead / War
THE RETURN, Tyfon / Black Mark BMCD 666-2 (1985)
Possessed / The Rite Of Darkness / Reap Of Evil / Son Of The Damned / Sadist / The Return... / Revelation Of Doom / Total Destruction / Born For Burning / The Wind Of Mayhem / Bestial Lust (Bitch)
UNDER THE SIGN OF THE BLACK MARK, Black Mark BMCD 666-3 (1986)
Nocturnal Obedience / Massacre / Woman Of Dark Desires / Call From The Grave / Equimothorn / Enter The Eternal Fire / Chariots Of Fire / 13 Candles / Of Doom..
BLOOD FIRE DEATH, Black Mark 666-4 (1988)
Oden's Ride Over Nordland / A Fine Day To Die / The Golden Walls Of Heaven / Pace 'Till Death / Holocaust / For All Those Who Died / Dies Irae / Blood Fire Death
HAMMERHEART, Black Mark BMCD 666-5 (1990)
Shores In Flames / Valhalla / Baptized In Fire And Blood / Father To Son / Song To Hall Up High / Home Of Once Brave / One Rode To Asa Bay
TWILIGHT OF THE GODS, Black Mark BMLP666-6 (1991)
Prologue - Twilight Of The Gods - Epilogue / Through Blood By Thunder / Blood And Iron / Under The Runes / To Enter Your Mountain / Bond Of Blood / Hammerheart
JUBILEUM VOLUME 1, Black Mark BMCD 666-7 (1992)
Rider At The Gate Of Dawn / Crawl To Your Cross / Sacrifice / Dies Irae / Through Blood By Thunder / You Don't Move Me (I Don't Give A Fuck) / Oden's Ride Over Nordland / A Fine Day To Die / War / Enter The Eternal Fire / Song To Hall Up High / Sadist / Under The Runes / Equimanthorn / Blood Fire Death
JUBILEUM VOLUME II, Black Mark 666-8 (1993)
The Return Of The Darkness And Evil / Burnin' Leather / One Rode To Asa Bay / The Golden Walls Of Heaven / Call From The Grave / Die In Fire / Shores In Flames / Possessed / Raise The Dead / Total Destruction / Bond Of Blood / Twilight Of The Gods
REQUIEM, Black Mark 666-10 (1994)
Requiem / Crosstitution / Necroticus / War Machine / Blood And Soul / Pax Vobiscum / Suffocate / Distinguish To Kill / Apocalypse
OCTAGON, Black Mark 666-11 (1995)
Immaculate Pinetreeroad / Born To Die / Psychpath / Sociopath / Grey / Century / 33 Something / War Supply / Schizianity / A Judgement Of Posterity / Deuce
BLOOD ON ICE, Black Mark BMCD666-12 (1996)
Intro / Blood On Ice / Man Of Iron / One Eyed Old Man / The Sword / The Stallion / The Wodwoman / The Lake / Gods Of Thunder Of Wind And Of Rain / The Ravens / The Revenge Of Blood On Ice
JUBILEUM VOLUME III, Black Mark (1998)
33 Something / Satan My Master / The Lake / Crosstitution / In Nomine Satanas / Immaculate Pinetreeroad #930 / War Machine / The Stallion / Resolution Greed / Witchcraft / Valhalla / Sociopath / Pax Vobiscum / Genocide / Gods Of Thunder Of Wind And Of Rain
DESTROYER OF WORLDS, Black Mark (2001)
Lake Of Fire / Destroyer Of Worlds / Ode / Bleeding / Pestilence / 109 / Death From Above / Krom / Liberty & Justice / Kill Kill Kill / Sudden Death / White Bones / Day Of Wrath

BATTLEFIELD (GERMANY)
Line-Up: Connie Ernst (vocals), Arthur Schilling (guitar), Frank Nitti (guitar), Patrick Renner (bass), Gerd Haußmann (drums)

BATTLEFIELD, a Power Thrash Metal quintet, was formed in 1987 by guitarists Arthur Schilling and Frank Nitti. The duo were joined by drummer Gerd Haußmann before adding bassist Andres Rückle and female vocalist Conny Ernst.

Following the bankruptcy of BATTLEFIELD's record label T.R.C. the band released a demo tape in 1990 aptly entitled 'Time To Rethink'. Ernst would join an early line up of IVANHOE. Vocalist Tanja Ivenz was fronting the band by the second album in a revised BATTLEFIELD line-up that also saw new faces in bassist Patrick Renner and drummer Stephan Fiedler.

The group played with the likes of PSYCHOTIC WALTZ, LIFE ARTIST and GYPSY KISS.

Singles/EPs:
We Come To Fight / Nuclear Death / Knock On Your Door / Grave Of The Unknown / Possessed Preacher, TRC 011 (1988) ('We Come To Fight' EP)

Albums:
STILL AND EVER AGAIN, Rising Sun IRS 972 223 (1991)
Experienced To Die / Still And Ever Again / Battlefield Of Misery / Red Rag / A Leap In The Dark / Experienced To Kill / Suction Of Eternity / If Our Earth Could Cry / Garden Of Stones
SPIRIT OF TIME, Rising Sun SPV 084-62162(1993)
Walls In Deformation / Heat In November / Living Skin / Through The Moment Of Changes / 7th Sky / There Ain't No Sorrow / Geradine / Spirit Of Time / Oh Moon

BEAST (NJ, USA)
Line-Up: Scott Ruthless (vocals), The Hinge (guitar), Ron Ace (guitar), Jeff Gross (bass), Doug Ryan (drums)

Singles/EPs:
Power Metal / Radical Man / Enemy Ace / The Shape, Mutha Records 006 (1983)

THE BEAST (USA)
Line-Up: The Beast (vocals), Guitar Pete (guitar), Joey Scumrot (bass), Creepy (drums)

THE BEAST adopted a new rhythm section for the second album 'Carnival Of Souls' of bassist John Sherry and drummer Tommy Diesel.
THE BEAST guitarist Guitar Pete (Pete Brasino) later launched GUITAR PETE'S AXE ATTACK issuing three albums before signing to major label Giant with his 1994 band SNAKEYED SUE. Brasino now operates as a Blues player.

Albums:
THE BEAST... HAS ARRIVED, Napalm

FLAME 001(1985)
The Beast Has Arrived / McDonalds Man / Kill Or Be Killed / Blood Bath / Death Rattle / World In Flames / Skull Butt / Poison Dart
CARNIVAL OF SOULS, Maze Music SPV08-600 (1988)
From Parts Unknown / Brain Dead / Horror Show / War Path / Bang! / Destroy / Carnival Of Souls / Frustration / Thrill Kill / Sex Club / Wreckless

BEAST PETRIFY (SINGAPORE)
Line-Up: Al Fahmi (vocals / guitar), Hairulnizam (guitar), Scyfrul (bass), Rosmawan Boy (drums)

Rooted in the 1993 Death Metal band BRUTAL BEAST. At this juncture BRUTAL BEAST's line-up cited frontman Al Fahmi, bassist Scyfrul, rhythm guitarist Yumos and drummer Hasni.
During 1995 ETHEREAL brought BRUTAL BEAST member Al Fahmi into the fold as their new vocalist / guitarist. However, his preference for Thrash Metal soon won the day and Al Fahmi along with his BRUTAL BEAST colleague bass player Scyfrul and ETHEREAL members guitarist Hairulnizam and drummer Rosmawan Boy adopted a whole new side venture. With the title of BEAST PETRIFY, the band played strictly in a Speed Metal direction made evident on their 1997 demo cassette 'In The Circle Of Time'. Later erstwhile guitar colleague Yumos would join the band and Shahril from OSSUARY took over the drum stool for recording of the 1999 album 'Dimensional Deranged Dilemma' BEAST PETRIFY splintered down to just a duo of Al Fahmi and Scyfrul.

Albums:
DIMENSIONAL DERANGED DILEMMA, Sonic Wave International (1999)
Dimensional Deranged Dilemma / Massive Irretrievable Burden / Slaves Of The Abyss / Impending Disaster / Revulsion After Discrimination / Pestiferous Betrayal / Obscure Obliteration (Extended Aggression Version) / The Pain Deep Within / In The Circle Of Time

BELIEVER (Colebrook, PA, USA)
Line-Up: Kurt Bachman (vocals / guitar), Dave Baddorf (guitar), Howe Kraft (bass), Joey Daub (drums)

Pennsylvanian Christian Death Thrashers formed in 1985 by drummer Joey Daub and vocalist Kurt Bachman together with guitarist Dave Baddorf and bassist Howe Kraft. Added new bassist Wyatt Robertson in mid 1990.

BELIEVER courted controversy by immersing themselves fully into the Thrash scene, wearing T shirts of non-secular acts and touring with the likes of BOLT THROWER.

During 1991 Bachman would produce the debut album from fellow Christian Thrashers LIVING SACRIFICE.

The 1994 album 'Dimensions' found BELIEVER with Jim Winter on bass and William Keller on lead vocals. Daub would forge a union with SACRAMENT members guitarist Mike DiDonato and bassist Erik Ney to create FOUNTAIN OF TEARS for a 1999 album.

Ex-BELIEVER members later founded SERAPH.

Albums:
EXTRACTION FROM MORTALITY, REX Music 000-137-8902D (1989)
Unite / Vile Hypocrisy / D.O.S. (Desolation Of Sodom) / Tormented / Shadow Of Death / Blemished Sacrifices / Not Even One / Extraction From Mortality / Stress
SANITY OBSCURE, RC Records RC 9312 (1991)
Sanity Obscure / Wisdom's Call / Non-Point / Idols Of Ignorance / Stop The Madness / Dies Irae (Day Of Wrath)/ Dust To Dust/ Like A Song
DIMENSIONS, Roadrunner RR 9101-1 (1994)
Gone / Future Mind / Dementia / What Is But Cannot Be / Singularity / No Apology / Trilogy Of Knowledge: Intro - The Birth, Movement I: The Lie, Movement II: The Truth, Movement III: The Key

BELLADONNA (New York, NY, USA)
Line-Up: Joey Belladonna (vocals), Al Romano (guitar), John McCoy (bass), Michael Sciotto (drums).

A short-lived liaison, following his split from ANTHRAX, vocalist Joey Belladonna teamed up with ex-GILLAN, McCOY and MAMMOTH bassist John McCoy having initially been sounded out by guitarist Al Romano to team up. Michael Sciotto left New York based Melodic Rockers FROM THE FIRE to round out the line-up pieced together in July 1992. The band looked strong on paper, but split after a handful of recording sessions, Romano going onward to team up with the ailing ex-BADLANDS / BLACK SABBATH vocalist RAY GILLEN in SUN RED SUN. His place was taken by former TRASH BROADWAY man Joe Stump.

Belladonna then re-forged the band with ex-AXIOM and HIPPIE JET guitarist Darin Scott, bassist Joe Andrews and drummer Scott Schroeter. This line up would record the debut album for the Belgian Mausoleum label. With steady rumours that Belladonna had ditched the trademark Thrash of ANTHRAX (he often cited JOURNEY as a great love) critics and fans were taken aback to discover the album was an uncompromisingly brutal piece of work. American dates supporting MOTÖRHEAD ensued to promote the record. Bad luck befell the band in the midst of recording a second album when the Mausoleum label collapsed. Ultimately BELLADONNA would fold. Scott teamed up with BULLETBOYS drummer Robby Karras in an act titled PAIN INC.

Some of the results of the ill-fated second round of recordings undertaken by BELLADONNA were released independently by the USG label in 1999. The band was credited as comprising guitarist Darin Scott, bassist Joe Andrews and drummer Scott Schroeter. John McCoy is listed as playing bass on 'Two Face' and 'Injun'.

Stump founded JOE STUMP'S REIGN OF TERROR. Sciotto journeyed through stints with ACE FREHLEY and VICK LECAR. Scott would re-emerge with SPIDER BABYS, a band comprising vocalist Gerry Schad, bassist Jeff Beebe and FOUR LARGE MEN drummer Mike Merrifield.

Albums:
BELLADONNA, Mausoleum 904170-2 (1995)
Blunt Man / Power Trip / Rob You Blind / Perfection / Two Face / Down & Out / R.I.P. / Last Call / Nothing To Hide / Taken By Force / Injun / Mixed Emotions / 1-900
SPELLS OF FEAR, USG 1029-2 (1999)
Stress Your Mind / Lost Control / Jokin' / Bad Memories / How Would You Know / Ultimate Threat / Don't Pin Me Down / Face You / Phony / Out Of Gas / I Don't Need / Cover Me / Long Way Down

BENEDICTION (UK)
Line-Up: David Ingram (vocals), Darren Brookes (guitar), Peter Rew (guitar), Frank Healy (bass), Ian Treacy (drums)

A Birmingham act formed in early 1989, BENEDICTION are sadly more noted in their home country for having supplied vocalist Barney Greenaway to NAPALM DEATH than their musical achievements. However, outside of Britain, BENEDICTION have garnered a sizeable following through ever improving albums and constant touring.

The group debuted with the 'Dreams You Dread' demo in June 1989 which secured the band a deal with German label Nuclear Blast.

Following the release of the first album, entitled 'Subconscious Terror', Dave Ingram stepped in for Greenaway on vocals and contributed to promotion activity during the year which included British supports to PARADISE LOST and AUTOPSY.

The band undertook a further British tour opening for BOLT-THROWER prior to recording their follow up effort 'The Grand Leveller'. Before the record came out the band undertook further headlining dates throughout 12 countries, capitalized on by selected British and German dates upon its release. 1991 shows included gigs with label mates DISMEMBER and MASSACARA.

The group endured another line-up change when bassist Paul Adams departed in late 1991, BENEDICTION favouring ex-CEREBRAL FIX man Frank Healy to take his place.

Toward the end of 1991 BENEDICTION released the 'Dark Is The Season' EP which featured a reworking of the old ANVIL chestnut 'Forged In Fire'. At the dawn of 1992 BENEDICTION hit the road once more with BOLT-THROWER on a bill including ASPHYX that enabled the band to play its first dates in Israel.

The 1993 album 'Transcend The Rubicon' opened up more new ground as BENEDICTION topped the bill of a European tour with ATHEIST and CEMETERY as support. Dates included visits to Ireland, Portugal and Mexico. The travelling cost the group the services of drummer Ian Treacy though, the skinsman quitting and being superseded by the 18 year old Neil Hutton.

In 1994 BENEDICTION supported BOLT-THROWER on their American club tour, but found themselves as headliners on latter dates as problems hit BOLT-THROWER forcing their withdrawal. BENEDICTION, with future MARSHALL LAW drummer Paul Brookes in tow, also appeared at the legendary 'Milwaukee Metalfest' during the same year, on a bill alongside fellow heavyweights BIOHAZARD and SLAYER.

During 1995 Neil Hutton and David Ingram formed the side project WARLORD UK, releasing the 'Maximum Carnage' album on Nuclear Blast in 1996. The album included covers of AMEBIX and SLAYER songs.

More recently frontman Ingram (now named Dave Bjerregaard Ingram after his marriage) lent a helping hand to BOLT-THROWER for a batch of live dates during 1997, when their vocalist Martin Van Drunen bailed out without warning. However, the 'helping hand' turned out to be more permanent. Ingram stayed the course for a series of festival appearances but by November of 1998 had bailed out.

BENEDICTION promptly pulled in former DETHRONED frontman Dave Hunt to fill the vacated vocal position. Latterly Ingram rejoined BOLT THROWER.

BENEDICTION's 1998 album 'Grind Bastard' included a cover of JUDAS PRIEST's 'Electric Eye'.

BENEDICTION would make a return with the September 2001 record 'Organised Chaos' produced by ex SABBAT guitarist Andy Sneap.

Singles/EPs:
Experimental Stage, Nuclear Blast NB057 (1992)
Foetus Noose / Forged In Fire / Dark Is The Shadow / Jumping At Shadows / Experimental Stage, Nuclear Blast NB059 (1992)
Return To The Eve, Nuclear Blast NB 058PDS (1992)
The Grotesque / Ashen Epitaph / Violation Domain (Live) / Subconscious Terror (Live) / Visions In The Shroud (Live), Nuclear Blast NB 088-2 (1994) ('The Grotesque - Ashen Epitaph' EP)

Albums:
SUBCONSCIOUS TERROR, Nuclear Blast NB033 (1990)
Intro - Portal To Your Phobias / Subconscious Terror / Artefacted Irreligion / Grizzled Finale / Eternal Eclipse / Experimental Stage / Suspended Animation / Divine Ultimatum / Spit Forth The Dead / Confess All Goodness
THE GRAND LEVELLER, Nuclear Blast 048 (1991)
Vision In The Shroud / Graveworm / Jumping At Shadows / Opulence Of The Absolute / Child Of Sin / Undirected Aggression / Born In A Fever / The Grand Leveller / Senile Dementia / Return To Eve
TRANSCEND THE RUBICON, Nuclear Blast NB073 (1993)
Unfound Mortality / Nightfear / Paradox Alley / Bow To None / Painted Skulls / Violation Domain / Face Without Soul / Bleakhouse / Blood From Stone / Wrong Side Of The Grave / Artefacted - Spit Forth
THE DREAMS YOU DREAD, Nuclear Blast NB120 (1995)
Down on Whores (Leave Them All For Dead) / Certified...? / Soulstream / Where Flies Are Born / Answer To Me / Griefgiver / Denial / Negative Growth / Path Of The Serpent / Saneless Theory / The Dreams You Dread
GRIND BASTARD, Nuclear Blast (1998)
Deadfall / Agonized / West Of Hell / Magnificat (Irenicon) / Nervebomb / Electric Eye / Grind Bastard / Shadow World / Bodiless / Carcinova Angel / We The Freed /

Destroyer / I
ORGANISED CHAOS, Nuclear Blast
NB0522 (2001)
Suicide Rebellion / Stigmata / Suffering
Feeds Me / Diary Of A Killer / The Temple Of
Set / Nothing On The Inside / Easy Way To
Die / Don't Look In The Mirror / This
Graveyard Earth / Charon / I Am The
Disease / Organised Chaos

BEOWÜLF (CA, USA)

Line-Up: Dale Henderson (vocals / guitar),
Mike Jensen (guitar),
Paul Yamada (bass), Michael Alvarado
(drums)

Formed in California during 1983, BEOWÜLF
debuted with a track inclusion on the
'Welcome To Venice' compilation. The band
released their self-titled debut in 1987 before
returning for a second stab a year later with
the more Punk oriented Speed Metal of 'Lost
My Head... But I'm Back On The Right Track'.
Post-BEOWÜLF, vocalist Dave Henderson
fronted KOOL WHIP. Guitarist Mike Jensen
would attend the Guitar Institute of
Technology before forging Hip Hop act THE
BONEYARD CREW. The guitarist would later
reunite with BEOWÜLF drummer Miguel
'Michael' Alvaredo to found the popular club
circuit act CREEPER in alliance with vocalist
'Fifty One', bassist 'Insect Dragster' and
erstwhile SUICIDAL TENDENCIES guitarist
Mike Clark.
Although CREEPER would undergo various
line up changes Jensen and Alvarado stuck
together for the 'Lost Dog' album.
BEOWÜLF bassist Paul Yamada would sadly
pass away in 1995.

Albums:
BEOWÜLF, Suicidal (1987)
Tool The Jewel / No Doubt / Drink, Fight,
Fuck / All I Need / Shoot Them Down / Taste
The Steel / Phuck / Get The Grind /
Americanizm / Down Till Dead / Belligerence
/ Don't Give A Damn / (My Life) Alcohol
**LOST MY HEAD... BUT I'M ON THE RIGHT
TRACK**, Caroline CAROL 1355 (1988)

BETRAYAL (San Francisco, CA, USA)

Line-Up: Chris Ackerman (vocals), Marcus
N. Colon (guitar), Bob McCue (guitar), Jeff
Lain (bass), Jeff Mason (drums)

A Bay Area Christian Thrash Metal act that
arrived on the scene with the 1989 demo
session 'The Reviling Darkness'. For the 1991
debut 'Renaissance By Death', recorded in
Chicago for Wonderland Records,
BETRAYAL cited a line up of vocalist Chris

Ackerman, erstwhile MARTYR guitarists
Marcus N. Colon and Matt Maners, bass
player Jeff Lain and drummer Brian Meuse.
By the sophomore 1993 effort 'The Passing'
Maners and Meuse were out of the picture,
new draftees being guitarist Bob McCue and
drummer Jeff Mason. Also contributing on
backing vocals would be DELIVERANCE
vocalist Jimmy Brown and Chris Scott of
PRECIOUS BLOOD.
Despite engendering a loyal fanbase
BETRAYAL folded in October of 1993. Post-
BETRAYAL both Colon and Mason would join
the highly regarded Christian Thrash act
DELIVERENCE.
During 2000 Colon and Maners resurrected
the BETRAYAL title for the Gothic inclined
effort 'Leaving Nevermore'. A compilation of
BETRAYAL and MARTYR archive material
'The Passing Of Time' preceded a further
Gothic / Industrial album 'In Remembrance Of
Me'.

Albums:
RENAISSANCE BY DEATH, Wonderland
(1991)
Renaissance By Death / The Invitation /
Fallen Deceived / More Faith Than Me /
Escaping The Altar / Assassin In The Midst /
Mortal Flesh / Stroll Thru A Wicked Age /
Prophets Of Baal / Plead The Blood
THE PASSING, Wonderland (1993)
Renouncement / The Usurper / Carnival Of
Madness / Ichabod / Forest Of Horrors /
Race Of Hypocrisy / As I Turned Away /
Whispers Of Chaos / Strength Of The
Innocent / Retaliatory Strike / Frantic
LEAVING NEVERMORE, Black & White
(2000)
THE PASSING OF TIME, Black & White
(2001)
IN REMEMBRANCE OF ME, Black & White
(2002)

BEYOND BELIEF (HOLLAND)

Line-Up: A.J. Van Drenth (vocals / guitar),
Robbie Woning (guitar), Ronnie Van Der Way
(bass), Jacko Westendorp (drums)

Formed in 1986, BEYOND BELIEF feature
two ex-DEADHEAD members guitarist
Robbie Woning and bassist Ronnie Van Der
Way. Having released the 'Remind The Skull'
demo in 1990, a further demo, 'Stranded',
followed in 1992.
BEYOND BELIEF toured their native Holland
with CREEPMINE, ANCIENT RITES and
DEADHEAD.

Albums:
TOWARDS THE DIABOLICAL

EXPERIMENT, Shark 029 RTD (1993)
Intro: Ave / Shapes Of Sorrow / Stranded /
The Experiment / The Nameless / Silent Are
The Holy / Fade Away / Untouched /
Prophetic Countdown / Kissing In XTC / The
Finishing Touch / Outro: Never
RAVE THE ABYSS, Shark 102 (1995)
Rave The Abyss / Cursed / Blood Beach /
High On The Moon / The Burning Of
Redlands / Crushed Divine / The Grand
Enigma / Tyrants Of The Sun / Lost

BEYOND POSSESSION (CANADA)

Calgary based Crossover act led by vocalist
Ron Hadley. Both the 1985 'Skaters Life' EP
and Metal Blade 'Is Beyond Possession'
album tracks would be assembled with
unreleased demos for the 2001 Melodiya
release 'Repossessed: 1985-1989'.

Singles/EPs:
Tell Tale Heart / What's The Matter /
Skater's Life / No Religion / Vengeance /
Dying Fast, Fango-Rooter (1985) ('Skaters
Life' EP)

Albums:
IS BEYOND POSSESSION, Metal Blade
72168 (1986)
Never Nothing New / Life Force / Dying Fast
/ Living To Tell You About It / Last Will And
Testament / You're So Important / Final Daze
/ Why? It's Youth / Beyond Possession /
Creeping Eruption / Hard Times / Attitude
Problem / Depression / Cinderella Syndrome
/ I'll Never Rest In Peace
REPOSSESSED: 1985-1989, Melodiya
(2001)

BEYOND THE EMBRACE
(New Bedford, MA, USA)
Line-Up: Shawn Gallagher (vocals), Alex
Botelho (guitar), Oscar Gouveia (guitar), Jeff
Saude (guitar), Adam Gonsalves (bass),
Mike Bresciani (drums)

BITTER END (Seattle, WA, USA)
Line-Up: Matt Fox (vocals / guitar), Russ
Stefanovich (guitar), Chris Fox (bass), Harry
Dearinger (bass)

Seattle's BITTER END started life as a trio in
1983. Debuted with a 1988 demo 'Meet Your
Maker'. Critics were almost universal in
comparing the 1990 Metal Blade debut 'Harsh
Realities' to Dave Mustaine's crew.

Albums:
HARSH REALITIES, Metal Blade ZORRO
10 (1990)

Sex And Death / Guilty (Until Proven
Innocent) / Just Say Yes / Beat The System /
Profits Of Doom / Meet Your Maker / Harsh
Realities / Save Us / Waiting For Death /
Living Hell

BLACK DEATH (USA)
Line-Up: Siki Spacek (vocals / guitar), Greg
Hicks (guitar), Darrel Harris (bass), Phil
Bullard (drums)

Singles/EPs:
Here Comes The Wrecking Crew /
Retribution, Auburn AU7-002 (1984)

Albums:
BLACK DEATH, Auburn AU 002 (1984)
Night Of The Living Death / The Hunger /
When Tears Run Red (From Love Lost
Yesterday) / Fear No Evil / The Scream Of
The Iron Messiah / Streetwalker / Black
Death

BLACKEND (GERMANY)
Line-Up: Michael Goldschmidt (vocals /
guitar), Manuel Unterhuber (guitar), Mario
Unterhuber (bass), Alex Mayer (drums)

Out and out Thrashers founded in their early
teens during 1991. At first BLACKEND crafted
their skill as a covers band honouring their
Bay Area favourites. The demo 'Contrast Of
Minds' led to a debut tech-Thrash album
'Sloth' in 1997. This outing scored
BLACKEND a deal with the Massacre label
for the 1999 'Mental Game Messiah' album.
The band unsurprisingly donated cover
versions to two of their mentors' tribute
albums with renditions of '...And Justice For
All' appearing on the METALLICA collection
'Phantom Lords' and TESTAMENT's 'Practice
What You Preach' on the tribute offering 'Jump
Into The Pit'.
BLACKENED folded during October of 2001.
Bassist Mario Unterhuber soon
teamed up with LOONATIKK for live work.

Singles/EPs:
The Eye Of The Observer / Freezing The
Skin / As The Sun Remains, Massacre
(1999) (Promotion release)

Albums:
SLOTH, MDD 12CD (1997)
Harmonies In Black / No More Confidence /
Regression / Not To Deny / Separate /
Retaliation Breed / Parts Of Peril / Virtual /
Streams Of Perfection
MENTAL GAME MESSIAH, Massacre MAS
CD0218 (1999)
The Eye Of The Observer / Detect The

Crack / Mental Game Messiah / Burn The Fuse / Beyond Forever / Liquid Surroundings / Freezing The Skin / Save Our Souls / Scars Can't Tell / As The Sun Remains
DEMO'95, Gutter (1999) (Split CD with LOONATIKK)
Absent-Minded / None / Lost Imaginations / Voices Of Reality
THE LAST THING UNDONE, Massacre MAS CD0275 (2001)
The Last Thing Undone / I Am The Chosen One / The More I Lie / Long Now / Exclude The Included / Darkest Day / The Dice Is Cast / Battle Between Minds

BLACK SHEPERD (BELGIUM)
Line-Up: Yvon Verhaegen (vocals), Igor Plint (guitar), Michel Oluf (guitar), Patrick Minnebier (bass), Alain Verhaegen (drums)

A Belgian Thrash act with Black Metal influences. Ex-BLACK SHEPERD guitarist Luc Vervelot created CONSPIRACY OF SILENCE.

Albums:
IMMORTAL AGGRESSION, Punk Etc (1988)
Immortal Aggression / State Of Decay / Make Love War / Corpses / Preacher Of Death / Trash / Another Day To Die / Kill The Priest / Animal / Lord Of The Darkness / I Am God / Evil Revenge

BLACKSTAR (UK)
Line-Up: Jeff Walker (vocals / bass), Carlo Regadas (guitar), Mark Griffith (guitar), Ken Owen (drums)

As CARCASS, the originators of Gore Metal, gradually evolved into a more traditional Hard Rock outfit the band's later works, such as 'Heartworks' and 'Swansong', found the band so distanced from the original concept that a split was inevitable.
Founder member and vocalist Jeff Walker resurfaced with BLACKSTAR, an act very much musically akin to latter day CARCASS. BLACKSTAR also featured two fellow erstwhile CARCASS members, guitarist Carlo Regadas and drummer Ken Owen, together with former CATHEDRAL guitarist Mark Griffiths.
BLACKSTAR cut cover versions of HÜSKER DÜ's 'The Girl Who Lives On Heaven Hill' and THIN LIZZY's 'Running Back' for the 1998 Peaceville compilation 'X'.

Albums:
BARBED WIRE SOUL, Peaceville CDVILE69 (1997)

Game Over / Smile / Sound Of Silence / Rock n' Roll Circus / New Song / Give Up The Ghost / Revolution Of The Heart / Waste Of Space / Deep Wound / Better The Devil / Instrumental

BLACK TASK (USA)
Line-Up: Warren Appleby (vocals), Steve Kristiansen (guitar), Gus Santiago (bass), Jim Trub (drums)

Pennsylvania Speed Metal act. BLACK TASK slowed the pace for 1986's 'Long After Midnight'. For this outing vocalist Warren Appleby became simply 'Warren Ay'.

Albums:
BLACK TASK, Damnation (1985)
Sex And Destruction / Kill Your Enemies / Firestorm / Smash Your Face
LONG AFTER MIDNIGHT, Axe Killer (1986)
Long After Midnight / Set To Explode / Knowledge Is Deadly / The Terminal Frost / This Road Burns / Shattered And Torn / Burning The Sky / Overload / In The Shadows / Rip!

BLACK VIRGIN (USA)
Line-Up: Kenny Lienhardt (vocals / guitar), Joe Cerna (bass), Cathy Burke (drums)

BLACK VIRGIN's debut privately pressed single featured a line-up that included vocalist Jimmy Strain. The band then pulled in Sean Vasquez on bass in 1984 who in turn would be superseded by Robbie Graham then Joe Cerna for the album. Kenny Lienhardt took the lead vocal role for the 'Most Likely To Exceed' record. Drummer Cathy Burke was previously a member of THE REACTORS.

Singles/EPs:
Feel The Steel / 44 Killer, Black Virgin (1983)

Albums:
MOST LIKELY TO EXCEED, Bellaphon (1987)
Nightriders / Most Likely To Exceed / Blood Brothers / Desperate Means / Life After Life / First To The Worst / Heavy Metal Mad / Hand Over Fist

THE BLAMED (USA)
Line-Up: Matt Switaj (vocals / guitar), Bryan Gray (guitar), Christopher Wiitala (bass), Trevor Wiitala (drums)

THE BLAMED are amongst the leading crop of Christian Hardcore Thrash acts.
THE BLAMED, then rooted in California and

fronted by vocalist Jeremy Moffit, bowed in with the 1994 '21' album, so titled because it took a mere 21 hours to record. Following the 1995 heavily Thrash orientated 'Frail' album THE BLAMED folded.

Guitarist Bryan Grey would go onto join SIX FEET DEEP and LEFT OUT but, utilising members of LEFT OUT, would resurrect THE BLAMED for the 1998 'Again' album on Grrr Records, a label division of the Chicago based 'Jesus People' organisation. The band at this juncture involved Gray, bass player Jeff Locke, CRUCIFIED / MORTAL drummer Jim Chaffin and Jeff Hansen.

1999's 'Forever' outing found THE BLAMED comprising Gray, Locke, Chaffin and vocalist / guitarist Matt Switaj. The record was noted for it's double tribal drumming between Chaffin and a guesting Lance Garvin of LIVING SACRIFICE. 'Forever' would also close with the Celtic flavoured '4/20/99' with guest female vocals courtesy of THE CROSSING's Hilde Bialach.

Yet another switch in personnel occurred for the 2001 record 'Isolated Incident'. Gray retained Switaj but enrolled the twins bassist Christopher and drummer Trevor Wiitala as a new rhythm section.

Matt Switaj decamped in February of 2002.

THE BLAMED have contributed a version of 'Soldiers Under Command' to a STRYPER tribute album.

Singles/EPs:
This Is For David / On Westnedge... In Amsterdam, Burnt Toast Vinyl (2000)
For Brian Wilson / At This Moment / Our Bazaar World / That's The Ticket, Computer Club Records CCRP1001 (2001) ('At This Moment' EP)

Albums:
21, Tooth & Nail (1994)
Abuse / Help Yourself / Testimony / Drunk, Separation / A State Of... / From Me To You / Rainbow / 3 a.m. / God Is Alive / Walkabout / The Ballad Of The Blamed
FRAIL, Tooth & Nail (1995)
Feeding The Ignorant / Weakness / For You / No Difference / Just Because / Breeze / Prove Your Excuse / Second Minded Friend / Torn / Guy In A Suit And The Pope / Declaration Dead
AGAIN, Grrr (1998)
Beginning / In The End / Casualty Of War / Rage / God Have Mercy / Don't Fall / Covered / Deny / Outer Crust / Crying Tree / The Pride / Experience / Live By Truth / D Sin Grate
FOREVER, Grrr (1999)
Dissonance / To Change / Pistol Whipped /

Reason Escapes / Satori / Degeneration / Conversations In The Mirror / Forever / Knock Me Down / New Seeds Of Contemplation / Seven Story Mountain / Beyond Your Passion In His Passion / 4-20-99
GERMANY, Grrr (2000)
Wounded - Overwhelmed / Discussed / Running Away Can Be An Ugly Thing / Darkness Is So Unforgiving / Last Time I Do This For The First Time / This Is It / At Last We Will Have Revenge
ISOLATED INCIDENT, Grrr (2001)
At This Moment / Social Calls / To See You How You Are Seen / Short Of A Miracle / At Least We Have Each Other / N.X.N.W. / Our Bazaar World / For Fifteen Bucks (And A Spot On The Floor) / The Piano Is Playing Our Song / The Bat Storm / The Finest Of Society's Philanderers / Talking Philosophy On The Streets Of Oslo / Ch-Ch-What's Missing Is You Are

BLESSED DEATH
(New York, NY, USA)
Line-Up: Larry Portelli (vocals), Jeff Anderson (guitar), Nick Fiorentiono (guitar), Kevin Powelson (bass), Chris Powelson (drums)

Alex Perialas and RAVEN drummer Rob Hunter produced 'Destined For Extinction'. A third BLESSED DEATH album was recorded but would have to wait a decade before its final release.

Albums:
KILL OR BE KILLED, Megaforce (1986)
Melt Down / Pig Slaughter / Omen Of Fate / Into The Ovens / Knights Of The Old Bridge / Eternal War / Blessed Death/ Napalm/ Kill Or Be Killed
DESTINED FOR EXTINCTION, Roadrunner RR 9688 (1988)
Digital War / Pain Killer / 10,000 Days / Incoming Wounded / Pray For Death / Death In The Sky / Curse Of Weapons / Alien Impregnation / Destruction's Eve
DOUBLE ATTACK, Old Metal (1998)

BLIND FURY (UK)
Line-Up: Lou Taylor (vocals), Steve Ramsey (guitar), Russ Tippins (guitar), Graeme English (bass), Sean Taylor (drums)

BLIND FURY arose from the ashes of Newcastle Metallers SATAN catering for the band's new found, mellower direction with new vocalist Lou Taylor (who had replaced Brian Ross). BLIND FURY, had been the moniker of one of Taylor's previous outfits.

SATAN fans did not appreciate the change in direction though, and, after one album for Roadrunner, the band promptly reverted back to SATAN, ousting Taylor in the process. Following a brief tenure with PERSIAN RISK the singer later formed TOUR DE FORCE in 1988 alongside guitarists Fred Avesque (ex-TROY / DRIVESHAFT) and Andy Warnock, bassist Mike Antoine and drummer Gary Burfort. TOUR DE FORCE, however, never recorded. Taylor has long since become one of London's leading Rock club DJ's.

Back in Newcastle, Steve Ramsey and Graeme English formed the successful Martin Walkyier fronted Folk Metal band SKYCLAD.

Albums:
OUT OF REACH, Roadrunner (1985)
Do It Loud / Out Of Reach / Evil Eyes / Contact Rock n' Roll / Living On The Edge / Dynamo (There Is A Place...) / Back Inside / Dance Of The Crimson Lady (Part One)

BLIND ILLUSION
(Richmond, CA, USA)
Line-Up: Marc Biedermann (vocals / guitar), Larry Lalonde (guitar), Les Claypool (bass), Mike Miner (drums)

Founded in 1978, Bay Area Thrashers BLIND ILLUSION date back further than the Thrash Metal movement's origins in the early '80s. BLIND ILLUSION ranked alongside then burgeoning acts such as METALLICA, ANVIL CHORUS and EXODUS on the San Francisco scene.

Guitarist Marc Biedermann formed the group with keyboard player Ben Heveroh but by 1984 the whole band had drifted apart leaving Biedermann solo. A new act was assembled in 1984 with Biedermann joined by guitarist Pat Woods, vocalist Dave Godfrey, bassist Geno Side and drummer Mike Mlhor. This line up soon fractured when Godfrey joined HEATHEN in 1985. Biedermann took over lead vocals for their next demo tape 'Blood Shower' / 'Smash The Crystal'.

BLIND ILLUSION was also then joined by bassist Les Claypool. Outside the confines of the group, Claypool would pursue a project band with guitarist Todd Huth being basically the prototype for PRIMUS titled PRIMATIVE. Claypool is also believed to have produced the album 'Plastic Rock For A Plastic World' from Pop Metal band THE GUMBYS.

BLIND ILLUSION recorded demos produced by METALLICA guitarist Kirk Hammet as a trio of Biedermann, Claypool and drummer Mike Mihor which secured a deal with British label Music For Nations subsidiary Under One Flag.

Prior to recording the band added second guitarist John Marshall. This liaison was short lived however, with Marshall (a guitar technician with METALLICA at the time) departing to fill in for an injured James Hetfield on a METALLICA tour before joining METAL CHURCH.

BLIND ILLUSION thus added ex-POSSESSED guitarist Larry Lalonde in May 1987 but the new guitarist joined Claypool decamping to create PRIMUS. PRIMATE man Todd Huth switched roles to join BLIND ILLUSION.

Biedermann contributed guest lead guitar parts to BLUE OYSTER CULT's 'Imaginos' album in 1988.

Albums:
THE SANE ASYLUM, Under One Flag FLAG 18 (1988)
The Sane Asylum / Bloodshower / Vengeance Is Mine / Death Noise / Kamakazi / Smash The Crystal / Vicious Visions / Metamorphosis Of A Monster

BLIND JUSTICE (HOLLAND)
Line-Up: Attila Szabo (vocals / guitar), Folkert Draisma (guitar), Dennis Van Melis (bass), Marco De Groot (drums), Mark Spring In't Veld (saxophone), Edith Mathot (violin)

Thrash act BLIND JUSTICE combine dark and heavy sounds with violins and saxophones making for a quite unusual concoction.

The band was formed in 1989 by vocalist / guitarist Attila Szabo and guitarist Folkert Draisma, both previously having had experience with school act HEAT WAVE, and bass player Dennis van Melis. Drummer Marco De Groot was inducted in 1989.

De Groot would depart in 1994, having his position filled by Nicolas Hamel. With this line up BLIND JUSTICE cut the 'In Equilibrium' opus which included a cover version of IRON MAIDEN's 'The Trooper'.

Dennis Van Melis decamped in 1995 as the band issued the 'Pissed' EP, a record which saw another cover version - this time THIN LIZZY's 'Massacre'. Promoting their 1996 album 'Hurt' BLIND JUSTICE would tour Holland as support to American all girl Rockers PHANTOM BLUE. The following year the band witnessed yet another switch on the drum stool with Andre Borgman taking Hamel's place. Further ructions ensued when founder member Draisma made his exit, BLIND JUSTICE duly filling the gap with Hans Hansen.

Borgman bailed out in 2000 taking up

membership of AFTER FOREVER and APOCALYPSE. An esteemed veteran of the Dutch Metal scene Ernst Van Ee, a man with credits ranging from THRENODY, HIGHWAY CHILE, VENGEANCE and HELLOISE, plugged the gap.

Singles/EPs:
Pissed... Again / Boulder / Massacre, Blind Justice BJ 0095 (1995) ('Pissed' EP)

Albums:
SAX &VIOLINS, Blind Justice (1993)
Intro / Down We Go / Sax And Violins (At The Fireplace) / Suffer / Time's Ticking / Mother Nature / Why Should We Care? / Relief
IN EQUILIBRIUM, Blind Justice BJ (1994)
CHILD'S PLAY, Blind Justice BJ (1995)
HURT, Killer Whale (1996)
This Is How It Begins / Why? / Hurt / Reality-V / Relief / Boulder / Child's Play / Post War Depression / Life's A Bitch / R.U. God? / Pissed (Again) / No Win War / Upset / Weird Science - So This Is How It Begins

BLITZKRIEG (UK)
Line-Up: Brian Ross (vocals), Jim Sirotto (guitars), Ian Jones (guitars), Steve English (bass), Steve Abbey (drums).

BLITZKRIEG are perhaps most noted for METALLICA's rendition of their theme song 'Blitzkrieg', featured on the B side of the Bay Area monsters 'Creeping Death' single.
Despite this notoriety and a strong cult following BLITZKRIEG releases have been few and far between, although this hasn't been for the lack of trying.
Vocalist Brian Ross is the guiding force behind the band and has a colourful career including auditions with TYGERS OF PAN TANG, requests to join SAMSON and E.F. BAND and forming, albeit very briefly, a band with ex-WHITESNAKE guitarist BERNIE MARSDEN.
BLITZKRIEG formed in October 1980 in Leicester, the line-up listed above being the original. Brian Ross answered an advert placed by SPLIT IMAGE comprising Jim Sirotto, Ian Jones, Steve English and Steve Abbey looking to replace their previous vocalist, Sarah.
Ross had previous form with KASHMIR (an act that featured WHITESNAKE's David Coverdale's cousin Kev Stevens on drums) and ANVIL. Upon Ross joining SPLIT IMAGE Jez Gilman suggested the new name of BLITZKRIEG, although various paying club gigs were still for a while performed under the old moniker.

The band's first product was a three track demo cassette, which led to a single for the Newcastle based Neat Records entitled 'Buried Alive'. The same year BLITZKRIEG also contributed the track "Inferno" to the Neat 'Leadweight' compilation.
In February 1981 the band underwent a line-up change adding ex-ELECTRIC SAVAGE guitarist John Antcliffe and bassist Mick Moore.
The latter had previously played in the Leicester outfit AXE VICTIM with Ian Jones and Moore tells the tale that the legendary 'Blitzkrieg' (the B-side of the 'Buried Alive' single) had originally been conceived by AXE VICTIM under the title 'Bitch'. Jones had taken the nucleus of the song to BLITZKRIEG with him, the riffs of which had been a lame attempt to duplicate those of Dutch outfit FOCUS' legendary 'Hocus Pocus'!
With a revised line-up BLITZKRIEG gained welcome press coverage by featuring in the very first issue of 'Kerrang!' and went on to record a show supporting TRUST in Newcastle for an officially released tape entitled "Blitzed Alive". However, the band spilt in December 1981 with Moore and Ross eventually forming AVENGER and Antcliffe joining CHROME MOLLY. Ross was to subsequently perform vocal duties with SATAN for a tour of Holland and wound up leaving AVENGER for the ranks of SATAN.
Ross kept in touch with Mick Moore and, along with Jim Sirotto, teamed up again as BLITZKRIEG to record the album 'Blitzkrieg - A Time Of Changes' with Sean Taylor of SATAN on drums and TYGERS OF PAN TANG guitarist Mick Proctor. At this point, Ross was also managing and singing for LONEWOLF.
The band, almost a pet project by this stage, underwent further reshuffling in June 1986 leaving Ross as the sole surviving member with Proctor teaming up with SPEAR OF DESTINY. BLITZKRIEG was reassembled with guitarists J.D. Binnie (ex-MANDORA) and Chris Beard, bassist Darren Parnaby and drummer Sean Wilkinson. This incarnation recorded a four track demo in 1987, but the band split once more at the close of 1987 with Wilkinson, Parnaby, Binnie and Beard staying together in a Glam Metal act called LIBERTY. Ross, after a rethink, started afresh in the summer of 1988. The singer gathered around him guitarists Glenn S. Howes and Steve Robertson, bassist Robbie Robertson and drummer Kyle Gibson, yet the only recorded product was a two track demo before BLITZKRIEG once more succumbed to another drastic line-up shuffle.
By August of 1989 only Ross and Howes remained from the most recent band,

augmented with new guitarist Tony J. Liddle - previously a member of SARATOGA, PREDATOR and VIOLET ERUPTION, bassist Glen Carey and former AVENGER drummer Gary Young. A video, 'At The Kazbah', was released and the long awaited second album '10 Years Of Blitzkrieg' on the Roadrunner label.

Inevitably there were to be more departures. In early 1991 Carey, Young and Howes quit to form HURRICANE. Ross turned to his old comrade Mick Moore together with ex SATAN drummer Sean Taylor and guitarist Paul Nesbitt, although Moore had left within a year, BLITZKRIEG trimming down to a quartet of Ross, Liddle, Taylor and former WHEELBARROWS FROM HELL bassist Dave Anderson. This line-up recorded the album 'Unholy Trinity' in 1992. However, it was not to be released until the close of 1995.

BLITZKRIEG undertook a short tour of Greece in early 1996 with yet more new members; bassist Steven Ireland and drummer Paul 'Sid' White. Liddle would decamp in January of 1997 for TENDAHUX - recording an as yet unreleased album - but further gigging found BLITZKRIEG on tour in their strongest market, Germany, during the winter of 1997. Ireland was unable to fulfil these dates and a stand in bassist Gavin Gray the same year the band recorded a Japanese language version of the track 'Blitzkrieg', the original version of which will forever remain the group's legacy.

During 1998 BLITZKRIEG were working on new material for Neat Metal Records although predictably the band line up had evolved once more. Joining Ross were a returning Howes on guitar, fellow guitarist Martin Richardson and drummer Mark Hancock. This line up put in a rare appearance at the Wacken Open Air festival in Germany

Early 1999 found BLITZKRIEG back in action performing their first American show in New Jersey sharing a billing with SWEET SAVAGE and RAVEN.

As 2002 drew in Ross announced not only the planning of a projected album to be titled 'Absolute Power' for the Metal Nations label but yet another completely revised BLITZKRIEG line up. Tony Liddle made a return to be joined by second guitarist Paul Nesbitt, bassist Andy Galloway and erstwhile WHATEVER and DISPOSABLE HEROES drummer Phil Brewis. With this line up BLITZKRIEG performed at the 'Motala Metal' festival in Sweden and would be confirmed for appearances at the 'Metal Meltdown' in Asbury Park, New Jersey and Germany's annual 'Wacken Open Air'.

Singles/EPs:

Buried Alive / Blitzkrieg, Neat NEAT 10 (1980)

Albums:

BLITZKRIEG - A TIME OF CHANGES, Neat 1023 (1985)
Ragnarok / Blitzkrieg / Pull The Trigger / Armageddon / Take A Look Around / Hell To Pay / Vikings / A Time Of Changes / Saviour
TEN YEARS OF BLITZKRIEG, Roadrunner RO9302 (1991)
Blitzkrieg / Buried Alive / Night Howl / The Sentinel / Nocturnal Vision
UNHOLY TRINITY, Neat Metal NM002 (1995)
Hair Trigger / Struck By Lightning / Taking Care Of Business / Field Of Dreams / Take A Look Around / After Dark / Crazy For You / Zip / Unholy Trinity / Calming The Savage Beast / The Wraith / Easy Way Out / All Hallows Eve / Countess Bathory / Jealous Love / House Of Pleasure / Return Of The Zip
TEN, Neat Metal NM 012 (1996)
Cavo D'Oro / Fighting All The Way To The Top / Buried Alive / The Sentinel / The Power Of The King / Night Howl / I'm Not Insane / Court In The Act / Blitzkrieg '96 / Nocturnal Vision
THE MISTS OF AVALON, Neat Metal NM032 (1998)
The Legend / Tranquil State / I Am The Doctor (Who Are You?) / Deceiver / Princess For The World / The Mighty 'A' / Smell Of Roses / Love's Too Late / Anasazi / Yesterdays (Hope For The Future) / Another Interview? / Vicious Rumours / I Was Having A Great Time And Stayed Longer Than I Should, So When I Got To The Railway Station The Train Had Gone!
ABSOLUTE POWER, Metal Nations (2002)

BLITZKRIEG (USA)

Line-Up: Don Ross (vocals), Eric Von Theumer (guitar), Jeff Johnson (guitar), Neil Moore (bass), Jeff Wills (drums)

As coincidences go, American Metal outfit BLITZKRIEG found themselves involved in one of the strangest.

Not content with sharing their band name with the infamous Newcastle based NWoBHM BLITZKRIEG group, the Americans also boasted a singer with the surname of Ross and a bassist called Moore, the same names as their British counterparts!

BLITZKRIEG's album was produced by KEEL's frontman Ron Keel.

Albums:

READY FOR ACTION, Talen / Greenworld GWD 90521 (1985)
Winner Takes All / Ready For Action / Young

73

Forever / First Strike / Let Me Know / Misbeliever

BLOOD (Torrance, CA, USA)
Line-Up: Robyn Kyle Basauri (vocals), Chris Howell (guitar)

RACER X's drummer Jeff Martin and bassist Greg Chaisson aided Californian Christian metallers BLOOD in the studio. Vocalist Robin Kyle Basauri would also spend terms with DIE HAPPY and JOSHUA.

Albums:
RED SEA, Rugged RGD 33012 (1994)
Soulshaker / Blood / Wolves At The Door / Dust To Dust / Last Days Of Winter / Walk On Fire / Shades Of Purple / Hellbound Train / Losin' My Way / Down Home Static / Tears Of Joy

BLOODCUM (USA)
Line-Up: Joey Hannemann (vocals) Bobby Tovar (guitar), George Hierro (guitar), John Araya (bass),
Jimmy Sotelo (drums)

BLOODCUM came to attention for featuring SLAYER siblings: vocalist Joey Hannemann being brother of SLAYER guitarist Jeff Hannemann and bassist John Araya playing the same instrument as his more famous brother and SLAYER frontman Tom Araya.

Albums:
BLOODCUM, Wild Rags (1987)
Son Of Sam / Harassment By Farm Animals / Belligerent Youth / Live To Kill / First To Die / Happily Married
DEATH BY A CLOTHES HANGER, Wild Rags (1988)
Happily Married / Son Of Sam / Live To Kill / Good Hearted Man / Treatment Of Death / Death By A Clothes Hanger / Belligerent Youth / Harassment By Farm Animals / First To Die / Sike-O-Path

BLOODFEAST (USA)
Line-Up: Gary Markovitch (vocals), Adam Tranquilli (guitar), Lou Starita (bass), Kevin Kuzma (drums)

Initially known as BLOODLUST in 1985. Released a 4 track demo 'Suicidal Mission' in February 1986 shortly after adding second guitarist Mike Basden. Changed names to BLOODFEAST before signing to New Renaissance Records. BLOODFEAST toured America in 1988 supporting DEATH ANGEL. Due to heavy demand for the debut 'Kill For Pleasure' album a four track EP, 'Face Fate'

was rush released which included a re-recording of 'Blood Lust' and remixes of 'Vampire' and 'R.I.P.'
The 'Kill For Pleasure' album would later be re-issued on CD format and by Shark Records in Germany as a double pack shared with KUBLAI KHAN.
The band parted company with guitarist Adam Tranquilli upfront of working on a new album announced as 'The Last Remains'. However, when it finally emerged this second album, which included a cover version of THE MIGHTY SPHINCTER's 'Hitler Painted Roses', was renamed as 'Chopping Block Blues'.
Tranquilli re-emerged in 1991 with his new outfit LAST REMAINS featuring Rich Caputo on vocals, Kurt Becker on second guitar, Ron McLynn on bass and drummer Adam Kieffer. With New Renaissance re-issuing the albums on CD for the first time BLOODFEAST would be tempted back into a full blown reformation for the 1999 'Metal Meltdown' festival in Asbury Park, New Jersey.

Singles/EPs:
Face Fate / Bloodlust / R.I.P. (Remix)
Vampire (Remix), New Renaissance NRR 35 (1988)

Albums:
KILL FOR PLEASURE, New Renaissance NRR 16 (1987)
Menacing Thunder / Kill For Pleasure / Cannibal / Vampire / Suicidal Mission / Venomous Death / The Evil / Darkside / R.I.P.
CHOPPING BLOCK BLUES, Flametrader FLAME 1016CD (1990)
The Last Remains / Hunted, Stalked And Slain / Chopping Block Blues / Hitler Painted Roses / Dropping Like Flies / Born Innocent / Turn To Dust / The Chemically Imbalanced / Spasmodic / Remnants

BLOODGOOD (USA)
Line-Up: Les Carlson (vocals), David Zaffiro (guitar), Mike Bloodgood (bass), Mark Welling (drums)

Christian Metal band fronted by former JOSHUA vocalist Les Carlson. Guitarist David Zaffiro's history stretches back through MORNING STAR and CYPRESS.
The band debuted with a 1983 promotional cassette entitled 'Metal Missionaries'. At the time the group's no holds barred Metal approach shocked much of the established Christian Rock audience. The opening track to their inaugural 1986 eponymous album 'Black Snake' was nothing short of pure

Thrash. Indeed, noted Christian Death Metal combo MORTIFICATION would cover the track on their 'Live Planetarium' record.

BLOODGOOD drafted ex-PERENNIAL drummer Mark Welling for the sophomore 'Detonation' album. This album too saw no let up in the musical aggression, album opener 'Battle Of The Flesh' quickly gaining status as a Speed Metal classic. The band promoted the album in Europe by putting in a performance at the British Christian Greenbelt festival in 1987.

BLOODGOOD's third effort was to prove a turning point. Not only did studio problems almost nullify the bass sound on the record but the band had opted for a change of direction to a melodic Hard Rock sound. Guitarist David Zaffiro departed prior to the recording of the 'Out Of The Darkness' album in 1989 and had his position taken by Paul Jackson. BLOODGOOD also added former WATCHMEN drummer Kevin Whistler after Welling was sacked and the group finally released 'Out Of The Darkness' late the same year. Welling would join Seattle act RAIL for a seven year term of duty.

In the early '90s BLOODGOOD added rhythm guitarist Craig Church for live work and keyboard player Brooke Lizotte. An extremely limited live album from a German tour, simply dubbed 'Live In Germany', emerged but in a strictly limited hand numbered release of a mere 990 copies.

DAVID ZAFFIRO released a solo album, 'The Other Side', virtually at the same time the new BLOODGOOD album was issued and went on to pursue a solo career and involved himself in the production of several other Christian Rock acts well into the late '90s.

The 1991 BLOODGOOD effort 'All Stand Together' saw Bloodgood and Carlsen joined by Jackson, keyboard player Tim Heintz and future GIANT man Dan Huff.

Carlsen would become a temporary frontman for esteemed Christian Thrashers TOURNIQUET, delivering lead vocals on their 1993 studio live album. Zaffiro would guest on the 1996 album by fellow Christians NOUVEAUX.

During January of 2002 there would surface strong rumours of a full BLOODGOOD reformation. These murmurings would turn out to be true, BLOODGOOD being found to be suitably rehearsing in a church with a line-up of Carlson, Bloodgood - now a fully fledged pastor, Jackson and new drummer Jeff McCormack.

Albums:
BLOODGOOD, Frontline FR 9002 (1986)
Accept The Lamb / Standing In The Light / Demon On The Run / Anguish And Pain / Awake / Soldier Of Peace / You Lose / What's Following The Grave / Killing The Beast / Black Snake

DETONATION, Frontline CO9019 (1987)
Battle Of The Flesh / Vagrant People / Self-Destruction / Alone In Suicide / Heartbeat (Of The City) / Eat The Flesh / Holy Fire / Crucify / The Messiah / Live Wire

ROCKIN' A HARD PLACE, Frontline RO9036 (1988)
Shakin' It / The Presence / What Have I Done? / Heaven On Earth / Do Or Die / She's Gone / The World (Keeps Moving Around) / Seven

OUT OF DARKNESS, Intense RO 9063 (1989)
Out Of The Darkness / Let My People Go / America / It's Alright / Top Of The Mountain / Hey You / Mad Dog World / Changing Me / New Age Illusion

ALIVE IN AMERICA - BLOODGOOD LIVE VOLUME ONE, Intense RO 9219 (1990)
Out Of The Darkness / Do Or Die / It's Alright / Hey You / Alone In Suicide / She's Gone / Heaven On Earth / Shakin' It / Soldier Of Peace / America / Never Be The Same / Demon On The Run / Killing The Beast / Battle Of The Flesh / Black Snake

SHAKIN' THE WORLD - BLOODGOOD LIVE VOLUME TWO, Intense RO 9220 (1990)
Let My People Go / Mad Dog World / Top Of The Mountain / Awake / Eat The Flesh / Holy Fire / Crucify/ The Sixth Hour / The Messiah / Accept The Lamb / Seven / New Age Illusion

ALL STAND TOGETHER, Broken Again CO8793 (1991)
S.O.S. / All Stand Together / Escape From The Fire / Out Of Love / Say Goodbye / Kingdom Come / Fear No Evil / Help Me / Rounded Are The Rocks / Lies In The Dark / Streetlight Dancer / I Want To Live In Your Heart

THE COLLECTION, Intense FLD9091 (1991)
Anguish And Pain / Battle Of The Flesh / Eat The Flesh / Never Be The Same / New Age Illusion / Crucify / The Messiah / What's Following The Grave / Shakin' It / Killing The Beast / Alone In Suicide / Out Of The Darkness / Do Or Die / The Presence / Top Of The Mountain / Black Snake

TO GERMANY WITH LOVE, SB (2000)
Intro- Kingdom Come / Heaven On Earth / Let My People Go / Out for Love / All Stand Together / Hey You! / Anguish and Pain / Escape From The Fire / I Want to Live In Your Heart / Self Destruction - Drum solo / Crucify / Intro - Messiah / Seven

BLOODLUST (USA)

Line-Up: Guy Lord (vocals), Anthony Romero (guitar), Earl Mendenhall (guitar), Sandy K. (bass), M.E. Cuestas (drums)

Following the release of their debut album BLOODLUST split with vocalist Guy Lord and added ex-ABBATOIR man Steve Gaines, brother of STRYPER bassist Tim Gaines. Further line up shuffles witnessed the departure of guitarist Anthony Romero and drummer M.E. Cuestas.

The 'Terminal Velocity' EP of 1988 saw BLOODLUST with a line-up of Gaines, guitarists Earl Mendenhall and John Lisi, together with bassist Sandy K. and drummer Craig Kasin.

BLOODLUST were later to recruit bassist Eric Meyer. In 1990 Sandy K. and John Lisi created LAST RITES.

Singles/EPs:
Terminal Velocity / City Of The Forgotten / C.T.R (Sunday's Liar) / Semper Fi / Guilty As Sin, Wild Rags WRR005 (1988)

Albums:
GUILTY AS SIN, Roadrunner RR 9744 (1985)
Soldier Of Fortune / Ride To Death /

Chainsaw / Tear It Up / Bleeding For You / Too Scared To Run / Rising Power

BLOODMONEY (UK)

Line-Up: Danny Foxx (vocals), Gramie Dee (guitar), Dale Lee (bass), Brett Avock (drums)

Manchester Thrash band BLOODMONEY brought together ex-GRITTER vocalist Danny Foxx, erstwhile WOLFSBANE men Gramie Dee (guitar) and Dale Lee (bass) plus ex-VERA CRUZ drummer Brett Avock.

The band's debut album, 'Red Raw And Bleeding' featured a delightful chainsaw n' blood sleeve.

After the second album, 'Battlescarred', appeared in 1987 the group eventually parted company. Danny Foxx formed BISON with guitarist Dave Kelly, before creating FOXX (who gained a 'Friday Rock Show' session from their 'Legion' demo of 1988 vintage).

FOXX later went through a long period of evolution, turning into ZIONOIZ and then SACRASANCT. Unfortunately, Danny Foxx's career was put on hold following a severe motorcycle accident, which put him in a coma for two weeks. Thankfully, a full recovery was made and the singer was last heard of fronting CHINA BEACH and was shortlisted for the vacant IRON MAIDEN vocalist position in 1994 which was ultimately won by WOLFSBANE's Blaze Bayley.

Albums:
RED RAW AND BLEEDING, Ebony EBON 41 (1987)
Metalyzed / Gor / NZFEDK / Lazarus / Red, Raw And Bleeding / Stormer / Taras Bulba / Deathsting / The Third Wish / Death Heavy
BATTLE SCARRED, Ebony EBON 46 (1987)
Battlescarred / Wolf Beat / Mutant / The Legend (Aghati) / Charnal House (House Of Death) / Shapeshifter / Caligula / Bird Or Beast / Atlantis / Evil Bitch

BLOOD RED ANGEL (GERMANY)
Line-Up: Klaus Spangenberg (vocals), Jens Pesch (guitar), Robert Balner (guitar), Bernd Groß (bass),
Adriano (drums)

Traditional Thrashers and proud of it. Erstwhile VERNISSAGE members guitarist Jens Pesch, bassist Bernd Groß and drummer Klaus Spangenberg would, with the latter adopting a lead vocal role, unite with ex-FERNGULLY guitarist Robert Balner to create retro Thrash Metal band BLOOD RED ANGEL in the late '90s. BLOOD RED ANGEL boast a drummer Adriano who reportedly "kicks the double bass drum like a true Lombardo believer".
BLOOD RED ANGEL debuted with a 5 track demo. This tape would land the band a deal with Gutted Records for the album 'The Language Of Hate' which received almost universal laudable reviews. Following the record's release in July 2000 BLOOD RED ANGEL toured as support to BLACKENED.

Albums:
THE LANGUAGE OF HATE, Cutter GUTCD0014 (2000)
THE STATE OF INSANITY, Gutter GUTCD0048 (2001)

BLUDGEON (Chicago, IL, USA)
Line-Up: Mark Duca (vocals / guitar), Carlos Alvarez (guitar), Eric Karol (bass), Matt Dezynski (drums)

Albums:
CRUCIFY THE PRIEST, Metal Blade (2002)
Smoke Screen / Idle Distinction / Tortured Through Lies / Zero Tolerance / Last Rites / Voluntary Manslaughter / Crucify The Priest / Abandoned / Bound / Inner Hell / Turmoil / Stained In Blood

BOLT THROWER (UK)
Line-Up: Karl Willetts (vocals), Barry Thomson (guitar), Gavin Ward (guitars), Jo-Anne Bench (bass), Andy Whale (drums)

Founded in Birmingham during 1986 BOLT THROWER gaining notoriety on the local Metal scene with a unique, war obsessed heaviness. At this time the band featured vocalist Alan West, guitarist Barry Thomson, bassist Gavin Ward and drummer Andy Whale. The name BOLT THROWER is taken from a siege device in a fantasy role playing game.
Following a 1987 demo 'Concessions In Pain' the fledgling band added bassist Jo-Anne Bench, shifting Gavin Ward to second guitar. A further demo ensued, which resulted in a Radio One session on the John Peel show. This airing led to an album deal with Vinyl Solution Records, but not before West's departure.
The band added vocalist Karl Willetts to record the debut album 'In Battle There Is No Law'. Having performed well on the Earache organised "Grindcrusher" tour of 1989 after contributing a track to the compilation album of the same name, the band then executed dates in Holland with AUTOPSY and PESTILENCE on the 'Bloodbrothers' tour.
The group's first album for Earache, 'Realm Of Chaos', was to sell in excess of 50,000 copies worldwide and utilised artwork from Games Workshop that carried on the theme of fantasy wargaming. Vinyl Solution would re-issue the debut on CD format, this variant coming complete with brand new artwork.
With the release of the 'Cenotaph' EP BOLT THROWER once more toured Europe, this time with support from NOCTURNUS. The release of the next studio affair, 'Warmaster', saw the band's first American dates before engaging in further European shows, where they were supported by BENEDICTION and ASPHYX. However, BOLT THROWER's first Australian tour in 1993 ended in debacle when the band were stuck without a flight home!
Eventually managing to make it back to Britain the Birmingham bunch undertook another American club tour in July 1994 with fellow brummies BENEDICTION as support, but failed to complete the schedule.
Ex-PESTILENCE, ASPHYX and SUBMISSION vocalist Martin Van Drunen joined the band in 1994 replacing the departed Willets and drummer Martin Kearn was added in the line-up shuffle.
Sovoring connections with Earache Records in early 1997 and signing to American label Metal Blade, before recording on a brand new album could commence, Van Drunen,

suffering from a disease which made his hair fall out, quit unexpectedly on the eve of some European festivals. BOLT THROWER killed time by throwing in a few live gigs with BENEDICTION's Dave Ingram guesting.

As BOLT THROWER went into the studio in late 1997 it was announced that 19 year old Alex Thomas had succeeded skinsman Kearns and that Willets had rejoined. With this line-up the band cut the 1998 album 'Mercenary' for new label Metal Blade Records. This offering, despite the lengthy hiatus between recordings, re-established BOLT THROWER's fanbase and gave the group a showing in the national German album charts too. Former label Earache Records weighed in at this opportune moment with the 'Who Dares Wins' compilation, a collection of early EP material. Although Willetts had performed on the album it would be a re-instated Dave Ingram, having recently quit BENEDICTION, who took up the vocal mantle for live work.

Confusingly Thomas would then leave and the drummer he had usurped in the first instance duly took over once again in time for BOLT THROWER's second showing at the major German 'Full Force' festival.

BOLT THROWER toured Europe in January 2001 supported by FLESHCRAWL and HEAVEN SHALL BURN.

Singles/EPs:
Cenotaph / Destructive Infinity / Prophet Of Hatred / Realm Of Chaos, Earache MOSH CD 33 (1991)
Spearhead / Crown Of Life / Dying Creed / Lament, Earache MOSH 73 (1993) ('Spearhead' EP)
Forgotten Existence / Attack In The Aftermath / Psychological Warfare / In Battle There Is No Law, Strange Fruit (1988) ('The Peel Sessions' EP)

Albums:
IN BATTLE THERE IS NO LAW, Vinyl Solution SOL 11 (1988)
In Battle There Is No Law / Challenge For Power / Forgotten Existence / Denial Of Destiny / Concession Of Pain / Attack In The Aftermath / Psychological Warfare / Nuclear Annihilation / Blind To Defeat
REALM OF CHAOS, Earache MOSH 13 (1989)
Eternal War / Through The Eye Of Terror / Dark Millennium / All That Remains / Lost Souls Domain' / Plague Bearer / World Eater / Drowned In Torment / Realm Of Chaos / Outro
WARMASTER, Earache MOSH 35 (1991)
Unleashed (Upon Mankind) / What Dwells

Within / The Shreds Of Sanity / Profane Creation / Final Revelation, Cenotaph, War Master / Rebirth Of Humanity / Afterlife
THE PEEL SESSIONS 1988-90, Strange Fruit DEI 8118-2 (1991)
Forgotten Existence / Attack In The Aftermath / Psychological Warfare / In Battle There Is No Law / Drowned In Torment / Eternal War / Realm Of Chaos / Domination / Destructive Infinity / Warmaster / After Life / Lost Souls Domain
THE FOURTH CRUSADE, Earache MOSH 70 (1993)
The Fourth Crusade / Icon / Embers / Where Next To Conquer / As The World Burns / This Time It's War / Ritual / Spearhead / Celestial Sanctuary / Dying Creed / Through The Ages (Outro)
FOR VICTO23RY, Earache MOSH 120 (1994)
War / Remembrance / When Glory Beckons / For Victory / Graven Image / Lest We Forget / Silent Demise / Forever Fallen / Tank (MK 1) / Armageddon Bound
MERCENARY, Metal Blade 14147 (1998)
Zeroed / Laid To Waste / Return From Chaos / Mercenary / To The Last.... / Powder Burns / Behind Enemy Lines / No Guts, No Glory / Sixth Chapter
WHO DARES WINS, Earache MOSH 208 (1998)
Cenotaph / Destructive Infinity / Prophet Of Hatred / Realm Of Chaos (Live) / Spearhead (Extended remix) / Crown Of Life - Dying / Creed / Lament / World Eater '94 / Overlord
HONOUR, VALOUR, PRIDE, Metal Blade (2001)
Contact Wait Out / Inside The Wire / Honour / Suspect Hostile / 7th Offensive / Valour / K-Machine / A Hollow Truce / Pride

BOMBTHREAT (GERMANY)
Line-Up: Christian Behrens (vocals), Maik Siegismund (guitar), Daniel Johring (bass), Matthias Wiele (drums)

An Aschersleben outfit that straddle the line between Thrash and Death Metal. BOMBTHREAT started life as the 1995 combo ETERNAL CURSE with a line up of Maik Siegismund on vocals and guitar, Nico Wasserberg on guitar, bassist Matthias Wiele and drummer Daniel Seecker.

By December of 1995 the group had evolved into AEON and would switch titles again to BOMBTHREAT. The line up by now had seen Wiele manouevering over to drums and the induction of bassist Daniel Johring and frontman Christian Behrens.

A succession of demos, 1997's 'The Last Warning' and 1998's 'The Eternal Curse' led up to the debut CD release 'Peacemaker'.

Albums:
PEACEMAKER, Bombthreat (1999)
Intro - Eternal Curse / Cold And Wet /
Nightmare / Agents Of Disease / Religious
Insanity / Forever / Peacemaker / Cryonic
Experiments / Peacemaker (Live) / Suspicion
Of Murder (Live) / Burst Command Til War
(Live) / Weihnachtslied (Live)

BRICK BATH (San Diego, CA, USA)
Line-Up: Joseph McCaw (vocals),
Eric Meyer (guitar), Pete Stone (bass), Scott
Babbel (drums)

San Diego Californian neo-Thrashers
founded in 1996 as EPITAPH. Previous to
BRICK BATH guitarist Eric Meyer had been a
member of SHOCKHEAD.
BRICK BATH debuted with the 'Scarred'
album for the Chainsaw label. However, the
record label folded shortly after the album
release. Undaunted, BRICK BATH set about a
heavy gig schedule opening for EXODUS,
TESTAMENT, FLOTSAM & JETSAM and
FORBIDDEN among others.
Adding bassist Pete Stone, a former member
of DFA and TEABAG, the band recorded the
self produced 'I Won't Live The Lie' album for
Crash Music.

Albums:
SCARRED, Chainsaw (1997)
I WON'T LIVE THE LIE, Crash Music CRAS
61014 (2002)
Inner Peace / Bone Dry / Pain My Friend /
Sick Of You / Undone / I Won't Live The Lie /
Crucified / Simple Life / So Wrong /
Oppression Kills / Need / Legacy / Erased /
Die Alone

BRIDE (Louisville, KY, USA)
Line-Up: Dale Thompson (vocals), Troy
Thompson (guitar / keyboards), Scott Hall
(bass), Stephan Rolland (drums)

Kentucky Christian rock act BRIDE debuted
with the 'Show No Mercy' album, a record of
considerable aggression bearing in mind its
lyrical stance. Musical progression over the
years has witnessed a development from out-
and-out Thrash attacks of earlier albums up to
an almost Rap Core stance for more recent
outings.
The formative BRIDE consisted of the
Thompson brothers vocalist Dale and
guitarist Troy, second guitarist Steve
Osbourne, bassist Scott Hall and drummer
Stophon Rolland. The band had initially
debuted as MATRIX but would later switch to
BRIDE when a secular Ohio based band was
also found to be using the MATRIX monicker.

BRIDE would sign to the Refuge subsidiary
label Pure Metal Records for their inaugural
offering 'Show No Mercy'.
By the second album 'Live To Die', produced
by Armand John Petri, Hall lost his position to
newcomer Frank Partipilo. The album caught
many Christian Rock fans off guard by
including an unaccredited final track of
screaming demons! (Actually a studio mix of
piano and vocal howling!)
BRIDE were back to a single guitar band for
the 'Silence Is Madness' album. Retaining
mainstay Troy Thompson the band utilized
additional studio guitar from Rob Johnson.
Record company politics would find BRIDE
relocating to the larger Christian Star Song
label after a buy out of Pure Metal.
By 1992 Rik Foley had occupied the bass
position. BRIDE undertook a bout of
European touring which would be captured
on the 'Bride Live In Germany' album. Fans
would move quickly to grab German import
copies, the record being limited to just 2000
copies. 1995's 'Drop', on new label Rugged,
found BRIDE in experimental sub-Grunge
mode. Foley had departed by this time, his
replacement on bass being Steve Curtsinger.
However, Foley made a return and for a
handful of gigs BRIDE manouevered
Curtsinger to guitar to allow their former
bassist's resumption of duties. This union was
not to last though and Foley would decamp
once again.
1997's 'The Jesus Experience', released by
the Oregon based Organic label, found the
band once more in collaboration with
KANSAS notables John and Dino Elefante
and boosting their studio sound with the
addition of guitarist Tim Bushong of
LOVEWAR.
Follow up 'Oddities' had Lawrence Bishop
occupying the bass position with Jerry
McBroom on drums and GUARDIAN's Tony
Palacios on guest guitar.
The 1999 live album was limited to just 700
copies and saw the Thompson brothers &
McBroom joined onstage by bassists Andrew
Wilkinson & Steve Curtsinger. BRIDE 2001
would number the Thompson siblings,
Lawrence Bishop on bass and Mike Loy on
the drum stool.
Archive MATRIX recordings from the pre-
BRIDE act of the Thompson brothers would
be issued in album format during 2001
entitled 'Lost Reels'.

Singles/EPs:
God Gave Rock And Roll To You /
Rattlesnake / Dust Through A Fan, Music
For Nations 12 KUT 156 (1994)

Albums:

SHOW NO MERCY, Pure Metal
SPCN7900601171 (1987)
Evil That Men Do / Now He Is Gone / Fly
Away / Forever In Darkness / Follow Your
Heart / Show No Mercy / I Will Be With You /
Thunder In The City / No Matter The Price /
The First Will Be The Last

LIVE TO DIE, Pure Metal (1988)
Metal Night / Hell No / Into The Dark / Out
For Blood / Live To Die / Fire And Brimstone
/ Whiskey Seed / Here Comes The Bride /
Heroes

SILENCE IS MADNESS, Pure Metal (1989)
Fool Me Once / Hot Down South Tonight /
Silence Is Madness / Until The End We Rock
/ Evil Dreams / Under The Influence / All
Hallow's Eve / No More Nightmares / Rock
Those Blues Away

BEST OF BRIDE - END OF THE AGE,
(1990)
Everybody Knows My Name / Hell No / Hot
Down South / Forever In Darkness / Heroes
/ Same Ol' Sinner / Thunder In The City /
Fire And Brimstone / Evil That Men Do / All
Hallow's Eve

KINETIC FAITH, Star Song (1991)
Troubled Times / Hire Gun / Ever Fallen In
Love / Love On The Mountain / Ski Masks
and Hand Guns / Everybody Knows My
Name / Young Love / Kiss The Train / Crimes
Against Humanity / Sweet Louise

SNAKES IN THE PLAYGROUND, Star Song
SSC 8261 (1992)
Rattlesnake / Would You Die For Me /
Psychedelic Super Jesus / Fallout / Saltriver
Shuffle / Dust Through A Fan / I Miss The
Rain / Don't Use Me / Picture Perfect / Love,
Money / Some Things Never Change /
Goodbye

SCARECROW MESSIAH, Star Song (1994)
Beast / Place / Murder / ScareCrow / Crazy /
Time / One / MomDad / Doubt / Thorns /
Questions

BRIDE LIVE IN GERMANY, (1994)
Would You Die For Me / Scarecrow /
Pychedelic Super Jesus / Hired Gun / Under
The Influence / Thorns / Everybody Knows
My Name / Hell No / Murder / Troubled
Times / Sweet Louise (Acoustic) / How Long
(Acoustic) / I Miss The Rain (Acoustic)

LOST REELS, (1994)
How Long / Fine Line / Only Hurts When I
Laugh / Lisa / Let the Son Shine / I Don't
Get It / Hollywood / Sugar / I'm The Devil /
Good Rock n' Roll / Dirty / 18 / Help / Could
You Live In My World / Think About Our
Future / Sleepy Southern Town / Pyramid /
Echoes Of Mercy / I Miss Dancing With You /
It's The Devil

DROP, Rugged RGD66012 (1995)
Personal Savior / Mamma / You Never Knew

Me / Life Is The Blues / Help / It Only Hurts
When I Laugh / Thrill A Minute / How Long /
Have You Made It / I'm Nobodies Hero / I'm
the Devil / Jesus Came Back

SHOTGUN WEDDING, Star Song (1995)
Psychedelic Super Jesus / Would You Die
For Me / Everybody Knows My Name /
Place / Fallout / Same Ol' Sinner / Time /
Rattlesnake / Trouble Times / Beast / Hired
Gun

THE JESUS EXPERIENCE, Organic-Word
ORCD-9703 (1997)
I Love You / The Worm / Till The End Of The
World / For You / Follow Me / Tell Me / Love-
Hate / Once Race / I Hear Words / Cosmic
Christ / One Last Glance

LOST REELS III, (1997)
Guilty / One Race / Break My Spine / Cosmic
Christ / Cover Dry Bones / What Am I
Supposed To Do? / I Believe / Days of Shame
/ I'm Trying To Tell You / What Are We? / I'm
Not Alone / Alive

ODDITIES, (1998)
I Ain't Coming Down / Why Won't He Break /
If I Told You It Was The End Of The World / I
Found God / Close To The Center Of The
Earth / Tomorrow Makes No Sense / Day By
Day / Spirit / It's Only When I'm Left Alone /
God's Human Oddities / Under The Blood /
Die A Little Bit Every Day / Restore Me

BRIDE LIVE, (1999)

BRIDE LIVE 2, (2000)
Everybody Knows My Name / Knockin' On
Heaven's Door / Hired Gun / Sweet Louise /
Show Them / Political Statement / Hell No /
Christian Rock Statement / Same Ol' Sinner
/ Rock Of Ages / Kiss The Train / Help /
Young Love / Hollywood

BRIDE LIVE AT CORNERSTONE 2001,
(2001)
Intro / Same Ol' Sinner / Fool Me Once /
Preaching About Drinking / Whiskey Seed /
First Will Be Last / Thunder In The City /
Until The End We Rock / Hell No / I Saw The
Light / Under The Influence / Amazing Grace
/ Jesus On The Mainline / I Have Decided

FISTFUL OF BEES, Absolute (2001)
Beginning Of The End / Bitter End /
California Sunshine / Do Your Own Time /
Dog The 9 / War / God / Jesus In Me / Never
Thought About / Soul Winner / Too Tired

BROCAS HELM
(San Francisco, CA, USA)
Line-Up: Bobbie B. Wright (vocals / guitar),
Tom Behney (guitar), Jim Schumacher
(bass), Jack Hays (drums)

First heard of with the Maiden influenced
jousting of their 1984 debut 'Into Battle',
strongly influenced by English medieval
imagery

BROCAS HELM released a demo in 1987 titled 'Black Death' which carried the tracks 'Fly High', 'Satan's Prophets', 'Hell's Whip' and 'Prepare For Battle', eventually releasing the tracks as a full-blown album two years later.

Quite sensationally BROCAS HELM would reform in 2000 issuing the limited edition red vinyl 'Blood Machine' 7" single. The band toured the Heavy Metal stronghold of Greece in the Autumn supported by domestic Metal bands DREAM WEAVER, RAGING STORM and BATTLEROAR.

Albums:
INTO BATTLE, First Strike (1984)
Metallic Fury / Into Battle / Here To Rock / Beneath A Haunted Moon/ Warriors Of The Dark/ Preludious / Ravenwreck / Dark Rider / Night Siege / Into The Ithilstone
BLACK DEATH, Gargoyle NO 13-8801 (1989)
Black Death Overture / Black Death / Prepare For Battle / Hell's Whips/ Satan's Prophets/ Fly High/ Prophet's Scream / The Chemist / Fall Of The Curtain

BRUTAL FEAR (SINGAPORE)
Line-Up: Andy (vocals), Hairy (guitar), Zul (bass), Eddie (drums)

A Thrash / Death Metal hybrid act forged during 1990 under the original banner of MULTICRANE. At this early stage the band comprised vocalist Andy, guitarist Hairy and bass player Zul. The transition to BRUTAL FEAR came in 1993. By 1997, with the addition of Eddie on drums, the group issued the debut demo 'Decayed Centuries'.

Albums:
FATALLURGICAL, Candlelight Productions (1999)
The Agony Of Suffocation / Infernal Crusher / Morbid Desperation / The Sombre Forest / Politician... Pig / Metal Flames / Gods Of War / Hail, Northern Steel / Farewell To The Flesh

BRUTALISED (BRAZIL)
Line-Up: José Antônio (vocals), Marcelo Quintanilha (guitar), Marcus Vinícius (guitar), Júnior (bass), Gabriel Teykal (drums)

Latecomers on the scene. BRUTALISED emerged in 2000 touting a two track cassette consisting of 'Assassinos' and 'Darkness'.

BRUTALITY (FL, USA)
Line-Up: Scott Reigal (vocals), Don Gates

(guitar), Jay Fernandez (guitar), Jeff Acres (bass), Jim Coker (drums)

BRUTALITY's debut album, recorded naturally at Morrisound studios, featured a line-up of vocalist Scott Reigal, guitarists Don Gates and Jay Fernandez, bassist Jeff Acres and drummer Jim Coker. Fernandez would make his exit to be replaced by Brian Hipp for 1995's 'When The Sky Turns Black'.

By the time of BRUTALITY's last outing 'In Mourning' Both Hipp and Gates had been superseded by former NASTY SAVAGE man Danny Gray and erstwhile DEGRADATION member Dana Walsh. However, pre-recording Gray made way for ex-EXECRATION guitarist Pete Sykes.

Ex-member Brian Hipp would enjoy a fleeting appearance with premier British Black Metal band CRADLE OF FILTH during 1995 and later resurfaced as a member of DIABOLIC.

Singles/EPs:
Hell On Earth, Gore GORE 007 (1991)
Sadistic, (1992)

Albums:
SCREAMS OF ANGUISH, Nuclear Blast NB 075 (1993)
These Walls Will Be Your Grave / Ceremonial Unearthing / Sympathy / Septicemia Plague / Crushed / Spirit World / Exposed To The Elements / Cries Of The Forsaken / Cryptorium / Spawned Illusion
WHEN THE SKY TURNS BLACK, Nuclear Blast NB115-2 (1995)
When The Sky Turns Black / Race Defects / Awakening / Electric Funeral / Foul Lair / Screams Of Anguish / Esoteric / Artistic Butchery / Violent Generation / Shrine Of The Master
IN MOURNING, Nuclear Blast (1996)
Obsessed / The Past / Destroyed By Society / Waiting To Be Devoured / Died With Open Eyes / In Mourning / Subjected To Torture / Calculated Bloodshed / Extinction

BRUTAL OBSCENITY (HOLLAND)
Line-Up: Kief (vocals), Ben Humpig (guitar), Luois Melger (guitar), Renske Van Baak (bass), Emil Hannik (drums)

Singles/EPs:
God Is A Fairytale / Defensor Minor / No More Feelings Left / Hangover D.D.D. / The Overtaking, Underground (1990) ('Demo series' EP)

Albums:
IT'S BECAUSE OF THE BIRDS AND THE FLOWERS, CMFT (1989)

Death Is A Damn Good Solution / ...It's Because Of The Birds And The Flowers / Straight And Stoned / Emotion Suicide / Mom Or Dad? / It's Cruel (Part I) / 1,2.3,... / Useless Immortality

DREAM OUT LOUD!, Prophecy PROPH 3-1 (1991)

Expect The Unexpected / Twisted Hearts / Children's Paradise / Maybe You're Right... / Fragile / Strength To Smile / Like / Nobody's Perfect / U.A.R. (It's Cruel 2) / Truus De Boer / My Utopia / Sea Of Luxury / Just A Bit Of Misery / Fading Dayglow / As Pretty As A Flower

BRUTAL TRUTH (USA)

Line-Up: Kevin Sharp (vocals),
Brent McCarty (guitar), Dan Lilker (bass),
Rich Hoak (drums)

BRUTAL TRUTH, Grindcore exponents with a definite thirst for speed, were created during a lull in NUCLEAR ASSAULT activities when bassist Dan Lilker (Previously with ANTHRAX / STORMTROOPERS OF DEATH) assembled a band to indulge his love of hardcore. Recruiting guitarist Brent McCarty and drummer Scott Lewis the line up was finalized with the addition of vocalist Kevin Sharp.

Recordings made by the band whilst still a trio were issued on the bootleg EP 'The birth of ignorance' on Liberated Records.

In time Lilker split NUCLEAR ASSAULT to concentrate fully on BRUTAL TRUTH. With Lilker's pedigree a deal was quickly on the table and the band signed to grindcore exponents Earache Records for their debut effort 'Extreme Conditions Demand Extreme Responses'. A 7" single 'Ill Neglect' also saw the light of day featuring a raucous cover of THE BUTTHOLE SURFERS 'The Shah Sleeps In Lee Harvey's Grave'.

BRUTAL TRUTH paid their live dues in America opening for CATHEDRAL, CARCASS and NAPALM DEATH prior to guesting for FEAR FACTORY in Europe. During the tour Lewis departed and was supplanted by former NINEFINGER man Rich Hoak.

Pushing the boundaries of extremity even further BRUTAL TRUTH forged a liaison with Coventry techno act LARCENY to record the 'Perpetual Conversion' 7", the B side of which featured a version of BLACK SABBATH's 'Lord Of This World'.

The 1994 album 'Need To Control' was formatted uniquely enough to make an impact with it being a boxed set of 5, 6, 7, 8 and 9 inch vinyl. Bonus cuts included CELTIC FROST's 'Dethroned Emperor' and PINK FLOYD's seminal 'Wish You Were Here'.

Even as this album was being released Lilker was dabbling in another project titled EXIT 13, together with Lewis, and guesting on the 'No Matter What The Cause' album by Germans HOLY MOSES up front of a BRUTAL TRUTH tour encompassing Australia, Japan and America.

The band, feeling that Earache Records did not have the necessary commitment, broke away from the label in search of another deal. It was to be a full two years before BRUTAL TRUTH signed up with American label Relapse Records. During this interim the quartet were far from inactive. A 1995 vinyl album 'Machine Parts' emerged which included no less than five different live versions of 'Collateral Damage' including takes with EXIT 13's Bill Yurkiewicz and NAPALM DEATH's Barney Greenaway on vocals. The band also contributed tracks to the 'Nothings Quiet On The Western Front' compilation and issuing a split EP with SPAZZ which included a version of DIE KREUZEN's 'Rumburs'.

In 1997 Hoak teamed up with CORROSION OF CONFORMITY's Mike Dean to record a project album under the band name of NINE FINGER.

BRUTAL TRUTH made an appearance in a porn movie 'Studio X' in 1997. The band played two songs live and even took a part in acting although not in some of the more 'animated' scenes. Lilker took time out to resurrect STORMTROOPERS OF DEATH as the original line up toured America one last time.

The '97 album 'Sounds Of The Animal Kingdom' broke BRUTAL TRUTH into fresh audiences and includes a somewhat unlikely cover of jazz maestro SUN RA's 'It's After The End Of The World'. The Japanese release added bonus cover versions of AGATHOCLES's 'Hippie Cult', NAUSEA's 'Cybergod' and BLACK SABBATH's 'Cornucopia'. The latter also appeared on a split EP on Hydrahead Records, a label that specializes in BLACK SABBATH covers! The band at this point were credited as being Sharp (grunts and groans), Gurn (fingers), Lilker (opposable thumbs) and Hoak (sticks and stones).

BRUTAL TRUTH undertook a demanding 90 date tour of America to wind up 1997 on a touring package combining CANNIBAL CORPSE, IMMOLATION and OPRESSOR.

Despite steady progress and increased sales BRUTAL TRUTH split following completion of an Australian tour in September 1998. Lilker resumed activity with STORMTROOPERS OF DEATH for their 'Bigger Than The Devil' album. The bassist also operates Black Metal band HEMLOCK.

Hoak re-emerged in 2000 with his subtly titled new band TOTAL FUCKING DESTRUCTION. BRUTAL TRUTH's epic swansong 'Goodbye Cruel World' comprised a twin CD set. The first CD featured a live show from Sydney, Australia which included covers of tracks by BLACK SABBATH, S.O.B., THE GERMS, THE MELVINS and AGATHOCLES whilst the second CD had bonus track rarities and the 'Machine Parts' recordings along with more live material from Japanese and New Zealand shows.

Singles/EPs:
Ill Neglect / The Shah Sleeps In Lee Harvey's Grave, Earache 7 MOSH 080 (1992)
Perpetual Conversion / Perpetual Larceny / Walking Corpse / Lord Of This World / Bedsheet, Earache MOSH 084CD (1993) (Split CD with LARCENY)
Godplayer, Earache (1994) (7" single)
B.I.T.B. / Dethroned Emperor / Painted Clowns / Wish You Were Here, Earache MOSH 110B (1994) (Free EP with 'No Need To Control' album)
Porkfarm / Rumburs / Foolish Bastard, Bovine (1996) (7" split single with SPAZZ)
Split, Deaf American (1997) (7" split single with RUPTURE)
Cornucopia, Hydrahead (1997) (Split EP with CONVERGE)

Albums:
EXTREME CONDITIONS DEMAND EXTREME RESPONSES, Earache MOSH 069 (1992)
P.S.P.I. / Birth Of Ignorance / Stench Of Prophet / Ill Neglect / Denial Of Existence / Regression - Progression / Collateral Damage / Time / Walking Corpse / Monetary Gain / Wilt / H.O.P.E. / Blockhead / Anti-Homophobe / Unjust Compromise
NEED TO CONTROL, Earache MOSH 110 (1994)
Collapse / Black Door Mine / Turn Face / Godplayer / I See Red / Iron Lung / Bite The Hand / Ordinary Madness / Media Blitz / Judgement / Brain Trust / Choice Of A New Generation / Mainliner / Displacement / Crawlspace
MACHINE PARTS, Deaf American (1995)
Spare Change / Machine Parts / Collateral Damage (Live) / Collateral Damage (Live) / Collateral Damage (Live) / Collateral Damage (Live) / Collateral Damage (Live) / Fucktoy / Kill Trend Suicide
KILL TREND SUICIDE, Relapse RR 6498 (1997)
Blind Leading The Blind / Pass Some Down / Lets Got To War / Hypocrite Invasion /

Everflow / Zombie / Homesick / Humanity's Folly / I Killed My Family / Kill Trend Suicide
SOUNDS OF THE ANIMAL KINGDOM, Relapse RR 6968 (1997)
Dementia / K.A.P. / Vision / Fuck Toy / Jiminez Cricket / Soft Mind / Average People / Blue World / Callous / Fisting / Die Laughing / Dead Smart / Sympathy Kiss / Pork Farm / Promise / Foolish Bastard / Postulate Then Liberate / Machine Parts / In The Words Of Sun Ra / Unbaptise / Cybergod
GOODBYE CRUEL WORLD! LIVE FROM PLANET EARTH+13, Relapse (1999)
Intro / Dementia / K.A.P. / Choice Of A New Generation / Birth Of Ignorance / Stench Of Profit / Walking Corpse / Sympathy Kiss / Pork Farm / Jemenez Cricket / Respect At Length / Media Blitz / Fucktoy / Ill-Neglect / Kill Trend Suicide / Cornucopia / Godplayer / I Killed My Family / Time / Denial Of Existence / Hippie Cult / Callous / Zodiac / No Sleep / Hippie Cult / Cybergod / Cornucopia / Born To Die / Spare Change / Machine Parts / Collateral Damage (Live) / Collateral Damage (Live) / Collateral Damage (Live) / Collateral Damage (Live) / Collateral Damage (Live) / Fucktoy / Kill Trend Suicide / Bubblbop Shop / Boredom's Cover No. 2 / Telly (With Bucky) / Blind Leading The Blind / Pass Some Down / Vision / Die Laughing / Let's Go To War / Zombie / Homesick / Everflow / Dead Smart / Dethroned Emperor / It's After The End Of The World / Callous / Average People / Black Door Mine / Promise / Foolish Bastard / Bite The Hand / Collateral Damage
FOR DRUG CRAZED GRINDFREAKS ONLY!, Solardisk (2000)
K.A.P. / Dead Smart / Blind Leading The Blind / Lets Go To War / Choice Of A New Generation / Walking Corpse / Fisting / Homesick / Stench Of Profit / Jemenez Cricket / Untitled

B-THONG (SWEDEN)
Line Up: Tony Jelencovich (vocals), Stefan Thuresson (guitar), Lars Häglund (bass), Morgan Petersson (drums)

Gothenburg Crossover Metallers B-THONG date to 1990 when the band was originally titled CONCRETE STUFF. Having released a self-financed single and demos, the group chose to go for the name change to B-THONG in 1993. Prior to the formation of the quartet, drummer Morgan Pettersson had recorded with BOULEVARD and MIDNIGHT BLUE.
B-THONG recorded and released the 'Skinned' debut album in 1994 and promoted it via a support tour to SKINTRADE the same

year.
After the emergence of second album 'Damage' frontman Tony Jelencovich quit B-THONG in November 1995 to form TRANSPORT LEAGUE (releasing the 'Stallion Showcase' album in early 1996), his position being filled for the 1997 'From Strength To Strength' album by Ralph Lennart.

Albums:
SKINNED, Mascot M7007-2 (1994)
SFM / Fatal Accusation / Godslave / Schizophrenic Pavement / No More / Violent Blows / Floodgate / Stained / My Opinion / Power Ranger / Days Of Blood / Taking You Home / Under My Nails / Justice Seeker
DAMAGE, Mascot M7013-2 (1995)
Seeking / Prison Mirror / Ropes / Last Way Wrong Home / Cockroach / Breath / Passive Control / Lost Emperor / My Wound / That Parts Part Dead / Blind Addiction / Weakness
FROM STRENGTH TO STRENGTH, Mascot M 7028-2 (1997)
Under Behind/ Cut Or Run / Falling Down / Lucified / The Ogre / Witch Waltz / Warphobia / Larghetto / Suntrip / In My Eyes / Cosmic Elvis / Welcome To Leave
THE CONCRETE COLLECTION, Mascot (2000)

BULLDOZER (ITALY)
Line-Up: Alberto Contini (vocals / bass), Andy Panigada (guitar), Rob K. Cabrini (drums)

Taking their cue from MOTÖRHEAD, Italian Metal merchants BULLDOZER were formed in 1980 by bassist Dario Carria and guitarist Andy Panigada. Forced to split in 1981 due to national service commitments the group nevertheless reformed in 1983 with drummer Don Andras, now influenced by the likes of VENOM and TANK. Indeed, BULLDOZER's debut album, The 'Day Of Wrath' was produced by TANK frontman Algy Ward.
Sadly, founder member Carria committed suicide.
From the 'IX' album onwards drums were handled by Rob Cabrini and, as a new decade dawned, the band's lyrical standpoint became increasingly devoid of any satanic references.
Contini was involved with ex-SLAYER drummer Dave Lombardo's classical Vivaldi album 'The Meeting' in 1999. The frontman would also donate narrative to the highly regarded debut from British Black Metal band THE MEADS OF ASPHODEL 'The Excommunication Of Christ'. The group would repay the favour by cutting a version of 'Neurodelini' for a BULLDOZER tribute EP assembled by Warlord Records.

Singles/EPs:
Fallen Angel / Another Beer, Bulldozer (1984)

Albums:
THE DAY OF WRATH, Roadrunner (1985)
The Exorcism / Cut Throat / Insurrection Of The Living Damned / Fallen Angel / The Great Deceiver / Mad Man / Whiskey Time / Welcome Death / Endless Funeral
THE FINAL SEPARATION, Roadrunner RR 9711 (1986)
The Final Separation / Ride Hard, Die Fast / The Cave / Sex Symbol's Bullshit / 'Don' Andreas / Never Relax! / Don't Trust The Saint / The Death Of Gods
IX - CIRCLE OF HELL, Discomagic LP328 (1988)
IX / Desert / Ilona The Very Best / Misogynist / Heaven's Jail / Rob 'Kilster' / The Derby / No Way / The Vision Never Fades
NEURODELIRI, Metal Master MET109 (1989)
Overture / Neurodeliri / Minkions / We Are... Italian / Art Of Deception / Ilona Had Been Elected /Impotence / More Tua-Vita Mea / Willful Death / You'll Be Recalled
ALIVE IN POLAND, Metal Master (1990)
IX / Desert / Ilona The Very Best / Impotence / The Derby / Heaven's Jail / Mikiens / Mors Tua Vita Mea / Overkill / Willful Death (You'll Be Recalled)
1983-1990 THE YEARS OF WRATH, Sound Cave (1999)

BURNT OFFERING
(Chicago, IL, USA)
Line-Up: Hal Shore (vocals), John Voll (guitar), Jim Martinelli (guitar), Paul Sroczynski (bass), Mitch (drums)

Chicago act BURNT OFFERING trod a fine line between Thrash Metal and proto-Death. Active in the late '80s BURNT OFFERING would fold following their debut. Guitarist Jim Martinelli briefly teamed up with Paul Speckmann's MASTER in 1990.
BURNT OFFERING would resurface in 1998 for live shows and a new album 'Walk Of The Dead'.

Albums:
BURNT OFFERING, Walkthrufyre (1989)
Kick Your Dirt / Leatherface / Prisoner Of War / Snow Death / Power Of Death / Beware The Axe / Desecration / Slaughterhouse Grizzle / Black Blasphemy / Graphic Violence / Pure Fuckin' Death

DEATH DECAY COMPLETE, Modern Day Recordings (1998)
Kick Your Dirt / Leatherface / Prisoner Of War / Snow Death / Power Of Death / Beware The Axe / Desecration / Slaughterhouse Grizzle / Black Blasphemy / Graphic Violence / P.F.D. / Leatherface (Demo) / Desecration (Demo) / Black Blasphemy (Demo) / Prisoner Of War (Demo) / Beware The Axe (Demo) / Power Of Death (Demo)

WALK OF THE DEAD, Sounds Of Death (1999)
Hell Is Yours / Thou Shalt Not Kill / With All The Blood / Nailed / Walk Of The Dead / Black Metal / The One / Mother's Shallow Grave / Time To Close Your Eyes / Snow Deadlier / Burnt Offering

CACOPHONY (USA)

Line-Up: Peter Marrino (vocals), Marty Friedman (guitar), Jason Becker (guitar), Jimmy O'Shea (bass), Atma Anur (drums)

CACOPHONY arrived with perfect timing in the mid '80s heightened interest in speed guitarists.

Guitarist MARTY FRIEDMAN had paid his dues with HAWAII and VIXEN and forging an alliance with another six string whizz kid JASON BECKER founded CACOPHONY with erstwhile LE MANS singer Peter Marrino. The resulting album 'Speed Metal Symphony' sparked considerable interest; enough for both guitarists to capitalize on it with solo outings. Friedman launched 'Dragon's Kiss' whilst Becker's 'Perpetual Burn' was released simultaneously.

Drummer Atma Anur departed prior to the second CACOPHONY album 'Go Off!' and was superseded by ex-LE MANS skinbasher Kenny Stavropoulos. However, drums on the album are in fact supplied by Dean Castronovo, most recognised for his work with WILD DOGS, HARDLINE, OZZY OSBOURNE and JOURNEY. Stavropoulos later joined STARSHIP.

Friedman was later to enjoy global recognition as part of MEGADETH and for his later solo workouts. Becker has also made a name for himself with a string of authoritative solo albums and an appearance in DAVID LEE ROTH's band.

Becker contributed guitar parts to DAVID LEE ROTH's 'A Little Ain't Enough' album but just as Becker seemed on the edge of the stardom he deserved the young guitarist was diagnosed as suffering with the crippling Lou Gehrig's disease commonly known as ALS. Tragically the disease left the guitarist completely without the use of his body Becker still composed music albeit with great difficulty using a computer scanner to read and his eyes to communicate to others. When the true extent of his predicament was learned his fellow musicians rallied around in a show of camaraderie resulting fresh recording interpretations of Becker's music to remind the world of his talent.

The tribute album, entitled 'Warmth In The Wilderness' and released by Lion Music on July 22nd 2001 (Becker's birthday), boasted a quite staggering array of guest contributors. Included were fellow guitarists MARTY FRIEDMAN, VINNIE MOORE, PAUL GILBERT, PATRICK RONDAT, NIGHTRANGER and MOTHERS ARMY man Jeff Watson, DEEP PURPLE's Steve Morse, ALEX MASI, MOGG/WAY's Jeff Kollman, LARS ERIC MATTSON and former MEGADETH member CHRIS POLAND. Also involved were DOKKEN's bassist Jeff Pilson. Erstwhile DANGER DANGER mentor Ted Poley, ROBIN McAULEY, MARK BOALS, Mark Mangold, Jeff Scheetz, Stuart Smith, EMPIRE's Rolf Munkes and Kenny Aaronson.

<u>Albums:</u>

SPEED METAL SYMPHONY, Roadrunner 349577 (1987)
Savage / Where My Fortune Lies / The Ninja / Concerto / Burn The Ground / Desert Island / Speed Metal Symphony

GO OFF!, Roadrunner RR 94991(1988)
X-Ray Eyes / E.S.P. / Stranger / Go Off! / Black Cat / Sword Of The Warrior / Floating World / Images

CALHOUN CONQUER
(SWITZERLAND)

Line-Up: Geri Christian Gerling (vocals), Chris Muzik (guitar), Bruce Muzik (guitar), Stefan Gerling (bass / drums)

Thrash Metallers CALHOUN CONQUER benefited from the on loan services of drummer Mark Halbheer, although the album track 'Lost In Itself' is the sole work of a drum computer. Other contributing musicians included guitarists Fritz Ott and Bruno Amatruda.

CALHOUN CONQUER's line-up later featured MEKONG DELTA, AIN'T DEAD YET and KROKUS drummer Peter Haas.

In 1992 sibling guitarists Bruce and Christian Muzik along with Haas and joined BABYLON SAD. Haas would team up with KROKUS again in 1999.

<u>Singles/EPs:</u>

Pathological Proportions / No Parallel With Eden / Outermost Consequences / Diane, Chainsaw Murder (1987) ('... And Now You're Gone' EP)

<u>Albums:</u>

LOST IN ONESELF, Aaarrg AAARRG 22 (1989)
Disgust And Hate / Fuckhead / You Mean Nothing / Torturer / Portals Of Delirium / Psycho Trap / Nothing (Has Killed Itself) / Outermost Consequences / Worlds In Collision / Diane

CALVARIA (MEXICO)

Line-Up: Mario Montano (vocals), Juan Pablo Agudelo (guitar), Oswaldo Blanco (guitar), Laszlo Kalloi (bass), Vincente Gazano (keyboards), Juan Pablo Ramirez (drums)

Albums:
CALVARIA, Argenta (2001)
El Rostro De La Muerte / Alas Al Viento / Destructor / Metalia / Requiem / El Heroe / Último Viaje / Salvame / Sigues Aquí / Náufrago Del Tiempo / Valle De Soledad

CANCER (UK)
Line-Up: John Walker (vocals / guitar), James Murphy (guitar), Ian Buchanan (bass), Carl Stokes (drums),

Telford based extreme Speed Metal band, CANCER's first gig was in Birmingham opening for BOMB DISNEYLAND and the initial demos were recorded at the legendary Pits studio, owned by STARFIGHTERS vocalist Steve Burton. Having been granted a deal by Vinyl Solution CANCER's debut album, 'To The Gory End', took a mere four days to record!
Erstwhile AGENT STEEL and OBITUARY guitarist JAMES MURPHY was enlisted to record the sophomore 'Death Shall Rise' and the platter was produced by noted Death Metal producer Scott Burns into the bargain. Amusingly, the album caused a great deal of controversy upon release in Europe when it was banned in Germany by the State body for censorship of works dangerous to the youth, on grounds that the album cover would incite youngsters to inflict violence upon each other! CANCER had recorded 'Death Shall Rise' in Scott Burns' Florida home state and chose to spend further working time in America by playing the 1991 'Milwaukee Metalfest' and also supporting DEICIDE and OBITUARY. However, by December 1991 James Murphy had quit the band to form DISINCARNATE, later joining TESTAMENT and Danes KONKHRA.
1993 was another particularly busy year for the band, releasing third album 'The Sins Of Mankind' and performing a European tour with openers CEREBRAL FIX. The group also was to tour Britain and America with DEICIDE.
In 1994 the band enrolled new guitarist Barry Savage and CANCER stepped up a level upon signing to major label East West Records. Following the release of the new album, 'Black Faith', which featured a caustic take on DEEP PURPLE's 'Space Truckin', the quartet toured Britain with support act MESHUGGAH.
During 1997 Carl Stokes would also find himself involved with NOTHING BUT CONTEMPT. The short lived act assembled by vocalist Barney Greenaway in his period away from NAPALM DEATH. This act included Greenaway, Stokes, NAPALM DEATH guitarist Danny Herrera and SACRIFICIAL

ALTAR / ASATRU guitarist Rob Engvikson. NOTHING BUT CONTEMPT folded when Greenaway rejoined NAPALM DEATH.
Stokes filled in for Telford Hardcore mongers ASSERT in 2000. The drummer also busied himself with a new Metal project titled REMISSION with Walker.
Guitarist Barry Savage would join the high profile LOCK UP in early 2002 as touring guitarist.

Albums:
TO THE GORY END, Vinyl Solution SOL 22 (1990)
Blood Bath / C.F.C. / Witch Hunt / Into The Acid / Imminent Catastrophe / To The Gory End / Body Count / Sentenced To The Gallows / Die Die
DEATH SHALL RISE, Vinyl Solution SOL28 (1991)
Hung, Drawn And Quartered / Tasteless Incest / Burning Casket / Death Shall Rise / Back From The Dead / Gruesome Tasks / Corpse Fire / Internal Decay
THE SINS OF MANKIND, Vinyl Solution SOL35 (1993)
The Sins Of Mankind / Cloak Of Darkness / Electro-Convulsive Therapy / Patchwork Destiny / Meat Train / Suffer For Our Sins / Pasture Of Delights At The End / Tribal Bloodshed Part I - The Conquest / Tribal Bloodshed Part II - Under The Flag
BLACK FAITH, East West 0630 10752-2 (1995)
Ants (Nemesis Ride) / Who Do You Think You Are / Face To Face / Without Cause / White Desire / Kill Date / Temple Song / Black Faith / Highest Orders / Space Truckin' / Sunburnt / Save Me From Myself

CANCEROUS GROWTH (USA)

Albums:
TODAY'S SOCIETY, Ax/ction ACT 4 (1986)
Branded / Ecology / The Demon And The Goddess / Today's Society / Late For The Grave
LATE FOR THE GRAVE, Nuclear Blast (1987)
HMMMNLMNLMM, Nuclear Blast (1988)

CANDIRIA (Brooklyn, NY, USA)
Line-Up: Carley Coma (vocals), Mike Maciovor (bass), Ken Schalk (drums)

Genre defying Brooklyn outfit created during 1992, delightfully named after the Brazilian fish that has a predilection for swimming up urine streams and lodging itself by means of retractable spines inside the penis, that effortlessly blend extreme Thrash and

Hardcore Metal with Jazz Dance beats and fusion. CANDIRIA's inaugural line-up comprised frontman Carley Coma, guitarists Chris Puma and Eric Matthews, bassist Mike Holt and drummer Kenneth Schalk.

The band debuted with the 'Subliminal' demo after which Holt made his exit. Two bassists in quick succession came and went - 'Eric' and 'Jimmy', before CANDIRIA resolved to persevere minus a bassist. CANDIRIA's first commercially available product would be the 7" EP 'Deep In The Mental' issued by Devastating Soundworks during 1995. Both single tracks 'Temple Of Sickness' and 'Elevate In Madness' would appear on the debut Too Damn Hype album 'Surrealistic Madness'. This album would witness a number of re-issues with differing artwork. The third such re-release also came with a different tracklisting skipping 'Infected Wisdom' and the instrumental 'Observing Highways' in favour of 'Purity Condemned' taken from the 'Subliminal' demo.

The sophomore 'Beyond Reasonable Doubt' album would witness lyrical and vocal contributions from Mark Scondotto of SHUTDOWN on lead track 'Faction' and the same degree of benevolence from MERAUDER's Jorge Rosado on the track 'Year One' and CUTTHROATS' Ryan Murphy on 'Tribes'. CANDIRIA also contributed 'Pull' featuring Tom of INDECISION and 'Statistics' to the 'New York's Hardest: Volume II' compilation album. At this stage CANDIRIA were still without a bassist.

Puma would leave to be supplanted by DEAD AIR's John Lamacchia. Shortly after another DEAD AIR member, Mike MacIvor - after a short spell with MERAUDER, joined the fold to complete the band. CANDIRIA's third album 'Process Of Self Development' would feature a further slew of guest artists including Jamey Jasta of HATEBREED, Paul of DISSOLVE, Phil of IRATE and Jorge Rosado once again.

CANDIRIA's tour plans for 2000 on a package billing with MADBALL and SHADOWS FALL were scuppered when projected road partners MADBALL decided to fold.

May of 2001 would see the release of CANDIRIA's '300% Density' record for the German Century Media label. The band would also be slated to play at the gargantuan extreme Metal 'Beast Feast' festival in Yokohama, Japan during August. CANDIRIA hooked up with BIOHAZARD and CLUTCH for a November package tour of the States during November. Touring the UK in late January 2002 would find the band packaged once again with CLUTCH and also RAGING SPEEDHORN.

CANDIRIA members, in keeping with their adventurous nature, also operate the Jazz improvisational side endeavour GHOSTS OF THE CANAL releasing the 1999 EP 'Sessions From The Flats'.

The band would re-issue their 1997 album 'Beyond Reasonable Doubt' via their own label C.O.M.A. label in May. Retitled 'C.O.M.A. Imprint', the re-release came as a double CD set, with the second CD featuring tracks from the band members assorted side projects.

Singles/EPs:
Temple Of Sickness / Elevate In Madness, Devastating Soundworks (1995) ('Deep In The Mental' EP)

Albums:
SURREALISTIC MADNESS, Too Damn Hype (1995)
Temple Of Sickness / Wind / Elevate In Madness / Infected Wisdom / Toying With The Insanities / Mental Crossover / Observing Highways / Pages / Weep / Red Eye Flight
BEYOND REASONABLE DOUBT, Too Damn Hype (1997)
Faction / Year One / Lost In The Forest / Paradigm Shift / Tribes / Molecular Dialect / Divided / Mental Politics / Riding The Spiral / Primary Obstacle / Intrusive Statements
THE PROCESS OF SELF DEVELOPMENT, MIA 1008 (1999)
Three Times Again / Onefortyeight / Pull / Method Of Expression / Temple Of Sickness / Mathematics / Work In Progress / Matter. Anti. Matter / Cleansing / Elevate In Madness / Down To The Last Element / The Process Of Self-Development / Leaving The Atmosphere
300% DENSITY, Century Media (2001)
300% Percent Density / Signs Of Discontent / Without Water / Mass / Constant Velocity Is Natural As Being At Rest / Words From The Lexicon / Channeling Elements / Advancing Positions / The Obvious Destination / Contents Under Pressure / Opposing Meter

CAPITOL PUNISHMENT (USA)

Industrious Punk Thrashers fronted by former HELL'S KITCHEN vocalist Jimi.

During 1995 Jimi founded STRYCHNINE in league with ex-FILTH personnel guitarist Len Rokk and bassist Mike-O-Psyco, erstwhile ECONOCHRIST drummer Markley Hart and second guitarist Damen Vernon.

Singles/EPs:
Jody Is My Bloody Love EP, Stage Dive (1983)
Glutton For Punishment EP, (1988)

WHEN PUTSCH COMES TO SHOVE, Stage Dive (1985)
Ballad Of A Broken Home / Capitol Punishment / Child Abuse / Walking Crying Dying / Elephant Man / God Of Greed / Racism Is Ignorance / Is This Justice / Smile / Poke Me With A Fork I'm Done.
SLUM WITH A VIEW, We Bite (1987)
ZIPYERPANTSUP, Destiny (198-)
BULWARKS AGAINST OPPRESSION, We Bite (1990)
Two Hands / Nytro / Fire And Brimstone / Bulwarks Against Oppression / Heavymetalmeltdown / The Pug / We're Not A Soundtrack For Violence / I'm Hungry / Bad Girl / Count The Basies / Strychnine / Jacknifed Rig / Severin / Everyday My Life's Living Hell / When You're Helpin' The Shepherd. You're Helpin' The Sheep / Old George Cloud
THE FIRST LINE UP, We Bite WBCD078166 (1993)
MESSIAH COMPLEX, We Bite 2005 (1995)
Manumit / Dagger In My Eyes / 7 Lucky Devils / The Postman Always Shoots Twice / Ethnic Cleansing / Cenobite Stomp / I'm Not Like Everybody Else / Tick Tick Tick / It's Gotta Come Out / Your Farts Are Like Frankincense To Me, I Wanna Be The Anti-Christ / Down
3 CHORD PILE UP, We Bite 13 (1996)

CAPRICORN (GERMANY)
Line-Up: Adrian Ergün (vocals / bass), David (guitar), Stefan Arnold (drums)

Previously known as GRINDER, this German outfit formed as CAPRICORN in 1991. Following the debut album CAPRICORN supported GRAVEDIGGER on a German tour.
Frontman Adrian Ergün guested on the 1996 album from CRASH MUSEUM.
Ergün would create NEMESIS for an eponymous 1997 album in collusion with guitarist Axel Katzmann and Arnulf Tunn of TANKARD.

Albums:
CAPRICORN, Shark SHARK 030 (1993)
Mob In The Hood / One Shot From Murder / Burn / Light Up Your Mind / Lonely Is The World / Mr. Voorhees / Bomb Eden / Shotdown Downtown / The Harder They Fall / Long Way Home / Exceeding The Limits Of Pain
INFERNO, (1995)
Iced Age / Claws Of The Mad / The Wire Fence / Dead Can Walk / Moonstruck / Iron Biter / Gun For Hire / A Call For Defiance /

You Can't Stop Rock n' Roll / Camp Blood / Inferno

CAPTURA (ITALY)
Line-Up: Alessandro Gusmerini (vocals), Enrico Degiovanetti (guitar), Andrea Mossini (guitar), Rome (bass), Giuseppe Gasparotti (drums)

Singles/EPs:
Vortice / Cenobio Isterico / Sguardi / M.Y.A., (2001) ('Cenebio Isterico' EP)

CARNAL FORGE (SWEDEN)
Line-Up: Jonas Kjellgren (vocals), Johan Magnusson (guitar), Jari Kuusisto (guitar), Petri Kuusisto (bass), Stefan Westerberg (drums)

The founding line-up of Thrashers CARNAL FORGE comprised DELLAMORTE man Jonas Kjellgren, drummer Stefan Westerberg of IN THY DREAMS and STEEL ATTACK personnel guitarist Jari Kuusisto and bassist Dennis Vestman. Following the debut album 'Who's Gonna Burn' Vestman departed to be replaced by another IN THY DREAMS man Petri Kuusisto.
Vocalist Jonas Kjellgren was temporary guitarist with CENTINEX between 1999 and September 2000.
In 2001 guitarist Johan Magnusson made his exit prompting bassist Petri Kuusisto to switch over to guitars whilst former SLAPDASH and ROSICRUCIAN man Lars Lindén assumed bass duty. Lindén already had a CARNAL FORGE connection being responsible for the band's website as well as providing artwork for second album 'Firedemon'
A fresh CARNAL FORGE album 'Please Die!' would be cut during the summer of 2001. The band would land a valuable European tour on a strong package billing with NILE, THE HAUNTED and THE FORSAKEN.

Albums:
WHO'S GONNA BURN, Wrong Again (1998)
Who's Gonna Burn / Sweet Bride / Twisted / Godzilla Is Coming Thru' / The Other Side / Part Animal - Part Machine / Born Too Late / Evilizer / Moggotman / Confuzzed
FIREDEMON, Century Media (2000)
Too Much Hell Ain't Enough For Me / Covered With Fire (I'm Hell) / I Smell Like Death (Son Of A Bastard) / Chained / Defacer / Pull The Trigger / Uncontrollable / Firedemon / Cure Of Blasphemy / Headfucker / The Torture Will Never Stop / A Revel In Violence
PLEASE... DIE!, Century Media 8099-2

(2001)
Butchered, Slaughtered, Strangled, Hanged / Hand Of Doom / Fuel For Fire / Totalitarian Torture / Everything Dies / Slaves / Welcome To Your Funeral / Please… Die! (Aren't You Dead Yet?) / Becoming Dust / No Resurrection / A World All Soaked In Blood / A Higher Level Of Pain

CARNIVORE (New York, NY, USA)

Line-Up: Peter 'Petrus Steele' Ratajczyk (vocals / bass), Keith Alexander (guitar), Louie Beateaux (drums)

Thrash act that showed the earliest inklings of Pete Steele's pre TYPE O NEGATIVE genius. As frontman for CARNIVORE Steele went under the stage name 'Petrus Steele' with drummer Louie Beateaux opting for 'Lord Petrus T'.

CARNIVORE's early gigs made quite an impact with former FALLOUT lead man Pete Steele (real name Peter Ratajczyk) often resorting to self mutilation carving crosses into his face. His talents in other areas were also much in demand as he is credited with penning the lyrics on the debut AGNOSTIC FRONT album.

Guitarist Keith Alexander left the fold in 1986 to create PRIMAL SCREAM together with ex-HELLICON vocalist Steve Alliano and former BLACK VIRGIN bassist Rob Graham. He was replaced by Marc Piovanetti.

Steele set about completely re-inventing the band through REPULSION to SUB ZERO evolving eventually into what would become the globally successful and controversial gothic outfit TYPE O NEGATIVE.

Piovanetti allied himself with THE CRUMBSUCKERS.

Albums:
CARNIVORE, Roadrunner RR9754 (1985)
Predator / Carnivore / Male Supremacy / Armageddon / Legion Of Doom / God Is Dead / Thermonuclear Warrior / World Wars III And IV
RETALIATION, Roadrunner RR9567 (1988)
Jack Daniel's And Pizza / Angry Neurotic Catholics / S.M.D. / Ground Zero Brooklyn / Race War / Inner Conflict / Jesus Hitler / Technophobia / Manic Depression / U.S.A. For U.S.A. / Five Billion Dead / Sex And Violence

CASBAH (JAPAN)

Line-Up: Taka Hatori (vocals), Ryo Murayama (guitar), Kouichi Mitani (bass), Takashi Usui (drums)

Japanese Thrash Metal band CASBAH

originally went under the title of EXPLOSION. As CASBAH the band featured on two compilation albums, 'Heavy Metal Forum 3' on Explosion Records and 'Devil Must Be Driven Out With Devil' for the Hold Up label. CASBAH then released a 1985 single 'Fear And Destruction'.

At this stage CASBAH comprised frontman Taka Hatori, guitarist Nariaki Kida, bassist Kouichi Mitani and drummer Takashi Usui. The self-financed 'Russian Roulette' single followed which saw Kida replaced by Ryo Murayama. A further demo session 'Infinite Pain' arrived in 1987.

The band put in a noteworthy live gig at the infamous New York CBGB's club during 1992 but would then undergo line-up changes. CASBAH signed to the Roadrunner label in 1996 issuing the 'Bold Statement' album the following year. A collection of archive material, 'Dinosaurs', arrived in 1998.

CASBAH vocalist Hatori would also deputise live for OUTRAGE.

Latterly CASBAH's rhythm section has witnessed a shift over to bass player Takatoshi Kodaira and drummer Suguru Kobayoshi. The latter would join SOLITUDE in late 2001.

Singles/EPs:
Fear And Destruction / Kill You All, Explosion (1985)
Russian Roulette / Death Metal, Music Visions (1986)
Mr. Mess / Decay / Paranoise / Spiral 2000, Roadrunner RRCA 9004 (1999) ('Barefooted On Earth' EP 1)
Speak / **Flying High** / Garden Of Roses / Bold Statement, Roadrunner RRCA 9005 (1999) ('Barefooted On Earth' EP 2)

Albums:
BOLD STATEMENT, Roadrunner (1997)
DINOSAURS, Roadrunner RRCA 1003 (1998)
Discharge / Low Intensity Warfare / No More Slaughter / The Cloning / Chain Gang / Infinite Pain / Gun Crazy / Swan Song / Kids On The Skids / Lock The Passion / Desperate War / The One's Left Behind / Russian Roulette / Death Metal

CATALEPSY (BELGIUM)

Brussels Thrashers CATALEPSY supported many acts such as SACRED REICH, CHANNEL ZERO and CRO-MAGS prior to recording their debut demo 'The Rope Of Life'. This was followed by a further tape, 'One Size Fits All', before the group was able to issue the 'House Of Despair' single in 1993.

The group has since followed up with two albums.

Singles/EPs:
House Of Despair / House Of Despair (Mix) / Hotdog And Beercanhill (Live) / Brick By Brick (Live), Electrip EL 108 (1993)

Albums:
FRUITCAKES WE HAVE KNOWN, Elecrtrip EL107CD (1993)
Brick By Brick / Hot Dog & Beercanhill / Civilised Genocide / House of Despair / Here Comes King Gossip / Miss Brainless / Tortured Minds / Clowns / Suicide Letters

CAULDRON (USA)
Line-Up: Varnom Ponville (vocals), Scott Shelby (guitar), Zeb Perkins (bass), Jason Thibodeaux (drums)

The erstwhile Texan Thrash duo vocalist Varnam Ponville and guitarist Scott Shelby of GAMMACIDE relocated to Louisiana to assemble the Doom styled Thrash outfit CAULDRON. They would be joined in this endeavour by bassist Zeb Perkins and drummer Jason Thibodeaux for the ensuing 1997 Tim Kimsey produced 'For The Love Of Pain' album.

Albums:
FOR THE LOVE OF PAIN, Brainticket (1997)
Acts Of God / Mindwarp / I'll Make You Beg / Blood On The Cross / For The Love Of Pain / Theater Of The Absurd / All That I See Is Red / Too Little Too Late / Lord Have Mercy / Overcome Evil / Endless / (Earth) After Forever

CAUSTIC (DENMARK)
Line-Up: Soren Jansen (vocals), Gert Lund (guitar), Rolf Hansen (guitar), Rune H. Andersen (bass), Carsten Gierlevsen (drums)

Death Metal band with Thrash influences CAUSTIC, founded in 1991, hail from Esbjerg releasing demo sessions 'An Integral Sense' and 'Timid Reality' the same year.

Singles/EPs:
Victim Of Ignorance / Moments In The Infinite / Lacrymose Progeny, Shiver Records SHR009 (1994) ('Moments In The Infinite' EP)

CELTIC FROST (SWITZERLAND)
Line-Up: Tom G. Warrior (vocals / guitar), Martin Eric Ain (bass), Reed St. Mark (drums)

A highly influential Zurich Thrash Metal act who pushed the musical boundaries of the genre to the limit, CELTIC FROST blended a fusion of extreme aggression with classical and jazz leanings to create a unique 'avant-garde' eclectic style. The band rapidly built a strong fan base and, at their peak, looked set to rival the big name American Speed Metal outfits for world domination.

CELTIC FROST had a strange genesis as mentor and renowned 'death grunter' Warrior and bassist Martin Eric Ain were members of what was generally acknowledged to have been one of the worst bands ever - HELLHAMMER. Tom himself started out musically in GRAVE HILL who were heavily influenced by the NWoBHM bands such as DIAMOND HEAD and VENOM.

The original CELTIC FROST, so named after a combination of song titles on a CIRITH UNGOL album sleeve, line-up in May 1984 comprised Warrior, Ain and drummer Isaac Darso. The latter lasted precisely one rehearsal before being usurped by SCHIZO's Stephen Priestly on a temporary basis as a session drummer for recording. At this stage CELTIC FROST were still working on NWoBHM favourites such as songs by ANGELWITCH and ARAGORN.

With HELLHAMMER's reputation preceding them (magazines reviews polarized at either the genius or dreadful end of the spectrum) CELTIC FROST retained their previous deal with Noise Records by submitting a master plan detailing the names of all future releases. The strategy called for an initial demo to be entitled 'A Thousand Deaths' but the label soon persuaded the band that this should form the basis of an opening commercially available product.

CELTIC FROST's first product, the mini-album, 'Morbid Tales' was recorded with Martin Eric Ain's former colleague in SCHIZO drummer Stephen Priestly. As soon as the sessions were completed Priestly decamped. CELTIC FROST set about negotiations with American drummer Jeff Cardelli of Seattle act LIPSTICK. However, the band hired another American, ex-CROWN drummer Reed St. Mark (real name Reid Cruickshank).

As with HELLHAMMER media views on 'Morbid Tales' ranged in their extremity from excellent to dire. The controversy stoked up by these opposing views would serve the band well. CELTIC FROST were still at this juncture wearing the stage make up later to be given the name 'corpse paint' by later generations of Black Metal bands. A further EP 'The Emperors Return' followed to equally polarized reviews and even condemnation from the band themselves. By now CELTIC FROST were being acknowledged as leaders in their field.

CELTIC FROST's inaugural live performances came with a run of shows opening for German bands BEAST and MASS in Germany and Austria. Planned shows in Italy with ASTAROTH were shelved. Ain had been asked to leave during recording of the next album 'To Megatherion' and CELTIC FROST pulled in Dominic Steiner of the Glam Rock act JUNK FOOD. The album, which saw the band utilizing timpanis, French horns and operatic vocals courtesy of Claudia-Maria Mokri, would be the first to be graced with lavish album sleeve artwork from the renowned artist H.R. Giger.

Friction between the band members resulted in Steiner's dismissal as soon as 'Into Mega Therion' had been completed. For CELTIC FROST's debut show outside of Europe at the November 1985 'World War Three' festival in Montreal alongside VOIVOD, POSSESSED, DESTRUCTION and NASTY SAVAGE with Martin Eric Ain back in the bass position.

Warrior also worked as producer for fellow Swiss Metal band CORONOR, a gesture they repaid by becoming CELTIC FROST's roadcrew!

1986 saw CELTIC FROST back on the live circuit touring Europe sharing billing with HELLOWEEN and GRAVE DIGGER. Later shows saw a headline at a Belgian festival, the band's debut in England in London with GRAVE DIGGER and HELLOWEEN supporting and also touring in America alongside RUNNING WILD and VOIVOD.

With CELTIC FROST's status rising sharply the 'Tragic Serenades' EP was issued to keep fans happy between albums. The EP consisted of remixed tracks from 'Into Megatherion' and new numbers.

'Into The Pandemonium' provided fans with another bizarre offering comprising tracks such as a cover of WALL OF VOODOO's 'Mexican Radio' and the Rap cut 'One In Their Pride'. Before the album had been recorded New York based guitarist Ritchi Desmond was briefly linked with a position in the band, but, having travelled to Switzerland to work with the group Desmond returned home citing "too many conflicting attitudes" as the reason why he failed to join CELTIC FROST. Warrior countered that Desmond brought uninvited family members along to the audition and looked nothing like his submitted photograph! Desmond was to front SABBAT for their 'Mourning Has Broken' album and subsequent disastrous tour.

During a break in recording the band played a series of European gigs with ANTHRAX, CRIMSON GLORY and even METALLICA.

For livework to promote 'Into The Pandemonium' CELTIC FROST added second guitarist Ron Marks and toured Britain in winter of 1987 with support from KREATOR then America on a bill with EXODUS and ANTHRAX. The tour succeeded in dumbfounding many of the band's established fans with such radical tracks as the aforementioned 'Mexican Radio' cover and the band was dogged throughout it's duration by legal wrangles with Noise Records. Disillusioned, Marks quit to be replaced by former JUNK FOOD guitarist Oliver Amberg.

Upon their return to Europe CELTIC FROST hit further problems when Martin Ain decided to abandon the music business entirely in favour of wedded bliss (!), so Warrior quickly drafted in Curt Victor Bryant.

CELTIC FROST was in a state of flux besieged by business and financial problems. Even an offer from director Ken Russell to lay down the soundtrack to the movie 'The Lair Of The White Worm' had to be declined because the group was in such disarray. However, the final blow to the classic line-up came when Reed St. Mark upped and left to join MINDFUNK and his position was filled by a returning Stephen Priestly. This was the line-up that was to record the disastrous 'Cold Lake' album produced by Tony Platt; a record that effectively killed the band's career in Europe.

With this effort CELTIC FROST appeared to ditch all of their former pretensions artistically and even adopted a new 'Glam' image, much to the horror of their most hardcore following. Tom dropped the 'Warrior' from his stagename and became plain old Thomas Gabriel Fischer, sporting an L.A. GUNS T-shirt on official press photos.

It was heavily rumoured that the band had, in a SPINAL TAP style move, adopted Tom's girlfriend as manager and that the new look was her masterplan for CELTIC FROST's step into the big league. CELTIC FROST themselves maintained that tracks like 'Teaze Me' were a parody of Glam Rock, but fans were outraged and the media universally attacked the album. The European tour fared badly with audiences deserting in droves. However, in America 'Cold Lake' was in actual fact making serious sales headway and a U.S. tour beginning in March 1989 was judged a success..

In late '89 the badly bruised CELTIC FROST announced a return to their former style and regrouped with Ron Marks. Martin Eric Ain was also persuaded to put down some guest bass tracks and contribute lyrics. The 'Vanity / Nemesis' Roli Mossiman produced album was cited by many as the band's best record to date, but the legacy of 'Cold Lake' still haunted the quartet to such a degree that sales suffered.

CELTIC FROST only managed minimal touring to back up the release of 'Vanity / Nemesis' including a British tour. By now Warrior was to be seen spotted playing a guitar emblazoned with his wife's name 'Michelle', the lady in question also having become a backing singer for the band.

New management hooked up a deal with major label BMG in America. However, the deal was shelved at the last minute leaving CELTIC FROST high and dry.

A further CELTIC FROST album did emerge titled 'Parched With Thirst Am I And Dying'. The record comprised rare material and completely reworked older tracks. Promoted as a new album it sold extremely well.

Warrior took the band into an even more radical direction when he mooted the idea of working with ex-THE TIME guitarist Jesse Johnson on a projected Funk-Metal project. Stephen Priestly meantime would perform drums for French act TREPONEM PAL's 1991 'Aggravation' album.

Following a 1992 four track demo, featuring the tracks 'Honour Thy Father', 'Seeds Of Rapture', 'Icons Alive' and 'Oh Father', the band searched in vain for a new deal. Initial tapes were laid down with Priestly on drums but sessions in Texas saw Reed St. Mark back behind the kit and Renée Hernz on bass. Nothing came of this latest venture and CELTIC FROST effectively split; Marks relocating to America to form STEPCHILD then SUBSONIC.

In 1992 Noise released a CELTIC FROST epitaph in the form of 'Parched With Thirst Am I And Dying'; a collection of rare and unreleased studio out-takes as the band bowed out.

In more recent years Martin Ain has produced the debut album from Doom band SADNESS in 1995, whilst Tom Warrior was found fronting APOLLYON'S SON In 1996.

Late 2001 would herald renewed rumours of a full-blown CELTIC FROST reunion with Tom G. Warrior, Martin Eric Ain and Reed St. Mark all participating.

Singles/EPs:
The Usurper / Jewel Throne / Return To Eve, Noise N0041 (1986) ('Tragic Serenades' EP)
Dethroned Emperor / Circle Of The Tyrants / Morbid Tales / Suicidal Winds / Visual Aggression, Noise N0042 (1986) ('Emperor's Return' EP)
I Won't Dance / One In Their Pride / Tristesses De La Lune, Noise N094 (1986) ('Emperor's EP)
Wine In My Hand (Third From The Sun) / Heroes / Descent From Babylon, Noise NO (1990)

Albums:
MORBID TALES, Noise N 0017 60-1673 (1984)
Into The Crypt Of Rays / Visions Of Mortality / Procreation (Of The Wicked) / Return To Eve / Danse Macabre / Nocturnal Fear
TO MEGATHERION, Noise N0031 (1985)
Innocence And Wrath / The Usurper / Jewel Throne / Dawn Of Megiddo / Eternal Summer / Circle Of Tyrants / (Beyond The) North Winds / Fainted Eyes / Tears In A Prophet's Dream / Necromantical Screams
INTO THE PANDEMONIUM, Noise N0065 (1987)
Mexican Radio / Mesmerised / Inner Sanctum / Sorrows Of The Moon / Babylon Fell / Caress Into Oblivion / One In Their Pride / I Won't Dance / Rex Irae (Requiem-Opening) / Oriental Masquerade
COLD LAKE, Noise NUK 125 (1989)
Intro - Human / Seduce Me Tonight / Petty Obsession / (Once) They Were Eagles / Cherry Orchards / Juices Like Wine / Little Velvet / Blood On Kisses / Downtown Hanoi / Dance Sleazy / Roses Without Thorns / Tease Me / Mexican Radio (New Version)
VANITY/NEMESIS, Noise-EMI EMC 3576 (1990)
The Heart Beneath / Wine In My Hand (Third From The Sun) / Wings Of Solitude / The Name Of My Bride / This Island Earth / The Restless Seas / Phallic Tantrum / A Kiss Or A Whisper / Vanity / Nemesis / Heroes
PARCHED WITH THIRST AM I AND DYING, Noise N 191-2 (1992)
Idols Of Chagrin / A Descent To Babylon / Return To The Eve / Juices Like Wine / The Inevitable Factor / The Heart Beneath / Cherry Orchards / Tristesses De La Lune / Wings Of Solitude / The Usurper / Journey Into Fear / Downtown Hanoi / Circle Of The Tyrants / In The Chapel In The Moonlight / I Won't Dance / The Name Of My Bride / Mexican Radio / Under Apollyon's Sun

CENTINEX (SWEDEN)
Line-Up: Mattias Lamppu (vocals), Kenneth Wiklund (guitar), Andreas Evaldsson (guitar), Martin Schulman (bass), Joakim Gustafsson (drums)

Renowned Death / Thrash Metal act that have increasingly bolstered their sound and imagery with Satanic lyrical references. CENTINEX opened their career in September 1990 issuing the debut demo cassette 'End Of Life' the following year. The band signed to Swedish label Underground for release of the album 'Subconscious Lobotomy' which saw a limited release of 1,000 copies. The CENTINEX line-up at this juncture comprised twin vocalists Erik and Mattias Lamppu, guitarist Andreas Evaldsson, bass player Martin Schulman and drummer Joakim Gustafsson.

A further three track demo session 'Under The Blackened Sky' followed. CENTINEX's next cassette release 'Transcend The Dark Chaos', released on the band's own novelly titled Evil Shit Productions, was repressed by Sphinx Records.

The second CENTINEX full-length album 'Malleus Malefaction' was recorded for the German Wild Rags label and produced by Peter Tägtgren of HYPOCRISY.

1996 saw the release of a shared 7" single 'Sorrow Of Burning Wasteland' in collusion with INVERTED and a fresh band line up retaining Lamppu, Schulman and Evaldsson but with new faces in UNCURBED guitarist Kenneth Wiklund and drummer Kalimaa. The band also featured on a split EP with Sweden's VOICES OF DEATH and German act BAPHOMET.

Early 1997 found CENTINEX on tour in Scandinavia as guests to CRADLE OF FILTH. However, a split in the ranks came the following year when both Lamppu and Evaldsson made their exit.

The 'Bloodhunt' album, issued in June 1999 by Repulse, would also be delivered by Oskorei Productions in a limited edition 10" vinyl format restricted to just 300 copies.

It was to be July 1999 before CENTINEX enrolled UNCANNY and DELLAMORTE drummer Kennet Englund. For touring later in the year CENTINEX pulled in DELLAMORTE and CARNAL FORGE man Jonas Kjellgren on guitar and UNCURBED and DELLAMORTE vocalist Johan Jansson.

The same year had CENTINEX contributing their version of 'Ripping Corpse' to a Full Moon Productions KREATOR tribute album.

2000 witnessed yet more ructions when Kjellgren and Englund decamped. Replacements were AZURE vocalist Robban Kanto and drummer Johan. In December of 2000 Japanese label Soundholic issued the 'Hellbrigade' album. The following year it would be picked up by Repulse for European release, World War III Records in America, Picoroco Records in South America and Irond Records in Russia. Nocturnal Music would also weigh in with a limited edition vinyl version.

2001 had CENTINEX sharing vinyl with the infamous American act NUNSLAUGHTER with their take on SODOM's 'Enchanted Land' for the 'Hail Germania' EP on the Belgian Painkiller label.

In October 2001 guitarist Kenneth Wiklund would break ranks. He would be replaced on a session basis by Johan Ahlberg of SUBDIVE.

Singles/EPs:

Sorrow Of Burning Wasteland / , Voices Of Death VOD003 (1996) (Split 7" single with INVERTED. 600 copies)

Shadowland / Eternal Lies, Oskorei Productions 004 (1998)

Apocalyptic Armageddon / Seeds Of Evil / Everlasting Bloodshed, Deadly Art DAP 095 (2000)

Enchanted Land / , Painkiller (2001) ('Hail Germania' Split 7" with NUNSLAUGHTER)

Albums:

SUBCONSCIOUS LOBOTOMY, Underground UGR05 (1992)
Blood On My Skin / Shadows Are Astray / Dreams Of Death / Orgy In Flesh / End Of Life / Bells Of Misery / Inhuman Dissections Of Souls / The Aspiration / Until Death Tear Us Apart

TRANSCEND THE DARK CHAOS, Sphinx SIXR 003 (1994)

MALLEUS MALEFACTION, Wild Rags WRR 043 (1995)
Upon The Ancient Ground / Dark Visions / Sorrow Of The Burning Wasteland / Transcend The Dark Chaos / Thorns Of Desolation / Eternal Lies / At The Everlasting Evil

REFLECTIONS, Diehard RRS 954 (1997)
Carnal Lust / Seven Prophecies / Before The Dawn / The Dimension Beyond / My Demon Within / In Pain / Undivined / Darkside / Into The Funeral Domain

REBORN THROUGH FLAMES, Repulse RPS 032CD (1998)
Embraced By Moonlight / Resurrected / Summon The Golden Twilight / The Beauty Of Malice / Under The Guillotine / Through Celestial Gates Molested / In The Arch Of Serenity

BLOODHUNT, Repulse RPS 042CD (1999)
Under The Pagan Glory / For Centuries Untold / Luciferian Moon / Bloodhunt / The Conquest Infernal / Like Darkened Storms / Mutilation

HELLBRIGADE, Repulse RPS 046CD (2001)
Towards Devastation / On With Eternity / The Eyes Of The Dead / Emperor Of Death / Last Redemption / Blood Conqueror / Neverending Hell / Nightbreeder / Hellbrigade

CEREBRAL FIX (UK)
Line-Up: Simon Forrest (vocals), Tony Warburton (guitar), Greg Fellows (guitar), Frank Healy (bass), Andy Baker (drums)
Birmingham's CEREBRAL FIX trod a fine line between Crossover Punk and Death style Thrash Metal. The band were founded at the

height of the Thrash explosion in 1988 with a line-up of vocalist Simon Forrest, guitarist Gregg Fellows, bassist Steve and drummer Ade none of whom had previous band experience.

CEREBRAL FIX's first demo landed them a deal with Vinyl Solutions Records for 1988's 'Life Sucks And Then You Die'. However, the band had appeared on a Sounds magazine flexi-sampler just before this with the track 'Maimed To Beg'. The same year the band got some serious touring under their belts sharing a bill in Britain with BOLT-THROWER, both acts promoting debut albums on the same label.

CEREBRAL FIX lost their rhythm section in 1990 as both Steve and Ade departed, ostensibly to form another act but this never materialized. Replacements were ex-NAPALM DEATH and SACRILEGE bassist Frank Healy and former VARUKERS and SACRILEGE drummer Andy Baker. This line-up turned in another demo to secure a fresh deal with Roadrunner Records.

CEREBRAL FIX set about touring once more guesting for NAPALM DEATH on their 'Harmony Corruption' dates up front of a second album 'Tower Of Spite'. Harking back to Healy and Baker's roots the bonus track on the CD was a cover of SACRILEGE's 'The Closing Irony'.

In May of 1990 the band gained the honours of supporting SEPULTURA at London's Marquee club.

1991 saw Baker leaving and in his place former VARUKERS and METAL MESSIAH man Kevin Frost for the 'Bastards' album. CD bonus tracks comprised 'Maimed To Beg', the GBH cover 'No Survivors' and the DAMNED's 'Smash It Up', the latter featuring WOLFSBANE's Blaze Bayley on vocals. Promoting the album found the band guesting in Britain to OBITUARY.

1992's 'Death Erotica' had a version of DISCHARGE's 'Never Again' with NAPALM DEATH's Barney Greenaway and POP WILL EAT ITSELF's Clint on guest vocals. NAPALM DEATH's bassist Shane Embury also added vocals to the track 'Too Drunk To Funk' whilst MARSHALL LAW's Andy Pyke and SHY and SIAM vocalist Tony Mills contributed to a version of the JUDAS PRIEST hit 'Living After Midnight'.

A 1992 tour with PARADISE LOST was followed up by a European tour in 1993 alongside CANCER and GOMORRAH. Healy had departed by this time and the band pulled in the bassist from DISCHARGE to fulfil the dates.

The band folded shortly after. Healy later teamed up with BENEDICTION. Frost is back with THE VARUKERS.

Albums:
LIFE SUCKS AND THEN YOU DIE, Vinyl Solution SOL 15 (1988)
Warstorm / Cerebral Fix / Looniverse / Give Me Life / Soap Opera / Behind The Web / Product Of Disgust / Life Sucks / Power Struggle / Go / Fear Of Death / Acid Sick / Skatedrunk / Zombie / Existing Not Living
TOWER OF SPITE, Roadrunner RO 9356 1 (1990)
Unite For Who? / Enter The Turmoil / Feast Of The Fools / Chasten Of Fear / Circle Of The Earth / Tower Of Spite / Injecting Out / Quest For Midian / Forgotten Genocide / Culte Des Mortes (I)
BASTARDS, Roadracer RO 92861 (1991)
Descent Into Unconsciousness / Veil Of Tears / Beyond Jerusalem / Return To Infinity / Sphere Born / I Lost A Friend / Ritual Abuse / Mammonite / Middle Third (Mono Culture) / Maimed To Beg / No Survivors / Smash It Up
DEATHEROTICA, Under One Flag FLAG 75 (1992)
Death Erotica / World Machine / Clarissa / Haunted Eyes / Mind Within Mine / Splintered Wings / Creator Of Outcasts / Angel's Kiss / Still In Mind / Ratt Of Medusa / Never Again / Too Drunk Too Funk / Burning/ Living After Midnight

CEREBUS (NC, USA)
Line-Up: Scott Board (vocals), Chris Pennel (guitar), Andy Huffine (guitar), Eric Burgess (bass), Joby Barker (drums)

Singles/EPs:
Like A Banshee On The Loose, Cerebus (1987)
On The Edge / Wasted Time / Invisible / Close The Door / The Offering, Rockduster (1991) ('Regression Progression' EP)

Albums:
TOO LATE TO PRAY, New Renaissance (1986)
Running Out Of Time / Taking Your Chances / Distant Eyes / Too Late To Pray / Rock The House Down / Catch Me If You Can / Talk Is Cheap / Longing For Home / She Burns

CESSATION OF LIFE
(Ventura, CA, USA)
Line-Up: Chris Violence (vocals), Travis Anderberg (guitar), Justin Harrison (bass), Ron Ostlund (drums)

A Ventura based trad Thrash act that has self-financed two full albums to date.

1999 saw the release of their debut album 'Aggressive By Nature, Destructive By

Choice' and the inclusion of the track 'Impalement' on the Black Light Records 'Escape The Furnace 3' compilation. CESSATION OF LIFE contributed their version of 'Wrathchild' to the IRON MAIDEN tribute album 'Children Of The Damned', released by the Italian Adrenaline label. This album would also see a CESSATION OF LIFE original, 'Synthetic Suicide', included.

CESSATION OF LIFE would support Thrash veterans TESTAMENT on their South West leg of the 'Ride The Snake' tour. Former HUNGSOLO and REALITY bassist Justin Harrison was inducted into the fold during February of 2002.

Albums:
AGGRESSIVE BY NATURE, DESTRUCTIVE BY CHOICE, (1999)
At One With The Dark / Synthetic Suicide / Don't Push / Tears Of The Dead / Witch Finder General / Angel Of Mercy / Impalement / Ready To Burn
KILL YOU AGAIN, (2002)
Forgotten / Long Awaited Secession / A Minute To Live / The Call / Kill You Again / A New Religion / Johnny Wants A Six Pack / I.F.T.W.M.F.A. / Pulverizing Vortex

CHAINSAW (GERMANY)
Line-Up: Frank Von Schmidt (vocals), Burkhardt Rautenberg (guitar), Andreas Klimowitsch (guitar), Gerd Gutsche (bass), Arndt Kermer (drums)

When this German speed Metal quintet sent out promo copies of their 'Hell's Burnin' Up' album the group ensured a miniature 'Action Man' size chainsaw was included in the package daubed with the band's logo!

Albums:
HELL'S BURNIN' UP, Bonebreaker BONE 2 (1986)
Hell's Burnin' Up / Dungeon / Last Fortress / Cut Loose / Rage And Revenge / Midnight Hunter / Born To Kill / He Knows You Are Alone / Ageless Force

CHANNEL ZERO (BELGIUM)
Line-Up: Franky De Smet Van Damme (vocals), Xavier Carion (guitar), Tino Olivier De Martino (bass), Phil Baheux (drums)

Brussels Thrash Metal act CHANNEL ZERO was created in 1990 by ex-CYCLONE members.

Having debuted in 1992 with an eponymously titled debut for Shark Records, the quartet stepped up a level with the follow-up 'Stigmatised For Life' album, which was produced by PANTERA drummer Vinnie Paul. Following its release the band toured Europe supporting BIOHAZARD, OBITUARY, PRO-PAIN, EXHORDER and NAPALM DEATH.

The band's third album, The 'Unsafe', (the second on Play It Again Sam) is notable for a guest vocal performance on one track by M.O.D.'s Billy Milano.

For recording of the ensuing 'Black Fuel' CHANNEL ZERO flew to Connecticut in America in order to record, but became disillusioned with the results. Deciding upon scrapping these recordings, CHANNEL ZERO returned to Europe to complete the album with producer Attie Bauw.

Guitarist Peter Iterbeke has a project band entitled MANTRA, also including drummer J.T. Scaglione and bassist Jimmy Preziosa from American Thrash Metal veterans WHIPLASH.

Singles/EPs:
Suck My Energy (Edit) / Suck My Energy / Repetition, Play It Again Sam 977. 847 (1995)
Help / Last Gasp / All For One / Man On The Edge, Play It Again Sam (1995)

Albums:
CHANNEL ZERO, Shark 032 (1992)
No Light (At The End Of The Tunnel) / Tales Of Worship / The Pioneer / Succeed Or Bleed / Never Alone / Inspiration To Violence / Painful Jokes / Save Me / Animation / Run With The Torch
STIGMATISED FOR LIFE, Play It Again Sam BIAS 259CD (1994)
Gold / Testimony / Unleash The Dog / Chrome Dome / Repetition / America / Stigmatised For Life / Play A Little / Big Now / Last Gap
UNSAFE, Play It Again Sam BIAS 290CD (1995)
Suck My Energy / Heroin / Bad To The Bone / Help / Lonely / Run W.T.T. / Why / No More / Unsafe / Dashboard Devils / Asa Boy / Man On The Edge
BLACK FUEL, Play It Again Sam BIAS 350 CD (1996)
Black Fuel / Mastermind / Call On Me / Fool's Parade / Self Control / Misery / The Hill / Love - Hate Satellite / Caveman / Put It In / Wasted / Outro
LIVE, Play It Again Sam (1998)
Black Fuel / As A Boy / Mastermind / Self Control / Fool's Parade / Bad To The Bone / Dashboard Devils / Call On Me / Run W.T.T. / Heroin / Suck My Energy / Help / Lonely / Man On The Edge

CIRITH UNGOL (Ventura, CA, USA)
Line-Up: Tim Baker (vocals), Jerry Fogle
(guitar), Greg Lindstrom (guitar), Michael Flint
(bass), Robert Garven (drums)

With a name inspired by Tolkien's Kirith Ungol
(the lair in which the spider Shelob made an
attempt to destroy Baggins in 'Lord Of The
Rings') and a semi-legendary logo featuring
two praying, kneeling skeletons. Ventura,
California's CIRITH UNGOL, based around
former TITANIC duo of guitarist Jerry Fogle
and drummer Robert Garven, mixed up a
bundle of varying influences and gained a
loyal, cult following in a career that had first
been established in the early '70s! The group
would, however, not record an album until
1981's 'Frost And Fire' on their own Liquid
Flames label.
Although CIRITH UNGOL's debut album
'Frost And Fire' sported an amazing piece of
cover artwork, the actual contents of the
record disappointed many potential fans. It
even featured a track, an instrumental entitled
'Maybe That's Why', that, through an error,
lyrics for appeared in the album packaging!
Following the album's release, CIRITH
UNGOL parted company with second
guitarist Greg Lindstrom and, amazingly,
many proclaimed the band's ensuing
contribution to the first 'Metal Massacre'
compilation album ('Death Of The Sun') as
rather listenable!
Metal Blade picked up the band for a second
album, the highly rated 'King Of The Dead'
emerging during 1984 (on Roadrunner in
Europe) and this record would not only show
a vast improvement in the standard of
songwriting and musicianship. It would push
the Californian mob further into the hearts of
the true believers, gaining a host of new
admirers along the way.
The group also began to become inspired the
work of novelist Michael Moorcock lyrically, a
fact that gained more prominence on 1986's
'One Foot In Hell' album.
Bearing in mind the almost universal derision
heaped upon their early albums the band
began to attain a cult status in mainland
Europe during the '90s. CIRITH UNGOL's
legacy took a bizarre twist in 1995 when a live
single was issued, financed by none other
than DECEASED's King Fowley.

Singles/EPs:
I'm Alive (Live) / Atom Smasher (Live), Old
Metal (1995)

Albums:
FROST AND FIRE, Liquid Flames HM
13666 (1981)

Frost And Fire / I'm Alive / A Little Fire /
What Does It Take / Edge Of A Knife / Better
Off Dead / Maybe That's Why
KING OF THE DEAD, Roadrunner RR 9832
(1984)
Atom Smasher / Black Machine / Master Of
The Pit / King Of The Dead / Death Of The
Sun / Finger Of Scorn / Toccatta In D / Cirith
Ungol
ONE FOOT IN HELL, Roadrunner RR9681
(1986)
Blood And Iron / Chaos Descends / The Fire
/ Nadsokar / 100 M.P.H. / War Eternal /
Doomed Planet / One Foot In Hell
PARADISE LOST, Restless 7-72510-2
(1991)
Join The Legion / The Troll / Fire / Heaven
Help Us / Before The Lash / Go It Alone /
Chaos Rising / Fallen Idols / Paradise Lost
SERVENTS OF CHAOS, Metal Blade (2001)
Hype Performance / Last Laugh / Frost And
Fire (Early version) / Eyes / Better Off Dead
(Alternate version) / 100 MPH (Alternate
version) / I'm Alive (Alternate version) / Bite
Of The Worm / The Twitch / Maybe That's
Why (original version) / Ill Met In Lankhmar /
Return To Lankhmar / Darkness Weaves /
Witchdance / Feeding The Ants / Obsidian /
Death Of The Sun (Remix) / Fire (Alternate
version) / Fallen Idols (Alternate version) /
Chaos Rising (Rehearsal) / Fallen Idols
(Rehearsal) / Paradise Lost (Rehearsal) /
Join The Legion (Rehearsal) / Before The
Lash (Rehearsal) / Atom Smasher (Live) /
Master Of The Pit (Live) / King Of The Dead
(Live) / Last Laugh (Live) / Cirith Ungol (Live)
/ Secret Agent Man / Ferrari 308QV On
Dyno At 8000 RPM

CLOWN ALLEY
(San Francisco, CA, USA)
Line-Up: David Duran (vocals),
Marc Deutrom (guitar), Lori Black (bass),
Justin Clayton (drums)

Both CLOWN ALLEY's guitarist Marc
Deutrom and bassist Lorl 'Lorax' Black -
daughter of screen icon Shirley Temple no
less, would later come to attention with the
MELVINS. The MELVINS would re-record
CLOWN ALLEY's 'Theme' for their 'Peel
Sessions' EP.
Albums:
CIRCUS OF CHAOS, Alchemy (1986)
The Lie / Unplugged / In The Cartoon / On
The Way Up / Uranium Miner's Daughter / Pet
Of A Pig / The Grey Men / Envy / Theme / The
Second Day / The Prey

COLD STEEL (NY, USA)
Line-Up: Troy Norr (vocals), Ave Casa

(guitar), Joe Shavel (guitar), Greg Hock (bass), Dom Mincieli (drums)

Progressive Thrash Metal. COLD STEEL drummer Hal Aponte would later come to the fore with Progressive Rock outfit ICE AGE.

<u>Albums:</u>
DEMO SERIES, Underground C.C.C. CCC004 (1990)
Crackdown / Pleasant Dreams / Dead By Dawn / Smashed!
FREAKBOY, Turbo 005CD (1992)
Truth Or Dare / The Worst Is Yet To Come / Bracing The Fall / Perfect Peace / Fool's Paradise / Freakboy / New World / What Are You Looking At? / Never Now, Never Will / DSM / Hazardous (To Your Health)
BRACING THE FALL, Turbo 008CD (1992)

CONCRETE SOX (UK)
Line-Up: John (vocals / drums), VicTim (guitar), Les (bass)

Nottingham/Derby Hardcore Thrash Metal act CONCRETE SOX originally started out as a straight Punk band in 1982. The group bowed in as a trio of vocalist / drummer John, bassist Les and guitarist VicTim.
The 'Your Turn Next' album was released by COR Records as well as the track 'Eminent Scum' appearing on a COR Records sampler 'Digging In Water' alongside SACRALIGE and HIRAX in 1985.
John would decamp to join HERESY and CITY INDIANS drummer Andy Sewell and vocalist Sean Cook were enrolled to plug the gap. With this line-up CONCRETE SOX shared a split album release with HERESY, being Earache Records very first release.
A heavy touring schedule followed after which the band switched to the Manic Ears label for 1987's 'Whoops, Sorry Vicar'. The band would also feature on the Manic Ears compilation 'The North Atlantic Noise Attack'. The 1989 'Sewerside' album was issued upfront of guitarist VicTim joining Glamsters SLEEZEPATROL.
Rick Button was drafted on guitar for European touring billed alongside DOOM. The band toured as support to AGNOSTIC FRONT in 1992.
A series of line-up tribulations would dog the band over the next few years. Both Cook and Button made their exit, substitutes being vocalist Lloyd and guitarist Ian. This version of CONCRETE SOX released the 'Lunched Out' live 7" single in America.
Ian would be next to leave and Mark Greenwell took the guitar position as the group signed to Lost And Found for the 'No World Order' album. CONCRETE SOX, complete with a returning Sean Cook, then undertook a tour of Japan and issued a split EP in alliance with NIGHTMARE.
After a ten year term Andy Sewell decided to vacate the drum stool. CONCRETE SOX ultimately folded. There would be a reformation comprising of Les, Lloyd, Mark Greenwell and drummer Pug for a burst of UK dates but once again the band split.
The band would be back for a series of UK shows in the summer of 1998. Swedish shows followed into 1999 with a CONCRETE SOX roster made up of Sean Cook, Mark Greenwell, new bass player Rick Lamell and drummer Andy Sewell.
An EP, simply titled 'The New EP', arrived on the Data label, the cover artwork being a clever 'South Park' spoof announcing "Oh my God - They killed Anarkenny!"

<u>Singles/EPs:</u>
Scape Anglican Attic, COR Records flexi (1985) (with SACRALIGE & HIRAX)
The New EP, Data DATA 008 (1999)

<u>Albums:</u>
YOUR TURN NEXT, COR Records GURT 10 (1986)
SPLIT LP, Earache (1986) (Split with HERESY)
Key To The Door / False Inside / Speak Siberian Or Die (For SOD) / Modernisation (A New Form Of Slavery) / Sustain The Orgy
WHOOPS, SORRY VICAR!, Manic Ears ACHE 11 (1987)
Prophecy / No Trust In Faith / Scientific Slaughter / Comparison / Rumour Well Out Of Hand / Think Now / False Insight / Dream / Salt Of The Earth / Facts / Moustache / Like A Maniac
SEWERSIDE, Big Kiss (1989)
NO WORLD ORDER, Lost & Found LF048 (1993)
Subliminal Thought Circumcision / Senile / Wretched Insertion / Disinfect / The Hate I Create / Bitter End / Alienation / Sometimes I… / Tracy's Song

CONDEMNED (AUSTRALIA)

CONDEMNED is a Thrash Metal project of members from DEATH SENTENCE, VICIOUS CIRCLE and ATTITUDE.

<u>Albums:</u>
HUMANOID OR BIOMECHANOID, Nuclear Blast (198-)

CONVICT (USA)

CONVICT were actually a totally fictitious band purposely made in the studio. Vocalist Gord Kirchin, previously with MAINSTREAM and FIST, cut the lead vocals anonymously. Kirchin was better known as his other pseudonym the shock Thrash Metal singer PILEDRIVER.

CONVICT's guitars were supplied by Conrad Taylor.

Kirchin later created DOGS WITH JOBS and SOFA Q.

Albums:
GO AHEAD MAKE MY DAY, Conra CL1002 (1985)
Evil Eyes / Manic Obsession / Edge Of The Sword / Bloodsucker / Bite The Hands That Feeds You / Metal Warriors / When Your Dreams Are Over / Don't Turn Away

CORONER (SWITZERLAND)

Line-Up: Ron Royce (vocals / bass), Tommy T. Baron (guitar),
Marquis Marky (drums)

Zurich Metal band CORONER achieved European success with a distinct brand of experimental avant-garde Metal in the tradition of CELTIC FROST. In the early part of their career, the band hardly toured, which added to their mystique.

Originally formed in 1984 with guitarist Oliver Amberg (later to join CELTIC FROST), Tom Warrior, mainstay of CELTIC FROST, contributed vocals to CORONER's first demo, 'Death Cult', before new guitarist Tommy T. Baron and drummer Marquis Marky joined CELTIC FROST's American 'Tragic Serenades' tour as road crew. From then on CORONER were continually blighted by comparisons to CELTIC FROST, not helped by Noise Records (CELTIC FROST's label) signing the Swiss trio for good measure!

CORONER's first album, 'RIP', received good reviews and went on to sell over 50,000 units in Europe, and the distinct lack of gigs was more by circumstance than planning. A proposed European tour supporting METHOD OF DESTRUCTION was cancelled by the headliners when protesters threatened to sabotage the tour.

The second album, 'Punishment For Decadence', was produced by Guy Bidmead and emerged a year after CORONER's 1987 debut, featuring a cover of the JIMI HENDRIX classic 'Purple Haze'. Once more the band were unable to tour properly to promote the album, with a planned American jaunt with SABBAT and RAGE being cancelled at the last minute and British dates postponed when the band were incarcerated by British customs for lack of work permits! CORONER did, however, manage to snatch a few support shows to SACRED REICH later in the year.

1989 brought CORONER's third album, 'No More Colour', produced by Pete Hinton and it would be in support of this release that the band finally toured Europe in 1990 with strong support from cult Texans WATCHTOWER.

In 1993 CORONER supported Canadians ANNIHILATOR on a British tour and, although still utilizing the services of Mark and Royce, CORONER had by 1995, to all intents and purposes, become a solo vehicle for Baron.

Marquis Marky turned up again in 1999 as part of Thomas Fischer's APOLLYON SON. Fortunately he had reverted to his real name of Mark Edelmann.

Singles/EPs:
Die By My Hand / Tunnel Of Pain, Noise NO136-6 (1989)
Purple Haze / Masked Jackal, Noise 7HAZE3 (1989)
I Want You (She's So Heavy) / Divine Step, Noise NO0177-7 (Limited Edition Promotion)

Albums:
R.I.P., Noise N0075 (1987)
Intro / Reborn Through Hate / When Angels Die / Intro (Nosferatu) / Nosferatu / Suicide Command / Spiral Dream / R.I.P. / Coma / Fried Alive / Intro (Totentanz) / Totentanz / Outro
PUNISHMENT FOR DECADENCE, Noise NUK 119 (1988)
Intro - Absorbed / Masked Jackal / Arc-Lite / Skeleton On Your Shoulders / Sudden Fall / Shadow Of A Lost Dream / Newbreed / Voyage To Eternity
NO MORE COLOR, Noise NUK 138 (1989)
Die By My Hand / No Need To Be Human / Read My Scars / D.O.A. / Mistress Of Deception / Tunnel Of Pain / Why It Hurts / Last Entertainment
MENTAL VORTEX, Noise N0177-1 (1991)
Divine Step (Conspectu Mortis) / Son Of Lilith / Semtex Revolution / Sirens / Metamorphosis / Pale Sister / About Life / I Want You (She's So Heavy)
GRIN, Noise NO2010-2 (1993)
Dream Path / The Lethargic Age / Internal Conflicts / Caveat (To The Coming) / Serpent Moves / Still Thinking / Theme For Silence / Paralized, Mesmerised / Grin (Nails Hurt) / Host
CORONER, Noise N0212-2 (1995)
Between Worlds / The Favorite Game / Shifter / Serpent Moves / Snow Crystal / Divine Step (Conspectu Mortis) / Gliding

Above While Being Below / Der Mussolini / Last Entertainment (TV Bizarre) / Reborn Through Hate / Golden Cashmere Sleeper (Part 1) / Golden Cashmere Sleeper (Part 2) / Masked Jackal / I Want You (She's So Heavy) / Grin (No Religion Remix) / Purple Haze (Radio Live Cut)

CORROSION OF CONFORMITY
(Raleigh, NC, USA)
Line-Up: Karl Agell (vocals),
Pepper Keenan (guitar), Woody Weatherman (guitar), Mike Dean (bass), Reed Mullin (drums)

CORROSION OF CONFORMITY may well justifiably lay claim to the title of America's first crossover act. The band effortlessly blend riffs of extreme magnitude with infectious hardcore.

Originally a trio titled NO LABELS the band was forged in 1982 by vocalist / bassist Mike Dean, guitarist Woody Weatherman and drummer Reed Mullin. The band augmented their line-up with lead vocalist Eric Eyke for first album 'Eye For An Eye' in 1984, an album that was later re-released by Caroline during 1990.

With 'Animosity' in 1985 the band veered more towards straight metal territory. However, the same year saw the departure of Dean and the band pulled in former UGLY AMERICANS singer Bob Sinister for the 'Technocracy' mini-album as the band, benefiting from the global upsurge of interest in Thrash, were now propelled to front runner status.

Sinister had left the fold by 1988 and CORROSION OF CONFORMITY were effectively put on ice until May 1989 when activity resumed with the addition of ex-SEIZURE / SCHOOL OF VIOLENCE frontman Karl Agell. During the interim a six track EP 'Six Songs With Mike Singing' was released to fulfill contractual obligations as Dean and guitarist Woody Weatherman created project band SNAKE NATION, releasing an album.

Although without a contract for a lengthy period CORROSION OF CONFORMITY, now with bassist Phil Swisher, still kept up the live work touring with DIRTY ROTTEN IMBECILES, DANZIG, SOUNDGARDEN and BAD BRAINS. The band added second guitarist Pepper Keenan upfront of the 1991 album but recording of 'Blind' was delayed as Keenan recovered from a broken hip sustained whilst stagediving!

With the album release the band set about a club tour of America with support from PRONG and BULLET LAVOLTA. These dates were to trigger a world tour that would last a

gruelling two years, an after which vocalist Karl Agell was asked to leave following a New York show with TROUBLE thus prompting the departure of Swisher. The departing duo would later create LEADFOOT releasing the 1997 album 'Bring it on'.

Christmas 1991 bore witness to a bout of recording between Keenan and an old friend PANTERA vocalist Phil Anselmo. The project, titled DOWN, was later to see a CD release.

The 1994 album 'Deliverance', with Keenan now lead vocalist, saw the return of Dean to the bass role from his interim act SPORE as the band embarked on an American tour with support from KEPONE. The band's sound had shifted once more, even echoing the vintage southern sound and twin guitar harmonies.

CORROSION OF CONFORMITY also opened the 1994 Castle Donington 'Monsters Of Rock' festival headlined by METALLICA.

Dean formed an alliance with BRUTAL TRUTH's Rich Hoak to give birth to a 1996 side project act titled NINEFINGER, releasing an album the following year.

Despite renewed interest in the band Columbia instructed the act to adopt more commercial leanings before funding further product. The band delivered a batch of mellowed out Southern flavoured demos but found themselves dropped anyway.

CORROSION OF CONFORMITY toured America in 2000 backed up by CLUTCH and SIXTY WATT SHAMEN. Mullin, suffering from back injuries, was replaced by EYEHATEGOD's Jimmy Bower.

Singles/EPs:
Eye For An Eye / Center Of The World / Citizen / Not For Me / What? / Negative Outlook, Product Inc. INCCD 002/3 (1988) ('Six Songs With Mike Singing' EP)
Vote With A Bullet / Condition A, Condition B / Future - Now / Break The Circle / Jim Beam And Coon Ass, Roadrunner RR 23886 (1992)

Albums:
EYE FOR AN EYE, Southern Studios (1984)
Tell Me / Minds Are Controlled / Indifferent / Broken Will / Rabid Dogs / L.S. / Redneckkk / Co-exist / Excluded / Dark Thoughts / Poison Planet / What? / Negative Outlook / Positive Outlook / No Drunk / College Town / Not Safe / Eye For An Eye / Nothing's Gonna Change
ANIMOSITY, Metal Blade ZORRO 44 (1985)
Loss For Words / Mad World / Consumed / Holier / Positive Outlook / Prayer / Intervention / Kiss Of Death / Hungry Child / Animosity

TECHNOCRACY, Metal Blade ZORRO53 (1987)
Technocrazy / Hungry Child / Happily Ever After / Crawling / Ahh Blugh
BLIND, Roadracer RO 9236-2 (1991)
These Shrouded Temples... / Damned For All Time / The Dance Of The Dead / Buried / Break The Circle / Painted Smiling Face / Mine Are The Eyes Of God / Shallow Ground / Vote With A Bullet / Great Purification / White Noise / Echoes In The Well / ....Remain
DELIVERANCE, Columbia 477683-2 (1994)
Heaven's Not Overflowing / Albatross / Clean My Wounds / Without Wings / Broken Man / Senor Limpio / Man De Mono / Seven Days / No. 2121313 / My Grain / Deliverance / Shale Like You / Shelter / Pearls Before Swine
WISEBLOOD, Columbia 484328-2 (1996)
43 UK
King Of The Rotten / Longwhip - Big America / Wiseblood / Goodbye Windows / Born Again For The Last Time / Drowning In A Daydream / The Snake Has No Head / The Door / Man Or Ash / Redemption City / Wishbone (Some Tomorrow) / Fuel / Bottom Feeder (El Que Come Abajo)
AMERICA'S VOLUME DEALER, Sanctuary (2000)

COUNTERBLAST (SWEDEN)
Line-Up: Martin Letell (vocals), Stefan Hakeskog (guitar), Andreas Ågren (bass), Håkan Paulsson (keyboards), Håkan Andersson (drums)

Apocalyptic blend of Thrash Hardcore and Crustcore.

Singles/EPs:
Prospect / Remain, Skuld SKULD023 (1995)

Albums:
BALANCE OF PAIN, Skuld E.B. 010 (1996)
Prelude Pain / Independence / Disembodiment / Balance Of Pain / Depression / In League With Baldrick / The European Empire Of Capitalism / Beneath The Surface

THE COUP DE GRACE (MN, USA)
Line-Up: James Mecherle (vocals / guitar), Steve Wresh (guitar), Kurt Gillespie (bass), Chris Westling (drums)

A Minneapolis based Metal band, THE COUP DE GRACE blended Thrash Metal with twin guitar British '70s Hard Rock influences and melodies. Their 1990 eponymous debut, which featured a line up of frontman James 'Jim' Mercerle, guitarist Steve Wresh, bassist Kurt Gillespie and drummer Chris Westling, would be produced by none other than Dave Pirner of SOUL ASYLUM.

Although highly rated by the media 'The Coup De Grace' failed to take off. A second low key album was delivered in 1995 'The Art Of Survival'. For this outing Mecherle, Wresh and Westling were joined by new bass player Kyle Lund.

A later line up of the band saw a brand new rhythm section of bassist Tommy Dee and drummer Brent Degendorfer. On guitar would be another new face, Mark Chaussee, later of Rob Halford's FIGHT and DANZIG.

Vocalist / guitarist James Mecherle would later join the band of controversial Rock artist ANDREW W.K.

Albums:
THE COUP DE GRACE, Twin Tone TRG 89182 (1990)
Daylight Dawning / Burning With Optimism / Sad But True / Bombs Away / Me, Myself & I / 'Til The Bitter End / All Of The Above / Barbed Wire / So Be It
THE ART OF SURVIVAL, (1995)
Ten Feet Tall / God Given / Helping Hand / It's Only Money / Not For Today / All Fall Dead / Grave World / Bonds That Bind / Warning Signs / Pride Ran Deep / Celtic Song

COURAGOUS (GERMANY)
Line-Up: Chris Staubach (vocals), Gerd Lucking (guitar), Olli Lohman (guitar), Jurgen Weiland (bass), Jan Mischon (drums)

Thrashers founded in 1988. COURAGOUS (unfortunately mispelt) scored valuable points by winning a 'Battle of the bands' contest, the prize for which was supporting JUDAS PRIEST at the 2001 Balingen 'Bang Your Head' festival.

COURAGOUS feature two RAWBONED members in Staubach and Lucking, the latter acting as drummer. Lucking also operates as drummer with LIGHTMARE and dexterously as bass player for MELANCHOLIC SEASONS.

COURAGOUS debuted with a 1996 demo 'Liar', capitalising on this with appearances on compilation albums such as 'Azathot' and 'Deathphobia V'. Their debut album 'Listen' was released in November 1998. Their 2002 follow up, 'Remember', was mastered by REBELLION man Uwe Lulis.

Albums:
LISTEN, (1998)

REMEMBER, (2002)

COVEN (Seattle, WA, USA)
Line-Up: Jay Clark (vocals), Paul Hash (guitar), Dean Babbitt (guitar) Gary Peebles (bass), Neal Babbitt (drums)

Albums:
BLESSED IS THE BLACK, Medusa 72243 (1988)
Blessed Is The Black / 666 / Burn The Cross / Out Of The Grave / Rock This Church / Iron Dick / The Monger / McDonaldland Massacre / Another Life / Creature Of Duty (And My Duty Is Death)
DEATH WALKS BEHIND YOU, Medusa (1989)
Too Late To Pray / Ministry Of Lies / Spellbinder / Succubus / Death Walks Behind You / Frozen Bones / Propoganda / Justified Suicide / Ted Bundy / Silent Night (Violent Night)

CREEPIN' DEATH (ITALY)
Line-Up: Luca Leoncini (vocals), Giancarlo Eusebio (guitar), Paolo Quarati (guitar), Paolo Testa (bass), Ricky Valo (drums)

Torino based Thrashers previously known as BLACK EVIL, CREEPIN' DEATH released a six song demo, 'No Privatation', in 1987 before the arrival of the debut 'Errare Humanum Est...' album two years later.

Albums:
ERRARE HUMANUM EST... LM LMO18 (1989)
Intro - Solitude / Rotten Press / I Want To Live... / Squirts Of Shout / Stop That Car / From The Dark / Black Horizon / Green White Red

CRIPPLE (SWEDEN)
Line-Up: Daniel Ruud (vocals / guitar), Anton Reborg (guitar), Mattias Lurgo Fransson (bass), Daniel Berg (drums)

Albums:
GREEN PILLOW, Crypta 8213-2 (1993)
I Turn Into God / Welcome To My Circus / The Crying Moon / Silent Library / Gangway / In Deep Sleep / Crispy Leaves / Shiver Through End Of Life / Breathe / 2 Lame 2 Understand

CRISIS (Salt Lake City, UT, USA)
Line-Up: Dave Thompson (vocals / bass), Jeff Cross (guitar), Bret Desmond (drums)

Guitarist Jeff Cross formed ROUGH NIGHT

in 1988 together with vocalist / bassist Dane Thomson and drummer Bob Wilson.

Albums:
ARMED TO THE TEETH, Bullet BULP 4 (1984)
Crank It Up / Diane / We're The Boys / Break The Action / Take It Or Leave It / Armed To The Teeth
KICK IT OUT, Crisis (1986)

CRO MAGS (New York, NY, USA)
Line-Up: John Joseph (vocals), Harley Flanagan (vocals / bass), Doug Holland (guitar), Parris Mitchell Mayhew (guitar), Mackie Jason (drums)

Seminal tattooed New York Hardcore Thrash Crossover act dating back to 1984 noted for plying aggressive music whilst professing peaceful Hare Krishna beliefs. CRO MAGS founder vocalist / bassist Harley Flanagan started out whilst a young teenager in punk band THE STIMULATORS prior to forming M.O.I. with guitarist Doug Holland and drummer Pete Hines.

The inaugural CRO MAGS line-up featured Flanagan, Holland (who had also had a previous stint in KRAUT), vocalist John 'Bloodclot' Joseph, guitarist Parris Mitchell Mayhew and drummer Mackie Jason.

Jason opted out and by 1988 was found in a variety of bands including BAD BRAINS, ICEMAN, URBAN BLIGHT and BLITZSPEER.

John Joseph departed in mid 1989 and Flanagan took over on lead vocals.

1990 saw turbulent times for the band as drummer Potio Hoinz departed in favour of the returning Mackie. Before long however Mackie was out turning up in BAD BRAINS once more. Further tribulation followed when long standing guitarist Doug Holland was replaced with Rob Buckley.

1992 album was crafted by a line-up of Flanagan, Holland, Joseph and new blood Gabby and Dave. However, the stability was not to last and by the 'Near Death Experience' album CRO MAGS had effectively become a duo of Flanagan and Joseph. Worse was to come though and Flanagan, keeper of the flame for so long, quit just prior to the album release.

1994's live album release provided fans with an overview of the band's recent history with a two disc set comprising a 1991 show from the Hollywood Palladium and a 1994 gig from Studio One in New Jersey.

Flanagan created WHITE DEVIL and was to produce and perform on the debut 1997 album from STIGMATA 'Hymns For An Unknown God'.

Joseph founded a fresh act BOTH WORLDS with ex-LEEWAY members for a 1998 album 'Memory Rendered Visible' Mayhew reunited with Flanagan the following year to create SAMSARA with ex-SUICIDAL TENDENCIES guitarist Rocky George.

CRO MAGS reformed in 2000 for European festival dates.

By early 2002 Flanagan had re-emerged touting a fresh act HARLEY'S WAR in union with ex-SUICIDAL TENDENCIES guitarist Rocky George and former WARZONE guitarist Jay Vento.

AGE OF QUARREL, GWR GWLP 9 (1987)
We Gotta Know / World Peace / Show You No Mercy / Malfunction / Street Justice / Survival Of The Streets / Seekers Of The Truth / It's The Limit / Hard Times / By Myself / Don't Tread On Me / Face The Facts / Do Unto Others / Life on My Own / Signs Of The times
BEST WISHES, Profile FILCD 274 (1989)
Death Camps / Days Of Confusion / The Only One / Down, But Not Out / Crush The Demoniac / Fugitive/ Then And Now / Age Of Quarrel
ALPHA-OMEGA, Century Media CM9730CD (1992)
See The Signs / Eyes Of Tomorrow / The Other Side Of Madness (Revenge) / Apocalypse Now / The Paths Of Perfection / Victims / Kuruksetra / Changes
NEAR DEATH EXPERIENCE, Century Media CM 77050-2 (1993)
Say Good-Bye To The Mother Earth / Kali-Yuga / War On The Streets / Death In The Womb / Time I Am/ Reflections / Near Death Experience / The Other Side Of Madness (Rat Soup version '93)
HARD TIMES IN AN AGE OF QUARREL - LIVE, Century Media CM 77072-2 (1994)
Intro / We Gotta Know / World Peace / Show No Mercy / Apocalypse Now / See The Signs / Malfunction / Survival Of The Streets / Days Of Confusion / Street Justice / The Only One / Crush The Demoniac / Changes / Down But Not Out / Seekers Of The Truth / It's The Limit / Life Of My Own / Signs Of The Times / Age Of Quarrel / Hard Times / Death Camps / Intro / See The Signs / World Peace / Show No Mercy / Say Good-Bye To Mother Earth / Malfunction / Path To Perfection / Other Side Of Madness / It's The Limit / Life Of My Own / Age Of Quarrel / Signs Of The Times / Seekers Of The Truth / Don't Tread On Me / Death Camps / We Gotta Know / Apocalypse Now / Crush The Demoniac / Down But Not Out / Hard Times

CRONOS (UK)

Line-Up: Cronos (vocals / bass), Mike Hickey (guitar), James Clare (guitar), Chris Patterson (drums)

After nine years fronting one of the archetypal Thrash Metal outfits VENOM mainman Conrad Lant (a.k.a. Cronos) left the group in 1988 to form CRONOS, the result of the disappointing sales of 1987's 'Calm Before The Storm' album.

Conrad took both VENOM guitarists Mike H. (real name Mike Hickey) and Jimi C. along with him and soon added drummer Chris P. (at this point the band's musicians were known only by the initial letters of their surnames).

Scheduled tours of America and Japan were postponed in late 1989 when Cronos sustained a broken hand in a car accident. The band later toured the east coast of America, but after the release of the 'Dancing In The Fire' debut album live activity became limited.

CRONOS were due to tour Britain on a double bill with WARFARE on the so-dubbed 'Dancing With The Firehammers' tour, but this was cancelled due to lack of interest! The band did, however, support MASSACRE at London's Marquee in 1992, by which time a second album, 'Rock n' Roll Disease' had appeared the previous year.

Lant guested on the 1994 album 'When War Begins... Truth Disappears' from German act WARPATH. Hickey emerged as temporary member of CATHEDRAL and then as live guitarist for CARCASS during 1994 touring to promote their 'Heartwork' album.

A third album was recorded during 1994, but Cronos decided - somewhat inevitably - to participate in the reformation of the original VENOM line-up in 1995 that headlined the 'Waldrock' festival.

A new CRONOS album was released during 1995 to record the 'Venom' album with a brand new membership that contained Cronos, Hickey and ex-CATHEDRAL drummer Mark Wharton. The album oddly featured re-workings of classic VENOM songs.

As VENOM geared up for their re-formation album 'Cast In Stone' and subsequent touring CRONOS was inevitably put on the back burner despite sessions for a planned fourth album titled 'Triumphirate' already being in the can.

DANCING IN THE FIRE, Neat ODIO48 (1990)
Fantasia / Terrorise / Dancing In The Fire / Speedball / I'll Be Back / Vampire / Chinese

Whispers / Old Enough To Bleed / Painkiller / My Girl / Hell To The Unknown
ROCK N' ROLL DISEASE, Neat D1051 (1991)
Messages Of War / Rock n' Roll Disease / Lost And Found / Midnight Eye / Sexploitation / Aphrodisiac / Sweet Savage Sex / Dirty Tricks Department / Bared To The Bone
VENOM, Neat Metal NM003 (1995)
In League With Satan / Superpower / Vempyr / Fire / 1000 Days In Sodom / Know Evil / Messages Of War / 7 Gates Of Hell / Painkiller / Don't Burn The Witch (In Nomine Satanas) / Ye Of Little Faith / Satanachist / At War With Satan / Babylon

CROSSFIRE (BELGIUM)

Line-Up: Peter De Wint (vocals), Marc Van Caelenberge (guitar), Rudy Van De Sjipe (guitar), Patrick Van Londerzele (bass), Chris De Brauwer (drums)

One of the first signings to the Mausoleum label, CROSSFIRE released two albums that were much lauded in the underground Metal press.
The band started out in 1980 as a Punk outfit entitled THE ONION DOLLS, with De Wint handling drums as well as lead vocals.
The band contributed two tracks to the Dutch 'Aardschock' magazine compilation album 'Metal Clogs' on the Rave-On label, although original CROSSFIRE guitarist Ner Neerinckx left the band and was subsequently jailed for the murder of a policeman (possibly documented in the lyrics of 'Killing A Cop' on CROSSFIRE's first album 'See You In Hell'?!?)
Enjoying strong album sales throughout Europe the group supported the likes of ACCEPT and IRON MAIDEN in their time and also played their first English dates in 1985, playing two dates in London; the first at the Wellington in Shepherd's Bush promoted by Shades Records.
Following the demise of the act De Wint and De Brauwer formed Melodic Rockers MYSTERY in 1989.

Albums:
SEE YOU IN HELL, Mausoleum SKULL 8314 (1983)
Demon Of Evil / Killing A Cop / Magnificent Night / Danger On Earth / Fly High / Lover's Game / Starchild / See You In Hell
SECOND ATTACK, Mausoleum SKULL (1985)
Second Attack / Feeling Down / Highway Driver / Atomic War / Master Of Evil / Scream And Shout / Running For Love

SHARPSHOOTER, Mausoleum SKULL (1986)
Break Out / Killer Queen / Metal Knifes / Motorcycles (Live) / Crossfire (Live) / Sound Of War
LIVE ATTACK, Bellaphon (1987)
Second Attack / Starchild / Killer Queen / Master Of Evil / Scream And Shout / Sound Of War / Fly High / Highway Driver / Feeling Down

THE CROWN (SWEDEN)

Line-Up: Johan Lindstrandt (vocals), Marcus Sunesson (guitar), Marko Trevonen (guitar), Magnus Osfelt (bass), Janne Saarenpaa (drums)

Previously known as CROWN OF THORNS. Although often confused with Jean Beuvoir's American Melodic Rock act, Sweden's CROWN OF THORNS, founded in 1990 by ex-IMPIOUS vocalist Johan Lindstrandt and very much in the Grindcore mould, were a much heavier proposition altogether. CROWN OF THORNS first hit the tape trading scene with an impressive demo, 1993's 'Forever Heaven Gone'. Shortly after its release the band got to play the Swedish Hultsfred festival alongside ENTOMBED and IGGY POP but lost guitarist Robert Österberg to Punk act ÖLHÄVERS. His replacement was Marcus Sunesson who cut his teeth with the 1994 demo 'Forget The Light'. This tape scored them a deal with Black Sun Records for the debut album 'The Burning'. CROWN OF THORNS also made their mark on the SLAYER tribute album 'Slaytanic Slaughter' contributing their take on 'Mandatory Suicide'. The band's sophomore outing 'Eternal Death' continued the trend and yet again the Swedes were adding to another tribute album, this time nailing a cover of 'Arise' for the SEPULTURA homage 'Sepultural Feast'.
Continued threat of litigation from the American CROWN OF THORNS resulted in the band adopting the title THE CROWN in 1997. Undaunted the band toured Europe in early 1998 on a billing with SACRILEGE resulting directly in a deal with American label Metal Blade for third album 'Hell Is Here'.
To promote the record THE CROWN embarked on further European dates on a Black Metal festival package bill of IMPALED NAZARENE, EMPEROR, MORBID ANGEL and PECCATUM. A further cover version ensued, this time a crack at BATHORY's 'Burnin' Leather' for the 'Power From The North' compilation.
THE CROWN toured Europe in December 2000 as part of an almighty Death Metal package that included ENSLAVED, MORBID ANGEL, BEHEMOTH, HYPNOS and DYING

THE CROWN Photo : Kenneth Johannsson

FETUS.
THE CROWN guitarist Marcus Sunesson would join THE HAUNTED for American touring in 2001. Drummer Janne Saarenpää would deputise for GOD DETHRONED for their 'No Mercy' festival appearances. A further round of American dates, commencing in Tampa, Florida on the 24th April 2002, saw support from DARKEST HOUR and ALL THAT REMAINS.

Albums:
THE BURNING, Black Sun (1995)
Of Good And Evil / Soulicide Demon-Might / Godless / The Lord Of The Rings / I Crawl / Forever Heaven Gone / Earthborn / Neverending Dreams / Night Of The Swords / Candles / Forget The Light
ETERNAL DEATH, Black Sun (1997)
Angels Die / Beautiful Evil Soul / In Bitterness And Sorrow / The Black Heart / World Within / The Serpent Garden / Kill (The Priest) / Misery Speaks / Hunger / Death Of God
HELL IS HERE, Metal Blade (1998)
The Poison / At The End / 1999- Revolution 666 / Dying Of The Heart / Electric Night / Black Lightning / The Devil And The Darkness / Give You Hell / Body And Soul / Mycterion / Death By My Side
DEATHRACE KING, Metal Blade (2000)
Deathexplosion / Executioner (Slayer Of The Light) / Back From The Grave / Devil Gate

Ride / Vengeance / Angel Rebel / I Won't Follow / Blitzkrieg Witchcraft / Dead Man's Song / Total Satan / Killing Star (Superbia Luxuria XXX)
CROWNED IN TERROR, Metal Blade 3984-14394-2 (2002)
Introduction / House Of Hades / Crowned In Terror / Under The Whip / Drugged Unholy / World Below / The Speed Of Darkness / Out For Blood / (I Am Hell) / Death Is The Hunter / Satanist / Death Metal Holocaust

CRUCIFEROUS (UK)

Old style retro Thrash from Dagenham, Kent outfit.

Singles/EPs:
Empyrean, Cruciferous (1997)

THE CRUCIFIED (Fresno, CA, USA)
Line-Up: Mark Saloman (vocals), Greg Minier (guitar), Jeff Bellew (bass), Jim Chaffin (drums)

Christian Crossover Thrashers THE CRUCIFIED started life as a straightforward Punk act but evolved into Thrash / Hardcore territory. The group made their entrance with the 1987 demo 'Take Up Your Cross', the band at this point comprising vocalist Marc Cooksey, guitarist Greg Minier, bassist Trevor Palmer and drummer Jim Chaffin. The 'Nailed' tape followed which saw THE CRUCIFIED with two new faces - vocalist Mark Saloman and bassist Mark Johnson. Finally a live tape surfaced dubbed 'Live At The New Order', by this juncture Johnson had made way for Jeff Bellew.

Signing to the Narrowpath label THE CRUCIFIED issued the eponymous inaugural album in 1988. The second album, 1991's 'The Pillars Of Humanity', is held in high regard as a classic of the genre.

Upon the band's demise the Ocean label issued the 1994 album 'Nailed', a collection of archive recordings from THE CRUCIFIED's Punk formative years. Although having folded in 1993 it appears that the group did reform for sporadic gigs in 1995.

Vocalist Mark Saloman would later found Alternative Rock act STAVESACRE. Following a spell with the industrially inclined CHATTERBOX bassist Jeff Belew also teamed up with STAVESACRE. The bassist would also share co-production credits for P.O.D.'s 'Snuff The Punk' record and contribute guest guitar to MORTAL's 'Fathom' opus. Saloman also guested on this latter release.

Drummer Jim Chaffin appeared with FASEDOWN and united with prolific Chicago Thrash act THE BLAMED.

Guitarist Greg Minier has also issued solo product. The 1990 MINIER album, released by the R.E.X. label, maintains a Thrash course whilst APPLEHEAD sees a shift into a Grunge direction.

Albums:
THE CRUCIFIED, Narrowpath (1988)
The Pit / Diehard / Your Image / Getting A Grip On Things / Hellcorn / Rise / One Demon To Another / Unity / A Guy In A Suite And The Pope / Back To The Cross / Confidence / The Insult Circus / Thread / Crucial Moment
THE PILLARS OF HUMANITY, Ocean 7018133505 (1991)
Intro / Hateworld / It's All About Fear / The Wrong One / Mindbender / Path To Sorrow / Fellowship Of Thieves / Focus / The Strength / Blackstone / So Called Living 1991 / The Pillars Of Humanity
NAILED, Ocean (1994)
I'm Not A Christian Punk / Death To Death / Your Image / God In A Cage / Crucified With Christ / Give It Up / Disposal /

CRUMBSUCKERS (USA)
Line-Up: Chris Notaro (vocals), Robbie Koebler (guitar), Chuck Lenihan (guitar), Gary Meskill (bass), Danny Richardson (drums)

Long Island's CRUMBSUCKERS formed as a quartet in 1983 playing New York's A7 club. Notaro was ex-KRACKDOWN.

Guitarist Robbie Koebler departed after recording 'Beast On My Back' and was replaced by CARNIVORE's Mark Piovanelli. The group also replaced original vocalist Chris Notaro with Joe Haggerty from ZERO HOUR but eventually settled on the unknown Craig Allen.

In late 1989 CRUMBSUCKERS became HEAVY RAIN in an attempt to pursue a more Hard Rock style.

Lenihan went on to forge shock S&M Metal merchants the GENITORTURERS and vampire rockers VASARIA. Haggerty joined Arizona's KNUCKLEHEAD.

The band's rhythm section of Meskill and Richardson joined heavyweights PRO-PAIN as other members founded HEAVY RAIN. Richardson later joined LIFE OF AGONY for their 1997 album 'Soul Searching Sun'.

Albums:
LIFE OF DREAMS, Rough Justice JUST4 (1986)
Just Sit There / Trapped / Interlude / Super Tuesday / Shits Creek / Return To The Womb / Longest War / Shot Down / Prelude / Life Of Dreams / Brainwashed / Face Of Death / Hubrub / Bullshit Society / Live To Work / Mr. Hyde
BEAST ON MY BACK (B.O.M.B.), Rough Justice JUST 9 (1988)
Breakout / Jimmie's Dream / Charge / Initial Shock / I Am He / Connection / Rejuvenate / Remembering Tomorrow / Beast On My Back

CRUSTACEAN (HOLLAND)
Line-Up: TMP (vocals / bass), MKK (guitar), RCS (guitar), JVI (drums)

A Dutch band heavily enthused by a love of eighties U.S. Thrash. CRUSTACEAN members pedigree includes both guitarists MKK and RCS having enjoyed terms of employment with Paul Speckmann's MASTER. RCS was also with ACROSTICHON and DISEMBOWEL.

MKK (Michael) was also a member of ACROSTICHON and fellow renaissance Thrashers OUTBURST. Vocalist / bassist TMP is an ex-MASTICATOR member whilst drummer JVI was with SPINA BIFIDA.

The group came together in 1989 as CRYSTAL LAKE, issuing a string of demos upfront of February 1994's 'Rip Off' session. At this juncture the band evolved into CRUSTACEAN.

Two tracks were included on the 'No Sleep 'Til

Burg' compilation album and the 1995 'Headcleaner' EP solidified their standing.

The Teutonic Existence label took CRUSTACEAN on for the debut album 'Burden Of Our Suffering'. A mini-album 'Satanized' ensued before the 2001 effort 'Insaniac'.

CRUSTACEAN members also operate on the club circuit as a SLAYER covers band. RCS also operates with BLACK MELODY.

Singles/EPs:
Tube Life / Of The Soil / Deranged / Levels / Go Away, (1995) ('Headcleaner' EP)

Albums:
BURDEN OF OUR SUFFERING, Teutonic Existence (2000)
Bitter State / Burden Of Our Suffering / Black Domain / Dark Crusade / Deathly Grin / Injected with Blood / Tomblike Silence / Devilish Enchantments / Evil Magick / Drawn From The Grave / Diabolical Contraptions - Deathmatch
SATANIZED, (2000)
Bloodshot / Satanizer / Soulsucker / Devilution / Lost (Head)
INSANIAC, Teutonic Existence (2001)
Arena (QIIIa) / Random Terror (Chemical Juggernaut) / Psycho 2001 / Satanizer / Deathtrap (Infiltration Part II) / Soulsucker / Bloodshot / Lost (Head) / Penance (Ad Infinitum) / Redeemer (Sanctum Sanctorum) / Foul Usurper / State Necropolis (The Very End Of You)

CRYPT (CANADA)

Line-Up: Rob Mainati (vocals), Marc Andrews (guitar), Dave Ledder (bass), Dennis Maio (drums)

CRYPT bassist Dave Ledden teamed up with noted Metal band EXCITER in 1990.

Albums:
STICK TO YOUR GUNS, Deadmeat Productions (1987)

CRYPTIC REBORN (FRANCE)

Line-Up: Oliver (vocals), Thibaud (guitar), Vincent (guitar), Florian (bass), Loki (drums)

Montpellier Thrashers founded in November of 1988.

Singles/EPs:
Timothy / Satan Stole My Teddy Bear / Overcome / Deadline / Redemption, (2001)

CRYPTIC SLAUGHTER
(Santa Monica, CA, USA)

Line-Up: Bill Crooks (vocals), Les Evans (guitar), Rob Nicholson (bass), Scott Peterson (drums)

Thrash Metal band CRYPTIC SLAUGHTER made their entrance with the 1985 'Life In Grave' demo tape. CRYPTIC SLAUGHTER actually broke up completely shortly after recording the 'Stream Of Consciousness' album as vocalist Bill Crooks and drummer Scott Peterson decided to give up the music scene altogether.

Guitarist Les Evans and bassist Rob Nicholson remained a unit and forged a new act with new recruits guitarist Eli Nelson and drummer Eddie. The latter was drafted by Evans' mother after she saw a kid walking down the road carrying a pair of drumsticks!

In May of 1989 Evans relocated to Portland, Oregon to have another stab at starting CRYPTIC SLAUGHTER anew. This revised version of the band, with WEHRMACHT / SWEATY NIPPLES drummer Brian Lehfeldt onboard, issued the 'Speak Your Piece' album. Evans would also guest on the SWEATY NIPPLES 'What's Your Funktion?' EP.

With completion of Autumn 1990 touring CRYPTIC SLAUGHTER folded. Lehfeldt would join EVERCLEAR as touring drummer in the '90s.

Albums:
CONVICTED, Roadrunner RR 9680 (1986)
M.A.D. / Little World / Sudden Death / Lowlife / Rage To Kill / Rest In Pain / Nuclear Future / State Control / Hypocrite / War To The Knife / Nation Of Hate / Black And White / Reich Of Torture / Convicted
MONEY TALKS, Roadrunner RR 9607 (1987)
Money Talks / Set Your Own Pace / Could Be Worse / Wake Up / Freedom Of Expression? / Menace To Mankind / Too Much, Too Little / Human Contrast / Tables Are Turned / Positively / All Wrong / American Heroes
STREAM OF CONSCIOUSNESS, Roadrunner RR9521 (1988)
Circus Of Fools / Aggravated / Last Laugh / Overcome / Deteriorate / See Through You / Just Went Black / Drift / Altered Visions / Addiction / One Last Thought
SPEAK YOUR PIECE, Metal Blade CDZORRO 6 (1990)
Born Too Soon / Still Born, Again / Insanity By Numbers / Co-Exist / Deathstyles Of The Poor And Lonely / One Thing Or Another / Divided Minds / Speak Your Piece / Killing Time

CULPRIT (Seattle, WA, USA)
Line-Up: Jeff L'Heureux (vocals),

John DeVol (guitar), Kjartan Kristoffersen (guitar), Scott Earl (bass), Bud Burrill (drums)

An exceedingly British influenced Seattle Metal band showing huge chunks of British influences in their raw, aggressive style.

During early 1979 North Seattle natives guitarist John DeVol, bassist Scott Earl and drummer Bud Burrill created ORPHEUS playing parties and local 'Battle of the bands' contests. Meantime AMETHYST, from the east of the city and including guitarist Kjartan Kristoffersen and vocalist Jeff L'Hereaux in their ranks were playing their favourite cover versions.

The two bands came into contact with AMETHYST supporting ORPHEUS at Mr. Bills club resulting in the headliner making a play for L'Heureaux's services. The singer was willing to join on the condition his colleague Kristofferson was part of the deal and CULPRIT was borne.

The band signed to Shrapnel Records after gigs in California with WILD DOGS and CINEMA before appearing on one of the label's series of 'U.S. Metal' compilations with the slightly Progressively tinged 'Players' and followed it up with the Mike Varney produced 'Guilty As Charged' album.

The band frequently gigged in their native Seattle, in particular the Metal stronghold of Bellevue, but would split when Krisoffersen and Earl joined local legends TKO in 1984. However, although the duo appeared on the cover of the 'In Your Face', the album was recorded long before the band were signed by Combat Records in the States (the album was released by Music For Nations in Europe) and the ex-CULPRIT pair had come on board.

Jeff L'Heureux would later turn up fronting another Seattle band, MISTRUST. The group appeared on the 'Pacific Metal Project' compilation before recording the 'Spin The World' album. John DeVol meantime re-emerged in 1987 with DeVOL, a group boasting a line-up of vocalist Terry Tandeski, bassist Dennis Quintella and drummer Jeff McCormack.

Following the TKO stint, Kristoffersen and Earl formed the Glam outfit BANG GANG, having relocated to Los Angeles in the late '80s. Earl would form SHAKE THE FAITH in 1992 although he was ousted by the recording of their solitary album.

Albums:
GUILTY AS CHARGED, Shrapnel 1008 (1983)
Guilty As Charged / Ice In The Back / Steel To Blood / I Am / Ambush / Tears Of Repentance / Same To You / Fight Back / Players

CURARE (GERMANY)
Line-Up: Falk (vocals / bass), Robby (guitar), Martin (guitar), Mario (drums)

Thrash Metal act CURARE issued a demo between their two albums.

Albums:
JUST A SCRATCH, Rail (1991)
Generations Talk / Place And Time / Distrust A Change / Fabula De Antigua Hora
MOMENTS BEFORE DETONATION, Curare (1995)
Raw Conversation / Inside My Head / Push! / Accident Dance / What's Up Now / The Death Waltz / Moments Before Detonation / Violence And Force / Bumble Bee / Peace Eater

CUTLASS
(Glendale Heights, IL, USA)
Line-Up: Jeff Hundriser (vocals), Victor Vasquez (guitar), Nick Cox (guitar)

Formed in 1989, CUTLASS finally issued their debut album during 1994 after a brace of EP releases and having won a new talent contest in American Rock mag Circus

Albums:
NO EXPLANATION NECESSARY, Eatin' ER 903 (1994)

CYANIDE (NJ, USA)

A New Jersey Thrash band.

Albums:
WORLD PEACE SIX FEET UNDER, Mutha MUTHA #034 (1990)

CYBERGRIND (USA)

CYBERGRIND, operating in Death- Thrash territory, was founded by erstwhile MORTIFICATION guitarist Mick Carlisle.

Albums:
TRANSCEND, Rowe Productions (1999)
Macrocosmic Portent / Portal (Intro) / Descend / Transcend / Tragedy Strikes / Brainwashed / Nauseating Sickness / Phantasmic Landscapes / Destiny / Cybergrind / E"no! / Rubber Chicken Reflection / Fiend Transformation / The Complaints of the Dead / Defensive Manouvers Pt. 1 (outro) / Lost Sea of Emoceans

JEFF L'HEUREUX of CULPRIT Photo : Nico Wobben

CYCLONE (BELGIUM)

Line-Up: Guido Gevels (vocals), Johnny Kerbush (guitar), Pascal Van Lint (guitar), Stefan Daamen (bass), Nicolas Lairio (drums)

Vilvoorde based Metallers released the 1985 demo 'In The Grip Of Evil' following a name change from CENTURION.

CYCLONE's debut gigs came as a support to ACID in 1984. Gigs with Germany's DESTRUCTION led to the inclusion of two tracks on the Roadrunner compilation 'Metal Race'.

CYCLONE supported ANTHRAX, ACID and AGENT STEEL and assorted members later formed CHANNEL ZERO.

Albums:

BRUTAL DESTRUCTION, Roadrunner RR 9687 (1986)
Prelude To The End / Long To Hell / Fall Under His Command / The Call Of Steel / Fighting The Fatal / In The Grip Of Evil / Take Thy Breath / Incest Love
INFERIOR TO NONE, Justice JR-CD02-90 (1990)
Convulsions (Intro) / Neurotic / So Be It / Paralysed / Throw The First Stone / The Other Side / I Am The Plague / Crown Of Thorns (Instrumental) / Slavery

CYCLONE TEMPLE (USA)

Line-Up: Brian Troch (vocals), Greg Fulton (guitar), Scott Schafer (bass), John Slattery (drums)

CYCLONE TEMPLE were previously known in their more studs n' leather period as ZNOWHITE. The band put in an appearance at the 1991 Milwaukee Metalfest but lost their record deal with Relativity.

In 1992 vocalist Brian Trach was replaced by Marco Salinas for the 'Building Errors In The Machine' mini-album. Yet another switch in singers came with third outing 'My Friend Lonely' in 1994. This record, fronted by Sonny DeLuca, comprised re-recorded tracks from 'Building Errors In The Machine' alongside new material.

Post CYCLONE TEMPLE both guitarist Greg Fulton and bass player Scott Schafer would move on to REBELS WITHOUT APPLAUSE in league with guitarist Mark Alarno and drummer Tony Heath issuing the 1997 EP 'Rip Hop Soulcore Crush'.

Albums:

I HATE THEREFORE I AM, Relativity (1991)
Why / Sister (Until We Meet Again) / Words Are Just Words / Public Enemy / In God We Trust / I Hate Therefore I Am / March For Me, Die For Me / Born To Lose / Silence So Loud
BUILDING ERRORS IN THE MACHINE, Polydisc (1993)
Hate Makes Hate / Me, Myself & I / Down The Drain / Killing Floor / Drug Of The Masses / The Law Of Relativity
MY FRIEND LONELY, Monsterdisc (1994)
Hate Makes Hate / Down The Drain / My Friend Lonely / Me, Myself & I / Drug Of The Masses / Comfortably Superficial / Killing Floor / Time Heals All / The Law Of Relativity

CYNIC (FL, USA)

Line-Up: Paul Masvidal (vocals / guitar), Jason Gobel (guitar), Tony Choy (bass), Sean Reinert (drums)

CYNIC were more noted for their individual members contributions to other acts.

Bassist Tony Choy contributed bass parts to the ATHEIST album 'Unquestionable Presence' before joining Dutch thrashers PESTILENCE for their 'Testimony Of The Ancients' album and following world tour. Guitarist Paul Masvidal and drummer Sean Reinert played on DEATH's 1992 album 'Human' then opted to join DEATH's 1992 American and European tour on a temporary basis.

Masvidal also contributed heavily to MASTER's 'And On The Seventh Day God Created Master' album. Guitarist Jason Gobel guests on MONSTROSITY's 'Imperial Doom' album and also filled in for live shows.

CYNIC recorded a 1992 three track demo for Roadrunner Records. Following the album release Masvidal reunited with DEATH on a permanent basis.

Reinert joined GORDION KNOT but by 2000 was involved with AGHORA. Malone also contributes to the debut AGHORA album.

Albums:

FOCUS, Roadrunner RR 91692 (1993)
Veil Of Maya / Celestial Voyage / The Eagle Nature / Sentiment / I'm But A Wave To… / Uroboric Forms / Textures / How Could I

DAM (UK)
Line-Up: Jason McLoughlin (vocals), John Bury (guitar), Elly (guitar), Dave Pugh (bass), Phil Bury (drums)

Morecambe Thrashers DAM, including ex-METAL HEART guitarist John Bury amongst their number, debuted with a three track demo, 'Human Wreckage', in 1988 and followed it with a second tape entitled 'Destruction And Mayhem'.

Whereas the original line-up featured bassist Liam Godden the four-string slot was subsequently filled by Andy Elliot until Dave Pugh got the nod.

DAM supported both TORANAGA and ACID REIGN in 1989 before a plethora of 1990 gigs opening for a European double billing of DARK ANGEL and NUCLEAR ASSAULT. It was during this tour that the band was captured on the '3 Way Thrash' video, by which time the 'Human Wreckage' debut album had been released through Noise Records.

Guitarist Elly quit in 1991 to form BURNT OAK, releasing the 'English Rock n' Roll' demo in 1993, whereas Dave Pugh would join SKYCLAD in 1992.

Albums:
HUMAN WRECKAGE, Noise NUK149 (1990)
MAD / Death Warmed Up / Killing Time / Left To Rot / Prophets Of Doom / Terror Squad / Total Destruction / Infernal Torment / Vendetta / Human Wreckage / Aliens / F.O.D.
INSIDE OUT, Noise N0162 (1991)
Man Of Violence / House Of Cards / Appointment With Fear / Winter's Tear / Innocent One / My Twisted Mind / No Escape / Beneath Closed Eyes / Inside Outro

DAMIEN (USA)
Line-Up: Randy Mikelson (vocals), Chuck Stohl (guitar), Fritz Adamshick (guitar), Kevin Kekes (bass), Johnny Cappelletty (drums)

DAMIEN's first brace of albums featured a stable line-up comprising vocalist Randy 'Wolf' Mickelson, lead guitarist Chuck Stohl, rhythm guitarist Fritz Adamshick, bass player Kevin 'Killer' Kekes and drummer Johnny 'Evil' Cappelletty.

DAMIEN reformed for a 1995 comeback album 'Angel Juice'. Joining Stohl and Kekes would be new members vocalist Scott Miller and drummer Rob Brug.

DAMIEN would still be active as late as 1996 but would eventually fold. Stohl created STOHL:N in league with vocalist Dennis Taylor, bassist John Conroy and drummer Dave Giles.

Cappelletty and Mikelson would retain their partnership in FETISH DOLL, a band rounded out by guitarists Harald Champnoise and Parker Harroun with bassist Matt Champnoise.

Both Keke and Brug would be found in BONES GARAGE. The ex-DAMIEN bassist would also gain credits with Cincinnati guitar guru CHASTAIN and his project offshoot SOUTHERN GENTLEMEN.

Meantime Scott Miller would later figure in BROTHERS GRIM.

Albums:
EVERY DOG HAS ITS DAY, Select (1987)
Wolf Dream / Possession / Serpents Rising / Give Me A Sign / Every Dog Has Its Day / World Affair / Season Of The Arrow / I Play For You / Glass City / Race To the End
STOP THIS WAR, ZYX (1989)
Stop This War / Breakout / Rising Down / Matilda / 30 St. Clair / Stormwind / Warlord / Always In Lust / The Priests Are Coming / Corpse Grinder
ANGEL JUICE, Mourning Star (1995)
Shadows In Darkness / Silent Rage / The Politics of Pain / The Rite / Broken Neck / Death March / Perpetual Sleep / The Awakening / Vlad / Retribution / Turn The Key / The Legend of Trotis

DAMIEN THORNE
(Chicago, IL, USA)
Line-Up: Justin Fate (vocals), Michael Monroe (guitar), Ken Starr (guitar), Sanders Pate (bass), B. Hurak (drums)

In 1987 DAMIEN THORNE left their American label Cobra Records recording a new four track demo featuring the tracks 'Vlad', 'Ra (The Curse Of Tutankhamen)', 'Caretaker' and 'Phantoms Of Fire'.

Albums:
THE SIGN OF THE JACKAL, Roadrunner RR9691 (1986)
The Sign Of The Jackal / Fear Of The Dark / The Ritual / Grim Reaper / Hell's Reign / Escape Or Die / Siren's Call / Damien's Possession (March Of The Undead)

DAMMAJ (San Jose, CA)
Line-Up: Greg Hill (vocals), Mick Gilbert (guitar), Rich Gilbert (guitar), Steve Gilbert (bass), Bob Newkirk (drums)

Albums:
MUTINY, Roadrunner RR9636 (1986)

Smuggler / Devil's And Angels / March Of
The Gladiators / Without You / Mutiny /
Leather Master / Clashes Of Steel / To The
Bitter End

DARK AGE (USA)
Line-Up: Robert Stevens (vocals), Johnny
Ljissacs (guitar), Alan Foley (guitar), Jimmy
Thaiger (bass),
Jeff Exx (drums)

Albums:
DARK AGE, Roadrunner (1984)
Metal Axe / Tales Of Medusa / Dark Age
(Rock Revelation) / The Execution:
Messenger Of Ascheron / Warrior / Viper

DARKANE (SWEDEN)
Line-Up: Andreas Sydow (vocals), Christofer
Malmstrom (guitar), Klas Ideberg (guitar),
Jörgen Löfberg (bass), Peter Wildoer (drums)

DARKANE founders guitarist Christofer
Malmstrom and drummer Peter Wildoer were
previously members of noted technical Metal
band AGREGATOR. The duo forged
DARKANE with the enlistment of second
guitarist Klas Ideberg, bassist Jörgen Löfberg
and singer Lawrence Macrory and bowed in
with the impressive 'Rusted Angel' record.
Ex-vocalist Lawrence Macrory would guest
session on the 1999 ANDROMEDA debut
album 'Extension Of The Wish'. He would
later found FORCEFEED, later changing this
band name to SEETHINGS.
DARKANE reconvened for a sophomore
Daniel Bergstrand produced opus entitled
'Insanity'. This outing also marked the debut

of new vocalist Andreas Sydow. Promoting
'Insanity' the band would put in their inaugural
United States show at the 'Milwaukee
Metalfest' in 2001. Japanese versions of the
album, released on the Toys Factory label,
would see a bonus track with a live rendition
of 'Convicted'.
Jörgen Löfberg and guitarist Klas Ideberg,
along with SOILWORK's drummer Henry
Ranta and vocalist Henrik Sjöwall and
guitarist Mattias Svensson would forge a
project band entitled THE DEFACED.

Albums:
RUSTED ANGEL, (1998)
::Iii:O:Iii::/ Convicted / Bound / Rape Of
Mankind / Rusted Angel / A Wisdoms Breed
/ Chase For Existence / The Arcane
Darkness / July 1999 / Frenetic Visions
INSANITY, Nuclear Blast NB 602 (2001)
Calamitas / Third / Emanation Of Fear /
Impure Perfection / Hostile Phantasm /
Psychic Pain / 000111 / The Perverted Beast
/ Distress / Inauspicious Coming / Pile Of
Hate / Inverted Spheres

DARK ANGEL
(Long Beach, CA, USA)
Line-Up: Ron Rinehart (vocals),
Eric Meyer (guitar), Jimmy Durkin (guitar),
Mike Gonzalez (bass),
Gene Hoglan (drums)

DARK ANGEL's inaugural effort of 1985 'We
Have Arrived' featured a line-up of vocalist
Jon Doty, guitarists Eric Meyer and Jimmy
Durkin together with bassist Robbie Yahn and
drummer Jack Schwartz. An early DARK

DARKANE Photo : Stefan Ideberg

ANGEL drummer, Bob Gourley, had graduated from a fleeting appearance in a fledgling SLAYER. Upon his departure from DARK ANGEL Gourling forged POWERLORD releasing a 1988 album 'The Awakening'.

DARK ANGEL benefited from a unique promotional release to back up the 'Darkness Descends' album. The track 'Merciless Death', released by Azra Records, came in a variety of bizarre shapes such as a skull, a wheel, a square, a black heart and even a Christmas tree!

The band itself had lost the services of Yahn and Schwartz and in their stead came a fresh rhythm section of bassist Mike Gonzalez and drummer Lee Rausch, the latter a former member of MEGADETH. However, Rausch's place was soon taken by WARGOD man Gene Hoglan.

New vocalist Ron Rinehar joined for 1988's 'Leave Scars' album. The album featured cover versions of LED ZEPPELIN's 'Immigrant Song' and FEAR's 'Action' and 'I Don't Care About You'. VIKING vocalist Ron 'Eriksen' Daniels would lend his vocal talents to 'Leave Scars' too, duetting with Rinehart on the song 'Promise Of Agony'.

During 1989 the group and Jim Durkin parted company, DARK ANGEL playing a few shows as a four-piece before drafting VIKING axeman Brett Eriksen on a stand-in basis.

DARK ANGEL undertook a tempestuous co-headline tour of America with DEATH in 1990. In late 1991 Brett Erikson was replaced by former SILENT SCREAM guitarist Chris McCarthy but DARK ANGEL folded shortly after

Rinehart became a Christian in 1992 although this did not stop his Metal endeavours as he founded OIL with former DECEIVER, DESIRE and CAPTAIN BLACK guitarist Blake Nelson. OIL issued the 'Refine' album for Kaluboné Records.

Hoglan joined DEATH in 1994 for their 'Individual Thought Patterns' album.

Durkin re-emerged in 2000 with his new act DREAMS OF DAMNATION and the 'Let The Violence Begin' album.

Singles/EPs:
Merciless Death / We Have Arrived, Azra MS 8602 (1986) (USA promotion)

Albums:
WE HAVE ARRIVED, Metalstorm MS 8501 (1985)
We Have Arrived / Merciless Death / Falling From The Sky / Welcome To The Slaughter House / No Tomorrow / Hell's On It's Knees / Vendetta

DARKNESS DESCENDS, Under One Flag FLAG 6 (1986)
Darkness Descends / The Burning Of Sodom / Hunger Of The Undead / Merciless Death / Death Is Certain (Life Is Not) / Black Prophecies / Perish In Flames
LEAVE SCARS, Under One Flag FLAG 30 (1988)
Leave Scars / Death Of Innocence / Promise Of Agony / Never To Rise Again / No One Answers / Worms / Immigrant Song / Cauterization / Older Than Time Itself / Action / I Don't Care About You.
LIVE SCARS, Under One Flag FLAG 42 (1990)
Leave Scars / The Burning Of Sodom / Never To Rise Again / The Promise Of Agony / We Have Arrived / Death Is Certain (Life Is Not) / The Death Of Innocence / I Don't Care About You
TIME DOES NOT HEAL, Under One Flag FLAG 54 (1991)
Time Does Not Heal / Pain's Invention, Madness / Act Of Contrition / The New Priesthood / Psychosexuality / An Ancient Inherited Shame / Trauma And Catharsis / Sensory Deprivation / A Subtle Induction
DECADE OF CHAOS (BEST OF), Under One Flag FLAG 70 (1992)
Darkness Descends / Never To Rise Again / Pain's Invention, Madness / Merciless Death / The Promise Of Agony / Death Is Certain / Leave Scars / Act Of Contrition / The Burning Of Sodom / We Have Arrived

DARKLIN REACH
(Chicago, IL, USA)
Line-Up: Alan Pangelinan (vocals / guitar), Ed Chapa (bass), Tony DiVozzo (drums)

High intensity Metal band DARKLIN REACH included former AMULANCE drummer Tony 'T-Bone' DiVozzo in the ranks. The solitary DARKLIN REACH album was produced by the esteemed SAVATAGE duo of Jon Oliva and Steve Wacholz.

DARKLIN REACH folded during September 2001 with DiVozzo going on to join BLACK CUNTRY ROCK.

Albums:
WHERE EVIL DWELLS, Corpse 005CD (1992)

DARKNESS (GERMANY)
Line-Up: Olli (vocals), Arnd (guitar), Pierre (guitar), Bruno (bass), Lacky (drums)

Straightforward Thrash band from Essen originating back to 1984 with their inaugural demo 'Devil Curse'. DARKNESS' second

113

demo, 'Titanic War' released in 1985 led to a 1987 live tape 'Attack The Darkness' which secured them a deal with Gama Records.
Second guitarist Andre was added to the ranks for the 'Death Squad' album.

Albums:
DEATH SQUAD, Gama (1987)
Invasion Sector 12 / Critical Threshold / Death Squad / Stasefeind / Tarsman Of Ghor / Faded Pictures / Iron Force / Burial At Sea / Phantasmagoria
DEFENDERS OF JUSTICE, Tales Of Trash (1988)
Bloodbath / Inverted Minds / Caligula / They Need A War / Locked / Defenders Of Justice / Predetermined Destiny
CONCLUSION AND REVIVAL, Hot Blood (1989)
Soldiers / The Omniscient / Under Control / Bass / Burial / Predetermined Destiny / Price Of Fame / All Left To Say / Beside My Grave
BROKEN HEART, (1991)

DAVIDIAN (GERMANY)
Line-Up: Chris Prendergast (vocals), Micha Weidler (guitar), Alex Schniepp (guitar), Tim Hinderer (bass),
Tobi Weidler (drums)

Traditional Thrash Metal act DAVIDIAN came together during 1997 with an original line-up of vocalist Benni Schniepp, guitarists Alex Schniepp and Micha Weidler, bassist Salli Indovina and drummer Tobi Weidler.
By 1998 Tim Hinderer had taken the bass position. The following year Benni Schniepp opted out, DAVIDIAN bringing in Chris Prendergast as replacement in time for their debut demo. A self-financed album 'In Pain' arrived during 2000.
In March of 2001 Weidler announced his exit. DAVIDIAN were brought back up to strength by November with the enlistment of erstwhile REQUIEM man Alex Scherf.

Albums:
IN PAIN, (2000)
Intro (Eternal Scream) / The Face You'll Never See Again / Crescent Nation / Burning Witches / Torture / Outro

DEADLY BLESSING (NJ, USA)
Line-Up: Larry Betson (vocals), Tony Sgro (guitar), Tom Bach (guitar), Mark Stavola (bass), Dan Pettalkina (drums)

New Jersey Thrashers DEADLY BLESSING replaced original vocalist Ski with 18 year old Larry Betson in late 1989 and released a four track demo in 1990 featuring the tracks 'As

Good As Dead', 'Psycho-Drama', 'Solitary Confinement' and 'Burial Dream'.

Singles/EPs:
Salem's Lot / Escape The Wrath / Cry Of Medusa, New Renaissance NRR89 (1987) ('Deadly Blessing' EP)

Albums:
ASCEND FROM THE CAULDRON, New Renaissance NRR37(1989)
Search And Destroy / Salem's Lot / Escape The Wrath / Cry Of Medusa / Deliver Us From Evil / Silent Madness / Mindbender / Deadly Blessing

DEAD ON (New York, NY, USA)
Line-Up: Mike Raptis (vocals), Michael Caronia (guitar), Tony Frazzitta (guitar), John Lindner (bass), Mike Caputo (drums)

DEAD ON toured Britain in November 1990 as support to ONSLAUGHT. Vocalist Mike Raptis lost his position after these dates to Carl Frazzitta.

Singles/EPs:
Different Breed, SBK CDP 560 203620-2 (1989) (Split EP with MEGADETH and DANGEROUS TOYS)
One 4 You / Everyday On Earth / Lost At Sea / Do What You Want, Mausoleum 367 0005-2 (1991)

Albums:
DEAD ON, SBK K2 93249 (1989)
Salem Girls / Beat A Dead Horse / The Widower / The Matador's Nightmare / Full Moon / Escape / Merry Ship / Different Breed / Dead On

DEAD ORCHESTRA (Wichita, USA)
Line-Up: Justin Crumbliss (vocals), Joel Hesser (guitar), Miles Pehde (guitar), Grant Smith (drums)

Albums:
GLOBAL LOBOTOMY, Steamhammer 008 76371 (1991)

DEAFAID (SWEDEN)
Line-Up: Ulf Blomberg (vocals / guitar), Marcus Angalsson (guitar), Dennis Nilsson (bass), David Wreland (drums) A Christian Thrash / Metalcore unit out of Husqvarna.
DEAFAID was founded in late 1997 debuting with an eponymous demo cassette in April of 1998. 'The Payment' EP followed in February of 1999.
Guitarist Marcus Angalsson left the band in 2000.

The Payment / R.I.P. / Why Destroy? /
Without Fear, (1999) ('The Payment' EP)

Albums:
INHALE, (2000)
Inhale / Miss Noself / This Shit / Kick n' Lick /
Scary Nothing / Bloodbound / Miss Noself
(Live) / Inhale (Live) / Inject (Remix)

DEAF DEALER (CANADA)
Line-Up: Michael Flynn (vocals), Ian Penn
(guitar), Marc Hayward (guitar), J.P. Forsyth
(bass), Dan McGregor (drums)

DEAF DEALER debuted with a track on the
'Metal Massacre IV' compilation album.
Vocalist Andy La Roche was replaced by
Michael Flynn before their solitary album
'Keeper Of The Flames'.

Albums:
KEEPER OF THE FLAMES, Neat NEAT
1035 (1986)
Don't Get It In My Way / Deaf Dealer / On
The Wings Of A Foxbat / The Fugitive / Dead
Zone / Sadist / Free And Easy / Getting
Ready To Go / Caution To Kill

DEARLY BEHEADED (UK)
Line-Up: Alex Creamer (vocals), Phil Stevens
(guitar), Steve Owens (guitar), Tim Preston
(bass), Rob Ryan (drums)

Manchester modern Power Thrash Metallers
DEARLY BEHEADED debuted with 'We The
Unwilling' demo in 1993.
Having performed a BBC 'Friday Rock Show'
session the group won MTV's best unsigned
act contest and signed to major label East
West to record debut EP. However, arguments
ensued regarding a proposed cover depicting
severed heads and the label's insistence that
DEARLY BEHEADED ditch their drummer.
The band were subsequently dropped, even
though they had recorded for East West, and
were picked up by Music For Nations
following a British support tour to EXTREME
NOISE TERROR in 1995.
The band's first album was produced by Colin
Richardson and engineered by ex-SABBAT
guitarist Andy Sneap.
For the second effort DEARLY BEHEADED
brought in former CRITICAL MASS guitarist
Darren Hough for a departing Phil Stevens.
Colin Richardson was chosen once more on
the production front as the band launched an
uncompromising album that even proudly
boasted of the absence of any guitar solos!
By 2000 Preston, Owens and Hough had
created SLEATH with vocalist Darren Hircock

and drummer Charly Moniz.

Singles/EPs:
In A Darkened Room / Break My Bones /
Never / The Season Of Lies, Music For
Nations CDKUT 168 (1995)

Albums:
TEMPTATION, Music For Nations CDMFN
302 (1996)
Behind The Sun / Witness / Temptation /
Between Night And Day / Leaving Them
Behind / We Are Your Family / Fuel For My
Hatred / Break My Bones / Break My
Restaurant / No Rest
CHAMBER OF ONE, Music For Nations
(1997)
A Thankless Task / A Moment Of Clarity /
The Escape / Chamber Of One /
Generations / Giving Up The Lies / Faceless
/ Tribal Convictions / Dead Issue / Haunting
Your Horizons

DEATH ANGEL (USA)
Line-Up: Mark Osegueda (vocals),
Rob Cavestany (guitar), Gus Pepa (guitar),
Dennis Pepa (bass),
Andy Galeon (drums)

DEATH ANGEL excited Thrash Metal fans
with their arrival in 1987 as the latest export
from the rapidly expanding Bay Area Metal
scene that threatened to engulf the world in
the late '80s. Although the band came
together in 1982 it would be five years before
their first album, the widely admired 'The
Ultra-Violence'.
The group returned in 1988 with the Enigma
released 'Frolic In The Park' album and
ventured over to Britain the same year to
support MOTÖRHEAD.
Band activities were suspended in 1990 when
DEATH ANGEL were involved in a road
accident in Arizona hospitalizing vocalist
Mark Osegueda and drummer Andy Galeon.
In 1991 Geffen records, believing the name
DEATH ANGEL was detrimental to the band's
interests, attempted to market the band under
the abbreviated monicker of D.A. to promote
the band through radio play but found little
interest and subsequently dropped the band.
The band soldiered on performing acoustic
sets billed as THE PAST but enduring a
further setback Osegueda departed in the
same year retiring from the music business
leaving guitarist Rob Cavestany to handle
lead vocals.
By the end of the year the band were going
under a new title THE ORGANISATION
releasing two albums 1994's 'Free Burning'
and the follow up 'Savor The Flavor'. Dennis

Pepa created THICK AS THIEVES.
During 1999 Osegueda, Cavestany and Galeon created THE SWARM with new bassist Michael Isiah.

Albums:
THE ULTRA-VIOLENCE, Under One Flag FLAG 14 (1987)
Thrashers / Evil Priest / Voracious Souls / Kill As One / The Ultra-Violence / Mistress Of Pain / Final Death/ I.P.F.S.
FROLIC IN THE PARK, Enigma CDENV 502 (1988)
3rd Floor / Road Mutants / Why Do You Do This? / Bored / Confused / Guilty Of Innocence / Open Up / Shores Of Sin / Cold Gin / Mind Rape / Devil's Metal
ACT III, Geffen 7599242802 (1990)
Seemingly Endless Time / Stop / Veil Of Deception / The Organisation / Discontinued / A Room With A View / Stagnant / EX-TC / Disturbing The Peace / Falling Asleep
FALL FROM GRACE - LIVE, Roadracer RO 93332 (1990)
Evil Priest / Why Do You Do This? / Mistress Of Pain / Road Mutants / Voracious Souls / Bored / Kill As One / Guilty Of Innocence / Shores Of Sin / Final Death / Confused

DEATHCORE (GERMANY)
Line-Up: Tschakk (vocals / guitar), Corre (bass), Simon (drums)

Speyer Metal act heavily influenced by Hardcore music. Vocalist Torsten Kater departed following the release of the debut album 'Spontaneous Underground'.

Albums:
SPONTANEOUS UNDERGROUND, Nuclear Blast (1991)
Into Death / Manati / Human Error / Guerilla / Annihilating War / Morbus Gravis / Spontaneous Combustion / Evil Death Slaughter / RU 486? / Regantanz / Religious Fanatics / Dolphin Instinct / Regantanz 2
MONOBROW, Spontaneous Underground (1994)

DEATHCULT (Los Angeles, CA, USA)

Extreme outfit DEATHCULT debuted with a 1992 demo 'Devoured In Holyness'.
Albums:
SODOMY: REPULSIVE IN MY WAYS, Wild Rags (1993)

DEATH IN ACTION (GERMANY)
Line-Up: Ralf Pfügler (vocals), Glenn Krügener (vocals / guitar), Udo Franke (bass), Willi Golus (drums)

Crossover Metal act DEATH IN ACTION lost all their members bar guitarist Glenn Krügener after the 'Toxic Waste' debut. For 1990's 'Just For Our Sake?' Krügener had built up the band strength with bassist Ralf Theilacher and drummer Robbi Balci. Krügener himself took over lead vocal duties. The band also operated under the shortened handle of D.I.A.

Albums:
TOXIC WASTE, We Bite 1-032 (1988)
Veins Of Fear / Brain Damage / Adapt Or Die / Negative Influences / Veins Of Fear / Toxic Waste / Nuclear Death
JUST FOR OUR SAKE?, We Bite WB062 (1990)
Paralyzed / Daily Cruel Death / Sale Of Surgery / Disgraced / Just For Our Sake / Creditors To Violence / Handle With Care / Deathly Blessing
STUCK IN TIME, We Bite WB 1-079 (1991)
SCHEITERHAUFEN BRENNT, WLCD DIA-04 (1996)
Todessehnsucht / Ignorance / Seelenruhe / Depths Of Soul / Scheiterhaufen Brennt / Soulless Son (Die Letzte Flut) / Way To Survive / Your Day

DEATH MASK (USA)
Line-Up: Steven Michaels (vocals), Benny Ransom (guitar), Chris Eichorn (bass), Lee Nelson (drums)

DEATH MASK's solitary release was produced by the musclebound Canadian THOR.

Albums:
SPLIT THE ATOM, Killerwatt KILP 4004 (1986)
Split The Atom / I'm Dangerous / The Reign / Lust For Fire / Tortured Mind / Nightmares (A Lesson For The Innocent) / Hell Rider / Walk Alone / Death Has No Boundaries / Commando

DEATHRASH (NJ, USA)
Line-Up: Tim Scherer (guitar), Pat Burns (bass), Pete Pollack (drums)

New Jersey thrashers DEATHRASH came into being when bassist Pat Burns severed ties with WHIPLASH. The band's three track 1986 demo featuring WHIPLASH (and later SLAYER) drummer Tony J. Scaglione comprised 'Lock Jaw', 'Blood For Blood' and 'Buried Alive'.
DEATHRASH added two new recruits in 1986 in the form of second guitarist Tim Scherer and drummer Peter Pollack. With this line up

the band contributed the track 'Buried Alive' to the 'Speed Metal Hell Volume 2' compilation album.

Burns parted ways with the band to forge a new alliance titled ZERO HOUR. Joining him in this venture were Scaglione on drums and former AGNOSTIC FRONT guitarist Gordon Ancis. This act soon folded with Scaglione joining LUDICHRIST.

Albums:
THE 10,000 R.P.M. GROOVE ORGY, Pigs Ear PIG 001 (1989)
Liqueur Whore / Sexbeast / Now I Wanna Make Some Noise / 50,000 M.P.H. / Disciples Of Sleaze / Mindtrashed And Loaded / True And Wild / I'm Your Man / Queen Of The Night / Death Trash Rock And Roll

DEATHRIDER (MN, USA)
Line-Up: Phillip Patton (vocals / guitar), Michael Soderstrom (guitar), Steve Sherman (bass), Craig Waters (drums)

Albums:
REQUIEM, (1991)
Burn Victim / Feel The Pain / Plague Of Death / Manslaughter / The Gate / I Can't Win / Scum Pit / Dum

DEATHROW (GERMANY)
Line-Up: Milo (vocals / bass), Sven Flugge (guitar), Thomas Priebe (guitar), Markus Hahn (drums)

Dusseldorf Thrash band DEATHROW was created when guitarist Sven Flugge and drummer Markus Hahn split from Bremen's HÖLLENHUNDE in 1983.
Relocating to Dusseldorf, the duo teamed up with vocalist / bassist Milo and second guitarist Priebe via advertisements in music magazines and formed SAMHAIN. However, an American act also existed of that name, so upon signing to Noise Records they changed monikers to DEATHROW.
The quartet's debut album was originally titled 'Riders Of Doom', but the album was repackaged with a different title ('Satan's Gift') after objections from the American market. DEATHROW toured Europe in 1986 with VOIVOD and POSSESSED.
DEATHROW's second album, 'Raging Steel', was another praiseworthy effort, but the band did little touring to back up it's release. Priebe left in late 1988 forcing the recruitment of former END AMEN / MEKONG DELTA man Uwe Osterlehner in time to play dates in Italy with CORONOR and record the third album 'Deception Ignored'.

Singles/EPs:
Towers In Darkness / Somewhere In This Night / We Can Change, Metal Machine (1991)

Albums:
RIDERS OF DOOM, Noise N 0044 (1986)
Winds Of Death / Satan's Gift / Riders Of Doom / Hell's Ascent / Spider Attack / Slaughtered / Violent Omen / Dark Tales / Samhain
RAGING STEEL, Noise N 0081 (1987)
The Dawn / Raging Steel / Scattered By The Wind / Dragon's Blood / The Thing Within / Pledge To Die / Mortal Dread / The Undead Cry / Beyond The Night
DECEPTION IGNORED, Noise NUK 128 (1989)
Events In Concealment / The Deathwish / Triocton / N.L.Y.H. / Watching The World / Narcotic / Machinery / Bureaucrazy
LIFE BEYOND, West Virginia 084-57222 (1992)
Life Beyond / Behind Closed Eyes / Towers In Darkness / Hidden Truth / Harlequins Mask / Homosapiens Superior / Suicide Arena / Deathrow / Reflected Mind / The Remembrance

DEATH S.S. (ITALY)
Line-Up: Vampire (vocals), Death (guitar), Zombie (guitar), Mummy (bass), Werewolf (drums)

Gothic horror Metal act DEATH SS date back to 1977 and have, over the years, become a cult institution, although the band has gone through various guises and titles; with the mainstay and lynchpin being founder Steve Sylvester. DEATH SS first made an impression with the 1981 demo tape 'Horned God Of The Witches'.
The first stable line-up of DEATH SS comprised vocalist Sylvester ('Vampire'), Paul Chain ('Death'), Claud Galley ('Zombie'), Danny Hughes ('Mummy') and Thomas Chaste ('Werewolf') and the group eventually debuted with a series of limited edition singles sold at gigs. Only 500 of each were pressed
In 1982 DEATH SS appeared on their first compilation album, 'Gathered', with the song 'Terror' and would then add the track 'Black And Violet' to the 1983 Italian Metal compilation album 'Heavy Metal Eruption'. However, DEATH SS split later the same year with Chain forming PAUL CHAIN VIOLET THEATRE. In the interim however Chain issued the 'Chains Of Death' single under the

STEVE SYLVESTER of DEATH SS Photo : Nico Wobben

title of DEATH SS minus Sylvester!

Sylvester himself went solo and issued an EP of his own, 'The Free Man', using the services of ex-DEATH SS members. Having since reformed DEATH SS Sylvester now fronts the mothership act and his spin-off solo outfit SYLVESTER'S DEATH.

The 1997 album 'Do What Thou Wilt', recorded in England, sees DEATH SS with a line up of Sylvester, guitarists Emil Bandera and Felix Moon, bassist Andrew Karloff and drummer Ross Lukather.

As a footnote, former DEATH SS drummer Mimmio Palmiotta is now a member of DOMINE appearing on their 1997 album 'Champion Eternal'.

Steve Sylvester guested on the 2000 TENEBRE album 'Mark Ov The Beast'. Chain founded LOOSIN 'O' FREQUENCIES in 1999 for the 'Regeneration' album.

DEATH SS cut their versions of 'Come To The Sabbat' and 'Ancient Days' to the BLACK WIDOW tribute album 'King Of The Witches'.

The 'Let The Sabbath Begin' album of 2001 comprised of new studio material, remixes and a live concert culled from the band's 2000 tour.

Erstwhile DEATH SS guitarist Steve Mineli would found NODE issuing the Thrash Metal 'Sterilized' mini album in 2001.

Singles/EPs:

Zombie / Terror, (198-) (Band pressing. 500 copies)

Night Of The Witch / Black Mummy (Live), (198-) (Band pressing. 500 copies)

The Profanation / Spiritualist Séance, (198-) (Band pressing. 500 copies)

In The Darkness / The Mandrake Root, (198-)

Chains Of Death / Inquizitor / Schizophrenic, Metal Eye (1983)

Kings Of Evil / Gethsemane / Murder Angel, Metalmaster MET 127 (1989)

The Cursed Singles, Avantgarde (1995) (Limited edition. 666 copies.]

Albums:

THE STORY OF DEATH SS 1977-1984, Minotaur DEA 101 (1988)

Terror / Murder Angels / Horrible Eyes / Cursed Mania / Zombie / Violet Overture / Chains Of Death / Inquisitor / Schizophrenic / Black And Violet / The Bones And The Grave

IN DEATH OF STEVE SILVESTER, Metalmaster MET111 (1989)

BLACK MASS, Metalmaster MET 120 (1990)

Kings Of Evil / Horrible Eyes / Cursed Mania / Buried Alive / Welcome To My Hell / Devil's

Rage / In The Darkness / Black Mass

HEAVY DEMONS FEATURE, Rosemary's Babydisc 002 (1992)

Walpurgisnacht / Where Have You Gone? / Heavy Demons / Family Vault / Lilith / Peace Of Mind / Way To Power / Baphomet / Inquisitor / Templar's Revenge / All Souls' Day / Sorcerrous Valley

THE CURSED CONCERT - LIVE, (1992)

FEAR OF EVIL, (199-)

HORROR MUSIC - THE BEST OF DEATH SS, Lucifers Rising (1996)

DO WHAT THOU WILT, Bossy Ogress 561 3016 20 BO (1997)

Liber I: The Awakening Of The Beast / Liber II: The Phoenix Mass / Liber III: Baron Samedi / Liber IV: Scarlet Woman / Liber V: The Serpent Rainbow / Liber VI: Crowley's Law / Liber VII: Guardian Angel / Liber VIII: The Shrine In The Gloom / Liber IX: The Way Of The Left Hand / Liber X: Liber Samekh PANIC, Dream Catcher (2000)

Paraphernalia / Let The Sabbath Begin / Hi-Tech Jesus / Lady Of Babylon / The Equinox Of The Gods / Ishtar / The Cannibal Queen / Rabies Is A Killer / Tallow Doll / Hermaphrodite / Panic / Auto Sacramental

LET THE SABBATH BEGIN, Lucifer Rising (2001)

Let The Sabbath Begin / Rim Of Hell / Let The Sabbath Begin (Pandemonium remix) / Hymn Of The Satanic Empire Or The Battle Hymn Of The Apocalypse / Ishtar (Great Mother Goddess Sexy Mix) / Let The Sabbath Begin (Live) / Baphomet (Live) / Lady of Babylon (Live) / Baron Samedi (Live) / Equinox Of The Gods- Ishtar (Live) / Medley: Black And Violet- Inquisitor - Cursed Mama - Chains Of Death - Where Have You Gone? - Family Vault (Live) / Scarlet Woman (Live)

DEATHWISH (UK)

Line-Up: Jon Van Doom (vocals), Dave Deathwish (guitar), Stuart Ranger (bass), Brad Sims (drums)

Formed in 1983, DEATHWISH offered straightforward British Thrash.

The band's initial demos secured a deal with Metalworks Records, although following the release of 'At The Edge Of Damnation', the band split for pastures new and promoted themselves sufficiently to gain major label interest in 1988, although they opted for manager Tom Doherty's GWR label.

In mid 1989 bassist Stuart Ranger left to be replaced by Ben Rumble.

Albums:

AT THE EDGE OF DAMNATION,

Metalworks VOV 667(1987)
Deathwish / In The Name Of God / For Evil
Done / Sword Of Justice / Demonic Attack /
Dance Of The Dead / Leaving Your Life
Behind / Exorcist / Forces Of Darkness /
Edge Of Damnation
DEMON PREACHER, Roadracer RO 9478 1
(1988)
Death Procession / Demon Preacher /
Carrion / Visions Of Insanity / Symptom Of
The Universe

DECADENCE (BELGIUM)

Thrash Metal band DECADENCE debuted
with a 1988 demo 'Reprisal'.

Albums:
GANG AND VICTIMS, Justice (1990)

DECEASED (VA, USA)
Line-Up: King Fowley (vocals), Mark Adams
(guitar), Mike Smith (guitar), Lez Snyder
(bass)

DECEASED band leader King Fowley also
owns Old Metal Records, a label specialising
in re-releasing '80s Metal underground
classics. DECEASED were founded in the
mid '80s and opened up proceedings with the
inaugural 1987 demo session 'Evil Side Of
Religion'. Pre DECEASED vocalist and
drummer Kingsly 'King' Fowley had paid his
dues with school band SLACK TYDE and the
1982 unit MESSENGER.
As DECEASED, Fowley, with guitarists Doug
Souther and Mark Adams, played their debut
gig in April 1986 performing a set of covers by
bands such as SODOM, BATHORY, SLAYER
and MOTÖRHEAD at a friends house.
Progress was swift and soon DECEASED
were becoming a draw on the local club
circuit.
However, tragedy would strike the band in
March of 1988 when bass player Rob Sterzel,
along with two friends of the band, was killed
in a hit and run incident. Stopping his car to
change a flat tyre the three friends were
mown down by a van driver. Needless to say
the media had a field day when it was
revealed Rob's band was titled DECEASED.
Following this huge setback the 1989 set 'One
Night In The Cemetary' ensued. Two further
cassettes ensued with 'Birth By Radiation'
and 1990's 'Nuclear Exorcist' before
DECEASED hooked up with Death Metal
specialists Relapse Records for the debut
album 'Luck Of The Corpse'. Frictions within
the band led to DECEASED recording the live
'Gutwrench' single minus Souther. Shortly
after recording Souther quit with Mike Smith

taking his place.
The 1995 release 'Death Metal From The
Grave' comprises early demo material with
live cuts and a cover version of VENOM's 'Die
Hard'.
DECEASED's 2000 album 'Supernatural
Addiction' was produced by Simon Effemey.
The band's live album includes a cover
version of KROKUS's 'Headhunter'.
DECEASED also cut various other covers for
tribute albums and laid down in quick
succession their takes on SODOM's 'Witching
Hour', AUTOPSY's 'Charred Remains' and
KREATOR's 'Tormentor'.
The 2002 album 'Zombie Hymns' would
virtually be a textbook of King Fowley's Heavy
Metal upbringing pulling together a collection
of cover versions. Honoured acts included
SLAYER with 'Chemical Warfare' and 'Die By
The Sword' VENOM's 'Black Metal' and 'Die
Hard', IRON MAIDEN's 'Wrathchild' and '2
Minutes To Midnight' and the MERCYFUL
FATE pairing of 'Nuns Have No Fun' and
'Doomed By The Living Dead'. Also included
would be the METAL CHURCH anthem 'Metal
Church', SAXON's 'Fire In The Sky',
IMPETIGO's 'Dis Organ Ised', VOIVOD's
'Blower', EXCITER's 'Violence And Force' and
OZZY OSBOURNE's 'S.A.T.O.' amongst
others. The solitary non-traditional Metal
offering would be a rendition of THE DOORS
'Not To Touch The Earth'.
Fowley also operates the Trad Metal act
OCTOBER 31 as well as DOOMSTONE.

Albums:
LUCK OF THE CORPSE, Relapse
(199-)
Fading Survival / The Cemetery's Full /
Experimenting With Failure / Futuristic Doom
/ Haunted Cerebellum / Decrepit Coma /
Shrieks From The Hearse / Psychedelic
Warriors / / Feasting On Skulls / Birth By
Radiation / Gutwrench
THE THIRTEEEN FRIGHTENED SOULS,
Relapse (199-)
The 13 Frightened Souls / Robotic Village /
Voivod / Planet Graveyard / Nuclear Exorcist
DEATH METAL FROM THE GRAVE, (1995)
Immune To Burial / Worship The Coffin /
Birth By Radiation / Vomiting Blood / Virus /
Deformed Tomorrows / Nuclear Exorcist /
Shrieks From The Hearse / A Trip To The
Morgue / After The Bloodshed / Sick Thrash
/ Futuristic Doom (Live) / Fading Survival
(Live) / Haunted Cerebellum (Live) / Robotic
Village (Live) / Die Hard
THE BLUEPRINTS FOR MADNESS, (1995)
Morbid Shape In Black / The Triangle / Island
Of The Unknown / The Blueprints For
Madness / The Creek Of The Dead / Mind
Vampires / Into The Bizarre / Alternate

Dimensions / Midnight / Negative Darkness /A Reproduction Of Tragedy
FEARLESS UNDEAD MACHINES, Relapse RR 6957 (1997)
The Silent Creature / Contamination / Fearless Undead Machines / From The Ground They Came / Night Of The Deceased / Graphic Repulsion / Mysterious Research / Beyond Science / Unhuman Drama / The Psychic / Destiny
SUPERNATURAL ADDICTION, Relapse (2000)
The Premonition / Dark Chilling Heartbeat / A Very Familiar Stranger / Frozen Screams / The Doll With The Hideous Spirit / The Hanging Soldier / Chambers Of The Waiting Blind / Elly's Dementia
UP THE TOMBSTONES - LIVE 2000, Thrash Corner (2000)
The Silent Creature / The Premonition / The 13 Frightened Souls / Robotic Village / The Triangle / Dark Chilling Heartbeat / Fearless Undead Machines / The Psychic / Headhunter / Sick Thrash
BEHIND THE MOURNER'S VEIL, (2001)
It's Alive / The Mausoleum / Zombie Attack / Reaganomics / New Age Of Total Warfare / Deathrider / Victims Of The Masterplan (I-V)
ZOMBIE HYMNS, Crook'D (2002)
Black Metal / Violence And Force / Witching Metal / 2 Minutes To Midnight / S.A.T.O. / Blower / Doomed By The Living Dead / Dis

Organ Ised / Die By The Sword / Not To Touch The Earth / Metal Church / Wrathchild / Bombs Of Death / Fire In The Sky / Nuns Have No Fun / Headhunter (Live) / Stay Clean / Die Hard / Tormentor / Chemical Warfare

DECEASED

DECEMBER WOLVES
(Salem, MA, USA)
Line-Up: Devon (vocals), Joe (guitar), Tim (guitar), Brian (bass), Scott DeFusco (drums)

DECEMBER WOLVES debuted with the 1994 demo 'Wolftread'. The band issued their Celtic

flavoured Black Thrash Metal debut album 'Til Ten Years' on the Korean label Hammerheart. Drummer Scott DeFusco, who also had a solo project TURAGHAN, would leave the band following the 'Completely Dehumanised' album.

DECEMBER WOLVES pulled in a fresh rhythm section in 2000 of bassist Dave Ebola and drummer Joe Kill.

Latterly members of DECEMBERS WOLVES have renounced any Black Metal connections.

<u>Singles/EPs:</u>
We Are Everywhere / Not With Tainted Blood, December Wolves (1997)

<u>Albums:</u>
'TIL TEN YEARS, Hammerheart (1996)
Ode To The Master Therion / The Night That I Died / Our Centuries Have Been Found / Lycanthropy: Yonder Through Ice Storms / 'Til Ten Years / When The Clouds Cry / Outro
COMPLETELY DEHUMANISED, Wicked World SICK03CD (1998)
Conditioned By The Thoughts That I Transmit To You / Completely Dehumanised / We Are Everywhere / Time Flies When You Wish You Were Dead / Friday The 13th / The Gard Division / My Bible / Not With Tainted Blood / To Kill Without Emotion

DECIMATOR (UK)
Line-Up: Dog (vocals), Lice Marshall (guitar), E Raunch Launcher (guitar), Metaldwarf (bass), Shawn Beaver (drums)

<u>Albums:</u>
CARNAGE CITY STATE MOSHPATROL, Neat (1989)
Raider / Mutoids / F.H. / Blood Island / C.C.S.M.P. / Devil's Bridge / Rogue Decimator / Dustbowl / Stealer Of Souls
DIRTY HOT AND HUNGRY, Neat D1052 (1993)
Red Eye / Dirty, Hot And Hungry / Sixteen Six / Flight 19 / Mutant Lieutenant / Carnage City Rocks / Stealer Of The Souls (The Renegade) / T.R.I.P. / Megazine

DECISION D (HOLLAND)
Line-Up: Edwin Ogenio (vocals), Stijn Bollinger (guitar), Daniel Bootsman (guitar), Gerard Vanderreee (bass), Peter Zaal (drums)

Dutch Thrashers DECISION D formed in 1986. A series of demos gained the quintet a deal with German label Inline Records subsidiary Crypta. In November 1994 DECISION D were able to tour America. The

year also saw the emergence of 'The Last Prostitute', a self financed effort.

<u>Albums:</u>
RAZON DE LA MUERTE, Crypta 8209-2 (1992)
Diabolic Shadows / World's Deception / Babylon's Kingdom / Holy Supper / Hymn Of The Refuge / Ecclesia Anorexia / Criticize / Reincarnation Of Death
MORATORIA, Crypta 8204-2 (1993)
Social Darkness / Devoted / Statues Of Deliberation / Slaughterslice Atmosphere / Devastation Of A Nation / Birth Of Cadaver / Bow Down In Suffocation / Bastard / Spiritu Santo
THE LAST PROSTITUTE, Bark Horse 95001 (1994)
Last Prostitute / Graffiti / Residence Of Dishonour / Women Of Injustice / Independent Remorse / Smoke / Accusations / Forsaken / You Ain't Nothing / Racist Behaviour

DED ENGINE (MI, USA)
Line-Up: Scott Litz (vocals), Doug Horstman (guitar), Marky De Sade (bass), G.H. Lorimer (drums)

DED ENGINE, who throughout their career were constantly blighted by comparisons to better known British Metal bands, were founded in 1981 but did not get an opportunity to release product until 1985 after the French label Black Dragon had picked up on the Michigan quartet

1988 saw DED ENGINE offering an album entitled 'Hold A Grudge' appropriately enough through the American independent company Grudge Records.

<u>Albums:</u>
DED ENGINE, Black Dragon BD014 (1985)
Scream / Kings Of The City / Renegade / Rabid / Bloodlust / Take A Hike / Hot Shot / Young And Hot / Reign Of Terror / Till Deaf Do Us Part
HOLD A GRUDGE, Grudge (1988)
High Rider / The Breed / Heads Down / Termination Day / South Of Hell / Hang Together / White Hot / Unleash The Beast / Ground Zero / Violence Is Golden

DEFENDER (HOLLAND)
Line-Up: Simon Meuting (vocals), Henk Verheul (guitar), Stef Köhler (guitar), Harm Noort (bass), Remco Bonsma (drums)

Mid '80s Speed Metal merchants. DEFENDER's demo 'Tales Of The Unexpected' garnered enough attention in the right places to land them the support to an AGENT STEEL European tour.

A further two years was to follow before the self-financed debut EP 'City Ad Mortis'.

DEFENDER then cut their own promotional album 'Journey To The Unexpected' before folding.

Singles/EPs:
City Ad Mortis / Die For You / In The Beginning / Counter Attack / Deadly Peril, Defender (1987)

Albums:
JOURNEY TO THE UNEXPECTED, Promo (1989)

DEFIANCE (San Francisco, CA, USA)
Line-Up: Ken Elkington (vocals), Doug Harrington (guitar), Jim Adams (guitar), Mike Kaufmann (bass), Matt Vander Ende (drums)

DEFIANCE's debut album was produced by ANNIHALATOR guitarist Jeff Walters. DEFIANCE arrived on the scene with the 1988 'Hypothermia' demo session. Although DEFIANCE were fronted by vocalist Ken Elkington for 'Product Of Society' by the following year Steev Esquivel had taken his place.

Third album was produced by Rob Beaton. In addition HEATHEN guitarist Lee Altus contributed guitar parts. Guitarist Brian Wenzel was drafted in late 1992.

DEFIANCE evolved into INNER THRESHOLD drafting former BLIND ILLUSION and HEATHEN vocalist Dave Godfrey. Another transition saw the band morph into UNDER as Godfrey formed part of the 2000 HEATHEN reunion.

Albums:
PRODUCT OF SOCIETY, Roadrunner (1989)
The Fault / Death Machine / Product Of Society / Forgotten / Lock Jaw / Insomnia / Deadly Intentions / Aftermath / Tribulation / Hypothermia
VOID TERRA FIRMA, Roadracer (1990)
Void Terra Firma / Deception Of Faith / Questions / Skitz - Illusions / Slayground / Killers / Steamroller / Checkmate / Buried Or Burned / Last Resort (Welcome To Poverty)
BEYOND RECOGNITION, Roadrunner (1992)
The Killing Floor / Step Back / Perfect Nothing / No Compromise / Dead Silence / Inside Looking Out / The Chosen / Power Trip / Promised Afterlife

DEFLESHED (SWEDEN)
Line-Up: Lars Löfven (vocals / guitar), Gustaf Jorde (bass), Matte Modin (drums)

DEFLESHED are purveyors of Thrash infused Death Metal, heavy on gross lyrics and unpenetratable vocals.

DEFLESHED was forged during 1991 with an inaugural line-up of guitarist Lars Löfven, Kristoffer Griedl and drummer Oskar Karlsson. This line-up managed an eponymous demo before fracturing. Second session 'Abrah Kadavrah' saw the inclusion of erstwhile CREMATORIUM bassist Gustaf Jorde and lead vocals from Johan Hedman. Progress was such that DEFLESHED were included on the Nuclear Blast 'Grindcore' compilation and had three tracks from the demo issued as a 7" courtesy of the Italian Miscarriage label.

Bassist Gustaf Jorde was added prior to recording of debut album 'Ma Belle Scalpelle' for the German Invasion Records concern. Karlsson left for GATES OF ISHTAR (also SCHEITAN and RAISED FIST) and in his stead came Matte Modin in time for the 'Abrah Kadavhrah' album.

In 1998 DEFLESHED contributed their version of SEPULTURA's 'Beneath The Remains' for a tribute album.

DEFLESHED toured Europe as support to CANNIBAL CORPSE in 1999. By 2000 Modin had bailed out to join DARK FUNERAL.

The band toured Japan during March of 2001.

Singles/EPs:
Obsculum Obscenum / Satanic Source / Phlegm, Miscarriage MS002 (1993)

Albums:
MA BELLE SCALPELLE, Invasion IR009 (1994)
Gathering Flies / Moribiance Blue Cafe / Simply Fall Towards / Many Mangled Maggots / Ma Belle Scalpelle
ABRAH KADAVRAH, Invasion IR019 (1995)
Beaten, Loved And Eaten / Mary Bloody Mary / With A Gambrel / In Chains And Leather / Abrah Kadavrah / Gone With The Feaces / Anatomically Incorrect / On Gorgeous Grounds / Body Art... / ...Pierced Through The Heart
UNDER THE BLADE, Invasion IR 032 (1997)
Farewell To The Flesh / Entering My Yesterdays / Eat The Meat Raw / Sons Of Spellcraft And Starfalls / Metalbounded / Under The Blade / Thorns Of A Black Rose / Cinderella's Return And Departure / Walking The Moons Of Mars / Metallic Warlust / Curse The Gods

DEATH... THE HIGH COST OF LIVING,
War Music (1999)
Entering My Yesterdays / Mary Bloody Mary /
Metallic Warlust / Under The Blade / Walking
The Moons of Mars / In Chains & Leather /
Thorns Of A Black Rose
FAST FORWARD, War Music (1999)
The Return Of The Flesh / The Heat From
Another Sun / Fast Forward / The Iron And
The Maiden / Proud To Be Dead /
Snowballing Blood / Wilder Than Fire /
Feeding Fatal Fairies / Lightning Strikes
Twice / Domination Of The Sub Queen /
Speeding The Ways

DEFORME (CHILE)

Line-Up: Leo Pozo (vocals / guitar), Eladio
Cordova (guitar), Carlos Alarcon (bass), Juan
Marambio (drums)

Death styled Thrashers DEFORME were
created during 1995 as the brainchild of
vocalist / drummer Leo Pozo. The band's
inaugural roster included guitarist Alejandro
Valenzuela and bassist Emilio Armero.
This latter pairing would decamp to allow in
new blood guitar player Octavio Meneses de
la Barra and bass player Carlos Alarcon. Pozo
would then switch to a guitar role when
DEFORME pulled in RITUAL drummer Juan
Marambio.
The band issued the 1998 demo tape
'Tiempos Cercaros' but would then fracture
once more, both Meneses de la Barra and
Marambio making their exit.
Valenzuela was re-recruited and Rodrigo
Asalgado occupied the drum stool for the
2000 EP release 'Tierra De Guerras'.
Latterly DEFORME comprises of Pozo,
Alarcon, a returning Marambio and guitarist
Eladio Cordova.

Singles/EPs:
Tu Raza / Esto Es Ahora / Deforme / Chupa
Cabras, (2000) ('Tierra De Guerras' EP)

DEHUMANIZED

(New York, NY, USA)
Line-Up: Sol Caceres (vocals / guitar), Chris
Jefferson (guitar), Jones (bass), Kevin
(drums)

New York Hardcore styled Death Metal act
DEHUMANIZED, originally fronted by vocalist
/ bassist Araena Sanchez, gained exposure
supporting the likes of British veteran Punk
acts UK SUBS and CHELSEA. The band
would issue an eponymous four track EP, one
of these songs, 'To You', also appearing on
the 'At War With Society' compilation.
The band appears to have undergone a
complete transformation with a later line up
credited as vocalist Jerry, guitarists Rich and
Tom, bassist Mike and drummer George
Torres.
Torres would join fellow New York Death Metal
crew SKINLESS during October 2001. Torres
would also add session vocals for IRATE.

Albums:
PROPHECIES FORETOLD, Pathos (1988)
Prophecies Foretold / Kingdom Of Cruelty /
Fade Into Obscurity / Solitary Demise /
Infinite Despair / Doomed To Die / Terminal
Punishment / Condemned / Drawn By Blood
PROBLEMS FIRST, New Red Archives
NRA76CD (1999)
Classified / Educators / Fee To Live /
Mommy's Killin' / Fuck You Where's My Brew
/ Confessions / Coo-Coos / Better Later
Days / Convenience / Everyday / Childish &
Cowardly / Tragic / To You / Gimme The
Scoop

DEKAPITATOR (USA)

Line-Up: Matt Hellfiend (vocals / guitar), Wes
Blackwülf (guitar), Dan Bulldoze (bass), Andy
Maniac (drums)

A retro 'Speed Renaissance' pure Thrash
band convened by EXHUMED members
vocalist Matt Harvey and drummer Andy 'Col'
Jones. DEKAPITATOR, incensed by what
they viewed as 'false Thrash' coming onto the
scene, apparently formed in an effort to show
the world what just real Thrash was. Judging
by the almost universal praise bestowed upon
the album 'We Will Destroy,... You Will Obey'
DEKAPITATOR appears to have succeeded
in their goal.
The original band name chosen was
HAMMERFALL but some enterprising
Swedes got to that one first. DEKAPITATOR
debuted as a trio of Hellfiend on "Killsaw &
Deaththroat", Bulldoze on "Thermo Nuclear
Bass Slaughter" and Atomic Maniac
supplying "Rapid Fire Drum Assault". This unit
delivered two tracks 'Make Them Die' and
'Haunted By Evil' to a 1997 split 7" single
shared with the notorious NUNSLAUGHTER.
The band signed to Blackmetal.com Records
for the album. Produced by Thrash veteran
guitarist JAMES MURPHY the record also
featured a holidaying Fredrik Soderberg of
Swedish act DAWN on backing vocals.
Hellfiend, Blackwulf and Maniac also operate
the side project CADAVERIZER.

Singles/EPs:
Make Them Die / Haunted By Evil, Midnight
(1997) ('Blood On Steel' EP. Split 7" single
with NUNSLAUGHTER)

Albums:
WE WILL DESTROY... YOU WILL OBEY,
Blackmetal.Com BM.C 66602 (1999)
One Shot, One Kill / Release The Dogs / We
Will Destroy... You Will Obey / Hell's Metal /
Make Them Die / Possessed With
Damnation / Thundering Legions /
Faceripper / Attack With Mayhem / T.F.S.
(Total Fucking Slaughter) / Haunted By Evil

DELIRIUM TREMENS (GERMANY)
Line-Up: Premutos (vocals), Sadistick Dick
Of Destruction (guitar), Death Tormentor
(bass), Christ Impaler (drums)

A less than serious '80s Thrash Metal
throwback named after the fatal alcohol
withdrawal. Certainly not to be confused with
the Puerto Rican Prog Ambient outfit of the
same title!
DELIRIUM   TREMENS   nevertheless
remained faithful to both the epoch and the
genre and pulled in commendable reviews for
their 'Violent Mosh Ground' album.
The band comprised vocalist 'Premutos'
(Christian Lindner) on "Vomiting throat",
guitarist 'Sadistick Dick Of Destruction'
(Christian Brehm) credited with "Massacre
guitar, leather death mask & high flames",
bassist 'Death Tormentor' (Ralf Enskat)
delivered "Distorted four string bass inferno"
and finally drummer 'Christ Impaler' (Jochen
Steger) with "M-16, uzi & bazooka".
Steger has previous experience with DRY
ROT, ABSORB and BLOOD OF MESSIAH.

Albums:
VIOLENT MOSH GROUND, (2000)
Seed Of Violence / Fuck Posers / Violent
Mosh Ground / Execution Command / Beer
Patrol / Bloody Harleyriders / Angel Fuck /
Night Of Terror / Hellfighters / B.O.D. / Get
Out Of My Way / Infernal Sex Slave
DELIVERANCE (UK)
Line-Up: Kris Krowe (bass / vocals), Sin
(guitar), Master Daniels (drums)

Albums:
DEVIL'S MEAT, Metalworks VOV666 (1987)
Desire / Your Death / Rotten To The Core /
Devil's Meat / R.I.P. / Killing For Jesus /
Deliverance / Twenty One Steps To Hell
EVIL FRIENDSHIP, AVM (1989)
Dies Irae / Tongues Of Lies / Lord Of Vice /
Bell, Book And Scandal / No Way Out / Alive
Forever / The Drowning / Turn Me To Stone /
Evil Friendship / Rabid / Trooper Of Death /
Requiem
BOOK OF LIES, Metalworks VOV 679
(1990)
The Devil's Instrument: Part 1 - Succubus,

Part 2 - Siren, Part 3 - Succubus / Nightmare
/ Sympathy / Book Of Lies / Runaway / The
Evil / Tear Down The Walls / R.I.P.
THE ULTIMATE REVENGE, Griffin GN
5931-2 (1993)
The Devil's Instrument (Succubus Part 1-3) /
Turn Me To Stone / Devil Friendship /
Deliverance / Bell Book & Scandle /
Runaway / Troopers Of Death / Alive Forever
/ R.I.P. / 21 Steps To Hell / The Evil / Vision /
Stealer Of Dreams / The Church Of
Deliverance

DELIVERANCE
(Los Angeles, CA, USA)
Line-Up: Jimmy P. Brown II (vocals / guitar),
Glenn Rogers (guitar), Brian Kharirullah
(bass), Chris Hyde (drums)

Los Angeles Christian Thrash Metal outfit
DELIVERANCE debuted in 1985 with the
'Greetings Of Death' demo tape. An
appearance on the important Christian Metal
compilation 'California Metal' on Regency
Records   would   follow   in   1987,
DELIVERANCE sharing space by donating
'Attack' and 'A Space Called You' with
MASTEDON, NEON CROSS, GARDIAN,
HERO and BARREN CROSS.
In 1989 delivered a Bill Metoyer produced
self-titled album. DELIVERANCE comprised
frontman Jimmy P. Brown II on vocals and
guitar, guitarist Glenn Rogers, bass player
Brian Khairullah and drummer Chris Hyde.
Guitarist Glenn Rogers would score co-
writing credits on the first VENGEANCE
RISING album 'Human Sacrifice'.
A sophomore effort 'Weapons Of Our
Warfare', generally acknowledged as a genre
classic, was released in 1990. The band
would benefit from heavy MTV rotation of the
video for the title track. Hyde would take time
out to session on the 1991 VENGEANCE
RISING album 'Destruction Comes'.
For the 'Weapons Of Our Warfare' album the
group dispensed with guitarist Rogers,
replacing him with RECON's George Ochoa.
The last DELIVERANCE album to deliver
Speed Metal would be the 1991 'What A Joke'
album. This album witnessed DELIVERANCE
hosting an entirely new rhythm section of
bassist Mike Grato - another RECON veteran,
and drummer Kevin Lee.
The transitional 'Stay Of Execution',
witnessed guitarist Mike Phillips supplanting
Ochoa. The former guitarist would figure as
part of the live line-up for the notorious Death
Metal act VENGEANCE RISING's last 'non-
secular' tour.
'Stay Of Execution', saw the beginnings of
DELIVERANCE's move into less angst ridden

music although the group did put in a sterling performance on the 1993 'Intense Live Series Vol. 1' release, which included a cover version of STRYPER's 'Surrender'. Khairullah made a return for this live in the studio recording.

Predictably the band switched members once again for the 'Learn' album. With only Brown remaining from the original line-up, DELIVERANCE now included guitarist Jon Maddux, bass player Manny Morales and drummer Jon Knox.

Much to the shock of many of their fans DELIVERANCE, now as a trio with new drummer Jeff Mason of BETRAYAL onboard and Brown handling all guitars, drifted into Alternative Rock territory with the 1994 'River Disturbance' album. Earlier Brown had lent guest vocals to two tracks on BETRAYAL's 'The Passing' album. The compilation, 'A Decade Of Deliverance', would include a cover version of BLACK SABBATH's 'After Forever'.

The harder edged 'Camelot In Smithereens' arrived in 1995. Both Morales and Mason were retained for this record with BETRAYAL guitarist Marcus Colon putting in a guest session.

Brown would eventually disband DELIVERANCE to found a fresh act FEARFUL SYMMETRY. Brown would put in a guest session with the Christian apocalyptic Progressive act SAVIOUR MACHINE. However, demand for DELIVERANCE remained high, Magdalene Records issuing archive and demo material in 2000. Brown would resurrect the band for a 2001 album 'Assimilation' for Dream Recordings. The new look DELIVERANCE had Brown heading a band of former bassist Manny Morales, SANCTIFIED SISTER guitarist Lael Conlon, drummer Ian Baird and FEARFUL SYMMETRY keyboard player David Gilbreath.

Ex-DELIVERANCE guitarist Glenn Rogers would announce the formation of MONTH OF SUNDAYS, a union with erstwhile REVEREND guitarist Brian Korban.

A brand new DELIVERANCE album 'The Sad Veil Of Tears' was expected in 2002.

Albums:
DELIVERANCE, Intense RO 9072 (1989)
Victory / No Time / Deliverance / If You Will / The Call / No Love / Blood Of The Covenant / Jehovah Jireh / Temporary Insanity / Awake
WEAPONS OF OUR WARFARE, Intense (1990)
Supplication / This Present Darkness / Weapons Of Our Warfare / Solitude / Flesh And Blood / Bought By Blood / 23 / Slay The Wicked / Greetings Of Death / If We Faint Not

WHAT A JOKE, Intense (1991)
Intro / Prophet Of Idiocy / Pseudo Intellectual / Cheeseburger Maker Du / What A Joke / Chipped Beef / After Forever / It's The Beat / A Product Of Society / Happy Star / J.P.D. / Pray / Silent Night / J.I.G. / Purgatory Sandwich With Mustard / Attack
STAY OF EXECUTION, Intense (1992)
Stay Of Execution / Windows Of The Soul / Words To The... / From Once Was / Self-Monger / Horrendous Disc / Lord Of Dreams / Ramming Speed / Entombed / Weapons Of Our Warfare (Remix)
INTENSE LIVE SERIES VOL. 1 - RECORDED LIVE, Intense (1993)
Surrender / No Love / This Present Darkness / Stay Of Execution / The Call / No Time
LEARN, Intense (1992)
Time / 1990 / Learn / Who Am I? / Renew / The Rain / Reflection / In The Will / Desperate Cries / Sanctuary
RIVER DISTURBANCE, Brainstorm (1994)
Belltown / After I Fell / River Disturbance / Now & Then / Speed Of Light / A Little Speed (w/ 12th Tribe) / Map / You Still Smile / Breathing Still
A DECADE OF DELIVERANCE, Intense (1994)
Victory / No Time / The Call / Flesh and Blood / This Present Darkness / Rescue / After Forever / Prophet Of Idiocy / Words To The... / Ramming Speed / Stay Of Execution / Learn / Desperate Cries / Sanctuary
CAMELOT IN SMITHEREENS, Intense (1995)
Somber Theme (Where Are You) / Lindsey / Not Too Good 4 Me / Anymore / Book Ends / Beauty & The Beast / Make My Bed In Hell / The Red Roof / In-U
BACK IN THE DAY: THE FIRST FOUR YEARS, Magdalene (2000)
Narration / Who Will Save The Children / Stand Up And Fight / Narration / No Time / Narration / Talk From The Stage / Fortress / Deliverance / Narration / Attack / A Space Called You / Narration / Hold On Tightly / J.I.G. / Temporary Insanity
GREETINGS OF DEATH, ETC, Magdalene (2001)
Victory / Greetings Of Death / No Time / J.I.G. / Speckled Bird / Awake / Attack / A Space Called You / Weapons Of Our Warfare / This Present Darkness / Greetings Of Death / Rescue / Slay The Wicked / Solitude / 23 / Radio interview (1992)
ASSIMILATION, Dream Recordings (2001)
The Limitless Light / From The Beginning / Assimilation / The Circle / Sell Your Soul... / The Search / The Learned Man / Between 2 Worlds / Impressions / Save Me From
LIVE AT CORNERSTONE 2001, Magdalene (2001)

126

Intro / Stay of Execution / Introductions / No Time / Learn / What A Joke / Belltown / Psalm 23 / Weapons of Our Warfare / Thanks / Victory / Words To The... / Sanctuary

DELLAMORTE (SWEDEN)
Line-Up: Jonas Kjellgren (vocals), Johan Jansson (guitar), Matthias Norrman (guitar), Daniel Ekeroth (bass), Sonny Svedlund (drums)

An infamous Death Metal act with a deeply rooted Thrash bias. DELLAMORTE was rooted in the 1990 band INTERMENT, established by erstwhile HATRED and ASOCIAL guitarist Johan Jansson. Vocalist Jonas Kjellgren is ex-PEXILATED.
During 1993 INTERMENT evolved briefly into MOONDARK before settling on DELLAMORTE. A 1995 demo, 'Drunk In The Abyss', landed a deal with the Finn label, recording in a mere 4 days the now very scarce but highly sought after album 'Everything You Hate'. The following year a 7" single, 'Dirty', emerged through the Yellow Dog label and prompted the interest of the Kron-H label, a subsidiary of French concern Osmose Productions. DELLAMORTE released the sophomore 'Uglier And More Disgusting' album, produced by Peter Tagtgren of HYPOCRISY, and set about promoting it as part of the 'World Domination' tour billed alongside DARK TRANQUILITY and ENSLAVED. Added exposure was garnered with the subsequent inclusion of DELLAMORTE on the follow up 'World Domination Live' CD and video.
1998 would witness both Jansson and vocalist Jonas Kjellgren, still retaining their allegiance to DELLAMORTE, joining the renowned Deathsters CENTINEX. Paradoxically though the duo would switch roles in CENTINEX, Jansson becoming a lead vocalist and Kjellgren adopting guitar. DELLAMORTE bassist Daniel Ekeroth would not be left on the sidelines when it came to side ventures, the four stringer joining INCISION.
Third album, 'Home Sweet Hell' produced once again by Peter Tagtgren, arrived in 1999. DELLAMORTE welcomed in new drummer Kennet Englund, a veteran of MOONDARK, UNCANNY and SUBDIVE. That same June Englund too would team up with CENTINEX. Besides DELLAMORTE and CENTINEX both Jansson and Kjellgren are members of the SIDEBURNERS. Jansson also busies himself with UNCURBED and Kjellgren too has another act in the high profile CARNAL FORGE.
Matthias Norrman would tour as bassist for

OPETH in 2001, a quiet year for DELLAMORTE with the band only putting in one gig during March.

Singles/EPs:
Dirty / Plug Me In / Suchastupid,disgustingfuckedupfuck Yellow Dog 006 (1997)

Albums:
EVERDAY YOU HATE, Finn 016 (1996)
Total Agony / Break The Limits / Fuck Off / Pieces / Empty / No Shit / In A Box / In Your Face / Never Bleed / Gotta' Explode / Monster / Syringe Kiss
UGLIER AND MORE DISGUSTING, Kron-H 09CD (1997)
Uglier And More Disgusting / Sex Machine / Miss Lords / Corpses / The Lies / Fallen Angel Crashes Dead / Dirty / Plug Me In / Wretched / As Much As You Hurt Me / 666 And Pentagrams / So Many Reasons
HOME SWEET HELL, Kron-H 14CD (1999)
Heart Of Darkness / Dellamortesque / Fucked / Home Sweet Hell / Into The Fire / The Tombs Of My Fear / Supercharged / Strategies Of Humanity / Bones / Faustian Soul / The Deathking / Motorkill / The Zoo / Rapes Of Wrath

DEMENTIA (HOLLAND)
Line-Up: Arno Burtner (vocals / guitar), Marc Faber (guitar), Ron Van Dijk (bass), Spike Baker (drums)

Den Haag Death Thrash metal men DEMENTIA came together at the tail end of the '80s. By the 'Watching At Dawn' album DEMENTIA had developed a pure Thrash style.

Albums:
WATCHING THE DAWN, Dementia (1995)
Ignorance Is Bullshit / Destiny / Inside Your World / Contradictory Emotions / C.T.P.K. / Thorn In Our Side / Regression

DEMENTIA (Sacramento, CA, USA)
Line-Up: James Torres (vocals), Anthony Gouvea (guitar), Brad Smith (bass), Daniel Davies (drums)
Previously a quintet before the departure of guitarist Laurin Lee, DEMENTIA formed in 1994 and have enjoyed a string of local successes including winning the Best Metal band award at Sacramento's 1997 Sammy Awards and gaining a track on the 'Sacramento Rocks Vol. 4' compilation.
The group also had six songs included on the soundtrack to a movie titled 'Gold Razor'.
In their short career, aggressive Metallers

DEMENTIA have opened up shows for L.A. GUNS, QUIET RIOT and Bay Area Thrashers EXODUS.

During 1997 DEMENTIA issued a 17 strong CD having previously recorded an eight track demo.

Albums:
MANIACAL, Brain Rotting Music (1997)
Smell The Coffee / Massive Mercy / Slice / Not This Time / Inside / You Looz / Ponr / Stories End / Happy Jam / No Point In Pretending / Buried Alive / Punk Junk / Zodiac / Idol Time / Child / Crucify / M.S.P.P.

DEMIGOD (FINLAND)
Line-Up: Esa Linden (vocals), Mika Naapasalo (guitar), Jussi Kiiski (guitar), Tero Laitinen (bass), Seppo Taatila (drums)

Black Thrash Metal act DEMIGOD first issued the demo 'Unholy Domain' prior to the 'Slumber Of Sullen Eyes' album. The act split after only one album. In 1993 Seppo Taatila joined ADRAMELCH. Esa Linden would also join ADRAMELCH in 1996.

Albums:
SLUMBER OF SULLEN EYES, Drowned DC008 (1993)
Apocryphal / As I Behold I Despise / Dead Soul / The Forlorn / Tears Of God / Slumber Of Sullen Eyes / Embrace The Darkness / Blood Of The Perished / Fear Obscures From Within / Transmigration Beyond Eternity / Toward The Shrouded Infinity / Perpetual Ascent / Darkened

DEMON DAGGER (PORTUGAL)
Line-Up: Pedro Mendes (vocals), Vitor Carvalho (guitar), José Figueiredo (bass), Miguel Carvalho (drums)

DEMON DAGGER date back to 1995. The band was founded as a quartet of vocalist Pedro Mendes, guitarist Vitor Carvalho, bassist José Silva and drummer Miguel Carvalho.

Silva departed in 1997. A 1997 demo featured W.C. NOISE guitarist Rodolfo Carduso as a guest.

Singles/EPs:
Soul Of Steel / A Stand Below, Recital (1999)

Albums:
AFTERSHOCK, Recital BOX002 (2000)
Etched Face / Sinking / Wrecking Wrench / A Stand Below / Broadmoor / Corundura Pursuit / Don't Look Back / Sinful Bles-sin / Sweet Turning Sour / Frenzy Wraith / Soul Of Steel

DEMON FLIGHT (USA)
Line-Up: Rick Gerard (vocals / guitar), H. Michael Osuna (guitar), Francis White (drums)

The Los Angeles band's name came to Rick Gerard as he was driving down the freeway, no doubt listening to a heavy dose of '70s British Metal along the route!

Singles/EPs:
Dead Of The Night / Search And Destroy / Flight Of The Demon, Metal Blade (1982)

DEMONSPEED (New York, NY, USA)
Line-Up: Matt Payne (vocals), Chris Shannon (guitar), Sal Villanueva (bass), Jim 'The Swing' King (drums)

Nothing if not original DEMONSPEED, musically the besuited quartet blend a bizarre amalgam of Rockabilly and Thrash that tops sinister lyrical content extolling the exploits of noted serial killers.

Albums:
SWING IS HELL, Black Pumpkin (1997)
Pogo / Fifth Of Satan / Green River / Zodiac / Threshold / Michael Landon's Ghost / King Catfish

DENATA (SWEDEN)
Line-Up: Tomas Andersson (vocals / guitar), Roger Blomberg (bass), Ponta Sjosten vocals / drums)

Retro Thrashers DENATA, comprising of former TOTAL DEATH members vocalist / drummer Ponta Sjosten and bassist Roger Blomberg alongside frontman Tomas Andersson, debuted with a 1998 EP of cover versions.

The 'Departed To Hell' album followed in 2000 before the Arctic Music Group signed DENATA for the 'Deathtrain' opus.

Singles/EPs:
Necro Erection / Stench In My Throat / The Ape At The Right Shelve / Man On The 3'rd Floor, Ghoul (1999)

Albums:
DEPARTED TO HELL, Ghoul (2000)
Intro / Necro Erection / Happy Days / Sent From Hell / Stench In My Throat / Kill You With A Saw / Mistress Of Buffalo Shit / Heavy Metal Highway / Saccharified And Grey / 666
DEATHTRAIN, Arctic Music Group (2002)
Intro / Deathtrain / 1349 / Slaughter Machine / The Black Lodge / Pentagram / Go To Hell /

Three Fingers / Upon The Hill / The Funeral / Hellish Surgery / Kill Your Roots

DENIAL (NC, USA)

<u>Albums:</u>
ANTI CHRIST PRESIDENT, Colossal NRC63 (1991)

DESECRATED DREAMS

(SLOVALKIA)
Line Up: Stano Konechy (vocals), Lubomir Michalovic (guitar), Milan Jozefek (guitar), Marek Navratil (bass), Andrej Simon (drums)

DESECRATED DREAMS deliver Death Metal with strong Thrash leanings. The band, founded in 1996 by former BARBAROSSA guitarists Lubomir Michalovic and Milan Jozefek, arrived on the scene in 1997 with the demo 'Waiting For The Last Sunset', capitalising on this with a further promotional tape 'Raven Forest' in 1998.

The opening DESECRATED DREAMS album, 2001's 'Feeling Of Guilt' issued by Metal Age Productions, saw the band fronted by Stano Konechy, with Marek Navratil on bass and Mizo Patz on drums.

Subsequently erstwhile EMBALMED and BLACK WIDOW drummer Andrej Simon would join the fold. In late 2001 Navratil

departed.

<u>Albums:</u>
FEELINGS OF GUILT, Metal Age Productions (2001)
Intro (...In The Darkest Forest) / Mirror Of Damnation / Animal / The Lost Faith / Impure / Mysteries Of The Spiritual World / Pavor Nocturnus / Angel's Whisper / Screaming Eyes / Fallen To The Sin / Breathing Fire

DESERT STORM (GERMANY)

Line-Up: Marco Scharfenort (vocals / bass), Oliver Delfs (guitar), Daniel Habenicht (guitar), Alex Spiekermann (drums)

Thrash act DESERT STORM first came to attention with their 1992 six song demo 'The Dark Half'. Featured a track on the 'Peace Eater Volume Three' compilation album. A split CD, 'Fade To Grey', was issued in 1993 prompting a full length album in 1994.

DESERT STORM played gigs in Germany with CANNIBAL CORPSE, MESSIAH, AGRESSOR and WARPATH.

The 1997 more groove orientated 'Walking Straight To The Moon' album saw the arrival of erstwhile KINGDOM COME drummer Mario Brodtrager. Post DESERT STORM Brodtrager would be involved with DR. SHIVAGO and, as 'Capt. Caracho', Nu-Metal band RISING DOWN.

Albums:
FADE TO GREY, Remedy (1993)
PERSPIRATION, Remedy 0022 (1994)
Perspiration / Stupefaction / Musical
Madness / Goblin / Desert Of Souls
WALKING STRAIGHT TO THE MOON,
Remedy (1997)
Imperil My Life / Long Way / Sucker /
Journey / Cold / Faceless / Succubi / Spirit
Of Now / Call It / The Dark Half

DESPAIR (GERMANY)
Line-Up: Robert Kampf (vocals), Marek
Grzeszek (guitar), Waldemar Sorychta
(guitar), Klaus Pachura (bass), Markus
Freiwald (drums)

DESPAIR formed in 1986 with vocalist Robert
Kampf, although the group swapped Kampf
shortly after the release of the Harris John's
produced 'History Of Hate' for new vocalist
Andreas Henschel in 1988 as the former
became head of record label Century Media.
DESPAIR were perennials on the German
Metal scene having opened for the likes of
DEATH and DEATH ANGEL even before
landing a deal. With a record under their belts
further touring in Europe ensued as guests to
acts such as ANNIHILATOR and OVERKILL.
Drummer Markus Freiwald joined FLAMING
ANGER then VOODOO CULT.
Guitarist Waldemar Sorychta founded GRIP
INC. with ex -SLAYER drummer DAVE
LOMBARDO and is also now an
accomplished producer in his own right.

Singles/EPs:
Slow Death (Live) / History Of Hate (Live) /
Young And Uncertain (Live), Century Media
(1991)

Albums:
HISTORY OF HATE, Century Media 08
9702-1 (1988)
The Enigma / Freedom Now / History Of
Hate / Constructing The Apocalypse / Slow
Death / Outconditioned / Slaves Of Power /
Joy Division / Never Trust
DECAY OF HUMANITY, Century Media 08
9712 (1990)
Decay Of Humanity / Cry For Liberty /
Delusion / Victims Of Vanity / A Distant
Territory / Silent Screaming / Radiated /
Satanic Verses
BEYOND ALL REASON, Century Media 08
9726 1 (1992)
Beyond Comprehension / Deaf And Blind /
Imported Love / The Day Of Desperation / In
The Deep / Rage In The Eyes / Burnt Out
Souls / Son Of The Wild / Crossed In Sorrow

DESTINY'S END (USA)
Line-Up: James Rivera (vocals), Dan Delucie
(guitar), Eric Halpern (guitar), Nardo Andi
(bass), Brian Craig (drums)

DESTINY'S END saw the return to action of
noted HELSTAR frontman James Rivera.
Joining him were former members of
SHADOW INSANE and NEW EDEN
drummer Brian Craig and bassist Nardo Andi
alongside erstwhile NEW EDEN, SECRET
WISDOM and CRAB NEBULA guitarist Dan
Delucie. Making up the full complement would
be guitarist Perry Grayson, a former member
of OBSCURE- an act which also included
PROTOTYPE personnel Mike Brew and
Kragen Lum alongside one time NEW EDEN
singer Mike Grant.
DESTINY'S END would sign up with Metal
Blade Records cutting their opening shot
'Breathe Deep The Dark' with producer Bill
Metoyer.
By 2000 Rivera was also fronting side outfit
RIVERA PROJECT. Despite DESTINY'S
END being announced as performing at the
German 'Bang Your Head' festival in May of
2000 Grayson decamped to concentrate on
literary work and forge a Progressive Thrash
act RELENTLESS. His place was swiftly
taken by Eric Halpern of Houston's Z LOT Z
and tribute act MINDCRIME. At 'Bang Your
Head' Rivera was even granted the honour of
performing onstage with the SCORPIONS for
a rendition of 'He's A Woman, She's A Man'.
Rivera would find himself invited back to the
'Bang Your Head' 2001 festival with a
HELSTAR reunion concert.
The band would record their second effort;
the Vivaldi infused conceptual 'Transition',
working with producer Joe Floyd of
WARRIOR. Mastering was handled by Ty
Tabor of KINGS X. However, the end results
were not initially as expected and the whole
record would be delayed for a remix in
November by Achim Kohler. 'Transition' would
eventually arrive in early 2001.
DESTINY'S END would also contribute their
take on 'Dressed In White' to a KING
DIAMOND tribute album on Necropolis
Records. It would be reported in August of
2001 that Rivera had joined FLOTSAM &
JETSAM after their longstanding vocalist Eric
A.K. departed.
Drummer Brian Craig would join Jack Frost's
SEVEN WITCHES project band in November
2001. The same month would witness a
return to action of former DESTINY'S END
man Perry M. Grayson together with vocalist
Mike Brew ('Mike Bear') with their new act
ARTISAN. Joining the duo for this new
venture would be RAPTURE guitarist Ana
Greco and drummer Matt Conley. In July of

130

ERIC HALPERN of DESTINY'S END
Photo : Nico Wobben

DAN DELUCIE of DESTINY'S END
Photo : Nico Wobben

2002 erstwhile frontman Rivera teamed up with SEVEN WITCHES, debuting with the band at the 'Classic Metal Fest II' in Cleveland, Ohio.

Albums:
BREATHE DEEP THE DARK, Metal Blade 14178 (1998)
Rebirth / Breath Deep The Dark / To Be Immortal / Idle City / The Fortress Unvanquishable / Sinister Deity / Unsolved World / Under Destruction's Thumb / Clutching At Straws / Where Do We Go? / The Obscure
TRANSITION, Metal Blade 14340 (2001)
Transition / The Watcher / A Passing Phase / The Suffering / From Dust To Life / Storm Clouds / First You Dream, Then You Die / The Legend / A Choice Of Graves / Vanished

DESTROYER (USA)
Line-Up: Michael L. Myers (vocals / guitar), Kjell Benner (bass), Mark O. Bennett (drums)

Albums:
OPTIMUM D.S.I., Screamin' Mini (1988)
Love Burns / Four On The Floor / Can We Try / Shout It Out / Grind Stone / Moron

DESTROYERS (POLAND)
Line-Up: Marek Loza (vocals / bass), Adam Stomkowski (guitar), Wojcieck Zieba (drums)

Thrash act DESTROYERS debuted with the album 'Noc Krolowej Zadzy' as a trio of frontman Marek Loza, guitarist Adam Stomkowski and drummer Wojcieck Zieba. Prior to releasing the album in an English version as 'A Night Of The Lusty Queen' album Speed Metal merchants DESTROYERS appeared on the legendary 'Metalmania' festival in Poland during 1987. The band also included four tracks on the 'Metalmania' compilation EP sharing space with fellow Poles HAMMER.
Loza would completely overhaul DESTROYERS for the follow up 'The Miseries Of Virtue' drafting guitarist Waldemar Lukoszek, bassist Waldemar Szyszko and drummer Tomasz Wlczewski.

Albums:
A NIGHT OF THE LUSTY QUEEN, Barricade (1989)
Introduction / A Terrible Anathema / Call Of Blood / Czarina's Warm Pubes / Wine And Sex / A Night Of The Lusty Queen / The Kingdom Of Evil / The Temple Of Pleasure / Angry / Bastard
THE MISERIES OF VIRTUE, Metal Muza (1991)
The Miseries Of Virtue / Histoire D'O / Oeachlet / Odyssey / Nymphomania / The Birth Of Courtesan / The Craft Of Tyranny / I Praise You, Lilith

DESTRUCTION

DESTRUCTION (GERMANY)

Line-Up: Marcel 'Schmier' Schirmer (bass / vocals), Michael Siffringer (guitar), Harold Wilkens (guitar),
Thomas Senmann (drums)

Formed in 1983 under their original title of KNIGHT OF DEMON this German Speed Metal band went on to win much acclaim and healthy album sales. The band made their recording debut when they recorded the 'Bestial Invasion' demo which featured the track 'Mad Butcher', which was to become so popular that it would feature as the leading title track on a 1987 issued EP.

The 'Eternal Devastation' album was produced by Manfred Neurer. The 'Mad Butcher' EP released in 1987 features a cover version of the PLASMATICS 'The Damned'. This release was the first with additional guitarist Harold Wilkens and new drummer Oliver Kaiser after Thomas Senmann quit the music business to become a policeman.

DESTRUCTION scored notable sales with the 'Mad Butcher' EP and with renewed fire opened for MOTÖRHEAD on their 1987 European tour including their first British show at the Brixton Academy. They kept up the momentum with their first shows in America including dates opening for SLAYER. 'Release From Agony', produced by Kalle Trapp, enabled DESTRUCTION to break into the worldwide market. DESTRUCTION returned to Britain once more in 1989 supporting CELTIC FROST promoting their live album 'Live Without Sense' which was

recorded at shows in Austria, Spain and Portugal.

In 1990 the band fired Schmier claiming his studio performances were below par. Schmier began negotiations with PAGANINI but ended up fronting a totally new outfit HEADHUNTER. Schmier's place was filled by former POLTERGEIST vocalist Andre and the resulting album 'Cracked Brain' provided fans with more of the same gut wrenching fare only let down by an appalling cover of THE KNACK's 'My Sharonna'.

In early 1991 ex-ARTILLERY vocalist Flemming Ronsdorf joined DESTRUCTION but lasted barely two weeks.

Schmier and Siffringer resolved their differences in 1999 and DESTRUCTION put in some triumphant return performances at European festivals. Sure enough the band, with new drummer Sven, signed to Nuclear Blast for the 2000 Peter Tägtgren produced album 'All Hell Breaks Loose'. As a bridge between the DESTRUCTION history of yore and the band's renewed position the classic 'Mad Butcher' track from the 1984 'Sentence Of Death' EP, a firm fan favourite, was answered with a new cut entitled 'The Butcher Strikes Back'.

Sales were strong and the album attained a number 67 position on the national German album charts. A brief warm-up tour led to European festival performances. DESTRUCTION would then hit the road as part of the 'Nuclear Blast Festival' roadshow packaged alongside HYPOCRISY, KATAKLYSM, CREMATORY and RAISE HELL. The partnership with Canadians KATAKLYSM was re-forged with American dates, which saw DYING FETUS as openers. During April 2001 the group once again entered Abyss Studios with Peter Tägtgren to record the follow up 'The Antichrist'. The album ran into a whole slew of production problems when finished copies were found to have the track order compiled incorrectly, sleeves printed in red instead of full colour and mysterious sound drop outs on the "hidden" bonus track 'Curse The Gods'. These initial mispressings would soon be snapped up by eager collectors. The problems did not end there though as the album would also be seized by Swiss customs officials but later released.

DESTRUCTION parted ways with drummer Sven Vormann during October, replacing him with Berliner Marc Reign, a veteran of ORTH and GUNJAH, in time for a nostalgic Thrash Metal mammoth tour of Germany with compatriots SODOM and KREATOR commencing 26th December in Ludwigsburg and running through into the new year.

DESTRUCTION's new studio album

MIKE of DESTRUCTION Photo : Nico Wobben

SCHMIER of DESTRUCTION Photo : Nico Wobben

projected for a 2002 release was announced as having the first 10,000 copies coming complete with a bonus CD compilation of up and coming Thrash acts.

Singles/EPs:
Mad Butcher / The Damned / Reject Emotions / The Last Judgement, Steamhammer SPV 601 897 (1987)
Decisions / I Kill Children / Things Of No importance / Smile, UAM 0447 (1994) ('Destruction' EP)

Albums:
SENTENCE OF DEATH, Steamhammer SPV NR60-1838 (1984)
Intro / Total Disaster / Black Mass / Mad Butcher / Satan's Vengeance / Devil's Soldiers
INFERNAL OVERKILL, Steamhammer SPV 081806 (1985)
Invincible Force / Death Trap / The Ritual / Tormentor / Bestial Invasion / Thrash Attack / Antichrist / Black Death
ETERNAL DEVASTATION, Steamhammer SPV 08-1885 (1986)
Curse The Gods / Confound Games / Life Without Sense / United By Hatred / Eternal Ban / Upcoming Devastation / Confused Mind
RELEASE FROM AGONY, Steamhammer SPV 087503 (1988)
Beyond Eternity / Release From Agony / Dissatisfied Existence / Sign Of Fear / Unconscious Ruins / Incriminated / Our Oppression / Survive To Die
LIVE WITHOUT SENSE (LIVE), Noise NUK126 (1989)
Curse The Gods / Unconscious Ruins / Invincible Force / Dissatisfied Existence / Reject Emotions / Eternal Ban / Mad Butcher / Pink Panther / Life Without Sense / In The Mood / Release From Agony / Bestial Invasion
CRACKED BRAIN, Noise NUK 136 (1990)
Cracked Brain / Frustrated / SED / Time Must End / My Sharrona / Rippin' You Off / Blind / Die A Day Before You're Born / No Need To Justify / When Your Mind Was Free
BEST OF, Steamhammer SPV 084-76482 CD (1992)
Intro / Total Desaster / Mad Butcher / Devil's Soldiers / Invincible Force / Death Trap / The Ritual / Tormentor / Black Death / Beyond Eternity / Release From Agony / Sign Of Fear / Incriminated / Our Oppression / Survive To Die / Confound Games / United By Hatred / Upcoming Devastation / Confused Mind / Curse The Gods / Unconscious Ruins / Thrash Attack / Reject Emotions / Mad Butcher / Pink Panther - Life

Without Sense / In The Mood - Relapse From Agony / Bestial Invasion
ALL HELL BREAKS LOOSE, Nuclear Blast (2000) **67 GERMANY**
Intro / The Final Curtain / Machinery Of Lies / Tears Of Blood / Devastation Of Your Soul / The Butcher Strikes Back / World Domination Of Pain / X-treme Measures / All Hell Breaks Loose / Total Desaster 2000 / Visual Prostitution / Kingdom Of Damnation
THE ANTICHRIST, Nuclear Blast NB0632 (2001)
Days Of Confusion / Thrash Till Death / Nailed To The Cross / Dictators Of Cruelty / Bullets From Hell / Strangulated Pride / Meet Your Destiny / Creations Of The Underworld / Godfather Of Slander / Let Your Mind Rot / The Heretic / Curse The Gods

DESTRUCTOR (USA)
Line-Up: Dave Overkill (vocals / guitar), Pat Rabid (guitar), Dave Holocaust (bass), Matt Flammable (drums)

Promising Thrash Metal band DESTRUCTOR emerged with the 1985 demo tape 'Smash Your Skull With Power'. Tragically bass player Dave Holocaust suffered an early death and DESTRUCTOR broke up.

Albums:
MAXIMUM DESTRUCTION, Auburn (1986)
Prelude In Sledge-Minor Opus 7 1st Movement / Maximum Destruction / Destructor / Take Command / Instrumental / Pounding Evil / Overdose / Iron Curtain / Hot Wet Leather / Bondage

DETENTE (San Francisco, CA, USA)
Line-Up: Dawn Crosby (vocals), Ross Robinson (guitar), Caleb Quinn (guitar), Steve Hochheiser (bass), Dennis Butler (drums)

Formed in Los Angeles in 1984 by ex-FIRST ATTACK and ALLIES frontwoman Dawn Crosby along with drummer Dennis Butler and guitarist Fred Tutone. Thrash outfit DETENTE recorded a demo tape and played around Los Angeles until the group's original bass player was fired along with Tutone. This line up shuffle heralding the arrival of the dual guitar team of Celeb Quinn and Ross Robinson plus new bassist Steve Hochheiser. This incarnation recorded the debut 'Recognize No Authority' album produced by VINNIE VINCENT INVASION bassist Dana Strum. However, following the album release DETENTE, obviously forgetting their band name, broke up in acrimonious circumstances. Guitarists Ross Robinson and

Caleb Quinn quit together with bassist Steve Hochheiser, claiming the band title for themselves. A bitter war of words ensued in which Crosby retained the DETENTE banner. Robinson later played with CATALEPSY and MURDERCAR.

The run of bad luck continued as Crosby's sole remaining band member drummer Dennis Butler was involved in a serious burn accident at a chemical plant putting the band out of action for several months. Upon his recovery DETENTE had effectively disintegrated so Butler busied himself jamming with local acts LOUD SENSELESS NOISE and VERMIN.

Crosby and Butler finally pulled DETENTE back together adding guitarists Mike Carlino and Gregg Cekalovich together with bassist George Rob.

In 1989 and now based in New Jersey, Crosby, Carlino, bassist Blair Darby recorded a three track demo 'All That Remains' in New York with Rob Hunter from RAVEN guesting on drums. The drumming stool was eventually filled a few months later by Eric Alpert.

The band would then evolve into FEAR OF GOD, an act of huge potential fronted by DÉTENTE members vocalist Dawn Crosby, guitarist Michael Carlino and bassist Blair Derby but blighted by an ever shifting line up. The band was actually signed to major label Warner Brothers by Roberta Peterson whilst still named DÉTENTE. As DETENTE they tested the market with a three track 1989 Alex Perialis produced demo tape comprising 'All That Remains', 'Deceased' and 'Waysted Time'. A further effort led by the track 'Love's Death' ensued the same year.

The band's line-up at the time included Rob 'Wacko' Hunter, drummer of NWoBHM stalwarts RAVEN. As negotiations with the label drew on Hunter bowed out and New Jersey's Eric Alpert was drafted. His tenure would be brief though and the band finally settled on Steve Cordova to occupy the drum stool.

It was discovered that the band name DÉTENTE had already been registered so initial recordings were convened under the band name SEDITION. The album tapes for 'Within The Veil' would be re-mixed for release by Andy Wallace and with due process of time the group evolved into FEAR OF GOD.

After a chaotic career FEAR OF GOD collapsed when Crosby's well documented reliance on drugs and alcohol caught up with her. On December 15th 1996 she died tragically young of acute liver failure.

Ross Robinson would go on to become a much sought after high profile producer being given large credit for the rising careers of acts such as KORN, MACHINE HEAD and

SLIPKNOT.

Albums:
RECOGNISE NO AUTHORITY, Roadrunner RR 9695 (1986)
Losers / Russian Roulette / It's Your Fate / Holy War / Catalepsy / Shattered Illusions / Life Is Pain / Blood I Bleed / Widows Walk / Vultures In The Sky

DETERIORATE (USA)

Line-Up: Mike Trush (vocals / bass), Joe Gorski (guitar), Frank Jerovante (guitar), Rich Yurgevich (drums)

A Pennsylvania Thrash / Death outfit founded during June of 1991 that, following line up changes after the debut 1993 album 'Rotting In Hell', would drift into Black Metal territory. The band issued a 1994 demo 'Gather The Nebbish' with a line up retaining only original guitarists Joe Gorski and Frank Jerovante. New faces would be vocalist Gannon, bass player Thorous and drummer Dark Woods. Tracks from the demo session would reappear as part of the 1996 album 'The Senectuous Entrance'.

Albums:
ROTTING IN HELL, JL America (1993)
Agonized Display / A Thousand Years Of Anguish / Cannibal Autopsy / Devoured / The Sufferance / Rotting In Hell / Asphyxiation Cremation / Shadows Of Death / Beyond The Grave / Decomposed Anatomy
THE SENECTUOUS ENTRANCE, Pulverizer (1996)
The Senectuous Entrance / In The Presence Of Eurus / Xipe Totec / Stealing Strength From The Ivory Boar / Kiev: 1237 / Religious Fatum / Ode To A Mortal / Davea Come... / Gather The Nebbish / Evaporated Battle Ground

DETONATION (HOLLAND)

Line-Up: Koen Romeijn (vocals / guitar), Mike Ferguson (guitar), Otto Schimmelpenninck (bass), Thomas Kalksma (drums)

Founded in 1997, originally entitled INFERNAL DREAM, the band evolved into DETONATION in 1998. The band's line up comprised ex-ENGORGE vocalist / guitarist Koen Romeijn, former GRASMOAIER guitarist Mike Ferguson and Thomas Kalksma of FLAMING FIST on drums. The band persevered without a bassist until ENTROPION's Otto Schimmelpenninck took on the role. DETONATION debuted with two tracks on the

January 1999 'Crushed Skull' compilation. A self financed four track EP, 'Lost Euphoria', followed.

DETONATION toured as support to ORPHANAGE in April of 2001. The band are projecting a full length album, provisionally titled 'An Epic Defiance', for 2002.

Singles/EPs:
Failure To Commit / Euphoric Loss / Reflections Of A Torn Spirit / Helplessness, (2000) ('Lost Euphoria' EP)

DETONATORS (USA)
Line-Up: Bruce Wartnell (vocals / guitar), Juan Camacho (guitar), Pat Fargher (bass), Eric Capucci (drums)

Albums:
JUST ANOTHER REASON, National Trust (1987)
Resistance / Something I Don't Believe / Just Another Reason / Charcoal Alley / Beyond Control / Child Psychology / Ammunition / Now / Gotta Be A Threat / Yer Child's War / Electroshock Therapy / Prison Bus / It's Safe

DETRITUS (UK)
Line-Up: Mark Broomhead (vocals / bass), Earl Morris (guitar), Andy Neal (guitar), Andy Bright (drums)

Bristol based Christian Thrash Metal band DETRITUS enrolled noted sleeve designer Rodney Matthews contributed to album cover artwork.

Despite attaining serious sales with the 'Perpetual Defiance' album DETRITUS folded after the 1993 effort 'If But For One'. Frontman Mark Broomhead would join up with another high profile Christian Thrash outfit SEVENTH ANGEL and, after that band's demise, founded LOVE LIES BLEEDING with erstwhile SEVENTH ANGEL and AMARANTH guitarist Simon Bibby. With the addition of drummer Adam Gallagher and keyboard player Scott James this band duly evolved into FIRE FLY issuing a 1999 EP 'Swings & Roundabouts'.

Albums:
PERPETUAL DEFIANCE, Under One Flag FLAG 55 (1991)
Subliminal Division / Point Of No Return / Playing With Fire / Taste The Blood / Morbid Curiosity / No Mercy / Child / Eviction / Derange / OTT
IF BUT FOR ONE, Kingsway ECD7030 (1993)
Masquerade / So Far Away / D.I.G.M. / Let Peace Begin With Me / Feel / Blindly

Rejected / If But For One / Sailor's Farewell / Father To Son / Painted Reality / As It Reigns / Subtle Shades

DEUCE (Laurel, MD, USA)
Line-Up: Tom Gattis (vocals / guitar), Timmy Meadows (guitar), Chris Hall (bass), Billy Giddings (drums)

Formed in 1978 by guitarist Tom Gattis, the Baltimore heavyweights' first line-up featured vocalist Eddie Day (hired because he was a soundalike for CHEAP TRICK's Robin Zander and quickly dispensed with!) guitarist MARTY FRIEDMAN, bassist Steve Leter and drummer Chris Tinto. The latter duo were soon replaced by Chris Hall and Billy Giddings respectively. Gattis took over vocal chores after Day's departure.

Friedman quit for the sunnier climate of Hawaii and eventually found fame as a member of MEGADETH via Hawaii acts VIXEN and HAWAII. His replacement, Timmy Meadows, joined the fold in 1980.

Meadows was the brother of ANGEL's Punky Meadows and had been a member of the ANGEL roadcrew in the '70s.

DEUCE released a self-financed single in 1981, quickly earning themselves comparisons with British Metal acts by merging viciously precise twin guitar work with raw NWoBHM like aggression.

In 1982 Hall left the group and DEUCE were thus joined by Mike Francis, a former compatriot of Meadows' on the ANGEL roadcrew. This line-up completely revamped a demo tape recorded after the single and both feature the DEUCE rendition of the Marty Friedman penned 'Angels In The Dust'

The band changed their name to TENSION prior to recording their proposed debut album. However, a Duluth, Georgia based record label titled O.P.M. Records released an album full of DEUCE demo material with the blessing of the band, despite having the appearance of a bootleg.

The first four tracks and tracks six to nine were recorded between 1978 and 1979 whilst tracks five and ten were cut between 1979 and 1980 with Timmy Meadows on guitar.

Gattis was last seen as a member of Heavy Metal band WARDOG touting the 'Scorched Earth' album. Post WARDOG Gattis announced the formation of a new band entitled AFTERBURN, a reunion with erstwhile TENSION colleague Tim O'Connor on bass, Bulgarian master guitarist Peter Petev and ex-VYPER and PRIZONER drummer Michael Scott . The title of this new venture would later be switched to BALLISTIC.

Singles/EPs:
I'm Saved / Bad Boys, (1981)

Albums:
DEUCE, OPM Records OPMR 1000 (1999)
Barnburner / Angels From The Dust / 72
Hours / One Nation Underground / Bad Boys
/ Atomic Age / Telemann's 3rd / Love's
Massive Suicide / Lords Of The Universe /
I'm Saved

DEVASTATION (TX, USA)
Line-Up: Rodney Runsmore (vocals), Dave
Burk (guitar), Edward Vasquez (bass), Jesse
Lopez (drums)

Not to be confused with the Chicago
Thrashers of the same name that evolved into
SINDROME.
The Texan DEVESTATION specialised in
intense Thrash metal. Bolstered their live
sound for the 'Signs of life' album by adding
second guitarist Henry Elizondo.
Drummer Louis Carrisalez quit in mid 1990.
He later turned up fronting DEATH for a short
spell on a British tour with KREATOR in 1990
when vocalist / guitarist Chuck Schuldiner
was unable to fulfill the dates.
Carrisalez's place was taken by David Lozano
for the 'Idolatry' album but the band had
reinstated Carrisalez by the time they played
the 'Milwaukee Metalfest'.

Albums:
VIOLENT TERMINATION, Zombo ZR 0269
(1986)
(Intro) Beginning Of The End / Massive
Devastation / Innocent Submission /
Syndrome Of Terror / Violent Termination /
Death Is Calling / Meet Your Maker / Insanity
/ Deceptive Slaughter / Beneath The Surface
SIGNS OF LIFE, Under One Flag CDFLAG
44 (1989)
Eye For An Eye / Desolation: Manic
Depressive / Signs Of Life / Retribution /
Tomorrow We Die / Contaminated / Fear Of
The Unknown / Escape To Violence
IDOLATRY, Combat (1991)
Deliver The Suffering / Freewill / Forsaken
Hatred / Souls Of Sacrifice / Idolatry /
Legacy Of Faith / Subconscious / Never
Believe

DEVIANT (UK)
Line Up: Jes 'Dredd' Williamson (vocals), Al
Hella (guitar), Izzy Rider (bass), Paul
Torquemada (drums)

Norfolk Speed Metal band DEVIANT were
formed in 1987 and released the
'Dreamscape' three track demo in 1988,
shortly followed by a further demo 'Lambs To
The Slaughter'.
The band had one of their songs, 'The Slayer',
featured on the 'Taste Of Armageddon'
compilation album in 1989.

Singles/EPs:
In Pursuit Of Happiness / Masquerade /
Say It To My Face, Deviant (1991)

DEVIANT Seattle, WA, USA)

Seattle Thrash Metal act DEVIANT emerged
with the 1988 demo tape 'Faces Of Death'.

Albums:
BALANCE OF POWER, Rumble Gully
(1991)

DEVIATE (BELGIUM)
Line-Up: Danny Mouethwil (vocals), Michael
Kirby (guitar), Xavier Decoster (bass),
Laurens Kusters (drums)

DEVIATE are the product of an amalgamation
between Thrash act SIXTY NINE and
Hardcore outfit MENTAL DISTURBANCE in
1991. DEVIATE industriously established
their own label, I Scream Records, to issue
the debut 1992 Frank von Bogaet produced
'Small Traces Of Life' debut. The band would
go on to tour Europe as support to FEAR
FACTORY in May 1993 and put in further
dates alongside EXCEL the September
promoting the second record, 'Crisis Of
Confidence' produced by Andr Gielen.
The 'Cold Prejudice' album was issued as a
Belgian only limited edition release, selling
out of it's pressing in a mere two weeks.
During 1996 the band, adding second
guitarist Jo, participated in the inaugural
'Vans Warped' tour. The same year DEVIATE
relocated to New York, releasing the Jamie
Locke produced 'Thorn Of The Living' album
the following year. MADBALL's Freddy Cricien
would lend his session vocals to the track
'Last Judgement'.
Touring in Europe found the band as part of
the December 'Mad X-Mas' tour billed
alongside BACKFIRE. The band enhanced
their reputation in Europe with a showing at
the infamous 'Dynamo' festival in Holland.
'State Of Grace' arrived in June 1999 and
subsequently licensed for American release
through Too Damn Hype Records. DEVIATE
toured Japan during September of 1999,
tapes from which spawned the live album
'One By One'.
The band put in a further date in Japan in
February 2002, performing at the mammoth
SLAYER headlined Yokohama 'Beast Feast'

festival.

Singles/EPs:
My Colour And Sickness, I Scream 900 0305 24 (1993)

Albums:
SMALL TRACES OF LIFE, I Scream 900 0300 21 (1992)
Intro / Step To Me / Small Traces Of Life / Children's Whispers / One Against / Across The Nation / I Judge / Extro
CRISIS OF CONFIDENCE, I Scream 900 0306 20 (1993)
Intro / Sickness / End Of A Fiction / Crisis Of Confidence / Mantrack / Case For The Prosecution / Oppression / In Order To Strike / Indicate The Reason / Deface / My Color
WRECK STYLE, I Scream 88 896 02 (1997)
Wreck Style / Sequel Of Arrogance / Spread A Threat / Strain / Falling Down / Face It / Crack-Down / Fearless State / Spoiled For Peace / Depth / Days Of Living / Conviction / Come Into View / Cold Prejudice / Inner Days / Neurotic / Only Nether World
COLD PREJUDICE, I Scream (1996)
Intro / Cold Prejudice / Inner Days / Neurotic / Only Neither World
THORN OF THE LIVING, I Scream (1997)
Thorn Of The Living / Darkened World / Redemption Days / Lawless Innocence / Last Judgement / Cold Snap / Surge To Victory / Disgraced / Sworn Chains / 21st Century / Eyewitness / Realness / Half-Life / Divisions Of Pain
DARKENED WORLD, I Scream (1998)
Crisis Of Confidence / Sickness / Spread A Threat / Sequel Of Arrogance / Cold Prejudice / Inner Days / Darkened World
ONE BY ONE, I Scream (1999)
Last Judgement / Thorn Of The Living / Cold Prejudice / Redemption Days / One By One / Spread A Threat / Only Neither World / After Time / Divisions Of Pain / 21st Century / Cold Snap / Wreck Style / Lawless Innocence
STATE OF GRACE, I Scream (1999)
Wounds Of Time / State Of Grace / Stepped Off / Empty World / Aftertime / Circle Of Friends / Dawn Of Mankind / Burned Out / One By One / Broken Angel / Low-Down / Walk With Death
RED ASUNDER, (2001)

DEVIL CHILDE (USA)
Line-Up: Lucifer (guitar), Matthew Hopkins (drums)

Anonymous Thrash outing. In reality guitarist 'Lucifer' is Jack Starr, previously a member of VIRGIN STEELE and presently with BURNING STARR whilst drummer 'Matthew Hopkins' is RAVEN / PENTAGRAM man Joe Hasselvander.

Albums:
DEVIL CHILDE, (1984)
Devil Childe / Rain Of Terror / Son Of A Witch / Repent Or Die / Thru The Shadow / Grave Robber / Beyond The Grave

DEW SCENTED (GERMANY)
Line-Up: Leif Jensen (vocals), Ralf Klein (guitar), Jörg Szittnick (guitar), Patrick Heims (bass), Taref Stinshoff (drums)

Germany's DEW SCENTED, despite their innocuous title, trade in a vicious amalgam of Thrash Hardcore Doom Heavy Metal.
DEW SCENTED made their intentions clear with the 1994 opening demo 'Symbolization'. Further exposure would be gained with the inclusion of the 'Poems Of Dirt' track on a 1995 Major Records compilation. These sessions would lead to a recording contract with the Steamhammer label for the 1996 'Immortelle' record.
The 'Innoscent' album would include a cover version of OVERKILL's 'Fatal If Swallowed'. During late 1999 DEW SCENTED drummer Uwe Werning would loan himself to NIGHT IN GALES for tour work.
DEW SCENTED returned in January 2001 with the 'Inwards' album, produced by ex-HOLY MOSES guitarist Andy Classen. The band would tour Japan during March of 2001 billed alongside NIGHT IN GALES and DEFLESHED. The group's 2001 release 'Inwards' would see a January 2002 issue in Japan courtesy of Soundholic Records. Japanese versions included an exclusive track, a cover of SLAYER's 'War Ensemble'.
DEW SCENTED's line-up shifted over the years, latterly the band comprising vocalist Leif Jensen, guitarist Florian Müller, bassist Patrick Heims and drummer Uwe Werning.
The band tagged onto the Thrash renaissance joining DESTRUCTION, KREATOR and SODOM on the 'Hell Comes To Your Town' tour for dates in Holland and Belgium during early 2002.

Albums:
IMMORTELLE, Steamhammer SPV 085-18262 (1996)
In Flames / Silenced / Black Is The Day / Thirst For The Sun / Unending / Afterlife / Afterlove / ...Yonder... / Beloved Elysium / For You And Forever / Poets Of Dirt / Native Soil Venus / Theory Of Harm
INNOSCENT, GSM (1998)
Shatteredinsanity / Bereaved / Burn With Me

DEW SCENTED

/ Starspangled / The Sicker Things / Everred / The Grapes Of Wrath / Aentity / Underneath / Fatal If Swallowed
ILL NATURED, GSM (1999)
Embraced By Sin / This Grace / Simplicity In Chaos / Apocalypse Inside / Defiance / Wounds Of Eternity / Idolized / Skybound / The Endless / Hear See Say No...
INWARDS, Nuclear Blast (2002)
Bitter Conflict / Unconditional / Life Ending Path / Inwards / Blueprints Of Hate / Locked In Motion / Degeneration / Terminal Mindstrip / Feeling Not / Reprisal

DIAMOND CLAW (USA)

Line-Up: Debra Lynn Billingsley (vocals),
Jenny Thornburg (guitar),
Mary Jo Godges (bass),
Pamela Renee Galloway (drums)

Albums:
NO HATE IN PARADISE, Blackjack (1987)
Hail To The Queen / No Hate In Paradise / Enhance Romance / Shooting Star / Danger Eyes

DIE KREUZEN (USA)

Line-Up: Danny Kubinski (vocals / guitar), Brian Egeness (guitar), Keith Brammer (bass), Erik Tunison (drums)

A truly innovative Wisconsin Crossover Metal act that covered a wider spectrum of genres than most. The band were notable for constantly shifting the parameters of their music with each successive release taking in Punk, Thrash and Hardcore elements. DIE KREUZEN was founded during 1981 by

vocalist Dan Kubinski and guitarist Brian Egeness who both relocated from Rockford, Illinois, with bassist Keith Brammer and drummer Erik Tunison. The title 'DIE KREUZEN' was apparently deliberately chosen to add to their mystique and avoid genre tagging.

The band's inaugural public offering would come in the form of four songs donated to the 'Noise' magazine cassette 'Charred Remains' compilation. This would be capitalised on by three further tracks as part of another compilation collection, 'The Master Tape'. The exposure afforded by these releases led in turn to the 7" EP 'Cows And Beer', issued by the Version Sound label in late 1982. This record soon sold out of it's initial 1,000 copy pressing, a second run of similar quantity also soon being swallowed up. DIE KREUZEN promoted the release by touring the West Coast and down South into the summer of 1983.

A debut full length album, released by the Touch & Go label in July 1984, proved an immediate seller and was the catalyst for a solid two years of road work.

A second album, 'October File', emerged in May 1986 followed by July 1988's 'Century Days'. After road work in Europe DIE KREUZEN cut a single 'Gone Away', one of the B sides for which was a rework of AEROSMITH's 'Seasons Of Wither'.

At this juncture various members indulged themselves in side concerns. Brammer and Kubinski busied themselves with Darren Brown and Eric Lunde's proto industrial band BOY DIRT CAR. Brammer would also perform with WRECK whilst the industrious Kubinski managed to also allocate time for IMPACT

TEST 1990, WAR ON THE SAINTS and THE MUCKRAKERS. Both Kubinski and Egeness formed part of CHEAP TRICK homage band CHICK TREAT. Eventually regrouping DIE KREUZEN delivered their fourth album for Touch & Go, 'Cement'.

In April of 1992 DIE KREUZEN opted to disband, apparently prompted by Egeness' decision to make an exit. The surviving trio soon re-gelled as CHAINFALL, pulling in S.O.D.A. and NERVE TWINS guitarist Charles Jordan. Other endeavours found Kubinski and Tunison as members of the quaintly titled FUCKFACE whilst Brammer dabbled with THE CARNIVAL STRIPPERS. Kubinski would later re-emerge touting a fresh act CUSTOM GRAND.

Singles/EPs:
The School / Think For Me / Hate Me / Pain / Don't Say Please / Enemies, Version Sound (1983) ('Cows And Beer' EP)
Gone Away / Different Ways (Live), Touch & Go (1988) (Limited edition white vinyl 7" single)
Gone Away / Seasons Of Wither / Man In The Trees (Live) / Bitch Magnet (Live) / Number Three (Live), Touch & Go T&G40 (1988) (12" single)
Pink Flag / Land Of Treason, Touch & Go T&G65 (1990)
Big Bad Days / Gone Away (Acoustic), Touch & Go T&G79 (1991)
Albums:
DIE KREUZEN, Touch & Go T&GLP4 (1986)
Rumors / This Hope / In School / I'm Tired / On The Street / Enemies / Get 'Em / Fighting / No Time / All White / Pain / Sick People / Hate Me / Live Wire / Not Anymore / Mannequin / Fuckups / Think For Me / Dirt And Decay / Don't Say Please / No Name
OCTOBER FILE, Touch & Go T&GLP7 (1987)
Man In The Trees / Uncontrolled Passion / It's Been So Long / Imagine A Light / Cool Breeze / Counting Cracks / Red To Green / Among The Ruins / Hear And Feel / Hide And Seek / Conditioned / There's A Place / Open Lines / Melt / Rumors / This Hope / In School / I'm Tired / On the Streets / Enemies / Get 'Em / Fighting / No Time / All White / Pain - Sick People / Hate Me / Live Wire / Not Anymore / Mannequin / Fuckups / Think For Me / Dirt And Decay / Don't Say Please / No Name
CENTURY DAYS, Touch & Go T&G30 (1988)
Earthquakes / Lean Into It / Different Ways / So Many Times / These Days / Elizabeth / Stomp / Slow / The Bone / Bitch Magnet / Number Three / Dream Sky / Halloween

GONE AWAY, Touch & Go T&G73CD (1990)
Gone Away / Seasons Of Whither / Pink Flag / Land Of Treason / Stomp / Cool Breeze / Man In The Trees / Bitch Magnet / Number Three / Different Ways / In School / Think For Me / Hate Me / Pain / Don't Say Please / Enemies / On The Street / All White / Fighting
CEMENT, Touch & Go T&G80 (1991)
Wish / Shine / Big Bad Days / Holes / Downtime / Blue Song / Best Goodbye / Heaven / Deep Space / Shake Loose / Over And The Edge / Black Song

DIGGER (GERMANY)
Line-Up: Chris Boltendahl (vocals), Uwe Lulis (guitar), Chris F. Brank (bass), Albert Eckhardt (drums)

Eschewing their more familiar Heavy Metal guise GRAVEDIGGER, pulling in former S.A.D.O. bassist Chris F. Brank, became DIGGER and attempted a much mellower direction. Career wise the album was an unmitigated disaster.

Vocalist Chris Boltendahl and guitarist Uwe Lulis then founded the short-lived HAWAII but failed to progress further than a solitary demo.

Inevitably they reformed GRAVE DIGGER and are still a going concern.

Albums:
STRONGER THAN EVER, Noise NO (1986)
Wanna Get Close / Don't Leave Me Lonely / Stronger Than Ever / Lay It On / Don't Need Your Love / Listen To The Music / Stay Till The Morning / Stand Up And Rock / Shadows Of The Past

DIMPLE MINDS (GERMANY)
Line-Up: Ladde (vocals), Speedy (guitar), Ole (guitar), Mao (bass), Martin P. (drums)

Created in 1986 DIMPLE MINDS have made themselves household names on the German rock scene with their alcoholic image and Heavy Prollcore music.

The band shifted some 500 copies of their debut demo enabling a deal with No Remorse Records and issuing the EP 'Blau Auf'm Bau'. By This time drummer Martin P. had been ousted by Todde Larisch. He in turn was to depart and in came Michael Hirch.

Following DIMPLE MINDS first headline tour of Germany with support acts LIAR and THE IDIOTS the band split away from No Remorse for a fresh deal with SPV Steamhammer.

The liaison proved fruitful for both parties as the next album 'Volle Kanne Live' sped straight into the national charts. A further album followed quickly and once more DIMPLE MINDS were out on the road this time with opening act KGB.

With the 'Helden Der Arbeit' album of 1991, produced by Charlie Bauerfeind, Hirch had quit and plugging the gap was Bangjamin Meier.

By 1996 Hirch had returned to the fold. DIMPLE MINDS had seemingly run out of lyrics connected with beer and drinking and were pursuing more cerebral themes.

Singles/EPs:
Blau Auf'm Bau / Feuer Und Eis / Alkoliker / Unter Strom / Außer Rand Und Band, No Remorse NRR 1002 (1988) ('Blau Auf'm Bau' EP)

Blau Auf'm Bau / Trinker An Die Macht, No Remorse (1989) (7" single)

Albums:
TRINKER AN DIE MACHT, No Remorse (1988)
Hausfrau / Böse Buben / 1.ooo Huren / Halb Mensch, halb Tier / Akne / Arme Teufel / Trinker an die Macht / Gummi & Leder / Nonnentanz / Krawattenmörder / Deutsche Gemütlichkeit / Im Suff

VOLLE KELLE LIVE, Steamhammer SPV (1990)
Intro (The Number Of Erwin) / Blau Auf'm Bau / Hausfrau / Böse Buben / Halb Mensch, Halb Tier / Außer Rand Und Band / Gummi Und Leder / Feuer Und Eis / Trinker An Die Macht / Nonnentanz / Deutsche Gemütlichkeit / Alkoholiker / Hausfrau (Demo Version)

DURSTIGE MÄNNER, Steamhammer SPV 008-76201 (1990)
Asozial / Hals Über Kopf / Gangster in Grün / Verbotene Früchte / Teenage Rebel / Durstige Männer / Erkannt, Erwischt, Entmündiget / 100 Kilo Fleisch / Wehr-Wolf / Meister Propper

HELDEN DER ARBEIT, Steamhammer SPV 084-76362 (1991)
Helden Der Arbeit / Keine Komplimente / Giggolo / Unternehmen Untergang / Immer Tiefer / Gossentraum / Spanische Fliege / Lesen Macht Dumm / Ex-Exhibitionist / Flucht Nach Vorn / Egel oder Engel / Party Pur

DIE BESTEN TRINKEN AUS, Steamhammer SPV (1993)
Die Besten Trinken Aus / Katastropenengel / Nachbarn / Amputator III / Tätowierter Taugenix / Zombies Auf Schnee / Pfandpiraten / Rauchende Colts / Die Nacht Zum Tag / Lebensmüde / Miss Godzilla / Somebody Put Something In My Drink /

Hoden Von Eisen / Blumenkinder

DURCH UND DURCH DURCH – LIVE IN ALZHEIM, Steamhammer SPV (1995)
Amputator III / Unternehmen Untergang / Katastrophengel / Gossentraum / Verbotene Früchte / Unter Strom / Lebensmüde / Tätowierter Taugemix / Asozial / Hoden Von Eisen / Pfandpiraten / Die Besten Trinken Aus / Im Suff... /Durstige Männer / Blau Auf'm Bau / Alkoholiker

MAXIMUM DEBILIUM, Steamhammer SPV 085-18332-2 (1996)
Denen Man Nichts Vergibt / Malen Nach Zahlen / Die Null In Mir / Schattenboxen / Schwarzer Frühling / Weiße Mäuse / Benzin / Unsichtbarer Feind / Wir Sind Debil / Falsche Freunde / Anders Sein / Hautnah / Prime Mover / Der Schrei

DRUNK ON ARRIVAL, Under Siege (1997)
Deposit Pirates / The Best Finish Their Drinks / Found, Filmed, Fucked / Gutterdream / Head Over Heals / Balls Of Iron / Operation Downfall / Hooked On Death And Pain / Thirsty Men / Sick Of Life / Forbidden Fruit / Tracy Lords / Smelly Tattooed Loser / White Trash / Somebody Put Something In My Drink

DER MAURER UND DER KOENIG, SPV (1998)
Hausfrau / Böse Buben / 1000 Huren / Halb Mensch, Halb Tier / Akne / Arme Teufel / Trinker An Die Macht / Gummi & Leder / Nonnentanz / Krawattenmörder / Deutsche Gemütlichkeit / Im Suff / Blau Auf'm Bau / Feuer Und Eis / Alkoholiker / Unter Strom / Außer Rand Und Band

HAPPY HOUR, SPV (1999)
Brotlose Kunst / Happy Hour / Was Wir Wollen / Verwundete / Krieger / Kamikaze Bleifuss / Kuschelpapst / Du Bist Schuld / Marlene / Dosenkavalier / Barfuss Oder Lackschuh / Hoffnungsloser Fall / James Dean / Quit Playing Games

MONSTER HITS - BEST OF, SPV (1999)
Durstige Männer / Wir Sind Debil / Pfandpiraten / Benzin / Die Besten Trinken Aus / Verbotene Früchte (Live) / Nonnentanz / Gossentraum / Unsichtbarer Feind / Hoden Von Eisen (Live) / Erkannt, Erwischt, Entmündigt / Helden Der Arbeit / Malen Nach Zahlen / Ausser Rand Und Band / Party Pur / Taetowierter Taugenix / Unternehmen Untergang / Blau Auf'm Bau (Live) / Alkoholiker (Live) / Im Suff (Live)

DISCIPLES OF POWER
(CANADA)
Line-Up: Hart Bachmier (vocals / guitar), Wes Sontag (guitar), Andy Smith (bass), Dean Relf (drums)

Founded in Medicine Hat, Alberta in 1985,

141

from the ashes of WARTHORN, DISCIPLES OF POWER are one of Canada's longest running Metal acts. The driving force behind the band has always been founder Hart Bachmier who relocated the band to Edmonton in 1987. After a quick demo called 'Kutulu' in 1987 and another called 'Power Of Death', they appeared on a local, vinyl compilation called 'Writing In Stone' in 1988. DISCIPLES OF POWER were early enough on the Metal scene to score a reasonably secure deal with Fringe Records and they relocated to Ottawa.

In 1989 they released their debut album 'Power Trap' and toured Canada. The band relocated again briefly to Vancouver where they produced a video for the track 'Crisis'. Yet another relocation and line-up change found the band back in Edmonton where they recorded their second Fringe album, 'Ominous Prophecy'. More touring followed and the over the next few years the band received critical acclaim for their Death-Thrash style. The band filmed a video for the track 'Nature's Fury' and hosted the 'Power Hour', Much Music's metal video specialty show.

After two releases on Fringe, the band decided to go the independent route releasing another album entitled 'Invincible Enemy' on their own Mindt Gash label. They shot another video followed for the track 'Before The End' and more touring followed. 1993 was a busy year for the band as DISCIPLES OF POWER released a total re-working of their debut 'Power Trap' also on Mindt Gash. Another video was shot in Edmonton this time for the title track of the re-issue subtitled, 'The Brutal Re-mix'.

In 1995 the band release their 4th full-length 'Mechanikill'. This album was not as well received and the band toured Western Canada very sporadically for the next several years while the band members pursue other projects. Despite many line-up changes the band has a solid reputation, not only for their intense, technical Death Metal but also for their professional image and attitude enhanced by steady touring, videos and the excellent artwork. Steve Chandler provided the art for the first two releases and the following three were done by Shane Hawco of THORAZINE.

In 2000 the band decided to regroup and began writing and touring a little more extensively including headlining the inaugural show of the 'Okanagan Metal Fest' in Oliver, BC. in the summer of 2001. A further album, 'In Dust We Trust', is projected for release also on the Mindt Gash label.

Albums:
POWER TRAP, Fringe (1989)
Shades Of Grey / Powertrap / Ice Demons / Slave To No One / Protector / Night Of The Priest / Crisis / Hidden Worlds / Bitch Of Doom / Disciples Of Power.

OMINOUS PROPHECY, Fringe (1992)
Chains Of Reason / Vindicator / Nature's Fury (Betrayed Earth) / Witch Of Lies / Sleeping Dead / The Rising / Skull March / Eternal Purgatory

INVINCIBLE ENEMY, Mindt Gash PPC003 (1993)
Afterbirth / Invincible Enemy / Infected Science / Born Unto Death / Injecticide / Lords Of Creation / Return From The Gates / Before The End

MECHANIKILL, Mindt Gash (1996)
Introvenus / Wings Of Suicide / Cast The First Stone / Inside (Circles Of Sickness) / Crypts Of The Frozen Soul / Swarming The Throne / Mechanikill / Symphonic Animosity / Waraphoric Structures (Part 1 & 2).

IN DUST WE TRUST, Mindt Gash (2002)
The Cursing Of Winter / Tripwire / Armoured Ring Of Skull / Widows Web / Pharmaceutical Suicide / In Dust We Trust / Dimensions Of The Dragon Sky / Wartorn

DISINCARNATE (USA)
Line-Up: Tomas Lindberg (vocals), James Murphy (guitar), Steve DiGeorgio (bass), Nick Barker (drums)

Although a veteran journeyman guitarist for hire on the Death scene guitarist JAMES MURPHY (whose credits include AGENT STEEL, DEATH, TESTAMENT, CANCER, OBITUARY and KONKHRA) also has time for his own act DISINCARNATE.

The band was reassembled in 1999 with a line-up of Murphy, ex-AT THE GATES singer Tomas Lindberg, SADUS / DEATH bassist Steve DiGeorgio and CRADLE OF FILTH drummer Nick Barker. Before any product could be issued Barker joined DIMMU BORGIR.

Murphy has issued two solo albums to date 'Convergence' in 1996 and 1999's 'Feeding The Machine'.

Albums:
DREAMS OF THE CARRION KIND, Roadrunner (1993)
De Profundis / Stench Of Paradise Burning / Beyond The Flesh / In Sufferance / Monarch Of The Sleeping Marches / Soul Erosion / Entranced / Confine Of Shadows / Deadspawn / Sea Of Tears / Immemorial Dream

DISSENSION (USA)

Albums:
WHY WORK FOR DEATH?, Metal Storm (1986)
Why Work For Death? / B.B.B. / Average American Kid / Hypocrite / Sole Survivor / Telling Me / Fate / Blackout / You Know Who / Dissension / Unoptional Conformity

DISTRUST (Plaistow, NH, USA)
Line-Up: Shawn Hutchins (vocals), Travis Horton (guitar), David Ulrich (bass), Kevin Royer (drums)

The original incarnation of New Hampshire's DISTRUST was founded in 1995 but had split by 1998. Vocalist Shawn Hutchins retained the name to assemble a fresh band cutting the 2000 'No Good Deed Shall Go Unpunished' album.

Albums:
NO GOOD DEED SHALL GO UNPUNISHED, (2000)
Personality Instability / Don't Wait For Dawn / No Government Cheese / Threshold / Forget The Past / Fleshless Bitch / Misery Is In Season / Bloodstorm / Breaking The Pain Barrier

DOFKA (USA)
Line-Up: Scot Edgell (vocals), Jim Dofka (guitar / bass / keyboards), Casey Culbreth (drums)

The DOFKA album was re-issued in America on CD in 1998.

Albums:
TOXIC WASTELAND, Black Dragon (1990)
Dragons / Vampire's Curse / Where The Monsters Live / Toxic Wasteland / Intro Solo / Guitar Opera / There Is No More / Speed Mental / Doctor Of Death / Taken All We Had / Pick Monsters / Can't Make It Alone

DOMINION (UK)
Line-Up: Michelle Richfield (vocals), Mass Firth (vocals / guitar),
Arno Cagna (vocals / guitar),
Danny North (bass), Bill Law (drums)

Starting life as Thrash influenced outfit BLASPHEMER in 1995 over numerous demo recordings BLASPHEMER evolved into DOMINION promoting session singer and erstwhile ballet student Michelle Richfield to the lead vocalist role. However, her angelic strains still compete in the mix with the Death growls of guitarists Mass Firth and Arno

Cagna.
The track 'Alive?' on the debut features MY DYING BRIDE's Ade on vocals.
DOMINION offered two bizarre cover versions to the 1998 Peaceville Records compilation album 'X' in TEARS FOR FEARS 'Shout' and the ROLLING STONES ' Paint It Black'.
Drummer Bill Law joined MY DYING BRIDE for their '34.788%... Complete' album in 1998.

Albums:
INTERFACE, Peaceville CDVILE63 (1996)
Tears From The Star / Millennium / Silhouettes / Alive? / Weaving Fear / The Voyage / Deep Into Me / Impulse / Conspire To Me / Hollowvision
BLACKOUT, Peaceville (1998)
Blackout / Release / Covet / Distortion / Ill Effect / Today's Tomorrow / Down / Prism / Threshold / Unseen / Fuelling Nothing

DOOMWATCH (USA)
Line-Up: Daniel Klasnick (vocals / guitar), Jeff Cherep (guitar),
Garry Mintz (bass), Blair Powell (drums)

Pittsburgh Thrash Metal band DOOMWATCH date to 1986. Following the 'Final Hour' EP a series of demos ensued prior to the 1989 'A Symphony Of Decadence' album.
In later years drummer Blair Powell would be spotted in the BAD GENES and as stand up bassist for Psychobilly band HIGHWAY 13.
Singles/EPs:
Final Hour / Guillotina / Drunk On Your Blood / Doomwatch / The Short, Happy Life Of... , Facemelt FM001 (1986)
Crankin' 21, B.U.F. (1990)

Albums:
A SYMPHONY OF DECADENCE, Strategic Combat (1989)
Notorious / Iconoclast / The Fourth Reich / A Waste Of Mind / Tragic Flow / Final Hour / Mass Media / Monstrosity / Rude Awakening / Legacy Of Death / Wretched Glory / Ballet Of Destruction / Asylum / Doomwatch / Blind Obedience / Maybe It'd Be Better

DORSAL ATLANTICA (BRAZIL)
Line-Up: Carlos Vândalo (vocals / guitar), Alexandre Farias (bass), Gugos (drums)

Thrash Metal act DORSAL ATLANTICA shared their inaugural 1985 split album 'Ultimatum' with METALMORPHOSIS. The band at this juncture comprised vocalist / guitarist Carlos Vândalo, bassist Claudio 'Cro-Magnon' Lopes and drummer Marcos 'Animal'. For 1980's 'Antos Do Fim' the band listed their drummer simply as 'Hardcore'. The 1989 release 'Searching For The Light' would receive an American release through the Wild Rags label.

Ângelo Arede would assume the bass position for the 1997 album 'Straight'. By 2002 DORSAL ATLANTICA had drafted Alexandre Farias on bass.

Singles/EPs:
Victory / Dweller In The Streets, Flight 18 (1988) (Swiss release)

Albums:
ULTIMATUM, Gravacoes Electricas (1985) (Split album with METALMORPHOSIS)
Imperio De Sata / Catastrofe / Armagedon / Princesa Do Prazer / Heavy Metal
ANTES DO FIM, Lunario Perpetuo Discos (1986)
Cacador Da Noite / H.T.L.V.-3 / Alcool / Depressao Suicida / Vorkuta / Joseph Mengele / Guerrilha / Inveja / Morte Aos Falsos
DIVIDIR E CONQUISTAR, Heavy Discos (1988)
Tortura / Vitoria / Violencia E Real / Metal Desunido / Lucrecia Borgia / Morador Das Ruas / Preso Ao Passado
CHEAP TAKES FROM DIVIDE AND CONQUER, Heavy Discos HV005 (1988)
Disunited Metal / Victory / Dweller Of The Streets / Lucrecia Borgia / Violence Is Real
SEARCHING FOR THE LIGHT, Wild Rags WRR026 (1989)
Hierarchic Democracy / Fighting In Gangs / Misery Spreads / Not To Leave The Power / Only One Of Them (Must Be Left) / Gathered Prisoners / Childish Boots And Steps / The Ones Left Scream / History Starts (To Take A Route)
MUSICAL GUIDE FROM STELLIUM, Heavy Discos 804573 (1992)
Razor's Edge / Recycle Yourself / The Hidden And Unexpected / Kali Yuga (From Vishnu Purana) / Seven Races / Rock Is Dead / Warrior / My Generation
ALEA JACTA EST, Cogumelo CD COG069 (1994)
Thy Kingdom Come / Give People A Chance / R.I.P. (Racism, Ignorance, Prejudice) / Straitgate / Raise The Dead / Human Rights / Virtual Reality / Last Act / Black Messiah / Loyal Legion Of The Admirers / Life Goes On (Vidcom Experiences) / Take Time / Summary Condemnation / Tribute To Gauguin
STRAIGHT, Cogumelo (1996)
6:45 P.M./ Sign Of The Times / God Complex / Rapist / Straight / Who The Fuck Do You Think You Are? / Dor / All The Women (I've Loved) / Black Mud / Carniceria / H.I.V. / Extreme Conditions / Corporate Discrimination / Madness / Seasons Of Decay / Walls / Bollocks / Blood Pact / In Line / Heretic (Jacques De Molay) / Mothers Of Tomorrow / Racial Patterns / Success And Fall

DOWNRIGHT MALICE (FRANCE)

Line-Up: Jean-Luc 'Cliff' Khelifa (vocals), Didier Bauer (guitar), Aristide 'Aris' Brigenti (bass), Nicholoas 'Nicky' Kapps (drums)

Saint Louis Power Thrash Metal mongers forged in 1987 by guitarist Didier Bauer. During 1991 DOWNRIGHT MALICE underwent internal ructions with drummer Christian Pfauwadel deciding on a career elsewhere as his position was taken by Nicholas Kapps and fresh face Jean-Luc Khelifa was enrolled too. Second guitarist Daniel Hauser was to pack his bags but undeterred the band soon after cut their debut six track demo 'Errare Humanum Est'.

During May of 1993 bassist Oliver Houdement quit to be substituted by Aristide Brigenti. A further cassette 'Criminal Insane' shifted some 650 copies landing the band at the French Rock festival 'Printemps De Borges '95'.

The album is both self-financed and self-produced.

Albums:
INNATION... DOCTRINE, Downright Malice DRM001 (1995)
Indoctrination / Sniper / Bloodbath In Symphony / Soldiers Of Genocide / Psychoes / Life Discrimination / Current Shocks / Desperation

DRAGON (POLAND)

Line-Up: St. Vitus (vocals), Gronoss (guitar), Acu (guitar), Demon (bass), Gabriel Bomber (drums)

DRAGON are one of the bands to benefit from inclusion on the influential 1987 Polish Metal compilation 'Metalmania'.

The band's debut 'Horda Goga' was re-recorded for the Western market as 'Horde Of Gog'.

Not content with ludicrous stage names Polish Death Metal act DRAGON further complicated matters when lead vocalist St. Vitus became Freddy and bassist Demon then wished to be known as Ziggy. Therefore it may come as some surprise that guitarist Spider, who performs on the first two albums, is not the same person known as his

144

replacement Acu.

HORDE OF GOG, Metal Master (1989)
The Priest Of Betray / Seven Bowls Of Wrath
/ Eternal Rest / Beliar / Horde Of Gog /
Cerveza / Innocent Blood / Here Comes The
Dragon / Armageddon
FALLEN ANGEL, Under One Flag FLAG 48
(1990)
Fallen Angel / I Spit In Your Face / Tears Of
Satan / Deceived / Simon Peter / Destructor:
Sewer Of Graves / Into The Dark / Crying
Woman
SCREAM OF DEATH, Under One Flag
FLAG 58 (1991)
Mutant / Memory / Altars Of Doom / Gallery
Of Void / Alley Of... / Forgotten By Death /
Scream Of Death / Prisoner / Song Of
Darkness / Final Introduction / Ashes Of A
Generation / Demon Of War

DRAGSTER (BRAZIL)
Line-Up: Tiago Torres (vocals / guitar),
Gabriel Spazziani (guitar), Armando
Benedetti (bass), Evandro Junior (drums)

Thrash Metal act DRAGSTER was forged in
1998, originally billed as BULLDOZER.
Renaming themselves DRAGSTER the band
issued a self financed four track EP 'New
Times'.

Singles/EPs:
Break Down / The Chase / Why Do You Kill?
/ New Times, (2001) ('New Times' EP)

DREAM DEATH (USA)
Line-Up: Brian Lawrence (vocals / guitar),
Terry Weston (guitar),
Ted Williams (bass), Mike Smail (drums)

Pittsburgh Thrashers DREAM DEATH arrived
in 1984 releasing a demo tape 'More
Graveyard Delving' two years later. After
DREAM DEATH's debut album was released
by the New Renaissance label in 1987 bassist
Ted Williams defected to the Pittsburgh
Thrash act EVICTION.
Guitarist Terry Weston, frontman Brian
Lawrence and drummer Mike Smail later
created premier Doom act PENANCE issuing
a string of highly commended albums.

Albums:
JOURNEY INTO MYSTERY, New
Renaissance (1987)
Back From The Dead / The Elder Race /
Bitterness And Hatred / Black Edifice /
Divine In Agony / Hear My Screams / Sealed
In Blood / Dream Death

DREAMS OF DAMNATION (USA)
Line-Up: Charlie Silva (vocals), Jimmy Durkin
(guitar), Al Mendez (drums)

DREAMS OF DAMNATION are led by former
DARK ANGEL guitarist Jimmy Durkin. The
band actually evolved as far back as 1992 but
would reform with a completely new line-up
for the 'Let The Violence Begin' album.
In September of 2001 Durkin took on extra
duties with the reformed Bay Area Thrashers
HIRAX. 2002 opened with DREAMS OF
DAMNATION announcing Loana Valencia as
their new vocalist.
Durkin also operates Hardcore band
BLISTER.

Albums:
LET THE VIOLENCE BEGIN, Necropolis
NR064 CD (2000)
Blood To Free A Soul / Unholy Invocations /
Cremation Day / Demonic Celebration /
Hammer Of Sickness / Release Me

D.R.I. (Houston, TX, USA)
Line-Up: Kurt Brecht (vocals), Spike Cassidy
(guitar), Josh Pappé (bass), Felix Griffin
(drums)

Founded during 1981 by guitarist Spike
Cassidy DIRTY ROTTEN IMBECILES (more
commonly known as simply D.R.I.) purveyed
a high energy brand of Hardcore and Punk
that veered toward more Metal territory with
every release.
Cassidy had moved from New York to Texas
and put the first incarnation of the group
together with vocalist Kurt Brecht, drummer
Eric Brecht (Kurt's brother) and bassist
Dennis Johnson. The three had been working
as SUBURBANITES with Spike's roommate
on guitar before he left and Spike joined up as
the band evolved into D.R.I. The name was
inspired by the father of the Brecht brothers
who would come home during a band
practice and shout abuse at the group for the
noise they were making, "dirty rotten
imbeciles" being one phrase he used with
regularity.
D.R.I. released their debut album through
their own label in 1983 before being picked up
by Metal Blade and concocting the
breakthrough 'Dealing With It' album on the
Death imprint during 1985.
By this time both Dennis and Eric had quit the
group (the latter joining HIRAX and then the
San Francisco based ATTITUDE) and Josh
Pappé and Felix Griffin had taken their
respective places. Metal Blade's Brian Slagel
got to hear D.R.I. after HIRAX vocalist Katon
Depena had passed on a tape enthusing

about the group's potential after seeing them perform a one-off show in Los Angeles.

For the 'Dealing With It' album only Kurt Brecht and Cassidy remained having enrolled a new rhythm section of bassist Mikey Offender and drummer Felix Griffin.

Following a 1989 tour supporting GANG GREEN the band suffered a setback when bassist Josh Pappe opted to join the headline act. His replacement was ex-MANTAS bassist John Menor who joined D.R.I. in time for further touring in Britain to promote the 'Thrash Zone' album with NASTY SAVAGE acting as the support band.

Drummer Felix Griffin was announced to have quit in 1990 to be replaced by ex-MEGADETH drummer Chuck Beehler. However, by the time of a European tour Griffin was back on the drumstool.

D.R.I. continue to tour although the release schedule has slowed down with the last album issue being 'Full Speed Ahead', recorded with bassist Chumley Porter, in 1995. Touring in 2001 found infamous Bay Area photographer Harold 'O' Oimoen inducted as bass player for dates in August and September supported by SWORN ENEMY. Latterly a rare 7" split single with RAW POWER was issued on the Killer Release label, limited to just 500 copies.

Singles/EPs:
Running Around / Couch Slouch / To Open Closed Doors / Violent Pacification, (1984) ('Violent Pacification' EP)
You Think For Yourself, Metal Blade 75022 (1988) (USA promotion)

Albums:
DIRTY ROTTEN LP, Rotten (1983)
I Don't Need Society / Commuter Man / Plastique / Why / Balance Of Terror / My Fate To Hate / Who Am I / Money Stinks / Human Waste / Yes Ma'am / Dennis' Problems / Closet Punk / Reagonomics / Sad To Be / War Crimes / Busted / Draft Me / F.R.D.C. / Capitalist Suck / Misery Loves Company / No Sense / Blockhead
DEALING WITH IT, Death 720691 (1985)
Snap / I'd Rather Be Sleeping / Marriage / Yes Ma'am / Soup Kitchen / Mad Man / Stupid, Stupid War / Counter Attack / Couch Slouch / God Is Broke / Karma / Nursing Home Blues / I Don't Need Society / Give My Taxes Back / The Explorer / Reagonomics / How To Cut / Shame / Argument Then War / Evil Minds / Slit My Wrist / Busted Again / Equal People / On My Way Home / Bail Out
CROSSOVER, Roadrunner RR9555 (1988)
The Five Year Plan / Tear It Down / A Coffin /

Probation / I.D.K.Y. / Decisions / Hooked / Go Die / Redline / No Religion / Fun And Games / Oblivion / Fade Out
FOUR OF A KIND, Roadrunner RR 9538 (1988)
All For Nothing / Manifest Destiny / Gone Too Long / Do The Dream / Shut Up! / Modern World / Think For Yourself / Slumlord / Dead In a Ditch / Suit And Tie Guy / Man Unkind
THRASH ZONE, Roadrunner RO 9429-2 (1989)
Thrashhard / Beneath The Wheel / Enemy Within / Strategy / Labelled Incurable / Gun Control / Kill The Words / Drown You Out / The Trade / Standing In Line / Give A Hoot / Worker Bee / Abduction / You Say I'm Scum
DEFINITION, Rotten ROT 2093CD (1992)
Acid Rain / Tone Deaf / Guilt Trip / Hardball / The Application / Paying To Play / Say It / Dry Heaves / Don't Ask / Time Out / Let It Go / You / The Target
LIVE, Rotten (1994)
Intro / Thrashard / Acid Rain / Mad Man / Couch Slouch / Argument Then War / The Application / I Don't Need Society / Hardball / Violent Pacification / Beneath The Wheel / The Explorer / Commuter Man / You Say I'm Scum / The 5 Year Plan / Suit And Tie Guy / Nursing Home Blues
FULL SPEED AHEAD, Rotten (1995)
Problem Addict / I'm The Liar / Under The Overpass / They Don't Care / Drawn And Quartered / No End / Wages Of Sin / Syringes In The Sandbox / Who Am I / Girl With A Gun / Dead Meat / Down To The Wire / Level 7 / Broke / Sucker / Underneath The Surface
DIRTY ROTTEN IMBECILES, Cleopatra (2001)
Who Am I / Commuter Man / Yes Ma'am / The Explorer / Violent Pacification / Argument Then War / Mad Man / Couch Slouch / Nursing Home Blues / Don't Need Society / A Coffin / Redline / Hooked / Probation / The Five Year Plan / No Religion

DRIFTER (SWITZERLAND)
Line-Up: Tommy Lion (vocals), Peter Wolff (guitar), Ivano Marcon (guitar), Sven Rosemann (bass), Guido Kirschke (drums)

DRIFTER formed in 1984 and released their debut five track demo 'Tales Of Dragonia' in 1986. They received glowing reviews with the debut of 1988's 'Reality Turns To Dust' album, a record that featured a guest appearance by MOTÖRHEAD guitarist Phil Campbell.

DRIFTER's second album includes a cover version of ROSE TATTOO's 'We Can't Be Beaten'.

Guitarists Ivano Marcon and Peter Wolff

created GODS OF NOISE in 1993.

Albums:
REALITY TURNS TO DUST, Frontrow
626763 (1988)
Dust To Dust / Reality Turns To Dust / Crime
Of A Lifetime / Spiritual Diary Of Oppression
/ No Fear Of The Future / Senseless Death /
Burning Circles / Highlander / Banners On
The Battlefield / La Bamba
NOWHERE TO HIDE, Frontrow (1989)
So Much Blood / Strontium Dog / Concrete
Jungle / King Corruption / Principle Of
Speed / Shame Of A Perfect Race / The
Elder / We Can't Be Beaten

DR. MASTERMIND
(Portland, OR, USA)
Line-Up: Dr. Mastermind (vocals), Kurt James
(guitar), Deen Castronovo (drums)

Project band summoned up by former WILD
DOGS drummer Deen Castronovo. The band
were set up originally with former FRENCH
KISS vocalist Ron Chick as he adopted the
nom de plume of Boris Mastermind'. It was,
however, to be ex-WILD DOGS / MAYHEM
vocalist Matt McCourt, originally set to be the
producer, going under the revised
pseudonym of DR. MASTERMIND that would
record vocals on the album.
Deen Castronovo also brought in ex-
STEELER guitarist Kurt James.
Castronovo later found mainstream success
with BAD ENGLISH, OZZY OSBOURNE,
DAMN YANKEES and JOURNEY.

Albums:
DR. MASTERMIND, Roadrunner RR 9605-
2(1988)
Domination / The Right Way / Man Of The
Year / The Villa (2631) / We Want The World
/ Control / Abuser / Black Leather Maniac / I
Don't Wanna Die

DRUNKEN STATE   (UK)
Line-Up: Robert Trash (vocals), David
Leishman (guitar), Douglas K. Smith (guitar),
Michael Brash (bass), Graeme Thompson
(drums)

Scottish Thrash act DRUNKEN STATE self-
financed their debut 'Bags Not To Carry The
Coffin' EP and would go onward to support
the likes of ONSLAUGHT, WOLFSBANE and
SABBAT. The group's album, 'Kilt By Death',
was produced by Frank 'Uncle Bastard'
Mitzen.

Singles/EPs:
Bags Not To Carry The Coffin, Blast
Furnace Kickass 003 (1989)

Albums:
KILT BY DEATH, Heavy Metal MMRLP 151
(1990)
Time To Stop / Blind Faith / Forgotten Ones /
Lament / Call To Arms / Resurrection / ERIC
/ Let Me Go / Deal With The Cliche /
Prophets In The Wind

DRY ROT   (GERMANY)
Line-Up: Volker Schmidt (vocals), Michael
Gerstlauer (guitar), Niko Singer (bass),
Jochen Steger (drums)

Thrash act DRY ROT was created during
1990 by guitarist Michael Gerstlauer. A batch
of six demos, including 'Fatal Glance' and
'Brave New World', a track inclusion on the
'Bullet In The Head Volume One' compilation
and an appearance at the 'Full Force' festival
led to a recording deal with the Sub Zero label
in 1998.
The eponymous debut, which included a
vicious re-working of the POLICE hit
'Message In A Bottle' complete with a
guesting Bernhard Schmitt of HATE SQUAD,
saw a release in February 1999. DRY ROT
toured Germany as support to CROWBAR,
TESTAMENT and 40 GRIT.
Latterly DRY ROT's rhythm section of bassist
Niko Singer and drummer Jochen Steger has
been replaced by Make and Basti
respectively. Steger turned up as 'Christ
Impaler' in the tongue in cheek retro Thrash
act DELIRIUM TREMENS.

Albums:
DRY ROT, Sub Zero SZ9903-2 (1999)
Two Faced / Guilty / Release / Raped / Face
Down / Message In A Bottle / Hate Means
Love / To Whom It May Concern / Respect /
All Hope Is Lost / I Will Give You Pain

DYMAXION   (Wadsworth, OH, USA)
Line-Up: Mark Agnesi (vocals / guitar), Jason
Venner (vocals / guitar), Matt Agnesi (bass),
Jeremy Kostko (drums)
Highly regarded complex Thrash Metal
purveyed by youthful Ohio quartet
DYMAXION. Guitarist Mark Agnesi was a
mere fifteen at the time of recording of the
debut 1996 album 'Awakened By Reality'.

Albums:
AWAKENED BY REALITY, Fortunate
(1996)
Third World / Relative Aggression / One Last
Chance / After Hours / Deliverance Of Denial
/ Awakened By Reality / Subconscious / The
Deceiver / Apocalypse / Quiet Chaos

DYSFUNCTION (USA)

DYSFUNCTION's debut album came as a limited edition of five hundred picture discs featuring the same five songs on each side.

Albums:
THE $235 DEMO, Metalstorm MS8816 (1989)
Anxiety / Get To Work / Nuclear Warfare / River Of Blood / Me And My Uzi

ELEKTRASH (PERU)
Line-Up: R. Franco Olivera (vocals / guitar), Alejandro Hernandez (bass), Dario Hernandez (drums)

Lima Thrashcore band borne out of the 1993 act QUIMERA. Citing a line-up of vocalist / guitarist Luis Pajuelo, guitarist R. Franco Olivera, bassist Peter Ramirez and Jorge Salveredy on drums the Hard Rock covers previously delivered by QUIMERA gave way to original Thrashcore upon the name switch to ELEKTRASH in January of 1994.

ELEKTRASH would then be assailed by line-up ructions. In September of 1994 Ramirez opted out, his place being taken by Oscar Bustamente. However, before long Bustamente would be forced out with health problems and Ramirez was invited back in. 1996 witnessed the withdrawal of Salveredy's services. For many months ELEKTRASH was put on ice minus a drummer but finally in March of 1997 Dario Hernandez plugged the gap. The band's problems were far from over though as then frontman Pajuelo made his exit. Oliveria added lead vocals to his duties as ELEKTRASH became a power trio. An album collecting together prior demos was issued in 1998 billed as 'Excusa Para Morir'. The band issued a second album, 'Filosofia De Casos' which included a cover of DEEP PURPLE's 'Bloodsucker', in April of 1999. During recording Ramirez decamped for the second time and Alejandro Hernandez assumed the role of bassist.

Albums:
EXCUSA PARA MORIR, (1998)
Excuse Para Morir / Actitude Inconsciencia / Aquiel Inferno / Grisacea / La Belleza De Dolor / Mundo Pasairo / Cultura De La Violencia / Pandemonium / Demente / Errate / Antro / Neurosis / Coma
FILOSOFIA DE CASOS, (1999)

EMBRYO KILLERS (GERMANY)
Line-Up: Manchild (vocals), Dr. Bucket (guitar), John Smith (guitar), Shitlips (bass). Bonecrusha (drums)

Spoof Thrash Metal. Bet the bass player is popular with the girls.

Albums:
EMBRYO KILLERS, Born Dead 013607-34 (1992)
The Devil Is My Plumber (In The Drain Pipe To Hell) / Uugh! / Inhuman Insanity / Coathanger Death/ Go Die! / Break Hymen / Evil Frog / Sewer Rat / Warbird / Demon In Blood / Shotgun Wedding / Psycho / Metal Monster / The Fastest Song / Necro Nun / Belzebub Hellbullies / I'm Gonna Eat My Head / Drivel / Lint / Blood Fart / At The Hop / T.R.O.T.S. Of The Evil Frog / Testicles (Don't Chop Off My...) / My Dick Is My Religion / Eeeeeee!!!! / I Got A Name / Sinterview

EMILS (GERMANY)

German Punk Thrashers EMILS named their band after their own favourite act SLIME merely spelling it backwards in tribute. EMILS shared a split live 7" single in 1991 with SUCKSPEED and CAPITOL PUNISHMENT.

Singles/EPs:
Blut For Oil, We Bite (1991)
Deutsch Und Gut / Pass Dich An / Abrechnung / Wer Frisst Wen ? / Dumm-Punk / Nein Nein Nein / When Does It Stop? / Kirche Nein / Wir Mussen Draussen Bleiben, We Bite (1991) (Split single with SUCKSPEED and CAPITOL PUNISHMENT)

Albums:
FIGHT TOGETHER FOR..., We Bite (1988)
ES GEHT UNS GUT, We Bite (1989)
Experiment / Kosaken Kaffee / Schizophren / Du Und Ich / Nein Nein Nein / Anonyme Philharmonie / Such Ihn / Rufmord / Hungerlied / Es Geht Uns Gut / Abrechnung
WER FRISST WEN?, We Bite (1990)
Mitgehangen Mitgefangen / Wer Frisst Wen? / Schwein / Keine Kompromisse / Geh Los / Deutsch Und Gut / Geld Rackt Kopfe Gerade / Gavur / Krieg Und Frieden / Freund Oder Feind
LICHT AM HORISONT, We Bite (1993)
Intro / Hippiescheisse / Hans / Darling / Schleim / Monopoly / Umweltschock / 93 / Moderne Zeit / Hype / Kampfsignal / Abschlussmelodie
DER SCHWARZE FLECK, We Bite (1995)
Kirche Nein / Kampfsignal / Viel Zu Langsam / Wer Frisst Wen / Experiment / Neonazis / Geld Ruckt Kopfe / Gerade / D'93 / Gerechtigkeit / Hype / Abrechnung / Deutsch Und Gut / Schizophren / Dummpunk / Gavur / Pass Dich An / Hippiescheisse / Rufmord / Hans

ENCHANTMENT (UK)
Line-Up: Paul Jones (vocals), Marc Gibson (guitar), Steve Blackmore (guitar), Mark Tierney (bass), Chris Sanders (drums)

A mixture of Gothic, Doom, Thrash and Death Metal ENCHANTMENT's debut recording, the demo tape 'A Tear For The Young Eloquence', was produced by Peaceville Records boss Hammy.

The group, based in Blackpool, was later snapped up by the German label Century Media.

Albums:
DANCE THE MARBLE NAKED, Century Media (1994)
Kneading With Honey / My Oceans Vast / The Touch Of A Crown / Carve Me In Sand / Summer For The Dames / God Send / Of Acorns That Gather / Meadows

ENCRYPTION (GERMANY)
Line-Up: Norbert Hartmann (vocals), Christian Klein (guitar), Stefan Muller (guitar), Oliver Goss (bass), Johannes Klein (drums)

Franconian Progressive Thrashers ENCRYPTION were founded as CRYPTIC during 1995, issuing 'The Cryptogram' demo the following year and a 1997 debut album 'Shrouded In Mystery'.

During the final recording stages of the second album CRYPTIC would be delivered two blows. Not only did founder member and guitarist Manfred Herzog depart but a Munich based band claimed legal right to the CRYPTIC band title. With artwork already completed for the record stickers were hastily made up bearing the new title of ENCRYPTION.

Second guitarist Stefan Muller was added to the ranks in August of 2001.

Albums:
SHROUDED IN MYSTERY, (1997)
Shrouded In Mystery / Lack Of Animosity / Brainchild / Oblivious Vapours / Predator One / My Messiah / Fog's Kiss / Throne Of Chaos
PERISHING BLACK LIGHT, (2000)
Perishing Black Light / Lambda Core / All Philistines / The Inmost Dance / Conquering The Night / Autumn Harvest

ENDLESS DISTRUST (GERMANY)

A Heavy, '80s style Thrash act with aggressive, modern neo Hardcore elements to their sound.

Singles/EPs:
Holy War / Buddy Go Home / Paradise / Change The Leading, Endless Distrust (1996) ('Conscience' EP)

ENDLESS TEARS (FRANCE)

Line-Up: Vince (vocals / guitar), Philippe (guitar), Francois (bass), Roulo (drums)

After the release of two demos this four piece band from Talant recorded their first, self-financed CD.

'Emotion' finds this Bi-lingual outfit (lyrics are in French and English) offering technical, melancholic Thrash Metal.

Albums:
EMOTION, Endless Tears ENT001 (1994)
Emotion / Sacrifice-Le Poete / Lies / Retour / Sister Love / L'Acte / Wait / Le Dernier Survivant

ENERTIA (Albany, NY, USA)
Line-Up: Scott Featherstone (vocals), Dave Stafford (guitar), Roman Singleton (guitar), Joe Paciolla (bass), Jeff Daily (drums)

Albany based Power inclined Thrash act ENERTIA came together during February of 1996 and have industriously embarked upon a programme of self releases ever since commencing with July 1996's 'Law Of Three' mini-album. ENERTIA reaped valuable exposure as part of the independent movie 'These Days', performing 'Real' from the 1999 'Flashpoint' album.

ENERTIA would also act as the backing band for a METALLICA tribute released by Perris Records. Amongst he songs covered would be 'Ride The Lightning' featuring WATCHTOWER vocalist Jason McMaster 'For Whom The Bell Tolls' and 'Master Of Puppets' fronted by erstwhile IRON MAIDEN singer PAUL DIANNO and 'Creeping Death' with vocals from Stevie Blaze. Also cut would be 'Welcome Home (Sanitarium)' and 'Sad But True', both with ENERTIA vocalist Scott Featherstone taking the lead. During 2002 ENERTIA set to work on recording a new album with famed Metal producer Neil Kernon.

Albums:
LAW OF THREE, Enertia (1996)
The Mirror / Child Now Lost / I Know Your Demons / Same Old Story / If I Were You
MOMENTUM, Enertia (1998)
Ripped Out / Dear God / And So You Fall / Six Weeks / Weight Of The World / You Know / Sever The Wicked / Walls
FLASHPOINT, Enertia (1999)
Victim Of Thought / Leave Me In Peace / Glitch / Crawling / Real / D.O.M. / Voices Without End / What Hurts Me... / Right To Die

ENFORCER (Chicago, IL, USA)
Line-Up: Doug Trevison (vocals),

Brian Lee (guitar), Chip Jurkovac (bass), Scot Tomaras (drums)

ENFORCER were a Metal band founded in 1982. A set of demos followed in 1984.

EPIDEMIC (San Francisco, CA, USA)
Line-Up: Carl Fulli (vocals), Erik Moggridge (guitar), Guy Higbey (guitar), Mark Bodine (bass), Bob Cochran (drums)

EPIDEMIC debuted with the 'Immortal Minority' demo. A further demo tape in 1989 secured an album deal with Metalcore Records. Second guitarist Guy Higbey bailed out following the 1992 'Decameron' album.
Guitarist Erik Moggridge would later found OLD GRANDAD in union with bassist Max Barnett and former MACHINE HEAD, WARFARE D.C. and BROOD drummer Will Carroll.

Albums:
THE TRUTH OF WHAT WILL BE, Metalcore CRE4CD (1990)
DECAMERON, Metal Blade CDZORRO 50 (1992)
Circle Of Fools / Insanity Plea / Vision Divine / Hate / Unknown / Live Your Death / Factor Red / Blown Doors / Territories / Tornado / Three Witches / Lord War
EXIT PARADISE, Metal Blade CDZORRO 79 (1994)
Void / Vulture / Deaden / Lament / Exit Paradise / Institution Of Ignorance / Section 13 / Everlasting Lie / Written In Blood / To Escape The Void
EPIDEMIC, Rage (1994)

ERIC STEEL (Chicago, IL, USA)
Line-Up: Bruce Hausfield (vocals), Dave Anderson (guitar), Michael Hobson (bass), Ronnie Stewart (drums)

Created in 1982 Chicago Metal act ERIC STEEL had built up a strong following in the Mid-West and could boast to have supported the likes of MOUNTAIN, KING KOBRA, QUIET RIOT and METALLICA in their time.
The group signed to Johnny Z's Megaforce label for their first album - issued on the off-shoot Avalanche imprint - but soon severed connections with the company feeling that Megaforce were too pre-occupied with their major acts at the time to give ERIC STEEL due attention
Brad Wickham, who played drums on the first album, was replaced by ex JOE PERRY PROJECT skinbasher Ronnie Stewart for second album 'Infectious'.
By 1991 ERIC STEEL had recruited a new

bassist in ex-HAMMERON and AFTERMATH member Danny Vega and a new frontman in former DIAMOND REXX vocalist Johnny Cattone.

Albums:
ERIC STEEL, Avalanche MARZ 2001 (1984)
Fantasy / Lady Luck / American Dream / Hypnotised / Heat Of The Night / High Roller / No Way Out / All Night Long/ Under The Gun / Take It Like A Man
INFECTIOUS, Passport PBC 6059 (1987)
Forever Yours / Since You've Been Gone / Wanted Man / Somewhere Sometime / Rescue Me / Wishing Well / In Cold Blood / When The Lights Go Out / After Midnight

EROSION (GERMANY)
Line-Up: Chris Zenk (vocals), Michael Hankel (guitar), Stefan Römhild (guitar), Peter Ewaldt (bass), Klaus Nowakowski (drums)

In their career this German outfit has undergone something in the region of twenty line-up changes! Musically EROSION have transformed themselves from a Hardcore style outfit to one performing a more Thrashier style, although the Hardcore roots are still evident.
Guitarists Stefan Römhild and Michael Hankel were also included in the ranks of ex-HOLY MOSES man Andy Classen and former WARPATH singer Dirk Weiss's project band RICHTHOFEN in 1997.

Singles/EPs:
Gunman EP, We Bite (1992)

Albums:
MORTAL AGONY, We Bite (1988)
Erosion / Way Of Force / The Unborn / Bilharzia / Aftermath / False Prophets / Paralyzed / Mortal Agony / Nuclear Frost / Into The Void / Humanity
THOUGHTS, We Bite (1990)
H / The Scourge / Thought / You Belong To Us / Are You God? / Nightmare / Strike / Change
EROSION III, We Bite (1992)
Erosion III / Erosive Life / Revenge / Body & Soul / Reality / Power Within / Enemy / MLH / Germany 2003 / 70th Floor / Love / Lonely / Dead Europe
DOWN, We Bite WB1-138-2 (1996)
Up / Silver / Four Walls / Sub Consciously / A New Day / The Cross / Temptation / The Mutants Kiss / Sisyphos / Trapped And Confused / Our Minns-Mavn

E.S.T. (RUSSIA)
Line-Up: Jean Sagadeev (vocals / bass),
Vasily Biloshitsky (guitar), Misha Sagel
(drums)

A Russian Metal act with plentiful live
experience, E.S.T. (ELECTRIC SHOCK
THERAPY) debuted in Western markets with
'The Taste Of The Knife' in 1989, a record
produced by KRUIZ guitarist Valeri Gaina.
The record sold 200,000 albums in Russia
and this provoked a surge of interest in the
group from Western record labels.
The second album appeared through the
independent Destiny label and followed a
successful bout of touring through Germany,
Austria and the Benelux nations.
E.S.T. were later to appear on a 'Monsters Of
Rock' bill in Europe with AC/DC, METALLICA,
the BLACK CROWES and PANTERA. This
performance was duly captured on the 'Live In
The Outskirts Of Moscow' album.
E.S.T. mellowed out somewhat for their 1995
'13' album with the addition of a keyboard
player.

Albums:
RUSSIAN VODKA, (1989)
KLINGENPROBE, (1991)
TASTE OF THE KNIFE, (1989)
ELECTRIC SHOCK THERAPY, Destiny
(1990)
Perestroika / Joker / Father / Knife /
Remember Kathy / Russian Vodka / Moscow
Outskirts / Fuckin' Lisa / 10 Holy Jolly Years /
Drunken Without Wine / Red Beast
LIVE IN THE OUTSKIRTS OF MOSCOW,
Mausoleum 904010-2 (1992)
Bully / Moscow Outskirts / Father / Bitch! /
10 Holy Jolly Years / Fuckin' Lisa /
Remember Kathy / Hush-Hush-Show / Hot
Poison / Good Night Brighton Beach / Let
Your Dogs Hunt / Sting With Your Bayonette
13, (1995)

ESTIGIA (SPAIN)
Line-Up: Sergio Barros (vocals),
Juan Antonio Bonachela (guitar), Borja
Asensio (bass), Adrian Barros (drums)

A Granada based Progressive Thrash act.

Albums:
TRIP TO NOWHERE, (1996)
One Way System / Trip To Nowhere /
Another View / The Restless Hearing / Split
Personality / Inserts

ETERNAL DIRGE (GERMANY)
Line-Up: Timo (vocals / guitar), Pethe
(guitar), Boelmi (bass), Ralf (drums)

This band, from Marl, Westfalia, was formed
in the mid '80s and released several demos
before 'We Are The Dead' led to a record deal.
Both of ETERNAL DIRGE's albums highlight
the group's brand of Death / Thrash Metal
with keyboard leanings on a grand scale.
Indeed, during the recording of the 'Khaos
Magick' album permanent keyboardist
Sascha R. joined the group.

Albums:
MORBUS ASCENDIT, HASS Production
(1994)
Out The Eons / The Crawling Chaos /
Exploring The Depths / Blind Idiot God / The
Decadence Within / We Are The Dead /
Sinustis Maxillaris / Evolved Mutations
KHAOS MAGICK, Moribund MR024 (1996)
I, Unnamable / The Threshold Of Sensation /
Anthem To The Seeds (Of Pure Demise) /
Feaster From The Stars / Rending The Veils
/ Kallisti / Like Roses In A Garden Of Weed /
In Praise Of Biocide / Hymn To Pan / My
Sweet Satan

ETHEREAL SCOURGE
(AUSTRALIA)
Line-Up: Jarod Murray (vocals), Asoka Bane
(guitar), Greg Smith (bass), Glenn Reseigh
(drums)

Adelaide based Christian Thrash Metal.

Albums:
JUDGEMENT AND RESTORATION, Rowe
Productions (1997)
Through The Waters / Warcry / Refuge /
Estranged From The Womb / Shroud Of Mist
/ Earthshaker / Hecatombs / Restoration /
Quiet Surround / Subconscious / Giver Of
Life

EULOGY (Tampa, FL, USA)
Line-Up: Jason Avery (vocals), Jarret
Pritchard (guitar), Jay Medina (guitar), Mike
Beardon (bass), Clayton Gore (drums)

EULOGY, despite only managing a solitary
mini album release 'The Essence', was a
renowned and influential force in the Florida
Thrash / Death Metal transitional scene
during the early '90s.
The band was originally established in
Virginia by vocalist Jason Avery, guitarist
Jarrett Pritchard and bass player Mike
Beardon. A debut demo was cut with the aid
of a drum machine before EULOGY relocated
to Florida in order to hook up with drummer
'Antar' Lee Coates, a veteran citing credits
such as NECROSIS, EXMORTIS and
IMPIETY. However, within weeks Coates was

out of the picture, duly replaced by Clayton Gore.

The band debuted on the live front in January of 1992, opening a gig in Tampa for MONSTROSITY and BRUTALITY. For a brief period EULOGY operated with second guitarist Jerry Mortillero, later of DIABOLIC, but back as a quartet the band recorded the 1992 Tom Harris produced demo session 'Dismal'. Following these recordings EULOGY introduced Jay Medina on guitar.

Later that same year a deal was scored with the Dutch Cenotaph label and recording commenced for the mini album 'The Essence'. However, in spite of fronting the money for these studio sessions themselves the record was massively delayed, surfacing as late as 1994. A tour of Florida ensued in alliance with GOREPHOBIA and IMMOLATION after which Medina exited. BRUTALITY's Jay Fernandez would deputize but then in another body blow Beardon decamped.

Down to the surviving trio of Pritchard, Avery and Gore EULOGY attempted to regroup bringing in Ed Webb on bass and Erik Rutan on guitar. Rutan soon bade his farewell to join premier act MORBID ANGEL and Dave Sawyer stepped into the breach for live work. A demo tape, 'Lesson In Fear', surfaced in January of 1995, a track from which, 'Human Harvest', appeared on the Metal Blade 'Metal Massacre MMXII' compilation.

Shortly after EULOGY folded. Avery became frontman for MONSTROSITY. Jarret Pritchard switched from guitar to bass in order to enroll in CANEPHORA. Beardon would found ANGEL TRUMPETS, a band that also saw contributions from Fernandez, Avery and Gore. The drummer would also enjoy a brief term with Erik Rutan's ALAS project band.

Webb teamed up with BRUTALITY before joining forces with formative EULOGY drummer Lee Coates in DIABOLIC. Later Webb, ex-EULOGY guitarist Dave Sawyer and the erstwhile BRUTALITY pairing of Pete Sykes and Jim Coker founded CONTORTED.

Albums:
THE ESSENCE, Cenotaph (1994)
The Essence / When The Heavens Bleed / Entombed By Belief / Consecration Of Fools

EVICTION (Pittsburgh, PA, USA)
Line-Up: Todd Porter (vocals), Dominic Fusca (guitar), Rob Tabachka (guitar), Ted Williams (bass), Ron Reidell (drums)

Pittsburgh Thrashers EVICTION were founded in 1986 by guitarists Rob Tabachka and Wes Harris, vocalist Todd Porter and

drummer Ron Reidell. Debuted with the 1987 demo tape 'Straggle Is Society'. The band added ex-DREAM DEATH bassist Ted Williams in early 1988.

EVICTION would fold in the mid '90s with guitarist Rob Tabachka and bassist Ted Williams founding the '70s influenced Rock n' Roll act PILSNER releasing the 'Autosuggestion' album. Tabachka would subsequently reunite with EVICTION mainman Todd Porter in SILVER TONGUED DEVIL.

Albums:
THE WORLD IS HOURS... AWAY!, Metal Blade CDZORRO 14 (1990)
Our World / Listen / Drunken State / Marching Off To War / Living In Emptiness / You Decide / Struggle With Society / Behind The Mask / Open Your Eyes / American Way

EVIL DEAD (USA)
Line-Up: Phil Flores (vocals), Juan Garcia (guitar), Albert Gonzales (guitar), Mel Sanchez (bass), Rob Alaniz (drums)

EVIL DEAD, a band who were unafraid to take Death Metal to new levels of extremity, were created by guitarist Juan Garcia after he abandoned AGENT STEEL in 1988. Garcia's previous credits also included ABATTOIR.

Indeed, the original version of EVIL DEAD included ex-ABATTOIR bassist Mel Sanchez and ex-NECROPHILIA drummer Rob Alaniz. ABATTOIR guitarist Mark Caro was invited to join early on but the liaison didn't pan out and he quickly left the scene after recording a three track demo tape.

Guitarist Albert Gonzalez and vocalist Phil Flores were added a year later and EVIL DEAD would go on to score a deal with the German label Steamhammer Records.

The group debuted with the 'Rise Above' EP in 1989 and followed it up with the full blown album 'Annihilation Of Civilization' the same year.

The Japanese version of 'Annihilation Of Civilization' included bonus tracks from the European only released EP.

EVIL DEAD fragmented before their second album, Albert Gonzales was fired and would join DEATH for touring duties.

Rob Alaniz walked out (forming RISE in the process) but Flores and Garcia regrouped by adding guitarist Dan Flores and bassist Karlos Medina (after Sanchez split) for 1991's 'The Underworld'. Drums on the album, which included a version of the SCORPIONS 'He's A Woman, She's A Man', were supplied by Doug Clawson and backing vocals by METAL CHURCH man David Wayne. DEATH drummer Gene Hoglan also guested.

Singles/EPs:
Rise Above / Run Again / Sloe Death / S.T. Riff, Steamhammer 557590 (1989)

Albums:
ANNIHILATION OF CIVILIZATION, Steamhammer 847603 (1989)
F.C.I.: The Awakening / Annihilation Of Civilization / Living God / Future Shock / Holy Trials / Gone Shooting / Parricide / Unauthorised Exploitation / B.O.H.I.C.A.
THE UNDERWORLD, Steamhammer 084 76362 (1991)
Intro (Comshell 5) / Global Warming / Branded / Welcome To Kuwait / Critic-Cynic / The 'Hood / The Underworld / He's A Woman, She's A Man / Process Elimination / Labyrinth Of The Mind / Reap What You Sow
LIVE... FROM THE DEPTHS OF THE UNDERWORLD, Steamhammer (1992)

EXCEL (Venice, CA, USA)
Line-Up: Daniel Clemente (vocals) Adam Siegel (guitar), Shaun Ross (bass), Greg Saenz (drums)

Californian Thrash Metal band EXCEL debuted with a 1985 demo 'Personal Onslaught'. EXCEL's 1989 album 'The Joke's On You' includes a raucous cover version of THE POLICE hit 'Message In A Bottle'.

Albums:
SPLIT IMAGE, Suicidal (1987)
Your Life, My Life / Insecurity / Split Image / Never Look Away / Wreck Your World / Social Security / Set Yourself Apart / The Joke's On You / Looking For You / Spare The Pain
THE JOKE'S ON YOU, Caroline (1989)
Drive / Fired (You're) / Tapping Into The Emotional Void / Affection Blends With Resentment / Sealing Insane / My Thoughts / I Never Denied / Message In A Bottle / Given Question / The Stranger / Blaze Some Hate

EXCELSIS (NORWAY)
Line-Up: Steinar Jorgenson (vocals / bass), Zahir (guitar), Geir (guitar), Magne (drums)

Sarpsborg Thrash act EXCELSIS released a limited edition 250 run of the 'Beginning Of The End' mini-album in 1995. Formed in 1991, initially known as BELFEGOR by guitarist Zahir, the group added vocalist/bassist Steinar Jorgenson in 1992. The group added further members in guitarist Geir (who joined in 1993 and drummer Magne (1994).

Singles/EPs:
Dreams Of Disease / Incurable / Master Of Misery / Blowing Mind, Excelcis EXCEL 195 (1995) ('Beginning Of The End' EP)

EXCIDIUM (SWITZERLAND)
Line-Up: Claudio Tolfo (vocals / guitar), Maurizio Dottore (guitar), Raphael Hofmänner (bass), Jürg Oehler (drums)

Heavy Power Rock outfit from Switzerland with plentiful Thrash influences.

Albums:
INNOCENT RIVER, Adipocere CD AR 035 (1995)
Innocent River / Why Should I / Choice Of Failure / Whisper Inside / Among The Same / What Else Do I Need / I Guess I Love / What To Leave Behind / Frigidity / Hands

EXCITER (CANADA)
Line-Up: Dan Beehler (vocals / drums), John Ricci (guitar), Allan Johnson (bass)

Canadian Metal trio EXCITER, founded in Ontario in 1979 and almost certainly named after the infamous show opening JUDAS PRIEST track, made their presence known with some gut crunching Metal blessed by the raucous vocals of drummer Dan Beehler. EXCITER first got noticed courtesy of their 'Heavy Metal Maniac' demo which quickly led to a deal with Mike Varney's Shrapnel label. EXCITER's 1984 'Violence And Force' album was produced by THE RODS drummer Carl Canedy and soon shifted a healthy 75,000 copies. Its follow up 'Long Live The Loud' saw production from Guy Bidmead. The band backed up this release by touring Europe as support to ACCEPT in early 1985.
1986's Guy Bidmead produced 'Unveiling The Wicked' found long term member guitarist John Ricci departing to found BLACKSTAR. His replacement was Brian McPhee. EXCITER pulled in former SILENT PARTNER / SIMMONDS vocalist Jimmy Kunes but this liaison did not gel. After dates in Brazil the band added vocalist Rob Malnati for 1989's 'OTT' record.
Beehler decided to put EXCITER on ice during 1990 forming a new act KILJOY. Joining him on demos were former CRYPT bassist David Ledden and guitarist Joe Desmond.
Ricci and Beehler decided to re-energize EXCITER once more bringing in bassist Ledden for the 'Kill After Kill' album produced by ex-AVALON man Manfred Leidecker. The latter, along with ex-AVALON guitarist Brian Sim, would also handle their follow up 'Better

EXCITER Photo : Nico Wobben

Live Than Dead'. For live work EXCITER utilized the talents of bassist Jeff McDonald. Recently the band returned with 'The Dark Command' issued on French Black Metal label Osmose Productions. The album was internationally given the thumbs up as a powerful return to form. Ricci had give new life to the band which now included an all new crew of vocalist Jacque Belanger, bassist Marc Charron and drummer Rick Charron. This unit solidified EXCITER's return with the 2000 'Blood Of Tyrants' opus. However, during September of 2001 it was learned that Belanger had bailed out.

Meantime Toronto Black Metal band MEGIDDO would pay homage by including a cover version of 'Violence And Force' on their 'The Devil And The Whore' album.

Further exposure would be garnered when up and coming American Metal band SEVEN WITCHES covered 'Pounding Metal' for their second album 'City Of Lost Souls'. The band has sustained enough interest to warrant a slew of live bootlegs including 'Devil's Soul', 'Live Beasts' and 'Night Of The Creeps'.

During early 2002 famed Virginian Heavy Metal band DECEASED would cover 'Violence And Force' on their 'Zombie Hymns' album.

Vocalist Jacque Belanger apparently left the band in May.

Singles/EPs:
Feel The Knife / Violence And Force, Music For Nations 12 KUT 113 (1985)

Albums:
HEAVY METAL MANIAC, Shrapnel (1983)
Holocaust / Heavy Metal Maniac / Mistress Of Evil / Rising Of The Dead / Cry Of The Banshee / Stand Up And Fight / Iron Dogs / Under Attack / Blackwitch
VIOLENCE AND FORCE, Music For Nations MFN 17 (1984)
Oblivion / Violence And Force / Scream In The Night / Pounding Metal / Evil Sinner / Destructor / Swords Of Darkness / Delivering To The Master / Saxons Of The Fire / War Is Hell
LONG LIVE THE LOUD, Music For Nations MFN 47 (1985)
Fall Out / Long Live The Loud / I Am The Beast / Victims Of Sacrifice / Beyond The Gates Of Doom / Sudden Impact / Born To Die / Wake Up Screaming
UNVEILING THE WICKED, Music For Nations MFN 61 (1989)
Break Down The Walls / Brainstorm / Die In The Night / (I Hate) School Rules / Shout It Out / Invasion - Waiting In The Dark / Living Evil / Live Fast, Die Young / Mission Destroy

O.T.T., Maze 854603 (1989)
Scream Bloody Murder / Back In The Night / Ready To Rock / O.T.T. / I Wanna Be King / Enemy Lines / Dying To Live / Playin' With Fire / Eyes In The Sky / Termination
KILL AFTER KILL, Noise N 0192-2 (1992)
Rain Of Terror / No Life, No Future / Cold Blooded Murder / Smashin' Em Down / Shadow Of The Cross / Dog Eat Dog / Anger, Hate And Destruction / Second Coming / Born To Kill (Live)
BETTER LIVE THAN DEAD - LIVE, Bleeding Hearts CDBLEED 5 (1993)
Stand Up And Fight / Heavy Metal Maniac / Victims Of Sacrifice / Under Attack / Sudden Impacts / Delivering To The Master / I Am The Beast / Blackwitch / Long Live The Loud / Rising Of The Dead / Cry Of The Banshee / Pounding Metal / Violence And Force
THE DARK COMMAND, Osmose Productions OPCD 059 (1997)
The Dark Command / Burn At The Stake / Aggressor / Assassins In Rage / Ritual Death / Sacred War / Let Us Prey / Executioner / Suicide Overdose / Screams From The Gallows
BLOOD OF TYRANTS, Osmose Productions OPCD 089 (2000)
Metal Crusaders / Rule With An Iron Fist / Intruders / Predator / Martial Law / War Cry / Brutal Warning / Weapons Of Mass Destruction / Blood Of Tyrants / Violator

EXCRUCIATE (USA)

Albums:
PASSAGE OF LIFE, Thrash THR019 (1993)

EXCRUCIATION (SWITZERLAND)
Line-Up: Eugi (vocals), Marc (guitar), Mick (bass), Andy (drums)

Swiss Thrash Metal band EXCRUTIATION emerged with a 1984 demo tape 'Prophecy Of Immortality'.

Singles/EPs:
At The Edge Of Madness / The Silence / Hateful Pain / Desperate End (Nuclear Nightmare) / Mirror Of Eternity, Chainsaw Murder CM 002 (1987) ('Last Judgement' EP)

Albums:
ANNO DOMINI - ANTHOLOGY OF THE PAST, Turbo (1991)

EXE (New York, NY, USA)
Line-Up: Joseph Palma (vocals), Rui 'Evil' Tavora (guitar), Adam 'Muammar' Marigliano (guitar), Ricky 'R.H' Boeckel (bass / vocals),

Charles Lopez (drums)

A Horror-Thrash band from New York, EXE's debut album was produced by Carl Canedy of THE RODS who also contributed guitar parts. The album was released in Britain on the Shades label.

Boeckel, a Long Island resident, had left the band before second album, 'Sicker Than I Thought', was recorded. His position was taken by Gus Silva. Further changes saw drummer Charles Lopez departing making way for Bill Gerdes and singer Joseph Palma handing in his cards leaving space for the incoming Tommy Lee Haley.

Albums:
STRICKEN BY MIGHT, Shatter (1987)
Slaughter Disorder / Stricken By Might / Autopsy / Metal Hell / Slayer / Martial Law / Warchild / Fatally Wounded / Seek And Destroy / Crib Death
SICKER THAN I THOUGHT, Shatter (1990)
Three Years Later: Dismembered / Another Chosen Life / Sexploitation / Innocent Betrayal / Chamber Of Sorrow / Second Coming / Horrors Of The Mind / No One To Pray To / I'm Sanctified

EXECUTIONER (USA)
Line-Up: Marc Johnson (vocals), Ari Vainio (bass), Dan Skannell (drums)

The second EXECUTIONER album saw new bassist Seth Putnam. Post EXECUTIONER Putnam would go on to create one of the most infamous names in the annals of extreme music with the less than subtly titled ANAL CUNT.

Albums:
IN THE NAME OF METAL, GWD 90538 (1986)
Victims Of Evil / Hell And Back / Death By The Blade / Nuclear Nightmare / Your Life Is Over / Annihilation / Stand Up And Fight / In A Silent Way / Genocide / Going Blind / Cyanide / In The Name Of Metal / Battlelands
BREAK THE SILENCE, New Renaissance NRR 24 (1987)
Death March / Break The Silence / Eye Of The Needle / Your Life Is Over / Terminally Ill / Hatred / Genocide / No One Left To Die / Victims Of Evil / Stand Up And Fight

EXEQUIA (COLUMBIA)
Line-Up: Juan Antonio Aperador (vocals), Fernando Morales (guitar), Felipe Lara (guitar), Javier Vargas (bass), Mauricio Torres (drums)

Albums:
BEGGARS OF SOULS, (2000)
For Your Acts / Death Society / Last Dream / Palabras De Profeta / Sobre Mis Ruinas / A Espadas Del Creador / Nieve Negra / El Resplandor / Beggars Of Souls / Terminal Action

EXHORDER (New Orleans, LA, USA)
Line-Up: Kyle Thomas (vocals), Vinnie La Bella (guitar), Jay Ceravollo (bass), Chris Nail (drums)

Following the debut album release EXHORDER lost bassist Andy Villaferra bringing in replacement Frank Sparcello. EXHORDER's 1992 album 'The Law' included a cover version of BLACK SABBATH's 'Into The Void'.

EXHORDER split in 1994 with vocalist Kyle Thomas creating PENALTY and bass guitarist Jay Ceravolo joining FALL FROM GRACE as replacement for departing Matt Thomas who had jumped over to CROWBAR. Thomas later fronted Chicago Doomsters TROUBLE and created FLOODGATE.

Albums:
SLAUGHTER IN THE VATICAN, Roadracer RO 93632 (1990)
Death In Vain / Homicide / Desecrator / Exhorder / The Tragic Period / Legions Of Death / Anal Lust / Slaughter In The Vatican
THE LAW, Roadracer RO 92342 (1993)

EXHUMED (CA, USA)
Line-Up: Matt Harvey (vocals),

Members of EXHUMED formed IMPALED to issue the CD 'The Dead Shall Dead Remain' in 2000.

Albums:
GORE METAL, Relapse (1988)
SLAUGHTERCULT, Relapse (2000)

EXOCET (GERMANY)
Line-Up: Dirk Mylius (vocals), Stephan Hämmerling (guitar), Patrick Stein (guitar), Tom Merker (bass), Steffan Kolditz (drums)

EXOCET, formed in 1989, first demoed in late 1992 with their 'Apocalyptic Visions' tape. The group subsequently played various support dates to the likes of CREMATORY, ATROCITY and POST MORTEM and also appeared at the 1994 'Thrash Against Trash' festival headlined by KREATOR. The 'Confusion' album was produced by former ANGEL DUST / SCANNER singer S.L. Coe. Supported CREMATORY on their 1995

European tour.

CONFUSION, Massacre MASSCD068 (1995)
Hypocrite / I Kill Now / Commercial Overkill / The Martyr / Abyss Of Sexuality / Chemical Profit War / In Hate / Apocalyptic Visions / Retaliation / My Nuclear Safety / Unborn / More Bass

EXODUS (San Francisco, CA, USA)
Line-Up: Paul Ballof (vocals), Rick Hunholt (guitar), Gary Holt (guitar), Rob McKillop (bass), Tom Hunting (drums)

San Franciscan Speed Metal band created in 1981 and featuring METALLICA guitarist Kirk Hammet in the original line-up. EXODUS was among the frontrunners of the legendary Bay Area Thrash Scene and highly regarded by fans and peers alike. Hammet was to depart prior to any recording and the debut EXODUS effort saw a line-up of vocalist Paul Baloff, guitarists Rick Hunholt and Gary Holt, bassist Rob McKillop and drummer Tom Hunting.

The CD version of 'Bonded By Blood' came with the bonus live tracks 'And Then There Were None' and 'A Lesson In Violence'. With this debut EXODUS were to catapult themselves into the thrash major league but steadily lost ground with each successive release despite no let up in quality.

Paul Baloff left, initially to team up with HIRAX for a brief liaison and turning down an offer from German thrashers DESTRUCTION, as EXODUS struggled to wriggle free from their American deal with Torrid Records. During the lull Holt busied himself producing a demo for San Francisco's FUHRER.

As 1988 drew in Baloff announced his new act PIRAHNA comprising guitarists Ron Shipes and ex-EXECUTION man Chuck Sedlak, bassist Bob Eggleston and drummer Fred Cotton. By 1988 Baloff had joined HEATHEN.

EXODUS meanwhile were soon back in the fray with a major deal with Capitol Records. 'Pleasures Of The Flesh' was the first album to include new vocalist Steve 'Zetro' Souza. The singer's previous act LEGACY was later to evolve into TESTAMENT.

Whilst on tour with ANTHRAX and HELLOWEEN drummer Tom Hunting was forced to leave the band due to a mysterious stomach virus (or so it was reported) and temporarily replaced by VIO-LENCE's Perry Strickland. The group wound up using ANTHRAX drum tech John Tempesta on a headlining American tour in 1989 and would take over full-time as Hunting opted out.

Hunting was later to involve himself in IR8, a demo project put together by METALLICA's Jason Newsted.

The group reformed for 1997's 'Another Lesson In Violence', a collection of live recordings of the band's 'classics' but also including the Kirk Hammet co-written 'Impaler', never previously available on record. The album was produced by ex-SABBAT guitarist Andy Sneap.

The reformed EXODUS featured Baloff, Hunholt, Holt and Hunting along with new bassist Jack Gibson. Holt had been working with Jack Gibson and Tom Hunting in WARDANCE prior to being involved in the reunited EXODUS.

Souza was operating his act DOG FACE with ex-REXXEN and HEATHEN guitarist Ira Black, later of VICIOUS RUMOURS.

The band subsequently appeared at the Dynamo Festival in Holland in the early Summer of 1997 but would yet again break up shortly after. The band name would be kept in the public eye in 2000 as Death Metal band SIX FEET UNDER covered 'Piranha' on their 'Graveyard Classics' album.

EXODUS buried the hatchet in August 2001 re-uniting for a one off gig at the 'Thrash Of The Titans' festival in aid of TESTAMENT frontman Chuck Billy's cancer treatment fund. Sadly Paul Baloff was to die after suffering a stroke in February 2002. The band, with Baloff as frontman, had only just reformed. Despite this huge loss EXODUS persevered pulling in old colleague Steve 'Zetro' Souza in order to fulfil February engagements in Anaheim and an appearance at the Whittier 'Hellfest' in March.

Objection Overruled / Free For All / Changing Of The Guard, Capitol 12CLPD 597 (1989)

BONDED BY BLOOD, Music For Nations MFN 44 (1985)
Bonded By Blood / Exodus / And Then There Were None / A Lesson In Violence / Metal Command / Piranha / No Love / Deliver Us To Evil / Strike Of The Beast
PLEASURES OF THE FLESH, Music For Nations MFN 77 (1987) **82 USA**
Deranged / 'Til Death Us Do Part / Parasite / Brain Dead / Faster Than You'll Ever Live To Be / Pleasures Of The Flesh / 30 Seconds / Seeds Of Hate / Chemi-Kill / Choose Your Weapon
FABULOUS DISASTER, Music For Nations MFN 90 (1988) **82 USA**
The Last Act Of Defiance / The Toxic Waltz /

Low Rider / Cajun Hell / Like Father, Like Son / Corruption / Verbal Razors / Open Season
IMPACT IS IMMINENT, Capitol CDEST 2125 (1989)
Intro / Impact Is Imminent / A.W.O.L. / The Lunatic Parade / Within The Walls Of Chaos / Objection Overruled / Only Death Decides / Heads They Win (Tails You Lose) / Changing Of The Guard / Thrash Under Pressure
GOOD FRIENDLY VIOLENT FUN, Roadracer RO 92351 (1991)
LESSONS IN VIOLENCE, Music For Nations MFN 138 (1992)
Bonded By Blood / Chemi-Kill / The Toxic Waltz / A Lesson In Violence / Piranha / Brain Dead / Fabulous Disaster / Low Rider / And Then There Were None
FORCE OF HABIT, Capitol CDEST 2179 (1992)
Thorn In My Side / Me, Myself And I / Force Of Habit / Bitch / Fuel For The Fire / One Foot In The Grave / Count Your Blessings / Climb Before The Fall / Architect Of Pain / When It Rains It Pours / Good Day To Die / Pump It Up / Feeding Time At The Zoo
ANOTHER LESSON IN VIOLENCE, Century Media 77173-2 (1997)
Bonded By Blood / Exodus / Pleasures Of The Flesh / And Then There Were None / Piranha / Seeds Of Hate / Deliver Us To Evil / Brain Dead / No Love / A Lesson In Violence / Impaler / Strike Of The Beast

EXORCIST (USA)
Line Up: Damien Rath (vocals), Marc Dorian (guitar), Jamie Locke (bass), Geoff Fontaine (drums)

EXORCIST are rumoured to be none other than trad metallers VIRGIN STEELE going under pseudonyms.

Albums:
NIGHTMARE THEATRE, Roadrunner RR 9700 (1986)
Black Mass / The Invocation / Burnt Offerings / The Hex / Possessed / Call For The Exorcist / Death By Bewitchment / The Trial / Execution Of The Witches / Consuming Flames Of Redemption / Megawatt Mayhem / Riding To Hell / Queen Of The Dead / Lucifer's Lament / The Banishment

EXTREMA (ITALY)
Line-Up: Gianluca Perotti (vocals), Andrea Boria (guitar), Tommy Massara (guitar), Alex Ghilardotti (bass), Christiano Dalla Pellegrina (drums)

The above EXTREMA line-up recorded the 'We Fuckin' Care' single and the group would tour in Italy as support to SLAYER on the American group's 'Reign In Blood' tour. Although a highly popular live act in their native country it took ten years for EXTREMA to issue their debut album in 1992, by which point the group comprised vocalist Tommy Massara, guitarist Gianluca Perotti and Giolio Loglio, bassist Mattioa Bigi and drummer Chris Dalla Pellegrina.
The live EP of 1993 vintage was only ever released in Italy and featured a cover of the DEAD KENNEDYS 'Too Drunk To Fuck'.
Guitarist Giolio Loglio quit the group before they recorded 1995's 'The Positive Pressure (Of Injustice)' album.

Singles/EPs:
We Fuckin' Care, Extrema (1988)
Lawyer's Inc. / Child O' Boogaow / Modern Times / Displaced / Join Hands / Too Drunk To Fuck, Rosemary's Baby Discs BABE 13 CD (1993) ('Proud, Powerful n' Alive' EP)

Albums:
TENSION AT THE SEAMS, Rosemary's Baby Discs 08-110052 (1992)
Join Hands / Child O' Boogaow / Displaced / Truth This Everybody / Modern Times / Double Face / Road Pirates / Lawyers Incx. / And The Rage Awaits / For Good The Die / Life
THE POSITIVE PRESSURE (OF INJUSTICE), Flying FLY 190 CD (1995)
This Toy / The Positive Pressure (Of Injustice) / Fear / Money Talks / Confusion / Grey / Like Brothers / To Hell / On Your Feet, On Your Knees / Tell Me

EXUMER (GERMANY)
Line-Up: Paul Arakai (vocals / bass), Bernie (guitar), Ray Mensch (guitar), Syke Bornetto (drums)

The debut EXUMER album, 'Possessed By Fire', featured original vocalist Mem Von Stein, but he had left by the time the German outfit's sophomore album, 'Rising From The Sea' emerged.
During 1987 EXUMER had been scheduled to support WARFARE in Britain for some hotly anticipated dates but were ultimately prevented from doing so by British customs who refused Arakai entry into the country for lacking a work permit.
In 1990 Syke Bornetto formed Q SQUAD in 1990 switching roles from that of a drummer to a lead vocalist.

Albums:

POSSESSED BY FIRE, Disaster 1005
(1986)
Possessed By Fire / Destructive Solution /
Fallen Saint / A Mortal In Black / Sorrows Of
The Judgement / Xiron Darkstar / Reign Of
Sadness / Journey To Oblivion / Silent Death
RISING FROM THE SEA, Disaster 10007
(1987)
Winds Of Death / Rising From The Sea /
Decimation / The First Supper / Unearthed /
Shadow Of The Past / Are You Deaf? / I
Dare You / Ascension Day

FACTORY OF ART
(GERMANY)
Line-Up: Gunter (vocals), Flecke (guitar), Joe F. Winter (guitar / keyboards), Ron (bass), Wolf (drums)

Founded as an 'Art' Rock act during 1990 and debuting with a self-financed EP, 'No Better World', in 1992. FACTORY OF ART's debut album, 'Grasp', features guest appearances by Alex Krull of ATROCITY and Chris Boltendahl of GRAVEDIGGER.
The band became known for their Progressive Power Metal style which they mixed with Speed Metal and Thrash.
FACTORY OF ART signed to the CCP Records label for a 2002 concept album 'The Tempter'. The band at this juncture cited lead vocalist Jens Schmikale, guitarists Heiko Flechsig and Joe Heiko Winter, bass player Ronald Losch, keyboard player Ekkehard Meister and drummer Ralph Marcel Dietrich.

Singles/EPs:
Wings Of Destiny / Twilight Zone / Touch Of Cold Rain / No Better World, Factory Of Art (1992) ('No Better World' EP)
The Point Of No Return / Crown Of Creation / Silent Crying, AFM Records 014 (1997)
Story Of Pain / The Mass / Twilight Zone, Factory Of Art (1999)

Albums:
GRASP!!!, AFM Records CD 34325-422 (1996)
Never Dying Hero (N.D.H.) / No Fixed Address / Until The End Of Time / Live Fast / Wings Of Destiny / Character Of Society / The Other Side / Queen Of Seduction / Solitary Soldier / Long Way To The Height

FAITH OR FEAR (NJ, USA)
Line-Up: Tim Blackman (vocals), Chris Bombeke (guitar), Bob Perna (guitar), C.J. Jenkins (bass), Rick Lohwasser (drums)

A Bay Area style Thrash band from New Jersey. Following the solitary 1989 Combat album 'Punishment Area' guitarist Bob Perna was usurped by Merrit Gant. FAITH OR FEAR splintered with Gant joining veteran Thrashers OVERKILL, other members would found WAGONHEAD in 1994.
Gant later re-emerged with BLOOD AUDIO.

Albums:
PUNISHMENT AREA, Combat 88561-2005-1 (1989)
Lack Of Motivation / C.D.S. / Punishment

Area / Rampage / Nothing Uncommon / Have No Fear / What Would You Expect / Darkside / Shadow Knows / Ripoffs / Time Bomb / Instruments Of Death

THE FALLEN
(Orange County, CA, USA)
Line-Up: Mike Granat (vocals / guitar), Mark Venier (guitar), Bryan Klinger (bass), Henry Higgs (drums)

Stoic Metal campaigners THE FALLEN, founded as THE CRESTFALLEN during 1992, endured nearly a decade of struggle and successive demo releases before finally landing a record deal in 2001. The group was convened as a trio of vocalist / guitarist Mike Granat, guitarist Mark Venier and drummer Max Wolff mixing traditional Metal with newer Death and retro Thrash influences. With the addition of bass player Bryan Klinger the band became known as THE FALLEN.
A demo cassette, 'The Perfect Darkness Of Death', arrived in 1993 which found the group fronted by lead vocalist Wagner Pierera. However, THE FALLEN was back to a quartet for 1994's 'Eventually Nothing Remained' session with Granet taking the lead vocal mantle. Wolff would be out of the picture by the band's third and fourth attempts, 1995's 'Turning Hollow' and the following year's 'Bloodletting: Victims Of The Order', drums being simply credited to 'Greg'. Keith Gordon took the drum stool for the 1997 'Bloodrush' session.
THE FALLEN, now with Henry Higgs placed on drums, committed to CD for the first time with their 1999 three track EP 'Sector- 7G'. A self-financed full-length album 'The Tones In Which We Speak' emerged in 2000 leading to a deal with the Metal Blade label and the subsequent Bill Metoyer produced 'Front Toward Enemy'.

Singles/EPs:
To Dust / Descend From Heaven / Bound In Thorns, (1999) ('Sector- 7G' EP)

Albums:
THE TONES IN WHICH WE SPEAK, (2000)
Suffer With It / The Tones In Which We Speak / All For None / Harbinger / Turning Hollow / Sunken Ploy / To Dust / Descend From Heaven / Bound In Thorns / Bloodwash

FANTOM WARRIOR (USA)
Line-Up: Keith Pires (vocals / guitar), Steve Schley (guitar), John Chernack (bass), James Jensen (drums)

161

Albums:
FANTASY OR REALITY, Token (1987)
Chosen Fate / Psychotic Mind / Don't
Criticize / Final Call / Backstabber / E.R.C. /
Not Sure / Kill Rip Destroy

FATAL OPERA
(Orange City, FL, USA)
Line-Up: Andy Freeman (vocals),
Billy Brehme (guitar), Stewart Samuelson
(guitar), Travis Karcher (bass), Gar
Samuelson (drums)

Drummer Gar Samuelson is ex-MEGADETH.
The debut FATAL OPERA album includes a
cover of the BEATLES classic 'Lucy In The
Sky With Diamonds'.

Albums:
THE ELEVENTH HOUR, Massacre MAS
PC0120 (1997)
Would You? / Nothing Is Everything / Once I
Was A Fly / Indiscretion / Inside-Outside /
Lucy In The Sky / Wrist Twister / Mindfuck /
Dredges (The Truth) / Three Steps / The End
Of Me / My Psychiatrist / Devil's Monkey /
Calling Of Lotar

FATAL ORDER (USA)
Line-Up:

Albums:
BRANDED FOR LIFE, Fatal Music
Publishing (1999)
Branded For Life / DNC / Spellmaker / Until
The End / I Dream / You'll Burn / Chasing
Time / Evil / Forever Rest In Peace / Kicked
In The Balls / No Sleep / Another Time
Another Place / Fatal Order / Torn Apart

FEAR OF GOD (USA)
Line-Up: Dawn Crosby (vocals), Michael
Carlino (guitar), Blair Darby (bass), Steve
Cordova (drums)

An act of huge potential fronted by ex-
DÉTENTE members vocalist Dawn Crosby,
guitarist Michael Carlino and bassist Blair
Derby, but blighted by an ever shifting line-up.
The band was actually signed to major label
Warner Brothers by Roberta Peterson whilst
still named DÉTENTE. As DETENTE they
tested the market with a three track 1989 Alex
Perialis produced demo tape comprising 'All
That Remains', 'Deceased' and 'Waysted
Time'. A further effort led by the track 'Love's
Death' ensued the same year.
The band's line-up at the time included Rob
'Wacko' Hunter, drummer of NWoBHM
stalwarts RAVEN. As negotiations with the
label drew on Hunter bowed out and New

Jersey's Eric Alpert was drafted. His tenure
would be brief though and the band finally
settled on Steve Cordova to occupy the drum
stool.
It was discovered that the band name
DÉTENTE had already been registered so
initial recordings were convened under the
band name SEDITION. The album tapes for
'Within The Veil' would be re-mixed for release
by Andy Wallace and with due process of time
the group evolved into FEAR OF GOD.
A month long trek across America to promote
the album caused internal frictions that would
cause Cordova to leave as soon as dates
were fulfilled. Drummer Brendan Etter of
Industrial act NATURE would figure in the
group's 1991 line-up for a showcase gig at the
'Foundations Forum' but would leave the
following year. Crosby would also replace
bassist Blair Darby having met his
replacement, a rastafarian named Jason
Levin, by way of a chance meeting on a train.
The band travelled to London's Battery
studios in early 1992 to work with producer
Chris Tsangerides FEAR OF GOD would
practically split up in the midst of recording a
projected second album for Warner Brothers
just upfront of a booked series of European
shows.
The FEAR OF GOD that European audiences
actually saw on stage would in fact only
involve Crosby from the previous line-up.
Assisting for these shows, which included a
prestigious appearance at the Dutch
'Aardschok' festival, was WRATHCHILD
AMERICA members guitarists Jay Abbene
and Terry Carter along with drummer
Shannon Larkin and HAVE MERCY /
JAKKPOT man Rob Michael on bass.
Whilst Larkin depped for the band a more
permanent member Douglas Sylvia,
previously with GENETICIDE and SKELETAL
EARTH, was brought into the fold. FEAR OF
GOD, retaining Michael and Sylvia but with
new guitarists Brandon Hefner and Randy
Bobzien, cut fresh demos for Warner Bros. In
a much more aggressive style. These tapes
would be re-recorded with new drummer John
Grden of HAVE MERCY. Warner Bros.
dropped the act still believing they were
heading into Death Metal territory and in
September of 1993 Hefner quit the ranks.
The band's second album 'Toxic Voodoo',
issued on the Pavement label in 1994,
sported another all new look to the band
structure. Guitars came courtesy of Chris
Kalandras and Randy Bobzien with a rhythm
section culled from HAVE MERCY being
bassist Robert Ian Michael (also a member of
JAKKPOT) and drummer John Grden.
However, Crosby's reliance on drugs and
alcohol had severely affected the recording

process putting yet further strains on the band.

Michael, Kalandras and Bobzien left the band en masse mere weeks prior to the 'Toxic Voodoo' tour. Replacements were hastily drafted in the form of guitarists Sparky Voyles and Bill Hayden together with former DESECRATION, SPINE and VOX HUMANA bassist Bruce Greig. This revised unit would set to work on a scheduled third album but Voyles would relinquish his position to Frank DiMauro.

The resulting album demo did not find favour with Pavement and yet more fractures occurred within the ranks with DiMauro being usurped by Tony Mallory of CHAPEL BLACQUE, who also took on keyboard duties. Grieg too would leave for NEXT STEP UP being replaced by Mike Schafer.

FEAR OF GOD's last outing was the cassette album 'Killing The Pain' in 1997.

Sadly Dawn Crosby was to die tragically young on December 15th 1996, of acute liver failure due to years of excessive alcohol abuse. The remaining members, including Mallory, Haydon and Grden, persevered billed simply as FOG.

John Grden would later show up in BLACK MASS and, along with Haydon, PESSIMIST. Sparky Voyles journeyed through SADISTIC TORMENT. M.O.D., DYING FETUS and by September 2001 was ensconced as a member of MISERY INDEX.

Albums:
WITHIN THE VEIL, Warner Bros. (1991)
All That Remains / Betrayed / Emily / Red To Grey / Diseased / Wasted Time / Love's Death / White Door / Drift
TOXIC VOODOO, Pavement (1994)
Beyond The Veil / Cloud Chamber / Swine Song / Burnt / Feed Time / Mercy / Santismo / U.V. / Will Of Evil / Worms
KILLING THE PAIN, (1997) (Cassette release)

FERTILIZER (GERMANY)
Line-Up: Daniel Wagner (vocals), Markus Münch (guitar), Marcus Beck (bass), Dennis Emmel (drums)

A Death / Thrash Metal quartet formed in 1990, FERTILIZER released the 'Environmental Glutton' demo a year later.
In 1993 guitarist Frank Lemmart joined the group and, in 1994, FERTILIZER issued their debut album.
The four piece have toured with PYOGENESIS, DISASTROUS MURMER and RU DEAD? throughout Germany.

Albums:
A PAINTING OF ANNOYANCE, Invasion / SPV 0077.141532 (1994)
Solar Vertigo / Traumstunde / T.U.S.C. / Feelharmony Melodream Overdose / Under The Oath Of... / 2nd Service / Time Dune

F.F.F. (FRANCE)
Line-Up: Marco (vocals), Yarol (guitar), Niktus (bass / samples), Felix (keyboards), Krichou (drums)

Thrash Funk band F.F.F. (FREE FOR FEVER) had their 'Free For Fever' album produced by Mark Wallis.

Albums:
BLAST CULTURE, Epic (1991)
New Funk Generation / Marco / Devil In Me / Tout Pour Le Kliff / La Compliante Du Plombier / Maman Krie / Doctor Love / Ac2n (Acid Rain) / Mama Fonck / Santa Claus / Requiem Pour Un Con / Kamarad / Trash A Muffin /
FREE FOR FEVER, Epic 474421-2 (1993)
Stone To The Bone / Des Illusions / Mouche A Miel (Jingle) / Silver Groover / La Camisole (Drugs) / Positive / Wreye Sem (Jingle) / Wiseman / R.U. Real / Tout Semble Flou / Shot 'Em Down / Leave Me Alone / Ou Tu Vas Y Aller (Jingle) / King Of Party / Free For Fever / Emotion / Back To The Bone (Jingle)
VIERGE, V2 (2000)
Alice / Leyaourt / Mauvais Fils / I Want You / On Avance / Come On / Fame / Tout Est Mou / God Bless The Family / Mon Desordre / Je Deteste Le Dimanche / On Le Fait / 7 Fois Dans Ma Bouche

FIGHT (UK / USA)
Line-Up: Rob Halford (vocals), Russ Parrish (guitar), Brian Tilse (guitar), Jay Jay (bass), Scott Travis (drums)

A joint Anglo / American, stripped down in-your-face Metal act FIGHT was created by JUDAS PRIEST vocalist Rob Halford, a man whose vocal prowess is almost legendary. Wishing to pursue a radical change of direction from the more classic, technical style of JUDAS PRIEST, Halford bowed out after 1991's hugely successful 'Painkiller' world tour. Longstanding JUDAS PRIEST fans were somewhat bemused by a shift in his traditional leather and studs image to one that mimicked PANTERA's vocalist Phil Anselmo. It came as no surprise then that Halford began guesting at PANTERA shows and cut a single, 'Light Out Of Black', with the band for a movie score.

163

Although the vocalist had the blessing of JUDAS PRIEST for this out of the blue project, a bitter verbal conflict ensued. As the accusations and counter-accusations flew, Halford's twenty year tenure abruptly came to and end as he formed FIGHT, taking JUDAS PRIEST drummer Scott Travis with him.

The eagerly awaited debut album was light years removed from JUDAS PRIEST, Halford toning down his vocal range and opting for much simpler songs. Many critics panned the release as a lame PANTERA copy but in the main Halford managed to take many former fans with him.

Live dates in England were marred by paltry attendance figures with many JUDAS PRIEST fans feeling almost betrayed by Halford's endeavours. The vocalist reacted by issuing vitriolic statements about the British media. In the States Halford enjoyed better response and FIGHT toured there opening for the mighty METALLICA.

The interim 'Mutations' mini-album included a raucous live rendition of JUDAS PRIEST's 'Freewheel Burning'. 1994's 'A Small Deadly Space' found Mark Chaussee in the group in place of ex-WAR & PEACE guitarist Russ Parrish.

Halford was also busying himself outside of FIGHT with his E.M.A.S. Management organization. Taking on Australian Thrashers ALLEGIANCE Halford secured a deal for the young act with major label Polygram.

FIGHT's days, however, were numbered. After a brief flirtation working with BLACK SABBATH guitarist TONY IOMMI (indeed, Halford had guested for BLACK SABBATH at the legendary Costa Mesa shows in late 1992 subbing for an absent Ronnie James Dio) the singer formed a new band under the title of HALFORD.

This later act retitled itself GIMP then TWO, emerging with a Trent Reznor of NINE INCH NAILS produced Industrial Rock album 'Voyeurs' that, it is true to say, left many of Halford's fans scratching their heads in bemusement. Even more so when the man, now sporting a stage image that alternated between Nosferatu and blue rubber romper suits, seemingly denounced Metal as dead and buried.

Chaussee joined DANZIG in 1996 but bailed out just prior to their world tour. By 2000 Parrish was a member of the acclaimed spoof covers band METAL SHOP along with former L.A. GUNS man Ralph Saenz. Parrish would also double duties with Alternative Rockers THE DUCKS.

Much to the relief of his long suffering fans, Rob Halford, now simply billed as HALFORD, resurrected his career in spectacular style during 2000 with the suitably titled 'Resurrection' album, a quite remarkable statement of Metal intent that charted internationally. HALFORD, signing up to IRON MAIDEN manager Rod Smallwood's firm for management and label, saw his profile rise sharply with a subsequent special guest slot to IRON MAIDEN's American dates.

Albums:
WAR OF WORDS, Epic 4745472 (1992)
Into The Pit / Nailed To The Gun / Life In Black / Immortal Sin / War Of Words / Laid To Rest / For All Eternity / Little Crazy / Contortion / Kill It / Vicious / Reality, A New Beginning
MUTATIONS, Epic 477243 2 (1993)
Into The Pit (Live) / Nailed To The Gun (Live) / Freewheel Burning (Live) / Little Crazy (Live) / War Of Words (Bloody Tongue Mix) / Kill It (Dutch Death Mix) / Immortal Sin (Tolerance Mix) / Little Crazy (Straight Jacket Mix)
A SMALL DEADLY SPACE, Epic 478400 2 (1994)
I Am Alive / Mouthpiece / Legacy Of Hate / Blowout In The Radio Room / Never Again / Small Deadly Space / Gretna Greene / Beneath The Violence / Human Crate

FINAL ASSAULT (USA)

Christian metal act FINAL ASSAULT's single came in a variety of formats including a heart and a Christmas tree.

Singles/EPs:
Final Assault / Messenger Of God, Azra (1987)

FLACMAN SPORT (GERMANY)
Line-Up: Mark Herges (vocals), Roland Walter (guitar), Jürgen Herrmann (guitar), Jörg Warken (bass), Günter Junker (drums)

A German Heavy Rock troupe with Thrash influences.

Albums:
AFTERLIFE, West Virginia SPV 084-57292 (1992)
Intro / Meaning Of Life / The Truth / Afterlife / The Fear / My Way / Prisoners Of War / Suicide / Katharsis / Age Of Fear / False Prophets

FLEGMA (SWEDEN)
Line-Up: Kalle Metz (vocals), Martin Olsson (guitar), Jörgen Lindhe (guitar), Richard Lion (bass), Martin Brorsson (drums)

Punk infused Thrash act. FLEGMA started life

FLESH MADE SIN
Photo : Nico Wobben

n 1987 citing a line up of vocalist Rother, guitarist Puschel, bass player Richard Lion and drummer Martin Brorsson. Having released their full blown debut album, 'Blind Acceptance' in 1992, FLEGMA added ex-OBSCURITY guitarist Jörgen Lindhe to the line-up following 1994's 'Flesh To Dust' album. This also found them offering a cover of the KISS track 'I Stole Your Love'.

In addition the band have contributed tracks to both VENOM and METALLICA tribute albums with 'Leave Me In Hell' on the VENOM tribute 'Promoters Of The Third World War' on Primitive Art Records and 'The Thing That Should Not Be' on Black Sun Records 'Metal Militia' METALLICA tribute album.

FLEGMA disbanded with vocalist Kalle Metz and Richard Lion founding the Gothic Metal act TENEBRE in league with FUNHOUSE guitarist Fredrik. Ex-FLEGMA man Martin Olsson contributed session work to the debut TENEBRE album 'XIII'.

Singles/EPs:
Eine Kleine Schlachtmusik, Insane
INSANE 001 (1990)

Albums:
BLIND ACCEPTANCE, Black Rose BRR001
(1992)
FLESH TO DUST, Black Rose BRR002
(1994)
Rotting Away / Crown Of Thorns / Drowning / Walk In Confusion / Shadow Of A Silhouette / Father / Enticed / As The World Watches / I Stole Your Love / Flesh To Dust

FLESH MADE SIN (HOLLAND)
Line-Up: Twan van Geel (vocals / guitar), Bjorn van Hamond (guitar), Marc van Stophort (bass), Marco Stubbe (drums)

With the opening track on their self-financed 'Scenery Of Death' EP entitled 'Thrash Is Back!' there would be no doubting FLESH MADE SIN's credentials. Vocalist Twan van Geel's credentials included a stint with SAURON whilst guitarist Bjorn van Hamond was previously a member of SPLATTER. Drummer Marco Stubbe had bashed the skins for ANTROMORPHIA.

A full length album, 'A Masterwork In Blood', was projected for 2002.

FLESH MADE SIN's rhythm section of Marc van Stophort and drummer Marco Stubbe also perform with Crossover act ANTRO.

Singles/EPs:
Thrash Is Back! / Sculpture Of Bones / Your Blood Is Mine / Scenery Of Death, (2001) ('Scenery Of Death' EP)

FLOTSAM AND JETSAM
(Phoenix, AZ, USA)
Line-Up: Eric A.K. (vocals), Ed Carlson (guitar), Mike Gilbert (guitar), Troy Gregory (bass), Kelly Smith (drums)

Founded in 1981 FLOTSAM AND JETSAM were to rise above the thrash melee with a strong debut album. However, the band are known more for being the source of METALLICA's Jason Newsted and despite major label back up have struggled to rid themselves of that stigma.

Newsted's first band was titled GANGSTER. This unit evolved into PARADOX with the addition of drummer Kelly David-Smith and then the Scottsdale based DOGZ with the recruitment of guitarists Mark Vasquez and Mark Horton. DOGZ added vocalist Eric A.K. in 1983 and Horton made way for Ed Carlson as the band retitled itself FLOTSAM AND JETSAM.

The band started the ball rolling by playing local support gigs to the likes of MALICE, AUTOGRAPH, ARMORED SAINT, MEGADETH and ALCATRAZ.

FLOTSAM AND JETSAM's demo tapes, starting with 1985's 'Metal Shock' followed by '1985 Bootleg', attracted the attention of several leading Metal indie labels resulting in the band debuting with tracks on the compilation albums 'Speed Metal Hell II' and 'Metal Massacre IV'. The inclusion on the latter led to a deal with Metal Blade Records (Roadrunner Records licensed the album for Europe). The band's first album 'Doomsday For The Deceiver', produced by Brian Slagel, was a well received release, chock full of quality aggressive metal.

With Newsted's departure to METALLICA the band carried out live commitments utilizing the temporary services of SACRED REICH's Phil Rind. Following these early post-Newsted live dates ex-SENTINAL BEAST bassist Mike Spencer was hired, FLOTSAM AND JETSAM were picked up by METALLICA's label Elektra and the group gained the valuable support slot on a European tour with MEGADETH in 1987.

However, Spencer lost his position in early 1988 to Troy Gregory. The 1988 album 'No Place For Disgrace' features a rip-roaring version of the ELTON JOHN hit 'Saturday Night's Alright For Fighting'. Although the band fared well opening for KING DIAMOND in America during 1988 by the end of the tour their major label deal with Elektra had been lost.

Some fifteen months later the group had bagged a new deal with MCA Records and began recording third album 'When The Storm Comes Down' with producer Alex

FLOTSAM AND JETSAM

Perialas in New York. The album was to appear in 1990.

1992's 'Cuatro' produced by Neil Kernon, although a solid release, did little to improve their sales figures. The band recorded a track co-written with Dave Ellefson of MEGADETH 'Date With Hate' although strangely this did not make the running order for the album. It only saw a release as the B side to the 'Swatting At Flies' single.

1995's Kernon produced 'Drift' saw the band out on tour in America supporting MEGADETH but MCA let the band go. Gregory bailed out to join PRONG. The four stringer would later found Psychedelic Rock act THE WITCHES.

FLOTSAM AND JETSAM returned to the scene after a lengthy absence reuniting ties with their former record company Metal Blade. The resulting album 'High' proudly stated the band's intentions towards true metal with song titles mimicking many household name band logos such as JUDAS PRIEST, KISS and AC/DC. The album also includes a version of LARD's 'Fork Boy'.

The band returned to live action debuting their new drummer Craig Neilson at the 'Bang Your Head' festival in Southern Germany prior to a lengthy bout of touring alongside ANVIL and EXCITER.

Upon their return the band drafted in a further new member guitarist Mark Simpson who made his debut on 1999's 'Unnatural Selection' album. Simpson did actually leave the band to join George Lynch's LYNCH MOB but had returned to the fold by the summer of 2000 as FLOTSAM AND JETSAM geared up for another album.

With FLOTSAM & JETSAM gearing up for release of a 2001 album 'My God' it was revealed that Eric A.K. was doing the club circuit with a Country & Western band titled THE A.K. CORRAL!

FLOTSAM AND JETSAM themselves commenced a short burst of American club dates kicking off with a Los Angeles Troubadour gig on 28th July. As August drew to a close it was reported that Eric A.K., the band's vocalist for more than twenty years, had departed. His speedily announced replacement would be James Rivera of DESTINY'S END and HELSTAR.

Singles/EPs:

Flotzilla / I Live You Die, Metal Blade RR 125471 (1987)

Saturday Night's Alright For Fighting / Hard On You (Live) / Misguided Fortune (Live) / Dreams Of Death (Live), Roadrunner

RR 24531 (1988)
Suffer The Masses, MCA (1990) (USA promotion)
The Master Sleeps / Interview, MCA CD45-18515 (1990) (USA promotion)
Never To Reveal / Double Zero / Wading Through The Darkness / (Ain't Nothing Gonna) Save The World, MCA MCA9P-2489 91992) (USA promotion)
Swatting At Flies / Date With Hate, MCA (1992)
Wading Through The Darkness / Wading Through The Darkness (Radio edit) / Wading Through The Darkness (Industrial mix), MCA (1992)(USA promotion)
Cradle Me Now (Radio edit) / Cradle Me Now (Album version, MCA (1992) (USA promotion)
Smoked Out (Radio edit) / Smoked Out (Album version), MCA MCA5P-3351 (1995) (USA promotion)
Blindside (Radio edit) / Blindside (Album version) / Fairies Wear Boots, MCA MCA5P-3447 (1995) (USA promotion)
Destructive Signs (Radio edit) / Destructive Signs (Album version), MCA MCA5P-3454 (1995)

Albums:
DOOMSDAY FOR THE DECEIVER, Roadrunner (1986)
Hammerhead / Iron Tears / Desecrator / Fade To Black / Doomsday For The Deceiver / Metalshock / She Took An Axe / Der Führer / Flotzilla
NO PLACE FOR DISGRACE, Roadrunner RR 9549 (1988)
No Place For Disgrace / Dreams Of Death / NE Terror / Escape From Within / Saturday Night's Alright For Fighting / Hard On You / I Live You Die / Misguided Fortune / PAAB / The Jones
WHEN THE STORM COMES DOWN, MCA DMCG 6084 (1990)
The Master Sleeps / Burned Device / Deviation / October Thorns / No More Fun / Suffer The Masses / 6, Six, VI / Greed / EMTEK / Scars / KAB
CUATRO, MCA MCD 10678 (1992)
Natural Enemies / Swatting At Flies / Message / Cradle Me Now / Wading Through The Darkness / Double Zero / Never To Reveal / Forget About Heaven / Secret Square / Hyperdermic Midnight Snack / Are You Willing / (Ain't Nothing Gonna) Save This world
DRIFT, MCA MCAD 11212 (1995)
Me / Empty Air / Pick A Window / 12 Year Old Boy With A Gun / Missing / Blindside / Remember / Destructive Signs / Smoked Out / Poet's Tell
HIGH - IT'S METAL SO FUCK OFF, Metal

Blade 3984-14126-2 (1997)
Final Step / Hallucinational / It's On Me / High Noon / YH (Your Hands) / Monster / Lucky Day / Toast / High / Everything / Fork Boy
UNNATURAL SELECTION, Metal Blade 3984-14184-2 (1999)
Dream Scrape / Chemical Noose / Promise Keepers / Liquid Noose / Falling / Fuckers / Brain Dead / Way To Go / Win, Lose Or Dead / Welcome To The Bottom

FLYING SKULL (GERMANY)
Line-Up: Achim Nohl (vocals), Roland Saager (guitar), Stefan Uschwa (guitar), Elmar Birlo (bass), Ralph Blankart (drums)

A Heavy Metal five-piece influenced by classic Speed and Power Metal.

Albums:
DARKNESS, Flying Skull 1st R. (1991)
Tommyknockers / Nightwalk / Lonesome Child / Darkness / Hawkeye / Child Of Icka / Annie / The Unknown Day
REVELATION, Flying Skull 2nd R. (1993)
Forgotten World (Genesis) / Red Death / 1912 / They / Take My Hand / Thumbs Down / Keep On Running

FORBIDDEN
(San Francisco, CA, USA)
Line-Up: Russ Anderson (vocals), Craig Loccicero (guitar), Tim Calvert (guitar), Matt Camacho (bass), Steven Jacobs (drums)

Known in 1985 initially as FORBIDDEN EVIL this San Francisco thrash act have weathered the storm that has seen so many of their contemporaries drift away.
The band's original line-up comprised vocalist Russ Anderson, guitarists Glen Alvelais and Craig Loccicero, bassist Matt Camacho and drummer Paul Bostaph. In their early days FORBIDDEN EVIL regularly played alongside the likes of EXODUS and TESTAMENT and demos secured a deal with Combat Records. Guitarist Rob Flynn also had a lengthy spell in the band before leaving for VIO-LENCE and later MACHINE HEAD.
Truncating their name to simply FORBIDDEN the band's first album of 1989 put the act firmly into the extreme metal end of the market. A tour of Europe, including an appearance at the 'Dynamo' festival, enhanced their live reputation. The 'Dynamo' show was recorded and tracks subsequently released on the live mini-album 'Raw Evil-Live At The Dynamo'.
Guitarist Glen Alvelais departed prior to the 'Twisted Into Form' album making way for ex-

MILITIA man Tim Calvert. The album also saw Andy Galeon. Dennis Pepa and Mark Osegueda of DEATH ANGEL on backing vocals.

FORBIDDEN toured guesting for EXODUS and SACRED REICH before the band were to unite with the DEATH ANGEL members again when FORBIDDEN played as support to DEATH ANGEL in America prior to their first British gig at London's Hammersmith Odeon alongside DEATH ANGEL and VICIOUS RUMOURS.

However, record company disputes put paid to FORBIDDEN's recording schedule in America and the band duly signed to German label G.U.N. Records at the same time welcoming new drummer Steve Jacobs for European dates opening for GOREFEST. Their 1994 album 'Distortion' included a remake of KING CRIMSON's '21st Century Schizoid Man'.

Bostaph later joined TESTAMENT for one album and more permanently SLAYER. Loccicero, Jacobs and Camacho founded MAN MADE GOD, a band that featured guitarist Ahrue Lister later of MACHINE HEAD.

Alvelais created BIZARRO with guitarist Nick St. Denis (later of PRO-PAIN) and drummer Paul Hopkins (later of SKINLAB). Alvelais then joined TESTAMENT for a tempestuous period before resuming activity with BIZARRO then forging LD/50 with ex-GEEZER vocalist Clark Brown.

Singles/EPs:
Victim Of Changes / Forbidden Evil / Chalice Of Blood / Through Eyes Of Glass, Under One Flag 12FLAG 108 (1989) ('Live at the Dynamo' EP)

Albums:
FORBIDDEN EVIL, Under One Flag FLAG 27 (1989)
Chalice Of Blood / Off The Edge / Through Eyes Of Glass / Forbidden Evil / March Into Fire / Feel No Pain / As Good As Dead / Follow Me
TWISTED INTO FORM, Under One Flag FLAG 43 (1990)
Parting Of The Ways / Infinite / Out Of Body (Out Of Mind) / Step By Step / Twisted Into Form / RIP / Spiral Depression / Tossed Away / One Foot In Hell
POINT OF NO RETURN - THE BEST OF, Under One Flag FLAG 73 (1992)
Chalice Of Blood / Out Of Body (Out Of Mind) / Feel No Pain / Step By Step / Off The Edge / One Foot In Hell / Through The Eyes Of Glass / Tossed Away / March Into Fire / Victim Of Changes

DISTORTION, Gun (1994)
Distortion / Hypnotized By The Rhythm / Rape / No Reason / Feed The Hand / Wake Up! / Mind's 'I' / All That Is / Undertaker / 21st Century Schizoid Man
GREEN, Gun 74321 44249-2 (1997)
What Is The Last Time? / Green / Phat / Turns To Rage / Face Down Heroes / Over The Middle / Kanaworms / Noncent$ / Blank / Focus

FORCED ENTRY (Seattle, WA, USA)
Line-Up: Tony Benjamins (vocals / bass), Brad Hull (guitar), Colin Mattson (drums)

Seattle based Progressive Thrash Metal band FORCED ENTRY first emerged with the 1987 demo 'Thrashing Helpless Down'.

Albums:
UNCERTAIN FUTURE, Relativity (1989)
Bludgeon / Kaleidoscope Of Pain / A Look Through Glass / Anaconda / Octoclops / Unrest They Find / Morgulon / Foreign Policy
AS ABOVE, SO BELOW, Relativity (1991)
Bone Crackin' Fever / Thunderhead Macrocosm, Microcosm / Never A Know, But The No / We're Dicks / Apathy / The Unextinguishable / As Of Yesterday / When One Becomes Two / How We Spent Our Summer Vacation
THE SHORE, Morning Wood (1995)

FORCEFED (CANADA)
Line-Up: Jeff Cool (vocals / guitar), Caughey Machine (guitar), The Bull (bass), Scantron (drums)

Pembroke, Ontario based Thrash / Crossover act. The band, created in December 1995 originally as a trio of frontman Jason Junop a.k.a. 'Jeff Cool', bassist Brandon Kennedy - 'The Bull' and drummer Chris Chartrand - known as 'Scantron', were initially known as LOUDMOUTH.

As LOUDMOUTH the band put in their debut live gig in February 1996 and issued the 14 track demo 'No Commercial Potential' the following month.

The group would augment their sound with the induction of second guitarist Caughey Machine for a second demo 'That Guy's Head'. A CD EP ensued entitled 'Chop Shop' but this would be limited in the extreme - to just 1 copy.

The band evolved into FORCEFED when it was learnt that a Chicago act already held the name LOUDMOUTH. A further demo session 'Special Places' would be the first product under the new name.

In August of 1998 Machine decamped to

169

attend college. For a brief period FORCEFED operated with Evan Lobeck filling in on second guitar but then reverted back to a trio. Both Junop and Kennedy also operate with CORPSEBIKE.

FORTE (OK, USA)
Line-Up: James Randel (vocals), Jeff Scott (guitar), Richard Sharpe (bass), Greg Scott (drums)

Oklahoma Thrash Metal act FORTE arrived with the 1990 demo tape 'Dementia By Design'. The band signed to Germany's Massacre Records for the debut album 'Stranger Than Fiction'. Line-up included former OLIVER MAGNUM singer James Randel, guitarist Jeff Scott, bassist Ghames Jones and drummer Greg Scott.
The 1994 album 'Division' witnessed a radical change in the band format with Roy Kelly introduced on bass and vocals now in the hands of Bill Dollins. The album included a cover version of ACCEPT's 'Fast As A Shark'. The 1997 'Destructive' record saw Dollins supplanted by David Thompson. Original singer James Randell made a return in November 1999.
Jones travelled on to BLACK SYMPHONY during 1997 and was ensconced in the MICHAEL SCHENKER GROUP for the German guitar guru's 2001 opus 'Be Aware Of Scorpions'.

Albums:
STRANGER THAN FICTION, Massacre (1992)
Coming Of The Storm / The Inner Circle / Stranger Than Fiction / G-13 (Devoid of Thought) / Mein Madness / Time and Time Again / Digitator / Between the Lies / The Last Word / The Promise
DIVISION, Massacre (1994)
Dischord / Inhuman / Thirteen Steps / Last Machine / E 2 M.N. / In This Life / One Flesh / Division / Legacy Of Silence / Ultimatum / Back To Zero / Fast As A Shark
DESTRUCTIVE, Massacre (1997)
Barcode / Deviate/ Hammer / Destructive / October / Heal Me / Strength / Never Sleep / The Hard Way / Art of War / Eternal / Far Away
RISE ABOVE, Massacre (1999)
Man Against Machine / Fading Away / Ninety Nine / Forgiven / Rise Above / Destroyer / Poison Tongue / Burn / Over My Head / Until the End of Time

MARTY FRIEDMAN (USA)

Marty Friedman fronted the multi platinum

MEGADETH throughout their commercially most successful period. Previous to MEGADETH the mop topped six stringer made his mark with HAWAII and CACOPHONY. His solo work is mainly instrumental, displaying the guitarist's inventiveness and penchant for Japanese and Arabian scales.
The 'Dragon's Kiss' album includes his former CACOPHONY colleagues guitarist JASON BECKER and drummer Deen Castronovo.
1997's 'True Obsessions' album features both Greg Bisonette, previously with DAVID LEE ROTH, and veteran ex-VANILLA FUDGE / CACTUS / KGB / KING KOBRA man CARMINE APPICE on drums, whilst the bass parts are supplied by MEGADETH colleague Nick Menza.
The album is also unusual in that it's the first of Friedman's solo efforts to feature vocals, although Friedman subcontracted the work out to Stanley Rose and NIGHTRANGER's Jesse Bradman.
The album also marked a more melodic approach by Friedman to his solo work and was written whilst Marty was out with MEGADETH on the 'Youthanasia' tour.
Friedman left MEGADETH in 2000.

Albums:
DRAGON'S KISS, Roadrunner RR 9529-2 (1988)
Saturation Point / Dragon Mistress / Evil Thrill / Namida (Tears) / Anvils / Jewel / Forbidden City / Thunder March
SCENES, Roadrunner CDRR 9104-2 (1992)
Tibet / Angel / Valley Of Eternity / Night / Realm Of The Senses / West / Trance / Triumph
TRUE OBSESSIONS, Metal Blade 3984 14219 2 (1997)
Rio / Espionage / Last September / Rock Box / The Yearning / Live And Learn / Glowing Path / Intoxicated / Farewell / Thunder March

FRONT (RUSSIA)

Thrashcore outfit FRONT had their first four albums only issued in cassette form.

Albums:
METALLISAZIJA, (1988)
LEBEN IM LEICHENHAUS, (1988)
KRESTY, (1989)
DER WASSER DER KÖLN, (1990)
MORTAL SURGERY, (1992)

FROZEN SUN (HOLLAND)
Line-Up: Boris Bouma (vocals), Jelle Bakker (guitar), Juliette Van Caspel (bass), Felix Van

Dommelen (keyboards), Richard Van Leeuwen (drums)

FROZEN SUN's first demo was issued in August 1995 and was followed by support slots to TIAMAT, LIFE OF AGONY and FEAR FACTORY locally.
Following the release of a second demo the group toured Holland with THE GATHERING and, in 1996, finally released their debut album 'Unspoken'.
Playing Neo Thrash with Industrial, Funk and Hardcore influences, a career highlight thus far has been a spot on the bill of 1996's 'Dynamo Festival'.

Albums:
UNSPOKEN, DSFA DSFA 1003 (1996)
Face Down / Heritage (Break The Chain) / This Identity / Leash / Womb / Dry Mouth / Gimmick / Cosmic Truth / Choke / Unspoken

FROZEN SUN (DENMARK)
Line-Up: Kenny Nielsen (vocals), Michael Kopietz (guitar), Nick Jensen (guitar), Henrik Kopietz (bass), Thomas Moller (drums)

Albums:
DIMENSIONS, Serious SE 004CD (1996)
Once And For All / Life In Misery / Obsession / Grey / Puss Gore n' Decay / Streetwalker Song / In The Shadow Of Your Soul / Censorship Equals / Defect Dimension Of Souls / Into The Outro

FURY (AUSTRALIA)
Line-Up: Michael O'Neill (vocals), Rick Boon (guitar), Darren McLennan (guitar), Steven Comacchio (bass), Derek Beauchamp (drums)

Thrashers FURY are almost unique in their field in that rhythm guitarist and driving force behind the band Ricky Boon, an erstwhile member of CLAUDIA'S GHOST, is completely blind. Boon initially founded FURY with guitarist Darren McLennan, a veteran of Gothic Rock act CHALICE, and DUNGEON vocalist Lord Tim. Before long Michael O'Neill, ex-singer with ACID and guitarist with BLOODLUST, came in to front the band as touring commenced with Aaron Dewsbery taking up bass and ACID's Ben Harris on drums.
FURY opted for a career relocation to Adelaide, drafting bassist Steven Comacchio and drummer Derek Beauchamp in the process. The latter already had a well documented past with acts such as NECROSIS, VALHULL and SLAYER tribute band MANDATORY SUICIDE. Beauchamp

also performs with Punk acts TOXIC SHOCK and N.F.I.
In March of 1999 FURY donated tracks to the Blacklight 'Time Capsule 2000' compilation as well as the Australian Metal collection 'Down Under Ground 3'. Dwell Records in America would pick up on the band too for their ongoing tribute album series and FURY duly delivered a cover of 'Symphony Of Destruction' for a MEGADETH tribute album. Further contributions to Dwell's tribute arsenal came with tracks for SUICIDAL TENDENCIES, DEATH and KING DIAMOND tributes. FURY would also manage to put in a showing at the American 'Metal Meltdown' festival.
A four track EP, 'Stigmatized', arrived in March of 2000 with the band's second full length album 'Slavekind' released the following year.

Singles/EPs:
Fallen Ones / Tempest Deceit / Stigmatised / Excuses, Fury FCD002 (2000) ('Stigmatized' EP)

Albums:
FURY, Fury FCD001 (1997)
Bleeding Me Dry / Lost In An Unknown Mind / Innocence / Forever / Save Me / Final Scream / 1814 (Empire's End) / Pay The Price / Fuck You
SLAVEKIND, Fury FCD003 (2001)
Shapes Of Three / Slavekind / One Thousand Pasts / Forsaken / Denying Fear / The Serpent's Kiss / Lies Of This Insanity

FURY (Hamilton, OH, USA)
Line-Up: Don Delph (vocals), Nick Rotundo (guitar), Pat Bishop (bass), Jim Dee Gadd (drums)

Singles/EPs:
Sharp Knives And Heavy Chains, Furyous (1984)

Albums:
FURY, Furious (1983)
Crossfire / Bonified Freak / Potted Delite / Time Waster / Closet Case / Flash Four

GAMMACIDE
(Arlington, TX, USA)

Arlington, Texas based "Ecological" Thrash band previously going under the title of WARLOCK. As GAMMACIDE the band issued one demo plus a solitary album for Wild Rags 'Victim Of Science' during 1989. The band would splinter during the early '90s. In 1992 erstwhile GAMMACIDE man Rick Perry founded the Industrial flavoured PUNCTURE in league with SOLITUDE AETURNUS guitarist John Perez, POST MORTEM STATEMENT sampler Per Nilsson and drummer Larry Moses of Punk acts WHY AM I? and DAYS OF DECISION. Meanwhile vocalist Varnam Ponville and guitarist Scott Shelby relocated to Louisiana to assemble the Doom styled Thrash outfit CAULDRON. They would be joined in this endeavour by bassist Zeb Perkins and drummer Jason Thibodeaux for the ensuing 'For The Love Of Pain' album.

Albums:
VICTIMS OF SCIENCE, Wild Rags WRR016 (1989)

GANG GREEN (Boston, MA, USA)
Line-Up: Chris Doherty (vocals / guitar), Fritz Ericson (guitar), Joe Gittleman (bass), Brian Betzger (drums)

Punk Speedcore Metallers GANG GREEN were previously known as DRUNKS AGAINST MAD MOTHERS. Created in the early eighties as a trio GANG GREEN made themselves instantly recognizable by their adoption of the Budweiser beer logo as their official emblem.
Vocalist / guitarist Chris Doherty and drummer Brian Betzger were members of JERRY'S KIDS in between an erratic early period for GANG GREEN but got the band rolling again as a priority in 1985.
GANG GREEN's first outing came with a track on the 1982 compilation album 'Boston Not L.A.' followed swiftly by inclusion on another compilation 'Unsafe At Any Speed'. The band fragmented shortly after with vocalist / guitarist Chris Doherty forming DRUNKS AGAINST MAD MOTHERS. A former GANG GREEN guitarist, Tony Nichols, formed trad Metal outfit MELIAH RAGE.
Doherty resurrected GANG GREEN in 1985 releasing the 7" single 'Alcohol'. In early 1986 a four track EP 'P.M.R.C. Sucks' surfaced followed up the same year with the band's first album 'Another Wasted Night'.
The brothers guitarist Chuck Stilpen and bassist Glenn Stilpen departed after the first album and by 1988 had forged an alliance with ex-STRAW DOGS members to form MALLET-HEAD releasing their self titled debut on Roadrunner Records.
GANG GREEN regrouped adding his JERRY'S KIDS colleague drummer Brian Betzger, bassist Joe Gittleman and guitarist Fritz Ericson.
The band performed a short British tour in late 1987 alongside CIRCLE JERKS. The third album title 'I81B4U' was a crafty sleight at the VAN HALEN album '0U812'.
GANG GREEN gained valuable experience touring as support to DIRTY ROTTEN IMBECILES in Europe. However, Gittleman was to quit before the live album. His position was taken by Josh Pappe, previously with tour mates DIRTY ROTTEN IMBECILES. Gittleman later surfaced once again with platinum Ska Rockers the THE MIGHTY MIGHTY BOSSTONES.
GANG GREEN went their separate ways in the early '90s but would reunite in 1997 for 'Another Case Of Brewtality'.

Singles/EPs:
Alcohol (1985)
P.M.R.C. Sucks (1986)
Living Loving Maid / We'll Give It You / Born To Rock, Roadrunner RR 2463-1 (1987)
We'll Give It To You / Skate Hell, Roadrunner RR 65470 (1987)
Bartender / Lost Chapter / Rent / Put Her On Top / Cum In U, Roadrunner RR 9500-1 (1988) ('I81B4U' EP)

Albums:
ANOTHER WASTED NIGHT, Taang! 856418 (1986)
Another Wasted Night / Skate To Hell / Last Chance / Alcohol / Have Fun / 19th Hole / Skate Hate / Let's Drink Some Beer / Protect And Serve / Another Bomb / Voices Carry / Sold Out Alabama
YOU GOT IT, Roadrunner RR 349591 (1987)
Haunted House / We'll Give It To You / Sheet Rock / Ballerina Massacre / Born To Rock / Bomb / L.S.D. / Whoever Said / Party With The Devil / Some Things / The Climb / Sick, Sex, Six
OLDER... BUDWEISER, Emergo EM 9464-2 (1989)
Church Of Fun / Just One Bullet / We Can Go / Tear Down The Walls / Flight 911 / Bedroom Of Doom / Casio Jungle / Why Should You Care / I'm Still Young / The Ballad
CAN'T LIVE WITHOUT IT - LIVE,

Roadrunner RR 9380-2 (1990)
Let's Drink Some Beer / Bartender / Lost
Chapter / We'll Give It To You / We Can Go /
Have Fun / Last Chance / Just One Bullet /
Born To Rock / Rabies / Voices Carry / Sold
Out / Bedroom Of Doom / Bomb / Alcohol
KING OF BANDS, Roadrunner RR 92542
(1991)
Thunder / Alcohol / We'll Give It To You /
Bartender / Ballad / Fuck In A / Just One
Bullet / Another Wasted Night / Put Her On
Top / Church Of Fun / Rub It In Your Face
**LET IT BURN (BECAUSE I DON'T LIVE
THERE ANYMORE)**, Roadrunner (1994)
BACK AND GACKED, Taang TAANG
133CD (1997)
Livin' In Oblivion / Time To Pay / You Tucked
It To Me / Here To Stay / Accidental
Overdose / Deflect And Swerve
PRE SCHOOL, Taang (1997)
Sold Out / Terrorize / Snob / Lie Lie / Don't
Know / Rabies / Narrow Mind / Kill A
Commie / Have Fun / Selfish
ANOTHER CASE OF BREWTALITY, Taang
TAANG 135CD (1997)
Eviction Party / Wash The Blood / Break The
Bottle / Hole (In The Road) / Death Of The
Party / I Missed It / Beach Whistle / Don't
You Know / Tricked Into Bed… Again /
Denied / This Job Sucks / Out On The
Couch / Weekend Millionaire / I'll Worry
About It Monday / Time To Pay / Say Good
Buy / Livin' In Oblivion / Accidental Overdose
/ 6,000 Crucified Slaves / Suspect Device /
Penalty Box / To The Point / Here To Stay

GARGANTUA SOUL
(New Haven, CT, USA)
Line-Up: Kris Keyes (vocals), Marc
Amendola (guitar), Jason Bozzi (guitar),
Brendan Kane Duff (bass), Tommy Hetz
(keyboards), Budzy (turntables), Opus
(drums)

GARGANTUA SOUL, fronted by former
BLIND JUSTICE vocalist Kris Keyes, are
making serious headway with their groove
orientated Thrash Rock style. The band
received huge exposure as part of the VH-1
movie 'At Any Cost' where GARGANTUA
SOUL performed as the fictional band 'The
Strange Divas', getting to perform an original
song 'Drive' to a TV audience of millions. The
band would also land a valuable appearance
at the MP3 stage at the 'Woodstock '99'
festival.
To date GARGANTUA SOUL have issued two
self financed albums, most recent being the
September 2001 'Impact'.

Albums:
THE FIRST, THE LAST, THE TRIBE,
Wonderdrug (2000)
The First / Drive / No Oasis / S.O.S. /
Prophet Of The Fire / Rat Pack / Angel Of
Apocalypse / Cover Me / Hands Of Life /
God My / Electrified
IMPACT, (2001)
Calling My America / Isabella Madonna / Far
Away / About Earth / Deep Cover /
Gargantua / Wolfvision / Rabbit Song / Jacob
/ Shankaracharya / Dark Knight

GARGOYLE (Portland, OR, USA)
Line-Up: Tim Lachman (vocals), Kevin
Sanders (guitar), Doug Smith (bass), David
Kendall (drums)

Founded in late 1981 by guitarist Kevin
Sanders and drummer David Kendall prior to
adding ex-MONARCH bassist Doug Smith.
With Kendall on lead vocals GARGOYLE
surfaced onto the tape trading scene in 1985
with a demo comprising 'Into The Darkness',
'The Man In Black' and 'Crimson Red'.
Vocalist Tim Lachman would later found
STATE OF THE ART in league with his
brother, future HALFORD / DIESEL
MACHINE guitarist Pat Lachman, future
RAISED BY ALIENS bassist Alex Sarabia
and drummer Dennis Kelly.
The Lachman siblings would later be found in
both ERROR 7 and ELEVENTH HOUR with
both of these acts donating tracks to an IRON
MAIDEN tribute album.
GARGOYLE drummer David Kendall would
later be located as a member of Portland Pop
Rockers COLORFIELD.

Singles/EPs:
The Burning / Look Homeward / Final
Victory, New Renaissance NRR 88 (1988)

Albums:
GARGOYLE, New Renaissance NRR88
(1988)
Nothing Is Sacred / The Burning / Aryan
Diplomacy / Final Victory / Look Homeward /
Out From The Shadows / Dark Mirror Dream
/ Blind Faith / Down To The Ground

GENOCIDE INC. (CANADA)

A mid '80s Canadian Thrash Metal band
GENOCIDE INC. included ex-members of
OUTBREAK. The band released the
'Chainsaw Slaughter Demo' in 1986 and its
1907 follow up 'Black List'.

GIGANDHI (DENMARK)
Line-Up: Jens Christiansen (vocals), Martin

Spanner Zimmermann (guitar), Kris B. Prasada Rao (guitar), Jacob Oxner (bass), Jens Hesselholdt (drums)

A Danish Thrash / Hardcore outfit.

Albums:
RAFFLESIA, Pingo TBA TBCD 003 (1996) Nashwari Pul / Last Wish / No Shame / Avoid / In My Head / Spasmodic / Scornful Lies / Gigandhi / Haze Before The Eyes / Slow Pain

GODFALL (FINLAND)
Line-Up: Jani Peippo (vocals), Sami Hämäläinen (guitar), Jere Kuukkanen (guitar), Antti Sjöblom (bass), Perttu Laakso (drums)

Formed in 1993, GODFALL started life as a Thrash Metal quartet featuring a band composed of Julle (vocals), Jere (guitar), Sami (guitar) and Perttu (drums). Unable to find a bassist the Finns decided upon switching Julle to the bass slot and adding Jani Peippo on vocals.
GODFALL, having released their first demo later on in 1993, quickly began to forge a more Death Metal direction, although Julle quit in late '94 and thus new bassist Antti joined the ranks.
Signed by Abstract Emotion in the summer of 1995, GODFALL released their debut EP later the same year.

Singles/EPs:
The Sound Of Robogroove EP, Abstract Emotion AE004 (1995)

GOD FORBID (Brunswick, NJ, USA)
Line-Up: Bryon Davis (vocals), Doc Coyle (guitar), Dallas Coyle (guitar), John Outcalt (bass), Corey Pierce (drums)

New Jersey's GOD FORBID, founded by drummer Corey Pierce and ex FEINT 13 guitarist Dallas Coyle issued early product on the independent 9 Volt label. The band had evolved from its earlier inception as MANIFEST DESTINY through to INSALUBRIOUS before settling on GOD FORBID. During May of 1997 GOD FORBID were joined by vocalist Bryon Davis and in September of the same year by erstwhile WOMB bassist John 'Beeker' Outcalt.
Guitarist Doc Coyle would deputize on a temporary basis for AS DARKNESS FALLS in 1998.
Upon signing to German concern Century Media for the highly praised 'Determination' album GOD FORBID upped their American

touring plans appearing with AMEN and SHADOW FALL for a March tour then hooking up with the NEVERMORE / OPETH / CHILDREN OF BODOM dates in April.

Singles/EPs:
Mind Eraser / Habeeber / Madman / Nosferatu / Inside, 9 Volt 9V001 (199-) ('Out Of Misery' EP)

Albums:
REJECT THE SICKNESS, 9 Volt 9V008 (1999)
Amendment / Reject The Sickness / N2 / No Sympathy / Assed Out / Ashes Of Humanity (Regret) / Dark Waters / Heartless / Weather The Storm / The Century Fades
DETERMINATION, Century Media (2001)
Dawn Of The New Millennium / Nothing / Broken Promise / Divide My Destiny / Network / Wicked / Determination Part I / Determination Part II / God's Last Gift / A Reflection Of The Past / Dead Words on Deaf Ears

GODHELPUS (Lockport, IL, USA)
Line-Up: Brian Leli (vocals), Andy Avezzano (guitar), Jeff Slawnikowski (bass), Ryan Blazek (drums)

Albums:
COME DAMNATION, Godhelpus (2000)
Godhelpus / Rage / Cleansed / 655-321 / Despair / Numb / The End...
DISABLE THE SUN, Godhelpus (2002)
The Harvest / The Lucid Decay / Disable The Sun / Immune / Suicide Christ

GODSEND (UK)
Line-Up: Bob Reid (vocals), Andy Sneap (guitar), Wayne Banks (bass), Mole (drums)

Nottingham trad Thrash Metal band, GODSEND featured ex-SABBAT men Andy Sneap and Wayne Banks and former SLEEZEPATROL drummer, Mole (real name Ian Etheridge)
Having released the 'Heavier Than A Death In The Family' four track demo in 1993 (comprising 'Self Sacrifice', 'Dressed In Skin', 'Realms' and 'Mind Flying', the group added new bassist Jason Birnie in early 1995 and recorded a new four track demo titled 'When Man Plays God'.
GODSEND broke up in 1996 despite offers of record deals. Mole later sessioned for WRAITH. Sneap continued an engineering and production career, gaining a credit on the 1996 release from DEARLY BEHEADED and later STUCK MOJO. Sneap is now a highly rated producer much in demand.

By 1998 Mole had his own tribute act on the circuit titled MOLETALLICA.

Albums:
GODSEND, Stay Free STAY 006CD (1994)

GOTHIC SLAM (NJ, USA)
Line-Up: Dan Gomex (vocals), Klaude Ryker (guitar), Bill Genese (guitar / keyboards), J.T. (bass), Dave Chavarri (drums)

Power metal outfit originally known as STRYKER in 1984. By 1988 the band title had changed to GOTHIC SLAM.
The second album, featuring a cover of THIN LIZZY's 'Thunder And Lightning', was produced by RAVEN drummer Rob 'Wacko' Hunter.

Albums:
KILLER INSTINCT, Roadrunner RR9554 (1988)
Skankin' / Living To Survive / Stryker / Bedlam / Tormentor / Killer Instinct / Stand Up And Fight / Fought For Death
JUST A FACE IN THE CROWD, Torrid / Roadracer RO94741 (1989)
Why Not? / Who Died And Made You God / Battered Youth / Thunder And Lightning / Feel The Pain / Cry Freedom / Violence

Imprisoned / Keep The Faith / Demented Obsession / Contract Killer

GRAVEDIGGER (GERMANY)
Line-Up: Chris Boltondahl (vocals), Peter Masson (guitar), Willi Lackman (bass), Albert Eckardt (drums)

GRAVEDIGGER formed in 1980 in Gladbeck and their debut album, 'Heavy Metal Breakdown', with keyboard contributions from Dietmar Dillhardt, sold more than 40,000 copies in Europe, although the band had initially made their recording debut supplying two tracks to the 'Rock From Hell' compilation album.
The original line-up of the band comprised vocalist / guitarist Peter Masson, bassist Chris Boltendahl and drummer Lutz Schmelzer, a trio that remained stable until 1982 when Schmelzer left and was replaced by Philipp Seibel. The following year a decision was taken for Masson to concentrate on guitar duties and allowing Boltendahl to take over the microphone. A new bassist, Willi Lackmann was promptly recruited.
By the time the band came to record the 'Heavy Metal Breakdown' debut album Siebel had been replaced on drums by Albert Eckhart, although Willi Lackmann soon

JENS BECKER of GRAVEDIGGER
Photo : Nico Wobben

CHRIS BOLTENDAHL of GRAVEDIGGER
Photo : Nico Wobben

MANNI SCHMIDT of GRAVEDIGGER
Photo : Nico Wobben

departed and Boltendahl filled the vacancy in order to record the 'Shoot Her Down' EP released after the album.

Although one Rene T. Bone (real name Rene Teichmann) is credited for playing bass on GRAVEDIGGER's second album, 1985's 'Witch Hunter', a brand new bassist, C.F. Brank had joined the band by the time Noise released the record. Indeed, bass duties were actually undertaken by both Boltendahl and Masson on the record as they had fired Teichmann during recording in March 1985.

GRAVEDIGGER's third album, 'Wargames', appeared in 1986. It was something of a disappointment to all concerned in terms of sales and led to the departure of Masson from the ranks.

Opting to go in a more commercial direction with new guitarist Uwe Lulis in tow the German outfit adopted the new title of DIGGER and recorded an album titled, rather misleadingly in hindsight, 'Stronger Than Ever'. Needless to say, the record flopped and the group split.

In the wake of the DIGGER disaster bassist Brank hooked up with S.A.D.O. whilst Lulis and Boltendahl opted to stay together and formed HAWAII with drummer Jochen Börner and bassist Rainer Bandzus, although the project never got beyond the demo stage.

In 1993 Boltendahl decided to reform GRAVEDIGGER, the new line-up featuring Boltendahl, Uwe Lulis, bassist Tomi Gottlich (ex-ASGARD and IRON ANGEL) and drummer Peter Breitenbach. This group released a four-track promo CD and 1993's 'The Reaper'. However, by 1994 Breitenbach was out, joining WARHEAD, in favour of the well travelled Jörg Michael (ex-AVENGER / MEKONG DELTA / RAGE / HEADHUNTER) GRAVEDIGGER recorded the album 'Symphony Of Death' before Michael joined RUNNING WILD and new drummer Frank Ulrich teamed up with the Gladbeck crew.

Ulrich's tenure with the band was to be relatively brief. Although he played on 1995's 'Heart Of Darkness' album he encountered personal differences with his bandmates and departed, being succeeded by former CAPRICORN and WALLOP drummer Stefan Arnold. Ulrich joined X WILD for their third album 'Savage Land'.

Returning to action with the conceptual 'Tunes Of War' record in 1996 the band toured Germany in 1997 with support from SINNER, the record having enjoyed several weeks in the loftier regions of the German national charts. GRAVE DIGGER's return to form came courtesy of 'Tunes Of War's ambitious concept. A conceptual piece based upon Scottish history and liberal in its use of that tried and trusted Heavy Metal instrument the bagpipes. The band also novelly invited the German Rock media on a trip through the ancient battlefields of Scotland.

GRAVE DIGGER stuck to the historical theme for 1998's 'Knights Of The Cross', an album based on the exploits of the knights Templar, this album providing further momentum to their revival. Japanese variants of the album saw bonus tracks in covers of BLACK SABBATH's 'Children Of The Grave' and RAINBOW's 'Kill The King'. Despite this welcome reversal of fortunes the man behind the revival Tomi Göttlich decamped and was superseded by ex-RUNNING WILD, X WILD and CROSSROADS man Jens Becker.

Touring found the band on the road in Europe with IRON SAVIOUR and American act IMAGIKA. Both Boltendahl and Lulis would both guest on IMAGIKA's '… And So It Burns' album.

GRAVE DIGGER toured Germany in January of 2000 supported by Italians WHITE SKULL. Lulis departed toward the end of the year being swiftly replaced by Manni Schmidt, previously with RAGE. GRAVE DIGGER's tenth studio album, the mediaeval themed 'Excalibur', would once again find the band with a strong presence in the national album charts. The band this time taking journalists by bus from Germany to Stonehenge and Tintagel castle for the pre-launch listening party. A limited digi-pack run of this outing would include an exclusive track 'Black Cat' whilst the Japanese release, in keeping with tradition, held one more bonus cut namely a cover of IRON MAIDEN's 'Running Free'.

GRAVE DIGGER would delve into cover territory once more in late 2001 cutting a version of LED ZEPPELIN's 'No Quarter'. The band's set at the annual 'Wacken Open Air' in Germany would see the light of day as the 2002 live album 'Tunes Of Wacken'.

GRAVE DIGGER, together with support from BRAINSTORM, undertook European touring to kick off 2002. However, following January dates in Germany and shows in Southern Europe the band's projected Belgian and Dutch gigs for March would be cancelled as Schmidt was incapacitated with a virus the guitarist had caught whilst on the Iberian continent.

Also in March of 2002 ex-members guitarist Uwe Lulis and bassist Tommi Göttlich returned to the fore with the adventurous conceptually based REBELLION, taking on no less than the Bard's 'Macbeth' as the theme for their opening shot 'A Tragedy In Steele'. Joining the ex-GRAVE DIGGER personnel for REBELLION would be WARHEAD frontman Bjorn Eilen on second guitar, drummer Randy Black from Canadian Thrashers ANNIHILATOR and vocalist

Michael Seifert from Osnabruck acts BLACK DESTINY and XIRON.

Singles/EPs:
Shoot Her Down / Storming The Brain / We Wanna Rock You, Noise N0016 50-1672 (1984)
Ride On / Spy Of Mason / Shadows Of A Moonless Night / Fight The Fight, Grave Digger (1993) (Promotion release)
Rebellion (The Clans Are Marching) / Truth / Dark Of The Sun / The Ballad Of Mary (Queen Of Scots), G.U.N. GUN 103 BMG (1996) (Promotion release)
Rebellion (Live) / The Dark Of The Sun / Heavy Metal Breakdown / Witchhunter / Headbanging Man, G.U.N. GUN 74321 48738 2 (1997) ('The Dark Of The Sun' EP)

Albums:
HEAVY METAL BREAKDOWN, Noise N007 08-1670 (1984)
Headbanging Man / Heavy Metal Breakdown / Back From The War / Yesterday / We Wanna Rock You / Legion Of The Lost / Tyrant / 2000 Lightyears From Home / Heart Attack
WITCHHUNTER, Noise N0020 (1985)
Witch hunter / Nightdrifter / Get Ready For Power / Love Is A Game / Get Away / Fight For Freedom / School's Out / Friends Of Mine / Here I Stand
WARGAMES, Noise N0034 (1986)
Keep On Rockin' / Heaven Can Wait / Fire In Your Eyes / Let Your Heads Roll / Love Is Breaking My Heart / Paradise / (Enola Gay) Drop The Bomb / Fallout / Playin Fools / The End
BEST OF THE EIGHTIES, Noise NO234-2 (1992)
Heavy Metal Breakdown / Shoot Her Down / Get Away / Paradise / (Enola Gay) Drop The Bomb / Fallout / Back From The War / Witch Hunter / Keep On Rockin' / 2000 Lightyears From Home / Heaven Can Wait / Headbanging Man / Night Drifter / We Wanna Rock You / Yesterday / Don't Kill The Children / Tears Of Blood / Girls Of Rock n' Roll
THE REAPER, G.U.N. GUN 032 BMG 74321 17142-2 (1993)
Tribute To Death / The Reaper / Ride On / Shadows Of A Moonless Night / Play Your Game (And Kill) / Wedding Day / Spy Of Mas'On / Under My Flag / Fight The Fight / Legion Of The Lost (Part II) / And The Devil Plays Piano / Ruler Mr. H. / The Madness Continues
SYMPHONY OF DEATH, G.U.N. GUN 039 BMG 74321 19908-2 (1994)
Intro / Symphony Of Death / Back To The

Roots / House Of Horror / Shout It Out / World Of Fools / Wild And Dangerous
HEART OF DARKNESS, G.U.N. GUN 060 BMG 74321 24746-2 (1995)
Tears Of Madness / Shadowmaker / The Grave Dancer / Demon's Day / Warchild / Heart Of Darkness / Hate / Circle Of Witches / Black Death
HEART OF DARKNESS, G.U.N. GUN 060 BMG 74321 24746-2 (1995) (Digi pack version)
Tears Of Madness / Shadowmaker / The Grave Dancer / Demon's Day / Warchild / Heart Of Darkness / Hate / Circle Of Witches / Black Death / My Life / Dolphin's Cry
TUNES OF WAR, G.U.N. GUN 74321 39035-2 (1996)
The Brave / Scotland United / The Dark Of The Sun / William Wallace (Braveheart) / The Bruce / The Battle Of Flodden / The Ballad Of Mary (Queen Of Scots) / The Truth / Cry For Freedom (James VI) / Killing Time / Rebellion (The Clans Are Marching) / Culloden Muir / The Fall Of The Brave
KNIGHTS OF THE CROSS, G.U.N. (1998)
Deus Io Vult / Knights Of The Cross / Monks Of War / Heroes Of This Time / Fanatic Assassins / Lionheart / The Keeper Of The Holy Grail / Inquisition / Baphomet / Over The Sea / The Curse Of Jacques / The Battle Of Bannockburn
EXCALIBER, G.U.N. (1999)
The Secrets Of Merlin / Pendragon / Excalibur / The Round Table (Forever) / Morgana Le Fay / The Spell / Tristan's Fate / Lancelot / Mordred's Song / The Final War / Emerald Eyes / Avalon
THE GRAVE DIGGER, Nuclear Blast (2001)
47 GERMANY
Son Of Evil / The Grave Digger / Raven / Scythe Of Time / Spirits Of The Dead / The House / King Pest / Sacred Fire / Funeral Procession / Haunted Palace / Silence / Black Cat
TUNES OF WACKEN, (2002)
Scotland United / Dark Of The Sun / The Reaper / The Round Table (Forever) / Excalibur / Circle Of Witches / Ballad Of Mary / Lionheart / Morgana Le Fay / Knights Of The Cross / Rebellion / HM Breakdown

GRAVEN IMAGE (USA)
Line-Up: Rob Griffin (vocals / guitar), Glenn Irwin (bass), Mike Clemens (drums)

The debut single features lead vocalist Mike Aldridge.

Singles/EPs:
People In Hell Want Ice Water: No Rest (For You) / Warn The Children, Rockhaus

America (1984)
Warn The Children / No Rest (For You) /
The House, Rockhaus America RRPD1
(1987)

THE GREAT KAT (USA)

Reckoned by many to be as mad as a March
hare, The Great Kat first reared her head in
1987 touting herself as the world's fastest
guitarist and only true musician.

Having attended the famed Julliard School Of
Music, Kat signed to Roadrunner and
recorded her debut album, the unsubtle
'Worship Me Or Die' to an interesting array of
opinion from the world's Metal press.

By 1989 Kat had seemingly found suitable
musicians in order to tour with, the lucky duo
being bassist Chip Marshall and drummer
Kevin Dedario.

Later releases have been short on duration if
crammed to the hilt with energy. The 1998
'Bloody Vivaldi' opus features a take on
Vivaldi's much loved 'Four Seasons', the 39
second hyper blast of 'Blood' and also
Sarasate's 'Carmen's Fantasy'. The 2000
release 'Rossini's Rape' plumbed even
deeper into the realms of the truly disturbing
with workouts of Rossini's 'William Tell
Overture' and Bazzini's 'The Road Of The
Goblins'.

Singles/EPs:
Satan Says EP, (1986)

Albums:
WORSHIP ME OR DIE, Roadracer RO
95892 (1987)
Metal Messiah / Kat Possessed / Death To
You / Satan Goes To Church / Worship Me
Or Die / Demons / Speed Death / Kill The
Mothers / Ashes To Dust / Satan Says /
Metal Massacre
BEETHOVEN ON SPEED, Roadracer RO
93732 (1990)
Beethoven On Speed / Flight Of The
Bumble-Bee / Funeral March / God / Sex
And Violins / Gripping Obsession /
Worshipping Bodies / Total Tyrant / Ultra-
Dead / Revenge Of The Mongrel / Kat Abuse
/ Made In Japan / Beethoven Mosh (5th
Symphony) / Paganinni's 24th Caprice /
Guitar Concerto In Blood Minor / Back To
The Future: For Geniuses Only
DIGITAL BEETHOVEN ON CYBERSPEED,
Great Kat (1996)
GUITAR GODDESS, Blood And Guts Music
(1997)
Rossini's The Barber Of Seville / Dominatrix
/ Feast Of The Dead / Sarasate's Gypsy
Violin Waltz Zigeuneriveisen

BLOODY VIVALDI, Great Kat (1988)
Vivaldi's 'The Four Seasons' For Violin,
Chamber Orchestra And Band / Torture
Chamber / Blood / Sarasate's 'Carmen
Fantasy' For Violin & Band
ROSSINI'S RAPE, TPR (2000)
Rossini's 'William Tell Overture' For
Symphony Orchestra & Band / Sodomize /
Castration / Bazzini's 'The Road Of The
Goblins' For Violin, Piano & Band

GRIFFIN (NORWAY)
Line-Up: Tommy Sebastian (vocals), Kai
Nergaard (guitar), Marcus Silver (guitar),
Johnny Wangberg (bass), Marius Karlsen
(drums)

A 1998 formation GRIFFIN, led by
BLOODTHORN guitarist Kai Nergaard and
who deal in retro style traditional Thrash style
Metal, was originally founded as a sideline to
the members priority acts BLOODTHORN,
DARK AGES and ATROX. A demo was duly
cut, which uniquely featured the sounds of
double bass and saxophone, but would
remain unreleased. A second attempt, the
'Conquers The World' session, scored the
band a deal with French label Season Of Mist
for the October 2000 debut album 'Wasteland
Serenades'.

GRIFFIN gained the valuable support slot to
MAYHEM's European tour, bringing onboard
new guitarist Marcus Silver shortly after. This
revised line up would cut a second GRIFFIN
album, the more Metal inclined April 2002
'The Sideshow'.

Albums:
WASTELAND SERENADES, Season Of
Mist SOM034 (2000)
Mechanized Reality / The Usurper / Spice
Keeps Me Silent / Obsession / New
Business Capitalized / Hunger Strikes /
Always Closing / Punishment Macabre / Exit
2000 / Wasteland Serenade / Dream Of The
Dreamers (Bliss 2)
THE SIDESHOW, Season Of Mist SOM063
(2002)
Prologue / Shadows Of Deception / Horrific /
Freakshow / The Last Rays Of A Dying Sun /
Death Row League / What If / A Distant
Shore / Vengeance Is Mine / Today's
Castaway / Cosmic Revelation / Epilogue

GRIFFIN (San Rafael, CA, USA)
Line-Up: Billy McKay (vocals), Mike 'Yaz'
Jastremski (guitar), Rick Cooper (guitar), Tom
Spraybery (bass), Rick Wagner (drums)

GRIFFIN came together when ex-METAL
CHURCH drummer Rick Wagner joined

forces with vocalist William Rodrick 'Billy' McKay and guitarist Rick Cooper in 1980. Recording their first demo in 1982 the band quickly progressed into one brought up on a staple diet of British Heavy Metal and, at one time, featured guitarist Henry Hewitt, formerly 'U.S. Metal' compilation participants EXXE.

The band's ten song deep second demo initially proved difficult to obtain directly from the band, GRIFFIN oddly reluctant to let potential fans in on the fun, but soon emerged on the thriving tape trading circuit.

In 1983 GRIFFIN relocated to San Francisco's Bay Area supplementing their line-up with guitarist Mike 'Yaz' Jastremski and bassist Thomas Sprayberry.

The material was quick to impress Shrapnel head Mike Varney who signed the group with 'Flight Of The Griffin' arriving in 1984. The album was a powerful statement of intent and second album 'Protectors Of The Lair' followed suit although minus Jastreemski and Sprayberry as GRIFFIN trimmed down to a trio.

Albums:
FLIGHT OF THE GRIFFIN, Shrapnel (1984) Hawk The Slayer / Heavy Metal Attack / Submission / Creeper / Flight Of The Griffin / Fire In The Sky / Hell Runneth Over / Judgement Day / Travelling In Time
PROTECTORS OF THE LAIR, Griffin (1986) Eulogy Of Sorrow: Awakening / Hunger / Infinite Voyage / Cursed Be The Deceiver / Entity: Watching From The Sky / Sanctuary / Truth To The Cross / Poseidon Society / Eulogy Of Sorrow (Reprise)

GRINDER (GERMANY)
Line-Up: Adrian (vocals / bass), Andy (guitar), Lario (guitar), Stefan Arnold (drums)

Metal band GRINDER debuted with the 'Sacred To Death' demo and included ex-WALLOP drummer Stefan Arnold. GRINDER's debut album 'Dawn For The Living' was produced by Kalle Trapp, whilst the third release, 'Nothing Is Sacred', is noted for production by Harris Johns and Tom Stiehler. GRINDER later evolved into CAPRICORN. Guitarist Andy joined RAWBONE.

Arnold joined GRAVE DIGGER for their 'Tunes Of War' album.

Singles/EPs:
Reeling On The Edge / Incarnation Off / Truth In The Hands Of Judas / Just Another Scar (Live) / Dawn For The Living (Live) / F.O.A.D. (Live), No Remorse NRR1011 (1990)

Albums:
DAWN FOR THE LIVING, No Remorse NRR 1003 (1988) Obsession / Dawn For The Living / Sinners Exile / Magician / Frenzied Hatred / Dying Flesh / Delirium / Traitor / F.O.A.D.
DEAD END, No Remorse NRR 1007 (1989) Agent Orange / Dead End / The Blade Is Back / Inside / Just Another Scar / Total Control / Why / Train Raid / Unlock The Morgue
NOTHING IS SACRED, Noise (1991) Drifting For 99 Seconds / Hymn For The Isolated / The Spirit Of Violence / Nothing Is Sacred / None Of The Brighter Days / Superior Being / Dear Mr. Sinister / Pavement Tango / The Nothing Song / NME

GRIP INC. (USA)
Line-Up: Gus Chambers (vocals), Waldemayr Sorychta (guitars), Jason Vie Brooks (bass), Dave Lombardo (drums)

GRIP INC. are most noted for their inclusion of ex-SLAYER drummer DAVE LOMBARDO, a man who whilst with his former unit often topped the 'best drummer' polls in magazines for many years. His relationship with his erstwhile band mates in SLAYER was known to be fragile and his departure was no surprise. However, it took a few years to re-emerge with GRIP INC.

The band also feature British ex-21 GUNS vocalist Gus Chambers, former HEATHEN bassist Jason Vie Brooks and ex-VOODOO CULT guitarist Waldemayr Sorychta. (Lombardo had met Sorychta whilst laying down drums on a VOODOO CULT album as special guest). A fledgling version of GRIP INC. also included ex-OVERKILL guitarist Bobby Gustafson but his tenure was a brief one.

Lombardo later enjoyed a stint with TESTAMENT and issued a solo album, the pseudo classical 'Vivaldi'. The drummer would also forge FANTOMAS with ex-FAITH NO MORE singer Mike Patton.

Vie Brooks formed part of the 2000 HEATHEN reunion.

Albums:
THE POWER OF INNER STRENGTH, SPV Steamhammer 085 76922 (1995) Uno / Savage Seas / Hostage To Heaven / Monster Among Us / Guilty Of Innocence / Innate Affliction / Colors Of Death / Ostracized / Cleanze The Seed / Heretic War Chant / Longest Hate
NEMESIS, SPV 085-18322 (1996) Pathetic Liar / Portrait Of Henry / Empress (Of Rancor) / Descending Darkness / War

GRIP INC.
Photo : Alex Solca

Between One / Scream At The Sky / Silent Stranger / The Summoning / Rusty Nail / Myth Or Man / Code Of Silence
SOLIDIFY, SPV 085-18592 (1999)
Isolation / Amped / Lockdown / Griefless / Foresight / Human? / Vindicate / Stresscase / Challenge / Verrater (Betrayer) / Bug Juice

GRUNGEON (AUSTRALIA)
Line-Up: Doug Dalton (vocals / guitar), Greg Morley (guitar), Glen Sullivan (bass), Wayne Campbell (drums)

Sydney Metal band founded by ex-SUICITY guitarist Doug Dalton and former MORTAL SIN drummer Wayne Campbell. GRUNGEON included tracks on the 'Redrum' and 'While My Guitar Gently Kills Your Mother' compilation albums.
Dalton and Sullivan left the fold in 1994 and their positions were filled by guitarist Anthony Hoffman and bassist Dave Collis for a support tour to BRUTAL TRUTH. GRUNGEON broke up shortly after.
Campbell rejoined MORTAL SIN in 1996.

GUITAR PETE'S AXE ATTACK (USA)
Line-Up: John Pisciotta (vocals), Pete Brasino (guitar), Rick Panzeka (bass), Mike Siro (drums)

'Guitar' Pete Brasino was previously a member of THE BEAST. His erstwhile colleague vocalist The Beast contributes backing vocals to the second album.

Albums:
DEAD SOLDIER'S REVENGE, Heavy Metal America (1985)
Won't Ease Up / Dead Soldier's Revenge / Road Warrior / Shattered Paradise / Satan's Twister / Ball Breaker / Thirsty For Blood / Gutter Rat / Diggin' For Gold
NIGHTMARE, Axe Killer (1986)
Axe Attack / Leather, Lace And Studs / Pushing Your Luck / Stand And Fight / Klimaxx / Nitemare (In Queens) / Rock n' Rollin' Thunder / Burning Hearts / She's A Killing Machine / Rockin' All Nite (In New York)

GURD (SWITZERLAND)
Line-Up: V.O. Pulver (vocals / guitar), Tommy B. (guitar), Marek (bass), Tobias Roth (drums)

GURD were formed in January 1994 by ex-POLTERGEIST guitarist V.O. Pulver. Guitarist Tommy B. is ex-EROTIC JESUS.
GURD have toured as support to KREATOR, CORONER, SODOM, PRO-PAIN and BODY COUNT. Their work ethic paid off and by 1996

the band had signed to Century Media releasing third album 'D-Fect' and a remix offering the following year.

Further extensive touring ensued with the likes of STUCK MOJO, PRO-PAIN and LIFE OF AGONY prior to the recording of 1998's 'Down The Drain' with producer Tomas Skogsberg. Further dates followed upon its release with PRO-PAIN.

GURD underwent a drastic overhaul though with three quarters of the band decamping leaving Pulver alone to carry on the name. He duly reforged GURD pulling in former SWAMP TERRORISTS personnel guitarist Spring and bassist Andrej. New face behind the drumkit for the 2000 album 'Bedlam' was ex-JERK man Tschibu.

Albums:
GURD, C&C CC 6243 (1995)
Get Up / You Won't Make It / I.O.U. Nothing / Enough / The Mant (Groovy) / Scum / Cut It Out / The Way You Want / Distinction / Gone So Far / Ceasefire / Don't Ask Me
ADDICTED, Major CC035 (1995)
HxHxHx / Learn / Chill Out / Feel The Silence / Ghost Dance / Face To Face / Red House / Give In / Down And Out / Too Vicious / Higher
D-FECT, Century Media 77150-2 (1996)
What Do You Live For / No Sleep / We've Been Told / Fever Of Pain / Bullshit / Human Existence / Go Go Go / Look Away / This Place / Read My Lips / Think / Heaven Sent / Lose Myself
D-FECT - THE REMIXES, Century Media 77176-2 (1997)
Get Up (Caveman remix) / Heaven Sent (Stop Denying edit) / Go Go Go (Vibe Master remix) / We've Been Told (Powder Rose remix) / Bullshit (Splatter remix) / Heaven Sent (Sweet remix) / Insane / 102
DOWN THE DRAIN, Century Media CD 77203-2 (1998)
Down The Drain / Head Full Of Shit / DeadOr Alive / Bow My Head / I Remember / My Future / T.R.T.L. / Time To Forget / Caught / Help Me / Survive / Skin Up!!
BEDLAM, Century Media (2000)
Masterplan / Big Shot / Bedlam / Stardust / Always / Rule The Pit / V.U.L.T. / Take My Hand / Golden Age / Shed No Tears / Defiance / We Will resist / War Machine

GUERRILA (GERMANY)
Line-Up: Timur Slapke (vocals / guitar), Pete Zimmermann (vocals / guitar), Andi Bauer (bass), Martin Below (drums)

A Thrash Hardcore hybrid founded during 1994. GUERRILLA started to introduce Death

Metal elements into their sound for a 1996 demo. Line-up changes during 1998 led to the recording of the 'Breed Us, Feed Us, Weed Us' album. 'On Target' arrived in 2001.

Albums:
BREED US, FEED US, WEED US, (1999)
ON TARGET, (2001)
Infected / Watchers Of The Sleep / This Time Its War! / City Of Sorrow / Red Moon Rising / Return Of The Repressed / Public Enemy / Blood Minor / Twisted Mind / Follow Me

GWAR (Richmond, VA, USA)
Line-Up: Oderus Urungus (vocals), Balsac, The Jaws Of Death (guitar), Flattus Maximus (guitar), Beefcake The Mighty (bass), Nippleus Erectus (drums)

GWAR burst onto the Metal scene flaunting some of the most outrageous stage costumes ever graced by a Rock band. Offering a heady brew of Sci Fi and a fixation with porn GWAR succeeded in shocking the establishment from the off and the high quality theatrics soon drew in legions of supporters.

The band claimed a lineage millions of years in antiquity as a group of rebel space pirates titled 'Scumdogs Of The Universe'. Supposedly banished to planet earth GWAR claimed responsibility for the extinction of the dinosaurs, the emergence of mankind and the destruction of Atlantis. For these heinous deeds they were imprisoned in Antarctica until their escape in time for debut album 'Hell-O' in 1989.

The outlandish costumes hid the alter ego personas of vocalist Dave Brockie ('Oderus Urungus'), guitarist Mike Derks ('Balsac, The Jaws Of Death'), guitarist Zack Blair ('Flattus Maximus') and bassist Casey Orr ('Beefcake The Mighty').

Needless to say their origins lay not in Antarctica but Richmond, Virginia. Pre GWAR Brockie had been a member of the Hardcore trio DEATH PIGGY which had released three single throughout the '80s 'Love War', 'Death Rules The Fairway' and 'R45'. In 1985 Brockie and DEATH PIGGY drummer Sean Sumner teamed up with director Hunter Jackson who was planning a movie entitled 'Scumdogs Of The Universe'. The costumes for this intended movie would provide the catalyst for the first GWAR incarnation. For a while both Brockie and Sumner divided their duties between DEATH PIGGY and GWAR but Sumner's lifestyle would finally catch up with him. The drummer was imprisoned for attempted murder.

In 1995 the full membership of GWAR released an album 'You Have The Right To

Remain Silent' under their real names billing themselves as the X-COPS. Touring to promote the album without revealing their identities as the GWAR characters proved a struggle. Tragically the year after original GWAR drummer Sean Sumner would take his own life.

Another former GWAR drummer Jim Thompson founded BIO RITMO for a Spanish language Metal album. For their 2000 American dates GWAR redrafted 'The Sexecutioner' and 'Sleazy P. Martini'. The dates were supported by AMEN and LAMB OF GOD.

The GWAR 2000 album 'Slave Gang Singles' was only issued to the bands fan club members.

In 2001 Dave Brockie emerged with his DBX (THE DAVE BROCKIE EXPERIENCE) project album 'Diarrhea Of A Madman'. Also featured in DBX were GWAR men guitarist Mike Derks and drummer Dave Roberts ('Jizmak Da Jusha'). Having first revealed the identity of the band to the media in order to avoid the previous calamity with their X-COPS venture DBX would tour America. Also on the billing for these shows was RAWG - actually the full compliment of GWAR sans costumes.

GWAR announced another bout of North American touring, billed as 'Blood Drive 2002' and commencing 16th January 2002, in alliance with GOD FORBID and SOILENT GREEN. However, these dates would be without the recently departed Sylmentsra Hymen. The tour was further hit when members of SOILENT GREEN suffered an auto accident. GOATWHORE took the newly vacant position.

Albums:
HELL-O, Shimmy Disc 010 (1989)
Time For Death / AEIOU / Americanised / I'm In Love (With A Dead Dog) / Slütman City / World O Filth/ War Toy / Captain Crünch / Püre As The Arctic Snow / Je M'Appelle J Cöusteaü / GWAR Theme / Bone Meal / Öllie North / Techno's Song / U Ain't Shit / Rock & Roll Pärty Töwn
SCUMDOGS OF THE UNIVERSE, Master MASCD 001 (1990)
The Salamaniser / Maggots / Sick Of You / Slaughterama / Kingqueen / Horror Of Yig / Vlad The Impaler / Black And Huge / Love Surgery / Sexecutioner
AMERICA MUST BE DESTROYED, Metal Blade ZORRO 037 (1991)
Ham On The Bone / Crack In The Egg / Gor-Gor / Have You Seen Me? / The Morality Squad / America Must Be Destroyed / Gilded Lily / Poor Ole Tom / Rock n' Roll Never Felt So Good / Blimey / The Road Behind /

Pussy Planet
THE ROAD BEHIND, Metal Blade 3984-17004-2 (1992)
The Road Behind / Overture In N Minor / Krakdown / Voodoo Summoning / Captain Crunch / Have You Seen Me? / SFW
THIS TOILET EARTH, Metal Blade ZORRO 63 (1994)
Saddam A Go-Go / Penis I See / Cat Steel / Jack The World / Sonderkommando / Bad Bad Men / Pepperoni / The Insidious Soliloquy Of Skulhedface / B.D.F. / Fight / The Issue Of Tissue (Spacecake) / Pocket Pool / Slap U Around / Krak Down / Filthy Flow / The Obliteration Of Flab Quarv 7
RAGNORAK, Metal Blade 3984-17001-2 (1995)
Meat Sandwich / The New Plague / Whargoul / Rag Na Rock / Dirty, Filthy / Stalin's Organs / Knife In Her Guts / Think You Outta Know This / Martyr Dumb / Nudged / Fire in The Loins / Surf Of Syn / Crush Kill Destroy / No One But The Brave
CARNIVAL OF CHAOS, Metal Blade 3984-14125-2(1997)
Penguin Attack / Let's Blame The Lightman / First Rule Is / Sammy / Endless Apocalypse / Billy Bad Ass / Hate Love Songs / Letter From The Scallop Boat / Pre-School Prostitute / If I Could Be That / In Her Fear / Back To Iraq / I Stuck On My Thumb / The Private Pain Of Techno Destructo / Gonna Kill U / Sex Cow / Antarctican Drinking Song / Don't Need A Man
WE KILL EVERYTHING, Metal Blade 14237 (1999)
Babyraper / FishFuck / The Performer / A Short History Of The End Of The World (Part VII: The Final Chapter - Abbr.) / Escape From The Mooselodge / Tune From Da Moon / Jiggle The Handle / Nitro Burnin' Funny Bong / Jagermonsta / My Girly Ways / The Master Has A Butt / We Kill Everything / Child / Penile Drip / Mary Anne / Friend / Fuckin' An Animal

HADES

(NJ, USA)
Line-Up: Paul Smith (vocals),
Joe Casilli (guitar), Dan
Lorenzo (guitar), Anthony Vitti
(bass), Tom Coombs (drums)

A renowned name in Metal circles. New Jersey's HADES have weathered the storms of line up changes and break ups to consistently deliver ever improving slabs of technical Heavy Metal. Having attained a worthy cult following on American soil, despite a sometimes overtly socio-politial lyrical stance, HADES have maintained a sturdy fanbase in Germany.

HADES underwent turbulent times in the early '80s. Vocalist Paul Smith left to join the army and for a brief tenure was replaced with John Callura. However, Callura was out within weeks. Bassist Lou Ciarlo also quit, leaving HADES as just a duo of guitarist Dan Lorenzo and drummer Tom Coombs.

Things stabilized somewhat with the addition of bassist Sandy Handsel and guitarist Scott LePage. As HADES found a new frontman in Alan Tecchio the band also pulled in ex-ATTACKER bassist Jimmy Schulman. This line-up recorded the 1985 'The Cross' single. A further live demo 'Live At The Fox' (one of a set of live tapes HADES released in 1986, others being 'Live At The China Club' and 'Live At Manhattans') secured HADES a deal with Torrid Records. HADES' objectives were again hindered though, when Schulman suffered a near fatal car crash putting live work on ice for a lengthy period.

LePage joined Hardcore Rappers MUCKY PUP on an amicable basis and HADES was soon up to strength again by including guitarist Ed Fuhrman.

Vocalist Allan Tecchio, opting to join Texan Progressive techno-metallers WATCHTOWER for their 'Control And Resistance' album, was supplanted by a returning Paul Smith.

Lorenzo founded NON FICTION, along with a returning Tecchio, releasing three albums, although HADES reunited for the 'Exist To Resist' album. Tecchio later fronted POWER in a guest capacity. All was running far from smoothly however as soon after recording various band members announced their intention never to record with HADES again.

During April of 1988 HADES, back with Tecchio and patching up their differences once more, began rehearsing and writing for a new album. LePage was reunited with the act to put down bass and in came new drummer Dave Lescindky.

Originally intended as a final farewell in 1995 the band issued 'Exist To Resist'. There are at least three versions of this compilation with the US, Black Pumpkin version adding four bonus tracks. The CD had some material recorded in 1989, at the very end of their first run. The US version also has alternate artwork as well.

Fan demand to re-issue the old demos resulted in the band releasing 'The Lost Fox Studio Sessions' during 1998. The band themselves admit the sound quality is terrible and recommends it only for die-hard fans!

The time was right and the band, spurred by the demand for classic Thrash, inked a deal with Metal Blade Records

HADES added drummer Ron Lipinski in August of 2000 and re-drafted Jimmy Schulman on bass. The band put in a valuable performance at the annual 'Wacken Open Air' festival in Germany. Their 2000 album 'The Downside' would see M.O.D. and S.O.D.'s larger than life frontman Billy Milano adding backing vocals and D.D. Verni of OVERKILL putting down session bass on the track 'Bitter Suite No. 1'.

HADES released their latest musical chapter 'DamNation' in June of 2001. 2002 saw an independent, 20th anniversary compilation release 'Hades1982-2002' featuring tracks from their entire career.

Singles/EPs:
Girls Will Be Girls / Social Disease, Hades (1982) ('Deliver Us From Evil' EP)
The Cross / Widow's Mite, Hades (1985)

Albums:
RESISTING SUCCESS, Torrid (1987)
On To Illiad / Legal Tender / Sweet Revenge / Nightstalker / Resist Success / Widows Mite / Cross? Masque Of The Red Death
IF AT FIRST YOU DON'T SUCCEED, Torrid (1988)
Opinionate / Process Of Elimination / King In Exile / In The Meantime / Rebel Without A Brain / Aftermath Of Rebellion / I Too Eye / Face The Fat Reality / Technical Difficulties
LIVE: ON LOCATION, Grand Slamm 38(1991)
The Leaders? / King In Exile / On To Illiad / In The Meantime / Opinionate! / Rebel With out A Brain / "A" / Rape Of Persephone / The Cross / Face The Fat Reality / I Too Eye / Aftermath Of Betrayal / Nightstalker / MES (Technical Difficulties) / Diplomatic Immunity
EXIST TO RESIST, Art Of Music 51002 (1995)
Exist To Resist / Rape Of Persephone / Doubt / Colorblind / Deter-My-Nation / Throughout Me, Threw Out You / Second Degree Sleepwalking/ A(G) / The Other / The Leaders '95

185

THE
DOWNSIDE

THE LOST FOX STUDIO SESSIONS, Black Pumpkin (1998)
The Leaders? / Sweet Revenge / Nightstalker / Resist Success / Gamblin' With Your Life / Deter My Nation / Rape Of Persephone / Not A Part Of Your Life / Bete Noir / Throughout Me, Threw Out You / Amerasian Reparation / King In Exile / Opinionate / A / Easy Way Out
SAVIOUR SELF, Metal Blade 3984- 14194-2 (1999)
Saviour Self / Decline And Fall Of The American Empire / Our Father / Active Contrition / To Know One / In The Words Of The Profit / The Agnostic / Y2K / End Of The Bargain / Fall / The Atheist
THE DOWN SIDE, Metal Blade (2000)
Ground Zero N.Y.C. / Align The Planets / Bitter Suite #1 / Hoax / Pay The Price / Hail To The Thief / Shove It / It's A Wonderful Lie / Become Dust / Responsible / The Me That Might Have Been / Ground Zero (Reprise)
DAMNATION, Metal Blade (2001)
Bloast / Out The Window / DamNation / Absorbed Force / Quit / Stressfest / Biocaust / This I Know / Momentary Clarity / California Song / Stop And Go / Bad Vibrations

HALL AFLAME (USA)
Line-Up: Ron Lowd (vocals), Kurdt Vanderhoof (guitar), Brian Smith (bass), Tom Weber (drums)

Having retired from active service in METAL CHURCH, guitarist Kurdt Vanderhoof surprisingly turned up in the IRS signed HALL AFLAME, a band replete with some seriously monstrous guitar work
Interestingly, METAL CHURCH vocalist Mike Howe supplies backing vocals.
In 1997 Vanderhoof re emerged united back with METAL CHURCH drummer Kirk Arrington releasing the outstanding Southern Rock flavoured VANDERHOOF self titled album on SPV Steamhammer Records. Somewhat inevitably Vanderhoof resurrected METAL CHURCH to close the century.

Albums:
GUARANTEED FOREVER, IRS EIRSA 1049 (1991)
Shake The Pain / Child Of Medicine / The Money Cold Wind / No How, No Way / Feed The Fire / One Time Winner / Pirate's Life / Pray To God / Slippin' Through My Fingers / Another Heartbeat / Country Angel

HALLOWS EVE (Atlanta, GA, USA)
Line-Up: Stacy Anderson (vocals), David Stuart (guitar), Tommy Stewart (bass), Tym Helton (drums)

Atlanta Thrash Metal act HALLOWS EVE date back to 1984 with an initial line-up of vocalist Stacy Anderson, guitarists David Stuart and Skellator, bassist Tommy Stewart and drummer Tym Helton. The band's debut appearance came with the inclusion of the track 'Metal Merchants' on the Metal Blade 'Metal Massacre IV' compilation.
Drummer Ronny Appoldt appeared on the debut album although Tym Helton handled the drums on the tracks 'Metal Merchants' and 'Hallows Eve'.
Drums for 'Monument', which included a cover version of QUEEN's 'Sheer Heart Attack', are by Rob Clayton although for live work Paul Kopchinski occupied the drumstool. By the third album Tym Helton was back in the fold.
The track 'D.I.E.' was a featured track on the Metal Blade issued soundtrack album for the 1988 movie 'Black Roses'.
The group appeared to have split in late 1988 as Anderson departed to Los Angeles although Tommy Stewart and David Stuart carried on into the following year looking for new members and writing material.
The duo eventually found new guitarist JAMES MURPHY (ex-AGENT STEEL) and drummer Tom Knight but the pair lasted barely a few months, Murphy joining DEATH and later playing with OBITUARY, CANCER, TESTAMENT, KONKHRA, DISINCARNATE as well as issuing solo product.
Tommy Stewart later turned up as a member of FRAGILE X.

Albums:
TALES OF TERROR, Roadrunner RR 9772 (1985)
Plunging To Megadeath / Outer Limits / Horrorshow / The Mansion / There Are No Rules / Valley Of The Dolls / Metal Merchants / Hallows Eve
DEATH AND INSANITY, Roadrunner RR 9676-1 (1989)
Death And Insanity / Goblet Of Gore / Lethal Tendencies / Obituary / Plea Of The Aged / Suicide / D.I.E. (Death In Effect) / Attack Of The Iguana / Nefarious / Nobody Lives Forever / Death And Insanity (Reprise)
MONUMENT, Metal Blade (1988)
Speedfreak / Sheer Heart Attack / Rot Gut / Monument To Nothing / Pain Killer / The Mighty Decibel / Righteous Ones / No Sanctuary

HAMMER (POLAND)
Line-Up: Rob Keller (vocals), Mick Savage (guitar), Peter Poland (guitar), Robert Joy (bass), Derek Cloud (drums)
Polish Thrash Metal band HAMMER adopted

anglicised stage names for the English version of their 1992 album 'Terror'. Vocalist Robert Köhler became Rob Keller, guitarist Maciej Sawicz adopted the name Mick Savage, fellow guitarist Jaroslaw Kopola turned into Peter Poland, bassist Robert Kurys was Robert Joy and drummer Tomasz Klimczak morphed into Derek Cloud. The band name would also undergo the same process adopting Teutonic umlauts to become HÄMMER.

Previously the band had debuted with four tracks on the 1987 compilation album 'Metalmania '87' sharing space with DESTROYERS. By 1989 an eponymous debut album saw the light of day.

Albums:
HAMMER, (1989)
TERROR, (1991)
TERROR, Shark 028 (1992) (English version)
Terror / Streetfighter / Shut Up / Inside Looking Out / Monsters / Angel's Wrath / This Is War / Old Man

HAMMER HEAD (Tacoma, WA, USA)
Line-Up: Peter Mainzer (vocals / keyboards), Greg Martin (guitar), Brett Haybell (bass), Dave Fender (drums)

Albums:
ROCK FOREVER, HHR 101 (1987)
Arakian Nightmares / Neighbors / Rock Forever / Stone Cold Crazy / Angel / Masters Of Frustration / Holocaust / Grounded / Pain / Point Nine

HAMMERS RULE (Denver, CO, USA)
Line-Up: Blade Duncan (vocals), Spunki Mechlinski (guitar), Shaun Henley (bass), Chuck Hohn (drums)

Denver Thrash Metal act founded in 1984 and including former BLITZKRIEG drummer Chuck Hohn. HAMMERS RULE boasted quite a stageshow. smashing skulls with a huge sledgehammer. The 'Show No Mercy' debut album was delivered in white vinyl format.
Hohn quit in 1986, turning up as a bassist in a Lounge band. He would later join PAXTON'S EMPIRE and NC-17.

Albums:
SHOW NO MERCY, Tangents (1984)
Prelude / The Calm / Before The Storm / After The Bomb / Pool Of Piranhas / Castle Walls / Hammer's Rule / If Only You Knew / Set Me Free / She's A Rocker / Little Girls / Sex, Drugs And Rock n' Roll
AFTER THE BOMB, W.E.B Pentagram HRT-

2 21983 D5 (1985)
Prelude / The Calm / Before The Storm / After The Bomb / Kamikaze / Mission of Death / Stop The World / If Only You Knew
SPONTANEOUS HUMAN COMBUSTION, Metal Enterprises (1991)
Marilyn Monroe / Spontaneous Human Combustion / Madman On The Loose / Shattered Glass / Icepick / Buried Alive / White Widow

HARTER ATTACK (USA)
Line-Up: Richard Harter (vocals / guitar), Kip Lemming (bass), Glenn Evans (drums)

HARTER ATTACK debuted with a four track demo in 1986. Bassist Kip Lemming is ex-RIOT whilst drummer Glenn Evans was also with NUCLEAR ASSAULT. Both Harter and Evans had previously been members of STRIKER.
HARTER ATTACK issued three self-financed singles on their own Arena Records prior to the album and a new line up of Harter and brothers George Chahalis on drums and Nick Chahalis on bass.
Harter's friendship with Evans stood the band in good stead as the HARTER ATTACK album was produced by the NUCLEAR ASSAULT drummer and also boasts guest contributions from fellow members bassist Dan Lilker and Anthony Bramante.

Singles/EPs:
Salt In The Wound / Top Of The World, Arena (1986)

Albums:
HUMAN HELL, Metalcore CORE1CD (1989)
Death Bells Of The Apocalypse / Last Temptation / Slaves Of Conformity / Message From God / Nuclear Attack / Human Hell / Culture Decay / Thugs Against Drugs / Symbol Of Hate / Let The Sleeping Dogs Lie

HATE SQUAD (GERMANY)
Line-Up: Burkhard Schmidt (vocals), Mark Künnemann (guitar), Tim Baurmeister (bass), Helge Dolgener (drums)

Formed in 1993 HATE SQUAD, a band displaying some Hardcore and Death Metal influences to their Thrash style, attracted the attention of G.U.N. Records with their 'Theater Of Hate' demo, leading to a deal and the recording of the 1994 debut album of the same title.
Ex SARGANT FURY and ZENITH bassist Bauke De Groot joined the group after the record hit the stores in order that Tim

Baurmeister could concentrate on guitar. His new axe partner Mark Künnemann would depart after second album 'I.Q. Zero' and was replaced by Markus Fenske for a tour with KREATOR.

1995's 'Sub Zero' album proved to be a collection of remixed tracks lent new life by artists such as ATARI TEENAGE RIOT, DIE KRUPPS, T.A.S.S. and GIGANTOR.

Following the release of 'Sub-Zero' both Bauermeister and De Groot quit (the former joining RYKERS); the band only replacing De Groot with former HEATHEN and GRIP INC. man Jason Vie Brooks in order to begin work on a proper third album.

Vie Brooks formed part of the 2000 HEATHEN reunion.

Singles/EPs:
Not My God / Terror / March Or Die (Stormtroopers Of Death Medley): A) March Of The Stormtroopers Of Death / B) United Forces / C) Freddy Krüger / D) The Ballad Of Jimi Hendrix, G.U.N. GUN 076 BMG 74321 31787-2 (1995) (Promotion release)

Albums:
THEATER OF HATE, G.U.N. GUN 049 BMG 74321 24672-2 (1994)
Cause And Effect / Self-Defence (Is No Offense) / Love-Hate / Theater Of Hate / Perverse Insanity / Bastards / Mindloss / Condemned To Die / Hardness Of Life / Free At Last
I.Q. ZERO, G.U.N. GUN 075 BMG 74321 31447-2 (1995)
Not My God / BDD / My Truth / IQ Zero / Dishonesty / Crucified / Different From You / Terror / Respect
SUB-ZERO, G.U.N. GUN 096 BMG 74321 37500-2 (1995)
Not My God (Die Krupps Remix) / BDD (The Speed Remix) / IQ Zero (TASS Remix) / Different From You (Biochip C Remix) / Every Second Counts (Gigantor Remix) / Not My God (Alec Empire Remix) / Every Second Counts
PZYCO!, G.U.N. GUN 129 BMG 74321 43582-2 (1997)
Who Dares Wins / Freedom Speaks / Mission Done / Psyco! / Synthetic Twins / Just A Dream / Change / Get Loaded / The Senseless Fall / B.T.C. 97

HATRIK (Chicago, IL, USA)
Line-Up: John McPhearson (vocals), Erik Baumman (guitar), John Bernardi (bass), Rich Ryan (drums)

The solitary HATRIK albums sees a cover of the GRAND FUNK RAILROAD hit 'We're An American Band'. In early 1988 HATRIK resurfaced under the new guise of TECHNOKILL.

Albums:
THE BEAST, Roadrunner RR 9761 (1985)
Rule Of War / We're An American Band / Moov / Play To Survive / Demon's Lair / The Beast / I Like To Eat Out / Little Fugue / S.O.S. / The Other Side Of Crazy / Still Of The Night

HATRIX (OH, USA)
Line-Up: Jeff Hatrix (vocals), Dave Felton (guitar), Kevin Skelly (bass), Steve Felton (drums)

Ohio Thrash Metal band HATRIX include ex members of SINISTER and former PURGATORY vocalist Jeff Hatrix in the ranks. Following the solitary HATRIX album most of the band founded MUSHROOMHEAD for a string of albums.

Albums:
COLLISION COURSE WITH NO PLACE, Massacre MASS 040 (1995)
It's Not Hard To Hate / Bad Religion / My Asylum / Psychoface / Deprivation / No One / Status / Soul Shock / Sick Of Myself / Reason To Be / Subliminal / What Comes Around / Joyride

THE HAUNTED (SWEDEN)
Line-Up: Marco Aro (vocals), Jensen (guitar), Anders Bjorler (guitar), Jonas Bjorler (bass), Per Moller Jensen (drums)

A Death / Thrash act with strong Black Metal links. THE HAUNTED was founded by former SÉANCE guitarist Jensen during the summer

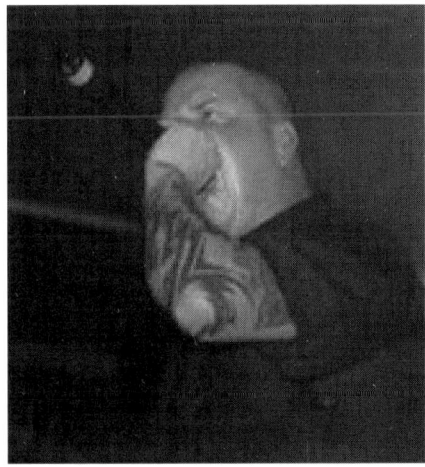

THE HAUNTED

of 1996 bringing in erstwhile INFESTATION, AT THE GATES and TERROR guitarist Anders Bjorler together with drummer Adrian Erlandsson. THE HAUNTED also drafted former DISSECTION and CARDINAL SIN man John Zweetsloot on bass. Zweetsloot's tenure would be brief and another ex AT THE GATES man Jonas Bjorler would take his place.

The band attempted to lure in a lead vocalist and discussions were held with Toxine of SATANIC SLAUGHTER and WITCHERY, and Rogga of MERCILESS. Ultimately it would be Peter Dolving of MARY BEATS JANE that landed the job.

During 1997 Erlandsson created the side project HYPERHUG. Within time he would decamp from THE HAUNTED to concentrate on this act full time. THE HAUNTED attempted to fill the drum position with DISSECTION and OPTHALAMIA man Ole Öhman. Fate intervened when HYPERHUG's singer damaged his hearing curtailing the group. Erlandsson rejoined his former colleagues.

A deal was soon struck with Earache Records and THE HAUNTED undertook touring in Europe with NAPALM DEATH. Shortly after Dolving quit to found ZEN MONKEY. His replacement was FACEDOWN's Marco Aro. With this new line up the band toured the European festival circuit in 1999.

THE HAUNTED was offered the support slot to TESTAMENT's American dates the same year but in mid rehearsal for these shows Erlandsson quit to join premier British Black Metal band CRADLE OF FILTH. The tour went ahead with Per Moller Jensen of KONKHRA and INVOCATOR fame.

Albums:
THE HAUNTED, Earache (1999)
Hate Song / Chasm / In Vein / Undead / Choke Hold / Three Times / Bullet Hole / Now You Know / Shattered / Soul Fracture / Blood Rust / Forensick
THE HAUNTED MADE ME DO IT, Earache (2000)
Dark Intentions / Bury Your Dead / Trespass / Leech / Hollow Ground / Revelation / The World Burns / Human Debris / Silencer / Under The Surface / Victim Iced

HAUNTED GARAGE (CA, USA)
Line-Up: Dukey Flyswatter (vocals), Johnny Ho (guitar), Gaby Godhead (guitar), King Dinosaur (bass), Stiff Slug (drums)

Schlock horror outfit launched by veteran splatter movie director Michael Sonye under the pseudonym of Dukey Flyswatter.

HAUNTED GARAGE also comprise of erstwhile X MEN guitarists Gaby Godhead and Johnny Ho, bassist King Dinosaur and former MAX & THE MAKE UPS / THE RAVONS / JUNKYARD / SAVAGE GRACE drummer Stiff Slug (real name Jon Howard). Guitarist Mike Alvarez of THE RAVONS and MAX & THE MAKE UPS also contributes.

Albums:
POSSESSION PARK, Metal Blade CDZORRO 27 (1991)
Theme / Welcome To Hell / She Freak / Bitch Like You / Psychotic Reaction / 976 Kill / Brain In A Jar / Torture Dungeon / Little Green Men / Dead And Gone / Party In The Graveyard / Hokey Pokey

HAVE MERCY (MD, USA)
Line-Up: Lonnie Fletcher (vocals), Nick Ellingson (guitar), Tom Maxwell (guitar), Rob Michael (bass), John Knoerlein (drums)

Metal band formed in late 1983. HAVE MERCY issued a debut demo the following year featuring vocalist Lee Dayton.

HAVE MERCY underwent line up shuffles with Dayton ousted in favour of Lonnie Fletcher and guitarist Nick Ellingson left the fold prior to the band attaining a deal and his place was filled by John Brenner. However, Brenner's stay was short-lived as Ellingson soon returned.

Albums:
ARMAGEDDON DESCENDS, Relativity (1986)
Intro / Mass Destruction / City Of Doom / Holy Dismissal / Faces Of Death / No Forgiveness

HAVOC (USA)
Line-Up: David Hughes (vocals), Mike Elwood (guitar), Frank Rodriguez (guitar), Matt Hodges (bass), Jeff Groerer (drums)

Albums:
THE GRIP, Auburn (1985)
Blazes / Thrasher / Screams / The Grip / The Force Within

HAVOC MASS (FL, USA)
Line-Up: Ray Wallace (vocals / bass), Ben Meyer (guitar), Andy Wallace (guitar), Curt Beeson (drums)

Thrash Metal band HAVOC MASS included ex-NASTY SAVAGE men guitarist Ben Meyer and drummer Curt Beeson along with former members of LAST RITES frontman Ray Wallace and guitarist Andy Wallace. The band emerged with the 1991 demo 'In Extremities'. A further effort entitled 'Unknown Origin' followed before the 1993 debut album.

The Wallace brothers would go on to create INHUMAN for a series of albums. Both Beeson and Curtis would stick together to found the 2000 act LOWBROW for the 'Victims At Play' album.

Albums:
KILLING THE FUTURE, Massacre MASSCD 019 (1993)
Intro / Scarred For Life / Burned / Prime Directive / All That Is Evil / Distant Signs / Pools Of Blood / Mark My Words / Into Nothingness

HAWAII (USA)
Line-Up: Gary St. Pierre (vocals), Marty Friedman (guitar), Tom Azcredo (guitar), Joe Galisha (bass), Jeff Graves (drums)

HAWAII were initially known as VIXEN in 1981 comprising vocalist Kim LaChance, ex-DEUCE guitarist MARTY FRIEDMAN, bassist Gary St. Pierre and drummer Jeff Graves. Shortly after their formation the band scored inclusion of their track 'Angels From The Dust' on the 'US Metal II' compilation album.

Further demos followed and a mini-album 'Made In Hawaii'. Strangely, the band's next compilation cut 'Heavy Metal Virgin' on the Metal Blade Records 'Metal Massacre II' was credited to a pseudonym of ALOHA.

Shrapnel Records Mike Varney signed the band for the poorly produced but frenetic 'One Nation Underground'. St. Pierre departed for pastures new to front VICIOUS RUMOURS.

Further releases followed as the band got steadily more commercial. The mini-album 'Loud, Wild & Heavy' saw Friedman and Graves alongside fresh recruits vocalist Eddie Day and Joey Galisa on bass. HAWAII expanded by bringing in second guitarist Tom Azevedo for 'The Natives Are Restless'.

Friedman eventually dissolved the band and would turn up as founder member of CACOPHONY as well as releasing solo instrumental albums and more significantly joining MEGADETH.

Albums:
ONE NATION UNDERGROUND, Shrapnel 1009 (1983)
Living In Sin / Silent Nightmare / Escape The Night / You're Gonna Burn / One Nation Underground / Nitro Power / The Pit And The Pendulum / Secret Of The Stars / Overture Volcanica
LOUD, WILD AND HEAVY, Hawaii (1985)
Bad Boys Of Metal / Loud, Wild And Heavy /

Escape The Night / Rhapsody In Black
THE NATIVES ARE RESTLESS, SPV Steamhammer (1985)
Call Of The Wild / Turn It Louder / V.P.H.B. / Beg For Mercy / Unfinished Business / Proud To Be Loud / Lies / Dynamite

HAYWIRE (USA)
Line-Up: Billy Rubin (vocals), Rick Greeno (guitar), John Bruce (bass), Vadim Rubin (drums)

Albums:
PRIVATE HELL, We Bite (1989)
So Good / Sword Swallower / Winding / D.T.E. / Bring The Power Down / Latest God / Private Hell / Pain / Looking Down / Bomber / Body Politic / Fiend Without A Face
PAINLESS STEEL, Nemesis (1989)
Winding Down / Bring The Power Down / Skin Diver / Sword Swallower
ABOMINATIONS, We Bite (1990)
Dropping Like Flies / Skin Diver / Murderers / Crash And Burn / Endtro / Writer's Camp / Incognito God / Two Faced Judas / Hand Job / Short Eyes

HEADHUNTER (GERMANY)
Line-Up: Marcel 'Schmier' Schirmer (vocals / bass), Uwe 'Schmuddel' Hoffmann (guitar), Jörg Michael (drums)

Initially titled CURSE upon their inauguration during 1990. Frontman Schmier had been the mentor behind successful Teutonic thrashers DESTRUCTION. Guitarist Uwe 'Schmuddel' Hoffmann was an erstwhile TALON member whilst drummer Jörg Michael had performed duties with AVENGER, LAOS, MEKONG DELTA, RUNNING WILD and RAGE. Michael continued to record and tour with ex-STEELER guitarist AXEL RUDI PELL in addition to his employment with HEADHUNTER.

Before entering the studio to record the debut album 'Parody Of Life' HEADHUNTER toured Japan in 1990 as well as supporting British veterans SAXON in Europe the same year. The record boasted the services of GAMMA RAY's inimitable Kai Hansen guesting on the track 'Cursed'.

Headline dates in 1993 witnessed ANTIDOTE and ACCUSER as strong support. The band had released the follow up record 'A Bizarre Gardening Accident' and 1995's 'Rebirth', after a very real, very bad and less bizarre car crash involving 'Schmuddel' Hoffmann. For some time it remained unclear as to whether the group would ever record again.

Michael's talents post HEADHUNTER have

191

seen his services retained by AXEL RUDI PELL as well as racking up credits with GRAVE DIGGER and STRATOVARIUS.

In 1998 Schmier successfully reforged DESTRUCTION to great anticipation in Europe.

Albums:
PARODY OF LIFE, CBH Virgin 261 151 (1991)
Parody Of Life / Ease My Pain / Plead Guilty / Kick Over Your Traces / Force Of Habit / Caught In A Spider's Web / Cursed / Crack Brained / Trapped In Reality
A BIZARRE GARDENING ACCIDENT, Major 018/043-2 (1993)
Oh What A Pleasure / Signs Of Insanity / Hit Machine / Born In The Woods / Two Faced Promises / Ramalama / Boozer / Domo / Pangs Of Remorse / Character Assassination / Rude Philosophy / Deadly Instinct / Sex And Drugs And Rock n' Roll
REBIRTH, Major CC024 (1995)
Auf Geht's / Army's Of The Blind / Warhead / Unhuman World / Mistreated / Mindless / Change / Disco / Scares / Adrenalin / Strucked / Don't Bogart

HEADSHOT (GERMANY)
Line-Up: Andi Bruer (vocals), Olaf Danneberg (guitar), Steffen Keuchel (bass), Moritz Hoffmeister (drums)

Thrashcore act HEADSHOT won the 'Braunschweiger Rockwettbewerb '95' contest. The band issued a self financed and financed debut the following year. HEADSHOT have in their time supported DESTRUCTION, JINGO DE LUNCH and HATE SQUAD.
Drummer Moritz Hoffmeister later joined UNDERWATER CIRCUS.

Albums:
BRAIN AT RISK, Headshot (1996)
Day Of The Dead / Mother Earth Meltdown / Two Minutes Hate / Break Lies / Blood On The Screen / Obedience / Sentenced / Struggle For Life / State Of Dependence / The Brain At Risk / Invader / Shadows Of Death

HEATHEN (USA)
Line-Up: Dave Godfrey (vocals), Lee Altus (guitar), Doug Piercy (guitar), Mike Jazstrempski (bass), Carl Sacco (drums)

Noted Tech-Thrash mob HEATHEN were already veterans of the notorious Bay Area Thrash scene by the time of their formation in the early '80s. Drummer Carl Sacco was previously with THE LEWD, METAL CHURCH and MURDER whilst vocalist Sam Kress ran the Metal fanzine 'Whiplash'. Completing the line-up was guitarist Lee Altus. Lacking a bassist HEATHEN soldiered on undertaking their first gigs without one. However, by April 1985 ex-SCEPTRE man Eric Wong had been enlisted. HEATHEN also drafted the scene veteran guitarist Doug Piercy, then a member of CONTROL but having previous credits with COBRA, DELTA and the highly influential ANVIL CHORUS.

After HEATHEN's first demo of 1986 Wong was ousted in favour of ex-GRIFFIN man Mike 'Yaz' Jastremski. Realising Kress was a better writer than a singer he bowed out in favour of former BLIND ILLUSION man Dave Godfrey.

Besides working with HEATHEN Piercy got his name around in 1986 by producing demos for such acts as MORDRED, LEGACY and ATTITUDE ADJUSTMENT.

Their debut album was produced by none other than veteran ex-MONTROSE guitarist RONNIE MONTROSE and included a version of SWEET's 'Set Me Free'. Sacco departed shortly after recording of 'Breaking The Silence' and in his stead came Darren Minter. Jazstrempski was next to go and HEATHEN, minus a permanent bassist, utilized the talents of BLIND ILLUSION guitarist Mark Biedermann to record the bass parts on the 'Victims Of Deception' album. Guest guitar parts came courtesy of ANVIL CHORUS man Thaen Rasmussen.

Breaking away from their American label Combat Records in 1987 HEATHEN purged Godfrey from the band after numerous interested labels expressed concerns over the band's frontman. Godfrey reacted by creating his own act LAUGHING DEAD. For a brief tenure in 1988 HEATHEN worked with erstwhile EXODUS and PIRANHA man Paul Ballof. HEATHEN also worked with David Wayne of METAL CHURCH but this liaison was even shorter. However, before long HEATHEN had re-enlisted Godfrey after Ballof had lasted less than a month. Swallowing their pride HEATHEN invited Godfrey back into the ranks and also recruited bass player Manny Bravo.

HEATHEN's line-up following the 'Victims Of Deception' album comprised Godfrey, Altus, Minter, Piercy and bassist Randy Laire. The album includes a cover of RAINBOW's 'Kill The King'.

In 1989 Altus auditioned for MEGADETH but shied off this possible union concerned with the lifestyle of Mustaine's crew at the time.

Piercy opted out joining ANGELWITCH in January 1991. HEATHEN, back with Piercy, then toured Europe as support to Brazilians

SEPULTURA. Tragedy struck though when Laire was killed in a car crash. Piercy later relocated to Germany to create THE COMPANY.

In 1992 Altus and Rasmussen united with VICIOUS RUMOURS drummer Larry Howe and MY VICTIM singer Jay to create BOMB THREAT touring the California clubs with a nostalgic set of NWoBHM covers.

Thaen Rasmussen took Piercy's place and Jason Vie Brooks took the bass role. Former REXXEN guitarist Ira Black was also inducted during 1992 but the band folded when Altus and Minter joined German Industrial Metal act DIE KRUPPS.

Godfrey joined INNER THRESHOLD, a band formed by ex-DEFIANCE members.

In 1995 Vie Brooks turned up as part of GRIP INC., the band created by ex-SLAYER drummer DAVE LOMBARDO and would later join HATE SQUAD. Black journeyed through ex-EXODUS man Steve Souza's DOG FACE, ex-TESLA guitarist Tommy Skeoch's UTERIS before joining VICIOUS RUMOURS in 2000.

HEATHEN reformed in 2000 with a line up of Godfrey, Altus, Rasmussen, Vie Brooks and Minter.

Singles/EPs:
Set Me Free / Goblin's Blade, Combat 88561 8182-1 (1987)
.

Albums:
BREAKING THE SILENCE, Music For Nations MFN 75 (1987)
Death By Hanging / Goblin's Blade / Open The Grave / Pray For Death / Set Me Free / Breaking The Silence / World's End / Save The Skull
VICTIMS OF DECEPTION, Roadrunner RO 93312 (1989)
Hypnotized / Opiate Of The Masses / Heathen's Song / Kill The King / Fear Of The Unknown / Prisoners Of Fate / Morbid Curiosity / Guitarony / Mercy Is No Virtue

HEATHEN'S RAGE (USA)
Line-Up: Rob Pizzauro (vocals), Rob Warner (guitar), Tony Lee (guitar), Mike Lepond (bass), Chris Teresyn (drums)

Singles/EPs:
Knights Of Steel / City Of Hell / Dark Storm, Rockdream (1986)

HELICON (GERMANY)
Line-Up: Uwe Heepen (vocals), Tom Kusters (guitar), Christian Guth (guitar), Silvester Walevski (bass), Andre Ostopezzo (drums)

Formed in 1986 and debuting with demo 'The Heimbach Tapes', HELICON released the 'Black And White' demo in 1989 and pressed this up as a self-financed single later in the year.

Hit line-up problems which were unresolved until mid 1992 when HELICON signed with Noise Records. In 1994 HELICON shared space with GAMMA RAY, RAGE and CONCEPTION on the live compilation album 'Power Of Metal Live'.

The band settled on a group comprising Heepen, Kusters, Ostapeschen and new guitarist Andy Geisler by 1995, although the group would eventually split in frustration when they lost their record deal.

Singles/EPs:
Black And White / Woman, Helicon (1989)

Albums:
HELICON, Noise N0213-2 (1993)
The Story About Helicon / Helicon Part II / It's Rock n' Roll / Junk / Victim Of Love / Freedom / Black Andite / Come On Rock / Woman / There Is No Rose Without Thorns
MYSTERIOUS SKIPJACK, Noise N0243-2 (1995)
American Fever / Streetgang / Power Magic / Wild Vice Woman / Mysterious Skipjack / Giant Heart / Darkness Of Love / Versatile / Fly In The Sky / Shuffle

HELLHAMMER (SWITZERLAND)
Line-Up: Satanic Slaughter (vocals / guitar), Savage Damage (bass), Bloodhunter (drums)

Formerly known as HAMMERHEAD, this bizarre and primitive extreme Metal outfit was founded in 1982.

Previous to HAMMERHEAD frontman Thomas Gabriel Fischer and bassist Steve had been involved with various fledgling acts emulating their NWoBHM heroes VENOM.

During the August of 1982 Fischer, transferring from bass to guitar, was now fronting a trio of Priestly and drummer Jörg Neubart. Inspired apparently by Newcastle NWoBHM band RAVEN and their Gallagher brothers team Fischer and Priestly adopted the joint stage surnames of 'Warrior'. Neubart became 'Bruce Day'.

Their debut demo, 'Triumph Of Death', was widely regarded as one of the worst examples of a Heavy Metal band ever! 'Metal Forces' magazine editor Bernard Doe in particular cited it as the most appalling thing he had ever heard. History however would dictate that HELLHAMMER would later be recognized as one of the root catalysts of the Black Metal genre.

Although in later years band members have admitted their knowledge of music was basic to say the least when the HELLHAMMER recordings were made nevertheless the band were in possession of an artistic vision which would undoubtedly shape the Metal scene over many years.

In 1983 HELLHAMMER enrolled bass player Martin Eric Ain and drummer Stephen Priestly from SCHIZO. However, invited to submit a fresh demo to Berlin's Noise Records HELLHAMMER very nearly split as Ain felt he did not have the necessary talent to go through with the session!

Still, positive or negative press encouraged Noise to sign the band and the Berlin based label released the 'Apocalyptic Raids' EP which had no details as to what RPM the record should be played at; sounding just as strange at 33RPM as it did at 45!

Metal Blade Records released the EP in America with an extra two tracks.

HELLHAMMER mainman 'Satanic Slaughter' later swapped identities to become Tom G. Warrior and started the avant-garde Metal legends CELTIC FROST in May of 1984 retaining the deal with Noise. CELTIC FROST issued a stream of critically praised outings before fizzling out.

Still an influence in some circles over ten years later, Sweden's ABYSS covered the HELLHAMMER track 'Massacra' on their 1995 album 'The Other Side'.

Warrior forged a new project in the late '90s billed as APOLLYON SUN.

Singles/EPs:
The Third Of The Storms (Evoked Damnation) / Massacra / Triumph Of Death / Horus / Aggressor, Noise N008 50-1668 (1984) ('Apocalyptic Raids' EP)

HELLION (Los Angeles, CA, USA)
Line-Up: Anne Boleyn (vocals), Alan Barlam (guitar), Ray Schenk (guitar), Bill Sweet (bass), Sean Kelly (drums)

HELLION, fronted by vocalist Ann Boleyn (who actually claimed some distance lineage to the decapitated former royal) made their mark on the Los Angeles circuit with a series of demos. One of these tapes was to emerge as the 'Hellion' mini-album and the band, now managed by Wendy Dio, were soon the focus of attention when the record was picked up in Europe by Music For Nations. However, disagreements between management and band were to break the band apart.

Barlam, Schenk and Kelly departed to form BURN after being convinced that a female lead singer was deterring major label attention. Retaining the HELLION name Boleyn soon regrouped to record a new album 'Screams In The Night' with a fresh line up comprising guitarist Chet Thompson, former LION bassist Alex Campbell and ex-DOKKEN drummer Greg Pekka.

Boleyn contributed the track 'Monster Mash' to the 1987 movie 'Return Of The Living Dead - Part II' soundtrack.

The 1988 mini album 'Postcards From The Asylum', with new bassist Dave Dutton, saw the reunion of original HELLION members Barlam and Kelly and features a cover of the JUDAS PRIEST classic 'Exciter'. Thompson meanwhile had a short spell with BRITTON.

The band put in a British club tour during early 1988 supported by MARSHALL LAW which saw the addition of former ALLEGANCE bassist Rex Tennyson, who would later join ex-CATS IN BOOTS vocalist Joel Ellis in HEAVY BONES.

'The Black Book' proved to HELLION's last outing to date. Boleyn published a novel to coincide with the release.

HELLION was resurrected in 1998 by Boleyn, Schenk and Kelly cutting a album the following year which awaits release. Fans were still waiting developments when it was learned in mid 2001 that Boleyn had recorded an album, produced by Mikey Davis, and was auditioning for an entire new band. This new unit, simply billed as ANN BOLEYN and comprising guitarists Mike Guererro and Chris Kessler, former RHINO BUCKET man Eric Becica on bass and drummer Vince Rage, toured Japan in October.

Singles/EPs:
Don't Take No (For An Answer) / Backstabber / Lookin' For A Good Time / Driving Hard, Bongos Lodus (1983) ('Hellion' EP)
Driving Hard / Black Night, Mystic (1983)
The Evil One / Exciter / Never More / Run For Your Life, Music For Nations MFN 82 (1987) ('Postcards From The Asylum' EP)

Albums:
HELLION, Music For Nations MFN 15 (1983)
Break The Spell / Don't Take No / Backstabber / Lookin' For A Good Time / Driving Hard / Up From The Depths
SCREAMS IN THE NIGHT, Music For Nations MFN 73 (1987)
Screams In The Night / Bad Attitude / Better Off Dead / Upside Down Guitar Solo / The Hand / Explode / Easy Action / Put The Hammer Down / Stick 'Em / Children Of The Night / The Tower Of Air
THE BLACK BOOK, Music For Nations CDMFN 108 (1990)

Breakdown / The Black Book / Stormrider / Living In Hell / The Discovery / Losing Control / Arrest... Jail... Bail / Daemon Attack / Conspiracy / Amnesia / The Warning / The Room Behind The Door / The Atonement / Immigrant Song

HELLOWEEN (GERMANY)
Line-Up: Andi Deris (vocals), Michael Weikath (guitar), Roland Grapow (guitar), Marcus Großkopf (bass), Uli Kusch (drums)

German Power Metal band HELLOWEEN quickly developed a large and loyal fan base built upon a series of strong Speed Metal album releases that culminated in the twin album project 'Keeper Of The Seven Keys'. Stylistically HELLOWEEN have trod a path from Speed Metal through an ill fated dalliance with injecting oddball humour through to career revival delivering consistent melodic Metal. However, in spite of two decades of maturity HELLOWEEN are still known to show their Speed Metal teeth on occasion.

Kai Hansen, Marcus Großkopf and Ingo Schwichtenberg had been playing together since 1980 in SECOND HELL then IRON FIST. Vocalist Peter Sielck departed IRON FIST in 1982 effectively putting the band on ice, so during this period of inactivity Hansen received an offer to join POWERFOOL, featuring guitarist Michael Weikath. As things turned out Hansen lured Michael to his own band and then changed the name to HELLOWEEN.

The group came to prominence upon their signing to leading German Metal label Noise Records and three tracks on the notorious 'Death Metal' compilation album in 1984. Their debut mini-album, 'Helloween', and first, full length album 'Walls of Jericho' provided HELLOWEEN with plenty of media attention and critical favour. The mid '80s saw a massive resurgence of interest in German Rock bands and HELLOWEEN quickly established themselves at the top of the heap with successive strong releases.

Following the release of the 'Judas' EP HELLOWEEN set about changing their musical direction, intending to add more scope to their music with the recruitment of PROPHECY's frontman MICHAEL KISKE, who took over vocal duties from Hansen. The band peaked with an elaborate brace of concept albums centred upon the 'The Keeper Of The Seven Keys' tale.

The first 'Keeper...' album, produced by VICTORY's Tommy Newton, was a useful vehicle in gaining popularity for the band outside Europe. Worldwide it went on to sell over half a million copies, shifting over 125,000 in Germany alone. Released in America on the RCA label it peaked at number 102 in the Billboard charts and its success enabled the band to appear as part of the 'Hell On Wheels' U.S. tour along with GRIM REAPER and ARMORED SAINT. RCA did not curry favour with the band though when they released the 13 minute track 'Halloween' as a 4 minute edited single!

These American dates were followed by the quintet's first tour of Japan prior to recording 'Keeper... Part 2' and, in 1988, HELLOWEEN appeared at the Castle Donington 'Monsters Of Rock' festival and toured as support to IRON MAIDEN throughout Europe before their own German headlining dates. In 1989 HELLOWEEN again toured America on the same bill as ANTHRAX and EXODUS. A live mini-album 'Live In The UK' charted in Great Britain but would provide ardent fans two more reasons to shell out for product as the record was issued in Japan as 'Keepers Live' with different artwork and in America as 'I Want Out - Live', again with completely different artwork.

However, stardom, and in particular touring, became anathema to the driving force behind HELLOWEEN, guitarist Kai Hansen. He left to form the studio project GAMMA RAY with former TYRAN PACE vocalist Ralph Scheepers with whom he had worked earlier in PROPHECY (and had previously offered the HELLOWEEN vocalist job to). Ironically, GAMMA RAY overtook HELLOWEEN in the popularity stakes shortly after. Hansen was replaced by ex-RAMPAGE guitarist Roland Grapow. Another shift in personnel saw the induction of drummer Riad 'Ritchie' Abdel-Nabi in November of 1992.

HELLOWEEN signed to IRON MAIDEN's management Sanctuary Music and, convinced that signing to a major label would further their career began efforts to extricate themselves from their Noise deal. The band signed to EMI and promptly landed themselves in a lengthy legal wrangle with Noise, who claimed that they were still under contract. During this period of inactivity the press speculated that Kiske was to join IRON MAIDEN.

Following all the delays, HELLOWEEN seemingly committed commercial suicide by releasing the ludicrously titled 'Pink Bubbles Go Ape' album. Supposed to show that the band had a sense of humour, the Chris Tsangarides produced album with song titles such as 'Heavy Metal Hamsters' only served to alienate their former fans. Indeed, worse was to come when Noise placed an injunction on the album, effectively stopping its release and any live work in Germany.

In 1993, EMI released the band's new album

'Chameleon', a record that was certainly not up to the standards of the past and found HELLOWEEN seriously lacking in direction.

HELLOWEEN, minus Abdel-Nabi who went on to create BABYLON 27 with ex-KINGDOM COME guitarist Heiko Radke-Siab, returned in the summer of 1994 signed to Rawpower, an offshoot of Castle Communications. As well as a new label the band had used their period away from the spotlight for a drastic rethink in both musical and personnel terms. Ingo Schwichtenberg and Michael Kiske both departed and in came former HOLY MOSES / GAMMA RAY member Uli Kusch and Andy Deris respectively, the latter being nabbed from the successful German outfit PINK CREAM 69.

Whilst MICHAEL KISKE released a solo album 'Instant Clarity' featuring Kai Hansen in 1996, fate was not as kind to Schwichtenberg who, suffering from depression and fighting a drug problem, committed suicide in 1995.

A new HELLOWEEN album, 'Keeper Of The Rings', ploughed a much more traditional path harking back to their Noise days. The album charted strongly in their home country and even reached the number 1 position in Japan. The group was forced to take a break in early 1995 when Deris suffered a throat infection forestalling any live work.

Still, the group returned in 1996 with the single, 'The Time Of The Oath', (which included covers of JEAN MICHEL JARRE's 'Magnetic Fields' and JUDAS PRIEST's 'Electric Eye') and an album of the same name, which found Tommy Hansen once more behind the desk. Touring with BRUCE DICKINSON and SKIN, HELLOWEEN were also to release 'High Live' during 1996.

HELLOWEEN made a triumphant return in 1998 with the 'Better Than Raw' album sounding heavier than ever. The album quickly racked up Japanese sales of quarter of a million plus. HELLOWEEN played selective European dates as guests to IRON MAIDEN.

Großkopf made space to execute a side endeavour SHOCKMACHINE during 1999. Joining in the proceedings for the eponymous album would be vocalist Olly Lugosi, X-13 guitarist Rolly Feldman, HELLOWEEN members drummer Uli Kusch and guitarist ROLAND GRAPOW and ROUGH SILK keyboard player Ferdy Doernberg.

Kusch too would get in on the action pursuing his project CATCH THE RAINBOW, a conglomeration of name German Rockers dedicated to paying homage to RAINBOW. An album, 'A Tribute To Rainbow', arrived in 1999 which featured the entire HELLOWEEN cast, alongside GAMMA RAY, PRIMAL FEAR and BRAINSTORM personnel as guests.

Großkopf contributed to EDGUY mainman Tobias Sammet's ambitious AVANTASIA eponymous project album of 2000.The same year saw the issue of a worthy HELLOWEEN tribute album 'The Keepers Of Jericho'. The album benefited from cover artwork by Uwe Karczewski, the man responsible for the sleeve artwork on HELLOWEEN classic albums 'Walls Of Jericho' and 'Keeper Of The Seven Keys'. The album included many of the European Metal scene's rising stars and saw reworkings by acts such as METALIUM, HEAVEN'S GATE, SONATA ARTICA and Italian acts RHAPSODY, DARK MOOR, LUCA TURILLI and LABYRINTH.

In August of 2001 the band suffered a major blow when both guitarist ROLAND GRAPOW and drummer Uli Kusch quit. The pair would soon be announced as having forged a fresh project with SYMPHONY X vocalist Russell Allen. However, news also leaked out that the duo had also assembled a project with the strange title of MR. TORTURE (later scrapped), cutting demos produced by ex-SABBAT guitarist Andy Sneap and confirming their intention to work with ex-HELLOWEEN vocalist MICHAEL KISKE. Later still it would transpire the Grapow / Kusch venture had been renamed MASTERPLAN and the pair were in cahoots with the highly rated erstwhile YNGWIE MALMSTEEN vocalist JORN LANDE.

By mid September it was announced that British drummer Mark Cross had joined the HELLOWEEN fold. Cross had a cosmopolitan range of credits across the Rock field with Greek acts SCRAPTOWN, MAGNA CARTA and SPITFIRE, occult Metal band NIGHTFALL and more recently KINGDOM COME and METALIUM.

GAMMA RAY guitarist Henjo Richter would also be in the running although apparently his services were offered on a temporary basis.

ANDI DERIS would donate his services to the GERMAN ROCK STARS October 2001 song 'Wings Of Freedom' in honour of the September 11th World Trade Center victims. Grosskopf would assist his erstwhile HELLOWEEN colleague Kai Hansen by filling in for an injured Dirk Schlachter of GAMMA RAY for October German gigs.

Singles/EPs:
Judas / Ride The Sky (Live) / Guardians (Live), Noise N0048-6 (1986)
Halloween / Halloween, Noise (1986) (USA promotion)
Judas / Ride The Sky / Guardians / Victim Of Fate (Live) / Cry For Freedom (Live), Noise (1987) ('Judas' EP)
Future World / Starlight / A Little Time, Noise (1987)
Dr. Stein / Savage / Livin' Ain't No Crime,

Roland Grapow, Markus Grosskopf, Andy Deris, Uli Kusch & Michael Weikath of HELLOWEEN Photo : Fin Costello

Noise HELLO 1 (1988) **57 UK**
Dr. Stein / Savage / Livin' Ain't No Crime /
Victim Of Fate, Noise NO116-5 (1988) (3"
CD single)
Dr. Stein / Savage, Noise NO116-6 (7"
single)
I Want Out / Don't Run For Cover / Save Us,
Noise NO126-3 (1988) **69 UK**
I Want Out / Don't Run For Cover, Noise
NO126-6 (1988) (7" single)
I Want Out / Save Us / Don't Run For Cover,
Noise NO126-5 (1988) (12" single)
Intro: Happy Halloween / I Want Out, Noise
(1988) (USA promotion)
Kids Of The Century / Blue Suede Shoes /
Shit And Lobster, EMI (1991) **56 UK**
Helloween / Keeper Of The Seven Keys,
Noise (1991) (Free 12" with 'The Best, The
Rest, The Rare' album)
Kids Of The Century / Blue Suede Shoes /
Interview, JVC Victor VICP 15005 (1992)
(Japanese release)
Number One / Les Hambourgeois Walkways
/ You Run With The Pack, EMI 72348 80146
25 (1992)
Windmill / Cut In The Middle / Introduction /
Get Me Out Of Here, EMI 7243 8 81065 2 8
(1993)
When The Sinner (Edit) / When The Sinner
(Album version) / I Don't Care, You Don't
Care, EMI 72438 805862 9 (1993)
When The Sinner (Edit) / I Don't Care, You
Don't Care / Oriental Journey, JVC Victor
VICP 15025 (1993) (Japanese release)
I Don't Wanna Cry No More / Red Socks
And The Smell Of Trees / Ain't Got Nothing
Better, Victor VICP 15029 (1993) (Japanese
release)
Step Out Of Hell / Cut In The Middle /
Introduction / Get Me Out Of Here, Victor
VICP 15030 (1993) (Japanese release)
Mr. Ego (Take Me Down) / Where The Rain
Grows / Star Invasion / Can't Fight Your
Desire, Rawpower CMS 6516-5 (1994)
Where The Rain Grows / Mr. Ego (Take Me
Down) / Can't Fight Your Desire / Invasion,
JVC Victor VICP 15035 (1994) (Japanese
release)
Perfect Gentleman / Cold Sweat,
Rawpower RAWX 1002 (1994)
Perfect Gentleman / Cold Sweat / Silicon
Dreams / Grapowski's Malmsuit, JVC Victor
VICP 15037 (1994) (Japanese release)
Cold Sweat Plus Interview, Rawpower
SPC 9526 (1994) (Free with Limited edition
version of 'Master Of The Rings' album)
Sole Survivor / In The Middle Of A
Heartbeat / I Stole Your Love / Closer To
Home, JVC Victor VICP 15044 (1995)
(Japanese release)
Steel Tormentor / A Million To One,
Rawpower RAWP 1017 (1996) (Promotion
release)
Power / We Burn / Rain / Walk Your Way,

Rawpower RAWX1014 (1996)
The Time Of The Oath / Magnetic Fields /
Electric Eye, Rawpower RAWX 1018 (1996)
Forever And One (Neverland) / In The
Middle Of A Heartbeat (Live) / Light In The
Sky / Time Goes By, Rawpower RAWX 1033
(1996)
I Can / A Handful Of Pain / A Game We
Shouldn't Play, JVC Victor VICP 60193
(1998) (Japanese release)
If I Could Fly (Edit) / Deliver Us From Evil /
If I Could Fly (Album version), Nuclear Blast
NB 532-2 (2000)
Mr. Torture, (2000) (Japanese release)

Albums:
HELLOWEEN, Noise NO0021 (1985)
Victim Of Fate / Cry For Freedom / Starlight /
Murderer / Warrior
WALLS OF JERICHO, Noise N0032 (1986)
Walls Of Jericho / Ride The Sky / Reptile /
Guardians / Phantoms Of Death / Metal
Invaders / Gorgar / Heavy Metal Is The Law /
How Many Tears
KEEPER OF THE SEVEN KEYS – PART I,
Noise NO061 (1987) **42 SWEDEN**
I'm Alive / Future World / Helloween / Twilight
Of The Gods
KEEPER OF THE SEVEN KEYS – PART II,
Noise NUK 117 (1988) **7 SWEDEN, 24 UK**
Invitation / Eagle Fly Free / You Always Walk
Alone / March Of Time / Dr. Stein / Rise And
Fall / We Got The Right / I Want Out /
Keeper Of The Seven Keys
HELLOWEEN, Noise NO0088 (1988)
(combines 'Helloween' Mini-album, 'Walls Of
Jericho' album and the 'Judas' EP in one
package)
Starlight / Murderer / Warrior / Victim Of Fate
/ Cry For Freedom / Walls Of Jericho / Ride
The Sky / Reptile / Guardians / Phantoms Of
Death / Metal Invaders / Gorgar / Heavy
Metal (Is The Law) / How Many Tears /
Judas
PUMPKIN TRACKS, Noise (1989) **30
SWEDEN**
Savage / Save Us / Victim Of Fate / Livin'
Ain't No Crime / Don't Run For Cover /
Judas / Future World / Murderer / Starlight /
Phantoms Of Death / A Tale That Wasn't
Right / I Want Out / March Of Time / I'm
Alive
KEEPERS LIVE, JVC Victor (1989)
(Japanese release)
A Little Time / Dr. Stein / Future World / Rise
And Fall / We Got The Right / I Want Out /
How Many Tears
I WANT OUT - LIVE, EMI (1989) (USA
release)
A Little Time / Dr. Stein / Future World / Rise
And Fall / We Got The Right / I Want Out /
How Many Tears

LIVE IN THE UK, EMI EMC 3558(1989) **25 SWEDEN, 26 UK**
A Little Time / Dr. Stein / Future World / Rise And Fall / We Got The Right / I Want Out / How Many Tears

THE BEST, THE REST, THE RARE, Noise NO176 (1991)
I Want Out / Dr. Stein / Future World / Judas / Walls Of Jericho / Ride The Sky / Helloween / Livin' Ain't No Crime / Save Us / Victim Of Fate / Savage / Don't Run For Cover / Keeper Of The Seven Keys

PINK BUBBLES GO APE, EMI EMC 3588 (1991) **14 SWEDEN, 41 UK**
Pink Bubbles Go Ape / Kids Of The Century / Back On The Streets / Number One / Heavy Metal Hamsters / Goin' Home / Someone's Crying / Mankind / I'm Doing Fine Crazy Man / The Chance / Your Turn

CHAMELEON, EMI 7 89368 2 (1993) **35 SWEDEN**
First Time / When The Sinner / I Don't Wanna Cry No More / Crazy Cat / Giants / Windmill / Revolution Now / San Francisco (Be Sure To Wear Flowers In Your Hair) / In The Night / Music / Step Out Of Hell / I Believe / Longing

KEEPER OF THE SEVEN KEYS - PART II, Noise NO240-2 (1994) (Re-issue, featuring bonus tracks)
Invitation / Eagle Fly Free / You Always Walk Alone / March Of Time / Dr. Stein / Rise And Fall / We Got The Right / I Want Out / Keeper Of The Seven Keys / Save Us / Don't Run For Cover / Livin' Ain't No Crime / Savage

MASTER OF THE RINGS, Rawpower RAW CSC 7150-2 (1994)
Irritation / Sole Survivor / Where The Rain Grows / Why? / Mr Ego (Take Me Down) / Perfect Gentleman / The Game Is On / Secret Alibi / Take Me Home / In The Middle Of A Heartbeat / Still We Go

THE TIME OF THE OATH, Rawpower PD109 (1996)
We Burn / Steel Tormentor / Wake Up The Mountain / Power / Forever And One (Neverland) / Before The War / A Million To One / Anything My Mama Don't Like / Kings Will Be Kings / Mission Motherland / If I Knew / The Time Of The Oath

HIGH LIVE, Rawpower RAW DF116 (1996)
We Burn / Wake Up The Mountain / Sole Survivor / The Chance / Why / Eagle Fly Free / The Time Of The Oath / Future World / Dr. Stein / Before The War / Mr. Ego (Take Me Down) / Power / Where The Rain Grows / In The Middle Of A Heartbeat / Perfect Gentleman / Steel Tormentor

PUMPKIN BOX, JVC Victor VICP 60 84-7 (1998) (Japanese release)
Starlight / Victim Of Hate / Cry For Freedom / Walls Of Jericho / Ride The Sky / Guardians / How Many Tears / Judas / Savage / Livin' Ain't No Crime / Save Us / Don't Run For Cover / Starlight (Michael Kiske version) / A Little Time (Version) / Victim Of Fate (Michael Kiske version) / Initiation / I'm Alive / Future World / Invitation / Eagle Fly Free / Rise And Fall / Dr. Stein / I Want Out / Halloween / Follow The Sign / Keeper Of The Seven Keys / Kids Of The Century / Mankind / The Chance / Don't Wanna Cry No More / First Time / When The Sinner / Windmill / Step Out Of Hell / A Little Time (Live) / Dr. Stein (Live) / Future World (Live) / How Many Tears (Live) / Interview with Kai Hansen / Halloween (Edit) / Interview with Michael Kiske, Michael Weikath and Roland Grapow / Eagle Fly Free (Edit) / Interview with Markus Grosskopf, Uli Kusch, Harrie Smits, Jorn Ellerbrock and Andy Deris / Power (Outro)

BETTER THAN RAW, Sanctuary (1998) **8 FINLAND**
Deliberately Limited Preliminary Prelude Period In Z / Push / Falling Higher / Hey Lord / Don't Spit On My Mind / Revelation / Time / I Can / A Handful Of Pain / Laudate Dominium / Back On The Ground / Midnight Sun

METAL JUKEBOX, Sanctuary 4505 (1999) **49 GERMANY, 51 SWEDEN**
He's a Woman-She's a Man / Locomotive Breath / Lay All Your Love On Me / Space Oddity / From Out of Nowhere / All My Loving / Hocus Pocus / Faith Healer / Juggernaut / White Room / Mexican

THE DARK RIDE, Nuclear Blast (2000) **32 FINLAND, 26 GERMANY, 38 SWEDEN, 68 SWITZERLAND**
Behind The Portal / Mr. Torture / All Over The Nations / Escalation 666 / Mirror Mirror / If I Could Fly / Salvation / The Departed / The Sun Is Going Down / I Live For Your Pain / We Damn The Night / Immortal / The Dark Ride

TREASURE CHEST, Metal-Is (2002)
Mr. Torture / I Can / Power / Where The Rain Grows / Eagle Fly Free / Future World / Metal Invaders / Murderer / Starlight / How Many Tears / Ride The Sky (Remix) / Halloween / A Little Time / A Tale That Wasn't Right / I Want Out / Keeper Of The Seven Keys (Remix) / Dr. Stein (Remix) / The Chance / Windmill / Sole Survivor / Perfect Gentleman / In The Middle Of A Heartbeat / Kings Will Be Kings / Time Of The Oath / Forever & One / Midnight Sun / Mr. Ego / Immortal / Mirror Mirror

HELLRAISER (RUSSIA)
Line-Up: Alexander Luov (vocals / guitar), Mike Djanov (vocals / bass), Paul Chinyakov

(drums)

Russian Thrash Metal band HELLRAISER covered MOTÖRHEAD's 'Killed By Death' and JUDAS PRIEST's 'Love Bites' on their 1996 'Live' album.

Albums:
WE'LL BURY YOU!, Metalagen (1990)
Rockets In The Air / I Got A Power / Dark Side Of You / I Wanna Be Free / Danger Zone / Win The Battle / Snakes In The Kitchen
NO BRAIN, NO PAIN, Triton (1994)
No Brain, No Pain / Vision Of Darkness / Killhead / Witch / See You In Hell / The Land Of Dead / Remembering / God Of War
LIVE, Moroz (1996)
03, (1997)
SKORAY POMOSH, (1998)

HELLWITCH (FL, USA)
Line-Up: Pat Raneiri (vocals / guitar), Tommy Mouser (bass), Joe Schnessel (drums)

HELLWITCH, formed in 1984, released a 1987 demo titled 'Mordrivial Dissemination'.

Albums:
SYZYGIAL MISCREANCY, Wild Rags WRE 902 (1990)
The Ascent / Nosferatu / Viral Ehogence / Sentient Transmography / Mordirivial Dissemination / Pyrophoric Seizure / Purveyor Of Fear
TERRASYMMETRY, Lethal LMCD 1111 (1993)
Terrasymmetry / Satan's Wrath / Dawn Of Apostasy

HELSTAR (USA)
Line-Up: James Rivera (vocals), Larry Barragan (guitar), Andre Corbin (guitar), Jerry Abarca (bass), Frank Ferriera (drums)

High octane Power based metallers HELSTAR, created in Houston during 1982, came to the fore on the underground tape trading scene with their debut 1983 demo. The band's original line up comprised ex-DEATHWISH / SCORCHER vocalist James Rivera, guitarists Larry Barragan and Robert Trevin, bassist Jerry Abarca and drummer Rene Lima.
The impact made by the demo soon landed HELSTAR a deal with Combat Records in 1984 and the resulting debut album, 'Burning Star', was produced by drummer Carl Canedy of THE RODS. Ructions hit the band soon afterwards though and Trevin and Lima opted out to make way for guitarist Andre Corbin and drummer Frank Ferriera, whilst Barragan

quit after a row with both the band's management and his colleagues. He intended forming a new band, BETRAYER, but was to quickly rejoin HELSTAR.
Following 'Remnants Of War' HELSTAR split from Combat and re-locating to Los Angeles signed a fresh deal with Metal Blade Records. 'A Distant Thunder' captured worthy reviews and HELSTAR proceeded to tour both America and then Europe opening for TANKARD and YNGWIE MALMSTEEN. Upon their return the band migrated back to their native Houston.
The 'Distant Thunder' album saw HELSTAR covering the SCORPIONS classic 'He's A Woman, She's A Man'.
A line-up change saw HELSTAR split asunder with only Rivera and Barragan remaining. Fresh blood was soon drafted in the form of guitarist Tom Rogers, bassist Paul Medina and drummer Hector Pavan.
Following the 'Nosferatu' release HELSTAR cut a further demo tape consisting of 'Social Circles', 'Scalpel In The Skin', 'Sirens Of The Sun' and 'Change with seasons'. The recording line-up was Rivera, Abaraca, Barragan and drummer Russel Deleon. Soon after Barragan withdrew from the metal scene totally finding a new calling with a Tex-Mex bar band. HELSTAR struggled on playing gigs on the local circuit but under a new title of VIGILANTE.
As VIGILANTE the band members began negotiation with MEGADETH bassist Dave Ellefson with the intention of recording a four track demo. However, circumstances forced their hand as, with the return of Abaraca and under pressure the band reverted back to their HELSTAR moniker. Also forcing the pace was MEGADETH's dumping from the support slot they had at the time with rock giants AEROSMITH. MEGADETH opted out of the tour at a Houston date when main man Dave Mustaine was unable to continue and Ellefson found himself with more time to work with HELSTAR, the planned demo then evolving into the 'Multiples Of Black' album.
By 1998 Rivera was fronting DESTINYS END for their 'Breathe Deep The Dark' album. The singer founded a new act in 2000 titled PROJECT RIVERA which comprised Z-LOT-Z guitarist Eric Halpern, MYSTIC CROSS guitarist Don LaFon, OUTWORLD bassist Brent Marches, VICTIM keyboard player Adam Rawlings and drummer Rick Ward from MIDNIGHT CIRCUS.
It would be reported in August of 2001 that Rivera had joined FLOTSAM & JETSAM after their longstanding vocalist Eric A.K. departed.

JAMES RIVERA of HELSTAR
Photo : Nico Wobben

Albums:
BURNING STAR, Combat MX007 (1984)
Burning Star / Towards The Unknown /
Witch's Eye / Run With The Pack / Leather
And Lust / Possession / The Shadows Of Iga
/ Dracula's Castle
REMNANTS OF WAR, Noise N 0043 (1986)
Unidos Por Trjsteza / Remnants Of War /
Conquest Of War / Evil Reign / Destroyer /
Suicidal Nightmare / Dark Queen / Face The
Wicked One / Angel Of Death
A DISTANT THUNDER, Roadrunner RR
95242 (1988)
King Is Dead / Bitter End / Abandon Ship /
Tyrannicide / Scorcher / Genius Of Insanity /
Whore Of Babylon / Winds Of Love / He's A
Woman, She's A Man
NOSFERATU, Roadrunner RO 94382
(1989)
Rhapsody In Black / Baptized In Blood / To
Sleep / Perchance To Scream / Harker's Tale
(Mass Of Death) / Perseverance And
Desperation / Curse Has Passed Away /
Benediction / Harsh Reality / Surling
Madness / Von Am Lebem Destro Sturm /
Aieliaria And Everon
MULTIPLES OF BLACK, Massacre
MASSCD 053 (1995)
No Second Chance / Will It Catch Again /
Lost To Be Found / When We Only Bleed /
Reality / Good Day To Die / Beyond The
Real Of Death / Save Time / Black Silhouette
Skies / Last Serenade
TWAS THE NIGHT OF A HELLISH XMAS,
Metal Blade 14306 (2000)
Swirling Madness / The King Is Dead / Evil
Reign / Abandon Ship / Baptized In Blood /
To Sleep, Perchance To Scream / Harker's
Tale / The Cursed Has Passed Away /
Scorcher / Angel Of Death

HERESY (UK)
Line-Up: Reevsy (vocals / guitar), Kalv
(bass), Steve (drums)

Nottingham Thrashcore act HERESY made
their mark courtesy of the then fledgling
Earache label with the debut 'Never Healed'
EP. Originally formed by Reevsy, Kalv and
Steve, Reevsy opted to concentrate on vocals
and the band added ex-CONCRETE SOX
drummer John. Later HERESY added ex-
SACRILEGE and UNSEEN TERROR
guitarist Mitch in favour of Reevsy who had
decided to quit. This version of the band
toured Europe and put in Radio One sessions
for the John Peel show.
Mitch would decamp and Baz of RIPCORD
took over for the 'Face Up To It' album which
included a medley of covers versions of the
likes of YOUTH OF TODAY and SIEGE.
Critics that had previously poured praise upon

HERESY found this new record lacking.
1989's 'Thirteen Rocking Anthems' comprised
two 'Peel Session' recordings. Post HERESY
Baz joined DUMBSTRUCK whilst Steve and
Kalv founded 666DEAD.

Singles/EPs:
Never Healed / Despair / Deathbitter /
Anguish Of War / More Blood Is Shed /
Dead, Earache EAR 1 (1985)
Whose Generation, In Your Face FACE04
(1989)

Albums:
HERESY, Earache MOSH 2 (1987) (Split LP
with. CONCRETE SOX)
Genocide / Belief / Visions In Fear / Nausea
/ Release / In Silence
FACE UP TO IT, In Your Face FACE 1 (1988)
Consume / Face Up To It / Too Close To
Home / Flowers In Concrete / Belief /
Network Of Friends / When Unity Becomes
Solidarity / Acceptance / Cornered Rat /
Dedication From Inspiration / Against The
Grain / Sick Of The Stupidity / Trapped In A
Scene / Believing A Lie / Into The Grey /
Build Up - Knock Down / Street Enters The
House / Make The Connection
THIRTEEN ROCKING ANTHEMS, In Your
Face FACE007 (1990)
Everyday Madness Everyday / Ghettoised /
Release / Consume / Face Up To It / Unity -
Solidarity / Open Up (D.Y.S.) / Break The
Connection / Network Ends / Genocide / Into
The Grey / Street Enters The House /
Cornered Rat
NEVER SPLIT THANKS, Toys Factory
(1990)
Never Healed / Despair / Deathbiter /
Anguish Of War / More Blood Is Shed / Dead
/ Genocide / Belief / Visions Of Fear /
Nausea / Release / In Silence / Genocide /
Belief / Visions Of Fear / Nausea / Release /
In Silence / Make The Connection / Trapped
In A Scene / Network Of Friends /
Acceptance
VOICE YOUR OPINION, Lost And Found
LF042CD (1992)
VISIONS OF FEAR, (1995)

HERETIC (Los Angeles, CA, USA)
Line-Up: Mike Howe (vocals), Brian Korban
(guitar), Bobby Marquez (guitar), Dennis
O'Hara (bass), Rick Merrick (drums)

HERETIC were amongst the fray when
California's Thrash scene erupted but made
their mark with some precise Speed Metal.
The band's original vocalist Mike Torres
departed prior to recording to team up with
ABBATOIR for their 'Only Safe Place' album.

The debut mini-album 'Torture Knows No Boundaries' featured singer Julian Mendez who lost his position to Mike Howe in late 1987.

Howe appeared on the 'Breaking Point' album but joined METAL CHURCH the same year. Two members of HERETIC, guitarist Brian Korban and bassist Dennis O'Hara would team up with ex-METAL CHURCH vocalist David Wayne's REVEREND. Korban recently forged Christian Metal act MONTH OF SUNDAYS in league with erstwhile DELIVERANCE guitarist Glenn Rogers.

Albums:
TORTURE KNOWS NO BOUNDARY, Roadrunner RR 9640 (1987)
Riding With The Angels / Blood Will Tell / Portrait Of Faith / Whitechapel / Torture Knows No Boundary
BREAKING POINT, Roadrunner RR 95341 (1988)
Intro/ The Heretic / And Kingdom Fall / The Circle / The Enemy Within / Time Runs Short / Pale Shelter / Shifting Fire / Let 'Em Bleed / Evil For Evil / The Search

HEXENHAUS (SWEDEN)
Line-Up: Tommie Agrippa (vocals), Mike Wead (guitar), Rick Meister (guitar), Jan Blomqvist (bass), Ralph Raideen (drums)

HEXENHAUS were originally titled MANNINYA BLADE, under which name they released one album.

Having adopted the new name in 1987, the band's line-up for the debut album ('A Tribute To Insanity') comprised of vocalist Nicklas Johansson, ex-CANDLEMASS guitarist Mike Wead (real name Mikael Vikström), second guitarist ex-DAMIEN man Rick Meister (real name Andreas Palm), bassist Jan Blomqvist and drummer Ralph 'Raideeen' Ryden.

In early 1989 Niclas Johansson left, to be superseded by ex-DAMIEN vocalist Tommie Agrippa (real name Thomas Lundin). 1990's 'The Edge Of Eternity' album also featured a fresh bassist in former NAGASAKI, DAMIEN and MANNYINA BLADE man Mårten Marteen (real name Mårten Sandberg).

MANNINYA BLADE reformed in 1990 with Rutström, Leif Eriksson, Blomqvist and drummer Johan Eriksson, although Leif was to leave after the band cut a new demo tape in 1995.

For the third HEXENHAUS album, 'Awakening', only Wead and Lundlin remained with the band's new members, being guitarist Marco A. Nicosia, ex-MEZZROW bassist Conny Welen and ex-PARASITE drummer John Billerhag.

After the album emerged Mike Wead created MEMENTO MORI then formed ABSTRAKT ALGEBRA with his old buddy, ex-CANDLEMASS bassist Lief Edling.

Marco Nicosia appeared on the 1997 album by FIFTH REASON 'Psychotic', a band founded by refugees from TAD MOROSE, ABSTRAKT ALGEBRA and MEMORY GARDEN.

Marteen joined MEMENTO MORI.

Albums:
A TRIBUTE TO INSANITY, Active ACTLP 6 (1988)
It / Eaten Alive / Delirious / As Darkness Falls: 1st Movement: a) Shades Of An Obscure Dream, b) A Fatal Attraction, c) In The Spiders Web. 2nd Movement: a) The Possession, b) The Damnation, 3rd Movement: a) On The Threshold Of Insanity, b) Behind Closed Doors, c) The Fall From Grace / Incubus / Death Walks Among Us / Memento Morie - The Dead Are Restless / Requiem
THE EDGE OF ETERNITY, Active ATVLP13 (1990)
Prelude / Toxic Threat / Prime Evil / Home Sweet Home / The House Of Lies / A Temple For The Soul / The Eternal Nightmare / At The Edge Of Eternity
AWAKENING, Active ATV19 (1991)
Shadows Of Sleep / Awakening / Betrayed (By Justice) / Necromonicon Ex Mortis / Code 29 / The Forthcoming Fall / Sea Of Blood / Paradise Of Pain / The Eternal Nightmare Act III / Incubus
DEJA VOODOO, Black Mark BMCD 98 (1997)
Dies Irae - Vreden's Dag / Reborn (At The Back Of Beyond) / Phobia / Nocturnal Rites / Dejavoodoo / From The Cradle To The Grave / Rise Babylon Rise

HEXX (CA, USA)
Line-Up: Manzo (vocals), Dan Watson (guitar), Bill Peterson (bass), Dave Schmidt (drums)

HEXX began life as PARADOX upon their formation in 1978. They evolved into HEXX during 1983. HEXX split apart after the debut 'No Escape' album. Remaining members guitarist Dan Watson, bassist Bill Peterson and drummer Dave Schmidt recruited fresh blood in the form of vocalist Dan Bryant and second guitarist Clint Bower.

Schmidt opted out for the 'Quest For Sanity' album and his position was filled by John Schafer.

The 1992 album was produced by METAL CHURCH guitarist John Marshall.

Watery Graves / Edge Of Death / Under The Spell, Wild Rags WRR025 (1990)

Albums:
NO ESCAPE, Shrapnel (1984)
Terror / Invader / The Other Side / Look To The Sky / Beware The Darkness / Night Of Pain / No Escape / Live For The Night / Fear No Evil
UNDER THE SPELL, Shrapnel (1986)
Hell Riders / A Time Of War / Edge Of Death / The Victim / Under The Spell / Out For Control / Suicide / The Hexx / Fever Dream / Midnight Sun
QUEST FOR SANITY, Under One Flag MFLAG 22 (1989)
Twice As Bright / Fields Of Death / Mirror Of The Past / Racial Slaughter / Sardonicus
MORBID REALITY, Century Media 84 9725-2 (1992)
Morbid Reality / The Last Step / Birds Of Prey / Blood Hunter / Fire Mushrooms / Persecution Experience / Watery Graves / Spider Jam

HIRAX (Buena Park, CA, USA)
Line-Up: Katon W. DePena (vocals), Scott Owen (guitar), Gary Monardo (bass), Eric Brecht (drums)

An undisputed underground Thrash legend. HIRAX were created in 1984 by vocalist Katon W. DePena, bassist Gary Monardo, guitarist Bob Savage and drummer Brian Keith from the defunct L.A. KAOS and KGB. The obligatory first demo was a much sought after item on the tape trading scene. Co-produced by the band and Y&T guitarist Joey Alves, the tape contained four tracks of Power Metal muscle and HIRAX made further inroads with a track on the compilation album 'Metal Massacre VI'.
The debut HIRAX album, 'Raging Violence', with drummer John Tabares, was a solid display of intense metal marred by a weak production. Soon after recording Tabares was asked to leave and the band drafted in ex-D.R.I. man Eric Brecht for the 'Hate, Fear And Power' mini-album. HIRAX garnered much laudable press but DePena quit to form PHANTASM, an act comprising former METALLICA bassist Ron McGoveney, HIRAX refugee John Tabares on drums and guitarists Rodney Nicholson and Carlos Guaico. Drummer Gene Hoglan, later of DARK ANGEL and TESTAMENT fame, also had a term with PHANTASM.
Following vocalist Paul Ballof's departure from EXODUS the band rehearsed with Ballof for a short while until his departure to form

PIRANHA.
The band persevered with erstwhile CORRUPTION singer Billy Wedgeworth. Before too long Monardo walked out and HIRAX folded. Brecht joined DEATH and ATTITUDE.
An attempt to revive the name with De Pena and Tabare was attempted in late 1987 and resulted in the original line-up of the band reforming and recording a three track demo in 1988. Tracks from this tape emerged on the 'Blasted In Bankok' single.
DePena, Tabare, Owen and Monardo finally reformed HIRAX in 2000. HIRAX returned to the recording studio to cut their comeback 'Barrage Of Noise' opus. Joining DePena for these sessions would be PRODIGAL SON guitarist James Joseph Hubler, guitarist Justin Lent from Colorado Punk act CLUSTERFUX and drummer Nick Sieblinger. Guitarist Jimmy Durkin of DARK ANGEL and DREAMS OF DAMNATION joined the new line-up in September 2001.
The band restructured itself yet again to consist of DePena, Hubler and Durkin with the TCHILDRESS rhythm section of bassist Mike Brickman and drummer Dan Bellinger.
During early 2002 famed Virginian Heavy Metal band DECEASED would cover 'Bombs Of Death' on their 'Zombie Hymns' album.

Singles/EPs:
Blasted In Bankok, Lautrec (1988)
Dying World (Shock), Pessimer Theologian (1997) (Split single with SPAZZ)
I See Blood Red / Slit Your Wrist, Black Death (2000) ('El Diablo Negro' EP. 7" Picture disc)

Albums:
RAGING VIOLENCE, Metal Blade (1985)
Demons / Evil Forces / Blitzkrieg Air Attack / Guardian Protector / Bombs Of Death / Defeat Of Amalek / Raging Violence / Call Of The Gods / Warlords Command / Suicide / Executed / The Gauntlet / Destruction And Terror / Destroy / Bloodbath
NOT DEAD YET, Metal Blade (1985)
Demons / Evil Forces / Bombs Of Death / Warlords Command / Bloodbath / Blind Faith / Criminal Punishment / Lightning Thunder / The Plague
HATE, FEAR AND POWER, Roadrunner RR 9675 (1986)
Hate, Fear And Power / Blind Faith / Unholy Sacrifice / Lightning Thunder / The Last War / The Plague / Imprisoned By Ignorance / Criminal Punishment
BARRAGE OF NOISE, Deepsix Records (2001)
Murder One / Barrage Of Noise / Walk Of

Death / Broken Neck / Jade / Mouth Sewn Shut / Beyond The Church (Part 1) / French Pearl

HOBB'S ANGEL OF DEATH
(AUSTRALIA)
Line-Up: Peter Hobbs (vocals/ guitar), Mark Wooley (guitar), Phillip Gresik (bass), Darren McMaster-Smith (drums)

HOBB'S ANGEL OF DEATH was one of the few Australian acts to employ Satanic overtones with '80s Thrash Metal. Peter Hobbs had started his musical career in 1984 with TYRUS, creating ANGEL OF DEATH in 1986. The following year saw the release of two demos 'Angel Of Death' and 'Virgin Metal Invasion From Down Under'. These sessions were recorded with the assistance of Melbourne act NOTHING SACRED guitarist Mark Wooley, Karl Lean and Sham.
These tapes came to the attention of German label Steamhammer and the 1988 eponymous album was produced by Harris Johns in Berlin. HOBB'S ANGEL OF DEATH had now solidified around Hobb's, NOTHING SACRED guitarist Mark Wooley, former MASS CONFUSION bassist Phil Gresik and ex-NEW RELIGION drummer Darren McMaster-Smith. Back home HOBB'S ANGEL OF DEATH put in their debut live show opening for MORTAL SIN.
By 1989 the band had splintered with Hobbs and Wooley enlisting bassist Dave Frew and drummer Bruno Canziani. Following touring the band was then put on ice resulting in Wooley and Frew founding HATRED.
Bassist Phil Gresik would later join the notorious Black Metal band BESTIAL WARLUST and later the equally infamous DESTROYER 666. Latterly he has found LONG VOYAGE BACK.
Reports in 2002 suggested that HOBB'S ANGEL OF DEATH had reformed with the return of guitarist Mark Wooley.

Albums:
HOBB'S ANGEL OF DEATH, Steamhammer (1988)
Jack The Ripper / Crucifixion / Brotherhood / Journey / House Of Death / Satan's Crusade / Lucifer's Domain / Marie Antoinette / Bubonic Plague / Cold Steel
INHERITANCE, Shock (1995)

HOLOCROSS (USA)
Line-Up: Char R.G. (vocals), P.J. Macin (guitar), Max Uzax (bass), Ray Molinari (drums)

Defunct Christian Thrash Metal.

Albums:
HOLOCROSS, New Renaissance (1988)
Wolf Pack / Bombardment / Warpath / B. Hive / Seizure / Manslaughter / Murder Cycle / Drill / Ptomaine / Battle Stations

HOLOSADE (UK)
Line-Up: Phillip De Sade (vocals), Jack Hammer (guitar), Gary Thomson (guitar), Mac (bass), Damien Lee (drums)

Darlington quintet HOLOSADE debuted in 1985 formed by ex-DARK HEART and REBEL vocalist Phillip De Sade. The band's first product was the cassette 'Vendetta', followed by a two track demo featuring 'Set Me Free' and 'Only In Love'. HOLOSADE also had the track 'Cries In The Night' featured on the Ebony Records compilation album 'The Metal Collection'.
Original bassist Kevin Hole was to depart in favour of ex-DARK HEART and ROULETTE man Colin Bell in early 1986, as the band also added ex-PHANTOM guitarist Jack Hammer. This revised line-up recorded another two track cassette featuring 'Love It To Death' and 'Vicious'.
A further demo, 'Psycho / Eternal life', produced by Evo of WARFARE, was recorded at Neat Record's Impulse studios during 1987. Drummer Michael Lee (a.k.a. Damien Lee) opted to jump ship to major signing LITTLE ANGELS later that year and was later to join THE CULT and ROBERT PLANT. Interestingly enough he was later to deny any involvement with HOLOSADE whatsoever!
Colin Bell also departed and was replaced by EXXPLODER and PHANTOM bassist Mac in late 1987.
Following the release of the 'Hellhouse' debut on Powerstation Records, HOLOSADE toured with DEMON and SKELETON CREW among others. Although a second album was planned, the band split from the label and HOLOSADE suffered a major blow when guitarist Jack Hammer (real name Simon Jones) went on to join SABBAT in early 1989. Bassist Mac teamed up with ACID REIGN. Substitutes were Paul Trotter and Chris Bently respectively. The band also added drummer Andy Barker.
Following the split from Powerstation and line-up reshuffling, HOLOSADE released a three track demo, 'The Return', but soon split and various members of later turned up during 1993 in new act DOMINION.
However, HOLOSADE reformed in 1994 with Simon Jones reverting back to his stage persona of Jack Hammer. A second album was recorded but never released.
By 1998 Barker was running Metal magazine 'Sound Barrier' and playing drums once more,

this time for INTENSE.

Singles/EPs:
Battleaxe, Other (1987)

Albums:
HELLHOUSE, Powerstation AMP16 (1988)
Look In The Mirror / Welcome To The
Hellhouse / Love It To Death / Madame
Guillotine / Psycho / Eternal Life / Bitter
Sweet / Nightmare Reality

HOLY MOSES (GERMANY)

Line-Up: Sabina Classen (vocals), Andy
Classen (guitar), Reiner Laws (guitar),
Thomas Becker (bass), Ulli Kusch (drums)

Formed in 1979 by Raymond Brusseler,
HOLY MOSES only got around to serious
action in 1984 when vocalist Sabina Classen
and guitarist Andy Classen were recruited, a
move that resulted in the demos 'Walpurgis
Nacht' and 'The Bitch'.

The band specialised in brutal Techno Thrash
of the highest order and created an impact
with a string of impressive albums and the
striking vocals (not to mention looks as well!)
of Sabina after scoring a deal with Aaaarrg
Records.

The band had recruited drummer Herbert
Dreger to record the 1986 debut 'Queen Of
Siam' and soon after its release bassist Andre
Chapelier joined, although the latters tenure
was short as he debuted on second album
'Finished With The Dogs' before he promptly
left.

Having opened for DIRTY ROTTEN
IMBECILES and HOLY TERROR on their
1987 European tour the band added second
guitarist Georgie and, still lacking a
permanent bassist, TARGET's Johan Susant
filled in for live dates before a new bassist was
found in ex-DARKNESS man Thomas Berker.
The recently added Georgie departed to join
LIVING DEATH, however but by July 1988 ex-
MAMMUT and RISK guitarist Thilo Herrmann
completed the line-up.

The band signed to major label Warner Bros.,
no doubt aided by Sabina's exposure as a TV
presenter on the 'Mosh' programme. HOLY
MOSES recorded their third album under the
guidance of producer Alex Perialas. Thilo
Herrmann left during the sessions to re-join
RISK and his place was taken by Reiner
Laws. Strangely, Laws did not contribute
musically to 'The New Machine Of
Lichtenstein' album, but did design the album
cover!

Herrmann later emerged as a member of
RUNNING WILD and GLENMORE.

Having released the album HOLY MOSES

performed at the 'Dynamo' open air festival in
1989 to 20,000 people, but strangely Warner
Bros. dropped the band! Undeterred, HOLY
MOSES carried on gigging, including dates in
East Germany and were signed to West
Virginia Records in order to release the Will
Reid Dick produced 'World Chaos' album in
1990.

Post HOLY MOSES drummer Ulli Kusch
teamed up with a reformed GRAVE DIGGER
then HELLOWEEN whilst Sabina Classen
formed TEMPLE OF THE ABSURD and
entered the world of television.

Andy Classen entered the world of production
gaining credits on albums by the likes of
ASPHYX, RYKERS and CRACK UP. In 1997
Classen created RICHTHOFEN with former
WARPATH singer Dirk Weiss.

During mid 2001 HOLY MOSES reformed for
high profile festival performances such as
'Wacken Open Air'. The band was announced
as forming part of the 2002 KREATOR /
DESTRUCTION / SODOM Thrash
extravaganza but would pull back to
concentrate on writing new music.

Singles/EPs:
Road Crew EP, Aaarrg ARG 10 (1986)
Too Drunk To Fuck / (You Gotta) Fight For
Your Right (To Part!) / Bloodsucker, West
Virginia 50 57019 (1991)

Albums:
QUEEN OF SIAM, Aaarrg ARG1 001-1
(1986)
Necropolis / Don't Mess Around With The
Bitch / Devil's Dancer / Queen Of Siam /
Roadcrew / Walpurgisnacht / Bursting Rest /
Dear Little Friend / Torches Of Fire
FINISHED WITH THE DOGS, Aaarrg ARG6
005-2 (1987)
Finished With The Dogs / Current Of Death /
Criminal Assault / In The Slaughterhouse /
Fortress Of Desperation / Six Feet Women /
Corroded Dreams / Life's Destroyer / Rest In
Pain / Military Service
THE NEW MACHINE OF LIECHTENSTEIN,
Warner Bros. 243 873-1 (1989)
Near Dark / Def Con II / Panic / Strange
Deception / Lucky Popster / Secret Service
Project / State: Catatonic / The Brood / Lost
In The Maze
WORLD CHAOS, West Virginia 084-57002
1990)
World Chaos / Diabolic Plot / Bloodsucker /
Education / Guns n' Moses / Summer Kills /
Deutschland (Remember The Past) /
Permission To Fire / Jungle Of Lies / Dog
Eat Dog / Too Drunk To Fuck / Fight For Your
Right
TERMINAL TERROR, West Virginia 084-

57102 (1991)
Nothing For My Mum / To Sides Terror / Terminal Terror / Creation Of Violation / Cool Of Blood / Distress And Death / Adultmachine / Malicious Race / Tradition Of Fatality
REBORN DOGS, West Virginia 084-57232 (1992)
Clash My Soul / Decapitated Mind / Welcome To The Real World / Reborn Dogs / Fuck You / Third Birth / Deadicate / Five Year Plan / Roses Of Pain / Reverse / Dancing With The Dead
TOO DRUNK TO FUCK - BEST OF, West Virginia 084-57012 (1993)
Too Drunk To Fuck / Fight For Your Rights / Nothing For My Mum / Theotoci / Distress And Death / Clash My Soul / Five Year Plan / Welcome To The Real World / Finished With The Dogs / World Chaos / Waste Or Try / Black Metal
NO MATTER WHAT THE CAUSE, Steamhammer SPV 84-76862 (1994)
Upon Your Tongue / A Word To Say / Step Ahead / Acceptance / Just Because / What's Up / Senseless One / Denial / Hate Is Just A 4 Letter Word / On You / I Feel Sick / No Solution / Bomber

HOLY TERROR
(Los Angeles, CA, USA)
Line-Up: Keith Deen (vocals), Kurt Kilfelt (guitar), Mike Alvard (guitar), Floyd Flanery (bass), Joe Mitchell (drums)

HOLY TERROR were the result of an amalgamation between guitarist Kurt Kilfelt, recently departed in less than amicable terms from metal eccentrics AGENT STEEL, former DARK ANGEL drummer Jack Schwartz, ex-BLACK WIDOW guitarist Mike Alvard, vocalist Keith Deen and former THRUST bassist Floyd Flanary. However, before long Schwarz had fled the fold and HOLY TERROR drafted Joe Mitchell in his stead.
HOLY TERROR toured America alongside DIRTY ROTTEN IMBECILES and KREATOR during 1988 as a remixed version of their debut album was released.
The band began work on a projected third album minus Alvard but were to fold during the sessions.

Albums:
TERROR AND SUBMISSION, Under One Flag FLAG 10 (1987)
Black Plague / Evil's Rising / Blood Of The Saint / Mortal Fear / Guardians Of The Netherworld / Distant Calling / Terror And Submission / Tomorrow's End / Alpha Omega

MIND WARS, Under One Flag CDFLAG25 (1988)
Judas Reward / Debt Of Pain / The Immoral Wasteland / A Fool's Gold / Terminal Humour / Mind Wars / Damned By Judges / Do Unto Others / No Resurrection / Christian Resistance

HOMICIDE (ITALY)

Italian Thrash Metal band HOMICIDE date from their inception in 1987. The band released an eponymous 1990 demo followed up by a further 1992 tape 'We On The Cross'. The band utilised the services of ALLIGATOR vocalist Gianluca Melino for their 'Self Determined Breed' sessions.
HOMICIDE, with new vocalist Clash, would veer off into an Industrial Metal direction for a 1997 demo.

Albums:
RETALIATION FALL, Homicide (1993)
SELF DETERMINED BREED, Wild Rags (1995)

HOMICIDE HAGRIDDEN (ITALY)
Line-Up: Max (vocals / guitar), Dave (bass), Steo (drums)

Singles/EPs:
Where Angels Work / The Inner Sinner / Violated / Eternal Rage, Homicide Hagridden (2000)

HORDE OF TORMENT
(Las Vegas, NV, USA)
Line-Up: Kevin Leonard (vocals / bass), Ahrue Luster (guitar), Scott Savich (guitar), Joey Capabianco (drums)

Thrashers HORDE OF TORMENT started life in 1987 named PESTILENCE releasing the demos 'Pestilence' and 1988's 'Infected'. Discovering the already established Dutch band of the same name the act morphed into HORDE OF TORMENT in 1989 for a further demo session 'Product Of A Sick Mind'.

Singles/EPs:
Inherit The Sun / Alive Within / Pain Asylum, Butcher (1990) ('Horde Of Torment' EP)

Albums:
DEMO SERIES, Underground (1989)
Product Of A Sick Mind / Viral Malignance / As I Lay Dying / Blood Justice
PRODUCT OF A SICK MIND, S.A. Butcher (1990)
Product Of A Sick Mind / Viral Malignance / As I Lay Dying / Blood Justice / Liquidation /

The Raven / Corruption / Final Solution

HORRORSCOPE (POLAND)
Line-Up: Adam Brylka (vocals), Krzystof Pistelok (guitar), Lech Smiechowicz (guitar), Tomasz Walczak (bass), Arek Kus (drums)

Thrash Metal band HORRORSCOPE originally assembled as a trio during 1997 to release the first demo tape 'Worship Game'. A further cassette release, 'Wrong Side Of The Road', followed in 1999. Signed by the Empire label in 2001 the band debuted with 'Pictures Of Pain'. Crash Music would license the album for the North American market.

Albums:
PICTURES OF PAIN, Empire EMP 005 (2001)
Rising / Inferno / Highway Of The Losts / Macabra Cadabra / Darkest Future / The Deal / Deal With The Devil / Read The Signs / The Aztec Sun / Aargh Leonus / Count The Dead / Pictures Of Pain

HOUSE OF SPIRITS (GERMANY)
Line-Up: Olaf Bilic (vocals), Uwe Baltrusch (guitar), Martin Hirsch (bass), Jörg Michael (drums)

HOUSE OF SPIRITS men Olaf Bilic and Martin Hirsch had both been members of JESTERS MARCH, whilst Uwe Baltrusch is ex MEKONG DELTA and drummer Jörg Michael was formally with MEKONG DELTA, RUNNING WILD, GRAVE DIGGER and RAGE.
Baltrusch departed after the debut album making way for Benjamin Schippritt. HOUSE OF SPIRITS collapsed with bassist Martin Hirsch joining HILTON then Deathsters MORGOTH. Bilic put in vocal sessions with both FAITH HEALER and FALCON.
A four track demo secured a new deal with the Century Media label and once more drums were supplied by Jörg Michael. However, Michael's commitments as full time member of STRATOVARIUS and AXEL RUDI PELL meant the recruitment of new drummer Michael Strichen for live work.

Singles/EPs:
In My Heart (Single Version) / The Eye Of The Storm (Single Version) / In My Heart / The Eye Of The Storm, G.U.N. Gun 043 BMG (1994) ('Get The Spirit' EP promotion release)

Albums:
TURN OF THE TIDE, G.U.N. Gun 044 BMG 74321 (1994)

Dawn / Turn Of The Tide / Wasteland / Keep Me From Dreaming / Close To The Edge / He Waited / In My Heart / The Eye Of The Storm / In A Daze / Final Mistake / Time Has Come
PSYCHOSPHERE, Century Media CD 77228-2 (1999)
Take Me To The Other Side / Back On My Own / History Is Repeating / World Full Of Pain / Voices / Voice Of My Heart / Save The Secret / Time Is Drawing / Oblivion Night's / Dark & Light / Back At The Double / Psychosphere

HYDRA VEIN (UK)
Line-Up: Mike Keen (vocals), Danny Ranger (guitar), Stephan Davis (guitar), Damon Maddison (bass), Nathan Maddison (drums)

A Brighton based act with Thrash leanings HYDRA VEIN emerged in late 1987 with original guitarist Jack Kartoffel, whose departure was forced on medical grounds.
The Maddison brothers had previously played with DEATHWISH and HYDRA VEIN added Danny Ranger and Stephan Davis in early 1988. Brighton based thrash act with obvious Bay Area leanings. In addition to the two albums listed below the group also recorded the four track demo 'The Reptilliad' in 1987

Albums:
RATHER DEATH THAN FALSE OF FAITH, Metalother OTH12 (1988)
The House / Rabid / Crucifier / Right To Die / Rather Death Than False Of Faith / Misanthropic / Harlequin / Guillotine
AFTER THE DREAM, RKT CMO 193 (1989)
7 USC / Pro-Patria / Born Through Ignorance / No Future / Turning Point / After The Dream

ICE AGE (SWEDEN)

Line-Up: Sabrina Kihlstrand (vocals / guitar), Pia Nyström (guitar), Vicky Larsson (bass), Tina Strömberg (drums)

An all female Thrash act ICE AGE toured consistently yet unfortunately never released any product despite a set of strong demos.

Formed in Gothenberg during early 1985 by Pia Nyström and Sabrina Kihlstrand and later adding Strömberg, Vicky Larsson joined in October 1986, replacing Kihlstrand's sister on bass.

KIM FOWLEY, the man responsible for putting the legendary American all girl band THE RUNAWAYS together in the mid '70s, did have a management interest in the group for a brief period before Englishman Dave Maile took on complete responsibility.

The band toured in Britain on a number of occasions, including dates at London's Marquee Club, scoring a great deal of press in all the right publications at the time. Sabrina Kihlstrand quit midway through a European tour, frustrated at a lack of progress and dissatisfaction with the band in general. The frontwoman was eventually replaced by American vocalist Debbie Gunn (ex-SENTINAL BEAST and ZNOWHITE), with ICE AGE also addeing a second guitarist in the Italian born Isabella Fronzoni.

However, the band cancelled their December 1989 British tour when Tina Strömberg suffered a broken jaw in an altercation outside a Gothenberg nightclub. At this point Fronzoni announced her decision to return to Italy and Larsen also quit.

In January 1990 US born Tammi Chiavarini joined the group on bass whilst fellow American, New Jersey native Lisa Decovolo succeeded Fronzoni. Having received some interest from CBS Records the band split up after the Americans wanted to relocate to New York which, it seems, they wound up doing, only not as members of ICE AGE.

Although tapes for a proposed album were recorded (indeed, the band had three albums worth of material lying around!) with the revised line-up, they were never released.

Fronzoni returned to Britain to join another all girl band ORIGINAL SIN in 1991 with ex-NO SHAME drummer Liz Watt. She was later part of a new ROCK GODDESS line-up.

Back in Sweden, Pia Nyström and Vicky Larsson were reunited with Sabrina Kihlstrand in IDIOTS RULE, a group that featured a male drummer and have, thus far, have only featured on a compilation album.

Gunn returned to America to front BRUTAL GROOVE.

ICED EARTH (USA)

Line-Up: Matt Barlow (vocals), John Schaffer (guitar), Randy Shawver (guitar), Steve DiGeorgio (bass), Richard Christy (drums)

The traditional, intense, no compromise style of overblown Metal purveyed by ICED EARTH has seen the band rise from an obscure mid '80s indie band to legend status in Germany and mainland Europe. Musically the band have developed from their formative years delivering Power Thrash to more refined, yet still none the less heavy, melodically charged Heavy Metal.

The band began life in 1985 titled PURGATORY with a teenage garage band line-up of vocalist Gene Adam, guitarists Jon Schaffer and Bill Owen, bassist Dave Abell and drummer Greg Seymour. Another ex-PURGATORY man bassist Richard Bateman also made a fleeting appearance and he was later to find prominence in AGENT STEEL and NASTY SAVAGE. As PURGATORY a demo 'Psychotic Dreams' was released.

As the transition from PURGATORY to ICED EARTH began the band were still very much a horror shock outfit wearing cassocks onstage and dousing their audience in liver and blood as part of the theatrics. Thankfully these tactics were soon resigned to the pase as ICED EARTH concentrated more on the music.

The first ICED EARTH recordings proper came in the form of the 'Horror Show' demo featuring one new composition 'Dracula' allied with two reworkings of PURGATORY tracks 'Jack' and 'In Jason's Mind', both from the 'Psychotic Dreams' demo.

ICED EARTH's next effort was the tape that secured their career and landed them a deal with Germany's Century Media Records. The 'Enter The Realm' demo consisting of tracks 'Colors', 'Enter The Realm', 'Nightmares', To Curse The Sky', 'Solitude' and 'Iced Earth'. ICED EARTH also made an appearance on the 'Metal Mercenaries' compilation album with a song produced by ex-SAVATAGE bassist Keith Collins.

Seymour was briefly replaced by Mike McGill for a European tour after which both McGill was unceremoniously fired and the band also brought in drummer Richie Secharri as ICED EARTH struggled to keep a tight rein on their drummers.

The second release 'Night Of The Stormrider', for which Schaffer took over the lead vocal role, also saw John Greeley on the drumstool although predictably his tenure was short.

1995's 'Burnt Offerings' sees Rodney Beasley on drums. For the groundbreaking 'Dark Saga' album ICED EARTH recorded minus a permanent drummer employing the services of studio engineer Mark Prator. Abell quit soon after this release.

1997 release 'Days Of Purgatory' is a collection of re-worked tracks from the band's 'Enter The Realm' demo and cuts from the first two albums.

1998 had ICED EARTH putting in an almost triumphant performance at the 'German Wacken Open Air' festival as the 'Something Wicked This Way Comes' album cracked the German charts at number 19. Follow up, the ambitious treble live album 'Live In Athens', recorded in front of 120,000 fans, gave ICED EARTH a Greek number one.

Quite spectacularly Schaffer's side project DEMONS & WIZARDS, a union with BLIND GUARDIAN's Hansi Kirsch blew the European charts wide open even scoring the guitarist a further number one in Greece. DEMONS & WIZARDS toured on the festival circuit with CONTROL DENIED / DEATH drummer Richard Christy.

By mid 2000, still without a permanent drummer, ICED EARTH pulled in Christy for live commitments. Ever industrious Christy also found time to commit to his side project band BURNING INSIDE with ACHERON's Michael Estes and BLACK WITCHERY's Steve Childers.

ICED EARTH's 'Horror Show' album found Christy being inducted into the ranks officially along with former DEATH / SADUS bassist Steve DiGeorgio. The interim 'Melancholy' mini-album included cover versions of BAD COMPANY's 'Shooting Star', BLACK SABBATH's 'Electric Funeral' and JUDAS PRIEST's 'The Ripper'.

Jimmy MacDonough joined the ICED EARTH clan as touring bassist for mid 2001. 'Horror Show' saw the band topping the Greek national charts yet again and with stronger than previous European chart positions in most territories.

Touring in America was to have stepped up significantly for the band when they were announced as openers to the JUDAS PRIEST and ANTHRAX tour. However, the terrorist attacks on the United States on September 11th resulted in the cancellation of this entire tour.

Century Media weighed in with the gargantuan 'Dark Genesis' box set to close 2001. The lavish package comprised of remastered versions of early albums, the 'Enter The Realm' demo plus a bonus tribute disc 'Tribute To The Gods'.

This latter disc would be released separately during 2002 and saw ICED EARTH taking on 'Creatures Of The Night' and 'God Of Thunder' by KISS, 'Number Of The Beast' and 'Hallowed Be Thy Name' by IRON MAIDEN, 'Highway To Hell' and 'It's A Long Way To The Top' by AC/DC, 'Burnin' For You' and 'Cities On Flame (With Rock n' Roll)' from BLUE OYSTER CULT, 'Screaming For Vengeance' by JUDAS PRIEST, 'Dead Babies' by ALICE COOPER and BLACK SABBATH's 'Black Sabbath'.

The band's headline 'Feel The Horror' European tour would commence in Hardenberg, Holland on the 17th January 2002. It would then be back to their homeland for a run of headline dates kicking off on April 8th at the Everson Theater in Indianapolis. Strong support on these shows would come from Colorado label mates JAG PANZER and Swedish Deathsters IN FLAMES.

Albums:
ICED EARTH, Century Media CM 7714-2 (1990)
Iced Earth / Written On The Walls / Colors / Curse The Sky / Life And Death / Solitude / Funeral / When The Night Falls
NIGHT OF THE STORMRIDER, Century Media 9727-2 (1994)
Angels Holocaust / Stormrider / The Oath I Choose / Before The Vision / Mystical End / Desert Rain / Pure Evil / Reaching The End / Travel In Stygian
BURNT OFFERINGS, Century Media 77093-2 (1995)
Burnt Offerings / Last December / Diary / Brainwashed / Burning Oasis / Creator Failure / The Pierced Spirit / Dante's Inferno: i) Denial, Lust, Greed, ii) The Prodigal, The Wrathful, Medusa, iii) The False Witness, Angel Of Light
THE DARK SAGA, Century Media CM 77131-2 (1996)
Dark Saga / I Died For You / Violate / The Hunter / The Last Laugh / Depths Of Hell / Vengeance Is Mine / The Suffering: Scarred / Slave To The Dark / A Question Of Heaven
DAYS OF PURGATORY, Century Media 77165-2 (1997)
Enter The Realm / Colors / Angels Holocaust / Stormrider / Winter Nights / Nightmares / Before The Vision / Pure Evil / Solitude / The Funeral / When The Night Falls / Burnt Offerings / Cast In Stone / Desert Rain / Brainwashed / Life And Death / Creator Failure / Reaching The End / Travel In Stygian / Dante's Inferno / Iced Earth
SOMETHING WICKED THIS WAY COMES, Century Media CD77214-2 (1998)
19 GERMANY
Burning Times / Melancholy (Holy Martyr) / Disciples Of The Lie / Watching Over Me / Stand Alone / Consequences / My Own Savior / Reaping Stone / 1776 (Instrumental) / Blessed Are You Something Wicked (Trilogy) / Prophecy / Birth Of The Wicked / The Coming Curse

ALIVE IN ATHENS, Century Media (1999)
1 GREECE
Burning Times / Vengeance Is Mine / Pure
Evil / My Own Savior / Melancholy (Holy
Martyr) / Dante's Inferno / The Hunter /
Travel In Stygian / Slave To The Dark / A
Question Of Heaven / Dark Saga / Last
Laugh / Last December / Watching Over Me
/ Angels Holocaust / Stormrider / Path I
Choose / I Died For You / Prophecy / Birth Of
The Wicked / The Coming Curse / Iced Earth
/ Stand Alone / Cast In Stone / Desert Rain /
Brainwashed / Disciples Of The Lie / When
The Night Falls / Diary / Blessed Are You /
Violate
MELANCHOLY, Century Media (2000)
Melancholy / Shooting Star / Watching Over
Me / Electric Funeral / I Died For You / The
Ripper / Colors (Live)
HORROR SHOW, Century Media (2001)
**32 AUSTRIA, 90 FRANCE, 30 GERMANY,
1 GREECE, 6 HOLLAND, 71 SWEDEN,
86 SWITZERLAND**
Wolf / Damien / Jack / Ghost Of Freedom /
Im-Ho-Tep (Pharaoh's Curse) / Jekyll & Hyde
/ Dragon's Child / Frankenstein / Dracula /
The Phantom Opera Ghost

IGNORANCE (UK)
Line-Up: Neil Duthrie (vocals), Marcus Stone
(guitar), Steve John (guitar), Stef Brooks
(bass), Niki Beric (drums)

Nottingham Thrash act that impressed with
their 'Why?' demo, IGNORANCE signed to
Metal Blade Records, recorded their debut
album in San Francisco with producer John
Cuniberti and drastically altered musical
direction to fit in with the then Funk-Metal
boom.
In 1991 the group opened proceedings at the
Dynamo Festival in Holland and supported
MORDRED in Germany.
The group toured Britain on a double bill with
NEW ENGLAND before guitarist Steve John
quit in early 1993.

Albums:
THE CONFIDENT RAT, Metal Blade ZORRO
17 (1991)
Questions / Sean / ...It's Never Wrong /
Momma Hocus / Hello & Goodbye / The
Confident Rat / The Garden / In My Hands /
Why / Funny!
POSITIVELY SHOCKING, Metal Blade
ZORRO 48 (1992)
Shocking / Two Sick Blokes / Blinded / Lesson
#12 / World Upside Down / Popscotch Mex
Man / True / Healing Hands / The Colour Blue
/ Slouch

IMAGIKA (San Carlos, CA, USA)
Line-Up: David Michaels (vocals), Steven D.
Rice (guitar), Michael Dargis (bass), Henry
Moreno (drums)

A Bay Area Thrash band, founded in 1993-94
and featuring ex-WICKED TRUTH drummer
Henry Moreno, that musically unashamedly
harks back to the tradition that put the area on
the Metal map. Taking their name from a Clive
Barker novel, IMAGIKA debuted in April of
1996 with an eponymous outing issued on
their own imprint, Headless Corpse Records.
Subsequently this album would be distributed
in Germany by the ABS concern. They would
then score a licensing deal with the Nuclear
Blast subdivision Radiation Records to
distribute their 'Worship' album before
switching to the Massacre label. The band
toured Germany during 1999 as openers to
GRAVE DIGGER and IRON SAVIOR.
Bass player Michael Dargis departed in 2000.
The album '... And So It Burns' featured
GRAVE DIGGER's Chris Boltendahl and Uwe
Lulis as guests. This album was re-released
with an additional three extra tracks culled
from the 'Worship' sessions by World War III
Records for America, although the album title
was oddly changed to simply 'So It Burns'.
IMAGIKA would hook up with World War III for
two tribute albums, donating versions of
METALLICA's 'Four Horsemen' and BLACK
SABBATH's 'Never Say Die'.
The band, splitting away from Massacre
Records, announced the recruitment of new
bassist Elena, previously with MOTHER
EARTH, for recording of a projected 2002
album 'Fallen God'.

Albums:
IMAGIKA, Headless Corpse A.B.S. TODAY
202 (1996)
Crush Your World / Murder 1 / Realize /
Chance To Survive / Caged And Shackled /
Vengeance Is Mine / Endings / If A Thought
Could Kill / Immortal Eyes / Life's Diseased /
Nightbreeder
WORSHIP, Massacre (1998)
Golgotha / The Conflict / Court Of Confusion
/ The Sky Is Falling / Worship / Hall Of
Desire / Devour / The Way / Precious Life /
Of Weaker Men / Redemption / Beyond
... AND SO IT BURNS, Massacre (2000)
Intro / Chaos To Murder / Fallen One / My
Dominion / Atrocity / Hell / It Burns /
Annihilate / Darkness Has Come / Fade
Away

IMPALER (St. Paul, MN, USA)
Line-Up: Bill Lindsey (vocals), Michael
James Torok (guitar), Court Hawley (bass),

Bob Johnson (drums)

A Shock Rock band fronted by the over the top antics of Bill Lindsey, Minnesota's IMPALER debuted in 1985 with the self-financed 'Rise Of The Mutants' EP, although a release through their own Blood label had been slated for 1984.

A mixture of Horror Schlock and 'The Night Of The Living Dead', IMPALER would quickly come to the attention of Combat Records thanks to increasing exposure in Metal magazines the world over, leading to the amusingly titled 'If We Had Brains We'd Be Dangerous' album in 1986.

Singles/EPs:
Shock Rock / Crack That Whip / Impaler / Heaven's Force, IRD (1985) ('Rise Of The Mutants' EP)

Albums:
IF WE HAD BRAINS WE'D BE DANGEROUS, Combat (1986)
Blood Bath / Puppet Master / City In Chains / Wasteland / Search And Destroy / Assassin / Speed Thrills / Witch Queen / Dancin' On The Edge / Metal Messiah

IMPERIUM (HOLLAND)
Line-Up: André Vuurboom (vocals), Michel Cerrone (guitar), Rob Cerrone (guitar), Remco Nijkamp (bass), Patrick Gerritzen (drums)

A combination of technical Thrash Metal and Progressive Power Metal forged by ex-SACROSANCT member guitarist Michel Cerrone. Dutch outfit IMPERIUM scored a deal with Mascot Records after one demo.

Albums:
TOO SHORT A SEASON, Mascot M 7005-2 (1993)
Too Short A Season / Play Of Passion / Chemical Dreams / Silenced / Left Meaningless / ...To The Things That Were.../ Messiah Mask / Slip Of The Tongue / Awakening

IMPIOUS (SWEDEN)
Line-Up: Martin Akesson (vocals), Valle Adzic (guitar), Robin Sorqvist (guitar), Erik Peterson (bass), Ulf Johansson (drums)

Trollhäten based Thrash orientated Death Motal act. Created in early 1994 by guitarists Vladimir 'Valle' Adzic and Martin Akesson IMPIOUS originally relied on a drum machine for initial demos. In late 1994 CROWN OF THORNS / THE CROWN vocalist Johan

Lindstrandt manned the drum stool and a temporary bassist was enlisted. IMPIOUS put in their inaugural gig in May 1995 supporting LORD BELIAL and got to grips with their debut publicly available demo session entitled 'Infernal Predomination'. The track 'Dominated By Tales' would also surface on the compilation album 'Vad Hander'.

In early 1996 Lindstrandt was drafted for his military service. This move put CROWN OF THORNS on ice temporarily but freed up their guitarist, Marko Trevonen, to replace Lindstrandt as the new IMPIOUS drummer! With this makeshift line-up a second demo tape 'The Suffering' was produced by KING DIAMOND guitarist Andy La Rocque. Shortly after recording Ulf Peterson took the drum stool on a more permanent basis. IMPIOUS would donate their version of SEPULTURA's 'Inner Self' to the Black Sun tribute album 'Sepulchural Feast'. A further cover saw the band tackling METALLICA's 'One' but more significantly the group's first album 'Evilized' saw release. Promotion witnessed a rash of dates in the low countries in cahoots with Dutch veterans SINISTER.

Akesson would then decide to concentrate on the lead vocal role and as such IMPIOUS manouevered Robin Sorqvist over to guitar. The numbers were made up with the induction of bass player Erik Peterson. This revised version of the band cut the 'Terror Succeeds' album which saw release in America by way of licensing to the Century Media label.

In March of 2002 drummer Ulf Johansson, opting out to become bass player for the TV series band TRIBAL INK, made way for Mikael Norén.

Albums:
EVILIZED, Black Sun (1998)
Dying I Live / Don't Kiss My Grave / Born To Suffer / Haven (A Leap In The Dark) / Facing The Nails / Anthem For The Afflicted / The Faded Paradise / Painted Soul / Extreme Pestilence / Inside / Evilization
TERROR SUCCEEDS, Black Sun BS21 (2000)
Soulexcursion / Terror God / Retaliation / Nuclear Storm Demise / The Punishment / Dimension Hell / Black Death / Diseased / The Loss Of Life / Nightmare Resurrection

IMPULSE MANSLAUGHTER
(Chicago, IL, USA)
Line-Up: Karl Patton (vocals), Chris Hanley (guitar), Nick Stevens (bass), Glen Herman (drums)

IMPULSE MANSLAUGHTER's 1988 album

'Logical End' included cover versions of MOTÖRHEAD's 'Stone Deaf Forever' and the ROLLING STONES 'Paint It Black'.

Albums:
BURN ONE NAKED AND NUKE IT,
Impulse Manslaughter (1986)
Sack O'Shit / Ratbag / Slithis / Nothing / Sedation / Chaos / Contradiction / Oatmeal
HE WHO LAUGHS LAST... , Nuclear Blast (1987)
Batman And The Oracle Of Pevile Savage / Vomit Heads / We're All Bored Here / Suffer In Silence / Walls / They Start The War / Premature Evacuation / Crimes / Too Late / Pills / This World / Sedation / Cheer Up You Fucker / Kein Spiel / Oatmeal II / 1987 Schitzoid Sam / Pattonstein's Disease / Piss Me Off
LOGICAL END, Walkthrufyre (1988)
Drag / Face It / Not Quite Sure / Missing Children / Gimme Shelter / Crimson Dreams / No Deals / Let Them Die / Stone Dead Forever / Borderline Retard
SOMETIMES, Nuclear Blast (1992)

INCANTATION (USA)
Line-Up: Craig Pillard (vocals / guitar), John McEntee (guitar), Ronnie Deo (bass), Jim Roe (drums)

A highly influential act that straddle the borderlines between Black, Thrash and Death Metal. INCANTATION are cited by many of today's acts as being a direct inspiration.
INCANTATION came together with a line up of erstwhile BLOOD THIRSTY DEATH members guitarist Brett Makowski and bassist Aragon Amori, ex-REVENANT man John McEntee and Paul Ledney, previously with G.G. Allin's CONNECTICUT COCKSUCKERS.
A major fall out occurred with McEntee being left alone as Makowski, Amori and Ledney decamped en masse to found the notorious Black Metal act PROFANATICA releasing a string of highly controversial EPs.
By March of 1990 INCANTATION was citing a line up of McEntee, bassist Ronnie Deo and the ex-DECAY pairing of guitarist Sal Seijo and drummer Peter Barnevic. This line-up cut INCANTATION's inaugural demo, a tape which included a cover version of HELLHAMMER's 'Third Of The Storm'. At this juncture McEntree was also acting as substitute guitarist for fellow Death Metal unit MORTICIAN. This union prompted MORTICIAN frontman Will Rahmer to act as guest vocalist for the 7" 'Entrantment Of Evil' single. After recording both Seijo and Barnevic parted ways with the band. By August of the same year INCANTATION was back up to strength having enrolled Bill Venner on guitar and Jim Roe on drums. Unfortunately Venner's tenure was fleeting although he did provide a worthy service in executing INCANTATION's now familiar logo. November of 1990 saw the induction of former PUTREFACT guitarist Craig Pillard. With Rahmer's commitments to MORTICIAN increasing his position was made vacant and Pillard subsequently stepped into the lead vocal role too. This line up released the single 'Deliverance Of Horrific Prophecies' and undertook the group's first American national tour billed alongside ANAL CUNT and PHLEGM. With the dates completed in November of 1992 Deo opted out.
INCANTATION brought in ex-CRUCIFER man Dan Kamp on bass for recording of the track 'Emaciated Holy Figure', donated to the tracklisting of the Nuclear Blast 'Death Is Just The Beginning Volume II' compilation. Further touring would see the band out on the road with AUTOPSY, VITAL REMAINS and MORGUE. However, both Roe and Kamp broke ranks following these shows.
It would be August of 1993 when INCANTATION announced the recruitment of a fresh rhythm section in NECROSION bassist Dave Niedrist and DETERIOROT drummer John Brody. With a tour awaiting in the wings and recording of the debut album 'Onward To Golgotha' to be completed the band solved matters by re-employing Roe to handle drums in the studio whilst Brody learnt the material for the live setting.
Following INCANTATION's debut album 'Onward To Golgotha' and European dates in conjunction with SINISTER and DEADHEAD frontman Craig Pillard broke away from the group. Before long bassist Ronnie Reo and drummer Jim Roe joined him to found WOMB, an act that evolved into DISCIPLES OF MOCKERY.
Competition between DISCIPLES OF MOCKERY and INCANTATION was so fierce that at the 1994 Deathstock festival in New York Pillard's band played a full set of INCANTATION numbers just before INCANTATION themselves took the stage! Confusion reigned in Death Metal circles when INCANTATION's 1994 album 'Mortal Throne Of Nazarene' was re-released under the new title of 'Upon The Throne Of Apocalypse' with a reversed track order and a sticker proclaiming 'Pagan Disciples Of Mockery'!! (Later Pillard's mob became WOMB again but reverted to DISCIPLES OF MOCKERY for the 1999 three track promotion CD).
Amidst all this INCANTATION regrouped

enlisting Duane Morris on vocals and guitar for a package tour in alliance with MORGUE, AFTERLIFE, ANAL CUNT and MORPHEUS DESCENDS. MALEVOLENT CREATION were originally slated as headliners but with their cancellation INCANTATION were elevated to headline status. With the tour wound up the band familiarly fractured yet again, this time Brody and Niedrist bidding their farewell.

INCANTATION relocated entirely to Ohio with only founder member John McEntree creating a completely revised line-up. Morris was retained as frontman with ex-BLOOD OF CHRIST bassist Randy Scott and ESCALATION ANGEL man Kyle Severn being recruited on drums.

An American tour with FEAR OF GOD and Swedes GRAVE was nearly curtailed when Scott decided not to go along for the ride. Stoically the band carried on without bass as a trio of McEntree, guitarist Duane Morris and drummer Kyle Severn. In March of 1995 Mike Donnelly of DISGORGED teamed up with the band as INCANTATION performed a short tour of Mexico in 1995 sharing a bill with IMMOLATION and ACID BATH. Further confusion followed as Morris then bailed out only to return shortly after. The problem re-occurred halfway through touring as Morris upped and left once again. Daniel Corchado of Mexican acts CENOTAPH and THE CHASM was hastily drafted to complete the dates.

Donnelly was next to leave and INCANTATION took on yet another guise by pulling in bassist Mary Ciullo, MORTICIAN and DEATHRUNE man Mike Saez on guitar and a re-enlisted Will Rahmer on vocals. This unit demoed and put in three shows in New York, Pennsylvania and Cleveland.

In March of 1996 McEntree and Severn were joined by MALIGNANCY bassist Kevin Hughes and vocalist / guitarist Nathan Russi of ROTTREVORE for American dates with MORTICIAN and ANAL CUNT. Russi would then bow out and former member Craig Pillard took the frontman mantle once again for recording of 'The Forsaken Mourning Of Angelic Anguish'. Mike Saez would also be involved in this line up on a session basis. Hughes took his leave and once more INCANTATION called on Daniel Corchado, this time acting in the bass role. The 1997 album, produced by Bill Korecky, features a cover of DEATH's 'Scream Bloody Gore'. Corchado would occupy the frontman spot for a burst of touring and Saez was invited onboard for American touring with VITAL REMAINS and European dates with AVULSED, ADRAMELECH and DEEDS OF FLESH. Saez would be unable to commit to later gigs and so, switching Corchado to guitar INCANTATION performed as a trio minus bass.

In April of 1998 Bob Yench, a veteran of MORPHEUS DESCENDS and BRIMSTONE, filled the bass position. INCANTATION set about touring with MORBID ANGEL and VADER but Corchado was obliged to leave mid way through these dates. With an appearance at the 'Milwaukee Metalfest' already booked the band took onboard Tom Stevens as vocalist / guitarist. Stevens had previous credits with SAVAGE DEATH, EXILE, BRIMSTONE, NOKTURNEL and MORPHEUS DESCENDS. This line-up was to undertake further shows in Canada with MORBID ANGEL but Severn was found to be ineligible to cross the Canadian border. Chris Dora of INTEGRITY, SOULLESS and DECREPIT quickly stepped in to save the day.

The band then suffered a major blow when, returning home from a gig in Dallas, Texas, their van overturned. Both McEntree and Severn were badly injured. Following the accident Severn decided to retire from the band. Clay Lytle of FATAL AGGRESSION would occupy the drum stool for INCANTATION's appearance at the 1998 'Chilean Metalfest'. Ranked alongside DEATH and CANNIBAL CORPSE the band performed to over 7,000 South American fans in one night. After the gig Lytle dropped out. INCANTATION moved bases to Pennsylvania, recruiting a new sticksman Rick Boast of NECROTOMIE. The band hooked up with ANGEL CORPSE and Brazilians KRISIUN for the nation-wide American 'Diabolical Extermination' tour before Boast also left. Chris Dora would once again act as stand in for the band's March 1999 'Metal March Meltdown' festival in New Jersey's Asbury Park. In April Mark Perry (a.k.a. 'Tophetareth') of Texan act DEATH OF MILLIONS became the latest in a long line of INCANTATION drummers. A headline tour of Canada ensued after which Perry opted out. In July of 1999 Stevens too took his leave in order to resurrect his NOKTURNEL act.

For a batch of dates in Argentina the reliable Chris Dora came in on drums and past member Mike Saez also rejoined as frontman. The 2000 album 'The Infernal Storm' was recorded with session drummer Dave Culross of MALEVOLENT CREATION and the band pulled in DEATH, CONTROL DENIED and ICED EARTH man Richard Christy for tour work.

Ex drummer Kyle Severn was back in the fold by August of 2000 for American gigs with NILE and IMPALED. Severn also involved himself with the high profile WOLFEN

SOCIETY project featuring ACHERON's Vincent Crowley, VITAL REMAINS singer Jeff Gruslin and DARK FUNERAL guitarist Lord Ahriman. Severn would also perform gigs with ACHERON and commit to studio sessions for a single.

INCANTATION geared up for a month long tour of the States in early 2001 in alliance with IMMOLATION and GOATWHORE. However, the dates would be abruptly curtailed at a gig in Queens, New York. The band's van was broken into outside the Voodoo Lounge venue before the show then various band members and friends became embroiled in a vicious fight. Saez had stepped in to prevent a fight involving his former DEATHRUNE bandmate Chris Shaw. As it turned out Shaw was stabbed in the back and face no less than seven times. The intervening Saez also received major wounds to his arm. Another friend Pete Schulz also received deep lacerations to the arm.

The attacker fled from the venue but was chased and caught by Kyle Severn who apprehended the man and held him until police caught up with him. The injuries to Saez were so severe that the tour was cancelled. Saez would later be rushed into hospital at a later date with stomach pains but would make a full recovery.

INCANTATION switched labels from Relapse to Necropolis and put in a series of hugely successful Brazilian shows with a guesting REBAELLION in May of 2001 after which Yench decided to exit the band. The Sao Paulo gig would be recorded, albeit only from the soundboard, for a live album 'Blasphemy In Brazil'. Released by Mutilation Records it would be limited to 2000 copies all of which quickly sold out.

Joe Lombard took over bass for a set of German dates in August.

Planned touring of Europe for February of 2002 backed up by INFERNAL POETRY and INIQUITY was postponed when Severn suffered a back injury.

The group would embark on a further round of American dates, headlined by CANNIBAL CORPSE and billed alongside DARK FUNERAL and PISSING RAZORS, commencing on the 24th April in Los Angeles.

Singles/EPs:
Entrantment Of Evil, Seraphic Decay (1990)

Albums:
ONWARD TO GOLGOTHA, Relapse (1992)
Golgotha / Devoured Death / Blasphemous Creation / Rotting Spiritual Embodiment / Unholy Massacre / Entrantment Of Evil /

Christening The Afterbirth / Immortal Cessation / Profanation / Deliverance Of Horrific Prophecies / Eternal Torture
MORTAL THRONE OF NAZARENE, Relapse (1994)
Demonic Incarnate / Emaciated Holy Figure / Iconclasm Of Catholicism / Essence Ablaze / Nocturnal Dominium / The Ibex Moon / Blissful Bloodshower / Abolishment Of Immaculate Serenity
TRIBUTE TO THE GOAT, (1997)
Devoured Death / Profanation / Unholy Massacre / Blissful / United in Repugnance / Nefarious Warriors / Twisted Sacrilegious Journey Into Our Darkest Neurotic Delirium / Abomination / Devoured Death / Entrantment Of Evil / Eternal Torture / Profanation
THE FORESAKEN MOURNING OF ANGELIC ANGUISH, Relapse RR 6974 (1997)
Shadows From The Ancient Empire / Lusting Congregation Of Perpetual Damnation (Extreme Eden) / Triumph In Blasphemy (Interlude) / Forsaken Mourning Of Angelic Anguish / Scream Bloody Gore / Twisted Sacrilegious Journey Into The Darkest Neurotic Delirium / Outro / The Ibex Moon / Blasphemous Cremation / Essence Ablaze / Blissful Bloodshower
DIABOLICAL CONQUEST, Relapse (1998)
Impending Diabolic Conquest / Desecration (Of The Heavenly Gracefullness) / Disciples Of Blasphemous Reprisal / Unheavenly Skies / United In Repugnance / Shadows From The Ancient Empire / Ethereal Misery / Masters Of Infernal Damnation / Horde Of Bestial Flames
BLASPHEMY IN BRAZIL, Mutilation (2000) (Limited edition of 2000)
THE INFERNAL STORM, Relapse (2000)
Anoint The Chosen / Extinguishing Salvation / Impetuous Rage / Sempiternal Pandemonium / Lustful Demise / Heaven Departed / Apocalyptic Destroyer Of Angels / Nocturnal Kingdom Of Demonic Enlightenment

INCUBUS (New Orleans, LA, USA)
Line-Up: Scot W. Latour (vocals / bass), Francis M. Howard (guitar), Moyses M. Howard (drums)

New Orleans Thrashers INCUBUS debuted with a 1987 demo 'Supernatural Death'. INCUBUS augmented their line-up with bassist Mark Lavenia for the 'Beyond The Unknown' album although he was to depart in 1992. Lavenia teamed up with ex-MASSACRE drummer Kam Lee and EQUINOX's Pete Slate to found project act CAULDRON in 2000.

During 1999 the band underwent a change of

name to OPPROBIUM to release the 2000 album 'Discerning Forces' produced by Harris Johns.

Singles/EPs:
God Died On His Knees, Gore (1988)

Albums:
SERPENT TEMPTATION, Metalworks VOV 674 (1988)
The Battle Of Armageddon / Voices From The Grave / Sadistic Sinner / Incubus / Blaspheming Prophets / Hunger For Power / Serpent Temptation / Underground Killers
BEYOND THE UNKNOWN, Nuclear Blast (1990)
Certain Accuracy / The Deceived Ones / Curse Of The Damned Cities / Beyond The Unknown / Freezing Torment / Massacre Of The Unborn / On The Burial Ground / Mortify

INCURSION DEMENTA (HOLLAND)
Line-Up: Benny V.D. Wal (vocals), Benny Meerstra (guitar), Sjoerd Van Slooten (guitar), Radboud Burgsma (bass), Douwe Leeuwen (drums)

A Power / Thrash Metal band from Holland. Following the break-up of the group Benny V.D. Wal and Benny Meerstra formed HIDEOUS SUN DEMONS.

Albums:
ALL THIS IS ALL, Incursion Dementa (1992)
All This Is All / Dirge / Chivy About / Self Conceit / Some Overdo It / The... End / Relapse / Warfare / Enigmatic Chamber / Cut This Live Off From Me

INDESTROY (MD, USA)
Line-Up: Mark Strassburg (vocals / guitar), Drew Adrian (guitar), Jeff Parsons (bass), Gus Basilika (drums)

Maryland Thrash Metal band INDESTROY, titled after a song by THE OBSESSED, debuted with the 1986 demo session 'Tortured By Fire'. The INDESTROY second album features a completely revised line-up of vocalist / guitarist Mark Strassburg and bassist Jeff Parsons together with guitarist Danny Kenyon and drummer Rob 'Cougin' Brannigan. For subsequent demo recordings Shawn Williams took the place of Kenyon.
Strassberg went missing on a cross country motorcycle trip during July 1989 having left Maryland for San Francisco and was planning to later head to Los Angeles in order to undertake promotion work for 'Senseless Noise'. He was reportedly found safe and well

although his family declined to disclose what had happened to him.
Parsons would later be found as a member of WRETCHED and UNORTHODOX. Drummer Gus Basilika too would appear on the first two WRETCHED albums after an initial spell in DELIRIUM.
Kenyon was a member of DREADNOT during 1990 and would journey into the Doom scene with VORTEX OF INSANITY in 1993. This band, which also included INDESTROY's Cougin on drums, would issue the 1994 'Social Decay' album for German label Hellhound. Kenyon and Basilika would reunite in 1998 founding another Doom project LIFE BEYOND, fronted by erstwhile CREEPSHOW, SILENT CRY and IMMORAL man Louis Strachan.
INDESTROY's name would be re-activated many years later as 'Senseless Theories' saw a release in 2001 on the New Renaissance label.

Albums:
INDESTROY, New Renaissance NRR10 (1987)
The Gate / U.S.S.A. / Ground Zero / Dead Girls (Don't Say No) / Fatal Sin / Brain Damaged / Justice Sucks / Shadowland / A.I.M.L.E.S.S. / Dismembered
SENSELESS NOISE, New Renaissance (1989)
Tortured By Fire / Living In Filth / Terminal Choice / Senseless Theories / Sam The Butcher / Instant Insanity
SENSELESS THEORIES, New Renaissance (2001)

INDESTRUCTIBLE NOISE COMMAND (CT, USA)
Line-Up: Dennis Gergeley (vocals / bass), Tony Fabrizi (guitar), Eric Barath (guitar), Gary Duguay (drums)

INDESTRUCTIBLE NOISE COMMAND date back to a 1983 covers band performing songs by the likes of JUDAS PRIEST and IRON MAIDEN. The following year the band adopted the title of GENOCIDE. Shortly after a further name change occurred as the band became GENOCIDE INC. before shortening that moniker to just I.N.C.
The second album was produced by Alex Perialas and RAVEN's Rob Hunter.

Albums:
RAZORBACK, Giant GRI 6003-1 (1987)
I.N.C. / The Grip Of Death / War Not Words / Anarchy (The Pursuit Of Happiness) / Razorback / Fists From The Mighty / Fear / Passageway Through Purgatory

THE VISITOR, Giant GRI 6025 (1988)
Dry Heaven / Bed Time Stories / What Are
You Looking At? / Thunderstruck / The Visitor
/ Hypo-Dermic Coastline / Scammed Again /
Just What I Needed / Candy-O

INFECTIOUS GROOVES (USA)
Line-Up: Mike Muir (vocals), Dean Pleasants
(guitar), Adam Siegal (guitar), Robert Trujillo
(bas), Brooks Wackerman (drums)

Diversion from SUICIDAL TENDENCIES
members vocalist Mike Muir and bassist
Robert Trujillo. Initially INFECTIOUS
GROOVES had drums supplied by former
JANES ADDICTION man Stephen Perkins.
Drummer Josh Freese of THE VANDALS,
also included in the ranks of SUICIDAL
TENDENCIES, enrolled in time for 1993's
'Sarsippius Ark'. Freese temped for America's
hottest ticket PEARL JAM during late 1994
and would also figure in GUNS N' ROSES
limbo years and the 2000 success story A
PERFECT CIRCLE.
INFECTIOUS GROOVES added the ex-BAD
FOR GOOD 17 year old Brooks Wackerman
on drums for 1994's 'Groove Family Cyco'.
Wackerman would later guest on JUDAS
PRIEST guitarist GLENN TIPTON's 'Baptism
Of Fire' solo album.
Bassist Robert Trujillo joined the OZZY
OSBOURNE band.

Albums:
**THE PLAGUE THAT MAKES YOUR BOOTY
MOVE (IT'S THE INFECTIOUS GROOVES)**,
Epic 4687292 (1991)
Punk It Up / Therapy / I Look Funny / Stop
Funkn' With My Head / I'm Gonna Be My
King / Closed Session / Infectious Grooves/
Infectious Blues / Monster Skank / Back To
The People / Turn Your Head / You Lie... And
Yo Breath Stank / Do The Sinister /
Mandatory Love Song / Infecto Groovalistic /
Thanx But No Thanx
SARSIPPIUS ARK, Epic 473591-2 (1993)
Intro / Turtle Wax (Funkaholics Anonymous) /
No Cover / 2 Drink Minimum / Immigrant
Song / Caca De Kick / Don't Stop Spread
The Jam / Three Headed Mind Pollution /
Slo-Motion Slam / Legend In His Own Mind
(Ladies Love 'Sip) / Infectious Grooves /
These Freaks Are Here To Party / Man
Behind The Man / Fame / Savor Da Flavor /
No Budget / Dust Off The 8 Track / Infectious
Grooves (2) / You Pick Me Up (Just Throw
Me Down) "Therapy" / Do The Sinister / Big
Big Butt By Infectiphibian / Spreck
GROOVE FAMILY CYCO, Epic 475929-2
(1994)
Violent And Funky / Boom Boom Boom /

Frustrated Again / Rules Go Out The
Window / Groove Family Cyco / Die Like A
Pig / Do What I Tell Ya / Cousin Randy / Why
/ Made It
MAS BORRACHO, XIII Bis (2000)
Citizen Of The Nation / Just A Lil Bit / Lock It
In The Pocket / Good For Nothing / Borracho
/ Good Times Are Out To Get You / Wouldn't
You Like To Know / Going, Going, Gone /
21st Century Surf Odyssey / Please Excuse
This Funk Up / Fill You Up / What Goes Up /
Leave Me Alone

INFERNAL (BRAZIL)
Line-Up: Marcelo Koehler (vocals), Luga
(guitar), Danilo Zolet (guitar), Covero (bass),
Mauricio Amorim (drums)

Curitiba based INFERNAL, founded in 1986,
trade in European influenced Thrash / Speed
Metal that would later give way to more Death
Metal persuasions. The group's initial
formation cited a line up of vocalist Paulo,
guitarists Danilo Zolet and Marcelo Dos
Anjos, bassist Covero (real name Renate
Augusto de Alburquerque) and drummer
Jonas. INFERNAL's inaugural gig, opening for
MX in 1988, would already signal the start of
a constant stream of line up ructions - new
faces for the show being guitar player Lineau
and frontman Marcelo Paulista.
In 1989 INFERNAL got around to cutting their
first demo session 'The First Stage' but ran
into immediate controversy with the media for
the lyric "Speak Portuguese Or Die" in the
track 'Brazoo'.
Another shift in line-up found Mano on guitar
and CREEPIN' DEATH / STEEL WAR man
Mauricio Amorim on drums the following year
for a sophomore cassette 'Cathedral Of
Despair'. The track 'Fear Of Death' also
garnered further exposure included on the
compilation album 'Vampiros De Curitiba'.
INFERNAL debuted commercially in 1991
with the 7" single 'Of Weakness And
Cowardice' but shortly after Mano decamped.
Juliano Oening would fill the vacant guitar
spot for a mammoth show in Araucária to over
4,000 people.
Paulista would be the next in line to leave
creating Black Metal band AMEN CORNER.
Marcelo Koehler would then take the mike
stand for the inaugural album 'Drowning In
The Chalice Of Sin'. For session work
INFERNAL drafted Mano of HECATOMB but
at the closure of recording ex-guitarist Mano
rejoined. The returning six stringer made it
back in time to lay down lead guitar solos on
the album. (Sadly Oening would later be killed
in a car accident).
A heavy gig schedule across Brazil then
ensued but Mano would bid farewell yet

again, creating Death Metal band IMPERIOUS MALEVOLENCE.

HECATOMB's Mano assisted in the interim until INFERNAL recruited ex HAMMERDOWN member Poyoka. However, following a gig in Asunción, Paraguay in May 1997 Poyoka also left. Daniel of SUBVERSIVE was to replace him but an injury to the new guitarist's left hand soon forced his dismissal. Ex-CYTOMEGALODEATH man Luis Gabriel Maluf da Silva a.k.a. 'Luga' took over for recording of a second album 'Ritual Humiliation'

Singles/EPs:
Prelude To The Feast / The Feast Divine / True Reality, (1991) ('Of Weakness And Cowardice' EP)

Albums:
DROWNING IN THE CHALICE OF SIN, (1993)
Smash Thy Enemy / Bloody Rain / Il Passagio - The Ends Of Hell / Morbid Dream / Reaping Lives / Drowning In The Chalice Of Sin / Eternal Battle / Insurrection Day / The Endless Well Of Torment / Cathedral Of Despair
RITUAL HUMILIATION, (2001)
Intro: Bestial Overture / Die (Slow, Painful Death) / Absent Light / Secret Code / Ritual Humiliation / A Study In Blood And Darkness / Before My Turn, Agonizing / Plains Of Desolation / Intermezzo: The Nightmare / Sights Of The Unreal / Unholy Life / Invitation To Delirium / Cities Of Horror / Like Men Bleed / Rise, Charge, Obliterate / Finale: P.M.L.T.R.C.

INFERNAL (USA)
Line-Up: Ronnie Galletti (vocals),

INFERNAL are led by vocalist Ronnie Galletti, previously better known as 'Nasty Ronnie' the wrestler and vocalist with '80s Metal band NASTY SAVAGE.
The 2000 release is in fact INFERNAL's demo recorded in 1995.

Albums:
INFERNAL, Crook' D (2000)

INFERNAL MAJESTY (CANADA)
Line-Up: Chris Bailey (vocals), Steve Terror (guitar), Kenny Hallman (guitar), Psychopath (bass), Rick Nemes (drums)

Following Thrash Metal band INFERNAL MAJESTY's debut 1987 album 'None Shall Defy' the band released the 'Nigresent

Dissolution' and 'Creation Of Chaos' demos. Dutch label Displeased re-issued the debut album with bonus tracks culled from the demo sessions. The 1999 'Chaos In Copenhagen' album added extra tracks of INFERNAL MAJESTY cover versions by CHRIST DENIED and DAWN.

Albums:
NONE SHALL DEFY, Roadrunner (1987)
UNHOLIER THAN THOU, Hypnotic HYP 1062 (1998)
Unholier Than Thou / The Hunted / Gone The Way Of All Flesh / Black Infernal World / Roman Song / Where Is Your God? / Death Toll / Art Of War
NONE SHALL DEFY, Displeased (1997)
Overlord / R.I.P. / Night Of The Living Dead / S.O.S. / None Shall Defy / Skeletons In The Closet / Anthology Of Death / Path Of The Psycho / Into The Unknown / Hell On Earth
CHAOS IN COPENHAGEN, Hypnotic (1999)
Birth Of Power / Unholier Than Thou / Where Is Your God? / R.I.P. / Night Of The Living Dead / S.O.S. / Night Of The Living Dead (DAWN) / Overlord (CHRIST DENIED)

INFERNÖ (NORWAY)
Line-Up: Aggressor, Necrodevil, Bestial Tormentor

A self proclaimed 'True' Metal band that includes in its rankings Carl Michael Eide ('Aggressor') of AURA NOIR, VED BUENS ENDE and also an ex-SATYRICON and ULVER member.
INFERNÖ debuted with a 1995 demo session 'Massacre In Hell'.
For INFERNÖ's 1996 album 'Utter Hell' the frightening personality named as "Hazardous Pussy Desecrator" was found to be contributing "Session Guts"!
Following the debut record INFERNÖ delivered tracks to the Primitive Arts EP 'Headbangers Against Disco'.
The vinyl version of 1998's 'Downtown Hades' included two live tracks recorded on the band's 'Euro Holocaust' tour with ABSU and ENSLAVED.

Albums:
UTTER HELL, Osmose Productions OPCD 044 (1996)
Intro From Hell / Satanic Overkill / Tormentor / Ripping Hell / Storming Metal / Infernal Invasion / Sodom (Burning The Flag) / Necroslut / Torment Her / Massacre In Hell / Infernö
DOWNTOWN HADES, Osmose Productions OPCD 060 (1998)
Straight From Hell / Utter Hell / Rot In Hell /

Roadkill / In Bed With Satan / Bulldozer / Alcoholocaust / Thrash Till Death / Metal Attack / Violator

INFERNO (FL, USA)

Albums:
PSYCHIC DISTANCE, Massacre MASS CD043 (1994)
PANELS, Massacre (1994)

INGRAINED (ITALY)
Line-Up: Antonio Gianfreda (vocals), Damiano Deparigi (guitar), Gianluigi Spalluto (guitar), Sandro Namavecchia (bass), Mario Vitale (drums)

Singles/EPs:
Disconnect-Dead / Dark Messiah / Erotikrist, Ingrained (2001) ('From The Eyes Of Pain' EP)

INHUMAN (USA)
Line-Up: Ray Wallace (vocals / bass / programming). Andy Wallace (guitar)

Ray and Andy Wallace had formed LAST RITES in the summer of 1989 and then, as HAVOC MASS in union with ex-NASTY SAVAGE members guitarist Ben Meyer and drummer Curt Beeson, the pair had a demo cut ('Tormented Souls') had featured on the 'Metal Massacre Volume XI' compilation album. Further demos led to a deal with Massacre Records for the 1993 album 'Killing The Future'.
However, HAVOC MASS eventually fell by the wayside and INHUMAN sprang up in its place.

Albums:
INHUMAN, Rawk IMCD 75 (1998)
The Light At The End / Live While You Can / Why I Hate / Slow Motion Murder / These Scars / To Kill Or Die / The Weak Shall Fall / When All Is Lost / Taken Away / Never Forget, Never Forgive
REBELLION, Exit (2000)

INQUISITOR (HOLLAND)
Line-Up: Alex (vocals), Erik (guitar), Hans (bass), Wim (drums)

Formed in 1992 from the merging of Dutch outfits MENTICIDE and DESULTORY. INQUISITOR soon became known for a style of hectic Thrash Metal with strong Death Metal influences.
Having debuted with the 'Blasphemous Accusations' demo after several line-up changes a second demo ('Your Pain Will Be

Exquisite') led to a deal with Shiver Records. The debut album caused problems however as the cover artwork was deemed obscene and was forced to be censored.
INQUISITOR became CENTURION in the late '90s debuting with the 'Of Purest Fire' EP.

Albums:
WALPURGIS - SABBATH OF LUST, Shiver (1996)
Damnation For The Holy / Consuming Christ / Condemned Saints / Trial Of Denial / Chaos In Eden / Jehova's Downfall / Crypt Of Confession / Unholy Seeds / Cry Of The Christians / Fallen Missionary / Inquisitor

INSANIAC (Bloomfield, NJ, USA)
Line-Up: Lou Fugaro (vocals), Tom Nolz (guitar), C.J. Sciosia (guitar), Tom Medcraft (bass), Eddie Scortly (drums)

INSANIC man Tom Nolz would found a later Power Metal band SOULSTORM for a 1992 demo.

Singles/EPs:
Quiet / Plead Insanity / Buy, Insaniac (1986)

INTRINSIC
(San Luis Obispo, CA, USA)
Line-Up: Garret Graupner (vocals), Mike Mellinger (guitar), Ron Crawford (guitar), Joel Stern (bass), Chris Binns (drums)

Founded in 1983 by guitarists Ron Crawford and Mike Millinger, INTRINISIC opened for MEGADETH and ARMORED SAINT before parting company with vocalist Garret Graupner shortly after the debut album release.
The Californians worked for a period with ex-METAL CHURCH vocalist David Wayne during 1988 but his tenure with the group was by no means lengthy and he was already dabbling with HEATHEN before he quit the INTRINSIC camp.
The second album, 'Distortion Of Perspective', found INTRINSIC fronted by a new vocalist Lee Dehmer and guitarist Ron Crawford out of the fold in favour of Garrett Craddock.
INTRINSIC made an unexpected return in 1997 with the 'Closure' album. The new line-up comprised Dehmer, Mellinger, Craddock, Binns, and bassist Mike McClaughlin.

Albums:
INTRINSIC, No Wimp 007 (1987)
Ahead Of The Game / Hit The Streets / Condo / Rip!! / Possessor / No Return / Leaving Insane / Wasted Life

DISTORTION OF PERSPECTIVE, Cheese
Flag (1990)
Distortion Of Perspective / Sail Into The Sun
/ Piracy / Maximator / Fear And Loathing
CLOSURE, Rokarola 728085004 (1997)
The Wheel / Up For The Slam / BKB / 3X0 /
Falling In / End Times / Nothing Special / I
Still Feel Ya / Bystander / Someone's Gotta
Pay / Try My Luck / Visceral / Brutally Frank /
The Reasons Why / Who Goes There?

INTRUDER (Nashville, TN, USA)

Singles/EPs:
Cover Up, Iron Works (1987)
Escape From Pain / 25 Or 6 To 4 / Cold
Blooded Killer / Kiss Of Death / T.M. (You Paid
The Price), Metal Blade (1990)

Albums:
LIVE TO DIE, Iron Works IW 1023 (1987)
Cover Up / Turn Back / Victory In Disguise /
Live To Die / Kiss Of Death / Cold Blooded
Killer / Blind Rage / T.M. (You Paid The
Price)
A HIGHER FORM OF KILLING, Roadracer
(1989)
Time Of Trouble / Martyr / Genetic Genocide
/ Second Chance / (I'm Not Your) Stepping
Stone / Killing Winds/ Sentence Is Death /
Agents Of The Dark (MIB)/ Antipathy
PSYCHO SAVANT, Metal Blade CDZORRO
25 (1991)
Face Of Hate / Gerl's Lament (When) / The
Enemy Within / It's A Good Life / Invisible /
Traitor To The Living / Final Word / N.G.R.I.

INTRÜDER (USA)
Line-Up: Krazy Lou Hilaire (vocals), Rotten
Ronnie Hanisco (guitar), Phil Mortelli (bass),
Jack Robbins (drums)

Singles/EPs:
Krush, Kill, Destroy / Give Me Metal, Hide-A-
Way (1986)

INVOCATOR (DENMARK)
Line-Up: Jacob Hansen (vocals / guitar),
Jacob Schultz (guitar), Jesper M. Jensens
(bass), Per M. Jensens (drums)

A pioneering Death / Thrash Metal band
dating back to 1986 that went under their
original title of BLACK CREED, the group's
first demo tape was 'Genetic Confusion' in
1988 followed by 'Alterations' the following
year. After gigs with EDGE OF SANITY and
ENTOMBED the band signed to Swedish
label Black Mark.
The band's debut album 'Excursion Demise'
sold around 10,000 copies in Europe,
prompting INVOCATOR to record a further
album 'Weave The Apocalypse' and they
opened for PARADISE LOST in Europe
during 1994.
1995's 'Early Years' album comprised the
band's original demo tapes plus covers of
ARTILLERY and DARK ANGEL tracks. The
same year found Jacob Hansen aiding fellow
Danish Death Metallers MERCENARY with
production on their 'Supremacy' EP.
Jacob Schultz was replaced by guitarist Perle
Hansen for the 'Dying To Live' album.
As a closing note to their career the band
released 'Early Years', essentially a re-issue
of their 1988 'Genetic Confusion' demo and
1989's 'Alterations' demo with two bonus
cover tracks. It also was released as a limited
edition in Scandinavia with a booklet including
a history of the band and many photos.

Albums:
EXCURSIONS DEMISE, Black Mark
BMCD12 (1992)
Excursion Demise (...To A Twisted Recess
Of Mind) / Forsaken Ones / The Persistence
From Memorial Chasm / Absurd Temptation /
Schismatic Injective Therapy / Occurrence
Concealed / Beyond Insufferable Dormancy /
Inner Contrarieties / Alterations
WEAVE THE APOCALYPSE, Black Mark
BMCD 34 (1993)
Through The Nether To The Sun / From My
Skull It Rains / Desert Sands / Condition
Critical / Breed Of Sin / Doomed To Be / Lost
At Birth / Land Of Misery / The Afterbirth /
Weave The Apocalypse
EARLY YEARS, Die Hard RRS943 (1995)
Dismal Serfage / Insurrected Despair /
Restraint Life / The Scars Remain /
Alterations / Occurrence Concealed / The
Persistence From Memorial Chasm / Pursuit
Of A Rising Necessity / The Eternal War /
The Promise Of Agony
DYING TO LIVE, Progress PCD20 (1995)
Dying To Live / Kristendom / Shattered Self /
King In A World Of Fools / Search / South Of
No North / Living Is It / Astray / For A While /
Hole

IRON ANGEL (GERMANY)
Line-Up: Dirk Schroder (vocals), Sven
Struven (guitar), Peter Wittke (guitar),
Thorsten Lohmann (bass), Mike Matthes
(drums)

Formed in 1983 by the former METAL GODS
triumvirate of drummer Mike Matthes, bassist
Thortsen Lohmann and guitarist Sven
Struven. IRON ANGEL issued their second
demo in 1984 'Legions Of Evil'. Added Jürgen
Blackmore, son of DEEP PURPLE and
RAINBOW guitarist RITCHIE BLACKMORE,

to the band in mid 1986.

In 1987 IRON ANGEL parted company with bassist Thorsten Lohmann manoeuvering guitarist Peter Witthe over to bass and recruiting a new guitarist Stefan Kleinow. The Portuguese Black Thrash act ALASTOR would cover IRON ANGEL's 'Sinner' for their December 2001 album 'Hellward'.

Albums:
HELLISH CROSSFIRE, Steamhammer SPV 08-1853 (1985)
The Metallion / Sinner / Black Mass / The Church Of Lost Souls / Hunter In Chains / Rush Of Power / Legions Of Evil / Wife Of The Devil / Nightmare / Heavy Metal Soldiers
WINDS OF WAR, Steamhammer SPV 08-1880 (1986)
Winds Of War / Metalstorm / Son Of A Bitch / Vicious / Born To Rock / Fight For Your Life / Stronger Than Steel / Sea Of Flames / Creatures Of Destruction / Back To The Silence

IRON CHRIST (USA)

Albums:
IRON CHRIST, New Renaissance (198-)
GETTING THE MOST OUT OF YOUR EXTINCTION, New Renaissance (1990)

IRON CROSS (IL, USA)

Albums:
CHURCH AND STATE, Turmoil (1987)

ISIDORE (TX, USA)

Black Thrash act ISIDORE is one of a triumvirate of solo projects from Endymion. Other operations include the ambient ENDYMION and the pre ISIDORE act HYLAS.

Albums:
SHADOW SEASON, Aphelion (1999) (Split album with HYLAS)

JACKHAMMER
(Bloomington, IN)
Line-Up: J.W. Baker (vocals), Edward Baun (guitar), D.J.M. (guitar), Damien (bass), Andy Snider (drums)

Early '90s Thrash Metal band JACKHAMMER hailed from Bloomington, Indiana.

JAG PANZER (CO, USA)
Line-Up: Harry 'The Tyrant' Conklin (vocals), Mark Briody (guitar), Chris Broderick (guitar), John Tetley (bass), Rikard Sternquist (drums)

Originally a covers band, JAG PANZER rose to enjoy true cult status on the American Metal scene and later amplified this into major appreciation on the European mainland later in their career. The band have delved into many styles in their career and have been assailed by line-up tribulations but have won through, finally stabilising their line-up and reaping the rewards during the '90s.

The band had been playing the local club circuit in their native Colorado for around two years before, legend has it, Briody heard a copy of the 'Monsters Of Rock' compilation album commemorating the first ever festival at Donington in 1980. The singer was blown away by the likes of a participating SAXON and RIOT. Promptly discovering NWoBHM bands such as ANGELWITCH, the fledgling band - then entitled TYRANT, set about recording a demo of their first song 'Tower Of Darkness'. Enthused by the results a further demo demos contained the tracks 'Battlezones' and 'The Crucifix' which, courtesy of a friend's persuasive efforts got into the hands of both Metal Blade and Azra in Los Angeles.

However, news also arrived of the already established Los Angeles Metal band TYRANT. With a name change in order the band decided they liked the sound of the Jagdpanzer WW II German tank destroyer but subtly reworked the name for an American audience as JAG PANZER. The band opted to sign with Azra - on the strength of a higher royalty offer and a colour cover for the debut offering - the 'Tyrants' EP was issued in 1983. The EP subsequently bore witness to a myriad of collectable versions, including various picture discs featuring a monster, a lady with chainsaw, a torture rack and a promotion release with a gas mask disc. Just prior to the release JAG PANZER had relocated to Los Angeles in an effort to crack the big time. Initially, before the release of the EP, gigs were hard to come by but as soon as

'Tyrants' was issued the group pulled over 400 people to their first gig.

In 1984 Azra released JAG PANZER's first fully fledged album and 'Ample Destruction' marked the recording debut of the newly recruited JOEY TAFFOLA, who teamed up with JAG PANZER's existing guitarist Mark Briody in a formidable frontline. The band put in support slots to acts as diverse as GRIM REAPER and SLADE. In an effort to establish a new recording deal JAG PANZER committed two new songs to tape, 'Shadow Thief' and 'Viper'.

Taffola, taking Carlson with him, quit for a solo career, eventually debuting with the 1987 album 'Out Of The Sun' on Shrapnel Records before teaming up with ALICE COOPER. In 1986 vocalist 'The Tyrant' (real name Harry Conklin) appeared fronting a black metal band SATAN'S HOST under the even stranger pseudonym of 'Leviathan Thesiren' releasing the album 'Metal from Hell'. Conklin reverted back to his real name to enjoy a fleeting tenure with New York cult rockers RIOT. At his first RIOT live performance Conklin unfortunately lost his voice and was dumped. Conklin would also assemble TITAN FORCE, issuing two albums - 1989's 'Titan Force' on the U.S. Metal label and 1991's 'Winner / Loser' for the German Shark Concern.

JAG PANZER regrouped drawing in guitarist Christian Lesegue and drummer Rikard Sternquist. A succession of vocalists then flowed through the ranks including Chris Cronk of KARIAN, Steve Montez and Bob Parduba of Denver Metal band ALLOY CZAR. With this line-up JAG PANZER self financed the recording of a fresh album's worth of material 'Chain Of Command' which included a re-make of IRON BUTTERFLY's groundbreaking '60s hit 'In A Gadda Da Vida'. On the live front the group guested for HELLOWEEN and MEGADETH. A contract with a major label was offered for 'Chain Of Command' but the band deemed it too restrictive and declined. Both Parduba and Lesegue left soon after.

Meantime the 'Ample Destruction' album was the subject of varying release formats with the Canadian release on Banzai Records being retitled 'License To Kill' and coming with an extra track 'Black Sunday'. The British release on Metalcore Records also added 'Black Sunday' but also squeezed in 'Eyes Of The Night' and 'Fallen Angel', the latter two tracks recorded at a different session and featuring new drummer Reynold 'Butch' Carlson, who replaced original skinsman Rick Hilyard.

With little activity officially interest in the band was sustained with the emergence in 1991 of an unofficial split album with MAJESTY and

CHRIS BRODERICK of JAG PANZER
Photo : Nico Wobben

HARRY CONKLIN of JAG PANZER
Photo : Nico Wobben

of the 'Shadow Thief' bootleg in 1992.
The band cut a 1994 album 'Dissident Alliance' with new singer Daniel Conca and guitarist Chris Kostka but unfortunately, despite having the extra promotional push of a single 'Jeffrey Behind The Gate', this record, released by Rising Sun in Europe and Pavement Music in America, was universally panned by critics. Nevertheless, the band did manage to tour Euope for the first time as openers to OVERKILL before their two newest recruits made their exit. Conca made his mark with GOTHIC SLAM.

JAG PANZER made a return to the scene in 1996 tempted no doubt by the burgeoning interest in retro-trad metal in Europe and Japan. The band, re-enlisting Harry Conklin, demoed the more traditionally aligned tunes 'Future Shock', 'Ready To Strike' and 'Shadow Thief', promptly landing a deal with the German Century Media label. The resulting album, 'The Fourth Judgement' issued in August of 1997, was hailed as a renaissance for the band and the European Rock media in particular enthused over JAG PANZER's return to form. Notably JOEY TAFFOLA contributed lead guitar solos to the record but would be unable to tour. Chris Broderick took the vacant guitar slot for European dates billed alongside HAMMERFALL and GAMMA RAY.

'The Age Of Mastery' album, a collection of re-recorded archive tracks as requested by a poll of fans, confirmed the validity of the band's comeback. A nationwide American

tour found JAG PANZER sharing stages with ICED EARTH. The band undertook a headlining tour of Germany to close off 1998 supported by ANGEL DUST, GLADIATORS and GB ARTS. Collectors would also be tempted by JAG PANZER's inclusion of a live version of 'Tyranny' on an 'Ungebrochen Metal' compilation.

Although 1999 would not deliver a new album JAG PANZER did offer up their rendition of 'Children Of The Sea' to the DIO 'Holy Dio' Century Media tribute album and put in a sterling set at the 'Wacken Open Air' festival. As the year drew to a close Century Media surprised fans by offering a download of Mark Briody and Harry Conklin's Christmas song 'Do You See What I See'.

JAG PANZER would make a return with the May 2000 'Macbeth' inspired 'Thane To The Throne' opus. The ambitious album track 'The Prophecies (Fugue In D Minor)' would see the veritable inclusion of the Moscow string quartet. With 'Thane To The Throne' the band managed to elevate itself above cult status making serious headway on the sales front. The following year a diversion saw hockey fans JAG PANZER reworking JUDAS PRIEST's 'You've Got Another Thing Comin' into 'You've Got Another Cup Comin', donated as a theme song to the Colorado Avalanches team. JAG PANZER's continued revival was bolstered by the arrival of the Jim Morris produced 'Mechanized Warfare' album in 2001.

JAG PANZER, alongside Swedish Deathsters

IN FLAMES, would lend strong support to ICED EARTH's April 2002 American tour. The band would make available for these shows an exclusive DVD package dubbed 'The Era Of Kings And Conflict' boasting feature videos and a bootleg live film of a show in Switzerland.

Conklin also fronts the IRON MAIDEN tribute band POWERSLAVE 2000 in union with ex-LESE MAJESTY bassist Paul Stickney.

Singles/EPs:
Death Row / Battle Zones / Metal Melts The Ice / Iron Shadows, Azra DTR 007 (1983)
Jeffrey Behind The Gate / Spirit Suicide / Jeffrey Behind The Gate (Remix), Rising Sun 050-62303CDS (1994)

Albums:
AMPLE DESTRUCTION, Iron Works IW 1001 (1984)
Licensed To Kill / Warfare / Symphony Of Terror / Harder Than Steel / Generally Hostile / The Watching / Reign Of Tyrants / Cardiac Arrest / Crucifix: i) The Possession, ii) Suffer Unto Me, iii) Apostles Of The Damned, iv) The Beast, v) Armageddon
CHAIN OF COMMAND, Auburn (1987)
Prelude / Chain Of Command / Shadow Thief / She Waits / Ride Through The Storm / In A Gadda Da Vida / Never Surrender / Burning Heart / Sworn To Silence / Dream Theme / Gavotte In D
DISSIDENT ALLIANCE, Rising Sun (1994)
Jeffrey Behind The Gate / The Clown / Forsaken Child / Edge Of Blindness / Eve Of Penance / Last Dying Breath / Psycho Next Door / Spirit Suicide / GMV-407 / The Church / Whisper God
THE FOURTH JUDGEMENT, Century Media 771722 (1997)
Black / Call Of The Wild / Despair / Future Shock / Recompense / Ready To Strike / Tyranny / Shadow Thief / Sonet Of Sorrow / Judgement Day
THE AGE OF MASTERY, Century Media 77225-2 (1998)
Iron Eagle / Lustful And Free / Twilight Years / Sworn To Silence / False Messiah / The Age Of Mastery / Viper / Displacement / Chain Of Command / Take This Pain Away / Burning Heart / The Moors
THANE TO THE THRONE, Century Media (2000)
Thane Of Cawdor / King At A Price / Bloody Crime / The Premonitions / Treachery's Stain / Spectres Of The Past / Banquo's Final Rest / Three Voices Of Fate / Hell To Pay / The Prophecies (Fugue In D minor) / Insanity's Mind / Requiem For Lady MacBeth / Face Of Fear / Fall Of Dunsinane / Fate's Triumph /

The Downward Fall / Tragedy Of MacBeth
MECHANIZED WARFARE, Century Media (2001)
Take To The Sky / Forever In Fear / Unworthy / The Silent / The Scarlet Letter / Choir Of Tears / Cold Is The Balde (And The Heart That Wields It) / Hidden In My Eyes / Power Surge / All Things Renewed

JAILOR (BRAZIL)
Line-Up: Flavio Wyrwa (vocals /guitar), Daniel Hartkopf (Guitar), Emerson Niederauer (bass), Sonne De Oliveira (drums)

Thrash revivalists JAILOR arrived on the scene during 1998. To date the band has issued two demo cassettes, 'Capitol Punishment' in February 1999 and 'Religious Unpurge' in April of 2001.

JELEZNY POTOK (RUSSIA)

Russian Thrash Metal band JELEZNY POTOK ('Iron River') released the 'Chernay Sila' ('Black Power') demo in 1989.

Albums:
ZNAMENIE, Rusky Disk (1992)
BESKONECHNAY BOL, Moroz (1993)
ZOVUSHAY VECHNOST, Moroz (1996)

JERK (SWITZERLAND)
Line-Up: Fri Reeder (vocals / guitar), Bruno Spring (guitar), Andrej A. (bass), Mauro C. (drums)

Albums:
SCREAMS AGAINST WALLS, Major CC 032/058-2 (1995)
Kill / Scream Against Walls / Religion / War / So Horny / Ballad / Shithead / X-Mas / We're Not The Same / Go For It / Dirty World

JERSEY DOGS (USA)
Line-Up: Lou Ciarlo (vocals / bass), Mike Benetatos (guitar), Jon Ilaw (guitar), Mike Sabatini (drums)

Formed from the ashes of New Jersey Metal outfit ATTACKER by bassist Lou Ciarlo and drummer Mike Sabatini. In 1990 the band released their full length debut on the small US label Grudge Records. Lack of distribution and fierce competition in the genre saw the band fold shortly after. The band's 'Don't Worry, Get Angry!' is reputedly both heavier and thrashier than ATTACKER's material.

The album features three originals plus covers of AC/DC's 'Dirty Deeds Done Dirt Cheap' and VAN HALEN's 'Somebody Get Me

A Doctor'.
Sabatini reformed ATTACKER in 2000 in direct competition to another version of the band led by former members.

Albums:
DON'T WORRY, GET ANGRY, Wild Rags WRR015 (1989)
Wasted World / Who's To Blame / Another Pretty Day / Dirty Deeds Done Dirt Cheap / Somebody Get Me A Doctor
THRASH RANCH, Grudge 4526-2-F (1990)
Posse Of Doom / Medicine Man / Why Is / Blood From A Stone / Who's To Blame / Wasted World / Games / Greasy Funk Chicken / Last Breath / Another Pretty Day

JESTERS OF DESTINY (USA)
Line-Up: Bruce Duff (vocals / bass), Eric Carlson (guitar), Ray Violet (guitar), Luie Schilling (drums)

Founded as a side project by THE MENTORS guitarist Eric Carlson. JESTERS OF DESTINY's drum stool was initially occupied by Dave Kuzma. The 1987 album 'In A Nostalgic Mood' comprises cover versions of well known acts such as BLACK SABBATH, LITTLE RICHARD, ELASTIC BAND and JIMI HENDRIX. Fresh recruits for this release were guitarist Michael Montana and drummer Dave Kuzma.

Albums:
FUN AT THE FUNERAL, Metal Blade (1986)
Diggin' That Grave / God Told Me To / Love Theme From 'Jesters On Parade' / I Hate Bruce / End Of Time / Attack Of The Jesters / Incubus / Happy Times / Crimson Umbrella / Love Dust / Ray's Theme
IN A NOSTALGIC MOOD, Metal Blade (1987)
Electric Funeral / Foxy Lady / Spazz / Fortunate Son / The Girl Can't Help It

JEWEL (HOLLAND)
Line-Up: Rick Ambrose (vocals), Henky Backer (guitar), Arwin Vergers (bass), Henkie Rammstein Mulder (drums)

A Melodic Thrash band along the lines of the '80s Bay Area outfits, JEWEL copied MEGADETH's attempts in covering NANCY SINATRA's 'These Boots...' on their debut album 'Revolution In Heaven'.

Albums:
REVOLUTION IN HEAVEN, Classic Trash CTRCD 9101 (1991)
Below The Belt / Dirty Bitch / These Boots... / Circle Of Despair / Blasting Glory / Lonely

Without You / High Speed Pursuit / Road To Katmandu / God's Heart Attack / Warpaint / the Vietnam Requiem: Part I: The Arrival, Part II: Ignorance & Heavy Combat, Part III: Second Tour, Part IV: Tunnel Warfare, Part V: Search And Destroy Mission, Part VI: Tet Offensive, Part VII: The Disillusion, Part VIII: The Awakening

JUGGERNAUT (USA)
Line-Up: Harlan Glenn (vocals), Eddie Katilus (guitar), Scott Womack (bass), Bobby Jarzombek (drums)

JUGGERNAUT were fronted by vocalist Steve Cooper for the second album.
Drummer Bobby Jarzombek later recorded the 'Thundersteel' album with the legendary New York outfit RIOT before founding SPASTIK INK then joining ROB HALFORD's band in 2000.

Albums:
BAPTISM UNDER FIRE, Metal Blade (1986)
Impaler / Slow Death / Cast The First Stone / Rains Of Death / Cut Throat / All Hallows Eve / Burn Tonight/ Juggernaut / Purgatory's Child / Blizzards / Hang 'Em High
TROUBLE WITHIN, Metal Blade (1987)
Without Warning / Vengeance / Russian Roulette / The Calm Before... / The Swarm / Trouble Within / Weeping In Fire / Onslaught Of The Hordes / The Pirate's Blade / Stellar Rubeae / Rap

KABÁT
(CZECH REPUBLIC)
Line-Up: Josef Vojtek (vocals), Tomás Krulich (guitar), Ota Vána (guitar), Milan Spalek (bass), Radek 'Hurvajs' Hurcik (drums)

Thrash Metal band KABÁT had their albums produced by VITACIT frontman and solo artist MILOS DOLEZAL. The band was founded in 1984 and first appeared on the 1990 compilation album 'Rockmapa II' issued by Supraphon Records.
Following the debut album 'Ma Ji Motorovu' KABAT would contribute the track 'Dej Mi Vic Sve Lasky' to an Olympic tribute album. Such was their standing KABAT put out a 1993 live album 'Zive' as their second proper release recorded at concerts in Brno and Toebie during 1992.

Albums:
MÁ JI MOTOROVU, Monitor (1991)
Dr. Bambus / Orgie / A Sek / Nechte Me Bejt / Fuck 'n' Roll / Mas To Zu Sebos / Ma Ji Motorovu / Skr Blik / Sexpervers / Rebel / Vasil / Sex, Drogy, Rock n' Roll / Pasik
ZIVE, Monitor (1992)
Onanie / Chlap Co Oval / Nechte Mi Bejt / Poat Ele Starnou Zase Jsem Na Mol / Uz Sou Zase Na Koni / V Utulcich Pro Ztraceny / Zizeo / Rumovej Rock n' Roll / Ma Ji Motorovu / Mas To Uz Za Sebou
DEVKY TY TO ZNAJ, Monitor (1993)
Uvod / Porcelanovy Prasata / Opilci V Dejinach / My Jsme Zamilovany / Aby Te Rakovina / Devky Ty To Znaj / Pro Nas Meni Misto V Raji / Tahni Dal / Uz Jsou Zose Na Koni / Jack Daniels I: Prolog / Jack Daniels II: Epilog / Oda Na Konopi / Joint / Pivrnec / Hej Moralisti / Tak To Ma Bejt / Zizen / Moderni Devce
COLORADO, Monitor (1994)
Rohyphol Po Tete / Cetrytuga / Nejsen Z Usa / Scerti Nejsou Zerty / Starej Bar / Colorado / Ou Ji Pe Je / Moje Holka Je Batman / Kdyby Zensky Nebyly / Sem Kidnej / Az Pro Me Prijdou
ZEMÉ PLNÁ TRPASLIKU, Monitor EMI (1995)
Piju Ja, Piju Rad / Uz Me Bijou / Daram Ti Jeden Den / Vsude Tu Sou / Jen Sem Ztratil Smer / Davno Uz Uim / Zeme Plna Tupasliku / Zhasnete Svetla / Zasypat To Vaprem / Silnej Jako Vul / Tak Teda Pojd / Vaclav Je Na Plech / Lada
CERT NA KOZE JEL, Monitor EMI (1997)
Satan Klaus / Raketoj Pes / Cert Na Koze Jel / Jabadabadu / Wonder / Sedlak / Kabat / Lady Jane / Cejeni / Boogie Ceskyho Sitare / Stvorenej Pro Acapulco / Balada O

Spinavejch Fuseklich / Tarantule V Trenkack / Blues Folsomske Veznice / Sem Tam Si Tahy Dam / Vs Echno Bude Jako Driv / Kra Lici
MEGA HU, Monitor EMI (1999)
Teta / Vite Jah To Boli / Ueitel / Obi Rucelevy / Bruce Willis / MagaHu / Label Asya / Eioani / Pohrony / Prdel Vody / Ja Si Kopu Vlastini Hrob / Chaoa S Rylou / Brouk Pytisk / Sama
GO SATANE GO, Monitor EMI (2000)
Snih Pada Snih / Go Satane Go / V Pekle Valej Sudy / Na Sever / Mravenci / Kanibal Hanibal / Rodnej Tank / Bara / Bum Bum Tequilla / Ber / Ohrozenej Druk / Odbilo Nam Klekani / Sliben Nezarmoutis / Rio Grande

KAMIKAZE (BRAZIL)
Line-Up: Guilherme Bizzoto (vocals), Reginaldo Silva (guitar), Gustave Duarte (bass), Joao Guimares (drums)

Albums:
KAMIKAZE, Cogumelo (198-)
Trilha Do Metal / Forca Motriz / Machado Guerra / Agora E Com Voce

KAT (POLAND)
Line-Up: Roman Kostrzewski (vocals), Poitr Luczyk (guitar), Wojciech Mrowiec (guitar), Tomasz Jagus (bass), Irseneusz Loth (drums)

KAT were amongst the first Polish Metal bands to make a breakthrough into Western European Rock circles in the mid '80s. KAT's debut Polish release '666' was reissued for the Western market in the toned down form of 'Metal And Hell'.
Following the 1989 album 'Oddech Wymarlich Swiatów' ('The Breath Of Dead Worlds') KAT underwent line-up changes. Losing guitarist Wojciech Mrowiec and bass player Tomasz Jagus the band would regroup with bassist K, Oset and guitar player J, Regulsji.
The 1992 'Bastard' album found KAT operating more furiously than ever before but the act calmed down considerably for the 1994 'Ballady' effort. Later work has seen KAT back on track.
The 1997 mini album 'Badz Wariatem, Zagraj Z Latem' ('Get Crazy, Play With Kat') the band reworked earlier material alongside new tracks and Techno remixes.
KAT vocalist Roman Kostrzewski has also issued a double album inspired by Anton La Vey's 'Satanic Bible'.

Singles/EPs:
Ostatni Tabor / Noce Szatana, MMPR (1985) (7" single)

Albums:
666, Silverton (1986)
METAL AND HELL, Ambush (1986)
Metal And Hell / Killer / Time To Revenge / Devil's House Part I / (You Got Me) Vampire / Devil's Child / Black Hosts / Oracle / Devil's House Part II / 666
38 MINUTES OF LIVE, Silverton (1988)
ODDECH WYMARLYCH SWIATÓW, Metal Mind (1994)
BASTARD, Silverton (1992)
BALLADY, Silverton (1994)
RÓZE MILOSCI NAJCHETNIEJ PRZYJMUJA SIE NA GROBACH, Silverton (1995)
BADZ WARIATEM, ZAGRAJ Z KATEM, Silverton (1997)
SZYDERCZE ZWIERCIADO, Silverton (1997)

KAZJUROL (SWEDEN)

Line-Up: Kjelle (vocals), Pontus (guitar), Tban (guitar), Hakan (bass), Bonden (drums)

KAZJUROL began as a purely amateur project by members of Hardcore band RESCUES IN FUTURE. The band's first commercial release came with a track on a German compilation single entitled 'Breaking The Silence' in 1986.
The interest generated by the single track prompted the recording of a demo cassette titled 'A Lesson In Love', which surfaced in 1988.
The band eventually released their debut album, 'Dance Tarantella', in 1990 which saw vocalist Kjelle replaced by Tomas Bengtsson. However, by the next release, the 'Bodyslam' EP KAZJUROL had found another frontman in Henka 'Gator' Ahlberg. The EP featured covers of tracks by BAD BRAINS, VENOM, STORMTROOPERS OF DEATH and CRO MAGS.
The band further displayed their Hardcore / Punk leanings with a cover of a DISCHARGE track on the Burning Heart Records 1991 compilation 'A Tribute Of Memories'.
However, KAZJUROL eventually split, with both guitarists forming Hardcore act BAD DREAMS ALWAYS.

Singles/EPs:
Messengers Of Death / Stagedive To Hell / Who Needs You?, Uproar UPROAR 004 (1987)
We Gotta Know / United Forces / Pay To Cym / Countless Bathory, Burning Heart Heartcore 001 (1991) ('Bodyslam' EP)
Hallucinations / DanceTarentella / Blue Eyed Devils, Burning Heart Heartcore 002

(1991)

Albums:
DANCE TARANTULA, Active ATV12 (1990)
A Clockwork Out Of Order / Moment 22 / Than / Honesty, The Right Excuse / Dance Tarantella / Blind Illusions / Three Minator / Echoes From The Past / Stagedive To Hell

KIL D'KOR (Seattle, WA, USA)

Line-Up: Shane Peck (vocals), Brian Coloff (guitar), Jeff Wilhelm (bass), Don Martin (drums)

Seattle Metal band KIL D'KOR contributed tracks to the compilation albums 'Northwest Connection' and 'Metal Meltdown'. A demo was issued in 1986.

KILLER (BELGIUM)

Line-Up: Shorty (vocals / guitar), Spooky (vocals / bass), Double Bear (drums)

Formed in 1980 by Shorty and drummer Fat Leo, both men previously with the more obscure MOTHERS OF TRACK, the pair teamed up with ex-TRASH vocalist / bassist Spooky to complete the trio.
KILLER signed to the Belgian arm of WEA Records to record two albums, 'Ready For Hell' and 'Wall Of Sound', and became well known throughout Europe for their appreciation by various biker organizations; probably due to their biker oriented image.
With their departure from WEA Records, KILLER were the first band to sign up to the newly formed Mausoleum label in April 1983. But, just prior to the signing, Fat Leo left the group to be replaced by the equally ridiculously monickered Double Bear.
Mausoleum re-issued both the WEA albums and put two new KILLER tracks on the compilation 'If It's Loud We're Proud' as a taster to the new Jos Kloek produced album 'Shockwaves'. KILLER actually made it over to Britain in 1984 when the trio debuted at the Walthamstow Royal Standard in East London and were also due to play the Kerrang! magazine rock festival at Great Yarmouth, but were scuppered by customs delays on their equipment.
The group reappeared in 1991 with a belated fourth album on the rejuvenated Mausoleum label entitled 'Fatal Attraction'.

Albums:
READY FOR HELL, WEA (1981)
Ready For Hell / Killer / Secret Love / I Know / Rock And Roll Fan / Backshooter / Laws Are Made To Break / It's Too Late / Dressed To Kill

WALL OF SOUND, Lark INL 3535 (1983)
Wall Of Sound / Battlescars / Blinded / No Future / Bodies And Bones / Maybe Our Interests Are The Same / Hellbreaker / Kleptomania
SHOCK WAVES, Mausoleum SKULL 8320 (1983)
Shock Waves / Scarecrow / In The Name Of The Law / King Kong / Blood On The Chains / Richter Scale 12 / In The Eye Of My Gun / Timebomb
FATAL ATTRACTION, Mausoleum 367 0001-2 (1991)
Middle Ages / Fatal Attraction / Break Down The Wall / Steel Meets Steel / Kick On Your Ass / Lift Me Up / Highway Killers / Hibernation / Evil On The Road / I'm On Fire

KILLING TIME (NY, USA)

Hardcore Thrash act KILLING TIME started life as RAW DEAL. Opted for the name change the same year for the 'Brightside' album.

Albums:
BRIGHTSIDE, In Effect (1988)

KILL VAN KULL (USA)

Singles/EPs:
Burn It Up, KVK (1988)

KINETIC DISSENT
(Atlanta, GA, USA)
Line-Up: Dwight Bales (vocals), Stephan Danyo (guitar), Rick McConnell (guitar), Troy Stephens (bass), Ed Reimer (drums)

Albums:
I WILL FIGHT NO MORE FOREVER,
Roadrunner (1991)
Cults Of Unreason / Banished / Melanin / 12 Angry Men / Social Syndrome / I Will Fight No More Forever / Novocaine Response / Testing Ground / Reworked

KNIGHTMARE
(Manchester, NH, USA)
Line-Up: Al Mead (vocals / bass), Tim Koukos (guitar), Steve Piaceczny (drums)

The 1985 single features drummer Bill Connell. KNIGHTMARE's album, 'Mindless Mayhem', featured scenes of depravity involving weapon wielding G.I. Joe figures looming large over dismembered Barbie dolls covered in blood.

Singles/EPs:
Still Insane After All This Treatment,

Knightmare (1983)
Battle From Within / The Power In My Soul, Knightmare (1985)

Albums:
MINDLESS MAYHEM, Beaner City KN86 (1987)
Lake Of Fire / The Hate In Me Grows / Complete Control / Never Be / The Wasteland / Trash / Technology / Possessed / Sonic Reducer / Mindless Mayhem / Land Of The Future

KNIGHTMARE II

(Seal Beach, CA, USA)
Line-Up: The Rod (vocals), Joe Kagle (guitar), Van Simmons (guitar), Gary Gillian (bass), Todd Ferguson (drums)

KNIGHTMARE II are fronted by The Rod, known to his parents as Dennis Carlock.
The debut single 'Warlord' featured a line up of guitarists Darrel Lofton and Dave Klinge, bassist Dave Massey and drummer Doug Craite.
The Rod ditched his whole band upfront of the first album bringing in a completely fresh team of guitarists Van Simmons and Joe Kagle and a rhythm section of Gary Gillian and Todd Ferguson.
KNIGHTMARE II's debut album, which comprises the same songs on both sides, boasts guest contributions from Q5's Floyd Rose and KINGDOM COME's Danny Stag. Drum duties are shared between Todd Ferguson and Alex Sfuentes.
Guitarists Joey Allen (then known as Joe Kagle) and Erik Turner, both later members of WARRANT, enjoyed terms in KNIGHTMARE II.

Singles/EPs:
Warlord / Probation Violation, Raucous RR001 (1984)
Razor Love / Metal Massacre, Raucous (1985)
Guillotine, Iron Works IW 1020 (1988)
Heart Of Stone, Masque (1988)
The Edge Of Knight, Iron Works (1988)
Body Heater, Raucous (1990) (as THE ROD SQUAD)

Albums:
DEATH DO US PART, Raucous (1985)
Razor Love / Crack The Whip / Promised Land / Cold Reception / Goin' Insane
THE EDGE OF KNIGHT, Masque (1988)
The Dark Side / Guillotine / Fear No Evil / Knightrider / Metal Massacre / Queen Of The Knight / Goddess / Make Me Scream / See You In Hell

KORZUS (BRAZIL)
Line-Up: Marcello Pompeu (vocals), Silvio
Golfetti (guitar), Heros Trench (guitar), Dick
Siebert (bass), Rodrigo (drums)

A Sao Paulo act conceived in 1983 citing an
original line-up of vocalist Marcello Pompeu,
guitarists Silvio Golfetti and Eduardo
Toperman bass player Dick Siebert and
drummer Mauricio Brian.
KORZUS debuted with two tracks on a 1985
compilation album 'SP Metal II' and their
opening album 'Korzus Ao Vivo' followed in
1986. This record included a cover version of
SLAYER's 'Evil Has No Boundaries'.
Shortly after KORZUS would be joined by a
new drummer Jose Mauro for recording of the
follow up 'Sonho Maniaco' album. However,
tragedy would strike the same October when
Mauro committed suicide.
KORZUS regrouped with new drummer
Roberto Sileci and guitarist Marcello Nicastro
for 1989's 'Pay For Your Lies', singing in
English for the first time.
'Mass Illusion' arrived in 1991, complete with
cover of BLACK SABBATH's 'Under The Sun',
giving the band increased exposure and
healthy sales. The reputation of KORZUS was
such that Golfetti would be asked to deputize
for Andreas Kisser on a SEPULTURA tour of
Germany. KORZUS themselves would later
tour the European continent.
Another change on the drum stool saw Sileci
departing to found MOSH and KORZUS
pulling in Ricardo Confessori. This latest
inductee would soon decamp though to join
the high profile Progressive Metal act
ANGRA. Fernando Schaefer filled the
drummer's role but then Nicastro bowed out.
New face on second guitar would be Marcelo
Nejem.
KORZUS issued the 'KZS' album in 1996
amply displaying no let up in speed or
aggression. Yet more changes found both
Schaefer and Nejem out of the picture,
creating TRETA. Rodrigo took on the
drummer's vacancy and in 1998 Heros Trench
augmented the guitar sound as KORZUS
gained the honours of appearing alongside
MEGADETH and SLAYER at the Brazilian
'Monsters Of Rock' festival.
2000 witnessed the departure of Rodrigo and
the induction of Kiko of NECROMANCIA on
drums. A live album culled from the 'Monsters
Of Rock' performance was released which
added new studio tracks. With Kiko's
commitments to NECROMANCIA Rodrigo
rejoined the band.

Singles/EPs:
Pay For Your Lies EP, Devil Discos (1989)

Albums:
KORZUS AO VIVO, (1986)
Guerreiros Do Metal (Metal Warriors) /
Príncipe Da Escuridão (Darkness Prince) /
Ataque Supremo (Supreme Attack) /
Caminhos Negros (Dark Ways) / Anjo Do
Mal (Angel Of Evil) / Evil Has No Boundaries
SONHO MANIACO, (1987)
Anjo Do Mal (Angel Of Evil) / Juízo Final
(Judgement Day) / Suícidio (Suicide) /
Caminhando Nas Trevas (Walking On
Darkness) / Sonho Maníaco (Maniac Dream)
/ Guerra Nuclear (Nuclear War) / Paraíso Da
Morte (Paradise Of Death)
MASS ILLUSION, (1989)
The Dark Side Of The Mind / Brain Wash /
Born To Kill / Elm Street / The World Is A
Stage / Under The Sun
KORZUS SP-SP, (1996)

KRANK (NJ, USA)
Line-Up: Frank Tyson (vocals), Mike Force
(guitar), Kevin Mercer (bass), Jack Hamer
(drums)

Albums:
HIDEOUS, Metal Blade Roadrunner RR9674
(1986)
Power / Til Hell Freezes Over / Evil / Nasty
Habits / Rock The House / Rented Heat /
Head Like A Rock / No More Lies / Don't
Fuck With Me / Hideous (Heavy Metal
Havoc)

KRATOS (OH, USA)
Line-Up: Bern Hanzel (vocals / guitar), Paul
Gregory (bass), Bob Hanzel (drums)

Singles/EPs:
Iron Beast / Armageddon / Chainsaw / Save
Their Souls, Kratos (1985)

KREATOR (GERMANY)
Line-Up: Mille Petrozza (guitar / vocals), Jörg
Tritze (guitar), Rob (bass),
Ventor (drums)

Essen based trio formed in 1982 as
TORMENTOR, and, having adopted the new
monicker of KREATOR, the German outfit
were to become much favoured by European
Thrash fans in the mid '80s.
KREATOR toured Europe and America
consistently, improving with each album
release and keen to augment their live sound
would spend time searching for a second
guitarist. Wulf from SODOM joined for a brief
period in 1986 and KREATOR were found
sharing the billing with RAGE and
DESTRUCTION that year, after which
guitarist Jorg Tritze was added to the line-up.

MILLE PETROZZA of KREATOR Photo : Nico Wobben

In 1987 KREATOR toured Britain opening for CELTIC FROST and America as support to DIRTY ROTTEN IMBECILES backed by a promotion video for 'Toxic Trace' that gained the band valuable MTV exposure. It ensured sales of the band's third album, 'Terrible Certainty', were racked up ever more and set the tone for the subsequent 'Into The Light' and 'Extreme Aggression' albums.

The latter album was produced by leading American based Thrash knob twiddler Randy Burns and, amongst all new KREATOR originals, featured a cover version of the RAVEN track 'Lambs To The Slaughter'.

Just prior to their 1989 American tour playing alongside SUICIDAL TENDENCIES Tritze was ousted in favour of SODOM's Frank Blackfire. This line-up would record 1990's 'Coma Of Souls' in Los Angeles; once again with Randy Burns at the production helm.

A rather bizarre incident occurred later the same year when KREATOR pulled out of their London Electric Ballroom show complaining that they would have to play with a decibel meter in attendance! Still, no such problems prevented the group from completing a successful South American tour in 1992 performing in Chile, Brazil and Argentina.

Having left Noise after a lengthy relationship of nearly ten years, KREATOR signed to G.U.N. Records in late 1994 with the first fruits of the new deal coming in the form of 1995's 'Cause For Conflict'. And the group also introduced a new line-up of Petrozza, Blackfire bassist Christian Giesler and ex-WHIPLASH drummer Joe Cangelosi. However, by the end of the year both Godszik and Cangelosi were to depart. The band filled the gap with guitarist Tommy Vetterli and drummer Jürgen Reil.

More recently, in addition to a brace of new records in 1996 and 1997, KREATOR contributed a version of JUDAS PRIEST's 'Grinder' to the 'Legends Of Metal Volume II' tribute album in 1996. The 1999 'Endorama' album would find KREATOR pursuing a distinctly Gothic tinged direction.

A tribute album to KREATOR emerged in 2000 titled 'Raise The Flag Of Hate'. Contributors included PAZUZU, ANGEL CORPSE, ACHERON, MYSTIFER and BLACK WITCHERY.

Vetterli was out of the picture for recording of the 2001 Andy Sneap produced album 'Violent Revolution'. He was supplanted by Sami Yli-Sirniö, the same figure who temporarily replaced him for live work earlier. Promoting the album, which landed in the German album charts at number 38, found KREATOR with running mates CANNIBAL CORPSE for European touring. KREATOR would form part of a nostalgic Thrash Metal mammoth tour of Germany with compatriots SODOM and DESTRUCTION commencing 26th December 2001 in Ludwigsburg and running through into the new year.

Singles/EPs:
Flag Of Hate / Take Their Lives / Awakening Of The Gods, Noise 0047 (1986) (12" single)
After The Attack, Noise (1986)
Behind The Mirror / Gangland, Noise 0084 (1987) (12" single)
Impossible To Cure / Lambs To The Slaughter / Terrible Certainty (Live) / Riot Of Violence (Live) / Awakening Of The Gods (Live), Noise NO118-4 (1988) ('Out Of The Dark... Into The Light' EP)
People Of The Lie, Noise (1990)
Lost / Hate Inside Your Head, G.U.N. GUN 072 BMG 74321 30960-2 (1995) (Promotion release)
Isolation / Men Without God, G.U.N. GUN 079 BMG 74321 33082-2 (1995) (Promotion release)
Chosen Few / Endorama / Children Of A Lesser God / Chosen Few (Video) / Endorama (Video), Drakkar (1999)

Albums:
ENDLESS PAIN, Noise NO025 (1985)
Endless Pain / Total Death / Storm Of The Beast / Tormentor / Son Of Evil / Flag Of Hate / Cry War / Bone Breaker / Living In Fear / Dying Victims
PLEASURE TO KILL, Noise NO037 (1986)
Intro (Choir Of The Damned) / Ripping Corpse / Death Is Your Saviour / Pleasure To Kill / Riot Of Violence / The Pestilence / Carrion / Command Of The Blade / Under The Guillotine / Flag Of Hate / Take Their Lives / Awakening Of The Gods
TERRIBLE CERTAINTY, Noise NO100 (1987)
Toxic Trace / No Escape / One Of Us / Behind The Mirror / Blind Faith / Storming With Menace / Terrible Certainty
INTO THE LIGHT, Noise NO200-2 (1988)
Impossible To Cure / Lambs To The Slaughter / Terrible Certainty / Riot Of Violence / Awakening Of The Gods / Flag Of Hate (Live) / Love Or Hate Us (Live) / Behind The Mirror
EXTREME AGGRESSION, Noise NO129 (1989)
Extreme Aggression / No Reason To Exist / Love Us Or Hate Us / Stream Of Consciousness / Some Pain Will Last / Betrayer / Don't Trust / Bringer Of Torture / Fatal Energy
COMA OF SOULS, Noise N1058 (1990)
When The Sun Burns Red / Coma Of Souls / People Of The Lie / World Beyond / Terror

Zone / Agents Of Brutality / Material World / Paranoia / Twisted Urges / Hidden Dictator / Mental Slavery
RENEWAL, Noise NO193 (1994)
Winter Martyrium / Renewal / Reflection / Brainseed / Karmic Wheel / Realiätskontrolle / Zero To None / Europe After The Rain / Depression Unrest
CAUSE FOR CONFLICT, G.U.N. GUN 071 BMG 74321 30002-2 (1995)
Prevail / Catholics Despot / Progressive Proletarians / Crisis Of Disorder / Hate Inside Your Head / Bomb Threat / Men Without God / Lost / Dogmatic / Sculpture Of Regret / Celestial Deliverence / Isolation
SCENARIOS OF VIOLENCE, Noise N0222-2 (1996)
Suicide In Swamps / Renewal / Extreme Aggression / Brainseed / Terrorzone / Ripping Corpse / Tormentor/ Some Pain Will Last / Toxic Trace / People Of The Lie / Depression Unrest / Coma Of Souls / Europe After The Rain / Limits Of Liberty / Terrible Certainty / Karmic Wheel
OUTCAST, G.U.N. GUN BMG 74321 45262-2 (1997)
Leave This World Behind / Phobia / Forever / Black Sunrise / Nonconformist / Enemy Unseen / Outcast / Stronger Than Before / Ruin Of Life / Whatever It May Take / Alive Again / Against The Rest / A Better Tomorrow
ENDORAMA, Drakkar (1999)
Golden Age / Endorama / Shadowland / The Chosen Few / Everlasting Flame / Passage To Babylon / Future King / Entry / Soul Eraser / Willing Spirit / Pandemonium / Tyranny
VOICES OF TRANSGRESSION - A '90s RETROSPECTIVE, (1999)
Lucretia (My Reflection) / The Chosen Few / Isolation / Leave This World Behind / Golden Age / Bomb Threat / Phobia / Whatever It May Take / Renewal / Lost / Hate Inside Your Head / Inferno / Outcast / State Oppression / Endorama / Black Sunrise / As We Watch The West
PAST LIFE TRAUMA, Noise (2000)
VIOLENT REVOLUTION, (2001)
Reconquering The Throne / The Patriarch / Violent Revolution / All Of The Same Blood (Unity) / Servant In Heaven - King In Hell / Second Awakening / Ghetto War / Replicas Of Life / Slave Machinery / Bitter Sweet Revenge / Mind On Fire / System Decay

KRIMSON KROSS

(Houston, TX, USA)
Line-Up: Daron Douglas (vocals), Jacl Mize (guitar), Joey Gamino (bass), Bryan Thornton (drums)

Singles/EPs:
Dogs Of War / God Bless The Damned, Krimson Kross (1984)

KRISIUN (BRAZIL)
Line-Up: Alex Carmago (vocals / bass), Moyses Kolesne (guitar / keyboards), Max Kolesne (drums)

Sao Paulo Death Metal merchants KRISIUN include plentiful old school Thrashing as part of their delivery. The band first offered their 1991 demo 'Evil Age'. A further tape 'Curse Of The Evil One' backed it up the following year leading to the band's first official product the 'Unmerciful Order' EP. Other releases included shared EP's with Germans HARMONY DIES and VIOLENT HATE. Signing to Germany's G.U.N. Records KRISIUN debuted proper with 1996's 'Black Force Domain'.
The band would make a significant impact upon European shores in 1998 ranked on tour alongside NAPALM DEATH, CRADLE OF FILTH and BORKNAGER before embarking on a series of headline dates with support act SOILWORK. The band would also gain further exposure with appearances on two tribute albums offering a vastly accelerated take on KREATOR's 'Total Death' and 'Nuclear Winter' to a SODOM homage.
February of 1999 had KRISIUN involved in their inaugural North American tour alongside INCANTATION and ANGEL CORPSE. Switching to Century Media Records KRISIUN's 2000 album 'Conquerors Of Armageddon' was produced by MORBID ANGEL's Eric Rutan. Touring to promote the album found the band sharing billing with SATYRICON, IMMORTAL and ANGEL CORPSE in America. As ANGEL CORPSE disintegrated mid tour with the departure of mainman Pete Helmkamp KRISIUN would obligingly loan out Carmago to fulfil vocal duties in order that ANGEL CORPSE could complete the run of dates. There would be no let up for the band, soon after engaged in European touring on a package billing in alliance with OLD MAN'S CHILD, GORGOROTH and SOUL REAPER.
The Tchello Martin produced 'Ageless Venomous' arrived in 2001 prompting a full scale global workout which saw KRISIUN performing in Europe, North America, South America, Russia and Japan. The band by now had risen to headliner status for the 'Thrash 'Em All' festivals throughout Poland and Russia topping a bill of VADER, LUX OCCULTA and BEHEMOTH. November of 2001 had the band on the road in the UK and Ireland for seven shows with CANNIBAL CORPSE and KREATOR, this union

transferring to Europe before hooking up with MARDUK, DARK FUNERAL, NILE and VOMITORY to participate in the hugely successful sold out 'X-Mas' festivals.

<u>Albums:</u>
UNMERCIFUL ORDER, (1993)
They Call Me Death / Unmerciful Order / Crosses Towards Hell / Agonize The Ending / Summons Of Irreligious / Meaning Of Terror / Infected Core / Insurrected Path (Depth Classic) / Rises From The Black
BLACK FORCE DOMAIN, G.U.N. GUN147 (1997)
Black Force Domain / Messiah Of The Double Cross / Hunter Of Souls / Blind Possession / Evil Mastermind / Infamous Glory / Respected To Perish Below / Meanest Evil / Obsession By Evil Force / Sacrifice Of The Unborn
APOCALYPTIC REVELATION, G.U.N. (1998)
Creations Scourge / Kings Of Killing / Apocalyptic Victory / Aborticide (In The Crypts Of Holiness) / March Of The Black Hordes / Vengeances Revelation / Rites Of Defamation / Meaning Of Terror / Rises From Black
CONQUERORS OF ARMEGEDDON, Century Media (2000)
Intro - Ravager / Abyssal Gates / Soul Devourer / Messiah's Abomination / Cursed Scrolls / Conquerors Of Armageddon / Hatred Inherit / Iron Stakes / Endless Madness Descends
AGELESS VENOMOUS, Century Media (2001)
Perpetuation / Dawn Of Flagellation / Ageless Venomous / Evil Gods Havoc / Eyes Of Eternal Scourge / Saviour's Blood / Serpents Specters / Ravenous Hordes / Diableros / Sepulchral Oath

KRONEN (USA)
Line-Up: Rik Wyryk (vocals), Steven Lesli (guitar), Jeff Brown (bass), Victor Price (drums)

<u>Singles/EPs:</u>
Wasted / Alone / No You Won't / Rock & Roll / Children Of Steel, Azra (1986)

KUBLAI KAHN
(Minneapolis, MN, USA)
Line-Up: Greg Handevidt (guitar / vocals), Kevin Idso (guitar), Mike Liska (bass), John Fedde (drums)

KUBLAI KAHN, created by former MEGADETH guitarist Greg Handevidt, debuted with a three track demo in 1986. The album was released in America by New Renaissance Records and licensed through Europe by Heavy Metal America.

<u>Albums:</u>
ANNIHILATION, Heavy Metal America HMUSA 95 (1987)
Death Breath / Mongrel Horde / Down To The Inferno / Liars Dice / Passing Away - Kublai Khan / Clash Of The Swords / Battle Hymn (The Centurion)

LÄÄZ ROCKIT
(San Francisco, CA, USA)
Line-Up: Michael Coons
(vocals), Aaron Jellum (guitar),
Phil Kettner (guitar), Willy Lange
(bass), Victor Agnello (drums)

LÄÄZ ROCKIT was formed by vocalist Michael Coons and guitarist Aaron Jellum who stole second guitarist Phil Kettner from a rival local outfit. The inaugural bass player Dave Starr actually named the band (after a sci-fi weapon in a Clint Eastwood movie) as in their formative days they were called DEPTH CHARGE.

Having added drummer Victor Agnello to the ranks LÄÄZ ROCKIT replaced Starr in 1983 with Willy Lange following a support slot to RATT. Starr created power trio BLACK LEATHER before joining VICIOUS RUMOURS.

LÄÄZ ROCKIT were originally signed to RATT manager Marshall Berle's Timecoast label, but Berle disbanded the company once his charges had been picked up by Atlantic, leaving the door open for Mark Leonard's Target concern to sign the group, releasing the debut 'City's Gonna Burn' album in September 1984.

LÄÄZ ROCKIT began a tour of America in support of their debut album as opening act to GRIM REAPER and EXCITER, but were unceremoniously removed after three shows. Lange would audition for the position of bassist for METALLICA in 1986.

With 'Know Your Enemy' gaining the band more media attention LÄÄZ ROCKIT managed some European shows opening for MOTÖRHEAD and a slot on the prestigious Aardschock Festival in Holland. Agnello departed, but returned in time for American dates. Further British shows saw the band opening for EXODUS.

The band toured Europe with support from Dutchmen OSIRIS in 1989. The 1991 album 'Nothing Sacred' saw Coons and Jellum joined by bassist Scott Dominguez, guitarist Scott Sargeant and drummer Dave Chavarri. Ex LÄÄZ ROCKIT guitarist Ken Savitch joined Illinois's SINDROME during 1991.

Sargeant joined KILLING CULTURE before teaming up with SKINLAB in 1998. Chavarri joined PRO-PAIN.

Singles/EPs:
Holiday In Cambodia / Mirror To Madness / Prelude To Death (Live) / Forced To Fight (Live), Roadracer RO 24361 (1990)

Albums:
CITY'S GONNA BURN, Target (1984)

City's Gonna Burn / Caught In The Act / Take No Prisoners / Dead Man's Eyes / Forced To Fight / Silent Scream / Prelude / Something More
NO STRANGER TO DANGER,
Steamhammer 081866 (1985)
Dreams Die Hard / I've Got Time / Town To Town / Backbreaker / Stand Alone / Spared From The Fire / Off The Deep End / Tonight Alive / Wrecking Machine
KNOW YOUR ENEMY, Music For Nations MFN 81 (1987)
Demolition / Last Breath / Euroshima / Most Dangerous Game / Shot To Hell / Say Goodbye M.F. / Self Destruct / Means To An End / I'm Electric / Mad Axe Attack / Shit's Ugly
ANNIHILATION PRINCIPLE, Enigma CDENV 521 (1989)
Mirror Into Madness / Chasin' Charlie / Fire In The Hole / Shadow Company / Holiday In Cambodia / Mob Justice / Bad Blood
NOTHING SACRED, Roadracer (1991)
In The Name Of The Father And The Gun / Into The Asylum / Greed Machine / Too Far Gone / Curiosity Kills / Suicide City / The Enemy Within / Nobody's Child / Silence Is A Lie / Necropolis
TASTE OF REBELLION (LIVE), (1991)
In The Name Of The Father And The Gun... / Greed Machine / Fire In The Hole / City's Gonna Burn / Leatherface / The Omen / Suicide City / The Enemy Within / Prelude To Death / Into The Asylum / Holiday In Cambodia / Curiosity Kills

LAZARUS SIN (OR, USA)

Albums:
INTERCRANIAL MASS, Lazarus Sin (1988)
Blood For Mercy / Apothecaries' Measure / 7734 / The Son Of The Jackal / Author Of Sorrow / Monument / Out Of The Box

LEGION (OH, USA)

Singles/EPs:
Legion Of Death, Realtime (1986)

LEGION OF DEATH (Colorado, USA)

Albums:
LEGION OF DEATH, L.O.D. (1988)

LESE MAJESTY
(Colorado Springs, CO, USA)
Line-Up: Joey Freeman (vocals), Rick Aligaen (guitar), Mick Nichols (guitar), Paul Stickney (bass), Pete Derbort (drums)

LESE MAJESTY bassist Paul Stickney would

later hook up with JAG PANZER vocalist Harry Conklin in the IRON MAIDEN tribute band POWERSLAVE 2000.

Albums:
SURVIVING, Iron Works IW 1029 (1988)
Surviving / Killing Freedom / Blinded By Vengeance / Dead Sea / Goodbye / Wake Up / Sell Jesus / No Escape (Kill Me) / Nobody Wins / Depression

LETHAL (Kentucky, USA)
Line-Up: Tom Mallicoat (vocals), Dell Hull (guitar), Eric Cook (guitar), Glen Cook (bass), Jerry Hartman (drums)

Kentucky Thrashers LETHAL, founded in 1982 by brothers Eric and Glen Cook, on guitar and bass respectively, boast the extreme vocal talents of Tom Mallicoat.

Albums:
PROGRAMMED, Metal Blade ZORRO 15 (1990)
Fire In Your Skin / Programmed / Plan Of Peace / Another Day / Arrival / What They've Done / Obscure The Sky / Immune / Pray For Me / Killing Machine
YOUR FAVOURITE GOD, Bullet (1993)
Swim Or Drown / Waiting On The Kill / The Page Before / Hard To Breathe / The Real / Balancing Act
POISON SEED, Massacre (1995)
Down / Bitter Taste / Born / Walking Wounded / Poison Seed / Watch Me Feed / Meaning / Now / Your Favorite God / Odd Shaped Pearl

LETHAL AGGRESSION (NJ, USA)
Line-Up: John Saltz (vocals), Rob De Froscia (guitar), George Yeck (bass), Ken Lund (drums)

A New Jersey Crossover Thrashcore act dating back to 1985. LETHAL AGGRESSION debuted with an infamous demo 'From The Cunt Of The Fucking Whore'. An inclusion of the track 'Corruption' on the 1987 'Complete Death II' compilation led to a 7" single 'We Just Killed Rock n' Roll' for the Colorado Premature Entombment Productions label. The 'Subliminal Erosion' album would arrive in 1990 courtesy of the French Virulence concern.
A projected album, 'Godservation', was recorded in 1991 but consigned to the vaults. The band issued a self issued collection of live material, outtakes and fan messages entitled 'The Studdering Skull Sessions' in 1992.
Relapse Records would combine the demo

and shelved album for a 2001 CD release. Only vocalist John Saltz would survive from the founding line-up, being joined by guitarist Dave, bass player Todd and drummer Kenny in 2001.

Singles/EPs:
Dicked Again! / Godservation / Lies / Hard Day / Regret End / We Just Killed Rock n' Roll, Premature Entombment Productions (1987)
Ripple On Ice / Tomorrow Comes Around / Stuck Fuk / D'So Shall D'Kay / Spooge 2 / At Last / Dyaneticide Ineluctable, Virulence (1990) ('Subliminal Erosion' EP)

Albums:
LIFE IS HARD - BUT THAT'S NO EXCUSE, Funhouse (1989)
Intro / Morbid Reality / No Scene / Fighting In The City / Spooge / War / K.D.D. / I'll Fight / Quick Pain / Wild Kingdom / Vodda Vodka / Outcast / Newscaster's Lies / Proud Johnny / F.D.A. / Cuntry Pig / Don't Break The Pack / No More Wasted Time / What You See Is What You Get / Face The Facts / Exit
FROM THE CUNT OF THE FUCKING WHORE, Relapse RLP6484 (2001)
Spooge / Vodda Vodka / Cuntry Pig / Morbid Reality / Anarcheology / Metallic Rage / Lust / L'Amour's Radio Spot / So Dead Alive / Regret / Godservation / Tomorrow Comes Around / Gone Fishin' / Co-exist Within Myself / ??? / Circle Of Hate / What Ya Tryin' To Do? / Lies / Stuk Fuck / Six Inches Of Steel / Dyaneticide / The Great One / Subconscious Nirvana / Ripple On Ice / Rye Whiskey / Drugcore / Brik Life / Beh Chicka Deh Det / Yes / Subliminal Erosion / Stuck In A Rut / Learn That Poem (Outro)

LETHAL DOSE (WA, USA)
Line-Up: Rick Danks (vocals), John Parkes (guitar), Barry Allen (bass), Bill Waters (drums)

Albums:
LETHAL DOSE, Ever Rat (1988)
Caught In Between / Abattoir / Made Of Metal / Written In Blood / Capturing Your Mind / The Evil / Not Afraid To Die / In The Mirror / Curse Of The Dark / Ridin'

LEVIATHAN (CO, USA)
Line-Up: Jeff Ward (vocals), Ronnie Skeen (guitar), John Lutzow (guitar), Derek Blake (bass), Trevor Heffer (drums)

Progressive Thrash out of Colorado and named after JAG PANZER vocalist Harry Conklin's pseudonym 'Leviathan' adopted whilst fronting his side act SATAN'S HOST. Musically LEVIATHAN's early works are somewhat akin to technical Euro Thrash but as the act's career moved forward they would tone down considerably.

LEVIATHAN was forged during 1989 by former SONIC FURY guitar players Steve Fugate and Ronnie Skeen. Fugate would decamp in 1991, making way for John Lutzow.

The debut 1992 album sees a line up of mainstay guitarists Ronnie Skeen and John Lutzow, vocalist Tom Braden and a rhythm section of bassist James Escobedo and drummer Ty Tammeus. For the sophomore 1994 record 'Deepest Secrets Beneath' Braden was usurped by Jack Aragon.

LEVIATHAN switched to the German Century Media concern for 1996's 'Riddles, Secrets, Poetry And Outrage'. The band had changed radically both musically and in the personnel department veering into a straight Progressive Rock direction fronted by new singer Jeff Ward. LEVIATHAN had also summoned up a fresh team of bass player Derek Blake and drummer Trevor Heffer.

Although LEVIATHAN would stabilise it's line up for 1997's 'Scoring The Chapter' little has been heard since.

Ronnie Skeen did venture outside of LEVIATHAN for a Prog Power Metal concept IRON FORTRESS in league with vocalist Tim Lawrence. This outfit released an eponymous album through Germany's Hellion label.

Albums:
LEVIATHAN, (1992)
Fear Of Change / Degenerating Paradise / Two Roads To Nowhere / Beast Of Burden / Leviathan
DEEPEST SECRETS BENEATH, RTN RTN 41201 (1994)
Confidence Not Arrogance / Sanctuary / The Calling / Painful Pursuit Of Passion And Purpose / Not Always Lost / The Falling Snow / Run Forever / Disenchanted Dreams (Of Conformity) / Speed Kills
RIDDLES, SECRETS, POETRY AND OUTRAGE, Century Media (1996)
Census Of Stars / Mindless Game Control / Madness Endeavor / Pages Of Time / Are First Loves Forgotten? / So Where Is God? / Confusion / Don't Look To Me / Passion Above All Else
SCORING THE CHAPTERS, Corrosive CRD 77362 (1997)
Salvation / Friends Imaginary / Paying The Toll / The Door / J. Christopher's Haunting / If These Walls Could Talk / All Sins Returned / Scar Barrow's Fare / The Last King Of The Highlands / Born Unto (But Don't Belong To Me) / Leftist Out / Turning Up Broken /

Failing Avalon / Apologies Wanting To Make Good / Legacy Departing

LIFE SENTENCE (USA)
Line-Up: Eric Brockman (vocals / guitar), Joe Losurdo (bass), Tom O'Connor (drums)

Albums:
LIFE SENTENCE, Walkthrufyre (1986)
Problems / Race To Die / Election Day / Men In Blue / Punks For Profit / Peacetime Death / Unemployment / In The Streets / Figured It Out / Take A Stand

LIVING DEATH (GERMANY)
Line-Up: Thorsten Bergmann (vocals), Reiner Kelch (guitar), Frank Fricke (guitar), Dieter Kelch (bass), Andreas Oberhoff (drums)

An Extreme Thrash Metal act that attracted a sizable European cult following despite being dismissed by many critics, LIVING DEATH were formed by the Kelch brothers (guitarist Reiner and bassist Dieter) and guitarist Frank Fricke. The group's debut album, 'Vengeance Of Hell', was produced by Alex Thubeauville. The 'Vengeance Of Hell' album is, naturally, very prehistoric in sound compared to what the group later achieved, so whilst Metal fans either loved its rawness or dismissed it as the worst record they'd ever heard, LIVING DEATH slowly but surely progressed. The Kelch brothers more than most, both later appeared anonymously as part of the MEKONG DELTA project albums.

Releasing the band's second album, 'Metal Revolution' in 1986 the group would eventually be signed to Aaarg Records, although the 'Back To The Weapons' EP was severely censored by the European record industry for its cover art depicting scenes of extreme violence. Copies without a rather large white circular sticker (which, if removed cause severe damage to the sleeve) covering the offending image are extremely hard to find.

By 1988 the band had truncated their title from LIVING DEATH to L.D. and issued the 'World's Neuroses' album. Shortly after it's release the Kelch brothers quit and ex-VIOLENT FORCE vocalist Lemmy joined the band.

LIVING DEATH adopted a name change to SACRED CHAOS in January 1989. By 1990 Fricke had created LAOS for a solitary album in collusion with ex-AVENGER, RAGE and MEKONG DELTA drummer Jörg Michael.

Ultimately, LIVING DEATH drummer Atomic Steif joined SODOM in 1994.

Singles/EPs:
Watch Out / You And Me / Heavy Metal
Hurricane / Night Light, Earthshaker ESM
4007 (1985)
Nuclear Greetings / Bloody Dance / The
Way (Your Soul Must Go) / Child Of Illusion,
Aargg AAARRG 2 (1986) ('Back To The
Weapons' EP)
Eisbein (Mit Sauerkraut) / Horrible
Infanticide / Vengeance, Aaarrg AAARRG 9
(1987)
Killing Machine (Live) / Grippin' A Heart
(Live) / Road Of Destiny (Live) / Screaming
From A Chamber (Live), Aaarrg AAARRG 12
(1988)

Albums:
VENGEANCE OF HELL, Mausoleum
SKULL 8360 (1984)
You And Me / Living Death / Nightlight / My
Victim / Labyrinth / Heavy Metal Hurricane /
Hellpike / Riding A Virgin / Vengeance Of
Hell
METAL REVOLUTION, Earthshaker ES
4012 (1986)
Killing Machine / Grippin' A Heart / Rulers
Must Come / Screaming From A Chamber /
Intro / Shadow Of The Dawn / Panic And
Hysteria / Road Of Destiny / Deep In Hell
PROTECTED FROM REALITY, Aaarrg

AAARRG 5 (1987)
Horrible Infanticide (Part One) / Manila Terror
/ Nature's Death / Wood Of Necrophiliacs /
Vengeance / Horrible Infanticide (Part Two) /
Intruder / The Galley / War Of Independence
/ Eisbein (Mit Sauerkraut)
WORLD'S NEUROSES, Aaarrg AAARRG
15 (1988)
Last Birthday / Die Young / Schizophrenia /
On The 17th Floor / Down / World's
Neuroses / Bastard At The Bus Stop /
Sacred Chao / Tuesday
KILLING IN ACTION, Intercord IRS 986.944
(1991)
Killing In Action / Hang 'Em High / Dire Weak
Up / Hearteater / Polymorphic / World
Weariness / Die For (For What We Lie For) /
Stand Up / Tribute Of Gutter / Daily Life
LIVING DEATH, Aaarrg ARG 28-051-2
(1995)
Nuclear Greetings / Bloody Dance / The Way
(Your Soul Must Go) / Child Of Illusion /
Horrible Infanticide (Part One) / Manila Terror
/ Natures Death / Wood Of Necrophiliac /
Vengeance (Horrible Infanticide Part Two) /
Intruder / The Galley / War Of Independence
/ Last Birthday / Die Young / Schizophrenia /
On The 17th Floor / Down / World's
Neuroses / Bastard (At The Bus Stop) / The
Testament Of Mr. George / Sacred Chao /

239

Tuesday / Killing Machine / Grippin' A Heart / Road Of Destiny / Screamin' From The Chambre
METAL REVOLUTION, ABS Classics 100 (1996) (Digitally remastered re-issue)
Killing Machine / Grippin' A Heart / Rulers Must Come / Screaming From A Chamber / Intro / Shadow Of The Dawn / Panic And Hysteria / Road Of Destiny / Deep In Hell

DAVE LOMBARDO (USA)

Cuban born drummer Dave Lombardo is a renowned figure in the Rock world for taking speed drumming to new levels with SLAYER. Lombardo later joined GRIP INC.
His first solo album, working with Lorenzo Arruga, is a brave experiment in unifying Vivaldi's classical music with Metal drumming.
The album includes contributions from Alberto Contini, former front man with Italian Thrash merchants BULLDOZER.
Lombardo would hook up with SLAYER once again in January of 2002, fulfilling dates on the 'God Hates Us All' tour, although both parties stressed this was a temporary arrangement.

Albums:
VIVALDI - THE MEETING, SPV 085-29572 CD (1999)
Un Apparizione / Una Sfida: La Tempesta D'estate / Preludo Alla Pena Amara / Vedrö Con Mio Diletto / Nel Profundo / Agitata Da Due Venti / Un Congedo: Il Canto Del Pastore

LONE RAGER (USA)

The anonymous LONE RAGER is in fact none other than Megaforce Records boss Johnny Zazula.

Singles/EPs:
Metal Rap, Megaforce (1984)

LORDS OF THE CRIMSON ALLIANCE
(USA)
Line-Up: Far Cry (vocals / guitar), Cutterjohn (guitar), Grom (bass), Zan Zan (drums)

Albums:
LORDS OF THE CRIMSON ALLIANCE, Grudge (1986)
Firedancer / Dragonslayer / Swords Of Zeus / Death Crusade / The Sorcerer / The Dungeon / In The Arms Of Morpheus / Clone Of The Wolf

LOW TWELVE (Bloomington, IL, USA)
Line-Up: Pete Alteri (vocals / bass), Tim McCleland (guitar), Les Aldridge (guitar), Wes Pollock (drums)

Bloomington, Illinois Metal band LOW TWELVE came together as a trio of vocalist / bassist Pete Alteri, guitarist Tim McCleland and drummer Steve Chestney in mid 1998. The band augmented their sound with the addition of second guitarist Les Aldridge in that December. In November of the following year Chestney was usurped by Wes Pollock, this revised line up cutting the debut demo 'Blunt Force Trauma'.
Reviews were solid and LOW TWELVE succeeded in selling over a 1000 copies of the demo, leading in turn to the EP 'Kill Floor'. The band has proved active on the live front, credited with over 100 gigs during 2000 including headline slots at such Midwest festival events as 'Stomp Fest '99', 'Poser Roast 2000' and the '9 Mile Mosh Fest'.
The band would self-finance the 'Flesh Of The Weak' album, adding four live recordings to the new studio material.

Albums:
FLESH OF THE WEAK, D-Day (2000)
Brutal World / Begging To Die / Twelve / Trench / Enemy Of The State / S-21 / Meltdown / Crawlspace / Kill Floor / Thin Skinned / Sex Sin Sermon / Kill Floor (Live) / S-21 (Live) / Begging To Die (Live) / Enemy Of The State (Live) / Twelve (Extended intro)

LUDICHRIST (New York, NY, USA)
Line-Up: Tommy Christ (vocals), Glen Cummings (guitar), Joe Butcher (guitar), Chuck Valle (bass), Al Batross (drums)

Crossover Punk metal act LUDICHRIST's first album boasts hardcore guests Roger Miret of AGNOSTIC FRONT plus LEE WAY's Eddie Sutton, NUCLEAR ASSAULT's John Connelly and CRUMBSUCKERS Chris Notaro.
The band fractured between albums retaining only vocalist Tommy Christ and guitarist Glen Cummings. For the 'Powertrip' effort they were joined by guitarist Paul Nieder, bassist Mike Walters and drummer Dave Miranda.
Ex-LUDICHRIST bassist Chuck Valle joined MURPHY'S LAW in 1989.
Following this release Miranda lost his position to former WHIPLASH / ZERO HOUR noted speed drummer Tony Scaglione who had just finished deputising for DAVE LOMBARDO in SLAYER. The liaison was brief however and Scaglione departed in October 1988 to join RAGING SLAB.

LUDICHRIST toured Europe supporting the likes of AGNOSTIC FRONT, SUICIDAL TENDENCIES and BAD BRAINS.

LUDICHRIST split in 1990 with Tommy Christ, Glenn Cummings and Paul Nieder forming SCATTERBRAIN to record a self-titled album for In-Effect.

Drummer Dave Miranda later found Progressive Jazz Rock trio THE MAGIC ELF, releasing two albums 'Elf Tales' and 'Live'. Miranda is also a member of SIX AND VIOLENCE.

Albums:

IMMACULATE DECEPTION, Combat Core (1986)
Fire At The Firehouse / Most People Are Dicks / Murder Bloody Murder / Blown Into The Arms Of Christ / Big Business / Only As Directed / Games Once Played / Green Eggs And Ham / Immaculate Deception / You Can't Have Fun / Government Kids / Legal Murder / Down With The Ship / Thinking Of You / Tylenol / Mengele / Young, White And Well Behaved / Last Train To Clarksville / God Is Everywhere

POWERTRIP, Combat 88561-8246-1 (1988)
Powertrip / Zad / Stuff To Fill Graves / The Tip Of My Mind / Damage Done / T.B.O.S. (Barbiere Di Siviglia) / This Party Sucks / Johnnypump / Yesterday For You / And So It Goes / The Well Dressed Man Disguise / Iwo Jima (That Manly Smell) / One For The Road

MACE (Everett, WA)
Line-Up: Kirk Verhey (vocals), Dave Hillis (guitar), Vern White (bass), Shane White (drums)

Washington Thrash act that debuted as a trio on the 'Metal Massacre V' album. MACE at that juncture, contributing the track 'Marching Saprophytes', comprised lead vocalist and drummer Vence De Rose, guitarist Dave Hillis and bassist Kirk Verhey. Verhey would take over the lead vocal position in time for 1985's debut 'Process Of Elimination'.

Shane White departed before the second album and MACE drafted drummer David Kopler.

Post MACE guitarist Dave Hillis would play an integral role in the rise of Seattle Grunge acting as producer for acts such as ALICE IN CHAINS, BLIND MELON and even PEARL JAM. Hillis would also co-found SNOWBALL with erstwhile FEMME FATALE vocalist Lorraine Lewis.

Albums:

PROCESS OF ELIMINATION, Restless (1985)
S.U.B.C. / Smoking Gun/ The Introduction / Violent World / Drilling Brains / Marine Corpse / Act Of War / Room 101 / M.A.C.E
THE EVIL IN GOOD, Black Dragon BD023 (1987)
Gutripper / Intent To Kill / The Evil In Good / Daddy's Girl / War / Thinning The Herd / Choose Your God / When The Screaming Stops / Poison Gases / Blonde Obsession

MACHINE HEAD

(OAKLAND, CA, USA)
Line-Up: Robb Flynn (vocals / guitar), Logan Mader (guitar), Adam Duce (bass), Chris Kontos (drums)

Oakland's brutal Metal act MACHINE HEAD were founded by ex-VIO-LENCE man Robb Flynn in 1992. Previous to VIO-LENCE Flynn had a lengthy spell with FORBIDDEN, although this was when the band was known pre-debut album as FORBIDDEN EVIL.

Drummer Chris Kontos is ex-of ATTITUDE ADJUSTMENT. However, an early incarnation of the band featured former POSSESSED drummer Walter Ryan. The band debuted live with an American tour opening for NAPALM DEATH and OBITUARY.

Following the release of 'Burn My Eyes' MACHINE HEAD toured America as part of the 'Divine Intervention' roadshow alongside BIOHAZARD and headliners SLAYER. The band continued with SLAYER as guests to

their November 1994 British tour re-releasing 'Burn My Eyes' with a bonus track, a cover of POISON IDEA's 'Alan's On Fire'. The group appeared at the 1995 'Monsters Of Rock' Castle Donington festival.

Chris Kontos joined Danes KONKHRA in 1996 and was replaced by Dave McClain. MACHINE HEAD toured Britain in April 1997 supported by veteran Grindcore merchants NAPALM DEATH and newcomers SKINLAB. Further dates had the band guesting for PANTERA in Europe and MEGADETH in America. Nevertheless, Flynn found time to add guest vocals to New York Straight Edge merchant's EARTH CRISIS 'Breed The Killers' album.

The band's line up troubles were far from over though, as early 1998 witnessed the bitter departure of Mader to SOULFLY (and later PALE DEMONS cum MEDICATION). His replacement was Ahrue Lister, a young veteran of such acts as MAN MADE GOD, HORDE OF TORMENT and PESTILENCE. As the group anticipated the recording of a third album Flynn revealed that a song tentatively pencilled in for inclusion on the new album, 'Devil With The King's Card' was written about "a certain person who recently left the band".

Rumours surfaced in late 2000 that drummer McClain had jumped ship to join SYSTEMATIC.

MACHINE HEAD reared up once more in late summer of 2001 touting a new album 'Supercharger'. The proposed accompanying single 'Crashing Around You' would include live versions of 'Silver' and 'Ten Ton Hammer' recorded in Sweden and produced by CANDLEMASS bassist Leif Edling. However, in the wake of the September 11th terrorist attacks, 'Crashing Around You's release, video and marketing campaign was cancelled for the American market and substituted by 'Deafening Silence'.

MACHINE HEAD put in a 'secret' San Francisco gig billed as TEN TON HAMMER in November. Bizarrely the group dressed up in MÖTLEY CRÜE stagegear and even performed 'Shout At The Devil' and 'Live Wire'!

In early 2002 a Californian court ruled that the band had the full rights to use the title 'MACHINE HEAD'. The group had faced legal action from a US sound design company, Dewey Global Holding, Inc., who claimed rights to the title dating back to 1991.

MACHINE HEAD announced a clutch of headline European festival dates for the summer of 2002 including the Finnish 'Tuska Metal' and 'Ilosaari' events, Germany's 'Full Force' and Belgium's 'Grasspop'. These gigs would be scheduled to promote the band's first live album, recorded at London's Brixton Academy in December of 2001.

Singles/EPs:
Infected / Protoplan, Roadrunner (1994)
Old / A Nation On Fire (Demo) / Real Lies - Fuck It All (Demo) / Old (Demo), Roadrunner (1995) **43 UK**
Old / Davidian (Live) / Hard Times (Live) / Death Church (Demo), Roadrunner (1995)
Old / Death Church (Convent mix) / Old (Eve Of Apocalypse mix) / The Rage To Overcome, Roadrunner (1995)
Death Church / A Nation On Fire (Demo), Roadrunner (1995) (10" single)
Death Church / Real Lies - Fuck It All (Demo) / Old (Demo), Roadrunner (1995) (CD single)
Death Church / Old (Mix) / The Rage To Overcome (Demo), Roadrunner (1995) (CD single)
Take My Scars / Negative Creep / Take My Scars (Live) / Blood For Blood (Live), Roadrunner RR 2257-3 (1997) (CD single) **73 UK**
Take My Scars / Negative Creep / Ten Ton Hammer (Demo) / Struck A Nerve (Demo), Roadrunner RR 2257-5 (1997) (CD single)
From This Day, Roadrunner (1999)

Albums:
BURN MY EYES, Roadrunner RR 90162 (1994) **25 UK**
Davidian / Old / Thousand Eyes / None But My Own / Rage To Overcome / Death Church / I'm Your God Now / Blood For Blood / Nation On Fire / Real Eyes, Realise, Real Lies / Block
THE MORE THINGS CHANGE..., Roadrunner RR8860-2(1997)
17 SWEDEN, 16 UK
Ten Ton Hammer / Take My Scars / Struck A Nerve / Down To None / Thew Frontlines / Spine / Bay Of Pigs / Violate / Blistering / Blood Of The Zodiac
THE BURNING RED, Roadrunner (1999) **17 SWEDEN**
Enter The Phoenix / Desire To Fire / Nothing Left / The Blood, The Sweat, The Tears / Silver / From This Day / Exhale The Vile / Message In A Bottle / Devil With The King's Card / I Defy / Five / The Burning Red
SUPERCHARGER, Roadrunner (2001)
The Declaration / Bulldozer / White Knuckle Blackout / Crashing Around You / Kick You When You're Down / Only The Names / All In Your Head / American High / Brown Acid / Nausea / Blank Generation / Trephination / Deafening Silence / Supercharger

MAD BUTCHER (GERMANY)
Line-Up: Harry Elbrecht (vocals / bass), Sidney Keller (guitar), Rolli Borchert (guitar), Rainer Gullan (drums)

A German Heavy Metal act, MAD BUTCHER released two albums in 1985 and 1990 respectively.

Albums:
METAL LIGHTNING ATTACK, Earthshaker (1985)
Rock Shock / Mad Butcher / Right Or Wrong / Night Of The Wolf / Zero Talk / Bad Chile' Runnin' / Burn It Down / Livin' In Sin / Speed Of Light / Fearless, Heartless
METAL MEAT, Metal Enterprise (1990)
Remember / Drivin' Drivin' / U Can't Stand It / Looser / Flesh In The Night / Freewind / Machine / Hypnotized / Silhouette In Red / Children Of Tomorrow

MADHATTER (MI, USA)
Line-Up: Tommy Mac (vocals), Rockin' Robin Miller (guitar), Brian Smith (guitar)

Albums:
SHUT UP AND SIT DOWN, Hardway HARC 112 (1989)

MAD POLTERGEIST (ITALY)
Line-Up: Max (vocals), Alex (guitar), Franco (guitar), Chico (bass), Mordyllo (drums)

A Genova based Thrash act dating from 1987, MAD POLTERGEIST released 'The Gambler' demo in 1989 before returning with an EP in 1990.

Singles/EPs:
Mad n' Damn, Metal News (1990)

MAD REIGN (CA, USA)
Line-Up: Ice (vocals), Ian Coup (guitar), Brent Turner (guitar), Morgan Siloh (bass), Howard Texman (drums)

Singles/EPs:
American Dream / You Be The Judge / Get Ready / Wham, Wham, Iron Works IW 1010 (1986) ('Salute The New Flag' EP)

MAD SLAUGHTER (GERMANY)
Line-Up: Axel Becker (vocals / guitar), Jens-Uwe Schnorr (guitar), Kai Saß (bass), Olli Gerds (drums)

Thrashers MAD SLAUGHTER released two demos, 'Crush It' in 1992 and 'What We Know' the following year. In 1994 they were finally in a position to issue debut product.

Albums:
M.I.X., LC 5459 (1994)
Friends / How To Go All Starry-Eyed / No Jukebox / Irritation / So What - It's Life / The Pack / Birth Defect / Mom Is Dead / Personal Winter

MAFIA (RUSSIA)

Russian Thrash Metal band MAFIA emerged with a 1989 demo entitled 'Racket'. The 1991 demo session 'Beregis Svoih Detei' ('Beware Your Children') followed. MAFIA's 1993 tape 'Ukol V Mozg' ('Brain Injection') led to the debut album.

Albums:
MAGICHESKIY ZOV, Moroz (1994)

MAGNUM CARNAGE
(Kaneohe, HI, USA)

Hawaiian Black, riff fuelled Thrash Metal led by vocalist / guitarist Kai Laigo. MAGNUM CARNAGE added guitar player Angelo Barquez in 2002.

Albums:
NIGHTMARE FACTORY, (2000)
Stay Insane / I Watched Them Die / Demons / Possessed / Psalm Of Transformation / Dragons Lair / Midnight / Deathscythe

MAKINA (MEXICO)
Line-Up: Javier Herrera (vocals / guitar), Janel De Polanco (guitar), Carlos De La Pena (bass), Victor 'Gismo' Reza (drums)

Mexico City Thrashers that express their politically charged objectives in English rather than the more familiar Spanish. The group was convened in 1990, originally billed as MAKINA NEGRA. Under this guise the band released a four track 7" single 'Al Borde De La Destruccion', the whole affair being recorded in a mere three hours. Bass player 'Nefasto' Quiroga would break ranks shortly after, relocating to Chile, and was replaced by Carlos De La Pena - a veteran of both CHRIST and GEISHA. At this juncture, with a line-up of vocalist / guitarist Paul Rivers, guitarist Hans Mues, De La Pena on bass and drummer Victor 'Gizmo' Reza the act truncated the band title to simply MAKINA.
Following the 1991 debut album 'Dilemma', issued by the independent Lejos De Paraiso label, MAKINA put in support gigs to the likes of visiting international artists NAPALM DEATH, SODOM and D.R.I.
However, MAKINA then underwent a series of line-up ructions. Firstly Rivers would depart

and then Mues. MAKINA filled the vocal position with erstwhile CRIPTA man Carlos Alejandro but he too swiftly decamped. Finally the roster was settled with the addition of ex-ACROSTIC personnel vocalist / guitarist Javier Herrera and guitar player Janel De Polanco. This version of the band scored a deal with Sony Music subsidiary Discos Rockotitlan for 1994's 'Anabiosis' opus scoring valuable MTV exposure to boot.
MAKINA's third effort 'Red', arrived in 1996. It would be co-produced by the band together with Matt Green and FAITH NO MORE's Billy Gould.
De Polanco left the ranks in 1997. He would later turn up as part of the PRAYING MANTIS PROJECT.

Singles/EPs:
Al Borde De La Destruccion, (1986)
Interview / K.F.S / Terror / Chorizo / Red / Tons Of Shit, Discos Manicomio (1996) ('Chorizo' promotion release)

Albums:
DILEMMA, Lejos De Paraiso (1991)
Citizen's Hate / Dreamtrapped / Criminal Confession / Official Misconduct / The Clown Of This Town / Ciudad De Cagadas / The Window / Antiwar / Profound Conviction / S.CH.C.M.E.U.P. / Edge Of Confusion
ANABIOSIS, Discos Rockotitlan (1994)
Suddenly Dawned (Negative) / Insomnia / Human Wasted / Silent Disease / Nosotoxicotosis / Perro / Pinches Cerdos / Mind Changes (Vegetal) / Lies / Ripe / Anabiosis / Nymphomanic
RED, Discos Manicomio (1996)
I Am / 2 Much 2 Much / U / K.F.S. / Terror / Chorizo / Red / The Left / La Fuerza De La Tierra / Tons Of Shit / Millennium / Faithless

MALACHAI (GERMANY)
Line-Up: Steve (vocals), Marco (guitar), Andreas (bass), Attila (drums)

A Thrash outfit from Braunschweig.

Albums:
COULD YOU STAND THE PAIN?, Malachai (1995)
Under The Gun / I Them All / Sick & Depraved / Falling Down / Bottom Of The Jug / Six Days In The Hole / N.P.S. / Redemption In Agony

MALACHIA (Los Angeles, CA, USA)
Line-Up: Ken Pike (vocals / guitar), Jeffrey James (guitar), Wade A. Little (bass), Steve 'Chima' Ayola (keyboards), Dave Devaughn (drums)

Albums:
RED SUN RISE,
Victoria Ltd. VLP-002 (1987)
In Christ We Rock / Red Sunrise / Lonely Is
The Night / Let It Go / Sightless Eyes /
Heaven Or Hell / Mark Of The Beast /
Master's Call

MALEDICTION (UK)
Line-Up: Shaun Stephenson (guitars), Rich
Mumford (guitars), Darren O'Hara (guitars),
Mark Fox (bass), Alisdair Dunn (drums)

Middlesborough Progressive Thrash-Death
Metal act that excited considerable
underground interest with their single
released on the French Thrash label.
MALEDICTION's early line up consisted of
vocalist Shaun Stephenson, guitarists Rich
Mumford and Darren O'Hara, bass player
Mark Fox and drummer Alistair Dunn. The
band debuted with a 1990 Grindcore demo
'Infestation' before the 'System Fear' 7"
release on the Thrash label the following year.
MALEDICTION released a demo 'Framework
Of Condition' in 1992, which besides new
studio tracks featured a live recording of a gig
supporting BOLT-THROWER. These sessions
were due to include keyboard contributions
from SIGH's Mira Kawashima but apparently
the band opted to take their Japanese guest
to the pub instead! O'Hara would decamp to
found Folk / Death Metal act CERECLOTH
and was replaced by Mark McGowan.
A makeshift live album 'Chronicles Of
Dissension' arrived in 1993 on the Gargle
With Blood label. Also emerging the same
year was the yellow vinyl 'Dark Effluvium' EP
on the American Psychoslaughter label,
although apparently released without the
band's knowledge. Phil Slack would take over
the drumstool but would soon relinquish his
position to a returning Dunn. During 1994 a
proposed split EP with American act
INCARNIS was recorded but never released.
MALEDICTION signed to the Arctic
Serenades label recording their projected
debut album 'The Millennium Cotillion'.
However, with the label's demise the album
was shelved. MALEDICTION duly folded.
The band was resurrected during 2000 by
Mumford, McGowan and Fox announcing
their return with the demo session 'Shades Of
Inequity'. The group plotted a new album, 'The
Return Of The Prodigal', for 2002.

Singles/EPs:
System Fear / Insect In The Infrastructure,
Mangled Beyond Recognition (1991) ('Mould
Of An Industrial Horizon' EP)
Infestation / Outro / Moulded From Within /

Waste, Thrash (1991) ('System Fear' EP)
Dark Effluvium / Weeping Tears Of
Covetousness / Framework Of Contortion,
Psychoslaughter (1993)

Albums:
THE TEARS THAT PRECEDE BIRTH,
(1993)
CHRONICLES OF DISSENSCION, Gargle
With Blood GWBCD 001 (1993)
Mould Of An Industrial Horizon / Weeping
Tears Of Covetousness / Infestation /
Framework Of Contortion / Long-term Result
/ System Fear / Doctrines Eternal Circles

MALISHA (Hawaii, USA)
Line-Up: Kim La Chance (vocals) Randy
Hano (guitar), Darry Shishado (bass), Joe
Silva (drums)

Formed by ex-VIXEN / HAWAII frontwoman
Kim La Chance in November of 1982.
MALISHA served up straightforward no frills
aggressive Metal on their debut 1983 demo.
MALISHA formed with a line-up of La
Chance, guitarist Randy Hano, bass player
Darry Shihado and drummer Ivar. The latter
would be superseded first by Craig Brooks
then Rick Dingman.
The track 'Valkyrie' on the 'Serve Your Savage
Beast' album would be dedicated to Janne
Stark, guitarist with Swedish outfit
OVERDRIVE.
Post MALISHA La Chance created the 1992
act DRIVEN STEEL comprising guitarist Julia
Roberts (presumably not the actress!),
bassist Kelly Heckart and drummer Franco
Geneta.

Singles/EPs:
Give It All You Got, Malisha (1983)

Albums:
SERVE YOUR SAVAGE BEAST, Shardan
Kane (1986)
Valkyrie / Love For The Day / Step Through
Eternity / Serve Your Savage Beast / What I
Believe / Power Flight / Metal Wars / Burning
Rage / Hands Of The Ripper

MALTESE FALCON (DENMARK)
Line-Up: Charlie (vocals), Martin Peterson
(guitar), Carsten Schmidt (guitar), Hasse
'Hal' Patino (bass), Stig Neilson (drums)

Vocalist Charlie and guitarist Martin Peterson
had previously both featured in the Danish
outfit DEADLINE, but formed MALTESE
FALCON in 1983, with the group originally
conceived as a Black Metal band. In fact the
group's first five track demo merited

comparisons to VENOM and MERCYFUL FATE by magazines at the time!

However, MALTESE FALCON (formed with guitarist Carsten Smith, bassist Hasse Patino and drummer Stig Nielsen) soon changed direction to a more straightforward Metal approach with a second demo featuring 'Headbanger', 'The Rebellion', 'Back With The Rock', 'Back In The Circle' and 'Stonehenge'. The band promptly signed to Roadrunner who released the debut 'Metal Rush' album in 1984.

The same year the band gained valuable supports to GARY MOORE and MANOWAR. Ex-DARK MISSION drummer Flemming Kenneth replaced Nielson in 1985. Hasse 'Hal' Patino later joined the ranks of KING DIAMOND.

Albums:
METAL RUSH, Roadrunner RR 9824 (1984)
Alive / Rats / Mamma's In Town / Heavy n' Loud / Rebellion / Headbanger / On Fire / Metal Rush

MANDATOR (HOLLAND)
Line-Up: Marcel Verdumen (vocals), Luit De Jong (guitar), Hette Bonnema (bass), Claus (drums)

MANDATOR were previously known as MYSTO DYSTO, releasing the 1986 album 'The Rules Have Been Disturbed'. Changing titles to MANDATOR in 1987, the band released the 'No A.I.D.S. in Hell' demo, which secured a deal with Disaster Records.

For the follow up album 'Perfect Progeny' drummer Claus left to have his position filled by Walter Tjwa.

Albums:
INITIAL VELOCITY, Disaster 10009 (1988)
Attilla / Black Rose / Faces Of Death / Jack Boots And Leather Caps / Power Of The Law / Evil Dead / Posers / I Will Be Your Last
PERFECT PROGENY, Disaster (1990)
Stick Your Knife / Coition Interuptus / Surrealistic Manoeuvres / An Invisible Disease Strikes / Brain Disease / Perfect Progeny / Automatic Artillery / Life Is Calling

MANIA (GERMANY)
Line-Up: Chris Klauke (vocals), Frank Nottelmann (guitar), Thies Bendixen (guitar), Didy Mackel (bass), Rainer Heubel (drums)

Featuring ex-PROPHECY vocalist Chris Klauke, for a short period of time guitarist Holger Wendt was a member of MANIA. Wendt wound up nine years later playing in R.A.W. with GLENMORE vocalist Jürgen Volk

and the former JEALOUS HEART rhythm section of bassist Werner Hauser and drummer Chris Grenzer.

MANIA's Chris Klauke later formed ABRAXAS.

Singles/EPs:
Message / Deliverance, Mania (1988)

Albums:
WIZARD OF THE LOST KINGDOM, Noise NUK 127 (1988)
Mufty's Arrival / Wizard Of The Lost Kingdom / Night Of The Blade / Gods Of Fire / Under The Sign Of The Cross / Break Out / Mufty's Departure
CHANGING TIMES, Noise NUK 139 (1989)
Prelude / The Expulsion / Turn Towards The Light / No Way Back / Be Strong / To The End Of The World / The Vision / Gambler / We Don't Need War / Violent Time

MANIA (Houston, TX, USA)
Line-Up: Stacey Richards (vocals), Steve Wilbanks (guitar), Joe Reyes (guitar), John Smith (bass), Jesse York (drums)

Texan Metal band MANIA are better remembered for their album cover depicting scantily clad model Kim Weaver cooing over a Flying V guitar in a child's cot!

Albums:
NO LULLABIES!!, Strategem SR SW 001 (1986)
Rock Hard / Treat Me This Way / Nightstalkers / Cut Ya Down To Size / Licensed To Kill / Promises / Go For Broke

MANIAC (GERMANY / AUSTRIA)
Line-Up: Mark Wederall (vocals), Christoph Justin (guitar), Markus Uberbacher (guitar), Werner Ranftl (bass), Peter Garattoni (drums)

The German and Austrian alliance that was MANIAC underwent a line-up shuffle for the 'Look Out' album, which emerged four years after the debut. The band had now been complemented with new members bassist Andy Marberger and ex AXEWORK and GURGELHAS CLAN man Tom Peroutka on drums.

Albums:
MANIAC, Hot Blood (1985)
You Don't Know It / Get Ready / Dressed To Kill / God Of Thunder / Ride On / Shout It Loud / Stage Free / We Swear At You

LOOK OUT, Koch (1989)
Evil / Cities Burn / Bell Of Doom / Hot Shots / Confused Hearts / Fighting The Ryche Of Mordor / Power Metal Addicts / Armageddon's Day / Lambs To The Slaughter

MANIAC WITHIN (AUSTRIA)
Line-Up: Grey (vocals / guitar), Dragon (bass), Pete (drums)

An Austrian Thrash Metal act.

Singles/EPs:
The Maniac Within / A Day / The Voice, CCP 100117-2 (1994)

MANIKIN LAFF (USA)
Line-Up: Kevin Michael Tobin (vocals), Dennis Fecko (guitar), Martin Feldman (bass), Drew Allen (drums)

Although credited on the sleeve guitarist Dennis Fecko and drummer Drew Allen joined the band after recording in place of ousted members Tim Ranow and Bill Olmsted on guitar and drums respectively.

Albums:
MANIKAN LAFF, Red Light (1990)
Blinded / Fear No Evil / Return To Me / Hungry Hearts / Rubber Room / Electric Street / Looking At You

MANIPULATED SLAVES (JAPAN)
Line-Up: Hisayoshi (vocals), Yutaka Kageyama (guitar), Kazushi Nomora (guitar), Takayoshi Saita (drums)

Osaka renaissance Thrashers MANIPULATED SLAVES was founded In April of 1994 by the now only surviving original member guitarist Yutaka Kageyama. Two demo tapes arrived the following year and the group debuted live in August at the 'Rocket' club in their home city.
MANIPULATED SLAVES underwent numerous line-up changes but still managed to issue further demo sessions in the 1997 set 'Burst Into Blue Flame' and, adding ex-SLEAZY WIZARD guitarist Kazushi Nomura, 1999's 'Seventh Island'.
MANIPULATED SLAVES signed to the Worldchaos Productions label to release the first album 'Burst Into Blue Flame' during March of 2000. The line-up at this juncture stood at Kageyama on vocals and guitar, Nomura on second guitar, bass player Shlro Matsuno and drummer Mitshuhiro Enomoto. New frontman Hisayoshi would take the lead vocal mantle for the August 2001 set 'The Legendary Black Jade'.
Drummer Takayoshi Saita is an erstwhile member of DAZZLE.

Albums:
BURST INTO BLUE FLAME, Worldchaos Productions KDM002 (2000)
Masters Of Illusion / Obey The Moon / Halfway To Heaven / Come Down From The Skies / Damnation's Edge / Greed / Burst Into Blue Flame / Silently Falling Asleep / The Lunatic Moon On the Dark Sea
THE LEGENDARY BLACK JADE, Worldchaos Productions KDM006 (2001)
Thrust Sword Into The Earth / The Way Of The Emperor / Woman In The Ironmask / The Broken Chain / Eyes Filled With Tears / Man From The Horizon / Capitol Punishment / Assault On The Enemy / Bearing The Final Pain

MANTAS (UK)
Line-Up: Pete Harrison (vocals), Mantas (guitar), Alistair Barnes (guitar), Mark Savage (drums)

VENOM guitarist Mantas' more melodic leanings are evident on this solo effort, released in the period prior to his re-involvement with the band. Mantas (real name Jeff Dunn) recruited guitarist Alistair Braacken for the project, with drums supplied by Mark Savage (ex-WAR MACHINE).
Mantas rejoined VENOM, requisitioning Barnes for the new line-up. Savage became lead vocalist for XLR8R.

Singles/EPs:
Deceiver / I'm On Fire / The Green Manalishi, Neat NEAT 60-12 (1989)

Albums:
WINDS OF CHANGE, Neat NEAT 1042 (1988)
Let It Rock / Deceiver / Hurricane / King Of The Ring / Western Days / Winds Of Change / Desperado / Nowhere To Run / Sayonara

MARAUDER (GERMANY)
Line-Up: Peter Siewert (vocals), Robert Nowak (guitar), Gregor Vogt (guitar), Patrick Semper (bass), Dirk Lewandowsky (drums)

Essen new breed of Thrash Metal. MARAUDER was founded in 1992 and paid their dues with support gigs to TANKARD, OVERKILL and THE GATHERING. The debut 'Eternal Exlstence' album was laid down in May of 1997.

Albums:
ETERNAL EXISTENCE, Marauder (1997)
Vision Of Truth / Distrust / Five To Twelve / Illusions / Common Grave / Divination / Eternal Existence / Marauder / Minds / Joy Of Anticipation / Screams Of Anguish / Dark Moon Rising / Misleaded / Regret

MASS (Boston, MA, USA)
Line-Up: Louis St. August (vocals), Gene D'Itria (guitar), Kevin Varrio (bass) Joey 'Vee' Vadala (drums)

Formed in 1981 and taking their name from their home state of Massachusetts. MASS inked a deal with A&M Records and recorded an album, produced by Tom Allom in Miami, Florida. The band then found themselves involved in an almighty battle with their management at the time resulting in the four-piece being dropped by the label and, consequently, the record never seeing the light of day.
Effectively bankrupt, it wasn't until 1985, free of any managerial contracts and disputes, that MASS re-emerged with the release of a self-financed, four track EP, quickly followed by an album, 'New Birth', on RCA, produced by Tony Platt and partly recorded in England. Following the release of the album RCA underwent a huge internal restructure with the results that MASS were effectively out in the cold once more. Although MASS had a two album deal they decided to look elsewhere
Upon the recommendation of STRYPER's Michael Sweet (MASS had opened for STRYPER on the East Coast and the two had become good friends) Enigma Records sought out the Boston based group and liked what they heard. MASS thus signed to the Californian label and the first fruits of this new liaison arrived in the form of a six track mini-album in 1988, a collection of demo tracks cut after 'New Birth' plus two songs from the four track EP totally reworked.
This was the 'Voices In The Night' album, produced by MICHAEL SWEET. The affiliation with Sweet and several religious connotations found in songs and cover artwork, even dating back to 'New Birth', gave rise to accusations that MASS were, effectively, a Christian Rock band. A charge denied by the band who, it was claimed, were Catholics with strong beliefs about God, but that they tended to write about strong, positive things rather than their personal beliefs.

Singles/EPs:
Looking Good / Pedal To The Metal / Holy

One / Still Of The Night, Mass Music CW1023 (1985) ('MASS' EP)

Albums:
NEW BIRTH, RCA NFL1-8055 (1985)
Too Far Gone / Crying Alone / Time / Back To Me / Do You Love Me / New Birth / Left Behind / Voyager (Look For The Edge) / Day Without You / Watch Her Walk
TAKE YOU HOME, Medusa 72270-1 (1988)
Can't Get Enough / Want It Back / Over You / Take You Home / Pedal To The Metal / Holy One
VOICES IN THE NIGHT, Enigma 773345-1 (1989)
Voices In The Night / Nine Tonight / Reach For The Sky / Chance To Love / Turn It All Around / Carry Your Heart / Miles Away / Follow Me / Call Out Your Name / Staying Alive

MASTER (RUSSIA)
Line-Up: Mikhail Seryshev (vocals), Andrei Boshakov (guitar), Sergei Popov (guitar), Alexander Granovsky (bass), Kirill Pokrovosky (keyboards), Igor Molchanov (drums)

MASTER were originally a straightforward Metal act, but by the time the Russian's issued their second album in 1990 they had transformed themselves into a Thrash outfit.
MASTER include former members of the hugely successful band ARIA in guitarist Andrei Boshakov, bass player Alexander Granovsky and drummer Igor Molchanov.
Boshakov would leave the band and MASTER adopted a much tougher Thrash style.

Albums:
MASTER, Melodia (1988)
Watch Out / Hands Off / Shield And Sword / It's Night Once Again / Will And Reason / Stand Up, Get Over Fear / Save Me / Who Will Win? / Master
WITH THE LEE ON A NECK, Melodia (1990)
We Don't Want / Executioners / Are We Not Slaves? / When I Die... / God Save Our Fury / Don't Care A Fig! / Amsterdam / Judas / War / Seven Circles Of Hell
TALK OF THE DEVIL, Moroz (1991)
Intro Golgotha / Talk Of The Devil / Danger / Fallen Angel / Live To Die / Tsar / Heroes / Romance (Bass Solo) / I Hate Your Sex / Paranoid
MANIAC PARTY, Death City (1994)
Beastie Generation / Maniac Party / Lock Them In Graves / Burning In Hell (Civil War Disaster) / Screams Of Pain / Time X (Bass Solo) / They Are Just Like Us / Punk Guys / Go

MASTER - LIVE, Moroz (1995)
Intro / Beastie Generation / Tsar / Danger /
Live To Die / Lock Them In Graves /
Screams Of Pain / Punk Guys / Executioners
/ Master / Will And Reason / Smoke On The
Water / Here The Metal Is Being Born
PESNI MYORTVYH, Flam (1996)
Songs Of The Dead / Wild Goose / Lights On!
/ Ashes In The Wind / Got Bored / Only You By
Yourself / I Don't Need The War / Tattoo /
Night / Ship Of The Fools
THE BEST - LIVE IN MOSCOW, (1997)
Songs Of The Dead / Ship Of The Fools / Got
Bored / I Don't Need The War / Dust In The
Wind / Tattoo / Danger / Lock Them In Graves
/ We Don't Want / The Nigh Once Again /
Master / Here The Metal Is Being Born / Will
And Reason / Bass Solo

MASTIFAL (ARGENTINA)
Line-Up: Miguel A. Maciel (vocals), Diego
Conte (guitar), Matias Munighini (guitar),
Guillermo Ricci (bass), Luis Sanchez (drums)

Thrash outfit dating back to 1995.
MASTIFAL's original line-up was as a quartet
of vocalist / guitarist Marcelo H. Barreto,
guitarist Diego Conte, bass player Andres
Barreto and drummer Ruben Barreto.
The 1998 debut 'Ebola' was followed by the
live 'En Vivo'. After a second studio outing,
2000's 'Holocausto Mental', MASTIFAL
suffered a series of line-up fluxes. MASTIFAL
would lose their frontman Miguel Maciel
during November of 2000 and duly drafted in
guitarist Matias Munighini and singer Miguel
Maciel to stem the gap.
In late 2001 both Barreto brothers would
decamp. Their replacements would be
erstwhile LETHAL man Luis Sanchez on
drums and former EREBUS bassist Guillermo
Ricci. MASTIFAL would enroll another new
drummer in April of 2002, ex-HEFESTOS
man Leonardo Fernandez.

Albums:
EBOLA, (1998)
Fabrica De Monos / Ebola / Devastación /
Apodado Hijo Del Diablo / Lenta Muerte /
Tierratas / Escupiendo Rabia
EN VIVO, (1999)
Indiferencia / Escupiendo Rabia / Lenta
Muerte / Holocausto Mental / Espectaculo
Macabro / Ebola / Fabrica De Monos /
Apodado Hijo Del Diablo / Desperate Cry
HOLOCAUSTO MENTAL, (2000)
Holocausto Mental / Devastacion /
Espectaculo Macabro / Apodado Hijo Del
Diablo / Privado De Libertad / Ebola /
Indiferencia / Lenta Muerte / Cuando El Sol
Crucifique Mi Nombre / Fabricia De Monos /

La Plegaria Del Obero

MAXX WARRIOR
(Charlotte, NC, USA)
Line-Up: Carl Snare (vocals), Scott Atkins
(guitar), Alton Edkins (guitar), Perry
Richardson (bass), Billy Dorey (drums)

Excellent Precision Metal band hailing from
North Carolina, managed by NANTUCKET
man Mike Uzzell. The quartet's four track EP
was subsequently picked up by the German
label U.S. Metal for release in Europe.
Following the break up of the band Snare and
Richardson would later join forces again in
the successful Melodic Rock group
FIREHOUSE.

Singles/EPs:
High On Metal / It's Alright / Taken By Forces
/ Burning Down The Gates Of Hell, Executive
MX4000 (1985)

MAYHEM (Portland, OR, USA)
Line-Up: Matt McCourt (vocals), Eric Olsen
(guitar), Craig Lower (bass)

MAYHEM featured the former WILD DOGS
and EVIL GENIUS vocalist Matt McCourt,
replacing original singer Nick Damis. The
group would record the 'Buried Alive' album
for French label Black Dragon and put in a
series of high profile supports to KING
DIAMOND and MEGADETH.
Post MAYHEM McCourt founded DR.
MASTERMIND for a series of albums before
resurrecting WILD DOGS. Later acts included
EASTSIDE STRANGLER, MEATHOOK and
THE VULTURES.
McCourt would unsuccessfully audition for
JUDAS PRIEST in 1993. Undeterred he then
forged a JUDAS PRIEST tribute band
BRITISH STEEL before pulling WILD DOGS
back out of the history books once more.

Singles/EPs:
Blood Rush, Vigilante (1985)

Albums:
BURIED ALIVE, Black Dragon BD027
(1988)

MAZE OF TORMENT (SWEDEN)
Line-Up: Erik Sahlstrom (vocals), Peter
Karlsson (guitar), Kalle Sjodin (bass), Kjell
Enblom (drums)

A Death Metal act named after a MORBID
ANGEL song and showing plenty of
renaissance Thrash influences. Originally
titled TORMENT upon the band's formation in

1994 by former HARMONY members drummer Kjell Enblom and guitarist Peter Karlsson. The duo was soon joined by VINTERLAND guitarist Pehr Larsson.

The trio, still operating under the name HARMONY, recorded a demo which came to the attention of Deviation Records based in Scotland. The band then switched titles to TORMENT for a three track demo. Upon signing to Corrosion Records the band title became MAZE OF TORMENT for the 1996 album 'The Force' produced by EDGE OF SANITY's Dan Swäno. The band line-up at this juncture comprised vocalist / bassist Pehr Larsson, guitarist Peter Karlsson and drummer Kjell Enblom.

Shortly after the release of 'The Force' a deal was struck with Thomas Nyqvist's Iron Fist Productions for the sophomore outing 'Faster Disaster'. Peter Janssen took over bass duties as Larsson concentrated on his lead vocal role.

Larsson was replaced by Erik Sahlstrom of SERPENT OBSCENE and THE MARBLE ICON. Jansson also lost his place to Kalle Sjodin. MAZE OF TORMENT's 2000 album 'Death Strikes', released by the American Necropolis label, was produced by Tomas Skogsberg.

MAZE OF TORMENT would be back for another round in March of 2002 with the Necropolis released 'The Unmarked Graves'. Included would be a cover version of THE MISFITS 'All Hell Breaks Loose'.

Albums:
THE FORCE, Corrosion CR 6-503-2 (1996)
Shapeless In The Dark / Dream Of Blood / Souls Been Left To Die / The Force / Brave The Blizzard / Battle Of The Dead / The Last Candle / Land Unknown
FASTER DISASTER, Iron Fist Productions (1999)
The Reality / Five Inch / Dead Soul / Horror Visions / Ancient Treasure / Faster Disaster / The Devil's Kill / Hide The Light / Bite The Dust
DEATH STRIKES, Necropolis NR056CD (2000)
Death Strikes / Sodomizing Death Spell / Intense Slaughter / This Is Death / Aggressive Bloodhunt / The Infernal Force / The Sadist / Angels From Hell / The Evil Beneath The Flames

MD 45 (USA)
Line-Up: Lee Ving (vocals), Dave Mustaine (guitar), Kelly Lemieux (bass), Jimmy DeGrasso (drums)

Project band assembled by MEGADETH main man Dave Mustaine and Lee Ving of FEAR. Drummer Jimmy DeGrasso's pedigree includes stints with Y&T, FIONA, ALICE COOPER and of course MEGADETH.

Albums:
THE CRAVING, Capitol 7243 8 36616 2 6 (1996)
Hell's Motel / Day The Music Died / Fight Hate / Designer Behaviour / The Creed / My Town / Voices / Nothing Is Something / Hearts Will Bleed / No Pain / Roadman

MEANSTREAK (New York, NY, USA)
Line-Up: Bettina France (vocals), Rana Sands (guitar), Marlene Apuzzo (guitar), Lisa Pace (bass), Diane Lee Keyser (drums)

An All female Thrash Metal band, MEANSTREAK were originally managed by the Loud And Proud organisation, who also managed WHITE LION, OVERKILL and TYKETTO.

The band made their recording debut, with the track 'Lost Stranger', on the 'L'Amour Rocks' compilation issued by Mercenary Records in 1987.

Formed in 1985 by guitarists Rana Sands (the girlfriend of ANTHRAX vocalist Joey Belladonna at the time) and Marlene Apuzzo. The girls avoided being stereotyped by the media by deliberately shying away from the kind of lyrical content all girl bands are 'supposed' to write

Playing shows in the Tri-State area with the likes of BATTLEZONE, ZEBRA, PROPHET and REMINGTON, the band recorded their 'Roadkill' debut with noted New York Metal producer Alex Perialas at the helm.

The album was released by Mercenary Records in America and picked up for a European release by Music For Nations. Shortly after the record was completed drummer Diane Keyser quit, due to time honoured musical differences, and was replaced by Yael Devan

Marlene has since married DREAM THEATER drummer Mike Portnoy, whilst Rana wed his bass playing bandmate John Myung. The couples met when the two bands attended the Concrete Foundations Forum during September 1989.

Albums:
ROADKILL, Music For Nations MFN 89 (1988)
Roadkill / Nostradamus / Lost Stranger / Congregation / Searching Forever / It Seems To Me / Warning

MEDIEVAL (Kalamazoo, MI, USA)

Line-Up: Timmy Ambuist (vocals / guitar), Elwood Chew (bass), Willjious Ambuist (drums)

Founded in 1981 MEDIEVAL released their debut twelve track cassette album in 1983. The band was rated highly for their almost pre-Grunge Thrash sound but ultimately became yet another New Renaissance Records casualty.

Albums:
MEDIEVAL, New Renaissance NRR20 (1986)
Death Is Beauty / Lords Of Darkness / Face Of Death / Hell Is Full (Cruncher) / Reign Of Terror
MEDIEVAL KILLS, New Renaissance NRR34 (1987)
Somnambulism / Rules Of Fools / All Knobs To The Right / Life After Death / The Seventh SeaLl / B.F.H. / Reign Of Terror / Peter Gunn Theme / Hell Is Full (Thrasher) / Blood And Anger / World War IV / Black Assassin / Death Is Beauty / Epitaph

MEDIEVAL STEEL (Tennessee, USA)

Line-Up: Bobby Franklin (vocals), John Roth (guitar), Chuck Jones (guitar), Jeff Boydstun (bass), Bill Jones (drums)

Almost ten years on from the 'Medieval Steel' album guitarist John Roth would be hired to replace Paul Taylor in melodic Rockers WINGER for their 'Pull' tour

Albums:
MEDIEVAL STEEL, Sur (1984)
Medieval Steel / Warlords / Battle Beyond The Stars / Echoes

MEGACE (GERMANY)

Line-Up: Melanie Bock (vocals), Jörg Schror (guitar), Klaus Florian 'Dirty' Möller (guitar), Christian Wulff (bass), Andreas Düwel (drums)

A progressively inclined Thrash act founded back in February of 1988 by the trio of vocalist Melanie Bock, guitarist Jörg Schror and bassist Michael Muller. A month later MEGACE was completed by the enrollment of guitarist Robin Kortt and drummer Thorsten Jungermann. The latter's tenure would be brief though and soon Kai Alex Spiekermann was manning the drum kit. Further changes in personnel occurred when ex-ANESTHESIA man Klaus Florian 'Dirty' Möller supplanted Kortt in September. With this line-up MEGACE cut their opening demo session

'The Sign Of The Ape'.

Spiekermann left in the summer of 1989 to hook up with fellow Thrash act DESERT STORM, his place duly being taken by KILGORE's Rainer Behn as MEGACE demoed tracks for Aarrrggg Records dubbed the 'Human Errors' sessions.

In December of the same year Muller made his exit, eventually being substituted by DROWNING IN REAL's Christian Wulff in February of 1990. Further ructions that same year found Behn out of the picture, although he did hang around to complete the 'This Is The News' demo. Engineered by GAMMA RAY's Kai Hansen 'This Is The News' garnered valuable press and saw track inclusions on the 'Brown Bottles Go Ape' compilation album. Following recording Carsten Schubert took over the drummer's role.

MEGACE's debut album 'Human Errors' emerged in July of 1991. The band hit yet more line-up problems in August of 1992 when both Schubert and Möller exited. Stefan Spiedel, another DROWNING IN REAL member, took over guitar whilst the group had to wait until April of 1993 before the drummer's vacancy was filled by ex-NURNBERGER PROZESS man Stephan Gora.

MEGACE then completed the 'Pseudo Identity' promotional tape, strengthening the GAMMA RAY connection with Dirk Schlachter acting as engineer. In May of 1994 Gora bade farewell and Andreas Düwel took up residency behind the kit.

The band's second album, 'Inner War', hit the stores during May of 1999. Ambitiously it included a cover version of 'Synchronicity' by THE POLICE.

In 2000 the band donated their take on 'The Dogs Of War' to a PINK FLOYD compilation 'Signs Of Life'. MEGACE would also feature on the 'Unbroken Metal' magazine split 7" EP with another cover, this time MOTORHEAD's 'Iron Fist' with lead vocals from Schror. Another MOTORHEAD cover 'Sacrifice', once more with Schror handling vocals, appeared on the 'Motormorphosis' tribute album.

In 2001 Schror took time out to aid GAMMA RAY on their Mexican dates substituting on bass for an injured Dirk Schlachter.

Albums:
HUMAN ERRORS, Magic 3770022 (1991)
Something Incomprehensible / Law Enforcement Agency / Repetitions Of Human Errors / Let Me Explain / Save Your Dignity / No Brain / No Pain / Discord / Monofaces / Better To Forget
INNER WAR, Angular SKAN 8217.AR (1999)

Cry / Schweissnaht / Two / Inner War / Ciphers / Synchronicity / Conclusion (Reprise) / Industrial Dictatorship / Guilty / First-Take- Ponka-Song / Instinct, Science, Faith / Affengesicht / ...Which Have Been Predicted / Rain

MEGADETH
(San Francisco, CA, USA)
Line-Up: Dave Mustaine (vocals / guitar), Al Pitrelli (guitar), Dave Ellefson (bass), Jimmy DeGrasso (drums)

MEGADETH is the vehicle for which METALLICA refugee Dave Mustaine, a guitarist and composer of unquestionable, if erratic, genius, has made his mark upon the world. The band went through many incarnations, although bassist Dave Ellefson has remained a central lynchpin, until settling on their most stable and commercially successful guise of Mustaine, Ellefson, guitarist MARTY FRIEDMAN and drummer Nick Menza.
Initially fuelled by anger, resentment and an out of control lifestyle driven by drugs and alcohol excess, Mustaine has cleansed himself in full public view, taking MEGADETH to the top echelons in the annals of metal history. By the late eighties the band could justifiably lay claim to their tag 'State of the art speed metal band'.
Mustaine's first act was titled PANIC, the band coming to a tragic end when a car crash, in which Mustaine was involved, killed the driver and band's drummer.
MEGADETH came together almost immediately after Mustaine's dismissal from METALLICA in April 1983, just four months before METALLICA were to record 'Kill 'Em All' (by his own admission for drunkenness) and the guitarist was quick to assemble another unit.
Local fanzines presumed the band to be titled FALLEN ANGEL, although in reality no hard and fast monickers were chosen. The FALLEN ANGEL concept fell by the wayside pretty swiftly and MEGADETH came into being with Mustaine, bassist Matt Kisselstein and drummer Lee Rausch.
This unit broke up after rehearsals and a fresh combo, including bassist Dave Ellefson, his room mate - Minnesota native Greg Handevidt - and Rausch was assembled. MEGADETH's debut live performance came with a show at San Francisco's Ruthie's club. Before long though Handevidt was out, with Mustaine citing the main reason for his dismissal being a lack of hair!
Handevidt, after a spell in a job washing turkeys, resurfaced in 1987 with the band KUBLAI KAHN, releasing a solitary album

'Annihilation'. He then opted out of the music business to become a military mortician.
With Rausch leaving for a brief tenure with DARK ANGEL the band then drafted in another drummer, Dijon Carruthers, but he too was to depart. Carruthers had persuaded the band, possibly motivated by fear of any racial prejudice, that his dusky complexion was a result of a Hispanic birth. The band discovered he was in fact black when his much darker brother, Kane Carruthers of the band THE UNTOUCHABLES was introduced to them at a party. The band duly fired Dijon, according to Mustaine: "Not because he was black, which didn't matter, but because he had lied to us".
The first recordings came in the form of a three track demo that included 'Love You To Death', 'Skull Beneath The Skin' and 'Mechanix'.
The band's first gigs on the club circuit, now including former jazz drummer Gar Samuelson, utilized SLAYER's Kerry King as stand in second guitarist before Chris Poland was enrolled.
Poland was previously with a female fronted pop act NO QUESTIONS, whose image involved jumpsuits and make-up, and had appeared on a 7" single 'Videobrat'. Poland had also been a member of WELKIN.
In a quite surreal twist of fate, the man who introduced both Samuelson and Poland to the band, Jay Jones, died in 1997, having been stabbed to death with a butter knife in a fight with his brother in law over a baloney sandwich!
MEGADETH's first album 'Killing Is My Business... And Business Is Good' was recorded on a shoestring budget, but still packed enough intensity to make the world's rock media sit up and take notice when issued by Combat in America and Music For Nations in Europe.
It was intended that MEGADETH was to have a lead vocalist at this point but, according to Mustaine: "The dickhead that came to sing for us turned up wearing eye-liner and carrying a six pack". The mystery vocalist was shown the door (but only after the band had downed the beer!) and Mustaine was forced to sing lead. Interestingly though, Mustaine had harboured thoughts of requesting the services of DIAMOND HEAD frontman Sean Harris, although this never got beyond the talking stage.
The album included the METALLICA track 'Mechanix' (retitled 'The Four Horsemen' for METALLICA's 'Kill 'Em All' album) and a twisted cover of the NANCY SINATRA hit 'These Boots Are Made For Walking'. Although marred by thin production, the debut was chock full of the trademark intense riffing

style that denoted MEGADETH as a unique entity in the rock field.

Poland was to depart and MEGADETH drafted the veteran former CAPTAIN BEEFHEART musician Mike Albert on guitar. The band undertook American dates with Canadians EXCITER, but within three months the situation was reversed, with Poland resuming his role in time for the second leg of the American 'Killing For A Living' tour. A New Year's show in San Francisco caught the band on a bill that included EXODUS, METAL CHURCH and, somewhat awkwardly, METALLICA.

The band's second album, produced by Mustaine and Randy Burns, was recorded prior to the band securing a major deal but would emerge remixed during 1986 as 'Peace Sells... But Who's Buying' on Capitol Records. The album had, in its original mixed form, been pressed up in a test batch by Music For Nations in anticipation of gaining the rights to release it, before the band announced that they had signed to Capitol. Thus white label copies do exist as one of the rarer MEGADETH collectibles.

The resulting tour, at first supporting MOTÖRHEAD (before friction between the two bands prompted MEGADETH's opting out), then as guests of ALICE COOPER,

began to wide a developing rift between the two Daves and Samuelson and Poland.

This was to rise to a head at MEGADETH's debut British gig headlining London's Hammersmith Odeon. The show, supported by METAL CHURCH, was to highlight the band's paper thin division between genius and chaos. With their gear impounded at customs and released only hours before the performance, combined with onstage resentment, MEGADETH's show had many wondering whether they had been in the presence of the next metal sensation or a bunch of sorry burn-outs.

During a break between road dates Mustaine was to earn production credits on the debut album from SANCTUARY 'Refuge Denied' before the gig schedule resumed. Dates in America saw KING DIAMOND and MAYHEM as support. By the tour's close in Hawaii, Samuelson, after numerous on the road disappearances and occasions where he would fall asleep at inopportune moments, was asked to leave. Poland persevered, but would lose his position as recording for a third album began.

It was to be many years before Samuelson re-emerged on the 1997 FATAL OPERA album 'The Eleventh Hour'. Poland issued the solo album 'Return To Metalopolis' before creating

DAMN THE MACHINE, then MUMBO'S BRAIN. (A further solo album 'Chasing The Sun' followed in 1999).

MEGADETH confirmed their revised line-up in November 1987. Alongside Mustaine and Ellefson were ex-BROKEN SILENCE guitarist Jeff Young and, from Detroit, MEANIES drummer Chuck Beehler, the latter having been Samuelson's drum technician. In fact, ex-SLAYER drummer DAVE LOMBARDO had been offered the vacant drum position before Beehler, but he turned the gig down because of Mustaine and Co's continuing drug problems.

Young had gained the position after he had taught ex-MALICE guitarist Jay Reynolds in order for his pupil to get the job. Although Reynolds briefly gained a place in MEGADETH, Young soon ousted him midway through recording of 'So Far, So Good… So What'.

With this fresh line-up, MEGADETH performed their second British show headlining the 'Christmas On Earth' festival atop a bevy of thrash acts including NUCLEAR ASSAULT, OVERKILL, LÄÄZ ROCKIT, VOIVOD and CRO-MAGS prior to American dates with DIO. By the tail end of these dates with the former RAINBOW / BLACK SABBATH singer, and their album nestling in the American top 30, MEGADETH had turned a - ticket sales wise- very slow tour into their own vehicle. A brief rest period was quickly curtailed by more headline shows, this time with Germans WARLOCK as openers.

The 'So Far, So Good... So What' album featured a cover version of the SEX PISTOLS track 'Anarchy In The UK', which was to chart in Britain, even boasted guest guitar from SEX PISTOLS guitarist STEVE JONES. Expectations were high as the thrash movement reached its zenith and MEGADETH's third album clocked up advance American sales of over 450,000.

The year could not go by though without controversy though. As the press stoked up the heat, numerous METALLICA vs. MEGADETH articles appeared alleging that Mustaine had put in a claim that METALLICA's track 'Leper Messiah' off their 'Master Of Puppets' album was in fact a thinly disguised reworking of an early track he wrote titled 'The Hills Ran Red'. METALLICA hit back with strong denials.

Back to business the same year MEGADETH went into the studio to re-record a fresh version of 'These Boots Are Made For Walking' for inclusion on the 'Dudes' soundtrack album.

1988 saw MEGADETH returning to Europe for a headline tour with support from Seattle's SANCTUARY.

Although many dates were sold out Mustaine threw the band straight into controversy when he made praising remarks about the IRA whilst onstage in Northern Ireland. Needless to say the audience were far from appreciative and began spitting at the frontman.

The troubled times were far from over however when after an impressive appearance at the Castle Donington 'Monsters Of Rock' festival MEGADETH once more split down the middle with Young and Beehler out, the drummer joining BLACK & WHITE. Young unsuccessfully auditioned for melodic Rockers DANGER DANGER.

Mustaine launched into a vitriolic stream of abuse about his former guitar partner even going so far as to suggest that Young was in love with WARLOCK chanteuse Doro Pesch and could not handle the fact that Pesch was supposedly writing love letters to Mustaine!

1988 had MEGADETH bouncing straight back and celebrating a top twenty British singles hit with their version of ALICE COOPER's 'No More Mr. Nice Guy' taken from the soundtrack to Wes Craven's 'Shocker' movie. Recording for this track was to be the first with new ex-RHOADS drummer Nick Menza.

Menza had coincidentally been Beehler's drum technician in the same way that Beehler had been Samuelson's. It took Menza three stabs to land the job though as, after two failed auditions, Mustaine persevered and taught the songs to Menza. It transpired that Menza's ability was there all along, but the prospect of joining an act like MEGADETH had reduced him to a bag of nerves at auditions.

The position of new lead guitarist for MEGADETH fuelled rumours concerning HEATHEN's Lee Altus, SAVATAGE's Criss Oliva, PANTERA's Diamond Darryl and Jeff Waters of ANNIHILATOR.

Waters nearly got the gig, but Darryl was in fact offered the position. The PANTERA guitarist insisted though that his brother, PANTERA drummer Vinnie, also be given a place and as such the negotiations broke down.

Mustaine pulled in old acquaintance CHRIS POLAND to perform on the demo recordings for a new album, but it was to be former DEUCE / VIXEN / HAWAII / CACOPHONY man MARTY FRIEDMAN who landed the job. The result of this union was 'Rust In Peace', produced by Mike Clink. Recording took place with Mustaine undergoing drug rehabilitation treatment, but the resultant album was to be their most mature effort to date giving them a further hit.

DAVE ELLEFSON of MEGADETH
Photo : Nico Wobben

MEGADETH forged part of the immense 'Clash Of The Titans' touring bill that caught the band appearing alongside fellow heavyweights ANTHRAX and SLAYER. The American dates, with openers ALICE IN CHAINS, proved a huge success with sell out attendances. The band dropped in a couple of San Francisco club shows billed as VIC & THE RATTLEHEADS and by October the 'Clash Of The Titans' touring package, now with support from TESTAMENT and SUICIDAL TENDANCIES, hit Britain and Europe. The live work was far from over however, as returning to America the band were to hook up with British metal legends JUDAS PRIEST for their 'Painkiller' tour.

Despite now enjoying heady success, Mustaine was still teetering on the edge. A 1993 support tour of America to AEROSMITH was curtailed when, in Houston, Texas, MEGADETH were forced out, Mustaine simply unable to perform. AEROSMITH themselves were also none too pleased at remarks Mustaine made about their age! The vocalist entered into a detox programme and in the lull Ellefson busied himself with production for Texan metal act HELSTAR for their 'Multiples Of Black' album.

With the pressure now off MEGADETH

reunited for two interim projects that were to give an indication as to future material, namely the 'Angry Again' track for the 'Last Action Hero' movie soundtrack and '99 Ways To Die' submitted for the Beavis & Butthead compilation album on Geffen. Friedman also found the time for a solo album.

MEGADETH relocated to Phoenix, Arizona to record the 'Youthanasia' album, even constructing a brand new studio titled Fat Planet in which to lay down tracks. The album was to break into the American top five and go double platinum as MEGADETH embarked on an almost year long world tour. Interestingly, the 'Youthanasia' album artwork was banned in Thailand, Malaysia and Singapore for depicting an old woman hanging babies out on a clothes line. The babies depicted in the video for the album track 'Train Of Consequences' were also censored by MTV worldwide!

With Mustaine's continual battle against addiction a harsh regime of no alcohol was put into force for all MEGADETH shows. The close of 1994 saw MEGADETH touring South America with support from British rockers THE ALMIGHTY.

1995 American dates saw FEAR FACTORY as openers. One obscure gig saw the band playing a one-off show in Tel Aviv. MEGADETH took a further foray into South America in September 1995 as part of the 'Monsters Of Rock' bill alongside OZZY OSBOURNE, ALICE COOPER, FAITH NO MORE and PARADISE LOST, to round off a gruelling eleven months on the road.

With the close of the tour Mustaine busied himself with the MD45 project, a punk industrial project in collaboration with FEAR's Lee Ving.

MEGADETH made a mighty return in 1997 with the 'Cryptic Writings' album which entered the American charts at number 10 selling 75,000 units in it's first week of release. The album was surprisingly produced by ex-GIANT man Dann Huff. Used to unrelenting recording schedules Mustaine was somewhat taken aback when Huff, a committed Christian, explained he could not work on Sunday as he had to take his family to Church. MEGADETH solved this potential personality problem by Mustaine attending church with his family too!

The band toured Britain in June 1997, supported by KILL II THIS, comfortably selling out venues. Returning to America where 'Cryptic Writings' remained firmly lodged in the album charts MEGADETH, with tour guests LIFE OF AGONY, set about touring with gusto to push the album past the platinum sales mark. Dates in Mexico had JUDAS PRIEST as special guests.

255

MEGADETH
Photo : Chapman Baehler

Nick Menza took a leave of absence in 1998 turning up on the FIREBALL MINISTRY album 'Ou Est La Rock?' with ex-THE OBSESSED and GOATSNAKE bassist Guy Pinhas in 1999. Brian Howe stood in on drums for the band's inclusion of 'I'll Get Even' to the Sci-Fi cartoon inspired soundtrack record 'Songs Of The Witchblade' in 1998.

Eventually a permanent replacement was located in ex-Y&T, SUICIDAL TENDENCIES and WHITE LION drummer Jimmy DeGrasso. The band put in a series of well attended American dates in 2000 as part of the 'Maximum Rock' tour alongside MÖTLEY CRÜE and ANTHRAX.

2000 saw ex-DANGER DANGER, ALICE COOPER, ASIA, WIDOWMAKER, SAVATAGE, BLUE OYSTER CULT and STEPHEN PEARCY guitarist Al Pitrelli replacing Friedman. Pitrelli, although highly respected as a musician, was acknowledged by many as a "guitar for hire" having been involved outside of the Rock community with artists as diverse as KOOL & THE GANG, CELINE DION and arch crooner MICHAEL BOLTON.

The band contributed their take on 'Never Say Die' for the BLACK SABBATH tribute album 'Nativity In Black 2'.

Mustaine would find a rare moment to donate a song to another artist. The unlikely recipient of 'The Day The Music Died' being the 'Get To You' album from JEANNINE ST. CLAIR.

MEGADETH would switch labels to the newly founded Sanctuary concern, led by IRON MAIDEN manager Rod Smallwood, for their 2001 release 'The World Needs A Hero'. With Mustaine promising a return to heavier past form the omens looked good as the lead single 'Motor Psycho' rocketed straight in at the number one position for American Rock radio plays in its first week of release. The album duly debuted high at number 16 in the American charts selling over 60,000 copies in its first week.

Meantime it was revealed that the singer now part owned a restaurant in Phoenix along with ALICE COOPER and a number of sports celebrities. The menu naturally included 'Megadeth Meatloaf'! Touring in the UK found MEGADETH supported by the Finnish 'Thrash cello' quartet APOCALYPTICA.

MEGADETH's projected Malaysian date as part of their 2001 Far Eastern dates at the Warp Club on August 2 in Kuala Lumpur was cancelled when the Malaysian government objected to the band's imagery deeming it "unsuitable for the youth of Malaysia". The band were warned off in the strongest terms and threatened with arrest if they attempted to play the concert.

The bands American bout of touring suffered no such problems commencing at the Saltair in Magna, Utah on September 7th and running through to a close in New York at the Irving Plaza on October 16th. Support band ENDO opened the proceedings and the headliners set list would fluctuate throughout as fans had been invited to vote for their favourite tracks. Despite numerous Rock acts finding the going tough on the American touring circuit MEGADETH overall retained their audience loyalty and kept up the pace undaunted by the September 11th terrorist attacks.

Meantime ex-member MARTY FRIEDMAN finally re-emerged touting his new project RED DYE #2. The guitarist would also collude with UFO guitarist Michael Schenker on an all instrumental studio project.

MEGADETH, riding on a renewed commercial high, would be the subject of strong rumours hinting at a joint METALLICA / MEGADETH tour in the future - possibly even involving a bi-partisan band unit dubbed 'META-MEGA' by Mustaine!

With the close of American dates Mustaine, along with producer Bill Kennedy, headed back into the studio undertaking a remix of the band's debut album 'Killing Is My Business... And Business Is Good'. The revised version would include tracks from earlier demos but initially not their take on NANCY SINATRA's 'These Boots Are Made For Walking', permission being denied from the original lyric writer following MEGADETH''s less than subtle change of words on their original session. As it transpired 'Boots...' did make the final running order as did bonus demo versions of 'Last Rites (Loved To Death)', 'Mechanix' and 'The Skull Beneath The Skin'.

As the year drew to a close, with MEGADETH now proudly sitting on a combined 15 million album sales to date, it would be revealed that Mustaine had embarked upon a studio project with DIAMOND HEAD guitarist Brian Tatler. Also in the works would be the MEGADETH's first live offering, a double CD and DVD affair entitled 'Rude Awakening' issued in March.

On April 3rd 2002 fans would be shocked to learn that Mustaine had suffered a severe nerve damage injury to his left arm and subsequently announced his departure from the band - to all intents and purposes folding MEGADETH. This announcement came only hours after conjecture that Mustaine was likely to pull out of the band after he had reportedly 'found God'. The fallout from this shock decision would be almost immediate with fast flowing rumours that Dave Ellefson

was to join METALLICA. The bassist was keen to get back to work though, writing songs for DRY KILL LOGIC's second album and acting as co-producer for the Canadian band WARMACHINE.

Meantime Al Pitrelli's next career move was so sudden it did not have time to generate any speculation, the guitarist announced on the 7th of April he was rejoining SAVATAGE, ousting previous incumbent Jack Frost. However, before taking up this post Pitrelli would undertake live work with former SKID ROW vocalist SEBASTIAN BACH.

Singles/EPs:
Wake Up Dead / Black Friday (Live), Capitol CL476 (1987) **65 UK**
Wake Up Dead / Black Friday (Live) / Devil's Island (Live), Capitol 12CL476 (1987) (12" single)
Anarchy In The UK / Liar, Capitol CL 480 (1988) **45 UK**
Anarchy In The UK / Liar / 502, Capitol 12CL 480 (1988) (12" single)
Mary Jane / Hook In Mouth, Capitol CL 489 (1988) **46 UK**
Mary Jane / Hook In Mouth / My Last Words, Capitol 12CL 489 (1988) (12" single)
No More Mr. Nice Guy, SBK SBK 4 (1988) **13 UK** (B side by DANGEROUS TOYS)
Holy Wars... The Punishment Due / Lucretia, Capitol CLP 588 (1990) **24 UK**
Holy Wars... The Punishment Due / Lucretia / Interview, Capitol 12CLP 588 (1990) (12" single)
Hanger 18 / The Conjouring (Live), Capitol CL 604 (1991) **26 UK**
Hanger 18 / The Conjouring (Live) / Hanger 18 (Live) / Hook In Mouth (Live), Capitol 12CLG 604 (1991) (12" single)
Foreclosure Of A Dream, Capitol (1992) (USA promotion)
Symphony Of Destruction / Peace Sells... But Who's Buying (Live), Capitol CLS 662 (1992) **15 UK**
Symphony Of Destruction / Peace Sells... But Who's Buying (Live) / Go To Hell / Breakpoint, Capitol CLS 662 (1992) (12" single)
Symphony Of Destruction / Skin O' My Teeth, Capitol 44886 (1992) **71 USA** (USA release)
Skin O' My Teeth / Holy Wars... The Punishment Due (General Norman Schwarzkopf mix), Capitol CL 669 (1992) **13 UK**
Skin O' My Teeth / Skin O' My Teeth (Version) / Lucretia, Capitol CDCL 669 (1992) (CD single)
Skin O' My Teeth / Holy Wars... The Punishment Due (Norman Schwarzkopf mix)

/ High Speed Drill Interview, Capitol 10LP 669 (1992) (10" single)
Sweating Bullets / Ashes In Your Mouth (Live), Capitol CL 692 (1993) **26 UK**
Sweating Bullets / Countdown To Extinction (Live) / Symphony Of Destruction (Gristle mix) / Symphony Of Destruction (Live), Capitol CDCL 682 (1993) (CD single)
Train Of Consequences / Crown Of Worms, Capitol CL 730 (1994) **22 UK**
Train Of Consequences / Crown Of Worms / Peace Sells.. But Who's Buying? (Live) / Anarchy In The UK (Live), Capitol CDCL 730 (1994) (CD single)
Train Of Consequences / Holy Wars… The Punishment Due (Live) / Peace Sells… But Who's Buying (Live) / Anarchy In The UK (Live), Capitol 12CL 730 (1994) (12" single)
A Tout Le Monde / Problems / New Wold Order (Demo), Capitol (1995) (USA release)
A Tout Le Monde / Symphony Of Destruction (Demo) / Architecture Of Aggression (Demo) / New World Order (Demo), Capitol (1995) (Dutch release)
Trust / Almost Honest / I'll Get Even / Use The Man, Capitol CDAS 118 (1997) (Promotion release)
Trust / A Secret Place / Tornado Of Souls (Live) / A Tout Le Monde (Live), Capitol (1997)
Skin O' My Teeth (Live) / Holy Wars (The Punishment Due) (Live) / Symphony Of Destruction (Live), Fan Club (1997)
Almost Honest, Capitol (1998)
Use The Man, Capitol (1998)
A Secret Place, Capitol (1998)
Crush 'Em, Capitol (1999)

Albums:
KILLING IS MY BUSINESS... AND BUSINESS IS GOOD, Music For Nations MFN 46 (1985)
Last Rites / Killing Is My Business... And Business Is Good / The Skull Beneath The Skin / Boots / Rattlehead / Chosen Ones / Looking Down The Cross / Mechanix
PEACE SELLS... BUT WHO'S BUYING?, Capitol TCEST 2022 (1986) **76 USA**
Wake Up Dead / The Conjuring / Peace Sells / Devil's Island / Good Mourning - Black Friday / Bad Omen / I Ain't Superstitious / My Last Words
SO FAR, SO GOOD... SO WHAT?, Capitol CDEST 2053 (1988) **37 SWEDEN, 18 UK, 28 USA**
Into The Lungs Of Hell / Set The World On Fire / Anarchy In The U.K. / Mary Jane / 502 / In My Darkest Hour / Liar / Hook In Mouth
RUST IN PEACE, Capitol CDEST 2132 (1990) **34 SWEDEN, 8 UK, 23 USA**
Holy Wars... The Punishment Due / Hanger 18 / Take No Prisoners / Five Magics / Poison

Was The Cure / Lucretia / Tornado Of Souls / Dawn Patrol / Rust In Peace.
COUNTDOWN TO EXTINCTION, Capitol CDESTU 2175 (1992)
10 SWEDEN, 5 UK, 2 USA
Skin O' My Teeth / Symphony Of Destruction / Architecture Of Aggression / Foreclosure Of A Dream / Sweating Bullets / This Was My Life / Countdown To Extinction / High Speed Dirt / Psychotron / Captive Honour / Ashes In Your Mouth
YOUTHANASIA, Capitol CDEST 2244 (1994) **6 UK, 4 USA**
Reckoning Day / Train Of Consequences / Addicted To Chaos / A Tout Le Monde / Elysian Fields / The Killing Road / Blood Of Heroes / Family Tree / Youthanasia / I Thought I Knew It All / Black Curtains / Victory
HIDDEN TREASURES, Capitol 33670 (1994) **28 UK, 90 USA**
No More Mr. Nice Guy / Breakpoint / Go To Hell / Angry Again / 99 Ways To Die / Paranoid / Diadems / Problems
CRYPTIC WRITINGS, Capitol 7243 8 38262 2 3 (1997) **15 SWEDEN, 38 UK, 10 USA**
Trust / Almost Honest / Use The Man / Mastermind / The Disintegrators / I'll Get Even / Sin / A Secret Place / Have Cool, Will Travel / She Wolf / Vortex / F.F.F.
LIVE TRAX, Capitol (1997) (Japanese release)
Tornado Of Souls / A Tout Le Monde / Reckoning Day / Angry Again / Use The Man / She-Wolf
RISK, Capitol 7243 4 99134 0 0 (1999) **29 UK**
Insomnia / Prince Of Darkness / Enter The Arena / Crush 'Em / Breadline / The Doctor Is Calling / I'll Be There / Wanderlust / Ecstasy / Seven / Time: The Beginning / Time: The End
CAPITOL PUNISHMENT: THE MEGADETH YEARS, Capitol 7243 5 25916 2 6 (2000)
Kill The King / Dread & The Fugitive Mind / Crush 'Em / Use The Man / Almost Honest / Trust / A Tout Le Monde / Train Of Consequences / Sweating Bullets / Symphony Of Destruction / Hanger 18 / Holy Wars… The Punishment Due / In My Darkest Hour / Peace Sells
THE WORLD NEEDS A HERO, Sanctuary (2001) **36 GERMANY, 38 SWEDEN, 16 USA**
Disconnect / The World Needs A Hero / Moto Psycho / 1000 Times Goodbye / Burning Bridges / Promises / Recipe For Hate... Warhorse / Losing My Senses / Dread And The Fugitive Mind / Silent Scorn / Return To Hangar 18 / When
RUDE AWAKENING, Sanctuary (2002)
Dread & The Fugitive Mind / Kill The King / Wake Up Dead / In My Darkest Hour / Angry

Again / She Wolf / Reckoning Day / Devil's Island / Train Of Consequences / A Tout Le Monde / Burning Bridges / Hangar 18 / Return To Hangar 18 / Hook In Mouth / Almost Honest / 1000 Times Goodbye / Mechanix / Tornado Of Souls / Ashes in Your Mouth / Sweating Bullets / Trust / Symphony Of Destruction / Peace Sells… But Who's Buying / Holy Wars… The Punishment Due

MEGAMOSH (GERMANY)
Line-Up: Beck (vocals), Steve (guitar), Matzer (guitar), Ussi (bass), Johnny (drums)

MEGAMOSH, founded as a quartet in 1987, supported PROTECTOR and WEHRMACHT on German tours in 1989 promoting their 'Fight The Epidemic Prince' EP.
MEGAMOSH pulled in second guitarist Steve in 1991 for a string of dates in Holland. Following release of the second album 'A Different Kind Of Meat' the band have guested for EXUMER, SODOM, CORONER and PESTILENCE amongst others.

Singles/EPs:
Fight The Epidemic Prince EP, (1989)

Albums:
CALL TO ACCOUNT, (1990)
A DIFFERENT KIND OF MEAT, Prophecy 22772 (1992)
I Am Trapped / Organ Dealer / Euphoria (Apoplexy II) / Killerflies / Struck By Blindness / Different / No More Mother / You Forced Me / No Cure In Sight / Set Me Free / When You Know You're Lost

MEGASLAUGHTER (SWEDEN)
Line-up: Emil Ilic (vocals), Kenneth Arnestedt (guitar), Alox Räfling (bass), Putte Räfling (drums)

MEGASLAUGHTER, formed in 1987, were initially known as DINLOYD. Their first demo as MEGASLAUGHTER, 'Death Remains' surfaced in 1989 and garnered the band a deal with French label Thrash Records.
After one album MEGASLAUGHTER split in 1992, with vocalist Emil Lilic resurfacing in 1997 fronting MURDER CORPORATION, a project band assembled by members of DERANGED that released the 'Blood Revolution 2050' album.

Albums:
CALLS FROM THE BEYOND, Thrash THR010 (1991)

MEKONG DELTA (GERMANY)
Line-Up: Wolfgang Borgmann (vocals), Uwe Baltrusch (guitar), Ralph Hubert (bass), Jörg Michael (drums)

MEKONG DELTA originally went under pseudonyms to protect their true identities; bassist Ralph Hubert being known as Bjorn Eklund for example. Drummer Jörg Michael was a member of RAGE at the time.
LIVING DEATH guitarists Frank Fricke and Reiner Kelch performed on the debut album under the guises of Vincent St. John and Rolf Stein. Ex-SODOM and U.D.O. guitarist Uwe Baltrusch played on the 'Principle Of Doubt' album.
Unable to attend the recording of 'The Gnome' EP Jörg Michael's place was taken by HOLY MOSES / GAMMA RAY drummer Uli Kusch. Michael's highly rated skills would find the stickman journeying through LAOS, HEADHUNTER, GLENMORE, GRAVE DIGGER and RUNNING WILD.
Vocalist Wolfgang Borgmann left in 1990 to be replaced by ex-SIREN singer Douglas Lee. Michael joined HEADHUNTER.
Another ex-MEKONG DELTA drummer Peter Haas of AIN'T DEAD YET and CALHOUN CONQUER later joined BABYLON SAD and KROKUS.

Singles/EPs:
The Gnome / The Hut Of Baba Yaga / Without Honour / The Cure, Aaarrg AAARRG 8 (1987)
Toccata / Black Betty / Interludium, Aaarrg AAARRG 17 (1989)

Albums:
MEKONG DELTA, Aaarrg AAARRG 4 (1987)
Without Honour / The Cure / The Hut Of Baba Yaga / Heroes Grief / Kill The Enemy / Black Sabbath
THE MUSIC OF ERICH ZANN, Aaarrg AAARRG 11 (1988)
Age Of Agony / True Lies / Confession Of Madness / Hatred / Interludium (Begging For Mercy) / Prophecy / Memories Of Tomorrow / I, King, Will Come / The Final Deluge / Epilogue
PRINCIPLE OF DOUBT, Aaarrg AAARRG 19 (1989)
A Question Of Trust (Cyberpunk) / The Principle Of Doubt / Once I Believed / Ever Since Time Began / Curse Of Reality / Twilight Zone (Lord Fouls Hort) / Shades Of Doom (Cyberpunk 2) / The Jester / El Colibri / No Friend Of Mine
DANCES OF DEATH (AND OTHER WALKING SHADOWS), Aaarrg ARG 23034-2 (1990)
Dances Of Death: I) Introduction, II)

Eruption, III) Beyond The Gates, IV) Outburst, V) Days Of Betrayal, VI) Restless, VII) Sanctuary, VIII) Finale / Transgressor / True Believers / Night On A Bare Mountain
KALEIDOSCOPE, IRS 986963 (1991)
I.N.N.O.C.E.N.T.? / Sphere Eclipse / Dance On A Volcano / Dreaming / Heartbeat / Shadow Walker / Sabre Dance / Misunderstanding / About Science
CLASSICS, Aaarrg ARG 27045-2 (1993)
Interludium (Begging For Mercy) (Part I) / Toccata / Twilight Zone / The Gnome / The Hut Of Baba Yaga / Night On A Bare Mountain / Interluduim (Part II) / El Colibri
LIVE AT AN EXHIBITION, Metal Machine RTD 3120042238 (1993)
The Cure / Transgression / True Believers / Night On A Bare Mountain / Memories Of Tomorrow / Hut Of Baba Yaga / Heroe's Grief / True Lies / Toccata
VISIONS FUGITIVES, Bullet Proof CDVEST 19 (1994)
Them / Imagination / Suite For Group And Orchestra: a) Introduction (The Danger In Dreams / The Chronicle Of Doubts - Book 3 / Chapter 1) / b) Preludium (Lord Kevin's Lament / The Chronicle Of Doubts - Book 2 / Chapter 8) / c) Allegro (Mhorams Victory / The Chronicle Of Doubts - Book 3 / Chapter 15) / d) Dance (The Corrupt / The Chronicle Of Doubts - Book 3 / Chapter 18) / e) Fugue (Knowledge / The Chronicle Of Doubts - Book 2 / Chapter 23 / f) Postludium (Lena's Daughter / The Chronicle Of Doubts - Book 2 / Chapter 21) / The Healer / Days Of Sorrow
PICTURES AT AN EXIBITION, Bullet Proof IRSCD993 626 (1996)
Promenade / Gnomus / Interludium / Il Vecchio Castello / Interludium / Tuileries (Dispute D'Enfants Apres Jeux) / Bydtlo / Interludium / Ballet Of The Unhatched Chicks / "Samule" Goldenberg And "Schmuyle" / Promenade / Lomoges: Le Marché (La Grande Nouvelle) / Catacombae (Sepulcrum Romancum) / Lingua Mortis / The Hut On Chicken's Legs / The Heroic Gate (In The Old Capital Of Kiev)

MEGATTACK (Orem, UT, USA)
Line-Up: Rick 'The Jack' Jackson (vocals), Jake Oslo (guitar), Parriah Hultquist (guitar), Patrick Carter (bass), Bryan Sorenson (drums)

MEGATTACK's first foray into the recording studio produced the three track demo in 1985 comprising 'Make It Rock', 'Earthshaker' and 'Take The Night'. For a short time ARMORED SAINT guitarist Phil Sandoval was linked to a vacant position in MEGATTACK, but this never transpired.

The group were picked up by the French based Dream label and released the 'Raw Delivery' album in 1986.

Albums:
RAW DELIVERY, Dream DRE 18365 (1986)
Never Surrender / Good Girls / Whisper In The Dark / Talk To Me / Kids Rock / Stay With Me / Carry On/ Make It Rock / Love Machine

MEGHAN (USA)
Line-Up: Meghan (vocals), Rowland McDaniel (guitar), Jacques Moriarty (guitar), Rick Eagle (bass), Scott Sherman (drums)

Albums:
MEGHAN, Pendragon (1987)
Don't Think Twice / I Don't Want To Know / Head Over Heels / Suicidal Lover / Well Of Souls / Radio Man

M-80 (Los Angeles, CA, USA)
Line-Up: Niki Buzz (vocals / guitar), Don Costa (bass), Sam Mann (drums)

M-80 were created by ex-VENDETTA guitarist Niki Buzz (real name Darrell Young) and bassist Don Costa, the latter being known as the man thrown out of OZZY OSBOURNE's band for being too outrageous. Pre-shredding his skin with a cheese grater onstage with Ozzy, Costa had trod the boards with a formative version of W.A.S.P.
Costa's stay in M-80 was short-lived (as was Mann's) In 1984 Buzz recorded with ex-BODINE bassist Jeronimo Bos and drummer Gerard Haitsma in Holland on a record tentatively titled 'Don't Feed The Animal'. He also put together the Dutch based NIKI BUZZ BAND with Arco Boomer (bass) and Robbie Fiffer (drums), playing Dingwalls in London during October.
by 1985 and the recording of 'The Maniac's Revenge' album, Buzz recruited ex-SAMSON bassist Chris Aylmer and drummer Ian Roberts.
Buzz would create the heavy Rap project THE ALARM before touring and playing with CURTIS KNIGHT. Latter bands included MIDNIGHT GYPSIES and LONE WOLF.

Singles/EPs:
M-80, Megaton (1983)

Albums:
M-80, Roadrunner (1984)
Face Cracker / Get Out Of Town / Supply And Demand / Frying Pan (Into The Fire) / Hollywood Chills / Stop In The Name Of Love

MANIAC'S REVENGE, Roadrunner RR 9801 (1985)
Maniac's Revenge / Get Outa My Face / You Drive Me Crazy / The Big Fiz / Nothing To Lose / The Winds Of Blowhuyven / Attention / Let's Rock / Stoplight / Forevermore / Love Is A Sacrifice

MELIAH RAGE (Boston, MA, USA)
Line-Up: Mike Munro (vocals), Jim Koury (guitar), Anthony Nichols (guitar), Jesse Johnson (bass), Stuart Dowie (drums)

Inspired by METALLICA's first ever visit to Boston in 1983, MELIAH RAGE were formed by guitarists Jim Koury (who had previously played in an AEROSMITH tribute group in partnership with STEEL ASSASIN axeman Mark Schulman, better known as MARC FERRARI of KEEL infamy!) and Anthony Nichols. The line-up had stabilised by 1986 with the addition of vocalist Mike Munro, bassist Jesse Johnson and drummer Stuart Dowie. The band name was a progression from the moniker of one of Koury's earlier bands MELIAH CRAZE.
After releasing a promising three track demo in 1987, MELIAH RAGE were picked up by Epic and debuted in 1988 with 'Kill To Survive' MELIAH RAGE featured guitarist Tony Nichols who was previously with Budweiser swilling Skate Rock band GANG GREEN.
The 1989 live album, 'Live Kill', was a one sided affair recorded at Harpo's club in Detroit. Micah Shevaloff contributes keyboards to the 'Solitary Solitude' album.
By 1996 MELIAH RAGE included bassist Dave Barcus and drummer Bob Mayo in the ranks. The band still remains somewhat active and released a fifth album called 'Unfinished Business' on their own label in 1999. The CD contained unreleased material recorded between the years 1992 and 1996. By this point Barcus and Mayo had been replaced bassist Clark Lush and drummer Sully Erna.

Albums:
KILL TO SURVIVE, Epic 463257-1(1988)
Beginning Of The End / Bates Motel / Meliah Rage / Deadly Existence / Enter The Darkness / Impaling Doom / The Pack
LIVE KILL, Epic 6E 45370 (1989)
Beginning Of The End / Kill To Survive / Bates Motel / Deadly Existence / The Pack
SOLITARY SOLITUDE, Epic 466675-1 (1990)
Solitary Solitude / No Mind / Decline Of Rule / Retaliation / Deliver Me / The Witching / Lost Life / Swallow Your Soul / Razor Ribbon
DEATH VALLEY DREAM, (1996)

UNFINISHED BUSINESS, Meliah Rage (1999)
Mind Stalk / Moment of Silence / Ruthless / Decade Dreams / Blacksmith / Possessing Judgement / Violent Force / Season To Kill

THE MENTORS (Seattle, WA, USA)
Line-Up: El Duce (vocals / drums), Sickie Wifebeater (guitar), Dr. Heathen Scum (bass)

Although their true identities remain a closely guarded secret, no small thanks in part to the black hoods the trio has always worn, the outrageous, politically incorrect scumbag Metal band THE MENTORS were originally formed in Seattle during 1977, before the group relocated to Los Angeles during 1979 / 1980. But 'success' eluded the trio, leaving bassist Dr Heathen Scum to opt out in order to attend University to major in Engineering.
Guitarist Sickie Wifebeater and bandleader vocalist / drummer El Duce continued the group with numerous other bassists, all going under the name Dr Heathen Scum it would seem!
The band's debut release, the 'Trash Bag' EP was unveiled by Mystic Records in 1983, with the live album 'Live At The Whiskey / Cathay De Grande' (so titled due to having separate live shows on either side) following soon after.
In 1985 the original Dr Heathen Scum, having graduated with honours, re-joined the group in time for their first studio album, the infamous 'You Asked For It', released by the Metal Blade offshoot Death label.
Metal Blade's Brian Slagel signed the band upon the recommendation of MALICE guitarist Jay Reynolds and the band swiftly engaged themselves in a lawsuit with Mystic Records over alleged unpaid royalties.
Signing to the Death label increased THE MENTORS notoriety to the extreme and their gigs became even greater targets for feminist groups to picket, in some instances the band had the plug pulled on their shows in protest by activists appalled at the extremely sexist lyrical content of MENTORS material.
THE MENTORS guitarist Eric Carlson also pursued a side project act JESTERS OF DESTINY releasing two albums.
Following the break up of the band El Duce released a solo album through Metal Blade in 1993, although the subject matter differed little from the material offered by THE MENTORS for the previous ten years!
Both 'You Axed For It' and 'Up The Dose' were re-issued by German label High Vaultage during 1997.

Singles/EPs:

Goin' Thru Your Purse / Get Up And Die / Peepin' Tom / Woman From Sodom, Mystic M12453 (1982)

Live In Frisco, Mystic (1983)

Adultery / Rock 'Em, Sock 'Em / Having Sickie's Baby, Mystic SS 7EP 214 (19870 (Free EP with re-release of 'Mentors' LP)

Albums:

MENTORS LIVE AT THE WHISKEY / CATHAY DE GRANDE, Mystic MLP 33107 (1983)
Adultery / Going Through Your Purse / Free Fix For A Fuck / Rock 'Em And Sock 'Em / Get Up And Die / Peepin' Tom / Woman From Sodom / Baby You'll Regret Me / Get Up And Die

YOU AXED FOR IT, Death 72036 (1985)
Sandwich Of Love / Shocked And Grossed / Four F Club / Herpes Two / Judgement Day / Sleep Bandits / Free Fix / Golden Showers / Clap Queen / My Erection Is Over

UP THE DOSE, Death 72172 (1986)
Heterosexuals Have The Right To Rock / Rock 'Em And Sock 'Em / White Trash Women / Adultery / On The Rag / Kick It Down / Secretary Hump / Couch Test Casting / SFCC / Up The Dose

SEX, DRUGSANDROCK N' ROLL, Medusa (1989)

NICK MENZA (USA)

Solo work from drummer NICK MENZA, for many years longterm drummer with Thrash veterans MEGADETH. The album, co-produced by the esteemed Max Norman, was issued on the musician's own Menzanations label exclusively through his website. For live dates in 2002 Menza pulled in erstwhile SUICIDAL TENDENCIES guitarist Anthony Gallo, GREAT WHITE and SAMANTHA 7 guitarist Ty Longley and bass player Jason Levin.

MEPHISTO (GERMANY)

Line-Up: Uwe Suerick (vocals / guitar), Andreas Hladik (guitar), Andreas Rippelmeier (guitar), Marc Schulz (bass), Wolfgang Mann (drums)

A German Speed Metal act, MEPHISTO's 'Megalomania' EP consisted of two demos originally recorded in 1986. Guitarist Andreas Rippelmeier and bassist Marc Schulz would later join HEAVENWARD.

Singles/EPs:

Megalomania EP, Wrong Again WAR (1996)

Albums:

MEPHISTO, Miracle (1988)
Prologue / Mephisto / X-Rays / In Dubio Contra Reum / Save Your Rights / Battle Of Kerovnia / Holy Child

IN SEARCH OF LOST REFUGE, Rockport SPV 08 96 421 (1991)
Intro - Nature / Aliens / Valley Of The Dolls / Unexpected Changes / Senseless Marching / A Fatal Development / The Final Chapter / Refugium (N.B.)

MERCENARY

(Salt Lake City, UT, USA)

Line-Up: Bryan Mehr (vocals), Todd Sundberg (guitar), Russ Millham (guitar), Rossi Iorg (bass), Chad Naylor (drums)

MERCENARY released an 11 track demo in 1985.

MERCENARY

(San Francisco, CA, USA)

Line-Up: Sven Soderlund (vocals), Danny White (guitar), Brooks Holland (bass), Slade Anderson (drums)

San Francisco Metal act MERCENARY became the stuff of folklore as the Bay Area Thrash scene developed almost mythical proportions on mainland Europe during the '90s. MERCENARY's legacy far outweighed their original achievements, the band having only cut one demo tape in 1986 and performed just two gigs.

The original incarnation of the band - vocalist Sven Soderlund, guitarist Danny White, bassist Brooks Holland and drummer Slade Anderson, folded in the fall of 1986. A reformation attempt was brought about in 1987 involving MORDRED guitarist Jim Sanguinetti and drummer Gannon Hall but after a miserly two live appearances MERCENARY imploded yet again in February of 1987. Both Hall and guitarist Danny White allied themselves with MORDRED. Following a spell at the Guitar Institute of Technology Sanguinetti would jump back to MORDRED too. Soderlund would go on to found MULTIPLY.

The band bowed to pressure for a reformation show on November 13th 2001 at the C.W. Saloon venue in San Francisco with plans to record this event for a live album.

The MERCENARY 2001 line-up consisted of founding members frontman Sven Soderlund and drummer Slade Anderson alongside erstwhile MY VICTIM and ULYSSES SIREN bassist J.R. Clegg and former HEATHEN, UTERIS, DOGFACE and current VICIOUS RUMORS guitarist Ira Black.

MERCY (SWEDEN)
Line-Up: Rick Wine (vocals), Andrija 'Witchking' Veljaca (guitar), Tom Mitchell (bass), Johan Norell (drums)

Swedish outfit MERCY, having evolved from Heavy Metal band TURBO, featured in their early days future CANDLEMASS vocalist Messiah Marcolin.
In their relatively short history the band underwent numerous line-up shuffles. The debut album, 'Swedish Metal', was recorded by guitarist Andrija Veljaca (sometimes going under the name of Yandriya Veechking or 'Witchking'), bassist Christian Karlsson (adopting the bizarre anglicised Christian C. Greenfood) and drummer Paul Gustavsson (as Paul G. Judas). Gustafsson later joined HIGH VOLTAGE then OVERHEAT, but by the self-financed 'Mercy' album only Veljaca remained alongside ex-ROUGH LIZZARDS vocalist Eddy Markulin (a.k.a. Messiah Marcolin) and guitarist Magnus Klinto.
Further ructions occurred as the band effectively split but reassembled, with new bassist Jörgen Holst in tow.
The line-up changed again for 'King Of Doom' with Veljaca now teamed with vocalist Rick Wine (Marcolin had quit to join CANDLEMASS), bassist Tom Mitchell and drummer Peter Svensson. After recording the album Svensson left for OVERHEAT and made way for new drummer Johan Norell.
This record was later re-released in Germany as 'Black Magic', formatted with different versions of songs and extra tracks.

Albums:
SWEDISH METAL, Metal Shock MCI 111 (1982)
State Of Shock / Don't Stop Heavy Guitar / Heavy Sound / Lost In Time / Stranger From The Dark
MERCY, Fingerprint FINGLP 008 (1984)
Heavy Metal Warriors / Dirty Love / Metal Mania / Tyrant / Master Of Disaster / Spanish Eyes / Zombie
WITCHBURNER, Fingerprint FINGLP013 (1984)
KINGDOOM, Mercy MCY112 (1988)
Death's Company / Tribulation / 1953-1988 / Black Magic / Evil Prepares / Memory / Heartbreak In Hell / Sorrows / Darkness
BLACK MAGIC, Imtrat (1989)
Death's Company / Tribulation / 1953-1988 / Black Magic / Evil Prepares / Memory / Heartbreak In Hell / Sorrows / Darkness / Mercy / Black Dead

MERCY RULE (USA)
Line-Up: Aaron Byrnes (vocals / guitar),

George Favazza (guitar), Bruce Tordrup (bass), Rich Favazza (drums)

Albums:
OVERRULED, R.E.X. 000-138-0893 (1989)
You Lied To Me / Cecilia / Real Love / Lonely Heart / Don't Cha Know / Black And White / Prodigal / If Only You Knew / There's A Love / Stand Up On The Rock

MERENDINE ATOMICHE (ITALY)
Line-Up: Luca Zandarin (vocals), David Bisson (guitar), Luca Securo (guitar), David Bianchi (bass), Luca Cerardi (drums)

Padova's MERENDINE ATOMICHE operate in old school Bay Area Thrash Metal territory. The group was forged in February of 1995 by drummer Luca Cerardi and vocalist Luca Zandarin. To stem an ever flowing tide of line-up changes the band drafted Cerardi's 13 year old sister Giulia on guitar! At this stage the group opted to become a METALLICA tribute band, enlisting a second guitarist David Bisson in May of 1998. A demo, naturally titled 'Tribute To Metallica', followed as did live shows opening for WHITE SKULL. David Bianchi would then be next in line for MERENDINE ATOMICHE membership, taking over the bass position in October of 1999. The group would tour Italy still performing METALLICA covers but then would cut the mini-album 'The Holy Metal' for No Brain Records comprising originals. During 2000 the group put in over 100 gigs and in August of 2001 also participated in a tour of Canada.
Rhythm guitarist Luca Securo would augment the band during October of 2001. MERENDINE ATOMICHE signed to the French Deadsun label, recording a 2002 album 'Walk Across Fire' at the famous Sunlight Studios in Sweden with Tomas Skogsberg manning production. Special guests on the album were projected to be Anders Lundemark of KONKHRA and Jeff Waters from ANNIHILATOR.

Albums:
THE HOLY METAL, No Brain NBR013 (2000)
War Or Peace / Holy Metal / The Truth / The Guardian / Mental Agony

MERSINARY (Nevada, USA)
Line-Up: Ice (vocals), Shawn Sherman (guitar), Eric Thompson (guitar), Steve Bray (bass), Dave Schiller (drums)

Singles/EPs:
Choose Death, Nomicon (1987)

Albums:

CHOOSE DEATH, Iron Works (1987)
Hunt You Down / Torn Apart / Medals / The
Pendulum / R.I.P. (Rest In Pieces) / Tear
Down The Walls
DEAD IS DEAD, Iron Works (1988)
The Pendulum / Tear Down The Walls / Hunt
You Down / Torn Apart / Medals / Dead Is
Dead / War Is Hell / Front Page / Shadowlord

MESHUGGAH (SWEDEN)

Line-Up: Jens Kidman (vocals), Fredric
Thordendal (guitar), Peter Nordin (bass),
Nicolas Lundgren (drums)

An experimental Thrash band boasting
guitarists that both employ seven string
guitars. Named after the Yiddish term for
'Crazy', MESHUGGAH formed in Umea
during 1987 as a trio of guitarist Fredrik
Thordendal (ex-bassist for MEMORANDUM),
bassist Peter Nordin and vocalist / guitarist
Jens Kidman. The band released a six song
demo EP 'Psykisk Testbild' in 1989.
Throughout their career MESHUGGAH have
established a reputation for adventurism and
non conformity in their approach to the Metal
genre.
Quite oddly, the quartet has often suffered
quite a few delays to their schedule thanks to
a catalogue of injuries to band members.
Guitarist Fredrik Thorendahl, a carpenter by
trade, has cut the top off a finger and
drummer Tomas Haake trapped his hand in a
lathe machine.
When MESHUGGAH toured Europe in 1995
supporting American outfit MACHINE HEAD
guitarist Mårten Hagstrom actually stepped in
for the headliner's guitarist Rob Flynn after
the American had suffered a hand injury. The
roles would be reversed when
MESHUGGAH, having lost their bassist,
opted to resume action as a quartet with
Thordendal playing bass - including lead
solos - through his guitar rig. Other gigs on
the tour just had two guitars with Mårten
playing through a pitch shifter shifted one
octave down.
In 1993 Thordendal appeared on the XXX
ATOMIC TOEJAM record 'A Gathering Of The
Tribes For The First/Last Human Be-In'.
It should be noted that the 1995 EP
'Selfcaged', although released by Nuclear
Blast in both Europe and America, sees a
completely different track listing for each
territory. The same year Thordendal would
donate a guitar solo to the BLENDER release
'Back To Planet Softcore'. The guitarist would
also figure on three tracks on the 1996
MATS/MORGEN album.
More recently, Fredric Thorendahl assembled
a side project with his former

MEMORANDUM colleague Petter Marklund
titled FREDRIK THORENDAHL'S MUSICAL
DEFECTS, recording an album in 1997.
MESHUGGAH's own 1997 release, the mini-
album 'The True Human Design', would
witness a remix of 'Future Breed Machine'
featuring CLAWFINGER's Jocke Skog.
The 1998 outing 'Chaosphere' would see a
MESHUGGAH line-up of vocalist Jens
Kidman, guitarists Fredric Thordendal and
Mårten Hagström, bass player Gustaf Hielm
and drummer Tomas Haake. Nicolas
Lundgren was to replace Haake as the band
toured America in 1999 supporting SLAYER.
The 2001 release 'Rare Trax' was compiled in
order to put the band's 1989 demo onto CD
format for the first time. Also included were
later demos and both studio and live video
footage.
MESHUGGAH received an enviable
opportunity in September of 2001 invited to
open for the September U.S. tour leg of
platinum artist TOOL.

Singles/EPs:

Cadaverous Mastication / Sovereigns
Morbidity / The Depth Of Nature, Garageland
BF 634 (1989)
Humiltitive / Sickening / Ritual / Gods Of
Rapture / Aztec Two-Step, Nuclear Blast
NB102-2 (1994) ('None' EP)
Selfcaged / Vanished / Suffer In Truth /
Inside What's Within Behind, Nuclear Blast
(1995)

Albums:

CONTRADICTIONS COLLAPSE, Nuclear
Blast NB049 (1991)
Paralyzing Ignorance / Erroneous
Manipulation / Abnegating Necessity /
Internal Evidence / Qualms Of Reality / We'll
Never See The Day / Greed / Choirs Of
Devastation / Cadaverous Mastication
DESTROY ERASE IMPROVE, Nuclear Blast
NB121 (1995)
Future Breed Machine / Beneath / Soul Burn
/ Transfixion / Vanished / Acrid Placidity /
Inside What's Within Behind / Terminal
Illusions / Suffer In Truth / Sublevels
THE TRUE HUMAN DESIGN, Nuclear Blast
NB 268-2 MCD (1997)
Sane / Future Breed Machine (Live) / Future
Breed Machine (Mayhem version) / Futile
Bread Machine (campfire version) / Quant's
Quantastical Quantasm (Ambient Techno by
Quant of DOT) / Friend's Breaking and
Entering (Ambient Techno by Friend of DOT)
/ Terminal Illusions (Video)
CHAOSPHERE, Nuclear Blast NB 3662
(1998)
Concatenation / New Millennium Cyanide

Christ / Corridor of Chameleons / Neurotica / The Mouth Licking What You've Bled / Sane / The Exquisite Machinery of Torture / Elastic
RARE TRAX, Nuclear Blast (2001)
War / Cadaverous Mastication / Sovereigns Morbidity / Debt Of Nature / By Emptyness Abducted / Don't Speak / Abnegating Cecity (1990 demo) / Internal Evidence (1990 demo) / Concatenation (remix) / Ayahuasca Experience / New Millennium Cyanide Christ (Video) / Elastic (Video - Live)

MESSIAH (SWITZERLAND)
Line-Up: Andy Kaina (vocals), R.B. Brogi (guitar), Patrick Hersche (bass),

Founded in 1984 by guitarist R. B. Brogi, MESSIAH built up impressive sales of their first two albums. 'Extreme Cold Weather' sold in excess of 12,000 units alone, prompting a deal with Noise Records.
MESSIAH's line-up changed in 1993 with the departure of vocalist Andy Kaina and bassist Patrick Hersche. The bass position was filled by Oliver Koll and a new vocalist was found in THERION man Christofer Johnsson.
Hersche subsequently joined AMON and then later Gothic Metal band SUCCUBUS.

Singles/EPs:
Birth Of A Second Individual /
Psychomorphia / Right For Unright / M.A.N.I.A.C., Noise N0244-3 (1994)
('Psychomorphia' EP)
The Ballad Of Jesus, Noise NO244-3 (1994)

Albums:
HYMN TO ABRAMELIN, Chainsaw Murder (1986)
Hymn To Abramelin / Messiah / Anarchus / Space Invaders / Thrashing Madness / Future Aggressor / Empire Of The Damned / Total Maniac / The Dentist
EXTREME COLD WEATHER, Chainsaw Murder 004 (1988)
Extreme Cold Weather / Enjoy Yourself / Johannes Paul Der Letzte (Dedicated In Hate To Pope John Paul II) / Mother Theresa (Dedicated In Love To Mother Theresa) / Hyper Bores / Radezky March: We Hate To Be In The Army Now / Nero / Hymn To Abramelin (Live) / Messiah (Live) / Space Invaders (Live) / Thrashing Madness (Live) / Golden Dawn (Live) / The Last Inferno (Live) / Resurrection (Live) / Ole Perversus (Live)
CHOIR OF HORRORS, Noise NO183-2 (1991)
Choir Of Horrors / Akasha Chronicle / Weeping Willows / Lycantropus Erectus / Münchhausen Syndrom / Cautio Criminalis / Northern Commands / Weena
ROTTEN PERISH, Noise CD084 04552 (1992)
Prelude: Act Of Fate / For Those Who Will Fail / Living With A Confidence / Raped Bodies / Lines Of Thought Of A Convicted Man / Conviction / Condemned Cell / Dreams Of Eschaton / Anorexia Nervosa / Deformed Creatures / Alzheimer's Disease / Ascension Of A Divine Ordinance
UNDERGROUND, Noise NO244-2 (1994)
Battle In The Ancient North / Revelation Of Fire / Underfround / Epitaph / The Way Of The Strong / Living In A Lie / Screams Of Frustration / The Ballad Of Jesus / Dark Lust / One Thousand Pallid Deaths / The End

MESSIAH FORCE (CANADA)

Line-Up: Lynn Renaud (vocals), Bastien Deschenes (guitar), Jean Tremblay (guitar), Eric Parise (bass), Jean-Francois Boucher (drums)

MESSIAH FORCE's solitary album, which saw keyboard contributions from Claude Champagne, was issued in America in 1989 on U.S. Metal Records with new cover artwork.

Singles/EPs:
The Sequel, Bold Reprieve 7 BRM021 (1988)

Albums:
THE LAST DAY, Haissem (1988)
The Sequel / Call From The Night / Watch Out / White Night / Spirit Killer / Silent Tyrant / Hero's Saga / The Last Day / The Third One

MESSIAH PROPHET (USA)

Line-Up: Charlie Clark (vocals), Brian Ncarry (guitar), Andy Strauss (guitar), Joe Shirk (bass), David Thunder (drums)

RAMAGE guitarists Bill Grabowski and Alexander Paul guest on the album.

Albums:
MASTER OF THE METAL, Pure Metal SPCN7900600485 (1986)
Hit And Run / Master Of The Metal / For Whom The Bell Tolls (Part 23) / Fear No Evil / Heavy Metal Thunder / The Friend / Battle Cry / Voice That's Calling

METAL CHURCH (Seattle, WA, USA)

Line Up: David Wayne (vocals), Craig Wells (guitar), Kurdt Vanderhoof (guitar), Duke Erikson (bass), Kirk Arrington (drums)

METAL CHURCH rank as one of the true founders of the early '80s American Thrash Metal scene. Guitarist Kurdt Vanderhoof created the band upon his departure from Punk act THE LEWD in 1981. As THE LEWD evolved into more of a Hardcore Thrash act Vanderhoof found himself more and more interested in the Metal scene. During a 1980 gig LEVIATHAN members guitarist Rick Condran and Aaron Zimpel got into a conversation with Vanderhoof and discussed the idea of an 'ultimate' Metal band. As Vanderhoof, Condran, bassist Steve Haat and drummer Aron Winer created ANVIL CHORUS - THE CHURCH OF METAL, the remnants of LEVIATHAN, Zimpel, bassist Bill Skinner and drummer Kenny Feragen

became Progressive Rock trio VIENNA.
The first Vanderhoof all instrumental demo comprised the LEVIATHAN track 'Red Skies', 'Heads Will Roll' and 'Merciless Onslaught'. The formative band went through numerous drummers (they even invited a pre-METALLICA Lars Ulrich to join).
A pair of other local musicians, guitarists Thaen Rasmussen (ex-VY-KING) and Doug Piercy (ex-COBRA / DELTA) liked the name ANVIL CHORUS so much they took it for themselves. They did however offer acknowledgement with the homage to their inspiration with the track 'Bow To The Church Of Metal'. Vanderhoof trimmed the name of his act down to simply METAL CHURCH.
SINISTER SAVAGE man Billy McKay fronted METAL CHURCH for a brief spell prior to founding GRIFFIN. Singer Ed Bull was invited to join the band but Condran objected. When the guitarist quit METAL CHURCH Bull was on the mike stand the very next day. With the abandonment of VIENNA Zimpel also joined forgoing his normal frontman position to become METAL CHURCH's drummer. With this line up METAL CHURCH cut their second demo. This four track affair included a rework of 'Heads Will Roll' titled 'Put The Chains On', an ANVIL CHORUS number 'Arab Nations', 'Wake Up And Die' and 'The Trap Is Set'. The latter track displayed the enmity between Bull and Condran as the singer's chorus of "Die Ricky, Die!" amply illustrates!
However, despite intensive tape trading, this early incarnation of METAL CHURCH folded, with Haat going on to a temporary stint with GRIFFIN then glamsters JETBOY. Bull founded CONTROL with guitarists Dino Scarposi and Bill Tuder. A later version of CONTROL featured another ex-ANVIL CHORUS man guitarist Doug Piercy, later of HEATHEN. ZImpel meantime joined the ranks of ANVIL CHORUS. Vanderhoof journeyed back to Seattle to create SCHRAPNEL. In 1983 this act had evolved into METAL CHURCH with a line-up of Vanderhoof, vocalist David Wayne, guitarist Craig Wells, bassist Duke Erikson and drummer Kirk Arrington. An earlier SCHRAPNEL vocalist Mike Murphy opened up the vacancy for Wayne by bailing out to join ROGUES GALLERY.
In 1984, METAL CHURCH signed to the Seattle based Ground Zero label and released the critically acclaimed, self-titled debut the same year. The band had previously contributed the track 'Deathwish' to the label's 'Northwest Metalfest' compilation album.
The debut album was to be re-issued by Elektra in 1985 following the signing of a major deal that would propel the group to the

forefront of the mid '80s Thrash Metal boom.

In 1986, METAL CHURCH released their second album, 'The Dark', an album that quickly warranted it's status as one of the premier Metal release of the '80s and probably the band's finest moment to date. However, in a band bust up Wayne was ejected, the frontman forming working with ex-LIZZY BORDEN guitarist Gene Allen, then REVEREND and later joining INTRINSIC. The singer also had a brief union with HEATHEN.

1988's 'Deadly Blessing' album saw METAL CHURCH now fronted by ex-HERETIC singer Mike Howe and with former BLIND ILLUSION man James Marshall augmenting Wells on guitar.

Vanderhoof's dislike of touring prompted his opting out. However, Vanderhoof was to remain a central character within METAL CHURCH as a songwriter and conspirator and regained his taste for playing by forming HALL AFLAME and releasing an album through IRS.

Initially the band drafted in guitarist Mark Baker to fulfill Vanderhoof's role for touring in America but added Marshall on a full time basis.

Howe had been suggested to the band by Vanderhoof, the guitarist having produced the debut HERETIC album.

In 1992 Howe got his name onto the second BOOTSAUCE album 'Bull' guesting on the track 'Touching Cloth'. Marshall meantime boosted the band's profile in an unusual manner when he was drafted into METALLICA on a temporary basis. Hetfield had burnt his hand and deputised his guitar duties to Marshall for much of their American tour. This was the second time Marshall had depped for Hetfield, the first was in 1987 when the frontman had broken his wrist skateboarding.

Following 1994's 'Hanging In The Balance', released on JOAN JETT's Blackheart label, METAL CHURCH fizzled out.

During 1997, Vanderhoof made his recording comeback in the modestly titled VANDERHOOF, a band that also included old METAL CHURCH colleague Kirk Arrington. Although the VANDERHOOF album surprised many with its undoubted quality under pressure from their German record label the classic 'The Dark' era METAL CHURCH reunited in mid 1998. The band heralded their return with probably their most over the top release to date with a live album culled from tapes recorded in the mid 1980s.

The band bounced back with a fresh studio album 'Masterpeace' (somewhat confusingly released with the track titles in completely the wrong order) touring Europe on a double

package with THUNDERHEAD.

By 2000 METAL CHURCH had a new rhythm section of bassist Brian Lake and drummer Jeff Wade, both members of VANDERHOOF. The story took a further twist when it emerged that Wayne had set up a fresh act titled DAVID WAYNE'S METAL CHURCH! Joining him were ex-WARRIOR guitarist Joe Floyd, former JOINT FORCES, GEEZER and THUNDERHEAD guitarist Jimi Bell and drummer B.J. Zampa, a veteran of YNGWIE MALMSTEEN, MVP, TONY MACALPINE and THUNDERHEAD. Bell also operates the covers band TATTERED TRAMPS.

Singles/EPs:

Fake Healer, Elektra PRO CD 8051 (1989) (USA promotion)

Watch The Children Pray, Elektra (1989) (USA promotion)

Badlands, Elektra (1989) (USA promotion)

Albums:

METAL CHURCH, Ground Zero (1984)
Beyond The Black / Metal Church / Merciless Onslaught / Gods Of Wrath / Hitman / In The Blood / (My Favorite) Nightmare / Battalions / Highway Star

THE DARK, Elektra 9 60493-2 (1986) **92 USA**
Ton Of Bricks / Start The Fire / Method To Your Madness / Watch The Children Pray / The Dark / Psycho / Line Of Death / Burial At Sea / Western Alliance

BLESSING IN DISGUISE, Elektra K 96087-2 (1989) **75 USA**
Fake Healer / Rest In Pieces / Of Unsound Mind / Anthem To The Estranged / Badlands / Spell Can't Be Broken / It's A Secret / Cannot Tell A Lie / Powers That Be

THE HUMAN FACTOR, Epic 4678162 (1991)
Human Factor / Date With Poverty / Final Word / In Mourning / In Harm's Way / In Due Time / Agent Green / Flee From Reality / Betrayed / Fight Song

HANGING IN THE BALANCE, Blackheart BH1001 (1994)
Gods Of Second Chance / Losers In The Game / Hypnotized / No Friend Of Mine / Waiting For A Saviour / Conductor / Little Boy / Down By The River / End Of The Age / Lovers And Madmen / A Subtle War

LIVE, SPV 085-18562 CD (1998)
Ton Of Bricks / Hitman / Start The Fire / Gods Of Wrath / The Dark / Psycho / Watch The Children Pray / Beyond The Black / Metal Church / Highway Star

MASTERPEACE, SPV 085-18702 CD (1999)
Sleeps With Thunder / Falldown / Into Dust /

Kiss For The Dead / Lb Of Cure / Faster Than Life / Masterpeace / All Your Sorrows / They Signed In Blood / Toys In The Attic / Sand Kings

METAL DUCK (UK)
Line-Up: Andy Parker Tortoise Gore (vocals), Fozzy Daniels Tarbuck Monkhouse Disneyland (guitar), Keith Tractor Safari 25 Minutes Robot (bass), Glam Dyno Rod Piella (drums)

A bizarre, yet short-lived Liverpool based humourus Thrash band, METAL DUCK were quickly eclipsed by LAWNMOWER DETH and ACID REIGN.
Having started life in 1985 as RAMPANT DUCK before adopting the METAL DUCK title and releasing 'Quack Core' demo in 1987. The group issued another demo with vocalist Andy (ex-ELECTRO HIPPIES) in 1988 before sharing a split LP on the Leicester based RKT label with LAWNMOWER DETH, featuring the line-up of: Dave (drums / vocals), Hutti (vocals), Fozzy (guitar / vocals) and Keith (bass / vocals)
A second, full album emerged in 1990 before the group went tail up.

Albums:
QUACK EM ALL, RKT CMO 192 (1989)
(Split LP with LAWNMOWER DETH)
Destruction Song / Stepping Stone To Hell / Pek-Yr-Ass / Bombay Duck / NxDxQxC / Cheese Puff Death Squad / March Of The Metal Ducks To The Ponds Of Hell / Rod, Jane & Freddys Total Noise Annihilation / Der, Der, Der / Ooerr I've Got A Sore Throat
AUTO DUCKO DESTRUCTO MONDO RKT CDMO 196 (1990)
Gore Literal / Duckula Assault / Drunk And A Flirt / Smell Of Sex / To Kill Again / Gate Of Asgard / Twilight Zone / Rod, Jane And Freddy (Part 2) / Mean, Green And Pink / Well Fu(n)ked Up / In Death / Apollyon Communiqué

METALLICA (Los Angeles, CA, USA)
Line-Up: James Hetfield (vocals / guitar), Kirk Hammett (guitar), Jason Newsted (bass), Lars Ulrich (drums)

Essentially the brainchild of Danish emigreé Lars Ulrich (born December 26, 1965), a self-confessed New Wave of British Heavy Metal fan. Ulrich gave up a potential career as a tennis pro in order to beat the living daylights out of the drums, METALLICA have unarguably been the leading lights of the Thrash Metal scene since their inception in the early '80s.

Although considered to be a San Francisco based group, the darlings of the Bay Area scene, METALLICA were actually formed by Ulrich in Los Angeles.
However, whilst Ulrich gets much of the credit for the rise of METALLICA, the band's roots essentially began the day one Ron McGoveney and the AEROSMITH obsessed James Hetfield (born August 3, 1963) had first met at Los Angeles East Middle School in 1977.
Hetfield's first act in 1979 was titled OBSESSION and covered classic Rock acts such as UFO (hence the band title), BLACK SABBATH and LED ZEPPELIN. OBSESSION comprised Hetfield on vocals and guitar, Jim Arnold on lead guitar, bassist Ron Valoz and drummer Rick Valoz. Hetfield's class mate Ron McGoveney roadied for the band. By 1980 Hetfield and Arnold had teamed up with Jim's brother Chris on drums to form the RUSH covers band SYRINX. This trio soon folded and downtime was filled by Hetfield and McGoveney jamming with drummer Dave Marrs.
The duo's next attempt was a more serious venture titled PHANTOM LORD with guitarist Hugh Tanner. This act evolved into LEATHER CHARM consisting of Hetfield on vocals, Troy James on guitar, McGoveney on bass and drummer Jim Mulligan. LEATHER CHARM began writing their own material and 'Hit The Lights' was borne out of these sessions. However, the band were still playing covers including the favourite 'Hollywood Teaze' by GIRL and IRON MAIDEN tracks.
Two other LEATHER CHARM songs 'Let's Go Rock n' Roll' and 'Handsome Ransom' would later be fused to become 'No Remorse'.
With the band's music beginning to adopt a far heavier stance parting of the ways with Jim Mulligan occurred and, responding to an add placed in the Los Angeles paper 'Recycler', LEATHER CHARM invited would-be drummer Lars Ulrich down to meet them. However, they quickly sent him away with a flea in his ear, unimpressed with this big-mouthed little Danish kid with an obsession for the New Wave of British Heavy Metal.
With his tail firmly between his legs, Ulrich returned to Europe where he would spend a few months following the likes of DIAMOND HEAD and MOTÖRHEAD's Lemmy around before flying back to Los Angeles intent on finally putting the band of his dreams together.
Having been somehow promised a spot on fanzine writer Brian Slagel's forthcoming compilation album 'Metal Massacre' on the newly formed Metal Blade Records (even though Ulrich didn't have a band at the time!), Ulrich used this to his advantage in gaining

favour with LEATHER CHARM.

Despite not being a particularly good drummer at the time, Ulrich convinced Hetfield & McGovney to recruit him to join him in this endeavour, eventually leading to the formation of METALLICA. This band title winning out over REDVETTE and BLITZER! Guitarist Lloyd Grant was drafted after replying to an advert.

It was this incarnation that featured on the first 'Metal Massacre' compilation album, eventually released on June 14 1982. Unfortunately, the group was credited as METTALICA on the first pressing. Both McGovney and Grant's names were also misspelled as 'Mcgouney' and 'Llyod' respectively. However, the album put together a whole host of names that would become greater forces in the future such as RATT, STEELER, BITCH, MALICE, AVATAR (SAVATAGE) and CIRITH UNGOL.

Grant's tenure with the group was cut short because, according to the man who replaced him, ex-PANIC guitarist Dave Mustaine, Lars Ulrich allegedly did not want a black musician in the group. This being one of the reasons as to why 'Hit The Lights' was re-recorded for the second pressing of the 'Metal Massacre' compilation album with Mustaine in the band. This version not only saw Grant's name

missing from the band line-up but featured the correct spelling of the band name. Needless to say, Mustaine's version of events would later be vigorously denied.

Grant was, however, to reappear in the mid '80s with a new act titled DEF CON contributing the track 'Red Light' to a 1986 compilation album.

Hetfield was still wary of his vocal talents so the band pulled in RUTHLESS vocalist Sammy Dijon although the union was brief and no gigs were performed with this line-up. METALLICA then got to work recording their first ever demo which featured the LEATHER CHARM track 'Hit The Lights', 'Killing Time' (originally by Irish band SWEET SAVAGE) and 'Let It Loose' by British band SAVAGE.

The band then gained the valuable support slot to SAXON in San Francisco. The Barnsley big teasers were playing two shows back to back and originally MÖTLEY CRÜE were scheduled to play. However, MÖTLEY CRÜE's status had exceeded the support position and they suggested METALLICA fill the slot instead with RATT opening up the other night.

Unfortunately METALLICA did not get to meet their heroes SAXON as their dressing room was closed to visitors harbouring as it did an inconsolable OZZY OSBOURNE still reeling

270

from the death of Randy Rhoads.

With Hetfield also assuming guitar duties, METALLICA cut the four track 'Power Metal' demo (comprising 'Hit The Lights', 'Mechanix', 'Jump In The Fire' and 'Motorbreath') before the decided to secure the services of a lead vocalist who could do a better job of fronting the group than Hetfield.

METALLICA performed as a five piece with vocalist Jeff Warner. The gig was apparently such a disaster the singer was immediately sacked. METALLICA also enlisted another guitarist Damien C. Phillips (real name Brad Parker) for a gig at the Concert Factory in Costa Mesa. The experience was so bad he was fired on the spot. Undaunted Parker created ODIN.

The band at first thought about the possibilities of requesting the services of ex-TYGERS OF PAN TANG vocalist Jess Cox, but by the time they had seen the singer's new look they rapidly changed their minds!

To compound their frustration, the one vocalist actually asked to fill the post, John Bush of ARMORED SAINT (and later ANTHRAX), turned the request down.

The Summer months of 1982 gave METALLICA another taste of recording, as Rocshire Records persuaded the band to go into the studio to record a proposed EP. However the label were shocked to discover the finished tapes were Metal and not Punk and shelved the deal. The resulting tapes were soon to surface on the underground tape trading scene as the 'No Life 'Til Leather' demo.

The demo comprised several tracks that would become legendary in 'Hit The Lights', 'The Mechanix', 'Motorbreath', 'Seek & Destroy', 'Metal Militia', 'Jump In The Fire' and 'Phantom Lord'.

By now, METALLICA, not wishing to be associated with the rising Los Angeles scene awash with bands like MÖTLEY CRÜE, relocated to San Francisco. The group had been garnering the most favour in 'Frisco, not least because of the support offered on a thriving underground level by the influential 'Metal Militia' fanzine run by Quintana. METALLICA's first gig in the city was on the same billing as BITCH filling in for a non appearance by CIRITH UNGOL.

However, before long McGovney departed. McGovney resurfaced in 1986 as part of PHANTASM, the act assembled by ex-HIRAX frontman Katon De Pena.

METALLICA added former TRAUMA bassist Cliff Burton (born February 10, 1962) in McGovney's place during December 1982 and METALLICA officially became residents of San Francisco after leaving Los Angeles on February 12, 1983.

JAMES HETFIELD of METALLICA
Photo : Andy Phillips

METALLICA were soon embroiled in discussions with Firesign Records, Shrapnel and Metal Blade.

In fact, way back when Slagel had first begun his 'Metal Massacre' series, the Metal Blade boss could well have just recorded a full album, but the funds just were not available to the company at the time and so the chance went begging.

Eventually the act were persuaded to contact the New Jersey based Megaforce Records, a label run by ANTHRAX manager and 'Rock n' Roll Heaven' record store owner Johnny Zazula.

METALLICA were by now firmly defining their unique sound. Rehearsals would see the band blasting through tracks by NWoBHM acts such as DIAMOND HEAD, BLITZKRIEG and SAVAGE. Oddly the latter act would be almost deleted from METALLICA's history with only a bootleg single bearing testament to the influence of the Mansfield Metal act.

However, after a show with VENOM and VANDENBERG in New York Mustaine was unceremoniously fired after a huge bust-up with Hetfield left Mustaine bruised, bloodied and out of a job. A replacement was swiftly found, as METALLICA's sound engineer also happened to manage the burgeoning Bay Area outfit EXODUS. The approach to EXODUS six stringer Kirk Hammett (born

271

CLIFF BURTON of METALLICA
Photo : Matt Sampson

November 18, 1962) was made and he was duly enrolled, virtually catching the next plane out of San Francisco to begin work on the debut METALLICA album. Mustaine meanwhile busied himself with creating his new act titled MEGADETH.

Mustaine completed one further gig with the band supporting THE RODS before being sent packing.

The 'Kill 'Em All' album was recorded in Rochester, New York and the album was released on Zazula's newly established Megaforce label, with distribution from the Relativity concern. The album was duly licensed to ex-Secret Records boss Martin Hooker's new Music For Nations company for release in Europe.

Amusingly, the record had been envisioned to be titled 'Metal Up Your Ass' and boasting a cover depicting an arm emerging from the depths of a toilet bowl menacingly wielding a rather large knife. Relativity persuaded the band that this idea wasn't exactly a good choice. Mind you, the eventual choice of 'Kill 'Em All' and accompanying cover were no more subtle!

T-shirts featuring a depiction of the album's original title and cover art would, however, be produced some while later.

In January 1984 Music For Nations issued 'Jump In The Fire' as a 12" single, backing it with supposedly live versions of 'Seek And Destroy' and 'Phantom Lord'. Both these tracks were actually re-recorded in the studio, MFN dubbing on applause from a London Marquee Club performance by Prog Rock band TWELFTH NIGHT.

The group set out on tour to support the 'Kill 'Em All' album, eventually making it over to Britain.

Originally the group had been booked to play through Europe between March 21st to April 3rd on a three band bill with Canadian power trio EXCITER and fellow American outfit THE RODS. Unfortunately, ticket sales were mysteriously poor and the tour scrapped.

However, the group nevertheless arrived in London and put in two headlining stints at the Marquee Club during late March as well as an earlier appearance at the 'Aardschok Festival' in Holland for good measure whilst on a tour of the continent with VENOM.

Following the shows, METALLICA moved up to Ulrich's native Denmark to begin work on their second album with producer Flemming Rasmussen, a man who had engineered on RAINBOW's 'Difficult To Cure' album in 1983. The band had specifically wanted to record in Europe and had apparently been impressed with Rasmussen's work on the RAINBOW album.

The new METALLICA album, titled 'Ride The Lightning', was recorded in a month and a half at Sweet Silence Studios in Copenhagen. Rasmussen recalled in a later magazine interview that the band were earnestly shopping for a major deal whilst in the throes of recording. At one point it looked highly likely that Bronze Records would sign the group until the label insisted that the band should scrap what they were doing and re-record the album in Britain. METALLICA, needless to say, refused.

'Ride The Lightning' was released in July 1984. Without any compromise in METALLICA's trademark ferocity the songs also were more accessible than previous efforts and was the first real step in infusing METALLICA's sound into the mainstream Rock audience. The accompanying single 'Creeping Death' was bolstered with two caustic cover versions of BLITZKRIEG's 'Blitzkrieg' and DIAMOND HEAD's 'Am I Evil'. Such was the impression made by these songs they would stay lodged in the band's live set for many years.

METALLICA's 1984 European tour was dealt a hammer blow that nearly curtailed the event. Whilst waiting for shipment, $40,000 of the band's equipment was stolen in Boston necessitating hasty negotiations to hire replacement gear.

With the band's burgeoning cult following rapidly spilling over into mainstream success major label Elektra were quick to buy out the Megaforce contract. This despite Megaforce having already shipped albums to the American stores and selling sufficient quantity to crack the Billboard top 200.

Elektra pulled out all the stops in promoting 'Ride The Lightning' maintaining sales levels as it was revealed that not only had METALLICA severed connections with Megaforce Records but also Johnny Z as manager. From now on the experienced Q Prime organisation would handle their affairs.

Mustaine was back in the ring in 1985 launching his debut album for MEGADETH. The album included the track 'Mechanix', a revised version of which appeared on METALLICA's debut as 'The Four Horsemen'.

During August 1985 Thrash Metal arrived in Donington thanks to METALLICA's inaugural appearance at the infamous 'Monsters Of Rock' festival held at the Donington Park racing circuit in Leicestershire. Playing a creditable fourth on a bill above Brit Pomp Rock outfit MAGNUM and San Diego Glamsters RATT and just below BON JOVI, MARILLION and a headlining ZZ TOP, METALLICA played a set lasting around 55 minutes and certainly impressed the gathered clans.

1985 was topped off with a crushingly heavy

New Year's Eve gig in San Francisco. Joining METALLICA on the bill were EXODUS, METAL CHURCH and, one suspects somewhat awkwardly, MEGADETH.

In downtime Hetfield and Burton assembled the kickabout band SPASTIC CHILDREN. With Hetfield on drums SPASTIC CHILDREN undertook club gigs with vocalist Fred Cotton and guitarist Jack McDaniel.

METALLICA had originally planned to record their third album in America retaining Flemming Rasmussen's services. However, a fruitless search for the perfect environment in Los Angeles led to the band returning to Sweet Silence in Copenhagen.

Hetfield dampened the momentum by breaking his wrist skateboarding. Undeterred the band enlisted METAL CHURCH man James Marshall and Hetfield's guitar tech to fill in on rhythm guitar while the bones healed. The resulting 'Master Of Puppets' album, released in March, proved to be a huge stride forward.

Despite the undoubted impact of 'Master Of Puppets' the glory was marred by Dave Mustaine putting in a claim that the song 'Leper Messiah' was in fact a reworked version of a cut titled 'The Hills Ran Red'. METALLICA flatly refuted the suggestion, admitting the song was based on an old riff but not one that Mustaine delivered. The American teen Metal press lapped it up offering regular METALLICA vs. MEGADETH articles.

'Master Of Puppets' was to hit the Gold mark in America during 1986, becoming the first Thrash era band to break the Billboard top 100, surely aided by their exposure out on the road in America opening for OZZY OSBOURNE.

Sadly, it came with a price, the tragic death of Cliff Burton in a road crash on the morning of Saturday, September 27 1986. Engaged on a headlining European tour supported by ANTHRAX, en route from Stockholm to Copenhagen, METALLICA's tour bus skidded off an icy road near the Swedish town of Ljungby, throwing the bassist out of the window near his bunk and tipped over on top of him, killing him instantly.

METALLICA actually received encouragement from Burton's parents to press on in the aftermath of the accident. Auditions were held with ARMORED SAINT's Joey Vera, LÄÄZ ROCKIT's Willy Lange, WATCHTOWER man Doug Keyser and Les Claypool. Eventually recruited was the Phoenix, Arizona based FLOTSAM AND JETSAM man Jason Newsted (born March 4, 1963) to fill the void left by Cliff's death. The band committing themselves to a previously scheduled Japanese tour, which opened on

November 12, a little over a month since the accident.

METALLICA wound up their European tour in Europe during January of 1987 before completing Scandinavian dates.

March proved to be trying for Hetfield as he broke his arm skate boarding. The guitarist vowed to give the sport up.

METALLICA went back into the studio to cut the 'Garage Days Revisted' EP. A novel homage to their inspirations and influences it fitted in well with the METALLICA ethos. Included were songs from DIAMOND HEAD, HOLOCAUST, BUDGIE and THE MISFITS. The Japanese version also had KILLING JOKE's 'The Wait'. Other tracks from these sessions BUDGIE's 'Breadfan' and DIAMOND HEAD's 'The Prince' would surface on subsequent single B sides.

The EP, a previously untested commercial move, was a solid success charting and lodging itself in the American charts for 8 weeks. 'Breadfan' in particular would dig its claws in as METALLICA opened up their live show with this old warhorse for many, many years to come.

In August 1987 METALLICA made a triumphant return to a rain sodden Castle Donington to appear third on a BON JOVI topped 'Monsters Of Rock' bill. METALLICA then joined the European leg of the festivals which were topped by DEEP PURPLE.

Newsted took time out in late 1987 to briefly reunite with his old act FLOTSAM AND JETSAM in Arizona when he performed an impromptu jam at a SACRED REICH show with his old band mates and SLAYER guitarist Kerry King.

METALLICA rounded off the year fittingly with the video 'Cliff 'Em All'.

Recording a successor to 'Master Of Puppets' began with GUNS N' ROSES studio man Mike Clink but within months longstanding ally Flemming Rasmussen had supplanted the big name producer and METALLICA started the album again from scratch.

Despite the problems in the studio METALLICA retained the fan awareness by clambering aboard the touring extravaganza that was the American 'Monsters Of Rock' roving package in 1988. Based upon the tried and tested British formula of the same name the American version, featuring a heavyweight package of VAN HALEN, SCORPIONS, METALLICA, DOKKEN and KINGDOM COME, it looked a winner but it was to eventually flounder due to high ticket prices. METALLICA themselves fared well even though the first month of the tour had them flying back to Bearsville, NY in a desperate race to finish mixing of the album that would become '...And Justice For All'.

JAMES HETFIELD of METALLICA
Photo : Matt Sampson

Newstead was to gain his first writing credit with the band for the lead track 'Blackened'.

The album was aired live secretly in Los Angeles as the band, dubbed, FRAYED ENDS, jammed out new material to a select few.

Upon the album's release METALLICA hit Europe starting with a show in Budapest, Hungary prior to a headlining American tour with strong support from QUEENSRYCHE.

February found the band invited to perform at the Grammy awards. METALLICA did not win but this inaugural foot in the door at the Grammys was a portent of what was to come. METALLICA completed their '...And Justice For All' world tour in South America during October 1989.

Together with 'Kerrang!' editor Geoff Barton, Lars compiled an album featuring some of his favourite New Wave of British Heavy Metal bands for the Vertigo label to celebrate the 10th anniversary of the movement.

In February of 1990 METALLICA returned to the Grammy awards once again. This time '...And Justice For All' won. A subsequent European tour beginning in May saw strong support from DIO prior to ensconcing themselves in the studio to begin the writing process for their next album.

The band picked up a further Grammy in February of 1991 for their take on QUEEN's 'Stone Cold Crazy'. By the start of the summer the Rock world was holding it's breath for the new album and when the simply titled 'Metallica' was launched it was apparent from the off that this was the record to propel METALLICA into the major league. Hitting the American number 1 position the album would doggedly retain its grip in the Billboard charts for a further staggering 85 weeks.

The first single culled from the album 'Enter Sandman' would be instantly hailed a classic and would quickly be recognised as one of the greatest songs of the genre.

In August METALLICA undertook the European 'Monsters Of Rock' festivals as special guests to AC/DC before an appearance in Moscow.

The band returned home to headline the San Francisco 'Day On The Green' festival before kicking off their 'Wherever I May Roam' would tour.

1992 was beckoned with METALLICA winning another in a long line of Grammy Awards. In April the band performed 'Stone Cold Crazy' at Wembley with QUEEN guitarist BRIAN MAY as part of the FREDDIE MERCURY tribute concert.

With both 'Nothing Else Matters' and 'Wherever I May Roam' continuing the band's presence in the charts METALLICA geared up for a strange pairing for an absolute leviathan American arena tour. METALLICA shared the headline slot with GUNS N' ROSES for a set of 'Monsters Of Rock' dates which many critics viewed as a complete mismatch. Support came from MOTÖRHEAD.

During these shows Hetfield was badly burned by a stage flare in Montreal. With their frontman unable to play guitar METALLICA drafted METAL CHURCH's John Marshall to fill in Hetfield's guitar parts to finish off the tour.

The 'Monsters Of Rock' extravaganza wound up in October but there was little respite as the band headed for Europe for further shows until the end of the year.

1993 rolled in with further awards accumulated at the American Music awards. The band were back on tour in March in the more far flung territories of Asia, Australia and South America before the 'Nowhere Else To Roam' dates in Europe. Some of these shows including MEGADETH as guests.

In November METALLICA launched their most ambitious release to date with the box set 'Live Shit: Binge & Purge'. Retailing at £75.00 the tin box included 3 live CDs and 3 live videos. Demand for METALLICA was so high these sets sold out almost immediately.

May 1994 had the road hungry METALLICA on the loose yet again. This time the shows were known collectively as the 'Live Shit' tour with support coming from DANZIG and CANDLEBOX. The band also appeared as one of the main attractions at the resurrection of the famous Woodstock festival during August before winding up the tour in Florida.

The winter months were spent writing for a new album. It would herald a radical new era for the band and test the loyalty of hardened Metal fans.

The bulk of 1995 found METALLICA in the studio working on a new album. Interim activities included a performance at the Castle Donington 'Monsters Of Rock' festival and a gig inside the Arctic circle with HOLE.

Newstead indulged in a further extra curricular project IR8 in 1995. Recorded at his home studio with ex-STEVE VAI / FRONTLINE ASSEMBLY man Devin Townshend and former EXODUS drummer Tom Hunting, tapes were laid down but the project got no further. Nevertheless these recordings made it onto the radio airwaves much to the chagrin of Hetfield and co.

With the impact of the 'Metallica' album still ringing in the industry's ears anticipation for 'Load' was high, so eager were fans for new material that the album shifted 680,000 copies in the first week of sale.

What devotees got with 'Load' though was a far cry from the METALLICA of yore. Band photographs issued for promotion shocked traditional metal fans to the core. Gone was the "none more black" dress code and de rigeour long hair as METALLICA now came across as a newly shorn set of people with a distinct identity crisis. Not only had Hammet taken to adopting a look more in keeping with a '70s pimp complete with batwing collared gaudy shirts and fur coats but Ulrich had taken to sporting eyeliner! With METALLICA on the surface aping U2's drag-popsters look fans who had religiously force fed themselves a diet of 'Metal Militia' and 'Whiplash' scratched their heads in amazement as Ulrich declared in an interview, albeit apparently tongue in cheek, "we're a Pop band". Newsted stayed out of the controversy while Hetfield, more and more acknowledged as the leader of the band, appeared to be more intent on hunting wild animals than involving himself in the press furore.

The music served to alienate some fans even more as the technical riffing of METALLICA's trademark sound had given way to a stripped down bluesey rock.

METALLICA also seemed to be pushing themselves out onto the margins as in various interviews little secret was made of their drug taking activities. Nonetheless METALLICA's status as bona fide rock giants was assured when the 'Load' American tour was announced as being the third biggest tour of the year for that territory grossing some $37 million dollars and only being surpassed by THE ROLLING STONES and U2.

'Load' was released in June and bolted straight to the American number 1 spot staying high in the charts for a tenacious 40 weeks. The band's touring plans also bore witness to their new approach as METALLICA headlined the touring 'Lollapalooza' festivals with support from SOUNDGARDEN and THE RAMONES. The band won another award at the MTV Video Music celebrations but were eager to get back out on the road again beginning their lengthy series of dates dubbed 'Poor Touring Me' in Europe during September.

The band's roguish intentions were still intact though in spite of their newly found Pop sensibilities. Pulling of a rip roaring versions of 'So What' and 'Last Caress' at the MTV awards complete with expletives got METALLICA banned from future events.

As the year closed METALLICA's touring plans merely rolled on as December ushered in the North American leg of 'Poor Touring Me'.

1997 started with a bang for METALLICA with a performance at the American Music Awards. The band also walking off by winning an award. February saw the release of the 'King Nothing' single and METALLICA finally wound down their 'Poor Touring Me' schedule the following month with a final show in Edmonton, Canada.

The band were soon back in action returning to the studio to begin work on 'Re-Load', only taking a break for European festival performances and for Hetfield's wedding in August. As the band wound up work on 'Re-Load' in October METALLICA put in an unusually low key showing by playing an acoustic benefit gig for the Bridge School in San Francisco.

In an attempt to get back to their roots METALLICA hosted a series of fan gatherings throughout Europe in November 1997. These events enabled the hardcore following to not only listen to a playback of the 'Re-Load' album but also catch the band playing a live set in an intimate club surrounding.

Keen to rekindle the '60s era of free festivals METALLICA announced their intentions for such a gig to launch their 'Re-load' promotion campaign. Initially though venues under consideration were unforthcoming with offers and eventually the band put in a performance in front of 50,000 non ticket paying fans in the car park of Philadelphia's Core States Arena. The show came a matter of days after an impromptu blast at London's Ministry of Sound club.

Debut single from 'Re-load', the melodramatic 'The Memory Remains', shot straight into the British and American charts and straight into fan debate too. Female backing vocals were provided by the ex-girlfriend of Mick Jagger and alleged abuser of mars bars MARIANNE FAITHFUL, the band having stopped off in Dublin especially to record her vocal parts. The album shot straight to number 1 in America as the band performed 'Fuel' and 'The Memory Remains' live on the famous American TV show 'Saturday Night Live'.

The year ended on a high with a performance at the Billboard awards and METALLICA adding another award to their collection, this time in the 'Best Hard Rock Band' category.

METALLICA got back into gear during 1998 with a fresh batch of cover versions assembled together with previous efforts under the title 'Garage Inc.'. New recordings included DIAMOND HEAD's 'It's Electric', BLUE OYSTER CULT's 'Astronomy', THIN LIZZY's 'Whiskey In The Jar' and a MERCYFUL FATE medley.

1998 also witnessed joyous events outside of METALLICA's creative and business parameters with both Hetfield and Ulrich becoming fathers. Cali Tee Hetfield was born in June and Myles Ulrich in August.

1999 found METALLICA winning a prestigious Grammy award for 'Better Than

You' in the 'Best Metal Performance' category. In April the band undertook an ambitious venture by performing two concerts with the San Francisco Symphony Orchestra. These shows would be collated for a double album release 'S&M' later in the year.

In the meantime the band set out on tour once more to promote 'Garage Inc.'

September was spent in production for 'S&M' and the album released in November. Opinion was sharply divided as to the merits of the album but needless to say worldwide sales were high. The band rounded off the year by performing 'Until It Sleeps' with full orchestra at the Billboard awards in December. METALLICA had also beaten another major act at their own game. German veterans the SCORPIONS had been planning a similar venture for some while.

Needless to say METALLICA had something special planned for the turn of the century headlining New York's Madison Square Gardens with support acts TED NUGENT and KID ROCK.

The new millennium started off well for METALLICA as they won another Grammy award for 'Best Metal Performance' for their rendition of 'Whiskey In The Jar'.

Hetfield appeared alongside Jim Martin on the track 'Eclectic Electric' on PRIMUS' 2000 album 'Antipop'. Newsted meantime busied himself with side project ECHOBRAIN, a power trio featuring guitarist Dylan Dokin and drummer Brian Sagrafena. Also contributing was the aforementioned Jim Martin and Hammet.

METALLICA contributed the new composition 'I Disappear' to the movie soundtrack for 'Mission Impossible 2'.

The band were also kept in the press the same year with a legal action brought by the band against internet company Napster. METALLICA accused Napster of depriving them of royalties by their download access of METALLICA tracks. Napster replied by posting an animated cartoon on their site featuring a Neanderthal Hetfield who could only mouth 'Money good!, Napster bad! Beer good!'.

A more complimentary tribute was made when GREGORIAN, a collection of Gregorian chanters, covered 'Nothing Else Matters' on their 'Masters Of Chant' album.

METALLICA spent mid 2000 on the road in America with their 'Summer Sanatorium' arena tour. Along for the ride were KID ROCK, KORN and POWERMAN 5000. By the end of the year it was announced that METALLICA had grossed over $40 million in tour receipts. The band's stability was rocked in February of 2001 when Newsted announced his departure. The bassist's frustrated attempts to instigate musical projects outside of the confines of METALLICA had been well documented.

Hetfield, Hammet and Ulrich resolved to record the band's next album as a trio although increased speculation put the spotlight firmly onto ex-OZZY OSBOURNE and ALICE IN CHAINS man Mike Inez as the potential new recruit. Another name dropped into the hat would be that of the original bass wildman Pete Way of UFO. (Inez though would join BLACK LABEL SOCIETY and Way resumed UFO activity).

The band, in typically unorthodox fashion, would also employ a novel method of auditioning bassists. Playing a website re-launch party in San Francisco on July 29th METALLICA would draw upon members of their official fan club to perform onstage with the band. The reaction of the audience would determine if the candidates got beyond the first song! The victor would be treated to a day out with the band and dinner. METALLICA got to grips with more personal internal affairs during the lay off upfront of a new album as their fan club announced that Hetfield was undergoing treatment for "alcoholism and other addictions."

Newsted, after a one off live gig with THE MOSS BROTHERS in San Francisco supporting SPINAL TAP, re-emerged with school friends vocalist / guitarist Dylan Donkin and drummer Brian Sagrafena as ECHO BRAIN, a band which had actually been a going concern for many years behind the scenes of METALLICA's unstoppable progress. Newsted also revealed plans to release material he had assembled over the years in alliance with such artists as Andreas Kisser of SEPULTURA, drummer Tom Hunting of EXODUS, DEVIN TOWNSEND and MACHINE HEAD's Robert Flynn.

ECHOBRAIN put in their debut live showing on August 19th 2001 as part of the 'Nadine's Wild Weekend' events in San Francisco. By September it had emerged that the ex-bassist was working in the studio with a re-united VOIVOD acting as producer and bassist. Meanwhile, with METALLICA on hold minus a bass player the band received an offer from MEGADETH's Dave Mustaine and bassist Dave Ellefson to found an interim live act to be dubbed META-MEGA!

For the fourth year running METALLICA fan club members would be rewarded with another 'Fan Can' release. '...And All This For You' included a live CD culled from a Dallas, Texas gig in 1989, a live video originally broadcast on German TV and various other goodies locked away in the by now obligatory tin can.

During January of 2002, As rumours spread

of involvement between Lars Ulrich and Kirk Hammet with former VAN HALEN star DAVID LEE ROTH, it was also learned that the METALLICA pair had collaborated with Rapper JA RULE for a track 'We Did It Again', included as part of a compilation album 'Ghetto Stories'. James Hetfield would get in on the action outside of METALLICA too, adding guest vocals on GOVT. MULE's 'Drivin' Rain' contribution to the all star NASCAR compilation album 'Crank It Up'.

The high profile Progressive Rock act DREAM THEATER added a rather novel twist to their touring activities in 2002. When booked for a two night consecutive venue run the band would perform the entirety of METALLICA's 'Masters Of Puppets' album live. Needless to say, fans who had not been made aware of DREAM THEATER's intentions, would be somewhat mystified.

When, in April Dave Mustaine made his announcement that MEGADETH was to fold due to a severe nerve injury the ex-METALLICA man had suffered to his left arm, the media rumour mill sprang into action, placing Mustaine's long serving bassist Dave Ellefson as a prospect for the still vacant position in METALLICA.

Whilst the Rock media concentrated on these developments other parties would be keeping an eye on Lars Ulrich's domestic position, the drummer putting his San Francisco abode on the market for $11 million and offloading some paintings at a further $11 million. Both Lars Ulrich and Kirk Hammet would unexpectedly take to the stage for famed 'Red Rocker' SAMMY HAGAR's last night of three gigs at the famous Bay Area Fillmore venue. The choice of material was a surprise too as Hagar and the METALLICA duo, alongside a guesting VAN HALEN bassist Michael Anthony, ripped through a set of MONTROSE songs.

Singles/EPs:
Jump In The Fire / Seek And Destroy (Live) / Phantom Lord (Live), Music For Nations 12KUT 105 (1984)
Creeping Death / Am I Evil / Blitzkrieg, Music For Nations 12KUT 112 (1984)
Master Of Puppets / Welcome Home (Sanatorium), Elektra (1986) (French release)
Helpless / The Small Hours / Crash Course In Brain Surgery / Last Caress - Green Hell, Vertigo METAL 112 (1987) **27 UK, 28 USA** ('$5.98 EP: Garage Days Revisited' EP)
Eye Of The Beholder / Breadfan, Elektra (1988) (USA release)
Harvester Of Sorrow / Breadfan / The Prince, Vertigo METAL 212 (1988) **20 UK**
One / The Prince, Elektra (1989) **35 USA**

(USA release)
One / Seek And Destroy (Live), Vertigo METAL 5 (1989) (7" single) **13 UK**
One / For Whom The Bell Tolls (Live) / Welcome Home (Sanatorium) (Live), Vertigo METAL 512 (1989) (12" single)
One (Album Version) / Seek And Destroy (Live), Vertigo METPD 510 (1989) (10" Picture Disc)
One (Demo Version) / For Whom The Bell Tolls (Live) / Creeping Death (Live), Vertigo METG 512 (1989) (12" single)
Harvester Of Sorrow (Live) / One (Live) / Breadfan (Live) / Last Caress (Live), Vertigo METAL 612 (1991) ('The Six And A Half Year Anniversary EP'. Limited edition released packaged with the 'Garage Days Revisited EP', 'Harvester Of Sorrows' and 'One' 12" singles packaged as 'The Good, The Bad And The Live')
Enter Sandman / Stone Cold Crazy, Vertigo METAL 7 (1991) (7" single)
14 SWEDEN, 5 UK, 16 USA
Enter Sandman / Stone Cold Crazy / Holier Than Thou / Enter Sandman (Demo), Vertigo METAL 712 (1991) (12" single)
Enter Sandman / Stone Cold Crazy / Enter Sandman (Demo), Vertigo METCD 7 (1991) (CD release)
The Unforgiven / Killing Time, Vertigo METAL 8 (1991) (7" single)
32 SWEDEN, 15 UK, 35 USA
The Unforgiven / Killing Time / So What / The Unforgiven (Demo, Vertigo METAL 812 (1991) (12" single)
Nothing Else Matters / Enter Sandman (Live), Vertigo METAL 10 (1992)
14 SWEDEN, 6 UK, 34 USA
Nothing Else Matters / Enter Sandman (Live) / Harvester Of Sorrow (Live) / **Nothing Else Matters (Demo)**, Vertigo METAL 1012 (1992) (12" single)
Enter Sandman (Live) / Sad But True (Live) / Nothing Else Matters (Live), Vertigo METCL 10 (1992) (Charity release, all royalties going to Phoenix Trust)
Wherever I May Roam / Fade To Black (Live), Vertigo METAL 9 (1992) (7" single)
28 SWEDEN, 25 UK, 82 USA
Wherever I May Roam / Medley (Live) / **Wherever I May Roam (Demo)**, Vertigo MET 912 (1992) (12" single)
Wherever I May Roam / Fade To Black (Live) / Wherever I May Roam (Demo), Vertigo METCD 9 (1992)
Sad But True / So What, Elektra 64696 (1992) **98 USA** (USA release)
Sad But True / Nothing Else Matters, Vertigo METAL 11 (1993) (7" single)
Sad But True / Nothing Else Matters (Elevator Version) / Creeping Death (Live) / Sad But True (Demo), Vertigo METAL 1112

(1993) (12" single. Also released on CD as METCD 11) **31 SWEDEN, 20 UK**
Sad But True / Nothing Else Matters (Live) / Sad But True (Live), Vertigo METCH 11 (1993)
Until It Sleeps / 2x4 (Live) / Until It Sleeps (Moby remix), Vertigo METAL 12 (1996) (10" single) **18 UK**
Until It Sleeps / Until It Sleeps (Herman Melville mix) / 2x4 (Live) / FOBD, Vertigo METCD 12 (1996) (CD single)
Until It Sleeps / Kill / Ride Medley: Ride The Lightning - No Remorse - Hit The Lights - The Four Horsemen - Phantom Lord - Fight Fire With Fire - (Live) / Until It Sleeps (Herman Melville Mix), Vertigo METCX 12 (1996)
Until It Sleeps / Overkill, Elektra 64276 (1996) **10 USA** (USA release)
Hero Of The Day / Mouldy / Hero Of The Day (Outta B Sides mix) / Overkill, Vertigo METAL 13 (1996) (12" single) **17 UK**
Hero Of The Day / Overkill / Damage Case / Hero Of The Day (Outta B Sides mix), Vertigo METCD 13 (1996) (CD single)
Hero Of The Day / Stone Dead Forever / Too Late Too Late / Mouldy, Vertigo METCX 13 (1996) (CD single)
Hero Of The Day / Overkill / Damage Case / Stone Dead Forever / Too Late Too Late, Vertigo METCY 13 (1996) (CD single)
Hero Of The Day / Kill 'Em All - Ride The Lightning medley, Elektra 64248 (1996) 60 USA (USA release)
Mama Said / Ain't My Bitch (Live), Vertigo METAL 14 (1996) **19 UK**
Mama Said / King Nothing (Live) / Whiplash (Live) / Mama Said (Edit), Vertigo METCD 14 (1996) (CD single)
Mama Said / So What (Live) / Creeping Death (Live) / Mama Said (Demo), Vertigo METCX 14 (1996) (CD single)
King Nothing, Elektra 64197 (1997) **90 USA**
The Memory Remains / For Whom The Bell Tolls (Haven't Heard It Yet Mix), Mercury MET 15 568 268-7 (1997) (7" single) **6 AUSTRALIA, 13 UK, 28 USA**
The Memory Remains / For Whom The Bell Tolls (Haven't Heard It Yet Mix), Mercury MET 15 568268-2 (1997)
The Memory Remains / Fuel For Fire (Work In Progress With Different Lyrics) / Memory (Demo Version), Mercury METCD 15 568 269-2 (1997)
The Memory Remains / The Outlaw Torn (Unencumbered By Manufacturing Restrictions Version) / King Nothing (Tepid Mix), Mercury MET DD15 568 271-2 (1997)
The Unforgiven II / Helpless (Live) / The Four Horsemen (Live) / Of Wolf And Man (Live), Mercury (1998) **15 UK, 59 USA**

The Unforgiven II / The Thing That Should Not Be (Live) / The Memory Remains (Live) / King Nothing (Live), Mercury (1998)
The Unforgiven II / No Remorse (Live) / Am I Evil? (Live) / The Unforgiven II (Demo), Mercury (1998)
Turn The Page / Stone Cold Crazy (Live) / The Wait (Live) / Bleeding Me (Live), Vertigo (1998)
Fuel, Vertigo (1998) 31 UK
Whiskey In The Jar, Vertigo (1999) **29 UK**
I Disappear, Hollywood (2000)

Albums:
KILL 'EM ALL, Music For Nations MFN 7 (1983)
Hit The Lights / The Four Horsemen / Motorbreath / Jump In The Fire / (Anesthesia) Pulling Teeth / Whiplash / Phantom Lord / No Remorse / Seek And Destroy / Metal Militia
RIDE THE LIGHTNING, Music For Nations (1984) **22 SWEDEN, 87 UK, 173 USA**
Fight Fire With Fire / Ride The Lightning / For Whom The Bell Tolls / Fade To Black / Trapped Under Ice / Escape / Creeping Death / The Call Of Ktulu
MASTER OF PUPPETS, Music For Nations (1986) **17 SWEDEN, 41 UK, 29 USA**
Battery / Master Of Puppets / The Thing That Should Not Be / Welcome Home (Sanatorium) / Disposable Heroes / Leper Messiah / Orion / Damage Inc.
MANDATORY METALLICA, Elektra (1988) (USA Promotion)
Master Of Puppets / For Whom The Bell Tolls / Seek And Destroy / Fade To Black / Welcome Home (Sanatorium) / The Thing That Should Not Be / Creeping Death
...AND JUSTICE FOR ALL, Vertigo (1988) **5 SWEDEN, 4 UK, 6 USA**
Blackened / ...And Justice For All / Eye Of The Beholder / One / The Shortest Straw / Harvester Of Sorrow/ The Frayed Ends Of Sanity / To Live Is To Die / Dyers Eve
METALLICA, Vertigo (1991) **4 SWEDEN, 1 UK, 1 USA**
Enter Sandman / Sad But True / Holier Than Thou / The Unforgiven / Wherever I May Roam / Don't Tread On Me / Through The Never / Nothing Else Matters / Of Wolf And Man / The God That Failed / My Friend Misery / The Struggle Within
LIVE SHIT: BINGE AND PURGE, Vertigo 518 726-2 (1993) **56 UK, 26 USA**
Enter Sandman / Creeping Death / Harvester Of Sorrow / Welcome Home (Sanatorium) / Sad But True / Of Wolf And Man / Guitar Doodle / The Unforgiven / And Justice For All / Solo / Through The Never / For Whom The Bell Tolls / Fade To Black /

Master Of Puppets / Seek And Destroy / Whiplash / Nothing Else Matters / Wherever I May Roam / Am I Evil / Last Caress / One / Battery / The Four Horsemen / Motorbreath / Stone Cold Crazy
LOAD, Elektra 61923 (1996) **1 USA**
Ain't My Bitch / 2 X 4 / The House Jack Built / Until It Sleeps / King Nothing / Hero Of The Day / Bleeding Me / Cure / Poor Twisted Me / Wasting My Hate / Thorn Within / Ronnie / The Outlaw Torn
RELOAD, Elektra (1997) **2 AUSTRALIA, 1 AUSTRIA, 5 BELGIUM, 2 CANADA, 2 DENMARK, 1 FINLAND, 3 FRANCE, 1 GERMANY, 3 HOLLAND, 6 ITALY, 12 JAPAN, 1 NORWAY, 3 SPAIN, 3 SWITZERLAND, 4 UK, 1 USA**
Fuel / The Memory Remains / Devil's Dance / The Unforgiven II / Better Than You / Slither / Carpe Diem Baby / Bad Seed / Where The Wild Things Are / Prince Charming / Low Man's Lyric / Attitude / Fixxer
METALLICA - BAY AREA THRASHERS, Get Back (1998)
Hit The Lights / Seek And Destroy / Motorbreath / Phantom Lord / Mechanix / Jump In The Fire / Metal Militia
GARAGE INC., Vertigo 538 351-2 (1998) **29 UK**
Free Speech For The Dumb / It's Electric / Sabbra Cadabra / Turn The Page / Die, Die My Darling / Loverman / Mercyful Fate / Astronomy / Whiskey In The Jar / Tuesday's Gone / The More I See / Helpless / The Small Hours / The Wait / Crash Course In Brain Surgery / Last Caress - Green Hell / Am I Evil / Blitzkrieg / Breadfan / The Prince / Stone Cold Crazy / So What / Killing Time / Overkill / Damage Case / Stone Dead Forever / Too Late Too Late
S&M, Vertigo 546 797-2 (1999) **33 UK, 2 USA**
The Ecstasy Of Gold / The Call Of Ktulu / Master Of Puppets / Of Wolf And Man / The Thing That Should Not Be / Fuel / The Memory Remains / No Leaf Clover / Hero Of The Day / Devil's Dance / Bleeding Me / Nothing Else Matters / Until It Sleeps / For Who The Bell Tolls / Human / Wherever I Amy Roam / Outlaw Torn / Sad But True / One / Enter Sandman / Battery

METALLIS (TX, USA)

Singles/EPs:
Lady Hunter / Hollow Winds Echo, Metallis (1986)

METAL MESSIAH (UK)
Line-Up: Jim Aspinall (vocals), Biff (guitar), Grem Darroch (guitar), Graham Kerr (bass), Kev Frost (drums)

A Nottingham Speed Metal act formed from the remains of Punk act VARUKERS, this group adopted new title of ARBITRATOR in 1987 before changing to METAL MESSIAH with the addition of ex-PARALEX vocalist Phil Ayling and guitarist Grem Darroch.
METAL MESSIAH recorded a 'Friday Rock Show' session in 1988 before cutting their first demo with vocalist Phil Ayling but he was replaced by Jim Aspinall (ex-WICKED) for the 'Mad Man' demo.
The group actually enjoyed brief interest from the major record companies until Thrash lost its appeal.

Albums:
HONOUR AMONG THIEVES, RKT CMO 195 (1990)
Intro / Mad Dogs Of War / Madman / Kiss Of Nosferatu / Honour Among Thieves / Metal Messiah / Curse Of The King / Nightwing / Awakening

METAL ONSLAUGHT (IL, USA)
Line-Up: Martti Payne (vocals / bass), Richard Godfrey (guitar), Ken Bretfors (guitar), James Coleman (drums)

METAL ONSLAUGHT's only album was also released in Germany as a double CD alongside SEPULTURA's 'Morbid Visions'.

Albums:
CEASE TO EXIST, Shark (1989)
Waiting For Death / Chester / Welcome To My Hell / Redneck / Victims Of The Axe / Cease To Exist / Run For Your Life / Death Do Us Part / Buttfuck

METAL VIRGINS (UK)
Line-Up: Steve (vocals / guitar), Gary (bass), Glenn (drums)

An early, British Thrash Metal mob.

Albums:
ANIMAL PEOPLE, Thrash Metal (1984)
Animal People / I'm For Real / Feelings / Virgins / Get Out / Rubber Dolls / Call My Name / Invasion

METAL WOLF (PA, USA)

Albums:
DOWN TO THE WIRE, Meta (1986)

METHEDRAS (ITALY)
Line-Up: Claudio Facheris (vocals), Massimiliano Ducato (guitar), Eros Muizzi (guitar), Andrea Bochi (bass), Carlo Radaelli (drums)

Milan retro-Thrashers METHEDRAS began life covering Thrash standards in 1996. The band line-up evolved from an initial duo of rhythm guitarist Massimiliano Ducato and vocalist / bassist Andrea Bochi over the course of two demo sessions, 1997's 'Cost Of Life' and an untitled 2001 effort. The latter recording still clearly demonstrates the band's influences, including cover versions of METALLICA's 'For Whom The Bell Tolls' and SLAYER's 'Seasons In The Abyss'.

MEZZROW (SWEDEN)
Line-Up: Uffe Petersson (vocals), Staffe Karlsson (guitar), Zebba Karlsson (guitar), Conny Welen (bass), Steffe Karlsson (drums)

A Swedish band very strongly influenced by the American 'Bay Area' Thrash scene, MEZZROW issued their debut album in 1990 but were dropped by Active Records and suffered the further indignation of bassist Conny Welen jumping ship to join HEXENHAUS then DRY DEAD RIVER. Opting not to replace Welen, MEZZROW struggled on with vocalist Uffe Petersson adopting bass duties. The band recorded a new four track demo in 1991, but would eventually split.
Uffe Petersson is now vocalist in ROSICRUCIAN.

Albums:
THEN CAME THE KILLING, Active ATV 11 (1990)
Then Came The Killing / Ancient Terror / The Final Holocaust / Frozen Soul / Distant Death / Prevention Necessary / Where Death Begins / The Cross Torment / Inner Devastation

MIDAS TOUCH (SWEDEN)
Line-Up: Patrick Wiren (vocals), Tomas Forshund (guitar), Lasse Gustavsson (guitar), Patrick Sporrong (bass), Bosse Lundstrom (drums)

A Speed Metal band formed in 1985 by Patrick Sporrong, Tomas Forshund and Bosse Lundstrom, MIDAS TOUCH added vocalist Patrick Wiren in 1987 to record the demo 'Ground Zero'.
This tape achieved a recording deal with Noise Records. Prior to recording the debut album, Forshund quit and MIDAS TOUCH drafted in Richard Sporrong as replacement. The resulting 'Presage To Disaster' album was produced by Roy Rowland.
Vocalist Patrick Wiren and bassist Patrik Sporrong formed HIGH TECH JUNKIES then

Wiren formed MISERY LOVES COMPANY in 1994. Guitarist Rickard Sporrong joined PEACE, LOVE AND PITBULLS.

Albums:
PRESAGE TO DISASTER, Noise NUK124 (1989) **40 SWEDEN**
The Arrival / Forcibly Incarcerated / Sinking Censorship / When The Boot Comes Down / True Believers Inc. / Reminiscence / Sepulchral Epitaph / Lost Paradise / Accessory Before The Fact / Accldama - Terminal Breath / Subhumanity (A New Cycle)

MIDEVIL (Cleveland, OH, USA)
Line-Up: Jon Pamblanco (vocals / guitar), Joe Mitchell (guitar), Scott Vesely (bass), Eugene Plascak (drums)

Albums:
EXPIRATION DATE, (1997)
Sounds Of Infinity / Expiration Date / Be Afraid / This World / The Game / Hands Across The Void / Zonk
THEE ALMIGHTY, (1999)
The Sounds Of Infinity II / My Sanity / Thee Almighty / Life's Casualties / Funky And The Melon / Sign Of The Times / Sinbound / The Red-Purple / Didi-Ups / Last Breath

MILITIA (TX, USA)
Line-Up: Mike Soliz (vocals), Tony Smith (guitar), Robert Willingham (bass), Phil Achee (drums)

In 1987 MILITIA vocalist Mike Soliz would join fellow Texans WATCHTOWER for recording of the 'Instruments Of Random Murder' demo.

Singles/EPs:
Objective: Termination / Salem Square / The Sybling: i) The Birth, ii) The Arrival, iii) The World Accepts Evil, iv) Evil Throughout The Ages, v) The Second Coming, Scythe NR 16356 (1986) ('The Sybling' EP)

MINDFUNK (New York, NY, USA)
Line-Up: Patrick R. Dubar (vocals), Jason Coppola (guitar), Louis J. Svitek (guitar), John Monte (bass), Reed St. Mark.

Originally intended to be named MINDFUCK, New York mob MINDFUNK were put together by bassist John Monte and ex-ZOETROPE guitarist Louie Svitek. The band ultimately recruited ex-UNIFORM CHOICE vocalist Patrick R. Dubar alongside guitarist Jason Coppola and former CROWN and CELTIC FROST drummer Reed St. Mark (real name Reid Cruickshank) before signing to Epic.

The name switch prompted confusion as the band's musical direction with many eager to tag the 'Funk Rock' tag onto the band no matter how uncomfortably it stuck.

John Monte had previously been with METHOD OF DESTRUCTION and, prior to his union with Billy Milano's mob, Monte had been in CHEMICAL WASTE with Jason Coppola, an act that released a 1987 demo 'Life's A Bitch'.

MINDFUNK were spectacularly dropped by Epic on the day they arrived at Bearsville Studios in upstate New York to begin work on their second album.

Help was at hand in the form of Megaforce Records' Johnny and Marsha Zazula. Already managing the band the husband and wife team arranged for the band to record at HEART's Bad Animals studio in Seattle with producer Terry Date, with the band naturally being signed to Megaforce.

The second album, cynically titled 'Dropped' following the Epic episode, by which point drummer Shawn Johnson had replaced Reed St. Mark and former NIRVANA / SOUNDGARDEN / OLD guitarist Jason Everman had stepped into Jason Coppola's shoes. Monte and St. Mark had both been fired in November 1991 following MINDFUNK's tour with SLAYER Monte later worked with CHEAP WINE and GRAFFITTI.

MINDFUNK toured Europe in May and June '93 with NUDESWIRL opening for them on many of the non festival dates.

A third album was recorded as MINDFUNK trimmed own to a quartet of Dubar, Svitek, a returning Johnson and ex-GENERATION WASTE / MIND OVER FOUR / TENSION WIRE bassist Frank Ciampi. Everman had quit the music scene to become an army ranger in the special forces!

Svitek later joined MINISTRY.

Singles/EPs
Touch You / Bang Time / Velvet Jane / Surprise Touch, Epic 657618 (1991)
Big House Burning / Sugar Ain't So Sweet, Epic XPR 1661 (1991) (Purple Vinyl USA Promotion)

Albums:
MINDFUNK, Epic 4677902 (1991)
Sugar Ain't Sweet / Ride And Drive / Bring It On / Big House Burning / Fire / Blood Runs Red / Sister Blue / Woke Up This Morning / Innocence / Touch You
DROPPED, Megaforce ZAZ 3 (1993)
Goddess / Closer / Drowning / In The Way Eye / Zootiehead / Wisteria / Mama, Moses And Me / 11 Ton Butterfly / Hogwallow / Billygoat / Hollow

PEOPLE WHO FELL FROM THE SKY, Music For Nations MFN 182 (1995)
Rift Valley Fear / Superchief / Seasick / Deep End / People Who Fell From The Sky / Weird Water / Aluna / 1000 Times / Kill The Messenger / Acrobats Falling

MINIER (USA)

A rare solo outing from Greg Minier, guitarist with Christian Thrashers THE CRUCIFIED. The R.E.X. label released this collection of demos which, although conspicuous by its absence of bass guitar, novelly credited "Me, Myself, I" for the credits.

Minier would also operate another solo project billed as APPLEHEAD.

Albums:
MINIER, R.E.X. (1990)
Do Not Be Deceived / The Skeptic / Price / Killing Of The Innocence / Prophecy / Philosophy Of Man / The Secret Song

MINOTAUR (GERMANY)
Line-Up: Andreas Richwein (vocals / guitar), Marco Schafenort (bass), Jorg Bock (drums)

A Hamburg Thrash Metal band that only failed to break through on the back of the '80s German Thrash Metal wave through sheer bad luck. MINOTAUR was created in 1983, issuing 'The Oath Of Blood' demo the following year. Further exposure was gained with the inclusion of a track on Roadrunner's 'Teutonic Metal Invasion Part 1' compilation album.

A further demo, 'The Slaughter Continues', arrived in 1987. Although Roadrunner offered a full album the band opted to self finance the 1988 'Power Of Darkness' album. A limited edition of 2,500, the record soon sold out.

MINOTAUR signed to the Turbo label for an EP but pulled out of this deal to go with Remedy Records. The resulting 'Eat Metal' EP was subsequently issued in 1909. Constant gigging with the major Thrash acts of the day continued. However, MINOTAUR would fold around 1992.

The band, now with Wikinger on bass, reformed for a projected 2002 album. MINOTAUR's early demos would be re-issued in CD format by T.T.D. Records.

Singles/EPs:
Towards My Eternity / Total Decay, Remedy (1989) ('Eat Metal' EP)
Intro / Total Decay / Daddschai / Tales Of Terror, T.T.D. (2001) ('The Oath Of Blood' EP)
Intro / Planed Head / Savage Aggressions /

Fall Of The Gods, T.T.D. (2001) ('The Slaughter Continues' EP)

Albums:
POWER OF DARKNESS, Minotaur (1988)

MISTREATER (Fontana, CA, USA)
Line-Up: Johnny Rainbow (vocals), Gregory Jay (guitar), Dane Alex (bass), Steven E (drums)

Singles/EPs:
Hell's Fire / Baby Blue, Too West (1980)

Albums:
MISTREATER, Erika (1985)
Quest / Liquid Windows / Deviated / Prowess / Mastermyth / Infernal Witch / Red Lights / Wild Child / Morality's Nightmare

MISTRUST (Seattle, WA, USA)
Line-Up: Jeff L'Heureaux (vocals), Michael Winston (guitar), Owen Wright (guitar), Tim Wolfe (bass), Chris Gohde (drums)

A Seattle Metal band formed by erstwhile CULPRIT vocalist Jeff L'Heureaux, MISTRUST first appeared contributing the track 'Running For My Life' to the compilation album 'Pacific Metal Project' in 1985.
Released on the Coma label, the record showcased a number of Seattle and Portland based Metal bands and led to an album deal with Coma. A full blown album, 'Spin The World', appeared two years later.
Guitarist Owen Wright and drummer Chris Gohde founded MY SISTER'S MACHINE. Gohde would later join LYE.

Albums:
SPIN THE WORLD, Coma (1987)

M.O.D. (New York, NY, USA)
Line-Up: Billy Milano (vocals), Tim McMurtrie (guitar), Ken Ballone (bass), Keith Davis (drums)

METHOD OF DESTRUCTION (M.O.D.) were created by former STORMTROOPERS OF DEATH vocalist Billy Milano.
The singer had wished to pursue the success of studio project band S.O.D. after the band folded when bassist Dan Lilker formed NUCLEAR ASSAULT and guitarist Scott Ian and drummer Charlie Benante opted to pursue ANTHRAX on a full time basis. M.O.D. carried on the S.O.D. tradition with short sharp hardcore bursts of metal. The initial line-up was completed by guitarist Tim McMurtrie, bassist Ken Ballone and drummer Keith Davis.

Debut album 'U.S.A. for M.O.D.', co-produced by Scott Ian - who also contributed acoustic guitar to the track 'Ode To Harry', created a media storm when some journalists labelled Milano a fascist. The lyrics, had been written in the third person of a character the singer had created called 'Corporal Punishment', and Milano steadfastly refuted the claims of racism. However, the furore could well have been worse as a song subtly titled 'Death to Hindus' was dropped from the record at the last minute. The controversy resulted in the record losing British distribution for a short period.
M.O.D. split in early 1988 with Milano opting to carry on with the name, McMurtrie, Davis and Ballone created a new act AMERICA'S CHOICE. Before long though McMurtie and Ballone were back with Milano in M.O.D.
M.O.D. performed a successful headline tour of America in 1988 with strong support from EXODUS. The band were knocked by some serious setbacks when McMurtie broke a leg in a stagediving accident. The guitarist endured and, not missing a show, was soon back in action performing from a wheelchair. Further injuries hit when Ballone broke his arm and had to be replaced by former CHEMICAL WASTE bassist John Monte for the duration of the tour.
M.O.D. announced a fresh look in mid 1988. Alongside Milano was now Monte, ex-ZOETROPE guitarist Louis Svitek and drummer Tim Mallare. However, in 1990 Monte and Svitek broke away to create MINDFUNK scoring a major deal with Epic Records. (Svitek later played with MINISTRY).
M.O.D.'s 1996 album 'Dictated Aggression' is essentially a Milano solo album. Other musicians include KILL BILLYS guitarist Joe Young and drummer Dave Chavarri. HEADLOCK's Bob McLynn adds guest vocals to the track 'Just Been Fired'.
Milano reformed S.O.D. for their late '90s album 'Bigger Than The Devil'. Following a highly successful S.O.D. tour Milano recreated M.O.D. (now apparently as MILANO'S ON DRUGS) with guitarist Joe Affe for a burst of American dates. These shows, curtailed due to illness on Milano's part, saw DYING FETUS guitarist Sparky Voyles in the line-up.
Chavarri teamed up with PRO-PAIN, SOULFLY and ILL NINO. By early 2002 Milano was announcing an M.O.D. reformation album handled by the production team of ANTHRAX / SEBASTIAN BACH guitarist Paul Crook and NUCLEAR ASSAULT bassist Scott Metaxas.

Surfin' U.S.A. / Surf's Up / Sargent Drexell Theme / Mr. Oofus, Roadrunner RR 2452-2 (1988)

Albums:
U.S.A. FOR M.O.D., Megaforce MOO89 (1987)
Aren't You Hungry / Get A Real Job / I Executioner / Don't Need The Bears / Ballad Of Dio / Thrash Or Be Thrashed / Let Me Out / Bubble Butt / You're Beat / Bushwackateas / Man Of Your Dreams / That Noise / Dead Men/ Most / Captain Crunch / Jim Gordon / Imported Society / Spandex Enormity / Short But Sweet / Parents / A.I.D.S. / Ruptured Nuptuals / Ode To Harry / Hate Tank
SURFIN' M.O.D., Megaforce (1988)
Goldfish From Hell / Totally Narley Talking By Katrina And Bill / Surfin' U.S.A. / More Narley Talking By Katrina And Bill / Surf's Up / Sargent Drexell Theme / Billy, Katrina And Alex Spot Oofus / Mr Oofus / Still More Narley Talk And The Party Crash Scene / Party Animal / Bill's Big Love Scene / Color My World / Bill And Katrina Split Up And The Big Party Scene / Shout / The Big Finale / Surfin' U.S.A. / Surf's Up / Sargent Drexell Theme / Mr Oofus / Party Animal / Color My World / Shout
GROSS MISCONDUCT, Noise NUK 133 (1989)
No Hope / No Glove No Love / True Colors / Accident Scene / Godzilla / E Factor / Gross Misconduct / Satan's Cronies / In The City / Come As You Are / Vents / Theme / P.B.M. / The Ride / Dark Knight
M.O.D. FOR U.S.A., Music For Nations MFN 126 (1991)
RHYTHM OF FEAR, Music For Nations MFN 145 (1992)
Objection - Dead End / Get Up And Dance / Step By Step / Rhymestein / Minute Of Courage / Irresponsible / Override Negative / I, The Earth / Spy Vs Spy / Intruder / Time / Jimmy's Revenge / Rally (N.Y.C.)
DEVOLUTION, Music For Nations MFN 163 (1994)
Land Of The Free / Devolution / Repent / The Angry Man / Resist / Crash n' Burn / Supertouch / Rock Tonite / Behind / Running / Time Bomb / Unhuman Race
LOVED BY THOUSANDS ... HATED BY MILLIONS, Megaforce (1995)
Noize / Aren't You Hungry / Spandex Enormity / A.I.D.S. / Hate Tank / Goldfish / Surfin' U.S.A. / Surf's Up / Mr. Oofus / No Glove No Love / True Colors / Livin' In The City / Get Up And Dance / Rhymestein / Irresponsible / Rally (N.Y.C.) / The Ballad Of Dio / Bubble Butt / Short But Sweet / Ode To Harry / Vents / Theme Song / Bonanza /

Buckshot Blues / Clubbin' Seals / U.S. Dreams / He's Dead Jim / Get The Boot / Color My World
DICTATED AGGRESSION, Music For Nations MFN 201 (1996)
Dictated Aggression / Silence Of Your Sin / Damaged / Shot Glass / Stand Or Fall / One Was Johnny / Nation / Empty Vision / In My Shoes / U.S. Dreams / Hippypottomus / Just Got Fired / Whiteout / Brutal Beats

MORDRED (San Francisco, CA, USA)
Line-Up: Scott Holderby (vocals), Danny White (guitar), Art Liboon (bass), Gannon Hall (drums)

In the midst of the San Francisco focus on homegrown thrash acts MORDRED stuck to their guns with their unique blend of aggressive Funk influenced Thrash Metal. The band was created in 1984 by bassist Art Liboon and guitarist Jim Sangvinetti. During turbulent early years Sangvinetti quit to join MERCENARY in 1986 and in a straight swap MERCENARY guitarist Sven Soderlund filled his shoes in MORDRED. During this period MORDRED were fronted by Steve Skates who was deposed by Chris Whitney.
Guitarist Danny White, who superseded Sangvinetti, and drummer Gannon Hall are both ex-MERCENARY. Sangvinetti undeterred joined the Guitar Institute of Technology and was later re-hired by the band.
The debut album was recorded using guitarist Jim Taffer. His tenure was short though as Sangvinetti returned for the second album.
1991's 'In This Life' had MORDRED experimenting with the thrash genre further by incorporating DJ Aaron 'Pause' Vaughn. The B side to the 'Falling Away' single saw a cover version of the THIN LIZZY track 'Johnny The Fox'.
The band's last effort found MORDRED now fronted by Paul Kimball.

Singles/EPs:
Every Day's A Holiday / Superfreak, Noise 7 MORD 5 (1989)
Falling Away / Lion's Den / Johnny The Fox, Noise 170-61-3 (1991)
Esse Quam Videri (Radio mix) / Intro - Killing Time (Live) / Every Day's A Holiday (Live), Noise N 01796 (1992)
Grand Summit / Lo Cal Hi Fiber / Acrophobia / The Pause (Public Domain), Noise (1994)

Albums:
FOOLS GAME, Noise CD NUK 135 (1989)
State Of Mind / Spectacle Of Fear / Every Day's A Holiday / Spellbound / Sever And

Splice / The Artist / Shatter / Reckless Abandon / Super Freak / Numb
IN THIS LIFE, Noise NO 159-2 (1991) **70 UK**
Esse Quam Videri / Downtown / Progress / Killing Time / Larger Than Life / High Potence / Falling Away / Window / In This Life / Strain
THE NEXT ROOM, Noise N 0211-2 (1994)
Skid / Crash / Splinter Down / Shut Over / Pauper's Wine / Acrophobia / Murray The Mover / In A Turn / The Trellis / The Next Room / Rubber Crutch

MORTAL SIN (AUSTRALIA)
Line-up: Mat Maurer (vocals), Paul Carwara (guitar), Mick Burke (guitar), Andy Eftichio (bass), Steve Hughes (drums)

As the Trash phenomenon swept the Rock world in the mid '80s Australia was not to be left out. Sydney's MORTAL SIN had been forged in 1985 consisting of vocalist Mat Maurer, guitarists Paul Carwara and Mick Burke, bassist Andy Eftichio and ex-WIZZARD drummer Wayne Campbell. Both Eftichio and Carwara are both ex-JUDGE members.
MORTAL SIN's career was given an enormous boost when editor Bernard Doe of British Metal magazine 'Metal Forces' was asked by the major Vertigo label which Thrash acts they should be looking at. Doe suggested MORTAL SIN and the band were soon signed up.
MORTAL SIN had, alongside SLAUGHTER LORD, been at the forefront of the Australian Thrash scene and it was their self-financed 'Mayhemic Destruction' album which had caught Doe's attention as he gave it 99 out of a 100 in his review. When SLAUGHTER LORD folded the path was clear for Although MORTAL SIN's and Vertigo quickly repackaged and reissued the album internationally.
MORTAL SIN's debut album featured former WIZZARD man Keith Krstin on guitar, he was superseded by SLAUGHTER LORD's Mick Burke for subsequent touring.
MORTAL SIN's next album, 'Face Of Despair' produced by Randy Burns, was issued in time for the band's support slot on METALLICA's 1989 Australian tour. In July of the same year drummer Campbell was replaced by another erstwhile SLAUGHTER LORD man Steve Hughes for European jaunts opening for EXODUS and FAITH NO MORE.
Campbell created WHITE TRASH then GRUNGEON with ex-SUICITY guitarist Doug Dalton.
In early 1990 Maurer bailed out to create OMEGA and the band plugged the gap with Steve Sly. MORTAL SIN effectively split in two later in the year when Carwana, Hughes and Burke all quit. Burke and Hughes formed PRESTO with singer Luke Pittman and bassist Aaron Hodge.
MORTAL SIN persevered filling the gaps with former ENTICER guitarist Dave DeFrancesco, ex-RAGS N' RICHES guitarist Alex Hardy and former WHITE WIDOW drummer Nash Hall. This line up guested for MEGADETH on their 1991 Australian trek although shortly after Tom Doustopil replaced Hardy.
MORTAL SIN cut a new record, the more Power Metal orientated 'Rebellious Youth' produced by Kevin Shirley, in 1991. The record was retitled 'Every Dog Has Its Day' for its European release on Music For Nations.
Struggling to survive MORTAL SIN folded in 1992. Eftichio was soon back in action with WHO'S GUILTY. Their sole release, the 1994 'Revenge' EP, featured Eftichio, vocalist Sean Bosco, guitarist Bruno Gerace, keyboard player Bob Wheatley and drummer Nick Pansini.
In 1996 MORTAL SIN reformed with Maurer, Eftichiou, Carwana, Campbell and Anthony Hoffman.

Singles/EPs:
I Am Immortal / Lebanon (Live) / Voyage Of The Disturbed, Vertigo VERX 47 (1990)
Every Dog Has Its Day, Virgin (1991)

Albums:
MAYHEMIC DESTRUCTION, Mega Metal AJLP 1016 (1987)
The Curse / Women In Leather / Lebanon / Liar / Blood, Death, Hatred / Mortal Slaughter / Into The Fire / Mayhemic Destruction
FACE OF DESPAIR, Vertigo 8363702 (1989)
Martyrs Of Eternity / Infantry Corps / Robbie Soles / Suspended Animation / For Richer, For Poorer / Voyage Of The Disturbed / Terminal Reward
REBELLIOUS YOUTH, Virgin (1991) (Australian release)
EVERY DOG HAS ITS DAY, Under One Flag CDFLAG61 (1991)

MORTUARY I.O.D. (HOLLAND)
Line-Up: Johannes Keekstra (vocals), Arnout Visser (guitar), Franke Kooistra (guitar), Germ Reitsma (bass), Douwe Talma (drums)

Berlikum Thrashers founded by then vocalist / guitarist Arnout Visser during 1995 as MORTUARY. The band folded in 1997 but reunited as MORTUARY I.O.D. ('Image Of Death') the following year.
The 2002 album 'Distorted Massacre: Fear

The Madness', actually recorded two years earlier, was produced by Jan Switters and erstwhile ELEGY frontman Eduard Hovinga.

Albums:
DISTORTED MASSACRE: FEAR THE MADNESS, (2002)

MOSHQUITO (GERMANY)
Line-Up: Olli (vocals), Ingo (guitar), Enrico (guitar), Rudi (bass), John (drums)

An East German Thrash act strangely rooted in the 1983 R&B act ARGUS. Slowly but surely ARGUS moved into Rock territory, becoming a Heavy Metal covers band, and by 1987 had adopted a full on Thrash approach and a new title of MOSHQUITO. As such a series of demos ensued starting with 'No Back To Inferno' then 'Mosh In Moscow' and 1991's 'Only Death Is For Nothing'. However, that same year MOSHQUITO would fold.
The band was reactivated during 1996, soon cutting the debut album 'Secrets' for the Noiseworks label. The album surfaced in 1998 and a follow up, 'World's End' for Morbid Records, in 2001.

Albums:
SECRETS, Noiseworks (1998)
WORLD'S END, Morbid (2001)
Animals / Do What You Want / Worlds' End / Hunting Demon / Cold Grave / Liquid Killer / No Respect / Your Pleasure Is Your Pain / Flesh

MOX NIX (Houston, TX, USA)
Line-Up: Johnny Duff (vocals / guitar), Bruce Tousinau (guitar), Robert Fernandez (bass), Joe Vernagalla (drums)

Houston Metal band MOX NIX started life in 1982 as a covers band citing a line-up of vocalist Thomas Rogers, guitarists Johnny Duff and Bruce Tousinau, bass player Robert Fernandez and drummer Donnie Bragg. In 1984, as MOX NIX made the transition to playing original material both Rogers and Bragg decamped necessitating Duff taking on the lead vocal role and the induction of new drummer Joe Vernagalla.
A demo tape scored laudatory reviews in European publications such as Holland's 'Aardschock' and Britain's 'Metal Forces', prompting a deal with the French Axe Killer label. Promoting the eponymous debut MOX NIX toured as support to WARLOCK, YNGWIE MALMSTEEN and ACCEPT.
The band signed to Shatter Records for a projected second album, recorded in New York and produced by Alex Perialis and

RAVEN drummer Rob Hunter. However, Shatter went under and the record was shelved.
Various members of MOX NIX now play in Alt-Rock act HIP CIRCLE.

Albums:
MOX NIX, Axe Killer 7023 (1985)
Fight Back / Ready Or Not / Reckless / Lost Sierra / Never Again / Steal The Show / Scream For Mercy / Make It / Kill Or Be Killed / Stand Alone

M PIRE (USA)
Line-Up: Michael O'Mara (vocals), Joshua Perahia (guitar), Pedler Rudling (guitar), Joey Rochrich (bass), Eric Stoskopf (drums)

M PIRE are led by guitar wizard Joshua Perahia. With his previous act JOSHUA the man was purported to be 'the fastest guitarist in the world'.

Albums:
CHAPTER ONE, Long Island (1995)
Concrete Jungle / You Want It All / Steady Weapon / One Night Is Not Enough / Long Way To Heaven / Dark Days / It Must Be Love / Tears Of Joy / Bad Man / Walk Into The Light / Devil's River / Right On Target

MUCKY PUP (NJ, USA)
Line-Up: Chris Milnes (vocals), Danny Nastasi (guitar), Dave (bass), Johnny (drums)

Crossover act MUCKY PUP featured ex-HADES guitarist Scott LaPage.
The line up for 1993's 'Lemonade' counted only vocalist Chris Milnes as a surviving founder member. Other musicians involved included guitarists John Milnes and Glen Cummings, bassist Marc DeBacker and drummer Kevin Powers.
Danny Nastasi founded NON FICTION, along with HADES Dan Lorenzo, releasing three albums until Lorenzo opted out as HADES reunited for their 'Exist To Resist' album.
In 1990 Nastasi found Hip Hop Rockers DOG EAT DOG as a side project fronted by MUCKY PUP roadie John Connor. DOG EAT DOG, debuting with the cheekily titled 'Warrant' EP would soon eclipse the parent act scoring a top ten single in Britain with 'No Fronts' in 1995. DeBacker would later shift from bass to guitar to replace Nastasi in DOG EAT DOG in 1996.
In 2001 a MUCKY PUP / DOG EAT DOG union entitled ALL BORO KINGS emerged citing a line-up of Dan Nastasi, guitarist Sean Kilkenny, bass player Dave Neabore and BLOODHOUND GANG drummer John Milnes.

Albums:
CAN'T YOU TAKE A JOKE?, Roadrunner
RR 9553 (1988)
Knock Knock / Nazichism / Caddy Killer /
M.B. (Ballad Of The Noron Bros.) /
Innocent's / Daddy's Boy (Theme Song) /
F.U.C.K. / U R Nothing/ A.I.D.S. / Life 4 Def /
Laughing In Your Face / Woody / Bush Pigs/
Mr. Prezident / I.R.S. / Shmbluh
A BOY IN A MAN'S WORLD, Torrid (1989)
U Stink / Batman / Someday / Homosexual /
Reagen Knew / Landscrapers / Never Again
/ Death By Cholesthorol / P.T.L. / A Boy In A
Man's World / Little Pigs / All's Cool / Jam It /
Whasky Wabbit / Big Freeze
NOW, Roadracer RO 9340 (1990)
Hippies Hate Water / Three Dead Gophers /
Jimmys / Baby / She Quieffed / Feeling Sick
/ A Headbanger's Ball And 120 Minutes / My
Hands, Your Neck / Face / Hotel Penitentiary
/ Mucky Pumpin' Beat / I Know Nobody /
Walkin' With The Devil / Yesterdays / To Be
Lonely
ACT OF FAITH, Century Media 08 9731-1
(1992)
Freakin' At The Peep Show / Mr. Hand /
Understand / Please Don't Burn The
Johnson / I Am / Summertime / Gotta Go /
Angry Song / Mucky Pumpkin Motion / The
Skinheads Broke My Walkman / Blowtorch /
Lonely As Me
LEMONADE, Century Media 77058-2 (1993)
Own Up For What You Say / Junkie Eyes /
Three Sides / Beautiful People / Mountain
Song / The TV's On Fire / Déjà Vu / Two
Little Men / If Wishes Were Fishes /
Confessions / Mountain Song 2 / Darkwave
Sleeps
FIVE GUYS IN A REALLY HOT GARAGE,
Century Media (1995)
This Ain't Workin' / Short Attention Span /
Messed Up / Jail / I've Got A Plan / You Know
/ Why Can't You Be More Like Your Picture /
You're Gonna Get It / Carter Farmer /
Straightman / You Smoke And I Eat Meat /
Fucked Up

MX MACHINE (USA)
Line-Up: Lee Kaiser (vocals), Mitch Rellas
(guitar), Diego Negrete (bass), Liquid Dan
(drums)

Albums:
MANIC PANIC, Restless (1988)
Kick You In The Face / Psychotic Killing
Machine / This Is No Drill / No Glam Fags /
Wild Bells / Manic Panic / Stay Clean / The
Longest Day / S.D.I. / Youth / Fuck The
Neighbours

MYTH (New Haven, CT, USA)
Line-Up: Rob Schwartz (vocals), Roger
Loiseau (guitar), Dan Lynch (bass), Mark
Minervini (drums)

A New Haven, CT based group certainly with
no connection to the group from Seattle that
would spawn QUEENSRYCHE vocalist Geoff
Tate, MYTH released their 'Metal To The
Pedal' single in 1984 and followed it up a year
later with a five-track demo.

Singles/EPs:
Metal To The Pedal / Rock Or Die, Metal
Force KS0001 (1984)

NAGLFAR (SWEDEN)
Line-Up: Jens Rydén (vocals), Andreas Nilsson (guitar), Kristoffer Olivius (bass), Morgan Hansson (drums)

A Black Metal band with strong Thrash influences, NAGLFAR's ex-drummer - Matte Holmgren - formed EMBRACING, releasing the 'I Bear The Burden Of Time' album in 1996 and would add vocals to the debut SKYFIRE demo 'Within Reach'. The AZURE 'Moonlight Legend' of 1998 also includes Holmgren on drums.
NAGLFAR's high profile second album saw Matthias Grahn taking on the drummer's role from previous incumbent Morgan Hansson. The parting of ways with Hansson could be viewed as acrimonious bearing in mind that the band pointedly offer him no thanks on the album cover and declare their former sticksman to be "mad"!
Ryden issued his solo project DEAD SILENT SLUMBER's 'Entombed In The Midnight Hour' album in 1999.

Albums:
VITTRA, Wrong Again WAR 008 (1996)
As The Twilight Gave Birth To The Night / Enslave The Astral Fortress / Through The Midnight Spheres / The Eclipse Of Infernal Storms / Emerging From Her Weepings / Failing Wings / Vittra / Sunless Dawn / Exalted Above Thrones
DIABOLICAL, War Music WAR 0005 (1998)
Horncrowned Majesty / Embracing The Apocalypse / 12th Rising / Into The Cold Voids Of Eternity / The Brimstone Gate / Blades / When Autumn Storms Come / A Departure In Solitude / Diabolical: The Devil's Child

NAKED TRUTH (Atlanta, GA, USA)
Line-Up: Doug Watts (vocals), Jimmie Westley (guitar), Kwame Boaten (bass), Bernard Dawson (drums)

NAKED TRUTH, although founded by Detroit born singer Doug Watts in Atlanta, Georgia would relocate to London, England in an attempt to crack the big time. NAKED TRUTH's brew of then topical Funk and Thrash style Metal landed management with Bernie Rhodes and a major deal with Sony Records.

Singles/EPs:
Head Between The Lines / Fight, Sony 658429-0 (1992) (10" single)
Black / Here Lies America, Sony 658949-6

(1993) (12" single)
Black / Here Lies America / Fight, Sony 658949-2 (1993) (CD single)

Albums:
GREEN WITH RAGE, Sony 469124-2 (1991)
Pan American Alive / King In My Home (Lovejoy) / Here Lies America / Downtown / Brood Flows / Harem Scares
FIGHT, Sony 472981-2 (1993)
Door / Tormented World / Downtown / Lovejoy / Black / Read Between The Lines / I Am He / Telepathy / Third Eye Spy / Red River

NAPALM (NY, USA)
Line-Up: Chris Liggio (vocals / guitar), Jeff Lombardi (guitar), Chris Weidner (bass), Bob Priomos (drums)

Crossover Thrash band NAPALM heralded their arrival with a 1985 demo session 'Let The Battle Begin'. The NAPALM 1986 EP featured a line-up of vocalist / guitarist Jeff Rossbach, bassist Chris Weidner and drummer Rex Rossbach.
The Rossbach brothers had left the fold by the time the full length album 'Cruel Tranquility' was issued. New faces were vocalist Chris Liggio, guitarist Jeff Lombardi and drummer Bob Proimos.
Oddly, the debut album was released as a two CD set in Japan, together with SIEGES EVEN's 'Life Cycle' album.
The 1990 effort witnessed a band that held none of its original members, with Weidner departing and coming in his stead bassist Brett Roth. Lombardi's position was taken by guitarist Kult.

Singles/EPs:
The Monarch / Tunnel Rat / All Out Assault / Evil Speak / Freedom Day, Combat Bootcamp (1986)

Albums:
CRUEL TRANQUILITY, Steamhammer 85-7565 (1989)
Mind Melt / AOA / Shake It Off / Gag Of Steel / Devastation / Combat Zone / Immoral Society / Attack On America / Re-Animate / Act Of Betrayal / Nightmare Administrator / Practice What You Preach / Kranked Up And Out
ZERO TO BLACK, Steamhammer 847622 (1990)
Teenage Illusion / Time And Time Again / Zero To Black / The Other Side Feels Grey / Pigs / Alternative Life Of Style / The Harder You Live / Crucified / Gone / Cut You Up

NARCOTIC GREED
(JAPAN / FRANCE)
Line-Up: Moreno Grosso (vocals), Hiroshi Yamashita (guitar), Yuuichi Senda (bass), Oliver Couturier (drums)

NARCOTIC GREED, centred upon the mask wearing guitarist 'Warzy' (a.k.a. Hiroshi Yamashita) debuted in Japan with the 1991 demo 'Absurd War'. A further tape, 1992's 'Crisis Of Ruins', led to the 1994 'Fatal' album issued by Lard Records. The band would adventurously put on a European tour in support of this record.

The following year NARCOTIC GREED drafted a fresh rhythm section of former JACQLINE ESS and DEATH COLOR drummer Kurata and bassist Riki of GELARD and DISGUST. Kurata bailed out in 1996 and Riki in 2000. Both would find re-employment that year in the ranks of SADISTIC EYES. Meantime NARCOTIC GREED issued 2000's oddly titled 'Twicet Of Fate' record. The band line up for this second album would be Yamashita, bassist Yuuichi 'Bomber' Senda, vocalist Ryouji Azuma and drummer Masayuki Higuchi.

Warzy and Senda would then relocate to France rebuilding NARCOTIC GREED in July 2001. Alongside the enterprising duo would be former CELTIC BLOOD and INHERITANCE singer Moreno Grosso and erstwhile WITCHES drummer Nicolas Borg. In January of 2002 KRISTENDOM drummer Olivier Couturier supplanted Borg.

Albums:
FATAL, Lard (1994)
TWICET OF FATE, World Chaos Productions (2000)
Don't Trust Anybody / Shotgun Highway / Deleted Illusion / 3: 16 / Thug City / Dulling Generation / Damn 'Em All / Operetta / Humanchain / End Is Near

NASTY SAVAGE (Brandon, FL, USA)
Line-Up: Nasty Ronnie (vocals),
Ben Meyer (guitar), David Austin (guitar),
Fred Dregischan (bass), Curtis Beeson (drums)

Fronted by professional wrestler Nasty Ronnie (real name Ronnie Galleti), NASTY SAVAGE were first formed in 1982 by guitarist Ben Mayer and bassist Fred Dregischan. First appeared with a debut four track demo entitled 'Wages Of Mayhem' in early 1984 consisting of the songs 'Unchained Angel', 'Savage Desire', 'Witches Sabbath' and 'XXX'. However, NASTY SAVAGE had trouble retaining bassists. Whilst the first album saw

co-founder Fred Dregischan very much involved he was replaced by Dezso Istvan Bartha for 'Indulgence', Chris Moorhouse was subsequently recruited for the 'Abstract Reality' EP and ex-PURGATORY / ICED EARTH and AGENT STEEL bassist Richard Bateman joined the band for 'Penetration Point'.

Drummer Curtis Beeson quit in the Spring of 1989 as NASTY SAVAGE ultimately folded. Both Beeson and Meyer would forge a union with erstwhile LAST RITES members to create HAVOC MASS for the 1993 album 'Killing The Future'.

By the mid '90s Galletti had founded INFERNAL, their 1995 demo being released commercially in 2000.

Bateman founded AFTER DEATH in 1999 together with erstwhile MORBID ANGEL and NOCTURNUS man Mike Browning. Beyer was to be found on SKULLVIEW's 1999 album 'Kings Of The Universe'.

Both Meyer and Beeson are members of LOWBROW with ex OBITUARY / SIX FEET UNDER vocalist Allen West and DEATH's Scott Carino. LOWBROW debuted with the 2000 album 'Victims At Play'.

Singles/EPS:
Abstract Reality / Unchained Angel / Eromantic Vertigo / You Snooze, You Lose, Roadrunner RR 9566 (1988)

Albums:
NASTY SAVAGE, Metal Blade (1985)
No Sympathy / Gladiator / Fear Beyond The Vision / Metal Knights / Asmodeus / Dungeon Of Pleasure / The Morgue / Instigator / Psycho Path / End Of Time
INDULGENCE, Metal Blade 72186-4 (1987)
Stabbed In The Back / Divination / XXX / Indulgence / Inferno / Hypnotic Trance / Incursion Dementia / Distorted Fanatic? ?
PENTRATION POINT, Roadracer RO 94181 (1989)
Welcome Wagon / Irrational / Ritual Submission / Powerslam / Sin Eater / Penetration Point / Puzzled / Horizertical / Family Circus

NECRODEATH (ITALY)
Line-Up: Ingo (vocals / guitar), Claudio (guitar), Paolo (bass), Peso (drums)

Originally known as GHOSTRIDER in a Doomier vogue before adopting Speed Metal for their 1985 demo 'The Shining Pentagram'. Italian Thrashers NECRODEATH's influence would be felt not only upon later generations of domestic acts but on the extreme Metal scene world-wide. NECRODEATH issued two albums between 1988 and 1989 before folding.

With interest in NECRODEATH remaining high the band emerged after a seven year break. Incredibly mainman Claudio had not even picked up a guitar during the extended lay off. NECRODEATH resumed activities with the 2000 album 'Mater Of All Evil', following it up with 2001's 'Black As Pitch'.

Albums:

INTO THE MACABRE, Nightmare (1988)
Agony - The Flag Of The Inverted Cross / At The Mountains Of Madness / Sauthencrom / Mater Tenebraum / Necrosadist / Infernal Decay / Graveyard Of The Innocents / The Undead - Agony (Reprise)
FRAGMENTS OF INSANITY, Metalmaster MET114 (1989)
Choose Your Death / Thanatoid / State Of Progressive Annihilation / Metampsychosis / Fragments Of Insanity / Enter My Subconscious / Stillbirth / Eucharistical Sacrifice
MATER OF ALL EVIL, Scarlet (2000)
The Creature / Flame Of Malignance / Black Soul / Hate And Scorn / Iconoclast / Void Of Naxir / Anticipation Of Death / Experiment In Terror / Serpent / At The Roots Of Evil / Fathers
BLACK AS PITCH, (2001)
Red As Blood / Riot Of Stars / Burn And Deny / Mortal Consequence / Sacrifice 2K1 / Process Of Violation / Anagaton / Killing Time / Saviours Of Hate / Join The Pain / Church's Black Book

NECROMONICON (GERMANY)

Line-Up: Volker Fredrich (vocals / guitar), Jürgen Weltin (guitar), Lars Heneck (bass), Axel Strickstock (drums)

A German Thrash act. Erna was to replace original guitarist Jürgen Weltin.

Albums:

NECROMONICON, Wave 941 452 (1986)
Dark Land / Possessed By Evil / Blood Revenge / Insanity / Blind Destruction / Hades Invasion / Magic Forest / Iron Charm
APOCALYPTIC NIGHTMARE, Scratchcore 085 269-938 (1987)
The Ancient One / Apocalyptic Nightmare / The Following Century (Darkland II) / Rhetorical Dictums / In Memory / Broken Illusions / Retributive Strike
ESCALATION, Scratch Core (1989)
Death Toll / Black Frost / Dirty Minds / Skeletal Remains / Murder Of Profit /
...And The Night Will Be Silent / Mosh The ABC / Cold Ages (Darkland III)

LIVE, Gamma (1990)
SCREAMS, D&S DSR CD022 (1995)
Final Course / Second Birth / Just Say No! / Bitter Sweet Perversion / Temptation / Crushing Defeat / How Long You Think... / Irreversible Destruction / Ruins (They Will Cry Tomorrow) / Groovy Mouth

NECROPHAGIA (CA, USA)

Line-Up: Eddie Santiago (vocals), Ruben Alverez (guitar), Tom Mukai (bass), Willie Mims (drums)

Albums:

NECROPHAGIA, Wild Rags (1987)
Wreckage / Bloodshed / Tear Off Your Face / The Final Solution / Feel My Knife

NECROPHOBIC (POLAND)

Polish Thrash Metal band NECROPHOBIC bowed in with the 1991 demo session 'Feeling Of Agony'.

Albums:
NO MORE LIFE, Carnage (1992)

NECROPOLIS (USA)

Line-Up: Keith Charron (vocals), Mel Ballard (guitar), Keith Eppinette (bass), David Randolph (drums)

Albums:

CONTEMPLATING SLAUGHTER, Bomp (1988)
Dark Despair / Waters Of Lathe / Ashes To Ashes / Contemplating Slaughter / Killing Kranium / Surrender To Death / Froze In Fear / Cease To Exist

NECROSIS (ARGENTINA)

Line-Up: Emiliano Arce (vocals), Martin Cluselia (guitar), Andres Hauch (guitar), Federico Ramos Mejia (bass), David Lanciani (drums)

Albums:

NECROSIS, (2000)
Mi Eterna Alma / Venganza Dela Realidad / Libert Ad / Inocentes / Sin Perdon / Criaturas De Dolor

NECROSIS (CHILE)

Chilean Thrash Metal band NECROSIS emerged with the 1987 'Kingdom Of Hate' demo.

Albums:
THE SEARCH, (1989)

NEVERMORE (Seattle, WA, USA)
Line-Up: Warrel Dane (vocals), Pat O'Brien (guitar), Jeff Loomis (guitar), Jim Sheppard (bass), Van Williams (drums)

Technical Speed Metal outfit NEVERMORE was created in 1995 by ex-SANCTUARY men vocalist Warrel Dane, guitarist Jeff Loomis, bassist Bill Sheppard and drummer Mark Arrington. Loomis had also been with EXPERIMENT FEAR.
Demos kindled the interest of renowned producer Neil Kernon who offered his servives promptly for further recordings. The resulting tapes landed NEVERMORE a deal with Germany's Century Media Records.
Kernon continued his relationship with the band producing extra tracks to make up NEVERMORE's eponymous February 1995 debut. Rave reviews followed and NEVERMORE, now augmenting their line-up with second guitarist Pat O'Brien, set out touring America alongside DEATH. It was during this tour that Dane's infamously long hair nearly proved to be his undoing. Falling drunkenly asleep next to the wheel of the band truck a roadie drove off not realizing the singer was there. Dane's mane caught in the axle of the vehicle as it dragged him 30 yards down the road. For the rest of the dates the vocalist had to walk with the aid of sticks.
Further dates, with Dane recovered, had the band supporting BLIND GUARDIAN in Germany winding up a world tour by appearing before 100,000 people at the prestigious Dynamo Festival in Holland.
An interim limited edition EP followed in July of the same year titled 'In Memory' that included radical reworks of BAUHAUS tracks 'Silent Hedges' segued with 'Double Dare'.
In late 1997, following a European tour alongside fellow Americans ICED EARTH, O'Brien joined gore mongers CANNIBAL CORPSE. His position was taken by former FORBIDDEN axeman Tim Calvert.
During 1998 NEVERMORE toured America with FLOTSAM & JETSAM prior to further European shows with OVERKILL.
NEVERMORE trimmed to a quartet for 2000's 'Dead Heart In A Dead World' with the loss of Calvert. The band, now with secondary guitars supplied by AGGRESSION CORE man Curran Murphy, toured America the same year sharing a package bill with FATES WARNING and PLANET X. A September 2001 run of dates in America would find NEVERMORE as guests to SAVATAGE. The band put in a further burst of dates as headliners kicking off at the L'Amour venue in Brooklyn on the 23rd November. Guests for these dates would be OVERKILL and SCAR CULTURE.

During November guitarist Curran Murphy bailed out to join Canadians ANNIHILATOR.

Singles/EPs:
Optimimist Or Pessimist / Matricide / In Memory / Silent Hedges - Double Dare / The Sorrowed Man, Century Media DIGICD 77121-2 (1995) ('In Memory' EP)

Albums:
NEVERMORE, Century Media CD77091-2 (1995)
What Tomorrow Knows / CBF / The Sanity Assassin / Garden Of Gray / Sea Of Possibilities / The Hurting Words / Timothy Leary / Godmoney
THE POLITICS OF ECSTASY, Century Media 77132-2 (1996)
Seven Tongues Of God / This Sacrament / Next In Line / Passenger / The Politics Of Ecstasy / Lost / The Tienanmen Man / Precognition / 42147 / The Learning
DREAMING NEON BLACK, Century Media 7891-2 (1999)
Ophidian / Beyond Within / The Death Of Passion / I Am The Dog / Dreaming Neon Black / Deconstruction / The Fault Of The Flesh / The Lotus Eaters / Poison Godmachine / All Play Dead / Cenotaph / No More Will / Forever
DEAD HEART IN A DEAD WORLD, Century Media (2000) **57 GERMANY**
Narcosynthesis / We Disintegrate / Inside Four Walls / Evolution 169 / The River Dragon Has Come / The Heart Collector / Engines Of Hate / The Sound Of Silence / Insignificant / Believe In Nothing / Dead Heart In A Dead World

NIGHTCRAWLER (OH, USA)

Albums:
SOLDIER IN TIME, Nightcrawler (1989)

NOKTURNEL (USA)
Line-Up: Tom Stevens (vocals / guitar), Lee Ribero (bass), Tophetareth (drums)

A Satanic Thrash act assembled by frontman Tom Stevens, a veteran of SAVAGE DEATH. The band came into being during 1989 when Stevens and fellow erstwhile SAVAGE DEATH cohort drummer Eric Young united with bassist Martin O'Connor.
This line-up issued two demos 'You Don't Stand A Chance' and 'Welcome To New Jersey' prior to a landing a deal with the J.L. America label for the 1993 debut 'Nothing But Hatred'. Although the sleeve artwork was amateurish the music won NOKTURNEL underground appeal.

Two tracks would be committed to the 'Anti Grunge' EP put together by Rage Records in 1994 before NOKTURNEL folded. Stevens would journey through a myriad of acts including EXILE, BRIMSTONE, MORPHEUS DESCENDS and INCANTATION.

Stevens would resurrect NOKTURNEL for a comeback record 'Fury Unleashed'. Assisting in the studio would be DEATH OF MILLIONS guitarist Lee Ribera handling bass duties and FOG drummer Tophetareth.

Albums:
NOTHING BUT HATRED, J.L. America (1993)
Human Termite / No 2nd Chance / Sliding Down The Razor / Global Suicide / Skonopolator / My Hell / Final Punishment / Target Planet / Revenge Of The Corpse / Welcome To New Jersey / Poltergeist
FURY UNLEASHED, Nokturnel Eclipse (2001)
Legend Of The Wolven / Taking Home To The Grave / Food Chain / I Remain Faithless / Visions Of The Haunted / Realm Of Possession / Forcefed Fear / Immortal Destroyer / A Collision Of Dimensions

NO MERCY (CA, USA)
Line-Up: Mike Muir (vocals), Mike Clark (guitar), Ric Clayton (bass), Sal Troy (drums)

With the burgeoning late '80s success of SUICIDAL TENDANCIES this side project of vocalist Mike Muir was released by the band's own label.

Albums:
WIDESPREAD BLOODSHED - LOVE RUNS RED, Suicidal (1987)
We're Evil / Crazy But Proud / Master Of No Mercy / Day Of The Damned / Controlled By Hatred / I'm Your Nightmare / Widespread Bloodshed- Love Runs Red / My Own Way Of Life / Waking The Dead

NUCLEAR ASSAULT
(New York, NY, USA)
Line-Up: John Connelly (vocals / guitar), Anthony Bramante (guitar), Dan Lilker (bass), Glenn Evans (drums)

With the mid '80s Thrash explosion, New York's NUCLEAR ASSAULT leapt to the fore due to the prime motivating force of ex-ANTHRAX bassist Dan Lilker. Although the gangly mop-topped bassist had severed ties with ANTHRAX in 1983, due to disagreements with then vocalist Neal Turbin, it took two and a half years to assemble his next project NUCLEAR ASSAULT. In the interim, Lilker had involved himself with the spoof Metal of STORMTROOPERS OF DEATH alongside ANTHRAX guitarist Scott Ian and METHOD OF DESTRUCTION vocalist Billy Milano.

NUCLEAR ASSAULT's line-up for the inaugural 'Brain Death' EP was Lilker, vocalist John Connelly, guitarist Anthony Bramante and ex-HARTER ATTACK / TT QUICK drummer Glenn Evans.

Despite NUCLEAR ASSAULT's rapidly growing profile on the crossover scene, Evans found time to invest in a new label, Arena Records. The first release on Arena was the 'Salt In The Wound' single by his previous outfit HARTER ATTACK.

1987's mini-album 'The Plague', a collection of old and new material including the infamous 'Buttfuck' (a song lyrically aimed at MÖTLEY CRÜE vocalist VINCE NEIL), was originally to be titled 'Cross Of Iron' and to have had a cross as the sleeve artwork. However, the American record company Combat cited possible objections that may have come from religious organizations. NUCLEAR ASSAULT's first foray into Europe came the same year, with dates alongside AGENT STEEL.

A return to Europe in 1988 as guests to SLAYER gave NUCLEAR ASSAULT access to far greater crowds and, fuelled by their reaction, the band returned for further dates as headliners, support being granted by ACID REIGN and RE-ANIMATOR. Further gigs saw the band opening for SEPULTURA in South America.

The band set about another American tour in 1992, bolstering their live sound by including former TT QUICK guitarist Dave DiPietro and ex-PROPHET guitarist Scott Metaxas. As Lilker announced details of his new act BRUTAL TRUTH the same year and an immediate signing with Earache Records, the demise of NUCLEAR ASSAULT became inevitable.

A last effort under the banner NUCLEAR ASSAULT came with 1993's 'Something Wicked' with the band now comprising Connelly, DiPietro, Metaxas and Evans.

Following a lengthy run of commendable Metalcore albums Lilker would disband BRUTAL TRUTH following completion of an Australian tour in September 1998. Lilker resumed activity with S.O.D. for their 'Bigger Than The Devil' album, the bassist also operating Black Metal band HEMLOCK as a side endeavour. Yet another venture found Lilker assembling THE RAVENOUS in 2000 for the 'Assembled In Blasphemy' album. Included were NECROPHAGIA's Killjoy and Chris Reifert of AUTOPSY. Lilker would surprisingly announce the reformation of the classic NUCLEAR ASSAULT line-up for an appearance at the 2002 'Wacken Open Air' Metal festival in Germany.

Singles/EPs:
Brain Death / Final Flight / Demolition, Combat 88561 8119-1 (1986)
Fight To Be Free / Equal Rights / Stand Up, Under One Flag 12 FLAG 105 (1989)
Fight To Be Free / Equal Rights / Stand Up / Brain Death / Final Flight / Demolition, Under One Flag CD12 FLAG 105 (1989)
Good Times, Bad Times / Hang The Pope (Live) / Lesbians / My America / Happy Days, Under One Flag 12 FLAG 107 (1989)
Critical Mass, Relativity (1989) (USA promotion)
Trail Of Tears, Relativity (1989) (USA promotion)

Albums:
GAME OVER, Under One Flag FLAG 5 (1986)
Live, Suffer, Die / Sin / Cold Steel / Betrayal / Radiation Sickness / Hang The Pope / After The Holocaust / Stranded In Hell / Nuclear War / My America / Vengeance / Brain Death
THE PLAGUE, Under One Flag MFLAG 13 (1987)
Game Over / Nightmares / Buttfuck / Justice / The Plague / Cross Of Iron
SURVIVE, Under One Flag FLAG21 (1988)
Rise From The Ashes / Brainwashed / F / Survive / Fight To Be Free / Got Another Quarter / Great Depression / Wired / Equal Right / P.S.A. / Technology / Good Times, Bad Times
HANDLE WITH CARE, Under One Flag FLAG 35 (1989)
New Song / Critical Mass / Inherited Hell / Surgery / Emergency / Funky Noise / F (Wake Up) / When Freedom Dies / Search And Seizure / Torture Tactics / Mother's Day / Trail Of Tears
OUT OF ORDER, Under One Flag FLAG 64 (1991)
Sign In Blood / Fashion Junkie / Too Young To Die / Preaching To The Deaf / Resurrection / Stop Wait Think / Doctor Butcher / Quocustodiat / Hypocrisy / Save The Planet / Ballroom Blitz
LIVE AT HAMMERSMITH ODEON, Roadracer RO 91672 (1992)
SOMETHING WICKED, Alter Ego ALTGOCD 003 (1993)
Something Wicked / Another Violent End / Behind Glass Walls / Chaos / Forge / No Time / To Serve Men / Madness Descends / Poetic Justice / Art / Other End
ASSAULT AND BATTERY, Receiver RRCD 244 (1997)

NUCLEAR DEATH (AZ, USA)
Line-Up: Lori Bravo (vocals / bass), Phil Hampson (guitar), Joel Whitfield (drums)

This cult-like Thrash/Death act has a certain reputation in the underground for paradoxically being both brutally bad and good at the same time. Founded in March 1986 in Tempe, Arizona the trio had a seldom seen phenomenon, a female vocalist and bassist. The band worked diligently in the underground and produced four demos 'Wake Me When I'm Dead' in 1986, 'Welcome To The Minds Of The Morbid' in 1987, a live ten track demo called 'A Symphony Of Agony' in November 1987 and finally in 1989 the session 'Caveat'.
By this time the band was signed to the then fledgling cult underground US Metal label, Wild Rags. The debut, 'Bride Of Insect' appeared in 1990. Staying with Wild Rags the band released 'Carrion For Worm' in 1991 which found Steve Cowan replacing Joel Whitfield on drums. The third release, 'For Our Dead' was delivered in 1992. It seems the band have been inactive ever since.

Albums:
BRIDE FOR INSECT, Wild Rags WRR017 (1990)
Necrobestiality / Corpse Of Allegiance / Feral Viscera / Stygian Tranquility / Place Of Skulls / Cremation / The Colour Of Blood / The Beloved Whore Celebration / Fetal Lament: Homesick / Bride Of Insect / The Misshapen Horror / Vultures Feeding
CARRION FOR WORM, Wild Rags WRR019 (1991)
Spawn Song / The Human Seed / Proposing To The Impaled / Moribund / Greenflies / Return Of The Feasting Witch / A Dark Country / Lurker In The Closet: A Fairy Tale / Cathedral Of Sleep / Homage To Morpheus / Carrion For Worm / Vampirism
FOR OUR DEAD, Wild Rags (1992)

NUCLEAR SIMPHONY (ITALY)
Line-Up: Gino (vocals / guitar), Ciro (guitar / bass), Giovanni (drums)

Albums:
LOST IN WONDERLAND, Steamhammer (1990)
Mister I.D.G.A.F. / Lustful For Desaster / Cry / Evil Spray / Mimmo The Bull / Where Eagles Reign / Rhapsody Of Sadness / Create Your Destiny / Die For Your Flag

NUMSKULL (IL, USA)
Line-Up: Skip McGullum (vocals), Tom Brander (guitar), Eric Seiller (guitar), Rob

Charrier (bass), Jeff McGullum (drums)

Thrash Metal act NUMSKULL emerged with a 1987 demo session 'Nums The World'. A further demo 'Thrash To The Bone' the following year secured a deal with the Enigma label for the 'Ritually Abused' album.
In 1995 a split album shared space with SEA OF TRANQUILITY.
NUMSKULL made a return with the 1996 album 'When Suffering Comes'. Band members guitarist Tom Brander and drummer Andy Vehnkamp would shortly after join EVIL INCARNATE.

Albums:
RITUALLY ABUSED, Enigma (1988)
The End / Ritually Abused / Death And Innocence / No Morals / Friday's Child / Off With Your Head / The Henchman / Pirate's Night / Turn Of A Screw / Kiss Me, Kill Me / Rigor Mortis
NUM SKULL, Rage (1995) (Split album with SEA OF TRANQUILITY)
WHEN SUFFERING COMES, Defiled (1996)
Eyes Of A Madman / The Gift Of Hate / Mercitron / In Sickness / Spill Your Guts / As The Dead Pile High / Inquisition Of The Guilty / Force Fed Lies / Buried Alive

OBLITERATION
(UK)
Line-Up: Lol Maycock (vocals),
Neil Chaney (guitar), Kev
Maycock (guitar), Rob
Maycock (bass), Darren Evans
(drums)

Albums:
OBSCURED WITHIN, Released Emotions
REM009 (1991)
Into The Void / Your Choice / Trenchmouth /
Inner Dreams / Claustrophobia / Macabre
Insanity / Void Existence / Parental Guidance

OBLIVEON (CANADA)
Line-Up: Stephane Pecard (vocals / bass),
Pierre Remillard (guitar), Martin Gagne
(guitar), Alain Demers (drums)

Canadian Thrash Metal act OBLIVEON,
formatively entitled OBLIVION, emerged in
1987 with the 'Whimsical Uproar' EP. The
band's line-up at this stage comprised
vocalist / bassist Stéphane Picard, guitarist
Martin Gagné and drummer Francis Giguère.
A further demo effort three years later 'Fiction
Of Veracity', seeing the departure of Giguère
and the upgrading to a quartet by enlisting
drummer Alain Demers and guitarist Pierre
Rémillard, led in turn to the debut album
'From This Day Forward' for the Active label.
Initially the record only saw European
distribution but would be picked up later for
Canada by Press Play.
Sophomore effort 'Nemesis' arrived in 1993. A
video clip of the live favorite 'Dynamo' was
shot and played on a regular basis on the
Canadian Much Music and Musique Plus
music television channels.
The following year Bruno Bernier was added
as lead vocalist, this incarnation of
OBLIVEON cutting the 'Cybervoid' album for
the A.S.A. label. During mid 1998 the
Soundscape Music label re-issued the band's
debut demo 'Whimsical Uproar' on CD format
to mark OBLIVEON's tenth anniversary. The
band also donated their version of OZZY
OSBOURNE's 'Suicide Solution' for the
Olympic Records tribute 'Legend Of A
Madman'.
Red Stream Records would re-issue the
band's debut demo on CD. Curiously
OBLIVEON issued as a promotion sampler a
version of the B-52's 'Planet Claire' in 1998.
OBLIVEON split in March of 2002.

Singles/EPs:
Whimsical Uproar / The Scrutinizer /
Undeserving Glory, Soundscape Music
(1997)

Planet Claire / Psychomatrix /
Biomecanique, (1998) (Promotion release)

Albums:
FROM THIS DAY FORWARD, Active (1990)
From This Day Forward / Fiction Of Veracity /
Droidomized / Imminent Regenerator / It
Should Have Stayed Unreal / Access To The
Acropolis / Chronocraze
NEMESIS, Obliveon (1993)
Nemesis / The Thinker's Lair / Obscure
Mindways / Dynamo / Frosted Avowals /
Factory Of Delusions / Estranging Abduction
/ Strays Of The Soul
CYBERVOID, Hypnotic (1995)
Cybervoid / Downward / Perihelion / Android
Succubus / Sequels / Subgod / Sombre
Phase / Biomécanique / Call Of Silence /
Deus Ex Machina / Psychomatrix / Drift Of
The Spheres
CARNIVORE MOTHERMOUTH, Hypnotic
(1999)
Technocarnivore Mothermouth / Love, Die,
Resurrect / Such A Quiet River / Devil In My
Eyes / Coercive Currents / Polarity / Vectors /
Glass Made Of Flesh / Fatal Induction /
Desert Incorporel

OBSESSION (CT, USA)
Line-Up: Mike Vescara (vocals), Bruce Vitale
(guitar), Art Maco (guitar), Matt Keragus
(bass), Jay Mezias (drums)

Metal band from Connecticut founded in
1983. OBSESSION debuted with a cut on the
Metal Blade 'Metal Massacre' compilation
series prompting their signature to the label
for a full length outing 'Marshall Law'.
Vescara's post OBSESSION career includes
a recording stint with Japanese metallers
LOUDNESS.
Following LOUDNESS' decision to recruit a
Japanese frontman back into the band,
Vescera was hired by YNGWIE MALMSTEEN
with whom he recorded and toured.
In 1997 he issued a Japanese release solo
album. Vescara also guests on HELLOWEEN
guitarist ROLAND GRAPOW's 'Kaleidoscope'
record and issued his own MVP album in
1999.

Albums:
MARSHALL LAW, Metal Blade MBR 1010
(1983)
Only The Strong Will Survive / Hatred Unto
Death / The Execution / Marshall Law
SCARRED FOR LIFE, Enigma ST3212
(1986)
Scarred For Life / Winner Take All / Losing
My Mind / In The End / Bang 'Em Till They
Bleed / Hy Lai 31568 - Take No Prisoners /

Taking Your Chances / Run Into The Night / Tomorrow Hides No Lies
METHODS OF MADNESS, Enigma ST-73262 (1987)
Four Play / Hard To The Core / High Treason / For The Love Of Money / Killer Elite / Desperate To Survive / Method Of Madness / Too Wild To Tame / Always On The Run / Panic In The Streets

ODIN (Los Angeles, CA, USA)
Line-Up: Randy O (vocals), Jeff Duncan (guitar), Aaron Samson (bass), Shawn Duncan (drums)

Probably more famous for their appearance in the Rockumentary 'The Decline And Fall Of Western Civilization Part II: The Metal Years' than any recorded product.
Guitarist Brad Parker appears on the 1983 EP. Under the pseudonym of Damien C. Phillips Parker had actually been a member of the fledgling METALLICA. His stay lasted just one gig.
After an abortive spell working with ex-HOLLAND guitarist Mike Batio in MICHAEL ANGELO during 1988, Randy O formed the LOST BOYS with Jeff Duncan.
Shawn Duncan played with MADAM X prior to that group's eventual demise in early 1989. Duncan later joined ARMORED SAINT before founding BIRD OF PREY.
In 2000 the Duncan siblings assembled side project band DC4 together with yet another Duncan family member bassist Matt.
Jeff Duncan is presently a member of the resurrected ARMORED SAINT.

Singles/EPs:
Caution / The Blade / Midnight Flight / Judgement Day, Duff (1983)

Albums:
DON'T TAKE NO FOR AN ANSWER, Half Wet GWD 1290509 (1985)
The Writer / One Day To Live / Shining Love / Solar Eye / Don't Take No For An Answer / Judgement Day
THE GODS MUST BE CRAZY, Victor (1988)

OIL (USA)
Line-Up: Ron Rinehart (vocals), Blake Nelson (guitar), Matthew Joy (bass), Jason Vander Pal (drums)

OIL are a Los Angeles based Christian Thrash Metal band fronted by former DARK ANGEL singer Ron Rinehart. The frontman became a Christian upon DARK ANGEL's dissolution in 1992.

OIL debuted with a self-financed EP during 1999. Also featured in the ranks of OIL is erstwhile DECEIVER, DESIRE and CAPTAIN BLACK guitarist Blake Nelson. For the full length album Jason Vander Pal took over on the drum stool from 'Eric'.
The 'Refine' album pulled in a generous helping of enthusiastic reviews for its honest, no frills Metal approach. The band managed to put in live gigs, including a showing at the STRYPER Expo, but unfortunately Rinehart received an injury shortly after the album release which put OIL on hold for nearly a year. Fully recovered, Rinehart and OIL got back into action being announced as special guests to DISCIPLE in April.

Albums:
REFINE, Kaluboné (1999)

OMEN (Los Angeles, CA, USA)
Line-Up: Kevin Goocher (vocals), Kenny Powell (guitar), Andy Haas (bass), Rick Murray (drums)

Traditional Heavy Metal band formed by ex-SACRED BLADE guitarist Kenny Powell. The band had been created during 1983 by Oklahoma natives guitarists Kenny Powell and Jody Henry along with drummer Steve Wittig. Unable to assemble a full band unit Powell took time out to work with SAVAGE GRACE. This tenure would be short-lived though and, brandishing a cassette of tapes originally scored for SAVAGE GRACE, Powell duly scored a deal with Brian Slagel and Metal Blade Records for OMEN.
The band line-up was completed with vocalist J.D. Kimball as OMEN debuted with the 'Battle Cry' album. Although blighted by an amateurish album cover OMEN's brand of Power Thrash style Metal won many converts world-wide.
A succession of albums ensued but OMEN were unable to extract themselves from a cult following into the mainstream.
The 1988 'Nightmares' mini-album contains a live version of the AC/DC classic 'Whole Lotta Rosie'. Kimball departed before this release and OMEN pulled in vocalist Coburn Pharr for the 'Escape To Nowhere' album which featured a version of GOLDEN EARRING's 'Radar Love'. Originally the album, produced by the esteemed Paul O'Neill, was to have been entitled 'Era Of Crisis' but many of the original tracks slated for the album would be rejected by O'Neill. Despite the tribulations OMEN scored valuable radio play with the track 'Thorn In Your Flesh'. Upon completion of a ten week run of live shows across America a disillusioned Powell decamped.

After the release of 1989's compilation 'Teeth Of The Hydra' Pharr opted out to join high profile Canadians ANNIHILATOR. Powell joined forces with vocalist Steve Kelley, bassist Andy Haas and drummer Doug Stevens to create STEP CHILD issuing a demo in 1991.

With a renaissance of '80s American Metal in Europe during the mid '90s OMEN was forced out of retirement due to fan pressure. Powell emerged with a new look OMEN that included his son Greg Powell on lead vocals and guitar, bassist Andy Haas and drummer Rick Murray.

This unit cut the comeback 'Reopening The Gates' album for Germany's Massacre Records and undertook a successful bout of European touring backing up FATES WARNING. After these dates Greg Powell embarked on his own career with STOMPING GROUND.

OMEN enlisted the services of Kevin Goocher and set to task on a new album projected for 2002 release titled 'Eternal Black Dawn'. Earlier in the year OMEN, with support band BATTLEROAR, had toured Greece to enthusiastic response.

Original OMEN bassist Jody Henry was touting a fresh act in 2002 billed as CELEBRITY CRUSH.

Albums:
BATTLE CRY, Roadrunner RR 9818 (1984)
Death Rider / The Axeman / Last Rites / Dragon's Breath / Be My Wench / Battle Cry / Die By The Blade / Prince Of Darkness / Bring Out The Beast / In The Arena
WARNING OF DANGER, Roadrunner RR 9738 (1985)
Warning Of Danger / March On / Ruby Eyes (Of The Serpent) / Don't Fear The Night / VBP / Premonition / Termination / Make Me Your King / Red Horizon / Hell's Gates
THE CURSE, Roadrunner RR 9661 (1986)
The Curse / Kill On Sight / Holy Martyr / Eye Of The Storm / S.R.B. / Teeth Of The Hydra / At All Cost / Destiny / Bounty Hunter / The Larch
NIGHTMARES, Metal Blade SQ-73266 (1987)
Nightmares / Shock Treatment / Dragon's Breath / Termination / Bounty Hunter / Whole Lotta Rosie (Live)
ESCAPE TO NOWHERE, Roadrunner RR 9544-2 (1988)
It's Not Easy / Radar Love / Escape To Nowhere / Cry For The Morning / Thorn In Your Flesh / Poisoned / Nomads / King Of The Hill / No Way Out
TEETH OF THE HYDRA, Metal Blade 3948 14206CD (1989)
Holy Martyr / Termination / Dragon's Breath /

Teeth Of The Hydra / Battle Cry / The Curse / Nightmares / Bounty Hunter / Thorn In Your Flesh / Die By The Blade / Hell's Gates
REOPENING THE GATES, Massacre MAS PCO124 (1997)
Dead March / Uneven Plow / Chained / Rain Down / Reopening The Gates / Everything / Well Fed / Crushing Day / Saturday Into The Ground

ONE BAD PIG (USA)
Line-Up: Carey Womack (vocals), Paul Q-Pek (guitar), Streak Wheeler (bass), Phillip Owens (drums)

One of the few Christian Thrash bands. The 'Swine Flew' album has guests including GIANT's Dan Huff, Phil Keaggy, Tommy Sims and guitar from Dale Oliver and Bob Hartman.

Albums:
SMASH, Pure Metal (1989)
Godarchy / Isiah 6 / Let's Be Frank / People Cry Out / Frat Rats / Smash The Guitar / Kingdom Come / Take A Flying Leap / I'm Not Getting Any Older / Looney Tune / Don't Be Fooled / Blow And Go
SWINE FLEW, Myrrh (1990)
See Me Sweat / Altar Ego / Hey Punk / Red River / Bowl Of Wrath / Big Stomach / Christmas Time / Judas Kiss / Thrash Against Sin / Swine Flew / When Your Love Died / We Want You

ONSLAUGHT (UK)
Line-Up: Sy Keeler (vocals), Nige Rockett (guitar), Rob Trotman (guitar), James Hinder (bass), Steve Grice (drums)

A Thrash act from Bristol. ONSLAUGHT stayed the course and had the majors running around after them for quite a while in an embarrassing period when major labels seemingly snapped up any old British Thrash act.

The band had initially been picked up upon by the magazine 'Metal Forces' after releasing the debut album 'Power From Hell' on the normally Punk handling Children Of The Revolution label. - indeed, the group initially started life as a Punk outfit in 1983 - and the exposure through the magazine prompted Music For Nations to sign the group to their Under One Flag imprint. Acknowledging the help given to them by the magazine, ONSLAUGHT would record the track 'Metal Forces' on second album 'The Force' in appreciation.

ONSLAUGHT's first, stable line-up settled on vocalist Sy Keeler, guitarists Nige Rockett and Jason Stallard, bassist Paul Mahoney and drummer Steve Grice, although the rawly produced debut album, 'Power From Hell', had been cut with Mahoney handling vocals and Stallard on bass. It was a record that sold 11,000 copies.

During 1986 bassist Paul Mahoney left enabling Jason Stallard to resume bass duties. A second guitarist, Rob Trotman, was added but departed soon after. ONSLAUGHT then drafted in bassist James Hinder, moving Stallard back to guitar once more.

In 1987, prior to releasing their first version of the AC/DC cover 'Let There Be Rock', the band sacked Stallard after supposedly recording him at a gig in Bristol and citing this as evidence he could not play well enough. A disgruntled Stallard refuted the claims and went on to form MILITIA, reverting to drums, with guitarists Darren Keeler (brother of Sy) and John Hinder (brother of Jim).

ONSLAUGHT eventually signed to London Records after being chased by a host of major labels, including A&M and CBS. The group's debut for the new label arrived in 1989.

'In Search Of Sanity' was originally recorded with vocalist Sy Keeler, but producer Stefan Galfas decided the man simply could not sing well enough, a fact that ended up prompting London to demand a change of vocalist. This naturally begged the question why did London's A&R department sign a band with a vocalist that could not sing in the first place? Nevertheless, Keeler departed to form MIRROR MIRROR with ex-PREYER drummer Lloyd Coates (an outfit that was later to support ONSLAUGHT!). Former GRIM REAPER singer Steve Grimmet joined the band to re-record the vocals on the album, injecting a much needed dose of class to the band. But, regrettably, it was all a hideous mismatch and after a low key European tour ONSLAUGHT was dropped by London.

The band drafted in new vocalist Tony O'Hara (ex-LARRAKIN and TORINO) in March 1990 and ONSLAUGHT took time out to regroup before for some dates with support acts DEAD ON and the aforementioned MIRROR MIRROR.

The best days of the group were behind them and ONSLAUGHT would ultimately perish, with Grice and Rockett later forming the Funk Rock outfit FRANKENSTEIN, managed by producer Pete Hinton. FRANKENSTEIN comprised the two ex-ONSLAUGHT men plus former RHODE ISLAND RED vocalist Tony Bryan, ex-TOKYO ROSE bassist Bob Presley and ex-MIRROR MIRROR guitarist Alan Jordan. FRANKENSTEIN achieved little beyond supporting SAXON on their poorly attended 1993 British tour.

Steve Grimmet, on the other hand, found a great deal of success in Japan with the more traditional Hard Rock delivered by his new group LIONSHEART.

Rockett turned up on the HORA-KANE 1999 album 'Eternal Infinity' fronted by ex-ONSLAUGHT and now PRAYING MANTIS vocalist Tony O'Hora.

Singles/EPs:
First Strike / State Control, Complete Control TROL 1 (1983)
Let There Be Rock / Metal Forces (Live) / Onslaught (Live) / Angels Of Death (Live), Under One Flag 12FLAG 103 (1987)
Shellshock / Confused / H-Eyes, London LONX 215 (1989)
Let There Be Rock / Shellshock (Live), London LON 224 (1989) (7" single) **50 UK**
Let There Be Rock / Shellshock (Live) / Metal Forces (Live), London LONX 224 (1989) (12" single)
Welcome To Dying / Nice n' Sleazy, London LON 198 (1989) (7" single)
Welcome To Dying / Atomic Punk / Nice n' Sleazy, London LONX 198 (1989) (12" single)

Albums:
POWER FROM HELL, C.O.R. GURT 2 (1985)
Damnation / Onslaught (Power From Hell) / Thermo Nuclear Devastation / Skullcrusher 1 / Lord Of Evil / Death Metal / Angels Of Death / Devil's Legion / Street Meets Steel / Skullcrusher 2 / Witch Hunt / Mighty Empress
THE FORCE, Under One Flag FLAG 1 (1986)
Let There Be Death / Metal Forces / Flight With The Beast / Demoniac / Flame Of The Antichrist / Contract In Blood / Thrash 'Til Death
IN SEARCH OF SANITY, London 828 142-2 (1989) **46 UK**
Asylum / Shellshock / Let There Be Rock / Welcome To Dying / In Search Of Sanity / Lightning War / Blood Upon The Ice / Powerplay
WHEN REASON SLEEPS, FM Revolver (1990)

OPERATION COUNTERSTRIKE
(GERMANY)
Line-Up: Meikal Rumper, Christopher Haut, Stephan Haut, Hendrik Schelenz, Kai Swillus

Hannover based old school Thrash resurgence Metal band. OPERATION COUNTERSTRIKE bowed in with the 'Bromelie' album.

BROMELIE, (1999)
With A Grin / Purify / Three Cards / Asses
For The Masses / Pitched, Nailed & Broken /
Outrage / Bromelie / Pull The Trigger /
Lesson Learned / Shub-Niggurath / Fading /
Operation Counterstrike
SURVEILLENCE, Metal Glory (2001)
And... / Surveillance / Interlude / Caged- The
Challenged / To Fucking Ass To Suffer / The
Cherry Stone Cucumber Massacre / Tymp
(Thinking Just Means Work & Pain)

ORIGINAL SIN (NY, USA)
Line-Up: Danielle Draconis (vocals), Cynthia
Taylor (guitar), Pandora Fox (bass), Darlene
Destructo (drums)

ORIGINAL SIN were an all girl Thrash band
produced by 'The Lion' (a.k.a. VIRGIN
STEELE's David DeFeis). The girls' album is
perhaps best known for its album cover,
featuring the barely clothed torso of model
Jody Roxx.
Vocalist Danielle Draconis had met guitarist
Cynthia Taylor at a VIRGIN STEELE show.
The pair joined forces with bassist Pandora
Fox and drummer Darlene Destructo on a
band project that would blossom into
ORIGINAL SIN after a furious period of
writing and rehearsing.
Through the VIRGIN STEELE connection,
ORIGINAL SIN were signed by the group's
then label, the Canadian based Cobra
Records.
The group were initially going to go under the
moniker of SATAN'S DAUGHTERS, although
the decision was made to eventually use the
ORIGINAL SIN tag.

Albums:
SIN WILL FIND YOU OUT, Cobra CL 1009
(1986)
Conjuration Of The Watcher / The Curse / To
The Devil A Daughter / A Slice Of Finger /
Bitches From Hell / Succubus / Pandora's
Box / Thunder War / Enchantress Of Death /
Disease Bombs

OSIRIS (HOLLAND)
Line-Up: Bram Oever (vocals), Geert
Kerrsies (guitar), Maurice Oudhof (guitar),
Rene Bronwasser (bass), Marc Fien (drums)

A very technical Thrash Metal band. OSIRIS
came together in 1985 with Robbie Woning of
DEADHEAD, but this incarnation would soon
split.
The only remaining original member of the
band, drummer Marc Fein, reassembled
OSIRIS with the above line-up in 1987. The
group recorded two demos - 'Inextricable
Reversal' in 1989 and 'Equivocal Quiescence'
in 1991 - before getting the chance to put an
album together.
1992's 'Futurity And Human Depressions'
turned out to be a highly complex Speed
Metal outing with histrionic vocals.
OSIRIS went on to support Americans LÄÄZ
ROCKITT on their 1992 European tour.

Albums:
FUTURITY AND HUMAN DEPRESSIONS,
Shark (1992)
Futurity (Something To Think About) / Mass
Termination / Inextricable / Out Of Inspiration
/ Inner Recession / Fallacy (The Asylum) /
Frozen Memory

OUTBREAK (ITALY)
Line-Up: Patrick Wire (vocals), Andrea
Angelini (guitar), Matt Treasure (guitar),
Francesco Bucci (bass), David Folchitto
(drums)

During March of 2002 the STORMLORD
Black Metal rhythm section of bassist
Francesco Bucci and drummer David
Folchitto announced an allegiance with
guitarist Andrea Angelini and the BEHOLDER
duo of vocalist Patrick Wire and guitarist Matt
Treasure to found the Thrash Metal side
venture OUTBREAK. This unit, citing
influences ranging from Swedish Death Metal
to classic '80s Bay Area Thrash, bowed in
promptly with a two track promo CD.

Singles/EPs:
Breakdown Overall / Slaughter Machine,
(2002)

OUTBURST (HOLLAND)
Line-Up: Tijn (vocals), Jos Van Der Brand
(guitar), Arvid (guitar), Tjerk Maas (bass),
Serge Smolders (drums)

Thrashers OUTBURST were founded in 1998
by former ACROSTICHON members
drummer Serge Smolders, guitarists Jos Van
Der Brand and Michael. Vocalist Tijn and
bassist Tjerk Maas were added shortly after
but Michael would soon depart to concentrate
on his priority act CRUSTACEAN. A
replacement was duly found in March 2001 in
Arvid. OUTBURST supported Swedes
DARKANE before recording the demo
'Victory For A Soul'.

OUT OF ORDER (USA)
Line-Up: Devon (vocals), Rade (guitar), Jim
(bass), Matt (drums)

Albums:
LOST PARADISE, Walkthrufyre (1986)
No Reaction / Green Eyed Monster / Suicide Lullaby / She Knew She'd Lose / Snubbed / Anal Aggression / Dead Or Alive / Survival Of The Fittest / Blessing In Disguise / I Don't Feel Like Laughing / Eric B. / When It's All Done / The Ripper / Wicked Ways / Paradise Lost / Gotham City

OUTRAGE (JΛPΛN)
Line-Up: Yoshihiro Yasui (vocals / bass), Yousuke Abe (guitar), Sinya Tange (drums)

Japanese Thrashers OUTRAGE, founded in 1982, show strong classic Bay Area influences. The 1990 limited edition version of the album 'The Great Blue' includes cover versions of THE RAMONES 'Blitzkrieg Bop' and IGGY POP's 'I Feel Alright'.
OUTRAGE would still be soldiering on in 2002 promoting the 'Play Loud' EP.

Singles/EPs:
Ethiopia / Six Feet Down / We Know - You Don't / Denial, (2002) ('Play Loud' EP)

Albums:
OUTRAGE, Piledriver (1987)
BLACK CLOUDS, Polydor POCP-1156

(1988)
Curtain Of History / Under Control Of Law / Slowly But Surely / Black Clouds / Bring Him Back / Eos / Edge Of Death / Peyote
BLIND TO REALITY, Polydor POCP-1157 (1989)
Blind To Reality / In His Steel Claw / Call Of The Hunter / Nowhere To Turn / Name Your Poison / Game Of Greed / What The Meaning Of Freedom / Lookin' At The Time
THE GREAT BLUE, Polydor POCP-1158 (1990)
Just Believe In Me / Rusty Door / Fall To Disorder / The Day Of Rage / Voyage Of… / Clay Liner / The Truth / Great Blue / Bearing Down
THE FINAL DAY, Polydor POCP-1140 (1991)
My Final Day / Madness / Follow / Wings / Sad Survivor / Visions / Veiled Sky / River / Fangs
SPIT, East West AMCM-4117 (1993)
Mr. Rightman / Faith / To You / The Smoke / How Bad / The Key / Never Make The Same / Live My Life / Inner Strength / Eagle
LIFE UNTIL DEAF, East West AMCM-4221 (1995)
Megalomania / Vanishing Fully From The World / Undertow / Midnite Carnival / In Union With Earth / Echo / Draggin' Me Down

(Fear Is) / You Suck / Concrete Mirror / Argument / Live Until You Die / Popcorn Song

DAYS OF RAGE - 1986-1991, Polydor POCP-7100 (1995)

Under Control Of Law / Blind To Reality / Madness / Just Believe In Me / Curtain Of History / River / Veiled Sky / The Day Of Rage / Name Your Poison / Edge Of Death / Black Clouds / My Final Day / Love Song / Step On It (1986 demo)

WHO WE ARE, East West AMCM-4281 (1997)

Broken Man / Let My Ass Go / The Ladder / After All / World Slow Down / Stuck Together / Shadow / We Suck / Descent / Who We Are / Lash Me To The Wheel / Donkey Ride

IT'S PACKED, East West AMCM-4308-9 (1997)

Donkey Ride (Live) / Under Tow (Live) / Broken Man (Live) / Madness (Live) / Megalomania (Live) / Under Control Of Law / Death Trap / Edge Of Death / Step On It

VOLUME ONE, FTMCD-0758 (2000)

This Zombie Nation / Brain Storm / Tough Shit / Ocean / A.T.B. / Tonight Is The Night

OVERDOSE (BRAZIL)

Line-Up: B.Z. (vocals), Sergio Cichovicz (guitar), Claudio David (guitar), Eddie Weber (bass), Andre Marcio (drums)

Bela Horizonte's OVERDOSE internationally are known for sharing their debut album 'Seculo XX' with Brazil's biggest Rock export SEPULTURA. This album witnessed an OVERDOSE line-up of vocalist Bozo, guitarists Claudio David and Ricardo Dos Santos Souza, bassist Fernando Pazzini and drummer Helinho 'Helium' Eduardo. Following this outing, which sold in excess of 15,000 copies, OVERDOSE secured a placing on the 'Metal Massacre 9' compilation album.

1987's first full length album 'Conscience' found the band trimmed down to a quartet with just Claudio David handling guitars. The fourteen year old Andre Marcio would take over on the drum stool for 1989's 'You're Really Big' effort.

A string of Brazilian release albums followed prior to 1994's 'Progress Of Decadence' being released in America on Fierce Recordings and Europe on Music For Nations. OVERDOSE spent the year touring America on a package bill with SKREW and SPUD MONSTERS prior to European dates including the Dynamo festival. Back home in Brazil the band undertook a headline tour before hooking up as guests to SKID ROW. OVERDOSE were back in America touring with MERCYFUL FATE then CROWBAR to promote the 'Scars' album. The band's 1993

'Circus Of Death' album was issued in America during 1999 by Pavement Records. In recent years OVERDOSE enlisted former SEPULTURA and THE MIST guitarist Jairo Guerez and ex-ANGEL HEART bassist Gustavo Monsanto.

Albums:

SECULO XX, Cogumelo (1985) (Split LP with SEPULTURA)

Angels Of The Apocalypse / Children Of The World / Century X.X.

CONSCIENCE, Cogumelo (1987)

God Save The Metal / Messenger Of Death / Children Of The War / Save Our Hearts / Peace / Ultima Estrela / Kharma / The Day After / Rebellion / Prison Of The Conscience

YOU'RE REALLY BIG, Cogumelo (1989)

Stone Land / Nuclear Winter / Big As The Universe / Age Of Aquarius / Let Us Fly / United We'll Be One / Fight For Our Dreams

ADDICTED TO REALITY, Cogumelo (1991)

Sweet Reality / Night Child / White Clouds / Pain / Your Way / Strangers In Our Own Land / Winds Of Change / A Great Dream

CIRCUS OF DEATH, Cogumelo (1993)

The Zombie Factory / Children Of War / Dead Clouds / Profit / The Healer / Violence / A Good Day To Die / Powerwish / Beyond My Bad Dreams

PROGRESS OF DECADENCE, Under One Flag CDFLAG 83 (1994)

Rio, Samba E Porrada No Morra / Street Law / Straight To The Point / Progress Of Decadence / Capitalist Way / Deep In Your Mind / Noise From Brazil / Al Uquisarrera / Farela / No Truce / Faithful Death / Stupid Generation / Zombie Factory

SCARS, Music For Nations CDMFN 213 (1996)

The Front / My Rage / Manipulated Reality / How To Pray / Scars / Still Primitive / Just Another Day / School / Last Words / Postcard From Hell / Who's Guilty??? / Out Of Control - A Fairy Tale / Nu Dos Otro E Refresco

OVERKILL (CA, USA)

Line-Up: Merril Ward (vocals), Jeff Dimmick (guitar), Ron Cordy (bass), Kurt Markham (drums)

Bassist Ron Cordy joined fellow Los Angeles Metallers BITCH.

Singles/EPs:

Hell's Getting Hotter, S.S.T. SST008 (1984)

Albums:

TRIUMPH OF WILL, S.S.T. SST038 (1985)

What Do You Want / Triumph Of The Will /

American Dream / Slaughter / No Holds Barred / Victimized / Ladies In Leather / Bad Boy / Chains / Addict / Lost Life / On The Loose / Don't Need A Reason / Head On

OVERKILL

(New Providence, NJ, USA)
Line-Up: Bobby 'Blitz' Elsworth (vocals), Bobby Gustafson (guitar), D.D. Vernie (bass), Sid Falck (drums)

Formed in 1981 by drummer Rat Skates and bassist D.D. Verni after the pair had left the Hardcore Punk outfit LUBRICUNTS. OVERKILL's original incarnation was completed by ex-D.O.A. vocalist Bobby 'Blitz' Elsworth and two unidentified guitar players and this newly established quintet began gigging locally with a mainly cover dominated set.

In 1983, with both guitarists out of the group, former DROPOUTS man Bobby Gustafson joined the existing trio of Elsworth, Verni and Skates in time to lay down the 'Power In Black' demo. A five track blast of undiluted metal the tape comprised 'Overkill', 'The Beast Within', 'There's No Tomorrow', 'Death Riders' and 'Raise The Dead'.

By 1984 exposure generated by the demo led to an appearance on Metal Blade's 'Metal Massacre V' compilation and another track included on the 'New York Metal '84' collection. Ever the opportunists, Azra Records signed the group for the release of the four track 'Overkill' EP in July 1985 before Johnny Z's Megaforce label snapped OVERKILL up for the band's full blown debut album, 'Feel The Fire' produced by Carl Canedy - drummer with THE RODS, released towards the end of the year.

Johnny Z had been a fan of OVERKILL since the release of the 'Power In Black' demo. He sold 1,500 copies of it through his New Jersey based record store Rock n' Roll Heaven' alone. The band were signed after seeing them open for ANVIL at the L'Amours club in Brooklyn, New York.

The quartet arrived in Europe during the first half of 1986 opening for label mates ANTHRAX, although they were not on the bill of the British show ANTHRAX performed at the Hammersmith Palais, having already returned to the States.

OVERKILL did, however, return to Europe later in the year opening for SLAYER.

1991's 'Horrorscope', which included a radical reworking of EDGAR WINTER's 'Frankenstein', was to be OVERKILL's last album with Gustafson. Internal disputes had prompted the guitarist's departure and to plug the gap OVERKILL pulled in former FAITH OR FEAR man Merritt Gant and their erstwhile guitar technician Rob Cannavino.

By the 1996 album OVERKILL had found themselves, due to a combination of tenacity and dogged refusal to compromise musically, with a huge cult following in Germany. The band now comprising Blitz, Verni, guitarists Sebastian Marino and ex-LIEGE LORD man Joe Comeau and drummer Tim Mallare. Former guitarist Merritt Gant founded BLOOD AUDIO.

'The Killing Kind' album garnered numerous 'album of the month' credits selling well enough for the band to undertake a headline German tour in February.

Elsworth also found time in 1996 to produce a promo CD for New Jersey act DIRT CHURCH.

1999 found OVERKILL treading a well worn path issuing an album of covers, the band offering their interpretations of tracks by BLACK SABBATH, JUDAS PRIEST, KISS, DEEP PURPLE and naturally MOTÖRHEAD's 'Overkill'.

Comeau joined Canadians ANNIHILATOR in 2000. Two ex-OVERKILL men, vocalist Joe Comeau and guitarist Sebastian Marino, would make their presence felt at the August 2000 'Wacken Open Air' festival participating in a one off LIEGE LORD reunion gig. OVERKILL toured Germany in November 2000 supporting HALFORD.

The band would put in a short burst of dates in America during late November of 2001 packaged with NEVERMORE.

The 2002 line-up of OVERKILL consisted of Elsworth, Verni, guitarist Derek Tailer, also a member of Dee Snider's SICKMUTHAFUCKERS, second guitarist Dave Linsk and drummer Tim Mallare. This unit cut recordings for a live DVD and album project at New Jersey's Asbury Park in March.

Singles/EPs:
Fuck You (Live) / Rotten To The Core (Live) / Hammerhead (Live) / Use Your Head (Live) / Electro-Violence (Live), Under One Flag 12 FLAG 104 (1987)

Albums:
OVERKILL, Azra (1985)
FEEL THE FIRE, Megaforce MRI 1469 (1985)
Raise The Dead / Rotten To The Core / There's No Tomorrow / Second Son / Sonic Reducer / Hammerhead / Feel The Fire / Blood And Iron / Kill At Command / Overkill
TAKING OVER, Megaforce Atlantic 781 735-1 (1987)
Deny The Cross / Wreckin' Crew / Fear His Name / Use Your Head / Fatal If Swallowed /

BOBBY 'BLITZ' ELSWORTH of OVERKILL
Photo : Nico Wobben

OVERKILL

Powersurge / In Union We Stand / Electro-Violence / Overkill II

UNDER THE INFLUENCE, Megaforce Atlantic 781 865-2 (1988)
Shred / Never Say Never / Hello From The Gutter / Mad Gone World / Brainfade / Drunken Wisdom / End Of The Line / Head First / Overkill III

YEARS OF DECAY, Megaforce Atlantic K7 82045-2 (1989)
Time To Kill / Elimination / I Hate / Nothing To Die For / Playing With Spiders - Skullcrusher / Birth Of Tension / Who Tends The Fire / The Years Of Decay / E.Vil N.Ever D.Ies

HORRORSCOPE, Megaforce East West 7567822832 (1991)
Coma / Infectious / Blood Money / Thanx For Nothin' / Bare Bones / Horrorscope / New Machine / Frankenstein / Live Young, Die Free / Nice Day... For A Funeral / Soulitude

I HEAR BLACK, Atlantic 756782476 2 (1993)
Dreaming In Colombian / I Hear Black / World Of Hurt / Feed My Head / Shades Of Grey / Spiritual Void / Ghost Dance / Weight Of The World / Ignorance And Innocence / Undying / Just Like You

10 YEARS OF WRECKING YOUR NECK - LIVE, C.M.C. CMC 7603 (1995)
Where It Hurts / Infectious / Coma / Supersonic Hate / wrecking Crew / Powersurge / The Wait - New High In Lows / Skullcrusher / Spiritual Void / Hello From The Gutter / Anxiety / Elimination / Fast Junkie / World Of Hurt / Gasoline Dream / Rotten To The Core / Horrorscope / Under One / New Machine / Thanx For Nothin' / Bastard Nation / Fuck You

THE KILLING KIND, Edel Concrete 0086502CTR (1996)
Battle / God-Like / Certifiable / Burn You Down (To Ashes) / Let Me Shut That For You / Bold Face Pagan Stomp / Feeding Frenzy / The Cleansing / The Mourning After - Private Bleeding / Cold, Hard Fact

FUCK YOU AND THEN SOME, SPV 085-18722 (1997)
Fuck You / Rotten To The Core (Live) / Hammerhead (Live) / Use Your Head (Live) / Electro-Violence (Live) / Fuck You (Live) / Hole In The Sky (Live) / Evil Never Dies (Live) / Rotten To The Core / Fatal If Swallowed / The Answer / Overkill

FROM THE UNDERGROUND AND BELOW, SPV 085-18772 (1997)
It Lives / I'm Alright / Genocya / Save Me / Half Past Dead / Little Bit Of Murder / Long Time Dyin' / The Promise / F.U.C.T. / The Rip n' Tear

NECROSHINE, SPV CD 085-18882 (1999)
Necroshine / My December / Let Us Prey / 80 Cycles / Revelation / Stone Cold Jesus / Forked Tongue / I Am Fear / Black Line / Dead Man

COVERKILL, SPV 085-21542 CD (1999)
Overkill / No Feelings / Hymn 43 / Changes / Space Truckin' / Deuce / Never Say Die / Death Tone / Cornucopia / Tyrant / Ain't Nothin' To Do / I'm Against It

BLOODLETTING, SPV (2000)
Thunderhead / Bleed Me / What I'm Missin' / Death Comes Out To Play / Let It Burn / I, Hurricane / Left Hand Man / Blown Away /

My Name Is Pain / Can't Kill A Dead Man /
We Gotta Get Out Of This Place

OVERLORDE (NJ, USA)
Line-Up: Pat O'Donnell (vocals), Mark
Edwards (guitar), John M. Bunucci (bass),
David L. Wrenn (drums)

A Metal band from New Jersey.

Singles/EPs:
Snow Giant / The Masque Of The Red
Death / Overlorde, Strike Zone SZR 101
(1987)

OVERTHROW (CANADA)
Line-Up: Derek Rockall (guitar), Ian Mumble
(guitar), Nick Sagias (bass), Wayne Powell
(drums)

This Scarborough, Ontario band was founded
by four friends in high school in 1989. The
band quickly put out a six song EP on the
small Epidemic label. OVERTHROW had
some quick buzz in the Ontario Thrash
underground scene doing quite well at local
area gigs and so on.
A second release came in 1990 called 'The
Suffering Within' also on Epidemic. The
Thrash band, while competent musicians with
decent lyrics, failed to spark the imagination
of the Thrash buying public and band
dissolved shortly after.

Singles/EPs:
Infection Overthrow / Chaos Incarnate /
Conformity Institute / Chemically Exposed /
Suppression / Corrupted Faith, Epidemic
EP89-1 (1989) ('Bodily Domination' EP)

Albums:
THE SUFFERING WITHIN, Epidemic (1990)

PANACEA (AUSTRIA)
Line-Up: Markus (vocals / guitar), Frank (guitar), Alex (bass), Olli (drums)

Thrash Metal act PANACEA date back to November 1990. A five track demo 'Forgotten Dreams' followed the year after which garnered positive press. A second cassette ensued in June 1992 but during recording the band opted to release these songs as a fully commercial release titled 'Is It Human?'.

A second album capitalised on their efforts in 1995.

PANDEMONIC (SWEDEN)
Line-Up: Micke Ullenius (vocals), Micke Jaconsson (guitar), Harry Virtanen (bass), Nicke Karlsson (drums)

A Vasby based second wave Thrash act convened in the spring of 1998. PANDEMONIC was created by a collection of Death Metal veterans including former INTERNAL DECAY guitarist Micke Jacobsson and ex-SOILS OF FATE drummer Nicke Karlsson. This duo would be joined by singer Micke Ullenius and bassist Janne Sokura, the latter making way for Harry Virtanen of DEFORMITY pedigree.

PANDEMONIC issued an opening demo 'Lycanthropy'. It would be followed up on by the werewolf themed 2000 album 'The Authors Of Nightfear'.

The band would lose Karlsson bringing in 'Mackan' as replacement. Before long though Marcus Jonsson, a veteran of MORTIFER, FLAGELLATION and GENOCRUSH FEROX, was announced as the man on the drum stool.

Music (2000)
The Hunter / Wolfman's Lullaby / Changeling Eve / Authors Of Nightfear / The Forging Of A Beast / Clad In Wolven Shape / The Coming Of Dawn / Lycanthropic Siege

PANIC (Tamarac, FL, USA)
Line-Up: Mike Craig (vocals), Hank Edney (guitar), Gavin Graves (guitar), Pete Joseph (bass), Jon Sumerlade (drums)

Created in 1985 Metal band PANIC issued a 1990 demo tape.

PANIC (Seattle, WA, USA)
Line-Up: Jeff Braimes (vocals), Martin Chandler (guitar), George Hernandez (bass), Jack Coy (drums)

Ex-PANIC vocalist Jeff Braimes later forged WATTS in union with erstwhile MONO MEN personnel guitarist Dave Crider and drummer Aaron Roeder.

PANTERA (USA)
Line-Up: Phil Anselmo (vocals), Dimebag Darrell (guitar), Rex Brown (bass), Vinnie Paul (drums)

Metal band formed by brothers 'Diamond' Darrell Abbott and Vinnie Paul Abbott alongside vocalist Terry Lee Glaze and bassist Rex 'Rocker' Brown.

PANTERA (Spanish for 'Panther') started live in 1981 on the Texan club scene performing cover sets of VAN HALEN and KISS songs. Diamond Darrell's enthusiasm to pick up the guitar came from having witnessed Ace Frehley. To this day he sports an ACE FREHLEY tattoo and KISS emblazoned guitars.

PANTERA quickly became cult favourites on the underground Metal scene with fans being constantly bemused by the band's undoubted quality against a series of truly horrendous amateur album covers and PANTERA's inability to break into the big time.

Nevertheless PANTERA soon became

adopted sons on their home turf, supporting the likes of STRYPER, DOKKEN and QUIET RIOT promoting thier debut album 'Metal Magic' in 1983. Glaze was to change his surname to Lee for the 'Projects In The Jungle' album, a record which captured PANTERA drifting away from the more obvious melodic influences.

'I Am The Night' was like thier previous albums, produced by "The Eldn" (in reality Darrell and Vinnie's father) at Pantego Studios. This release found the band in a heavier mood, boosted their profile and scored maximum marks with much or the world's Metal press. PANTERA were still suffering from poor distribution, many fans being forced to pay extortionate import prices for the album. Consequently the album struggled to sell 25,000 copies.

Soon after 'I Am The Night's release Lee split from the band to form LORD TRACY (originally called TRACI LORDS) and PANTERA retreated into the shadows. A series of vocalists followed including Matt L'Amour (who later joined DIAMOND) and David Peacock.

These liaisons were short however and PANTERA re-emerged fronted by Louisiana native and ex-SAMHAIN and RAZORWHITE singer Phil Anselmo. The latter act also had in their ranks future CROWBAR man Matt Thomas and FALL FROM GRACE's Wil Buras.

Despite finding their frontman PANTERA were still blighted by problems. Their new record label Gold Mountain, tipped off about the band's prowess by KEEL guitarist MARC FERRARI, who had met PANTERA when KEEL had played in Dallas with LOUDNESS during 1985, tried to manouvere the band into commercial territory. Undaunted PANTERA recorded their heaviest album to date: 'Power Metal' and negotiated for a release on their own Metal Magic label.

MARC FERRARI guests on the album with PANTERA returning the favour by recording Ferrari's 'Proud To Be Loud'. Although 'Power Metal' was undoubtedly a much harder record than previous attempts it was nothing compared to what was to come...

PANTERA drew back away from the limelight during which time the band came close to splintering. Darrell had auditioned for the vacant guitar position in MEGADETH and was offered the post. However, Darrell insisted that Vinnie was part of the package and MEGADETH, who already had a drummer in Nick Menza, backed off, recruiting Marty Friedman instead.

Negotiations with Atco Records ensued upon their re-emergence. PANTERA surprised many with a new look (Anselmo now sporting

a close shorn haircut and numerous tattoos) and a radical change in direction. PANTERA's 'Cowboys From Hell' album offered bludgeoning Hardcore riffs, the solid intensity of their new songs burying any comparisons to their more melodic predecessors.

The 'Cowboys From Hell' tour opened in America with a touring bill that saw the Texans sharing the stage with EXODUS and SUICIDAL TENDENCIES. Later dates had PANTERA alongside MIND OVER FOUR and PRONG. In the midst of a Canadian tour JUDAS PRIEST vocalist ROB HALFORD joined the band onstage for versions of JUDAS PRIEST's 'Grinder' and 'Metal Gods'. This union was to aid PANTERA later the same year as they performed their first ever European shows in 1991 opening for the British metal Gods. Bearing in mind JUDAS PRIEST's status future events became quite bizarre as PRIEST frontman Rob Halford seemingly metamorphasised into Anselmo both vocally and image wise for his FIGHT project.

Two and a half years on the road had convinced PANTERA to pursue their new found harder direction with even more vigour and the resulting 1992 album 'A Vulgar Display Of Power' silenced all critics as it broke the band worldwide charting in both Britain and America.

PANTERA were by now openly opinionating their desire to exceed any aural ferocity that had gone before. Many rock fans believed the band to have lost the essence of songwriting in their hunt for extremity but many more fans lapped it up. The band meantime were confessing to recording albums almost spontaneously whilst under the influence.

Quite incredibly for a record of such ferocity 'Far Beyond Driven', complete with a cover of BLACK SABBATH's 'Planet Caravan', entered at the Number 1 position in the American Billboard album charts. PANTERA were quick to fling themselves headlong into a bout of touring with guests CROWBAR. South American shows were conducted to near ecstatic sold out crowds, dates in Argentina had ANIMAL and LETHAL as openers and in Brazil DR. SIN were the guests. July saw a strengthening of the touring package as PANTERA were now topping a bill comprising SEPULTURA and BIOHAZARD. By the close of the tour, including a Donington 'Monsters Of Rock' performance, a September British tour with support from DOWNSET and later American shows having PRONG as openers, the band had put in some 90 dates.

The Donington show was slightly marred by an ugly incident the night before at Nottingham's Rock City club where both Darrell and Vinnie were involved in altercations with journalists Morat of Kerrang! and Paul Rees of Raw respectively, the latter due to the drummer having once been portrayed by the magazine in cartoon form as Obelisk, Asterix The Gaul's fat partner.

The May 1994 single '5 Minutes Alone' came backed with a B side cover version of POISON IDEA's 'The Badge', the song originally having been cut for the band's contribution to 'The Crow' movie soundtrack.

1995 began with a continuation of live work but by March PANTERA had landed themselves in trouble when at a Canadian gig in Montreal a radio DJ perceived some of Anselmo's onstage raps to be of a racist tone. Anselmo was forced into issuing a public retraction purporting that his drunken remarks were off the cuff and ill advised.

1995 also saw the release of Anselmo's DOWN knockabout act's album 'Nola'. The front man had recorded a batch of brutal songs in some PANTERA downtime together with friends Pepper Keenan from CORROSION OF CONFORMITY, CROWBAR's Kirk Windstein and Todd Strange and EYEHATEGOD's Jimmy Bower.

Anselmo, billing himself as 'Anton Crowley' would also turn up as guitarist for the reformed NECROPHAGIA for the 1999 'Holocausto De La Morte' album.

2000 found Anselmo involved in the Black Metal 'star' side project EIBON. With a low key track inclusion on the 'Moonfog 2000' compilation album EIBON consisted of SATYRICON's Satyr Wongraven, DARKTHRONE's Fenriz, Maniac of MAYHEM and NECROPHAGIA's Killjoy.

PANTERA's 2000 European tour found SATYRICON as openers. American dates were curtailed when Anselmo broke two ribs at an early gig.

Another of Anselmo's 'Anton Crowley' side projects the Black Metal act VIKING CROWN also issued the 'Innocence From Hell' album the same year.

PANTERA got down to business in early 2001, touring to promote the new album. Following a batch of American headliners winding up in Anchorage, Alaska the band struck out to Seoul in Korea prior to Australasian gigs supported by CORROSION OF CONFORMITY. Not content to rest there PANTERA assembled a billing entitled 'Extreme Steel' for a further American leg strongly bolstered by MORBID ANGEL, SLAYER, STATIC X and SKRAPE.

However European festival billings, dubbed the 'Tattoo The Planet' dates originally in alliance with SLAYER, BIOHAZARD, VISION OF DISORDER and STATIC X, were far from trouble free. Following the September 11th terrorist attacks PANTERA pulled out of the tour leaving SLAYER to remain behind as headliners.

Toward the close of the year Anselmo seemingly took his passion for side ventures into overdrive declaring a further two bands to his ever lengthening list of side projects. SOUTHERN ISOLATION, which featured Anselmo's girlfriend Stephanie Opal as lead vocalist, saw Anselmo acting as guitarist. The band was rounded out by CHRIST INVERSION keyboard player Ross Karpelman, Kevin Bond of CHRIST INVERSION, CROWBAR and SUPERJOINT RITUAL on bass guitar and Sid Montz on drums. A four track EP was issued in October 2001 on the Baphomet label.

Also announced was another collaboration with Killjoy of NECROPHAGIA billed as ENOCH. This band also boasted the inclusion of Mirai from cult Japanese Black Metal band SIGH.

Vinnie Paul and Dimebag Darrel would pursue side activities too, although of a rather unexpected nature, forging an affiliation with Country & Western artist DAVID COE ALLEN. This Southern Rock styled venture would emerge billed as GASOLINE.

Singles/EPs:
Mouth For War / Rise, Atco A 5845 (1992) (7" single) **73 UK**
Mouth For War / Rise / Cowboys From Hell / Heresy, Atco A 5845CD (1992) (CD single)
Mouth For War / Mouth For War (Superloud mix) / Domination / Primal Concrete Sledge, Atco A 5845T (1992) (12" single)
Walk / Cowboys From Hell / Psycho Holiday (Live), Atco B 6076T (1993) (12' single) **34 UK**
Walk / Fucking Hostile / By Demons Be Driven, Atco B 6076CD (1993) (CD single)
Walk / No Good (Attack The Radical) / A New Level / Walk (Extended version), Atco B 6076CDX (1993) (CD single)
I'm Broken / Slaughtered, Atco B 5932T (1994) (12" single) **19 UK**
I'm Broken / Domination (Live) / Primal Concrete Sledge, Atco B 5932CD2 (1994) (CD single)
I'm Broken / Cowboys From Hell (Live) / Psycho Holiday (Live), Atco B 5932CD3 (1994) (CD single)
I'm Broken / Walk (Cervical edit) / Fuckin' Hostile, Atco B 5932X (1994) (12" single)
5 Minutes Alone / Badge, Atlantic A 8293 (1994) (7" white vinyl single)
Planet Caravan / 5 Minutes Alone, Atco A 5836 (1994) (7" single) **26 UK**
Planet Caravan / The Badge / Cowboys From Hell (Live) / Heresy (Live), Atco A 5836T (1994) (12" single)
Planet Caravan / The Badge / New Level

(Live) / Becoming (Live), Atco A 5836CD
(1994) (CD single)
Planet Caravan / The Badge / Domination
(Live) / Hollow (Live), Atco A 5836CD2
(1994) (CD single)

Albums:
METAL MAGIC, Metal Magic MMR 1283
(1983)
Ride My Rocket / I'll Be Alright / Tell Me If
You Want It / Latest Lover / Biggest Part Of
Me / Metal Magic / Widowmaker / Nothin' On
(But The Radio) / Sad Lover / Rock Out!
PROJECTS IN THE JUNGLE, Metal Magic
MMR 1984 (1984)
All Over Tonite / Out For Blood / Blue Lite
Turnin' Red / Like Fire / In Over My Head /
Projects In The Jungle / Heavy Metal Rules!
/ Only A Heartbeat Away / Killers / Takin' My
Life
I AM THE NIGHT, Metal Magic MMR 1985
(1985)
Hot And Heavy / I Am The Night / Onward
We Rock / D.G.T.T.M. / Daughters Of The
Queen / Down Below / Come-On Eyes /
Right On The Edge / Valhalla / Forever
Tonight
POWER METAL, Metal Magic MMR 1988
(1988)
Rock The World / Power Metal / We'll Meet
Again / Over And Out / Proud To Be Loud /
Down Below / Death Trap / Hard Ride /
Burnnn! / P.S.T. 88
COWBOYS FROM HELL, East West
7567913722 (1990)
Cowboys From Hell / Primal Concrete
Sledge / Psycho Holiday / Heresy /
Cemetery Gates / Domination / Shattered /
Clash With Reality / Medicine Man /
Message In Blood / The Sleep / The Art Of
Shredding
A VULGAR DISPLAY OF POWER, Atco
756791782 (1992) **64 UK, 44 USA**
Mouth For War / New Level / Walk / Fucking
Hostile / This Love / Rise / No Good For No
One / Live In A Hole / Regular People / By
Demons Be Driven / Hollow
FAR BEYOND DRIVEN, Atco 756792302-2
(1994) **3 UK, 1 USA**
Strength Beyond Strength / Becoming / 5
Minutes Alone / I'm Broken / Good Friends
And A Bottle Of Pils / Hard Lines, Sunken
Cheeks / Slaughtered / 25 Years / Shedding
Skin / Use My Third Arm / Throes Of
Rejection / Planet Caravan
THE GREAT SOUTHERN TRENDKILL,
Atco 7559 61908-2 (1996) **17 UK, 4 USA**
Drag The Waters / War Nerve / It Can't
Destroy My Body / 13 Steps To Nowhere /
Sandblasted Skin / Underground In America
/ Suicide Note (Part 1) / Suicide Note (Part
2)

100% OFFICIAL LIVE, Atco 7559-62068-2
(1997) **32 SWEDEN, 15 USA**
New Level / Walk / Becoming / 5 Minutes
Alone / Sandblasted Skin / Suicide Note Pt.
2 / War Nerve / Strength Beyond Strength /
Doom-Hollow / This Love / I'm Broken /
Cowboys From Hell / Cemetery Gates /
Hostile / Where You Come From / I Can't
Hide
REINVENTING THE STEEL, Atco 62451
(2000)
Hell Bound / Goddamn Electric / Yesterday
Don't Mean Shit / You've Got To Belong To It
/ Revolution Is My Name / Death Rattle /
We'll Grind That Axe For A Long Time / Up
Lift / It Makes Them Disappear / I'll Cast A
Shadow

PANZER (BRAZIL)
Line-Up: Élcio Cruz (vocals), André Pars
(guitar), Jan Leonardi (bass), Edson Graseffi
(drums)

Thrash Metal act PANZER was initially
founded as a trio during 1992 but had
collapsed a few years later. The name was
resurrected in 1998 for recording of the album
'Inside', which featured cover versions of both
JUDAS PRIEST's 'Nightcrawler' and the KISS
staple 'Detroit Rock City'. The JUDAS
PRIEST track would also show up on the
compilation 'The Loudest Times - A Tribute To
'80s Metal' issued in America by the ProgArt
label.
PANZER followed the debut with 'The
Strongest' in 2001 for Spiral Noise. Both
albums would subsequently be picked up for
Japanese distribution by the Arco Iris label.

Albums:
INSIDE, Destroyer (1999)
Limitations / Rejected / N.S.A / Breaking /
Despair / Detroit Rock City / Clowns Of Dust
/ Enough! / Pressure / Ethnic Ghetto /
Despair II / Night Crawler
THE STRONGEST, Spiral Noise (2001)
Fake Game Of Heroes / Red Days / Affliction
/ Show Me! / Box / Speedy / My Night / Your
Blood / The Strongest / Fear Of God / House
Of Decadence / The Strongest (Reprise)

PANZER DIVISION
(Washington DC, USA)
Line-Up: J.D. Feldstein (vocals), Dave
Bradley (guitar), Jimmy Crockett (bass),
John Tutko (drums)

PANZER DIVISION issued a demo in 1984.

PANTOKRATUR (GERMANY)
Line-Up: Eddy Kloß (vocals / bass), Hansi

Makowski (guitar), Chreddy Riepert (guitar), Karin Groß (keyboards), Arthur Gramsch (drums)

A Gothic Death Metal band with a great deal of Thrash influence and a penchant for abstract philosophy. PANTOKRATUR has been previously listed as a Christian band.
The group was created in 1989, a demo 'Faces Of Fate' following in 1991. Line-up changes, including the recruitment of Karin Groß on keyboards, ensued upfront of the 'Act' EP.

Singles/EPs:
Trip To The Other Side / Act / Sarcastic Lies / Flight Of Life, Pantokratur (1993) ('Act' EP)

PARADOX (GERMANY)
Line-Up: Charly Steinhauer (vocals / guitar), Markus Spyth (guitar), Roland Stahl (bass), Axel Blaha (drums)

A late '80s Speed Metal band, PARADOX debuted with the Roadrunner issued 'Product Of Imagination', produced by Kalle Trapp, in 1988. Founder members frontman Charly Steinhauer and drummer Axel Blaha are both ex-WARHEAD.
A new look PARADOX recorded the second Harris Johns produced album, 'Heresy', the band having drafted new guitarist Dieter Roth and bassist Matthias Schmitt. Erstwhile CRONOS TITAN guitarist Kai Paseman was recruited in November of 1989 but shortly after PARADOX would go into a period of hibernation. Paseman founded the KRAUTS, an act which evolved into DECLARATION OF DEPENDENCE issuing two albums.
PARADOX was reunited for a 'Wacken Open Air' show in August of 1999. Joining Steinhauer and Paseman were the esteemed SIEGES EVEN sibling rhythm section of bass player Oliver and drummer Alex Holzwarth. Besides making their mark with Progressive Metal band SIEGES EVEN the brothers have contributed to many other high profile acts - Oliver to BLIND GUARDIAN and Alex to Italian Symphonic Metal act RHAPSODY and Brazilians ANGRA.
The revised PARADOX released the 'Collision Course' album, which included a rendition of the SCORPIONS 'Dynamite', through the AFM Records label in 2000. Japanese versions of the album came with no less than three extra tracks: 'Pray To The Godz Of Wrath', 'Paradox' and 'Execution'. The band also contributed to a Nuclear Blast ABBA tribute album.
Oliver Holzwarth later teamed up with DEMONS & WIZARDS.

Albums:
PRODUCT OF IMAGINATION, Roadrunner RR9563 (1988)
Opening Theme / Paradox / Death, Screaming And Pain / Product Of Imagination / Continuation Of Invasion / Mystery / Kill That Beast / Pray To The Gods Of Wrath / Beyond Space / Wotan II
HERESY, Roadracer RO 9506-1 (1989)
Heresy / Search For Perfection / Killtime / Crusaders Revenge / The Burning / Massacre Of The Cathars / Serenity / 700 Years On / Castle In The Wind
COLLISION COURSE, AFM CD 042 (2000)
Decade Of Sorrow / Collision Course / Rearrange The Past / Path Of Denial / Savior / Blamed For Nothing / Prostitution Of Society / Shattered Illusions / Sadness / Overshadowed / Dynamite

PARALEX (UK)
Line-Up: Phillip Ayling (vocals), Kev Bower (guitar), Neil Bryan (drums), Ian Dobbs (bass), Mark Gibson (guitar)

A Nottingham NWoBHM band that have been cited by METALLICA as an early influence, the roots of PARALEX trace back to the 1978 act TOKIO ROSE, a band comprising bassist Tony Speakman, drummer Tim Bowler, guitarists Nigel Revell and Howard Ccooper and singer Nick Shipley.
In their short period together TOKIO ROSE replaced Nigel Revell with Mick Hartshorn before the group split, with Speakman joining SOVEREIGN and Bowler joining Grantham act OVERLORD. With SOVEREIGN's demise Speakman joined PARALEX, replacing Ian Dobbs.
Together with vocalist Phil Ayling, guitarist Mark Gibson and drummer Neil Bryan, Speakman recorded the rare green vinyl 'White Lightning' single. A further cassette single followed featuring the tracks 'Getting Somewhere', 'Rock The Force', 'Justice' and 'Lionheart'.
PARALEX formed a band co-operative with two other local acts RACE AGAINST TIME and RADIUM and played many gigs together. Eventually the band folded with Speakman and Bower leaving to form Black Metal pioneers HELL with ex-RACE AGAINST TIME vocalist Dave G. Halliday and ex-TOKIO ROSE drummer Tim Bowler.
PARALEX vocalist Phil Ayling later turned up in mid '80s Thrash merchants METAL MESSIAH.

Singles/EPs:
White Lightning / Black Widow / Travelling Man, Reddingtons Rare Records DAN004 (1980)

PARAZITE (SWEDEN)
Line-Up: Larsa Bengtsson (vocals), Ola Renske (guitar), Linkan Andersson (guitar), Martin Karlsson (bass), Geron Fritofsson (drums)

Singles/EPs:
Live In Pain / A Different Kind Of Livin' / Bastard / Cry Baby, Parazite PZCD001 (1994)

PARIAH (UK)
Line-Up: Mick Jackson (vocals), Steve Ramsey (guitar), Russ Tippins (guitar), Graeme English (bass), Sean Taylor (drums).

Formed from SATAN, a band that achieved great success in Europe on the German Steamhammer label, PARIAH was basically the same band, but a name change was thought in order due to the connotations of the old monicker.
The first album was recorded with producer Roy Rowland. Unfortunately, 'The Kindred' was never given a British release as PARIAH concentrated on the lucrative European market.
The second album, recorded at Horus Studios and produced by the band, built upon the success of the debut and proved that the name change had been the correct move as PARIAH albums sold in greater numbers than previous SATAN records. However, PARIAH folded amidst financial wranglings with their record company, even though a third album was recorded at Links Studios in Newcastle during 1993. It remained unreleased, but the band that recorded it featured guitarists Steve Ramsey and Russ Tippins, bassist Graeme English, ex SATAN and BATTLEAXE drummer Ian McCormack and former TYSONDOG vocalist Alan Hunter.
As Ramsey and English went on to form the excellent Folk Metal band SKYCLAD erstwhile drummer Sean Taylor joined BLITZKRIEG.
The 1993 recordings were finally issued by the band members themselves as 'Unity' in 1997.

Albums:
THE KINDRED, Steamhammer 08-7526 (1988)
Gerrymander / The Rope / Scapegoat / Foreign Bodies / La Guerra / Inhumane / Killing For Company / Icons Of Hypocrisy / Promise Of Remembrance
BLAZE OF OBSCURITY, Steamhammer SPV 85-7595 (1989)
Missionary Of Mercy / Puppet Regime /

Canary / Blaze Of Obscurity / Retaliate! / Hypochondriac / Enemy Within / The Brotherhood
UNITY, (1997)
Unity / Reactionary / Walking Wounded / No Exit / Snakes & Ladders / One Of Us / Saboteurs / Mutual Street / The Jonah / Learning To Crawl

PARIAH (Brandon, FL, USA)
Line-Up: Garth Egger (vocals), Shaun Egger (guitar), Wayne Derrick (bass), Chris Egger (drums)

Albums:
TAKE A WALK, Moshroom 20002 (1988)
Take A Walk / King Of The Night / Running Scared / Loser's Ground / Evil / Breakfree / Frustrated Obsession / Speedball

PATRIARCH (BELGIUM)
Line-Up: Herman Cambre (vocals), Jan Geerts (guitar), Freddy Mylemans (guitar), Paul Verboven (bass), Herman Cambre (drums)

Originally known as PARIAH and formed by guitarist Freddy Mylemans in March 1983, issuing a self titled demo the same year followed in 1984 by a second four track tape 'Evil Wings'. The band had to be put on ice in 1988 when bassist Jan T'Seyen was killed in a road accident. However, before the end of the year the band had reformed (confusingly with a vocalist and drummer that share the same name!), but due to press coverage of the British version of PARIAH opted to change titles to PATRIARCH. A new demo secured a deal with German label Shark Records.
Following two albums PATRIARCH split with their label and underwent a massive line-up change. Only guitarist Freddy Mylemans remained from the original group as he was joined by new members in vocalist Erik Rinkes, guitarist Jan Van Bulck, bassist Paul Verboven and drummer Frank Dresselaers.
This line-up released a demo in 1995 featuring 'Parade Of Fools', 'The End Of The Day', 'I Machine' and 'Changing Matter'.

Albums:
PROPHECY, Shark 016 (1991)
At The Warlord's Command / Dance / Children Of The Moon / Shadowland / Father Kreator / Castle Of Darkness / Kmar-Q-Luque / Island Of Insanity / Prophecy / Pilgrims Of The Dark Age
WORLD WITHIN WORLDS, Rock Power R.P. 003 (1993)

Leviathans / The Watching Eve / Lady Of The Lines / Steleas Of Ghorfa (instrumental) / World Within Worlds / Decadence Within / Burning Grounds / Forsaken Wisdom / Strange Reality

P.C.P. (Vineburg, CA, USA)
Line-Up: Nasty Nate Clark (vocals), Jeffro Belly (guitar), Mick Thomas (bass), Brian Durham (drums)

Southern Bay Area Thrashers P.C.P. comprising sole surviving founder member 'Nasty' Nate Clark on vocals and bass guitar, Jefro Belly on guitar and Brian 'Bandit' Durham on drums. The group originally came together in 1994 with a line up of Nate Clark, Mike Leahy, Sam Moore and Craig Bingham, a union of erstwhile personnel from acts such as PROPHECY and INIFINITY PERCENT. However, a succession of line-ups eventually settled with the present trio. Brian Durham, a veteran of such acts as RINGWORM, EXCELSIOR and PADURHAM, was inducted during 1995. Guitarist Jeffro Belly joined in 1996, citing credits with SOCIETY'S PRODUCT and even THE BEVERLEY BEER BELLYS.
P.C.P. issued their debut album, 'Evilhatemotherfucker', during 2000. Bass player Mick Thomas, a former member of CONFUSED, was added in April of 2002.
Clark also operates with VENGEANCE whilst both Durham and Thomas are involved with THE DJN PROJECT.

Albums:
EVILHATEMOTHERFUCKER, (2000)

PENDEMIA (UK)

Cumbrian Thrash band PENDEMIA added drummer Jim Harley in 1988, although guitarist Jonathan Sharpe left in 1989 to form DISSENTION.
Nevertheless, PENDEMIA issued a self-financed album in 1990.

Albums:
NARCOTIC RELIGION, CMFT CMFT4 (1990)

PERSONAL WAR (GERMANY)
Line-Up: Matthias Zimmer (vocals / guitar), Sascha Kerschgens (guitar), Frank Buchwalter (bass), Martin Buchwalter (drums)

A deliberately 'Bay Area' styled Thrash band PERSONAL WAR, previously known in their formative days as CROSSING SKULLS, forged part of the retro Thrash movement in Germany during the mid '90s.
PERSONAL WAR first came to attention with a demo 'Fear Of Death'. A later demo track 'Putrefaction' would also pull in valuable exposure with its inclusion on the 'Rock Hard' magazine 'Unerhort' compilation CD for unsigned bands.
PERSONAL WAR would issue the debut 1998 album 'The Inside' through the Gernhart label, following this with a move to B. Mind Records for May 2000's 'Newtimechaos'. The record included guest guitar solos courtesy of RAGE's Victor Smolski.

Albums:
THE INSIDE, Gernhart (1998)
NEWTIMECHAOS, B.Mind (2000)
Newtime Bitch / Questions / Nothing Remains At All / Area Black / The Unknown / Voices / Mother Darkness / Angels / The Bag Of Bones / Dying Times

PESTILENCE (HOLLAND)
Line-Up: Patrick Mameli (vocals / guitar), Patrick Uterwyck (guitar), Tony Choy (bass), Marco Foddis (drums)

A popular Death-Thrash Grindcore Metal outfit that have seen considerable album sales in Europe in spite of an ever fluctuating line-up, PESTILENCE were conceived in spring 1986 and were originally a trio of guitarist Randy Meinhard, drummer Marco Foddis and vocalist / guitarist Patrick Mameli. As a three piece PESTILENCE released their first demo 'Dysentery'.
The group later added vocalist / bassist Martin Van Drunen, who assumed vocal duties from Mameli, and cut another demo entitled 'The Penmance'. The debut album, 'Malleus Malificarum', was produced by Kalle Trapp.
In January 1989 PESTILENCE underwent a major line-up reshuffle with Foddis and Meinhard quitting. Mcinhard, replaced by former THERIAC man Patrick Uterwijk, joined SACROSANCT and later SUBMISSION. Van Drunen concentrated from this point purely on vocals and the band drafted in the aptly named Bass on bass guitar.
In early 1993 the band recruited new bassist Jereon Thesseling. Vocalist Van Drunen quit following 'Consuming Impulse' to join ASPHYX, SUBMISSION and later BOLT-THROWER.
For 'Testimony Of The Ancients' PESTILENCE employed the services of Florida's CYNIC bassist Tony Choy and Dutchman Jeroen Thesseling joined PESTILENCE as a permanent bassist in late

1993. The same year saw the release of the band's last album 'Spheres'. Following European dates with CYNIC the band folded.

Albums:
MALLEUS MALIFICARUM, Roadrunner RR95191 (1988)
Malleus Malificarum / Antromorphia / Parricide / Subordinate To The Domination / Extreme Unction / Commandment / Chemotherapy / Bacterial Surgery / Cycle Of Existence / Orculum Infame / Systematic Instruction
CONSUMING IMPULSE, Roadrunner RR 9421 (1989)
Dehydrated / Process Of Suffocation / Suspended Animation / The Trauma / Chronic Infection / Out Of The Body / Echoes Of Death / Deify Thy Master / Proliferous Souls / Reduced To Ashes
TESTIMONY OF THE ANCIENTS, Roadracer RO 9285 (1991)
The Secrecies Of Horror / Bitterness / Twisted Truth / Darkening / Lost Souls / Blood / Land Of Tears / Free Us From Temptation / Prophetic Revelations / Impure / Testimony / Soulless / Presence Of The Dead / Mindwarp / Stigmatized / In Sorrow
SPHERES, Roadrunner RR9081 (1993)
Mind Reflections / Multiple Beings / The Level Of Perception / Aurian Eyes / Soul Search / Personal Energy / Voices From Within / Spheres / Changing Perspective / Phileas / Demise Of Time
MIND REFLECTIONS – THE BEST OF PESTILENCE, Roadrunner RR 8996 (1995)
Out Of The Body / Twisted Truth / The Process Of Suffocation / Parricide / Mind Reflections / Dehydrated / Land Of Tears / Hatred Within / The Secrecies Of Horror / Subordinate To The Domination / Dehydrated (Live) / Chemotherapy (Live) / Presence Of The Dead (Live) / Testimony (Live) / Chronic Infection (Live) / Out Of The Body (Live)

PHALANX (GERMANY)
Line-Up: Dennis (vocals), Waips (guitar), Holger Simon (guitar), Chris (bass), Carsten 'Cazy' Jercke (drums)

PHALANX, formed in 1986 and secured a deal with D&S Records from their 1991 demo 'Towards The Pearly Gates'.
'The Judas Touch' debut arrived in 1993. PHALANX's second album included a cover of METALLICA's 'Enter Sandman' but miscredited it simply as 'Sandman'.

Albums:
THE JUDAS TOUCH, D&S Records DSR CD 003 (1993)
Do You Think / The Seeds We Plant / Towards The Pearly Gates / I Will Devour / The Judas Touch / A Winterplay's Thought / Lethal Toy / Closed Eyes / On The Beach
LOOK BEHIND THE MASK, D&S Records DSR CD 025 (199-)
Silent Consent / Searching For Comfort / Face The Facts / State Of Mind / Yanus / Scratch The Surface / Why Speak? / Remnants / Listening To Yourself / Sandman (Charleston mix)

PHANTOM LORD (BELGIUM)
Line-Up: Simon Berger (vocals / guitar), Gunther Wassel (guitar), Klaus Schwartzen (bass), Wolfgang Gundermann (drums)

Albums:
PHANTOM LORD, Pentagram (1985)
Live Fast, Rock Hard / Mad Bash / Hang Tough / I'm In H.E.A.T. / Mach Ten / Speed Kills / Fight The Thunder / Phantom Lord / White Fire
EVIL NEVER SLEEPS, LSR (1986)
Speed Demons / Highway Of Death / Call Of The Wild / Battle Zone (Guitar Solo) / Evil Never Sleeps / Mercy Killer / Wicked World / Avenging Angels

PHYSICAL ATTRACTION (SWEDEN)
Line-Up: Anders Palme (vocals), Peter Lindell (guitar), Tobbe Nyberg (guitar), Räven Alisic (bass), Martin Palme (drums)

A Hardcore Thrash act in the style of many similar New York based acts, PHYSICAL ATTRACTION featured ex-members of REFUSE.

Albums:
THE FOOL LEAD THE BLIND, Progress PCD 15 (1995)
Stones Are Cold / The Fool Lead The Blind / Your Obligation / Life In Pain / People With Power / Complete Deafness / I Hate You More... / Someone Else's Words / Master Of Disaster / Brainkilled / Undress Your Soul

PIECE DOGS (Atlanta, GA, USA)
Line-Up: Greg Anderson (vocals), Mike Grimmett (guitar), Kyle Sanders (bass), John Connolly (drums)

Atlanta Thrashers PIECE DOGS would contribute to Nu-Metal history with bassist Kyle Sanders subsequently joining SKREW then MEDICATION in August of 2001. Meantime drummer John Connolly was later to be found in the ranks of SEVENDUST.

EXES FOR EYES, Energy (1992)
Devxl Dog / Sxck Of Xt / Mornxn Sun Burnxn / The Outcast / Death Chant / Who's Got Xt / Mentally Sound / Hxgh Anxxety / Rxdxn Hxgh / Broken Wxng / Hatrxsm

PIERCE (NY, USA)

Albums:
PIERCE, Screamin' SKULL (1989)

PILEDRIVER (CANADA)

Infamous Thrash Metal band. The figure known as PILEDRIVER was in fact one Gord Kirchin, previously a bass player and singer with INCOGNITO, MAINSTREAM, a 1982 incarnation of FIST and also U.N.

MAINSTREAM vocalist Louise Remy aided on lyrics for the album whilst MAINSTREAM's Leslie Howe recorded guitar. Although originally planned as a pure money making exercise PILEDRIVER's use of bondage artwork and deliberately provocative song titles could not hide the fact that the songs were actually rather well done. Consequently the album sold exceptionally well and was licensed worldwide.

The totally fictitious band was listed as Piledriver, guitarists Bud Slaker and Knuckles Akimbo with drummer Former Lee.

In America the song titles were deemed too obscene hence 'Alien Rape' became 'Alien Dead', 'Sex With Satan' became 'Devil's Lust' and 'Sodomize The Dead' was changed to 'Twister'.

After recording of 'Metal Inquisition' Kirchin joined ICE but was recalled to perform on another PILEDRIVER album. 'The sophomore effort 'Stay Ugly' included anonymous contributions from VIRGIN STEELE men David DeFeis and Eddie Pursino.

Once again fake musicians names were used in guitarists Bruizer Bernette and John Savage, bassist Sal Gibson and drummer Hammer.

Kirchin planned to take PILEDRIVER on the road and drafted vocalist guitarist Jim Doherty and guitarist Sean Abbott. By 1989 PILEDRIVER had a new look with Randy Deeg on guitar and Bend Quieser on drums. The latter soon departed as sessions for a future third PILEDRIVER album to be titled 'Shock' was written with Kirchin's brother Randy on second guitar. The last PILEDRIVER incarnation included the Kirchin brothers, guitarist Dave Copeland and drummer Ruston Baldwin.

Kirchin would also contribute anonymously to the CONVICT album 'Go Ahead Make My Day'. Kirchin and Copeland, with new drummer Shawn Tilley, would later use this projected PILEDRIVER material in his new act DOGS WITH JOBS.

Following two DOGS WITH JOBS albums Kirchin created SOFA Q. The '90s reissue of 'Metal Inquisition' on High Vaultage Records in Germany included an interview with 'Piledriver'.

Albums:
METAL INQUISITION, Cobra CL1001 (1985)
Metal Inquisition / Sex With Satan / Sodomize The Dead / Witch Hunt / Piledriver / Human Sacrifice / Alien Rape
STAY UGLY, Cobra CL1002 (1986)
The Incubus / Metal Death Racer / The Fire God / Chaos / The Warning / Lord Of Abominations / Flowers Of Evil / The Executioner

P.I.T.T. (SOUTH AFRICA)
Line-Up: Marco (vocals), Stefan (guitar), Alex (bass), Kerryn (drums)

A Johannesburg Thrash / Hardcore act that relocated to London in February of 2001. In South Africa P.I.T.T. have been prolifically active on the live scene and supported CRYOGENIC during October of 1998.

P.I.T.T. was created in 1996 originally featuring a rhythm section of bassist Andrew and drummer Caleb. These two would leave in February of 1997. A succession of bassists followed including Steven, Bernard (who lasted two gigs), Filippo and the female four stringer Tamlyn who, upon joining in August of 1998 stuck the course for three years.

P.I.T.T. issued two self-financed albums in 2000, 'Three And A Half Years In The Making' in March, comprising archive material, and 'Forced Illusion' in December.

Albums:
THREE AND A HALF YEARS IN THE MAKING, (2000)
The Hand That Feeds / Gathering Of Introverts / Little White Room / The Dreamer / Prison / Rogue Trooper
FORCED ILLUSION, (2000)

PLEUROSIS (SPAIN)

A Spanish Thrash band who prefer to sing in their native tongue.

Albums:
NO MAS NUCLEAR, (19--)

CHRIS POLAND (USA)

Ex-MEGADETH guitarist. Upon his ousting from MEGADETH Poland issued the solo album 'Return To Metalopolis' featuring his brother Mark on drums and ex-ARCADE man John Mason on vocals.

The Poland brothers and Mason's next step was to form DAMN THE MACHINE, an act that lasted one album.

The '90s found Poland with a new avant-garde Metal act MUMBO'S BRAIN before issuing a further solo effort 'Chasing The Sun'. Poland also has a live act entitled OHM. Mark Poland has also performed live with WHITE ZOMBIE drumming on a Japanese tour.

Albums:
WELCOME TO METALOPOLIS,
Roadrunner RR 9348-2 (1990)
Club Ded / Alexandria / Return To Metalopolis / Heinous Interruptus / The Fall Of Babylon / Row Of Crows / Theatre Of The Damned / Beelzebub Bop / Apparition Station / Khazad Dum
CHASING THE SUN, Grooveyard 001 (1999)
Chasing The Sun / Hip Hop Karma / Wendell's Place / Robostomp / Straight Jacket / Cosmo's Thumb / Lu Lu's Dream / Salvador / Interference Blues / Alphabet City / Mercy / Song For Paul (31 Summers / Alexandria '99
RARE TRAX, Grooveyard 002 (1999)

POLLUTED INHERITANCE
(HOLLAND)
Line-Up: Ronald Camonier (vocals / guitar), Erwin Wesdorp (guitar), Menno De Fouw (bass), Friso Van Wijk (drums)

A Death / Thrash band, POLLUTED INHERITANCE's debut album was produced by ex-HOLY MOSES man Andy Classen.

Albums:
ECOCIDE, West Virginia WVR SPV 084-57312 (1992)
Faces / Dissolved / Eaten / Memories Of Sadness / Substance Of Existence / Fear / Stillborn / After Life / Rottings / Look Inside
BETRAYED, Displeased DSFA 1002 (1996)
Intro / Forgotten Cause / Mental Connection / Elimination / Betrayed / Emptiness / Drowning (In Faith) / Indulge / Never To Be Free / Need Me / My Voice

POLTERGEIST (SWITZERLAND)
Line-Up: Andre (vocals), V.O. Pulver (guitar), Tom (bass), Walt (drums)

Heavily influenced by German Thrash Metal, this Swiss quartet came together in 1985 and released their debut three track demo in 1988, produced by Schmier of DESTRUCTION.

In the wake of Schmier's departure from DESTRUCTION Andre contributed lead vocals to the DESTRUCTION album 'Cracked Brain'.

POLTERGEIST evolved into Neo-Thrashers GURD during the mid '90s, recording some four albums on Century Media Records up to 1998's 'Down The Drain'.

AIN'T DEAD YET, BABYLON SAD and KROKUS drummer Peter Haas has also sessioned for POLTERGEIST. Ex-POLTERGEIST bassist Marek Felis founded CHURCHILL.

Singles/EPs:
You've Leaned Your Lesson, Century Media (1989) (Split flexidisc with LIAR. Free with 'Rock Hard' magazine)

Albums:
DEPRESSION, Century Media 9705-2 (1989)
Three Hills / Depression / Inner Space / Writing On The Wall / Wheels Of Sansara / You've Learned Your Lesson / Prophet / Ziita / Shooting Star
BEHIND MY MASK, Century Media CM 9715 (1991)
We Are The People / Behind The Mask / Act Of Violence / Prey / Delusion / Drilled To Kill / Make Your Choice / Chato's Land / Still Alive / Driftin' Away
NOTHING LASTS FOREVER, Haunted House 084-55812 (1994)
Only You Remain / Empty Inside / Those Were Better Days / Just Doin' My Job / Never Again / Haunted House / Nothing Lasts Forever / You've Seen Your Future / Tell Me / Darken My Mind / Living For The Games

POROSITY OF MIND (GERMANY)
Line-Up: Marcus (vocals), Olli (guitar), Korfe (bass), Eike (drums)

A Hardcore / Thrash act with lyrics in both German and English.

Albums:
SHOW YOUR FAITH, Raiser RM 9026 (1996)
Heile Welt / Voices / No Escape / Dich / Get Fucked / I Don't Care / Gewissen / Bad Influence / Rise To Power / Menschenwürde / Nightmares / Aim
IMPROVEMENT, Raiser RM 9018 (1998)

Embarrassment / Your Fault / The Flow / Mitleid / Open Your Mind / Wand Aus Stahl / I regret / Rough Time / Scheig! / Trust / Tief In Mir / Ozelot / Between The Lines

POSEIDON (GERMANY)
Line-Up: Konde (vocals), Thommi (guitar), Markus (bass), Holger (drums)

<u>Singles/EPs:</u>
The Final Gate: BTSGOH / Freedom Of Thought / Violence, Poseidon (1989)

POSSESSED
(San Francisco, CA, USA)
Line-Up: Jeff Beccara (vocals / bass), Larry LaLonde (guitar), Mike Tarrao (guitar), Mike Sus (drums)

One of the instigators of the Bay Area Thrash scene. Founded as teenagers during 1983 POSSESSED were originally fronted by singer Barry Fisk. Tragedy struck the band early in their career though when Fisk committed suicide.
With Jeff Beccara replacing Fisk the band, including guitarists Mike Tarrao and Brian Montana with drummer Mike Sus, cut a 1984 demo which excited the interest of Metal Blade Records. The label gave an inclusion to POSSSESSED's 'Swing Of The Axe' to their 'Best Of Metal Massacre' compilation but did not sign the band up for an album.
This honour fell to Combat Records although not before Montana was fired, apparently for disagreeing with the bands image of leather, studs and inverted crosses. Larry LaLonde took his place for the debut 'Seven Churches'.
POSSESSED toured Europe with VOIVOD in 1986. The 'Beyond The Gates' album, produced by Carl Canedy of THE RODS, came wrapped in a lavish fold out sleeve, a rare extravagance for a Thrash act.
The follow up mini-album 'The Eyes Of Horror' was produced by none other than guitar guru JOE SATRIANI and found the group mellowing out slightly.
POSSESSED fractured leaving Tarrao to carry on the name. LaLonde would join BLIND ILLUSION then create the offbeat but commercially successful PRIMUS. Beccara suffered the misfortune of being shot by two drug addicts and was paralyzed from the waist down.
POSSESSED resurfaced in 1992 comprising of Tarrao, guitarist Mark Strausberg, bassist Bob Yost and drummer Walter Ryan. The band supported MACHINE HEAD the same year and cut a three song demo. POSSESSED's last incarnation came in 1993. Former POSSESSED guitarist Mike

Hollman joined hardcore merchants PRO-PAIN in 1994.
Ryan joined MACHINE HEAD. Torrao later forged IKONOCLAST.
Although their career was short the band's music is now held in high regard in particular by today's Black Metal legions.

<u>Albums:</u>
SEVEN CHURCHES, Roadrunner RR 9757 (1985)
Exorcist / Burning In Hell / Seven Churches / Holy Hell / Fallen Angel / Pentagram / Evil Warriors / Satan's Curse / Twisted Minds / Death Metal
BEYOND THE GATES, Under One Flag FLAG 3 (1986)
Heretic / Tribulation / March To Die / Phantasm / No Will To Live / Beyond The Gates / Beast Of The Apocalypse / Séance / Restless Dead / Dog Fight
THE EYES OF HORROR, Under One Flag FLAG 16 (1987)
Confessions / My Belief / The Eyes Of Horror / Swing Of The Axe / Storm In My Mind

POST MORTEM (MA, USA)
Line-Up: John McCarthy (vocals / bass), John Alexander (guitar), Mark Kelley (bass), Rick McIver (drums)

PHANTOM BLUE guitarist Michelle Meldrum guests on the 'Missing Link' album alongside Andrew Donheiser and Phil Williams.
By 1988 POST MORTEM had ousted guitarist John McCarthy in favour of Rich Goyette. The band were in the press the same year for all the wrong reasons when it was alleged that an unidentified POST MORTEM member was arrested in Boston for "indecent exposure for public masturbation"!

<u>Albums:</u>
CORONERS OFFICE, New Renaissance NRR 11 (1986)
Armies Of The Dead / Waiting For The Funeral / Ready To Die / No Time / Concealed / (It Was) Just A Thought / Syncopated Jazz / Soupy Sales / Coroners Office / Death To The Masses / I Want To Die / Run Amok
THE MISSING LINKS, New Renaissance NRR 19 (1987)
Caveman / Organized Crime / Fetus Man Quietus / Charnel House
FESTIVAL FOR FUN, Post Mortem (199-)
DESTINED FOR FAILURE, Red Light (1993)

POWERLORD (OK, USA)
Line-Up: Dane Cook (vocals), Tony Gourley

(guitar), Brian Massey (bass), Bob Gourley (drums)

Drummer Bob Gourley had actually missed the boat pre-POWERLORD as his early liaisons included stints with then fledgling outfits SLAYER and DARK ANGEL.

Albums:
THE AWAKENING, Shark 008CD (1986)
Masters Of Death / Malice / Silent Terror / The Invasion Of The Lords / Merciless Tyrants / (The Awakening) Powerlord

POWERMAD (MN, USA)
Line-Up: Joel Dubay (vocals / guitar), Jeff Litke (bass), Todd Haug (guitar), Adrian Liberty (drums)

Guitarist Todd Haug superseded Bill Hill who appears on the debut.

Albums:
POWERMAD, Combat Boot Camp (1986)
Chasing The Dragon / Terminator / Plastic Town / Nice Dreams / Blind Leading The Blind
THE MADNESS BEGINS, Reprise (1988)
Terminator / Hunter Seeker / Gimme Gimme Shock Treatment
ABSOLUTE POWER, Reprise (1989)
Slaughterhouse / Absolute Power / Nice Dreams / Returning From Fear / Test The Steel (Powermad) / Plastic Town / B.N.R. / Failsafe / Brainstorm / Final Frontier

POWERSURGE (Tampa, FL, USA)
Line-Up: James Marra (vocals), Eddie Rice (guitar), Todd Boese (guitar), Todd Dyer (bass), Rudy Goryance (drums)

Tampa's POWERSURGE pulled in solid reviews if little sales. Their 1988 demo tape included drummer Hal Loo.

Albums:
POWERSURGE, Roadrunner RR 93112 (1991)
Words / Pulled Over / Call Me / Engine Rail / Battle Call / Burning Revenge / Tear Up The Pavement / Shock Wave / Wall Of Power / Stress Attack

POWERTRIP (CA, USA)
Line-Up: Jeff Dahl (vocals), Mike Bailey (guitar), John Duffy (bass), John Bliss (drums)

Drummer John Bliss sadly died of a heart attack in June 1988 aged 32.

Albums:
WHEN CUT WE BLEED, Public (1983)
Demons / Lab Animal / Have A Nice Day / No Place / Caught In The Act / Powertrip / Flight Of The B.B.,'s/ Die / Iron Horse / Permanent Damage / Living Like A Dog / I've Got A Right

PREACHER (CA, USA)
Line-Up: Moses (vocals / bass), Jeff (guitar), Curtis (drums)

Albums:
TRAPPED IN HELL, Wild Rags (1987)
Excruciating Pain / Blood Angel / Trapped In Hell / Cry Of The Demon / Sacrifice Whore
HARDCORE DEMO SERIES, Wild Rags WRR004 (1988)

PREDATOR (USA)
Line-Up: Jeff Prentice (vocals / guitar), Kurt Dudley (guitar), Eddie Close (bass), Matt Johnson (drums)

Albums:
EASY PREY, Metal Blade (1985)
Prelude/ Easy Prey / Shrieks Of Terror / Masters Of The Night / Hawk Mistress / Siberia / Over The Edge / Road To Glory / Demon Witch / Tortured

PRESTIGE (FINLAND)
Line-Up: Aku (vocals / bass), Arska (guitar), Örkki (guitar), Tero (drums)

Albums:
ATTACK AGAINST GNOMES, Poko PALP 98 (1990)
Intro / It's Over / Force Of My Hate / Dead By Drugs / Attack Against Gnomes / Rotten Angel / Gods / Punishment / Brain Outburst / Rabb-It / Angels Cry / This World
SELLING THE SALVATION, Poko (1991)
Species To Pieces / Maggots / Help The Science / I Don't Wanna Play With Teddy / Selling The Salvation / Prestige / Bed Time Story / Miserable Life / Sexual Education / Naughty Granny / Violence / Makes No Sense

PRIMAL SCREAM (NY, USA)
Line-Up: Steve Alliano (vocals / drums), Keith Alexander (guitar), Rob Graham (bass)

Albums:
VOLUME ONE, Mercenary (1987)
State Of The State / War And Sin / Last Breath / Scream Till You Bleed / Kill The Light / Poisoned / Ignorance Is No Excuse / Megaton / Mr. McCreedy / Shot On Sight

PRIME EVIL (New York, NY, USA)
Line-Up: Andy Eichhorn (vocals), Gary Day (guitar), Mike Usifer (guitar), Mary Ciullo (bass), Tad Leger (drums)

PRIME EVIL marked their entrance onto the Metal scene in 1986 with an eponymous demo tape. The following year 'The Manifestation' cassette was release followed by a 7" single for Rage Records. Drummer Tad Leger was replaced by Todd Gukelberger in 1988. However, PRIME EVIL folded in 1992.
Battlezone Records, owned by DECEASED vocalist King Fowley, would release a collection of PRIME EVIL's works entitled 'Unearthed' in 2002.

Albums:
UNEARTHED, Battlezone (2002)

PRONG (New York, NY, USA)
Line-Up: Tommy Victor (vocals / guitar), Mike Kirkland (bass), Ted Parsons (drums)

With their arrival New York's PRONG prompted much well deserved praise due to their avant-garde approach. Early works displayed a distinct Thrash approach but the band would introduce more Industrial elements with each passing release. Founded by guitarist Tommy Victor, sound engineer for the legendary CBGB's club, ex-DAMAGE bassist Mike Kirkland and former SWANS drummer Ted Parsons.
1991's 'Prove You Wrong' was produced by Mark Dodson although apparently not to the band's liking. Subsequent releases came with a Terry Date production credit. Following the album's release the band pulled in former FLOTSAM & JETSAM man Troy Gregory on bass.
The album of remixes 'Whose Fist Is It Anway' saw PRONG being joined by KILLING JOKE / MURDER INC. bassist Paul Raven and FOETUS man Jim Thirlwell.
PRONG gained the valuable opening position for PANTERA's 'Far Beyond Driven' American tour. The band even had time to form a makeshift pseudo-death metal spoof band with PANTERA vocalist Phil Anselmo under the title of YETI.
The band drafted former SUFFER / DROWN bassist Rob Nicholson. However, PRONG folded when Victor joined DANZIG in 1996. Parsons teamed up with GODFLESH.
Nicholson also teamed up with DANZIG in 1997 then journeyed onto WHITE ZOMBIE under the new guise of 'Blasko'. For live work PRONG pulled in STEEL PROPHET bassist Vince De Juan Dennis who returned to his parent act upon completion of touring.

Singles/EPs:
Third From The Sun (Extended version) / Third From The Sun / Mind The Gap, Spigot SPT 3 (1989)
Defiant / Decay / Senseless Abuse / In My View, Strange Fruit SFPSCD 078 (1990) ('Peel sessions' EP)
Snap Your Fingers, Snap Your Neck / Another Worldly Device / Prove You Wrong / Beg To Differ, Dragnet DRA 660062 (1994)

Albums:
PRIMITIVE ORIGINS, Spigot SPT1 (1986) Disbelief / Watching / Cling To Life / Denial / Dreams Like That / In My Veins / Climate Control / Persecution
FORCE FED, Spigot SPT 2 (1988) Freezer Burn / Forgery / Senseless Abuse / Primitive Origins / Aggravated Condition / The Coliseum / Decay / It's Been Decided / Force Fed / The Taming / Look Up At The Sun / Drainpipe / Third From The Sun / Mind Gap
BEG TO DIFFER, Epic 4663751 (1990) For Dear Life / Steady Decline / Beg To Differ / Lost And Found / Your Fear / Take It In Hand / Intermenstrual D.S.B. / Right To Nothing / Prime Cut / Just The Same / Third From The Sun (Live)
PROVE YOU WRONG, Epic 4689452 (1991) Irrelevant Thoughts / Unconditional / Positively Blind / Prove You Wrong / Hell If I Could / Pointless / Contradictions / Torn Between / Brainwave / Territorial Rites / Get A Grip (On Yourself) / Shouldn't Have Bothered / No Way To Deny It
WHOSE FIST IS IT ANYWAY, Epic 658000-2 (1992) **58 UK**
Prove You Wrong (Fuzzbuster mix) / Hell If I Could / Get A Grip On Yourself / Irrelevant Thoughts (Safety mix) / Talk Talk (Xanax mix)
CLEANSING, Epic 474796-2 (1994) **71 UK** Another Worldly Device / Whose Fist Is This Anyway / Snap Your Fingers, Snap Your Neck / Cut-Rate / Broken Peace / One Outnumbered / Out Of This Misery / No Question / Not Of This Earth / Home Rule / Sublime / Test
RUDE AWAKENING, Epic 483651-2 (1996) Controller / Caprice / Unfortunately / Face Value / Avenue Of The Finest / Slicing / Without Hope / Mansruin / Innocence Gone / Dark Signs / Close The Door / Proud Division

PRO-PAIN (New York,NY)
Line-Up: Gary Meskil (vocals / bass), Tom Klimchuck (guitar), Rob Moschetti (guitar), Dan Richardson (drums)

PRO-PAIN were founded by CRUMBSUCKERS refugees vocalist / bassist Gary Meskill and drummer Dan Richardson in 1991. Meskill post CRUMBSUCKERS founded HEAVY RAIN prior to creating PRO-PAIN. The original plan was to have METHOD OF DESTRUCTION / STORMTROOPERS OF DEATH's larger than life frontman Billy Milano lead the band but this never materialized and Meskill took over the vocalist's role.

With the release of 'Foul Taste Of Freedom' guitarist Tom Klimchuck departed in favour of Nick St. Denis, previously a member of ex-FORBIDDEN / TESTAMENT guitarist Glen Alvelais' act BIZARRO. Heavy touring followed including shows with BODY COUNT. For second album 'The Truth Hurts' PRO-PAIN added ex-POSSESSED rhythm guitarist Mike Hollman. ICE T. guests on the track 'Put The Lights Out'. The cassette version of 'The Truth Hurts' had added extra tracks 'Death On The Dancefloor', 'Pound For Pound' and 'Foul Taste Of Freedom'.

The band also pulled in ex-LÄÄZ ROCKIT drummer Dave Chavarri.

Klimchuck made a return to the band during 1995 as PRO-PAIN shuffled their line-up yet again, also drafting former METHOD OF DESTRUCTION guitarist Rob Moschetti.

PRO-PAIN toured Europe in early 1998 with support from GURD, FURY OF FIVE and PISSING RAZORS. Their efforts paid off as the band were then invited to open for BÖHSE ONKELZ, one of Germany's biggest bands, which saw PRO-PAIN playing to huge arena audiences.

Albums:
FOUL TASTE OF FREEDOM, Roadrunner RR 90682 (1992)
Foul Taste Of Freedom / Death On The Dance Floor / Murder 101 / Pound For Pound / Every Good Boy Does Fine / Death Goes On / Rawhead / The Stench Of Piss / Picture This / Iragnophobia / Johnny Black / Lesson Learned / God Only Knows
THE TRUTH HURTS, Roadrunner RR 89852 (1994)
Make War (Not Love) / Bad Blood / Truth Hurts / Put The Lights Out / Denial / Let Sleeping Dogs Lie / One Man Army / Down In The Dumps / Beast Is Back / Switchblade Knife
CONTENTS UNDER PRESSURE, Energy (1996)
Crush / Shine / State Of Mind / Gunya Down / The Mercy Killings / Contents Under Pressure / Against The Grain / Box City / Odd Man Out / Political Suicide
PRO-PAIN, High Gain (1997)
Get Real / Time / No Love Lost / Don't Kill

Yourself To Live / Love / H8 / Life's Hard / Mark My Words / My Time Will Come / Smokin' Gun / Godsize / Blood Red
ACT OF GOD, High Gain (1998)
Stand Tall / In For The Kill / Act Of God / On Parade / Love And War / Pride / I Remain / Time Will Tell / Hopeless? / Burn / All Fall Down

PROPHECY (Missoula, MT, USA)
Line-Up: Douglas Koester (vocals / guitar), Gordy Robertson (vocals / drums), Brent Magstadt (guitar), Tracy Sprain (bass)

Albums:
PROPHECY, Metal Arc (1984)
Don't Tease Me Please / The Experience / Killer / Is It True? / Killin' Machine / Demon In Disguise / Night Of The Executioner / Key To Confusion / Endless Melody / Weeklong Love Affair

PROTECTED ILLUSION (FINLAND)
Line-Up: Rytkönen (vocals), Rami (guitar), Tapi (guitar), Jari (bass), Koffi (drums)

Singles/EPs:
Intro / Method Of Manipulation / Rude Awakening / Lie On A Bed Of Roses / Swimming In The Moonlight / Plain Pain, Real Illusion EP 4,70 (1989) ('Swimming In The Moonlight' EP)

PROTECTOR (GERMANY)
Line-Up: Martin Missy (vocals), Hansi Muller (guitar), Ede Belichmeier (bass), Michael Hasse (drums)

Thrashers PROTECTOR emanate from Wolfsburg and date to their formation in 1986 by guitarist Hansi Muller and drummer Michael Hasse. Having added vocalist Martin Missy and bassist Ede Belichmeier in March 1987, the group recorded their first two song demo. This tape led to a deal with Atom H Records and the first mini-album, 'Misanthropy', the same year.

1988's 'Golem' featured SODOM's Angel Ripper on the track 'Space Cake' and PROTECTOR toured Germany to support the album guesting for American act WEHRMACHT.

Unfortunately, vocalist Missy quit and was replaced by Olli Wiebel but Missy rejoined in time to record 'Urm The Mad'.

The group released another mini-album, 'Leviathan's Desire', in 1990 and toured Germany once more, this time as support to NAPALM DEATH. However, line-up problems hit the band prior to recording 'A Shedding Of Skin'. Belichmeier quit - having his position filled by bassist Matze Grün - and Muller also departed leaving Wiebel to record guitar parts as PROTECTOR became a trio.

Tragedy struck in February 1992 when Hasse died as a direct result of his drug addiction. Although PROTECTOR would eventually find a new drummer in Marco Pappe and toured alongside D.V.S. and CRUSHER.

PROTECTOR split after recording 'The Heritage' in 1994.

Albums:
MISANTHROPY, Atom H (1987)
Misanthropy / Holy Inquisition / Agoraphobia / The Mercenary / Kain And Abel / Holocaust
GOLEM, Atom H H007 (1988)
Delerium Tremens / Apocalyptic Revelations / Golem / Germanophobe / Protector Of Death / Operation Plagma Extrema / Meglomania / Only The Strong Survive / Omnipresent Aggression / Space Cake
URM THE MAD, Atom H (1989)
Capitalism / Sliced, Hooked And Grinded / Nothing Has Changed / The Most Repugnant Antagonist Of Life / Quasimodo / Urm The Mad / Decadence / Atrocities / Molotov Cocktail
LEVIATHAN'S DESIRE, Atom H (1990)
Intro / Humanised Leviathan / Subordinate / Mortal Passion / Kain And Abel
A SHEDDING OF SKIN, Major C&C CC016 038-3 (199-)
Intro / Mortuary Nightmare / A Shedding Of Skin / Face Fear / Retribution In Darkness / Doomed To Failure / Thy Will Be Done / Whom Gods Will Destroy / Necropolis / Tantalus / Death Comes Soon / Unleashed Terror / Toward Destruction
THE HERITAGE, Major C&CCC020 046-2 (1994)
Mental Malaria / Scars Bleed Life Long / The Heritage / Lost Properties / Convicts On The Streets / Projective Unconsciousness / Paralizer / Chronology / Palpitation / Outro
LOST IN ETERNITY, Major CC030 057-2 (1995)
Misanthropy / Protector Of Death / Tantalus / Mental Malaria / A Shedding Of Skin / Lost Properties / The Mercenary / Golem / Kain And Abel / Doomed To Failure / The Heritage / Humanised Leviathan / Germanophobe / Holocaust / Convicts On The Street / Palpitation

PROWLER (New York, NY, USA)
Line-Up: Steve Fienroth (vocals), Chris Carrol (guitar), Mike Mano (guitar), Meinghis Rhoding (bass), Jerry Whitney (drums)

A Power Thrash Metal band from New York.

Singles/EPs:
Thrash And Bang / Sudden Death / Back On The Rack, Tursha (1986)

Albums:
PROWLING DEATH SQUAD, New Renaissance NRR59 (1988)
Thrash And Bang / Sudden Death / In Your Boots / Back On The Rack / Lick The Knife

PSYCHO (CANADA)
Line-Up: Mike Meilleur (vocals / guitar), Gerald Butler (bass), Danny LaRiviere (drums)

Albums:
ON THE LOOSE, Polaris (1988)
Deadly Mass / Red Lightning / Attack And Kill / Motorized / Hammerhead / Burn You Down / On The Loose / Down In Dungeon

PSYCHO HOLIDAY (AUSTRIA)
Line-Up: Thomas Metzler (vocals / guitar), Johannes Leierer (bass), Joe Künz (drums)

An Austrian Hardcore Thrash band.

Singles/EPs:
Nature Strikes Back / Is This Life? / Kill Joy / Devil's Elixir / Heaven And Hell, Publica PRCD 9403 (1994) ('Nature Strikes Back' EP)

PSYCHOTRON (GERMANY)
Line-Up: Matze Morbitzer (vocals), Matze Braun (guitar), Kai Huissel (guitar), Frank Herold (bass), Gert Kopf (drums)

Retro '80s styled Thrash act out of Stuttgart. PSYCHOTRON came into being in 1995, issuing an opening eponymous demo in January of 1996. The self-financed 'Cosmic Chaos Tome' album emerged in May of 1999 to positive reviews.

The band would lose lead guitarist Andi Konstandaras to SPIRAL TOWER and duly filled the vacancy with Stefano Zanolli. However by March of 2000 Zanolili too bade his farewell and Jurgen Schmid was drafted. PSYCHTRON saw another switch in their lead guitar department during April of 2001. The new man being erstwhile DESERTION six stringer Kai Huissel.

Albums:
CHAOS COSMIC TIME, Psychotron (1999)
Intro / Psychotron / This Illusion / Alternative Suicide / Melancholia / Eternal Stream / The Raging Pit / Belief / Waiting For Last Summer / The Crossroads / Autumn Suite / In Dark Red Minor

PUNISHMENT (USA)
Line-Up: Doug Higson (vocals / bass), Logan Hall (guitar), Soren Appoldt (guitar), Isaac Hatch (drums)

Albums:
VICTORY OR DEATH, (2000)
Battle Axe / Skull And Crossbones / The Saint Of Sin / Retaliate / Escape From Darkness Lyrics

PURGATORY (UK)

Weston-Super-Mare based Thrashers, PURGATORY supported SUICIDAL TENDENCIES in Bristol during 1988. The band recorded a number of demos before contributing the track 'Warring Factions' to the 'Taste Of Armageddon' compilation album in 1989.

PURGATORY (OH, USA)
Line-Up: Jeff Hatrix (vocals), Greg Perry (guitar), Randy Gonce (guitar), Mark Alexander (bass), Kenny Easterly (drums)
Ex-members of PURGATORY would later create HATRIX for a 1994 album on Germany's Massacre label.

Singles/EPs:
Purgatory, JUF (1985)

Albums:
TIED TO THE TRAX, Auburn (1986)
Tied To The Trax / Deep Into The Red / Screamin' Machine / Night Crawler Bitch / Fear Of The Night / Crush The Black Cross / Lost Angels / Valley Of The Shadow Of Death / Purgatory (Shattered Vision)

PYRACANDA (GERMANY)
Line-Up; Hansi Nefen (vocals), Dennis Vaupel (guitar), Sven Fischer (guitar), Dieter Wittbecker (bass), Elmar Gehenzig (drums)

A German Thrash Metal act, PYRACANDA's Sven Fischer was to later join RAGE.

Albums:
TWO SIDES TO A COIN, No Remorse NRR1010 (1990)
Top Gun / Democratic Terror / Delirium Tremens / Challenge Cup / Rigor Mortis / Welcome To Grablouse City / Goodbye Mary Ann / Don't Get Infected / Looser
THORNS, Aaarrg ARG 251039-2 (1991)
At The Abyss / The Dragons Cult / Shut Up / Two Sides Of A Coin / Soulstrip / 18 Degrees / Montezumas Revenge / Bad Conscience / Senile Decay / Thorns

Q

QUO VADIS (CANADA)
Line-Up: Arie Itman (vocals / guitar), Bart Frydrychowicz (vocals / guitar), Remy Beauchamp (bass), Yanic Bercier (drums)

Albums:
FOREVER, Earth AD (1996)
Legions Of The Betrayed / As I Feed The Flames Of Hate / Carpae Deum / Mystery / Inner Capsule (Element Of The Ensemble Part II) / Pantheon Of Tears / Zero Hour / The Day The Universe Changed / Nocturnal Reflections / Sans Abris
DAY INTO NIGHT, Hypnotic (2000)
Absolution (Element Of The Ensemble III) / Dysgenics / Hunter-Killer / Hunter-Killer: Endgame / Let It Burn / Dream / On The Shores Of Ithaka / Night Of The Roses / I Believe / Mute Requiem / Cadences Of Absonance
PASSAGE IN TIME, (2001)
Vital Signs 2000 / As One / The Hunted (Hunter-Killer remix) / Dysgenics (Live) / Point Of No Return - Mute Requiem (Live) / Elements Of The Ensemble / Sons Of Greed / Vital Signs / Sadness

RAGE (GERMANY)
Line-Up: Peter 'Peavey' Wagner (vocals / bass), Victor Smolksi (guitar), Mike Terranna (drums)

RAGE were formed from the rampant Heavy Metal band AVENGER with a line-up of Peter Wagner, guitarists Jochen Schroeder and Thomas Gruning and drummer Jörg Michael. AVENGER released the 'Prayer Of Steel' album and 'Depraved To Black' EP on Wishbone Records before adopting the title of RAGE in 1986, due to confusion with the English AVENGER.
Signing to Noise Records to release 'Reign Of Fear', RAGE toured Germany on a bill with KREATOR and DESTRUCTION in 1986. Shortly after the tour, Gruning left and his position was filled by ex WARLOCK guitarist Rudy Graf. Michael also operated in the high profile side project MEKONG DELTA during 1987.
By 1988 both Graf and Michael were out, superceded by guitarist Manni Schmidt and drummer Chris Efthimiades. Michael would become the permanent drummer for AXEL RUDI PELL and rack up credits with HEADHUNTER, GRAVE DIGGER, GLENMORE and RUNNING WILD.
1988's 'Perfect Man' album enjoyed considerable critical success with the media and went on to sell over 30,000 copies in Europe. In 1990 RAGE toured Germany as support to RUNNING WILD.
Having released 'Reflections Of A Shadow' in 1991 RAGE's 1992 album, 'Trapped', featured a cover of the renowned ACCEPT classic 'Fast As A Shark' and Japanese issues also added two bonus cuts in 'Innocent Guilty' and 'Marching Heroes - The Wooden Cross'. The group would subsequently fulfil the ambition of touring in Japan and later joined SAXON and MOTÖRHEAD in Europe on the 'Eagles And Bombers' tour in Europe.
RAGE undertook further touring in 1993 on a bill alongside GAMMA RAY and Norwegians CONCEPTION as they were surely about to unleash the album of their career in 'A Missing Link'
In 1994 guitarist Schmidt left the band. His position was filled by Spiros Efthimiadis and ex-PYRACANDA man Sven Fischer and the ensuing 'Ten Years In Rage' album featured new cuts alongside old favourites.
RAGE split from Noise Records in 1994 following many other German acts to G.U.N. Records, an arm of major label BMG. The band undertook a short burst of seven dates during June 1995 in their homeland supported by GLENMORE.

After their debut for G.U.N. Records RAGE played a series of 'Summer Metal Meetings' together with RUNNING WILD, GRAVEDIGGER, GAMMA RAY, GLENMORE and ICED EARTH and, in 1996, released the 'Lingua Mortis' album. The record saw the band joined by the Symphony Orchestra of Prague playing some of their best cuts.
RAGE suffered a mass walkout in 1999 when both the Efthimiades brothers and second guitarist Sven Fischer decamped leaving Peavey Wagner flying solo. Undaunted Wagner pulled in former BEAU NASTY, YNGWIE MALMSTEEN, ARTENSION, METALIUM drummer American Mike Terranna and Russian guitar virtuoso VICTOR SMOLSKI, quickly bowing back in with the 'Ghosts' album. In Germany this new incarnation of RAGE would debut at the 'Wacken Open Air' festival then set off on an extensive tour of Russia.
2000 found Wagner guesting on the GB ARTS album 'The Lake'. Smolski too would session outside of RAGE contributing lead solos to the PERSONAL WAR 'Newtimechaos' outing.
2000 found Wagner guesting on the GB ARTS album 'The Lake'. Ex-RAGE man Manni Schmidt joined GRAVE DIGGER in December of 2000.
RAGE's 2001 album 'Welcome To The Other Side' would land the group an unexpected bonus when the track 'Straight To Hell' would be chosen for the soundtrack to the movie 'Der Schuh Des Manitu', a film which would turn out to be one of the most commercially successful German language films ever.
Terranna would also be found sessioning, in his case on the DRIVEN project album put together by ex-DIO guitarist Tracy G. The drummer would also regroup with ARTENSION for a 2002 comeback album 'Sacred Pathway' as well as putting in an appearance on German guitar guru AXEL RUDI PELL's 2002 'Shadow Zone' album.
RAGE meantime were back in the studio with producer Charlie Bauerfiend for their new opus 'Unity' projecting shows in Moscow and St. Petersburg during April as well as appearances at the 'Swedish Rock' festival and the Portuguese event 'Seixal Attack'.

Singles/EPs:
Invisible Horizons / Lost Side Of The World / Law And Order, Noise NO136-6 (1989) ('Invisible Horizons' EP)
Woman / Ashes / Battlefield / Waiting For The Moon / What's Up, Noise NO169-3 (1991) ('Extended Power' EP)
Beyond The Wall / Bury All Life/ On The Edge / I Want You / (Those Who Got) Nothing To Lose / Last Goodbye / Light Into The

Darkness / Dust, Noise NO202-3 (1992) ('Beyond The Wall' EP)
The Crawling Chaos / Black In Mind / Alive But Dead / Shadow Out Of Time, G.U.N. GUN 061 BMG (1995) (Promotion release)

Albums:
REIGN OF FEAR, Noise NO038 (1986)
Scared To Death / Deceiver / Reign Of Fear / Hand Of Glory / Raw Energy / Echoes Of Evil / Chaste Flesh / Suicide / Machinery / Scaffold
EXECUTION GUARANTEED, Noise NO073 (1987)
Down By Law / Execution Guaranteed / Before The Storm / Street Wolf / Deadly Error / Hatred / Grapes Of Wrath / Mental Decay / When You're Dead
PERFECT MAN, Noise N0112 (1988)
Wasteland / In The Darkest Hour / Animal Instinct / Perfect Man / Sinister Thinking / Supersonic Hydromatic / Don't Fear The Winter / Death In The Afternoon / A Pilgrim's Path / Time And Place / Round Trip / Between The Lines
SECRETS IN A WEIRD WORLD, Noise NO0137 (1989)
Intro (Opus 32 No. 3) / Time Waits For No One / Make My Day / The Inner Search / Invisible Horizons / She / Light Into The Darkness / Distant Voices / Without A Trace
REFLECTIONS OF A SHADOW, Noise N0160 (1991)
Introduction (A Bit More Of Green) / That's Human Bondage / True Face In Everyone / Flowers That Fade In My Hand / Reflections Of A Shadow / Can't Get Out / Waiting For The Moon / Saddle The Wind / Dust Nobody Knows
TRAPPED, Noise N0189 (1992)
Shame On You / Solitary Man / Enough Is Enough / Medicine / Questions / Take Me To The Water / Power And Greed / The Body Talks / Not Forever / Beyond The Wall Of Sleep / Baby, I'm Your Nightmare / Fast As A Shark / Difference / Innocent Guilty / Marching Heroes - The Wooden Cross
THE MISSING LINK, Noise NO217 (1994)
The Firestorm / Nevermore / Refuge / The Pit And The Pendulum / From The Underworld / Certain Days / Who Dares? / Wake Me When I'm Dead / Lost In The Ice / Her Diary's Black Pages / The Missing Link / Raw Caress
TEN YEARS IN RAGE, Noise N0219-2 (1994)
Vertigo / She Killed And Smiled / Destination Day / Take My Blood / No Sign Of Life / Submission / The Unknown / Dangerous Heritage / Prayers Of Steel / The Blow In A Row.
BLACK IN MIND, G.U.N. GUN 062 BMG

74321 27743-2 (1995)
Black In Mind / The Crawling Chaos / Alive But Dead / Sent By The Devil / Shadow Out Of Time / Spider's Web / In A Nameless Time / The Icecold Hand Of Destiny / Forever Until I Die / The Rage / The Price Of War / Start / All This Time
PRAYERS OF STEEL / DEPRAVED TO BLACK, G.U.N. GUN 062 BMG 74321 24484-2 (1995) (3,000 only Limited edition free with the 'Black In Mind' Album. Previously released under as AVENGER)
Battlefield / Southcross Union / Prayers Of Steel / Halloween / Faster Than Hell / Adoration / Rise Of The Creature / Sword Made Of Steel / Bloodlust / Assorted By Satan / Depraved To Black / Down To The Bone / Prayers Of Steel (Live) / Faster Than Hell (Live)
LINGUA MORTIS, G.U.N. GUN 090 BMG 74321 36667-2 (1996)
In A Nameless Time / Alive But Dead / Medley a) Don't Fear The Winter, b) Black In Mind, c) Firestorm, d) Sent By The Devil, e) Lost In The Ice / All This Time / Alive But Dead
END OF ALL DAYS, G.U.N. GUN 101 BMG 74321 39036-2 (1996)
Under Control / Higher Than The Sky / Deep In The Blackest Hole / End Of All Days / Visions / Desperation / Voice From The Vault / Let The Night Begin / Fortress / Frozen Fire / Talking To The Dead / Face Behind The Mask / Silent Victory / Fading Hours / The Sleep / The Trooper
THIRTEEN, G.U.N. GUN 74321 56314-2 (1998)
Overture / From The Cradle To The Grave / Days Of December / Sign Of Heaven / Incomplete / Turn The Page / Heartblood / Over And Over / In Vain (I Won't Go Down) / Immortal Sin / Paint It Black / Just Alone
GHOSTS, G.U.N. (1999) **31 GERMANY**
Beginning of the End / Back In Time / Ghosts / Wash My Sins Away / Fear / Love And Fear Unite / Vanished In Haze / Spiritual Awakening / Love After Death / More Than A Lifetime / Tomorrow's Yesterday / End Of Eternity
WELCOME TO THE OTHER SIDE, G.U.N. (2001)
Trauma / Paint The Devil On The Wall / The Mirror In Your Eyes / R.I.P. (Tribute To Dishonour Part 1) / One More Time (Tribute To Dishonour Part 2) / Requiem (Tribute To Dishonour Part 3) / I'm Crucified (Tribute To Dishonour Part 4) / No Lies / Point Of No Return / Leave It All Behind / Deep In The Night / Welcome To The Other Side / Lunatic / Riders On The Moonlight / Straight To Hell / After The End / Sister Demon
BEST OF ALL G.U.N. YEARS, G.U.N. (2001)

Straight To Hell / Days Of December / Back In Time / Alive But Dead / Deep In The Blackest Hole / The Mirror In Your Eyes / Black In Mind / Higher Than The Sky / Spiritual Awakening / The Crawling Chaos / Six Feet Under Ground / Just Another Wasted Day / From The Cradle To The Grave / Medley: Don't Fear The Winter-Black In Mind - Firestorm - Send By The Devil - Lost In The Ice
UNITY, G.U.N. (2002)
All I Want / Insanity / Down / Set This World On Fire / Dies Irae / World Of Pain / Shadows / Living My Dream / Seven Deadly Sins / You Want It, You'll Get It / Unity

RAISE HELL (SWEDEN)
Line-Up: Jonas Nilsson (vocals / guitar), Torstein Wickberg (guitar), Niklas Sjostrom (bass), Dennis Ekdahl (drums)

Much lauded Death-Thrash Metal combo founded in 1995 as IN COLD BLOOD by vocalist / guitarist Jonas Hilsson, bass player Niklas Sjöström and guitarist Torstein Wickberg. The following year drummer Dennis Ekdahl completed the rankings. The band, very much rooted in the Black Metal scene, were all still in their mid teens by the time the band was finalized leading to jibes about them being "the Death Metal HANSON".
In the summer of 1997 IN COLD BLOOD issued their only demo 'Nailed'. A record company bidding war erupted, which included the Earache label, after which Germany's Nuclear Blast emerged as the victors. However, at this point an American Hardcore act of same title was discovered hence the name switch to RAISE HELL.
By the time debut 'Holy Target' arrived RAISE HELL's average band member age was just 18. The record displayed a remarkable maturity for an act so young blending Death and Thrash Metal with unashamed anti-Christian lyrics. The group got straight into gear touring Europe to promote the album alongside DISMEMBER, AGATHODAIMON, NIGHT IN GALES and CHILDREN OF BODOM.
The 2000 album 'Not Dead Yet' found RAISE HELL maneuvering away from their Black Metal roots.
Ekdahl also drums for SINS OF OMISSION.

Albums:
HOLY TARGET, Nuclear Blast (1998)
The March Of Devil's Soldiers / Raise The Dead / Beautiful As Fire / Holy Target / Legions Of Creeps / The Red Ripper / Black Visions / Mattered Out / Superior Powers
NOT DEAD YET, Nuclear Blast NB 443-2 (2000)

Dance With The Devil / Babes / Back Attack / Devilyn / Not Dead Yet / No Pulse / User Of Poison / He Is Coming / Soulcollector

RAMP (PORTUGAL)
Line-up: Rudi Darte (vocals), Ricardo Mendonca (guitar), To-Ze (guitar), Jao (bass), Paulinho (drums)

One of Portugal's biggest Rock acts, Seixal based Thrashers RAMP began life in 1988 with an inaugural line-up of guitarists Ricardo Mendonca and To-Ze (Antonio), bassist Miguel and drummer Paulinho. To show their solidarity the group was named after their initials. A lead vocalist was recruited but quickly dismissed and second time around RAMP settled on frontman Rui Duarte.
The band's debut live performance came with a 1989 support to MORTIFERA and THE COVEN. MORTIFERA's bassist Jao would subsequently supplant Miguel.
An acclaimed 1991 demo tape swiftly secured a deal with major label Polygram for a six track EP 'Thought's. In March of 1992 RAMP supported FUDGE TUNNEL and SEPULTURA. Support from the Metal community in Portugal resulted in Polygram re-releasing 'Thoughts' on CD format complete with an extra three songs.
1993 proved a trying year for the band, the majority of its members undertaking their compulsory military service and RAMP severing ties with Polygram.
1994 found renewed momentum as RAMP opened for a visiting PARADISE LOST and signed to the Uniao Lisboa label for a second album 'Intersection'. With this release the band were able to put in festival appearances such as the Faro 'Super Rock' with THE EXPLOITED and RATOS DE PORAO and the 'Ultrabrutal' event at Penafiel alongside BENEDICTION and DISMEMBER. RAMP also made an impression in front of 30,000 people at the 'Festa Do Avante' organised by the Portuguese Communist Party. Other gigs included guest slots to NAPALM DEATH and FEAR FACTORY upfront of festivals in Belgium, France and the Czech Republic. RAMP undertook these latter gigs despite Jao being indisposed with a plastered broken leg.
In 1998 RAMP's third album, the Simon Efemy produced 'Evolution, Devolution, Revolution', arrived. The following year found the band gigging hard as openers to MANOWAR, MOTORHEAD, MONSTER MAGNET, the ROLLINS BAND and even METALLICA.

Albums:
THOUGHTS, Polygram (1992)
The Commediants / Desilluisions / March To Death / Thoughts / The Last Child / Try Again / In The Beginning / Out Of This World / Behind The Wall
INTERSECTION, Uniao Lisboa (1995)
All Men Taste Hell / Own Way / Black Tie / So You Say / Fate / Like You / Unpointless Name / Win / Trip / Friendly Word / Through
EVOLUTION, DEVOLUTION, REVOLUTION, (1998)
Dawn / Helping Hands / Hallelujah / Noone / Future / How / Old Times / D.T.A. / Apathy / For A While / Come
RAMP - LIVE, (2000)
Dawn / Helping Hands / Black Tie Apathy / So You Say / Noone / Walk Like An Egyptian / Hallelujah / How / For A While / Come / Out Of This World / All Men Taste Hell / Old Times / Through / Last Child / Behind The Wall / Try Again

RAPTURE (GERMANY)
Line-Up: Helge Fritsche (vocals / guitar), Christian Schmidt (guitar), Marko Teutge (bass), Nico Pohlmann (drums)

Speed Thrash with interesting Blues influences.

Singles/EPs:
Melt And Fly Away / After Four / Metaphor Of Honesty / Metamorphosis, Rabaz 4757 (1996) ('Metamorphosis' EP)

RAVAGE (Chicago, IL, USA)
Line-Up: Kyle Michael (vocals), D.D. Rand (guitar), Jayson Gray (bass), Dale Clark (drums)

Albums:
WRECKING BALL, Roadrunner RR 9672 (1986)
69 / Bloodshot / Battle Stations / Fire And Fury / Killer On The Loose / Keeper Of The Night / Kissing The Black / Passion Web / Raise Some Hell / Snake Bite

RAVEN (UK)
Line-Up: John Gallagher (vocals / bass), Mark Gallagher (guitar), Rob 'Wacko' Hunter (drums)

Newcastle "Athletic Rock" outfit that made a huge impact on the NWoBHM but sadly failed to live up to initial promise in their home country despite recognition abroad. Their early efforts are manic metal sprints through excellent riffs and high pitched distinctive vocals. Despite waning popularity in Britain

RAVEN command respect and a healthy fanbase across the world witnessed by sizeable followings in Germany and Japan as well as cult status in America.

RAVEN date back to 1974 with an initial line-up of brothers John and Mark Gallagher and Paul Bowden. However. at this fledgling stage RAVEN had only one classical guitar between them! Santa Claus came to the rescue and in December of that year the band got electric guitars for Christmas.

RAVEN's first live date in December 1975 was memorable if not only for the fact that both Gallagher brothers managed to fall offstage. By this point the band had added drummer Paul Sherrif. Within months Sherrif was out in favour of Mick Kenworthy. In this incarnation RAVEN opened for THE STRANGLERS and THE MOTORS locally. One of RAVEN's early headlining gigs included a Hells Angels convention where the band were ordered to play 'Born to be wild' no less than ten times in the pouring rain. The band only stalled the show by Mark faking an electric shock!

Kenworthy drifted away in late 1977 to be replaced by Sean Taylor. Bowden also departed in 1979 having his position filled by Pete Shore. RAVEN suffered another blow when Taylor quit, eventually to join SATAN.

RAVEN augmented the band line-up once more with the addition of drummer Rob Hunter, whose previous act FASTBREEDER also included future DURAN DURAN guitarist ANDY TAYLOR. RAVEN cut their first two track demo featuring "She Don't Need Your Money" and 'Wiped Out'. Courtesy of TYGERS OF PAN TANG manager Tom Noble this tape secured the band a deal with local Newcastle label Neat Records.

RAVEN's debut single 'Don't Need Your Money' created a huge swell of interest in the band and helped the first album reach the British charts. During 1980 RAVEN also had a track 'Let It Rip' on the 'Brute Force' compilation album. At the time RAVEN were certainly originators of the fast and powerful approach.

Album number two 'Wiped Out' saw the songs getting faster and the band honing their direction. Regrettably the intended mixes for the album were not used and substituted for a mix unapproved by the band. However, the band's fans were still impressed. RAVEN's first American shows in 1982, alongside RIOT and ANVIL, were promoted by Johnny Zazula of the 'Rock n' Roll Heaven' record store in New Jersey.

Producer Michael Wagner was drafted in for 'All for One' as RAVEN sought a more mature sound. It was also their first American release for Zazula's Megaforce label. This affiliation led to RAVEN's first 36 date American tour with opening act METALLICA. Further tours had EXODUS and ANTHRAX supporting.

At RAVEN's 1984 New York show the band headlined above METALLICA and ANTHRAX. Rumour has it that an A&R representative for Elektra Records was suitably impressed by RAVEN but upon inquiring as to the band's name was informed it was METALLICA. Once signed the same person was confused to find the band he had signed were now a quartet and not a trio. Allegedly...

With Megaforce's connection to Atlantic Records 1984 saw RAVEN ink a major deal. Atlantic, however, manouvered the band away from their speed attack towards a more mainstream approach even getting the band to wear bizarre spacesuit stage gear. RAVEN's audience were by now finding it hard to equate the killer live act with a succession of records that were ever more experimental, even drafting in horn sections at one point. RAVEN undertook a 1985 American tour utilizing JUDAS PRIEST's 'Screaming For Vengeance' stage set. The show included a pyro rocket firing guitar that set fire to the venue roof in San Diego.

RAVEN also contributed two tracks to the movie soundtrack of 'Hot Moves'. Songs cut were 'Hot Moves' and 'Ladykiller'.

'The Pack Is Back' was produced by Eddie Kramer but did little to stop the rot. RAVEN toured once more with support from fellow Brits TANK. Further shows supporting TWISTED SISTER where to follow but the headliner pulled out at the last minute. 1986 saw RAVEN opening for JUDAS PRIEST in America before headline dates. The tour ended with support shows to YNGWIE MALMSTEEN.

To promote 'Life's A Bitch' RAVEN made up a three band touring package including SLAYER and W.A.S.P. RAVEN fared well in front of rabid SLAYER fans intent on demoralizing W.A.S.P.

Hunter departed without warning in 1987 following Atlantic severing all ties with the band and RAVEN found an able replacement in ex-SIMMONDS, BURNING STARR and PENTAGRAM drummer Joe Hasselvander prior to signing a new deal with Combat Records.

RAVEN were back out on the road in America for headlining dates promoting 'Nothing Exceeds Like Excess' before another batch of gigs with TESTAMENT through into 1989. The band's first European tour for many years was offered with KREATOR, a German act that had recently covered a RAVEN track. Impressed by KREATOR's organization RAVEN soon signed to their management

and record label.

In 1990 John Gallagher assembled an extracurricular project entitled SLIDER comprising of former BLUE CHEER, SIMMONDS and SHAKIN' STREET guitarist Duck McDonald, ex-RODS and SIMMONDS bassist Gary Bordonaro and session player Bob Fortunato. The band issued one album 'The Slider Project' on Feedback Records in 1990.

The 'Architect Of Fear' album was a welcome return to previous heaviness. RAVEN set out on European dates with RUNNING WILD. However, RAVEN was to go on ice shortly after.

John Gallagher formed KILLERS with ex-IRON MAIDEN vocalist PAUL DIANNO, ex-TANK guitarist Cliff Evans, ex-DRIVE SHE SAID guitarist Ray Ditone and former PERSIAN RISK drummer Steve Hopgood for a proposed tour of South America. A rehearsal tape, recorded in an empty venue in New York and featuring Gallagher, later surfaced as the 'South American Assault' album.

The 1992 EP 'Heads up' prompted yet more European dates with support act RISK. 1993 proved a disastrous year for the band as John's house burned down as well as having all his guitars stolen.

In 1994 RAVEN performed at the Los Angeles Foundations Forum in an effort to secure a new deal. Before long RAVEN had signed to Japanese label Zero recording 'Glow' the same year. Hungry for the road the band performed American dates in early 1995 with WIDOWMAKER and ANVIL before headline shows of Japan. One of these shows became the 'Destroy All Monsters - Live In Japan' album.

The band toured Germany alongside TANK and newcomers HAMMERFALL during 1997. The band returned with renewed vigour during 1999 with a fresh studio album 'One For All' produced by Michael Wagener. The album would be issued in Europe by Massacre Records and the following year licensed into America via Metal Blade. A retrospective box set, provisionally entitled 'Stark Raven Mad', would also be announced but fell by the wayside. The band therefore took matters into their own hands issuing a collection of demos and rarities billed 'Raw Tracks'. Various territories saw differing track listings with the American version closing on a take of QUEEN's 'Tie Your Mother Down'. Japanese variants ended with 'All For One' and 'Young Blood' whilst the European imprint's last tracks would be 'Architect Of Fear' and 'Enemy'.

RAVEN toured Germany in early 2000 as guests to U.D.O. The two acts would unite once again for a series of American mid summer 2001 dates.

Singles/EPs:

Don't Need Your Money / Wiped Out, Neat NEAT 06 (1980)

Hard Ride / Crazy World, Neat NEAT 11 (1980)

Crash, Bang, Wallop / Firepower / Run Them Down / Rock Hard, Neat NEAT 15 (1981)

Break The Chain / Ballad Of Marshall Stack, Neat NEAT 28 (1983) (with UDO DIRKSCHNEIDER)

Born To Be Wild / Inquisitor, Neat NEAT 29 (1983) (with UDO DIRKSCHNEIDER)

Born To Be Wild / Inquisitor / Break The Chain, Neat NEAT 29-12 (1983) (12" single) (with UDO DIRKSCHNEIDER)

On And On / On And On, Atlantic PR702 (1984) (USA Promotion)

Pray For The Sun / On And On / The Bottom Line, Atlantic 786901 (1985)

Speed Of The Reflex / Do Or Die / How Did Ya Get So Crazy / Seen It On The TV / Gimme Just A Little, Atlantic 81670 (1986) ('Mad' EP)

Gimme Some Lovin', / One On, Atlantic A9453 (1986)

Albums:

ROCK UNTIL YOU DROP, Neat NEAT 1001 (1981) **63 UK**
Hard Ride / Hell Patrol / Don't Need Your Money / Over The Top / 39/40 / For The Future / Rock Until You Drop / Nobody's Hero / Hell Raiser / Action / Lambs To The Slaughter / Tyrant Of The Airways

WIPED OUT, Neat NEAT 1004 (1982)
Faster Than The Speed Of Light / Bring The Hammer Down / Firepower / Read All About It / To The Limit - To The Top / Battlezone / Live At The Inferno / Star War / U.X.B. / 20-21 / Hold Back The Fire / Chainsaw

ALL FOR ONE, Neat NEAT 1011 (1983)
Take Control / Mind Over Metal / Sledgehammer Rock / All For One / Run Silent, Run Deep / Hung, Drawn And Quartered / Break The Chain / Take It Away / Seek And Destroy / Athletic Rock

LIVE AT THE INFERNO, Megaforce MRI 969 (1984)
Live At The Inferno / Take Control / Mind Over Metal / Crash Bang Wallop / Rock Until You Drop / Faster Than The Speed Of Light / All For One / Forbidden Planet / Star War / Tyrant Of The Airways / Run Silent, Run Deep / Crazy World / Let It Rip / G.A.R.B.O. / Wiped Out / Firepower / Don't Need Your Money / Break The Chain / Hell Patrol / Live At The Inferno

STAY HARD, Atlantic 81241-1 (1985)
Stay Hard / When The Going Gets Tough / On And On / Get It Right / Restless Child / The Power And The Glory / Pray For The Sun / Hard Ride / Extract The Action / The Bottom Line

THE DEVIL'S CARRION, Rawpower LP003 (1985)
Hard Ride / Bring The Hammer Down / Inquisitor / All For One / Hellraiser / Action / Live At The Inferno / Crash Bang Wallop / The Ballad Of Marshall Stack / Crazy World / Rock Until You Drop / Don't Need Your Money / Hell Patrol / Rock Hard / Faster Than The Speed Of Light / Wiped Out / Break The Chains / Read All About It / Firepower / Athletic Rock / Run Silent, Run Deep

THE PACK IS BACK, Atlantic 81629 (1986)
The Pack Is Back / Gimme Some Lovin' / Screaming Down The House / Young Blood / Hyperactive / Rock Dogs / Don't Let It Die / Get Into Your Car And Drive / All I Need / Nightmare Ride

LIFE'S A BITCH, Atlantic 81734 (1987)
The Savage And The Hungry / Pick Your Window / Life's A Bitch / Never Forgive / Iron League / On The Wings Of An Eagle / Overload / You're A Liar / Fuel To The Fire / Only The Strong Survive / Juggernaut / Playing With The Razor / Finger On The Trigger

NOTHING EXCEEDS LIKE EXCESS, Under One Flag FLAG 28 (1988)
Behemoth / Die For Allah / Gimme A Break / Into The Jaws Of Death / In The Name Of Death / Stick It / Lay Down The Law / You Got A Screw Loose / Thunderlord / The King / Hard As Nails / Kick Your Ass

UNRELEASED TRACKS, Teichiku TECP 25450 (1990) (Japanese release)
Crash, Bang, Wallop / Rock Hard / Run Them Down / Don't Need Your Money / wiped Out / Crazy World / Born To Be Wild / Inquisitor / ...Plus Surprising Message

ARCHITECT OF FEAR, Steamhammer SPV 008 76281 (1991)
Intro / Architect Of Fear / Disciple / Got The Devil / Part Of The Machine / Under The Skin / White Hot Anger / Can't And Hide / Blind Leading The Blind / Relentless / Just Let Me Go / Heart Attack / Sold Down The River

RADIO HELL, Raw Fruit FRSCD009 (1992) (including VENOM & WARFARE tracks)
Lambs To The Slaughter / Hold Back The Fire / Hard Ride / Chainsaw

HEAD'S UP, Steamhammer 76-76392 (1992)
Hell On Earth / World Comes Tumbling / Stay Human / All For One / Into The Jaws Of Death / Can't Run And Hide

MIND OVER METAL, Success 16088 (1994)
GLOW, Steamhammer SPV 084-12092
(1995)
Watch You Drown / Spite / True Believer / So
Close / Altar / The Dark Side / The Rocker /
Turn You On / Far And Wide / Victim /
Gimme A Reason / Slip Away
**DESTROY ALL MONSTERS - LIVE IN
JAPAN**, SPV 085-12132 (1995)
Victim / Live At The Inferno / Crash, Bang,
Wallop / True Believer / Into The Jaws Of
Death / Hard As Nails / Die For Allah / Guitar
Solo / Speed Of The Reflex / Run Silent,
Run Deep / Mind Over Metal / Gimme A
Reason / Inquisitor / For The Future / Bass
Solo / Architect Of Fear / White Hot Anger /
Drum Solo / Break The Chain
EVERYTHING LOUDER, Fresh Fruit SPV
CD 085-12162 (1997)
Blind Eye / No Pain, No Gain / Sweet Jane /
Holy Grail / Hungry / Insane / Everything
Louder / ??? / Between The Wheels / Losing
My Mind / Get Your Finger Out / Wilderness
Of Broken Glass / !!! / Fingers Do The
Walking / Bonus
ONE FOR ALL, Massacre MASCD0206
(1999)
Seven Shades / Double Talk / Roll With The
Punches / Get Your Motor Running / To Be
Broken / Derailed / The Hunger Inside / Top
Of The World / In The Line Of Fire /
Kangaroo / New Religion / Last Ride
RAW TRACKS, (1999)
Firepower / Don't Need Your Money / Savage
& The Hungry / Nightmare Ride / Get It Right
/ On & On / Extract The Action / Barbarian /
Thunderlord / Gimme A Break / Move Over /
White Hot Anger / Altar / Tie Your Mother
Down

RAZOR (CANADA)
Line-Up: Bob Reid (vocals), Dave Carlo
(guitar), Jon Armstrong (bass), Rich
Oosterbosch (drums)

RAZOR made their album debut in 1984
comprising vocalist Stace 'Sheepdog'
McClaren, guitarist Dave Carlo, bassist Mike
Campagnolo and drummer M-Bro.
For 1988's 'Violent Restitution' only Carlo and
McLaren remained. New faces were bassist
Adam Carlo and drummer Rob Mills. The
album saw a release in Japan through
Teichiku Records although as part of a
strange double package with Australian act
HOBBS ANGEL OF DEATH.
McLaren quit before the album was released
and Bob Reid was quickly pulled in to fill the
gap.
RAZOR reunited in 1997. Meantime Toronto
Black Metal band MEGIDDO would pay
homage by including a cover version of 'Take

This Torch' on their 'The Devil And The Whore'
album.

Albums:
ARMED AND DANGEROUS, Voice (1984)
The End / Killer Instinct / Hot Metal / Armed
And Dangerous / Take This Torch / Ball And
Chain / Fast And Loud
EXECUTIONER'S SONG, Roadrunner RR
9778 (1985)
Take This Torch / Fast And Loud / City Of
Damnation / Escape The Fire / March Of
Death / Distant Thunder / Hot Metal /
Gatecrasher / Deathrace / Time Bomb / The
End
EVIL INVADERS, Roadrunner RR 9732
(1985)
Nowhere Fast / Cross Me Fool / Legacy Of
Doom / Evil Invaders / Iron Hammer / Instant
Death / Cut Throat / Speed Merchants /
Tortured Skull / Thrashdance
MALICIOUS INTENT, Roadrunner RR 9698
(1986)
Tear Me To Pieces / Night Attack /
Grindstone / Cage The Ragers / Malicious
Intent / Rebel Onslaught / AOD / Challenge
The Eagle / Stand Before Kings / High
Speed Metal / KMA
CUSTOM KILLING, Fist Fight FPL 3042
(1987)
Survival Of The Fittest / Shootout / Forced
Annihilation / Last Rites / Snake Eyes /
White Noise / Going Under / Russian Ballet
VIOLENT RESTITUTION, SPV
Steamhammer 087 569(1988)
The Marshall Arts / Hypertension / Taste The
Floor / Behind Bars / Below The Belt / I'll
Only Say It Once / Enforcer / Violent
Restitution / Out Of The Game / Edge Of
The Razor / Eve Of The Storm / Discipline /
Fed Up / Soldier Of Fortune
SHOTGUN JUSTICE, Fringe FPL 3094
(1990)
Miami / United By Hatred / Violence
Condoned / Electric Circus / Meaning Of
Pain / Stabbed In The Back / Shotgun
Justice / Parricide / American Luck / Brass
Knuckles / Burning Bridges / Concussion /
Cranial Stomp / The Pugilist
DECIBELS, Hypnotic HYP 1058 (1997)
Decibels / Jimi The Fly / Life Sentence / Liar/
The Game / Great White Lie / Open Hostility
/ Ninedead / Goof Soup / Violence... Gun
Control

REACTOR (CANADA)
Line-Up: Mike Ceminara (vocals), Dave Galea
(guitar), Grant Ormack (bass), Mike Whattie
(drums)

Montreal Thrash band issued a demo in 1991.

REALM (Milwaukee, WI, USA)
Line-Up: Mark Antoni (vocals), Paul Laganowski (guitar), Takis Kinis (guitar), Steve Post (bass), Mike Olson (drums)

Milwaukee Thrash Metal band REALM issued the demos 'Perceptive Incentive' in 1986 and the following years 'Final Solution'. Guitarists Paul Laganowski and Takis Kinis along with bass player Steve Post founded WHITE FEAR CHAIN with former LAST CRACK vocalist Buddo.

Albums:
ENDLESS WAR, Roadracer RO 9509-2 (1988)
Endless War / Slay The Oppressor / Eminence / Fate's Wind / Root Of Evil / Eleanor Rigby / This House Is Burning / Second Coming / All Heads Turn To The Hunt / Mang / Poisoned Minds / Theseus And The Minotaur
SUICIETY, Roadracer RO 9406-2 (1990)
Cain Rose Up (Scream Bloody Murder) / Fragile Earth / Energetic Discontent / Gateway / Final Solution / The Brainchild / La Flamme's Theory / Dick / Knee Deep In Blood / Suiciety

REANIMATOR (UK)
Line-Up: Mike Abel (guitar), Kev Ingleson (guitar), Mark Mitchell (bass), John Wilson (drums)

Yorkshire thrashers that undertook a severe left turn in their brand of music adopting then in vogue Funk for third album 'Laughing'. Toured as support to EXODUS, ACID REIGN and NUCLEAR ASSAULT. Managed initially by Music For Nations owner Martin Hooker then NUCLEAR ASSAULT manager Paul Loasby. Guitarist joined POP GODS.

Albums:
DENY REALITY, Under One Flag FLAG 32
Deny Reality / Follow The Masses / Fatal Descent / OPC/ DUAF/ Re-Animator
CONDEMNED TO ETERNITY, Under One Flag FLAG 37
Low Life / Chain Of Command / Room 101 / Condemned To Eternity / Shock Treatment / Buried Alive / Techno Fear / What The Funk / Say Your Prayers
LAUGHING, Under One Flag FLAG 53 (1991)
Rude Awakening / Laughing / Kipper n' / Another Fine Mess / Too Drunk To Fuck / Monkey See Monkey Dance / Don't Pastronize Me / Instrumental / Time And Tide / Big Black Cloud
THAT WAS THEN, THIS IS NOW, Under One Flag FLAG 67
Take Me Away / 2CV / Cold Sweat / Hope / Last Laugh / Kick Back / Listen Up / Sunshine Times / That Was Then... This Is Now / D.U.A.F.

RECIPIENTS OF DEATH (CA, USA)
Line-Up: Dead Rich G. (vocals / bass / guitar), Zac Taylor (guitar), Albert Gomez (guitar), Chris Broguiere (drums)

For the second album guitarists Albert Gomez and Zac Taylor were substituted by John Lisi.

Albums:
RECIPIENTS OF DEATH, Wild Rags WRE 905CD (1988)
Raping Death / Seizure / Necropolis (City Of The Dead) / Carnage / Gunned Town / The Aftermath / Fleshburn
FINAL FLIGHT, Wild Rags (1990)
Final Flight / Behind Closed Doors / Recrimination / F.O.A.D. (Intro) / Democratic Lie

RECON (USA)
Line-Up: Vett Roberts (vocals), George Rene Ochoa (guitar), Eddie Starline (guitar), Mike Grato (bass), John Christianson (drums)

A Christian Thrash Metal band that debuted publicly with a brace of tracks on the 'California Metal II' compilation album. The 'Behind Enemy Lines' album, regarded by many as a 'lost classic' of the genre, bore heavy connections to DELIVERANCE which would come to affect the band subsequently. DELIVERANCE mainman Jimmy Brown not only produced 'Behind Enemy Lines' but co-wrote the title track and performed lead guitar on the song 'Alive'. Roger Martinez of VENGEANCE RISING also contributed backing vocals.
RECON guitarist George Rene Ochoa would join fellow White Thrashers DELIVERANCE for their 1990 'Weapons Of Our Warfare' album. Bassist Mike Grato joined Ochoa in DELIVERANCE for the 1991 'What A Joke' record. Drummer John Christianson would also become involved with DELIVERANCE.
Ochoa later figured in the highly controversial VENGEANCE RISING, figuring in the live band for their last 'non secular' tour.
Vett Roberts would later be found as session vocalist for the esteemed MORTIFICATION's 1995 album 'Primitive Rhythm Machine'. A further RECON connection found Ochoa as producer of this record, as well as contributing much of the guitar work.
RECON would reform for an appearance at

the famed Christian 'Cornerstone' festival. RECON at this juncture comprised vocalist Vett Roberts, guitarist George Rene Ochoa, bass player Mike Grato, keyboard player Ronson Webster and drummer John Gonzales. This show would be captured for a subsequent live CD which also included tracks from the band's opening 1989 demo session.

Magdalene Records, specialists in archive Christian Rock, would re-issue 'Behind Enemy Lines' during 2001 albeit on a limited run of 1000 pressings. Added to the re-release would be six bonus tracks in 'Light The Fire' and 'Dreams' taken from 1988's 'California Metal II' compilation album and demo sessions of 'Light The Fire', 'Dreams', Alive' and 'Eternal Destiny'.

Albums:
BEHIND ENEMY LINES, Intense RO 9201 (1990)
In The Beginning / Lost Soldier / Ancient Of Days / Choose This Day / Dreams / Take Us Away / Holy Is The Lord / Alive! / Eternal Destiny / Behind Enemy Lines
LIVE AT CORNERSTONE 2001, Millennium Eight (2001)
Take It Away / Eternal Destiny / Choose This Day / Lost Soldier / Preaching / The Chosen Few / Alive / Dreams / Light The Fire (Demo) / Dreams (Demo) / Alive (Demo) / Eternal Destiny (Demo)

THE REIGN OF TERROR (USA)
Line-Up: Mike Vescara (vocals), Joe Stump (guitar), Jay Rigney (bass), Matt Scurfield (drums)

Joe Stump's THE REIGN OF TERROR was the melodic Speed Metal project of solo artist and former TRASH BROADWAY and SHINING HEMLOCK guitarist JOE STUMP. Stump, although credited with five solo albums, felt the need for a full band endeavour convening REIGN OF TERROR in the mid '90s, initially for the Japanese market. The 1995 album 'Light In The Sky' features ZANISTER vocalist Brian Sarrela as frontman.

The 1999 record 'The Second Coming' would be officially credited to JOE STUMP'S REIGN OF TERROR.

By the 2001 record 'Sacred Ground' Stump had been joined by the EVENT rhythm section of bassist Jay Rigney and drummer Matt Scurfield. Lead vocalist was none other than the highly rated Mike Vescara, veteran of YNGWIE MALMSTEEN, OBSESSION, LOUDNESS and MVP. The album, which included a cover of RAINBOW's 'Kill The

King', also saw guest keyboard playing from Mats Olausson of YNGWIE MALMSTEEN's band.

Albums:
LIGHT IN THE SKY, (1995)
Don't Look Back / Broken Heart / Highway Star / I Need Your Love / Better Off Dead / Don't Play Fair / Heartless / Guitar Concerto In D Minor / Day By Day / Take A Little / Light In The Sky
THE SECOND COMING, Leviathan (1999)
Sonata Hypnotica / Devil's Playground / You Turn My World Around / Hold On To Your Dreams / Speed Kills / Enchanted Sleep / All Things Must End / Take Your Life / Change / Hell And Back / Tapping Toccata
SACRED GROUND, Leviathan (2001)
Save Me / Sacred Ground / The Unknown / Paginini's Purgatory / Set Us Free / When Will We Know / Last Time / Undercover / Hellbound / Dante's Danza / Still Holding On / Kill The King

REQUIEM (GERMANY)
Line-Up: Boris Grgic (vocals / bass), Nicolas Flores (guitar), Roland Jacob (guitar), Patrick Fleischer (drums)

Frankfurt Thrash band created in 1989. With the addition of drummer Patrick Fleischer in 1992 REQUIEM stabilized their line-up and toured as support to AOK.

A 1993 demo secured a deal with Shark Records for the Wolfgang Stach produced 'Soul Machine' album.

Albums:
REQUIEM, Requiem BAMOT 201 (1992)
Intro / Inside My Dreams / The Visit / Living Out Of Life / Screams From Inside
SOUL MACHINE, Shark 105 (1993)
Lost Ground / Closer To Da Thing / Inside My Dreams / Soul Machine / Just A Spark / Acid Reign / This Is You / Vacuum Room / Screams From Inside / Places I Know

RESISTANT MILITIA (CA, USA)
Line-Up: Don, Russel, Hector, Anthony

RESISTANT MILITIA would develop from Crossover Thrashcore roots as displayed on their Wild Rags 1987 album through to a complete overhaul into RESISTANT CULTURE, a Nu-Metal band employing world influences and instrumentation with an array of guesting musicians.

The band added guitarist Katina Cuevas during 1993 and former SWINSIDE CIRCLE drummer Vic.

331

Singles/EPs:
Hardcore Demo Series, Wild Rags
WRR003 (1987)
The Rhythm And The Noise, Wild Rags
(1987)
Living By Law, Ironworks (1989)

Albums:
RESISTANT MILITIA, Wild Rags (1987)
Rotten Slave / Slaves / Soldiers Of Life / Don't
Let It Be / Life Process

REVENANT (NJ, USA)

Line-Up: Henry Veggian (vocals / guitar),
Dave Jengo (guitar), Tim Scott (bass), Will
Corcoran (drums)

Not to be confused with the Washington DC
REVENANT, previously operating as
OVERCAST.

Singles/EPs:
Distant Eyes / Degeneration, Thrash (1989)

Albums:
PROPHECIES OF A DYING WORLD,
Nuclear Blast (1991)
Prophecy Of A Dying World / Spawn /
Ancestral Shadows / The Unearthly /
Asphyxiated Time / Distant Eyes /
Valedictions

REVENGE (FL, USA)

Albums:
FIRST BLOOD, REI (1988)
FREEDOM OF CHOICE, REI (1989)

REVEREND (CA, USA)

Line-Up: David Wayne (vocals), Stuart
Fujinama (guitar), Brian Korban (guitar),
Dennis O'Hara (bass), Rick Basha (drums)

The history of REVEREND, HERETIC and
METAL CHURCH are truly intertwined in a
"holy trinity" (pun fully intended) of Thrash
Metal. In an odd twist of fate after the
dissolution of HERETIC which saw singer
Mike Howe leave to join METAL CHURCH,
the band evolved into REVEREND and
recruited ex-METAL CHURCH vocalist David
Wayne. Guitarists Stuart Fujinami and Brian
Korban along with bassist Dennis O'Hara
were all members of HERETIC. Joining them
would be drummer Stuart Vogel. By the 1990
album Vogel had made way for drummer Rick
Basha.
After the success of the debut EP on Caroline
Records and capitalizing on Wayne's history
with METAL CHURCH the band signed with
Charisma, a small but stable record label. The

Charisma full-length debut, 'World Won't Miss
You', was a rampaging affair, cranking the
brutality up just a notch above and beyond
either of the previous acts. The album was
dedicated to Dave Pritchard of ARMOURED
SAINT and featured Rocky George of
SUICIDAL TENDENCIES as a guest as well
as Chris Goss of MASTERS OF REALITY.
Late 1990, early 1991 saw some big changes
in the line-up with Fujinama, O'Hara and
Basha all departing with Angelo Espino
joining to play bass and Jason Ian appearing
on drums. The album, 'Play God', was
another punishing opus, and the band had
utilized a second guitarist in the studio by the
name of Tommy "V" Verdonck. The release
also featured a ripping cover of the
CREEDENCE CLEARWATER REVIVAL tune
'Fortunate Son' and also had Juan Garcia of
EVIL DEAD providing some backing vocals.
Unfortunately, with the onset of grunge and
alternative music, Thrash started to loose
momentum and the band capped the first
stage of their career with a six-song Live EP
simply called 'Live'. 1992 saw the addition of
Ernesto F. Martinez on guitar for the live
recording. The short punchy live EP was
considered to be a nice cap on the career of
REVEREND as the band entered a period of
inactivity.
With Wayne's departure from METAL
CHURCH post their comeback 'Masterpeace'
opus the singer reactivated REVEREND. A
limited edition four track EP, 'A Gathering Of
Demons', was made available solely through
the band's website.
Wayne would then found a further act simply
titled WAYNE. Cutting an album billed as
'Metal Church', complete with the
characteristic guitar-cross icon and the
WAYNE logo rendered in METAL CHURCH's
own familiar font left no doubting to which
audience the frontman was pitching.
During 2000 Wayne and WARRIOR guitarist
Joe Floyd would produce the BYFIST
'Adrenalin' EP.
This connection was strengthened when
BYFIST guitarists Davey Lee and Notch Vara
duly joined Wayne's REVEREND supplanting
guitarist Chris Nelson and bassist John
Stahlman.
After several years of inactivity and spurred
perhaps by the global resurgence in Metal,
REVEREND re-emerged in 2001 with an
independent 4 song EP called 'A Gathering
Of Demons'. The EP was notable for the song
'Legion' which was a reworking, both
musically and lyrically, of the METAL
CHURCH song 'Fake Healer'. The line-up
now consisted of Wayne and newcomers
guitarist Chris Nelson, bassist John Stalman
and Todd Stolz on drums. It was the heaviest

recording by the band to date.

Singles/EPs:
Massacre The Innocent / Down / Stealing My Mind / Legion, Neck Damage (2001) ('A Gathering Of Demons' EP)

Albums:
REVERAND, Caroline (1989)
Power Of Persuasion / Dimensional Confusion / Wretched Excess / Ritual
WORLD WON'T MISS YOU, Charisma (1990)
Remission / Another Form Of Greed / Scattered Wits / Desperate / Leader Of Fools / World Won't Miss You / Rude Awakening / Gunpoint / Killing Time / 11th Hour / Hand Of Doom
PLAY GOD, Charisma (1991)
Butcher Of Baghdad / Heaven On Earth / Fortunate Son / Blessings / Promised Land / Play God / Warp The Mind / What You're Looking For / Blackened Thrive / Death Of Me / Far Away
LIVE, Charisma 92149-2 (1992)
Gunpoint / World Won't Miss You / Scattered Wits / B.O.B / Promised Land / The Power Of Persuasion

RIFF RAFF (GERMANY)
Line-Up: Franz Potreck (vocals), Jan Potreck (guitar), Michael Hamann (guitar), Sven Löbl (bass), Henning Rohweder (drums)

Kiel's Speed Metal act RIFF RAFF date to 1991 releasing two demos 'Be Shit And Life' and 'Deep Frustration'. In September of 1992 bassist Tulpe departed, his position taken by Sven for the 'Recently Deceased' album.

Albums:
RECENTLY DECEASED, D&S Records (1993)
Deep Frustration / Death Zone / Brainshake / Evil In White / Melissa / Fright Night / Education / Fuck Off / Schizophrenia / Blinded By The Light

RIGOR MORTIS (Arlington, TX, USA)
Line-Up: Bruce Corbitt (vocals), Mike Scaccia (guitar), Casey Orr (bass), Harden Harrison (drums)

RIGOR MORTIS were snapped up by major label Capitol Records hot on the heels of their acquisition of EXODUS in the scramble for thrash acts in the late eighties.
Vocalist Doyle Bright had taken Bruce Corbitt's place for the 1989 mini-album 'Freaks'.

Singles/EPs:
Demons, Capitol (1988)

Albums:
RIGOR MORTIS, Capitol C1-48909 (1988)
Welcome To Your Funeral / Demons / Bodily Dismemberment / Condemned To Hell / Wizard Of Gore / Shroud Of Gloom / Die In Pain / Vampire / Re-Animator / Slow Death
FREAKS, Metal Blade (1989)
Freaks / Cattle Mutilation / The Haunted / Six Feet Under / Worms Of The Earth / Chained In The Attic
RIGOR MORTIS VS THE WORLD, Tripple X (1990)

RIGOR MORTIS (NY, USA)
Line-Up: Robert Vigna (guitar), Thomas Wilkinson (guitar),

Two erstwhile RIGOR MORTIS members guitarists Robert Vigna and Thomas Wilkinson would later found IMMOLATION.

Singles/EPs:
Holocaust / Warriors Of Doom, Seraphic Decay (1990)

RIGOR MORTIS (CA, USA)

Albums:
THE CONVEYED MESSAGE, Tabb (1986)

RITUAL (Cleveland, OH, USA)
Line-Up: Juan Ricardo (vocals), Bob Allerton (guitar), Mike Ruzsbanzki (guitar), Jack Kilcoyne (bass), Emery Ceo (drums)

Ohio Thrash Metal act RITUAL were founded in 1988 as TORMENTOR issuing a demo 'Addicted To Fire' in 1992. Adopted the new title RITUAL in 1992.
RITUAL's debut album was produced by Torsten Hartmann.

Albums:
TORMENTOR, (1991)
TRIALS OF TORMENT, Massacre MAS CD011 (1992)
She Rides The Sky / Where I Belong / Espionage / Addicted To Fire / The Forgotten / Pain Of It All / In The Dungeon / Dementia / Obscured By Twilight / City Of The Dead

RUMBLE MILITIA (GERMANY)
Line-Up: Staffi (vocals / guitar), Hacki (guitar), Klomman (bass), Olli (drums)
A politically inclined Thrash outfit known for its uncompromising lyrical stance. The 1994 album 'Hate Me' was recorded at Morrisound studios in Florida.

Singles/EPs:
No Nazis / Nazis Raus / Liebe / Bang 'Til
Death / Can't Understand (Live) / Full Of
Commercial (Live) / A.M.F. (Live) / No Nazis
(Live), Century Media 9710-1 (1991)
('Destroy Fascism' EP)
Chile Under Pinochet / The Great Rock n'
Roll Swindle / Never Trust A Business Pig /
Rise And Fight, Atom H (1988) ('En Nombre
Delley' EP)
Wieviel Hass Wollt Ihr Noch? / You're Sure
/ No Nazis / Nazis Raus / Die Erde Getränkt
In Blut / Völkermord / Ist Das Der Grund
(Outro), Century Media 76 9742-2 (1994)
('Wieviel Hass Wollt Ihr Noch?' EP)

Albums:
FUCK OFF COMMERCIAL, Atom H (1987)
Full Of Danger / Treason / Dead End Kids /
Bang 'Til Death / Nuclear Warfare - The First
/ Fright Of Stupidity / Rumble Attack /
Nuclear Warfare - The Last / Full Of
Commercial
THEY GIVE YOU THE BLESSING, Century
Media (1990)
The Church Crien / No Promises To No One
/ No Nazis / The Return Of The Commercial
Bastards / A.M.F. / The Earth Is Turning Red
/ Genocide / Is This The Reason? / Can't
Understand / Mirror Of Fortune
STOP VIOLENCE AND MADNESS, Century
Media (1991)
Intro / Boys In Blue / Reflection Of Your
Videoprogramme / You're Sure / Stop This
Shit / Save Yourself / Way Of Violence /
Kindergarden ('82) / Waiting For Death /
Stop Violence And Madness
HATE ME, RTD 312 1001 2 (1994)
Human Being / Solution / Life Goes On / RM
Family / Profit Thru' Addiction / Sweet World
/ Accused / Hate Me / Life Is Like A Trip /
Love And Peace Muthafucka / Full Of
Commercial

RUNNING WILD (GERMANY)
Line-Up: Rock n' Rolf (vocals / guitar), Majk
Moti (guitar), Jens Becker (bass), Iain Finlay
(drums)

Hamburg's RUNNING WILD debuted with the
album 'Gates To Purgatory', a record laden
with nonsensical occultism, but soon
developed a unique, if bizarre, image based
around pirates which they have fostered to
the present day. Led by Rock n' Rolf (real
name Rolf Kasparek) RUNNING WILD have
proved to be a mainstay of the German Metal
scene with consistently high profile albums
and tours.
The band started out in the early '80s billed
as GRANITE HEART, switching to RUNNING

WILD for their first demo in 1982. The band's
first line-up consisted of Rock n' Rolf, guitarist
Uwe Bendig, bassist Michael Hoffmann and
drummer Jörg Schwarz. By the band's
second tape the following year only Rock n'
Rolf remained. Fresh blood was provided by
guitarist Preacher, bassist Stephan Borisso
and drummer Hasche Haggemann.
RUNNING WILD's third demo 'Heavy Metal
Like A Hammerblow' secured a deal with
Noise Records.
The release of 1985's 'Branded And Exiled'
album, with new guitarist Majik Moti, saw
RUNNING WILD receive an invitation to open
for American Glam Rockers MÖTLEY
CRÜE's German 'Theatre Of Pain' tour dates.
One of the first German Thrash bands to tour
America, RUNNING WILD undertook a
lengthy club tour with CELTIC FROST and
VOIVOD, although following the release of the
popular 'Under Jolly Roger' album drummer
Hasche quit (and now works for the
Rockfabrik club in Ludwigsburg), being
substituted by Stefan Scwarzmann. The band
yielded to another blow shortly after when
bassist Stephan Borisso departed to join
U.D.O. Before long Schwarzmann followed for
the same destination.
The rhythm section was re-established with
the recruitment of bassist Jens Becker and
English drummer Iain Finlay for the 'Death Or
Glory' album. German dates in 1990 found
RAGE supporting.
The line-up would remain less than stable as
guitarist Majk Moti departed in early 1991 and
was replaced by Axel Morgan.
The 'Pile Of Skulls' album in 1992 saw the
addition of ex-U.D.O. rhythm section bassist
Thomas Smuszynski and the return of
drummer Stefan Schwarzmann and was
recorded in Studio M in Hildesheim. Becker
deputized for touring partners
CROSSROADS the same year.
RUNNING WILD would effectively split down
the middle with Becker, Schwarzmann and
Morgan creating X WILD, an outfit that lasted
for three albums. Becker was later to join
GRAVE DIGGER.
Two years later the group released their
eighth album, 'Black Hand Inn', the record
featuring the fifteen minute epic 'Genesis',
RUNNING WILD's alternative view on the
theory of evolution.
1995 yielded 'Masquerade' - recorded with
Gerhard 'Anyway' Wölfe at Horus Sound in
Hannover. The group immediately played the
'Summer Metal Meetings' with the likes of
RAGE and GRAVE DIGGER.
With the band inoperative for a period new
guitarist Thilo Hermann, previously with HOLY
MOSES and RISK, joined GLENMORE for
live work but would return to RUNNING WILD

the following year. Schwarzmann continued his musical chairs by emerging once again as the man behind the kit for U.D.O. in 1997.

The same year Herrmann put together the side project HÖLLENHUNDE for the 'Alptraum' album with GLENMORE drummer Dany Löble. Herrmann. When HÖLLENHUNDE dissolved the same year as the album release Herrmann resumed activities with RUNNING WILD.

For the 1997 release, which saw RUNNING WILD switching to the G.U.N. label, Rock n' Rolf was joined by Smuszynski, Hermann and drummer Jörg Michael, the latter boasting credits with AVENGER, RAGE, MEKONG DELTA, LAOS, HEADHUNTER, GRAVE DIGGER and AXEL RUDI PELL.

1998 found the band returning with a brand new studio affair. The 'Victory' album had Rolf, Herrmann and Smuszynski joined by Angelo Sasso, the latter being a pseudonym for a non 'Metal' drummer not wishing to be associated with the genre!

For touring RUNNING WILD pulled in erstwhile RAGE drummer Chris Efthimiades as Michael had committed himself fully to STRATOVARIUS.

Singles/EPs:

Victim Of States Power / Walpurgis Night (The Sign Of Women's Fight) / Satan, Noise N0010 (1984) ('Walpurgis Night' EP)

Bad To The Bone / Battle Of Waterloo / March On, Noise EM 116 (1989) ('Bad To The Bone' EP)

Wild Animal / Chains And Leather / Tear Down The Walls / Störtebeker, Noise NO173-3 (1990) ('Wild Animal' EP)

Little Big Horn / **Billy The Kid** / Genocide, Noise (1991) ('Little Big Horn' EP)

Lead Or Gold / Hanged, Drawn And Quartered / Win Or Be Drowned, EMI 8 80248-2 (1992)

The Privateer EP, EMI (1994)

Albums:

GATES TO PURGATORY, Noise N0012 08-167 (1984)

Victim Of States Power / Adrian (Son Of Satan) / Preacher / Black Demon / Soldiers Of Hell / Genghis Khan / Prisoner Of Our Time / Diabolical Force

BRANDED AND EXILED, Noise NO0030 (1985)

Branded And Exiled / Gods Of Iron / Realm Of Shades / Mordor / Fight The Oppression / Evil Spirit / Marching To Die / Chains And Leather

UNDER JOLLY ROGER, Noise NO064 (1987)

Under Jolly Roger / War In The Gutter / Raw Ride / Beggar's Night / Raise Your Fist / Land Of Ice / Diamonds In The Black Chest / Mercyless Game

READY FOR BOARDING (LIVE), Noise NO0108 (1988)

Hymn Of Long John Silver / Under Jolly Roger / Genghis Khan / Raise Your Fist / Purgatory / Mordor / Diabolic Force / Raw Ride / Adrian (S.O.S.) / Prisoner Of Our Time

PORT ROYAL, Noise NO122-2 (1988)

Port Royal / Raging Fire / Into The Arena / Uaschitschun / Final Gates / Conquistadores / Blown To Kingdom Come / Warchild / Mutiny / Calico Jack

DEATH OR GLORY, Noise NO172-2 (1990)

Riding The Storm / Renegade / Evilution / Running Blood / Highland Glory (The Eternal Fight) / Marooned / Bad To The Bone / Tortuga Bay / Death Or Glory / Battle At Waterloo / March On

BLAZON STONE, Noise NO171 (1990)

Blazon Stone / Lone Wolf / Slavery / Fire And Ice / Little Big Horn / Over The Rainbow / White Masque / Rolling Wheels / Bloody Red Rose / Straight To Hell / Head Or Tails / Billy The Kid / Genocide

THE FIRST YEARS OF PIRACY, Noise N184-1 (1991)

Under Jolly Roger / Branded And Exiled / Soldiers Of Hell / Raise Your Fist / Walpurgis Night / Fight The Oppression / Marching To Die / Raw Ride / Diamonds Of The Black Chest / Prisoner Of Our Time

PILE OF SKULLS, Electrola EMI 7 80651-2 (1992)

Chamber Of Lies / Whirlwind / Sinister Eyes / Black Wings Of Death / Fistful Of Dynamite / Roaring Thunder / Pile Of Skulls / Lead Or Gold / White Buffalo / Jenning's Revenge / Treasure Island

BLACK HAND INN, EMI 7 80651-2 (1994)

The Curse / Black Hand Inn / Mr. Deadhead / Soulless / The Privateer / Fight The Fire Of Hate / The Phantom Of The Black Hand Hill / Freewind Rider / Powder And Iron / Dragonmen / Genesis (The Making And Fall Of Man)

MASQUERADE, Noise NO261-2 (1995)

The Contract / The Crypts Of Hades / Masquerade / Demonized / Black Soul / Lions Of The Sea / Rebel At Heart / Wheel Of Doom / Metalhead / Soleil Royale / Men In Black / Underworld

THE RIVALRY, G.U.N. GUN 155 (1997)

March Of The Final Battle (The End Of All Evil) / The Rivalry / Kiss Of Death / Firebreather / Return Of The Dragon / Resurrection / Ballad Of William Kidd / Agents Of Black / Fire And Thunder / The Poison. Adventure Galley / Man On The Moon / War And Peace

VICTORY, G.U.N. GUN CD 74321 71502-2 (2000)
Fall Of Dorkas / When Time Runs Out / Timeriders / Into The Fire / Revolution / The Final Waltz / Tsar / The Hussar / The Guardian / Return Of The Gods / Silent Killer / Victory
SINGLES COLLECTION, (2000)
Walpurgis Night (Demo) / Satan (Demo) / March On / Hanged, Drawn And Quartered / Win Or Be Drowned / Wild Animal / Tear Down The Walls / Störtebeker / Billy The Kid / Genocide / Chamber Of Lies - White Buffalo / Poisoned Blood / Dancing On The Minefield / Genesis (The Making And The Fall Of Man)
THE BROTHERHOOD, G.U.N. (2002)
Welcome To Hell / Soulstripper / The Brotherhood / Powerride / Siberian Winter / Detonator / Pirate Song / U-Nation / Dr. Horror / The Ghost / Crossfire / Faceless

RUTHLESS (CA, USA)

Albums:
METAL WITHOUT MERCY, Ironworks (1984)
DISCIPLINE OF STEEL, Axe Killer (1986)

RYKER'S (GERMANY)
Line-Up: Kid D. (vocals), Iggy (guitar), Chris (bass), Meff (drums)

A Hardcore Thrash band formed in Kassel in 1992, RYKER'S involved ex-HOLY MOSES drummer Meff. Indeed, the band's producer was ex-HOLY MOSES man Andy Classen.
After recording the 1995 issued 'First Blood' album guitarist Iggy was replaced by newcomer Grobi.
RYKER'S folded in late 2000 with Meff opening a tattoo shop and Chris concentrating on his record label Kingfisher.
The retrospective live album 'From The Cradle To The Grave' would feature versions of VENOM's 'Witching Hour' and 'YOUTH OF TODAY's 'Together', this latter track even seeing YOUTH OF TODAY's Ray Cappo on guest vocals. An accompanying bonus CD added a drum n' bass remix of 'End Of Line' courtesy of MICRO B, two video tracks and a further slew of covers including GIRLSCHOOL's 'C'mon Let's Go' featuring THUMB's Claus Grabke on lead vocals, AC/DC's 'Dirty Deeds Done Dirt Cheap', BAD BRAINS 'Attitude' and ACCEPT's 'London Leatherboys'.

Singles/EPs:
Kickback EP, Ryker's (1993) (7" single)

Ryker's, Lost & Found (1993) (Split 7" with PITTBULL)
Ryker's, Lost & Found (1994) (Split 7" with POWER OF EXPRESSION)
Hunting Season / Where Were You, RAW WEA 0630-14517-7 (1996)

Albums:
PAYBACK TIME, Lost & Found (1993) (Including "Kickback" EP)
Beg To Differ / Threshold / Prove Yourself / Kickback / Truth / Eye For An Eye / Never Know Nothing / For A Trick / Nothing To Regret / (This Is) My Justice
BROTHER AGAINST BROTHER, Lost & Found LF 102/CD (1994)
Loyalty / Brother Against Brother / Up To You / Try / Once I Believed / Guilty / Beg To Differ / Enough Is Enough / Wrong / Thin Line / Below Zero / Brothers In Arms / True Colours / The Edge
BROTHER AGAINST BROTHER, Lost & Found (1994) (Split Double LP with SICK OF IT ALL)
Loyalty / Brother Against Brother / Up To You / Try / Once I Believed / Guilty / Beg To Differ / Enough Is Enough / Wrong / Thin Line / Below Zero / Brothers In Arms / True Colours / The Edge
FIRST BLOOD, Lost & Found LF 187 (1995)
First Blood / Stranghold / Slowly / Ricochet / What We Once Said / Together (YOUTH OF TODAY)
GROUND ZERO, RAW WEA 0630-14519-2 (1996)
I Reject / Lifeline / This Separation Mine / Without A Second Thought / When There"s No Divide / Hunting Season / Lowlife / Imbalance / Prove Yourself / Engine / Ground Zero / The Cause / Loose Ends / My Clear Moment / Absolution Ninety-Five / Witching Hour
A LESSON IN LOYALTY, WEA PRCD601 0630-18928-2 (1997)
Test Of Faith / As The Laughter Dies / Lesson In Loyalty / Naturally / Still / Triggered / Cold, Lost, Sick / 25 / Gutless / Sober / Shadowplay / Straight / The Peak / Finally / Emergency / Who Laughs Last (Laughs Alone)
LIFE'S A GAMBLE... SO IS DEATH, Century Media (1999)
Forever And A Day / End Of Line / Gone For Good / And None Shall Live / To Whom It May Concern / Violence Is Golden / Calculated / Past The Point / Bombs Of Death / A Dream Gone Bad / Cataclysmic / What It Means / Loss For Words / Stagnant / King / When Tigers Fight / You'll Never Walk Alone
FROM THE CRADLE TO THE GRAVE, Century Media 215655 (2000)

Intro - First Blood / Lowlife / End Of Line /
Truth / To Whom It May Concern / Lifeline /
Past The Point / Stranglehold / Gone For
Good / Hunting Season / Forever And A Day
/ Nothing To Regret / As The Laughter Dies /
Cold Lost Sick / True Love / Witching Hour /
You / Slowly / What We Once Said / My
Justice / Once I Believed / Together / Brother
Against Brother / Beg To Differ / Judas
Reward / From The Cradle To The Grave /
Sad Done / Attitude / C'mon Let's Go / Don't
Threat On Me / Dirty Deeds / London
Leatherboys / End Of Line (remix) / Beg To
Differ (Video) / True Love (Video)

SABBAT (JAPAN)
Line-Up: Gezol (vocals / bass),
Temis Osmond (guitar),
Zorugelion (drums)

Extremely Primitive and raw Thrash Black Metal band. In keeping with Japanese stereotypes SABBAT are seemingly armed with an inexhaustible work ethic. However, their industry is tempered by the fact that most of their releases are issued in strictly limited amounts as low as 100. Indeed, SABBAT's first four albums were restricted to a mere 500 copies. SABBAT formed in 1983 with a line-up of frontman Gezol, guitarists Elizaveat and Ozny with drummer Valvin. The band had previously been titled EVIL with singer Toshiya but upon his departure the title SABBAT was adopted. In 1985 Valvin departed to be superseded by Samm (sometimes known as 'Gero'). Ozny left the following year trimming SABBAT down to a trio.

In 1989 SABBAT united for a one off gig and tried out the services of vocalist Possessed Hammer and guitarist Barraveat.

Further ructions witnessed the departure of Samm in 1990 being replaced by Zorugelion. Temis Osmond took the guitarists position in 1991 in time for the 'Bloody Countess' demo sessions.

The 1994 compilation of re-recorded early material 'Black Up Your Soul' included a version of 'Satan's Serenade' by English NWoBHM band QUARTZ. The same year SABBAT contributed a bilingual version of 'Black Fire' and a remix of 'Satanic Rites' to the compilation 'Far East Gate In Inferno'.

1995 saw SABBAT revisiting more old songs for the album 'For Satan And Sacrifice'. They also chose another NWoBHM cover version, this time 'Kiss Of Death' by SATAN. The band proved that they had a sense of humour by re-recording their earlier 'Panic In The Head' retitled and with new lyrics as 'Baby Disco Is Fuck' as part of their contribution to the infamous 'Headbangers Against Disco' EP alongside GEHENNAH, BESTIAL WARLUST and INFERNO.

SABBAT are noted for their run of international flavoured 'Harmageddon' series of singles which comprise songs in different languages including rather novelly a Swahili version of 'Black Fire'! The 'South American Harmageddon' outing was made up exclusively of cover versions of fellow Japanese artists JURASSIC JADE and SACRIFICE.

The 1999 'Live Panica' and 2000's 'Live Revenge' albums were both limited to 100 copies. 2000 also saw SABBAT cutting their take of Italian '80s Thrash act BULLDOZER's

'Whisky Time' on a split tribute single shared with IMPERIAL. Live dates witnessed a successful return to Scandinavian soil.

2001 would see no let up in the ambitious release schedule of shared singles and ultra limited edition live albums such as 'Live Meltdown' and 'Live Nuts'. The Iron Pegasus label in particular would fuel the craving of SABBAT fans with a glut of picture disc re-releases, all limited editions and many with extra tracks.

The 'Antarctic Harmageddon' album proved of particular interest as, amongst the expected SABBAT tracks, was material from SATANAS, the band drummer Samm formed upon SABBAT's temporary hiatus in 1987. Also included were tracks from DISARM, Zorugelion's 1986 High School band and Samm's side project MAGNESIUM.

Singles/EPs:
Black Fire / Mion's Hill, Evil 666-01 (1985) ('Sabbat' 7" single)
Satanic Rites / Curdle The Blood / Poison Child, Evil 666-02 (1987) ('Born By Evil Blood' 7" single)
Welcome To Sabbat / Crest Of Satan / Children Of Hell / Darkness And Evil, Evil 666-03 (1988) ('Desecration' 7" single)
Hellfire / Immortality Of The Soul, Evil 666-04 (1989) ('The Devil's Sperm Is Cold' 7" single)
Possessed The Room (Kanashibari) / Sacrifice Of Angel / Crying In Last, Evil 666-05 (1990) ('The Seven Deadly Sins' 7" single)
All Over The Desolate Land / Blacking Metal / Witch's Mill / Rage Of The Mountains, Holycaust SIN001 (1994) ('Sabbatical Devilucifer' EP)
Satanican / Gok Kan Ma, Merciless MREP004 (1997) (7" single) ('European Harmageddon' 7" single) (German release)
Bleeding From The Ear / Reek Of Cremation (Live) / Jumu, Primitive Art PAR 014 (1997) ('Scandinavian Harmageddon' 7" single) (Swedish release)
Sabbat / Snow Woman, View Beyond VB0018 (1998) ('East European Harmageddon' 7" single) (Czech release)
The Well Of Krath (Kanashibari 6) / Another Collector (Dwelling II), Holycaust S810 (1998) ('American Harmageddon' 7" single) (USA release)
Takaightenshow / Rinnereighshi, Evil J001ER666-HS6 (1998) ('Asian Harmageddon' 7" single) (Chinese release)
Black Fire (Swahili version) / Splatter '98, Mganga UCHAIVI001 (1998) ('African Harmageddon' 7" single) (Tanzanian release)
Satanic Rites (Live) / Disembodys To The Abyss (Live) / Curdle The Blood (Live) /

Dead March (Live), Way Of Life WOLR1 (1999) ('Oceanic Harmageddon' 7" single) (Australian release)

Terror Beast / Hello Darkness / Destroy - Witch Hunt / Friday Nightmare, Mega Therion MTSS1 (1999) ('South American Harmageddon' 7" single) (Brazilian release)

Angel Of Destruction / Satan Bless You / Kamikaze Bomber / Darkness And Evil, View Beyond (1999) ('Sabbatical Demonslaught' Czech release)

Incubus Succubus / Possessed Hammer (Tribute To Possessed Hammer) / Whisper Of Demon '99, Sadistic Sodomizer SS-001 (2000) ('Sabbatical Magicurse - Baltic Harmageddon' 7" single) (Latvian release)

Whisky Time, Warlord (2000) (Split 7" single with IMPERIAL)

Envenom Into The Witch's Hole / Ghost Train, Hibernia Productions HB02V (2000) ('Iberian Harmageddon' 7" single) (Portuguese release)

Elixir De Vie (Nouvelle version) / Les Flammes De L'Enfer ('Hellfire' Version Francais), EAL Productions (2000) ('French Harmageddon' 7" single) (French release)

Transmigration Of The Soul / , Iron Pegasus IP03 (2001) ("Sabbatical Splitombstone' split EP with UNPURE. Limited edition of 666 copies)

Poison Child (Live) / Black Fire (Live), Berzerker BRZRK 666 (2001) ('Dietsland Harmageddon - Sabbatical Magicrest' EP. Limited edition of 333 copies)

Orochie (Live) / Devil Worship (Live), Infernal Thrash ITR-003 (2001) ('Minami-Kyushu Harmageddon - Sabbatical Magichaos' EP. Green vinyl, limited to 120 copies)

Rain Of Terror, View Beyond (2001) (Split single with GORGON)

Hellfire (Live), The Sky Is Red 001 (2001) (Split single with UNHOLY GRAVE. Limited edition of 1000 copies)

Le Feu Noir ('Black Fire', French version) / Darkness And Evil (Live) /, Legions Of Death 001 (2001) (Split single with TEROR SQUAD. Limited edition of 300 copies)

Albums:

ENVENOM, Evil 666-06 (1991)
Bewitch / The 6th Candle / Satan Bless You / Evil Nations / Devil Worship / Reek Of Cremation / Deathtemptation (Kanashibari Part II) / King Of Hell / Eviler / Carcassvoice / Deadmarch / Reminiscent Bells

EVOKE, Evil 666-07 (1992)
Dance Du Sabbat / Envenom Into The Witch's Hole / Godz Of Satan / Total Necro... / Torment In The Pentagram / Beyond The River / The Whisper Of Demon / Hellhouse / The Curse Of Pharaoh / Metalucifer And

Evilucifer

DISEMBODY, Evil 666-08 (1998)
The Seven Crosses Of Damnation / Bird Of Ill Omen / Metamorphosis / Diabolicalborn / Unknown Massacre / Evoke The Evil / Flower's Red / Reversed Bible / Hungarian Death No. 5 / Ghost In The Mirror

FETISHISM, Evil 666-09 (1994)
Disembody In The Abyss / In Satan We Trust / Satan Is Beautiful / Sausine / Elixir De Vie / Lost In The Grave / Burn The Church / Ghost Train / The Exorcism / Evanescent Quietude

BLACK UP YOUR SOUL, Evil 666-0A (1994)
Welcome To Sabbat / Black Fire / Poison Child / Rage Of The Mountains / Possessed The Room / Darkness And Evil / All Over The Desolate Land / Satan's Serenade / Mion's Hill / Black Fire / Hellfire / Bird Of Ill Omen / Danse Du Sabbat / Envenom Into The Witch's Hole / Carcassvoice / Bewitch

LIVE IN BLOKULA, Evil 666-00B (1995)
The Seven Crosses Of Damnation / Satan Bless You / Possessed The Room- Dead March / Bird Of Ill Omen / Reversed Bible / Evoke The Evil / Evil Nations / Total Necro... / Envenom Into The Witch's Hole / Disembody To The Abyss / Satan Is Beautiful / Hellfire / Ghost In The Mirror / Black Fire

FOR SATAN AND SACRIFICE, Evil 666-0C (1995)
Witch's Mill - Curdle The Blood / Satanic Rites - Crest Of Satan / The Egg Of Dapple / Acid Angel / Immortality Of The Soul / Gideon / Kiss Of Death / Mion's Hill / Sodoomed / Disembody To The Abyss / Unknown Massacre / Whisper Of Demon / Satan Bless You / Remiscent Bells

BLOODY COUNTESS, Holycaust SIN002 (1996) (USA release)
Splatter / Satan's Night / Bloody Countess / Panic In The Head / Madara No Tamago / Poison Child / Children Of Hell / Kanashibari Part 1 / Bloody Countess

THE DWELLING: THE MELODY OF DEATH MASK, Evil 666-10 (1996)
The Swelling - Melody Of The Death Mask

LIVE 666 - JAPANESE HARMAGEDDON, Evil 666-HS1 (1996)
In Satan We Trust / Total Necro... / Beyond The River / Satan Bless You / Bird Of Ill Omen / Mion's Hill / Black Fire

LIVE CURSE, Heavy Metal Super Star HMSS CD001 (1999)
Satanic Rites / Curdle The Blood / Crest Of Satan / Poison Child / Immortality Of The Soul / Devil's Sperm Is Cold / Black Fire / Mion's Hill / Intro: Welcome To Sabbat / Poison Child / Children Of Hell / Black Fire / Immortality Of The Soul / Mion's Hill

SABBATICAL RITES, Iron Pegasus IP04 (1999) (German release)

Black Fire / Mion's Hill / Satanic Rites /
Curdle The Blood / Poison Child (Mix) /
Darkness And Evil (Full version) / Welcome
To Sabbat / Crest Of Satan / Children Of Hell
/ Immortality Of The Soul (Mix) / Hell Fire
(Mix)
KARISMA, Iron Pegasus IP05 (1999)
(German release)
Karisma / Bowray Samurai (Samurai
Zombies) / Orochie / Harmageddon /
Makutsu (Den Of Hades) / Okiko Ningyo
(Okiku Doll Of The Devil) / Yoochuu
(Japanese Revelation)
LIVE KINDERGARDEN, Heavy Metal Super
Star HMSS CD-02 (1999)
Welcome To Sabbat / Black Fire / Hell Fire /
Possessed The Room / dead March /
Envenom Into The Witch's Hole / Beyond
The River / Evil Nations / Satan Bless You
LIVE PANICA, Heavy Metal Super Star
HMSS CD-03 (1999)
Welcome To Sabbat / Panic In The Head /
Wolfman / Splatter / Bloody Countess
LIVE DEVIL, Heavy Metal Super Star HMSS
CD-03 (2000) (Promotion release)
Sabbat Tribes / Gok Kan Ma / The Seven
Crosses Of Damnation / Satan Bless You /
Evil Nations / Whisper Of Demon / Evoke
The Evil / Panic In The Head / Mion's Hill /
Black Fire / Darkness And Evil
SATANASWORD, Iron Pegasus IP010
(2000) (German release)
Charisma / Angel Of Destruction / Kiss Of
Lilleth / Death Zone / The Gate / Dracula /
Nekromantik / Jealousy Carnage
LIVE REVENGE, Heavy Metal Super Star
HMSS CD-05 (2000)
Black Fire XX / Splatter / Children Of Hell /
Black Fire / Gok Kan Ma / Immortality Of The
Soul / Kanashibari / Poison Child / Mion's Hill
LIVE MELTDOWN, Heavy Metal Super Star
Records HMSS CD-06 (2001) (Limited
edition picture disc of 100 numbered copies)
Danse Du Sabbat / Satan Bless You / Evil
Nations / Charisma / Devil Worship /
Transmigration Aggressor / Japanese
Revelation / Baby, Disco Is Fuck /
Outroduction
LIVE NUTS, Heavy Metal Super Star
Records HMSS CD-08 (2001) (Limited vinyl
only edition of 80 copies)
Total Necro / Seven Crosses /
Metamorphosis / Evoke The Evil / Reversed
Bible / Satan Bless You / Evil Nations / Black
Fire / Poison Child
ANTARCTIC HARMAGEDDON, Heavy
Metal Super Star HMSS CD-010 (2001)
Night Of The Living Dead / Flame On The
Circle / Black Fate (VOIDD cover) / Hellfire
(Japanese version) / Bloodstained Holy
Cross (SATANAS) / Magnesium Lady
(MAGNESIUM) / Enola Gay (DISARM) /

Stop (DISARM) / Black Fire

SABBAT (UK)
Line-Up: Martin Walkyier (vocals), Andy
Sneap (guitars), Frazer Craske (bass), Simon
Negus (drums)

SABBAT - A Nottingham based 'Satanic
Opera' styled quartet - formed in June 1985
from a previous act entitled HYDRA. The
Line-up for HYDRA featured vocalist Martin
Walkyier, guitarist Adam Ferman, bassist
Frazer Craske and drummer Mark Daley. This
quartet soon added second guitarist Andy
Sneap, but Ferman and Daley quit and a
name change to SABBAT was agreed.
SABBAT were noted for their onstage
theatrics (heavily influenced by another
Nottingham act HELL) and the creative lyrical
talents of Walkyier. The band debuted live at a
young offenders institute in Doncaster before
recording their 'Fragments Of A Faith
Forgotten' demo that gained the band much
critical praise and ultimately led to a deal with
Germany's Noise Records. Once offered the
deal SABBAT had to wait for guitarist Andy
Sneap to turn 18 before they could sign the
contracts!
The first commercially available record was a
flexi disc for 'White Dwarf' magazine entitled
'Blood For The Bloodgod', produced by ex-
HELL and PARALEX guitarist Kev Bower.
SABBAT's debut album 'History Of A Time To
Come' launched the band onto the forefront of
the British Thrash Metal scene with Walkyier's
distinct pagan themes interwoven into its
impressive epic songs. The album went on to
sell in excess of 60,000 copies.
SABBAT played both Dynamo and Eindhoven
festivals in 1988 as part of a very successful
European tour. Shortly after, SABBAT added
second guitarist Simon Jones - previously
known as Jack Hammer from HOLOSADE -
to replace touring guitarist Richard Scott (on
loan from NO EXCUSE) who accompanied
the band on the European tour.
The group's second album, 'Dreamweaver',
produced by Roy Rowland, was an
opportunity for Walkyier to really let his
imagination fly as SABBAT launched the
crucial release in the form of a concept album
based on the Brian Bates book 'The Way Of Wyrd'.
SABBAT subsequently toured Europe heavily,
including support dates to MANOWAR in
Spain.
Surprisingly, Walkyier and Craske quit after
internal disputes and the vocalist went on to
form the highly successful and industrious
Folk Rock act SKYCLAD, whilst Craske opted
out of the music business returning to a
printing career.
American vocalist Richie Desmond (who had

341

previously been guitarist in CELTIC FROST for a very short period) joined SABBAT in 1990. The band's line-up at this point comprised Sneap, Desmond, guitarist Neil Watson and bassist Wayne Banks. However, both record company and fans were not impressed with the resulting album 'Mourning Has Broken' which sorely lacked Walkyier's more innovative input.

Noise dropped the band and, after two disastrous British dates, Sneap pulled the plug on the tour and the band. Negus joined local act GLORY BOYS. Sneap and Banks went on to form GODSEND. As GODSEND dissolved after a batch of demos Sneap began carving out a niche for himself in the production role making quite a name for himself with some high profile bands such as STUCK MOJO and MACHINE HEAD.

In 1995 there were rumours of a SABBAT reformation between Walkyier and Sneap, but this came to nothing.

SABBAT reared its head again though in 2000 when Britain's leading Black Metal exponents CRADLE OF FILTH covered 'For Those Who Died' with Walkyier providing guest vocals.

As 2001 dawned an announcement was made that a band entitled RETURN TO THE SABBAT was planned for a one off live show comprising Walkyier, Craske, Jones in alliance with former TALION guitarist Pete Wadeson and SKYCLAD and UNDERGROOVE drummer Jay Graham. However, Wadeson would decamp even before the groups debut gig, a warm up for the Derby 'Bloodstock' festival. Walkyier would put in his last show with SKYCLAD the same evening.

As the situation developed it became clear that RETURN TO THE SABBAT was indeed a long term proposition. Graham too parted ways with SKYCLAD as RETURN TO THE SABBAT announced their intentions for further live dates.

In early 2002 Jones parted ways with the band due to family commitments, his replacement being Andy Newby.

Swedish Black Metal act IN AETURNUM weighed in with their appreciation of SABBAT by recording their rendition of 'By Thy Command' culled from the original SABBAT demo 'Magik In Theory And Practice'.

Singles/EPs:
Blood For The Blood God, Games Workshop (1988)
Wildfire / The Best Of Enemies (Wulf's Tale), Noise (1989) (Flexidisc)

Albums:

HISTORY OF A TIME TO COME, Noise N0098 (1988)
Intro / A Cautionary Tale / Hosanna In Excelsis / Behind The Crooked Cross / Horned Is The Hunter / I For An Eye / For Those Who Died / A Dead Man's Robe / The Church Bizarre

DREAMWEAVER – REFLECTIONS OF OUR YESTERDAYS, Noise N0132 (1989)
The Beginning Of The End / The Clerical Conspiracy / Advent Of Insanity / Do Dark Horses Dream Of Nightmares? / The Best Of Enemies / How Have The Mighty Fallen? / Wildfire / Mythistory / Happy Never After

MOURNING HAS BROKEN, Noise N0162-2 (1991)
The Demise Of History / Theological Void / Paint The World Black / Dumbstruck / The Voice Of Time / Dreamscape / Without A Trace / Mourning Has Broken

SACRAMENT (GERMANY)
Line-Up: Alex Wiener (vocals / bass), Jürgen Kretschmann (guitar), Bernd Müller (guitar), Stefan Meyer (drums)

The avant-garde Thrash band SACRAMENT was formed by Alex Wiener, Bernd Müller and Stefan Meyer in 1988. The group would be completed two years later with the addition of Jürgen Kretschmann and have stuck to the same roster ever since.

In 1990 the quartet achieved top honours at a new band festival in Erlangen and were offered the chance to record a debut demo, followed by DIMPLE MINDS and SIEGES EVEN support slots.

In 1995 the first album, 'Agony', was produced by Wolfgang Eller, whilst producer Charlie Bauerfieind heavily assisted the group in a number of areas.

Albums:
AGONY, C.C.C. (1995)
Agony / Barren Cross / Scan The Dark Eyes Aglow / Maze Of Anger / Thin End Of The Wedge / Guilty / Feed The Memory / Prophets Of Doom / Where All Darkness Reveals / Seeds Of Scorn

SACRAMENT (PA, USA)
Line-Up: Rob Wolfe (vocals), Brian Toy (guitar), Erik Ney (bass), Paul Graham (drums)

A Christian Metal band. SACRAMENT's 1990 album 'Testimony For Apocalypse' featured vocalist Mike Torane and guitarist Mike DiDonato. The latter would depart and Torane was replaced by Rob Wolfe.

DiDonato joined forces with SACRAMENT

bassist Erik Ney and BELIEVER drummer Joe Daub to create FOUNTAIN OF TEARS.

Albums:
TESTIMONY OF APOCALYPSE, R.E.X. (1990)
Testimony Of Apocalypse / Slave To Sin / Hellfire Denied / Repentance / Valley Of Dry Bones / Mortal Agony / Conquer Death / Absence Of Fear / The Risen / Blood Bath
HAUNTS OF VIOLENCE, R.E.X. (1992)
Haunts Of Violence / Carry The Corpse / Destructive Heresies / The Wicked Will Rot / Supplication Of The Destitute / Souls In Torment / Separate From Iniquity / Seared Consciences / Under Threat Of Death / Portraits Of Decay

SACRED DENIAL (NJ, USA)
Line-Up: Janus (vocals), Ant (guitar), Mike (guitar), Ken (bass), Dave (drums)

New Jersey Thrashcore. Another SACRED DENIAL line-up is cited as Janus on vocals, Guido on guitar, Anthony Trance on bass and drummer Bill.

Albums:
NORTH OF THE ORDER, Forefront SD003 (1987)
SIFTING THROUGH REMAINS, Nuclear Blast NB 101 (1988)
Sifting Through Remains / When I Sleep / Brothers Inventions / Some Curiosity / Birdie Talk / Conquer / Root Of All Evil / No Way / Surrender / Take A Look Around / Violent Affection
EXTRA STRENGTH, Nuclear Blast NB 102941 (1989)
EXHUMED, Nuclear Blast NB 102942 (1989)

SACRED FEW (OH, USA)

Singles/EPs:
Sacred Few / Low Rider, Skull (1982)

Albums:
BEYOND THE IRON WALLS, Skull (1984)

SACRED OATH (USA)
Line-Up: Rob Thorne (vocals / guitar), Glen Criuciani (guitar), Pete Altieri (bass), Kenny Evans (drums)

Albums:
A CRYSTAL VISION, Mercanery (1987)
Two Powers / The Ferryman's Lair / Message To The Children / The Beginning / Rising From The Grave / a Crystal Vision / Magick Son / Shadow Out Of Time / The Omen /

The Reign

SACRED REICH (Phoenix, AZ, USA)
Line-Up: Phil Rind (vocals / bass), Wiley Arnett (guitar), Jason Rainey (guitar), Greg Hall (drums)

One of the frontrunners of the '80s Thrash boom SACRED REICH scored notable success particularly in Europe with their 'Surf Nicaragua' mini-album.
SACRED REICH were founded in 1985 by vocalist / bassist Phil Rind, guitarists Jeff Martinek and Jason Rainey and drummer Greg Hall. By 1987 Martinek had lost his place to Wiley Arnett for the debut 'Ignorance' album.
The stop-gap 'Surf Nicaragua' mini-album (that included 'Draining You Of Life' from SACRED REICH's demo and a version of BLACK SABBATH's 'War Pigs') was issued and was strangely the release that set SACRED REICH onto the world market. Such was the response to this record that SACRED REICH would find themselves upon a previously unplanned rollercoaster world tour. American dates kicked in during 1988 with ATROPHY and then FORBIDDEN, prior to European dates with MOTÖRHEAD before hooking up once more with FORBIDDEN through Europe in 1989.
The 'Independent' album on the new Hollywood label saw a SACRED REICH line up of Rind, guitarists Wiley Arnett and Jason Rainey and drummer Dave McClain.
Although SACRED REICH remained relatively quiet during 1995 they did submit their version of BLACK SABBATH's 'Sweet Leaf' to the 'Hempilation' album. The band also cut a version of JUDAS PRIEST's 'Rapid Fire' that included a guest vocal from ROB HALFORD which to date remains unreleased.
Shortly after 1996's 'Heal' Hall rejoined the fold, McClain teamed up with MACHINE HEAD, but it was to be stand in man Chuck Fitzgerald who took the drumstool for the band's world tour. Greg Hall was back in the band by 1997.
Arnett, in alliance with former ST. MADNESS vocalist Patrick Flannery, would be located during 2001 assembling a fresh band project entitled THE HUMAN CONDITION. However, these plans were put back when on 2nd August Arnett rolled his car while driving to Phoenix. The guitarist suffered several cracked ribs, bruising of his spleen, bruises and abrasions.
Meantime Hall temporarily joined SOULFLY for studio sessions during October 2001.

Singles/ EPs:
A Question / Let's Have A War / Who's To Blame, Metal Blade (1991)

Albums:
IGNORANCE, Roadrunner RR 9578 (1987)
Death Squad / Victim Of Demise / Layed To Rest / Ignorance / No Believers / Violent Solutions / Rest In Peace / Sacred Reich / Administrative Decisions
SURF NICARAGUA, Roadrunner RR 9512-2 (1988)
Surf Nicaragua / One Nation / War Pigs / Draining You Of Life
ALIVE AT THE DYNAMO, Roadracer RO 94312 (1989)
Surf Nicaragua / Violent Solutions / War Pigs / Death Squad
THE AMERICAN WAY, Roadracer RO 93922 (1990)
Love... Hate / Crimes Against Humanity / I Don't Know / State Of Emergency / The American Way / Way It Is / Flavors
INDEPENDENT, Hollywood HR 61369-2 (1993)
Independent / Free / Just Like That / Supremacy / If Only / Crawling / Pressure / Product / I Never Said Goodbye / Open Book / Do It
HEAL, Metal Blade 3984-14106-2 (1996)
Blue Suit, Brown Shirt / Heal / Break Through / Low / Don't / Jason's Idea / Asked / Who Do You Want To Be? / Seen Through My Eyes / I Don't Care / The Power Of The Written Word
STILL IGNORANT - LIVE (1987-1997), Metal Blade 3894-14145-2 (1997)
American Way / Administrative Decisions / One Nation / Independent / State Of Emergency / The Power Of The Written Word / Heal / Blue Suit, Brown Shirt / Who's To Blame / Violent Solutions / War Pigs / Death Squad / Surf Nicaragua

SACRED RITE (Hawaii, USA)
Line-Up: Mark Kaleiwahea (vocals / guitar), James Caterine (guitar), Peter Crane (bass), Kevin Lumm (drums)

SACRED RITE guitarist James Caterine went under the nom de guerre of Jimmy Dee on later releases. Second album 'The Ritual' has one side of live tracks recorded in Olomana, Hawaii during 1985.

Albums:
SACRED RITE, Sacred Rite (1984)
Wings Of Pegasus / Angels Never Die / White Boy / The Blade / Executioner / R.I.P. / Revelation
THE RITUAL, Megaton (1985)

Teaser / Ritual / Headfirst / 1812: The Battle / Witch's Fury (Live) / Executioner (Live) / Second Row (Live) / Revelation (Live)
IS NOTHING SACRED, Megaton (1986)
Cold Hearted Girl / I've Seen The Wizard / I Will Survive / Take Me To The Kingdom / NI 4 NI / Eleanor Rigby / The Last Rites / As It Was Told

SACRED WARRIOR (IL, USA)
Line-Up: Ray Perra (vocals), Bruce Swift (guitar), Steve Watkins (bass), Rick Macias (keyboards), Tony Velazquez (drums)

A Christian Speed inclined Heavy Metal band. SACRED WARRIOR debuted in 1988 with the 'Rebellion' album.
Roger Martinez of VENGEANCE RISING would guest on the 1989 'Master's Command' album. The 'Obsessions' album, which saw keyboard player Rick Macias absent but second guitarist John Johnson introduced, proved to be SACRED WARRIOR's last. The band, with Joe Petit now on keyboards, soldiered on until a swansong concert in Germany during March of 1993.
SACRED WARRIOR reformed for the 2001 Christian Metal 'Cornerstone' convention, this event being captured for a live album.

Albums:
REBELLION, Intense SSR 8116 (1988)
Black Metal / Mad, Mad World / Stay Away From Evil / He Died / Children Of The Light / Rebellion / Day Of The Lord / The Heaven's Are Calling / Famine / Master Of Lies / Sword Of Victory
MASTER'S COMMAND, Intense RO 9075 (1989)
Master's Command / Beyond The Mountain / Evil Lurks / Bound In Chains / Unfailing Love / Paradise / Uncontrolled / Many Will Come / Onward Warriors / The Flood / Holy, Holy, Holy
WICKED GENERATION, Intense (1990)
No Happy Endings / Little Secrets / Standing Free / Are You Ready / Minister By Night / Miss Linda / Warlords / Wicked Generation / War Torn Hero
OBSESSIONS, Intense (1991)
Wings Of A Dream / Sweet Memories / Turning Back / Obsessions / Kamikaze / Remember Me / Fire From Heaven / Temples On Fire / Mad Man
LIVE AT CORNERSTONE 2001, Millennium Eight (2001)
Intro / Children Of The Light / Remember Me / Rebellion / Holy Holy Holy / Little Secrets / Wicked Generation / Heavens Are Calling / Come On / Day By Day / Prince Of Peace / Temples Of Fire

SACRIFICE (CANADA)

Line-Up: Rob Urbinati (vocals / guitar), Joe Rico (guitar), Scott Watts (bass), Gus Pynn (drums)

Toronto's SACRIFICE left an indelible legacy on the extreme Metal scene inspiring legions of American acts. Drummer Gus Pynn made way for ex-HERICK pounder Darren Foster in 1991.

Frontman Rob Urbinati later created INTERZONE for the 1999 'Cydonia' album. By late 2002 Urbinati was touting a fresh act entitled TENET comprising Death Metal veterans drummer Gene Hoglan of DARK ANGEL and DEATH fame, STRAPPING YOUNG LAD guitarist Jed Simon and erstwhile GRIP INC. bassist Stuart Carruthers.

Albums:

TORMENT IN FIRE, Metal Blade 72159 (1986)
The Awakening / Sacrifice / Turn In Your Grave / Homicidal Breath / Warrior Of Death / Infernal Visions / Burned At The Stake / Necromonicon / The Exorcism / Possession / Decapitation / Beyond Death
FORWARD TO TERMINATION, Diabolic Force (1987)
Forward To Termination / Terror Strikes / Re-Animation / Afterlife / Flames Of Armageddon / Cyanide / Light Of The End / Pyrokinesis
SOLDIERS OF MISFORTUNE, Diabolic Force (1991)
As The World Burns / Soldiers Of Misfortune / In Defiance / Existence Within Eternity / Pawn Of Prophecy / Lost Through Time / A Storm In The Silence / Truth / After The Rain
APOCALYPSE INSIDE, Metal Blade 14267 (1999)
My Eyes See Red / Apocalypse Inside / Flesh / Salvation / Beneath What You See / Incarcerated / Ruins Of The Old / The Lost / Freedom Slave

SACRIFICIAL (DENMARK)

Line-Up: John Hansen (vocals), Kraen Meier (guitar), Sebastian Nordqvist (guitar), Asmus Thomsen (bass), Lukas Meier (drums)

A revered Jutland based Danish transitional Death-Thrash quintet assembled by the Meier siblings guitarist Kraen and drummer Lukas, during 1990. The remainder of the band included singer John Hansen, guitarist Sebastian Nordqvist and bassist Asmus Thomsen.

SACRIFICIAL embarked upon their career path by first offering up the rehearsal tape 'Sacrificial Combustion' followed up by the studio recording 'Lords Of Torment'. The group debuted commercially with the well received 1993 album 'Forever Entangled' but despite an appearance at the prestigious Roskilde festival the following year the band found it tough going. Vocalist John Hansen departed and SACRIFICIAL soldiered on with a replacement, Stefan Steenholdt, for a further demo session, 1994's 'Sadistic Slam'. A 1996 tape 'Authority', featuring Steenholdt on vocals and new bassist Heine Paaske, emerged although SACRIFICIAL maintained a low profile. Some two years later the band, back with Hansen at the microphone and Thomsen on bass, put on an intended one off reunion show. This gig would be enough for the Mighty Music label to offer a contract for the comeback record, January 2001's 'Erect: Eloquent: Extinct'.

As SACRIFICIAL entered the studio to commence work on a third album projected for 2002 release they discovered that Hansen had serious problems with his vocals. This situation got so desperate that Torsten from AUTUMN LEAVES was drafted to try out as a possible replacement. Hansen's voice though would recover just in time.

Hansen and Thomsen also operate the side act SLUGS in collusion with guitarist Tommy Christensen and drummer Martin Pagaard.

Albums:

FOREVER ENTANGLED, Trechoma TRP001CD (1993)
Edmund, A Butler's Tale / I Fall In Temptation / Contents Of Logical Disbelief / Destitute Of Compassion / Acknowledged By Life / This I Cry / Conducted Strain
ERECT: ELOQUENT: EXTINCT, Mighty Music PMZ009-2 (2001)
Trespass / Mass Conduct / Cold / Credit / Beyond / Falling / Hidden Agenda / A New Order / Stolen / In Pieces / Ethnic Cleansing

SACRILEGE (UK)

Line-Up: Lynda 'Tam' Simpson (vocals), Damien Thompson (guitar), Tony May (bass), Spikey T. Smith (drums).

Birmingham thrash metal band SACRILEGE date back to 1984 fronted by female vocalist Tam. The group's debut product, 'Behind The Realms Of Madness', shifted a respectable 7000 copies, although soon after recording the first album original guitarist Mitch and bassist Tony May left the band to pursue more Hardcore projects. SACRILEGE were then approached by FM Revolver Records, but this ultimately led nowhere.

Undeterred, the band again recorded, this

time with the assistance of Rob Bruce at Birmingham's famous Rich Bitch studios. Recording was completed for 'Within The Prophecy', with producer Mike Ivory in January 1987, when MFN stepped in with a deal.

At this juncture the band recruited new bassist Paul Morrisey and second guitarist Frank Healey, although in late 1987 drummer Andrew Baker was replaced by Paul Brookes. The third album, 'Turn Back Trilobite', saw SACRILEGE move away from mainstream Thrash and starting to explore slower, more Doom orientated material with a bit of Folk thrown in for good measure. At this point the band's line-up consisted of Tam, Thompson, Frank Healey on bass and Spikey T. Smith on drums.

Regrettably, the band turned in very few live appearances which resulted in a fairly stagnant career, despite the obvious maturity and increased sales on successive albums.

Post SACRILEGE both Healy and Baker founded CEREBRAL FIX and Healy later went on to BENEDICTION. Brookes joined BENEDICTION then Metal band MARSHALL LAW in 1999.

Albums:
BEHIND THE REALMS OF MADNESS, Children Of The Revolution GURT 4 (1985)
Life Line / Shadow From Mordor / At Death's Door / A Violation Of Something Sacred / The Closing Irony / Out Of Sight Out Of Mind
WITHIN THE PROPHECY, Under One Flag FLAG 15 (1987)
Sight Of The Wise / The Fear Within / Winds Of Vengeance / The Captive / Spirit Cry / Flight Of The Nazgul / Insurrection / Search Eternal
TURN BACK TRILOBITE, Under One Flag FLAG 29 (1989)
Father Time (Beneath The Gaze) / Silent Dark / Soul Search / Awaken (Suryanamaskar) / Key To Nirvana / Into The Sea Of Tranquility / Equinox

SACRILEGE B.C. (USA)
Line-Up: Stephan Taylor (vocals), Gary Wendt (guitar), Tim Howell (guitar), Scan (bass), Matt Fillmore (drums)

Albums:
BEYOND THE REALMS OF MADNESS, Cor (1985)
PARTY WITH GOD, Alchemy VM 102 (1986)
Azemeroth / Crucified / Fun With Napalm / Born Of Hell / Time To Die / Skinned Alive / Cancer / Judge Death / Death Toll / Words Of God / Final Rites / Slaughterhouse / Victimized

TOO COOL TO PRAY, GWR GWLP 47 (1988)
Cold / Where Are We Going / Snake Pit / Between / Revenge / Party With God / Ripping Apart / Too Cool To Pray / Mistake / Feed Off Me / Front Seat Funky

SACROSANCT (HOLLAND)
Line-Up: Michel Lucarelli (vocals), Randy Meinhard (guitar), Michel Cerrone (guitar), Christian Colli (bass), Marco Foddis (drums)

Meinhard and Foddis were both previously with PESTILENCE. SACROSANCT toured Germany in 1992 as support to DARK ANGEL following which Michael Lucarelli and Gerrit Knol departed, although this didn't prevent the group from contributing the song 'Shining Through' to the 'Stop War' compilation album.

The 'Tragic Intense' album featured ex-PHARAO musicians vocalist Collin Kock and guitarist Mike Kock and was produced by then TORCHURE vocalist S.L. Coe.

SACROSANCT's 1992 line-up comprised the Kock brothers, Meinhard, Colli and drummer Haico Van Atticum.

In 1994 both Meinhard and Colli joined SUBMISSION, the short lived band assembled by ex-PESTILENCE and ASPHYX vocalist Martin Van Drunen.

Guitarist Michel Cerrone created IMPERIUM for a 1993 album.

Albums:
TRUTH IS - WHAT IS, No Remorse NRR 1009 (1990)
Dimension Of Violence / Execrated (They Will Be) / Skin To Skin / The Sickened Thrill / Terminal Suicide / Disputed Death / Catalepsy / Truth Is - What Is / The Die Is Cast / Injured
RECESSES FOR THE DEPRAVED 1MF (1991)
Illusive Supremacy / Like Preached Directions / Astrayed Thoughts / Mortal Remains / Hidden Crimes Untold / Enter The Sanctum / With Malice Pretense / The Silence Of Being
TRAGIC INTENSE, 1MF 377.003-2 (1993)
From Deep Below / Godforsaken / Shining Through / Fainted / At Least Pain Lasts / The Gathering Of The Tribes / The Breed Within

SADUS (Antioch, CA, USA)
Line-Up: Darren Travis (vocals / guitar), Rob Moore (guitar), Steve DiGeorgio (bass), Jon Allen (drums)

SADUS came together as a quartet in 1984 of vocalist Darren Travis, guitarist Rob Moore, bassist Steve DiGeorgio and drummer Jon Allen although it was to be two years until the first fruits of this liaison came into being with the 1986 'D.T.P.' demo tape. These sessions led directly to the inclusion of two tracks on the 1987 'Raging death' compilation album.

Quick to capitalise on this achievement SADUS stuck their hands in their pockets to self finance the debut album pulling in METAL CHURCH guitarist John Marshall as producer.

The pace of progress was quickened as a deal with label Roadrunner Records was secured resulting in a further album 'Swallowed In Black' and touring with the likes of SEPULTURA and OBITUARY.

SADUS was put on ice for 1991 as DiGeorgio opted to assist DEATH for their 'Human' album. With this added exposure Roadrunner re-released the 'Illusions' debut retitled 'Chemical Exposure' as SADUS regrouped for a summer American tour opening for MORBID ANGEL.

Although a further album for Roadrunner, 1992's 'A Vision Of Misery', resulted in a European headline tour SADUS found themselves labelless upon their return. Further setbacks occurred when DiGeorgio was inticed back to DEATH for the 'Individual Thought Patterns' album and a subsequent year long bout of touring. DiGeorgio was to return for club shows with SADUS but before any momentum could be gained Moore bailed out.

SADUS continued as a trio crafting the Scott Burns produced 'Elements Of Anger' in 1997. The in demand DiGeorgio along with drummer Jon Allen also operated a side project DRAGONHEART with ex-VICIOUS RUMOURS and present day TESTAMENT guitarist Steve Smyth and his fellow TESTAMENT six stringer Eric Peterson. DiGeorgio teamed up with ICED EARTH in late 2000.

Albums:
ILLUSIONS, Sadus (1988)
Certain Death / Undead / Sadus Attack / Torture / And Then You Die / Hands Of Fate / Twisted Face / Fight Or Die / Illusions (Chemical Exposure)
SWALLOWED IN BLACK, Roadracer RO 93682 (1990)
Black / Man Infestation / Last Abide / The Wake / In Your Face / Good Ridn'z / False Incarnation / Images / Powers Of Hate / Arise / Oracle Of Omission
CHEMICAL EXPOSURE, Roadrunner RO 92592 (1991)
Certain Death / Undead / Sadus Attack / Torture / And Then You Die / Hands Of Fate / Twisted Face / Fight Or Die / Illusions /

Chemical Exposure
A VISION OF MISERY, Roadrunner (1992)
Through The Eyes Of Greed / Valley Of Dry Bones / Machines / Slave To Misery / Throwing Away The Day / Facelift / Deceptive Perceptions / Under The Knife / Echoes Of Forever
CHRONICLES OF CHAOS, Mascot M 7025-2 (1997)
Certain Death / Undead / Sadus Attack / Torture / Hands Of Fate / Illusions / Man Infestation / Good Rid'nz / Powers Of Hate / Arise / Oracle Of Obmission / Through The Eyes Of Greed / Valley Of Dry Bones / Slave To Misery / Facelift / Deceptive Perceptions / Echoes Of Forever
ELEMENTS OF ANGER, Mascot M 7026-2 (1997)
Aggression / Crutch / Words Of War / Safety In Numbers / Mask / Fuel / Power Of One / Stronger Than Life / Unreality / In The End

SALEM'S WYCH (USA)

Albums:
BETRAYER OF KINGS, Metal War (1986)

SAN ANTONIO SLAYER
(San Antonio, TX, USA)
Line-Up: Steve Cooper (vocals), Ron Jarzombek (guitar), Art Villarreal (guitar), Don Van Stavern (bass), Dave McClain (drums)

SAN ANTONIO SLAYER, previously known simply as SLAYER, this Texan based band prefixed their title with the name of their home city when confusion arose with the more prominent Los Angeles thrashers of the same name.

Between albums, bassist Don Van Stavern forged the MARK REALE PROJECT with RIOT guitarist Mark Reale. This project then became known as NARITA, as vocalist Steve Cooper and drummer Dave McClain also became involved. Von Stavern would join RIOT once Reale had resurrected his cult outfit.

Guitarist Art Villarreal was supplanted by Bob Catlin for the 'Go For The Throat' album.

Guitarist Ron Jarzombek reared his head again in 1997 with the SPASTIC INK album 'Ink Complete' and would later join RIOT and ex-JUDAS PRIEST vocalist ROB HALFORD for his 2000 touring band.

Don Van Stavern turned up in 1998 as one of the instigators behind the Industrial Techno outfit PITBULL DAYCARE.

Albums:
PREPARE TO DIE, Rainforrest (1983)

The Door / Warrior / Prepare To Die / The Final Holocaust / Unholy Book / To Ride The Demon Out
GO FOR THE THROAT, Under Den Linden D.D.L.-1 (1988)
Go For The Throat / Upon Us, The End / If You Want Evil / Off With Their Heads / Ride Of The Horsemen / Ancient Swords / T.L.O. 22 / The Witch Must Burn / Hell Will Be Thy Name / Power To Burn

SANCTUARY (Seattle, WA, USA)
Line-Up: Warrel Dane (vocals), Lenny Rutledge (guitar), Sean Blosl (guitar), Jim Sheppard (bass), Dave Budbill (drums)

SANCTUARY, dating back to 1985, may just hold the record for the band with the longest hair in the world. The speed Metal group came to prominence with the inclusion of a brace of demo cuts on the 'Northwest Metalfest' compilation album. Immediately apparent was that vocalist Warrell Dane was in possession of one of the most powerful throats on the Metal scene.
The debut album, produced by MEGADETH mainman Dave Mustaine, features a rather weighty cover of JEFFERSON AIRPLANE's acid daze classic 'White Rabbit'. SANCTUARY proceeded to tour Europe as support to MEGADETH, before recording the impressive 'Into The Mirror Black'.
SANCTUARY broke up with Dane forging NEVERMORE finding cult success in Europe. Dane's name was tenuously linked with the then vacant vocal position in JUDAS PRIEST during 1996.

Albums:
REFUGE DENIED, Epic 460 811-2 (1987)
Battle Angels / Termination Force / Die For My Sins / Soldiers Of Steel / Sanctuary / White Rabbit / Ascension To Destiny / The Third War / Veil Of Disguise
INTO THE MIRROR BLACK, Epic 465 876-2 (1990)
Future Tense / Taste Revenge / Long Since Dark / Epitaph / Eden Lies Obscured / The Mirror Black / Seasons Of Destruction / One More Murder / Communion

SANCTUS (Los Angeles, CA, USA)
Line-Up: Jason McCrarey (vocals), Royce Hsu (guitar), Mike O' Meara (guitar), Brent Gobson (bass), Adrian Ross (keyboards), Michael Chi (drums)

California act SANCTUS were created in 1998 under the name of PANTHEON, issuing a demo under this name. Scoring a deal with Metal Blade Records the band duly adopted

SANCTUS

the new title of SANCTUS.
Bassist Brent Gibson decamped in March of 2002.

Albums:
AEON SKY, Metal Blade (2000)
Empyreal / If We Fall... / Odyssey / November / Tired Of The Pain / Thought I Saw Your Wings / Thy Desolation / Remnants

SARCOFAGO (BRAZIL)
Line-Up: Wagner Lamounier (vocals / guitar), Gerald Minelli (bass), M. Joker (drums)

A veteran act on the South American Death Metal scene. The Satanically inspired SAROFAGO employ Death Metal with distinct Punk leanings allied to blasphemous lyrics.
Rather alarmingly guests on the 'Rotting' album included Oswaldo Pussy Ripper and Eugenio Dead Zone. Adverts for the album announced "Formed by Wagner Antichrist who left SEPULTURA because they were too commercial!"
SARCOFAGO debuted with the 1986 demo 'Satanic Lust' leaving no pretensions as to which musical direction the band was headed. The equally to the point demos 'The Black Vomit' and 'Christ's Death' ensued upfront of the first full length album 'I.N.R.I.'.
For 1991's 'The Laws Of Scourge' the band comprised of vocalist / guitarist Wagner 'Antichrist' Lamounier, guitarist Fabio Jhosko, bass player Gerald 'Incubus' Minelli and drummer Lucio Olliver. OVERDOSE mainman Claudio David provided backing vocals.

Albums:
I.N.R.I., Cogumelo (1987)
Satanic Lust / Desecration Of Virgin / Nightmare / I.N.R.I. / Christ's Death / Satanas / Ready To Fuck / Deathrash / The Last Slaughter / Recrucify / The Black Vomit
ROTTING, Cogumelo (1989)
The Lust / Alcoholic Coma / Tracy / Rotting / Sex, Drinks And Metal / Nightmare
THE LOST TAPES OF COGUMELO,

348

Cogumelo (1990)
THE LAWS OF SCOURGE, Under One Flag
CDFLAG 66 (1991)
The Laws Of Scourge / Piercings / Midnight
Queen / Screeches From The Silence /
Prelude To A Suicide / The Black Vomit /
Secrets Of A Window / Little Julie / Crush,
Kill, Destroy
HATE, Cogumelo (1995)
DECADE OF DECAY, Cogumelo (1996)
The Lost of Innocence / Orgy Of Flies / Hate
/ The God's Faeces / Song For My Death /
Midnight Queen / Screeches From The
Silence / Piercings / Crush, Kill, Destroy /
Nightmare / Rotting / INRI / Desecration Of
Virgin / Recrucify / The Black Vomit / Satanic
Lust / Christ's Death / The Anal Rape Of
God / Satanas / Third Slaughter
THE WORST, Cogumelo (1997)
The End (Intro) / The Worst / Army Of The
Damned / God Bless The Whores / Plunged
In Blood / Satanic Lust / The Necrophiliac /
Shave Your Head / Purification Process

SARKOMA (USA)

Line-Up: Brian Carter (vocals), Mike Hilleburg
(guitar), Stuart Johnson (guitar), Tony
Chisman (bass), Aaron Ingram (drums)

Albums:
COMPLETELY DIFFERENT, Impetus GC
18905 (1992)
INTEGRITY, Bulletproof CDVEST16 (1994)
Tuesdays / Tabula Rasa / Hoveldaze /
George / Universal Footsteps / Blue Horizon
/ 7 Mortamer / Paper / Less By One / Tung

SATAN (UK)

Line-Up: Lou Taylor (vocals), Russ Tippins
(guitar), Steve Ramsey (guitar), Graham
English (bass), Sean Taylor (drums),

Newcastle Heavy Metal act SATAN began life
in 1979 and would create a huge cult interest
for themselves in Europe and the West coast
of America with their first album, 1983's 'Court
In The Act'.
The original SATAN line-up included guitarist
Russ Tippins and Steve Ramsey, vocalist
Andrew Frepp, bassist Steven Bee and
drummer Andy Read. Frepp, however, was
soon replaced by Paul Smith.
At this stage SATAN was still a school act.
Bee was superceded on bass by Graham
English and Steve Allsop took over on vocals.
Read's position behind the drumstool was
relinquished to Ian McCormack who was to
be usurped in favour of ex-RAVEN man Sean
Taylor and would later turn up in BATTLEAXE.
Read, meantime, still served the band as a
roadie.

The group's first demo, 'Into The Fire',
featured vocalist Trevor Robinson, but
following the debut single 'Kiss Of Death' in
1979 Robinson departed in favour of Lou
Taylor.
Taylor would stick with the group until just
prior to the recording of 'Caught In The Act'.
His position was taken by Ian Swift before he
too was replaced by ex-BLITZKREIG and
AVENGER vocalist Brian Ross for recording,
as Swift filled Ross' boots in the AVENGER
ranks.
Curiously, Brian Ross was replaced by the
returning Lou Taylor following 'Court In The
Act', the band claiming that a lack of image
onstage as the main reason that Ross was
asked to leave. Incidentally, during this period
drummer Sean Taylor was also drumming for
WARRIOR as a sideline.
Shortly after this latest change of vocalists in
1985, SATAN renamed themselves after
Lou's previous band BLIND FURY and
recorded the far more commercial 'Out Of
Reach' which saw sales slide.
Meanwhile the 'Court In The Act' album was,
as mentioned, fast becoming a cult classic on
the West coast of America. The band
promptly kicked out Lou and renamed
themselves SATAN, citing American interest
in 'Court In The Act' for this change back to a
more Metallic approach. SATAN recruited
vocalist Mick Jackson (ex-ROUGH EDGE) in
the process.
Following his final departure Lou Taylor went
on to front TOUR DE FORCE and PERSIAN
RISK and later became a known figure on the
London club scene as a Rock DJ. English and
Ramsey later found European success with
the innovative SKYCLAD, whilst Tippins is
now a member of Folk Rock act McALLUM
and is also in an ABBA covers band!
A Ross / Tippins / Ramsey / English / Taylor
SATAN reunion album was on the cards at
one point, but this project was allegedly
shelved by one of the musician's wives!! A
further stab at a reformation came when
Brian Ross attempted to resurrect the band
for a one off appearance at the German
'Wacken Open Air' Festival but it was to no
avail.

Singles/EPs:
Kiss Of Death / Heads Will Roll, Guardian
GRC 145 (1979)
Key To Oblivion / Hear Evil, See Evil,
Speak Evil / Fuck You / The Ice Man,
Steamhammer SPV 60-1898 (1986) ('Into
The Future' EP)

Albums:
COURT IN THE ACT, Roadrunner RR 9894

(1983)
Into The Fire / Trial By Fire / Blades Of Steel / No Turning Back / Broken Treaties / Break Free / Hunt You Down / Dark side Of Innocence

SUSPENDED SENTENCE,
Steamhammer 08-1837 (1987)
92nd Symphony / Who Dies Wins / 11th Commandment / Suicidal Justice / Vandal (Hostile Youth) / SCUM (Socially Condemned Undesirable Misfits) / Avalanche Of A Million Hearts / Calculated Execution (Driller Killer)

SATANIC SLAUGHTER (SWEDEN)

Line-Up: Toxine (vocals), Ztephan Dark (vocals / guitar), Patrick Jensen (guitar), Richard (guitar), Goat (bass), Mique (drums)

SATANIC SLAUGHTER, deeply rooted in old school Thrash traditions, are one of Scandinavia's older Black Metal acts having formed in 1985. Previous to this date the band went under the politically incorrect name of EVIL CUNT. Of the original line-up only guitarist Ztephan Dark remains. Original bassist Goat became a pyromaniac and now resides in a mental hospital!

SATANIC SLAUGHTER released their demo 'One Night In Hell' during 1988. Vocalist Moto was replaced by Andy. In December of the following year the band was put on ice as Dark was imprisoned, convicted of assault. The man would later join MORBIDITY, CRUZIFIED ANGEL and MORGUE.

The band got back together in 1992 with members of SÉANCE, including vocalist Toxine, drummer Mique and guitarists Patrick Jensen and Richard were involved.

However, in 1997 SATANIC SLAUGHTER collapsed yet again, this time due to time honoured musical differences. Dark resolved himself to pick up the pieces with all the other ex-members creating the high profile act WITCHERY. Jensen also became a member of THE HAUNTED.

In 1999 SATANIC SLAUGHTER brought in former TRIUMPHATOR drummer Martin Axenroth to replace previous incumbent Robert Eng. The 2000 line-up comprised Dark, Axenroth, guitarist Christian Ljungberg, vocalist Andreas Deblén and bassist Filip Carlsson.

Albums:

SATANIC SLAUGHTER, Necropolis NR004 (1995)
Immortal Death / Forever I Burn / Dark Ritual / Into The Catacombs / Breath Of The Serpent That Rules The Cold World / On Black Wings / Nocturnal Presence / Legion

Of Hades / Divine Exorcism / I'll Await My Lord / Embraced By Darkness / Domine Lucipheros

LAND OF THE UNHOLY SOULS,
Necropolis NR014 (1997)
Intro / Hatred Of God / Servant Of Satan / Satanic Queen / Demons Feast / Forever I Burn / Legion Of Hades / Breath Of The Serpent That Rules The Cold World / Immortal Death / Land Of The Unholy Souls / One Night In Hell / Dark Ritual / Forever I Burn

AFTERLIFE KINGDOM, Loud n' Proud LNP012 (2000)
The Arrival - Afterlife Kingdom / Nocturnal Crimson Nightmare / When Darkness Prevails / Divine Repulsion / Through The Dark Profound / Autumn / Ad Noctum / Flag Of Hate

SATAN'S HOST (USA)

Line-Up: Leviathan Thisiren (vocals), Stan Patrick Evil (guitar), Belial (bass), D. Lucifer Stele (drums)

SATAN'S HOST vocalist Leviathan Thisiren is none other than JAG PANZER's Harry 'The Tyrant' Conklin who, later (under his real name) fronted RIOT for just one gig.

Conklin eventually made a return to JAG PANZER as the band bounced back for a renaissance series of comeback albums.

One legacy of SATAN'S HOST is that another Colorado band, LEVIATHAN, took their band name from Conklin's stage name.

Albums:

METAL FROM HELL, Web (1986)
Prelude: Flaming Host / Black Stele / In The Veil / Metal From Hell / King Of Terror / Strongest Of The Night / Standing At Death's Door / Hell Fire / Souls In Exile

SAVAGE (UK)

Line-Up: Chris Bradley (vocals / guitar), Andy Dawson (guitar), Wayne Renshaw (guitar), Mark Brown (drums)

At one time this lot were touted in the same breath alongside METALLICA. Indeed, there are early tapes of METALLICA covering SAVAGE songs and an American bootleg METALLICA single featuring the proto-Thrash SAVAGE track 'Let It Loose'.

Mansfield's premier Metal act first surfaced in 1976 having been put together by the then 15 year old bass guitarist Chris Bradley, vocalist Chris Gent, guitarist Lee Statham and drummer Mick Percival. This inaugural line-up lasted nine months in which time they performed just one gig.

By 1979 Bradley had got together a new SAVAGE with his brother Simon on drums, guitarists Andy Bradbury and Andy Dawson. The band debuted on a local sampler highlighting four local acts alongside TYRANT, SPARTA and PANZA DIVISION titled 'Scene Of The Crime' with new members, rhythm guitarist Wayne Renshaw and ex-WILDLIFE drummer Dave Lindley, before landing a deal with Hull's Ebony Records. Lindley was supplanted by former TYRANT drummer Mark Brown and later teamed up with DAWNTRADER.

SAVAGE's first release was a track on the 'Metal Fatigue' compilation album before the single 'Ain't No Fit Place' / 'China Run'. The resultant good reviews led Ebony to finance their classic debut album 'Loose n' Lethal', probably one of the finest British Metal albums ever released.

The album, despite being recorded in a tiny room at the back of producer Darryl Johnston's house, displayed a very aggressive punch, razor-sharp guitars and some fine Lynnot-esque narrative style lyric writing. Lacking any cohesive management backing the band failed to capitalise on the album's enormous potential and rave reviews despite appearing at many European festival dates, including 'Aardschock' alongside METALLICA and VENOM, French festivals with SORTILEGE, and many a London Marquee date.

With Ebony's inability to satisfactorily promote such a fine debut globally (the album racked up sales of about 25,000, mainly on import) the band fled for pastures new and Zebra Records. The first fruit of this liaison was the impressive 12" single 'We Got The Edge'.

The excellent reviews continued, quickly followed by the second album 'Hyperactive', which initially sold well. Serious backing and organisation was still sorely lacking however and the band could never break out of the club scene. Nevertheless, SAVAGE recorded a further demo tape, the slower paced 'This Means War', before throwing in the towel.

Dawson, Renshaw and Brown went on to form REBEL with bassist Stuart Corden and ex-NIGHTVISION vocalist Harry Harrison, cutting some very fine demos and putting in an appearance at the Birmingham 1988 'Rockfest', but this outfit disbanded without a deal. Corden joined GLORY BOYS as Renshaw returned to his day job at the local Metal Box factory.

After a long hiatus Bradley formed XL with local Mansfield musicians. XL recorded a 'Friday Rock Show' session with Dawson on stand in guitar but never secured a record deal.

Dawson and Harrison recorded again with CLOWNHOUSE - very much in the Pop Rock mould - before forming a Grunge inspired QUANGO then HUSK. Both these last two acts featured vocalist Harrison, who much later joined the resurrected WITCHFYNDE.

Bootleg versions of 'Loose n' Lethal' appeared in Europe during 1993 on the Reborn Classics label and in mid 1995 Dawson resurrected SAVAGE to record a new album 'Holy Wars' with Bradley and Lindley. Japanese versions of the album had two cover versions as extra tracks: namely UFO's 'Hot n' Ready' and THIN LIZZY's 'Are You Ready'.

The group added ex-STORMTRIBE and XL man Andy Wilson on second guitar in 1996 for live work and would perform their first ever German gig in April at the 'Bang Your Head' festival alongside TOKYO BLADE, GLENMORE and BLIND GUARDIAN. Unfortunately the band could only follow this up with a show in a local Mansfield pub!

However, Lindley departed prior to recording of 'Babylon' (later playing live with THE LUTHER BELTZ BAND) and in came another erstwhile XL member on drums Richard Kirk. Meantime 'Loose n' Lethal' finally achieved an official re-release through Neat Metal, the album containing three never before released demo tracks 'No Cause To Kill' and 'The Devil Take You' from 1980 and the 1979 recording 'Back On The Road'. The British Steel label would get in on the act re-issuing the band's 1985 opus 'Hyperactive', this too boasting extra material from the 'We Got The Edge' EP. SAVAGE recorded a fresh album 'Xtreme Machine' throughout 1998 as Dawson also worked with Wilson and Harrison and drummer Paul Comeroy once more on another project band. When 'Xtreme Machine' arrived in stores it soon fired up the grapevine between METALLICA fans as SAVAGE had cheekily included the METALLICA demo of their song 'Let It Loose' as a bonus track!

Singles/EPs:
Ain't No Fit Place / China Run, Ebony EBON 10 (1982)
We Got The Edge / She Don't Need You / Running Scared, Zebra 12 RA4 (1984)
Cardiac / Hard On Your Heels, Black Dragon (1986) (French release)

Albums:
LOOSE N' LETHAL, Ebony EBON 12 (1983)
Let It Loose / Cry Wolf / Berlin / Dirty Money / Ain't No Fit Place / On The Rocks / The China Run / White Hot
HYPERACTIVE, Zebra ZEB 4 (1985)
We Got The Edge / Eye For An Eye / Hard

On Your Heels / Blind Hunger / Gonna Tear Ya Heart Out / Stevie's Vengeance / Cardiac / All Set To Sting / Keep It On Ice

HOLY WARS, Neat Metal NM004 (1995)
Headstrong (Cult Of One) / Anthem / How? / This Means War / Down n' Dangerous (Machine Gun) / Suffer The Children / Fashion By Force / Twist / Streets Of Fire / Let The World Go Crazy / Glory Boys / Let It Loose '95

BABYLON, Neat Metal NM016 (1996)
Space Cowboy / Temple Of Deceit / Babylon / Rainmaker / Snakedance / Cyberhead / TV Nation / Sister Sleaze / No Ordinary Day

XTREME MACHINE, Neat Metal NM042 (2000)
Control Freak / Smiling Assassin / Choke / Extreme Machine / Promised Land / Drowning Man / Creepshow / Living With Uncertainty / Thorns / New Messiah / Evil We Can Do / Hyde / Let It Loose (by METALLICA)

SAVAGE DEATH

(East Rutherford, NJ, USA)
Line-Up: Joe Barrows (vocals / guitar), Tom Stevens (guitar), Tony Labosco (bass), Dave Marks (drums)

SAVAGE GRACE

(Los Angeles, CA, USA)
Line-Up: Mike Smith (vocals), Chris Logue (guitar), Mike Marshall (guitar), Brian East (bass), Dan Finch III (drums)

SAVAGE GRACE evolved from the band MARQUIS DE SADE, created in 1981. With the addition of guitarist Kenny Powell in February of 1983 the band decided on a name switch to SAVAGE GRACE, the first line-up being guitarists Powell and Christian Logue, bassist Brian East and drummer Don Finch.
Brian East had relocated to Los Angeles from Seattle where he had recorded a couple of singles with the semi-Glam troupe ALLEYBRAT.
SAVAGE GRACE debuted with a cut 'Sceptors Of Deceit' on the Metal Blade Records compilation album 'Metal Massacre II'. An EP, 'The Dominatress' quickly followed. Wishing to augment their sound SAVAGE GRACE pulled in lead vocalist John Birke in time for recording of 'The Dominatress' EP.
Birke departed to pursue mellower music. Birke, whose last shows with the band included gigs in San Francisco with SLAYER and EXODUS, actually found out about his dismissal second hand, the band announcing it on air during a radio interview. SAVAGE GRACE also lost guitarist Kenny Powell

shortly after. Powell went on to create power metallers OMEN.
SAVAGE GRACE were soon back up to full strength bringing in vocalist Mike Smith and former AGENT STEEL guitarist Mike Marshall. However, the guitar parts on the 'Master Of Disguise' album were performed by Logue as Marshall was added some two months after recording.
The 'After The Fall From Grace' album saw the supplanting of drummer Dan Finch III by Mark Marcum.
The 1987 single saw East replaced with bassist Brian Peace.

Singles/EPs:
The Dominatress / Live To Burn / Too Young To Die / Fight For Your Life / Curse The Night, Metal Blade (1983)
Ride Into The Night / We March On / The Healing Hand / Burn, Semaphore 1012 (1987)

Albums:
MASTER OF DISGUISE, Black Dragon 001 (1985)
Lion's Roar / Bound To Be Free / Fear My Way / Sins Of The Damned / Into The Fire / Master Of Disguise / Sons Of Iniquity / No One Left To Blame / Guitar Solo
AFTER THE FALL FROM GRACE, Black Dragon (1986)
A Call To Arms / We Came, We Saw, We Conquered / After The Fall From Grace / Trial By Fire / Palestinia / Age Of Innocence / Flesh And Blood / Destination Unknown / Tales Of Mystery

SAVAGE STEEL (CANADA)

Line-Up: Paul Gleneicki (vocals), Marshall Birch (guitar), Mark Taluitie (bass), Brian Vella (drums)

SAVAGE STEEL's debut album, on the California based New Renaissance label owned by HELLION vocalist Ann Boleyn, came in blue vinyl. Bassist Mark Taluitie was substituted by Stephan Turrer for the 'Do Or Die' album, produced by SAGA man Steve Negus.

Albums:
BEGINS WITH A NIGHTMARE, New Renaissance (1987)
Hit From The Rear / The Betrayal / Chambers Of Darkness / On The Attack / Nightprowler / Streets Of Indecision / A Night On The Horizon / Switchblade Man
DO OR DIE, Maze Music (1988)
Mind Over Matter / It's Do Or Die / Enough Is Enough / Time After Time / Better Late

Than Never / Men Of War / Evil Eye / Get Me Out Of Here

SAVANT (BRAZIL)
Line-Up: Leo D'Costa (vocals), Antonio Vargas (guitar), Monika Reeve (guitar), Joe Thunder (bass), Rogerio Abittan (drums)

Rio De Janeiro Thrashers created in November of 1994 and originally billed as ORACULO. The band switched titles to SAVANT in 1998 for the 'Portrait Of Reality' EP.
Following recording the band underwent a radical overhaul of its line-up with vocalist Wanderson Silveira, bassist Helios Lambais and drummer Felipe Palmer all exiting. Fresh blood was found in frontman Leo D'Costa, bass player Joe Thunder and Rogerio Abbitan on the drums.

Singles/EPs:
Think About This / Portrait Of Reality / Bad Boys Factory / Diadema / Caos, Varda (1999) ('Portrait Of Reality' EP)

SCARIOT (NORWAY)
Line-Up: Inge J. Tobiassen (vocals), Ronni Thorsen (vocals), Daniel Olaisen (guitar), Frank Orland (guitar), Stefan Schulz (bass), Freddy Bolso (drums)

SCARIOT was created by erstwhile SATYRICON guitarist Daniel Olaison and Anders Kobro of IN THE WOODS and CARPATHIAN FOREST. Also featured was TRAIL OF TEARS "growling" vocalist Ronnie Thorsen and "clean" vocals courtesy of GUARDIAN OF TIME frontman Bernt Fjellstad with session members guitarist Hugo Isaksen and bassist Bonne Thorson.
After the debut album 'Deathforlorn' SCARIOT trimmed down to a duo of Olaisen and Thorsen. The band by early 2001 had been brought back up to strength with Olaisen joined by ODYSSEY guitarist Frank Orland, vocalist Inge J. Tobiassen, INHERIT bassist Stefan Schulz and drummer Freddy Bolso.
Olaisen also operates, albeit under the guise of 'Dod', with the retro Death Metal project BLOOD RED THRONE with former SATYRICON and EMPEROR member Tchort. Thorsen would guest on BLOOD RED THRONE's inaugural demo 'Deathmix 2000'. The band would cut a new album 'Tongueless God' for 2001 release. SCARIOT, now with APOSTASY and OPUS FORGOTTEN man Tor A. Andersen on the drums, would dispense with the services of Tobiassen in November of 2001, announcing the induction

of a new singer, Oddleif Stensland of CLAIRVOYA and INGERMANLAND, in the Spring of 2002.

Albums:
DEATH FORLORN, Demolition DEMCD 017 (2000)
Crimson Tears / Sister / The Bad Man / Within / False Power / Resurrection / Remains Of Dreams / Cruisin'
TONGUELESS GOD, (2001)
Clear Mind / The Last Frontier / The Cynic / Death Request / Close To Hell / Tongueless God / Closing The Gates / Misery Fields / Darkenized

SECOND HELL (HOLLAND)
Line-Up: Evert Dekker (vocals), Mark Staffhorst (guitar), Viron Lymberopoulos (guitar), Robin Buenk (bass), Peter Van De Veen (drums)

Albums:
METAL DEADNESS, Killer Elite (1986) (Split LP with SKULL CRUSHER)
Prophets Of Hell / Trench Devils / Homicide / Face The Truth / Assignment To Kill

SENSELESS REMAINS (GERMANY)
Line-Up: Carsten David (vocals), Martin Ellebracht (guitar), Christian Cronenberg (guitar), Mike Walter (bass), Ulrich Körner (drums)

A German Thrash Metal quintet.

Albums:
REVENGE & HATE, Mega Blaster MBCDS 7932 (1995)
The Communist's Lie / Revenge & Hate / Free / Weak Charakter Burning / She Enemy / Forbidden Humor / Who Cares?

SENTENCED (FINLAND)
Line-Up: Ville Laihiala (vocals), Miika Tenkula (guitar), Sami Lopakka (guitar), Taneli Jarwa (bass), Sami Kukkohovi (bass), Vesa Ranta (drums)

An Oulu based Death Metal band that leaned more towards the classic NWoBHM '80s Thrash sound as each album progressed until later works shifted ground to a Doom-Death direction. Indeed, the band's classic British Rock influences were so evident the 1994 EP even went so far as to cover IRON MAIDEN's 'The Trooper'.
SENTENCED was created during 1989 by the trio of guitarists Miika Tenkalu and Sami Lopakka along with drummer Vesa Ranta. In

this incarnation the band cut their inaugural demo sessions the following year dubbed 'When Death Joins Us'. After recording SENTENCED's numbers were brought up to full strength with the addition of vocalist / bassist Taneli Jarwa as they scored a deal with the French Thrash label for the 1991 debut album 'Shadows Of The Past'. This effort garnered the band praiseworthy media coverage internationally prompting a fresh deal with the domestic Spinefarm label. 1993's sophomore outing 'North From Here' would see the band adding a greater degree of melody to their work whilst retaining the technical edge.

'The Trooper' EP, for new label Century Media, kept the faithful happy until the arrival of 'Amok'. This album succeeding in selling of 30,000 units.

SENTENCED toured Europe with TIAMAT and SAMAEL as Century Media re-released the bands first brace of albums to a wider audience.

Ever eager to experiment the 1995 EP 'Love And Death' included a version of BILLY IDOL's 'White Wedding'.

Jarwa often toured as bassist for IMPALED NAZARENE when the SENTENCED schedule allowed. Jarwa had departed following the 'Love And Death' EP.

Jarwa's place was filled by former BREED man Ville Laihiala for the 1996 Waldemar Sorychta produced 'Down' album. Backing vocals came courtesy of Vorph of SAMAEL. The bands new lead vocalist brought another new dimension to the SENTENCED sound as Laihiala opted for a clean vocal style better suited to the more recent, doomier outings. Global touring had SENTENCED hitting their stride with dates in Europe, America and Japan. SENTENCED also formed part of the billing for the December 1996 'Dark Winter Nights' touring festival alongside DEPRESSIVE AGE, LACRIMOSA, THE GATHERING and DREAMS OF SANITY.

The 1998 opus 'Frozen', which found bassist Sami Kukkohovi of BREED and MYTHOS added to the roster, would once again be produced by Sorychta.

The 2000 'Crimson' album would lend recognition to SENTENCED's status as it reached the coveted Number 1 position in the Finnish album charts. Later in the same year the album would be re-launched on picture disc vinyl format.

Meantime erstwhile frontman Jarwa resurfaced fronting THE BLACK LEAGUE the same year.

In February of 2001 Century Media repackaged the 'Amok' and 'Love & Death' records on a single CD re-release. Laihiala was also to be revealed as in collaboration with Jesper Stromblad of IN FLAMES on an extracurricular band project.

Singles/EPs:
The Trooper / Desert By Night / In Memoriam / Awaiting The Winter Frost, Spinefarm SPI 015 (1993) ('The Trooper' EP)
The Way I Wanna Go / Obsession / Dreamlands / White Wedding / Love And Death, Century Media 77101-2 (1995) ('Love And Death' EP)

Albums:
SHADOWS OF THE PAST, Thrash THR015-NR340 (1992)
When The Moment Of Death Arrives Rot To Dead / Disengagement / Rotting Ways To Misery / The Truth / Suffocated Beginning Of Life / Beyond The Distant Valleys / Under The Suffer / Descending Curtain of Death
NORTH FROM HERE, Spinefarm SPI13CD (1993)
My Sky Is Darker Than Thine / Wings / Fields Of Blood / Harvester Of Hate / Capture Of Fire / Awaiting The Winter Frost / Beyond The Wall Of Sleep / Northern Lights / Epic
AMOK, Century Media CD77076-2 (1994)
The War Ain't Over! / Phoenix / New Age Messiah / Forever Lost / Funeral Spring / Nepenthe / Dance On The Graves (Lil 'Siztah') / Moon Magick / The Golden Stream Of Lapland
DOWN, Century Media 77146-2 (1996)
Intro - The Gate / Noose / Shadegrown / Bleed / Keep My Grave Open / Crumbling Down (Give Up Hope) / Sun Won't Shine / Ode To The End / 0132 / Warrior Of Life (Reaper Redeemer) / I'll Throw The First Rock
STORY - GREATEST KILLS, Spinefarm SPI44CD (1997)
Noose / Nepenthe / Sun Won't Shine / Dance On The Graves / The Way I Wanna Go / White Wedding / My Sky Is Darker Than Thine / The Trooper / Desert By Night / In Memoriam / Awaiting The Winter Frost / The Truth
FROZEN, Spinefarm (1998)
Kaamos / Farewell / Dead Leaves / For The Love I Bear / One With Misery / The Suicider / The Rain Comes Falling Down / Grave Sweet Grave / Burn / Drown Together / Let Go (The Last Chapter) / Mourn
CRIMSON, Century Media 77346-2 (2000)
Bleed In My Arms / Home In Despair / Fragile / No More Beating As One / Broken / Killing Me, Killing You / Dead Moon Rising / The River / One More Day / With Bitterness And Joy / My Slowing Heart

SENTINAL BEAST (USA)

Line-Up: Debbie Gunn (vocals), Mark Koyasako (guitar), Barry Fischel (guitar), Mark Spencer (bass), Scott Awes (drums)

Following the demise of SENTINAL BEAST vocalist Debbie Gunn linked up with the Chicago outfit ZNOWHITE before travelling to England to join Swedish all female Thrashers ICE AGE and, although working on demos and gaining a reasonably high press profile, the band failed to gain a recording deal.

Albums:
DEPTHS OF DEATH, Roadrunner RR9694 (1986)
Depths Of Death / Mourir / Dogs Of War / Corpse / Evil Is The Night / Sentinel Beast / Revenge / The Keeper / Phantom Of The Opera

SEPULTURA (BRAZIL)

Line-Up: Max Cavalera (vocals / guitar), Andreas Kisser (guitar), Paulo Jr. (bass), Igor Cavalera (drums)

SEPULTURA rank as the undisputed leaders of Brazilian bands on the international Rock scene. Created in Bela Horizonte during 1983 SEPULTURA's initial albums were timed perfectly to benefit from the Thrash explosion of the early '80s. Although the act's early albums were far from sensational, the fact that the band more than looked the part allied to their professed influences of British Punk and American Metal stood them in good stead until the breakthrough 'Arise' album.

The band took on typical death metal noms de guerre for the early part of their career, Max Cavalara being known as "Max Possessed", Jairo T. calling himself "Tormentor", Igor Cavelara as "Igor Skull Crusher" and Paulo D. known as "Destructor". Jairo was superseded following 'Morbid Visions' by erstwhile PRESILENCE man Andreas Kisser.

Jairo would at first announce he no longer had any interest in Metal but emerged in 1990 as a member of Thrashers THE MYST for the 'Phantasmagoria' album. The band had other SEPULTURA connections with vocalist Korg (previously with CHAKAL) credited for the lyrics to SEPULTURA's 'To The Wall' and bassist Marcello Diaz being a SEPULTURA roadie.

Kisser had risen through the ranks of local amateur Metal bands such as SPHINX, an outfit that took on covers by acts such as SLAYER and JUDAS PRIEST before injecting original material and retitling themselves PESTILENCE.

Although 1989's 'Beneath The Remains' signalled the first move away from the standard Thrash fare for the band it was to be 'Arise', with cover artwork from noted Sci-Fi artist Michael Whelan, that took SEPULTURA into new realms of creativity. The band had extricated itself from the familiar run of the mill Thrash acts to create a unique album. By now the act's raucous live shows were also beginning to build a solid fanbase. SEPULTURA had become national heroes in Brazil putting in a worthy performance at the 1990 'Rock In Rio' festival sharing the same stage with major league international acts.

1993's 'Chaos A.D.' saw SEPULTURA stripping down their sound to Punk basics, the band's lyrical stance now becoming far more openly political. America too was now coming under the SEPULTURA spell and 'Chaos A.D.' broke the Billboard charts.

Demos for the 'Roots' album were recorded by FUDGE TUNNEL's Alex Newport. SEPULTURA then took the brave step of recording tracks deep in the Brazilian jungle with the Xavante indians. The resulting album took the band's aesthetic into totally new areas of operation as they offered the Rock world an album of unrelenting Metal infused with their own cultural heritage and ethnicity. 'Roots' proved to be their biggest seller to date going top 5 in Britain.

1997's filler album 'Blood Rooted' gave fans more than the usual interim product in anticipation of the new look SEPULTURA and SOULFLY albums. Featured were a barrage of live tracks and also the cut 'Mine' with FAITH NO MORE's Mike Patton on lead vocals plus 'Lookaway' with KORN's Jonathon Davis and Patton once more. Other rare cuts included the band's cover of CELTIC FROST's 'Procreation (Of The Wicked)', DEAD KENNEDY's 'Drug Me' and BLACK SABBATH's 'Symptom Of The Universe'.

With the media attention firmly focused on SOULFLY for a lengthy period the spotlight was pointed firmly back into the SEPULTURA camp when it was announced that Cavalera's position had finally been filled. The new recruit was the black goliath Derrick Green, formerly of ALPHA JERK, OVERFIEND and OUTFACE.

'Against' continued the tradition of tribalism with the inclusion of the Kodo drummers on the track 'Kamaitachi'. A reworking of the track, retitled 'Diary Of A Drug Fiend' with vocals from FAITH NO MORE's Mike Patton, was at the last minute removed from the album for fear of a sales backlash due to it's lyrical content.

The band tested the waters with American shows billed as TROOPS OF DOOM. SEPULTURA proper got to grips with promoting the 'Against' album fully with an American support tour opening for SLAYER. The single from the album 'Choke' featured versions of BAD BRAINS tracks 'Gene Machine' and 'Don't Bother Me'. The band also contributed a track to the 1999 BAD BRAINS tribute album 'Never Give In'. Green meantime turned up as a guest on INTEGRITY 2000's self titled album of the same year.

In April of 2000 Swedish label Black Sun released a SEPULTURA tribute 'Sepulchral Feast' which included honours paid by artists such as SACRAMENTUM, SWORDMASTER, DEATHWITCH, GARDENIAN, CHILDREN OF BODOM, LORD BELIAL, DEFLESHED, THE CROWN and IMPIOUS.

SEPULTURA returned in 2001 with the Steve Evetts produced 'Nation' album. Recorded in Brazil the record saw such diverse guest performances from JELLO BIAFRA on 'Politricks', Reggae artist Dr. Israel, the noted Finnish cello quartet APOCALYPTICA on the mellow 'Valtio' and HATEBREED's Jamey Jasta.

March of 2002 brought the news that drummer Igor Cavalera was pursuing a side venture in league with BIOHAZARD guitarist Billy Graziadei and Brazilian DJ Patife. Other outside activities found Cavalera and guitarist Andreas Kisser credited with material for a soundtrack album entitled 'No Coracao Dos Deuses'. Originally cut in 1999 the recordings would be made available in Europe by Mascot Records. The material includes a guest appearance from ex FAITH NO MORE frontman Mike Patton on the track 'Procura O Cara'. Meantime, Max Cavalera's last concert with SEPULTURA was slated for a 2002 release under the title 'Live At Brixton'.

Singles/EPs:
Under Siege (Regnum Irae) / Orgasmatron / Troops Of Doom (New version), Roadracer RO 2424-6 (1991)
Arise / Troops Of Doom (Live) / Inner Self (live), Roadrunner RR 2406-6 (1992)
Territory / Policia, Roadrunner RR 2382-7 (1993) **66 UK**
Refuse - Resist / Inhuman Nature / Propaganda, Roadrunner RR 2377-8 (1994) **51 UK**
Slave New World / Desperate Cry, Roadrunner RR 2374-2 (1994) 46 UK (CD single)
Slave New World / Crucifacados Pelo System / Drug Me / Orgasmatron (Live), Roadrunner RR 2374-8 (1994) (12" single)
Roots Bloody Roots / Symptom Of The Universe, Roadrunner RR 2320-7 (1996) **19 UK**

Roots Bloody Roots / Procreation (Of The Wicked) / Refuse-Resist (Live) / Territory (Live), Roadrunner RR 2320-2 (1996) (CD single)
Roots Bloody Roots / Propaganda (Live) / Beneath The Remains (Live) / Escape To The Void (Live), Roadrunner RR 2320-5 (1996) (CD single)
Ratamahatta / Mass Hypnosis (Live), Roadrunner RR 2314-7 (1996) (7" single) **23 UK**
Ratamahatta / War / Slave New World (Live) / Amen - Inner Self (Live), Roadrunner RR 2314-2 (1996) (CD single)
Ratamahatta / War / Roots Bloody Roots (Demo) / Dusted (Demo), Roadrunner RR 2314-5 (CD single)
Attitude / Dead Embryonic Cells, Roadrunner RR 2299-7 (1996) (7" single) **46 UK**
Attitude / Lookaway (Master Vibe mix) / Mine, Roadrunner RR 2299-2 (1996) (CD single)
Attitude / Kaiowas (Tribal Jam) / Clenched Fist (Live) / Boitech Is Godzilla (Live), Roadrunner RR 2299-5 (1996) (CD single)
Choke / Gene Machine / Don't Bother Me / Against (Demo), Roadrunner (1998)

Albums:
BESTIAL DEVASTATION, Cogumelo (1984) (Split LP with OVERDOSE)
Bestial Devastation / Antichrist / Necromamcer / Warriors Of Death
MORBID VISIONS, Cogumelo (1985)
Morbid Visions / Mayhem / Troops Of Doom / War / Crucifixion / Show Me The Wrath / Funeral Rites / Empire Of The Damned / The Curse
SCHIZOPHRENIA, Roadrunner (1987)
Intro / From The Past Comes The Storms / To The Wall / Escape From The Void / Inquisition Symphony / Screams Behind The Shadows / Septic Schizo / The Abyss / RIP (Rest In Peace) / Troops Of Doom
BENEATH THE REMAINS, Roadrunner (1989)
Beneath The Remains / Mass Hypnosis / Inner Self / Lobotomy / Sarcastic Existence / Slaves Of Pain / Primitive Future / Hungry / Stronger Than Hate
ARISE, Roadracer RO 9328-2 (1991) **40 UK**
Arise / Dead Embryonic Cells / Desperate Cry / Murder / Subtraction / Altered State / Under Siege (Regnum Irae) / Meaningless Movements / Infected Voice
CHAOS A.D., Roadrunner (1993) **11 UK, 32 USA**
Refuse-Resist / Territory / Slave New World / Amen / Kaiowas / Propaganda / Biotech Is Godzilla / Nomad / We Are Not As Others / Manifest / The Hunt / Clenched Fist / Policia

/ Inhuman Nature
ROOTS, Roadrunner RR 8900-2 (1995)
4 UK, 27 USA
Roots Bloody Roots / Attitude / Cut-Throat / Ratamahatta / Breed Apart / Straighthate / Spit / Lookaway / Dusted / Born Stubborn / Jasco / Itsari / Ambush / Endangered Species / Dictatorshit / Chaos B.C / Symptom Of The Universe / Kaiowas (Live)
BLOOD ROOTED, Roadrunner RR 8821-2 (1997)
Procreation (Of The Wicked) / Inhuman Nature / Policia / War / Crucificados Pelo Sistema / Symptom Of The Universe / Mine / Lookaway (Master Vibe Mix) / Dusted (Demo version) / Roots Bloody Roots (Demo version) / Drug Me / Refuse-Resist (Live) / Slave New World (Live) / Propaganda (Live) / Beneath The Remains - Escape To The Void (Live) / Kaiowas (Live) / Clenched Fist (Live) / Biotech Is Godzilla (Live)
AGAINST, Roadrunner (1998)
Boycott / Choke / Old Earth / Floaters In Mud / Boycott / Rumors / Tribus / Common Bonds / F.O.E. / Rezu / Kamaitachi / Unconscious / Drowned Out / Hatred Aside / T3rcrmillenium
NATION, Roadrunner (2001)
Sepulnation / Revolt / Border Wars / One Man Army / Vox Populi / The Ways Of Faith / Uma Cura / Who Must Die / Saga / Tribe To A Nation / Politricks / Human Cause / Reject / Water / Valtio

SERAPH (AUSTRIA)
Line-Up: Christian Kalns (vocals), Michael Kainberger (guitar), Manuel Inhester (bass), Hannes Vordemayer (drums)

A Salzburg Thrash Metal band formulated in August of 1996 with an initial line-up of ex-DYING ANGEL vocalist Christian Kalns, former DECORUM guitarist Michael Kainberger, bassist Dietmar Matzek, guitarist Andreas Haas and drummer Hannes Vordemayer. In September of the same year Matzek quit and was replaced by Manuel Inhester.
Haas decamped the following year but SERAPH would perform their first live gig in March of 1997.
The band launched a debut album 'Strong Impressions' in 1999 and garnered a valuable support slot to SOULFLY. In January of 2002 SERAPH also opened for the mighty 'Thrash 'Til Death' SODOM, KREATOR and DESTRUCTION tour.

Albums:
STRONG IMPRESSIONS, (1999)

SEVENTH ANGEL (UK)
Line-Up: Ian Arkley (vocals / guitar), Scott Rawson (guitar), Simon Bibby (bass), Mark Ruff (drums)

A West Midlands Christian Thrash band, SEVENTH ANGEL's 1989 demo featured tracks such as 'In The Name Of Christ We Rock' and 'Heed The Warning'.
The group would eventually release two albums through Music For Nations' Thrash label Under One Flag in the early '90s.
Frontman Ian Arkley created ASHEN MORTALITY in 1993 releasing two albums to date.

Albums:
THE TORMENT, Under One Flag (1990)
Tormented Forever / The Charmer / Forbidden Desires / I Of The Needle / Expletive Deleted / Dr. Hatchet / Locked Up In Chains / Acoustic Interlude / Katie / Epilogue
LAMENT FOR THE WEARY, Under One Flag FLAG 55 (1992)
Recollections Of A Life Once Lived / Life In All Its Emptiness / No Longer A Child / Full Of Blackness / Lament For The Weary / Woken By Silence / Falling Away From Reality / Dark Shadows / Passing Of Years / Secure In Eternity / Farewell To Human Cries

SEVERE WARNING OH, USA)

Albums:
DEATH TO FALSE METAL, New Renaissance (1987)

SGM (USA)
Line-Up: Mike Loser (vocals), Bitchard Louis (guitar), Kriss Quinn (guitar), Captain Blackout (bass), Pablo (drums)

Albums:
AGGRESSION, Modusa (1988)
Back In Circulation / Acid Rain / Power / Blow Job / Gutter Of Pain / Tap The Keg / Bascus Eroticus / Graveyard / Aggression / Fags Of Denial / Do Me ('Til I Die) / Mrs. Brown / She

SHAH (RUSSIA)
Line-Up: Antonio Garcia (vocals / guitar), Anatoly Krupnov (bass), Andrei Sazenov (drums)

SHAH was probably the toughest sounding act post perostroyka that were granted a Western release. SHAH debuted with a 1988 cassette album titled 'Escape From Reason'. Bass player Anatoly Krupnov was superseded by Miguel S.

Albums:
BEWARE, Atom H (1989)
Total Devastation / Beware / Coward /
Bloodbrothers / Save The Human Race /
Age Of Dismay / Threshold Of Pain / Say 'Hi'
To Anthrax
TERROR COLLECTION, SNC (1991)
P.S.I.H.O., (1993)
ESCAPE FROM MINDS, Moroz (1994)

SHARKRAGE (GERMANY)
Line-Up: Richie Meier (vocals), Rene Tornier
(guitar), Gerrit Staps (guitar), Thomas Junk
(bass), Kai Bergbolt (drums)

SHARKRAGE of Mainz tread the boundaries
between Thrash and Power Metal. The band,
founded during 1995, is centred upon lead
vocalist Richie Meier and guitarist Rene
Tornier. SHARKRAGE made their entrance
with the December 1995 promotional
cassette 'Surgeon Of Sorcery' which found
Meier and Tornier joined by guitarist Klaus
Erpenbach, bassist Jens Wagner and
drummer Peter Roth.
SHARKRAGE would switch drummers to
Martin Angres in 1996 upfront of undertaking
their debut gig in Offenbach alongside
FRACTURE. Before the year was out the
group had issued the first album
'Moonlandscape' but had lost the services of
Erpenbach. In 1997 keyboard player Christine
Schulte augmented the SHARKRAGE sound
for the sophomore 'Dreamland Area 51' mini-
album. Schulte would then decamp to Black
Metal band AGATHODAIMON. A further
shuffle would see Angres making way in
favour of Andreas Schmitt.
The third album 'Bloody Vengeance' saw
release in 2000. In 2001 SHARKRAGE's
longstanding bassist Jens Wagner bowed
out. His place would Thomas Junk. The drum
position would find Marian Kovacik holding
down the position for a brief spell before he
was usurped by Kai Bergbolt.

Albums:
MOONLANDSCAPE, (1996)
Moonlandscape / Secret Of Silence / Lucifer
/ Atheist / The Jaws / Jaws Part II
DREAMLAND AREA 51, (1998)
Who Are You / Magic Word / Dreamland
Area 51 / Cold As Ice / In My Dreams
BLOODY VENGEANCE, (2000)
Seventh Sign / Devil's Son / Bloody
Vengeance / Seed Of Aggression / Welcome
To Death / Atheist / Under The Blade / In
The Name Of JC / Forgotten Time /
Moonlandscape

SHEER TERROR (NY, USA)
Line-Up: Paul Bearer (vocals), Alan Blake
(guitar), Mark Neuman (bass), Jason Martin
(drums)

Infamous Thrashcore with strong Punk
persuasions. SHEER TERROR weighed in
with two cassette albums 'No Grounds For
Pity' in 1986 and 'Fall From Grace' during
1987. Guitarist Alan Blake decamped in 1990,
allegedly because of SHEER TERROR's
cover version of a song by THE CURE! He
would found DARKSIDE in 1992. DARKSIDE
would subsequently re-record some SHEER
TERROR material.
The 1995 album 'Love Songs For The
Unloved' was co-produced by Tommy Victor of
PRONG.
Former vocalist / bassist Barron Joseph
Misuraca founded DESECRATOR then
vampire rock act VASARIA during 1997 in
collusion with GENITORTURERS guitarist
Chuck Lenihan.
Frontman Paul Bearer would guest on the
1999 25 TA LIFE album 'Triple Crown'. During
2000 Bearer was fronting a new act JOE
COFFEE.

Singles/EPs:
Live At CBGB's, Blackout (1989)
I Need Lunch, Blackout (1990) (Split single
with CRAWLPAPPY)

Albums:
NYHC WHERE THE WILD THINGS ARE,
Blackout (1989)
JUST CAN'T HATE ENOUGH, Starving
Missile (1989)
Hear To Stay (F.Y.A.) / Twisting And Turning /
Ashes, Ashes / Cup 'O Joe / Ready To Halt /
Just Can't Hate Enough / Roses / Owe You
Nothing / Walls / Only 13 / Burning Time
UGLY AND PROUD, Maze (1991)
Three Year Bitch / Time Don't Heal A Thing /
Lulu Roman / Yesterday's Sweetheart /
Tumblin' Down / Sin Of Pride / A. No. 1 / I,
Spoiler / Close My Eyes / Blowout On
Indiana Avenue / Don't Hate Me 'Cause I'm
Beautiful / Done All Wrong / Young Punks In
Love / Bulldog
THANKS FER NUTHIN', Blackout (1992)
Three Year Bitch / Time Don't Heal A Thing /
Yesterday's Sweetheart / Don't Hate Me
'Cause I'm Beautiful / I, Spoiler / Close My
Eyes / Lulu Woman / Hymn 43 / Bulldog
LOVE SONGS FOR THE UNLOVED,
Blackout (1995)
Love Songs For The Unloved / A Tale Of
Moran / Jimmy's High-Life / Not Waving,
Drowning / Rock Bottom On The Kitchen
Floor / Skinhead Girl / Drunk!, Divorced!,

And Downhill Fast / Broken / Outro / College Boy / For Rudy The Kraut / Walnut St. / Be Still My Beating Heart (You're Killing Me)
BULLDOG EDITION, Blackout (2000)
Here To Stay / Twisting And Turning / Ashes, Ashes / Cup O' Joe / Just Can't Hate / Roses / Owe You Nothing / Ready To Halt / Walls / Only Thirteen / Burning Time / I, Spoiler (Live) / Just Can't Hate Enough (Live) / Boys Don't Cry (Live) / I Need Lunch / Walls / Broken / Everything's Fine / Goodbye, Farewell / I Still Miss Someone / Three Year Bitch / Time Don't Heal A Thin / Yesterday's Sweetheart / Don't Hate Me 'Cause I'm Beautiful / Spoiler / Close My Eyes / Lulu Roman / Hymn 43 / Bulldog / Howard Unruh / Not Giving Up / Into My Life / Everything And Nothing / Fashion Fighter / Smile, For A Price / Rome Song / Obsoletion / You Can't Put Your Arms Around A Memory / Said And Done

SHELLSHOCK (LA, USA)
Line-Up: Greg (vocals), Hatch Boy (guitar), Chris (bass), Goner (drums)

Singles/EPs:
No Holes Barred / Wake Me, Splatter (1986)

Albums:
WHITES OF THEIR EYES, Splatter (1986)
Whites Of Their Eyes / Can You Survive? / Alone In The Dark / Hyperdrive / Born To Be Wild / Two Face / Wake Me (When I'm Dead) / Fit To Be Tied / Living In A Hell Hole / Slipping Through My Fingers / Movie Maker (Live)

SHIT FOR BRAINS (GERMANY)
Line-Up: Michael Hohr (vocals), Matthias Hochler (guitar), Gernot Leinert (bass), Sanjai Shah (drums)

Thrash Metal band SHIT FOR BRAINS' members were previously with ANALEX and SHIT & RUBBISH. A self-produced album was released during 1993.
The 1996 album 'Vortex Cordis' was produced by Andy Classen of HOLY MOSES.
Classen utilised the talents of SHIT FOR BRAINS men drummer Sanjah Shah and bassist Gernot Leinart for recording of his 1997 RICHTHOFEN 'Seelenwalzer' album.

Albums:
LUKEWARM, Shit For Brains (1993)
Book Of Condolence / Playing God / Act Of Grace / Subsonic Friction / Recoil / Me, Myself And I
VORTEX CORDIS, Rawk RTD 397.0025.2

(1996)
Vortex Cordis / Bloodmoney / Playing God / Global Assessment Score / Lubrication / Act Of Grace / Perfection Failed / Bloodmoney (Acoustic) / Septic Selves / Pep Talk / Recoil / Me, Myself And I

SIEGES EVEN (GERMANY)
Line-Up: Greg Keller (vocals), Wolfgang Zenk (guitar), Oli Holzwarth (bass), Börk Keller (keyboards), Alexander Holzworth (drums)

A Progressive, Thrash inclined Metal band from Munich, SIEGES EVEN's first trio of albums were recorded with Marcus Steffen on guitar. However, having left the group in 1992 he was replaced by Wolfgang Zenk. The first two albums ('Life Cycle' and 'Steps') also featured the vocal work of Franz Herde, but 'Sense Of Change' witnessed the recruitment of Jogie Kaiser.
Oddly, Kaiser opted to pursue a career in musicals and left the group after recording the album, SIEGES EVEN eventually replacing him with Greg Keller. This was a man who had previously recorded with METRICAL CHARM, a quite well known band on the German underground Metal scene at the time.
Following Greg's relocation from Cologne to Munich SIEGES EVEN set to work on the new album 'Sophisticated', produced by noted Metal knob twiddler Charlie Bauerfeind (the man having also produced the two previous band efforts).
During 1996 SIEGES EVEN were augmented with the arrival of Greg's brother Börk Keller on keyboards. Börk had also been a member of METRICAL CHARM.
Drummer Alex Holzwarth joined Italian Symphonic Metal act RHAPSODY. Bassist Oliver Holswarth joined BLIND GUARDIAN and toured with the DEMONS AND WIZARDS project band.
The Holzwarth brothers united in 2000 with guitarist Markus Steffan to found LOOKING GLASS SELF. They would also session on the reformation album by PARADOX 'Collision Course' the same year.

Albums:
LIFE CYCLE, Steamhammer 08 7558 (1988)
Las Palabras Secreto De Libertad (Repression And Resistance) / Life Cycle / Apocalyptic Disposition / The Roads To Illiad / David / Straggler From Atlantis / Arcane
STEPS, Steamhammer 084 76212 (1991)
Tangerine Windows Of Solace: I) Alba, II) Epitome, III) Apotheosis, IV) Seasons Of

Seclusion (The Prison), V) An Essay Of Relief (A Tangerine Dream), VI) Disintegration Of Lasting Hope, VII) Elegy (Window Of Perception) / Steps / Corridors / The Vacuum Tube Processor / An Act Of Acquiescence / Anthem Chapter I / Anthem Chapter II

A SENSE OF CHANGE, Steamhammer 084 76212 (1995)
Prelude: Ode To Sisyphus / The Waking Hours / Behind Closed Doors / Change Of Seasons / Dimensions / Prime / Epigram For The Last Straw / These Empty Places

SOPHISTICATED, Under Siege Semaphore CD 32683 (1995)
Reporter / Trouble Talker / Middle Course / Sophisticated / Dreamer / As The World Moves On / Wintertime / Water The Barren Tree / War / Fatal / / The More The Less

UNEVEN, Semaphore 37746-422 (1997)
Disrespectfully Yours / What If? / Trainsong / Rise And Shine / Scratches In The Rind / Different Pace / What's Up God? / Love Is As Warm As Tears

SILENCER (Denver, CO, USA)
Line-Up: Keith Spargo (vocals / guitar), Ritchie Wilkison (guitar), Jeff Alexis (bass), Nick Seelinger (drums)

Denver Thrash act SILENCER, founded in 1998 by ex-PARAGON frontman Keith Spargo, have made a major impact in a relatively short span of time. The group's rhythm section comprised ex-PSYCHOTIC INSIGHT bassist Jeff Alexis and former DRUDGERY and BLYND JUSTICE drummer Nick Seelinger. During the band's formative months SILENCER operated with stand in bassists in the form of Chris Marye of the SLEWHOUNDS and Dale Storm from BLEEDING FAITH. The group delivered their opening shot, the 'Kozmos' mini-album, upfront of a split live affair shared with SERBERUS. These recordings would include a version of IRON MAIDEN's 'Wrathchild' with a guesting Harry Conklin of JAG PANZER on vocals.
The band would contribute a version of BLACK SABBATH's 'Into The Void' to the WWIII tribute album 'Hail To The Stonehenge Gods'.
In December of 2001 guitarist Mat Bollen decamped. Latterly the band has added second guitarist Ritchie Wilkison, a veteran of DROP DEAD and international acts ANGEL DUST and DEMONS & WIZARDS.
Upon completion of SILENCER's Spring 2002 dates both Wilkison and Seelinger would journey to Europe for tour work with ANGEL DUST.

Albums:
KOZMOS, (2001)
Mourning Star / Kozmos / Easter Island / Missing Hope / Industrial Command

BLACK FLAMES AND BURNING WORLDS, Crash Inc. (2002) (Split album with SERBERUS)
Intro: Easter Island / The Error Of Your Ways / Industrial Command / Missing Hope / Descending The Ziggurat / Cold War / Wrathchild

SINDROME (Highland Park, IL, USA)
Line-Up: Troy 'Dickslurp' (vocals), Chris Mittelbrun (guitar), Erv Brautigam (guitar), Shaun Glass (bass), Tony Ochoa (drums)

SINDROME were forged in 1988 by an alliance of members from name Chicago Thrash acts. Guitarist Chris Mittelbrun is erstwhile MASTER, both vocalist Troy 'Dickslurp' and guitarist Erv Brautigam are formerly with DEVESTATION whilst bassist Shaun Glass was with TERMINAL DEATH. The band added former LÄÄZ ROCKIT guitarist Ken Savitch in 1991.

Albums:
VAULT OF INNER CONSCIENCE, (1991)
Descending Into Madness / E.S.W. / Astral Projection / Against Infinity / Exit Screaming

SINFUL (New York, NY, USA)
Line-Up: Dana Albert (vocals), Jimmy Ambrose (guitar), Nars Lopez (bass), Al Garay (keyboards), Rick Schafer (drums)

New York's SINFUL mini-album was compiled using three tracks on side one that had drums by supplied by original skinsman Nelson Onofre.
The record was issued through the recently established Shades label formed by the Heavy Metal specialist store of the same name based in central London.
Unfortunately, whilst collectors of this kind of stuff could appreciate the record, reviews in the major Rock magazines weren't particularly kind. What's more, vocalist Dana Albert didn't do himself any favours in the band photo on the rear of the album by looking like a cross between a pirate and 'Coronation Street' character Ena Sharples!

Albums:
GONNA RAISE HELL, Shades (1985)
Burn Your Eyes / Wasteful Youth / Midnite Sun / You Gotta Rock / Teenage Overdose

SIREN (Tampa, FL, USA)
Line-Up: Doug Lee (vocals), Rob Phillips (guitar), Gregg Culbertson (bass), Brian Law (drums)

Tampa Bay thrash act founded in 1981 centred around vocalist Doug Lee who joined the following year. The 1984 self-financed single saw SIREN with a line up of Lee, guitarist Ron Phillips, bassist Ben Parrish and teenage drummer Ed Aborn.

Following the single release Parrish made way for bassist Edward Amyx and recording the January 1985 four track demo tape 'Iron Coffins'. Songs include the title track, 'Over The Rainbow', 'Before The Storm' and 'Shadow Of A Future Past'.

This exposure prompted Pennsylvania based Sanity Records to include the SIREN track 'Over The Rainbow' on their 'Start To Stardom' compilation album.

For the debut album SIREN revamped their rhythm section adding Gregg Culbertson on bass and drummer Brian Law.

Lee completely rebuilt SIREN for the second outing drafting guitarist Brian C. Hendrickson, bassist Les Talent and drummer David Smith. Not to be confused with the other Florida SIREN based in Miami.

Singles/EPs:
Terrible Swift Sword / Metro Mercenary, Siren (1984)

Albums:
NO PLACE LIKE HOME, Flametrader (1986)
Black Death / So Far To Go / Over The Rainbow / Shadows Of The Future Past / The Mine / Terrible Swift Sword / Burning Bridges / Another Lost Love / A Place In Time / Iron Coffins
FINANCIAL SUICIDE, Aaaarrrg (1989)
Kreator Of Dreams / Unsung Hero / Lines Of Steel / This Machine (Runs On Hate) / Locked And Chained / Like A Bullet / Digital Clock / Power March

SITHLORD (AUSTRALIA)
Line-Up: Saundies (vocals / guitar), Scott McMahon (guitar), Jay Saunders (bass), Snorkelbender (drums)

Melbourne, Victoria's SITHLORD are nothing if not original in their concept. A deliberately retro outfit combining large doses of '80s German Thrash Metal with modern Black Metal and named after a 'Star Wars' movie evil heirachy.

Founded in 1998, originally billed as ENMITY, by former CHRISTBAIT and ABRAMELIN drummer Jason 'Snorkelbender' Dutton and erstwhile RANCOR guitarist Saunders. The band, switching to the SITHLORD title after chancing upon the discovery of an already existing English ENMITY, added bassist

Gash who lasted for just one gig in 1999. His replacement would be Jay Saunders, also an operative member of ANATOMY.

The debut album, 'Labyrinth To The Gods', arrived through the Australian Bleed label in 1999. SITHLORD would then sign to the German Barbarian Wrath label for the follow up 'The Return Of Godless Times' set for 2002 release.

Albums:
LABYRINTH TO THE GODS, Bleed BLEED 006 (1999)
Intro / Labyrinth To The Gods / Disinterred Faith / Angelique / Enslaved To Hades / Outro / Dawning Of The New Millennium In Darkness
THE RETURN OF GODLESS TIMES, Barbarian Wrath WRATH666-020 (2002)

SKANNERS (ITALY)
Line-Up: Claudio Pisoni (vocals), Fabio Tenca (guitar), Dino Lucchi (guitar), Corrado Gasser (bass), Luigi Sandrini (drums)

An Italian Speed Metal mob, SKANNERS date back to 1982 and have been known to have supported DIO, TWISTED SISTER, HELLOWEEN, MOTÖRHEAD and MANOWAR on home turf.

Having had the track 'Dirty Armada' featured on the 1984 compilation album 'Rock News Of Vienna'. Guitarist Massimo Quinzio departed in early 1987 to be replaced by Dino Lucchi, and SKANNERS scored a track ,'Turn It Louder Now', on the 1988 compilation album 'Metal Shock'.

Ex-SCRATCH bassist Roberto Vajente superceded Covado Gasser in 1990.

Albums:
DIRTY ARMADA, (1986)
PICTURES OF WAR, CGD 20720 (1988)
Pictures Of War / Something Very Special / Drowning Down The Drain / She's Like A Boy / Fight Back / Turn It Louder Now / We Are Night / Wild / One Night
THE MAGIC SQUARE, Südton 95008-2 (1996)
Undertaker / Beyond Death / Trimurti / Magic Square / On My Way / Without You / You Feel The Power / Insane / Metal Party / Angel / Ciara Teobaldo / True Stories

SKEPTIC SENSE (GERMANY)
Line-Up: Conny (vocals), Stiefel (guitar), Ritchie (guitar), Krödel (bass), Illy (drums)

A Techno Thrash quintet from Southern Germany.

Albums:
PRESENCE OF MIND, Gorgon 8255-2 (1994)
Structures And Interruptions / Harmony Of Souls / Human Indulgence / Raped / Downfall / Norm Always Wins / Last Moments / Capital Punishment

SKELETAL EARTH (FL, USA)

Albums:
EULOGY FOR A DYING FETUS, Foundation 2000 (1990)

SKITZO (USA)

Line-Up: Lance Ozanix (vocals / guitar), John Crowhurst (guitar), Kurt Houser (bass), Dave Ostwald (drums)

A notorious name amongst Bay Area Thrash / Crossover circles. SKITZO are as renowned for their outrageous stage shows and publicity moves as, allegedly, having one of Thrash Metal's elite making a huge success out of one of their 1983 demo songs without giving due credit.

Frontman Lance Ozanix has proven to be the mainstay of the band which has issued a prodigious body of mostly self-financed work. Ozanix gained fame by vomiting onto a groupie on the 'Jerry Springer' TV show, causing the Canadian authorities to ban the offending show. His exploits have also been featured on 'Ripley's Believe It Or Not'. Onstage the band employs "Puke groupies" Octavia and Sunny Delight.

Various SKITZO albums are available as limited edition mail order only porno sleeve versions. 'Got Sick' in particular sporting an alarming carnivorous vagina!

The band toured California with another infamous act THE MENTORS during 1983. However, guitarist Kenny Springer was killed the following year in an auto incident. The band persevered substituting the late Springer with a mannequin named 'Greg Stiff'. The 1997 line up, included the mannequin as well as bassist Sherri Stewart and percussionist Beaver Hensely.

Ozanix also doubles duties appearing as 'Ozzy Osbourne' in the BLACK SABBATH tribute bands PARANOID and SWEET LEAF, the latter in union with VICIOUS RUMORS and TESTAMENT guitarist Steve Smyth. Smyth and erstwhile FAITH NO MORE guitarist JIM MARTIN would contribute guitar to the 1999 album 'Got Sick'.

Latterly SKITZO comprises Ozanix, Ostwald and bassist Kelly Gillis.

Albums:
WRATHAGE, Crowtown (1986)
MOSH TILL MUSH, Crowtown (1987)
DERRANGEROUS, IRS (1989)
THE SKULLING, Tomakazi (1990)
HAUNTING BALLADS, Tomakazi (1991)
EVILUTION, Tomakazi (1992)
CORPSE AND GRIND, Tomakazi (1993)
SYNUSAR SUKUS, Mourning Star (1994)
PSYCHO BABBLE, Mourning Star (1996)
Confessions / Heavenly Rain / Sneakin Out Of The House / I Spit On Your Grave / Last Depression / Maggie Maggot / Skulling II / Neuro Fesis / Somber Junction / Macuba Sex Slave / Uptight Suburbanites
GOT SICK, Mourning Star (1999)
Gates Of Hell / Decapitated Head / Parade / Class Dismembered / Kill With a Vengeance / Loner / P.O.A. (Prisoner Of America) / Political Entrails / Prom Night / Richard Killed Polly Sylvania / Unibomber / Cannibal Girl Island / Color Me / Blood Red Say Metal Monster Stomp / Intro
OLD SKOOL METAL, Mourning Star (2000)

SKYCLAD (UK)

Line-Up: Martin Walkyier (vocals), Steve Ramsey (guitar), Dave Pugh (guitar), Fritha Jenkins (violin / mandolin), Graeme English (bass), Keith Baxter (drums)

Formed in 1991 by vocalist Martin Walkyier, following his break from highly successful Nottingham Thrash act SABBAT. The singer was undoubtedly the unique factor in SABBAT and with SKYCLAD he was now able to push his extraordinary talents and unique inspirations to the fore. SKYCLAD contain such diverse elements as traditional Metal riffing, electric Folk violin and the distinctive pagan lyrical stance and imagery of the man himself.

Forged with ex-PARIAH and SATAN guitarist Steve Ramsey, SKYCLAD's initial demo for Noise Records consisted of purely Walkyier, Ramsey and a drum machine. Soon after gaining a deal former SATAN bassist Graeme English and drummer Keith Baxter were added, followed by ex-DAM guitarist Dave Pugh and fiddler Fritha Jenkins.

The group's debut album, 'Wayward Sons Of Mother Earth', illustrated Walkyier's original approach to Metal music, combining his noted lyrical twists with the classic Thrash inspired Metal riffing of Ramsey. The group toured Europe alongside GAMMA RAY, THUNDERHEAD and OVERKILL.

In late 1991 Ramsey suffered a fractured skull in a fall and the band were forced to cancel a string of British dates. The band hit back with 1992's 'Burnt Offering For The Bone Idol' and '93's 'Jonah's Ark' albums. For live work ex-

MARTIN WALKYIER of SKYCLAD

VELVET VIPER guitarist Dave Moore joined the band on a temporary basis.

1994 saw SKYCLAD undertaking a highly successful European tour on the back of the 'Prince Of The Poverty Line' release. The tour included dates opening for Swedish axe God YNGWIE MALMSTEEN before shows in Germany with FREAK OF NATURE. At the conclusion of the tour violinist Cath Howells (who had succeeded Fritha Jenkins) left to concentrate on studying and was replaced by Georginia Biddles.

During recording of 1995's 'The Silent Whales Of The Lunar Sea' album SKYCLAD were beset by problems. Ramsey collapsed in the studio and had to undergo hospital treatment for a heart complaint. Later in recording, Lynx Studios was broken into and recording equipment stolen.

Still, the album was eventually completed and a brand new SKYCLAD debuted in early 1995 with gigs in Greece, although the band once more hit line-up problems in April with both Pugh and Baxter quitting. Swift replacements were found in two ex-INNER SANCTUM members guitarist Dave Ray and drummer Jed Hawkins. Pugh turned up later in LOADSTONE with brother Brian on drums and bassist Trevor Beckitt.

Whilst SKYCLAD's 1996 album 'Oui Avant-Garde A Chance' included a cover of DEXY'S MIDNIGHT RUNNERS 'Come On Eileen', the group were back in the studio the following year to come up with the more folkified 'The Answer Machine' for 1997. Meantime German acts such as SUBWAY TO SALLY would be taking SKYCLAD's innovation in Folk-Metal to the masses. The British act were forced to hit back with T shirts bearing the legend "Originators of Folk Metal".

1999 had SKYCLAD back to the fore with a much harder release 'Vintage Whine' as the band put in no less than five German tours during the year on top of many prestigious festival performances. An appearance at the 'Wacken Open Air' festival was blighted though when Ramsey, also acting on the day as temporary guitarist for Prog Metal band MINDFEED (whose live sound engineer happened to be none other than Kevin Ridley), was beaten up by over zealous backstage security suffering a bloody head injury.

The band signed to Nuclear Blast Records later that year for the 'Folkemon' album. The limited digipack versions would add a cover of TENPOLE TUDOR's 'Swords Of A Thousand Men' whilst the Japanese edition boasted the exclusive 'Locomotion' instrumental.

German Black Metal act SUIDAKRA covered 'The One Piece Puzzle' on their 2000 album 'The Arcanum'. The same year found Walkyier

guesting on CRADLE OF FILTH's version of the SABBAT chestnut 'For Those Who Died'.

As 2001 broke rumours spread that founder member Walkyier had quit the band. However, SKYCLAD were announced as being scheduled to perform at the Derby 'Bloodstock' festival during May. This show was also scheduled to feature a one off showing of RETURN TO THE SABBAT, a SABBAT reformation of sorts with Sneap's would be role being filled by ex-TALION guitarist Pete Wadeson.

By April the band indeed confirmed that Walkyier had left and that 'Bloodstock' would be the farewell show. SKYCLAD themselves resolved to carry on with Ridley taking over on lead vocals. The new look band debuted with shows in Europe acting as openers to FISH.

As fans patiently waited to see just if SKYCLAD could survive without the figurehead of Walkyier it became apparent that the band had every intention of persevering. The act established their own label, Demolition Records, for release of a live album 'Another Fine Mess'. Being SKYCLAD's first official live release, tracks featured material culled from the band's 1995 Dynamo festival appearance.

The traditional round of touring in Germany also continued unabated although Jay Graham decamped to RETURN TO THE SABBAT. His swift replacement would be former AXIS and STICKY FINGERS drummer Arron Walton.

In October SKYCLAD also launched a single version of the TENPOLE TUDOR cover 'Swords Of A Thousand Men', even roping Eddie Tenpole in as session guest. The single package would also include a freshly re-worked version of the stage favourite 'The Widdershin's Jig'.

Singles/EPs:
Emerald / A Room Next Door / When All Else Fails / The Declaration Of Indifference / Spinning Jenny / Skyclad, Noise NO0194-3 (1992) ('Tracks From The Wilderness' EP)
Thinking Allowed? / Cradle Will Fall / The Widdershins Jig, Noise NO209-3 (1993)
Schadenfreude / Earth Mother, The Sun And The Furious Host / It Wasn't Meant To End This way, Noise (1993) (Promotion release)
Vintage Whine / Inequality Street / Constance Eternal / Building A Ruin / Sins Of Emission (Unplugged version), Massacre (1999) ('Classix Shape' shaped CD EP)
Swords Of A Thousand Men / The Widdershin's Jig, Demolition (2001)
Albums:
WAYWARD SONS OF MOTHER EARTH,

Noise NO0163-2 (1991)
The Sky Beneath My Feet / Trance Dance /
A Minute's Piece / The Widdershins Jig / Our
Dying Island / Pagan Man / The Cradle Will
Fall / Skyclad / Moongleam And
Meadowsweet / Terminus
BURNT OFFERING FOR THE BONE IDOL,
Noise NO0186-2 (1992)
Ware And Disorder / A Broken Promised
Land / Spinning Jenny / Salt Of The Earth
(Another Man's Poison) / Karmageddon (The
Suffering Silence) / Ring Stone Round / Men
Of Straw / R Vannith / The Declaration Of
Indifference / Alone In Death's Shadow
JONAH'S ARK, Noise NO0209-2 (1993)
Thinking Allowed / Cry Of The Land /
Schadenfruede / A Near Life Experience /
The Wickedest Man In The World / Earth
Mother, The Sun And The Furious Host /
The Ilk Of Human Blindness / Tunnel
Visionaries / A Word To The Wise /
Bewilderbeast / It Wasn't Meant To End This
Way
PRINCE OF THE POVERTY LINE, Noise
NO239-2 (1994)
Civil War Dance / Cardboard City / Sins Of
Emission / Land Of The Rising Slum / The
One Piece Puzzle / A Bellyful Of Emptiness /
A Dog In The Manger / Gammadion Seed /
Womb Of The Worm / The Truth Famine
**THE SILENT WHALES OF THE LUNAR
SEA**, Noise N0228-2 (1995)
Still Spinning Shrapnel / Just What Nobody
Wanted / Art Nazi / Brimstone Ballet / A
Stranger In The Garden / Another Fine Mess
/ Turncoat Rebellion / Halo Of Flies /
Desperanto (A Song For Europe?) / The
Present Imperfect.
IRRATIONAL ANTHEMS, Massacre MASS
CD (1996)
Snake Charming / My Mother In Darkness /
Penny Dreadful / The Wrong Song / I
Dubious / The Sinful Ensemble / No Deposit,
No Return / Quantity time / Inequality Street
/ Science Never Sleeps / History Lessons /
Sabre Dance / The Spiral Starecase
OUI AVANT - GARDE A CHANCE,
Massacre MASSCD0104 (1996)
If I Die Laughing, It'll Be An Act Of God /
Great Blow For A Day Job / Constance
Eternal / Postcard From Planet Earth /
Jumping My Shadow / Bombjour! / History
lessons (The Final Examination) / A Badtime
Story / Come On Eileen / Master Race /
Bombed Out / Penny Dreadful (Full Shilling
Mix)
OLD ROPE – THE BEST OF SKYCLAD,
Noise N0275-2 (1996)
The Widdershins Jig / Skyclad / Spinning
Jenny / Alone In Death's Shadow / Thinking
Allowed / The Wickedest Man In The World /
Earth Mother, The Sun And The Furious

Host / Cardboard City / Land Of The Rising
Son / The One Piece Puzzle / Just What
Nobody Wanted / Brothers Beneath The Sun
/ The Present Imperfect / Cradle Will Fall /
The Declaration Of Indifference / Ring Stone
Round / Men Of Straw
THE ANSWER MACHINE?, Massacre Swan
Lake MAS CD0128 (1997)
A Clown Of Thorns / Building A Ruin / Worn
Out Sole To Heel / Single Phial / Helium /
The Thread Of Evermore / Eirenarch /
Troublesometimes / Tainting By Numbers /
My Naked I / Catherine At The Wheel / Dead
Angels On Ice
VINTAGE WHINE, Massacre MAS CD0178
(1999)
Kiss My Sweet Brass / Vintage Whine / On
With Their Heads! / The Silver Cloud's Dark
Lining / A Well Beside The River / No Strings
Attached / Bury Me / Cancer Of The Heart /
Little Miss Take / Something To Cling To / By
George
FOLKEMON, Nuclear Blast 27361 65022
(2000)
The Great Brain Robbery / Think Back And
Lie Of England / Polkageist / Crux Of The
Message / The Disenchanted Forest / The
Antibody Politic / When God Logs-Off / You
Lost My Memory / Deja Vu Ain't What It Used
To Be / Any Old Irony?
HISTORY LESSONS, Massacre MAS
CD0296 (2000)
Penny Dreadful (Full Shilling Mix) / The
Silver Cloud's Dark Lining / Isle Of Jura / No
Deposit, No Return / Brimstone Ballet /
Constance Eternal / Building A Ruin /
Emerald / I Dubious / Jumping My Shadow /
A Bellyful Of Emptiness / Kiss My Sweet
Brass / Bury Me / Single Phial / By George
ANOTHER FINE MESS, Demolition
DEMCD112 (2001)
Intro / Another Fine Mess / Cardboard City /
Art-Nazi / The Wickedest Man In The World /
The One Piece Puzzle / Still Spinning
Shrapnel / Just What Nobody Wanted / Sins
Of Emission / Land Of The Rising Slum /
Alone In Deaths Shadow / Spinning Jenny
NO DAYLIGHTS NOR HEELTAPS, (2002)
Penny Dreadful / Inequality Street / Spinning
Jenny / The Cry Of The Land / Another Fine
Mess / Sins Of Emission / The Widdershins
Jig / History Lessens / The Land Of The
Rising Slum / Single Phial.

SLAMMER (UK)
Line-Up: Paul Tunnicliffe (vocals), Enzo
Annecchini (guitar), Milo Zivanic (guitar),
Russell Bertram (bass), Andy Gagic (drums)

Thrash Metal band fronted by former
EXCALIBUR and STEEL vocalist Paul
Tunnicliffe.

SLAMMER debuted with the 'Controlled Kaos' demo in 1988 and the following year the Bradford Thrash act recorded a 'Friday Rock Show' session with newly recruited ex-DEADLINE bassist Russell Bertram. In the American Thrash explosion which saw 'the big four' break worldwide, the British record companies were falling over themselves to sign homegrown Thrash acts little realising the scene had already peaked. In the meleé, London Records picked up ONSLAUGHT and Warner Bros. opted for SLAMMER.

What seemed like a dream come true for the fledgling Thrashers turned into a nightmare as the Rock media universally rounded on them for supposedly being signed for their being simply any old Thrash act rather than an individual talent.

SLAMMER toured hard with plenty of record company support, playing with ONSLAUGHT, Hardcore Americans SACRILIGE B.C. and a European jaunt with the CRUMBSUCKERS, although the debut Mark Dodson produced album was hammered by the critics who saw SLAMMER as nothing more than average wannabees.

By 1990 Bertram had split to form BITTER AND TWISTED with ex-ACID REIGN and future CATHEDRAL guitarist Adam Lehan.

NEW MODEL ARMY bassist Stuart Morrow joined the band but would leave for LOUD in 1992.

SLAMMER guitarist Milo Zivanic returned to the scene in early 2002 touting a METALLICA tribute band DAMAGE INC. for a tour of Holland.

Singles/EPs:
Born For War / Hellbound / If Thine Eye Offend Thee / Fight Or Fall, WEA SLAM 1 (1989) (Promotion release)
Insanity Addicts / Bring The Hammer Down / Maniac / I.O.U., Heavy Metal XD66 (1990)

Albums:
WORK OF IDLE HANDS, WEA 246000-2 (1989)
Tenement Zone / If Thine Eye / Johnny's Home / Razor's Edge / Hellbound / Hunt You Down / God's Prey / Fight Or Fall / No Excuses / Born For War
NIGHTMARE SCENARIO, Heavy Metal HMR XD170 (1991)
What's Your Pleasure / Greed / In The Name Of God / Just Another Massacre / Architect Of Pain / Every Breath / I Know Who I Am / Corruption / Think For Yourself / L'Ultima

SLAMMER (PA, USA)
SLAMMER drafted in new vocalist Denny Litman in order to record their debut single 'M.I.A.'

Ex-SLAMMER vocalist Todd Giornesto formed the Thrash Metal outfit GIORNESTO and demoed a selection of songs with this new band in 1988 before it evolved into CHILLING VISION the following year.

Singles/EPs
M.I.A. / Metal Anguish, Sledgehammer (1986)

SLAVEN (CA, USA)

Albums:
SLAVE TO THE HEART, Maniac (1985)

SLAYER (Huntington Beach, CA, USA)
Line-Up: Tom Araya (vocals / bass), Kerry King (guitar), Jeff Hannemann (guitar), Paul Bostaph (drums)

SLAYER are without question the most sinister of the acts to break out onto the world stage from the early '80s American thrash phenomena. With an unwillingness to compromise they have seemingly defied all the odds to place themselves in the position of regular chart breakers.

SLAYER's music is unrelentingly intense, initially fuelled by drummer DAVE LOMBARDO (often voted as the 'World's best drummer' in many Metal mags), the mainstay lethal twin guitars of Kerry King and Jeff Hanneman together with the almost inhuman vocals of bassist Tom Araya (a former hospital respiratory therapist). This union made

SLAYER Photo : Arto Lehtinen

SLAYER not only mould-breakers but an act faithfully plagiarized by countless lesser bands. Lyrically they are unafraid to venture into the realms of the most despicable and overtly controversial. Satanism and Nazism are familiar territories for SLAYER.

Initial recordings were marred by inadequate production and thus universally dismissed as derisory by the world's rock media. Even hardened thrash fans found SLAYER's inaugural bursts of speed noise, when compared with rising stars such as MEGADETH, ANTHRAX and METALLICA, difficult to stomach.

Founded in 1981 by uniting former SABOTAGE drummer Lombardo, King and Araya from QUITS and Hanneman, SLAYER were originally titled DRAGONSLAYER. At first they pursued a traditional heavy metal stance musically but debuting with the fast track 'Aggressive Perfector' on the 'Metal Massacre IV' compilation album on Metal Blade Records persuaded the band to adopt a more intense leaning. A three track demo tape followed comprising 'Fight 'Til Death', 'Black Magic' and 'The Antichrist' which rapidly became a much traded item on the underground metal scene.

King teamed up with fellow Los Angeles speed metal band MEGADETH performing live gigs on a temporary basis. During this period of flux Lombardo was briefly supplanted by drummer Bob Gourley, later to join DARK ANGEL then create POWERLORD.

Brian Slagel, Metal Blade mentor, was quick to notice the reaction and duly signed the band up putting them in the studio to record 'Show No Mercy' whilst Lombardo graduated from high school. The press hated it, proclaiming it to be an unintelligible mess it but it still sold.

The band got out on the road, even putting in an English appearance at London's Marquee club, before setting off on the 'Haunting North America' tour. SLAYER's no compromise approach saw them using inverted crosses onstage and King wearing leather armbands encrusted with nails.

With second album 'Hell Awaits' SLAYER provided ample defiance to those that sneered with the music easily equal in ferocity to the debut. SLAYER were clawing their way up and the British rock magazine 'Metal Forces' readers poll was a case of SLAYER sweeping the board gaining honours for best band, best live band, best album and best drummer.

SLAYER began to make serious headway when Rick Rubin, Owner and producer of Def Jam Records, signed the band in 1986. First fruit of this liaison was the 28 minute 'Reign In Blood' opus, a pure Thrash album that took the genre to new levels of extremity. Quite incredibly the album was to break into the American Billboard top album 100 charts, the first of many.

'Reign In Blood' also embroiled SLAYER into political condemnation almost immediately for the lyrics to the opening track 'Angel Of Death'. The song dealt with the infamous SS Auschwitz extermination camp doctor Joseph Mengele and many were quick to accuse SLAYER of fascist sentiments. The mighty CBS corporation, distributors of Def Jam, refused to handle the album.

The band retorted that this was merely an observation and not a belief, citing that Araya himself was far from being an all American white boy. The obviously Ayran Hanneman compounded the problem however by frequently wearing SS collar patches, iron crosses and insignia in photos and by adorning one of his guitars with cuff titles of notorious SS panzer divisions such as 'Totenkopf' and 'Das Reich'. SLAYER's tour T-shirts of the time proudly declared that the band were 'Slaytanic Wehrmacht' and featured a skull encased in a World War II German helmet. SLAYER seemed quite content to be stoking up their reputation as number 1 bad boys.

The band provoked further adverse reaction by their use of a new logo, a nazi eagle with the swastika replaced with the SLAYER logo. The furore over 'Angel Of Death' was so great that British distributor Geffen, owned by the Jewish entrepreneur David Geffen, dropped the album from their schedules. Ironically Geffen had been quick to capitalize on SLAYER's earlier dumping by CBS.

SLAYER heralded their first celluloid performance captured at New York's Studio 54 club alongside EXODUS and VENOM for 'The Ultimate Revenge' video. SLAYER, on the 'Reign In Pain' tour for the first time enjoying the comforts of a tour bus, toured America with OVERKILL before European dates with openers MALICE. Such was the extreme loyalty of the headliner's fans that MALICE were very often the subject of ugly scenes, having to endure booing and, sadly, more often than not, spitting.

With the band's burgeoning popularity former label Metal Blade were quick to capitalize releasing 'Live Undead', a picture disc live album with tracks culled from 1984 American shows.

Between albums and whilst in the midst of an American tour Lombardo announced he was quitting in December 1986. Rumours circulated that the cause of the split was an argument over Lombardo's wife being on the road. Nonetheless, SLAYER continued with

SLAYER Photo : Arto Lehtinen

substitute T.J. Scaglione of WHIPLASH. As the tour rolled on SLAYER hooked up with W.A.S.P., an ill fated union that witnessed a bitter war of words between the two bands as to which act viewed itself as selling the more tickets.

SLAYER were back in the headlines once more in 1987 for all the wrong reasons when they pulled out of a headlining slot at the prestigious 'Aardschock' Festival in Holland at the eleventh hour. A great degree of ill feeling was generated until the band explained that with the cancellation of METALLICA (due to the death of Cliff Burton) SLAYER had no intentions of performing but their agency had neglected to inform the relevant parties.

Lombardo, who during his sabbatical had turned down the opportunity to join MEGADETH, was enticed back into the band in April 1987 in time to record the next album. The reinstated drummer did however nearly miss a batch of British dates when his work permit had been refused.

SLAYER plugged the gap between albums by covering IRON BUTTERFLY's 'In A Gadda Da Vida' for the movie soundtrack 'Less Than Zero'.

1988's 'South Of Heaven', which saw SLAYER slowing the pace somewhat and included a cover of JUDAS PRIEST's 'Dissident Aggressor', gave SLAYER increased sales yet again. With the band seemingly attempting to extricate themselves from their previous Black Metal trip, oddly Rubin was to insist that the word 'Satan' appear on the record and at the last minute Araya reworked the lyrics to 'Read Between

The Lies' to include a reference to Ol' Nick.

American dates kicked off with support from NUCLEAR ASSAULT then SLAYER finally got the opportunity to play the major American arenas at the end of 1988 when they were invited to join JUDAS PRIEST as guests.

SLAYER took a lengthy break of some two years after the world tour during which time they severed ties with their British record company London Records. SLAYER had been far from amused when the single 'Mandatory Suicide' had been released on the very last date of the British tour.

1990 saw SLAYER in what some envisaged as an unholy union on the 'Clash Of The Titans' festival touring package. Three out of 'The big four', SLAYER, MEGADETH and ANTHRAX teamed up for a series of monumental shows across arenas in America and Europe. For the stateside dates ALICE IN CHAINS opened, whilst for the eighteen shows in Europe ANTHRAX were supplanted by SUICIDAL TENDENCIES and TESTAMENT opened.

One result of these dates is that Araya was invited to guest on ALICE IN CHAINS 'Dirt' album. His contribution comes in the form of a Slayeresque scream on an untitled track.

In May 1992 Lombardo quit for good. His first project being recording with VOODOO CULT then the formation of GRIP INC. with VOODOO CULT guitarist Waldemar Sorychta, a band that has released two albums to date. Lombardo's substitute was ex-FORBIDDEN man Paul Bostoph.

During 1994 SLAYER teamed up with

SLAYER Photo : Arto Lehtinen

gangster rapper ICE T to cut a track for the soundtrack to the movie 'Judgement Night', a cover of British punk act THE EXPLOITED's 'Disorder'.

SLAYER shot back to their previous status with 'Divine Intervention' in 1995. The album blasted into the Billboard top 100 at an incredible number 8 and the band geared up for a world tour with openers BIOHAZARD and MACHINE HEAD prior to a fourth on the bill showing at the 'Monsters Of Rock' festival headlined by METALLICA.

'Divine Intervention' was quick to achieve gold sales status and SLAYER's longevity was confirmed when 'Reign In Blood', 'South Of Heaven' and 'Seasons In The Abyss' were all confirmed gold too.

The subsequent tour had SLAYER appearing on an all star 'Monsters Of Rock' bill in South America alongside KISS and BLACK SABBATH.

SLAYER paid homage to their musical heroes in 1996 by cutting the 'Undisputed Attitude' (originally titled 'Selected And Exhumed') album made up of favourite punk tunes and three SLAYER original compositions including the more metal orientated 'Gemini' and 'D.D.A.M.M.'. Songs covered included those by T.S.O.L., England's G.B.H., and no less than three MINOR THREAT tracks. The Japanese version added SUICIDAL TENDENCIES 'Memories Of Tomorrow'. The event was marred for the band though when after recording Bostoph made his exit to concentrate on a jazz career. Drummerless SLAYER were forced to cancel South American and European tours.

Coincidentally while SLAYER were offering tribute to their mentors a series of Swedish compilation albums 'Slaytanic Slaughter' were released where Scandinavian acts covered their favourite SLAYER song.

SLAYER resumed activity with the addition of erstwhile TESTAMENT drummer John Dette. However his tenure was fleeting as Bostoph was reinstated, Dette returning to the TESTAMENT camp.

In his time away from the band Bostoph had formed THE TRUTH ABOUT SEAFOOD (and a stint with TESTAMENT!).

1996 also found the band pushed back into the public arena once more although unwittingly when the band's music was cited in a lawsuit as being a direct influence on the 1995 murder of a 15 year old girl. The teenager was kidnapped, tortured and killed by three members of a Black Metal band HATRED. The prosecution alleging that the band members were influenced by and inspired by SLAYER's lyrics from the track 'Necrophiliac'. The findings of the court were due to be heard in 2001.

Undeterred SLAYER came up with new product in 1998 with the 'Diabolus' album and appeared on the bill of the 'Ozzfest Show' at Milton Keynes during June. The group had been scheduled to appear on the American dates but the spot on the bill eventually went to MEGADETH.

In 1999 SLAYER teamed up with Berlin Techno-Punks ATARI TEENAGE RIOT to mould the track 'No Remorse (I Wanna Die)' for the 'Godzilla' movie soundtrack. 2000 saw SLAYER contributing their take on 'Hand Of Doom' for the BLACK SABBATH tribute album 'Nativity In Black 2'. Araya has also been writing material with Max Cavalera of SOULFLY, the track 'Terrorist' being featured on SOULFLY's 2000 album. Not to be outdone King features a guest guitar solo on the cut 'Goddamned Electric' from PANTERA's 2000 album 'Reinventing The Steel'.

SLAYER included the track 'Bloodline' on the movie soundtrack album 'Dracula 2000'.

As 2001 broke the bands relief that the case against them for having influenced the death of the teenager in 1995 was swiftly curtailed when another similar case was brought against the band. The parents of Elyse Pahler accused SLAYER of having directly influenced the death of their daughter. As these troubles broke, SLAYER themselves were rooted in the recording studio in Vancouver laying down the Matt Hyde produced new album prior to hooking up with PANTERA for the 'Extreme Steel' American tour.

Early leaks that the album was to be titled 'Soundtrack To The Apocalypse' proved false as the succinct 'God Hates Us All' was duly chosen. The album cover artwork was apparently deemed unacceptable to display in many major retail outlets and so many copies had the original concept disguised by a false cover depicting four gold crosses on a plain white background.

European festival billings, dubbed the 'Tattoo The Planet' dates originally in alliance with PANTERA, BIOHAZARD, VISION OF DISORDER and STATIC X, were far from trouble free. Following the September 11th terrorist attacks PANTERA pulled out of the tour leaving SLAYER to remain behind as headliners.

Guitarist Kerry King rounded off the year by guesting on the track 'Final Prayer For The Human Race' on the 2002 HATEBREED album 'Perseverance'. Less welcome news for Bostoph would be an aggravating wrist condition which forced his exit from the band. SLAYER kept it in the family by re-inducting their illustrious former colleague DAVE LOMBARDO back into the fold, albeit announcing this move as a temporary measure.

It would soon emerge that the hot contender to secure the job would be none other than Proscriptor McGovern (né 'Emperor Proscriptor Magikus' a.k.a. Russ Givens), leader of ancestral Black Metal band ABSU.

SLAYER, complete with Lombardo manning the drum kit, would donate a cover version to the NASCAR sponsored 'Crank It Up' compilation in the summer of 2002. DEEP PURPLE's 'Highway Star' was apparently first choice but then switched to the aptly titled ALICE COOPER vintage classic 'Under My Wheels'. Within days SLAYER's choice of cover for this soundtrack had changed again to STEPPENWOLF's 'Born To Be Wild' whilst TYPE O NEGATIVE took over the mantle for 'Highway Star'.

Singles/EPs:

Haunting The Chapel / Chemical Warfare / Captor Of Sin, Roadrunner RR 1255087 (1984)

Criminally Insane / Aggressive Perfector / Post Mortem, London LONX 133 (1987) **64 UK**

South Of Heaven / Mandatory Suicide / In A Gadda D Vida, London LONX 201 (1988)

Seasons In The Abyss (Live) / Aggressive Perfector (Live) / Chemical Warfare (Live), Def American DEFAC 9 (1991) **51 UK**

Ditto Head / Serenity And Murder, American ALASKA1 (1995) (USA promotion)

Witching Hour / Ditto Head / Divine Intervention, American 74321 38325-2 (1996) (Free CD single with 'Undisputed Attitude' album)

Serenity In Murder / Raining Blood / Dittohead / South Of Heaven, Def American 74321262347 (1995)

Serenity In Murder / At Dawn They Sleep / Dead Skin Mask / Divine Intervention, Def American 74321262342 (1995) (CD single)

Serenity In Murder / Angel Of Death / Mandatory Suicide / War Ensemble, Def American 74321312482 (1995) (CD single)

Abolished Government / Superficial Love, Sub Pop SP368 (1996) (Split single with T.S.O.L.)

Bitter Peace, American (1998) (Promotional release)

Albums:

SHOW NO MERCY, Roadrunner RR 9868 (1984)
Evil Has No Boundaries / The Anti-Christ / Die By The Sword / Fight Till Death / Metalstorm / Face The Slayer / Black Magic / Tormentor / The Final Command / Crionics / Show No Mercy

HELL AWAITS, Roadrunner RR 97951 (1985)
Hell Awaits / Kill Again / At Dawn They Sleep / Praise Of Death / Necrophiliac / Crypts Of Eternity / Hardening Of The Arteries

REIGN IN BLOOD, London LONPP 34 (1986) **47 UK, 94 USA**
Angel Of Death / Piece By Piece / Necrophobic / Jesus Saves / Altar Of Sacrifice / Criminally Insane / Reborn / Epidemic / Post Mortem / Raining Blood

LIVE UNDEAD, Roadrunner RR 9574 (1987)
Black Magic / Die By The Sword / Captor Of Sin / The Antichrist / Evil Has No Boundaries / Show No Mercy / Aggressive Perfector / Chemical Warfare

SOUTH OF HEAVEN, London LONLP 63 (1988) **50 SWEDEN, 25 UK, 57 USA**
South Of Heaven / Silent Scream / Live Undead / Behind The Crooked Cross / Mandatory Suicide / Ghosts Of War / Cleanse The Soul / Read Between The Lies / Dissident Aggressor / Spill The Blood

SEASONS IN THE ABYSS, Def American 84968712 (1990) **47 SWEDEN, 18 UK, 40 USA**
War Ensemble / Blood Red / Spirit In Black / Expendable Youth / Dead Skin Mask / Hallowed Point / Skeletons Of Society / Temptation / Born Of Fire / Seasons In The Abyss

DECADE OF AGGRESSION - LIVE, Def American 5106052 (1991) **29 UK**
Hell Awaits / The Anti-Christ / War Ensemble / South Of Heaven / Raining Blood / Altar Of Sacrifice / Jesus Saves / Dead Skin Mask / Seasons In The Abyss / Mandatory Suicide / Angel Of Death / Hallowed Point / Blood Red / Die By The Sword / Black Magic / Captor Of Sin / Born Of Fire / Post Mortem / Spirit In Black / Expendable Youth / Chemical Warfare / Black Magic

DIVINE INTERVENTION, American 74321236771 (1994) **15 UK, 8 USA**
Killing Fields / Sex, Murder, Art / Fictional Reality / Dittohead / Divine Intervention / Circle Of Beliefs / SS III / Serenity In Murder / Two-Thirteen / Mind Control

UNDISPUTED ATTITUDE, American 74321357591 (1996) **31 UK, 34 USA**
Disintegration - Free Money / Verbal Abuse - Leeches / Abolish Government - Superficial Love / Can't Stand You / D.D.A.M.M. / Guilty Of Being White / I Hate You / Filler - I Don't Want To Hear It / Spiritual Law / Sick Boy / Mr. Freeze / Violent Pacification / Richard Hung Himself / I Wanna Be Your God / Gemini

DIABOLUS IN MUSICA, American 4913022 (1998) **27 UK, 31 USA**
Biter Peace / Stain Of Mind / Love To Hate / Death's Head / Screaming From The Sky /

Overt Enemy / Scrum / In The Name Of God / Perversions Of Pain / Desire / Point

SLAYER (USA)

Albums:
DANGEROUS APPETITE, Slayer (1982)

SODOM (GERMANY)
Line-Up: Tom Angelripper (vocals / bass), Frank Blackfire (guitar), Chris Witchunter (drums)

Lambasted throughout much of their career the legacy of German Thrash outfit SODOM has witnessed a renaissance of appreciation for their brutal almost primitive Death Metal attack. SODOM debuted as a trio consisting of Angelripper, Witchunter and Agressor with the demo 'Witching Metal' in 1983.

In 1984 a second demo, 'Victims Of Death', included the original tracks boosted with the addition of four new songs. The demo began to receive a great deal of positive press, although Agressor would choose to opt out. He was eventually replaced by Grave Violator and the new line-up debuted for the first time at the 'Black Metal Night' in Frankfurt.

After a further show with DESTRUCTION and IRON ANGEL, SPV signed the band and would swiftly release SODOM's debut EP entitled 'In The Sign Of Evil'.

Grave Violator left at the end of 1985 and the debut, full blown 'Obsessed By Cruelty' album featured an additional guitarist in Ahathoor on the track 'After The Deluge'. Immediately after the record was released Destructor quit to join KREATOR. Blackfire replaced him.

During a lull in 1986 Witchhunter travelled to Sweden to rehearse with BATHORY for a proposed European tour with CELTIC FROST and DESTRUCTION. The tour was shelved and the drummer returned to SODOM.

SODOM toured Europe as co-headliners with WHIPLASH in 1987, promoting the Harris Johns produced 'Persecution Mania' album, but Blackfire also quit the band to join KREATOR on an American tour on the eve of the 'Agent Orange' tour with SEPULTURA in 1989. The band found a temporary replacement to fulfill the dates in MEKONG DELTA's Uwe Baltrusch. Still, the latest album, 'Agent Orange', sold strongly shifting in excess of 90,000 units in Europe. In January 1990 SODOM recruited new guitarist Michael Hoffman (ex-ASSASSIN) and the ensuing 'Better Off Dead' produced by Harris Johns, included a cover of the THIN LIZZY classic 'Cold Sweat'. For the 1994 album 'Get What You Deserve' album SODOM drafted in a new drummer in the shape of ex-LIVING

DEATH / VIOLENT FORCE / SACRED CHAO man Atomic Steif.

Angelripper issued a solo album of drinking songs 'Ein Schöner Tag' in 1995 whilst SODOM were put on ice for a while. Back with the main band, the man formed a new line-up comprising guitarist Bornemann and his ex-CROWS / RANDALICA colleague, drummer Bobby Schottkowski in order to record the new studio album 'Til Death Do Us Unite' for new label G.U.N. Records.

'Til Death Do Us Unite' featured a drastically reworked version of the PAUL SIMON tune 'Hazy Shade Of Winter' (as made popular by THE BANGLES). The original version of the album also sported a wonderful cover photograph juxtaposing a pregnant woman with a male beer belly. Sadly this clever image was banned.

SODOM continued their resurgence with the Harris Johns produced 'Code Red' on fresh label Drakkar. The millennium seems likely to herald a SODOM tribute album.

Singles/EPs:
Outbreak Of Evil / Sepulcharal Voice / Blasphemer / Witching Metal / Burst Command Til War, Steamhammer SPV 60-2120 (1984) ('In The Sign Of Evil' EP)
Sodomy And Lust / The Conquerer / My Atonement, Steamhammer SH 0061 (1987) ('Expurse Of Sodomy' EP)
Ausgebombt / Don't Walk Away (Live) / Incest (Live), Steamhammer S1 7604 (1989)
The Saw Is The Law / Tarred And Feathered / The Kids Wanna Rock, Steamhammer 050 76305 (1991)
Aber Bitte Mit Sahne / Sodomised / Abuse / Skinned Alive, Steamhammer CDS 055-76723R (1993)
Get What You Deserve / Yabba The Hut / Delight In Slaying / Die Stumme Ursel / Eat Me, Steamhammer SPV GET 1 (1993) (Promotion release)

Albums:
OBSESSED BY CRUELTY, Steamhammer SPV 08-2121 (1986)
Deathlike Silence / Brandish The Sceptre / Proselytism Real / Equinox / After The Deluge / Obsessed By Cruelty / Fall Of Majesty Town / Nuctemeron / Pretenders To The Throne / Witchhammer / Volcanic Slut
PERSECUTION MANIA, Steamhammer 076-75092 (1988)
Nuclear Winter / Electrocution / Iron Fist / Persecution Mania / Enchanted Land / Procession To Golgotha / Christ Passion / Conjuration / Bomberhagel
MORTAL WAY OF LIFE (LIVE), Steamhammer SPV DO 807575 (1988)

Persecution Mania / Outbreak Of Evil / Conqueror / Iron Fist / Obsessed By Cruelty / Nuclear Winter Electrocution / Blasphemer / Enchanted Land / Sodomy And Lust / Christ Passion / Bombenhagel / My Atonement

AGENT ORANGE, Steamhammer 076-75972 (1989)
Agent Orange / Tired And Red / Incest / Remember The Fallen / Magic Dragon / Exhibition Bout / Ausgebombt / Baptism Of Fire

BETTER OFF DEAD, Steamhammer 08 76261 (1991)
An Eye For An Eye / Shellfire Defense / The Saw Is The Law / Turn Your Head Around / Capture The Flag / Bloodtrails / Never Healing Wound / Better Off Dead / Resurrection / Stalnorgel

TAPPING THE VEIN, Steamhammer 076-76542 (1993)
Body Parts / Skinned Alive / One Step Over The Line / Deadline / Bullet In The Head / The Crippler / Wachturn / Tapping The Vein / Back To War / Hunting Season / Reincarnation

GET WHAT YOU DESERVE, Steamhammer SPV CD 084-76762 (1994)
Get What You Deserve / Jabba The Hut / Jesus Screamer / Delight In Slaying / Die Stumme Ursel / Freaks Of Nature / Eat Me / Unbury The Hatched / Into Perdition / Sodomised / Fellows In Misery / Moby Dick / Silence Is Consent / Erwachet / Gomorrah / Angel Dust

MAROONED LIVE, Steamhammer 084-76852 (1994)
Intro / Outbreak Of Evil / Jabba The Hut / Agent Orange / Jesus Screamer / Ausgebombt / Tarred And Feathered / Abuse / Remember The Fallen / An Eye For An Eye / Tired And Red / Eat Me / Die Stumme Ursel / Sodomised / Gomorrah / One Step Over The Line / Freaks Of Nature / Aber Bitte Mit Sahne / Silence Is Consent / Wachturm Erwachet / Stalinhagel / Fratricide / Gone To Glory

MASQUERADE IN BLOOD, Steamhammer SPV 085-76962 (1995)
Masquerade In Blood / Gathering Of Minds / Fields Of Honour / Braindead / Verrecke! / Shadow Of Damnation / Peacemaker's Law / Murder In My Eyes / Unwanted Youth / Mantelmann / Scum / Hydrophobia / Let's Break The Law

TEN BLACK YEARS – BEST OF, Steamhammer SPV DCD 086-18342 (1996)
Tired And Red / The Saw Is The Law / Agent Orange / Wachturm / Erwachet / Ausgebombt / Sodomy And Lust / Remember The Fallen / Nuclear Winter / Outbreak Of Evil / Resurrection /

Bombenhagel / Masquerade In Blood / Bullet In The Head / Stalinorgel / Shellshock / Angel Dust / Hunting Season / Abuse / 1000 Days Of Sodom / Gomorrah / Unwanted Youth / Tarred & Feathered / Iron Fist / Jabba The Hut / Silence Is Consent / Incest / Shellfire Defense / Gone To Glory / Fraticide / Verrrecke! / One Step Over the Line / My Atonement / Sodomized / Aber Bitte Mit... / Die Stumme Ursel / Mantelmann

'TIL DEATH DO US UNITE, G.U.N. GUN 199 BMG 74321 39034-2 (1997)
Frozen Screams / Fuck The Police / Gisela / That's What An Unknown Killer Diarised / Hanging Judge / No Way Out / Polytoximaniac / 'Til Death Do Us Unite / Hazy Shade Of Winter / Suicidal Justice / Wander In The Valley / Sow The Seeds Of Discord / Master Of Disguise / Schwerter Zu Pflugscharen / Hey, Hey, Rock n' Roll Star

CODE RED, Drakkar 74321 67384 2 (1999)
Intro / Code Red / What Hell Can Create / Tombstone / Liquidation / Spiritual Demise / Warlike Conspiracy / Cowardice / The Vice Of Killing / Visual Buggery / Book Burning / The Wolf And The Lamb / Addicted To Abstinence

M-16, (2001)
Among The Weirdcong / I Am The War / Napalm In The Morning / Minejumper / Genocide / Little Boy / M-16 / Lead Injection / Cannon Fodder / Marines / Surfin' Bird

SOILWORK (SWEDEN)
Line-Up: Bjorn Strid (vocals), Peter Vicious (guitar), Ludvig Svartz (guitar), Ola Flink (bass), Carlos Del Olmo (keyboards), Jimmy Persson (drums)

SOILWORK blend a heady mixture of Thrash and Death Metal. The 1998 album 'Steel Bath Suicide' was produced by Fredrik Fredman'. Frontman Bjorn Strid goes under the name of 'Speed' whilst guitarist Peter Vicious' real name is Peter Wichers. The latter would add session guitar to CONSTRUCDEAD's 2000 EP 'Turn'.
SOILWORK have also previously employed drummer Henry Ranta and guitarist Ola Flenning. The band signed to Germany's Nuclear Blast label for the 'A Predator's Portrait' album. They would return to the studio in October 2001 with producer DEVIN TOWNSEND.
Members of SOILWORK, in alliance with DARKANE personnel and CONSTRUCDEAD drummer Erik Thyselius also operate the project band TERROR 2000.

Albums:
STEEL BATH SUICIDE, Listenable POSH012 (1998)

SOILWORK
Photo : Nico Wobben

Entering The Angel Diabolique / Sadistic Lullaby / My Need / Skin After Skin / Wings Of Domain / Steelbath Suicide / In A Close Encounter / Centro De Predomino / Razorlives / Demon In Veins / The Aardvaarl Trail

THE CHAINHEART MACHINE, Listenable (1999)

The Chainheart Machine / Bulletbeast / Millionflame / Generation Speedkill / Neon Rebels / Possessing The Angels / Spirits Of Future Sun / Machine Gun Majesty / Room No 99

A PREDATOR'S POSTCARD, Nuclear Blast (2001)

Bastard Chain / Like An Average Stalker / Needlefeast / Neurotica Rampage / The Analyst / Grand Failure Anthem / Structure Divine / Shadowchild / Final Fatal Force / A Predator's Portrait

NATURAL BORN CHAOS, Teichiku TKCS-85037 (2002)

Follow The Follow / As We Speak / The Flameout / Natural Born Chaos / Mindfields / The Bringer / Black Star Deceiver / Mercury Shadow / No More Angels / Soilworker's Song Of The Damned / Kwlcksllver

SOLITARY (UK)

Line-Up: Richard Sherrington (vocals / guitar), Matthew Costello (guitar), Dave Marshall (bass), Roy Miller (drums)

A stoic British Metal band that has endured more than its fair share of line-up ructions over the course of years. SOLITARY came together in July of 1995 citing a line-up of frontman Richard Sherrington on vocals and guitar, guitarist Dave Herbert, bass player Rob Hewitt and drummer Tristan Callaghan. In this incarnation SOLITARY cut an inaugural demo entitled 'Desolate'. Songwriting contributions for this effort, released in March of 1995, were on hand from Chris Astley of XENTRIX.

A second promotional cassette 'Fear' followed in January of 1996. In July Paul Mortimer took the bass position as SOLITARY got to grips with a further demo 'The Human Condition'. Most of these tracks would subsequently emerge as an EP of the same name. Herbert would opt out in the September for a career as a policeman. The vacant guitar spot was duly filled by Matthew Costello and shortly after Jason Clark was enrolled as SOLITARY's new drummer.

The band signed a record deal with the Holier Than Thou concern the following year as yet more line up fluctuations hit home. Anthony Cox would replace Clark and Julian Heywood was the new man on bass guitar. The turbulence did not end there though as in February of the following year Cox departed and Simon Tomlinson came in on drums.

Just as SOLITARY were gearing up for recording of the debut album Heywood decamped and Gareth Harrop became the group's latest four stringer. A UK club tour was undertaken in the summer pre-empting the release of 'Nothing Changes' which arrived in November. Welcome support gigs to the likes of REIGN, KILL II THIS and Swedes DERANGED found Chris Gaughan now occupying the guitarist's role, but by the following February erstwhile member Matt Costello rejoined the ranks.

Negotiations were finalised for the Dutch label Roxson to license the album for Europe but predictably SOLITARY hit further membership problems as Tomlinson bade farewell in June. Roy Miller was the next drummer on call. In adverse times SOLITARY learnt that Roxson had gone into receivership as had their UK label's distributor. A UK tour also had more than its fair share of bad luck with 5 out of 9 dates being cancelled.

During 2000 SOLITARY's line-up remained in a state of flux. Costello departed yet again but his substitute, Stuart Armriding, remained with the band only briefly with an acrimonious split resolving itself with the induction of guitarist Paul Morrison. It would be a familiar tale for 2001. Dave Marshall took over on bass whilst Matt Costello rejoined for his third tenure. SOLITARY would soon lose Costello's services yet again though, replacing him with erstwhile VOID and SOMA guitarist Gaz Wilkinson.

Albums:
NOTHING CHANGES, Holier Than Thou (1999)
Within Temptation / Clutching Straws / The Downward Spiral / No Reason / A Second Chance / Twisted / Bitterness / Fear / Nothing Changes

SOLITUDE (Delaware, USA)
Line-Up: Keith Saulsbury (vocals / guitar), Dan Martinez (guitar), Rodney Cope (bass), Mike Hostler (drums)

Delaware's SOLITUDE, forged in 1985, made an impact on the tape trading scene with their 'Focus Of Terror' demo in 1987 and the following year's 'Sickness' recording. A final demo 'Fall Of Creation' led directly to a deal with Red Light Records and a license with a subsequent England's Music For Nations label.

SOLITUDE have toured alongside CELTIC

FROST, DEATH ANGEL and SACRED REICH.

Albums:
FROM WITHIN, Bulletproof CDVEST 18 (1994)
Twisted / No Future / Tipping The Balance / Alter The Red / Mind Pollution / From Within / The Afterlife / A Loss Of Blood / The Empty / Poisoned Population / In This Life / Side Winder

SORROW (New York, NY, USA)
Line-Up: Andy Marchione (vocals / bass), Brent Clarin (guitar), Billy Rogan (bass), Mike Hymson (drums)

Previously known as APPARITION. New York's SORROW delivered a blend of Thrash styled Death-Doom. Various members went onto create JOURNEY INTO DARKNESS.

Albums:
FORGOTTEN SUNRISE, Roadrunner (1991)
Awaiting The Savior / Eternally Forgotten / Curse The Sunrise / A Waste Cry For Hope
HATRED AND DISGUST, Roadrunner (1992)
Insatiable / Forced Repression / Illusion Of Freedom / Human Error / Separative Adjectives / Unjustified Reluctance

SOULSCAR (CANADA)
Line-Up: Andrew Staehling (vocals / guitar), Brent McKenzie (bass), Chris Warunki (drums)

Vancouver's SOULSCAR employ Death Metal with a healthy injection of prime era Thrash influences. The band came together in 1997 issuing a stream of demos in 1998's 'Lost In Life', 1999's 'Escaping' and 2000 'Abandoned'.

The 2000 album release is a collection of earlier demo tracks produced by Jeff Waters of ANNIHILATOR.

Albums:
ABANDONED, (2000)
S.S.R.I. (Intro) / Cutter / Your Absence, My End / Abandoned / Ever Alone / This Was My Life / Selfmutilation / Bliss Killer / Escaping / Terminal Prayer / Deathbringer-Surrender / Escaping / Lost In Life

SOUND BARRIER (USA)
Line-Up: Bernie K. (vocals), Spacey T. (guitar), Stanley E. (bass), Dave Brown (drums)
The all black SOUNDBARRIER evolved from the demise of the R&B oriented, seven-piece

strong COLOUR in 1979.

COLOUR had steadily become more Rock oriented thanks to the recruitment of Tinton Falls, New Jersey born guitarist Spacey T. However, alongside COLOUR drummer Dave Brown, Spacey formed the Metal band he had always longed for in SOUND BARRIER.

The first line-up included bassist Keith Roster in a group that, initially, went for more of a Progressive feel until Roster departed and was replaced with Stanley E., rounding out a line-up fronted by vocalist Bernie K.

Despite laudable press for the debut album SOUND BARRIER were duly dropped by MCA Records. Undaunted, they retained the momentum with the independent mini-album on Pitbull Records which highlighted more than anywhere the band's preference for the colours red and black and contained a cover of STEPPENWOLF's 'Born To Be Wild'.

The band was picked up by Metal Blade for third release 'Speed Of Light', by which time Stanley E., joining LIBERTY, had been succeeded by ex-TERRIF bassist Emil Lech. The album includes a cover of THIN LIZZY's 'Hollywood (Down On Your Luck)'.

The band fell apart once Italian six string hotshot Alex Masi got into the band and set about taking control leaving the remaining original members no option but to quit the SOUND BARRIER ship. Soon enough the band evolved into MASI.

After a period in late 1986 working with BLACK SHEEP bassist Willie Basse in SPACEY T'S LIBERTY, original SOUND BARRIER guitarist Spacey T briefly joined MOTHER'S FINEST in the early '90s on their initial European touring stint in support of the 'Black Radio Won't Play This Record' album. However, he had been replaced by a keyboard player, surely in a bid to get back to the days of Mike Keck in the '70s by the time they returned.

Lech turned up in JOSHUA whilst Brown formed TOTAL ECLIPSE with ex-BUSBOYS guitarist Victor Johnson, who had guested on the 'Speed Of Light' album. By 1998 Johnson was a member of SAMMY HAGAR's touring band THE WABORITAS.

Albums:
TOTAL CONTROL, MCA 5396-1 (1983)
Other Side / Total Control / Rock Without The Roll / Mayday / Second Thoughts / Nobody Cares / Don't Put Me On Hold / Hey U / Rock On The Wild Side
BORN TO ROCK, Pit Bull PBR 002 (1984)
Conquer The World / Born To Be Wild / Raging Heart / Born To Rock / Do Or Die
SPEED OF LIGHT, Metal Blade 72114 (1986)
Speed Of Light / Gladiator / On The Level (Head Banger) / What Price Glory? /

Hollywood (Down On Your Luck) / Fight For Life! / Aim For The Top / Hard As A Rock / On To The Next Adventure

SPERMBIRDS (GERMANY)
Line-Up: Lee Hollis (vocals), Roger Ingenthon (guitar), Frank Rahm (guitar), Markus Weilmann (bass), Matthias Gotte (drums)

A much favoured Kaiserlauten Punk act that infused their sound with plenty of American Crossover and Thrash influences. Founded in 1980 as ERADICATION the band, fronted by American singer Lee Hollis, adopted the title of SPERMBIRDS in 1982. The remainder of the group comprised guitarists Roger Ingenthon and Frank 'Cream' Rahm, bass player Markus 'While Man' Weilmann and drummer Matthias Gotte. First product would be a split album with WALTER 11.

The band soon pulled in a ready audience and mounting record sales but Hollis would quit during 1993 following recording of the 'Joe' album, later founding STEAKKNIFE. The SPERMBIRDS drafted another American, Ken Haus, as replacement but the group would ultimately fold in 1996.

Gotte went on to KICK JONESES whilst Rahm emerged with SUPER GOUGE.

The SPERMBIRDS would reunite with Hollis during 1999 for a series of 5 nostalgia concerts.

Albums:
DON'T FORGET THE FUN, (1984) (Split album with WALTER 11)
My God Rides A Skateboard / Shit Rolls Downhill / She's Got VD
SOMETHING TO PROVE, (1987)
Something To Prove / What A Bitch Is / You're Not A Punk / Playboy Subscriber / Kill Me Quick / What Do You Want? / My God Rides A Skateboard / Americans Are Cool / Get On The Stage / No Punks In K-town / Scumbag / Shit Job / Bed Tool / Try Again / Bloodstains
NOTHING IS EASY, (1989)
Die Sgt Landry / Your Problem / Nothing Is Easy / Cave / Another Dead Friendship / It's Just An Excuse / Light's Out / My Brother / 12 8 Pack / Texas Cowboy / We Don't Care / Americans Are Cool / What Do You Want? / Try Again
THANKS - LIVE, Dead Eye (1990)
Something To Prove / Common Thread / Nothing Is Easy / Stronger / Two Feet / Kill Me Quick / With A Gun / Get On The Stage / Dangers Of Thinking / Only A Phase / You're Not A Punk / Americans Are Cool / Texas Cowboy / Try Again
COMMON THREAD, X-Mist XM022 (1991)

Melt The Ice / Open Letter / Two Feet / Stronger / Only A Phase / One Chance / With A Gun / Common Thread / Truth Of Today / Victim Of Yourself

EATING GLASS, X-Mist XM032 (1992)
Eating Glass / Just A Moment / Static Energy / We Are All (Political Prisoners) / You're Fired / Fine / Waiting For The Bomb To Drop / You're Only As Good As Your Last War / Stalemate / Back In Time / Fragment / Souled Out

JOE, X-Mist XM034 (1992)
Crucifried / Real Life (Digging A Hole)/ Got Your Number / Tell Me About It / Dead / We Are One / My God Rides A Skateboard / Shit Rolls Downhill / She's Got VD / I'm Trapped / 12XU / Truth Of Today

SHIT FOR SALE, G.U.N. (1994)
Shit For Sale / Media Bullshit / You're Not Perfect / KKK Rep / I Feel Old Part 1 / I Feel Old Part 2 / Feed My Ego / L-Word / Cold Busted / Rich Man's High / In Many Way / Alike Your Opinion

FAMILY VALUES, G.U.N. (1995)
What Dad Says / Mr Cynical / Family Values / Pop Song / Bad Things / Disagree / Nervous Anxiety / All I Want / Desires And Wishes / Hate / In The Eyes Of Old People / Running Circle / Kaiserlautern Uber Alles

GET OFF THE STAGE, G.U.N. (1996)
You're Not Perfect / Mr. Cynical / Media Bullshit / Bad Things / KKK Rep / Shit For Sale / Pop Song / Nervous Anxiety / L-Word / Disagree / What Dad Says / Your Opinion / Family Values / Something To Prove / You're Not A Punk / My God Rides A Skateboard / Nothing Is Easy / Americans Are Cool / Melt The Ice / Shit Job / Die Sgt. Landry / Cruzifried / No Punks In K-Town / Kill Me Quick / Bloodstains / Get On The Stage / Try Again / Only A Phase / All I Want / Texas Cowboy / Truth Of Today / Lights Out

COFFEE, HAIR & REAL LIFE, Warner Bros. (1996)
She's got V.D. / Something To Prove / Americans Are Cool / You're Not A Punk / My God Rides A Skateboard / Try Again / Bed Tool / Get On The Stage / What Do You Want Ronald Reagan? / Nothing Is Easy / Another Dead Friendship / Texas Cowboy / It's Just An Excuse / Melt The Ice / Truth Of Today / Only A Phase / 2 Feet / With A Gun / Stronger / Victims Of Yourself / Back In Time / Eating Glass / Fine / Crucifried / Excess Bleeding Heart

BEST OF, G.U.N. (1999)

SQUEALER (GERMANY)
Line-Up: Andy Henner (vocals), Lars Doring (guitar), Michael Schiel (guitar), Michael Kasper (bass), Mike Terrana (drums)
Metal outfit SQUEALER's first product was the 1987 demo 'Ready To Fight' followed by a further demo in 'One Beer Too Much' in 1988. Initially a straight ahead Hard Rock act SQUEALER progressively developed into the accelerated Speed Metal of Thrash. Latter day releases found SQUEALER slowing the pace somewhat.

SQUEALER were in a position to offer an EP, 'Human Traces', in 1989 although it would be four years before a debut album arrived.

In early 1995 drummer Franky Wolf decamped. Tobias Exxel, previously a member of teen band HERESY, would be inducted as bassist but would in fact contribute both bass and guitar to the 1995 album 'Wrong Time, Wrong Place?'

1998 would witness Tobias Exxel's departure. The guitarist set to work on a project band entitled TARAXACUM, combining this endeavour with his enrollment as bass player into EDGUY.

The 1999 album 'The Prophecy' saw SQUEALER with guitarists Lars Doring and Michael Schiel, drummer Martin Winter and keyboard services donated by Tilo Rockstroh. EDGUY's Tobias Sammet guests on the track 'Friends For Life'. Quite bizarrely SQUEALER covered DEPECHE MODE's 'Enjoy The Silence' too. Released on AFM Records in Europe 'The Prophecy' would be licensed to Metal Blade for North America in July of 2000. The 2000 album 'Made For Eternity' has guest appearances from drummer Mike Terrana, a veteran of ARTENSION, YNGWIE MALMSTEEN and fellow German act RAGE, alongside HELLOWEEN guitarist ROLAND GRAPOW. SQUEALER committed their version of 'Victim Of Fate' to the HELLOWEEN tribute album 'Keepers Of Jericho'.

Terrana would commit to the band for European touring alongside EDGUY.

In 2001 ex-drummer Frank Wolf would guest on the ambitious TARAXACUM project album 'Spirit Of Freedom' conceived by EDGUY and erstwhile SQUEALER man Tobias Exxel. SQUEALER would spend the latter half of 2001 recording a new album 'Under The Cross' under the guidance of producers ex-VICTORY guitarist Tommy Newton and ex-SABBAT guitarist Andy Sneap. An odd inclusion on this record would be a cover of the '70s Pop hit 'In Zaire'.

Singles/EPs:
The Casualty / Lose Of Independence / Bereft Of Senses / I Will Fight / Insanity, Squealer (1989) ('Human Traces' EP)

378

MAKE YOUR DAY, AFM Records 21477 (1993)
A Little Piece Of Death / Behold The Lion / Make Your Day / Thoughts / The Wanderer / Tears Of Hate / RAP / Scaring The Winds / The Man Who Never Was

WRONG TIME, WRONG PLACE?, AFM Records 25702 (1995)
Intro / Liar / Wrong Time Wrong Place / Time Doesn't Wait / Hellcome In Heaven / Love To Hate You / Dying Forbidden! / Don't Wanna Be Like You / Whose Afraid Of Yellow Snow?

THE PROPHECY, AFM Records CD026 (1999)
The Prophecy (The Final Sign) / Friends For Life /...But No One Cares / Live Everyday / Hold On Tight / To Die For (...Your Sins) / Nowhere To Hide / I See The World / The Meaning Of Life / Enjoy The Silence / The Prophecy (Follow Me)

MADE FOR ETERNITY, AFM Records (2000)
End Of The World / The Final Daylight / Nothing To Believe / Don't Fear Your Life / The Eternity Of A Day / Show Me The Way / No One To Blame / People Are People / Free Your Mind / Hellcome In Heaven

UNDER THE CROSS, AFM (2002)
Painful Lust / Facing The Death / My Last Goodbye / Thinking Allowed! / Under The Cross / Rules Of Life / Down And Out / Fade Away / Out Of The Dark / In Zaire / Low Budget Heroes

STEELER (GERMANY)
Line-Up: Peter Burtz (vocals), Axel Rudi Pell (guitar), Thomas Eder (guitar), Volker Krawczak (bass), Jan Yildaral (drums)

STEELER emerged during a particularly golden period in the history of German Metal and would provide a worthy legacy of some finely crafted Metal albums and provide the launch pad for noted guitarist AXEL RUDI PELL.

Formed in Bochum, STEELER had originally used the name SINNER, and the band was put together by guitarist Axel Rudi Pell and bassist Volker Krawczak.

Pell joined his first band at the age of 14 between 1974 and 1975 with whom he took his first tentative steps. The band, a school outfit called SILVER STONES, at least taught Pell the art of tuning a guitar, evolving into FIREBIRD.

With the group splitting in 1976 Pell took a hiatus from music until joining a local act called MERCY and, subsequently, DEVIL'S DEATH, with whom he proceeded to play the regional school and club circuits.

Having formed STEELER with Krawczak, the duo recruited FALLEN ANGEL guitarist Thomas Eder and a drummer in Siggi Wiesemöller. The fledgling group recorded their first demo during 1982, utilizing the services of vocalist Karl Holthaus, on loan from local act NEMO (although he had also been known to have fronted a group called GLADIATOR).

STEELER took the demos to SCORPIONS producer Dieter Dierks who chose not to pursue his original interest in the band, although the tape fell into the hands of ACCEPT who were having problems with Udo Dirkschneider at the time and were covertly auditioning possible replacements. ACCEPT auditioned Holthaus, but eventually settled their differences with Dirkschneider without the press getting wind of the original problem.

Having received a fair amount of interest from demo track 'Call Her Princess' being aired on Tony Jasper's Rock show on the British Forces Broadcasting Service (BFBS) radio station STEELER not only recruited a permanent singer in Thomas Eder's former FALLEN ANGEL band mate Peter Burtz, they also hooked up with the newly formed Earthshaker label for a two record deal, releasing the debut 'Steeler' album in 1984.

STEELER's first album, recorded in a mere eleven days and with new drummer Jan Yildiral, sold a respectable 9,000 copies, although a proposed tour with WARLOCK turned into a disaster due to problems with WARLOCK's manager and petty jealousy existing between the two groups.

The band's second album, 'Rulin' The Earth', took between 14 or 15 days and was laid down at Horus Sound in Hanover and would sell 18,000 copies as the group proceeded to play every 'toilet' they could in a bid for greater recognition.

With the Earthshaker deal now over with STEELER signed to SPV, although legal problems with Earthshaker would persist for some time afterward especially concerning the payment of royalties. Having begun working on demo tapes of songs for the proposed third album STEELER parted company with Volker Krawczak. As the subject of the band's image had come up it had been decided that the unfortunate bassist, a portly chap, did not particularly fit into the scheme of things and the band felt it had no choice but to replace him. Krawczak would refuse to speak with his former colleagues for a good three years afterwards! Volker's place was taken by French bassist Herve Rossi, previously with ANTHRACITE and a friend of drummer Jan Yildiral. Whilst Rossi certainly fitted STEELER's concept on the image front, it was quickly discovered that he was rather lacking in any prowess as a musician. Rossi may have been hired for looking like the renowned bassist Nikki Sixx, but he didn't play a note on the third album, 1986's 'Strike Back', a guesting Tommy Newton from VICTORY doing the honours.

The album was produced by ELOY's Frank Bornemann, although Axel Rudi Pell claims the majority of the work was in effect carried out by Czech born engineer Jan Nimec. Ex-SCORPIONS guitarist ULI JON ROTH was in the same studio at the time and Pell took the opportunity of inviting him to play on a track that appeared on a 'Metal Hammer' compilation album at the time.

Having dispatched Rossi back to France STEELER recruited ex-AXE VICTIMS rhythm guitarist Roland Hag as the band's new bass player and hit the road, managing to add some shows in Holland and Switzerland to the regular German commitments.

'Strike Back', benefiting from better material, improved musicianship and a polished production, picked up sales in the region of 33,000 and set the mood for the recording of fourth album 'Undercover Animal'.

Despite touring Germany with SAXON the 'Undercover Animal' only wound up selling 21,000 copies. It would be during the writing of songs for the planned fifth album that AXEL RUDI PELL decided to leave the group, disenchanted at the band's more pop chorus oriented direction, officially departing on November 11th 1988.

STEELER opted to continue without Pell, hiring a guitarist from the Frankfurt area known as Vic and firing Jan Yildiral. The group recorded a three track demo and played a comeback show at Bochum's Zeche club, but split three or four months down the line.

Wheras Pell chose to pursue what turned out to be a very successful solo career (having teamed up with his old pal Volker Krawczak once more!), his former colleagues have engaged themselves in a variety of other careers. At one time Peter Burtz was the editor of German Metal magazine 'Metal Hammer' before taking the opportunity to work in the upper echelons of the EMI record label. Drummer Jan Yildiral now runs a travel agency, whilst Thomas Eder is working for a radio station reporting on events in the local courts.

Singles/EPs:
Night After Night / Waiting For A Star, Steamhammer 01-1884 (1986)
Undercover Animal, Steamhammer (1988)

Albums:
STEELER, Earthshaker ES 4001 (1984)
Chains Are Broken / Gonna Find Some Place In Hell / Heavy Metal Century / Sent

From The Evil / Long Way / Call Her Princess / Love For Sale / Hydrophobia / Fallen Angel
RULIN' THE EARTH, Earthshaker ES 4009 (1985)
The Resolution / Ruling The Earth / Shellshock / Let The Blood Run Red / Heading For The End / Maniac / Run With The Pack / S.F.M. 1 / Turning Wheels
STRIKE BACK, Steamhammer SPV 08-1890 (1986)
Chain Gang / Money Doesn't Count / Danger Comeback / Icecold / Messing Around With Fire / Rockin' The City / Strike Back / Night After Night / Waiting For A Star
UNDERCOVER ANIMAL, Steamhammer SPV 08-7510 (1988)
(I'll Be) Hunter Or Hunted / Undercover Animal / Shadow In The Redlight / Hard Breaks / Criminal / Rely On Rock / Stand Tall / The Deeper The Night / Knock Me Out / Bad To The Bone

STEEL FURY (USA)
Line-Up: Tim Casin (vocals / bass), Tim Berryhill (guitar), Dana Lauderdale (drums)

A Thrash trio with one album to their credit.

Albums:
LESSER OF TWO EVILS, New Renaissance 08-9801 (1989)
Justice Day / No More / The Cage / This Old Man / Choose Death / Nowhere To Hide / Synchronized / Too Fast / Private Room

STEEL PROPHET
(Van Nuys, CA, USA)
Line-Up: Rick Mythiasin (vocals), Steve Kachinsky-Blakmoor (guitar), John Pons (guitar), Vince Du Juan Dennis (bass), Pete Parada (drums)

The highly respected STEEL PROPHET deliver technically minded Progressive Heavy Metal. Previous to the release of the 1997 album STEEL PROPHET lost two members with guitarist Horacio Colmenares forging NEW EDEN. The album itself is composed of numerous re-workings of earlier material including 'Passage Of Time (Amber Leaves)' from the band's 1987 demo and a cover of IRON MAIDEN's 'Purgatory'.

Guitarist Bernie Versye contributes to the song 'Hate'.

Recording bassist Vince Du Juan Dennis was loaned to PRONG for a nationwide tour. STEEL PROPHET were far from over however with vocalist Rick Mythiasin being admitted to drug rehabilitation centres twice during actual recording, the song 'Death Of

STEEL PROPHET Rick Mythiasin, Jim Williams, Vince Dennis, Carl Rosqvist and Steve Kachinsky Photo : Alex Solca

Innocence' even missing a whole verse and chorus because Mythiasin was too sick to perform it. The bad luck continued as Du Juan Dennis was shot in the chest after the album's completion. The bassist survived.

During 1999 STEEL PROPHET cut their homage to JUDAS PRIEST with their take on 'Dream Deceiver' appearing on the 'Hell Bent For Metal' tribute album.

STEEL PROPHET's 2000 release 'Genesis' comprises the band's 1989 'Inner Ascendance' demo together with various cover versions of tracks by JUDAS PRIEST, IRON MAIDEN, METALLICA, BLACK SABBATH and surprisingly SIMPLE MINDS! STEEL PROPHET drafted new members Jim Williams on guitar and Karl Rosqvist on drums the same year replacing Kevin Cafferty and John Pons. Mythiasin would embark on a side project assembled by Tobias Exxel of German act EDGUY. This union, the 'Spirit Of Freedom' album, was released under the TARAXACUM banner in 2001. The singer would also session on the late 2001 REDEMPTION project assembled by guitarist Nick Van Dyk.

Albums:

INTO THE VOID (HALLUCINIGENIC CONCEPTION), Art Of Music 70410 (1997)
The Revenant / Death Of Innocence / Trapped In The Trip / Your Failure Inscribed

In Stone / Passage Of Time (Amber Leaves...) / Of The Dream / Ides Of March-Purgatory / What's Behind The Veils? / Idols / Hate

DARK HALLUCINATIONS, Nuclear Blast NB350-2 (1999)
Montag / New Life / Strange Encounter / The Secret / We Are Not Alone / Betrayal / Look What You've Done / Scarred For Life / Spectres

MESSIAH, Nuclear Blast (2000)
The Ides Of March / Messiah / Vengeance Attained / Mysteries Of Iniquity / Dawn Of Man / Earth And Sky / Goddess Arise / Unseen / 07/03/47 / Rapture / Ghosts Once Past

GENESIS, Nuclear Blast NB 546-2 (2000)
Death / Sleep Of Despair / Inner Ascendance / Life / Nihilisms Spell / Technocricide / Fast As A Shark / Gangland / Ides Of March- Purgatory / Fade To Black / Dream Deceiver / Neon Knights / Don't You Forget About Me

BOOK OF THE DEAD, Nuclear Blast NB 558-2 (2001)
When Six Was Nine / Tragic Flaws / Escaped / Soleares / Church Of Mind / Burning Into Blackness / The Chamber / Locked Out / Ruby Dreams (Faith And Hope) / Phobia / Anger Seething / Oleander

STEEL VENGEANCE (MI, USA)

Line-Up: Scott Carlson (vocals), Bob Lindstrom (guitar), Michael Wickstrom (guitar / keyboards), Steve Cavalier (bass), Andy Anderson (drums)

This semi-legendary cult Metal band have undergone more than a few line-up changes over the years. By the time the group recorded their 'Call Off The Dogs' debut album for the French Black Dragon label original vocalist Rock Rothweiler, guitarist Jay Carr and bassist Jeff Way had all quit from the line-up that had recorded a three track EP in 1984. STEEL VENGEANCE issued a demo tape earlier the same year which included drummer Carl Elliot.

Carr's replacement, Bob Lindstrom, was replaced himself by Tracy Kerbuski for the 'Prisoners' album, which also saw the arrival of Tom Vileho on drums in place of Andy Anderson.

In early 1987 the group were reported to have recruited a 14 year old drummer in the form of Tim Gilderloos.

The fourth album, 1989's 'Never Lettin' Go', found new vocalist Scott Nocon fronting STEEL VENGEANCE who also boasted a new guitarist in Glenn Rogers and a brand new rhythm section comprising bassist Killer Cerogatti and drummer John Draper. Guitarist / keyboardist Michael Wickstrom was thus the only original member of the band.

However, 1991's 'Live: Among The Dead' found Jason Saige on vocals on a recording of performances captured at shows in Ventura and San Diego during 1990.

Singles/EPs:
Your Time Has Come / Back Street Girl / Black Leather, Kingdom (1984)

Albums:
CALL OFF THE DOGS, Black Dragon (1985)
Night Turns To Day / Dreams Come True / Time To Live, Time To Die / Devil's Lair / 3 O' Clock In The Morning / Victim Of Love / Midnight Machine / Queen Of The Night / Will Not Be Defeated / Our Love Was Yesterday
SECOND OFFENSE, Black Dragon BD 017 (1986)
Beware The Wizard / She Moves In The Night / Eyes That Cannot See / Useless Information / Breakin' Away / Open The Door / Don't Waste It On Me / Pleasure With Pain / Just One More Time / Dead Or Alive
PRISONERS, Black Dragon BD028 (1988)
Burned Out / Destroy / Streets Of Gold / She'll Never Tell / Under World / Prisoners / Run From The Law / Till Tomorrow /

Vengeance Is Mine / Can't Stop The Rain
NEVER LETTIN' GO, Black Dragon (1989)
Epitaph / Beware The Wizard / Hard Man / She's Back / Never Lettin' Go / Victim Of Sin / Sing It Out / Your Time Has Come / I Surrender
LIVE: AMONG THE DEAD, Black Dragon (1991)
Pariah / Standing Alone / Nightfall / In For The Kill / Our Love Was Yesterday / Go To Hell From School / Scarred / No More / Mind Over Matter / Never Lettin' Go / Time To Live, Time To Die / Stalemate / I Bring You Lies / Right Side Of The Track

STEEL WARRIORS (NY, USA)

Albums:
STEEL WARRIORS, Warrior (1984)
ON THE ROAD TO HELL, Warrior (1985)

STEFFAN RODD (Newark, NJ, USA)

Line-Up: Steffan Rodd (vocals / guitar), John Pellicheto (guitar), Harry Blade II (bass), Pinky (drums)

New Jersey Metal band STEFFAN RODD opened a demo which included drummer Chuck Terrill and bassist Riff Thunder.

Pulling in new drummer Pinky and bassist Harry Blade II STEFFAN RODD opened officially with a self-financed EP followed by a 1984 demo tape.

Albums:
STEFFAN RODD, Steffan Rodd (1984)

STENAY (FRANCE)

Line-Up: Jeff (vocals), Loic (guitar), Jacque (guitar), Marc (bass), Juanjo (drums)

A French Thrash act dating back to 1989. It was not until 1995 that STENAY stabilised a line-up of singer Jeff, guitarists Loic and Jacque, bassist Laurent and drummer Fred, committing themselves to their first live gig in 1996.

That same year STENAY lost the services of their rhythm section in quick succession, Jacques leaving in April and Fred in May. Nevertheless, the 'Odin' demo was recorded before bassist Marc came on board. The drum position was finally settled in 1998 with the introduction of Spaniard Juanjo. STENAY then released a self-financed four track EP.

Singles/EPs:
Attendre / Salem / Odin / Serial Killer, Stenay (1999) ('Stenay' EP)

ST. MUCUS (FINLAND)
Line-Up: Janne Kerminen (vocals / guitar), Pekka Kulmala (guitar), Toni Grönroos (bass), Sauli Sumolainen (drums)

A Finnish Metal act who adopted a rather Bay Area Thrash Metal sound. The band evolved into AM I BLOOD having the second album re-released by Nuclear Blast under the new band title. The group members also all adopted new English sounding pseudonyms. AM I BLOOD issued the 1998 album 'Agitation'.

Albums:
NATURAL MUTATION, Stupido Twins (1995)
Time / Pit / Turn Away / Fall / Purpleslave / Energy / Misleading Sights / It's About / I'm Insane / No / Meanman / Motorchild / Religion / Exterior
AM I BLOOD, Tug Rec TUG 049 (1996)
Battlefreak / Disgrace / Cannot Feel / Endless Energy / Emotions / Immaterial / Frayed Chime / No Friend / Lust / Things You Hate / Determined Anger / Awake / Love Yourself / Ceremony To Fear

STONE (FINLAND)
Line-Up: Janne Joutsenniemi (vocals / bass), Roope Latvala (guitar), Nirri (guitar), Pekka Kasari (drums)

Outrageously successful in their native Finland STONE scored a number 1 hit with their 'Back To The Stoneage' EP in 1988 and were picked up by the MCA affiliated Mechanic Records for the release of a self-titled debut album in territories outside Finland.
Indeed, with backing from the label STONE toured America as support to TESTAMENT before returning home and adding ex-AIRDASH guitarist Nirri in 1990.
By 1992 the MCA deal was history and the 'Emotional Playground' album found the Finns signed to Black Mark, with a live album released the following year.
Although nothing appears to have been heard from STONE since, drummer Pekka Kasari joined AMORPHIS for their 1996 album 'Elegy'.

Singles/EPs:
Back To The Stone Age EP, (1988)

Albums:
STONE, Mechanic MCA 42175 (1988)
Get Stoned / No Commands / Eat Your Pride / The Day Of Death / Reached Out / Real Delusion / Brain Damage / Escape / Final Countdown / Overtake
NO ANASTHESIA, Megamania (1988)
Sweet Dreams / Empty Corner / Back To The Stone Age / Concrete Malformation / No Anaesthesia / Light Entertainment / Kill The Dead / Meat Mincing Machine
NO ANASTEHESIA, Megamania (1988) (Japanese release)
Sweet Dreams / Empty Corner / Back To The Stone Age / Concrete Malformation / No Anaesthesia / Light Entertainment / Kill The Dead / Meat Mincing Machine / Get Stoned / No Commands / Eat Your Pride / The Day Of Death / Reached Out / Escape / Final Countdown
EMOTIONAL PLAYGROUND, Black Mark BMCD13 (1992)
Small Tales / Home Bass / Last Chance / Above The Grey Sky / Mad Hatter's Den / Dead End / Adrift / Haven / Years After / Time Dive / Missionary Of Charity / Emotional Playground
FREE - LIVE, Black Mark BMCD 38 (1993)
Get Around / Empty Corner / Small Tales / Mad Hatter's Den / Sweet Dreams / Above The Grey Sky / Real Delusion / The Day Of Death / Last Chance / White Worms / Haven / Emotional Playground / No Commands / Missionary Of Charity / Overtake / Vengeance Of The Ghostrider

STORMTROOPERS OF DEATH
(New York, NY, USA)
Line-Up: Billy Milano (vocals), Scott Ian (guitar), Dan Lilker (bass), Charlie Benante (drums)

As side projects go, STORMTROOPERS OF DEATH proved to be extremely successful, a band that merged the talents of ANTHRAX men guitarist Scott Ian and drummer Charlie Benante with METHOD OF DESTRUCTION frontman Billy Milano. Completing the line-up was NUCLEAR ASSAULT / BRUTAL TRUTH (and ex-ANTHRAX) bassist Dan Lilker.
S.O.D., with the original line-up, resurrected themselves signing to German label Nuclear Blast, for 1999's 'Bigger Than The Devil'. The artwork of the album betrayed the humour inside, Sgt D. becoming larger than IRON MAIDEN's infamous Eddie.
The band's 2000 video and DVD's artwork was a wry take on the GUNS N' ROSES cross logo.
Lilker assembled a side project THE RAVENOUS in 2000 for the 'Assembled In Blasphemy' album. Included were NECROPHAGIA's Killjoy and Chris Reifert of AUTOPSY.

Albums:
SPEAK ENGLISH OR DIE, Roadrunner RR 9725 (1985)

STORMTROOPERS OF DEATH Scott Ian, Danny Lilker, Billy Milano and Charlie Benante

March Of The S.O.D. / Sergeant D And The S.O.D. / Kill Yourself / Milano Mosh / Speak English Or Die / United Forces / Chromatic Death / Pi Alpha Nu / Anti-Procrastination Song / What's The Noise / Freddy Krueger / Milk / Pre-Menstrual Princess Blues / Pussy Whipped / Fist Banging Mania

LIVE AT BUDOKAN, Music For Nations MFN 144 (1992)

Intro / March Of The Stormtroopers Of Death / Sargeant D. And The S.O.D. / Kill Yourself / Momo / Pi Alpha Nu / Milano Mosh / Speak English Or Die / Chromatic Death / Fist Banging Mania / The Camel Boy / No Turning Back / Milk / Vitality / Fuck The Middle East / Douche Crew / Get A Real Job / The Ballad Of Jimi Hendrix / Livin' In The City / Pussy Whipped / Stigmata / Thieves / Freddy Krueger / Territorial Pissings / United Forces

BIGGER THAN THE DEVIL, Nuclear Blast NB 383-2 (1999)

Bigger Than The Devil / The Crackhead Song / Kill The Assholes / Monkeys Rule / Skool Bus / King At The King / Evil Is In / Black War / Celtic Frosted Flakes / Charlie Don't Cheat / The Song That Don't Go Fast / Shenanigans / Dog On The Tracks / Make Room, Make Room / Free Dirty Needles / Fugu / We All Bleed Red / Frankenstein And His Horse / Every Tiny Molecule / Aren't You Hungry? / L.A.T.K.C.H. / Ballad Of Michael H. / Ballad Of Phil H. / Moment Of Truth

STRETTA (GERMANY)

Line-Up: Raphael Piatkowski (vocals), Norbert Kramarek (guitar), Andreas Ühlein (guitar), Peter Teicher (bass), Martin Kunz (drums)

A Thrash influenced German Metal band.

<u>Albums:</u>

ALONE IN THE BLUE, Rockwerk CD 1 (1991)

2BNNME / The Cup Of Reason / Fallacy / Among Thorns / Birthcrime / Hilidaze In Prisoncells / Big Letters

STYGIAN SHORE (Wichita, KS, USA)

A group produced by Mark Shelton of MANILLA ROAD. STYGIAN SHORE offered a four track EP during 1984 that was expected to be followed with a full length album. However, it's not known whether a follow up record was ever made.

<u>Singles/EPs:</u>

Stygian Metal / Luv Ta Rock You / Tidal Wave / Don't Look Now, Roadster SS2001 (1984) ('Stygian Shore' EP)

SUCKSPEED (GERMANY)

Line-Up: Michael Bothe (vocals / bass), Stoffi Krebs (guitar), Guido Steichen (guitar), Ollie Bertram (drums)

A German Crossover act hailing from Hannover, SUCKSPEED added ex-TERRY HOAX guitarist Ingo Schröder after the debut album.

In 1992 SUCKSPEED won a German Sony sponsored talent contest. Ex-SUCKSPEED guitarist Schröder founded BARFLY in march of 1993 and was replaced by Jochen Gutsch.

Singles/EPs:
Stormbringer / Step Out, We Bite (1990)
Stormbringer / Step Out / The Raid, We Bite WB 60 (1990) (12" single)

Albums:
THE DAY OF LIGHT, We Bite WB 1-059 (1989)
The Raid / Circumstances / Comin I.N.C. / Down And Out / Stay Aside / Alive And Dead / Day Of Light / Leader's Game / Stay In Line / One Time / Dark Side Of Your Mind
SLOW MOTION, We Bite (1991)
Try Harder / Steppenwolf / In My Bed / Guernica / What's To Come / Trash Movie - Slow Motion / Luxury Town / Get Away / Till The Next Time
END OF DEPRESSION, We Bite WB1-090 (1992)
Wild East / House Of Sin / Prove Me Wrong / Saw You Waiting / Bourbon Street / Bitching / More / After Dark / End Of Depression
UNKNOWN GENDER, We Bite WB1-099 (1993)
Bewitched / Destination / Boring But-Butt / Back To Me / Hollow Glow / Unknown Gender

SUICIDAL TENDENCIES
(Venice Beach, CA, USA)
Line-Up: Mike Muir (vocals), Grant Estes (guitar), Louiche Mayorga (bass), Amery Smith (drums)

SUICIDAL TENDENCIES, created in 1982 by vocalist Mike Muir, are one of the few Hardcore acts to break out onto the world circuit. Muir and his cohorts often appeared in photographs in the distinctive Los Angeles gang culture dress style of eyes hidden behind bandannas and check shirts held by the neck button. Later this image would develop through the skateboard culture fuelled by songs such as 'Possessed To Skate'.

Amongst the underground Hardcore circles the self-titled debut was recognized as a classic but as the band grew more conventional rock sensibilities would come to the fore.

Signing to major label Virgin in 1986, MTV support for the video to 'Institutionalized' raised the band's profile considerably, pulling them clear of their Indie Hardcore roots and breaking the charts on both sides of the Atlantic.

'Join The Army' saw the departure of Estes and Smith as the band debuted guitarist Rocky George and drummer R.J. Herrera.

Bassist Louiche Mayorga joined his erstwhile band mates Estes and Smith to form UNCLE SLAM, debuting the new act with the 'Say Uncle' album on Caroline Records during 1988.

The Mark Dodson produced 'How Will I Laugh...' saw the band being enlarged with the addition of ex-NO MERCY rhythm guitarist Mike Clark and bassist Bob Heathcote.

As SUICIDAL TENDENCIES were seemingly in ascendancy into the big league their controversial name made them ripe targets for the moral majority. California's police department, fearing Muir's crew was merely a front for a Los Angeles gang, even went so far as to ban the band performing in their hometown. The notorious moral campaigner Tipper Gore led pressure group P.M.R.C. kept up a campaign against the band claiming that a number of teenage suicides were directly attributable to the band.

SUICIDAL TENDENCIES brought in bassist Rob Trujillo for 'Lights, Camera... Revolution'. The album track 'Send Me Your Money', a forthright attack on American television evangelists proved a huge hit with the fans and quickly became a staple of live shows.

Both Muir and Trujillo captured more than their fair share of the limelight at this juncture creating side project act INFECTIOUS GROOVES together with erstwhile JANE'S ADDICTION drummer Stephan Perkins. This side project band that would go on to release two well received albums and test the duo's stamina as INFECTIOUS GROOVES often opened the show for SUICIDAL TENDENCIES.

Perhaps wishing to amend previous mistakes the band's next album 'Still Cyco After All These Years' was actually a complete re-recording of their debut.

Noted producer Peter Collins was utilized for what was to be SUICIDAL TENDENCIES's highest selling record reaching Number 52 in the Billboard charts for the 'Art Of Rebellion' album. The band once more announced a new recruit in VANDALS drummer Josh Freece, who incidentally took over the drumstool in INFECTIOUS GROOVES too.

'Suicidal For Life' had SUICIDAL TENDENCIES recording without a permanent drummer. Freese joined the limbo bound GUNS N' ROSES then PEARL JAM and A PERFECT CIRCLE. WHITE LION and Y&T man Jimmy DeGrasso deputised for the

SUICIDAL TENDENCIES Mike Muir, Brooks Wackerman, Mike Clark and Dean Pleasants

album sessions before he joined up full time with MEGADETH.

SUICIDAL TENDENCIES folded after this release. Rocky George created SAMSARA with CRO MAGS members Harley Flanagan and Parris Mayhew. Trujillo found himself part of the OZZY OSBOURNE band having an interim stint with PALE DEMON.

Guitarist Mike Clark would found CREEPER, an alliance with former BEOWÜLF and THE BONEYARD CREW guitarist Mike Jensen, BEOWÜLF drummer Miguel 'Michael' Alvarado, vocalist 'Fifty One' and bassist 'Insect Dragster'.

SLAYER covered 'Memories Of Tomorrow' for inclusion on their 'Undisputed Attitude' covers album. However, the track only made it onto the Japanese pressing.

The band returned in 1999 signed to Germany's Nuclear Blast label. In mid 2001 Brooks Wackerman returned to the ranks back from his touring stint filling in with A PERFECT CIRCLE. Drummer Josh Freese would also re-enlist.

By early 2002 Rocky George had re-emerged touting a fresh act HARLEY'S WAR in union with ex-CRO-MAGS frontman Harley Flanagan and former WARZONE guitarist Jay Vento. Meantime ex-SUICIDAL TENDENCIES guitarist Anthony Gallo re-emerged as part of ex-MEGADETH drummer Nick Menza's new band project.

Singles/EPs:

Possessed To Skate / Human Guinea Pig, Virgin VS 967 (1987) (7" single)
Possessed To Skate / Human Guinea Pig / Two Wrongs Don't Make A Right (But They Make Me Feel Better), Virgin VS 967-12 (1987) (12" single)
Institutionalized / War Inside My Head / Cycxo, Virgin VST 1039 (1988) (12" single)
Trip At The Brain / Suicyco Mania, Virgin VST 1127 (1988) (12" single)
Send Me Your Money / You Can't Bring Me Down / Waking The Dead / Don't Give Me Your Nothing, Epic 6563326 (1990)

Albums:

FIRST ALBUM, Frontier FLP1011 (1987)
Suicide's An Alternative / You'll Be Sorry / I Shot The Devil / Won't Fall In Love Today / Memories Of Tomorrow / I Saw Your Mommy... ? I Want More / Two Sided Politics / Subliminal / Institutionalised / Possessed / Fascist Pig / Suicidal Failure
JOIN THE ARMY, Virgin V2424 (1987) **81 UK, 100 USA**
Suicidal Maniac / Join The Army / You Got, I Want / Little Each Day / Prisoner / War Inside My Head / I Feel Your Pain And Survive / Human Guinea Pig / Possessed To Skate / No Name, No Words / Cyco / Two Wrongs Don't Make A Right (But It Makes Me Feel Better) / Looking In Your Eyes

HOW WILL I LAUGH TOMORROW WHEN I CAN'T EVEN SMILE TODAY, Virgin CDV 2551 (1988)
Trip At The Brain / Hearing Voices / Pledge Your Allegiance / How Will I Laugh Tomorrow / Miracle / Surf And Slam / If I Don't Wake Up / Sorry / One Too Many Times / Feeling's Back / Suicyco Mania
CONTROLLED BY HATRED - FEEL LIKE SHIT... DEJA VU, Epic 4653992 (1989)
Master Of No Mercy / How Will I Laugh Tomorrow / Just Another Love Song / Walking The Dead / Controlled By Hatred / Choosing My Own Way Of Life / Feel Like Shit... Déjà Vu / It's Not Easy / How Will I Laugh Tomorrow ('Heavy Emotion' version)
LIGHTS, CAMERA... REVOLUTION, Epic 4665692 (1990) **59 UK**
You Can't Bring Me Down / Lost Again / Alone / Lovely / Give It Revolution / Get Whacked / Send Me Your Money / Emotion No. 13 / Disco's Out, Murder's In / Go n' Breakdown
SUICIDAL TENDENCIES, Virgin OVED 384 (1991)
Suicide's An Alternative / You'll Be Sorry / Two Sided Politics / I Shot The Devil / Subliminal / Won't Fall In Love Today / Institutionalised / Memories Of Tomorrow / Possessed / I Saw Your Mommy... / Fascist Pig / I Want More / Suicidal Failure / Possessed To Skate / Human Guinea Pig / Two Wrongs Don't Make A Right (But It Makes Me Feel Better)
THE ART OF REBELLION, Epic 4718852 (1992) 52 USA
Can't Stop / Accept My Sacrifice / Nobody Hears / Tap Into The Power / Monopoly On Sorrow / We Call This Mutha Revenge / I Wasn't Meant To Feel This / Asleep At The Wheel / Gotta Kill Captain Stupid / I'll Hate You Better / Which Way To Be Free / It's Going Down / Where's The Truth
STILL CYCO AFTER ALL THESE YEARS, Epic 473749-2 (1993)
Suicide's An Alternative / Two Sided Politics / Subliminal / I Shot The Devil / Won't Fall In Love / Institutionalised / War Inside My Head / Don't Give Me Your Nothin' / Memories Of Tomorrow / Possessed / I Saw Your Mommy... / Fascist Pig / Little Each Day / I Want More / Suicidal Failure
SUICIDAL FOR LIFE, Epic 476885-2 (1994) 82 USA
Invocation / Don't Give A Fuck / No Fuckn' Problem / Suicyco Muthafucka / Fucked Up Just Right / No Bullshit / What Else Could I Do / What You Need's A Friend / I Wouldn't Mind / Depression And Anguish / Evil / Love v Loneliness / Benediction
PRIME CUTS, Epic 484123-2 (1997)
You Can't Bring Me Down / Join The New

Army / Lovely / Institutionalised / Gotta Kill Captain Studio / Berserk / I Saw Your Mommy / Pledge Your Allegiance / Feeding The Addiction / I Wasn't Meant To Feel This / Asleep At The Wheel / Send Me Your Money / No Fuck'n Problem / Go Skate / Nobody Hears / How Will I Laugh Tomorrow
FREEDUMB, Nuclear Blast (1999) **90 GERMANY**
Freedumb / Ain't Gonna Take It / Scream Out / Half Way Up My Head / Cyco Vision / I Ain't Like You / Naked / Hippie Killer / Built To Survive / Get Sick / We Are Family / I'll Buy Myself / Gaigan Go Home / Heaven
FREE YOUR SOUL... SAVE YOUR MIND, Nuclear Blast NB 528-2 (2000) **92 GERMANY**
Self Destruct / Sue Casa Es Mi Casa / No More No Less / Free Your Soul / Pop Songs / Billenium / Animal / Straight From The Heart / Cyco Speak / Start Your Brain / Public Dissention / Children Of The Bored / Got Mutation / Charlie Monroe / Home

SUICIDE SQUAD (Seattle, WA, USA)
Line-Up: Brad Sinsel (vocals), Rick Pierce (guitar), Rick Bradley (bass), Richard Stuverud (drums)

A post TKO project from the Seattle group's vocalist Brad Sinsel and former colleague Rick Pierce (then in Q5), SUICIDE SQUAD recorded a one-off EP that was released in Europe on Music For Nations.
Whilst Pierce went on to put together NIGHTSHADE with his Q5 colleague Jonathan K, Sinsel gained a deal from Columbia with his WAR BABIES outfit. The group also included SUICIDE SQUAD associate Richard Stuverud on drums, who would later record with THREE FISH, the Epic Records signed side project from PEARL JAM guitarist Jeff Ament.

Singles/EPs
No Solution / Bad Boys Blues / Live It While You Can / Can't Use Ya', MFN 85M (1988) ('Live It While You Can' EP)

SUICITY (GERMANY)
Line-Up: Jörg Holzhauser (vocals / guitar), Michael Cichoki (guitar), Klaus Bergermann (bass), Andy Nahrstedt (drums)

A Thrash Metal act with a bit of a Hardcore touch. SUICITY was originally named DESERT PLANES becoming SUICITY upon the recording of their debut 1989 demo.
Two further demos led up to the album 'The Strategy Of Hate' namely 1990's 'Badtime Stories' and 1992's 'For Those Who Suffer'.

THE STRATEGY OF HATE, Crypta Inline
55C-8787-011 (1993)
Home Video Target Range / Face The Facts /
The Harder They Fall / R.A.T.S. / 2000 A.D. /
The Prophecy / Brother Hate - Sister Pain /
Suicide Mission

SWEET DISTORTION (CANADA)
Line-Up: Jerome (vocals), Mark Tremblay
(guitar), Antoine Fafard (bass), Marc
Laflamme (drums)

Montreal Nu-Thrash act SWEET
DISTORTION self financed their April 2001
album 'Missing Link'. To appease the Quebec
French language 65% radio quota SWEET
DISTORTION duly delivered two radio
unfriendly tracks in 'Va Donc Chier' ('Fuck
Off') and the more surreal 'Mange De La
Marmalade'.

Albums:
MISSING LINK, (2001)
The Pit / I Refuse To Loose / Join The Hunt /
Fly High / Sweet Distortion / Loud Mouth /
Kiss My Ass / Riot / Brand New Breed / Sun
Of A Gun / Up Again The Wall / Emptiness /
Prophecy 2000

SWORDMASTER (SWEDEN)
Line-up: Andreas Bergh (vocals), Emil
Nödtveidt (guitar), Kenneth Gagfner (bass),
Tobias Kjellgren (drums)

SWORDMASTER date to 1993 and their
foundation by guitarist Nightmare (real name
Emil Nödtveidt). Nightmare also plays with
OPTHALAMIA and is the brother of the
imprisoned DISSECTION mentor Jon.
Following the mini album release on Florida's
Full Moon Productions, drummer Tobias
Kjellgren joined DECAMERON. He would
eventually rejoin DISSECTION for their
December 1995 European tour. His
temporary replacement in SWORDMASTER
was another ex-DISSECTION member, Ole
Öhman.
The 'Wrath Of Time' mini-album was re-
released on vinyl format in 1996, limited to
1000 copies and with two extra tracks;
'Metallic Devastation' and 'Claws Of Death
(Conspiracy)'. The band signed to Osmose
Productions the same year but would start to
draw themselves away from Black Metal and
into straightforward Thrash tinged Heavy
Metal with each successive release.
Presently the band are credited as vocalist
Whiplasher, guitarists Nightmare and Beast
Electric, bassist Thunderbolt and drummer
Terror.

Singles/EPs:
Wraths Of Time / Upon Blood And Ashes /
Conspiracy - Preview / Outro, Full Moon
Productions FMP004 (1995) ('Wraths Of
Time' EP)

Albums:
POST MORTEM TALES, Osmose
Productions OPCD055 (1997)
Indeathstries - The Master's Possession /
Crust To Dust / Postmortem Tales / Past
Redemption / Claws Of Death / Blood Legacy
/ The Serpent Season / Metallic Devastation /
Black Ace
DEATHRAIDER, Osmose Productions (1999)
Deathraider 2000 / Firefall To The Fireball /
Necronaut Psychout / Iron Corpse / Stand For
The Fire Demon
MORIBUND TRANSGORIA, Osmose
Productions OPCD084 (1999)
Deathspawn Of The Eibound / Towards The
Erotomech Eye / The Angel And The Masters
/ Metalmorphosis - The Secret Of Cain /
Sulphar Skelethrone / Moribund Transgoria /
Doom At Motordome / The Grotesque
Xtravaganza

TAIST OF IRON
(Tacoma, WA, USA)
Line-Up: Lorraine Gill (vocals),
Wylum Pearson (guitar), Mark
Glabe (bass), Jeff Massey
(drums)

Female fronted Metal band from Washington
State.

Albums:
RESURRECTION, Iron IR1313 (1984)
Resurrection / The Gates / Victim Child / We
Give Life / M.O.R.R. / Feeling You / Love &
Pain / Metal Taco / Evil / Bloody Axe / Cross
Of Fire / Ouija

TAKASHI (New York, NY, USA)
Line-Up: Danny Stanton (vocals), Craig
Khoury (guitar), Bob Simonson (guitar), Tom
Cangemi (bass), Chuck Khoury (drums)

A fairly powerful Heavy Metal band typical of
the period, TAKASHI was amongst a handful
of groups on the independent Mongol Horde
label operating in the early '80s.
Chuck Khoury quit to join fellow New York
outfit HITTMAN.

Albums:
KAMIKAZE KILLERS, Mongol Horde 1
(1983)

TALIÖN (UK)
Line-Up: Graeme Wyatt (vocals / guitar), Pete
Wadeson (guitar), Phil Gavin (bass), Johnny
Lee Jackson (drums)

TALIÖN guitarist Pete Wadeson and frontman
Graeme Wyatt were originally in TROJAN, a
band that released the Guy Bidmead
produced album 'Chasing The Storm' on
Roadrunner Records in 1987.
The duo's first project after TROJAN split was
titled LETHAL, with ex-WOLFPACK and
SALEM bassist Phil Gavin. After demoing
material at Twilight studios in Manchester in
1988, the band settled on the name TALIÖN
and signed to Major (a subsidiary of
Peaceville) in April 1989, promptly recording
the album 'Killing The World' with producer
Kevin Ridley (later of SKYCLAD).
The sound of this album turned out to be fast
and aggressive, bordering on Thrash but with
plenty of melody, the group following its
release with a trip, in early 1990, overseas to
appear at the 'Public Against Violence' festival
in Czechoslovakia alongside BONFIRE and
STORMWITCH.
Gavin and Lee Jackson quit the band in late
1991 prompting the recruitment of new

guitarist Andy J. in mid 1992 whilst Wadeson
took time out to contribute the solo track 'Thrill
Of The Chase' to the Japanese released
compilation 'Metal For Muthas '92'
compilation.
Following the demise of TALIÖN Wadeson
recorded a solo demo entitled 'Play With Fire'
in 1992. In 1994 Wadeson formed
BETRAYED.
In 1995 he issued an instrumental demo,
'Burnout', before later turning up as a Rock
journalist for Brazil's 'Rock Brigade'
magazine. 1999 found the man
unsuccessfully auditioning for ex-IRON
MAIDEN vocalist Blaze Bayley's new band
and for MARSHALL LAW.
By 2001 Wadeson's perseverance had paid
off as he joined the RETURN TO THE
SABBAT resurrection act assembled by ex-
SKYCLAD / SABBAT vocalist Martin Walkyier.
His tenure would be brief.

Albums:
KILLING THE WORLD, Major WADES1CD
(1989)
Killing The World / Sanctuary / Living On The
Edge / Speed Thrills / Laws Of Retaliation /
Screamin' For Mercy / Premonition

TANK (UK)
Line-Up: Algy Ward (vocals / bass), Mick
Tucker (guitar), Gary Taylor (drums)

Formed in Croydon during 1980, TANK
debuted as a trio of Algy Ward (ex-SAINTS
and the DAMNED), and the brotherly duo of
guitarist Pete Brabbs and drummer Mark
Brabbs. It was only inevitable that they would
quickly establish a reputation for themselves
as a power trio in the MOTÖRHEAD mould.
Some felt they were too close to close to
Lemmy and co. for comfort, especially on the
debut album 'Filth Hounds Of Hades', which
was produced by MOTÖRHEAD's guitarist
FAST EDDIE CLARKE.
In spite of the detractors TANK forged ahead
with strong sales and were quick to build up a
loyal fanbase particularly in Europe and
Japan.
After consistently touring opening for the likes
of GIRLSCHOOL, MOTÖRHEAD and
DIAMOND HEAD throughout the next two
years the unveiling of a second album,
entitled 'Power Of The Hunter' met with strong
sales and established a loyal fan base.
Changes were afoot for TANK by the time
their conceptual third album emerged in 1983,
the group having aligned themselves with
Music For Nations after the demise of
Kamaflage Records.
'This Means War', debuted TANK's new,

second guitarist Mick Tucker, previously with AXIS and WHITE SPIRIT, and the JOHN VERITY produced album also featured guest backing vocals by Jody Turner of ROCK GODDESS and Denise Dufort of GIRLSCHOOL. However, after just one gig promoting 'This Means War' Pete Brabbs was sacked and Mark Brabbs left to join DUMPY'S RUSTY NUTS (and later UK) shortly after.

Brabbs created a short-lived band with erstwhile ORE members bassist Dave Boyce and guitarist Dave Howard. 1986 found Brabbs as a member of SAMSON.

Meantime Ward and Tucker chose to enlist ex-CHICKENSHACK and HEADFIRST guitarist Cliff Evans and former WHITE SPIRIT drummer Graeme Crallan for a revised version of TANK. During late 1984 TANK supported METALLICA on a European tour. Later shows included gigs in America supporting RAVEN prior to further headline shows of their own.

Having recorded a second album for Music For Nations - 1985's 'Honour And Blood' - TANK replaced Graeme Crallen with ex-STREETFIGHTER Gary Taylor. Crallen joined London act BRITTON, then by 1987 PANAMA, reuniting with his erstwhile WHITE SPIRIT colleague keyboard player Toby Sadler.

Following the 'Tank' album (recorded in 1986 with Mick Tucker but only seeing a release in 1988), the band's line-up was back down to the trio, consisting of Algy Ward, Cliff Evans and Gary Taylor. Evans would later join KILLERS after Ward decided to bring TANK to a conclusion. Taylor travelled to America to form Punk Sleaze act SHOTGUN RATIONALE with ex-PLASMATICS man Chris Romanelli.

In 1993 there was some talk of a reunion album in the works, but nothing came of this. Ward spent time recording the 'Black Metal supergroup' album titled NECROPOLIS with ex-FASTWAY drummer Steve Clark and ASIA guitarist KEITH MORE among others, before joining Clark's Jazz Rock act NETWORK for the 'Refusal To Comply' album. He would also appear on the later NETWORK album 'L.N.C.' Ward resurfaced in London club band CONSPIRACY during 1994 before joining WARHEAD, a project assembled by ex-MOTÖRHEAD guitarist WURZEL and WARFARE mainman Evo.

In 1996 Ward rejoined the DAMNED, but before long the continental fascination for cult, early '80s acts had caught up with TANK and, offered a recording deal, the band duly reformed. The 1997 TANK line-up showed up at the 'Wacken Open Air' Festival in Germany, then undertook a tour of the country sharing a bill with HAMMERFALL and RAVEN. For most of the latter dates on this trek Ward took to the stage with the aid of a walking stick! The NECROPOLIS album finally saw a belated release in 1997.

The late '90s incarnation of TANK (Ward, Evans, Tucker and ex-PERSIAN RISK, JAGGED EDGE and BATTLEZONE drummer Steve Hopgood) issued the live album 'The Return Of The Filth Hounds' for Rising Sun Records and put in a further German showing at the 1998 'Bang Your Head' Festival.

TANK also got to play in Japan during early 1999 on a NWoBHM billing including PRAYING MANTIS as Evans also began work on a fresh KILLERS project.

Singles/EPs:
Don't Walk Away / Shellshock / Hammer On, Kamaflage KAM 1 (1981)
Don't Walk Away (Live) / The Snake, Kamaflage KAM F1 (1981)
Turn Your Head Around / Steppin' On A Landmine, Kamaflage KAM3 (1982)
Crazy Horses / Filth Bitch Boogie, Kamaflage KAM 7 (1982)
(He Fell In Love With A) Stormtrooper / Blood Guts And Beer, Kamaflage KAP 1 (1982)
Echoes Of A Distant Battle / Man That Never Was, Music For Nations KUT 101 (1983) (7" single)
Echoes Of A Distant Thunder / Man That Never Was / Whichcatchewedmycuckoo, Music For Nations KUT 101 (1983) (12" single)

Albums:
FILTH HOUNDS OF HADES, Kamaflage KAMLP 1 (1982) **33 UK**
Shellshock / Struck By Lightning / Run Like Hell / Blood, Guts And Beer / That's What Dreams Are Made Of / Turn Your Head Around / Heavy Artillery / Who Needs Love Songs / Filth Hounds Of Hades / Stormtrooper
POWER OF THE HUNTER, Kamaflage KAMLP 3 (1982)
Walking Barefoot Over Glass / Pure Hatred / Biting And Scratching / Some Come Running / T.A.N.K. / Used Leather (Hanging Loose) / Crazy Horses / Set Your Back On Fire / Red Skull Rock / Power Of The Hunter
THIS MEANS WAR, Music For Nations MFN3 (1983)
Just Like Something From Hell / Hot Lead Cold Steel / This Means War / Laughing In The Face Of Death / (If We Go) We Go Down Fighting / I (Won't Ever Let You Down) / Echoes Of A Distant Battle
HONOUR AND BLOOD, Music For Nations MFN26 (1985)

The War Drags Ever On / When All Hell Freezes Over / Honour And Blood / Chain Of Fools / W.M.I.A. / Too Tired To Wait For Love / Kill

ARMOUR PLATED, Rawpower RAWLP009 (1985)
Don't Walk Away / Power Of The Hunter / Run Like Hell / Filth Hounds Of Hades / (He Fell In Love With A) Stormtrooper / Red Skull Rock / The Snake / Who Needs Love Songs / Steppin' On A Landmine / Turn Your Head Around / Crazy Horses / Some Come Running / Hammer On / Shellshock / That's What Dreams Are Made Of / Biting And Scratching / Used Leather (Hanging Loose) / Blood, Guts And Beer / Filth Bitch Boogie / T.A.N.K.

TANK, GWR GWCD23 (1988)
Reign Of Thunder / March On, Sons Of Nippon / With Your Life / None But The Brave / The Enemy Below / Lost / (The Hell They Must) Suffer / It Fell From The Sky

THE RETURN OF THE FILTH HOUNDS LIVE, Rising Sun 008203 2 RS (1998)
This Means War / Echoes Of A Distant Battle / That's What Dreams Are Made Of / And Then We Heard The Thunder / Don't Walk Away / Honour And Blood / Power Of The Hunter / Shellshock / In The Last Hours Before Dawn (Studio) / And Then We Heard The Thunder (Studio)

TANKARD (GERMANY)

Line-Up: Andreas Geremia (vocals), Axel Katzmann (guitar), Andreas Bulgaropulos (guitar), Frank Thorwath (bass), Arnulf Tunn (drums)

A Frankfurt Metal act lyrically obsessed by the subject of alcohol, TANKARD's second album, 'Chemical Invasion', was close to being a crusade against the introduction of foreign chemicals into German beers!
The band was created during 1982 with an original line-up of vocalist Gerre, guitarists Axel Katzmann and Andy Boulgaropulas, bassist Frank Torwarth and drummer O.W. (Oliver Werner). This line-up cut the first demo in 1984 'Heavy Metal Vanguard' capitalised on by a second effort 'Alcoholic Metal'.
TANKARD's debut album, 1986's 'Zombie Attack', provided a useful sales base of 10,000 copies before 'Chemical Invasion' exceeded that figure three times over.
TANKARD's early drummer Oliver Werner was superseded by Arnulf Tunn. Werner went on to created CHASED CRIME and DARK STAR.
In 1988 TANKARD toured Europe heavily playing dates in Germany, Holland and Belgium before performing at festivals in Germany alongside VENDETTA and

HELSTAR. The interim 'Alien' EP was promoted in Germany by dates with DEATHROW. The group later recorded 'The Meaning Of Life' album in 1990, their first to enter the German national charts as TANKARD hit the road again, this time with RUMBLE MILITIA and NAPALM in tow. Shows in Bochum and Frankfurt were recorded for the band's debut live album 'Fat, Ugly & Live'.
1992 found TANKARD's popularity extending outside of Germany and the act's touring schedule was widened to include territories such as Turkey and Bulgaria where they played with support acts MEGLOMANIAX and Englishmen XENTRIX.
Following recording of 1994's 'Two Faced' album drummer Arnulf Tunn departed and in his stead came Olaf Zissel. This new line-up soon got back into action releasing an album of cover versions 'Angetankt' for a Germany only release in 1994 adopting the moniker TANKWART.
Before the next album Katzmann left the group due to health problems and TANKARD chose not to replace him but remain as a quartet. The group promptly recorded 'The Tankard' as a four-piece.
In 1996 the second TANKARD side project album was released through Century Media. Titled 'Himbeergeist Zum Frühstuck', the group would tour playing material from both this album and TANKARD material.
Katzmann and Tunn would create NEMESIS for an eponymous 1997 album in collusion with frontman Adrian Ergün of CAPRICORN.
The millennium saw no let up in TANKARD's alcohol fuelled activities with the 'Kings Of Beer' album, released by Century Media, selling well. For 2002, the band's 25th anniversary TANKARD set to work on the aptly titled 'B-Day' album for new label AFM Records with HOLY MOSES guitarist Andy Classen acting as producer.

Singles/EPs:
Alien / 666 Packs / Live To Die / Remedy / Empty Tankard, Noise NO131-3 (1987)
Stone Cold Sober / Broken Image / Mindwild, Noise N 190-9 (1992)
Ich Brauch Meinen Suff / Up From Zero, Noise N0233-3 (1993)

Albums:
ZOMBIE ATTACK, Noise N0046 8-4401 (1986)
Zombie Attack / Acid Death / Mercenary / Maniac Forces / Alcohol / Empty Tankard / Thrash 'Til Death / Chains / Poison / Screamin' Victims
CHEMICAL INVASION, Noise N084452 (1987)

Intro / Total Addiction / Tantrum / Don't Panic / Puke / For A Thousand Beers / Chemical Invasion / Farewell To A Slut / Traitor / Alcohol

THE MORNING AFTER, Noise N0123 (1989)
Commandments / Shit Faced / TV Hero / FUN / Try Again / The Morning After / Desperation / Feed The Lohicia / Help Yourself / Mon Cheri

HAIR OF THE DOG, Noise N0150 (1990)
The Morning After / Alien / Don't Panic / Zombie Attack / Chemical Invasion / Commandments / Tantrum / Maniac Forces / Shit Faced / Empty Tankard

MEANING OF LIFE, Noise N0156 (1990)
Open All Night / We Are Us / Dancing On Our Grave / Mechanical Man / Beermuda / The Meaning Of Life / Spacebeer / Always Them / Wheel Of Rebirth / Barfly

FAT, UGLY AND LIVE, Noise N0166-1 (1991)
The Meaning Of Life / Mercenary / Beermuda / Total Addiction / Live To Dive / Poison / Chemical Invasion / The Morning After / Space Beer / Alcohol / Puke / Mon Cheri / Wonderful Life / Empty Tankard

STONE COLD SOBER, Noise N0190-2 (1992)
Stone Cold Sober / Jurisdiction / Broken Image / Mindwild / Ugly-Beautiful / Centrefold / Behind The Back / Lost And Found (Tantrum Part Three) / Sleeping With The Past / Freiber / Of Strange People Talking Under Arabian Skies

TWO FACED, Noise N0233 (1994)
Death Penalty / R.T.V. / Betrayed / Nation Over Nation / Days Of The Gun / Cities In Flames / Up From Zero / Two Faced / Ich Brauch Meinen Suff / Cyberworld / Mainhatten / Jimmy B Bad

THE TANKARD, Noise N 0529-2 (1995)
Grave New World / Minds On The Moon / The Story Of Mr. Cruel / Close Encounter / Poshor Golovar / Mess In The West / Atomic Twilight / Fuck Christmas / Positive / Hope?

DISCO DESTROYER, Century Media 77209-2 (1998)
Serial Killer / Planetwide-suicide.com / Hard Rock Dinosaur / Queen Of Hearts / U-R-B / Mr. Superlover / Tankard Roach Motel / Another Perfect Day / Death By Whips / Away! / Face Of The Enemy / Splendid Boys / Disco Destroyer

KINGS OF BEER, Century Media 77274-2 (2000)
Flirtin' With Desaster / Dark Exile / Hot Dog Inferno / Hell Bent For Jesus / Kings Of Beer / I'm So Sorry! / Talk Show Prostitute / Incredible Loudness / Land Of The Free / Mirror, Mirror / Tattoo Coward

TANKWART (GERMANY)
Line-Up: Andreas Geremia (vocals), Axel Katzmann (guitar), Andreas Bulgaropulos (guitar), Frank Torwath (bass), Arnulf Tunn (drums)

TANWART is the side project arm of the less than serious beer swilling TANKARD crew. TANKWART's 1994 debut album 'Aufgetrankt' covered a number of German hits from the notorious 'Neue Deutsche Welle' era of Pop music from the early '80s. Included were 'Liebesspieler' by DIE TOTEN HOSEN, 'Elke' by DIE ÄRTZE, 'Sternenhimmel' by HUBERTKAH, 'Hurra, Hurra Die Schule Bennt' from EXTRABEIT and 'Skandal Im Sperrbezirk' from the SPIDER MURPHY GANG.

Albums:
AUFGETANKT, Noise NZ 003-2 (1994)
Libesspieler / Pogo In Togo / Hurra, Hurrra, Die Schule Brennt / Herr D / Sternenhimmel / König Von Deutschland / Elke / Skandal Im Sperrbezirk / Billiger Slogan

HIMBEERGEIST ZUM FRÜHSTÜCK, Century Media 77145-2 (1996)
Schöne Maid / Viva Espana / Tanze Samba Mit Mir / Ein Bißchen Spaß Muß Sein / Paloma Blanca / Am Tag, Als Conny Kramer Starb / Himbeergeist Zum Frühstück / Dschinghis Khan / Sieben Fässer Wein / Mendocino / Fiesta Mexicana / Fahrende Musikanten / Blau Blüht Der Enzian

TEFILLA (HOLLAND)
Line-Up: Jaap Heeling (vocals), Leo Van Gilst (guitar), Jeroen Wilts (guitar), Edwin Van de Laan (bass), Johnny Van Dijk (drums)

Stadskanaal based Christian Thrash Metal outfit.

Albums:
GRIEVOUS ANGUISH, (1998)
Sanguis / Grievous Anguish / The Judge / The Pillar / Exorators / Chapel / Funeral Of Death / Horn Of Salvation

TENEBRA (GERMANY)
Line-Up: Darius S. Sarbandi (vocals / bass), Sascha Krüger (guitar), Heiko Schröer (guitar), Gerald Jarausch (drums)

A Thrash Metal band formed in Bielefeld during 1991. TENEBRA recorded a demo entitled 'Exposed Senses' during 1992 before eventually gaining a deal with D&S Records.
Albums:
TENEBRA, D&S Records DSR CD 008 (1994)

Whatever / Urges / Innocent Culprit / Pellucid Viscera / Among / Hurt / Mother's Gate / Exposed Senses / Lost / Re-Reborn / Breach Of Trust / Threatening Questions

TENSION (Baltimore, MD, USA)

Line-Up: Tom Gattis (vocals), Timmy Meadows (guitar), Tim O'Connor (bass), Billy Giddings (drums)

Previously known as DEUCE, Baltimore's TENSION finally gained a long awaited deal with Torrid Records having impressed many under their original moniker with some rather tasty demos.
Led by founder Tom Gattis and including ANGEL legend Punky Meadows' brother Timmy on guitar, TENSION took their place amongst a new wave of American Thrash Metal bands.
The DEUCE demo material was actually released on vinyl by an extremely small independent label with the blessing of the band.
Tom Gattis went on to front WARDOG.

Albums:
BREAKING POINT, Torrid 88561-8098 (1986)
One Nation / Wreckin' Crew / Reach For Your Sword / Angels From The Past / W.O.C. / Shock Treatment / The Downfall Of Evil / Metal Paranoia / Seduced

TERRASPHERE (USA)

Albums:
THIRD IN ORDER OF THE SUN, New Renaissance NRR60 (1991)

TERROR SQUAD (JAPAN)

Line-Up: Udagawa (vocals), Ozeki (guitar), Joker (drums)

Thrash Metal band created in 1992 by vocalist Udagawo and guitarist Ozeki. TERROR SQUAD debut demo 'The Birth Of The New Rage' followed in 1994 and Joker was added on drums the year after.
A split 7" 'Disco Bloody Disco - Die Hard Metal' was issued in 1997 on Primitive Art Records. TERROR SQUAD also included their track 'Blood Fire Metal' to a Necropolis Records 1999 compilation 'Thrashing Holocaust'.
The band donated the track 'Fist Banging Mania' to a 2000 compilation 'Speak Japanese Or XXX'. A split single with SABBAT would also be in the works.

Singles/EPs:
Disco Bloody Disco - Die Hard Metal, Primitive Art (1997) (Split 7" single)

Albums:
THE WILD STREAM OF ETERNAL SIN, World Chaos Productions (1999)
Straight To Hell / Disco Bloody Disco / Order Of Lone Wolf / Chain Of The Damned / Nightmare Rider / Blood Fire Metal / Wild Disorder - Eternal Sin

TESTAMENT

(San Francisco, CA, USA)
Line-Up: Chuck Billy (vocals), Alex Skolnick (guitar), Eric Peterson (guitar), Greg Christian (bass), Louie Clemente (drums)

Founded as LEGACY in the infamous Bay area melting pot of Metal in 1983. As LEGACY the band had issued a demo titled 'Testament'.
LEGACY comprised Steve 'Retro' Souza on vocals, guitarists Eric Peterson and Derek Ramirez, bassist Greg Christian and drummer Louis Clemente. However, Souza bailed out to join fellow Bay Area thrashers EXODUS.
Upon the signing to major label Atlantic, via Johnny Z's Megaforce imprint, the band switched names (avoiding legal problems with another LEGACY) and drafted in new recruits vocalist Chuck Billy and guitarist Alex Skolnick.
During 1990 TESTAMENT, promoting the 'Souls Of Black' album, found themselves grabbing the opening spot on the mammoth 'Clash Of The Titans' touring package with MEGADETH, ANTHRAX and SLAYER.
Following 1992's 'The Ritual' Skolnick opted out to join SAVATAGE but by 1995 he had received a better offer to join OZZY OSBOURNE. However, the guitarist only lasted for one gig, a secret bash at Nottingham's Rock City. Skolnick founded ATTENTION DEFICIT with PRIMUS drummer Tim Alexander for a 1998 album.
TESTAMENT meanwhile failed to maintain a stable line-up for 1993's 'Return To Apocalyptic City'. New man on the drum stool was the highly respected ex-FORBIDDEN and SLAYER drummer Paul Bostoph and in came ex-FORBIDDEN guitarist Glen Alvelais. 1994's 'Low' featured Death Metal journeyman guitarist JAMES MURPHY whose credits include AGENT STEEL, DEATH, OBITUARY, DISINCARNATE and CANCER and EXODUS drummer John Tempesta. Shortly after recording Tempesta teamed up with WHITE ZOMBIE.
The line-up for the 'Live At The Fillmore'

album, recorded at a sell out show at the notorious Haight-Ashbury venue, comprised Billy, guitarists Peterson and Murphy, bassist Greg Christian and former EVIL DEAD drummer John Dette.

Down to a duo of Billy and Peterson TESTAMENT actually folded for a short period as the original pairing announced a new band DOG FACED GOD. These sessions would ultimately emerge as the new TESTAMENT album.

1997's 'Demonic' saw Billy and Peterson fronting a quartet completed by Ramirez on bass and ex-DEATH drummer Gene Hoglan. Prior to recording Dette had vacated his position making a move to SLAYER. Bass was now in the hands of ex-DEATH and SADUS man Steve DiGeorgio.

Another quick change ensued on the drumstool after 'Demonic's release as Hoglan took up an offer to fulfill live work with STRAPPING YOUNG LAD leaving a gap for the reinstatement of Dette whose brief tenure in SLAYER had lasted a matter of weeks. TESTAMENT drafted in Alvelais once more to boost their guitar sound. Chuck Billy meantime put in an appearance on Murphy's solo album 'Feeding The Machine'.

1998 found the newly formed Mayhem Records issuing a compilation album featuring a selection of the group's finest moments. The band meanwhile underwent a dramatic line-up change with guitarist Glen Alvelais being given his marching orders again. Filling the absent spot was guitarist JAMES MURPHY once more and former SLAYER drummer DAVE LOMBARDO on the drumstool for 1999's 'The Gathering'. As it transpired Dette regained his position although this was predictably brief.

Late 1999 found further ructions within the band as Murphy and Dette were ousted in favour of Steve Jacobs and VICIOUS RUMOURS guitarist Steve Smyth. Murphy's removal signalled the beginning of a run of health-generated bad luck for the band. Apparently the guitarist had been acting out of character for some time prompting his dismissal. Only later, after extensive surgery to remove a brain tumour, was the cause of Murphy's behavioural problems revealed.

Smyth, DiGeorgio and Peterson have a side project named DRAGONHEART with SADUS drummer Jon Allen. DiGeorgio later joined ICED EARTH. This band switched titles to DRAGONLORD. Smyth also doubles duties appearing as 'Zakk Wylde' in the BLACK SABBATH tribute band SWEET LEAF in union with SKITZO frontman Lance Ozanik. Smyth would also contribute guitar to the SKITZO 1999 album 'Got Sick'.

By 2000 Alvelais was fronting LD/50, a band including bassist Oddie McLaughlin, drummer Jeremy Colson and ex-GEEZER vocalist Clark Brown.

On the TESTAMENT front news emerged in early 2001 that Chuck Billy had been diagnosed with cancer. The enigmatic singer got stuck straight into a regime of treatment to defeat the disease and was aided in spirit by the announcement of a benefit concert in his name dubbed 'Thrash Of The Titans'. The highly anticipated concert, held August 11th at the San Francisco Maritime Hall, pulled together many of the most notorious Thrash names such as HEATHEN, FLOTSAM & JETSAM, STORMTROOPERS OF DEATH, ANTHRAX, FORBIDDEN EVIL reformations of EXODUS, VIO-LENCE and DEATH ANGEL and even a reformation of LEGACY. A retrospective studio album of TESTAMENT classics was also began in earnest with former vocalist Steve Souza committed to guest on tracks.

Singles/EPs:
Trial By Fire / Nobody's Fault / Reign Of Terror, Atlantic A 9092 T (1988)

Albums:
THE LEGACY, Megaforce Atlantic 781 741-1 (1987)
Over The Wall / Haunting / Burnt Offerings / Raging Waters / Curse Of The Legions Of Death / First Strike Is Deadly / Do Or Die / Alone In The Dark / Apocalyptic City
LIVE AT EINDHOVEN, Megaforce Atlantic 780 226-1 (1987)
Over The Wall / Burnt Offerings / Do Or Die / Apocalyptic City / Reign Of Terror
THE NEW ORDER, Megaforce Atlantic 781 849-2 (1988) **49 SWEDEN, 81 UK**
Eerie Inhabitants / New Order / Trial By Fire / Into The Pit / Hypnosis / Disciples Of The Watch / Preacher / Day Of Reckoning / Musical Death (A Dirge)
PRACTICE WHAT YOU PREACH, Megaforce Atlantic WX 297CD (1989) **40 UK, 77 USA**
Practice What You Preach / Perilous Nation / Envy Time / Time Is Coming / Blessed In Contempt / Greenhouse Effect / Sins Of Omission / Ballad (A Song Of Hope) / Nightmare (Coming Back To You) / Confusion Fusion
SOULS OF BLACK, Megaforce Atlantic 7567821432 (1990) **35 UK, 73 USA**
Beginning Of The End / Face In The Sky / Falling Fast / Souls Of Black / Absence Of Light / Love To Hate / Malpractice / One Man's Fate / Legacy / Seven Days In May
THE RITUAL, East West 756782392-2 (1992) **48 UK. 55 USA**

Sermon / As The Seasons Grey / Ritual / Deadline / So Many Lies / Let Go Of My World / Agony / Troubled Dreams / Signs Of Chaos / Electric Crown / Return To Serenity
RETURN TO APOCALYPTIC CITY, WEA 756782392-2 (1993)
Over The Wall / So Many Lies / Disciples Of The Watch / Reign Of Terror / Return To Serenity
LOW, East West 7567 82645-2 (1994)
Low / Legions (In Hiding) / Hail Mary / Trail Of Tears / Shades Of War / PC / Dog Faced Gods / All I Could Bleed / Urotsukidoji / Chasing Fear / Ride / Last Call
LIVE AT THE FILLMORE, Music For Nations CDMFN 186 (1995)
The Preacher / Alone In The Dark / Burnt Offerings / Musical Death (A Dirge) / Eerie Inhabitants / The New Order / Low / Urgesukidoji / Into The Pit / Souls Of Black / Practice What You Preach / Apocalyptic City / Hail Mary / Dog Faced Gods / Return To Serenity / The Legacy / Trail Of Tears
DEMONIC, Music For Nations CDMFN 221 (1997)
Demonic Refusal / The Burning Times / Together As One / Jun-Jun / John Doe / Murky Waters / Hatreds Rise / Distorted Lives / New Eyes Of Old / Ten Thousand Thrones / Nostrovia
SIGNS OF CHAOS: THE BEST OF TESTAMENT, Mayhem 11120-2 (1998)
Signs Of Chaos / Electric Crown / The New Order / Alone In The Dark / Dog Faced Gods / Demonic Refusal / The Ballad / Souls Of Black / Trial By Fire / Low / Practice What You Preach / Over The Wall / The Legacy / Return To Serenity / Perilous Nation / Sails Of Charon / Draw The Line
THE GATHERING, USG 1033-2 (1999)
DNR / Down For Life / Eyes Of Wrath / True Believers / 3 Days In Darkness / LOTD / Careful What You Wish For / Riding The Snake / Allegiance / Sewn Shut Eyes / Fall Of Siple Dome

THANATOS (HOLLAND)
Line-Up: Stephen Gebedy (vocals / guitar), Mark Staffhorst (guitar), Erwin De Brouwer (bass), Remo Vonarnhem (drums)

Dutch Death-Thrash band THANATOS tend to stand out from the crowd with some inventive songs. The group debuted with a 1987 demo entitled 'The Day Before Tomorrow', notable for featuring the live track 'Progressive Destructor'. Following their album for Shark Records they released another demo in 1991 featuring five tracks before Shark came up with a second record in 1992.
THANATOS returned in 2000 with ex-

CREMATION guitarist Paul Baayens in the ranks for the 'Angelic Encounters' album.
<u>Albums:</u>
EMERGING FROM THE NETHERWORLDS, Shark 015 (1990)
Dawn Of The Dead / Outward Of The Inward / Bodily Dismemberment / Infernal Deceit / The Day Before Tomorrow / War / Rebirth / Progressive Destructor / Imposters Infiltration / Omnicoitor / Dolor Satanae
REALMS OF ECSTASY, Shark 025 (1992)
Intro - And Jesus Wept / Tied Up Sliced Up / Realm Of Ecstasy / Mankind's Afterbirth / In Praise Of Lust / Perpetual Misery / Human Combustion / Reincarnation / Terminal Breath
ANGELIC ENCOUNTERS, Hammerheart (2000)
Angelic Encounters / In Utter Darkness / Sincere Chainsaw / Salvation / Infuriated / The Howling / Gods Of War / The Devil's Concubine / Speed Kills / Thou Shall Rot / Corpse Grinder
BEYOND TERROR, (2002)

THRASHER (New York, NY, USA)
Line-Up: Brad Sinsel (vocals), Dan Beehler (vocals), Rhett Forrester (vocals), Maryann Scandiffio (vocals), Andy McDonald (guitar), Dan Spitz (guitar), Kenny Aaronson (bass), Gary Bordonaro (bass), Mars Cowling (bass), Billy Sheehan (bass), Gary Driscoll (drums), Carl Canedy (drums), Dickie Peterson (drums) James Rivera (drums)

The THRASHER project was put together by an assortment of New York based musicians upon the instigation of Combat Records.
Produced, directed and arranged by THE RODS drummer Carl Canedy in partnership with BLUE CHEER's guitarist Andy 'Duck' McDonald, the 'Burning At The Speed Of Light' album was issued in Britain through Music For Nations.
The majority of the material appeared to be sung by TKO vocalist Brad Sinsel, but the album also boasted lead performances from EXCITER's Dan Beehler, ex-RIOT man RHETT FORRESTER and BLACK LACE's Maryann Scandiffio.
Musicianship was supplied by the aforementioned Canedy and McDonald. Joining them were TALAS bassist Billy Sheehan, VIRGIN STEELE's Jack Starr, ANTHRAX's Dan Spitz, H.S.A.S. bassist Kenny Aaronson, PAT TRAVERS / FLYING HAT BAND associate Mars Cowling, SAVOY BROWN's Kim Simmonds, ex-ELF and RAINBOW drummer Gary Driscoll, HELSTAR's James Rivera, BLUE CHEER's Dickie Peterson and THE RODS bassist Gary

Bordonaro.

Albums:
BURNING AT THE SPEED OF LIGHT,
Music For Nations MFN 45 (1985)

THRASH QUEEN (USA)
Line-Up: Princess Die (vocals), Vikki Stone (guitar), Nikki Santos (bass), J.K. Johnson (drums)

Albums:
MANSLAYER, Landslyde (1985
THE QUEEN IS DEAD – GOD SAVE THE QUEEN, D.A.M. Landslyde (1987)

THRUST (Chicago, IL, USA)
Line-Up: John Bonata (vocals), Ron Cooke (guitar), C.B. Sebastian (guitar), Price Sowers (bass), Ross Cristao (drums)

The THRUST 'Fist Held High' album was re-issued by the German High Vaultage label in 1998 complete with five extra tracks.

Albums:
SOLIDARNOSEROCK, Erect (1982)
FIST HELD HIGH, Roadrunner RR9807 (1984)
Fist Held High / Overdrive / Freedom Fighters / Metallic Attack / Heavier Than Hell / Thrasher / Torture Chamber / Posers Will Die!

THRUSTER (USA)

Singles/EPs:
Back In Time / Excellorator, Thruster (1985)

TIANANMEN (AUSTRIA)
Line-Up: Christian Unger (vocals / bass), Andreas Kalaschek (guitar), Mirko Matkovits (drums)

An Austrian Thrash trio. The band has toured heavily supporting the likes of such diverse acts as TYKETTO, METAL CHURCH, HELLOWEEN, KROKUS and HYPOCRISY.

Singles/EPs:
The Tell Tale Heart / Are We To Blame / Screams Of Pain / Doomsayer, Tiananmen (1993) ('The First… To Throw The Stone' EP)

Albums:
TIANANMEN, Whorehouse WHO 10295 (1995)
Listen To Me / The Preacher / Waiting For Tomorrow / Changes / Homesick / Peace
THE IRONY OF FATE, Whorehouse WHO 10796 (1996)

Another Day / Irony Of Fate / Once Again / Circles / Drowning / Attitude / Neuland / Childish / Haunted / The Principle / The Days / Seconds New World / Humananimal / The Cage / Irony Of Fate... Revisited / The Preacher

TITAN FORCE (Denver, CO, USA)
Line-Up: Harry Conklin (vocals), Mario Flores (guitar), Bill Richardson (guitar / keyboards), John Flores (bass), Stefan Flores (drums)

Band formed by ex-JAG PANZER, SATAN'S HOST and RIOT vocalist Harry Conklin. The singer returned to JAG PANZER upon their reformation.
The Flores siblings created covers band HIP POCKET.

Albums:
TITAN FORCE, US Metal US017CD (1989)
Chase Your Dreams / Master Of Disguise / Lord Desire / Toll Of Pain / Will O' Wisp / Blaze Of Glory / Wings Of Rage / New Age Rebels / Fool On The Run
WINNER / **LOSER**, Shark SHARK 021CD (1991)
Fields Of Valor / Shadow Of A Promise / Winner/Loser / Face To Face / Eyes Of The Young / One And All / Small Price To Pay / Dreamscape

TORANAGA (UK)
Line-Up: Mark Duffy (vocals), Andy Mitchell (guitar), Andy Burton (bass), Steve Todd (drums)

Bradford based Thrashers TORANAGA formed in 1985 and benefited from the late '80s British Thrash upsurge.
Created with a line-up including ex-RIVAL bassist Andy Burton and erstwhile CHARGER drummer Steve Todd, vocalist Mark Duffy joined in February 1988 from MILLENNIUM.
The band's first product was the Kevin Ridley produced mini-album 'Bastard Ballads', but the band's progress was stifled by Peaceville's distributor Red Rhino going bust just as the album was released. Nevertheless, the record secured the band enough attention to warrant a 'Friday Rock Show' session and serious interest from Chrysalis A&R man Alistair Cunningham.
Confusion arose when Duffy lent his vocals to MAJOR THREAT for their 1988 demo under the pseudonym of Dark Murphy. Peaceville Records were none too pleased and TORANAGA had to issue a statement to the effect that Duffy was still a full time member of the band and had not joined MAJOR

THREAT.

In 1989 TORANAGA performed in Europe opening for VENOM in Holland and later for MANOWAR.

In 1993 Duffy formed the more industrial flavoured THE SEED releasing a demo in 1995. This band subsequently evolved into X-SEED issuing a 1996 album 'Desolation' through the Bleeding Hearts label.

Singles/EPs:
Eden - Beauty And The Beast / Eternity's End / Pleasure From Pain / Oh Well, Chrysalis (1991)

Albums:
BASTARD BALLADS, Peaceville VILE 5 (1988)
Sentenced / Dealers In Death / Bastard Ballad / Soldiers Be Brave / Time To Burn / Retribution
GOD'S GIFT, Chrysalis (1990)
The Shrine / Psychotic / Sword Of Damacles / Hammer To The Skull / Food Of The Gods / Disciples / Last Breath Of Life / Black Is The Mask

TORCH (SWEDEN)
Line-Up: Dan Dark (vocals), Chris J. First (guitar), Claus Wildt (guitar), Ian Greg (bass), Steve Streaker (drums)

TORCH were a powerful, traditional yet unrelentingly fast paced Metal act that garnered lots of praise in their time.
Guitarist Claus Wildt relocated to America to join MASI. Wildt's guitar partner Chris First and drummer Steve Streaker (real name Hakan Hedlund) are now ensconced in CRYSTAL PRIDE.
Vocalist Dan Dark (real name Östen Bidebo) later fronted a cover act titled BLÄÄSTERS.

Singles/EPs:
Bad Girls / The Serpent / Cut Throat Tactics, Record Pool MAXIPOOL001 (1983)

Albums:
FIRERAISER, Tandan TEP001 (1983)
Beyond / Fireraiser / Pain / Mercenary / Retribution
TORCH, Sword LP001 (1984)
Warlock / Beauty And The Beast / Watcher Of The Night / Rage Age / Beyond The Threshold Of Pain / Battle Axe / Hatchet Man / Sweet Desire / Sinister Eyes / Gladiator
ELEKTRIKISS, Sword LP004 (1985)
Thunderstruck / Elektrikiss / Hot On Your Heels / Runnin' Riot / Victims Love / Bad Girls / Cut Throat Tactics / When The Going

Gets Tough... / Limelight

TORMENT (GERMANY)
Line-Up: Jörn 'Kannixx' Rüter (vocals / bass), Carsten 'Tumanixx' Overbeck (guitar), Rudi 'Daswirdnixx' Olhanson (drums)

Hamburg's TORMENT underwent various line-up changes from their inception in 1984 and released two self-financed singles before signing to Steamhammer. The debut album includes a cover of MOTÖRHEAD's theme song 'Motorhead'.
TORMENT's 1999 album 'Not Dead Yet' saw another MOTÖRHEAD cover version with 'We Are The Road Crew' and a medley cover section of DEATH, VENOM and RAZOR songs.

Singles/EPs:
State Of Torment / Bestial Sex / Deaf Metal / Chainsaw Massacre / What Shall We Do With A Drunken Torment, Torment (1987)
Das Neue / Shop 'Til Ya Drop, Remedy RP 18 085 (1989)
Sie Kam Zu Mir Am Morgen, (1992) ('Blood in urine' coloured vinyl!!)

Albums:
EXPERIENCE A NEW DIMENSION OF FEAR, Steamhammer SPV 084-76332 (1991)
Intro / Acid Rain / Religious Insanity / Shop 'Til Ya Drop / Bestial Sex / Motörhead / Chainsaw Massacre / Drunken Torment / Cry For Justice / Slaves Of Technology / Das Neue / Crucifixion / Ballad Of Peter's Dog / State Of War / Liebe Freunde Von Torment
TORMENT, (1993) (Split LP with MINOTAUR & DESERT STORM)
SPERMATIZED, Hellion HELLI049 (1997)
We Still Die / I'm The Doctor / Laws Of The Street / What You Don't Know / Our Own Way / The Hammer / The Prophecy / Rollo Der Wikinger
NOT DEAD YET, Hellion HELLI0308 (1999)

TORTOISE CORPSE (UK)
Line-Up: Tony Calvert (vocals), Tim Hamill (guitar), Steve Hamill (bass), Ivan Hoe (drums)

A Welsh Thrash band that first came to attention with their 1988 three track demo 'Tally Ho', TORTOISE CORPSE originally had vocalist Tony Calvert also handling drums before the addition of the ludicrously named Ivan Hoe.

Albums:
WORLD'S GOT A PROBLEM, Tombstone CORPS LP001 (1991)

Atomic Attack / Visions Of Lust / In God's Name / World's Got A Problem / Psychotaff / Loony Toon (Wake Up Mad) / E.F.N.I.S.I.E.N. / I Fell In Love (W.W.S.) / Under The Blade / The Legacy
STANDARD OF MISERY, Communiqué CMG CD 012 (1998)

TORTURE (TX, USA)
Line-Up: Tom Hicks (vocals / guitar), J.D. Robins (guitar), Deric Gunter (bass), Jerry 'Gonzlaught' Norland (drums)

Albums:
TERROR KINGDOM, Beta (1987)
STORM ALERT, Core (1989)

TOURNIQUET
(Los Angeles, CA, USA)
Line-Up: Luke Easter (vocals), Aaron Guerra (guitar), Victor Macias (bass), Ted Kirkpatrick (drums)

Christian Progressive Thrash Metal band TOURNIQUET was founded by vocalist Greg Ritter, guitarist Greg Lanaire and drummer Ted Kirkpatrick. The band have developed from Speed Metal to a harsher, more abrasive style musically but have retained their trademark almost esoteric lyrical value. Although at first TOURNIQUET's message may seem rather obscure the lyrics are in fact always taken from biblical passages.
For their debut record Mark Lewis was on hand for extra guitarwork. Lewis, along with Erik Jan James, would appear on the band photograph on the album sleeve in order to present TOURNIQUET as more of a complete band and not just the actual trio that they were.
Guitarist Erik Mendez was drafted for TOURNIQUET's 1991 album 'Psycho Surgery', which included a cover version of TROUBLE's 'The Tempter'.
Ritter departed in 1993 as did Mendez. The live 1993 album saw a guesting Les Carlsen of BLOODGOOD fame sessioning lead vocals.
Luke Easter took the vocal reins for the 'Vanishing Lessons' album and subsequent touring found second guitar player Aaron Guera of FINAL NOTICE enrolled. Longstanding member Lenaire opted out in 1996 shortly after the release of the 'Collected Works' compilation.
Bassist Victor Macias felt compelled to leave TOURNIQUET for 'theological' reasons as the band's activities did not sit easy with his Russian orthodox religion. The band finally replaced him in December of 1997 with Vince Dennis, although by 1999 he too departed.

Latterly Ritter and Lenaire have reunited in a new act ECHO HOLLOW. A 2002 re-release of the debut 'Stop The Bleeding' album added both live and demo bonus tracks.

Albums:
STOP THE BLEEDING, Intense (1990)
The Test For Leprosy / Ready Or Not / Ark Of Suffering / Tears Of Korah / The Threshing Floor / You Get What You Pray For / Swarming Spirits / Whitewashed Tomb / Somnambulism / Virgin Widow And The Harlot Bride
PSYCHO SURGERY, Intense (1991)
Psycho Surgery / A Dog's Breakfast / Viento Borrascoso (Devastating Wind) / Vitals Fading / Spineless / Dysfunctional Domicile / Broken Chromosomes / Steotaxic Atrocities / Officium Defunctorum
PATHOGENIC OCULAR DISSONANCE, Metal Blade CDZORRO 63 (1991)
Impending Embolism / Pathogenic Ocular Dissonance / Phantom Limb / Ruminating Virulence / Spectrophobic Dementia / Gelatinous Tubercles Of Purulent Ossification / Incommensurate / Exoskeletons / Theodicy On Trial / Descent Into The Maelstrom / En Hakkore / The Skeezix Dilemma / The Tempter
INTENSE PRESENTS VOL. 2: TOURNIQUET LIVE, Intense (1993)
Phantom Limb / Medley: Ark Of Suffering - Stereotaxix Atrocities / Whitewashed Tomb / The Skeezix Dilemma / The Tempter / The Messiah
VANISHING LESSONS, Intense (1994)
Bearing Gruesome Cargo / Pecking Order / Drowning Machine / Pushin' Broom / Vanishing Lessons / My Promise / Acid Head / K517 / Twilight / Your Take / Sola Christus
CARRY THE WOUNDED, (1995)
Carry The Wounded / When The Love Is Right (To Lizett) / Oh Well / My Promise / Heads I Win, Tails You Loose
THE COLLECTED WORKS, Intense (1996)
Perfect Night For A Hanging / Vanishing Lessons / Pathogenic Ocular Dissonance / Twilight / Psycho Surgery / You Get What You Pray For / Acidhead / Broken Chromosomes / Viento Borrascoso / Carry The Wounded / Bearing Gruesome Cargo / The Skeezix Dilemma / Ark Of Suffering / The Hand Trembler
CRAWL TO CHINA, Benson (1997)
Claustrospelunker / Crawl To China / Enveloped In Python / White Knucklin' The Rosary / If I Was There / The Tell Tale Heart / Bats / Proprioception: The Line Knives Syndrome / Tire Kicking / If Pigs Could Fly / Crank (The Knife) / Stumblefoot / Imaginary Friend / Going, Going... Gone / America

ACOUSTIC ARCHIVES, (1998)
Viento Borrascoso / Vanishing Lessons / Claustrospelunker / Bearing Gruesome Cargo / Phantom Limb / Bats / Heads I Win, Tails You Lose / Twilight / If Pigs Could Fly / Trivializing The Momentous, Complicating The Obvious
MICROSCOPIC VIEW OF A TELESCOPIC REALM, Metal Blade 14289 (2000)
Besprinkled In Scarlet Horror / Drinking From The Poisoned Well / Microscopic View Of A Telescopic Realm / The Tomb Of Gilgamesh / Servant of The Bones / Erratic Palpitations Of The Human Spirit / Martyr's Pose / Immunity Vector / Indulgence By Proxy / Caixa De Raiva / The Skeezix Dilemma Part II (The Improbable Testimony Of The Pipsisewah)

TOXIC SHOCK (GERMANY)
Line-Up: Uwe Dießenbacher (vocals), Tim Atwater (guitar), Manuel Kriessig (guitar), Geoff Atwater (bass), Klaus Kreissig (drums)

A German Thrash act initially boasting the brotherly duo of Tim and Geoff Atwater, both had left the group after the release of the 'Change From Reality' album in 1988. Atwater later saw action with the Stuttgart act CHERRY RED.
Uwe Dießenbacher briefly combined bass and vocal duties before the band dispensed with his services altogether and drafted in Phillip Kneule (bass) and Kai Weber (vocals) as TOXIC SHOCK switched to Nuclear Blast for 1990's 'Welcome Home... Near Dark' album.
1992's 'Between Good And Evil' saw a further switch to Massacre and a heavier direction, TOXIC SHOCK now coming across as more of a Death Metal unit.

Albums:
CHANGE FROM REALITY, Mind Control (1988)
Breakout / Burning Down Your Life / Forbidden Lust / Mad Sounds / State Of Madness / Overloaded / Raging Speed / Left To Die / United Forces
WELCOME HOME... NEAR DARK, Nuclear Blast NB027 (1990)
Intro / Behind The Guillotine / Change From Reality / Dragon's Eye (The Story Part One) / World Power Rules / True Insanity / One End / Welcome Home... Near Dark (The Story Part Two) / Termination / The Challenge
BETWEEN GOOD AND EVIL, Massacre CD008 (1992)

TOXIK (New York, NY, USA)

Line-Up: Mike Sanders (vocals), Josh Christian (guitar), Brian Bobini (bass), Tad Legar (drums)

TOXIK added second guitarist John Donnely prior to beginning work on their second album, 'Think This', in Florida.
A few months later vocalist Mike Sanders was replaced by Charlie Sabin

Singles/EPs:
There Stood The Fence / Out On The Tiles, Roadracer (1989)

Albums:
WORLD CIRCUS, Roadrunner RR 349572 (1988)
Heart Attack / Social Overload / Pain And Misery / Voices / Door To Hell / World Circus / 47 Seconds Of Sanity / False Prophets / Haunted Earth / Victims
THINK THIS, Roadracer RO 94602 (1989)
Think This / Creed / Spontaneous / There Stood The Fence / Black And White / WIR NJN 8 (In God) / Machine Dream / Shotgun Logic / Time After Time / Technical Arrogance / Out On The Tiles

TOXIMA (New York, NY, USA)

Albums:
WAR, Kiva (1987)

TOXIN (GERMANY)
Line-Up: Frank Ungewickel (vocals / guitar), Andreas Wendel (vocals / bass), Jendrik Pieck (guitar), Michael Kramer (vocals / drums)

A German Thrash act, between the two albums TOXIN replaced drummer Jendrik Pieck with ex-ACCEPT drummer Stefan Kaufmann. The 1991 album 'Misanthropy' was produced by Heimi Mikus of RISK.
Kaufmann was to team up with U.D.O. in 1997.

Albums:
APHORISMS, Black Fantasy HM 201 (1989)
Dismembered Illusions / Aphorisms / The Prophecy / Land Of Despair / Lord Of The Flies / Daily Infernal
MISANTHROPHY, Black Fantasy NW 113 (1991)
Two Sided Existence / Misanthropy / Retrospective / Disintegration / Destructive Ways / Lust For Life / Two Wishes / Wings Of Death / XTC

TOXODETH (MEXICO)
Line-Up: Raul Guzman (guitar)

Albums:

MYSTERIES ABOUT LIFE AND DEATH,
Wild Rags WRE 903CD (1990)
Intro / The Beacon / Phantasm / Visit Of The
Dead / Doom Predictions / Graveyard /
Mausoleum / Seeing To Our Ages / Tale
From The Beyond

TRANSMETAL (MEXICO)
Line-Up: Mauricio Torres (vocals), Juan
Partida (guitar), Ernesto Torres (guitar),
Lorenzo Partida (bass), Javier Partida
(drums)

Centred upon the erstwhile TEMPLE DE
ACERO triumvirate of: Partida siblings
guitarist Juan, bassist Lorenzo and drummer
Javier, TRANSMETAL are amongst the very
biggest of Mexican Rock acts. This studs n'
leather bedecked band, founded during
January of 1987, have stuck to their Thrash /
Speed Metal stance over nearly twenty
Spanish language albums.
Upon their formation TRANSMETAL were
fronted by vocalist Alberto Pimentel who
featured on the 1988 debut 'Muerto En La
Cruz', produced by DARK ANGEL's Eric
Meyer, and the follow up 'Desear Un Funeral'.
In 1990 Pimentel departed to found
LEPROSSY. Alejandro Gonzales of
ILLUSION would fill the vacancy before Juan
Carlos Camaiena took the role of second
guitarist. The band featured on the high profile
'New Titans Over Mexico' tour of 1991 sharing
billing with SEPULTURA, SACRED REICH
and NAPALM DEATH. In May of 1992
TRANSMETAL appeared as part of the
'Mexican Mosh' festival alongside SICK OF IT
ALL, DEICIDE and NUCLEAR ASSAULT.
1992 witnessed the departure of these latest
two recruits and Alberto Pimental resumed
activities with the band on a stand in basis. A
successful Mexican tour during October
found TRANSMETAL headlining over
MORTUARY and INQUISIDOR. The band's
status would engender a further slot at the
March 1993 'Mexican Mosh' festival event,
this time sharing honours with OVERKILL,
KREATOR and MONSTROSITY among
others.
The following year TRANSMETAL, together
with fellow native acts ANGELS DE
INFIERNO and RATA BLANCA, represented
Mexico at the June 1994 'Monstruos De Rock'
gathering in Spain.
Pimentel would opt out yet again to forge
another version of LEPROSY (spelt with one
'S' on this occasion) assembling a new band
including RAMSES guitarist Julio Marquez
and ex-INQUISIDOR drummer Felipe
Chacon.
TRANSMETAL took onboard the esteemed

former LUZBEL and HUIZAR frontman Arturo
Huizar as their lead vocalist but by February
of 1998 two members of PANIC, vocalist
Mauricio Torres and guitarist 'Eric Towers'
(a.k.a. Ernesto Torres) stabilised the band.
Lorenzo Partida and ex-TRANSMETAL
vocalist Alejandro Gonzales would create the
side project ULTRATUMBA.
TRANSMETAL, armed with a new album
'Sadness De Lucifer', toured South America
during 2000.

Albums:
MUERTO EN LA CRUZ, Denver DCD 3058
(1988)
DESEAR UN FUNERAL, (1989)
SEPELIO EN EL MAR, Denver DSD 3039
(1990)
Desear Un Funeral / El Llamado De La
Muerte / Obscuridad Atroz / El Profanador /
Temor A La Cruz / Camino Al Cementerio /
Exhumado / Atormentado Del Cerebro /
Sepelio En El Mar
ZONA MUERTA, Denver DSD 3061 (1991)
Invasores / Toxico Industrial / Tus Dias Estan
Contados / Zona Muerta / Sufrimiento
Quimico / El Unico Oscuro / Prediccion
Terrestre / Mundo Quemado
AMANECER EN EL MAUSELEO, Denver
DSD 3060 (1992)
EN VIVO. VOL. 1, Denver DSD 3062 (1992)
EN VIVO. VOL. 2, Denver DSD 3063 (1992)
El Llamado De La Muerte / Killers / Tus Dias
Estan Contados / El Infierno De Dante /
Simon El Enterrador / Prediccion / Terrestre /
Atormentado Del Cerebro / Sufrimiento
Quimico / Zona Muerta
BURIAL AT SEA, Grindcore International
89804-2 (1992)
Wishing A Funeral / The Call Of Death /
Atrocious Obscurity / Profaner / Fear Of The
Cross / The Road To The Graveyard /
Exhumed / Tormented Brain / Burial At Sea
DANTE'S INFERNO, Denver DSD 3046
(1993)
Dante's Inferno / Abysmal Emptiness /
Flames Of Purification / Septic Veneration /
Magnificent Height / Hymn For Him / Damned
Pits / Mystichal Universe Stars / Re-
encounter With Beatriz / Last Day's Shadow
CHRONICAS DE DOLOR, (1994)
Subyugado / Aborrecer Al Forense /
Regodearse En La Gula / The Call Of The
Woman / Muerte Violenta / La Ley Del Talion
/ Deceso Espiritual / Transmetal
VELOZ Y DEVASTADOR METAL, (1995)
MEXICO BARBARO, (1996)
Mexico Barbaro / Dios Nos Agarre
Confesados / Arboleda De Ahorcados /
Llanto En El Paraiso / Poder Y Pudricion /
Angel Enfermo / Fariseos / Mito De La
Sangre / Miserable / Ceveline / Rio Rojo /

Elegiaco
EL LLAMADO DE LA HEMBRA, (1996)
El Llamado De La Hembra / Muerte Violenta / Toxico Industrial / Poder Y Pudricion / Angel Enfermo / Killers / Invasores / Elegiaco / El Infierno De Dante
LAS ALAS DEL EMPERADOR, J.S.C. Productions (1998)
Tumbas De Insomnio / Celdas De La Divinidad / Perpetua Monstruosidad / Iglesia Interior / XIII / Las Alas Del Emperador / Santisimo Sufrimiento / Cenizas Humanas / Sombras Del Purgatorio / Monarca De Los Sonambulos / Jardin Seco / Orgasmatron
DE BAJO DE LOS CIELOS PARPURA, Denver DSD 6106 (1999)
Debajo De Los Cielos Parpura / Replicante / Humanidad De Mairmol / Marcado Por El Demonio / Decorado Con Clavos / Glorificacian De La Fornicacian / Espantosa Enfermedad / Parricida / Clacinado Por Pecados / La Pas De Mi Dolor
SADNESS DE LUCIFER, Denver DSD 6186 (2000)

TRAUMA (San Francisco, CA, USA)
Line-Up: Donny Hillier (vocals), Michael Overton (guitar), Ross Alexander (guitar), Lucas Advincula (bass), Kris Gustofson (drums)

The band that spawned METALLICA's late bassist Cliff Burton, Bay Area outfit TRAUMA were signed to an album deal with Shrapnel Records for 1984's 'Scratch And Scream', the record appearing almost coincidentally with local rivals EXODUS' 'Bonded By Blood' debut.

Albums:
SCRATCH AND SCREAM, Shrapnel SH 1017 (1984)
The Day All Hell Broke Loose / Bringin' The House Down / I Kill For Less / Scratch And Scream / The Warlock / Lay Low / In The End / We Are Watching You / The Flight Of The Raven

TREPONAM PAL (FRANCE)
Line-Up: Marco Neves (vocals), Michael Bassin (guitar), Laurent B. (guitar), Stephane Cressend (bass), Didier Serbourdin (drums)

TREPONAM PAL were formed in 1986 as an Industrial band including samplers prior to the inclusion of twin guitarists Bassin and Laurent B. Earlier works proved to be in a no pretence Thrash Metal mould but the band would diversify with each successive release. The debut album (which included the spectacularly and bizarrely titled 'Soft Mouth

Vagina') was recorded without the services of Bassin due to his country's national service requirements.

For 1991's 'Aggravation' the band used the services of producer Roli Mossiman and in came new bassist Stephane Cressend and drummer Didier Serbourdin (although CELTIC FROST drummer Steve Priestly played on the album). 'Aggravation' is noted for including a bizarre cover of German Techno band KRAFTWERK's 'Radioactivity'. TREPONAM PAL toured Europe supporting YOUNG GODS, PRONG and GODFLESH and Bassin and Neves joined MINISTRY on a temporary basis in June 1992 for the American 'Lollapolooza' tour.

A third album arrived during 1993.

Singles/EPs:
Pushing You Too Far (Edit) / Pushing You Too Far (Tribal Mix) / Pushing You Too Far (Com Trance Mix), Roadrunner RR23816 (1994)

Albums:
TREPONAM PAL, Roadracer RO9456-2 (1989)
Silico / Embodiment Of Frustration / Prettiest Star / In Out / Low Man / Soft Mouth Vagina
AGGRAVATION, Roadracer RO 9332 (1991)
Rest Is A War / What Does It Mean / Love / Out With No Flag / Fugitive Soul / Sweet Coma / TV Matic / Radioactivity / You Got What You Deserve
EXCESS AND OVERDRIVE, Roadrunner RR 9076 (1993)
Out Of Reach / Push You Too Far / Excess And Overdrive / For Progress / Crimson Garden / Stoned On Your Hate / Nowhere Land / Blow Me Out / Sometimes / Full Moon / Excess Remix
HIGHER, Mercury 534 526-2 (1997)
Cyberfreak / Renegade / Unchained / The Struggle / Lose Control / Panorama / Freetribe / Funk Me / Sick Train / Belief / Sweet Vibes / Psycho Rising / Funky Town

TRIFFID (New York, NY, USA)
Line-Up: John Chiara (vocals), Alan Payette (guitar), Dan Farnach (bass), Joe Von Stetina (drums)

Albums:
INVASION, Neon (1985)
Inside Out / Jolly Roger / By The Light Of Love / Danger

TSUNAMI (San Jose, CA, USA)
Line-Up: Doug Denton (vocals), Tatsuya Miyazaki (guitar), Tomataka Yammoto (guitar), Max Load (bass), Scott Sherman (drums)

An intriguing San Jose Metal band that featured two Japanese guitarists. TSUNAMI certainly impressed with their debut album but seemed unable to capitalise on this initial momentum.

Vocalist Doug Denton quit in 1986.

The second album, 'Tough Under Fire' recorded for the German Intercord label, found Max Load (going under the name of Salvador Max?) as the sole survivor from the debut, the band being rounded out by new musicians comprising vocalist / guitarist Koshi Shioya ('K.O.'), guitarist Jamie Francis and drummer Steven Tsutsumi. However, shortly after this release TSUNAMI folded.

TSUNAMI apparently reformed of late with a line up of Max Load (now billed as 'Maximus Load'), Shioya and Tsutsumi.

Albums:

TSUNAMI, Universe / Music For Nations MFN 9 (1983)
TOUGH UNDER FIRE, Intercord (1990)
Lost In Motion / Same Old Thing / The Runaround / Tough Under Fire / Room Of Doom / Money / Love To Hurt You / Love & War / In The Rain / World Without Walls

TT QUICK (Osbornville, NJ, USA)
Line-Up: Mark Tornillo (vocals), David Dipietro (guitar), Walt Fortune (bass), Glenn Evans (drums)

A renowned force on the New York club scene TT QUICK impressed many and soon built up a sizable cult following. Guitarist David Dipietro's skills were especially singled out, as a guitar tutor the man had taught both ZAKK WYLDE of the OZZY OSBOURNE band and SKID ROW's Dave Sabo.

The opening 'TT Quick' mini-album featured a rendition of JOHN FOGERTY's 'Fortunate Son'.

As drummer Glen Evans joined NUCLEAR ASSAULT former HELLCATS man Erik Ferro replaced him for the 'Metal Of Honor' album, which surprisingly included a cover of the DAVE CLARK FIVE's 'Glad All Over'. Internationally, TT QUICK peaked with the crunching 'Metal Of Honor', the album landing many commendable reviews, wide ranging media coverage and healthy sales. Touring saw TT QUICK opening for such major acts as ACCEPT, METALLICA, MEGADETH, MOTORHEAD and IRON MAIDEN.

The band hit a major stumbling block when Ferro was forced out due to family illness. Unable to replace their drummer TT QUICK disbanded. Dipietro also later joined NUCLEAR ASSAULT.

TT QUICK would reform with the original line-up sporadically over the intervening years, these reunions resulting in the 1989 'Sloppy Seconds' album and the live 'Thrown Together Live' opus recorded in 1990.

The band, retaining the classic line-up, reformed on a permanent basis in 2000 for the tattoo themed 'Ink' album.

Albums:

TT QUICK, Avalanche MARZ 2002 (1984)
Go For The Throat / Fortunate Son / Child Of Sin / Metal Man / Victims
METAL OF HONOR, Megaforce / Island ILPS 9847 (1986)
Metal Of Honor / Front Burner / Hard As Rock / Child Of Sin / Asleep At The Wheel / Come Beat The Band / Hell To Pay / Queen Of The Scene / Glad All Over / Siren Song
SLOPPY SECONDS, Halycon 65431 (1989)
Eye Of The Storm / Deliver Me / Save Some For Me / Method Or Madness / Rock You Over / Isolation Booth / White Spots / Rule The World
THROWN TOGETHER LIVE, Halycon (1992)
Intro - Kickin' Ass & Talkin' Names / Metal Man / Eye Of The Storm / Asleep At The Wheel / Deliver Me / Front Burner / Isolation Booth / Child Of Sin / Beat The Band / Metal Of Honor / Go For The Throat
INK, Ocean (2000)
Ink / Subterrania / Whippin' Time / World On Display / Run / Age Of Treachery / Thick As Thieves / Stone Dirt Cowboy / Water Song / Back To The Bottom / Take A Lickin'

2 TON PREDATOR (SWEDEN)
Line-Up: Mogge (vocals), Petter Freed (guitar), Tobbe (bass), Mathias Borg (drums)

2 TON PREDATOR started life during 1993 billed as WEDGE. Founded by vocalist Mogge and bass player Tobbe WEDGE was soon brought up to strength the addition of two erstwhile MANIFEST musicians, guitarist Petter 'Mazza' Freed and drummer Mathias Borg. The same year the band cut an opening demo with Dan Swano of EDGE OF SANITY at the production helm.

WEDGE's career would be interrupted by the imprisonment of Mogge. However, the remaining band members stayed loyal and upon his release Mogge resumed his position. Changes would be afoot though as the group opted for a new title of 2 TON PREDATOR. A 1998 demo 'Burned '98' secured a deal with the Danish Diehard label resulting in the 1999 Tue Madsen produced 'In The Shallow Waters'. A second album 'Boogie' arrived in August of 2001 and 2 TON PREDATOR duly promoted its release with a European tour as guests to ENTOMBED and

CATHEDRAL during September.
Borg also plies his trade with a side band, the Punk Rock act GENOCIDE SUPERSTARS.

Albums:
IN THE SHALLOW WATERS, Diehard PCD-39 (1999)
Still Remains / Hole In My Mind / Burned / The Bitteraftertaste / From Her Eyes / Rage Out Of Silence / Backstabbed / Get Out / Some Way / Lynch Mob / How
BOOGIE, Diehard (2001)
Boogie / Duct Tape Story / Broken Bond / Pumpjack Pleasure / Hail From Sweden / Freak 2000 / Downright Evil / 4 Tongues Strong / Turning Point / September Flu / Last Boost / Empty Chambers

TYNATOR (Phoenix, AZ, USA)

TYNATOR was fronted by former STRATUM guitarist Steve Bashford.

Albums:
LIVING IN PAIN, CCG (1990)

TYRANNICIDE (CA, USA)
Line-Up: Jeff Hill (vocals / guitar), Tim Narducci (guitar), Rick Berry (bass), Mike Serafin (drums)

A Thrashcore act convened on Halloween 1984. TYRANNICIDE marked their arrival with a demo and an appearance on the 'Eastern Front' compilation album. Although receiving numerous label deals TYRANNICIDE opted to self release the 'God Save The Scene' album.
The band broke up in 1991 with guitarist Tim Narducci going on to SYSTEMATIC. The band recently reformed for a one off live gig.

Albums:
GOD SAVE THE SCENE, Bad Taste (1988)

TYRANNY (CA, USA)
Line-Up: Robert Mirabilio (vocals), J.P. (guitar), Serrate Dillon (bass), Matt Wolf Chazin (drums)

Albums:
MANIPULATOR, Canyon (1987)
Tyranny / Doctor Deceiver / Echo Away From Here / Skirt The World / Manipulator / Toxic Wastelands / Addict / Living Your Way / Fight For Freedom

TYRANT (GERMANY)
Line-Up: Kermit (vocals), Carl Tomaschko (guitar), Holgar Thiele (guitar), Andre Papack (bass), Micky Budde (drums)

A German Metal band, TYRANT were fronted by the hilariously named Kermit and issued a number of independent albums through the mid to late '80s.
For their fourth album, 'Ruling The World', TYRANT underwent a major line-up change by ditching a guitarist and their rhythm section. The band's new recruits were guitarist Phil Zanell, bassist Chris Peterson and drummer Dieter Behle.

Singles/EPs:
Wanna Make Love / Look Out, Tyrant (1984)

Albums:
MEAN MACHINE, Corona (1985)
Free For All / We Stay Free / Making Noise And Drinking Beer / I'm Ready / Wanna Make Love / Tyrant / Invaders / Grapes Of Wrath / Blondsuckin' Woman / Killer cat
FIGHT FOR YOUR LIFE, Scratch 941308 (1986)
Dark Eyes Of London / Up The Hammer / Fight For Your Life / Metal Rules / Streetfighter / Two Down One To Go / Goddess / Danger / Can't Stand Still / We Will Rock
RUNNING HOT, Scratch (1986)
Rock Your Bottom / Breakout / Taste Of Paradise / When The Raven Flies Again / Running Hot / Fire At Sea / Take The Most Dangerous Way / Get Ready / She's A Killer / Starlight
RULING THE WORLD, Scratch (1988)
Burn You / Blind Revolution / Set 'Em On Fire / Killing The Peace We Fall / Wild Cats / She Makes Me Hot (Hot) / Wild And Free / Ruling The World / Beat It / On The Wings Of Endless
LIVE & CRAZY, (1990)

TYRANT (Temple City, CA, USA)
Glen May (vocals), Rocky Rockwell (guitar), Greg May (bass), G. Stanley Burtis (drums)

Californian Power Thrash Metal act TYRANT was formed by bassist Greg May and vocalist Doug Anderson in Pasadena, California during. Previous to TYRANT guitarist Rocky Rockwell had operated the act VISIONS which included a pre-STRYPER Tim Gaines. By 1982 Anderson's position had been taken by Glen May.
TYRANT would then be approached by Brian Slagel of Metal Blade Records with a proposition to appear on the 'Metal Massacre III' compilation album. TYRANT duly accepted, submitting the impressive Bill Metoyer produced 'Battle Of Armageddon'. Response was such that Metal Blade signed the band up for a full album deal. Metoyer

would handle production duties for the group's debut 'Legions Of The Dead' album released in August of 1985. Another Metoyer crafted record, 'Too Late To Pray' with G. Stanley Burtis taking Roy's place on the drum stool, arrived the following year.

Reportedly TYRANT was offered support slots to acts of such weight as SLAYER, SAVATAGE and MERCYFUL FATE but apparently declined these offers.

The band would be put on ice for many years until interest was re-sparked with the 1994 CD re-issue of 'Metal Massacre III'. The German label Art Of Music snapped the band up and TYRANT duly delivered the 1996 comeback effort 'King Of Kings'. Both previous albums would also be re-issued but on the eve of promotional touring Rockwell backed out. The vacancy was filled by Anthony Romero, an ex-member of BLOODLUST.

TYRANT would commit further tracks to tape in 1997 as well as contributing songs to Dwell Records tribute albums to MOTÖRHEAD and BLACK SABBATH.

Albums:
LEGIONS OF THE DEAD, Roadrunner RR 9765 (1985)
TOO LATE TO PRAY, Roadrunner RR 9658 (1988)
Tyrants Revelation II / Too Late To Pray / Beyond The Grave / Valley Of Death / Nazarene / Bells Of Hades / Into The Flames / Babylon / Verdalack / Beginning Of The End / Eve Of Destruction
KING OF KINGS, Semaphore 60607 (1996)
Tyrant's Revelation III / King Of Kings / Fast Lane / Dance With The Devil / Ancient Fire / Nowhere To Run / When Night Falls / Tighten The Vice / Coast To Coast / War

TYRANT'S REIGN (IL, USA)

Line-Up: Randy Barron (vocals), Karl Miller (guitar), Chris Nelken (guitar), Phil Fouch (bass), Gabriel Anthony (drums)

TYRANT'S REIGN issued a solitary self-financed and now extremely rare mini-album. Guitarist Jeff Baghepour would make his exit just prior to recording of the album.

Vocalist Randy Barron was later to found WINTERKILL releasing the 1997 album 'A Feast For A Beggar'. Drummer Gabriel Anthony was to join MOTHERFUNK whilst guitarist Karl Miller plys his trade with PSYCHOSIS.

Ex-TYRANT's REIGN men guitarist Jeff Baghepour and bassist Phil Fouch would unite with Russ Barron (Randy's sibling), keyboard player Michelle O'Day and drummer

Donny Mizanira to found the Power Metal band PHOENIX RISING. This act, after a name change to CRYPTIC VISION, later recorded an album.

Albums:
YEAR OF THE TYRANT, Cynical (1987)
Tyrant's Reign / Jack The Ripper / Untamed / Deadly Eyes / Reign Of Terror / Fadeaway

TYSONDOG (UK)

Line-Up: Clutch Carruthers (vocals), Paul Burdis (guitar), Alan Hunter (guitar), Kevin Wynn (bass), Ged Wolf (drums).

Newcastle Heavy Metal band TYSONDOG amusingly took their name from the bassist's girlfriend's dog!

The band originally came together in 1982, although guitarist Alan Hunter left in mid 1984. Ged Wolf quit immediately after recording the debut album to team up with ATOMKRAFT and was replaced by Rob Walker.

Although 'Beware Of The Dog' was produced by Cronos of VENOM, the man himself proclaimed afterwards that he thought the band were "shit" and nothing more than JUDAS PRIEST imitators, stating that he had done it purely as a favour because Wolf was the brother of VENOM manager Eric Cook!

In early 1986 the band parted company with Clutch Carruthers and Hunter. TYSONDOG eventually split in early 1987 with Wynn teaming up with ex-TYGERS OF PAN TANG vocalist Jess Cox in TYGER TYGER.

Alan Hunter performed vocals on the third PARIAH album, recorded in 1993, which, until recently, remained unreleased. It would be issued under the SATAN band banner in 2000.

Singles/EPs:
Eat The Rich / Dead Meat, Neat NEAT 33 (1984)
Shoot To Kill / Changeling / Hammerhead / Back To The Bullet, Neat NEAT 46 (1985)
School's Out / Don't Let The Bastards Grind Ya Down / Back To The Bullet, Neat NEAT 56 (1986)
School's Out / Don't Let The Bastards Grind Ya Down, Neat NEAT 56 (1986) (7" single)

Albums:
BEWARE OF THE DOG, Neat NEAT 1017 (1985)
Hammerhead / Dog Soldiers / Demon / The Inquisitor / Dead Meat / Painted Heroes / Voice From The Grave / The Butcher / In The End

CRIMES OF INSANITY, Neat NEAT 1031
(1986)
Taste The Hate / Don't Let The Bastards
Grind Ya Down / Blood Money / The Machine
/ School's Out / Street Thunder / Hotter Than
Hell / Judgement Day / Eat The Rich /
Smack Attack

UNAUTHORISED
(HOLLAND)

Dutch Death Metal with strong Thrash overtones.

Albums:
BLACK SKY, (2001)
Bothered / Blacksky / Falling / Guilty As Charged / Confessions / Bulletproof

UNCLE SAM (Rochester, NY, USA)
Line-Up: David Gentner (vocals), Larry Miller (guitar), Bill Purol (bass), Jeff Mann (drums)

The Rochester, New York based Crossover act UNCLE SAM enjoyed the majority of their fame thanks to the release of their debut album 'Heaven Or Hollywood' in 1988.
Actually, if truth be told, it wasn't so much the record but the album cover that attracted attention to the group formed by guitar playing milkman Larry Miller. The cover depicted a razor handed, naked unidentified female seemingly about to transform an intimate part of her anatomy into what's known in the trade as a shaven haven.
The band had formed earlier as Garage Rock act THE ATTICS. When original drummer Tom Shippers left the fold to join IMMACULATE MARY the band pulled in drummer Glenn 'G. Avery' Brisk and switched titles to UNCLE SAM.
The line-up of the group that recorded the first album was completed by vocalist Scott Cessna, bassist David Gentner and drummer G. Avery Brisk.
UNCLE SAM grabbed tons of coverage in the likes of 'Kerrang!' with the debut, leading to a European deal with (ironically enough) Razor Records. The first album certainly made an impact, going on to sell over 10,000 copies. Touring saw Ron K. taking the drum role before Jeff Mann made the position more permanent.
In April 1989 Cessna was reported to have quit and was replaced on lead vocals by bassist David Gentner. Gentner's brother, Bill Purol, was enlisted to fill his shoes in the four string position!
UNCLE SAM's next album 'Letters From London' was preceded by a 7" single 'Whiskey Slick', the B side of which featured a cover version of LINK WRAY's 'Rumble'.
A third album, 'Fourteen Women... Fifteen Days', based upon the exploits of Rochester serial killer Arthur Shawcross, did not emerge until after the band's demise in 1993.
Gentner went on to form THE VEINS, re-recording UNCLE SAM's 'Fallout Shelter' from the last album.

Singles/EPs:
Whiskey Slick / Rumble, Skeller 3MT 12 (1990)

Albums:
HEAVEN OR HOLLYWOOD, Skeller 3M TA3 (1988)
Live For The Day / Don't Be Shy / Alice D. / No Reason Why / Candy Man / Don't You Ever / All Alone / Peace Of Mind, Piece Of Body / Under Sedation / Heaven Or Hollywood / Steppin' Stone / Train Kept A Rollin'
LETTERS FROM LONDON, Skeller UK 3M55 (1990)
Letters From London / Whiskey Slick / Dreams Of Money / Red Shirt / Stranger / Goodbye Mr Mary / Crystal / Ain't No Valentino / Room For One / Lexington Blues
FOURTEEN WOMEN... FIFTEEN DAYS, Communiqué CMGCD 010 (1993)
Long Gun / Stripped Of Innocence / Caretaker / Carnival Knowledge / Dirty & Co. / Your Hotel Or Mine / Draggin The Coffin / Every Grey / Fallout Shelter / Fourteen Women... Fifteen Days

UNGOD (GERMANY)
Line-Up: Infamist Of Tumulus (vocals), Ancient Blasphemic Grave Invocator (guitar), Angel Of Blasphemy (guitar)

A Black Metal act with plenty of old school Thrash influence to their sound. UNGOD made their presence felt with their 1993 demo tape titled 'Magicus Tallis Damnatio'. Following the debut album 'Circle Of The Seven Infernal Pacts' UNGOD released a brace of shared 7" singles combining forces with DESASTER and CABAL.
UNGOD issued a split album in 1997 shared with IMPENDING DOOM.

Singles/EPs:
Renaissance Of The Dark Arcade, Merciless (1995) (Split single with CABAL)
Split, Merciless (1995) (Split single with DESASTER)

Albums:
CIRCLE OF THE SEVEN INFERNAL PACTS, Merciless M.R. CD001 (1994)
Silence In The Golden Halls Of Endless Hope / Circle Of The Seven Infernal Pacts / Land Of Frozen Tears / Magicus Tulis Damnatio / Dark Winds Around The Throne Of Blood / Lost Beast Born In Darkness / A Journey Through Forgotten Myth / The Grotesque Vision Of A Dying Moon / Black Clouds Beyond The Fullmoon
CONQUERING WHAT ONCE WAS OURS,

Merciless (1997) (Split album with
IMPENDING DOOM)
I Am The Chaos / Firestorm, Ashes,
Genocide / Conquering What Once Was Ours
/ Via Reducta / Anatomy Of Human
Destructivity

THE UNHOLY
(Minneapolis, MN, USA)
Line-Up: Wade Laszlo (vocals / guitar), Chris
Magras (bass), Tom Croxton (drums)

THE UNHOLY was borne out of Wade
Laszlo's frustration with his then band
ACHERON. Following recording of
ACHERON's debut album 'Prophecies
Unholy' he split off to found THE UNHOLY in
1991 and was soon joined by other
ACHERON members bassist Mark Belliel on
bass and drummer Tom Croxton. For some
time THE UNHOLY's rhythm section would
share duties with both camps.
In 1992 Laszlo enlisted a fresh band
comprising bassist Chris Magras and
drummer John Ryan for the demo 'Darkness
Dawns'. Following the debut album 'Garden
Of Sorrows' Ryan exited and original member
Tom Croxton reassumed his old position.
In 1998 Croxton joined up with IMPALER
whilst retaining links to THE UNHOLY. He also
has a side project KREPITUS.

Albums:
GARDEN OF SORROWS, Kaleidoscope
(1995)
Rite Of Spring / Raven Of Dispersion /
Through My Hands / The Magician / Not
Heaven Borne / The Tempter / Feast Of The
Beast / Scyldings / History
TRINITY, Kaliedoscope (1997)
Hammer Of Thor / Lucifer's Flame / Jakarta /
13 / Aeon / Flawed / Wicca Rising
NIGHTSHADE, Scylding Music (1998)
Welcome To Hell / Night Of Time /
Somewhere East Of Paradise / Maggot /
Familiar / Lost Souls Lament / Succubus /
Two Hours / Benediction
AS ABOVE SO BELOW, Scylding Music
(1999)
Hammer Of Thor / Lucifer's Flame / Jakarta /
13 / Aeon / Flawed / Wicca Rising / Welcome
To Hell / Night Of Time / Somewhere East Of
Paradise / Maggot / Familiar / Lost Souls
Lament / Succubus / Two Hours /
Benediction
ASH WEDNESDAY, Scylding Music (1999)
Hexe / Bloody Earth / Osculam Infame /
Goddamned / Lion Of May / Heaven's Burning
/ The Portrait / The Pact / Shrine / Raven Of
Dispersion (Roots II Re-make)
THE DEVIL'S CUT, Scylding Music (2000)

UNITED (JAPAN)
Line-Up: Masatoshi Yuasa (vocals), Yoshifumi
Yoshida (guitar), Shingo Ohtani (guitar),
Akhiro Yokoyama (bass), Yusuke Nakamura
(drums)

Bay Area style Thrashers UNITED, named
after the JUDAS PRIEST anthem, was found
in 1981 and operated primarily as a JUDAS
PRIEST cover band for many years. The act
finally got around to releasing original
material with February 1985's 'Destroy Metal'
EP, capitalized on in December 1986 by a
further effort 'Beast Dominate'. UNITED
would also contribute the track 'Emergency
Dominate' to a compilation album.
The band would re-enlist a former member,
guitarist Shingo Ohtani, from his interim act
EMPEROR in 1990. During October of 1990
UNITED signed a deal with the Howling Bull
Entertainment label, the first fruits of which
was the 'Bloody But Unbowed' album.
The 'Beast Dominate '92' was issued up-front
of a support tour to American Metal band
LÄÄZ ROCKIT. Another album, 'Human Zoo',
would arrive the same year.
Such rapid progress would spark the interest
of the major labels and in 1994 UNITED
announced a signing with the JVC Victor
label. 'N.O.I.Q.', produced by Pat Regan,
emerged in 1995. SLAYER manager Rick
Sales would take an active part in managing
the band globally at this juncture. UNITED
would lend valuable support to MACHINE
HEAD's Japanese dates as 'N.O.I.Q.' saw an
American release through the Metal Blade
label. UNITED would travel to California to
perform their debut gig on American soil at
the Foundations Forum trade event. However,
longstanding vocalist Yoshiaki Furui parted
ways with the band toward the close of the
year.
In March of 1996 UNITED declared Furui's
replacement to be the striking dreadlocked
figure and exceptionally tall newcomer
Shinichi Inazu. By October UNITED was back
in America cutting a new album 'Reload' with
producer Vincent Wojno.
UNITED would maintain the partnership with
Wojno for 1998's 'Distorted Vision' album.
Promotion would include an appearance at
the Akasada Blitz 'Live Undead' Metal festival
headlined by SLAYER.
Drummer Hirokazu Uchino was forced out
due to health problems, but would soon be
back in action with the DUFFLES. The band
returned with 2001's 'Infectious Hazard'.
UNITED sported a new vocalist and drummer
in former DEATH FILE man Masatoshi Yuasa
and Yusuke Nakamura respectively.

U.N.I.T.E.D. / Skill / Sniper, NRR-E003 (1985) ('Destroy Metal' EP)
S.R.S. / Do You Wanna Die? / Holy Dive Screamer / Combat, NRR-E010 (1986) ('Beast Dominate' EP)
Reload / Burst / Revenger / Violence Jack / Sniper, JVC Victor VICP-60007 (1997)

Albums:
BLOODY BUT UNBOWED, Howling Bull HBR-F0001 (1991)
Sniper / Welcome To Amazing World / The Plague / Power Rage / Don't Trust / (It's So) Hard To Breathe / Take A Bite Of Crime / Suck Your Bone / Unavoidable Riot
BEAST DOMINATES '92, Howling Bull HBR-M0006 (1992)
S.R.S. / Do You Wanna Die? / Holy Dive Screamer / Combat / Ultra / Yesterday's Heroes
HUMAN ZOO, Howling Bull HBR-F0009 (1992)
Human Zoo / Violence Jack / Machinery Days / Jungle Land / False Majesty / The Sea Of Silence / Can't See The Silence / Over The Ocean / Brothers In Arms / Don't Let Peace Break Out
N.O.I.Q., JVC Victor VICP-5500 (1995)
Revenger / Bad Habit / Run Through The Night / Kill Yourself For Business / Hit Me / One More Card / Words In Disguise / Outta My Way / Obsession
BEST RARE TRACKS FROM UNDER GROUND, JVC Victor VICP-5522 (1995)
Combat / Don't Trust! / Machinery Days / S.R.S. / Welcome To Amazing World / Holy Dive Screamer / (It's So) Hard To Breathe / Jungle Land / Don't Let Peace Break Out / False Majesty / Unavoidable Riot / Human Zoo / Violence Jack
RELOAD, JVC Victor VICP 5821 (1997)
Untied / Skin-Deep / Shameless / Thrill Kill / Monkey Brains / Mourning / L.O.U. / Ex-Friend / Suicide? / Mata / Slave / Style
DISTORTED VISION, JVC Victor (1998)
Flash Back / Trust Yourself / Color / Who I Am / Sick & Angry / Locked Inside / So Damn Low / Tiger / Change
INFECTIOUS HAZARD, Howling Bull HWCA-1039 (2001)
Cross The Line / The Ruin Of A Memory / Temporary Insanity / Sonic Sublime / Blackened Lies / Mosh Crew / Solid Ground / Penetrate / Low Dealer / Distorted Vision

UNLEASHED (IL, USA)

Singles/EPs:
Unleashed EP, DKP (1987)

USURPER (Chicago, IL, USA)
Line-Up: Diabolical Slaughter (vocals), Rick 'Rigor' Scythe (guitar), Jon Necromancer (bass), Apocalyptic Warlord (drums)

Black Metal outfit USURPER, founded by former ARMAGEDDON members guitarist Rigor and vocalist Diabolical Slaughter, debuted with the 1994 demo 'Visions From The Gods'. Drummer Apocalyptic Warlord retired from the band in March 1996. Following a period with a temporary sticksman former FUNERAL NATION and DISINTER drummer Dave Chiarella joined the fold renaming himself Dave Hellstorm.
USURPER toured Europe with ENTHRONED, HECATE ENTHRONED and later as guests to CRADLE OF FILTH supporting their 2000 album 'Necronemesis'. The album included guest vocals from ABSU mentor Proscriptor McGovern.
For live work USURPER's sound was fattened out by former ETERNAL HATRED and HATE ETERNAL guitarist Carcass Chris. Strangely, this was the same individual USURPER had gone into a dispute with some years earlier when he had, according to some reports, claimed credits for work on earlier albums.

Albums:
DIABOLOSIS, Head Not Found (1997)
Hypnotic Void / Blood Passion / Fullmoon Harvest / Nulla Sallus Extra Eccelcium / Deep In The Forest / The Infernal Storm / Diabolosis / The Ruins Of Gomorrah
THRESHOLD OF THE USURPER, Necropolis (1998)
Necrocult Part I - The Metal War / Slavehammer / Black Funeral / The Dead Of Winter / Threshold Of The Usurper
SKELETAL SEASON, Necropolis NR032 (1999)
Shadowfiend / Dismal Wings Of Terror / Skeletal Season / Embrace Of The Dead / Prowling Death - The Demi Goddess / Cemetarian / Birmstone Fist / Wolflord
VISIONS FROM THE GODS, Necropolis NR051 CD (2000)
Soulstalker '96 / Deep In The Forest / Visions From The Gods / Dusk / Soulstalker (Original version) / Charon / Bonefire / Wolflord (Night Stalker version) / Blood Passion (Live)
NECRONEMESIS, Necropolis NR063 CD (2000)
The Incubus Breed / Slaughterstorm / In Remembrance / Necronemesis / 1666 AD / Warriors Of Iron And Rust / Deathwish / Full Metal Maelstrom / Funeral Waters / Into The Oblong Box

VADER (POLAND)
Line-Up: Piotr Wiwczarek (vocals / guitar), Jackie (bass), Docent (drums)

Polish Thrash band with intense drumming and unashamed reliance on esoterica as a staple of their subject matter, VADER came together in 1986 with a line-up of vocalist guitarist Peter, bassist Jackie and drummer Docent.

The band soon released their first demo tape, 'Necrolust', and this gained VADER a deal with Carnage Records. A deal was struck to subsequently distribute the 1990 demo 'Morbid Reich'. A 1991 demo featured the tracks 'The Final Massacre', 'Reign Carrion', 'Breath Of Centuries' and 'Vicious Circle'.

Upon the release of their debut album, 'The Ultimate Incantion', VADER toured Europe with BOLT-THROWER and GRAVE. Further dates in America followed with DEICIDE, SUFFOCATION and DISMEMBER.

'The Darkest Age - Live', which includes a cover of SLAYER's 'Hell Awaits', was recorded in front of a home crowd in Krakow. June 1995 found VADER out on the road in Europe once more touring alongside CRADLE OF FILTH, MALEVOLENT CREATION, OPPRESSOR, DISSECTION and SOLSTICE.

The 'Sothis' EP witnessed another cover, BLACK SABBATH's anthem 'Black Sabbath', as well as a complete reworking of VADER's 1989 track 'The Wrath'.

Having added DIES IRAE guitarist China to augment their live sound, VADER undertook a full European tour in the spring of 1996 as guests to CANNIBAL CORPSE. In 1996 Docent would unite with Cezar of CHRIST AGONY to found a Black Metal side venture MOON. Docent would appear on the first MOON album before relinquishing the role to concentrate on VADER.

The band would be joined by another DIES IRAE man, guitarist Mauser, during 1997.

Wiwczarek produced the debut album by fellow Poles DECAPITATED during 2000. VADER themselves headlined the European 'No Mercy' festivals alongside American' VITAL REMAINS, Brazilians REBAELLIUN and Germany's FLESHCRAWL.

Mauser would find the opportunity to re-activate the DIES IRAE name in 2000 drafting his VADER colleague Docent on drums, SCEPTIC guitarist Hiro and frontman Novy of DEVILYN. This new version of DIES IRAE entered the recording studio in June of 2000 with producer Szymon Czech for the debut 'Immolated' album

September of 2001 found VADER on the look out for a new bassist as previous occupant of the position Shambo had departed. They found their man with Simon, an ex member of HUNTER. The band would figure as part of the gargantuan European 'No Mercy' touring festival package in March and April of 2002. Also on the billing would be IMMORTAL, CATASTROPHIC, DESTROYER 666, HYPOCRISY, DISBELIEF, MALEVOLENT CREATION and OBSCENITY.

Singles/EPs:
Hymn To The Ancient Ones / Sothis / De Profundis / Vision And The Voice / The Wrath / R'Lyeh / Black Sabbath, Massive MASS 001 MCD (1995) ('Sothis' EP)

Albums:
THE ULTIMATE INCANTATION, Earache (1992)
Creation / Dark Age / Vicious Circle / The Crucified Ones / Final Massacre / Testimony / Reign Carrion / Chaos / One Step To Salvation / Demon's Wind / Decapitated Saints / Breath Of Centuries
THE DARKEST AGE - LIVE '93, Arctic Serenades SERE 007 (1994)
Macbeth (intro) / Dark Age / Vicious Circle / Crucified Ones / Demon's Wind / Decapitated Saints / From Beyond (Intro) / Chaos / Reign-Carrion / Testimony / Breath Of Centuries / Omen (Outro) / Hell Awaits
DE PROFUNDIS, System Shock IRC 067 (1995)
Silent Empire / An Act Of Darkness / Blood Of Kings / Incarnation / Sothis / Revolt / Of Moon, Blood, Dream And Me / Vision And The Voice / Reborn In Flames
FUTURE OF THE PAST, System Shock IRC 092 (1996)
Outbreak Of Evil / Flag Of Hate / Storm Of Stress / Death Metal / Fear Of Napalm / Merciless Death / Dethroned Emperor / Silent Scream / We Are The League / IFY / Black Sabbath
BLACK TO THE BLIND, Impact IR-C-104 (1997)
Heading For Internal Darkness / The Innermost Ambience / Carnal / Fractal Light / True Names / Beast Raping / Foetus God / The Red Passage / Distant Dream / Black To The Blind
KINGDOM, Metal Mind (1998)
Creatures Of Light And Darkness / Breath Of Centuries / Kingdom / Anamnesis / Inhuman (Disaster mix) / Quicksilver (Blood mix)
LIVE IN JAPAN, System Shock IRC 132-2 (1999)
Damien / Sothis / Distant Dream / Black To The Blind / Silent Empire / Blood Of Kings / Carnal / Red Passage / Panzerstoss / Reborn In Flames / Fractal Light / From

Beyond / Crucified Ones / Foetus God / Black Sabbath / Reign In Blood / Omen / Dark Age
LITANY, Metal Blade 14297 (2000)
Wings / The One Made Of Dreams / Xefer / Litany / Cold Demons / The Calling / North / Forward To Die!! / A World Of Hurt / The World Made Flesh / The Final Massacre
REIGN FOREVER WORLD, Metal Blade CD 076-103182 (2001)
Reign Forever World / Frozen Paths / Privilege Of The Gods / Total Disaster / Rapid Fire / Freezing Moon / North (Live) / Forwards To Die!! (Live) / Creatures Of Light And Darkness (Live) / Carnal (Live)

VAMPYR (GERMANY)
Line-Up: Wolfgang Schwarz (vocals), Ralf Hollmer (guitar), Ironhead Sterzik (guitar), Nil Conan Mayr (bass), Roman Sterzik (drums)

A German Heavy Metal act with plentiful Speed Metal influence.

Albums:
CRY OUT FOR METAL, Hot Blood (1985)
Oath / Sinner / Indianapolis / Hell Bent Angels / Scytherman / Mercy Killing / Metal Hymn '86 / Warrior / Breakin' Metal / Vampyr

V.A.R. (CZECH REPUBLIC)
Line-Up: Pavel Berger (vocals), Martin Smejc (guitar), Jan Brtko (guitar), Jiri Vycital (bass), Jan Janota (drums)

Czechs V.A.R. (VRATISLAVICE ALCOHOLIC ROAR) deal in pure unbridled Thrash Metal. The band, named after a famous Czech beer brand, have retained a stable line-up since their inception in 1989. V.A.R. debuted with a 1990 demo 'Nen Se Kam Skryt' followed by a further session 'Brutalni Chaos' the following year. The band also featured with two songs on the Monitor label compilation 'Ultrametal'.
The release of V.A.R.'s inaugural album was delayed when the band suffered a major car accident. The group would all recuperate though and 'Personal Destruction' arrived in 1992. The album included a spoof on HELLOWEEN with the track 'Keeper Of The Seven Beers'.
The 1999 album 'Under Water' included Czech vocal versions of tracks by KISS, BLACK SABBATH and R&B Rockers DR. FEELGOOD.

Albums:
PERSONAL DESTRUCTION, Monitor (1992)
Brutální Chaos / Sebevra_da / Není Se Kam Skr_t / Krvav_ K_eft / Prdel Evropy / Konec

Svìta / Èeská Tragédie / Vratislav / Bez Tváøe / PodivnejJ_ivot / Útik Do Tmy / Nov_ M_tus / Moje Stará Je Dìvka / Proti Vizím / Keeper Of The Seven Beers / Káèulovo zrození
DEPENDENCE, Taga (1995)
Závislost Gama / Projdi Svou Zdí / Agent 00 / Je Po V_em / Lítáme Jak Spla_en_ / Mocná Síla / Dech Mrtv_ Milenky / Kamsto_láps? / Otrava / Kremace / Pár Slov / Vratislav (Techno remix)
UNDER WATER, 1K (1999)
Jednou Nás Sejmou / Zpátky K Stádu / Kù_ièka Století / Tango Na _iletkách / Requiem Pro Praseèí Hlavu / Pod Vodou / Mezitro / Poslední Sen 2 / Ba_ina / Kosmodrom Rostock / Dítì Temnot / Madìra

VECTOM (GERMANY)
Line-Up: Christian Buchner (vocals), Horat Gutz (guitar), Steafan Kroll (guitar), Ralf Simon (bass), Wolfgang Sonhutter (drums)

Considered to be one of the most brutal Metal bands to have risen from Germany, VECTOM offered fast, uncompromising Thrash.

Albums:
SPEED REVOLUTION, Hot Blood 941317 (1986)
Speed Revolution / In Nomine Satanas / Damned Love / The Exterminator / Loudness And Speed / Black Viper / Day Of Execution / Open The Coffin / Satan's Colours / Too Fast For Hell
RULES OF MYSTERY, Scratchcore 805 034 (1986)
Der Anfang / Prisoner's Back / Dipsomania / Metallic War / Why Am I Alive? / Outlaw / Feelings Of Freedom / Caught By Insanity / Evil Run / This Is The End

VEIL (GERMANY)
Line-Up: Raoul, Nils, Jens, Flo

A Hannover Thrash Act with Hardcore influences created in 1994. Toured Europe as support to BIOHAZARD prior to 1998's 'Words Vs Nothing' album.

Singles/EPs:
No One / Everyday, Threesome (1996)

Albums:
THE BURDON OF LIFE, Frontline Front 02 CD (1996)
Tomorrow / No One / The Stand / Seclusion / In This World / Insanity / Everyday / Bury / In Vain
VEIL, Lifeforce (1997)
WORDS VS. NOTHING, Kingfisher 008-2

(1998)
Intro / Heal / 9 To 5 / Without A Name / Place To Be / Shell / Another Wall / In Offence / Hold / The Last Facade / Gain / Stand To Fall

VENDETTA (GERMANY)
Line-Up: Daxx Homerlein (vocals / guitar), Micky (guitar), Klaus 'Heiner' Ullrich (bass), Samson (drums)

An unpretentious Thrash Metal mob, VENDETTA supported both HELSTAR and TANKARD on the back of the Harris Johns produced debut album 'Go And Live... Stay And Die'.
VENDETTA reformed in 1998. In 2002 the band was citing a line-up of Daxx and Heiner alongside vocalist Mario, guitarist Frank and drummer Thomas 'Lubber'.

Albums:
GO AND LIVE... STAY AND DIE, Noise N0102-1 (1988)
Suicidal Lunacy / Go And Live... Stay And Die / Traitor's Fate / System Of Death / Drugs And Corruption / Revolution Command / On The Road
BRAIN DAMAGE, Noise NUK 121 (1989)
War / Brain Damage / Conversation / Precious Existence / Never Die / Love Song / Fade To Insanity / Dominance Of Violence / Metal Law

VENGEANCE (CA, USA)

Singles/EPs:
Way Past Go / Driving Force, Mystic (1983)

Albums:
VENGEANCE, Azra (1986)

VENGEANCE RISING
(Los Angeles, CA, USA)
Line-Up: Roger Martinez (vocals / guitar), Jamie Mitchell (guitar), Joe Monsorb'nik (bass), Jonny Vasquez (drums)

Although one of the leading lights of the Christian Death-Thrash Metal scene for a lengthy period VENGEANCE RISING would become embroiled in bitter recriminations as vocalist Roger Martinez, now solo, has reportedly disowned his previous beliefs. Martinez, who is reported to be planning another anti-Christian VENGEANCE RISING album to be titled 'Realms Of Blasphemy' as well as an exposé treatise 'The Lixivium Letters', claims to have been duped into believing in and promoting God.
The band was created in 1985 by former SACRIFICE members along with guitarists Larry Farkas and Doug Thieme and drummer Glenn Mancaruso. Martinez, previously with PROPHET, was enrolled as singer the following year. The band was initially billed as VENGEANCE but another act of the same name was discovered. The album sleeves, which featured a close up of a nailed crucified hand - actually that of Pastor Bob Beeman, for the Caesar Kalinowski produced debut 'Human Sacrifice' had to be reprinted with the new logo.
Following the 1990 Ron Goudie produced 'Once Dead' album promotional tour the band splintered. Only Martinez remained to carry on with the name as Farkas, Mancaruso and bassist Roger Dale Martin all quit. Martin founded Biker Blues band TRIPLE ACE whilst the others created DIE HAPPY.
Meantime Martinez enrolled guitarist Derek Sean and drummer Chris Hyde of DELIVERANCE for the 'Destruction Comes' opus.
For the 1992 'Released From The Earth' album Martinez employed guitarist Jamie Mitchell, bass player Joe Monsrb'nik and drummer Jonny Vasquez. Backing vocals came courtesy of MORTIFICATION's Steve Rowe, TOURNIQUET men Victor Marcios and David Vasquez and Jimmy Brown of DELIVERANCE (the latter under the pseudonym of 'Simon Dawg'). Jonny Vasquez would then join MORTIFICATION for touring.
Touring upon the album release saw DELIVERANCE guitarist George Ochoa as live guitarist. Apparently upon completion of these dates, sometime between 1995 and 1997, Martinez became an atheist.
Undeterred by the scandal Christian Deathsters ULTIMATUM would cover 'Burn' for their third album 'The Mechanics Of Perilous Times'.
Martinez has been hinting at a new VENGEANCE RISING album 'Realms Of Blasphemy' for many years now but this has still yet to see the light of day. The VENGEANCE RISING website does offer a free album to American military personnel. Needless to say VENGEANCE RISING remains a hot topic of debate on the Christian music scene to this day.

Albums:
HUMAN SACRIFICE, Intense SSR 8115 (1989)
Human Sacrifice / Burn / Mulligan Stew / Receive Him / I Love Hating Evil / Fatal Delay / White Throne / Salvation / From The Dead / Ascension / He Is God / Fill This Place With Blood / Beheaded
ONCE DEAD, Intense (1990)
Warfare / Can't Get Out / Cut Into Pieces /

Frontal Lobotomy / Herod's Violent Death / The Whipping Post / Arise / Space Truck'in / Out Of The Will / The Wrath To Come / Into The Abyss / Among The Dead / Interruption
DESTRUCTION COMES, Intense (1991)
You Can't Stop It / The Rising / Before The Time / The Sword / He Don't Own Nothing / Countless Corpses / Thanatos / You Will Bow / Hyde Under Pressure / Raeqoul
RELEASED UPON THE EARTH, Intense (1992)
Help Me / The Damnation Of Judas And The Salvation Of The Thief / Released Upon The Earth / Human Dark Potential / Instruments Of Death / Lest You Be Judged / Out Of Bounds / Bishop Of Souls / Tion / You Will Be Hated
ANTHOLOGY, Intense (1993)

VENOM (UK)

Line-Up: Cronos (vocals / bass), Mantas (guitars), Abaddon (drums)

The Black Metal band that unwittingly inspired a plethora of imitators as part of the growing '80s extreme Metal scene in Europe and America. Newcastle trio VENOM was initially discounted for their early albums, although these records were later to be declared classics of the genre, in spite of their primitive approach.

VENOM's roots lay in the Newcastle late '70s acts GUILLOTINE, ALBUM GRACIA, OBERON and DWARFSTAR. In 1978 Lant was guitarist with ALBUM GRACIA. Members from this band including vocalist Keith Ballard and drummer Kevin Robson decamped to found a new act the same year entitled DWARFSTAR. Meantime another local band GUILLOTINE, featuring guitarist Jeffrey Dunn retitled themselves VENOM in 1979. The inaugural line-up of this group being Dunn, vocalist Dave Blackman, second guitarist Dave Rutherford, bassist Dean Hewitt and drummer Chris Mercaters. Both Blackman and Mercater lost their places in August of that year to former OBERON members drummer Tony Bray and singer Clive Archer. OBERON would play a further part in VENOM's later career when guitarist Eric Cook would wind up as manager of the band. The new look VENOM, also with a fresh bassist Alan Winston, were to pull in Lant as replacement for Rutherford in November. However, mere days before the band's debut gig in Wallsend Winston bailed out forcing Lant to take over the bassist's role. This he did by necessity plugging a bass guitar into a lead guitar amp.

By 1980 the proto-VENOM had decided upon the satanic image, rechristening the band members in suitable fashion. Archer became 'Jesus Christe', Lant 'Mr. Cronos', Bray 'Abbadon' and Dunn "Mantas". A three song demo was cut in April featuring early work outs of 'Angel Dust', 'Raise The Dead' and 'Red Light Fever'. A second session, recorded for a miserly £50, laid down six more tracks with Lant taking lead vocals for 'Live Like An Angel'. Archer packed his bags soon after and the unholy triumvirate of VENOM was born.

The band adopted the position of marrying Lant's Punk influences with direct inspiration from some of the global Rock giants. In early interviews the band professed the desire to have the energy of JUDAS PRIEST with the theatrics of KISS.

Having, naturally, been signed by Neat Records VENOM debuted in 1980 with the 'In League With Satan' single and immediately came to the attention of 'Sounds' journalist Geoff Barton.

Barton's championing of the group certainly brought VENOM to the attention of the Metal loving public, although the trio had yet to play a gig.

1981 summoned the group's first album, 'Welcome To Hell', followed in 1982 by the seminal 'Black Metal' set.

VENOM's third album found the Geordie triumvirate of Metal taking huge strides forward, especially abroad, as the semi-conceptual 'At War With Satan' hugely increased the band's following.

VENOM's first European live date came in Belgium (the group's initial live performance having ensured they would never play a club again as the event was marked by a handmade stage prop falling over and firing pyrotechnics into the audience!) where they headlined above PICTURE and ACID. It was only on the continent where the band were able to translate their mystique into material success with a series of major festival appearances and tours (including a trek through Europe in 1984 with METALLICA as the support act!) VENOM were virtually shunned by the UK audience where a succession of announced tours were scrapped, although the 'Seventh Date Of Hell' video did arise from the group's spectacular debut at Hammersmith Odeon in London on the 'At War With Satan' tour.

Before going in to record fourth album 'Possessed', Cronos produced fellow Neat label act TYSONDOG's first album, although somewhat bizarrely he then announced to the world that it was 'shit'!

1985 began disastrously for the band. The 'Possessed' album was roundly chastised and a planned Canadian/American tour was thrown into turmoil as Mantas succumbed to glandular fever. The dates were put back and, as his health worsened, VENOM recruited

AVENGER guitarist Les Cheetham and FIST guitarist Dave Irwin to fill the shoes of Mantas. The band's New York Studio 54 show (with EXODUS and SLAYER), their most prestigious date on the tour, was less than successful as Mantas, now with restored health, was denied access to America due to passport problems.

1986 saw the departure of the guitarist following American dates with support act HIRAX. Mantas resurfaced shortly after with his own MANTAS project that issued one album, but he soon retired to concentrate on building up a martial arts centre. Cronos busied himself producing the 1986 album from WARFARE 'Mayhem Fucking Mayhem'.

Mantas was to be replaced by two guitarists, Jimmy C. and Mike H., who performed their debut live shows with VENOM touring Brazil with support act EXODUS.

This new line-up recorded the lukewarm Nick Tauber / Kevin Ridley produced 'Calm Before The Storm' for RCA subsidiary Filmtrax. The album saw the band endeavouring to pursue a more finely crafted, mature approach rather than the bludgeoning ferocity of yore, but merely succeeded in alienating existing fans.

In 1988 Mantas appeared again, this time as guest guitarist on WARFARE's 'A Conflict Of Hatred' album.

Cronos quit in 1989 to form CRONOS with ex-VENOM members. VENOM regrouped once more in 1989, enticing original guitarist Mantas back into the fold alongside the drumming lynchpin of Abaddon, bassist / vocalist Tony Dolan and rhythm guitarist Al Barnes.

Barnes had worked previously with Mantas on his solo album 'Winds Of Change', whilst Dolan was ex-ATOMKRAFT. This line-up debuted with 'Prime Evil', once more produced by Tauber and Ridley.

VENOM took to the UK stages again in late 1989, billed under the pseudonym of SONS OF SATAN which included a "secret" London Marquee gig which attracted only a handful of followers giving ample indication as to the apathy towards the band in their home country.

Their 1990 album 'Tear Your Soul Apart' featured Mantas, Abaddon and Dolan and included a bizarre cover of JUDAS PRIEST's 'Hell Bent For Leather' classic. Dolan quit, citing Abaddon's claims in the press linking VENOM with Satanism as the main reason.

In 1994 a VENOM tribute album featuring such acts as PARADISE LOST and ANATHEMA was released. Cronos also came out of the shadows, lending backing vocals to rising UK Black Metal band CRADLE OF FILTH's 'Dusk And Her Dark Embrace' album. Meanwhile ex-VENOM guitarist Mike Hickey teamed up with arch goremongers CARCASS in 1994, would later form part of CRONOS and also performed bass duties for CATHEDRAL. Latterly Hickey, now dubbed 'Mykas Lord Of Metal', operates GOATREIGN.

Following no less than three years of negotiations, the original band line-up reformed in 1995, to nothing less than ecstatic European media response, to headline the 'Eindhoven Waldrock' and 'Eindhoven Dynamo' festivals.

During the latter event VENOM used so much pyro that one particular blast proved so powerful the band's backdrop came to rest over the drumkit midway through the set! An edited form of this show was released as the video / CD package 'The Second Coming'.

VENOM spent a large chunk of 1997 recording their ninth studio album, 'Cast In Stone', only interrupting proceedings to headline the 'Metal Invader Festival' in Athens, Greece.

The protracted nature of the recording was to be drawn out even further when, upon nearing completion, the band actually scrapped all previous efforts, opting to re-record the entire body of work.

Upon eventual release, initial copies of 'Cast In Stone' came with recent re-recordings of VENOM classics from the early days.

VENOM made a return to America in '97 headlining the notorious 'Milwaukee Metalfest', but end of year European dates supported by HAMMERFALL were cancelled due to Cronos having to undergo surgery for vocal nodes.

The 2000 Charlie Bauerfiend produced VENOM album 'Resurrection' saw Abbadon, who issued a somewhat bizarre industrial solo album 'I Am Legion', replaced by Antton. The band put in two bombastic showings at European festivals prior, In time honoured fashion, to canceling remaining dates.

Cronos would contribute guest vocals to FOO FIGHTERS man Dave Grohl's Metal elite PROBOT project album of 2001.

During early 2002 famed Virginian Heavy Metal band DECEASED would cover both 'Black Metal' and 'Die Hard' on their 'Zombie Hymns' album.

Singles/EPs:
In League With Satan / Live Like An Angel (Die Like A Devil), Neat NEAT 08 (1980)
Bloodlust / In Nomine Satanas, Neat NEAT 13 (1981)
Die Hard / Acid Queen / Burning Out, Neat NEAT 27 12 (1983) (12" single)
Die Hard / Acid Queen, Neat NEAT 27 (1983) (7" single)
Warhead / Lady Lust, Neat NEAT 38 (1984)

(7" single, released in three different sleeves)
Warhead / Lady Lust / The Seven Gates Of Hell, Neat 38 12 (1984) (12" single)
Manitou / Woman / Dead Of The Night, Neat NEAT 43 12 (1984) (12" single)
Manitou / Woman, Neat NEAT 43 (1984) (7" single)
Nightmare / Satanarchist / FOAD / Warhead (Live), Neat NEAT 47 12 (1985) (12" single)
Nightmare / Satanarchist, Neat NEAT 47 (1985) (7" single)
Witching Hour (Live) / Teacher's Pet (Live) / Poison (Live) / Teacher's Pet (Live), Neat NEAT 53-12 (1985) ('Hell At Hammersmith' EP)
Skool Daze / Bursting Out / The Ark / Civilized / Angel Dust / Hellbent (Live), Under One Flag MFLAG 50 (1990) ('Tear Your Soul Apart' EP)
7 Gates Of Hell / Welcome To Hell / In Nomine Satanas / Black Metal / The Evil One (New '96 track), Venom (1996) ('Venom '96' EP)
In Nomine Satanas, 2956 (1999) (Green vinyl 6" single. Russian release)
Schizo, 2934 (1999) (Brown vinyl 6" single. Russian release)
1000 Days In Sodom, 3064 (1999) (Blue vinyl 6" single. Russian release)
To Hell / Women, Leather And Hell, 3211 (1999) (Yellow vinyl 6" single. Russian release)
To Hell / Aarrrggh, 3224 (1999) (Red vinyl 6" single. Russian release)
The Other New One, 4016 (1999) (Yellow vinyl 6" single. Russian release)
Welcome To Hell, 4415 (1999) (Red vinyl 6" single. Russian release)
Satanachist, 4418 (1999) (Green vinyl 6" single. Russian release)
Under A Spell, 4462 (1999) (Clear vinyl 6" single. Russian release)
Muscle, 4466 (1999) (Blue vinyl 6" single. Russian release)
Dominus Mundi, 4537 (1999) (Clear vinyl 6" single. Russian release)
Kings Of Evil, 4542 (1999) (Green vinyl 6" single. Russian release)
Mortals, 4543 (1999) (Blue vinyl 6" single. Russian release)

Albums:
WELCOME TO HELL, Neat NEAT 1002 (1981)
Sons Of Satan / Welcome To Hell / Schizo / Mayhem With Mercy / Poison / Live Like An Angel / Witching Hour / One Thousand Days In Sodom / Angel Dust / In League With Satan / Red Light Fever
BLACK METAL, Neat NEAT 1005 (1982)
Black Metal / To Hell And Back / Buried Alive / Raise The Dead / Teacher's Pet / Leave Me

In Hell / Sacrifice / Heaven's On Fire / Countess Bathory / Don't Burn The Witch / At War With Satan (Preview)
AT WAR WITH SATAN, Neat NEAT 1015 (1984) **48 SWEDEN, 64 UK**
At War With Satan / Rip Ride / Genocide / Cry Wolf / Stand Up And Be Counted / Women, Leather And Hell / Aaaaarghhhh
POSSESSED, Neat NEAT 1024 (1985)
99 UK
Moonshine / Harmony Drive / Wing And A Prayer / Voyeur / Satanarchist / Mystique / Possessed / Suffer Not The Children / Hellchild / Fly Trap / Powerdrive / Too Loud For The Crowd / Burn This Place To The Ground
AMERICAN ASSAULT, Combat (1985) (USA release)
Rip Ride / Bursting Out / Dead Of The Night / The Seven Gates Of Hell (Live) / Countess Bathory (Live) / Welcome To Hell (Live)
CANADIAN ASSAULT, Banzai (1985) (Canadian release)
Die Hard (Live) / Welcome To Hell (Live) / In Nomine Satanas (Live) / Warhead / Woman / The Seven Gates Of Hell
FRENCH ASSAULT, Now (1985) (French release)
Nightmare / Bloodlust / In Nomine Satanas / Countess Bathory (Live) / Powerdrive / Bursting Out
SCANDINAVIAN ASSAULT, Neat (1985)
Nightmare (Live) / Too Loud (For The Crowd) (Live) / Die Hard (Live) / Bloodlust / Powerdrive / Warhead
JAPANESE ASSAULT, VAP R 35177 25 (1985) (Japanese release)
In League With Satan / Live Like An Angel (Die LLike A Devil) / Bloodlust / In Nomine Satanas / Die Hard / Witching Hour (Live) / Bursting Out / Warhead / Manitou / Dead Of The Night / The Seven Gates Of Hell
EINE KLEINE NACHTMUSIK, Neat NEAT 1032 (1986)
Too Loud For The Crowd / Seven Gates Of Hell / Leave Me In Hell / Nightmare / Countess Bathory / Die Hard / Schitzo / In Nomine Satanas / Witching Hour / Black Metal / The Chanting Of The Priests / Satanarchist / Fly Trap / Warhead / Buried Alive / Love Amongst The Dead / Welcome To Hell / Bloodlust
OBSCENE MIRACLE, Demon APKPD 12 (1986)
FROM HELL TO THE UNKNOWN, Rawpower (1986)
Sons Of Satan / Welcome To Hell / Schizo / Mayhem With Mercy / Poison / Live Like An Angel (Die Like A Devil) / Witching Hour / 1000 Days In Sodom / Angel Dust / In League With Satan / Red Light Fever / Bursting Out / At War With Satan

(Introduction) / Die Hard (Live) / Manitou / Senile Decay / Black Metal / Possessed / The Seven Gates Of Hell (Live) / Buried Alive / Too Loud (For The Crowd) / Radio Interview

THE SINGLES '80 - '86, Rawpower LP024 (1986)
In League With Satan / Live Like An Angel, Die Like A Devil / Blood Lust / In Nomine Satanas / Die Hard / Acid Queen / Busting Out / Warhead / Lady Lust / Seven Gates Of Hell / Manitou / Dead Of Night

SPEED REVOLUTION, Powerstation 941317 (1986)

GERMAN ASSAULT, Roadrunner RR9659 (1987)
Nightmare / Black Metal / Too Loud (For The Crowd) / Radio Interview / Witching Hour / Powerdrive / Buried Alive

LIVE – OFFICIAL BOOTLEG, American Phonograph (1987)
Intro / Leave Me In Hell / Countess Bathory / Die Hard / The Seven Gates Of Hell / Bass Solo / Buried Alive / Don't Burn The Witch / In Nomine Satanas / Welcome To Hell / Warhead / Stand Up And Be Counted / Guitar Solo / Bloodlust

CALM BEFORE THE STORM, Filmtrax MOMENT C115 (1987)
Black Xmas / The Chanting Of The Priests / Metal Punk / Under A Spell / Calm Before The Storm / Fire / Krackin' Up / Beauty And The Beast / Deadline / Gypsy / Muscle

PRIME EVIL, Under One Flag FLAG 36 (1989)
Prime Evil / Parasite / Blackened Are The Priests / Carnivorous / Skeletal Dance / Megalomania / Insane / Harder Than Ever / Into The Fire / School Daze / Live Like An Angel

TEMPLES OF ICE, Under One Flag FLAG 56 (1991)
Tribes / Even In Heaven / Trinity MCMXLV 0530 / In Memory Of (Paul Miller 1964-90) / Faerie Tale / Playtime / Acid / Arachnid / Speed King / Temples Of Ice

IN MEMORIUM, MCI VNM 1 (1991)
Angel Dust / Raise The Dead / Red Light Fever / Buried Alive / Witching Hour / At War With Satan / Warhead / Manitou / Under A Spell / Nothing Sacred / Dead Love / Welcome To Hell / Black Metal / Countess Bathory / 1000 Days In Sodom / Prime Evil / If You Wanna War / Surgery

THE WASTELANDS, Under One Flag FLAG 72 (1991)
Cursed / I'm Paralyzed / Black Legions / Riddle Of Steel / Need To Kill / Kissing The Beast / Crucified / Shadow King / Wolverine / Clarisse

ACID QUEEN, Marble Arch (1991)

Acid Queen / Dead Of Nite / Live Like An Angel (Die Like A Devil) / Die Hard / Manitou / Bloodlust / Warhead / Seven Gates Of Hell

SKELETONS IN THE CLOSET, Castle CMC 3082 (1992)
Your Intro Tape / Welcome To Hell / Dead On Arrival / Snots Shit / Black Metal / Hounds Of Hell / At War With Satan / Bitch Witch / Intro Tapes / Possessed / Sadist (Mistress Of The Whip) / Manitou / Angel Dust / Raise The Dead / Red Light Fever / Venom Station

THE BOOK OF ARMAGEDDON, Relativity (1992)
Witching Hour / Countess Bathory / Rip Ride / Live Like An Angel (Die Like A Devil) / Teacher's Pet / Black Metal / Manitou / 1000 Days Of Sodom / Blood Lust / Buried

METAL PUNK LIVE, Soundwings 111 1101-2 (1993)
Black Xmas / The Chanting Of The Priests / Metal Punk / Under A Spell / Calm Before The Storm / Fire / Crackin' Back / Beauty And The Beast / Deadline / Gypsy / Muscle

LEAVE ME IN HELL, Success 16089 (1994)
Leave Me In Hell / Black Metal / Burn This Place To The Ground / Buried Alive / Schizo / Witching Hour / Teachers Pet / Too Loud (For The Crowd) / Welcome To Hell / Satanarchist / Flytrap / Sons Of Satan / Poison / Hellchild / Angel Dust / Powerdrive

KISSING THE BEAST, (1994)
Black Metal / Die Hard / Flatline / Welcome To Hell / In Nomine Satanas / Witching Hour / Angel Dust / Fragile Life / Bloodlust / Countess Bathory / Buried Alive / Burstin' Out

OLD, NEW, BORROWED AND BLUE, Bleeding Hearts BLEED 7 (1994)
Countess Bathory / Skeletal Dance / Speed King / Welcome To Hell / Playtime / Die Hard / Clarisse / Hell Bent For Leather / Prime Evil / Teacher's Pet / School Daze / Faerie Tale / Megalomania / Temples Of Ice / The Witching Hour

THE SECOND COMING, Hardware CMA 001 (1996)
The Seven Gates Of Hell / Die Hard / Welcome To Hell / Leave Me In Hell / Countess Bathory / Buried Alive / Don't Burn The Witch / In Nomine Satanas / Schitzo / Nightmare / Black Metal / Witching Hour

BLACK REIGN, Receiver RRCD 212 (1996)
Insane / Civilized / Die Hard / In Nomine Satanas / If You Want A War / Countess Bathory / Harder Than Ever / Welcome To Hell / Carnivorous (Live) / Angel Dust / Fragile Life / Teacher's Pet / Skool Daze / Buried Alive / Blood Lust / Surgery / Black Metal / Flat Line / Blackened Are The Priests / Prime Evil / Bursting Out / Witching Hour

FROM HEAVEN TO THE UNKNOWN, Snapper Music SMDCD120 (1997)

Welcome To Hell / Witching Hour / Angel Dust / Red Light Fever / Black Metal / Buried Alive / Teacher's Pet / Countess Bathory / Don't Burn The Witch / At War With Satan / Rip Ride / Cry Wolf / Women, Leather And Hell / Satanarchist / Possessed / Hellchild / Mystique / Too Loud (For The Crowd) / In League With Satan / Live Like Ann Angel / Bloodlust / In Nomine Satanas / Die Hard / Bursting Out / Warhead / Lady Lust / 7 Gates Of Hell / Manitou / Dead Of The Night / Dead On Arrival / Hounds Of Hell / Bitch Witch / Sadist / Black Metal / Snots Shit

CAST IN STONE, CBH Steamhammer CD 8000136 (1997)

Evil One / Raised In Hell / All Devil's Eve / Bleeding / Destroyed And Damned / Domus Mundi / Flight Of The Hydra / God's Forsaken / Mortals / Infectious / Kings Of Evil / You're All Gonna Die / Judgement Day / Swarm

VENOM CLASSICS, CBH Steamhammer CD (1997) (Free CD with 'Cast In Stone' of re-recorded 'classics')

Intro / Bloodlust / Die Hard / Acid Queen / Burstin' Out / Warhead / Ladylust / Manitou / Rip Ride / Venom

LIVE 1996, Aspire (1999)

7 Gates Of Hell / Welcome To Hell / In Nomine Satanas / Black Metal / The Evil Due

BURIED ALIVE, Receiver (1999)

Welcome To Hell / Burstin' Out / Countess Bathory / Skeletal Dance / Civilized / Megalomania / Black Metal / Buried Alive / Blackened Are The Priests / Faerie Tale / Die Hard / Carnivorous / If You Want A War / Angel Dust / Playtime / Hell Bent For Leather / Clarisse / Speedking / Temples Of Ice / Witching Hour / Teachers Pet / Insane / Prime Evil / Harder Than Ever / School Daze / Surgery

NEW, LIVE AND RARE, Bleeding Hearts (2000)

Harder Than Ever / Skeletal Dance / Speed King / Welcome To Hell / Blackened Are The Priests / Playtime / Carnivorous / Die Hard / Hell Bent For Leather / Burstin' Out / Prime Evil / Black Metal / Megalomania / Faerie Tale / Civilized / Clarrise / Temples Of Ice / Angel Dust / Teacher's Pet / Witchin' Hour

RESURRECTION, SPV 085 21752 (2000)

Resurrection / Vengeance / War Against Christ / All There Is Fear / Pain / Pandemonium / Loaded / Firelight / Black Fire Of Satan / Control Freak / Disbeliever / Man, Myth And Magic / Thirteen / Leviathan

THE COURT OF DEATH, Receiver (2000)

Cursed / Need To Kill / In Memory Of (Paul Miller) / Wolverine / Arachnid / I'm Paralysed / Crucified / Live Like An Angel - Die Like A Devil / Into the Fire / Riddle Of Steel / Shadow King / Trinity MCMXLV 0530 / Black Legions / Parasite / Acid Queen / Tribes / Even In Heaven / Kissing The Beast

THE COLLECTION, Connoisseur (2000)

Temples Of Ice / Tribes / Arachnid / Speed King / Even In Heaven / Prime Evil / Parasite / Insane / Harder Than Ever / Wolverine / Shadow King / Riddle Of Steel / I'm Paralysed / Kissing The Beast / Welcome To Hell / Countess Bathory / Black Metal / Teachers Pet

BEAUTY AND THE BEAST, Dressed To Kill (2000)

Black Xmas / Chanting Of The Priests / Metal Punk / Under A Spell / Calm Before The Storm / Fire / Krackin' Up / Beauty And The Beast / Deadline / Gypsy / Muscle

ARCHIVE, Receiver (2001)

Speed King / Flatline / Bloodlust / Into The Fire / Kissing The Beast / Shadow King / Insane / Civilised / Parasite / Trinity MCMXLC 0530 / The Ark / Crucified / Need To Kill / Tribes / Skool Daze / Countess Bathory / Harder Than Ever / Wolverine

A TRIPLE DOSE OF VENOM, Big Eye Music (2001)

Black Xmas / Chanting Of The Priests / Metal Punk / Under A Spell / Calm Before The Storm / Fire / Krackin' Up / Beauty And The Beast / Deadline / Gypsy / Muscle / Intro / Too Loud (For the Crowd) / 7 Gates Of Hell / Leave Me In Hell / Nightmare / Countess Bathory / Die Hard / Schitzo / Guitar Solo / In Nomine Satanas / Witching Hour / Black Metal / Chanting Of The Priests / Satanachist / Fly Trap / Warhead / Buried Alive / Love Amongst The Dead / Bass Solo / Welcome To Hell / Bloodlust

VERDICT (GERMANY)

Line-Up: Daniel Baptista (vocals), Heiko Montkovski (guitar), Marius Pack (guitar), David Helmstetter (bass), Florian Bauer (drums)

Founded in 1990, VERDICT operated as a Death Metal band until substantial line-up changes during 1997 shifted the musical emphasis over towards Thrash Metal. During 2001 VERDICT lost the services of guitarist Peter Klaucke and drummer Michael Zobel. VERDICT recorded a debut album 'Reflections Of Pain' in February for 2002 release.

VEXED (ITALY)

Line-Up: Mik (vocals), Rob (guitar), Claud (guitar), Winx (bass), Moreno (drums)

Founded in 1996, VEXED are a Black Metal band consciously rooted in '80s Thrash traditions. Releasing the 1999 cassette 'Abyss Of Agony' VEXED comprised line-up citing vocalist Mik, guitarist Jex, bass player Kyle and drummer Mike. However, during 2000 both Kyle and Mike made their exit to join SINE MACULA.

The group regrouped quickly, pulling in replacements bassist Winx and drummer Moreno as well as second guitar player Claud. New material was demoed in December of 2000 with John of NECRODEATH at the production helm. With the songs laid down Jex left the band, being replaced by Rob.

A deal was struck with Witchhammer Records to release these sessions on CD format in 2002. The same songs would also be issued as a split single in league with Brazilian Thrashers FARSCAPE on Deathstrike Records.

Touring found VEXED as opening act for DESASTER, NECRODEATH and TANKARD. A further split tape release, 'Italian Thrash Metal Assault', in alliance with HATEWORK would be distributed globally through Deathstrike in Germany, Metal Psycho in Ecuador and Witchhammer in Thailand.

A second full length album provisionally titled 'Nightmare Holocaust' is projected for 2002 release.

Albums:
ENDLESS ARMAGEDDON, Witchhammer (2002)

VICIOUS BARREKA (PA, USA)
Line-Up: Jo Jo Monroe (vocals / guitar), Chris Chaparro (guitar), Brian Ciccone (bass), Tony Dalmes (drums)

Albums:
OUTRAGE, INSANITY AND PROFANITY, Axe Killer 7022 (1985)

VICIOUS RUMORS (CA, USA)
Line-Up: Geoff Thorpe (vocals / guitar), Steve Smyth (guitar), Tommy Sisco (bass), Larry Howe (drums)

A Power / Thrash Metal band of great repute, VICIOUS RUMORS formed in San Francisco in the early '80s, co-founded by guitarist Geoff Thorpe. Finding a niche market on the European mainland during the '90s VICIOUS RUMORS would develop their sound into a more streamlined melodic Metal style.

The band would quickly be taken under the wing of guitar guru and Shrapnel Records boss Mike Varney, Thorpe meeting the man through Varney's ROCK JUSTICE project.

At the time of their meeting Varney was in the process of putting the Shrapnel Records label together, a company that first made its name with the 'U.S. Metal' series of compilation albums that pushed the playing of the guitarists in the individual bands concerned well to the fore.

VICIOUS RUMORS line-up of 1983 comprised vocalist Mark Tate, guitarists Geoff Thorpe and Jim Cassero, bass player Jim Barnacle and drummer Jim Lange. The latter had supplanted Walt Perkins. At this stage VICIOUS RUMORS were heavily reliant on image with co-ordinated black and blue stage costumes and with their singer entering the stage held aloft in a coffin borne by monks!

Bassist Dave Starr had been a member of fellow Metal band LÄÄZ ROCKIT, actually a founder member having renamed that act from their previous title of DEPTH CHARGE. Fired from LÄÄZ ROCKIT in 1983 Starr created a power trio titled BLACK LEATHER with guitarist Rick Richards and drummer Jim Wells. The following year Starr formed part of the regrouped VICIOUS RUMORS completing a line-up of ex-HAWAII singer Gary St. Pierre, guitarist Geoff Thorpe and drummer Charles Emmil.

During this period VAIN guitarist Jamie Rowe (then titled 'Chuck Mooney') made some recordings with VICIOUS RUMORS. Drummer for this period was Don Selzer.

VICIOUS RUMORS made their first recorded appearance on 'U.S. Metal Volume III' with the track 'Ultimate Death'. At the time Thorpe had been looking for the perfect guitar partner and getting nowhere. Former BLACK LEATHER man Rick Richards filled in for one gig. Varney introduced him to a discovery of his from Delaware called VINNIE MOORE. In no time at all, Moore was in the group and the group were put in the studio by Varney to record a debut album for Shrapnel in 1985.

That first record 'Soldiers Of The Night', released in Europe through a licensing deal with Roadrunner, featured St. Pierre on vocals, Moore and Thorpe on guitar, bassist Dave Starr and drummer Larry Howe.

Moore, only ever a temporary member, would quit to pursue his goal of solo stardom and RUMORS promptly picked up former TYRANT man Terry Montana as a quick replacement. Montana lasted a year, recording demos and actually toured promoting the first album.

After Montana's services were dispensed with, Alameda, California raised Mark McGee came into the frame. Formerly a member of local act OVERDRIVE (in the dual role of vocalist and rhythm guitarist), McGee had also spent a period of time in the ranks of fading Pomp Rock outfit STARCASTLE.

McGee made his debut with VICIOUS RUMORS on 1988's 'Digital Dictator' album, a record that also premiered ex-RUFFIANS /

IRA BLACK of VICIOUS RUMORS
Photo : Nico Wobben

CORNBREAD of VICIOUS RUMORS
Photo : Nico Wobben

VILLIAN vocalist Carl Albert in place of the departed Gary St. Pierre.

VICIOUS RUMORS hooked up with SAVATAGE manager Robert Zemsky and consequently with major label Atlantic Records for the eponymous 1990 album. The record title was originally 'Immortal Battalion'. RUMORS toured America on a headlining club jaunt prior to European dates with DEATH ANGEL and FORBIDDEN as well as a performance at the prestigious Dynamo festival in Holland.

For 1991's 'Welcome To The Ball' the band toured Europe with SAVATAGE and put in further headline club gigs in America. Japanese dates resulted in the live 'Plug In And Hang On - Live In Tokyo' album.

The following year VICIOUS RUMORS were dealt two body blows. Not only were they dropped by Atlantic but Thorpe was found to be suffering from Carpal tunnel syndrome and had to undergo surgery for his condition. For a short while the band operated as a quartet without him. Howe filled his downtime by creating side project BOMB THREAT with HEATHEN members Lee Altus and Thaen Rasmussen with singer Jay from MY VICTIM. BOMB THREAT toured the California clubs playing a nostalgic set of NWoBHM covers.

By mid 1993 Thorpe was recovered enough to get out on the road again but by November line-up problems beset the band with Starr being fired.

In April 1995 VICIOUS RUMORS took another hammer blow when Albert was killed in an accident. The singer hung onto life for a few days but was eventually pronounced braindead. McGee also quit the band eventually uniting with GREGG ALLMAN.

Thorpe took over lead vocals for the 1996 album 'Something Burning' as the band was also bolstered by guitarist Steve Smyth. The following year VICIOUS RUMORS drafted vocalist Brian O'Connor. High profile European dates would see the group guesting for ACCEPT. Back in America further gigs were put in as openers to established artists such as THIN LIZZY, RAINBOW and BLUE OYSTER CULT. The band would play to their biggest audiences though during 1998, billed as special guests to Germany's BLIND GUARDIAN on their European tour.

In 1999 VICIOUS RUMORS announced their new vocalist to be ex-HIGH TREASON and MEGATON BLONDE man Morgan Thorn. Smyth joined TESTAMENT in the same year. The band bounced back in 2001 with the 'Sadistic Symphony' album. VICIOUS RUMORS new look comprised Thorn. Thorpe, guitarist Ira Black, bassist Cornbread and drummer Atma Anur.

Black's history traces back through REXXEN,

the 1992 incarnation of HEATHEN, UTERIS (featuring ex-TESLA guitarist Tommy Skeoch) and DOGFACE with erstwhile EXODUS man Steve Souza.

Bassist Cornbread is ex-BIZARRO, the band founded by ex-FORBIDDEN / TESTAMENT guitarist Glen Alvelais whilst drummer Atma Anur boasts numerous studio appearances with diverse acts such as DAVID BOWIE, JOURNEY, TONY MACALPINE and MARTY FRIEDMAN.

It would leak out that both Thorn and Cornbread had actually split away from the band in early 2001 but had resolved whatever differences of opinion there were and re-joined the fold.

Former VICIOUS RUMORS personnel bassist Dave Starr and drummer Larry Howe would both join CHASTAIN in 2001. Meantime Ira Black delved into nostalgia by forming part of the reunion of '80s Thrash act MERCENARY.

With the release of the 'Sadistic Symphony' album VICIOUS RUMORS once again changed tack, re-employing Brian O'Connor on vocals. The band hooked up with SAVATAGE and BLAZE for European tour dates commencing in Sweden during January 2002 but would soon pull out citing friction with BLAZE.

It would be learned in April that erstwhile VICIOUS RUMORS personnel bassist Dave Starr and drummer Larry Howe had joined CHASTAIN.

Albums:
SOLDIERS OF THE NIGHT, Roadrunner RR 9734 (1986)
Premonition / Ride (Into The Sun) / Medusa / Soldiers Of The Night / Murder / March Or Die / Blitz The World / Invader / In Fire / Domestic Bliss / Blistering Winds
DIGITAL DICTATOR, Roadrunner RR 9571 (1988)
Replicant / Digital Dictator / Minute To Kill / Towns On Fire / Lady Took A Chance / Worlds And Machines / The Crest / R.L.I I./ Condemned / Out Of The Shadows
VICIOUS RUMORS, Atlantic 7567820752 (1990)
Don't Wait For Me / World Church / On The Edge / Ship Of Fools / Can You Hear It / Down To The Temple / Hellraiser / Electric Twilight / Thrill Of The Hunt / Axe And Smash
WELCOME TO THE BALL, Atlantic 75682276121 (1991)
Abandoned / You Only Live Twice / Saviour From Anger / Children / Dust To Dust / Raise Your Hands / Strange Behaviour / Six Stepsisters / Mastermind / When Love Comes Down / Ends Of The Earth

PLUG IN AND HANG ON - LIVE IN TOKYO, Atlantic (1992)
WORD OF MOUTH, SPV Steamhammer 084-62232 (1994)
Against The Grain / All Rights Reserved / The Voice / Thinking Of You / Thunder And Pain (Part 1) / Thunder And Pain (Part 2) / No Fate / Sense Of Security / Dreaming / Building No. 6 / Ministry Of Fear / Music Box
SOMETHING BURNING, Massacre MASSCD091 (1996)
Ball Hog / Mouth / Out Of My Misery / Something Burning / Concentration / Chopping Block / Perpetual / Strip Search / Make It Real / Free To Go
CYBERCHRIST, Massacre CD0142 (1998)
Cyberchrist / Buried Alive / Kill The Day / No Apologies / Fear Of God / Gigs Eviction / Barcelona / Downpour / Candles Burn / Fiend / Faith
SADISTIC SYMPHONY, (2001)
Break / Sadistic Symphony / March Of The Damned / Blacklight / Puritan Demons / Born Again Hard / Neodymium Man / Elevator To Hell / Cerebral Sea / Ascension / Liquify

VIKING (Los Angeles, CA, USA)
Line-Up: Ron Eriksen (vocals), Brett Eriksen (guitar), James Lareau (bass), Matt Jordan (drums)

VIKING were a hard hitting Speed / Thrash Metal act out of Los Angeles. The band had a blistering rise over two highly praised albums before dropping out of the scene entirely when half of the band became born again Christians. VIKING was founded in the Spring of 1986 by guitarist Ron Daniels of the HAGS, drummer Matt Jordan of BARRIER and bass player James Lareau of Punk act LETHAL GENE.

This trio, along with singer Tony Spider, founded TRACER releasing one demo session. TRACER, now minus Spider, evolved into VIKING when Daniels discovered he could sing whilst jamming SLAYER songs at a rehearsal. Guitarist Brett completed the line-up.

As VIKING the band opted to promote the appropriate image and therefore both Daniels and Brett took the stage name 'Eriksen'. After just two gigs VIKING were signed to the Metal Blade label, committing the track 'Hellbound' to the 'Metal Massacre VIII' compilation then launching a full blown album 'Do Or Die'. Critics enthused over the sheer heaviness of the band and Ron Eriksen's vocals were singled out for particular praise.

Ron Eriksen would lend his vocal talents to the DARK ANGEL album 'Leave Scars', duetting with Ron Rinehart on the song 'Promise Of Agony'.

VIKING would go into the studio to cut a second album 'Man Of Straw' with engineer Bill Metoyer. However, Daniels had recently converted to Christianity and would re-write a large degree of the lyrics just prior to recording.

In May of 1990 both Daniels and Jordan would exit citing a conflict of interests between the Heavy Metal lifestyle and their faith. VIKING folded. These days Daniels is Pastor at Calvary Chapel, Cheyenne.

Albums:

DO OR DIE, Metal Blade 72225 (1988)
Warlord / Hellbound / Militia Of Death / Prelude - Scavenger / Valhalla / Burning From Within / Berserker / Killer Unleashed / Do Or Die
MAN OF STRAW, Caroline 1396 (1989)
White Death / They Raped The Land / Twilight Fate / The Trial / Case Of The Stubborns / Winter / Hell Is For Children / Creative Divorce / Man of Straw

VILLIAN (USA)

Line-Up: Carl Albert (vocals), Leon B. Smith (guitar), Greg E. Noll (guitar), Tommy Sisco (bass), Rob Quiellen (drums)

The late Carl Albert, an ex-member of RUFFIANS, joined VICIOUS RUMORS.

Albums:

ONLY TIME WILL TELL, Relentless (1986)
Kamikaze / Only Time Will Tell / Tie Your Mother Down / She'll Make You Fall (In Love) / Kids Of Crime / Just Close Your Eyes / Thrills In The Night

VIOGRESSION (USA)

Line-Up: Brian DeNeffe (vocals), Eric Johnston, Leon Schendel, Barry Jaeger, Bryan Jaeger (drums)

VIOGRESSION would tour America supporting DEATH and PESTILENCE during 1995.
Post VIOGRESSION vocalist Brian DeNeffe would serve a term with CYNIC. Drummer Bryan Jaeger would hook up with ex-ACROPHET members Rob Anthony and Dave Bauman in a Country Rock band.

Albums:

EXPOUND & EXHORT, Tombstone (1991)
Maggot Synod / Nothing (Psychomatic Insanity) / Puritan Flames / Wind Of Death / Fragmented Carcass / Cross Spells / As You Die / Limb From Limb / Transmigration / Choir Of Loudin / Circle Of The Divine / Choir Of Loudin - The Chantina

VIO-LENCE
(San Francisco, CA, USA)
Line-Up: Sean Killian (vocals), Robb Flynn (guitar), Phil Demmel (guitar), Dean Dell (bass), Perry Strickland (drums)

Relative latecomers in the Thrash explosion Bay Area's VIO-LENCE nevertheless managed to scramble onto a major deal offered by MCA Mechanic during 1988.
The genesis of the band can be found in DEATH PENALTY, a unit founded in 1985, consisting of guitarist Phil Demmel, drummer Perry Strickland, second guitarist Troy Fua, bassist Ed Billy and vocalist Jerry Burr. A rapid name change to VIO-LENCE took place but within months Billy had opted to pursue further education and in his stead came Dean Dell. The following year Birr departed the band filling the gap with Killian. The last member change found Fua being supplanted by Rob Flynn in early 1987.
Upon the debut's release VIO-LENCE undertook touring duties across America on a billing that included TESTAMENT and SANCTUARY. Flynn would later be replaced by Ray Vegas.
Rob Flynn created MACHINE HEAD whilst Demmel, Vegas and Dell founded TORQUE for an eponymous 1996 album.

Singles/EPs:
Eternal Nightmare, MCA Mechanic VOMIT1 (1988)

Albums:
ETERNAL NIGHTMARE, MCA Mechanic DMCF 4323 (1988)
Eternal Nightmare / Serial Killer / Phobophobia / Calling In The Coronor / T.D.S. / Take It As You Will / Bodies On Bodies / Kill On Command
OPRESSING THE MASSES, Megaforce 82105-2 (1990)
I Profit / Officer Nice / Subterfuge / Engulfed By Flames / World In A World / Mentally Afflicted / Liquid Courage / Oppressing The Masses
NOTHING TO GAIN, Bleeding Hearts CDBLEED4 (1993)
Atrocity / 12 Gauge Justice / Ageless Eyes / Pain Of Pleasure / Virtues Of Vice / Killing My Words / Psychotic Memories / No Chains / Welcoming Party / This Is System / Color Of Life

VIOLENT FORCE (GERMANY)
Line-Up: Lemmie (vocals / guitar), Stachel (guitar), Waldy (bass), Hille (drums)

VIOLENT FORCE frontman Lemmie would

later join SACRED CHAO. Drummer Hille departed to be replaced by Atomic Steif. However, Steif was to decamp to join SACRED CHAO also.

Steif later teamed up with SODOM.

Albums:
MALEVOLENT ASSAULT OF TOMORROW, Roadrunner (1987)
Dead City / Soulbursting / Vengeance And Venom / Malevolent Assault Of Tomorrow / What About The Time After? / Sign Of Evil / Violent Force / The Night / Destructed Life / S.D.I.

VIOLENT PLAYGROUND
(Fort Lauderdale, FL, USA)
Line-Up: Manny (vocals), Rocko (guitar), The Son (guitar), Gerrit (bass), Bobby Sheehan (drums)

A rather Blues oriented Speed Metal band from Florida, VIOLENT PLAYGROUND's 'Thrashin' Blues' debut was produced by THE RODS drummer Carl Canedy.

Albums:
THRASHIN' BLUES, Big Chief (1988)
Thrashin' Blues / I Hate My Boss Blues / Poverty Sucks / Toe Tag / Doctor Feelfine / Mr Dandy / Lame From The Neck Up / Play To Kill / 21st Century Bluesmen (Boogie Chilluh) / Anvil Head

VIPER (BRAZIL)
Line-Up: Pit Passarell (vocals / bass), Yves Passarell (guitar), Felipe Machado (guitar), Renato Graccia (drums)

A heavily Euro influenced Speed Metal act created durlng 1985 by teenage brothers guitarist Yves and bassist Pit Passarell. Joining them would be the equally youthful vocalist Andre Matos, second guitar player Felipe Machado and drummer Casi Audi.
VIPER announced their presence with the 'Killara Sword' demo which soon snagged a deal with the domestic Rock Brigade label. Promoting the debut 'Soldiers Of Sunrise' album VIPER would support MOTÖRHEAD.
For 1989's 'Theatre Of Fate' opus VIPER switched drummers, bringing in Sergio Facci. However, Guilherme Martin would be drafted on the drumstool for tour work and then the position was finally settled by Renato Graccia.
At this juncture Andre Matos split away from the band, apparently over a conflict of interest in stylistic direction. The erstwhile vocalist would found the immensely successful Progressive Metal act ANGRA. Pit Passarell took over the vocal mantle as VIPER trimmed down to a quartet.
By now VIPER's reputation had spread internationally with the 'Theatre Of Fate' album licensed to Japan in 1991 and Europe the following year. 1992 would also see VIPER scoring a huge Brazilian radio hit with the track 'Rebel Maniacs'.
The 1994 'Live - Maniacs In Japan' album would include the band's cover version of QUEEN's 'We Will Rock You' alongside a take of the RAMONES 'I Wanna Be Sedated'.
The 'Coma Rage' record, released in 1995, saw strong Hardcore elements being introduced into the band's sound.
Yves Passarel would unite onstage for a slice of nostalgia with former vocalist Andre Matos in 2001 as Matos debuted his post ANGRA outfit SHAMAN.

Singles/EPs:
Rebel Maniacs, (1992)

Albums:
SOLDIERS OF SUNRISE, Rock Brigade (1987)
Knights of Destruction / Nightmares / The Whipper / Wings Of The Evil / H.R. / Soldiers Of Sunrise / Signs Of The Night / Killera (Princess Of Hell) / Law Of The Sword
THEATRE OF FATE, (1989)
Illusions / At Least A Chance / To Live Again / A Cry From the Edge / Living For the Night / Prelude To Oblivion / Theatre Of Fate / Moonlight
EVOLUTION, (1992)
Coming From The Inside / Evolution / Rebel Maniac / Dead Light / The Shelter / Still the Same / Wasted / Pictures Of Hate / Dance Of Madness / The Spreading Soul / We Will Rock You
VIPERIA SAPIENS, (1993)
Acid Heart / Silent Enemy / Crime / Wasted Again / Killing World / The Spreading Soul (Acoustic version)
LIVE - MANIACS IN JAPAN, (1994)
Intro - Coming From the Inside / To Live Again / The Shelter / A Cry From The Edge / Dead Light / Knights Of Destruction / We Will Rock You / Acid Heart / Still The Same - Drum Solo / Evolution / Nao Quero Dinheiro / Living For the Night / Rebel Maniac / I Wanna Be Sedated
COMA RAGE, (1995)
Coma Rage / Straight Ahead / Somebody Told Me You're Dead / Makin Love / Blast! / God Machine / Far And Near / The Last Song / If I Dle By Hate Day Before / 405 South / A Face In The Crowd / I Fought the Law / Keep The Words
TEM PRA TODO MUND), (1996)

425

Dinheiro / Crime Na Cidade / 8 De Abril / Sabado / Not Ready To Get Up / Quinze Anos / Na Cara Do Gol / The One You Need / Lucinha Bordon / Alvo / Um Dia / Mais Do Mesmo

THE BEST OF VIPER - EVERYBODY, EVERYBODY, (1999)

Not Ready To Get Up / Dead Light / I Fought The Law / Rebel Maniac / 8 De Abril / Coma Rage / Não Quero Dinheiro (Live in Tokyo) / The One You Need / Killing World / Crime Na Cidade / A Cry From The Edge (Live) / Evolution / Living For The Night / The Shelter / Keep The Words / Soldiers Of Sunrise

VIRUS (UK)

Line-Up: Henry Heston (vocals), Cokie (guitars), Damien Hess (bass), Terry Kaylor (drums)

Formed in London in 1987 with a primitive brand of Thrash that improved as albums progressed. VIRUS toured alongside acts such as DEATH ANGEL, CELTIC FROST and SUICIDAL TENDENCIES.

VIRUS also gained a slot at the prestigious Leeds thrash festival alongside MEGADETH. They were due to tour America with DEATH but tour cancelled.

In 1991 Heston and Kaylor formed SAVAGE CIRCLE with vocalist / bassist J.D. Cooper and guitarist Syd Sholley.

Albums:
PRAY FOR WAR, Metalworks (1987)
Pray For War / To The Death / Malignant Massacre / Thermonuclear Thrash / Night Siege / Risen From Death / Scarred For Life / Neo Warlords / Cannibal Holocaust
FORCE RECON, Metalworks VOV 669 (1988)
Testify To Me / Visual Warfare / Force Recon / Release The Devil / No Return / B.S.S.D. / Hungry For Blood
LUNACY, Metalworks (1989)
Seeing is Believing / Lunacy / Bad Blood / The Pain Will Ease / State Of The Art / My Life / A Sense Of Freedom / Don't Get Even
WARMONGER - THE COMPILATION, MIA Records (1994)

VITAMIN F (New Fairfield, CT, USA)

Line-Up: John Rich (vocals / bass), Renato Ghio (guitar), Marcello Muraca (drums)

A Connecticut Speed Metal band. VITAMIN F debuted in 1997 with the five song EP 'Nobody Cares'.

Singles/EPs:
Nobody Cares EP, (1997)

VIXEN (Oahu, Hawaii, USA)

Line-Up: Kim La Chance (vocals), Marty Friedman (guitar), Paul Escorpeso (bass), Jeff Graves (drums)

Quite possibly Hawaii's first ever Metal band, VIXEN resulted from ex-DEUCE guitarist MARTY FRIEDMAN's decision to relocate from Baltimore, Maryland to the sunnier Pacific climate.

Moving to Hawaii in 1981, Friedman had hooked up with drummer Jeff Graves and began jamming with other local musicians, soon picking up bassist Paul Escorpeso and female vocalist Kim La Chance.

VIXEN quickly began to build up a cult following on the strength of their five track demo tape. VIXEN would eventually secure a one-off deal with the Los Angeles label Azra Records. The material for the mini-album was recorded in April 1982, but the record company failed to issue the one-sided 'Made In Hawaii' until well into 1983, long after the group had split.

Still, Friedman's guitar histrionics had not gone unnoticed, Shrapnel Records' Mike Varney offered VIXEN a slot on the first 'U.S. Metal' compilation album with a new version of the DEUCE track 'Angels In The Dust'.

But all was not well in paradise, as the band became progressively heavier VIXEN parted company with Kim La Chance and replaced Escorpeso with Kimo.

The group had been offered a spot on Metal Blade's 'Metal Massacre II' album and hired Lisa Ruiz to record 'Heavy Metal Virgin' for the album under the new moniker of ALOHA. But the new band was shortlived, Friedman and Graves ultimately chose to form the even heavier HAWAII and gain a deal with Shrapnel.

Kim La Chance, on the other hand, formed MALISHA after her departure from VIXEN. The group (comprising guitarist Rrat, ex-EXCALIBUR bassist Delian Shishido and drummer Joe Sylva) recorded a four track demo that was more along the lines of Y&T and SAMMY HAGAR. However, nothing appears to have been heard from Kim since.

MARTY FRIEDMAN of course carved out a worthy solo career and came to prominence in the '90s with MEGADETH.

Albums:
MADE IN HAWAII, Azra DTR 64 (1983)
(One-sided record only)
The Young And The Reckless / Living In Sin / Escape The Night / Rocking Me Hard / Beg For Mercy

VODU (BRAZIL)
Line-Up: Claudio Victorazzo (vocals), Andre
Cagni (bass),

Sao Paulo Thrashers forged in 1984 with an
initial line-up of ex-WITCHCRAFT vocalist
Jefferson Forcinito, guitarist Bruno Bontempi,
bassist Andre Cagni and drummer Sergio
Facci. Forcinito would decamp in favour of
Claudio 'Vicky' Victorazzo for the 1989
sophomore album 'Seeds Of Destruction'.
VODU released a mini-album 'No Way' in
1990 comprising new material, live tracks and
a cover version of THE CLASH. The band
broke up in 1991, reformed the following year
but split once again. Facci subsequently
joined VOLKANA.

Albums:
THE FINAL CONFLICT, (1987)
SEEDS OF DESTRUCTION, Rock Brigade
(1988)
NO WAY, (1990)
ENDLESS TRIP, (1993)

VOIVOD (CANADA)
Line-Up: Denis 'Snake' Belanger (vocals /
bass), Denis 'Piggy' D'Amour (guitar), Jean-
Yves 'Blacky' Theriault (bass), Michael 'Away'
Langevin (drums)

Jonquierer based avant-garde Thrash Metal
'Cyberpunk' act VOIVOD mixed Punk,
extreme Metal and Sci-Fi in a unique
combination that won them many fans during
the mid '80s Thrash boom.
The French speaking VOIVOD were
assembled in 1983 by frontman Snake (Denis
Belanger), guitarist Piggy (Denis D'Amour),
bassist Blacky (Jean-Yves Theriault) and
drummer Away (Michael Langevein). Initial
VOIVOD gigs had the band including
numerous cover versions in their set from the
likes of JUDAS PRIEST, MOTÖRHEAD and
VENOM.
The band's first forays into the recording
studio resulted in the 1984 'To The Death'
demo, quickly followed by a live tape 'Morgoth
Invasion'.
From the band's official debut in 1984 with a
track on one of the infamous 'Metal Massacre'
compilations and the inaugural 'War And Pain'
album VOIVOD immediately set themselves
apart from the Thrash bandwagon.
VOIVOD were forced to pull out of their
'Dimension Hatross' world tour when Piggy
was diagnosed with a brain tumour.
VOIVOD toured Europe with support from
POSSSESSED. 1989's 'Nothingface' features
the band's take on PINK FLOYD's 'Astronomy
Domine'.

VOIVOD's tenacity and reluctance to
compromise was rewarded with a major label
deal via MCA Records subsidary Mechanic
for 1991's 'Angel Rat', although Blacky had by
this time been replaced by Pierre St. Jean.
Snake backed out for 1995's 'Negatron'
forcing Piggy and Away into a rethink on the
band's future. Deciding to continue as a trio
the band pulled in ex-LIQUID INDIAN /
THUNDER CIRCUS vocalist / bassist Eric
Forrest.
1997's 'Phobos' included a cover version of
KING CRIMSON's '21st Century Schizoid
Man'. Unfortunately, during touring to promote
the album Forrest was severely injured during
a road accident on tour in Germany during
1998.
The band's Montreal show in late 1999
reunited VOIVOD with Snake for one gig, the
former frontman guesting with the band.
The 2000 live album 'Lives', recorded at the
Dutch Dynamo Festival and the renowned
New York CBGB's club, includes a cover of
VENOM's 'In League With Satan'.
During early 2002 famed Virginian Heavy
Metal band DECEASED would cover 'Blower'
on their 'Zombie Hymns' album.
Recently VOIVOD have committed to
recording a new album with Snake, the whole
affair being produced by erstwhile
METALLICA bassist Jason Newsted. The
renewed line-up debuted on the 30th
December at the Foufounes Electrique venue
in Montreal, the band performing a set
entirely comprising SEX PISTOLS covers.
Denis 'Piggy' D'Amour would be announced
as guesting on the 2002 studio album 'Black
Light District' from premier Dutch avant-garde
Rockers THE GATHERING.

Singles/EPs:
Thrashing Rage / Slaughter In A Grave /
Helldriver / To The Death, Noise N N0050PD
(1986) ('Thrashing Rage' EP)
Cockroaches / Too Scared To Scream,
Noise NPD 085 (1987) (12" picture disc)
Astronomy Domine (Radio edit) / The
Unknown Knows, MCA Mechanic L33-17980
(1989) (Promotional release)
Into My Hypercube / Missing Sequences,
MCA Mechanic CD45 18196 (1989)
(Promotional release)
Clouds In My House (Remix) / The Prow
(Remix) / Angel Rat / Panorama, MCA
Mechanic CD45 2000 (1991) (Promotion
release)
Fix My Heart / Fix My Heart (Radio edit),
MCA MCASP 2822 (1993) (Promotional
release)
Lost Machine / Jack Luminous, MCA
MCASP 2684 (1993) (Promotional release)
The Nile Song / Tribal Convictions (Live),

MCA MCASP 2926 (1994) (Promotional release)
Nanoman / Erosion / Vortex, Mausoleum MAJC 60018-2 (1996) (Promotional release)

Albums:
WAR AND PAIN, Roadrunner RR 9825 (1984)
Voivod / Warriors Of Ice / Suck Your Bone / Iron Gang / War And Pain / Blower / Live For Violence / Black City / Nuclear War
RRROOOAAARRR, Noise N0040 (1986)
Korgull The Exterminator / Fuck Off And Die / Slaughter In A Grave / Ripping Headaches / Horror / Thrashing Rage / Helldriver / Build Your Weapons / To The Death!
DIMENSION HATROSS, Noise N0106-1 (1988)
Prolog... Experiment / Tribal Convictions / Chaosmongers / Technocratic Manipulators / Epilog... Macrosolutions To Megaproblems / Brain Scan / Psychic Vacuum / Cosmic Drama
NOTHINGFACE, Noise N 0142-2 (1989)
The Unknown Knows / Nothingface / Astronomy Domine / Missing Sequences / X Ray Mirror / Inner Combustion / Pre- Ignition / Into My Hypercube / Sub Effect
ANGELRAT, MCA MCD 10293 (1991)
Shortwave Intro / Panorama / Clouds In My House / The Prow / Best Regards / Twin Dummy / Angel Rat / Golem / The Outcast / Nuage Fractal / Freedoom / None Of The Above
THE BEST OF VOIVOD, Noise NO 196-2 (1992)
Voivod / Ripping Headaches / Korgull The Exterminator / Tornado / Ravenous Machine / Cockroaches / Tribal Convictions / Psychic Vacuum / Astronomy Domine / The Unknown Knows / Panorama / The Prow
THE OUTER LIMITS, MCA MCD 10701 (1993)
Fix My Heart / Moonbeam Rider / Le Pont Noir / The Nile Song / The Lost Machine / Time Warp / Jack Luminous / Wrong Way Street / We Are Not Alone
NEGATRON, Hypnotic HYP001CD (1995)
Insect / Project X / Nanoman / Reality / Negatron / Planet Hell / Meteor / Cosmic Conspiracy / Bio TV / Drift / DNA (Don't No anything)
PHOBOS, Hypnotic HYPCD 1057 (1997)
Catalepsy I / Rise / Mercury / Phobos / Bacteria / Temps Mort / The Tower / Quantum / Neutrino / Forlorn / Catalepsy II / M-Body / 21st Century Schizoid Man
KRONIK, Hypnotic HYP 1065 (1998)
Forlorn / Nanoman / Mercury / Vortex / Drift / Erosion / Ion / Project X / Cosmic Conspiracy / Astronomy Domine / Nuclear War

LIVES, Century Media 77282 (2000)
Insect / Tribal Convictions / Nanoman / Nuclear War / Planet Hell / Negatron / Project X / Cosmic Conspiracy / Ravenous Medicine / Voivod / In League With Satan

VOODOO CULT (GERMANY / USA)
Line-Up: Phillip Boa (vocals), Gabby Abularach (guitar), Taif Ball (bass), Markus Freiwild (drums)

Metal project founded by VOODOO CLUB's Phillip Boa in collusion with SLAYER and GRIP INC. drummer DAVE LOMBARDO, Mille of KREATOR, GRIP INC. man Waldemar Sorychta and DEATH's esteemed frontman Chuck Schuldiner. The debut album, produced by Sorychta, provided enough impact for the band to tour and after these dates Boa decided on assembling a permanent version of VOODOO CULT for further work.
Pulling in guitarist Gabby Abularach, bassist Taif Ball and ex-DESPAIR drummer Markus Freiwald (all of whom had worked on the debut album) Boa laid down the 'Voodoocult' record of 1995, production being handled by ex- VICTORY man Tommy Newton. Guest musicians included ex-FAITH NO MORE guitarist JIM MARTIN.

Singles/EPs:
Metallized Kids / Killer Patrol / My Game Is Dracula / Ringleader, Motor 835 023-2 (1994)

Albums:
JESUS KILLING MACHINE, Motor (1994)
Killer Patrol / Metallized Kids / Jesus Killing Machine / Born Bad And Sliced / Albert Is A Headbanger / Hellatio / Death Don't Dance With Me / Art Groupie / Blood Surfer City / Voodoocult / Bitchery Bay
VOODOO CULT, Motor 527188-2 (1995)
Welcome To a New Season Of Deathwish / King Of The Beautiful Cockroach / The Stranger / I Close My Eyes Before I Bleed To Death / When You Live As A Body / Exorcized By A Kiss / Cliffhanger On A Bloody Sunday / Violenca / Egomania / Die Erotik der Machine / Electrified Scum

VOPO'S (HOLLAND)
Line-Up: Ronny Vopo (vocals), Frans Vopo (guitar), Borris Vopo (bass), Theo Vopo (drums)

Heavy Metal quartet with Speed Metal overtones.

Albums:

428

CONQUER, Solid (1983)
Hard And Loud / Tonight / In The Book /
Nuclear War / Warrior / Conquer / Get Me /
Speedbanging Babies / 007 / Short Joy

VULCANO (BRAZIL)
Line-Up: Angel (vocals), Flavio (guitar), Soto
Jr. (guitar), Zhema (bass), Laudir Piloni
(drums)

An esteemed name on the South American
Thrash front. VULCANO, centred upon
bassist Zhema, was formulated in 1982
following a precursor act ASTAROTH.
As VULCANO the band bowed in with a four
track single sung in Portuguese. Shortly after
Zhema completely reconstituted the band
drafting singer Angel, guitarists Flavio and
Soto Jr. and drummer Laudir Piloni. Switching
to English lyrics VULCANO blasted back with
'Bloody Vengeance', supporting both VENOM
and EXCITER in Brazil the same year.
A later VULCANO line-up saw Zhema joined
by singer Luiz Carlos, guitarist Mauricio and
drummer Jair. Further changes had guitarist
Johnny Hansen and drummer Renato
involved.
There are reports that latterly Zhema makes
his living with a CREEDANCE CLEARWATER
REVIVAL covers band! Guitarist Soto Jr.
would pass away in early 2002.

Singles/EPs:
Om Pushne Namah, (1983)

Albums:
LIVE!, Cogumelo (1985)
BLOODY VENGEANCE, Cogumelo CG0041
(1986)
Dominios Of Death / Ready To Explode /
Holocaust / Spirits Of Evil, Death Metal /
Voices From Hell / Incubus / Bloody
Vengeance
ANTHROPOPHAGY, Cogumelo (1987)
WHO ARE THE TRUE?, South Attack (1988)
RATRACE, Metalcore (1990)

WARDANCE

(GERMANY)
Line-Up: Sandra
Schumacher (vocals),
Thomas Heyer (guitar),
Franz Romer (guitar),
Markus Wawgraich (bass),
Stefan Humbert (drums)

Speed Metal with female vocals from the suitably named Sandra Schumacher.

Albums:
CRUCIFIXION, Wardance (1988)
Intro: Crucifixion / Neverending Nightmare / Choudas Dream / Killing Snow / Don't Play With Fire / Friday The 13th / Ernst Neger Und Seine Moshenden Eierachander / Outro: Fuck Off
HEAVEN IS FOR SALE, No Remorse 1013 (1990)
Heaven's For Sale / Destroyer / Believe / Neverending Nightmare / I Don't Love You Anymore / Overture / Don't Play With Fire / Death Caress / Paris In Fear / House Of The Rising Sun

WARDOG (USA)

Line-Up: Tom Gattis (vocals / guitar), Chris Catero (vocals / bass), John Herrera (drums)

WARDOG frontman Tom Gattis is ex-DEUCE and TENSION. The 'Scorched Earth' album sees drum duties shared between John Herrera and Ross Martinez. The band put in an appearance at the 1998 'Bang Your Head' Festival in Germany where they were joined onstage by a guesting IRON MAIDEN vocalist BRUCE DICKINSON.

Albums:
SCORCHED EARTH, Metal Blade 3984-14112-2 (1997)
Scorched Earth / Sounds Of War / Broken But Not Dead / Seeing Is Believing / Nothing Left / Killing Speed / Bucket O' Beer / Cuz / Tomb Of The Slain / Beast Of Damnation

WARFARE (UK)

Line-Up: Evo (vocals / drums), Gunner (guitar), Zlaughter (bass)

Mainman Evo is ex-ANGELIC UPSTARTS, MAJOR ACCIDENT and THE BLOOD. The debut album 'Pure Filth' was produced by TANK's Algy Ward who features, alongside members of VENOM, on the track 'Rose Petals Fall From Her Face'.

'Metal Anarchy' was produced by MOTÖRHEAD's mainman LEMMY and Guy Bidmead and features guitar contributions from WURZEL of MOTÖRHEAD.

Following the single's release Evo took time out to play drums for punk act MAJOR ACCIDENT on their 1985 American tour. Allegedly upset after being offered the support to METALLICA's London Hammersmith Odeon show then being asked for a buy on WARFARE performed an impromptu gig on the back of a lorry outside the venue on the night of the gig. Resultant damage caused by Evo throwing his mike stand at the Odeon manager's car and further cars damaged by the lorry saw the drummer in court on a criminal damage charge.

Bassist Falken quit after the release of 'Metal Anarchy' and was replaced by Zlaughter for the 'Mayhem Fucking Mayhem' album produced by VENOM vocalist Cronos. 'Mayhem...' sold over 40,000 copies despite lack of serious gigging.

Quick to follow up 'A Conflict Of Hatred' followed. Guesting was MANTAS of VENOM and rather obliquely LINDISFARNE's Marti Craggs on saxophone and former PRELUDE vocalist Irene Hume.

Gunnar quit in late 1990 and was replaced for live work by J.J. Dunn. WARFARE were popular on the European underground circuit despite only performing twice on the continent. In 1989 Evo uprooted the band from the Neat label signing a deal with Hammer Film Music releasing the 'Hammer Horror' album through FM Revolver. Alleged lack of promotion led to a heavier second version of the album with more tracks, totally re-recorded featuring Algy Ward on guitar, appearing on Silver Screen Records. This version also featured a classical piece co-written with former TYGERS OF PAN TANG guitarist Fred Purser which was later used as part of the soundtrack to the movie 'Vlad The Impaler'.

In mid 1993 Evo dabbled with the WARHEAD project incorporating MOTÖRHEAD guitarist Wurzel and TANK bassist Algy Ward.

Evo now makes a highly successful un-metallic living operating fairground attractions!

Singles/EPs:
Burn The King's Road / The New Age Of Total Warfare / Noise, Filth And Fury, Neat NEAT 41 (1984) ('Noise, Filth And Fury' EP)
Two Tribes (Metal Mix) / Hell / Blown To Bits, Neat NEAT 45-12 (1984)
Metal Anarchy / Rape / Burning Up / Destroy, Neat 49-12 (1985) ('Total Death' EP)
Mayhem Fucking Mayhem, Neat (1986)
Addicted To Love / Hungry Dogs (Live), Neat NEAT 58 (1987) (Promotion release)

Albums:

PURE FILTH, Neat 1021 (1984)
Warning / Total Armageddon / This Machine
Kills / Let The Show Go On / Noise, Filth
And Fury / Collision / Rabid Metal / Dance
Of The Dead / Limit Crescendo / Rose
Petals Fall From Her Face

METAL ANARCHY, Neat 1029 (1986)
Intro / Electric Mayhem / Warfare / Death
Vigilance / Wrecked Society / Disgrace /
Living For The Last Days / Military Shadow /
Metal Anarchy / Psycho Express /
Commando

MAYHEM FUCKING MAYHEM, Neat NEAT
1040 (1986)
Abortion Sequence / Hungry Dogs /
Generator / You've Really Got Me / Extreme
Finance / Projectile Vomit / Mayhem Fuckin'
Mayhem / Atomic Slut / Machine Gun Breath
/ Murder On Melrose

A CONFLICT OF HATRED, Neat NEAT
1044 (1988)
Wax Works / Hate To Create / Revolution /
Dancing In The Flames Of Insanity /
Evolution / Fatal Vision / Deathcharge
(Doomsday) / Order Of The Dragons / Elite
Forces / Rejoice The Feast Of Quarantine /
Noise, Filth And Fury Requiem

ANNIHILATION ANESTHETISED, Warfare
(1989) (Cassette only release available from
fan club)

HAMMER HORROR, FM Revolver REV6LP
147 (1990)
Hammer Horror / Plague Of The Zombies /
Ballad Of The Dead / Baron Frankenstein / A
Velvet Rhapsody / A Solo Of Shadows /
Prince Of Darkness / Tales Of The Gothic
Genre / Scream Of The Vampire

**HAMMER HORROR - A ROCK TRIBUTE
TO THE STUDIO THAT DRIPPED BLOOD**,
Silva Screen FILM CD 130 (1991)
Intro - Dracula Theme / Baron Frankenstein
/ A Velvet Rhapsody / Phantom Of The Opera
/ Scream Of The Vampire: Part 1 / Vlad The
Impaler / Scream Of The Vampire: Part 2 /
Funeral In Carpathia / Hammer Horror /
Plague Of The Zombies / Ballad Of The
Dead / A Solo Of Shadows / Prince Of
Darkness / Tales Of The Gothic Genre /
Dance Of The Dead / Phantom Of The
Opera (Hammer House Of Horror Remix)

DEATHCHARGE LIVE, RKT CMO 198
(1991)
Deathcharge / Elite Forces / Fear Zone /
Scream Of The Vampire / Baron
Frankenstein / Burn Down The Kings Road /
Blown To Bits

CRESCENDO OF REFLEXIONS, Kraze
3725-1108/-2 (1992) (USA release)
Warning / New Age Of Total Warfare / Burn
Down The Kings Road / Metal Anarchy /
Blown To Bits / Military Shadow / Elite Forces

/ Disgrace / Deathcharge / Living For The Last
Days / Dance Of The Dead / Prince Of
Darkness

DECADE OF DECIBELS, Bleeding Hearts
BLEED 8 (1993)
Warning / New Age Of Total Warfare / Burn
Down The King's Road / Metal Anarchy /
Blown To Bits / Military Shadow / Elite Forces
/ Disgrace / Deathcharge / Living For The Last
Days / Dance Of The Dead / Prince Of
Darkness

WARHAMMER (GERMANY)
Line-Up: Volker Frerich (vocals), Marco
Hoffmann (guitar), Rainer Filipiak (guitar),
Frank Krynojewski (bass), Rolf Meyn (drums)

WARHAMMER are openly blatant about their
appreciation to the cult legends
HELLHAMMER. So much so in fact that their
music is a deliberate homage to the Swiss
forefathers. The band debuted with the demo
session 'Towards The Chapter Of Chaos'.
WARHAMMER drafted second guitarist
Rainer Filipiak for the 1999 'Deathchrist'
outing.

Singles/EPs:

Riders / Blood And Honour / Alone /
Warhammer, (199-) ('Riders' EP)

Albums:

THE WINTER OF OUR DISCONTENT,
Voices Productions (1997)
Beyond Forgiveness / Damned For
Extinction / The Shape Of The Enemy /
Warzones / Drowned In Blackness /
Devastation Of Silent Resistance / Under
The Wings Of The Cross / Imposter Of All
Times / The Void Inside The Darkness / The
Winter Of Our Discontent / The Horror

DEATHCHRIST, Grind Syndicate Media
(1999)
This Graveyard Earth / Mankinds Darkest
Day / The Thorn Of Damnation / Deathchrist
/ The Capacity Of Tragic / Defy The Dark /
The Demon's Breed / Among The Dead /
The Tempter Of Destruction / The Realm Of
Torment

THE DOOM MESSIAH, Nuclear Blast NB
603-2 (2000)
Remorseless Winter / Shadow Of The
Decapitator / Cries Of The Forsaken / Hell Is
Open... / Cruel Transcendency / The Doom
Messiah / The Serpents Tantrum / Cruel And
Dying World / In Pain We'll Burn / The
Skullcrusher

WARHEAD (BELGIUM)
Line-up: Patrick 'The Beast' (vocals), Didier
'Wall Of Sound' (guitar), 'Firedamp' (bass),

Pierre (drums)

Albums:
SPEEDWAY, Mausoleum (1985)
Speedway / Kill The Witch / Driver / Devil's Child / Attack Of The Shark / The Alliance / Attack And Kill / First Light Of The Apocalypse
THE DAY AFTER, Mausoleum (1986)
Legions Of Hell / Evil Night / Devil's Church / The Day After / Black Time / Last Night / Fall Out

WARHEAD (UK)
Line-up: Evo (vocals / drums), Würzel (guitar), Algy Ward (guitar), Alan Ward (bass), Chris Labron (keyboards)

Extracurricular band project of MOTÖRHEAD guitarist WURZEL. Bassist Algy Ward is ex-TANK and DAMNED whilst Evo is ex-WARFARE.
By 1995 Ward was bank in the DAMNED then formed a resurrected TANK whilst Wurzel, having quit MOTÖRHEAD and after playing the London clubs with THE GANG SHOW, was a member of punk band DISGUST.

Albums:
WARHEAD, Communiqué CMGCD011 (1995)
Fear Zone / Dancing The Unknown / Touching Imagination / Dark Victory / Artistic Decline / Atmospheric Chill / Solitaire Dementia / Dream Rehearsal / Damned / Ever Eternal / Some Weird Sin

WAR MACHINE (UK)
Line-Up: Bernadette Mooney (vocals), Steve White (guitar), Lez Fry (bass), Brian Waugh (drums)

Outfit put together by former ATOMKRAFT guitarist Steve White in 1983 with original drummer Steve Smith who was superseded by Brian Waugh for the album. Waugh was later to depart and in came drummer Chris Buggy.
In 1989 WAR MACHINE regrouped to record a three track demo after which Mooney departed. Buggy also left to be replaced by Mark Savage who in turn performed drum duties on VENOM guitarist MANTAS solo album. Savage now fronts for XLR8R as lead vocalist.

Albums:
UNKNOWN SOLDIER, Neat NEAT 1036 (1986)
Sacred Hold / On The Edge / Power / No Time / Dangerous / Can't Wait / No Place To Hide /

Warrior

WARPATH (GERMANY)
Line-Up: Dicker (vocals), Ozzy (guitar), Schröder (guitar), Maurer (bass), Krid (drums)

Hamburg's WARPATH first contributed two tracks to the West Virginia Records compilation album 'Cries Of The Unborn' prior to being offered a deal. The debut album, produced by Andy Classen of HOLY MOSES, features guest vocals from CRONOS mainman Conrad Lant and Sabina Classen of HOLY MOSES.
In their time WARPATH toured alongside SODOM, FORBIDDEN and GOREFEST. The 1996 album 'Kill Your Enemy' includes a cover version of CRO-MAGS 'Sign Of Hard Times'. Vocalist 'Dicker' (Dirk Weiss) created RICHTHOFEN in 1997 with ex-HOLY MOSES guitarist Andy Classen.

Albums:
WHEN WAR BEGINS... TRUTH DISSAPEARS, West Virginia 084-57162 (1994)
Resistance Is Useless / Die In Grief / Forest Of Anima / Last Vacation / Wardance / Absolution / You Are The Sickness / Those Crawling Insects / Tightrope Walk / The Ballad Of H / Hypocrite / Black Metal
AGAINST EVERYONE, Steamhammer SPV 084-76812 (1994)
Gate Crasher / In Rage / Against Everyone / Terminus / Give A Shit / I Hate / Night On Earth / Paranoia / Vote Of Censure / That's For Me / Mind Commits Murder / End Of Salvation
MASSIVE, Steamhammer SPV 085-76672 (1995)
Intro / Massive / Pain / Race War / Ambivalence / Save Me From The Wreckage / Fears Of The Past / Remember My Name / Always Near You / Thoughts Begin To Bite / Reason Enough To Die
KILL YOUR ENEMY, Steamhammer SPV 085-18252 (1996)
Kill Your Enemy / A Matter Of Fact / Die Maschine / Frustration Grows / Outburst Of Rage / The Struggle / Sign Of Hard Times / Stomp / Overrollin' / Kill Your Enemy II

WASTELAND (GERMANY)
Line-Up: Tobias Schmalfeld (vocals), Tobias Kramer (guitar), Stephan Kern (guitar), André Ipfling (bass), Frank Gottschalk (drums)

WASTELAND rank as one of the new breed of pure Thrash Metal acts. The group was assembled during 1995 with a line-up comprising guitarists Stephan Kern and Tobias Kramer, bass player Frank Neugebauer and drummer Frank Gottschalk. Tobias Schmalfeld was soon added as lead vocalist. However, Kramer decamped in April of 1995 but would return by the November.

WASTELAND debuted with the privately issued 'Mare Tranquillitatis' mini-album but would be shaken when, in January of 1996, Neugebauer announced his departure. Within 24 hours WASTELAND had plugged the gap drafting André Ipfling.

In September of 1997 the band went back into the studio to record the full length 'Genuine Parts' album. Released in May of 1998 'Genuine Parts' garnered healthy press reports enabling WASTELAND to put in live appearances at festivals such as the 'Schweizer Garten' in Wittenberg in March 1997 and the 'Fuck the Commerce II' festival in 1998.

WASTELAND have contributed to various compilation collections including 'Deathophobia IV', 'Bullet In The Head I' and 'European Deathophobia'. During 1999 the band cut a whole slew of cover tracks for the American Dwell label contributing versions of 'Reckoning Day' to a MEGADETH tribute, 'Evil Dead' to a DEATH homage, 'Time Is Coming' to a TESTAMENT album. The group even donated AC/DC's 'Riff Raff' and LED ZEPPELIN's 'Wearing And Tearing' to tribute collections.

Albums:
MARE TRANQUILLITATIS, (1995)
Lavatory Charwoman / Dead End / Revelation Of Fear / How To Get Mentally Cracked / Chemikills - Wasted Land
GENUINE PARTS, (1998)
Infernal Heart / Winter Bloodthirst / Remains / Mania / Agony Of Christ / My Own Requiem / Blackherder Demon / 2nd Intergalactical Cyclone / Forever / Shadow The God / First Knife

WATCHTOWER (Austin, TX, USA)
Line-Up: Alan Tecchio (vocals), Ron Jarzombek (guitar), Doug Keyser (bass), Rick Colaluca (drums)

Metal band renowned for their inventiveness and complexity. Formed by drummer Rick Colaluca and bassist Doug Keyser in 1981, the original incarnation of WATCHTOWER also included vocalist Jason McMaster and guitarist BILLY WHITE.

WATCHTOWER debuted with an out of place track on a hardcore compilation record 'A Texas Hardcore Compilation: Cottage Cheese From The Lips Of Death'. The band also recorded a proposed debut album for Rainforest Records. The label went bust and the tapes subsequently became highly sought after on the tape trading scene.

McMaster's talents were well regarded and in 1986 the man turned down an offer from PANTERA. Whilst McMaster recorded with WATCHTOWER on their debut album and stuck with them for five months, one of his side bands, DANGEROUS TOYS, eventually got picked up by Columbia. Jason, naturally, quit. Keyser meantime auditioned for METALLICA following the loss of Cliff Burton, reportedly getting into the final placings.

McMaster was eventually replaced by ex-MILITIA and ASSAILANT singer Mike Soliz. The man's tenure was short though and after a 1987 demo 'Instruments Of Random Murder' former HADES frontman Alan Tecchio took the position. Tecchio had actually been tipped off about the vacancy by McMaster, urging his fellow singer to put in a call to Keyser.

Billy White joined DON DOKKEN's solo group and would later form the BILLY WHITE TRIO in the mid '90s. WATCHTOWER recruited Ron Jarzombek, who previously played with SAN ANTONIO SLAYER and Mark Reale's NARITA, to the ranks three years before the recording of the second album took place in 1989. Amusingly, the band was known at one point for playing a live, Metallic rendition of MICHAEL JACKSON's 'Billie Jean'!

WATCHTOWER guested for CORONOR on a 1990 European tour after which Tecchio bailed out to join NON FICTION in June. WATCHTOWER were for a short period fronted by Scott of CONFESSOR.

Tecchio would rejoin his original act HADES for a reformation whilst post DANGEROUS TOYS McMaster would appear on albums from BROKEN TEETH and GODZILLA MOTOR COMPANY.

Keyser and Colaluca were to be found in the ranks of RETARDED ELF.

Albums:
ENERGETIC DISASSEMBLY, Zombo 44452 (1985)
Violent Charge / Asylum / Tyrants In Distress / Social Fears / Energetic Disassembly / Argonne Forest / Cimmerian Shadows / Meltdown
CONTROL AND RESISTANCE, Noise N 0140-2 (1990)
Instruments Of Random Murder / Eldritch / Mayday In Kiev / Fall Of Reason / Control And Resistance / Hidden Instincts / Life Cycles / Dangerous Toy

433

WAYNE (USA)

Line-Up: David Wayne (vocals), Jimi Bell (guitar), Craig Wells (guitar), Mark Franco (bass), B.J. Zampa (drums)

A twist in the tale of renowned and highly respected Thrash veterans METAL CHURCH. Following the comeback studio album 'Masterpeace' METAL CHURCH, not for the first time in their career, parted ways with singer David Wayne. The man had originally fronted the band from 1983 onwards lending his distinctive bellow to what many regard as METAL CHURCH's finest moments, the debut 'Metal Church' and the mammoth second effort 'The Dark'.

Wayne would decamp at the pinnacle make or break juncture of METAL CHURCH's success in what many analysts at the time perceived was a rash move. Years later it would be revealed the singer had bailed out in order to clean up from drug abuse. Wayne resurfaced with REVEREND issuing a further string of commendable, if not commercially successful, albums. METAL CHURCH persevered turning in solid and even inspiring works with Wayne's replacement Mike Howe but would ultimately bite the dust.

The band, complete with Wayne and much of the classic line-up, reunited for the 'Masterpeace' album but fractures began to show yet again. With the METAL CHURCH membership in disarray at the turn of the millennium it emerged that Wayne had set up a fresh act initially titled DAVID WAYNE'S METAL CHURCH! Joining him were METAL CHURCH colleague and guitarist Craig Wells, former JOINT FORCES, GEEZER and THUNDERHEAD guitarist Jimi Bell and drummer B.J. Zampa, a veteran of YNGWIE MALMSTEEN, MVP, TONY MACALPINE and THUNDERHEAD. Bell also operates the covers band TATTERED TRAMPS.

The resulting album, released by the German Nuclear Blast label and naturally called 'Metal Church', not only witnessed the re-introduction of METAL CHURCH's famous guitar-cross device on the cover art but sported a WAYNE icon in the exact logotype as METAL CHURCH. The record would also sport a cover version of MOUNTAIN's 'Mississippi Queen'.

Wayne would not neglect his duties with REVEREND, gearing up for a new album release in 2002.

Albums:
METAL CHURCH, Nuclear Blast (2001)
The Choice / The Hammer Will Fall / Soos Creek Cemetery / Hannibal / Burning At The Stake / D.S.D. / Nightmare Part II / Vlad / Ballad For Marianne / Mississippi Queen

WEHRMACHT (Portland, OR, USA)

Line-Up: Tito Matos (vocals), Marco Zorich (guitar), John Duffy (guitar), Shann Mortimer (bass), Brian Lehfeldt (drums)

Infamous Speed Metal 'Beer-Core' act out of Portland. WEHRMACHT would ultimately fold due to drummer Brian Lehfeldt's success with his side projects SWEATY NIPPLES and CRYPTIC SLAUGHTER.

Originally intended as a joke band the subsequent ascendancy of SWEATY NIPPLES, a union with future EVERCLEAR guitarist David Luprinzi, would preclude Lehfeldt from his prior WEHRMACHT commitments. Latterly Lehfeldt has dabbled with FLOOD BUCKET and is now ensconced with VOLCANIC and TV: 616.

Albums:
SHARK ATTACK, New Renaissance NRR 23 (1987)
Shark Attack / Blow You Away / S.O.P. / Jabberjaw / Barrage Of Skankers / United Shoebrothers / (Puking) Part II / Go Home / Anti / Napalm Shower / Crazy Ways People Die / Fretboard Gymnastics / Terminator
BIERMACHT, Shark SHARK 009 (1988)
You Broke My Heart / Gore Fix / Beer Is Here / Drink Beer, Be Free / Everb / Micro E / Balance Of Opinion / Suck / Drink Jack / Radical Dissection / Beermacht / Outro

WHIPLASH (Passaic, NJ, USA)

Line-Up: Warren Conditi (vocals / guitar), Tony Portaro (guitar), Jimmy Preziosa (bass), Bob Candella (drums)

WHIPLASH initially made their mark as a ferocious trio out of New Jersey founded by ex-TOXIN guitarist Tony Portaro and drummer T.J. Scaglione in 1984. True to form the band was titled after the landmark METALLICA song of the same name.

WHIPLASH was formed from the amalgamation of their two previous acts JACKHAMMER and TOXIN to form a fresh act fronted by vocalist Mike Orosz and including bassist Rob Harding. As a quartet WHIPLASH unveiled themselves with the 'Full Force' demo tape prior to Orasz and Harding leaving the ranks. The remaining duo, with Portaro handling bass and vocals, kept the momentum going with a further cassette 'Thunderstruck'.

For recording of the next session the band drafted bassist Tony Bono and after unsuccessfully attempting to locate a lead vocalist settled on the trio format with Portaro taking the singing duties. Their third tape featured five songs and was titled 'Looking

Death In The Face'. Quite remarkably Portaro recorded these cuts with his arm in plaster having suffered a broken arm in a car accident. Nonetheless, the combination of their latter two tapes secured WHIPLASH a deal with Roadrunner Records for their commercial debut 'Power And Pain'.

In 1986 an 18 year old Scaglione received an offer he could not refuse from Thrash meisters SLAYER. Scaglione's skills would be put to the test in full public gaze replacing DAVE LOMBARDO, renowned as one of the very finest drummers of the genre. WHIPLASH drafted Joe Cangelosi on the drum stool for the 1987 album 'Ticket To Mayhem"

During late 1988 WHIPLASH added vocalist Glen Hanson and, retaining Cangelosi on drums, began to gather together material for a third album titled 'Insult To Injury'. Former drummer Scaglione was announced as the new drummer in Southern infused retro Rockers RAGING SLAB around the same period. The drummer would later affiliate with Hardcore units CAUSE FOR ALARM and SHEER TERROR.

Cangelosi would later unite with German Thrash veterans KREATOR for their 'Cause For Conflict' album.

Bono joined Hardcore unit INTO ANOTHER, fronted by ex-YOUTH OF TODAY vocalist Richie Birkenhead, for their eponymous 1992 album. Scaglione and Portaro would find themselves as members of the same band once more in 1993 when the duo acted as touring musician's for Billy Milano's M.O.D. European dates.

WHIPLASH conjoined with label mates SKYCLAD for a 1996 European tour and, although WHIPLASH's intense brand of retro Thrash seemed an uneasy bed partner for SKYCLAD's increasingly whimsical folk metal, the tour fared well for both acts. Drums were now in the hands of Rob Candella.

Pressures of the road were soon to show though as Gonzo was unceremoniously fired upon the tour's completion and WHIPLASH duly manouvered Conditi into the lead vocal position. The band issued the 'Thrashback' album in 1998, a collection of archive material re-recorded. One of these early tracks, 'Chained Up, Strapped Down', would be lyrically switched to become 'Nails In Me Deep'. Some critics took issue with the alteration of deemed classics and especially the cleaner vocal sound but overall the return of WHIPLASH was universally welcomed.

During 1999 Dutch label Displeased would re-package the first two albums as a double pack CD and release a collection of demos and rarities entitled 'Messages In Blood - The Early Years'. Another CD set, 'Insult To Injury',

comprised live tracks recorded in 1986 at the legendary CBGB's club in New York.

Scaglione these days operates with Hardcore acts the NORTH SIDE KINGS, ZERO SRI and MANTRA, a band led by CHANNEL ZERO guitarist Peter Iterbeke and also including erstwhile WHIPLASH colleague bassist Jimmy Preziosa.

Albums:

POWER AND PAIN, Roadrunner RR 9718 (1985)

Stage Dive / Red Bomb / Last Man Alive / Message In Blood / War Monger / Power Thrashing Death / Stirring The Cauldron / Spit On Your Grave / Nailed To The Cross

TICKET TO MAYHEM, Roadracer RO 95962 (1987)

Perpetual Warfare / Walk The Plank / Last Nail In The Coffin / Drowning In Torment / The Burning Of Atlanta / Eternal Eyes (Last Nail In The Coffin Part II) / Snake Pit / Spiral Of Violence / Respect The Dead / Perpetual Warfare

INSULT TO INJURY, Roadracer RO 9482-2 (1989)

Voice Of Sanity / Hiroshima / Insult To Injury / Dementia B / Essence Of Evil / Witness To The Terror / Battle Scars / Rape To The Mind / Ticket To Mayhem / 4 ES / Pistolwhipped

CULT OF ONE, Massacre MASS CD087 (1996)

Such Is The Will / No One's Idol / No Fear To Tread / 1,000 Times / Wheel Of Misfortune / Heavenaut / Lost World / Cult Of One / Enemy / Apostle Of Truth

SIT, STAND, KNEEL, PRAY, Massacre MAS PC0129 (1997)

Climb Out Of Hell / Left Unsaid / Hitlist / Cyanide Grenade / Jane Doe / Knock Me Down / Lack Of Contrition / Word To The Wise / Strangeface / Catharsis / Sit, Stand, Kneel, Pray

THRASHBACK, Massacre MAS DP0148 (1998)

Temple Of Punishment / Stab / This / Killing On Monroe Street / King With The Axe / Strike Me Blind / Memory Serves / Resurrection Chair / House With No Doors / Thrash 'Til Death / Nails In Me Deep

MESSAGES IN BLOOD - THE EARLY YEARS, Displeased D-00067 (1999)

King With The Axe / Spit On Your Grave / Thrash 'Til Death / Chained Up, Strapped Down / Burning Of Atlanta / Stirrin' The Cauldron / Respect The Dead / Last Man Alive / Spit On Your Grave / Killing On Monroe Street / Eternal Eyes / Respect The Dead / Stirrin' the Cauldron / Burning Of Atlanta / Nailed To The Cross / War Monger / Message In Blood / Nailed To The Cross / Stagedive

INSULT TO INJURY - LIVE CBGB'S 1986,

Displeased D-00064 (1999)

WILCZY PAJAK (POLAND)
Line-Up: Leszek Szpigiel (vocals), Piotr Mánkowski (guitar), Maciej Matuszak (guitar), Mariusz Przbylski (bass), Tomasz Goehs (drums)

Thrash act WILCZY PAJAK would evolve into the more familiar WOLFSPIDER for two albums 'Kingdom Of Paranoia' and 'Drifting In The Sullen Sea'.
The 1987 album was preceded by a live split affair with fellow Poles DRAGON.

Albums:
WILCZY PAJAK, (1987)

WITCHERY (SWEDEN)
Line-Up: Toxine (vocals), Patrick Jensen (guitar), Ricard Corpse (guitar), Sharlee D'Angelo (bass), Mique (drums)

Trad Metal merchants WITCHERY were created in 1997 from the ashes of SÉANCE and SATANIC SLAUGHTER. The band has set itself apart from the crowd by blending elements of Black, Death and retro 'Thrashback' styled Metal, this amalgamation seeing WITCHERY rapidly attaining solid international sales. Musically WITCHERY are unafraid to show their influences as made evident by the frequent '80s Metal cover versions that letter their catalogue.
Both vocalist Toxine and drummer Mique had also been members of TOTAL DEATH whilst Mique had also been involved in MORGUE together with guitarist Ricard Corpse.
WITCHERY came together when SATANIC SLAUGHTER vocalist Ztephan Dark fired his entire band just days before a scheduled album recording. Undaunted the quartet stuck together to found WITCHERY enlisting MERCYFUL FATE and ILLWILL bassist Sharlee D'Angelo. The latter's priority commitments to MERCYFUL FATE meant that recording of the debut WITCHERY album was delayed until the Autumn of 1997.
The band put in their debut show in April 1998 at Copenhagen's 'Rock Amar' club although minus Ricard who was too ill to perform.
The 1999 mini-album 'Restless And Dead' comprises originals plus various covers including ACCEPT's 'Restless And Wild', BLACK SABBATH's 'Neon Knights', W.A.S.P.'s 'I Wanna Be Somebody' and JUDAS PRIEST's 'Riding On The Wind'.
WITCHERY put in a showing at the renowned German 'Wacken Metal' festival in 1999.
Guitarist Patrick Jensen, also operates with THE HAUNTED. Toxine and Corpse also busy

themselves with INFERNAL. Mique has a side project entitled RHOCA GIL.
Latterly WITCHERY have cut versions of KING DIAMOND's 'The Shrine' and the SCORPIONS 'China White' for tribute albums.

Albums:
RESTLESS AND DEAD, Necropolis NR029 (1998)
The Reaper / Witchery / Midnight At The Graveyard / The Hangman / Awaiting The Exorcist / All Evil / House Of Raining Blood / Into Purgatory / Born In The Night / Restless And Dead
WITCHBURNER, Necropolis NR034 (1999)
Fast As A Shark / I Wanna Be Somebody / Riding On The Wind / Neon Knights / The Howling / The Executioner / Witchburner
DEAD, HOT AND READY, Necropolis (2000)
Demonication / A Paler Shade Of Death / The Guillotine / Resurrection / Full Moon / The Dead And The Dance Done / Dead, Hot And Ready / The Devil's Triangle / Call Of The Coven / On A Black Horse Thru Hell...
SYMPHONY FOR THE DEVIL, Necropolis (2001)
The Storm / Unholy Wars / Inquisition / Omens / Bone Mill / None Buried Deeper / Wicked / Called For By Death / Hearse Of The Pharaohs / Shallow Grave / Enshrined / The One

WITCHHAMMER (BRAZIL)
Line-Up: Paulo Henrique (vocals / guitar), Leandro (guitar), Casito (bass), Teddy (drums)

WITCHHAMMER debuted with the less than tactfully titled 'Weekend In Auschwitz' demo session of November 1987 and gained further exposure with their inclusion on the 'Warfare Noise III' compilation album. Signing to the Brazilian Cogumelo label WITCHHAMMER debuted with 1988's 'The First And The Last'. 1990's 'Mirror My Mirror' would follow and finally the 1992 swansong 'Blood On The Rocks'.

Albums:
THE FIRST AND THE LAST, Cogumelo COG018 (1988)
MIRROR MY MIRROR, Cogumelo (1990)
BLOOD ON THE ROCKS, Cogumelo COG048 (1992)

WITCHHAMMER (NORWAY)
Line-Up: Per Ståle Pettersen (vocals), Tor Erik Håkonsen (guitar), Peder Kjøs (guitar), Finn C. Gjerlaugsen (bass), Jan Erik Eide (drums)
Thrashers WITCHHAMMER, despite leaving

a solitary legacy of one self financed album, made quite an impression on the Scandinavian Metal scene. The band came into being during August of 1986 being boosted to a quintet with the enrollment of bassist Finn C. Gjerlaugsen just prior to their inaugural gig. Bass had originally been the domain of lead vocalist Per Ståle Pettersen, WITCHHAMMER being rounded out by guitarists Tor Erik Håkonsen and Peder Kjøs alongside drummer Jan Erik Eide. The band's singer had already carved out a considerable reputation for himself albeit not in the Metal world but as lead actor in productions such as 'Les Miserables' and 'Jesus Christ Superstar'. Projected demo recordings would in fact provide the catalyst for recording of a full length album, a project which was finalised in September of 1988. As WITCHHAMMER touted the tapes to labels in search of a deal, a tour with ARTCH was finalised. However, Kjøs decamped with little warning. WITCHHAMMER swiftly inducted Frank Wilhelmsen as replacement. With the culmination of the ARTCH dates WITCHHAMMER headlined an annual Thrash Metal festival in Bergen. Wilhelmsen would then depart in order to join METAL THUNDER and in a paradoxical turn of events METAL THUNDER six stringer Morten Skute duly teamed up with WITCHHAMMER. The '1497' album finally arrived in March of 1990 to positive reviews internationally. A headline Norwegian tour as well as Swedish gigs bolstered the band's reputation and once again WITCHHAMMER topped the bill at the Bergen Thrash festival. Valuable exposure would also be garnered when an Oslo show was broadcast on national television.

A follow up album was recorded later the same year but in September Skute made his exit. The album tapes would remain consigned to the vaults for a decade as WITCHHAMMER remained inactive, eventually resurfacing in 2000 billed as 'The Lost Tapes'.

Recently WITCHHAMMER have reformed for live work.

Albums:
1487, Witchhammer W001 (1988)
Intro / Transylvania / Kill All In Sight / Burning Court / The Whore Of Babylon / Enola Gay / Hallow's Eve / My Execution / By This Axe I Rule / Curiosity About Death
THE LOST TAPES, Dazed (2000)
Human Rights / Confrontation / No Name / Deliver Us From Evil / Beware The Child / The Ultimate Constellation / Be All End All / On My Own / Touch Of An Angel

WITCHMASTER GENERAL
(CANADA)
Line-Up: Randy Chase (vocals), Mark Beaudoin (guitar), Dan McNamara (guitar), Bryant Dale (bass), Tom Kavanagh (drums)

Ottawa Thrash Metal band WITCHMASTER GENERAL released a 1992 demo.

WOLFPACK (UK)

Ex-members of WOLFPACK founded SALEM for a 1988 demo tape.

Albums:
TOTAL HEAD REMOVAL, Chain Reaction CRE 101 (1987)
Full Scale Attack / Hell On Earth / Vigilante / Devil's Child / Maniac / Death By Default / Evil Lives / Traitors Gate

WOLFSPIDER (POLAND)
Line-Up: Jacky (vocals), Mankover (guitar), Popcorn (guitar), Jeff (bass), Tommy G. (drums)

Polish Thrash act previously titled WILCYY PAJAK. In this guise the band issued a split album with fellow Poles DRAGON.

Albums:
KINGDOM OF PARANOIA, Under One Flag FLAG 49 (1990)
Manifestants / Pain / Black n' Whites / Foxes / Waiting For Sense / Desert / Sickened Nation / Nasty-ment / Survive
DRIFTING IN THE SULLEN SEA, Under One Flag FLAG 63 (1991)
Blind Faith / Liberated Woman / Inclined / My Home / Drifting In A Sullen Sea / King Of The Animals / Freedom / Black And White (Part Two) / Enterprising Man / Orphanage

WIZZARD (FINLAND)
Line-Up: Teemu Kautonen (vocals / bass), Dan (guitar), Grobi (drums)

Black Thrash Metal with a prevalent '80s stance. WIZZARD mainman Teemu Kautonen is ex-DARKWOODS MY BETROTHED and NATTVINDENS GRAT. WIZZARD debuted with the demo 'I Am The King'. Although recorded in 1996 financial uncertainties with the band's German label resulted in a three year delay before the release of the debut album.

WIZZARD's early line-up comprised Kautonen, guitarist Hellboozer, second guitarist Demonos Sora of BARATHRUM and drummer Ville. After recording of the first record Wellu took over the drum position before Kautonen relocated to Germany establishing WIZZARD as an all new trio rounded off by THARGOS members guitarist Dan and drummer Grobi. By August of 1997 though the man was back in Finland laying down the sophomore 'Devilmusick' album for Spinefarm Records.

Line up for this release was Kautonen, guitarist Wilska Torquemada and drummer J. Crow. For live work another DARKWOODS MY BETROTHED man, drummer Tero, joined the fold. A package tour of Finland with BARATHRUM, HORNA and BABYLON WHORES was undertaken with JeeJee on second guitar and Torquemada switched to bass.

Further Finnish dates in April 1998 witnessed the departure of Tero and inclusion of erstwhile NIGHTWISH guitarist Samppa. With Pasi making up the numbers on drums a third album was recorded for Near Dark Productions but fiscal matters once more dogged the band and the album would be shelved. Fortunately for WIZZARD Massacre Records sub division Gutter Records licensed the album 'Songs Of Sin And Decadence' for 2000 release.

WIZZARD's 2000 EP 'Tormentor' sees a cover of JUDAS PRIEST's 'Breaking The Law'. Kautonen relocated back to Germany and also resurrected his union with Dan and Grobi for a further incarnation of WIZZARD.

Singles/EPs:
Songs Of Sin and Decadence / I Am The King / Breaking The Law / Get Slaughtered, Gutter (2000) ('Tormentor' EP)

Albums:
DEVILMUSICK, Spinefarm (1997)
Rock n' Roll (Devil's Music) / Feathers Burn, Leather Doesn't / One Way Ticket To Hell / Little Lyndsey / … Down The Pit Of Doom / Iron, Speed, Metal / Dirty As Fuck / Satan's Blues (In A Minor) / Vultures Over Golgotha / Revenge Of The Witch
WIZZARD, Nasgûl's Eyrie Productions NEP016 (1999)
Black Leather And Cold Metal / Fenris Is Loose! / Demons Blood / The Lord Of Shadows / I Am The King / Get Your Kicks On Route 666 / Possessed By Inferno / Thou Daughter Of Fire / Pestilence / Saviours Of Metal / When The Sun Goes Down / My Unholy Witch / Leather, Booze And Rock n' Roll / Hot Lead / Sabbath
SONGS OF SIN AND DECADENCE, Gutter (2000)
Sins Of A Past Life / Temple Of Eternal Evil / A Midnight Rendezvous / The Fire Of Volcanus / Angel De La Barthe / Sundown

Over Lavenham / Tormentor / Nacht Der Verdammten Seele / The Left Hand Of Eternity / Harbingers Of Metal
BLACK HEAVY METAL, Gutter (2001)
Black Heavy Metal / Maleficium / 1590 / The Tell-Tale Heart / Red Eyes In The Night / Soul Of A Devil / Under Eastern Sun / Friday The Thirteenth / 54 Stakes / The Grandmaster's Curse

WORLD WAR III (PA, USA)
Line-Up: Tipa Sparrs (vocals), Gary 'Sledge' Hammer (guitar), Dan Hammer (bass), Johnny DiTeodoro (drums)

The songwriting credits on the single are noted as S. Hammer, P. Taku and D. Drury.
Drummer Johnny DiTeodoro was mistakenly credited on the album cover. He would join the chaotic Pete Way led WAYSTED before returning to Philadelphia to team up with Glam Rockers BRITNY FOX. An earlier WORLD WAR III drummer Dean Davidson would switch to vocals, founding BRITNY FOX.
WORLD WAR III vocalist Tipa Sparrs had joined WHITEFOXX by 1987.

Singles/EPs:
Intensive Care / Come And Get It, Dorcas WW001 (1982)

Albums:
WORLD WAR III, Axe Killer 7009 (1985)
War Is Hell / Final Solution / Call Of The Wild / Steal The Night Away / Gypsy Eyes / Red Alert / Playin' With Fire

WRATH (NEW ZEALAND)
Line-Up: Dan Reed (vocals), Bevan Elliot (guitar), Jon Brooking (bass), Cameron Blackett (drums)

New Plymouth, Taranaki based modern Hardcore Metal band led by vocalist Dan Reed. The band would be the first New Zealand group to stream a live concert to the internet. WRATH was founded in 1994 with an initial line-up of Shane Fever on vocals, Bevan Elliot on guitar, ex-AFTERTHOUGHT bassist Dan 'Boone' Phillips and ex-SACRILEGE man Cameron Blackett on drums. With the departure of Fever WRATH inducted frontman Ari, but this latest frontman left in 1996. The band pulled in rhythm guitarist Dean Hoete and new vocalist Dan Reed in the September. WRATH debuted commercially with 'Rage' included on the 'Demon Nation Volume 1' compilation album. Phillips quit in late 1999, substituted by FEASTUS bassist Jon 'Thumb' Brooking.

Hoete would be the next to go, in 2000.
WRATH trimmed down to a single guitar band during 1999. Both guitarist Bevan Elliot and drummer Cameron Blackett operate as members of CYNICAL PLOY. Blackett is also bassist with N.N.B. and drummer with WOLFSBLADE. Dan Reed also doubles his duties with MOOK and NIMBUS.

Blackett received the 'Best drummer' award at the 2001 Auckland 'Battle Of The Bands' competition finals and supported Australians MISERY. WRATH issued their debut EP 'Feel My Pain' in March of 2002.

Singles/EPs:
Wretch / Fuel My Hate / Gobblefuck / Fexture / You Say / Feel The Pain / Biohazard, Digidiba Studios (2002) ('Feel The Pain' EP)

WRATH (Chicago,IL, USA)
Line-Up: Gary Golwitzer (vocals), Scott Nyquist (guitar), Mike Nyrkkanen (guitar), Gary Modica (bass), Dave Sollman (drums)

Chicago Thrash act WRATH debuted with the 1986 opus 'Fit Of Anger', an album noted for the uniqueness of vocalist Gary Golwitzer's performance. WRATH's 1987 follow up album 'Nothing To Fear', which witnessed drummer Mike Fron replaced by Rick Rios, merited production from guitar veteran RONNIE MONTROSE.

Third outing 'Insane Society' brought forth two new members, vocalist Kurt Grayson and drummer Dave Sollman.

Golwitzer founded STYGIAN for two EPs and an album with drummer Dennis Lesh from fellow Chicago Metal band TROUBLE.

Albums:
FIT OF ANGER, Megaton 0015 (1986)
In The Wake / Children Of The Wicked / What's Your Game / Abuse It / Bones / Fanatics / Fallen Angel / Machine / Vigilante Killer / Breakdown / Sudden Death
NOTHING TO FEAR, Medusa 72222-1 (1987)
R.I.P. (Ripped Into Pieces) / Mutants / Hell Is Full / Painless / Fear Itself / Sudden Death / Incineration - Caustic Sleep / When World's Collide / Victims In The Void
INSANE SOCIETY, Medusa (1989)
Killmania / Panic Control / Test Of Faith / Swarm / War Of Nerves / Insane Society / Low Of Liers / 11th Hours / Closed Doors
WRATH, Medusa MID 94011 (1990)

WYZARD (TX, USA)

Post WYZARD vocalist Buster would found RITUAL in alliance with guitarist Manuel Rajas, keyboard player Mike Johnson and erstwhile WYZARD colleagues Rene on bass and Art on drums. By 1991 Buster was fronting BLIND DATE.

Albums:
KNIGHTS OF METAL, Pazazu (1984)
THE FINAL CATASTROPHE, Mandrake Root (1997)

 **-CRETIA** (BELGIUM)

<u>Albums:</u>
PATRONIZING THE HETERODOX, Torpo (1986)
David Slays Goliath / Exaggerated / Destructive Outfit / The Laws Of Gravitation / The Wild One / Oblivion / The Heterodox / Talks About Morality / The X-Cretia Banzai Mosh

XENTRIX (UK)

Line-Up: Chris Astley (vocals / guitar), Kristian Harrard (guitar), Paul McKenzie (bass), Denis Gasser (drums)

Leyland speed metal act formed in 1986 previously known as SWEET VENGEANCE with vocalist Dacaw Hough. As SWEET VENGEANCE the band recorded various demos and contributed a track to an Ebony Records compilation and released the demo 'Hunger For Death'. Toured with SABBAT in Britain during 1989 during which time bassist Steve Hodgson was temporarily replaced by Mel Gasser prior to Paul McKenzie's appointment. Signed to Roadrunner on the strength of a three track demo in early 1989 as the British thrash explosion peaked. Thier debut album was produced by John Cunibert. The spectre of the 'Ghostbusters' single haunted the band who throughout their career endeavoured to shake off the image connotations and be viewed as a far more serious proposition.
XENTRIX's 1992 single 'The Order Of Chaos' featured a B side rendition of TEARDROP EXPLODES 'Reward'.
XENTRIX added new singer Simon Gordon, previously with RAWHEAD, and guitarist Andy Rudd and were still doing the rounds of club gigs in late 1994. XENTRIX signed to Heavy Metal Records in 1995 for a low key comeback album 'Scourge'.

<u>Singles/EPs:</u>
Ghostbusters / Nobody's Perfect / Interrogate, Roadracer RO 24352 (1990)
Pure Thought / Shadow Of Doubt / Balance Of Power (Live) / Crimes (Live) / Ghostbusters (Live), Roadracer RO 9320 (1991)
The Order Of Chaos / All Bleed Red / Reward, Roadracer (1992)

<u>Albums:</u>
SHATTERED EXISTENCE, Roadracer RO94441 (1989)
No Compromise / Balance Of Power / Crimes / Back In The Real World / Dark Enemy / Bad Blood / Reasons For Destruction / Position Of Security / Heaven Cent
FOR WHOSE ADVANTAGE, Roadracer RO 9366 (1990)
Questions / For Whose Advantage / The Human Condition / False Ideals / The Bitter End / New Beginnings / Desperate Remedies / Kept In The Dark / Black Embrace
KIN, Roadracer RO 9196 (1992)
The Order Of Chaos / A Friend To You / All Bleed Red / No More Time / Waiting / Come Tomorrow / Release / See Through You / Another Day
SCOURGE, Heavy Metal HMR XD 198 (1996)
13 Years / Scourge / Incite / Caught You Living / Strength Of Persuasion / Never Be / The Hand That Feeds Itself / Blood Nation / Creed / Breathe

X-SEED (UK)

Line-Up: Mark Duffy (vocals), Malcolm Spence (guitar), Doug McKendrick (guitar), Paul Thompson (bass), Craig Ward (drums)

X-SEED was founded by vocalist Mark Duffy, former frontman for MILLENIUM and TORANAGA. The 'Desolation' album was produced by SKYCLAD guitarist cum vocalist Kevin Ridley.

<u>Albums:</u>
DESOLATION, Bleeding Hearts (1996)
Get A Life / Freedom / Confrontation / Bleed Me Dry / Desolation / When The Bullets Fly / Consume / Crack Of Doom / Disarray

ZIONOIZ (UK)
Line-Up: Danny Foxx (vocals), Mark J. Mynett (guitar), David John Englund (bass), Craig Beattie (drums)

Manchester Thrash band originally recorded their demo 'Living In Samson's Dreams' and Friday Rock Show radio session in 1988 under the name FOXX, resulting in a record deal with Noise. Record label suggested the name change. Foxx was formerly with BLOODMONEY.

Mynett and Fox (dropping the second 'x') later forged AOR band CHINA BEACH. This band would undergo a drastic musical overhaul to become Nu-Metal crew KILL II THIS.

ZNOWHITE (Chicago, IL, USA)
Line-Up: Nicole Lee (vocals), Ian Tafoya (guitar), Scott Schafer (bass), Sparks Tafoya (drums)

For a relatively short period Chicago Metal band ZNOWHITE used the traditional method of spelling their moniker and performed as SNOWHITE, the irony being at the time that, apart from frontwoman Nicole Lee, the group consisted of black musicians.

ZNOWWHITE was a vehicle for the undoubted talents of guitarist Ian Tafoya. Nicole Lee had originally been engaged as the band's manager but was persuaded to front the group by Tafoya. They were joined in the ranks by his brother Sparks (drums) and cousin Nicky Tafoya (bass) all of whom had played together in a number of previous groups. After the recording of early demos Nicky departed to be briefly replaced by the mysteriously titled Amp Dawg.

After rave reviews, particularly in Europe, ZNOWHITE would sign to the (what appeared to be) German affiliated EMA label after a debut vinyl appearance on the 'Metal Massacre III' compilation with the track 'Hellbent'.

In truth, EMA Polydisc was ZNOWHITE's own label. Having self-financed the recording of an album under the belief that Megaforce would be signing the group, the band decided to release product themselves after the deal fell through. Obtaining manufacturing and distribution channels through Enigma in America, a three track, red vinyl flexidisc was made available to fans through specialist record stores or via the band (the EP contained three tracks from ZNOWHITE's demo tape). ZNOWHITE's debut album, 'All Hail To Thee' was released in 1984 and boasted an unknown guest guitarist on the opening 'Sledgehammer'.

A second album, 'Kick 'Em When They're Down', was released a year later followed by 1986's 'Live Suicide' album. This record was taken from a show in Cleveland, Ohio during December the previous year. By this time the band had been augmented on tour by bassist Scott Schafer.

1988's 'Act Of God' would be the Chicago group's one and only album with Roadrunner Records. At this point Schafer had replaced Sparks Tafoya on the drums and Alex Olivera took over on bass as Ian Tafoya became the sole black musician in the ranks.

Unfortunately, Nicole Lee split the ranks after 'Act Of God' hit the stores. ZNOWHITE, having hired new drummer, ex-TOOLS OF IGNORANCE man John Slattery for the tour after Olivera quit (and was briefly succeeded by Scott Schafer) replaced her with ex-SENTINAL BEAST vocalist Debbie Gunn.

A proposed ZNOWHITE album with Gunn, 'Land Of The Greed, Home Of The Depraved', was never recorded as the singer was out of the band by April 1989. Gunn later moving to Britain in the early '90s to join the Swedish all-girl outfit ICE AGE. She was replaced by Brian Troch as Ian Tafoya chose to work with a male vocalist for the first time.

The 'All Hail To Thee' album eventually made it to CD in 1998 in remastered form on Axe Killer. The 'Kick 'Em When They're Down' opus featured as bonus tracks.

Troch, Scafer and Slattery founded CYCLONE TEMPLE with guitarist Greg Fulton for the 1991 album 'I Hate Therefore I Am'.

Singles/EPs:
Live For The Weekend / Never Felt Like This / Vengeance, EMA Germany 1007ZW (1983) (Red vinyl flexidisc)

Albums:
ALL HAIL TO THEE, EMA Polydisc / Enigma E-1077 (1984)
Sledgehammer / Saturday Night / Somethin' For Nothin' / Bringin' The Hammer Down / Do Or Die / Never Felt Like This / Rock City Destination
KICK 'EM WHEN THEY'RE DOWN, EMA Polydisc / Enigma 72024-1 (1985)
Live For The Weekend / All Hail To Thee / Run Like The Wind / Too Late / Turn Up The Pain
LIVE SUICIDE, EMA Polydisc / Erika ZER606 (1986)
Hell Bent / Bringin' The Hammer Down / There's No Tomorrow / Too Late / Rock City Destination / Night On Parole / Rest In Peace
ACT OF GOD, Roadrunner RR9587-1 (1988)
To The Last Breath / Baptised By Fire / Pure

Blood / War Machine / Thunderdome / Rest In Peace / Disease Bigotry / A Soldier's Creed / Something Wicked (This Way Comes)

ZOETROPE (Chicago, IL, USA)
Line-Up: Barry Stern (vocals / drums), Kevin Michael (guitar), Ken Black (guitar), Calvin 'Willis' Humphrey (bass)

A self-styled 'Street Metal' band from Chicago, ZOETROPE (pronounced e-trop) debuted with the self-financed 'The Right Way' single in 1980. It would be the 'Metal Log Volume I' demo of 1983 that really brought the band to the attention of the masses thanks to its popularity on the tape trading circuit.
The group had a track included on Metal Blade's 'Metal Massacre Volume 4' compilation.
The band's debut album 'Amnesty' (prior to release it was to be titled 'Break Your Back') finally arrived in 1985 and included new interpretations of 'Member In A Gang' and 'Kill The Enemy' from the 'Metal Log...' demo, the group taking on a heavier, Thrashier hue by this point.
Asked once why they preferred to have Barry Stern singing lead whilst performing drum duties Ken Black was quoted as saying: "We don't want no guy with a headband shakin' his ass in front of the stage!"
ZOETROPE's second album was produced by Randy Burns. Louie Svitek had replaced Ken Black, although the departing guitarist had hung around long enough to play on the track 'Unbridled Energy'.
However, things went a little pear shaped after Barry Stern was tempted away with an offer to join TROUBLE and Louie Svitek followed him out of the band around the same time to hook up with METHOD OF DESTRUCTION and later stints with MINDFUNK and MINISTRY.
Kevin Michael and Calvin Humphrey recruited guitarist Mike Garret, ex-SGT. ROCKS drummer Drew Kristoff and vocalist Pete Montswillo

Singles/EPs:
The Right Way / Call "33", Zoetrope (1980)

Albums:
AMNESTY, Combat MY 8025 (1985)
Indecent Obsessions / Kill The Enemy / Mercenary / Amnesty / Member In A Gang / Break Your Back / Another Chance / Creatures / Trip Wires
A LIFE OF CRIME, Music For Nations MFN 76 (1987)
Detention / Seeking Asylum / Promiscuity / NASA / Unbridled Energy / Prohibition / Company Man / Pickpocket / Hard To Survive

Also available from

CHERRY RED BOOKS

Rockdetector
A-Z of
BLACK METAL

Garry Sharpe-Young

ISBN 1-901447-30-8

Throughout the history of Rock no other genre has pushed the boundaries of aural extremity and social rebellion quite like Black Metal. Many of the bands in this book operate way beyond the parameters of the established Rock scene carving their own left hand path in the darkest depths of true underground music.

Over a decade Black Metal has spawned legions of bands making up a truly global rebellion. For the first time ever this ultimate authority documents detailed biographies, line-ups and full discographies with track listings of over 1,000 groups.

Included are in-depth treatises on the major artists such as CRADLE OF FILTH, DIMMU BORGIR, EMPEROR, MAYHEM, IMMORTAL and MARDUK as well as spanning out to include sub-genres such as Viking Metal, the Black Ambient scene and even the ultimate irony of Christian Black Metal. Also chronicled are the originators such as VENOM, WITCHFYNDE, BATHORY and MERCYFUL FATE.

Paper covers, 416 pages, £14.99 in UK

www.cherryred.co.uk

Rockdetector
A-Z of
DEATH METAL
Garry Sharpe-Young

ISBN 1-901447-35-9

Reviled and revered in equal measure since its inception over a decade ago the phenomenon known as Death Metal has pushed Hard Rock music to the very edge of acceptability and way beyond. Born out of the Thrash Metal eruption, Death Metal took vocals to the realms of the unintelligibly insane, drove the blastbeats harder and pushed guitar riffs into a swarming blur. The familiar mythical subject matter of its parent Heavy Metal, and its bastard offspring Grindcore, has become the pariah of the music world as much as the depths of the underground scene has fostered and nurtured its steady growth to this day with each band striving to achieve renewed goals of sickness.

From the founding fathers such as NAPALM DEATH, CARCASS, DEATH, INCANTATION, IMPETIGO and MORBID ANGEL to the rise of Swedish Death Metal legends IN FLAMES, CARNAGE and AT THE GATES, the Death Metal of MARDUK, the Christian Death Metal of MORTIFICATION and the politically charged Noisecore of AGATHOCLES. All genres old and new are analyzed in depth with full career histories and detailed discographies.

No area of the globe has provided a safe haven and this book documents the burgeoning uprise of Death Metal bands in the Far East, Eastern Europe and South America.

Be warned - even though some of the band names are not for the faint-hearted the song titles will leave you reeling.

Paper covers, 416 pages, £14.99 in UK

Rockdetector
A-Z of
POWER METAL
Garry Sharpe-Young

ISBN 1-901447-13-8

Power Metal is Heavy Metal taken to the absolute, surgically precise, limit. When the major Metal institutions staked their claim they engendered a whole legion of followers in their wake. These up and coming acts were not simply content to match the volume levels of their forefathers though. Riffs evolved into complex, labyrinthine proportions, vocals scorched higher altitudes and, yes, they even managed to crank out some more volume as part of the formula. Power Metal had been born.

The acceleration of aggression afforded by the Thrash Metal movement helped boost the rise of Power Metal. As the first wave of Thrash waned, a ready audience of Metal fans lay waiting for something just as heavy but with sophistication. The British guard such as IRON MAIDEN and JUDAS PRIEST had opened the door, now a whole flood of American Metal flooded through ATTACKER, JAG PANZER, ICED EARTH, SAVATAGE and QUEENSRYCHE. In Europe bands rooted in Thrash matured at an alarming rate with HELLOWEEN, GAMMA RAY, BLIND GUARDIAN, RUNNING WILD and GRAVE DIGGER establishing lengthy careers. In latter years Power Metal itself has branched off on its own evolutionary trail spawning Symphonic Metal and Progressive Metal. A recent upsurge in the fortunes of bands such as SONATA ARTICA from Finland, ANGRA from Brazil and RHAPSODY from Italy illustrates just how global the reach of Power Metal has become. Cult acts from the 80s have been reforming at an alarming rate in order to cope with demand.

This book documents the full scope of the world-wide Power Metal phenomenon, tracing the lineage of the bands that paved the way, the first 80s wave of bands, the stoic survivors, the new breed and the myriad spider web like side projects. All with exhaustive, unique histories and detailed discographies.

Paper covers, approx 450 pages £14.99 in UK

Rockdetector
A-Z of
DOOM, GOTH & STONER METAL
Garry Sharpe-Young

ISBN 1-901447-14-6

Laboured, mournful and crushingly heavy. The anaesthetising, sloth like riffs of Doom Metal, the bong fuelled lazy retro Rock that is Stoner and the melancholy strains of Gothic Metal- it's all here. Rooted in ancient instigators such as PENTAGRAM, ATOMIC ROOSTER and the mightiest of the mighty- BLACK SABBATH, Doom has defied all the odds to spawn a huge global fanbase.

The impact of Doom can be felt not only in the respect afforded to faithful cult acts such as THE OBSESSED and TROUBLE but in burgeoning enormity of both the BLACK SABBATH legend and sheer scale of album sales. The rude health of those that have been handed on the flame, the new breed such as MY DYING BRIDE, CATHEDRAL, PARADISE LOST, NOVEMBER'S DOOM and CANDLEMASS, has morphed the genre into one of their own making.

In recent years Doom has taken a left turn into the desert wastelands of America and returned as Stoner. Bands like KYUSS, FU MANCHU, ALABAMA THUNDERPUSSY, IRONBOSS and hundreds of others pulling in legions of fans. The Europeans meantime added Electronica into the blend to create Darkwave and hordes of Metal bands discovered that adding a female vocalist, a Gothic touch and the introduction of avant garde instrumentation lent a whole new lease of life. Numerous artists placed firmly in genres such as Death Metal and Black Metal readily experiment with Doom and Gothic whilst groundbreaking artists such as RAIN FELL WITHIN and AUTUMN'S TEARS lend the whole scene ongoing re-invigoration.

Each and every band is included with an enormous wealth of historical detail and full global discography. From the full, weighty and unedited account of BLACK SABBATH'S tortured history and spanning Stoner, Gothic and Darkwave this book is the first to chronicle the underground world wide phenomena that is Doom.

Paper covers, approx 450 pages £14.99 in UK

Rockdetector
OZZY OSBOURNE
THE STORY OF THE OZZY OSBOURNE BAND
(AN UNOFFICIAL PUBLICATION)
Garry Sharpe-Young

ISBN 1-901447-08-1

Until 1978 THE original and definitive Heavy Metal band BLACK SABBATH was fronted by the irrepressible Ozzy Osbourne. With Osbourne at the helm BLACK SABBATH sold tens of millions of albums. When he finally broke away to fly solo Ozzy would achieve the unthinkable. Not only would he deliver one of the seminal Rock records ever crafted to mark his resurrection but he also used it as a career-making catalyst that would see him trounce his former band mates and evolve into a cult icon.

Along the way Ozzy displayed an enviable knack of choosing a series of groundbreaking guitarists such as Randy Rhoads, Jake E. Lee and Zakk Wylde. There would also be the unsung heroes such as songwriter extraordinaire Bob Daisley and a series of world renowned bassists, drummers and keyboard players.

This then is the story of the Ozzy Osbourne band - in their own words and detailed exclusively here for the first time.

Chronicled with first-hand interviews, this is the real story of the first prototype Blizzard of Ozz band, how Ozzy met Randy Rhoads, the painful saga of Rhoads' replacement Bernie Tormé and the torturous audition processes for successive guitarists and drummers told by both successful and unsuccessful candidates.

The Ozzy Osbourne story - as told by Bob Daisley, Lee Kerslake, Tommy Aldridge, Bernie Tormé, Brad Gillis, Steve Vai, Phil Soussan, Carmine Appice and many, many more.

Garry Sharpe-Young has interviewed more than twenty Ozzy band members and associates solely for this work thus making it the most detailed account of Ozzy's career so far.

"Ozzy Osbourne's solo career would prove spectacular, bizarre and extremely lucrative…" ROUGH GUIDE TO ROCK

Paper covers 368 pages £14.99 in UK

www.cherryred.co.uk

Rockdetector
BLACK SABBATH
Garry Sharpe-Young

FORTHCOMING EARLY 2003
ISBN 1-901447-16-2

Over a full decade Black Sabbath had dominated Heavy Metal. As much as Led Zeppelin scorned the term, Black Sabbath embraced it. In an age of bona fide super-groups Sabbath were unquestionably the heaviest thing stalking the planet and quite remarkably had remained a solid unit where others around them suffered ongoing membership fall-outs and line-up re-incarnations. Tony Iommi, Geezer Butler, Ozzy Osbourne and Bill Ward had weathered internal storms just as ferocious as every other band out on the circuit but had remained resolute. They had conquered the globe, sold close to 50 million albums and without concession had not pulled back one iota from delivering absolute, pure Heavy Metal.

In 1977 the unthinkable happened. Ozzy Osbourne decamped. He would be lured back for one last album "Never Say Die", before flying solo, rapidly building a band unit that would equal the repute of the mothership. The Iommi / Butler / Ward triumvirate at first bounced back in quite spectacular fashion by re-inventing themselves courtesy of their new frontman, the highly gifted Ronnie James Dio. Two classic albums followed but then the picture shattered. For the next two decades Black Sabbath faltered on a rocky path between all too brief moments of genius and fallow desperation. Only Tony Iommi stuck to his guns, the lynchpin amidst a tangled web of chaos. A succession of vocalists took up the challenge- Ian Gillan, Jeff Fenholt, David Donato, Glenn Hughes, Ray Gillen, Tony Martin and Ronnie James Dio once again. Harried by the press at every turn, Tony Iommi nevertheless succeeded in breathing new life into Black Sabbath time and time again. With the band's back catalogue still in heavy demand, those albums crafted in these times of adversity are now recognised as some of Sabbath's finest moments and the huge array of players that travelled through the ranks is now a constant source of fascination and rumours for Sabbath fanatics. Here, for the very first time with exclusive interviews conducted for this book including ones with the late Ray Gillen and Cozy Powell as well as the highly controversial figure of Jeff Fenholt and mysterious Dave Donato, is the definitive account of those years. The auditioning, song writing and recording processes of albums such as "Born Again", "Eternal Idol" and "Seventh Star" are examined in depth making this the definitive account. Author Garry Sharpe-Young is editor in chief at www.rockdetector.com the world's biggest Rock devoted database.

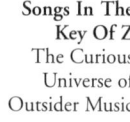

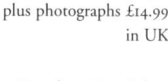
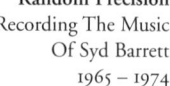

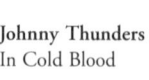

DRAGSTER
N.W.O.B.H.M. Revisited – The Very Best Of Dragster
So This Is England / Destiny / Heartbeat / Bite The Bullet / Ambitions / Mirror Image / Running / Here Comes The Weekend / You Win Again / Running (Version 2) / Bite The Bullet (Version 2) / Ambitions (Volume 2) / Running With The Pack / Until The Morning / Showtime / Action / I Didn't Know I Loved You / Hot legs / Hellraiser

A first time CD release for New Wave of British Heavy Metal legends Dragster. This 19 track compilation features all their fans favourites including "Bite The Bullet", "Running" and "Ambitions".

CDMETAL 17

GASKIN
End Of The World / No Way Out
Sweet Dream Maker / Victim Of The City / Despiser / Burning Alive / The Day Thou Gavest Lord Hath Ended / End Of The World / On My Way / Lonely Man / I'm No Fool / Handful Of Reasons / Dirty Money / Free Man / Just Like A Movie Star / Say Your Last Word / Broken Up / Ready For Love / Come Back To Me / High Crime Zone / Queen Of Flames / No Way Out

Gaskin were one of the most influential N.W.O.B.H.M. bands, to this day bands cite them as a major influence. In 1991 Lars Urich of Metallica included Gaskin on the "NWOBHM '79 Revisited" compilation he released. This double album on one CD features two extremely rare and collectable albums from the band. The original artwork is re-produced, with a full discography.

CDMETAL 6

THE HANDSOME BEASTS
Beastiality
Sweeties / David's Song / Breaker / One In A Crowd / Local Heroes / Another Day / Tearing Me Apart / High Speed / BONUS TRACKS: The Mark Of A Beast / All Riot Now / Sweeties (Single Version) / You're On Your Own

First time on CD for this legendary LP, originally issued as the first release by Wolverhampton based Heavy Metal Records. The original 9 track album has now been joined by four bonus cuts including the singles "All Riot Now" and "Sweeties" to give the definitive Handsome Beasts collection.

CDMETAL 5

MYTHRA
The Death & Destiny LP
Paradise / England / Warrior Of Time / Vicious Bastard / Heaven Lies Above / At Least They Tried / The Death Of A Loved One / The Age Of Machine / Death & Destiny / Killor / Overlord / UFO / Blue Acid

In their short-lived career at the start of the 1980's Mythra managed to gain themselves a reputation that now sees them as one of Britains Heavy Metal treasures. Cited as a 'revolutionary record' by Iron Pages' Matthias Mader this album includes tracks never released on CD format before.

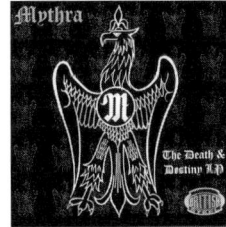

CDMETAL 16

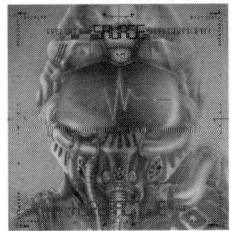

SAVAGE
Hyperactive
We Got The Edge / Eye For An Eye / Hard On Your Heels / Blind Hunger / Gonna Tear Your Heart Out / Stevies Vengeance / Cardiac / All Set To Sting / Keep It On Ice / BONUS TRACKS Runnin' Scared / She Didn't Need You / We Got The Edge (Single Version)

Savage are one of the leading cult bands of the whole New Wave Of British Heavy Metal movement that happened in the early eighties. This seminal album also includes the Mansfield based band's ultra rare three track 12" "We Got The Edge" as a bonus.

CDMETAL 10

WITCHFYNDE
The Best Of Witchfynde

Give 'Em Hell / Unto The Ages Of The Ages / Ready To Roll / Leaving Nadir / Getting' Heavy / Pay Now/ Love Later / Stage Fright / Wake Up Screaming / Moon Magic / In The Stars / The Devil's Playground / I'd Rather Go Wild / Cloak And Dagger / Cry Wolf / Stay Away / Fra Diabolo

Witchfynde was part of the New Wave Of British Heavy Metal of the early 80's that spawned the likes of Iron Maiden, Def Leppard and Judas Priest. Witchfynde still have a great significance on the later generations of Heavy Metal artists, Metallica and Paradise Lost regularly state the band as an influence. This CD includes 16 prime cuts that include the singles, "Give Em Hell", "In The Stars" and "I'd Rather Go Wild" as well as the best tracks from their rare LP's Give Em Hell, Stagefright and Cloak And Dagger. Iron Page's journalist Matthias Mader, an expert in the field has written the liner notes for this release.

CDMETAL 1

HEAVY METAL RECORDS
Singles Collection Vol. 1 : Various Artists

THE HANDSOME BEASTS *All Riot Now / The Mark Of The Beast / Breaker / Crazy / One In A Crowd /* BUFFALO *Battle Torn Heroes / Women Of The Night /* DRAGSTER *Ambitions / Won't Bring You Back /* LAST FLIGHT *Dance To The Music / I'm Ready /* SPLIT BEAVER *Savage / Hound Of Hell /* SATANIC RITES *Live To Ride / Hit And Run*

This is a fifteen track round-up of the first batch of singles released by Heavy Metal Records, the legendary Metal label of the early 80's. Again a highly collectable and expensive package when originally released, with rare and collectable tracks from Buffalo, Dragster, Last Flight, Split Beaver, Satanic Rites and Handsome Beasts. This release appears on CD for the first time, with a full colour booklet that contains a full discography, detailed liner notes and pictures of each of the sleeves.

CDMETAL 3

NEW ELECTRIC WARRIORS
Various Artists

TURBO *Running /* BUFFALO *Battle Torn Heroes /* STREETFIGHTER *She's No Angel /* STORM TROOPER *Grind And Heat /* TAROT *Feel The Power /* BASTILLE *Hard Man /* OXYM *Hot Rain /* DAWN WATCHER *Firing On All Eight /* VARDIS *If I Were King /* SILVERWING *Rock And Roll Are Four Letter Words /* RHABSTALLION *Chain Reaction /* COLOSSUS *Holding Back Your Love /* JEDEDIAH STRUT *Workin' Nights /* WARRIOR *Still On The Outside /* KOSH *The Hit /* RACE AGAINST TIME *Bedtime*

This was the first compilation album to feature bands from the N.W.O.B.H.M. Originally released 17 years ago, the album is now available for the first time on CD. Contributing bands include, Silverwing, Oxym, Buffalo and Streetfighter which was the first band to feature John Sykes of future Thin Lizzy- Whitesnake fame.

CDMETAL 13

N.W.O.B.H.M. METAL RARITIES VOL. 3
Various Artists

GIRLSCHOOL *Take It All Away / It Could Be Better* TWISTED ACE *I Won't Surrender / Firebird* SOLDIER *Sheraleer / Force* JAGUAR *Back Street Woman / Chasing The Dragon* DENIGH *No Way / Running* STATIC *Voice On The Line / Stealin'* SEVENTH SON *Metal To The Moon / Sound & Fury* WHITE LIGHTNING *This Poison Fountain / Hypocrite* DRAGONSLAYER *I Want Your Life / Satan Is Free / Broken Hearts*

The latest in the British Steel series, collecting many ultra rare single releases from the late 70's/ early 80's New Wave Of British Heavy Metal movement, most of which have never appeared on CD before. Vol. 3 includes bands such as Twisted Ace, Soldier and Jaguar, plus the very first single by Girlschool.

CDMETAL 14

ROXCALIBUR
Various Artists

BLACK ROSE *No Point Runnin'/ Ridin' High* BRANDS HATCH *Brands Hatch/ No Return* BATTLEAXE *Burn This Town/ Battleaxe* SATAN *Oppression/ The Executioner* MARAUDER *Battlefield/ Woman Of The Night* UNTER DEN LINDEN *Wings Of Night/ Man At The Bottom* SKITZOFRENIK *Exodus/ Keep Right On.*

Originally issued via Guardian Records in 1982, all fourteen cuts are unique to this album which gathered together some of the New Wave of British Heavy Metal scenes rising stars and includes contributions from Black Rose, Marauder, Battleaxe and Skitzofrenik.

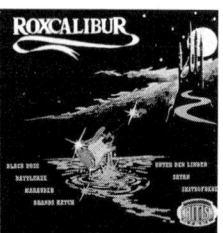

CDMETAL 15

ROCKDETECTOR: A TO Z OF THRASH METAL – FREE CD

1. SCARIOT - The Cynic (Daniel Olaisen & Scariot)
© 2001. Courtesy of Scariot. From the album TONGUELESS GOD

2. VICIOUS RUMORS - All Rights Reserved
(G.Thorpe / C.Albert / M.McGee / L.Howe)
© 1994 Courtesy of Vicious Rumors / Headless Butchers Songs
/ Zomba Music (ASCAP). From the album WORD OF MOUTH

3. ATOMIZER - Now That's Fuckin' Evil (Atomizer)
© 2002 Courtesy of Atomizer. From the album THE END OF FOREVER

4. DECEASED - It's Alive (Deceased)
© 2001 Courtesy of Relapse Records

5. MERENDINE ATOMICHE - Mental Agony (Luca M. & Merendine Atomiche)
© 2000 Courtesy NoBRAIN. From the album THE HOLY METAL

6. GRIFFIN - Death Row League (Griffin)
© 2002 Courtesy of Season Of Mist. From the album THE SIDESHOW

7. SOLITARY - 15 Years(Exclusive Version) (Sherrington / Miller)
© 2002 Courtesy of Copro Records. From the as yet untitled forthcoming album

8. NEVERMORE - The Heart Collector (Loomis / Dane)
© 2000 Courtesy of Century Media Records, Magic Art Publishing
From the album DEAD HEART IN A DEAD WORLD

9. ARCH ENEMY - Ravenous (Michael Amott / Christopher Amott / Angela Gossow)
© 2002 Courtesy of Century Media Records, Magic Arts Publishing.
From the album WAGES OF SIN

10. EXODUS - Piranha (Live) (Gary Holt / Paul Baloff)
© 1997 Courtesy of Century Media Records, Feeding Frenzy / No
Integrity Music. From the album ANOTHER LESSON IN VIOLENCE

11. CARNAL FORGE - Hand Of Doom (Carnal Forge)
© 2001 Courtesy of Century Media Records, Magic Arts Publishing.
From the album PLEASE...DIE

12. GOD FORBID - Nothing (God Forbid)
© 2001 Courtesy of Century Media Records,
Magic Arts Publishing. From the album DETERMINATION

13. HADES - Exist To Resist (Tecchio / Lorenzo)
© 1995 Courtesy of Exist To Resist / ASCAP. From the album 1982 TO 2002

14. AGENT STEEL - New Godz (B.Versailles / B.Hall)
© 1999 Courtesy of Agent Steel. From the album OMEGA CONSPIRACY

15. DENATA - Deathtrain (Denata)
© 2001 Courtesy of Arctic Music Group, Soaring Lori Music(ASCAP)
From the album DEATHTRAIN

16. SAVAGE - We Got The Edge (Bradley / Dawson)
© 1985 Courtesy of Zebra / Cherry Red Records, Complete Music Publishing
From the album HYPERACTIVE

17. WRATH - Wretch (Wrath)
© 2002 Courtesy of Wrath. From the album FEEL THE PAIN